EDITION 7

International Business

EDITION 7

International Business

Michael R. Czinkota
Georgetown University

Ilkka A. Ronkainen
Georgetown University

Michael H. Moffett
*Thunderbird, The American
Graduate School of
International Management*

THOMSON
™
SOUTH-WESTERN

Australia · Canada · Mexico · Singapore · Spain · United Kingdom · United States

THOMSON

SOUTH-WESTERN

International Business, 7e

Michael R. Czinkota, Ilkka A. Ronkainen, and Michael H. Moffett

VP/Editorial Director:
Jack W. Calhoun

VP/Editor-in-Chief:
Michael P. Roche

Senior Publisher:
Melissa S. Acuña

Executive Editor:
John Szilagyi

Developmental Editor:
Emma F. Guttler

Marketing Manager:
Jacquelyn Carrillo

Production Editor:
Emily S. Gross

Manufacturing Coordinator:
Rhonda Utley

Media Developmental Editor
Kristen Meere

Media Production Editor:
Karen Schaffer

Design Project Manager
Stacy Jenkins Shirley

Photography Manager:
John Hill

Photo Researcher:
Darren Wright

Production House:
Stratford Publishing Services

Cover Designer:
Grannan Graphic Design, Ltd.

Cover Images
Courtesy of ©Alamy

Internal Designer:
Grannan Graphic Design, Ltd.

Printer:
Quebecor World Dubuque
Dubuque, IA

Dedication

To all the Czinkotas: Ilona, Margaret, Ursula,
Mihaly, Birgit, Sarah and Thomas
—MRC

To Sirkka and Alpo Ronkainen
—IAR

To Bennie Ruth and Hoy Moffett
—MHM

Preface

We are grateful for the leadership position the market has awarded to this book. We are keenly aware of the fact that best-selling status in the educational field also imposes an obligation to deliver cutting-edge innovations and improvements in terms of content as well as presentation. We honor your trust by doing our best to delight you through our presentation of conceptually sound, reality-based knowledge and by easing your task of teaching and learning about international business. In this spirit of innovation, we offer you yet more value—*International Business*, 7th Edition.

This textbook is unique in its approach to international business. Our experience teaching managers and advising companies, both large and small, allows us to share with you the realities of the battle in the international marketplace. Due to our ongoing policy work with both national and international organizations, we are able to give you a firsthand perspective of government activities in international business. Through our research leadership, we can provide you with insights at the forefront of global thinking. As a result, this book offers the perspective of the multinational corporation as well as that of the small international start-up firm. It helps you understand how and why governments intervene in markets and suggests alternatives for working with governments to achieve corporate goals. This book provides you with a strong theory base but also fully reflects the managerial concerns of those who work on the front lines in the business world. Finally, ongoing improvements in pedagogy, presentation, and writing continue to make this a fun book from which to teach and learn.

Changes in the Seventh Edition

This new edition is even more user friendly. Important issues, such as investment flows, are now presented early in the text. The topics of transparency and governance are covered more thoroughly to echo the changing times in which we live. Multinational corporate issues, together with cooperative modes of market development, are presented in the context of international business entry and strategic planning. Countertrade is covered in conjunction with multinational financial management. The specific changes in this edition are explained below.

CURRENT COVERAGE

Today, change happens at breakneck speed. Keeping on top of the evolving world of international issues and their impact on international business can be difficult. This text addresses instructors' and students' needs for contemporaneous information with current perspectives on contemporary topics not yet available in other international business texts.

In preparing this edition, we have listened closely to our market in order to deliver an outstanding product. We begin by presenting the impact of international business on countries, corporations, and individuals.

We reflect more fully on some of the controversies in international business today, including the role of international institutions such as the World Trade Organization, the World Bank, and the International Monetary Fund. We discuss why some groups are disenchanted with increased globalization. Also presented are some of the links between and areas of friction in international business and development, such as payment for intellectual property rights, distribution of patented medication to poor countries, and development of genetically engineered foods. We address the issues of bribery and corruption and the benefit of good governance; in-depth attention is paid to the role of culture, policies, and politics. The dimensions of ethics, social responsibility, and diversity are fully reflected through examples and vignettes.

The text consistently adopts a truly global approach. Attention is given to topics that are critical to the international manager yet so far have eluded other international texts. This coverage includes chapters on supply-chain management, international service trade, and doing business with newly emerging market economies under conditions of privatization.

NEW AND IMPROVED TOPIC COVERAGE AND ORGANIZATION

International Business, 7th Edition, is organized into seven parts, and contains 20 chapters. These seven parts allow the text to flow logically from introductory material to the international environment to marketing and financial considerations in the international marketplace.

Part 1 deals with the impact of globalization, and provides an overview of the key issues facing international business today.

Part 2 covers the environment, and focuses on the similarities and differences between cultures, and how global politics and laws both influence and are influenced by these same factors

Part 3 shifts to the conceptual foundations surrounding international trade and investments.

Part 4 explores markets and institutions, including the discussion of international financial management and market entry.

Part 5 explains strategic management issues.

Part 6 is devoted to international operations, investigating strategic management issues.

Part 7 concludes with a look towards the future horizons of the field and of the student.

Among the new material in the text is the following:

Chapter 1 has a new focus on the issue of globalization. It addresses the pros and the cons, highlights the opportunities for individuals and firms but also presents the past shortcomings of economic institutions, which have led to problems and difficulties. The chapter covers the migration of manufacturing from developed nations to developing countries, discusses the highly charged issue of international sweatshops for the sake of low prices and also reflects some of the new political divisiveness which has affected trade issues, such as the rift between the United States and Europe.

Chapter 2 Culture emphasizes not only the importance of preparation for differences but also how culture can be used a competitive tool. The availability of new learning tools, such as those in the virtual environment, make acquiring culture-specific knowledge and sensitivity more feasible and effective.

Chapter 3 now offers coverage of the new international trade discussions in the Doha Round. It highlights the failure of negotiators to agree on an agenda due to disparate views among the 148 WTO members. Difficulties within trading blocs, such as NAFTA are discussed, as are new efforts aimed at export promotion.

Chapter 4 now has an additional focus on Africa and the prevailing corruption and lack of transparency which have made economic progress difficult. Substantial coverage is added on the issue of terrorism and its effect on world business. There is now coverage of the international need for managerial and corporate virtue, vision, and veracity if the market force model is to be acceptable around the globe.

Chapter 5 tracks how the theories of international economic relations—both trade and investment—have evolved in the past two centuries. In addition to presenting the various theories in a manner which allows the readers to compare and contrast their fundamental assumptions, the chapter moves the reader towards a more complete understanding of how international trade and investment are increasingly a single subject, their structures, implications, and strategies for companies and governments intertwined.

Chapter 6 on the balance of payments has been updated to promote a more intuitive basis to student understanding of this critical, yet historically dry subject. The extended discussions of the Asian Crisis and capital mobility in general provide a more life-like landscape for the reader attempting to interpret the daily deluge of balance of trade and balance of capital data reports.

Chapter 7 examines the theoretical drivers of exchange rates and international capital markets. The discussion includes the history, principles and practices of these markets, paying specific attention to the institutional characteristics of how currencies are traded and capital raised. Added discussion highlights the renewed vigor of the euro and its implications.

Chapter 8 The evolution and future development of trading blocs is updated to take into account the expansion of the European Union and the prospects for the Free Trade Area of the Americas. Economic alliances in emerging and developing countries contribute in a major way to these markets' integration into the world economy.

Chapter 9 contains increased coverage of China, both as a source of supplies and as a market. The benefits and difficulties encountered by the WTO membership of China are highlighted. In addition, the role of international business in improving the quality of life in less-developed markets by serving the four billion underprivileged customers is presented in a new section.

Chapter 10 explores how firms attempt to identify and respond to new trends around the world. It also addresses the dilemma that researchers encounter when it comes to the sharing of research findings in a climate of concern about abuses, terrorists and lack of respect for intellectual property rights. The importance of translation equivalence and of privacy issues is highlighted and a new section on the use of web technology for research is introduced.

Chapter 11 has increased coverage of a transaction cost perspective when it comes to international market entry choices. The rising frequency of "born global" firms is addressed, as is the "liability of foreignness" encountered by investors.

Chapter 12 Global strategy focuses on leveraging resources across markets. This means taking advantage of converging market trends by being able to maximize economies of scale or concentrating activities where they can be carried out most effectively. Large companies may have extensive operations worldwide. Many new players transcend nationality altogether by making many operations virtual.

Chapter 13 Organizational structures have to reflect changes in the environment and companies' adjustment to these changes. Implementation of global strategy, especially from the point of view of cross-market coordination of programs is discussed using centers of excellence and management of global knowledge networks as examples.

Chapter 14 now contains an updated discussion of companies' adjustment to the globalization of markets; i.e., how to incorporate local and regional elements into worldwide programs. The discussion on the role of e-commerce has been expanded to reflect the role of the e-dimension in testing new concepts and both new distribution modes.

Chapter 15 Services discusses how job shifts are not just occurring in the manufacturing sector. The globalization of service industries will increasingly lead to more global sourcing of service talent. The importance of international education and learning is discussed, as are the increasing constraints imposed by government policies.

Chapter 16 Logistics and Supply Chain Management explains how outsourcing requires the formation of new distribution strategies. Issues of infrastructure are raised, as is their influence on corporate strategies. An entire new section on Logistics and Security is presented which highlights how corporations have had to revise their sourcing and distribution activities to reflect the slow-down of transportation flows. Also new is a section on the supply chain and the internet which explains the emergence of new, global performance benchmarks.

Chapter 17 Multinational Financial Management now begins with a detailed discussion of the differences between stockholder wealth maximization as pursued in the United States and United Kingdom versus corporate wealth maximization as traditionally followed in Continental Europe and Japan. In addition to updated discussions of countertrade and import-export financing, the discussion of managing currency exposures and cash flows internationally has been streamlined and updated.

Chapter 18 Corporate Governance, Accounting, and Taxation has undergone a substantial revision to include the critical topics of corporate governance, shareholder rights, and transparency which have been so topical in the post-Enron business environment. The discussion details both the theory and the reality in practice of how corporate governance provides accountability to corporate stakeholders, and enumerates the many different principles and practices employed across countries.

Chapter 19 International Human Resource Management explains the importance of the expatriate phenomenon both from the individual and corporate points of view. Latest survey data on individual challenges faced as well as corporate preparatory programs for overseas assignments are included.

Chapter 20 is based on a completely new global Delphi study carried out by the text's authors. The continued economic difficulties forcast for Africa are explained as are the new opportunities arising in China and India. The issue of population balance is explained, where government policies and family preferences may lead to the eventual emergence of polyandry—where a wife has two or more husbands at the same time. The difficulties of future trade negotiations are presented, as are the opportunities for developing a new trade and security regime. Finally, an updated series of websites for international employment is offered.

Innovative Learning Tools

USE OF WORLDWIDE EXAMPLES

Drawing on worldwide examples, trends, and data rather than just on U.S.-based information makes this a global book. For example, many of the data sets presented and sources recommended come from Europe and Asia.

We also ensure the reality and pragmatism of our content by always addressing the issue of "What does this mean for international business?" As an example, we explain how to use cultural variables for segmentation purposes in order to create new competitive tools.

BLENDING CURRENT THEORY AND APPLICATION

Our theory section presents the latest thinking both from business researchers and leading economists. We also present the interdependence and linkages between the different theories so that students gain an appreciation of the overall context of international business thought. All tables, figures, and maps were updated to present the most current information.

RESEARCH EMPHASIS

This edition includes a greatly strengthened research chapter. An in-depth information appendix enhances the student's ability to conduct independent research, primarily by using web sites and other resources of the Internet. We devote a new section to the issue of data privacy and to research on the internet, where we highlight best practices of firms and provide a comparison of the different approaches to privacy in Europe and in the United States.

We also focus on "born global" firms, which have a global orientation from their inception, and differentiate the levels of internationalization of these firms. We offer a new model of the internationalization process, reflecting the latest in research findings. We show how firms can receive export help from their governments and provide Internet information for the leading export promotion organizations from around the globe. A new section highlights how leading-edge firms are developing "export complaint management systems" in order to stay close to their customers, adapt products quickly, and regain control of export channels.

TECHNOLOGY, ELECTRONIC COMMERCE, AND THE INTERNET

Issues surrounding technology in the international workplace are integrated throughout the text. In addition, Web-based questions and research exercises at the end of each chapter permit immersion in ongoing international business issues and communicate the excitement of rapid change.

We have developed a strong focus on Internet-based research, but also discuss the strengths and weaknesses of electronic databases. We highlight, for example, the fact that culture has a major effect on technology use and content expectations, and that search engines tend to pick only a small portion of actual work carried out and are still heavily biased toward English-language publications. We also show how new technology can help even very small firms reach out to international markets and compete successfully abroad.

UP-TO-DATE COVERAGE OF THE EUROPEAN UNION, ASIA, AND TRANSITION ECONOMIES

We have streamlined the discussion of the international monetary system, included the effects of the greater acceptance of the euro, and expanded the discussion of financial markets. We provide in-depth coverage of the new developments in the European Union together with the changing roles of Mercosur and APEC. In discussing the latest changes in transition economies, we are, due to our direct involvement in founding three business-learning institutions in Russia, able to highlight the human and leadership dimensions inherent in the change to a market economy.

ART AND PHOTO PROGRAM

Photos and advertisements have been updated to ensure currency of visual aids in illustrating key points. Throughout the text, concepts are depicted through tables, figures, and graphics. Artwork is designed to reiterate key concepts as well as to provide a pleasing format for student learning.

Distinguishing Pedagogical Features

GEOGRAPHY

To enhance the geographic literacy of students, the text includes many full color maps covering the social, economic and political features of the world. In addition, several chapters have maps particularly designed for this book, which integrate the materials discussed in the text and reflect a truly "global" perspective. They provide the instructor with the means to visually demonstrate concepts such as political blocs, socioeconomic variables, and transportation routes. A list of maps appears on page xxxiv. An appendix, dealing specifically with the impact of geography on international marketing, is part of Chapter 1. Each text is packaged with a fold out map by Rand McNally.

CONTEMPORARY REALISM

Each chapter offers a number of Focus on Issues boxes that describe actual contemporary business situations. These issues include Politics, Ethics, e-Business, Culture, and Entrepreneurship. These boxes are intended to serve as reinforcing examples, or minicases. As such, they will assist the instructor in stimulating class discussion and aid the student in understanding and absorbing the text material.

TAKE A STAND!

These end-of-chapter exercises ask students to read a short paragraph outlining a situation, and to make an educated decision about the outcome for the scenario. They can be used as a homework exercise, a personal assessment, or for classroom discussion.

CHAPTER SUMMARY AND REVIEW QUESTIONS

Each chapter closes with a chapter summary of key points that students should retain, organized by learning objective. The discussion questions are a complementary learning tool that will enable students to check their understanding of key issues, to think beyond basic concepts, and to determine areas that require further study. All these tools help students discriminate between main and supporting points and provide mechanisms for classroom activity or at-home review.

ON THE WEB

Each chapter contains several Internet exercises to involve students in the high-tech world of cyberspace. Students are asked to explore the Web to research topics related to materials covered in each chapter. This hands-on experience helps to develop Internet, research, and business skills.

EXEMPLARY CASE SELECTION

To further link theory and practice, we present twenty-one cases, more than half of which are new or updated. We draw case materials from firms around the world to offer truly global business scenarios, ranging from Vietnam and Russia to Iceland and Turkey. The cases deal not only with established manufacturing industries, such as Ford, but also with Yao Ming, the Chinese basketball player. We present some of the controversy emanating from diamond industry, and we also focus on the human dimension that is so highly important for expatriates. Challenging questions accompany each case. Some of our best cases from previous editions are also available on the text support site (http://czinkota.swlearning.com) for instructor use. They encourage in-depth discussion of the material covered in the chapters and allow students to apply the knowledge they have gained and allow instructors to retain the use of favorite teaching tools.

Comprehensive Learning Package

Instructor's Manual (0-324-23631-X) The text is accompanied by an in-depth *Instructor's Manual*, devised to provide major assistance to the professor. The material in the manual includes the following:

- **Teaching Plans** Alternative teaching plans and syllabi are presented to accommodate the instructor's preferred course structure and varying time constraints. Time plans are developed for the course to be taught in a semester format, on a quarter basis, or as an executive seminar.
- **Discussion Guidelines** For each chapter, specific teaching objectives and guidelines to help stimulate classroom discussion are presented.
- **End-of-Chapter Questions** All questions for discussion are fully developed in the manual to accommodate different scenarios and experience horizons. Where appropriate, the relevant text section is referenced. In addition, each chapter includes two or more Internet-based questions offering the students the opportunity to explore the application of new technology to international business on their own.
- **Cases** Detailed answers are provided for all discussion questions that follow the cases that appear in the text.

Test Bank (0-324-23632-8) Fully revised and expanded from the previous edition, this Test Bank consists of more than 2,000 true/false questions, multiple-choice questions, and short answer and essay questions. The questions are also available electronically on the text support site.

ExamView Available on the Instructor's Resource CD, ExamView contains all of the questions in the Test Bank. This program is easy-to-use test-creation software compatible with Microsoft Windows. Instructors can add or edit questions, instructions, and answers, and select questions (randomly or numerically). Instructors can also create and administer quizzes online, whether over the Internet, a local-area network (LAN), or a wide-area network (WAN).

PowerPoint Lecture Presentations An asset to any instructor, the lectures provide outlines for every chapter, graphics of the illustrations from the text, and additional examples providing instructors with a number of learning opportunities for students. The PowerPoint Lecture Presentations are available on the IRCD in Microsoft 2000 format and as downloadable files on the text support site.

Instructor's CD-ROM (0-324-23633-6) Key instructor ancillaries (Instructor's Manual, Test Bank, ExamView, and PowerPoint slides) are provided on CD-ROM, giving instructors a key tool for customizing lectures and presentations.

Overhead Transparencies (0-324-23341-8) Created from artwork in the text, as well as outside materials, the full color acetate package of 100 transparency acetates is available with this text. These transparencies can supplement lectures by displaying the key concepts from the text.

Videos (0-324-20354-3) Videos compiled specifically to accompany *International Business, 7th Edition* utilize real-world companies to illustrate international business concepts as outlined in the text. Focusing on both small and large businesses, the video gives students an inside perspective on the situations and issues that global corporations face. Please contact your local Thomson sales representative.

Companion Web Site *International Business*'s Web site at http://czinkota.swlearning. com/ provides a multitude of student resources. Additional supplementary materials for instructors are included on a password-protected site.

Student Resources

- Online quizzes for each chapter are available on the Web site for those students who would like additional study materials. After each quiz is submitted, automatic feedback tells the students how they scored and what the correct answers are to the questions they missed. Students are then able to e-mail their results directly to their instructor if desired.
- Students can download the PowerPoint presentation slides from the web site.
- Links to news articles and hot marketing topics are provided for extra student research.

Instructor Resources

- Downloadable Instructor's Manual and Test Bank files are available in Microsoft Word 2000 format and Adobe Acrobat format.
- Downloadable PowerPoint presentation files are available in Microsoft PowerPoint 2000 format.
- An online database of additional cases is supplied for adopters of the text at the instructor resources page. Go there to find tried and true case studies from previous editions.

TextChoice: Management Exercises and Cases TextChoice is the home of Thomson Learning's online digital content. TextChoice provides the fastest, easiest way for you to create your own learning materials. South-Western's Management Exercises and Cases database includes a variety of experiential exercises, classroom activities, management in film exercises, and cases to enhance any management course. Choose as many exercises as you like and even add your own material to create a supplement tailored to your course. Contact your South-Western/Thomson Learning sales representative for more information.

ECoursepacks Create a tailor-fit, easy-to-use, online companion for any course with eCoursepacks, from Thomson companies South-Western and Gale. eCoursepacks give educators access to content from thousands of current popular, professional, and academic periodicals, as well as NACRA and Darden cases, and business and industry information from Gale. In addition, instructors can easily add their own material with the option of even collecting a royalty. Permissions for all eCoursepack content are already secured, saving instructors the time and worry of securing rights.

eCoursepacks online publishing tools also save time and energy by allowing instructors to quickly search the databases to make selections, organize all the content, and publish the final online product in a clean, uniform, and full-color format. eCoursepacks is the best way to provide current information quickly and inexpensively. To learn more visit: http://ecoursepacks.swlearning.com.

InfoTrac College Edition Included with each new copy of the text is four months of free access to InfoTrac College Edition, an online library of more than 4,000 academic journals and periodicals. Through its easy-to-use search engine and other user-friendly features, InfoTrac College Edition puts cutting edge research and the latest headlines at students' fingertips.

PERSONAL SUPPORT

We personally stand behind our product and we will work hard to delight you. Should you have any questions or comments on this book, please contact us and provide us with your feedback.

Michael R. Czinkota	Ilkka A. Ronkainen	Michael H. Moffett
Czinkotm@georgetown.edu	Ronkaii@georgetown.edu	Moffettm@t-bird.edu

Acknowledgments

We are grateful to many reviewers for their imaginative comments and criticisms and for showing us how to get it even more right:

Kamal M. Abouzeid
Lynchburg College

Yair Aharoni
Duke University

Zafar U. Ahmed
Minot State University

Riad Ajami
Rensselaer Polytechnic Institute

Joe Anderson
Northern Arizona University

Robert Aubey
University of Wisconsin–Madison

David Aviel
California State University

Josiah Baker
University of Central Florida

Marilynn Baker
*University of North Carolina–
   Greensboro*

Bharat B. Bhalla
Fairfield University

Julius M. Blum
University of South Alabama

Sharon Browning
Northwest Missouri State University

Peggy E. Chaudhry
Villanova University

Ellen Cook
University of San Diego

Lauren DeGeorge
University of Central Florida

Luther Trey Denton
Georgia Southern University

Dharma deSilva
Wichita State University

Gary N. Dicer
The University of Tennessee

Peter Dowling
University of Tasmania

Carol Dresden
Coastal Carolina University

Derrick E. Dsouza
University of North Texas

Massoud Farahbaksh
Salem State College

Runar Framnes
Norwegian School of Management

Anne-Marie Francesco
Pace University–New York

Esra F. Gencturk
University of Texas–Austin

Debra Glassman
University of Washington–Seattle

Raul de Gouvea Neto
University of New Mexico

Antonio Grimaldi
Rutgers, The State University of New Jersey

John H. Hallaq
University of Idaho

Daniel Himarios
University of Texas at Arlington

Veronica Horton
Middle Tennessee State University

Basil J. Janavaras
Mankato State University

Michael Kublin
University of New Haven

Diana Lawson
University of Maine

Jan B. Luytjes
Florida International University

John Manley
Iona College

David McCalman
Indiana University–Bloomington

Tom Morris
University of San Diego

James Neelankavil
Hofstra University

V. R. Nemani
Trinity College

Moonsong David Oh
California State University–Los Angeles

Sam C. Okoroafo
University of Toledo

Diane Parente
State University of New York–Fredonia

Mike W. Peng
Ohio State University

William Piper
Piedmont College

Jesus Ponce de Leon
Southern Illinois University–Carbondale

Jerry Ralston
University of Washington–Seattle

Peter V. Raven
Eastern Washington University

William Renforth
Florida International University

Martin E. Rosenfeldt
The University of North Texas

Tagi Sagafi-nejad
Loyola College

Rajib N. Sanyal
Trenton State College

Ulrike Schaede
University of California–Berkeley

John Stanbury
Indiana University–Kokomo

John Thanopoulos
University of Akron

Douglas Tseng
Portland State University

Robert G. Vambery
Pace University

C. Alexandra Van Nostrand
Palm Beach Atlantic College

Betty Velthouse
University of Michigan–Flint

Heidi Vernon-Wortzel
Northeastern University

Steven C. Walters
Davenport College

James O. Watson
Millikin University

George H. Westacott
SUNY–Binghamton

Jerry Wheat
Indiana University Southeast

Tim Wilkinson
University of Akro

Kitty Y. H. Young
Chinese University of Hong Kong

Many thanks to those faculty members and students who helped us in sharpening our thinking by cheerfully providing challenging comments and questions. Several individuals had particular long-term impact on our thinking. These are Professor Bernard LaLonde, of the Ohio State University, a true academic mentor; the late Professor Robert Bartels, also of Ohio State; Professor Arthur Stonehill, of Oregon State University; Professor James H. Sood, of American University; Professor Arch G. Woodside, of Tulane University; Professor David Ricks, of University of Missouri, St. Louis; Professor Brian Toyne, of St. Mary's University; and Professor John Darling, of Mississippi State University. They are our academic ancestors.

Many colleagues, friends, and business associates graciously gave their time and knowledge to clarify concepts; provide us with ideas, comments, and suggestions; and deepen our understanding of issues. Without the direct links to business and policy that you have provided, this book could not offer its refreshing realism. In particular, we are grateful to Secretaries Malcolm Baldrige, C. William Verity, Clayton Yeutter, and William Brock for the opportunity to gain international business policy experience and to William Morris, Paul Freedenberg, H. P. Goldfield, and J. Michael Farrell for enabling its implementation. We also thank William Casselman, Lew Cramer of Summit Ventures, and Reijo Luostarinen of HSE.

Our elite team of student researchers provided valuable assistance. They made important and substantive contributions to this book. They dig up research information with tenacity and relentlessness; they organize and analyze research materials, prepare drafts of vignettes and cases, and reinforce everyone on the third floor of Old North with their can-do spirit. They are Sabrina Nguyen, Angie Kang, Shannon Antonio, Sofina Qureshi, Ida Shea, Ruthie Braunstein, and Jessie Sze-Ting Cheung, all of Georgetown University. We appreciate all of your work.

A very special thank you to the people at South-Western College Publishing. Thanks to Mike Roche, Vice President/Editor-In-Chief; Melissa Acuña, Senior Publisher; John Szilagyi, Executive Editor; Emma Guttler, Developmental Editor; Jacquelyn Carrillo, Marketing Manager; Stacy Shirley, Design Project Manager; Emily Gross, Production Editor; John Hill, Photography Manager; and Darren Wright, Photo Researcher.

Foremost, we are grateful to our families, who have had to tolerate late-night computer noises, weekend library absences, and curtailed vacations. The support and love of Ilona Vigh-Czinkota and Margaret Victoria Czinkota, Susan, Sanna, and Alex Ronkainen, Megan Murphy, Caitlin Kelly, and Sean Michael Moffett gave us the energy, stamina, and inspiration to write this book.

Michael R. Czinkota
Ilkka A. Ronkainen
Michael H. Moffett
February 2004

About the Authors

MICHAEL R. CZINKOTA

is on the faculty of marketing and international business of the Graduate School and the Robert Emmett McDonough School of Business at Georgetown University. He has held professorial appointments at universities in Asia, Australia, Europe, and the Americas.

Dr. Czinkota served in the U.S. government as Deputy Assistant Secretary of Commerce. He also served as head of the U.S. Delegation to the OECD Industry Committee in Paris and as senior trade advisor for Export Controls.

Dr. Czinkota's background includes eight years of private-sector business experience as a partner in an export-import firm and in an advertising agency. His research has been supported by the U.S. government, the National Science Foundation, the Organization of American States, and the International Council of the American Management Association. He has been listed as one of the three most published contributors to international business research in the *Journal of International Business Studies* and has written several books, including *Best Practices in International Marketing* and *Mastering Global Markets* (Thomson). He is also the co-author of the *STAT-USA/Internet Companion to International Marketing*, an official publication of the U.S. Department of Commerce.

Dr. Czinkota served on the Global Advisory Board of the American Marketing Association and on the Board of Governors of the Academy of Marketing Science. He is on the editorial boards of *Journal of the Academy of Marketing Science*, *International Marketing Review*, and *Asian Journal of Marketing*. For his work in international business and trady policy, he was named a Distinguished Fellow of the Academy of Marketing Science and a Fellow of the Chartered Institute of Marketing in the United Kingdom. He has been awarded honorary degrees from the Universidad Pontificia Madre y Maestra in the Dominican Republic and the Universidad del Pacifico in Lima, Peru. He is an elected Fellow of the Royal Society of Arts, Manufacturers, and Commerce (RSA).

Dr. Czinkota serves on several corporate boards and has worked with corporations such as AT&T, IBM, GE, Nestlé, and US WEST. He also serves as advisor to the United Nations and World Trade Organization's Executive Forum on National Export Strategies. Dr. Czinkota is often asked to testify before Congress and is a sought-after speaker and advisor to corporations.

Dr. Czinkota was born and raised in Germany and educated in Austria, Scotland, Spain, and the United States. He studied law and business administration at the University of Erlangen-Nürnberg and was awarded a two-year Fulbright Scholarship. He holds an MBA in international business and a Ph.D. in logistics from The Ohio State University.

ILKKA A. RONKAINEN

is a member of the faculty of marketing and international business at the School of Business at Georgetown University. From 1981 to 1986 he served as Associate Director and from 1986 to 1987 as Chairman of the National Center for Export-Import Studies. Currently, he directs Georgetown University's Hong Kong Program.

Dr. Ronkainen serves as docent of international marketing at the Helsinki School of Economics. He was visiting professor at HSE during the 1987–1988 and 1991–1992 academic years and continues to teach in its Executive MBA, International MBA, and International BBA programs. He is currently the chairholder of the Saastamoinen Foundation Professorship in International Marketing.

Dr. Ronkainen holds a Ph.D. and a master's degree from the University of South Carolina as well as an M.S. (Economics) degree from the Helsinki School of Economics.

Dr. Ronkainen had published extensively in academic journals and the trade press. He is coauthor of a number of international business and marketing texts, including *Best Practices in International Marketing* and *Mastering Global Markets* (Thomson). He serves on the review boards of the *Journal of Business Research*, *International Marketing Review*, and *Journal of Travel Research* and has reviewed for the *Journal of International Marketing* and the *Journal of International Business Studies*. He served as the North American coordinator for the European Marketing Academy, 1984–1990. He was a member of the board of the Washington International Trade Association from 1981–1986 and started the association's newsletter, *Trade Trends*.

Dr. Ronkainen has served as a consultant to a wide range of U.S. and international institutions. He has worked with entities such as IBM, the Rank Organization, and the Organization of American States. He maintains close ties with a number of Finnish companies, working with them on their internationalization and educational efforts.

MICHAEL H. MOFFETT

is currently Associate Professor of Finance and International Business at the American Graduate School of International Management (Thunderbird). Dr. Moffett has a B.A. in Economics from the University of Texas at Austin (1977), an M.S. in Resource Economics from Cololado State Univeristy (1979), and M.A. and Ph.D. in International Economics from the University of Colorado–Boulder (1985).

Dr. Moffett has lectured at a number of universities around the world, including the Aarhus School of Business (Denmark), the Helsinki School of Economics and Business Administration (Finland), the Norwegian School of Economics (Norway), and the University of Ljubljana (Slovenia). Dr. Moffett has also lectured at a number of universities in the United States, including Trinity College, Washington, DC, and the University of Colorado–Boulder. He is a former visiting research fellow at the Brookings Institution, and completed a two-year visiting professorship in the Department of International Business at the University of Michigan–Ann Arbor.

Michael Moffett's research publications have appeared in a number of academic journals, including the *Journal of International Money and Finance*, the *Journal of Financial and Quantitative Analysis*, *Contemporary Policy Issues*, and the *Journal of International Financial Management and Accounting*. He is coauthor of *Multinational Business Finance*, tenth edition, 2004, with David Eiteman and Arthur Stonehill, as well as coeditor with Arthur Stonehill of *Transnational Financial Management* for the United Nations Centre for Transnational Corporations, 1993. He is a continuing contributor to numerous collective works in the fields of international finance and international business, incluidng the *Handbook of Modern Finance* and the *International Accounting and Finance Handbook*. Dr. Moffett has also consulted with a number of private firms both in the United States and Europe.

Brief Contents

P A R T 7 | FUTURE   685

Contents

Chapter 6 The Balance of Payments, 180

PART 4 | MARKETS   215

Chapter 7   Financial Markets, 216

Chapter 8   Economic Integration, 248

Chapter 11   Entry and Expansion, 348

Chapter 12   Strategic Planning, 378

Chapter 13   Organization, Implementation, and Control, 404

PART 6 | OPERATIONS

467

Chapter 14 Marketing, 468

Chapter 15 Services, 504

Chapter 16   Logistics and Supply-Chain Management, 526

Chapter 17   Financial Management, 560

Chapter 18   Corporate Governance, Accounting, and Taxation, 590

Chapter 19   Human Resource Management, 624

PART 7 | FUTURE

685

Maps

The globalization of business brings new opportunities and threats to governments, firms, and individuals. The challenge is to compete successfully in the global marketplace as it exists today and develops tomorrow.

Part 1 sets the stage by introducing the effects of international business and demonstrating the need to participate in international activities.

PART

Impact

1

1   The International
    Business Imperative

CHAPTER

1

The International Business Imperative

Learning Objectives

- To understand the history and impact of international business

- To learn the definition of international business

- To recognize the growth of global linkages today

- To understand the U.S. position in world trade and the impact international business has on the United States

- To appreciate the opportunities and challenges offered by international business

Globalization: Opportunity or Threat?

Globalization of business is seen by many as creating wealth that benefits nations and individuals worldwide. Peter Woicke, of the World Bank, credits globalization with providing essential ingredients of success to entrepreneurs and corporations in developing regions. A multinational firm brings a reliable electricity source to local farmers, manufacturers, and businesses by building a hydroelectric dam in Uganda. A banana grower in Ecuador expands his agribusiness into Russia and China, allowing him to channel profits to protect a local tropical rain forest. World Bank loans support a network of entrepreneurs in South Africa and upgrade bank services in Latin America. "Globalization," Woicke concludes, "can help would-be industrialists change the labels of their countries from developing to developed."

However, entry into the world economy also causes its share of problems. Critics of globalization believe that international business mainly increases the wealth of corporations and investors at the expense of the poor. They say that it supports dictators, fails to relieve the massive debts of developing countries, spoils the environment, and causes terrorism. There are growing protests over labor exploitation and the export of jobs, and questions have been raised about the value and morality of the trade precepts guiding the world. In what seems to quickly have become a tradition, opponents of globalization regularly disrupt the meetings of the World Trade Organization. Protestors, police, and policy-makers also encounter ongoing clashes at meetings of the International Monetary Fund (IMF) and the World Bank. In June 2003, thousands of protestors disrupted the G8 Summit in Evian, France.

Proponents of globalization believe it is simplistic to blame globalization for worldwide poverty. The causes of poverty are numerous and complex, including war, disease (such as the African AIDS pandemic), corruption, illiteracy, and lawlessness. However, as a result of protests, many international firms and organizations have begun to revise some of their practices, suggesting that a middle ground might be found.

In 2003, the IMF released a report that stated that countries that follow IMF suggestions often suffer a "collapse in growth rates and significant financial crises," and admitted it was considering changes in its practices. Since the protests began, the World Bank has also made changes to the way it operates by shifting its focus away from government loans to microcredit schemes, and increasing the input from locals in countries it is trying to help. As the worldwide process of adjustment to globalization continues, the negotiations between those who benefit from it and those who lose out will continue.

Sources: Simon English, "IMF Says its Policies Seldom Work," *The Daily Telegraph,* March 20, 2003, 31; "Globalization and Its Critics," *The Economist,* September 27, 2001, http://www.economist.com, accessed February 4, 2002; Dan Ackman, "Davos Go Home," February 4, 2002, http://www.forbes.com; "Going Global," *The Economist Global Agenda,* February 1, 2002; Paul Blustein, "A Quiet Round in Qatar?" *Washington Post,* January 30, 2001, E1.

The Need for International Business

You are about to begin an exciting, important, and necessary task: the exploration of international business. International business is exciting because it combines the science and the art of business with many other disciplines, such as economics, anthropology, geography, history, language, jurisprudence, statistics, and demography. International business is important and necessary because economic isolationism has become impossible. Failure to become a part of the global market assures a nation of declining economic influence and a deteriorating standard of living for its citizens. Successful participation in international business, however, holds the promise of improved quality of life and a better society, even leading, some believe, to a more peaceful world.

On an individual level, most students are likely to become involved with international business enterprises during their careers. Manufacturing firms, as well as service companies such as banks, insurance, or consulting firms are going global. Artwork, films, and music are already widely exposed to the international market. Many of the future professional colleagues and competitors of today's students will come from around the world. In an era of open borders, niche marketing, instant communications, and virtually free ways of reaching millions of people, there emerges an unprecedented opportunity for individuals to enter the international business arena. Start-up firms can challenge the existing, long-dominant large competition. Speed, creativity, and innovation have often become more important to international success than size. Understanding international business is therefore crucial in preparing for the opportunities, challenges, and requirements of a future career.

International business offers companies new markets. Since the 1950s, the growth of international trade and investment has been substantially larger than the growth of

Anti-globalization activists protest against the World Trade Organization in Bangkok, Thailand, in September 2003. Many protesters believe that the WTO has too much power to advance globalization at the expense of democracy, claiming that free trade does not equal fair trade. There is concern that discussions and resolutions are reached behind closed doors, with no opportunity for public appeal.

© EPA PHOTO/EPA/VINAI DITHAJOHN

domestic economies. Technology continues to increase the reach and the ease of conducting international business, pointing to even larger growth potential in the future. A combination of domestic and international business, therefore, presents more opportunities for expansion, growth, and income than does domestic business alone. International business causes the flow of ideas, services, and capital across the world. As a result, innovations can be developed and disseminated more rapidly, human capital can be used better, and financing can take place more quickly. International business also offers consumers new choices. It can permit the acquisition of a wider variety of products, both in terms of quantity and quality, and do so at reduced prices through international competition. International business facilitates the mobility of factors of production—except land—and provides challenging employment opportunities to individuals with professional and entrepreneurial skills. At the same time, international business reallocates resources, makes preferential choices, and shifts activities on a global level. It also opens up markets to competition, which, in many instances has been unexpected and is difficult to cope with. As a result, international business activities do not benefit everyone to the same degree. Just like Janus, the two-faced god of the Romans, international business can bring benefits and opportunity to some, while delivering drawbacks and problems to others. The international firm and its managers, as well as the consumers of international products and services, need to understand how to make globalization work for them, as well as think about how to ensure that these benefits are afforded to a wide variety of people and countries. Therefore, both as an opportunity and a challenge, international business is of vital concern to countries, companies, and individuals.

A Definition of International Business

International business consists of transactions that are devised and carried out across national borders to satisfy the objectives of individuals, companies, and organizations. These transactions take on various forms, which are often interrelated. Primary types of international business are export-import trade and direct foreign investment. The latter is carried out in varied forms, including wholly owned subsidiaries and joint ventures. Additional types of international business are licensing, franchising, and management contracts.

The definition of international business focuses on transactions. The use of this term recognizes that doing business internationally is an activity, not merely a passive observation. Closely linked to activity is the term "satisfaction." It is crucial that the participants in international business are satisfied. Only if they feel they are better off after the transaction than they were before, will individual business transactions develop into a business relationship. The fact that the transactions are *across national borders* highlights a key difference between domestic and international business. The international executive is subject to a new set of macroenvironmental factors, to different constraints, and to quite frequent conflicts resulting from different laws, cultures, and societies. The basic principles of business are still relevant, but their application, complexity, and intensity vary substantially.

Subject to constant change, international business is as much an art as a science. Yet success in the art of business depends on a firm grounding in its scientific aspects. Individual consumers, policymakers, and business executives with an understanding of both aspects will be able to incorporate international business considerations into their thinking and planning. They will be able to consider international issues and repercussions and make decisions related to questions such as these:

- How will our idea, good, or service fit into the international market?
- Should we enter the market through trade or through investment?
- Should I obtain my supplies domestically or from abroad?
- What product adjustments are necessary to be responsive to local conditions?
- What threats from global competition should be expected and how can these threats be counteracted?

When management integrates these issues into each decision, international markets can provide growth, profit, and needs satisfaction not available to those that limit their activities to the domestic marketplace. To aid in this decision process is the purpose of this book.

A Brief History

Ever since the first national borders were formed, international business has been conducted by nations and individuals. In many instances, international business itself has been a major force in shaping borders and changing world history.

As an example, international business played a vital role in the formation and decline of the Roman Empire, whose impact on thought, knowledge, and development can still be felt today. Although we read about the marching of the Roman legions, it was not through military might that the empire came about. The Romans used the **Pax Romana,** or Roman peace, as a major stimulus. This ensured that merchants were able to travel safely and rapidly on roads built, maintained, and protected by the Roman legions and their affiliated troops. A second stimulus was the use of common coinage, which simplified business transactions and made them comparable throughout the empire. In addition, Rome developed a systematic law, central market locations through the founding of cities, and an effective communication system; all of these actions contributed to the functioning of the marketplace and a reduction of business uncertainty.

International business flourished within the empire, and the improved standard of living within the empire became apparent to those outside. Soon city-nations and tribes that were not part of the empire decided to join as allies. They agreed to pay tribute and taxes because the benefits were greater than the drawbacks.

Thus, the immense growth of the Roman Empire occurred mainly through the linkages of business. Of course, preserving this favorable environment required substantial effort. When pirates threatened the seaways, for example, Pompeius sent out a large fleet to subdue them. Once this was accomplished, the cost of international distribution within the empire dropped substantially because fewer shipments were lost at sea. Goods could be made available at lower prices, which in turn translated into larger demand and greater, more widely available benefits.

The fact that international business was one of the primary factors that held the empire together can also be seen in the decline of Rome. When "barbaric" tribes overran the empire, again it was not mainly through war and prolonged battles that Rome had lost ground. Rather, outside tribes were attacking an empire that was already substantially weakened at its foundations because of infighting and increasing decadence. The Roman peace was no longer enforced, the use and acceptance of the common coinage had declined, and communications no longer worked as well. Therefore, affiliation with the empire no longer offered the benefits of the past.

Former allies, who no longer saw any benefits in their association with Rome, willingly cooperated with invaders rather than face prolonged battles.

Similar patterns also can be seen in later eras. The British Empire grew mainly through its effective international business policy, which provided for efficient transportation, intensive trade, and an insistence on open markets.[1] More recently, the United States developed a world leadership position largely due to its championship of market-based business transactions in the Western world; the broad flow of ideas, goods, and services across national borders; and an encouragement of international communication and transportation. Some say that the period from 1945 to 1990 for Western countries, and since then, for the world, has been characterized by a **Pax Americana,** an American sponsored and enforced peace.

The importance of international business has not always persisted, however. For example, in 1896, the Empress Dowager Tz'u-hsi, in order to finance the renovation of the summer palace, impounded government funds that had been designated for Chinese shipping and its navy. As a result, China's participation in world trade almost came to a halt. In the subsequent decades, China operated in almost total isolation, without any transfer of knowledge from the outside, without major inflow of goods, and without the innovation and productivity increases that result from exposure to international business.

Withholding the benefits of international business has also long been a tool of national policy. The use of economic coercion by nations or groups of nations, for example, can be traced back to the time of the Greek city-states and the Peloponnesian War. In the Napoleonic Wars, combatants used naval blockades to achieve their goal of "bringing about commercial ruin and shortage of food by dislocating trade."[2] Similarly, during the Civil War period in the United States, the North consistently pursued a strategy of denying international business opportunities to the South in order to deprive it of needed export revenues.

The importance of international business linkages was highlighted during the 1930s. At that time, the **Smoot-Hawley Act** raised import duties to reduce the volume of goods coming into the United States. The act was passed in the hope that it would restore domestic employment. The result, however, was retaliation by most trading partners. The ensuing worldwide depression and the collapse of the world financial system were instrumental in bringing about the events that led to World War II.

World trade and investment have assumed a heretofore unknown importance to the global community. In past centuries, trade was conducted internationally but not at the level or with the impact on nations, firms, and individuals that it has recently achieved. In the past 30 years alone, the volume of international trade in goods and services has expanded from $200 billion to more than $7.5 trillion.[3] As Figure 1.1 shows, during almost all of that time, the growth in the value of trade has greatly exceeded the level of overall world output growth.

During the same time, foreign direct investment stock mushroomed to more than $6.6 trillion by 2001. The sales of foreign affiliates of **multinational corporations** are now twice as high as global exports.[4] As Table 1.1 shows, many of these corporations have their origins in developing economies as well. Nonetheless, foreign direct investment is highly selective. In 2001, global foreign direct investment (FDI) inflows reached $735 billion; while developed countries received $503 billion, or about 68 percent of those inflows, the 49 least developed countries received less than 1 percent.[5] Individuals and firms have come to recognize that they are competing not only domestically but in a global marketplace. As a result, the international market has taken on a new dynamic, characterized by major change.

FIGURE 1.1

Growth of World Output and Trade, 1992–2004

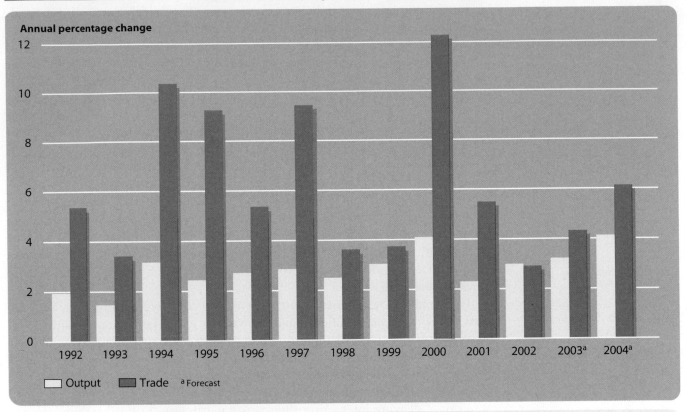

Annual percentage change

Legend: ☐ Output ■ Trade ᵃ Forecast

Sources: UN World Economic and Social Survey 2003, New York: United Nations, 2003. *World Economic Outlook*, Washington, DC: IMF, 2003, http://www.imf.org.

Global Links Today

International business has forged a network of **global links** around the world that binds us all—countries, institutions, and individuals—much closer than ever before. These links tie together trade, financial markets, technology, and living standards in an unprecedented way. A freeze in Brazil and its effect on coffee production are felt around the world. The sudden decline in the Mexican peso affected financial markets in the United States and reverberated throughout Poland, Hungary, and the Czech Republic. The economic turmoil in Asia influenced stock markets, investments, and trade flows in all corners of the earth.

These linkages have also become more intense on an individual level. Communication has built new international bridges, be it through music or the watching of international programs transmitted by CNN (http://www.cnn.com). New products have attained international appeal and encouraged similar activities around the world—we wear jeans; we dance the same dances; we watch the same movies; we eat hamburgers, pizzas, and sushi. Transportation links let individuals from different countries see and meet each other with unprecedented ease. Common cultural pressures result in similar social phenomena and behavior—for example, more dual-income families are emerging around the world, which leads to more frequent, but also more stressful, shopping.[6]

TABLE 1.1

The Top 25 Nonfinancial TNCs from Developing Economies, Ranked by Foreign Assets (millions of dollars and number of employees)

RANKING BY Foreign Assets	Corporation	Home economy	Industry	ASSETS		SALES		EMPLOYMENT	
				Foreign	Total	Foreign	Total	Foreign	Total
1	Hutchison Whampoa	Hong Kong, China	Diversified	41,881	56,610	2,840	7,311	27,165	49,570
2	Cemex	Mexico	Non-metallic mineral products	10,887	15,759	3,028	5,621	15,448	25,884
3	LG Electronics	Korea, Republic of	Electrical & electronic equip.	8,750	17,709	9,331	18,558	20,072	46,912
4	Petroleós de Venezuela	Venezuela	Petroleum expl./ref./distr.	8,017	57,089	49,780	53,234	5,458	46,920
5	Petronas	Malaysia	Petroleum expl./ref./distr.	7,690	36,594	11,790	19,305	3,808	23,450
6	New World Development	Hong Kong, China	Diversified	4,578	16,412	565	2,633	800	23,530
7	Samsung Corporation	Korea, Republic of	Diversified/trade	3,900	10,400	8,300	40,700	175	4,740
8	Samsung Electronics	Korea, Republic of	Electrical & electronic equip.	3,898	25,085	23,055	31,562	16,981	60,977
9	Neptune Orient Lines	Singapore	Transport and storage	3,812	4,360	4,498	4,673	6,840	8,734
10	Companhia Vale Do Rio Doce	Brazil	Mining & quarrying	3,660	10,269	758	4,904	6,285	17,634
11	Sappi	South Africa	Paper	3,239	4,768	3,601	4,718	9,399	19,276
12	COFCO	China	Food & beverages	2,867	4,543	4,767	12,517	350	26,000
13	Guangdong Investment	Hong Kong, China	Diversified	2,852	4,605	460	634	6,837	7,875
14	China National Chemicals, Imp. & Exp.	China	Chemicals	2,603	4,701	10,755	18,036	600	8,600
15	Hyundai Motor	Korea, Republic of	Motor vehicles	2,488	25,393	4,412	25,814	6,532	84,925
16	Keppel	Singapore	Diversified	2,293	22,180	338	3,657	5,910	16,389
17	First Pacific	Hong Kong, China	Electrical & electronic equip.	2,116	2,322	652	809	8,511	8,560
18	Citic Pacific	Hong Kong, China	Construction	2,076	4,022	981	2,058	7,118	11,354
19	Grupo Carso	Mexico	Diversified	2,043	8,827	4,000	9,315	19,542	89,954
20	South African Breweries	South Africa	Food & beverages	1,966	4,384	1,454	5,424	15,763	48,079
21	Orient Overseas International	Hong Kong, China	Transport and storage	1,819	2,155	2,382	2,395	3,792	4,414
22	Singtel	Singapore	Telecommunications	1,790	8,143	N/A	2,845	2,500	12,640
23	Posco	Korea, Republic of	Metal and metal products	1,777	15,901	2,311	10,873	2,741	26,261
24	San Miguel	Philippines	Food & beverages	1,738	3,061	300	1,861	3,091	14,864
25	Jardine Matheson	Hong Kong, China	Diversified	1,641	10,339	7,148	10,354	50,000	130,000

Source: UNCTAD, World Investment Report 2002: Transnational Corporations and Export Competitiveness, table IV.10.

Large firms are expanding around the globe. They may become so well entrenched that they are thought of as local firms.

International business has also brought a global reorientation in production strategies. Only a few decades ago, for example, it would have been thought impossible to produce parts for a car in more than one country, assemble it in another, and sell it in yet other countries around the world. Today, such global strategies, coupled with production and distribution sharing, are common. Consumers, union leaders, policymakers, and sometimes even the firms themselves are finding it increasingly difficult to define where a particular product was made, since subcomponents may come from many different nations. As Focus on Politics explains, the lack of such information may make the tools of the international business activist—such as boycotts—much more blunt than ever before. Firms are also linked to each other through global supply agreements and joint undertakings in research and development. Figure 1.2 gives an example of how such links result in a final consumer product.

In addition to the production of goods, service firms are increasingly part of the international scene. Consulting firms, insurance companies, software firms, and universities are participating to a growing degree in the international marketplace. Firms and governments are recognizing production's worldwide effects on the environment common to all. For example, high sulfur emissions in one area may cause acid rain in another. Pollution in one country may result in water contamination in another. Service activities can have cross-national impacts as well. For example, weaknesses in

Focus On ⬇

POLITICS

Name That Country!

Using economic levers to reward friends and punish foes is nothing new in American foreign politics. But with the U.S.- and Allied Forces-led Operation Iraqi Freedom, consumers' purchasing decisions are becoming a form of political protest. A poll directed by Supermarket Guru, a leading analyzer of consumer and marketing trends, notes that 71 percent of Americans agree that political disagreements should carry over to the trade arena, while 73 percent believe U.S. consumers should boycott French- and German-made goods.

American consumers exercising "purchasing protests" can easily find Californian, Australian, Spanish, Portuguese, and Chilean products as substitutes for French champagne. Danish and British cheeses are fine surrogates for French varieties, and perceived "American" and "Japanese" luxury cars may well be on par with "German" Mercedes-Benz and BMW.

But before U.S. customers become gung-ho about anti-French and German purchases, maybe a little research would be useful. If they're to bypass the bottled water of Perrier, Vittel, and Evian, maybe a closer look at household tap water would be interesting: It may well be purified by Culligan, a 65-year-old French water-treatment firm. While RCA stands for Radio Corporation of America, it's actually owned by the France-based Thales Group, 33 percent of which is owned by the French government. Consumers won't be tempted to buy Renault, Citroen, or

Peugeot cars since those are not exported to the United States anymore. But what about those purchases of "Japanese" Nissans? Renault holds 44.4 percent of Nissan's equity. Once they buy those Nissans, what about the tires? Of course, Michelins will be avoided, and B.F. Goodrich and Uniroyal "patriotic purchases" will be made. Wait a minute. Haven't both those firms been acquired by French companies? Let's assume they'll be tired of driving and opt to fly. Air France may surely be avoided, but how often will the distinction between an Airbus A300 and a Boeing 737 be made? After all, the French have a major stake in EADS, parent firm of Airbus.

Not only will consumers have difficulty finding the "right" goods to boycott, American-owned firms also run the risk of being wrongly identified. Take Grey Poupon, for example. Its name and advertisement models may have a French flair, but the mustard has been made in the United States since 1946 by Kraft Foods, a U.S. firm. What about the "All-American" Dannon versus Yoplait, "France's *c'est si bon*" yogurt? Some consumers may be shocked to learn that Yoplait is made by American food giant General Mills, while Dannon is made by a subsidiary of Groupe Danone of France. The maker of French's mustard, U.S.-owned Reckitt Benckiser, took no chances and issued a press release: "For the record, French's would like to say there's nothing more American than French's mustard."

Source: Caroline Mayer, "Identity Crisis in Aisle 7," *The Washington Post,* April 2, 2003, E1; "Consumers Support a Boycott of French-Made Products," *PR Newswire Association,* March 17, 2003.

FIGURE 1.2

THE GLOBAL COMPONENTS OF A BIG MAC IN UKRAINE

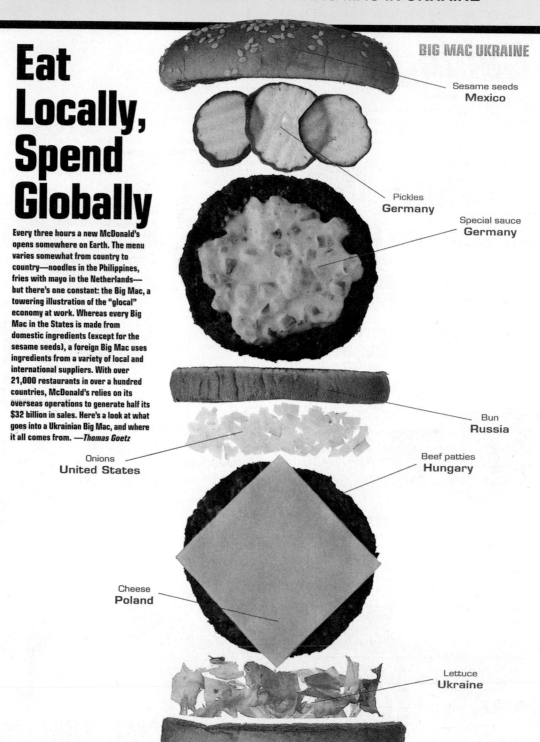

Eat Locally, Spend Globally

Every three hours a new McDonald's opens somewhere on Earth. The menu varies somewhat from country to country—noodles in the Philippines, fries with mayo in the Netherlands—but there's one constant: the Big Mac, a towering illustration of the "glocal" economy at work. Whereas every Big Mac in the States is made from domestic ingredients (except for the sesame seeds), a foreign Big Mac uses ingredients from a variety of local and international suppliers. With over 21,000 restaurants in over a hundred countries, McDonald's relies on its overseas operations to generate half its $32 billion in sales. Here's a look at what goes into a Ukrainian Big Mac, and where it all comes from. —*Thomas Goetz*

BIG MAC UKRAINE

Sesame seeds
Mexico

Pickles
Germany

Special sauce
Germany

Bun
Russia

Onions
United States

Beef patties
Hungary

Cheese
Poland

Lettuce
Ukraine

Source: Used with permission from McDonald's Corporation.

International Trade as a Percentage of Gross Domestic Product

MAP

Total Gross Domestic Product by Region
(in millions of U.S. $)

United States

$10,445,600*

Western Europe

$8,137,318

Japan

$4,841,584

East Asia and Pacific

$2,059,100

Latin America and Caribbean

$2,000,500

China and India

$1,536,938

Eastern Europe and Central Asia

$942,100

Canada

$687,882

Middle East and North Africa

$659,700

South Asia

$596,800

Sub-Saharan Africa

$322,700

*http://www.bea.doc.gov (accessed March 3, 2003).
SOURCE: Based on *The Little Data Book 2002*, The World Bank.

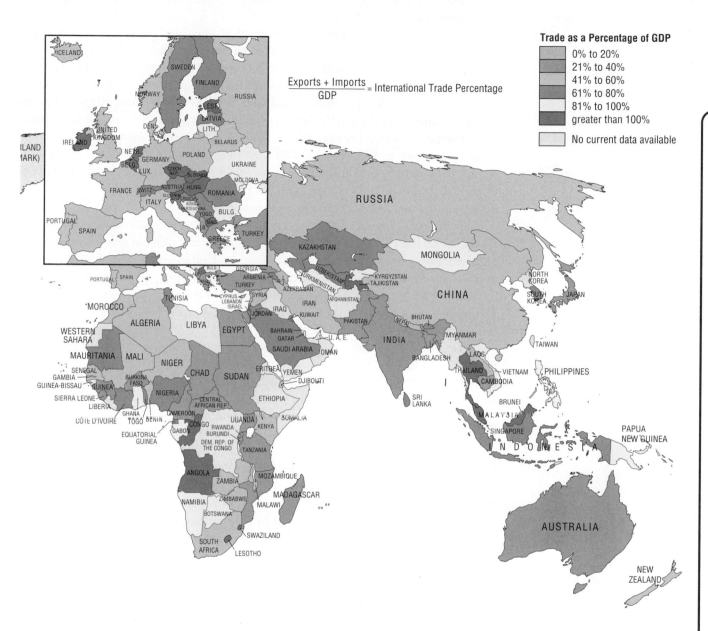

$$\frac{\text{Exports} + \text{Imports}}{\text{GDP}} = \text{International Trade Percentage}$$

Trade as a Percentage of GDP

- 0% to 20%
- 21% to 40%
- 41% to 60%
- 61% to 80%
- 81% to 100%
- greater than 100%
- No current data available

some currencies, due to problems in a country's banking sector, can quickly spill over and affect the currency values of other nations. The deregulation of some service industries, such as air transport or telephony can thoroughly affect the structure of these industries around the world.

All these changes have affected the international financial position of countries and the ownership of economic activities. For example, the United States, after having been a net creditor to the world for many decades, has been a world debtor since 1985. This means that the United States owes more to foreign institutions and individuals than to U.S. entities. The shifts in financial flows have had major effects on international direct investment into plants as well. U.S. direct investment abroad in 2002 had a market value of more than $2.3 trillion; foreign direct investment in the United States had grown to $2.8 trillion.[7] More than 1.1 million of the workers in the U.S. chemical, computer, and transportation industries toil for foreign owners.[8] The opening of plants abroad increasingly takes the place of trade. All of these developments make us more and more dependent on one another.

This interdependence, however, is not stable. On an ongoing basis, realignments take place on both micro and macro levels that make past orientations at least partially obsolete. For example, for its first 200 years, the United States looked to Europe for markets and sources of supply. Despite the maintenance of this orientation by many individuals, firms, and policymakers, the reality of trade relationships has changed. U.S. two-way merchandise trade across the Pacific totalled $650 billion in 2002, $225 billion more than trade across the Atlantic.[9]

At the same time, entirely new areas for international business activities have opened up. The East-West juxtaposition had for more than 40 years effectively separated the "Western" economies from the centrally planned ones. The lifting of the Iron Curtain presents a new array of trading and investment partners.

Concurrently, an increasing regionalization is taking place around the world, resulting in the split up of countries in some areas of the world and the development of country and trading blocs in others. Over time, firms may find that the free flow of goods, services, and capital encounters new impediments as regions become more inward looking.

Not only is the environment changing, but the pace of change is accelerating. Atari's Pong was first introduced in the early 1980s; today, action games and movies are made with computerized humans. The first office computers emerged in the mid 1980s; today, home computers have become commonplace. E-mail was introduced to a mass market only in the 1990s; today, many college students hardly ever send personal notes using a stamp and an envelope.[10]

These changes and the speed with which they come about significantly affect countries, corporations, and individuals. For example, the relative participation of countries in world trade is shifting. Over the past decades, in a world of rapidly growing trade, the market share of western Europe in trade has been declining. For the United States, the export share has declined while the import share has increased. Concurrent with these shifts, the global market shares of Japan, Southeast Asian countries, and China have increased.

The **composition of trade** has also been changing. For example, from the 1960s to the 1990s, the trade role of primary commodities has declined precipitously while the importance of manufactured goods has increased. This has meant that those countries and workers who had specialized in commodities such as *caoutchouc* (rubber plantations) or mining were likely to fall behind those who had embarked on strengthening their manufacturing sector. With sharply declining world market prices for their commodities and rising prices for manufactured goods, their producers were increasingly unable to catch up.

More recently, there has been a shift of manufacturing to new nations. In the mid 1800s, manufacturing accounted for about 17 percent of employment in the United States. This proportion grew to almost 30 percent in the 1960s, only to decline at a rising rate. At the beginning of the new millennium, U.S. manufacturing employment, at 14.8 percent, had decreased below the levels of when it was first officially measured. In the past 30 years, German manufacturing employment dropped by more than 13 percentage points, while in Japan the decrease was 6.5 percent. All these shifts in employment reflect a transfer of manufacturing away from the industrialized nations toward the emerging economies. During the times of decline in the United States, Germany, and Japan, the proportion of manufacturing of GNP has more than doubled in Malaysia, Thailand, and Indonesia.[11]

Increasingly, substantial shifts are also occurring in the area of services trade. Activities that were confined to specific locales have become mobile. The global transmission of radiology charts to physicians in India may be a portent of new shifts in trade composition in the future.

The Current U.S. International Trade Position

From a global perspective, the United States has gained in prominence as a market for the world but has lost some of its importance as a supplier to the world. In spite of the decline in the global market share of U.S. exports, the international activities of the United States have not been reduced. On the contrary, exports have grown rapidly and successfully. However, many new participants have entered the international market. In Europe, firms in countries with war-torn economies following World War II have reestablished themselves. In Asia, new competitors have aggressively obtained a share of the growing world trade. U.S. relative export growth was not able to keep pace with the total growth of world exports.

U.S. exports as a share of the GDP have grown substantially in recent years. However, this increase pales when compared with the international trade performance of other nations. For example, Japan, which so often is maligned as the export problem child in the international trade arena, exports less than 10 percent of its GDP.[12] Table 1.2 shows

TABLE 1.2

Exports and Imports of Goods and Services per Capita for Selected Countries

Country	Exports per Capita	Imports per Capita
Australia	$4,296	$4,525
Brazil	379	428
China	222	199
Japan	4,165	3,622
Kenya	91	125
United Kingdom	4,767	5,500
United States	3,472	4,962

Sources: World Factbook, http://www.cia.gov, accessed August 8, 2003, and World Bank 2002 World Development Indicators, Washington, DC, 2002.

the degree to which the United States comparatively "underexports and overimports" on a per capita basis.

THE IMPACT OF INTERNATIONAL BUSINESS ON THE UNITED STATES

Why should we worry about this misaligned participation in trade? Why not simply concentrate on the large domestic market and get on with it? Why should it bother us that the largest portion of U.S. exports is attributed to only 2,500 companies? Why should it concern us that the U.S. Census Bureau estimates that less than 2 percent of all U.S. firms export?[13] Why should it be of concern that many U.S. e-tailers don't accept orders from outside their home market and 55 percent of U.S. web merchants will not even ship to Canada?[14]

U.S. international business outflows are important on the **macroeconomic level** in terms of balancing the trade account. Lack of U.S. export growth has resulted in long-term trade deficits. In 1983, imports of products into the United States exceeded exports by more than $70 billion. While in the ensuing years exports increased at a rapid rate, import growth also continued. As a result, in 2002, the U.S. trade deficit in goods and services had risen to $418 billion.[15] Ongoing annual trade deficits in this range are unsupportable in the long run. Via the capital account, such deficits add to the U.S. international debt, which must be serviced and eventually repaid. Exporting is not only good for the international trade picture but also a key factor in increasing employment. It has been estimated that $1 billion of exports supports the creation, on average, of 11,500 jobs.[16] Imports, in turn, bring a wider variety of products and services into a country. They exert competitive pressure for domestic firms to improve. Imports, therefore, expand the choices of consumers and improve their standard of living.

On the **microeconomic level,** participation in international business can help firms achieve economies of scale that cannot be achieved in domestic markets. Addressing a global market greatly adds to the number of potential customers. Increasing production lets firms ride the learning curve more quickly and therefore makes goods available more cheaply at home. Finally, and perhaps most important, international business permits firms to hone their competitive skills abroad by meeting the challenge of foreign products. By going abroad, firms can learn from their foreign competitors, challenge them on their ground, and translate the absorbed knowledge into productivity improvements back home. Firms that operate only in the domestic market are at risk of being surprised by the onslaught on foreign competition and thus seeing their domestic market share threatened. Research has shown that U.S. multinationals of all sizes and in all industries outperformed their strictly domestic counterparts—growing more than twice as fast in sales and earning significantly higher returns on equity and assets.[17] Workers also benefit. As Figure 1.3 shows, exporting firms of all sizes pay significantly higher wages than nonexporters.[18]

The United States as a nation and as individuals must therefore seek more involvement in the global market. The degree to which Americans can successfully do business internationally will be indicative of their competitiveness and so help to determine their future standard of living.

Most U.S. firms are affected directly or indirectly by economic and political developments in the international marketplace. Firms that refuse to participate actively are relegated to reacting to the global economy. Consider how the industrial landscape in the United States has been restructured in the past decade as a result of international business.

FIGURE 1.3

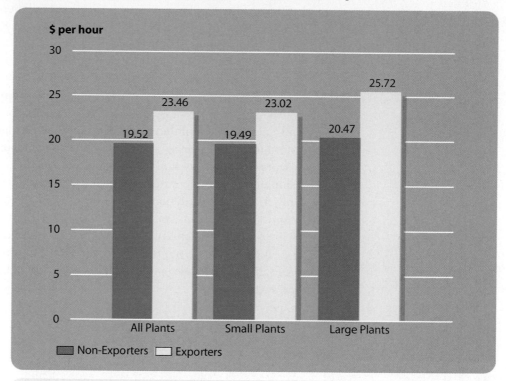

Average Plant Salary and Wages (per worker, dollars per hour)

Source: Business America, Vol. 117, No. 9, September 1996, p. 9.

Many industries have experienced the need for international adjustments. U.S. farmers, because of high prices, exchange-rate inequities, increased international competition, trade-restricting government actions, and unfair foreign trade practices, have lost world market share. U.S. firms in technologically advanced industries, such as semiconductor producers, saw the prices of their products and their sales volumes drop precipitously because of global competition. As a result of competition, many industries have adjusted, but with great pain. Examples abound in the steel, automotive, and textile sectors of the U.S. economy.

Still other U.S. industries never fully recognized what had happened and, therefore, in spite of attempts to adjust, have ceased to exist. VCRs are no longer produced domestically. Only a small percentage of motorcycles are manufactured in the United States. The shoe industry is in its death throes.

These developments demonstrate that it has become virtually impossible to disregard the powerful impact that international business has on all of us. Temporary isolation may be possible and delay tactics may work for a while, but the old adage applies: You can run, but you cannot hide. Participation in the world market has become truly imperative.

Global activities offer many additional opportunities to business firms. Market saturation can be delayed by lengthening or rejuvenating the life of products in other countries. Sourcing policies that once were inflexible have become variable because plants can be shifted from one country to another and suppliers can be found on every continent. Cooperative agreements can be formed that enable each party to bring its major strength to the table and emerge with better goods, services, and ideas than it could on its own. Consumers all over the world can select from among a greater variety of products at lower prices, which enables them to improve their choices and lifestyles. As Focus on Ethics shows, it is also easy to stir up controversy through international business. Consumers are paying much greater attention to products and they increasingly have the resources to check whether the firms producing them are exploiting their workers or harming the environment.

All of these opportunities need careful exploration if they are to be realized. What is needed is an awareness of global developments, an understanding of their meaning, and a development of the capability to adjust to change. Judging by the global linkages found in today's market and the rapid changes taking place, a background in international business is highly desirable for business students seeking employment. **Globalization** is the watchword that increasingly looms large in all walks of life, not only in our entertainment, our fashions, and the products we buy, but also in our morals, belief systems, and our very sense of being a human species. For the first time in history, the availability of international products and services has reached beyond the elite to become the reasonable expectation of the masses. The global market is inevitable, inescapable, and here. This book will help you understand it, cope with it, and succeed in it.[19]

The Structure of the Book

This book is intended to enable you to become a better, more successful participant in the global businessplace. It is written for both those who want to obtain more information about what is going on in international markets in order to be well-rounded and better educated and for those who want to translate their knowledge into successful business transactions. The text melds theory and practice to balance conceptual understanding and knowledge of day-to-day realities. The book, therefore, addresses the international concerns of both beginning internationalists and multinational corporations.

The beginning international manager will need to know the answers to basic, yet important, questions: How can I find out whether demand for my product exists abroad? What must I do to get ready to market internationally? These issues are also relevant for managers in multinational corporations, but the questions they consider are often much more sophisticated. Of course, the resources available to address them are also much greater.

Throughout the book, public policy concerns are included in discussions of business activities. In this way, you are exposed to both macro and micro issues. Part 1 of the book introduces the importance of international business and its global linkages. Part 2 presents the environment of international business, addressing culture, policies, politics, and law. Part 3 provides coverage of the theory of international trade and investment and presents balance of payments issues. In Part 4 we discuss markets, and highlight financial systems, economic integration, and emerging market concerns.

Focus On ⬇

Students Against Sweatshops

In November 1997, students at Georgetown, Harvard, Duke, and Holy Cross universities began to look at the labels of logo merchandise in their campus bookstores to get an idea of where the clothing was made. Their goal was to find ways to improve the working conditions of peole who made their caps and shirts.

In April 1998, UNITE, a union of textile workers, sponsored two workers from a Korean-owned apparel factory in the Dominican Republic for a tour of U.S. college campuses. Kenia Rodriguez and Roselio Reyes, both college-age, described the terrible conditions at the BJ&B factory where goods featuring the logos of major American colleges like Georgetown, Brown, Duke, Harvard, and Princeton were made.

They explained that workers had to cope with rancid drinking water, locked bathrooms, sweltering conditions, and intimidation. Men and women had unequal pay scales and workers were fired when they tried to start a union. None of the workers, who all worked 75 hours a week, earned more than one third of what the Dominican government considers sufficient for "the most basic life necessities."

In response, students at Georgetown and other universities began pressuring their administrations to adopt basic labor standards for any factories where school apparel would be made. Students wanted licensees to agree to pay workers enough to live on and disclose the locations of all of their factories. To help schools monitor factory conditions for themselves, students formed an independent organization called the Workers Rights Consortium (WRC).

Over the next two years, students used tactics such as petitions, faculty and student government resolutions, and rallies to persuade their administrations to sign on to the WRC. Some schools, such as Duke and the University of Wisconsin, held sit-ins when other tactics were not successful. At Georgetown, students occupied the office of the university's president for more than 100 hours before the administration agreed to sign on to the WRC and endorse a code of conduct that students felt was stringent enough.

Student groups across the United States continued to form and agitate for change on their campuses. As of January 21, 2003, 112 colleges and universities in the United States had joined. WRC income in 2002–2003 was more than one million dollars: 25 percent from affiliate schools and 75 percent from grants and other nonprofit donors. The organization had eight full-time employees who conduct 10–12 investigations per year in places such as Mexico, Indonesia, the Dominican Republic, and New York City. The WRC also maintains a searchable database of factory locations for all its member schools on its web site, so students can easily find out where their school's apparel is made.

In March 2003, the WRC announced a major victory at the factory where Kenia and Roselio had worked. The FEDOTRAZONAS union and the management of the BJ&B factory signed the first collective bargaining agreement in the factory's 17-year history, in part because of the WRC's efforts. The WRC continues to work to improve the conditions of factory workers who make licensed college apparel.

Sources: http://www.workersrights.org, accessed April 26, 2003; http://www.georgetown.edu/organizations/solidarity/info.html, accessed April 26, 2003; Interview with Andrew Milmore, former Solidarity Committee president, April 22, 2003 and April 26, 2003.

Part 5 presents the strategy considerations surrounding international business. The research activities required to properly prepare for international business, and the options for market entry and expansion are discussed. Strategic planning and the organizational and control issues surrounding global market penetration are the subsequent focus. Part 6 targets the operational issues surrounding international business, using an implementation-oriented perspective. Part 7 concludes the book with a focus on the future of the field and the reader's career.

We hope that upon finishing the book, you will not only have completed another academic subject but also be well versed in the theoretical, policy, and strategic aspects of international business and therefore will be able to contribute to improved international competitiveness and a better global standard of living.

Summary

International business has been conducted ever since national borders were formed and has played a major role in shaping world history. Growing in importance over the past three decades, it has shaped an environment that, due to economic linkages, today presents us with a global marketplace.

In the past three decades, world trade has expanded from $200 billion to more than $7.5 trillion, while international direct investment has grown to $6.6 trillion. The growth of both has been far more rapid than the growth of most domestic economies. As a result, nations are much more affected by international business than in the past. Global links have made possible investment strategies and business alternatives that offer tremendous opportunities. Yet these changes and the speed of change also can represent threats to nations, firms, and individuals.

Over the past 30 years, the dominance of the U.S. international trade position has gradually eroded. New participants in international business compete fiercely for world market share. Individuals, corporations, and policymakers around the globe have awakened to the fact that international business is a major imperative and offers opportunities for future growth and prosperity. International business provides access to new customers, affords economies of scale, and permits the honing of competitive skills. Performing well in global markets is the key to improved standards of living, higher profits, and better wages. Knowledge about international business is therefore important to everyone, whether it is used to compete with foreign firms or simply to understand the world around us.

Questions for Discussion

1. Will future expansion of international business be similar to that in the past?
2. Does increased international business mean increased risk?
3. Is it beneficial for nations to become dependent on one another?
4. Discuss the reasons for the increase in Chinese world trade market share.
5. With wages in some countries at one-tenth of U.S. wages, how can America compete?
6. Compare and contrast domestic and international business.
7. Why do more firms in other countries enter international markets than do firms in the United States?

Internet Exercise

1. Using World Trade Organization data (shown on the International Trade page of its web site, (http://www.wto.org), determine the following information: (a) the fastest growing traders; (b) the top ten exporters and importers in world merchandise trade; and (c) the top ten exporters or importers of commercial services.

Take a Stand

The term "globalization" describes the increased mobility of goods, services, labor, technology, and capital throughout the world. Although globalization is not a new development, its pace has increased with the advent of new technologies that make it easier for people to travel, communicate, and do business internationally.

For Discussion

Recent antiglobalization protests have revealed significant differences between businesses and the public in terms of how they view globalization and its effects. Some point out that globalization brings modern medicines, western communications technology, and better education and jobs for women. Others feel that globalization leads to cultural homogenization and are concerned about its effects on human rights and the environment. Can globalization be doing more harm than good?

Appendix I

Geographic Perspectives on International Business

The dramatic changes in the world of business have made geography indispensable for the study of international business. Without significant attention to the study of geography, critical ideas and information about the world in which business occurs will be missing.

Just as the study of business has changed significantly in recent decades, so has the study of geography. Once considered by many to be simply a descriptive inventory that filled in blank spots on maps, geography has emerged as an analytic approach that uses scientific methods to answer important questions.

Geography focuses on answering "Where?" questions. Where are things located? What is their distribution across the surface of the earth? An old aphorism holds, "If you can map it, it's geography." That statement is true, because one uses maps to gather, store, analyze, and present information that answers "Where?" questions. But identifying where things are located is only the first phase of geographic inquiry. Once locations have been determined, "Why?" and "How?" questions can be asked. Why are things located where they are? How do different things relate to one another at a specific place? How do different places relate to each other? How have geographic patterns and relationships changed over time? These are the questions that take geography beyond mere description and make it a powerful approach for analyzing and explaining geographical aspects of a wide range of different kinds of problems faced by those engaged in international business.

Geography answers questions related to the location of different kinds of economic activity and the transactions that flow across national boundaries. It provides insights into the natural and human factors that influence patterns of production and consumption in different parts of the world. It explains why patterns of trade and exchange evolve over time. And because a geographic perspective emphasizes the analysis of processes that result in different geographic patterns, it provides a means for assessing how patterns might change in the future.

Geography has a rich tradition. Classical Greeks, medieval Arabs, enlightened European explorers, and twentieth-century scholars in the United States and elsewhere have organized geographic knowledge in many different ways. In recent decades, however, geography has become more familiar and more relevant to many people because emphasis has been placed on five fundamental themes as ways to structure geographic questions and to provide answers for those questions. Those themes are (1) location, (2) place, (3) interaction, (4) movement, and (5) region. The five themes are neither exclusive nor exhaustive. They complement other disciplinary approaches for organizing information, some of which are better suited to addressing specific kinds of questions. Other questions require insights related to two or more of the themes. Experience has shown, however, that the five themes provide a powerful means for introducing students to the geographic perspective. As a result, they provide the structure for this discussion.

Location

For decades, people engaged in real estate development have said that the value of a place is a product of three factors: location, location, and location. This statement also highlights the importance of location for international business. Learning the location and characteristics of other places has always been important to those interested in conducting business outside their local areas. The drive to learn about other kinds of places, and especially their resources and potential as markets, has stimulated geographic exploration throughout history. Explorations of the Mediterranean by the Phoenicians; Marco Polo's journey to China; and voyages undertaken by Christopher Columbus, Vasco de Gama, Henry Hudson, and James Cook not only improved general knowledge of the world but also expanded business opportunities.

Assessing the role of location requires more than simply determining specific locations where certain activities take place. Latitude and longitude often are used to fix the exact location of features on the Earth's surface, but to simply describe a place's coordinates provides relatively little information about that place. Of much greater significance is its location relative to other features. The city of Singapore, for example, is between 1 and 2 degrees North latitude and is just west of 104 degrees East longitude. Its

Note: This appendix was contributed by Thomas J. Baerwald. Dr. Baerwald is senior science advisor at the National Science Foundation in Arlington, Virginia. He is co-author of *Prentice Hall World Geography*—a best-selling geography textbook.

most pertinent locational characteristics, however, include its being at the southern tip of the Malay Peninsula near the eastern end of the Strait of Malacca, a critical shipping route connecting the Indian Ocean with the South China Sea. For nearly 150 years, this location made Singapore an important center for trade in the British Empire. After attaining independence in 1965, Singapore's leaders diversified its economy and complemented trade in its bustling port with numerous manufacturing plants that export products to nations around the world.

An understanding of how location influences business therefore is critical for the international business executive. Without clear knowledge of an enterprise's location relative to its suppliers, to its market, and to its competitors, an executive operates like the captain of a fog-bound vessel that has lost all navigational instruments and is heading for dangerous shoals.

Place

In addition to its location, each place has a diverse set of characteristics. Although many of those characteristics are present in other places, the ensemble makes each place unique. The characteristics of places—both natural and human—profoundly influence the ways that business executives in different places participate in international economic transactions.

Natural Features

Many of the characteristics of a place relate to its natural attributes. **Geologic characteristics** can be especially important, as the presence of critical minerals or energy resources may make a place a world-renowned supplier of valuable products. Gold and diamonds help make South Africa's economy the most prosperous on that continent. Rich deposits of iron ore in southern parts of the Amazon Basin have made Brazil the world's leading exporter of that commodity, while Chile remains a preeminent exporter of copper. Coal deposits provided the foundation for massive industrial development in the eastern United States, the Rhine River Basin of Europe, in western Russia, and in northeastern China. Because of abundant pools of petroleum beneath desert sands, standards of living in Saudi Arabia and nearby nations have risen rapidly to be among the highest in the world.

The geology of place also shapes its **terrain.** People traditionally have clustered in lower, flatter areas, because valleys and plains have permitted the agricultural development necessary to feed the local population and to generate surpluses that can be traded. Hilly and mountainous areas may support some people, but their population den-

sities invariably are lower. Terrain also plays a critical role in focusing and inhibiting the movement of people and goods. Business leaders throughout the centuries have capitalized on this fact. Just as feudal masters sought control of mountain passes in order to collect tolls and other duties from traders who traversed an area, modern executives maintain stores and offer services near bridges and at other points where terrain focuses travel.

The terrain of a place is related to its **hydrology.** Rivers, lakes, and other bodies of water influence the kinds of economic activities that occur in a place. In general, abundant supplies of water boost economic development, because water is necessary for the sustenance of people and for both agricultural and industrial production. Locations like Los Angeles and Saudi Arabia have prospered despite having little local water, because other features offer advantages that more than exceed the additional costs incurred in delivering water supplies from elsewhere. While sufficient water must be available to meet local needs, overabundance of water may pose serious problems, such as in Bangladesh, where development has been inhibited by frequent flooding. The character of a place's water bodies also is important. Smooth-flowing streams and placid lakes can stimulate transportation within a place and connect it more easily with other places, while waterfalls and rapids can prevent navigation on streams. The rapid drop in elevation of such streams may boost their potential for hydroelectric power generation, however, thereby stimulating development of industries requiring considerable amounts of electricity. Large plants producing aluminum, for example, are found in the Tennessee and Columbia river valleys of the United States and in Quebec and British Columbia in Canada. These plants refine materials that originally were extracted elsewhere, especially bauxite and alumina from Caribbean nations like Jamaica and the Dominican Republic. Although the transport costs incurred in delivery of these materials to the plants is high, those costs are more than offset by the presence of abundant and inexpensive electricity.

Climate is another natural feature that has profound impact on economic activity within a place. Many activities are directly affected by climate. Locales blessed with pleasant climates, such as the Côte d'Azur of France, the Crimean Peninsula of Ukraine, Florida, and the "Gold Coast" of northeastern Australia, have become popular recreational havens, attracting tourists whose spending fuels the local economy. Agricultural production also is influenced by climate. The average daily and evening temperatures, the amount and timing of precipitation, the timing of frosts and freezing weather, and the variability of weather from one year to the next all influence the kinds of crops grown in an area. Plants producing bananas and sugar cane flourish in moist tropical areas, while cooler climates are more conducive for crops such as wheat and potatoes. Climate influences other industries, as well. The aircraft manufacturing industry in the United States developed largely in warmer, drier areas where conditions for test and delivery flights were most beneficial throughout the year. In a similar way, major rocket-launching facilities have been placed in locations where climatic conditions and trajectories are most favorable. As a result, the primary launch site of the European Space Agency is not in Europe at all but rather in the South American territory of French Guiana. Climate also affects the length of the work day and the length of economic seasons. For example, in some regions of the world, the construction industry can build only during a few months of the year because permafrost makes construction prohibitively expensive the rest of the year.

Variations in **soils** have a profound impact on agricultural production. The world's great grain-exporting regions, including the central United States, the Prairie Provinces of Canada, the "Fertile Triangle" stretching from central Ukraine through southern Russia into northern Kazakhstan, and the Pampas of northern Argentina, all have been blessed with mineral-rich soils made even more fertile by humus from natural grasslands that once dominated the landscape. Soils are less fertile in much of the Amazon Basin of Brazil and in central Africa, where heavy rains leave few nutrients in upper layers of the soil. As a result, few commercial crops are grown in those areas.

The **interplay between climate and soils** is especially evident in the production of wines. Hundreds of varieties of grapes have been bred to take advantage of the different physical characteristics of various places. The wines fermented from these grapes are shipped around the world to consumers, who differentiate among various wines based not only on the grapes but also on the places where they were grown and the conditions during which they matured.

Human Features

The physical features of a place provide natural resources and influence the types of economic activities in which people engage, but its human characteristics also are critical. The **population** of a place is important because farm production may require intensive labor to be successful, as is true in rice-growing areas of eastern Asia. The skills and qualifications of the population also play a role in determining how a place fits into global economic affairs. Although blessed with few mineral resources and a terrain and climate that limit agricultural production, the Swiss

have emphasized high levels of education and training in order to maintain a labor force that manufactures sophisticated products for export around the world. In recent decades, Japan and smaller nations such as South Korea and Taiwan have increased the productivity of their workers to become major industrial exporters.

As people live in a place, they modify it, creating a **built environment** that can be as or more important than the natural environment in economic terms. The most pronounced areas of human activity and their associated structures are in cities. In nations around the world, cities have grown dramatically during the twentieth century. Much of the growth of cities has resulted from the migration of people from rural areas. This influx of new residents broadens the labor pool and creates vast new demand for goods and services. As urban populations have grown, residences and other facilities have replaced rural land uses. Executives seeking to conduct business in foreign cities need to be aware that the geographic patterns found in their home cities are not evident in many other nations. For example, in the United States, wealthier residents generally have moved outward and as they established their residences, stores and services followed. Residential patterns in the major cities of Latin America and other developing nations tend to be reversed, with the wealthy remaining close to the city center while poorer residents are consigned to the outskirts of town. A store location strategy that is successful in the United States therefore may fail miserably if transferred directly to another nation without knowledge of the different geographic patterns of that nation's cities.

Interaction

The international business professional seeking to take advantage of opportunities present in different places learns not to view each place separately. How a place functions depends not only on the presence and form of certain characteristics but also on interactions among those characteristics. Fortuitous combinations of features can spur a region's economic development. The presence of high-grade supplies of iron ore, coal, and limestone powered the growth of Germany's Ruhr Valley as one of Europe's foremost steel-producing regions, just as the proximity of the fertile Pampas and the deep channel of the Rio de la Plata combine to make Buenos Aires the leading economic center in southern South America.

Interactions among different features change over time within places, and as they do, so does that place's character and its economic activities. Human activities can have profound impacts on natural features. The courses of rivers and streams are changed, as dams are erected and meanders are straightened. Soil fertility can be improved through fertilization. Vegetation is changed, with naturally growing plants replaced by crops and other varieties that require careful management.

Many human modifications have been successful. For centuries, the Dutch have constructed dikes and drainage systems, slowly creating polders—land that once was covered by the North Sea but that now is used for agricultural production. But other human activities have had disastrous impacts on natural features. A large area in Ukraine and Belarus was rendered uninhabitable by radioactive materials leaked from the Chernobyl reactor in 1986. In countless other places around the globe, improper disposal of wastes has seriously harmed land and water resources. In some places, damage can be repaired, as has happened in rivers and lakes of the United States following the passage of measures to curb water pollution in the past four decades, but in other locales, restoration may be impossible.

Growing concerns about environmental quality have led many people in more economically advanced nations to call for changes in economic systems that harm the natural environment. Concerted efforts are under way, for example, to halt destruction of forests in the Amazon Basin, thereby preserving the vast array of different plant and animal species in the region and saving vegetation that can help moderate the world's climate. Cooperative ventures have been established to promote selective harvesting of nuts, hardwoods, and other products taken from natural forests. Furthermore, an increasing number of restaurants and grocers are refusing to purchase beef raised on pastures that are established by clearing forests.

Like so many other geographical relationships, the nature of human-environmental interaction changes over time. With technological advances, people have been able to modify and adapt to natural features in increasingly sophisticated ways. The development of air conditioning has permitted people to function more effectively in torrid tropical environments, thereby enabling the populations of cities such as Houston, Rio de Janeiro, and Jakarta to multiply many times over in recent decades. Owners of winter resorts now can generate snow artificially to ensure favorable conditions for skiers. Advanced irrigation systems now permit crops to be grown in places such as the southwestern United States, northern Africa, and Israel. The use of new technologies may cause serious problems over the long run, however. Extensive irrigation in large parts of the U.S. Great Plains has seriously depleted groundwater supplies. In central Asia, the diversion of river water to irrigate cotton fields in Kazakhstan and Uzbekistan has reduced the size of the Aral Sea by more

than one-half since 1960. In future years, business leaders may need to factor into their decisions additional costs associated with the restoration of environmental quality after they have finished using a place's resources.

Movement

Whereas the theme of interaction encourages consideration of different characteristics within a place, movement provides a structure for considering how different places relate to each other. International business exists because movement permits the transportation of people and goods and communication of information and ideas among different places. No matter how much people in one place want something found elsewhere, they cannot have it unless transportation systems permit the good to be brought to them or allow them to move to the location of the good.

The location and character of transportation and communication systems long have had powerful influences on the economic standing of places. Especially significant have been places on which transportation routes have focused. Many ports have become prosperous cities because they channeled the movement of goods and people between ocean and inland waterways. New York became the largest city in North America because its harbor provided sheltered anchorage for ships crossing the Atlantic; the Hudson River provided access leading into the interior of the continent. In eastern Asia, Hong Kong grew under similar circumstances, as British traders used its splendid harbor as an exchange point for goods moving in and out of southern China.

Businesses also have succeeded at well-situated places along overland routes. The fabled oasis of Tombouctou has been an important trading center for centuries because it has one of the few dependable sources of water in the Sahara. Chicago's ascendancy as the premier city of the U.S. heartland came when its early leaders engineered its selection as the termination point for a dozen railroad lines converging from all directions. Not only did much of the rail traffic moving through the region have to pass through Chicago, but passengers and freight passing through the city had to be transferred from one line to another, a process that generated numerous jobs and added considerably to the wealth of many businesses in the city.

In addition to the business associated directly with the movement of people and goods, other forms of economic activity have become concentrated at critical points in the transportation network. Places where transfers from one mode of transportation to another were required often were chosen as sites for manufacturing activities. Buffalo was the most active flour-milling center in the United States for much of the twentieth century because it was the point where Great Lakes freighters carrying wheat from the northern Great Plains and Canadian prairies were unloaded. Rather than simply transfer the wheat into rail cars for shipment to the large urban markets of the northeastern United States, millers transformed the wheat into flour in Buffalo, thereby reducing the additional handling of the commodity.

Global patterns of resource refining also demonstrate the wisdom of careful selection of sites with respect to transportation systems. Some of the world's largest oil refineries are located in places like Bahrain and Houston, where pipelines bring oil to points where it is processed and loaded onto ships in the form of gasoline or other distillates for transport to other locales. Massive refinery complexes also have been built in the Tokyo and Nagoya areas of Japan and near Rotterdam in the Netherlands to process crude oil brought by giant tankers from the Middle East and other oil-exporting regions. For similar reasons, the largest new steel mills in the United States are near Baltimore and Philadelphia, where iron ore shipped from Canada and Brazil is processed. Some of the most active aluminum works in Europe are beside Norwegian fjords, where abundant local hydroelectric power is used to process imported alumina.

Favorable location along transportation lines is beneficial for a place. Conversely, an absence of good transportation severely limits the potential for firms to succeed in a specific place. Transportation patterns change over time, however, and so does their impact on places. Some places maintain themselves because their business leaders use their size and economic power to become critical nodes in newly evolving transportation networks. New York's experience provides a good example of this process. New York became the United States's foremost business center in the early nineteenth century because it was ideally situated for water transportation. As railroad networks evolved later in that century, they sought New York connections in order to serve its massive market. During the twentieth century, a complex web of roadways and major airports reinforced New York's supremacy in the eastern United States. In similar ways, London, Moscow, and Tokyo reasserted themselves as transportation hubs for their nations through successive advances in transport technology.

Failure to adapt to changing transportation patterns can have deleterious impacts on a place. During the middle of the nineteenth century, business leaders in St. Louis discouraged railroad construction, seeking instead to maintain the supremacy of river transportation. Only after it became clear that railroads were the mode of preference did St. Louis officials seek to develop rail connections for the city, but by then it was too late; Chicago had ascended to a dominant position in the region. For about 30 years during the middle part of the twentieth century, airports at Gander, Newfoundland, Canada, and Shannon, Ireland, became important refueling points for trans-Atlantic flights. The development of planes that could travel nonstop for much longer distances returned those places to sleepy oblivion.

Continuing advances in transportation technology effectively have "shrunk" the world. Just a few centuries ago, travel across an ocean took harrowing months. As late as 1873, readers marveled when Jules Verne wrote of a hectic journey around the world in 80 days. Today's travelers can fly around the globe in less than 80 hours, and the speed and dependability of modern modes of transport have transformed the ways in which business is conducted. Modern manufacturers have transformed the notion of relationships among suppliers, manufacturers, and markets. Automobile manufacturers, for example, once maintained large stockpiles of parts in assembly plants that were located near the parts plants or close to the places where the cars would be sold. Contemporary auto assembly plants now are built in places where labor costs and worker productivity are favorable and where governments have offered attractive inducements. They keep relatively few parts on hand, calling on suppliers for rapid delivery of parts as they are needed when orders for new cars are received. This "just-in-time" system of production leaves manufacturers subject to disruptions caused by work stoppages at supply plants and to weather-related delays in the transportation system, but losses associated with these infrequent events are more than offset by reduced operating costs under normal conditions.

The role of advanced technology as a factor affecting international business is even more apparent with respect to advances in communications systems. Sophisticated forms of telecommunication that began more than 150 years ago with the telegraph have advanced through the telephone to facsimile transmissions and electronic mail networks. As a result, distance has practically ceased to be a consideration with respect to the transmission of information. Whereas information once moved only as rapidly as the person carrying the paper on which the information was written, data and ideas now can be sent instantaneously almost anywhere in the world.

These communication advances have had a staggering impact on the way that international business is conducted. They have fostered the growth of multinational corporations, which operate in diverse sites around the globe while maintaining effective links with headquarters and regional control centers. International financial operations also have been transformed because of communication advances. Money and stock markets in New York, London, Tokyo, and Frankfurt now are connected by computer systems that process transactions around the clock. As much as any other factor, the increasingly mobile forms of money have enabled modern business executives to engage in activities around the world.

Regions

In addition to considering places by themselves or how they relate to other places, regions provide alternative ways to organize groups of places in more meaningful ways. A region is a set of places that share certain characteristics. Many regions are defined by characteristics that all of the places in the group have in common. When economic characteristics are used, the delimited regions include places with similar kinds of economic activity. Agricultural regions include areas where certain farm products dominate. Corn is grown throughout the "Corn Belt" of the central United States, for example, although many farmers in the region also plant soybeans and many raise hogs. Regions where intensive industrial production is a prominent part of local economic activity include the manufacturing belts of the northeastern United States, southern Canada, northwestern Europe, and southern Japan.

Regions can also be defined by patterns of movement. Transportation or communication linkages among places may draw them together into configurations that differentiate them from other locales. Studies by economic geographers of the locational tendencies of modern high-technology industries have identified complex networks of firms that provide products and services to each other. Because of their linkages, these firms cluster together into well-defined regions. The "Silicon Valley" of northern California, the "Western Crescent" on the outskirts of London, and "Technopolis" of the Tokyo region all are distinguished as much by connections among firms as by the economic landscapes they have established.

Economic aspects of movement may help define functional regions by establishing areas where certain types of economic activity are more profitable than others. In the early nineteenth century, German landowner Johann Heinrich von Thünen demonstrated how different costs for transporting various agricultural goods to market helped to define regions where certain forms of farming would occur. Although theoretically simple, patterns predicted by von Thünen can still be found in the world

today. Goods such as vegetables and dairy products that require more intensive production and are more expensive to ship are produced closer to markets, while less demanding goods and commodities that can be transported at lower costs come from more remote production areas. Advances in transportation have dramatically altered such regional patterns, however. Whereas a New York City native once enjoyed fresh vegetables and fruit only in the summer and early autumn when New Jersey, upstate New York, and New England producers brought their goods to market, New Yorkers today buy fresh produce year-round, with new shipments flown in daily from Florida, California, Chile, and even more remote locations during the colder months.

Governments have a strong impact on the conduct of business, and the formal borders of government jurisdictions often coincide with the functional boundaries of economic regions. The divisive character of these lines on the map has been altered in many parts of the world in recent decades, however. The formation of common markets and free trade areas in Western Europe and North America has dramatically changed the patterns and flows of economic activity, and similar kinds of formal restructuring of relationships among nations likely will continue in this century. As a result, business analysts increasingly need to consider regions that cross international boundaries.

Some of the most innovative views of regional organization essentially have ignored existing national boundaries. In 1981, Joel Garreau published a book titled *The Nine Nations of North America*, which subdivided the continent into a set of regions based on economic activities and cultural outlooks. Seven of Garreau's nine regions include territory in at least two nations. In the Southwest, "Mexamerica" recognized the bicultural heritage of Anglo and Hispanic groups and the increasingly close economic ties across the U.S.–Mexican border that were spurred by the *maquiladora* and other export-oriented programs. The evolution of this region as a distinctive collection of places has been accelerated by the passage of the North American Free Trade Agreement (NAFTA). Another cross-national region identified by Garreau is "The Islands," a collection of nations in the Caribbean for which Miami has become the functional "capital." Many business leaders seeking to tap into this rapidly growing area have become knowledgeable of the laws and customs of those nations. They often have done so by employing émigrés from those nations who may now be U.S. citizens but whose primary language is not English and whose outlook on the region is multinational.

In a similar vein, Darrell Delamaide's 1994 book entitled *The New Superregions of Europe* divides the continent

The New Superregions of Europe

Source: Darrell Delamaide. *the New Superregions of Europe.* New York: Dutton, 1994.

The Nine Nations of North America

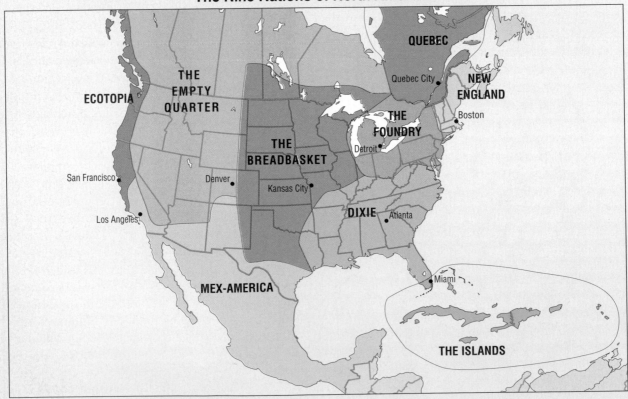

Source: Joel Garreau, *The Nine Nations of North America.* New York: Houghton Mifflin, 1981.

into ten regions based on economic, cultural, and social affinities that have evolved over centuries. His vision of Europe challenges regional structures that persist from earlier times. Seen by many as a single region known as Eastern Europe, the formerly communist nations west of what once was the Soviet Union are seen by Delamaide as being part of five different "superregions": "The Baltic League," a group of nations clustered around the Baltic Sea; "Mitteleuropa," the economic heartland of northern Europe; "The Slavic Federation," a region dominated by Russia with a common Slavic heritage; "The Danube Basin," a melange of places along and near Europe's longest river; and "The Balkan Peninsula," a region characterized by political turmoil and less advanced economies.

Delamaide's book has been as controversial as Garreau's was a decade earlier. In both cases, however, the value of the ideas they presented was not measured in terms of the "accuracy" of the regional structures they presented, but rather by their ability to lead more people to take a geographic perspective of the modern world and how it functions. The regions defined by Garreau and Delamaide are not those described by traditional geographers, but they reflect the views of many business leaders who have learned to look across national boundaries in their search for opportunities. As business increasingly becomes international, the most successful entrepreneurs will be the ones who complement their business acumen with effective application of geographic information and principles.

References Cited

Darrell Delamaide. *The New Superregions of Europe.* New York: Dutton, a division of Penguin Books, 1994.

Joel Garreau. *The Nine Nations of North America.* New York: Houghton Mifflin Co., 1981.

Take one 22-year old basketball player with a trait you can't teach—a physique of 296 pounds spread over 7 feet, 6 inches. Stir in sleek midrange jump shots, smooth passing skills, shot-blocking ability, court speed, and a plethora of low-post moves. Add charisma with a dash of humor. And one more thing: Make him from China, the world's most populous nation, with an untapped market of 1.3 billion people. From central casting comes Yao Ming— "The Next Big Thing" for international services and global business.

Ming, the Next Big Thing

Straight from China's Basketball Association, Yao was the first international player ever selected as the number one overall pick in the NBA, by the Houston Rockets. Although a lengthy adjustment period was expected, Yao was a solid contributor to the Rockets almost immediately. In a November game against the Lakers, Yao scored 20 points; four days later, he had 30 points and 16 rebounds against the Mavericks. On December 3, against the Spurs and two of the NBA's foremost "big men," David Robinson and Tim Duncan, Yao dazzled again: 27 points, 18 rebounds, and 3 blocks. Within five short months, Yao had become a star— ranking second in the league in shooting with 56 percent accuracy and averaging 14 points per game.

His NBA stardom stems not only from his talents but also from his personality. Yao's self-deprecating charisma and humor make him hard to dislike. While describing a dunk he missed, Yao told his teammates, "When you have pitiful moments that makes the good

Sources: This case was written by Sabrina Nguyen of Georgetown University, under the guidance of Professor Michael R. Czinkota. Barron, David, "The Marketing Machine Behind Yao Ming," *The Houston Chronicle,* November 3, 2002, A1; "Basketball Star Yao Ming Goes Wireless," *Business Wire,* January 7, 2003, http://www. businesswire.com; Blineburg, Fran, "The Book on Yao Is Not a Quick Read," *Houston Chronicle,* September 4, 2002; Law, Niki, "Yao Wows Fans," *South China Morning Post,* January 21, 2003, *Section News,* 5; Luo, Michael, "Yao Ming Carries Asians to New Heights," *Associated Press,* February 6, 2003; McCallum, Jack, "Sky Rocket," *Sports Illustrated,* February 10, 2003; Pasick, Adam, "Rookie Yao Ming, Apple of Advertisers' Eye," *Reuters News,* February 2, 2003; Thomsen, Ian, "The New Mr. Big," *Sports Illustrated,* October 28, 2002; Wang, Gene, "The Golden Bridge," *The Washington Post,* February 27, 2003, D1.

moments more valuable." When fellow NBA star O'Neal said to a reporter "Tell Yao Ming, 'Ching chong yang wah ah soh'" while making kung fu moves, Yao quipped that Chinese is a very difficult language to learn. With his talent and personality, Yao is the new center of attention of two continents and making hearts pound and cash registers ring in both.

Global Ming Mania

With fans' interest in the NBA plummeting since the championship run of the Chicago Bulls, Yao arrived none too soon. In the United States, the Rockets' television ratings and ticket sales have increased 65 percent. The Rockets distribute Yao "Growth Charts" and plaster the city with billboards bearing his image. ESPN runs commercials showing him dangling out of a tiny bunk bed and performing tai chi with the Rockets' mascot.

Perhaps more significantly, Yao has become a culture's hero by breaking the Hollywood portrayal of Asian males as inscrutable and subservient and dispelling the popular stereotype of the Asian American as bookish, slight, unathletic, and overachieving premed students. In 2002, Asian-American ticket purchases accounted for less than 1 percent of Houston's total sales, but with Yao's entrance a year later, it has grown to 14 percent. "Ming Mania" isn't only domestic: Ripple effects are showing even in Toronto, Canada, home of the Raptors and 500,000 Chinese: CCBC, the Raptors' local Chinese radio broadcaster, hired a Mandarin reporter for postgame interviews, and ticket purchases by the Chinese-Canadian Youth Athletic Association have increased by 150 percent.

NBA Going Global

As the world's number two team sport, behind soccer, NBA commissioner David Stern has been laying the groundwork for global penetration for nearly 15 years, broadcasting to and recruiting from the international scene. Fans' strong positive response to the influx of players from Germany (Dallas' Nowitzki), Yugoslavia (Sacramento's Stojakovic), and Spain (Memphis' Gasol) propelled the NBA to recruit globally. And "Yao came at the perfect time to the perfect league," as noted by Rich

Thomaselli, sports marketing expert. "The NBA has wanted exponential global growth. Other foreign players have helped, but Yao, who is truly unique because of his size, personality, and background will lead the way."

What better country to begin "exponential global growth" than in China, home to 1.3 billion people? The Rockets and the NBA couldn't be more grateful for the "Ming Mania." As Rockets President and CEO George Postolos enthuses, "It's incredible. In one week when we drafted Yao, we got more international attention than either of our two NBA championships. We think we're on our way to becoming the most-watched team in the world."

Postolos was right—the international viewership is astounding. Yao's NBA debut against the Indiana Pacers in October 2002 reached 287 million Chinese households—in contrast to 105 million in the United States. On a weeknight in December 2002, an NBA game between two strong teams drew television viewership of 1.1 million Americans. Compare that to an 8 a.m. broadcast game between the Rockets and the league's worst team, the Cavaliers, which pulled in 6 million Chinese viewers. Another 11.5 million tuned in for a repeat of the game that night—even a live broadcast of an NBA finals game doesn't attract that size audience in the United States.

A decade ago, fans in China were lucky to see one NBA game per week, usually from a month-old tape mailed to Beijing. Now, the average Chinese viewer can watch four games weekly, and many can catch a fifth game on Hong Kong-based satellite channels. But the NBA isn't just reeling in "Ming Mania" fans for the short-term: With a six-fold increase in NBA broadcasting, only a quarter are Rockets' games showing Yao. "The league wants to use the interest in Yao to build interest in all its teams," Michael Denzel, managing director of NBA Asia, asserts. "We're not the Rockets Channel. Even when the Chicago Bulls were at their peak, we didn't focus exclusively on one team. We're trying to create bounce."

Corporate "Courtship"

Regardless of the NBA's long-term aspirations, the short-term effect is clear: Millions of Chinese, young and old, basketball buffs and novices, are dodging work, skipping class, and losing sleep to catch a glimpse of their hometown hero's performance on the NBA stage. Clearly, the Asian market isn't going to only watch, it's also going to buy. "Asian and Asian-American consumers haven't plugged into sneakers and sports apparel," says Thomaselli. "I could see a whole Yao line." With the

first batch of NBA-licensed goods arriving in China in April 2003, signature jerseys of the usuals—Kobe, Shaq, and Iverson—and of the greatly anticipated Rocket's Number 11 are expected to fly off shelves. Unlike other pro leagues, the NBA has long had a global vision, but now, at least in Asia, it has the main ingredient to help reach that aspiration.

For the corporate scene, Yao is more than just a Chinese import to hit the United States. He's the perfect vehicle for multinational corporations to enter the Land of 1.3 billion potential consumers. With the 2008 Olympics in Beijing, the country is on the fast track to modernize. Markets are opening, and young people are starting to express themselves with purchasing power. One of the best ways to capture youth's purchasing power has been through sports figures. In the past, a few Asian athletes, such as Michael Chang and Michelle Kwan, have attained prominence, but in individual sports. It's marquee basketball players like Yao who command the most lucrative and successful endorsements. Yet, unlike in the United States, where endorsement figures like Tiger Woods and Michael Jordan are familiar, Yao is a marketing figure that can dominate China's still-emerging market without competition.

Just halfway through his rookie season, Yao is everywhere: He sized up Austin Powers' Mini-Me in TV ads for Apple computers; he played the confused New York tourist in a Visa commercial that also features Yogi Berra, and he graced Sports Illustrated's cover twice in only four months. In China, he is the centerpiece of Nike's and Gatorade's new print campaign.

China is the most elusive market for the wireless industry, having the world's largest mobile-phone subscriber base with 200 million users and the highest percentage of online gamers. With a Chinese public that idolizes the athlete and embraces mobile technology, wireless companies are quick to enlist Yao as their spokesman. After signing a $5 million contract, Yao will hawk wireless service for China's Unicom while Sorrent, a California-based technology firm will combine the best of both cell phone and gaming worlds by developing and marketing "Yao Ming Basketball," a mobile-phone game that renders the latest 3D animations.

Challenges for the "Great Wall"

For all that Yao has accomplished, one stark difference remains between him and "The Legends"—proven athletic ability that commands sky-high endorsement figures.

As Ray Clark, CEO of Marketing Arm, notes, "For an athlete to move products in America and abroad, he needs to perform extremely well or be recognized as the reason his team does." For all his potential, Yao is not yet the foremost center-position player, and despite the growing number of TV and arena fans, the number of Rocket games remaining in the season is contingent upon their play in the "hellish NBA Western Conference."

In comparison to Michael Jordan, the NBA's "sole influencer" and member of a six-time NBA champion team, two gold-medal-winning U.S. Olympic teams, and a seven time leading scorer, Yao's figures on and off the courts become meager. Michael Jordan's impact on the U.S. economy is estimated at $10 billion since he join the NBA in 1984. Nike sold more than $2.6 billion in Jordan-related products. While at the start of his career, the Bulls averaged only 6,365 fans per game, in his third season, the team began a string of sellouts that reached 542 consecutive games, culminating in $165 million in ticket revenue and netting another $366 million in NBA merchandise.

Then there's Yao's slowly progressing English. In public, he rarely speaks without the help of his interpreter, Colin Pine, and although Apple and Visa endorsements capitalized on his "smile that transcends language," how often can you use "nonverbal ads," asks Bon Williams, president of Burns Sports and Celebrities.

"The Golden Bridge"

Despite the media's attention on Yao's statistics, basketball fundamentals, and endorsement contracts, the NBA's international services strategy reveals that Yao's appeal instead is far more substantial. "Chinese citizens are closely following Yao for symbolic reasons not related to basketball," said Steven Lewis, an Asia expert at the Baker Institute for Public Policy. "They are wondering: 'Yao is a Chinese person going abroad to live and work among foreigners.'" Along with their hometown hero, the Chinese are watching and participating as their nation opens up to the world.

Questions for Discussion

1. Discuss the statement: "Yao Ming isn't just China's best basketball player. He's the most persuasive symbol of globalization."
2. Consider China's current international business issues such as intellectual property rights and logistical infrastructure. How should an international business manager consider these concerns before entering the potentially profitable yet elusive Chinese market?
3. **Internet Question:** Please assess Asian participation in basketball by going to http://www.asian-basketball.com.

In order to succeed in international business, one needs to be able to manage conflicts between cultures. This in turn requires an understanding of cultural differences in language, religion, values, customs, and education, so that one can develop cross-cultural competence. The chapter on culture addresses these dimensions.

To achieve an understanding of the political and legal dimensions which affect international business, this section highlights the policy issues surrounding the corporate decision maker and discusses the effect of politics and laws on business, together with the agreements, treaties, and laws that govern the relationships between home and host countries.

PART
Environment

2

CHAPTER

2

Culture

Learning Objectives

■ To define and demonstrate the effect of culture's various dimensions on business

■ To examine ways in which cultural knowledge can be acquired and individuals and organizations prepared for cross-cultural interaction

■ To illustrate ways in which cultural risk poses a challenge to the effective conduct of business communications and transactions

■ To suggest ways in which businesses act as change agents in the diverse cultural environments in which they operate

Crossing Cultures: Balancing the Global with the Local

MTV has emerged as a significant global medium, with more than 375 million households in 164 countries subscribing to its services. The reason for its success is simple—MTV offers consistent, high-quality programming that reflects the tastes and lifestyles of young people. While admired for its global reach, MTV has drawn the ire of critics, who accuse the teen-savvy network of being a cultural imperialist, trampling regional and local values and preferences.

MTV has shrewdly deflected such criticism and downplays its role as an exporter of American culture. To cater to the 80 percent of MTV viewers who reside outside of the United States, the company has a policy of 70 percent local content. Early in MTV's international expansion in the 1980, using American imagery was trendy, but the 1990s brought about a need to give the brand local imagery. As a result, MTV Russia now has a show called "12 Angry Viewers," in which intellectuals and others debate music videos. In Brazil, "Mochilao," a backpack-travel show, is hosted by a popular Brazilian model. In China, MTV Mandarin broadcasts "Mei Mei Sees TV," which features a virtual disc jockey. MTV India features "Silly Point," which includes short films poking fun at how cricket gear can be used in everyday life.

Digital compression allows the number of services offered on satellite feed to be multiplied. MTV has used this capacity to complement pan-regional programming and play lists, customizing them to local tastes in key areas. For example, MTV Asia launched MTV India and has five hours of India-specific programming during the 24-hour satellite feed to the subcontinent.

For various reasons, MTV is now embarking on a strategy to develop shows for more than one overseas market at a time. MTV has a big infrastructure of 76 channels in 17 languages and feels that it is time to leverage resources and develop programming that can not only cross borders but even have global appeal. One reason for this is pragmatic: an average production may cost as much as $350,000 per 30-minute episode. "Famous Last Minutes," a concept for an animated show on rock stars' imagined last minutes dreamed up by MTV Germany, is too expensive to be produced only for that market. Among other shows being piloted, MTV U.K. has "Heroes," in which pop stars interview their idols. "Mash," a program that "mashes" two videos together (e.g., Madonna and Lenny Kravitz), was launched in Europe in 2003 as part of a $75 million sponsorship deal with Motorola.

Under the new plan, local managers will not give up the power to make local programming decisions. The goal is to encourage cooperation among country units to develop new ideas that can be used in multiple countries. One incentive to do so is a centralized pool of money that national channels can tap into and use for program development. Such cooperation is not entirely new. Some shows from the United States have later been produced in localized versions, including the dating show "Dismissed" and "Cribs," a look inside the homes of stars.

MTV's goal is to derive 40 percent of revenue from overseas markets in the medium- to long-term future (share in 2003 was 16 percent). The trick will be to create programming that both individual and multiple markets can relate to. Expensive new cross-border shows can easily fail because of cultural differences and various traditions.

Sources: "MTV Seeks Global Appeal," The Wall Street Journal, July 21, 2003, B1, B3; "Think Local," The Economist, April 13, 2002, 12; Claudia Penteado, "MTV Breaks New Ground," Advertising Age Global, March 2002, 8; "MTV's World," Business Week, February 18, 2002, 81–84; "MTV Asia's Hit Man," Advertising Age Global, December 2001, 10; and Claire Murphy, "Global MTV Deal Trips Up Local Identity Drive," Marketing, June 18, 1998, 15.

The ever-increasing level of world trade, opening of new markets, and intensifying competition have allowed—and sometimes forced—businesses to expand their operations. The challenge for managers is to handle the different values, attitudes, and behavior that govern human interaction. First, managers must ensure smooth interaction of the business with its different constituents, and second, they must assist others to implement programs within and across markets. It is no longer feasible to think of markets and operations in terms of domestic and international. Because the separation is no longer distinguishable, the necessity of culturally sensitive management and personnel is paramount.

As firms expand their operations across borders, they acquire new customers and new partners in new environments. Two distinct tasks become necessary: first, to understand cultural differences and the ways they manifest themselves and, second, to determine similarities across cultures and exploit them in strategy formulation as highlighted in the opening vignette. Success in new markets is very much a function of cultural adaptability: patience, flexibility, and appreciation of others' beliefs.[1]

Recognition of different approaches may lead to establishing best practice; that is, a new way of doing things applicable throughout the firm. Ideally, this means that successful ideas can be transferred across borders for efficiency and adjusted to local conditions for effectiveness. Take the case of Nestlé. In one of his regular trips to company headquarters in Switzerland, the general manager of Nestlé Thailand was briefed on a summer coffee promotion from the Greek subsidiary, a cold coffee concoction called the Nescafe Shake. The Thai Group swiftly adopted and adapted the idea. It designed plastic containers to mix the drink and invented a dance, the Shake, to popularize the activity.[2]

To take advantage of the global marketplace, companies have to have or gain a thorough understanding of market behavior, especially in terms of similarities. For example, no other group of emerging markets in the world have as much in common as those in Latin America. They share a Spanish language and heritage; the Portuguese language and heritage are close enough to allow Brazilians and their neighbors to communicate easily. The Southern Florida melting pot, where Latin Americans of all backgrounds mix in a blend of Hispanic cultures, is in itself a picture of what Latin America can be. Tapping into the region's cultural affinities through a network-scale approach (e.g., regional hubs for production, and pan-Latin brands) is not only possible but advisable.[3]

Cultural competence must be recognized as a key management skill. Cultural incompetence, or inflexibility, can easily jeopardize millions of dollars through wasted negotiations; lost purchases, sales, and contracts; and poor customer relations. Furthermore, the internal efficiency of a multinational corporation may be weakened if managers and workers are not "on the same wavelength." The tendency for U.S. managers is to be open and informal, but in some cultural settings that may be inap-

tion

propriate. **Cultural risk** is just as real as commercial or political risk in the international business arena.

The intent of this chapter is to analyze the concept of culture and its various elements and then to provide suggestions for not only meeting the cultural challenge but making it a base of obtaining and maintaining a competitive advantage.

Culture Defined

Culture gives an individual an anchoring point, an identity, as well as codes of conduct. Of the more than 160 definitions of culture analyzed by Kroeber and Kluckhohn, some conceive of culture as separating humans from nonhumans, some define it as communicable knowledge, and some as the sum of historical achievements produced by man's social life.[4] All of the definitions have common elements: Culture is learned, shared, and transmitted from one generation to the next. Culture is primarily passed on from parents to their children but also transmitted by social organizations, special interest groups, the government, schools, and churches. Common ways of thinking and behaving that are developed are then reinforced through social pressure. Geert Hofstede calls this the "collective programming of the mind."[5] Culture is also multidimensional, consisting of a number of common elements that are interdependent. Changes occurring in one of the dimensions will affect the others as well.

For the purposes of this text, culture is defined as an *integrated system of learned behavior patterns that are characteristic of the members of any given society.* It includes everything that a group thinks, says, does, and makes—its customs, language, material artifacts, and shared systems of attitudes and feelings.[6] The definition, therefore, encompasses a wide variety of elements from the materialistic to the spiritual. Culture is inherently conservative, resisting change and fostering continuity. Every person is encultured into a particular culture, learning the "right way" of doing things. Problems may arise when a person encultured in one culture has to adjust to another one. The process of **acculturation**—adjusting and adapting to a specific culture other than one's own—is one of the keys to success in international operations.

Edward T. Hall, who has made some of the most valuable studies on the effects of culture on business, makes a distinction between high- and low-context cultures.[7] In **high-context cultures,** such as Japan and Saudi Arabia, context is at least as important as what is actually said. The speaker and the listener rely on a common understanding of the context and what is not being said can carry more meaning than what is said. In **low-context cultures,** however, most of the information is contained explicitly in the words. North American cultures engage in low-context communications. Unless one is aware of this basic difference, messages and intentions can easily be misunderstood. As an example, performance appraisals are typically a human resources function. If performance appraisals are to be centrally guided or conducted in a multinational corporation, those involved must be acutely aware of cultural nuances. One of the interesting differences is that the U.S. system emphasizes the individual's development, whereas the Japanese system focuses on the group within which the individual works. In the United States, criticism is more direct and recorded formally, whereas in Japan it is more subtle and verbal.

Few cultures today are as homogeneous as those of Japan and Saudi Arabia. Elsewhere intracultural differences based on nationality, religion, race, or geographic areas have resulted in the emergence of distinct subcultures. The international manager's task is to distinguish relevant cross-cultural and intracultural differences and

Mutual awareness of cultural differences is essential in international business. Levels of formality vary greatly among cultures. In most situations, restraint equals respect.

then to isolate potential opportunities and problems. Good examples are the Hispanic subculture in the United States and the Flemish and the Walloons in Belgium. On the other hand, borrowing and interaction among national cultures may narrow gaps between cultures. Here the international business entity acts as a **change agent** by introducing new products or ideas and practices. Although this may only shift consumption from one product brand to another, it may also lead to massive social change in the manner of consumption, the type of products consumed, and social organization. Consider, for example, that the international portion of McDonald's annual sales has grown from 13 percent to 58 percent.[8] In markets such as Taiwan, one of the 119 countries on six continents entered, McDonald's and other fast food entities dramatically changed eating habits, especially of the younger generation.

The example of Kentucky Fried Chicken in India illustrates the difficulties companies may have in entering culturally complex markets. Even though the company opened its outlets in two of India's most cosmopolitan cities (Bangalore and New Delhi), it found itself the target of protests by a wide range of opponents. KFC could have alleviated or eliminated some of the anti-Western passions by tailoring its activities to the local conditions. First, rather than opting for more direct control, KFC should have allied itself with local partners for advice and support. Second, KFC should have tried to appear more Indian rather than using high-profile advertising with Western ideas. Indians are ambivalent toward foreign culture, and its ideas may not always work well there. Finally, KFC should have planned for competition, which came from small restaurants with political clout at the local level.[9]

Many governments have taken action to protect their culture-specific industries. A specific example is provided in Focus on Politics, which highlights the European Union's attempt to protect the quality and reputation of regional, and often very culture-specific, products. The industry that many countries (such as Brazil, Canada, France, and Indonesia) protect is entertainment, mainly cinema and music. The WTO agreement that allows restrictions on exports of U.S. entertainment to Europe is justified by the Europeans as a cultural safety net intended to preserve national and

Indian Muslim restaurant owners spill American soft drinks to protest US led attacks on Afghanistan in Bombay, India, October 2001. Various Muslim organizations in Bombay have called for a ban on American and British products.

AP PHOTO/SHERWIN CRASTO

Focus On ↓

POLITICS

Protecting Mozzarella

If European negotiators in the World Trade Organization get their way, food names associated with specific regions—Parma ham from Italy, Stilton cheese from the United Kingdom, and Marsala wine from Italy—would be reserved solely for companies located in the respective regions; i.e., through so-called geographic indications. European Union (EU) officials argue that mozzarella, for example, is made according to exacting standards only in that particular part of Italy.

EU Trade Commissioner Pascal Lamy summarized the European point of view in this way: "Geographical indications offer the best protection to quality products which are sold by relying on their origin and reputation and other special characteristics linked to such an origin. They reward investment in quality by our producers. Abuses in other countries undermine the heritage of EU products and create confusion among consumers." Furthermore, Europeans fear that they may not be able to use their own names selling abroad in the future. A company in Canada, for example, could trademark a product named for a European place, preventing the rightful European originator from selling his goods in that market. The European Union has adopted geographic-indication laws governing 600 products sold inside the EU. Most recently, a ruling was issued that only Greek companies (which use goat's milk and specific production methods) can sell Feta cheese inside the EU. Now the EU wants to expand such a list worldwide and establish a multilateral register to police it.

For many, the European idea is bald-faced protectionism and has no merit in protecting cultural values. "This does not speak of free trade; it is about making a monopoly of trade," said Sergio Marchi, Canada's ambassador to the WTO. "It is even hard to calculate the cost and confusion of administering such a thing." Others argue that the Europeans are merely trying to cover up for inefficient production practices. Some even make the argument that multinational companies are the ones who have built up the value of the product names on the list—not the small producers in the regions in question.

The debate is still in its early stages. It is not clear how many names the Europeans will eventually want to have on the list, especially with the expansion of the EU to 10 new countries in 2004. The definition of geographic indications is not altogether clear in that some countries want to protect the adjectives found on product labels (such as "tawny" or "ruby" to describe Portuguese port wine). Other countries have their own lists as well; for example, India wants basmati rice to be protected even though "basmati" is not a place name.

Sources: "WTO Talks: EU Steps Up Bid for Better Protection of Regional Quality Products," *EU Institutions Press Releases,* August 28, 2003, DN:IP/03/1178; "Ham and Cheese: Italy Wins EU Case," *CNN.com,* May 20, 2003; "Europe Says, 'That Cheese is No Cheddar!'" *The Wall Street Journal,* February 13, 2003, B1; and "USTR Supports Geographic Indications for Drinks," *Gourmet News,* January 2003, 3.

regional identities.[10] In June 1998, Canada organized a meeting in Ottawa about U.S. cultural dominance. Nineteen countries attended, including Britain, Brazil, and Mexico; the United States was excluded. At issue were ways of exempting cultural goods from treaties lowering trade barriers, on the view that free trade threatened national cultures. The Ottawa meeting followed a similar gathering in Stockholm, sponsored by the United Nations, which resolved to press for special exemptions for cultural goods in the Multilateral Agreement on Investment.[11]

Even if a particular country is dominant in a cultural sector, such as the United States in movies and television programming, the commonly suggested solution of protectionism may not work. Although the European Union has a rule that 40 percent of the programming has to be domestic, anyone wanting a U.S. program can choose an appropriate channel or rent a video. Quotas will also result in behavior not intended by regulators. U.S. programming tends to be scheduled more during prime time, while the 60 percent of domestic programming may wind up being shown during less-attractive times. Furthermore, quotas may also lead to local productions designed to satisfy official mandates and capture subsidies that accompany them. Many emerging markets are following suit; in Cambodia, for example, local TV stations are requested by the Information Ministry to show local films three times a week.[12]

Popular culture is not only a U.S. bastion. In many areas, such as pop music and musicals, Europeans have had an equally dominant position worldwide. Furthermore, no market is only an exporter of culture. Given the ethnic diversity in the United States (as in many other country markets), programming from around the world is made available. Many of the greatest successes of cultural products of the past five years in the United States were non-U.S.; e.g., in television programming, "Who Wants to Be a Millionaire?" and "Weakest Link" are British concepts, as is the best-seller in children's literature, *Harry Potter*. In cartoons, Pokémon hails from Japan.

The worst scenario for companies is when they are accused of pushing Western behaviors and values—along with products and promotions—into other cultures, and this results in consumer boycotts and even destruction of property. McDonald's, KFC, Coca-Cola, Disney, and Pepsi, for example, have all drawn the ire of anti-American demonstrators for being icons of globalization. Similarly, noisy boycotts and protests targeted many multinational companies in the wake of the invasion of Iraq. In the United States, those protests were aimed at French and Germans, while opponents of the war focused on U.S. companies.[13]

The Elements of Culture

The study of culture has led to generalizations that may apply to all cultures. Such characteristics are called **cultural universals,** which are manifestations of the total way of life of any group of people. These include such elements as bodily adornment, courtship rituals, etiquette, concept of family, gestures, joking, mealtime customs, music, personal names, status differentiation, and trade customs.[14] These activities occur across cultures, but they may be uniquely manifested in a particular society, bringing about cultural diversity. Common denominators can indeed be found across cultures, but cultures may vary dramatically in how they perform the same activities.[15] Even when a segment may be perceived to be similar across borders—as in the case of teenagers or the affluent—cultural differences make dealing with them challenging. For example, European teens resent being treated like Americans with an accent by U.S. companies.[16]

Observation of the major cultural elements summarized in Table 2.1 suggests that these elements are both material (such as tools) and abstract (such as attitudes). The sensitivity and adaptation to these elements by an international firm depends on the firm's level of involvement in the market—for example, licensing versus direct investment—and the good or service marketed. Naturally, some goods and services or management practices require very little adjustment, while some have to be adapted dramatically.

TABLE 2.1   **Elements of Culture**

- Language
  - Verbal
  - Nonverbal
- Religion
- Values and attitudes
- Manners and customs
- Material elements
- Aesthetics
- Education
- Social institutions

LANGUAGE

Language has been described as the mirror of culture. Language itself is multidimensional by nature. This is true not only of the spoken word but also of what can be called the nonverbal language of international business. Messages are conveyed by the words used, by how the words are spoken (for example, tone of voice), and through nonverbal means such as gestures, body position, and eye contact.

Very often mastery of the language is required before a person is accultured to a culture other than his or her own. Language mastery must go beyond technical competency, because every language has words and phrases that can be readily understood only in context. Such phrases are carriers of culture; they represent special ways a culture has developed to view some aspect of human existence.

Language capability serves four distinct roles in international business.[17]

1. Language aids in information gathering and evaluation. Rather than rely completely on the opinions of others, the manager is able to see and hear personally what is going on. People are far more comfortable speaking their own language, and this should be treated as an advantage. The best intelligence on a market is gathered by becoming part of the market rather than observing it from the outside. For example, local managers of a multinational corporation should be the firm's primary source of political information to assess potential risk.
2. Language provides access to local society. Although English may be widely spoken and may even be the official company language, speaking the local language may make a dramatic difference.
3. Language capability is increasingly important in company communications, whether within the corporate family or with channel members. Imagine the difficulties encountered by a country manager who must communicate with employees through an interpreter.
4. Language provides more than the ability to communicate. It extends beyond mechanics to the interpretation of contexts that may influence business operations.

The manager's command of the national language(s) in a market must be greater than simple word recognition. Consider, for example, how dramatically different English terms can be when used in the United Kingdom or the United States. In negotiations, for U.S. delegates, "tabling a proposal" means that they want to delay a decision, while their British counterparts understand the expression to mean that immediate action is to be taken. If the British promise something "by the end of the day," this does not mean within 24 hours, but rather when they have completed the job. Additionally, they may say that negotiations "bombed," meaning that they were a success, which to an American could convey exactly the opposite message. Other languages are not immune to this phenomenon either. Goodyear has identified five different terms for the word "tires" in the Spanish-speaking Americas: *cauchos* in Venezuela, *cubiertas* in Argentina, *gomas* in Puerto Rico, *neumaticos* in Chile, and *llantas* in most of the other countries in the region. The company has to adjust its communications messages accordingly.[18]

The advertising campaign presented in Figure 2.1 highlights the difficulties of transferring advertising campaigns across markets. Electrolux's theme for vacuum cleaners is taken literally in the United Kingdom, but in the United States, slang implications interfere with the intended message. Another example is the adaptation of an advertisement into Arabic. When this is carried out without considering that Arabic reads from right to left, the creative concept can be destroyed.

FIGURE 2.1

Example of Ad That Transferred Poorly

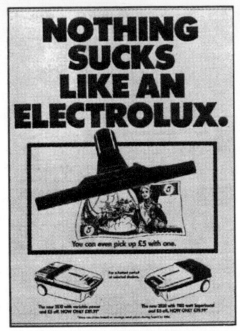

The role of language extends beyond that of a communication medium. Linguistic diversity often is an indicator of other types of diversity. In Quebec, the French language has always been a major consideration of most francophone governments, because it is one of the clear manifestations of the province's identity vis-à-vis the English-speaking provinces. The Charter of the French Language states that the rights of the francophone collectivity are: (1) the right of every person to have the civil administration, semipublic agencies, and business firms communicate with him or her in French; (2) the right of workers to carry on their activities in French; and (3) the right of consumers to be informed and served in French. The Bay, a major Quebec retailer, spends $8 million annually on translation. It has even changed its name to La Baie in appropriate areas. Similarly, in trying to battle English as the *lingua franca*, the French government has tried to ban the use of any foreign term or expression wherever an officially approved French equivalent (e.g., *mercatique*, not *un brain-storming*, and *jeune-pousse*, not *un start-up*) exists.[19] This applies also to web sites that bear the "fr" designation; they have to be in the French language.

Other countries have taken similar measures. Germans have founded a society for the protection of the German language from the spread of "Denglish." Poland has directed that all companies selling or advertising foreign products use Polish in their advertisements. In Hong Kong, the Chinese government is promoting the use of Cantonese rather than English as the language of commerce, while some people in India—with its 800 dialects—scorn the use of English as a lingua franca since it is a reminder of British colonialism.[20]

Despite the fact that English is encountered daily by those on the Internet, the "e" in e-business does not translate into English. In a survey, European users highlighted the need to bridge the language gap. One-third of the senior managers said they will not tolerate English online, while less than 20 percent of German middle managers and less than 50 percent of French ones believe they can use English well. Being

forced to use nonlocalized content was perceived to have a negative impact on productivity among 75 percent of those surveyed.[21] A truly global portal works only if the online functions are provided in a multilingual and multicultural format.

Dealing with language invariably requires local assistance. A good local advertising agency and a good local market research firm can prevent many problems. When translation is required, as when communicating with suppliers or customers, care should be taken in selecting the translator. The old saying, "If you want to kill a message, translate it," is true in that what needs to be conveyed is a feeling, which may require dramatically different terms than is achieved through a purely technical translation. In this context, translation software can generate a rough translation (it is 85 percent accurate) which then can be proofread and edited.[22] To make sure, the simplest method of control is **backtranslation**—translating a foreign language version back to the original language by a different person than the one who made the first translation. This approach may be able to detect only omissions and blunders, however. To assess the quality of the translation, a complete evaluation with testing of the message's impact is necessary.[23] A significant benefit of the Internet is accessibility to translation services worldwide to secure best quality and price.

Language also has to be understood in the historic context. Nokia launched an advertising campaign in Germany for the interchangeable covers for its portable phones using a theme "*Jedem das Seine*" ("to each his own"). The campaign was withdrawn after the American Jewish Congress pointed out that the same slogan was found on the entry portal to Buchenwald, a Nazi-era concentration camp.[24] The Indian division of Cadbury-Schweppes incensed Hindu society by running an advertisement comparing its Temptations chocolate to war-torn Kashmir. The ad carried a tagline: "I'm good. I'm tempting. I'm too good to share. What am I? Cadbury's Temptations or Kashmir?" The ad also featured a map of Kashmir to highlight the point. To add insult to injury, the ad appeared on August 15th, Indian Independence Day.[25]

NONVERBAL LANGUAGE

Managers also must analyze and become familiar with the hidden language of foreign cultures.[26] Five key topics—time, space, material possessions, friendship patterns, and business agreements—offer a starting point from which managers can begin to acquire the understanding necessary to do business in foreign countries. In many parts of the world, time is flexible and not seen as a limited commodity; people come late to appointments or may not come at all. In Hong Kong, for example, it is futile to set exact meeting times, because getting from one place to another may take minutes or hours depending on the traffic situation. Showing indignation or impatience at such behavior would astonish an Arab, Latin American, or Asian. Understanding national and cultural differences in the concept of time is critical for an international business manager.

In some countries, extended social acquaintance and the establishment of appropriate personal rapport are essential to conducting business. The feeling is that one should know one's business partner on a personal level before transactions can occur. Therefore, rushing straight to business will not be rewarded, because deals are made on the basis of not only the best product or price but also the entity or person deemed most trustworthy. Contracts may be bound on handshakes, not lengthy and complex agreements—a fact that makes some, especially Western, businesspeople uneasy.

Individuals vary in the amount of space they want separating them from others. Arabs and Latin Americans like to stand close to people when they talk. If an American, who may not be comfortable at such close range, backs away from an Arab, this might incorrectly be taken as a negative reaction. Also, Westerners are often taken aback by the more physical nature of affection between Slavs—for example, being kissed squarely on the lips by a business partner, regardless of sex.

International body language must be included in the nonverbal language of international business. For example, an American manager may, after successful completion of negotiations, impulsively give a finger-and-thumb OK sign. In southern France, the manager would have indicated that the sale was worthless and, in Japan, that a little bribe had been requested; the gesture would be grossly insulting to Brazilians. An interesting exercise is to compare and contrast the conversation styles of different nationalities. Northern Europeans are quite reserved in using their hands and maintain a good amount of personal space, whereas southern Europeans involve their bodies to a far greater degree in making a point.

RELIGION

In most cultures, people find in religion a reason for being and legitimacy in the belief that they are of a larger context. To define religion requires the inclusion of the supernatural and the existence of a higher power. Religion defines the ideals for life, which in turn are reflected in the values and attitudes of societies and individuals. Such values and attitudes shape the behavior and practices of institutions and members of cultures.

Religion has an impact on international business that is seen in a culture's values and attitudes toward entrepreneurship, consumption, and social organization. The impact will vary depending on the strength of the dominant religious tenets. While religion's impact may be quite indirect in Protestant northern Europe, its impact in countries where Islamic fundamentalism is on the rise (such as Algeria) may be profound.

Religion provides the basis for transcultural similarities under shared beliefs and behavior. The impact of these similarities will be assessed in terms of the dominant religions of the world, Christianity, Islam, Hinduism, Buddhism, and Confucianism. Other religions may have smaller numbers of followers, such as in the case of Judaism with 14 million followers around the world, but their impact is still significant due to the centuries they have influenced world history. While some countries may officially have secularism, such as Marxism-Leninism as a state belief (for example, China, Vietnam, and Cuba), traditional religious beliefs still remain a powerful force in shaping behavior.

International managers must be aware of the differences not only among the major religions but also within them. The impact of these divisions may range from hostility, as in Sri Lanka, to barely perceptible historic suspicion, as in many European countries where Protestant and Catholic are the main divisions. With some religions, such as Hinduism, people may be divided into groups, which determines their status and to a large extent their ability to consume.

Christianity has the largest following among world religions, with more than 2 billion people.[27] While there are many subgroups within Christianity, the major division is between Catholicism and Protestantism. A prominent difference between the two is the attitude toward making money. While Catholicism has questioned it, the Protestant ethic has emphasized the importance of work and the accumulation of wealth for the glory of God. At the same time, frugality was emphasized and the residual accumulation of wealth from hard work formed the basis for investment. It has been proposed that the work ethic is responsible for the development of capitalism in the Western world and the rise of predominantly Protestant countries into world economic leadership in the twentieth century.[28]

Religions of the World: A Part of Culture

Religious beliefs among 70% or more of the population

Atheist	Hindu
Buddhism	Indigenous
Confucian	Judaism
Christian, other	Muslim
Christian, Roman Catholic	Orthodox, no major sects

MAP

Source: *The World Factbook 2000*

Major holidays are often tied to religion. Holidays are observed differently from one culture to the next, to the extent that the same holiday may have different connotations. Christian cultures observe Christmas and exchange gifts on either December 24 or December 25, with the exception of the Dutch, who exchange gifts on St. Nicholas Day, December 6. Tandy Corporation, in its first year in the Netherlands, targeted its major Christmas promotion for the third week of December with less than satisfactory results. The international manager must see to it that local holidays, such as Mexico's Dìa De Los Muertos (October 31 to November 2), are taken into account in scheduling events ranging from fact-finding missions to marketing programs and in preparing local work schedules.

Islam, which reaches from the west coast of Africa to the Philippines and across a broad band that includes Tanzania, central Asia, western China, India, and Malaysia, has more than 1.2 billion followers.[29] Islam is also a significant minority religion in many parts of the world, including Europe. Islam has a pervasive role in the life of its followers, referred to as Muslims, through the Sharia (law of Islam). This is most obvious in the five stated daily periods of prayer, fasting during the holy month of Ramadan, and the pilgrimage to Mecca, Islam's holy city. While Islam is supportive of entrepreneurship, it nevertheless strongly discourages acts that may be interpreted as exploitation. Islam is also absent of discrimination, except against those outside the religion. Some have argued that Islam's basic fatalism (that is, nothing happens without the will of Allah) and traditionalism have deterred economic development in countries observing the religion.

The role of women in business is tied to religion, especially in the Middle East, where women do not function as they would in the West. This affects the conduct of business in various ways; for example, the firm may be limited in its use of female managers or personnel in these markets, and women's role as consumers and influencers in the consumption process may be different. Access to women in Islamic countries may only be possible through the use of female sales personnel, direct marketing, and women's specialty shops.[30] Religion impacts goods and services, as well. When beef or poultry is exported to an Islamic country, the animal must be killed in the "halal" method and certified appropriately. Recognition of religious restrictions on products (for example, alcoholic beverages) can reveal opportunities, as evidenced by successful launches of several nonalcoholic beverages in the Middle East. Other restrictions may call for innovative solutions. A challenge for the Swedish firm that had the primary responsibility for building a traffic system to Mecca was that non-Muslims are not allowed access to the city. The solution was to use closed-circuit television to supervise the work. Given that Islam considers interest payments usury, bankers and Muslim scholars have worked to create interest-free banking that relies on lease agreements, mutual funds, and other methods to avoid paying interest.[31]

Hinduism has 860 million followers, mainly in India, Nepal, Malaysia, Guyana, Suriname, and Sri Lanka. In addition to being a religion it is also a way of life predicated on the caste, or class to which one is born. While the caste system has produced social stability, its impact on business can be quite negative. For example, if it is difficult to rise above one's caste, individual effort is hampered. Problems in workforce integration and coordination may become quite severe. Furthermore, the drive for business success may not be important if followers place value mostly on spiritual rather than materialistic achievement.

The family is an important element of Hindu society, with extended families being a norm. The extended family structure affects the purchasing power and consumption of Hindu families, and market researchers, in particular, must take this into account in assessing market potential and consumption patterns.

Buddhism, which extends its influence throughout Asia from Sri Lanka to Japan, has 360 million followers. Although it is an offspring of Hinduism, it has no caste system. Life is seen as filled with suffering, with achieving nirvana—a spiritual state marked by an absence of desire—as the solution. The emphasis in Buddhism is on spiritual achievement rather than worldly goods.

Confucianism has over 150 million followers throughout Asia, especially among the Chinese, and has been characterized as a code of conduct rather than a religion. However, its teachings, which stress loyalty and relationships, have been broadly adopted. Loyalty to central authority and placing the good of a group before that of the individual may explain the economic success of Japan, South Korea, Singapore, and the Republic of China. It also has led to cultural misunderstandings: Western societies often perceive the subordination of the individual to the common good as a violation of human rights. The emphasis on relationships is very evident in developing business ties in Asia. Preparation may take years before understanding is reached and actual business transactions can take place.

VALUES AND ATTITUDES

Values are shared beliefs or group norms that have been internalized by individuals.[32] Attitudes are evaluations of alternatives based on these values. Differences in cultural values affect the way planning is executed, decisions are made, strategy is implemented, and personnel are evaluated. Table 2.2 provides examples of how U.S. values differ from other values around the world and how this, in turn, affects management functions. These cultural values have to be accommodated or used in the management of business functions.

The more rooted values and attitudes are in central beliefs (such as religion), the more cautiously one has to move. Attitude toward change is basically positive in industrialized countries, as is one's ability to improve one's lot in life; in tradition-bound societies, however, change is viewed with suspicion—especially when it comes from a foreign entity.

The Japanese culture raises an almost invisible—yet often unscalable—wall against all *gaijin* (foreigners). Many middle-aged bureaucrats and company officials believe that buying foreign products is downright unpatriotic. The resistance is not so much to foreign products as to those who produce and market them. Similarly, foreign-based corporations have had difficulty hiring university graduates or midcareer personnel because of bias against foreign employers. Even under such adverse conditions, the race can be run and won through tenacity, patience, and drive.

Cultural attitudes are not always a deterrent to foreign business practices or foreign goods. Japanese youth, for instance, display extremely positive attitudes toward Western goods, from popular music to Nike sneakers to Louis Vuitton haute couture to Starbuck's lattes. Even in Japan's faltering economy, global brands are able to charge premium prices if they tap into cultural attitudes that revere imported goods. Similarly, attitudes of U.S. youth toward Japanese "cool" have increased the popularity of authentic Japanese "manga" comics and animated cartoons. Pokémon cards, Hello Kitty, and Sony's tiny minidisc players are examples of Japanese products that caught on in the United States almost as quickly as in Japan.[33]

Dealing in China and with the Chinese, the international manager will have to realize that making deals has more to do with cooperation than competition. The Chinese believe that one should build the relationship first and, if successful, transactions will follow. The relationship, or *guanxi*, is a set of favor exchanges to establish trust.[34]

TABLE 2.2

Effect of Value Differences on Management Practice

Value of U.S. Culture	Alternative Value	Management Functions Affected
The individual can influence the future (where there is a will there is a way).	Life follows a preordained course, and human action is determined by the will of God.	Planning and scheduling
We must work hard to accomplish our objectives (Protestant ethic).	Hard work is not the only prerequisite for success. Wisdom, luck, and time are also required.	Motivation and reward system
Commitments should be honored (people will do what they say they will do).	A commitment may be superseded by a conflicting request or an agreement may only signify intention and have little or no relationship to the capacity of performance.	Negotiating and bargaining
One should effectively use one's time (time is money that can be saved or wasted).	Schedules are important but only in relation to other priorities.	Long- and short-range planning
A primary obligation of an employee is to the organization.	The individual employee has a primary obligation to his family and friends.	Loyalty, commitment, and motivation
The best qualified persons should be given the positions available.	Family considerations, friendship, and other considerations should determine employment practices.	Employment, promotions, recruiting, selection, and reward
Intuitive aspects of decision making should be reduced, and efforts should be devoted to gathering relevant information.	Decisions are expressions of wisdom by the person in authority, and any questioning would imply a lack of confidence in his judgment.	Decision-making process
Data should be accurate.	Accurate data are not as highly valued.	Record keeping
Company information should be available to anyone who needs it within the organization.	Withholding information to gain or maintain power is acceptable.	Organization communication, managerial style
Each person is expected to have an opinion and to express it freely even if his views do not agree with his colleagues.	Deference is to be given to persons in power or authority, and to offer judgment that is not in support of the ideas of one's superiors is unthinkable.	Communications, organizational relations
A person is expected to do whatever is necessary to get the job done (one must be willing to get one's hands dirty).	Various kinds of work are accorded low or high status and some work may be below one's "dignity" or place in the organization.	Assignment of tasks, performance, and organizational effectiveness
Change is considered an improvement and a dynamic reality.	Tradition is revered, and the power of the ruling group is founded on the continuation of a stable structure.	Planning, morale, and organization development

Source: Adapted from Philip R. Harris and Robert T. Moran, *Managing Cultural Differences* (Houston, TX: Gulf Publishing, 1996), Table 4.1.

A manager must be careful not to assume that success in one market using the cultural extension ensures success somewhere else. For example, while the Disneyland concept worked well in Tokyo, it had a tougher time in Paris. One of the main reasons was that while the Japanese are fond of American pop culture, the Europeans are quite content with their own cultural heritage.[35]

MANNERS AND CUSTOMS

Changes occurring in manners and customs must be carefully monitored, especially in cases that seem to indicate a narrowing of cultural differences among peoples. Phenomena such as McDonald's and Coke have met with success around the world, but this does not mean that the world is becoming Westernized. Modernization and Westernization are not at all the same, as can be seen in Saudi Arabia, for example.

Understanding manners and customs is especially important in negotiations, because interpretations based on one's own frame of reference may lead to a totally incorrect conclusion. To negotiate effectively abroad, all types of communication should be read correctly. Americans often interpret inaction and silence as negative signs. As a result, Japanese executives tend to expect that their silence can get Americans to lower prices or sweeten a deal. Even a simple agreement may take days to negotiate in the Middle East because the Arab party may want to talk about unrelated issues or do something else for a while. The aggressive style of Russian negotiators and their usual last-minute change requests may cause astonishment and concern on the part of ill-prepared negotiators. Some of the potential ways in which negotiators may not be prepared include: (1) insufficient understanding of different ways of thinking; (2) insufficient attention to the necessity to save face; (3) insufficient knowledge and appreciation of the host country—its history, culture, government, and image of foreigners; (4) insufficient recognition of the decision-making process and the role of personal relations and personalities; and (5) insufficient allocation of time for negotiations.[36]

One area where preparation and sensitivity are called for is in the area of gift giving. Table 2.3 provides examples of what and when to give. Gifts are an important part of relationship management during visits or recognizing partners during holidays. Care should be taken how the gift is wrapped; i.e., in appropriately colored paper. If

TABLE 2.3   When and What to Give in Gifts

China	India	Japan	Mexico	Saudi Arabia
Chinese New Year (January or February)	*Hindu Diwali festival (October or November)*	*Oseibo (January 1)*	*Christmas/New Year*	*Id al-Fitr (December or January)*
✓ Modest gifts such as coffee table books, ties, pens	✓ Sweets, nuts, and fruit; elephant carvings; candleholders	✓ Scotch, brandy, Americana, round fruit such as melons	✓ Desk clocks, fine pens, gold lighters	✓ Fine compasses to determine direction for prayer, cashmere
✗ Clocks, anything from Taiwan	✗ Leather objects, snake images	✗ Gifts that come in sets of four or nine	✗ Sterling silver items, logo gifts, food baskets	✗ Pork and pigskin, liquor

✓ recommended
✗ to be avoided

Source: Kate Murphy, "Gifts Without Gaffes for Global Clients," *Business Week,* December 6, 1999, 153.

delivered in person, the actual giving has to be executed correctly; e.g., in China, by extending the gift to the recipient using both hands.[37]

Managers must be concerned with differences in the ways products are used. General Foods' Tang is positioned as a breakfast drink in the United States; in France, where fruit juices and drinks are not usually consumed at breakfast, Tang is positioned as a refreshment. To shake powdered-soup domination in Argentina, Campbell markets its products as "the real soup," stressing its list of fresh ingredients. In Poland, where most soup consumed is homemade, Campbell promotes to mothers looking for convenience. The questions that the international manager has to ask are, "What are we selling?" "What are the benefits we are providing?" and "Who or what are we competing against?" Care should be taken not to assume cross-border similarities even if many of the indicators converge. For example, a jam producer noted that the Brazilian market seemed to hold significant potential because per capita jelly and jam consumption was one-tenth that of Argentina, clearly a difference not justified by obvious factors. However, Argentines consume jam at tea time, a custom that does not exist in Brazil. Furthermore, Argentina's climate and soil favor growing wheat, leading it to consume three times the bread Brazil does.[38]

Approaches that would not be considered in the United States or Europe might be recommended in other regions; for example, when Conrad Hotels (the international division of Hilton Hotels) experienced low initial occupancy rates at its Hong Kong facility, they brought in a *fung shui* man. These traditional "consultants" are foretellers of future events and the unknown through occult means, and are used extensively by Hong Kong businesses.[39] In Hilton's case, the *fung shui* man suggested a piece of sculpture be moved outside the hotel's lobby because one of the characters in the statue looked like it was trying to run out of the hotel. The hotel later reported a significant increase in its occupancy rate.

Meticulous research plays a major role in avoiding these types of problems. Concept tests determine the potential acceptance and proper understanding of a proposed new product. **Focus groups,** each consisting of 8 to 12 consumers representative of the proposed target audience, can be interviewed and their responses used as disaster checks and to fine-tune research findings. The most sensitive products, such as consumer packaged goods, require consumer usage and attitude studies as well as retail distribution studies and audits to analyze the movement of the product to retailers and eventually to households.

The adjustment to the cultural nuances of the marketplace has to be viewed as long term and may even be accomplished through trial and error. For example, U.S. retailers have found that U.S.-style retail outlets baffle overseas consumers with their size and warehouse-like atmosphere. Office Depot reduced the size of its Tokyo store by one-third, crammed the merchandise closer together, and found that sales remained at the same level as before.[40]

MATERIAL ELEMENTS

Material culture refers to the results of technology and is directly related to how a society organizes its economic activity. It is manifested in the availability and adequacy of the basic economic, social, financial, and marketing infrastructure for the international business in a market. The basic **economic infrastructure** consists of transportation, energy, and communications systems. **Social infrastructure** refers to housing, health, and educational systems prevailing in the country of interest. **Financial** and **marketing infrastructures** provide the facilitating agencies for the international firm's operation in a given market—for example, banks and research firms. In some parts of the world, the international firm may have to be an integral partner in developing the various infrastructures before it can operate, whereas in others it may greatly benefit from their high level of sophistication.

The level of material culture can aid segmentation efforts if the degree of industrialization of the market is used as a basis. For companies selling industrial goods, such as General Electric, this can provide a convenient starting point. In developing countries, demand may be highest for basic energy-generating products. In fully developed markets, time-saving home appliances may be more in demand.

While infrastructure is often a good indicator of potential demand, goods sometimes discover unexpectedly rich markets due to the informal economy at work in developing nations. In Kenya, for example, where most of the country's 30 million population live on less than a dollar a day, more than 770,000 people have signed up for mobile-phone service during the last two years; wireless providers are scrambling to keep up with demand. Leapfrogging older technologies, mobile phones are especially attractive to Kenya's thousands of small-time entrepreneurs—market stall owners, taxi drivers, and even hustlers who sell on the sidewalks. For most, income goes unreported, creating an invisible wealth on the strets. Mobile phones outnumber fixed lines in Kenya, as well as in Uganda, Venezuela, Cambodia, South Korea, and Chile. For companies this development is attractive as well given the expense of laying land lines.

Technological advances have been the major cause of cultural change in many countries. Increasingly, consumers are seeking more diverse products as a way of satisfying their demand for a higher quality of life and more leisure time. For example, a 1999 Gallup survey in China found that 44 percent of the respondents were saving to buy electronic items and appliances, which was second only to saving for a rainy day.[41] With technological advancement comes also **cultural convergence.** Black and white television sets extensively penetrated U.S. households more than a decade before similar levels occurred in Europe and Japan. With color television, the lag was reduced to five years. With video cassette recorders, the difference was only three years, but this time the Europeans and Japanese led the way while the United States was concentrating on cable systems. With the compact disc, penetration rates were equal in only one year. Today, with MTV available around the world and the use of the Internet increasing, no lag exists.[42]

Material culture—mainly the degree to which it exists and how it is esteemed—has an impact on business decisions. Many exporters do not understand the degree to which Americans are package conscious; for example, cans must be shiny and beautiful. In foreign markets, packaging problems may arise due to the lack of materials, different specifications when the material is available, and immense differences in quality and consistency of printing ink, especially in developing markets. Ownership levels of television sets, radios, and personal computers have an impact on the ability of media to reach target audiences.

AESTHETICS

Each culture makes a clear statement concerning good taste, as expressed in the arts and in the particular symbolism of colors, form, and music. What is and what is not acceptable may vary dramatically even in otherwise highly similar markets. Sex, for example, is a big selling point in many countries. In an apparent attempt to preserve the purity of Japanese womanhood, however, advertisers frequently turn to blond, blue-eyed foreign models to make the point. In introducing the shower soap Fa from the European market to the North American market, Henkel extended its European advertising campaign to the new market. The main creative difference was to have the young woman in the waves don a bathing suit rather than be naked as in the German original.

Color is often used as a mechanism for brand identification, feature reinforcement, and differentiation. In international markets, colors have more symbolic value than in domestic markets. Black, for instance, is considered the color of mourning in the United States and Europe, whereas white has the same symbolic meaning in Japan and most of the Far East. A British bank was interested in expanding its operations to Singapore and wanted to use blue and green as its identification colors. A consulting firm was quick to tell the client that green is associated with death in that country. Although the bank insisted on its original choice of colors, the green was changed to an acceptable shade.

With the global reach of the World Wide Web, symbols used have to be tested for universal appropriateness. The e-mailbox with its red flag is baffling to users outside of the United States and Canada. Similarly, the trash can on the e-mail interface may look to some like the British-styled mailbox. A British software application used the owl as a help icon only to find that in some countries it was not a symbol of wisdom but of evil and insanity.[43]

International firms, such as McDonald's, have to take into consideration local tastes and concerns in designing their outlets. They may have a general policy of uniformity in building or office space design, but local tastes often warrant modifications. Respecting local cultural traditions may also generate goodwill toward the international marketer. For example, McDonald's painstakingly renovated a seventeenth-century building for their third outlet in Moscow.

EDUCATION

Education, either formal or informal, plays a major role in the passing on and sharing of culture. Educational levels of a culture can be assessed using literacy rates, enrollment in secondary education, or enrollment in higher education available from secondary data sources. International firms also need to know about the qualitative aspects of education, namely, varying emphases on particular skills and the overall level of the education provided. Japan and South Korea, for example, emphasize the sciences, especially engineering, to a greater degree than do Western countries.

Educational levels also affect various business functions. For example, a high level of illiteracy suggests the use of visual aids rather than printed manuals. Local recruiting for sales jobs is affected by the availability of suitably trained personnel. In some cases, international firms routinely send locally recruited personnel to headquarters for training.

The international manager may also need to overcome obstacles in recruiting a suitable sales force or support personnel. For example, the Japanese culture places a premium on loyalty, and employees consider themselves members of the corporate family. If a foreign firm decides to leave Japan, its employees may find themselves stranded in midcareer, unable to find their place in the Japanese business system. Therefore, university graduates are reluctant to join any but the largest and most well-known foreign firms.

If technology is marketed, the product's sophistication will depend on the educational level of future users. Product adaptation decisions are often influenced by the extent to which targeted customers are able to use the good or service properly.

SOCIAL INSTITUTIONS

Social institutions affect the ways people relate to each other. The family unit, which in Western industrialized countries consists of parents and children, in a number of cultures is extended to include grandparents and other relatives. This affects consumption patterns and must be taken into account, for example, when conducting market research.

The concept of kinship, or blood relations between individuals, is defined in a very broad way in societies such as those in sub-Saharan Africa. Family relations and a strong obligation to family are important factors to consider in human resource management in those regions. Understanding tribal politics in countries such as Nigeria may help the manager avoid unnecessary complications in executing business transactions.

The division of a particular population into classes is termed **social stratification.** Stratification ranges from the situation in northern Europe, where most people are members of the middle class, to highly stratified societies in which the higher strata control most of the buying power and decision-making positions.

An important part of the socialization process of consumers worldwide is **reference groups.** These groups provide the values and attitudes that influence behavior. Primary reference groups include the family and coworkers and other intimate acquaintances, and secondary groups are social organizations where less-continuous interaction takes place, such as professional associations and trade organizations. In addition to providing socialization, reference groups develop a person's concept of self, which is manifested, for example, through the choice of products used. Reference groups also provide a baseline for compliance with group norms, giving the individual the option of conforming to or avoiding certain behaviors.

Social organization also determines the roles of managers and subordinates and how they relate to one another. In some cultures, managers and subordinates are separated explicitly and implicitly by various boundaries ranging from social class differences to separate office facilities. In others, cooperation is elicited through equality. For example, Nissan USA has no privileged parking spaces and no private dining rooms, everyone wears the same type of white coveralls, and the president sits in the same room with a hundred other white-collar workers. Fitting an organizational culture to the larger context of a national culture has to be executed with care. Changes that are too dramatic may disrupt productivity or, at the minimum, arouse suspicion.

Although Western business has impersonal structures for channeling power and influence—primarily through reliance on laws and contracts—the Chinese emphasize personal relationships to obtain clout. Things can get done without this human political capital, or *guanxi*, only if one invests enormous personal energy, is willing to offend even trusted associates, and is prepared to see it all melt away at a moment's notice.[44] For the Chinese, contracts form a useful agenda and a symbol of progress, but obligations come from relationships. McDonald's found this out in Beijing, where it was evicted from a central building after only 2 years despite having a 20-year contract. The incomer had a strong *guanxi*, whereas McDonald's had not kept its in good repair.[45]

Sources of Cultural Knowledge

The concept of cultural knowledge is broad and multifaceted. Cultural knowledge can be defined by the way it is acquired. Objective or factual information is obtained from others through communication, research, and education. **Experiential knowledge,** on the other hand, can be acquired only by being involved in a culture other than one's own. A summary of the types of knowledge needed by the international manager is provided in Table 2.4. Both factual and experiential information can be general or country-specific. In fact, the more a manager becomes involved in the international arena, the more he or she is able to develop a metaknowledge; that is, ground rules that apply whether in Kuala Lumpur, Malaysia, or Asunción, Paraguay. Market-specific knowledge does not necessarily travel well; the general variables on which the information is based do.

In a survey of managers on how to acquire international expertise, they ranked eight factors in terms of their importance, as shown in Table 2.5. The managers emphasized the experiential acquisition of knowledge. Written materials played an important but supplementary role, very often providing general or country-specific information before operational decisions were made. Interestingly, many of today's international managers have precareer experience in government, the Peace Corps, the armed forces, or missionary service. Although the survey emphasized travel, a one-time trip to London with a stay at a very large hotel and scheduled sightseeing tours does not significantly contribute to cultural knowledge. Travel that involves meetings with company personnel, intermediaries, facilitating agents, customers, and government officials, on the other hand, does contribute.

However, from the corporate point of view, global capability is developed in more painstaking ways: foreign assignments, networking across borders, and the use of multicountry, multicultural teams to develop strategies and programs. At Nestlé, for example, managers move around a region (such as Asia or Latin America) at four- or five-year intervals and may serve stints at headquarters for two to three years between such assignments. Such broad experience allows managers to pick up ideas and tools to be used in markets where they have not been used or where they have not been necessary before. In Thailand, where supermarkets are revolutionizing consumer-goods marketing, techniques perfected elsewhere in the Nestlé system are being put to effective use. The experiences then, in turn, are used to develop newly emerging markets in the same region, such as Vietnam.

Managers have a variety of sources and methods to extend their knowledge of specific cultures. Most of these sources deal with factual information that provides a necessary basis for market studies. Beyond the normal business literature and its anecdotal information, country specific studies are published by the U.S. government,

---

| **TABLE 2.4** | **Types of International Information** |

Source of Information	TYPE OF INFORMATION	
	General	**Country Specific**

Objective	Examples:
	  Impact of GDP
	  Regional integration
		Examples:
		  Tariff barriers
		  Government regulations

Experiential	Example:
	  Corporate adjustment
	  to internationalization
		Examples:
		  Product acceptance
		  Program appropriateness

TABLE 2.5

Manager's Ranking of Factors Involved in Acquiring International Expertise

Factor	Considered Critical	Considered Important
1. Assignments overseas	85%	9%
2. Business travel	83	17
3. Training programs	28	57
4. Nonbusiness travel	28	54
5. Reading	22	72
6. Graduate courses	13	52
7. Precareer activities	9	50
8. Undergraduate courses	1	48

Source: Data collected by authors from 110 executives, by questionnaire, February, 2003.

private companies, and universities. The U.S. Department of Commerce's (http://www.ita.doc.gov) *Country Commercial Guides* cover more than 133 countries, while the Economist Intelligence Unit's (http://www.eiu.com) *Country Reports* cover 180 countries. *Culturegrams* (http://www.culturegrams.com), which detail the customs of people of 174 countries, are published by the Center for International and Area Studies at Brigham Young University. Many facilitating agencies—such as advertising agencies, banks, consulting firms, and transportation companies—provide background information on the markets they serve for their clients. These range from Runzheimer International's (http://www.runzheimer.com) international reports on employee relocation and site selection for 44 countries, the Hong Kong and Shanghai Banking Corporation's (http://www.hsbc.com) *Business Profile Series* for 22 countries in the Asia-Pacific, to *World Trade* (http://www.worldtrademag.com) magazine's "Put Your Best Foot Forward" series, which covers Europe, Asia, Mexico/Canada, and Russia.

Specialists who advise clients on the cultural dimensions of business are available as well. Their task is not only to help avoid mistakes but to add culture as an ingredient of success in country- or region-specific programs. An example of such a service provider is shown in Figure 2.2

Blunders in foreign markets that could have been avoided with factual information are generally inexcusable. A manager who travels to Taipei without first obtaining a visa and is therefore turned back has no one else to blame. Other oversights may lead to more costly mistakes. For example, Brazilians are several inches shorter than the average American, but this was not taken into account when Sears erected American-height shelves that block Brazilian shoppers' view of the rest of the store.

International business success requires not only comprehensive fact finding and preparation but also an ability to understand and fully appreciate the nuances of different cultural traits and patterns. Gaining this **interpretive knowledge** requires "getting one's feet wet" over a sufficient length of time. Over the long run, culture can become a factor in the firm's overall success.

FIGURE 2.2

An Example of Culture Consulting

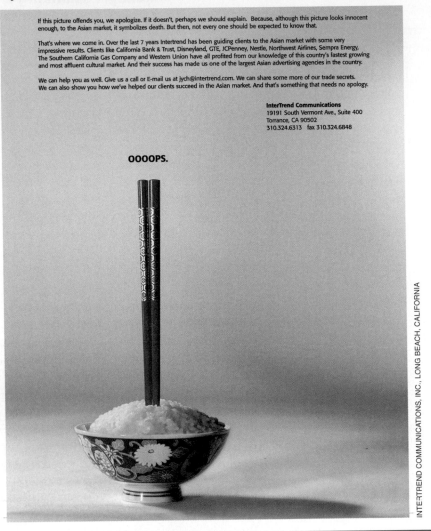

If this picture offends you, we apologize. If it doesn't, perhaps we should explain. Because, although this picture looks innocent enough, to the Asian market, it symbolizes death. But then, not every one should be expected to know that.

That's where we come in. Over the last 7 years Intertrend has been guiding clients to the Asian market with some very impressive results. Clients like California Bank & Trust, Disneyland, GTE, JCPenney, Nestle, Northwest Airlines, Sempra Energy, The Southern California Gas Company and Western Union have all profited from our knowledge of this country's fastest growing and most affluent cultural market. And their success has made us one of the largest Asian advertising agencies in the country.

We can help you as well. Give us a call or E-mail us at jych@intertrend.com. We can share some more of our trade secrets. We can also show you how we've helped our clients succeed in the Asian market. And that's something that needs no apology.

InterTrend Communications
19191 South Vermont Ave., Suite 400
Torrance, CA 90502
310.324.6313   fax 310.324.6848

OOOOPS.

INTERTREND COMMUNICATIONS, INC., LONG BEACH, CALIFORNIA

Cultural Analysis

To try to understand and explain differences among and across cultures, researchers have developed checklists and models showing pertinent variables and their interaction. An example of such a model is provided in Figure 2.3. Developed by Sheth and Sethi, this model is based on the premise that all international business activity should be viewed as innovation and as producing change.[46] After all, multinational corporations introduce management practices, as well as goods and services, from one country to others, where they are perceived to be new and different. Although many question the usefulness of such models, they do bring together all or most of the relevant variables on how consumers in different cultures may perceive, evaluate, and adopt new behaviors. However, any manager using such a tool should periodically cross-check its results against reality and experience.

FIGURE 2.3

A Model of Cross-Cultural Behavior

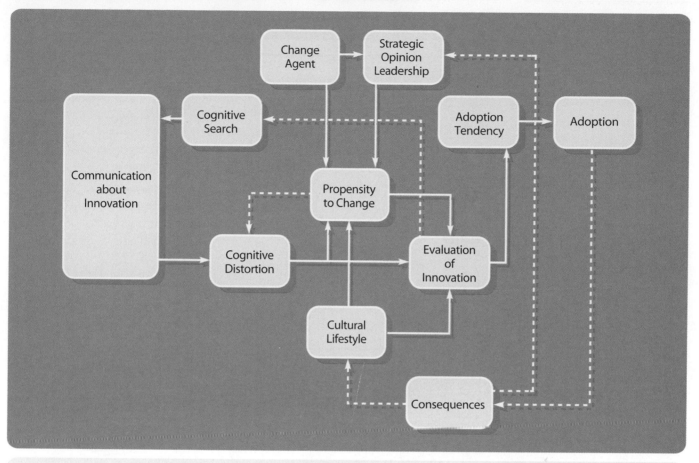

Source: Adapted by permission of the publisher from "A Theory of Cross-Cultural Buying Behavior," by Jagdish N. Sheth and S. Prakash Sethi, in *Consumer and Industrial Buyer Behavior,* eds. Arch G. Woodside, Jagdish N. Sheth, and Peter D. Bennett, 1977, 373. Copyright 1977 by Elsevier Science Publishing Co., Inc.

The key variable of the model is propensity to change, which is a function of three constructs: (1) cultural lifestyle of individuals in terms of how deeply held their traditional beliefs and attitudes are, and also which elements of culture are dominant; (2) change agents (such as multinational corporations and their practices) and strategic-opinion leaders (for example, social elites); and (3) communication about the innovation from commercial sources, neutral sources (such as government), and social sources, such as friends and relatives.

It has been argued that differences in cultural lifestyle can be explained by four dimensions of culture.[47] The dimensions consist of: (1) individualism ("I" consciousness versus "we" consciousness); (2) power distance (levels of equality in society); (3) uncertainty avoidance (need for formal rules and regulations); and (4) masculinity (attitude toward achievement, roles of men and women). Figure 2.4 presents a summary of 12 countries' positions along these dimensions. A fifth dimension has also been added to distinguish cultural differences: long-term versus short-term orientation.[48] All of the high-scoring countries are Asian (e.g., China, Hong Kong, Taiwan, Japan, and South Korea), while most Western countries (such as the United States and Britain) have low scores. Some have argued that this cultural dimension may explain

FIGURE 2.4

Culture Dimension Scores for Twelve Countries (0 = low; 100 = high)

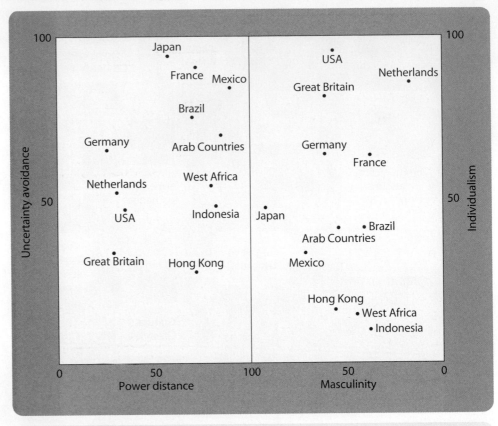

Source: Data for the figure derived from Geert Hofstede, "Management Scientists Are Human," *Management Science* 40, no. 1 (1994): 4–13.

the Japanese marketing success based on market share (rather than short-term profit) motivation in market development.

Knowledge of similarities along these four dimensions allows us to cluster countries and regions and establish regional and national marketing or business programs.[49] An example is provided in Table 2.6, in which the European market is segmented along cultural lines for the development of programs. Research has shown that the take-off point for new products (i.e., when initial sales turn into mass-market sales) is six years, on average, in Europe. However, in northern Europe new products take off almost twice as fast as they do in southern Europe.[50] Culturally, consumers in Cluster 1 are far more open to new ideas. Cluster 2, consisting of southern Europe, displays the highest uncertainty avoidance and should therefore be targeted with risk-reducing marketing programs such as extended warranties and return privileges.[51] It is important to position the product as a continuous innovation that does not require radical changes in consumption patterns.[52] Since the United States highly regards individualism, promotional appeals should be relevant to individual empowerment. Also, in order to incorporate the lower power distance, messages should be informal and friendly. In opposite situations, marketing communications have to emphasize that the new product is socially accepted. However, if the product is imported it can

TABLE 2.6   Culture-Based Segmentation

	Size (Million)	CULTURAL CHARACTERISTICS				Illustrative Marketing Implications
		Power Distance	Uncertainty Avoidance	Individualism	Masculinity	
Cluster 1						
Denmark, Sweden, Finland, Netherlands, Norway	37	Small	Low	High	Low	Relatively weak resistance to new products, strong consumer desire for novelty and variety, high consumer regard for "environmentally friendly" marketers and socially conscious firms
Cluster 2						
Belgium, France, Greece, Portugal, Spain, Turkey	182	Medium	Strong	Varied	Low-Medium	Appeal to consumer's status and power position, reduce perceived risk in product purchase and use, emphasize product functionality
Cluster 3						
Austria, Germany, Switzerland, Italy, Great Britain, Ireland	203	Small	Medium	Medium-High	High	Preference for "high-performance" products; use "successful-achiever" theme in advertising; desire for novelty, variety, and pleasure; fairly risk-averse market

(handwritten annotation near Cluster 1: "more open to new ideas")

(handwritten annotation near Cluster 2: "risk reducing marketing programms")

Source: Adapted from Sudhir H. Kale, "Grouping Euroconsumers: A Culture-Based Clustering Approach," *Journal of International Marketing* 3, 3 (1995): 42.

sometimes utilize global or foreign cultural positioning. For example, in China, individualism is often used for imported products but almost never for domestic ones.[53]

Understanding the implications of the dimensions helps businesspeople prepare for international business encounters. For example, in negotiating in Germany one can expect a counterpart who is thorough, systematic, very well prepared, but also rather dogmatic and therefore less flexible and willing to compromise. Efficiency is emphasized. In Mexico, however, the counterpart may prefer to address problems on a personal and private basis rather than on a business level. This means more emphasis on socializing and conveying one's humanity, sincerity, loyalty, and friendship. Also, differences in the pace and business practices of a region have to be accepted. Boeing Airplane Company found in its annual study on world aviation safety that countries with both low individualism and substantial power distances had accident rates 2.6 times greater than those at the other end of the scale. The findings naturally have an impact on training and service operations of airlines.[54]

Communication about innovation takes place through the physical product itself (samples) or through experiencing a new company policy. If a new personnel practice, such as quality circles or flextime, is being investigated, results may be communicated in reports or through word of mouth by the participating employees. Communication content depends on the following factors: the good's or policy's relative advantage over existing alternatives; compatibility with established behavioral patterns; complexity, or the degree to which the good or process is perceived as difficult to understand and use; trialability, or the degree to which it may be experimented with without incurring major risk; and observability, which is the extent to which the consequences of the innovation are visible.

Before a good or policy is evaluated, information should be gathered about existing beliefs and circumstances. Distortion of data may occur as a result of selective attention, exposure, and retention. As examples, anything foreign may be seen in a negative light, another multinational company's efforts may have failed, or the government may discourage the proposed activity. Additional information may then be sought from any of the sources or from opinion leaders in the market.

Adoption tendency refers to the likelihood that the product or process will be accepted. Examples are advertising in the People's Republic of China and equity joint ventures with Western participants in Russia, both of them unheard of a decade ago. If an innovation clears the hurdles, it may be adopted and slowly diffused into the entire market. An international manager has two basic choices: to adapt company offerings and methods to those in the market or to try to change market conditions to fit company programs. In Japan, a number of Western companies have run into obstructions in the Japanese distribution system, where great value is placed on established relationships; everything is done on the basis of favoring the familiar and fearing the unfamiliar. In most cases, this problem is solved by joint ventures with a major Japanese entity that has established contacts. On occasion, when the company's approach is compatible with the central beliefs of a culture, the company may be able to change existing customs rather than adjust to them. Initially, Procter & Gamble's traditional hard-selling style in television commercials jolted most Japanese viewers accustomed to more subtle approaches. Now the ads are being imitated by Japanese competitors. However, this is not to be interpreted to mean that the Japanese will adapt to Western approaches. The emphasis in Japan is still on who speaks rather than on what is spoken. That is why, for example, Japan is a market where Procter & Gamble's company name is presented as well in the marketing communication for a brand, rather than only the product's brand name, which is customary in the United States and European markets.[55]

Although models such as the one in Figure 2.3 may aid in strategy planning by making sure that all variables and their interlinkages are considered, any analysis is incomplete without the basic recognition of cultural differences. Adjusting to differences requires putting one's own cultural values aside. James A. Lee proposes that the natural **self-reference criterion**—the unconscious reference to one's own cultural values—is the root of most international business problems.[56] However, recognizing and admitting this are often quite difficult. The following analytical approach is recommended to reduce the influence of cultural bias:

1. Define the problem or goal in terms of the domestic cultural traits, habits, or norms.
2. Define the problem or goal in terms of the foreign cultural traits, habits, or norms. Make no value judgments.
3. Isolate the self-reference criterion influence in the problem, and examine it carefully to see how it complicates the problem.

4. Redefine the problem without the self-reference criterion influence, and solve for the optimum-goal situation.

This approach can be applied to product introduction. If Kellogg Co. wants to introduce breakfast cereals into markets where breakfast is traditionally not eaten or where consumers drink very little milk, managers must consider very carefully how to instill the new habit. The traits, habits, and norms concerning the importance of breakfast are quite different in the United States, France, and Brazil, and they have to be outlined before the product can be introduced. In France, Kellogg's commercials are aimed as much at providing nutrition lessons as they are at promoting the product. In Brazil, the company advertised on a soap opera to gain entry into the market because Brazilians often emulate the characters of these television shows.

Analytical procedures require constant monitoring of changes caused by outside events as well as the changes caused by the business entity itself. Controlling **ethnocentrism**—the tendency to consider one's own culture superior to others—can be achieved only by acknowledging it and properly adjusting to its possible effects in managerial decision making. The international manager needs to be prepared and able to put that preparedness to effective use.

The Training Challenge

International managers face a dilemma in terms of international and intercultural competence. The lack of adequate foreign language and international business skills have cost U.S. firms lost contracts, weak negotiations, and ineffectual management. A UNESCO study of 10- to 14-year-old students in nine countries placed Americans next to last in their comprehension of foreign cultures. The terrorist attacks of September 11, 2001, for instance, alerted the U.S. government not only to the national lack of competence in foreign language skills, but to the nation's failure to educate its population to cultural sensibilities at home and around the world.[57]

The increase in the overall international activity of firms has increased the need for cultural sensitivity training at all levels of the organization. Further, today's training must encompass not only outsiders to the firm but interaction within the corporate family as well. However inconsequential the degree of interaction may seem, it can still cause problems if proper understanding is lacking. Consider, for example, the date 11/12/04 on a telex; a European will interpret this as the 11th of December, an American as the 12th of November.

Some companies try to avoid the training problem by hiring only nationals or well-traveled Americans for their international operations. This makes sense for the management of overseas operations but will not solve the training need, especially if transfers to a culture unfamiliar to the manager are likely. International experience may not necessarily transfer from one market to another.

To foster cultural sensitivity and acceptance of new ways of doing things within the organization, management must institute internal education programs. The programs may include: (1) culture-specific information (data covering other countries, such as videopacks and culturegrams); (2) general cultural information (values, practices, and assumptions of countries other than one's own); and (3) self-specific information (identifying one's own cultural paradigm, including values, assumptions, and perceptions about others).[58] One study found that Japanese assigned to the United States get mainly language training as preparation for the task. In addition, many companies use mentoring, whereby an individual is assigned to someone who is experienced and who will spend time squiring and explaining. Talks given by returnees and by visiting lecturers hired specifically for the task round out the formal part of training.[59] At Samsung, several special interest groups were formed to focus on issues such as Japanese society and business practices, the Chinese economy, changes in Europe, and the U.S. economy. In addition, groups also explore cutting-edge business issues, such as new technology and marketing strategies. And for the past few years, Samsung has been sending the brightest junior employees abroad for a year.[60]

The objective of formal training programs is to foster the four critical characteristics of preparedness, sensitivity, patience, and flexibility in managers and other personnel. The programs vary dramatically in terms of their rigor, involvement, and, of course, cost.[61] A summary of the programs is provided in Figure 2.5.

Environmental briefings and cultural-orientation programs are types of **area studies** programs. The programs provide factual preparation for a manager to operate in, or work with people from, a particular country. Area studies should be a basic prerequisite for other types of training programs. Alone, area studies serve little practical purpose because they do not really get the manager's feet wet. Other, more involved, programs contribute context in which to put facts so that they can be properly understood.

FIGURE 2.5

Cross-Cultural Training Methods

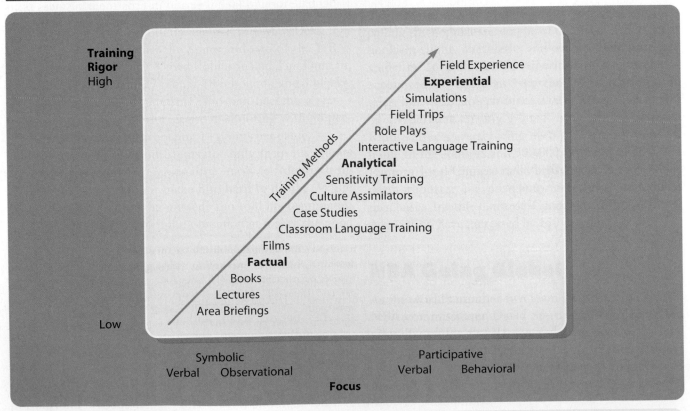

Source: J. Stewart Black and Mark Mendenhall, "A Practical but Theory-Based Framework for Selecting Cross-Cultural Training Methods," in *International Human Resource Management,* eds. Mark Mendenhall and Gary Oddou (Boston: PWS-Kent, 1991), 188.

The **cultural assimilator** is a program in which trainees must respond to scenarios of specific situations in a particular country. The programs have been developed for the Arab countries, Iran, Thailand, Central America, and Greece. The results of the trainees' assimilator experience are evaluated by a panel of judges. This type of program has been used most frequently in cases of transfers abroad on short notice.

When more time is available, managers can be trained extensively in language. This may be required if an exotic language is involved. **Sensitivity training** focuses on enhancing a manager's flexibility in situations that are quite different from those at home. The approach is based on the assumption that understanding and accepting oneself is critical to understanding a person from another culture. While most of the methods discussed are best delivered in face-to-face settings, web-based training is becoming more popular as seen in Focus on e-Business.

Finally, training may involve **field experience,** which exposes a manager to a different cultural environment for a limited amount of time. Although the expense of placing and maintaining an expatriate is high (and, therefore, the cost of failure is high), field experience is rarely used in training. One field experience technique that

Focus On ⬇

e-BUSINESS

Online Cultural Training

The Internet can play an important role in preparing marketing people for the international marketplace. While it cannot replace real-life interaction as an experiential tool, it does provide a number of benefits including comparisons between cultural ways of behaving and can provide an opportunity to develop the skills needed to interact successfully with people from other cultures. Many companies use online learning as an addition to existing instructor-led programs. When time is at a premium (due to a fast-approaching assignment/project or to a manager's overall schedule), the role of this learning approach becomes even more critical.

Companies typically rely on the following elements in designing web-based training:

1. **Detailed Scenarios.** Much of the training material consists of a detailed, realistic story that is tied into elements of the learner's background; i.e., the session becomes more than a briefing; it becomes a narrated experience full of learning moments for participants. This is made possible by the ability of the web to store and circulate a lot of information instantaneously around the world.

2. **Gradual Delivery.** The ability to control the flow of information to the participant supports the learning process in a number of ways. First, the participant is allowed to fit the training into his/her schedule. Secondly, the real-life flow of information is mimicked and a higher degree of realism is achieved.

3. **Support.** A set of detailed materials is provided to the participants 24 hours a day. At any hour and at any location, participants can check their perceptions against the materials, reinforce learning from a dimly recalled lesson, or seek feedback on an important point or issue.

4. **Relevant Exercises.** Participants can be provided topical exercises and activities the level of which can be adjusted depending upon how the participant has invested in the training.

5. **Online Discussions.** Sessions can be simulcast to hundreds of participants around the world. The lack of face-to-face interaction can be remedied by having discussion groups where participants can share their experiences with each other. The pooled learning experience is stronger than one with a solitary participant.

Online cross-cultural programs focus on preparing international managers for the host of business scenarios they will encounter overseas. Training is often specific to a location, priming managers for posts in the Asian Pacific, Latin America, Europe, or the Middle East. There are also online programs that prepare international managers for repatriation into the United States. Using a range of training tools, from compelling case studies that are revealed over time to web-based activities and exercises, programs cover such topics as intercultural adaptation, recognizing differences in communication styles, negotiation strategies, and practical information on aspects of business and daily life.

Source: Mike Bowler, "Online Learning is Fastest Growing Segment of Higher Education," *Knight Ridder Tribune Business News,* August 17, 2003, 1; "On-line Learning," Special Advertising Section, *Fortune,* July 1, 2002, S1–S19; Peter T. Burgi and Brant R. Dykehouse, "On-Line Cultural Training: The Next Phase," *International Insight,* Winter 2000, 7–10. See also http://www.runzheimer.com; IOR Global Services, www.ioworld.com, accessed February 6, 2002.

has been suggested when the training process needs to be rigorous is the host-family surrogate. This technique places a trainee (and possibly his or her family) in a domestically located family of the nationality to which they are assigned.[62]

Regardless of the degree of training, preparation, and positive personal characteristics, a manager will always remain foreign. A manager should never rely on his or her own judgment when local managers can be consulted. In many instances, a manager should have an interpreter present at negotiations, especially if the manager is not completely bilingual. Overconfidence in one's language capabilities can create problems.

Making Culture Work for Business Success

Culture should not be viewed as a challenge, but rather as an opportunity that can be exploited. This requires, as has been shown in this chapter, an understanding of cultural differences and their fundamental determinants. Differences can quite easily be dismissed as indicators of inferiority or viewed as approaches to be changed; however, the opposite may actually be the case. Best practice knows no one particular origin, nor should it acknowledge boundaries. The following rules serve as a summary of how culture and its appreciation may serve as a tool to ensure success.

Embrace local culture. Many corporate credos include a promise to be best possible corporate citizens in every community operated in.[63] For example, in 3M's plant near Bangkok, Thailand, a Buddhist shrine, wreathed in flowers, pays homage to the spirits Thais believe took care of the land prior to the plant's construction. Showing sensitivity to local customs helps create local acceptance and builds employee morale. More important, it contributes to a deeper understanding of the market and keeps the company from inadvertently doing something to alienate constituents.

Build relationships. Each country-market has its own unique set of constituents who need to be identified and nurtured. Establishing and nurturing local ties at the various stages of the market-development cycle develops relationships that can be invaluable in expansion and countering political risk. 3M started preparing to enter the China market soon after President Nixon's historic visit in 1972. For ten years, company officials visited Beijing and entertained visits of Chinese officials to company headquarters in Minneapolis-St. Paul. Such efforts paid off in 1984, when the Chinese government made 3M the first wholly owned venture in the market. Many such emerging markets require long-term commitment on part of the company.

Employ locals in order to gain cultural knowledge. The single best way to understand a market is to grow with it by developing the human resources and business partnerships along the way. Of the 7,500 3M employees in Asia, fewer than ten are from the United States. In fact, of the 34,000 3M employees outside of the United States, fewer than 1 percent are expatriates. The rest are locals who know local customs and purchasing habits of their compatriots. In every way possible, locals are made equals with their U.S. counterparts. For example, grants are made available for 3M employees to engage in the product-development process with concepts and idea development.

Help employees understand you. Employing locals will give a marketer a valuable asset in market development (i.e., in acculturation). However, these employees also need their own process of adjustment (i.e., "corporatization") in order to be effective. At any given time, more than 30 of 3M's Asian technicians are in the United States, where they learn about the latest product and process advances while gaining insight into how the company works. Also, they are able to develop personal ties with people they may work with. Furthermore, they often contribute by infusing their insights into company plans. Similar schemes are in place for distributors. Distributor advisory councils allow intermediaries to share their views with the company.

Adapt products and processes to local markets. Nowhere is commitment to local markets as evident as in product offerings. Global, regional, and purely local products are called for and constant and consistent product-development efforts on a market-by-market basis are warranted to find the next global success. When the sales of 3M's famous Scotchbrite cleaning pads were languishing, company researchers interviewed housewives and domestic help to determine why. Traditionally, floors are scrubbed with the help of rough shells of coconuts. 3M responded by making its cleaning pads brown and shaping them like a foot. In China, a big seller for 3M is a composite to fill tooth cavities. In the United States, dentists pack a soft material into the cavity and blast it with a special beam of light, making it as hard as enamel in a matter of seconds. In China, dentists cannot afford this technology. 3M's solution was an air-drying composite that achieved similar effects in a matter of minutes, with minimal expense.

Coordinate by region. The transfer of best practice is critical, especially in areas that have cultural similarities. When 3M designers in Singapore discovered that customers used its Nomad household mats in their cars, they spread the word to their counterparts throughout Asia. The company encourages its product managers from different parts of Asia to hold regular periodic meetings and share insights and strategies. The goal of this cross-pollination is to come up with regional programs and "Asianize" or even globalize a product more quickly. Joint endeavors build cross-border esprit de corps, especially when managers may have their own markets' interests primarily at heart.[64]

Summary

Culture is one of the most challenging elements of the international marketplace. This system of learned behavior patterns characteristic of the members of a given society is constantly shaped by a set of dynamic variables: language, religion, values and attitudes, manners and customs, aesthetics, technology, education, and social institutions. To cope with this system, an international manager needs both factual and interpretive knowledge of culture. To some extent, the factual knowledge can be learned; its interpretation comes only through experience.

The most complicated problems in dealing with the cultural environment stem from the fact that to truly become part of a culture, one has to live in it. Two schools of thought exist in the business world on how to deal with cultural diversity. One is that business is business the world around, following the model of Pepsi and McDonald's. In some cases, globalization is a fact of life; however, cultural differences are still far from converging.

The other school proposes that companies must tailor business approaches to individual cultures. Setting up policies and procedures in each country has been compared to an organ transplant; the critical question centers around acceptance or rejection.

The major challenge to the international manager is to make sure that rejection is not a result of cultural myopia or even blindness.

The internationally successful companies all share an important quality: patience. They have not rushed into situations but rather built their operations carefully by following the most basic business principles. These principles are to know your adversary, know your audience, and know your customer.

Questions for Discussion

1. Comment on the assumption, "If people are serious about doing business with you, they will speak English."

2. You are on your first business visit to Germany. You feel confident about your ability to speak the language (you studied German in school and have taken a refresher course), and you decide to use it. During introductions, you want to break the ice by asking "Wie geht's?" and insisting that everyone call you by your first name. Speculate as to the reaction.

3. Q: "What do you call a person who can speak two languages?"
A: "Bilingual."
Q: "How about three?"
A: "Trilingual."
Q: "Excellent. How about one?"
A: "Hmmmm. . . . American!"
Is this joke malicious, or is there something to be learned from it?

4. What can be learned about a culture from reading and attending to factual materials?

5. Provide examples of how the self-reference criterion might manifest itself.

6. Is any international business entity not a cultural imperialist? How else could one explain the phenomenon of multinational corporations?

Internet Exercises

1. Various companies, such as GMAC Relocation Service, are available to prepare and train international managers for the cultural challenge. Using GMAC's web site (http://www.gmacglobalrelocation.com), assess their role in helping the international manager.

2. Compare and contrast an international company's home pages for presentation and content; for example, Coca-Cola (at http://www.coca-cola.com) and its Japanese version (http://www.cocacola.co.jp). Are the differences cultural?

Take a Stand

France's Ministry of Culture is worried about the threat that the United States presents, especially to French cinema. However, the threat is perceived to be broader. Hollywood is seen as the Trojan horse bringing Disneyland Paris, fast-food chains, and advertising for U.S. products ranging from clothes to rock and country music. "The United States is not only interested in exporting movies," says Giles Jacob, the head of the Cannes Film Festival, "but it is also exporting its way of life." While the United States may not make the most movies in the world, it is the only one whose movies have global reach. Of any year's top-50 grossing movies, typically 48 or 49 are made in the United State. In the European Union, U.S. movies hold a 70 percent market share, up from 50 percent only 15 years ago. Marketing budgets for U.S. movies easily surpass an average European movie's total budget. At the same time, overseas markets, Europe in particular, have become critical to studios as production budgets have grown.

The French government has launched an offensive against what they see as American cultural hegemony. The French convinced the European Union to decree that 40 percent of TV programs be domestic. The government has also strengthened their substantial system of support, which, for example, taxes cinema tickets to help local film production, by extending subsidies to television.

In addition to criticism from the United States about these policies, some influential individuals in France have also spoken against this system of subsidies and quotas. Jeanne Moreau, the doyenne of French actors, argues that French film producers should stop relying on protectionism and start believing in themselves again.

For Discussion

1. Is American culture, like a horror-movie monster's foot, about to crush the world?
2. What constructive steps can governments take to protect their own cultural heritage in areas such as the cinema?

CHAPTER

3

Trade and Investment Policies

Learning Objectives

- To see how trade and investment policies have historically been a subset of domestic policies

- To examine how traditional attitudes toward trade and investment policies are changing

- To see the effects of global links in trade and investment on policymakers

- To understand that nations must cooperate closely in the future to maintain a viable global trade and investment environment

The World Bank Fights Poverty

Poverty is traditionally defined as a situation where a person's consumption or income levels fall below some minimum level necessary to meet basic needs. Extreme economic poverty is defined as living on less than $1 per day. Since "basic needs" vary from country to country and evolve as time progresses, the definition of poverty also keeps changing. For example, living standards have risen dramatically. Whereas per capita private consumption growth in developing countries averaged about 1.4 percent a year between 1980 and 1990, the growth rate averaged 2.4 percent per year between 1990 and 1999.

The growing population of developing countries has yielded an increasing number of people being born into poverty. The population of developing countries has risen from 2.9 billion in 1970 to 5.2 billion in 2000. Of these 5.2 billion, 2.8 billion live on less than $2 a day. Analysts predict that total world population will increase by another 1 billion between 2000 and 2015, with 97 percent of this increase occurring in developing countries.

The World Bank attempts to address the multidimensional nature of poverty by taking several factors into consideration: levels of income and consumption, social indicators, and indicators of vulnerability to risks and of sociopolitical access. There are seven major international development goals regarding the reduction of poverty: (1) to reduce the proportion of people living in extreme poverty by half by 2015; (2) to enroll all children in primary school by 2015; (3) to make progress toward gender equality and empowering women by eliminating gender disparities in primary and secondary education by 2005; (4) to reduce infant and child mortality rates by two thirds by 2015; (5) to reduce maternal mortality ratios by three quarters by 2015; (6) to provide access for all who need reproductive health services by 2016; and (7) to implement national strategies for sustainable development by 2005 so as to reverse the loss of environmental resources by 2015. In order to reach these goals, the World Development Report proposes three strategies: promoting opportunity, facilitating empowerment, and enhancing security.

In fiscal year 2002, the World Bank provided more than $19.5 billion in loans to its client countries. It works with more than 100 developing countries, providing financing and ideas to support poverty reduction. The World Bank's "Bottom-Up Participatory Approach" encourages governments to find the root causes of poverty, thus allowing the appropriate policy prescriptions to be developed. Despite the fact that it has access to vast oil reserves, Nigeria is among the 20 poorest countries in the world, with roughly 66 percent of its population living below the poverty line. Gross national product (GNP) per capita has decreased from $370 in 1985 to $260 today. Many of Nigeria's woes stem from economic mismanagement, corruption, and excessive dependence on the oil sector. Nigeria's large reserves of human and natural resources make its potential for overcoming poverty large. In June 2002, the Bank approved loans worth $237 million to Nigeria for socioeconomic improvement. In total, the World Bank supports ten projects in Nigeria with commitment of about $783 million in the areas of HIV/AIDS, community-driven development, privatization, power transmission, education, and water.

Source: World Bank's World Development Report Overview, *Attacking Poverty: Opportunity, Empowerment, and Security.* http://www.worldbank.org.

This chapter discusses the policy actions taken by countries. All nations have international trade and investment policies. The policies may be publicly pronounced or kept secret, they may be disjointed or coordinated, or they may be applied consciously or determined by a laissez-fiare attitude. Trade policy actions become evident when measures taken by governments affect the flow of trade and investment across national borders.

Rationale and Goals of Trade and Investment Policies

Government policies are designed to regulate, stimulate, direct, and protect national activities. The exercise of these policies is the result of **national sovereignty,** which provides a government with the right and burden to shape the environment of the country and its citizens. Because they are "border bound," governments focus mainly on domestic policies. Nevertheless, many policy actions have repercussions on other nations, firms, and individuals abroad and are therefore a component of a nation's trade and investment policy.

Government policy can be subdivided into two groups of policy actions that affect trade and investment. One affects trade and investment directly, the other indirectly. The domestic policy actions of most governments aim to increase the **standard of living** of the country's citizens, to improve the **quality of life,** to stimulate national development, and to achieve full employment. Clearly, all of these goals are closely intertwined. For example, an improved standard of living is likely to contribute to national development. Similarly, quality of life and standard of living are closely interlinked. Also, a high level of employment will play a major role in determining the standard of living. Yet all of these policy goals will also affect international trade and investment indirectly. For example, if foreign industries become more competitive and rapidly increase their exports, employment in the importing countries may suffer. Likewise, if a country accumulates large quantities of debt, which at some time must be repaid, the present and future standard of living will be threatened.

In more direct ways, a country may also pursue policies of increased development that mandate either technology transfer from abroad or the exclusion of foreign industries to the benefit of domestic infant firms. Also, government officials may believe that imports threaten the culture, health, or standards of the country's citizens and thus the quality of life. As a result, officials are likely to develop regulations to protect the citizens.

Nations also institute **foreign policy** measures designed with domestic concerns in mind but explicitly aimed to exercise influence abroad. One major goal of foreign policy may be national security. For example, nations may develop alliances, coalitions, and agreements to protect their borders or their spheres of interest. Similarly, nations may take measures to enhance their national security preparedness in case of international conflict. Governments also wish to improve trade and investment opportunities and to contribute to the security and safety of their own firms abroad.

Policy aims may be approached in various ways. For example, to develop new markets abroad and to increase their sphere of influence, nations may give foreign aid to other countries. This was the case when the United States generously awarded Marshall Plan funds for the reconstruction of Europe. Governments may also feel a need to restrict or encourage trade and investment flows in order to preserve or enhance the capability of industries that are important to national security.

Each country develops its own domestic policies, and therefore policy aims will vary from nation to nation. Inevitably, conflicts arise. For example, full employment

Cattle in Europe are raised without hormones. Since 1989 hormone-fed beef has been banned in European countries, effectively restricting imports of U.S. beef. A WTO review of the hormones found the ban was not based on scientific evidence, but despite threats of sanctions, the ban has not been lifted.

© GETTY IMAGES/PHOTODISK

policies in one country may directly affect employment policies in another. Similarly, the development aims of one country may reduce the development capability of another. Even when health issues are concerned, disputes may arise. One nation may argue that its regulations are in place to protect its citizens, whereas other nations may interpret the regulations as market barriers. An example of the latter situation is the celebrated hormone dispute between the United States and the European Union. U.S. cattle are treated with growth hormones. While the United States claims that these hormones are harmless to humans, many Europeans find them scary. Given the differences in perspectives, there is much room for conflict when it comes to trade policies, particularly when the United States wants to export more beef and the European Union attempts to restrict such beef imports.

The trade disagreement between the United States and Japan in the automotive sector is another example. While the United States claimed that Japanese firms prevent the importation and sale of U.S.-made auto parts, Japan's government blamed quality concerns and lack of effort by U.S. firms. Such disagreements can quickly escalate into major trade conflicts.

Differences among national policies have always existed and are likely to erupt into occasional conflict. Yet, the closer economic links among nations have made the emergence of such conflicts more frequent and the disagreements more severe. In recognition of this development, efforts have been made since 1945 to create a multilateral institutional arrangement that can help to resolve national conflicts, harmonize national policies, and facilitate increased international trade and investments.

Global Trade Regulation Since 1945

In 1945, the United States led in the belief that international trade and investment flows were a key to worldwide prosperity. Many months of international negotiations in London, Geneva, and Lake Success (New York) culminated on March 24, 1948, in Havana, Cuba, with the signing of the Havana Charter for the **International Trade Organization (ITO).** The charter represented a series of agreements among 53 countries. It was designed to cover international commercial policies, restrictive business practices, commodity agreements, employment and reconstruction, economic development and international investment, and a constitution for a new United Nations agency to administer the whole.[1]

Even though the International Trade Organization incorporated many farsighted notions, most nations refused to ratify its provisions. They feared the power and bureaucratic size of the new organization—and the consequent threats to national sovereignty. As a result, this most forward-looking approach to international trade and investment was never implemented. However, other organizations conceived at the time have made major contributions toward improving international business. An agreement was initiated for the purpose of reducing tariffs and therefore facilitating trade. In addition, international institutions such as the United Nations, the World Bank, and the International Monetary Fund were negotiated.

The **General Agreement on Tariffs and Trade (GATT)** has been called a "remarkable success story of a postwar international organization that was never intended to become one."[2] It started out in 1947 as a set of rules to ensure nondiscrimination, transparent procedures, the settlement of disputes, and the participation of the lesser-developed countries in international trade. To increase trade, GATT used tariff concessions, through which member countries agreed to limit the level of tariffs they would impose on imports from other GATT members. An important tool is the **Most-Favored Nation (MFN)** clause, which calls for each member country to grant every other member country the same most favorable treatment that it accords to any other country with respect to imports and exports.[3] MFN, in effect, provides for equal, rather than special, treatment.

The GATT was not originally intended to be an international organization. Rather, it was to be a multilateral treaty designed to operate under the International Trade Organization (ITO). However, because the ITO never came into being, the GATT became the governing body for settling international trade disputes. Gradually it evolved into an institution that sponsored various successful rounds of international trade negotiations with an initial focus on the reduction of prevailing high tariffs. Headquartered in Geneva, Switzerland, the GATT Secretariat conducted its work as instructed by the representatives of its member nations. Even though the GATT had no independent enforcement mechanism and relied entirely on moral suasion and on frequently wavering membership adherence to its rules, it achieved major progress for world trade.

Early in its history, the GATT accomplished the reduction of duties for trade in 50,000 products, amounting to two-thirds of the value of the trade among its participants. In subsequent years, special GATT negotiations such as the Kennedy Round, named after John F. Kennedy, and the Tokyo Round, named after the location where the negotiations were agreed upon, further reduced trade barriers and improved dispute-settlement mechanisms. The GATT also developed better provisions for dealing with subsidies and more explicit definitions of roles for import controls. Table 3.1 provides an overview of the different GATT rounds.

The latest GATT negotiations, called the Uruguay Round, were initiated in 1987. Even though tariffs still were addressed in these negotiations, their importance has been greatly diminished due to the success of earlier agreements. The main thrust of negotiations had become the sharpening of dispute-settlement rules and the integration of the trade and investment areas that were outside of the GATT. After many years of often contentious negotiations, a new accord was finally ratified in early 1995. The GATT was supplanted by a new institution, the **World Trade Organization**

TABLE 3.1   Negotiations in the GATT

Round	Dates	Numbers of Countries	Value of Trade Covered	Average Tariff Cut	Average Tariffs Afterward
Geneva	1947	23	$10 billion	35%	n/a
Annecy	1949	33	Unavailable		n/a
Torquay	1950	34	Unavailable		n/a
Geneva	1956	22	$2.5 billion		n/a
Dillon	1960–1961	45	$4.9 billion		n/a
Kennedy	1962–1967	48	$40 billion	35%	8.7%
Tokyo	1973–1979	99	$155 billion	34%	4.7%
Uruguay	1987–1995	124	$300 billion	38%	3.9%
Doha	2001–	148	TBN[a]	TBN[a]	n/a

[a]To be negotiated

Source: John H. Jackson, *The World Trading System* (Cambridge, Mass.: MIT Press, 1989) and *The GATT: Uruguay Round Final Act Should Produce Overall U.S. Economic Gains.* U.S. General Accounting Office, Report to Congress, Washington, DC, July 1994, http://www.gao.gov.

(WTO), which now administers international trade and investment accords (http://www.wto.org). These accords will gradually reduce governmental subsidies to industries and will convert nontariff barriers into more transparent tariff barriers. The textile and clothing industries eventually will be brought into the WTO regime, resulting in decreased subsidies and fewer market restrictions through the General Agreement on Trade in Services (GATS). An entire new set of rules was designed to govern the service area, and agreement also was reached on new rules to encourage international investment flows.

In 2001, a new round of international trade negotiations was initiated. Since the agreement to do so was reached in the city of Doha (Qatar), the negotiations are now called the "Doha Round." The aim was to further hasten implementation of liberalization to help particularly the impoverished and developing nations. In addition, the goal was to expand the role of the WTO to encompass more of the trade activities where there were insufficient rules for its definition and structure. This was due to either purposeful exclusion by governments in earlier negotiations or due to new technology changing the global markeplace. Examples are trade in agricultural goods, antidumping regulations, and electronic commerce. For example, in the agricultural sector it was proposed to reduce average global tariffs on farm products from 62 percent to 15 percent and to remove $100 billion in global-trade-distorting subsidies. Cutting barriers to trade by one third could boost the world economy by $613 billion, which is like adding an economy the size of Canada to the world economy.[4]

The beginning of the negotiations was quite slow, since U.S. negotiators did not have "fast track" authority, where Congress could either approve or disapprove proposed trade agreements, but not amend or change them. However, in the summer of 2002 such authority was granted to the President, and prospects for the Doha Round improved rapidly. A conclusion of the round is expected by 2006.

The GATT and now the WTO have made major contributions to improved trade and investment flows around the world. The success of the GATT and the resulting increase in welfare has refuted the old postulate that "the strong is most powerful alone." Nations have increasingly come to recognize that international trade and investment activities are important to their own economic well-being.

Nations also have come to accept that they must generate sufficient outgoing export and incoming investment activities to compensate for the inflow of imports and outgoing investment. In the medium and long term, the balance of payments must be maintained. For short periods of time, gold or capital transfers can be used to finance a deficit. Such financing, however, can continue only while gold and foreign assets last or while foreign countries will accept the IOUs of the deficit countries, permitting them to pile up foreign liabilities. This willingness, of course, will vary. Some countries, such as the United States, can run up deficits of hundreds of billions of dollars because of political stability, acceptable rates of return, and perceived economic security. Yet, over the long term, all nations are subject to the same economic rules.

Changes in the Global Policy Environment

Three major changes have occurred over time in the global policy environment: a reduction of domestic policy influence, a weakening of traditional international institutions, and a sharpening of the conflict between industrialized and developing nations. These three changes in turn have had a major effect on policy responses in the international trade and investment field.

REDUCTION OF DOMESTIC POLICY INFLUENCES

The effects of growing global influences on a domestic economy have been significant. Policymakers have increasingly come to recognize that it is very difficult to isolate domestic economic activity from international market events. Again and again, domestic policy measures are vetoed or counteracted by the activities of global market forces. Decisions that were once clearly in the domestic purview now have to be revised due to influences from abroad. At the same time, the clash between the fixed geography of nations and the nonterritorial nature of many of today's problems and solutions continues to escalate. Nation-states may simply no longer be the natural problem-solving unit. Local government may be most appropriate to address some of the problems of individuals, while transnational or even global entities are required to deal with larger issues such as economics, resources, or the environment.[5]

Agricultural policies, for example—historically a domestic issue—have been thrust into the international realm. Any time a country or a group of nations such as the European Union contemplates changes in agricultural subsidies, quantity restrictions, or even quality regulations, international trade partners are quick to speak up against the resulting global effects of such changes. Focus on Politics shows some of the effects of embargoes and tariffs. When countries contemplate specific industrial policies that encourage, for example, industrial innovation or collaboration, they often encounter major opposition from their trading partners, who believe that their own industries are jeopardized by such policies. Those reactions and the resulting constraints are the result of growing interdependencies among nations and a closer link between industries around the world. The following examples highlight the importance of international business and trade.

- U.S. services exports support more than 4 million U.S. jobs—jobs in both the services and manufacturing sectors.[6]
- In the United States, jobs supported by the export of goods pay wages that average 13 to 18 percent above the U.S. national average wage.[7]
- Thailand exported $1.9 billion worth of rice and $1.7 billion worth of canned fish in 2000.[8]
- Each month, 10 million kilos of California almonds, and $100 million worth of paintings leave the United States and arrive in London, Antwerp, Dublin, Lisbon, Milan, Oslo, and Helsinki.[9]
- The United States imports 1 million clocks, 3 million liters of French Champagne, and 2,600 German violins.[10]
- In 2001, South Africa's bottled-wine exports reached the 200 million liter mark.[11]
- European firms hold some $3.3 trillion in U.S. assets, accounting for more than two thirds of total foreign assets in the United States. There is more European investment in Texas alone than all U.S. investments in Japan.[12]

To some extent, the economic world as we knew it has been turned upside down. For example, trade flows used to determine **currency flows** and therefore the exchange rate. In the more recent past, currency flows have taken on a life of their own, increasing from an average daily trading volume of $18 billion in 1980 to $1.2 trillion per day in 2001.[13] As a result, they have begun to set the value of exchange rates independent of trade. These exchange rates in turn have now begun to determine the level of trade. Governments that want to counteract these developments with monetary policies find that currency flows outnumber trade flows by more than ten to one. Also, private sector financial flows vastly outnumber the financial flows that can be marshaled by governments, even when acting in concert. The interactions between global and domestic financial flows have severely limited the freedom for governmental

Focus On ⬇

Some Effects of Embargoes and Tariffs

In March 2002 the Russian Government imposed a ban on all poultry imports from the United States. According to Russian officials, the ban was in response to salmonella found in some imported poultry and also due to discrepancies in veterinary documents. This ban was lifted one month later, after the United States agreed to stricter veterinary controls and to harsher penalties for companies that export bacterially tainted poultry. The Russian poultry embargo had substantial repercussions. In the United States, "the embargo prompted stores to offer bargain prices on chicken and turkey [in order] to sell the unexported supply. Consumers [then] opted to take advantage of the lower prices and buy poultry over beef and pork, resulting in an excess supply [and lower prices] for those products," said Iowa State University economist Mike Duffy. Consumers benefited because the price of meat was low, but meat manufacturers were harmed because their profits decreased.

Prices for beef, live hog, and cattle sank in response and remained low even when word of an end to the embargo reached the markets.

The U.S. government had claimed that there was no scientific basis for the embargo and accused Moscow of protectionism. Though not officially mentioned, there was suspicion that the embargo was in direct response to the U.S. imposition of tariffs on steel imports in late 2001, which hurt the Russian steel industry. Very often a political decision to support one part of an economy can adversely affect another. The U.S. decision to impose a tariff on steel imports helped the steel industry but may have indirectly injured the meat-supplying industries because of the retaliatory embargo put in place by the Russian government. The export of U.S. food products may suffer as other countries react to the tariffs. U.S. farmers in particular could end up paying a good portion of the price for the government's attempt to subsidize the steel industry.

Sources: The International Herald Tribune, "Russians agree to lift embargo on US poultry," Associated Press, April 1, 2001, http://www.iht.com, accessed April 3, 2002; "Pork, beef prices dropping after Russian embargo U.S. exports," *The New York Times,* April 18, 2002, http://www.yorknewstimes.com/stories/04182/nat_0418020034.shtml, accessed September 2, 2002.

action. For example, if the European Central Bank or the Federal Reserve of the United States changes interest rate levels, these changes will not only influence domestic activities, but also trigger international flows of capital that may reduce, enhance, or even negate the domestic effects. Similarly, rapid technological change and vast advances in communication permit firms and countries to quickly emulate innovation and counteract carefully designed plans. As a result, governments are often powerless to implement effective policy measures, even when they know what to do.

Governments also find that domestic regulations often have major international repercussions. In the United States, for example, the breakup of AT&T resulted in significant changes in the purchasing practices of the newly formed Bell companies. Overnight, competitive bids became decisive in a process that previously was entirely with the firm. This change opened up the U.S. market to foreign suppliers of telecommunications equipment, with only limited commensurate market developments abroad for U.S. firms. Therefore, U.S. telecommunications firms found themselves suddenly under much greater competitive pressures than did their foreign counterparts.

Legislators around the world are continually confronted with such international links. In some countries, the implications are understood, and new legislation is devised with an understanding of its international consequences. In other nations, legislators often ignore the international repercussions and side effects of their actions. Yet, given the links among economies, this is an unwarranted and sometimes even dangerous view. It threatens to place firms at a competitive disadvantage in the international marketplace or may make it easier for foreign firms to compete in the domestic market.

Even when policymakers want to take decisive steps, they are often unable to do so. In the late 1980s, for example, the United States decided to impose **punitive tariffs** of 100 percent on selected Japanese imports to retaliate for Japanese nonadherence to a previously reached semiconductor agreement. The initial goal was clear. Yet the task became increasingly difficult as the U.S. government developed a list of specific imports to be targeted. In many instances, the U.S. market was heavily dependent on the Japanese imports, which meant that U.S. manufacturers and consumers would be severely affected by punitive tariffs. Many Japanese products are actually produced or assembled in the United States. To halt the importing of components would throw Americans out of work.

Other targeted products were not actually produced in Japan. Rather, Japanese firms had opened plants in third countries, such as Mexico. Penalizing these product imports would therefore punish Mexican workers and affect Mexican employment, an undesirable result.

More and more products were eliminated from the list before it was published. In two days of hearings, additional links emerged. For example, law enforcement agencies testified that if certain fingerprinting equipment from Japan was sanctioned, law enforcement efforts would suffer significantly. Of the $1.8 billion worth of goods initially considered for the sanctions list, the government was barely able to scrape together $300 million worth. Figure 3.1 illustrates how far such links have progressed

FIGURE 3.1

Who Builds the Boeing 777?

INTERNATIONAL SUPPLIERS

1	Radome
7	Dorsal fin
9	Rudder
10	Elevator
16	Flaperon
17	Flap support fairings
18	Outboard flap
19	Aileron
20	Wing tip assembly
28	Main landing gear
29	Engine
31	Nose landing gear
32	Nose landing gear doors

JAPANESE SUPPLIERS

3	Cargo doors
4	Fuselage panels
13	Wing-to-body fairing
24	In-spar ribs
26	Wing center section
27	Main landing gear doors
30	Passenger doors

U.S. SUPPLIERS

6	Fixed trailing edge
12	Floor beams
14	Spoilers
15	Inboard flaps
23	Leading edge slats
29	Engine

BOEING

2	Nose section
5	Trailing edge panels
8	Vertical fin
11	Horizontal stabilizer
21	Fixed leading edge
22	Wing box
25	Nocelles, struts, and fairings

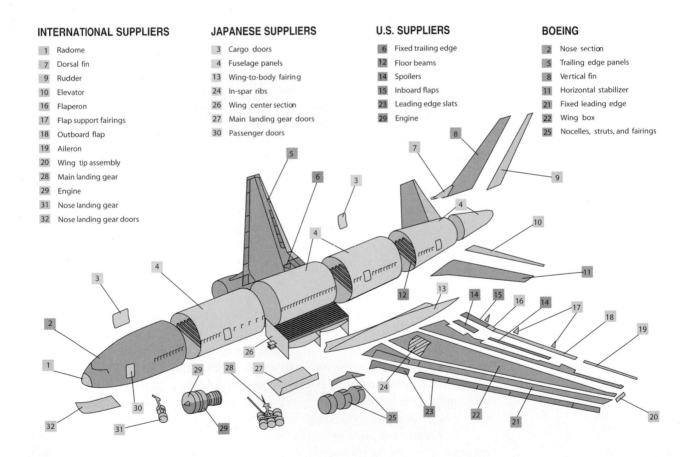

Source: Data compiled from http://www.boeing.com.

in the aircraft industry. With so many product components being sourced from different countries around the world, it becomes increasingly difficult to decide what constitutes a domestic product. In light of this uncertainty, policy actions against foreign products become more difficult as well.

Policymakers find themselves with increasing responsibilities, yet with fewer and less effective tools to carry them out. More segments of the domestic economy are vulnerable to international shifts at the same time that they are becoming less controllable. To regain some power to influence policies, some governments have sought to restrict the influence of world trade by erecting barriers, charging tariffs, and implementing import regulations. However, these measures too have been restrained by the existence of international agreements forged through institutions such as the WTO or bilateral negotiations. World trade has therefore changed many previously held notions about the sovereignty of nation-states and extraterritoriality. The same interdependence that made us all more affluent has also left us more vulnerable.

WEAKENING INTERNATIONAL INSTITUTIONS

The intense links among nations and the new economic environment resulting from new market entrants and the encounter of different economic systems are weakening the traditional international institutions and are therefore affecting their roles.

The formation of the WTO (http://www.wto.org) has provided the former GATT with new impetus. However, the organization is confronted with many difficulties. One of them is the result of the organization's success. Historically, a key focus of the WTO's predecessor was on reducing tariffs. With tariff levels at an unprecedented low level, however, attention now has to rest with areas such as nontariff barriers, which are much more complex and indigenous to nations. As a consequence, any emerging dispute is likely to be more heatedly contested and more difficult to resolve. A second traditional focus rested with the right to establishment in countries. Given today's technology, however, the issue has changed. Increasingly, firms will clamor for

Working together at agricultural talks aimed at capping tariffs and reducing subsidies, the US and 21 other member economies meet with the World Trade Organization. The discussion focused on cutting industrial tariffs with the biggest cuts aimed at highest tariffs with exceptions made for developing countries. This proposal intended to bolster negotiations on market access for industrial goods in the ongoing round of global trade negotiations. Developing countries would be allowed to cut their tariffs less than developed countries, based on their economic status and their commitment to bind their rates.

the right to operations in a country without seeking to establish themselves there. For example, given the opportunities offered by telecommunications, one can envision a bank becoming active in a country without establishing a single office or branch.

Another key problem area results from the fact that many disagreements were set aside for the sake of concluding the negotiations. Disputes in such areas as agriculture or intellectual property rights protection continue to cause a series of trade conflicts among nations. If the WTO's dispute settlement mechanism is then applied to resolve the conflict, outcries in favor of national sovereignty may cause nations to withdraw from the agreement whenever a country loses in a dispute.

A final major weakness of the WTO may result from the desire of some of its members to introduce "social causes" into trade decisions. It is debated, for example, whether the WTO should also deal with issues such as labor laws, competition, and emigration freedoms. Other issues, such as freedom of religion, provision of health care, and the safety of animals are being raised as well. It will be very difficult to have the WTO remain a viable organization if too many nongermane issues are loaded onto the trade and investment mission. The 146 governments participating in the WTO have diverse perspectives, histories, relations, economies, and ambitions. Many of them fear that social causes can be used to devise new rules of protectionism against their exports. Then there is also the question of how much companies—which, after all, are the ones doing the trading and investing—should be burdened with concerns outside of their scope.

To be successful, the WTO needs to be able to focus on its core mission, which deals with international trade and investment. The addition of social causes may appear politically expedient, but will be a key cause for divisiveness and dissent, and thus will inhibit progress on further liberalization of trade and investment. Failure to achieve such progress would leave the WTO without teeth and would negate much of the progress achieved in the Uruguay Round negotiations. It might be best to leave the WTO free from such pressures and look to increased economic ties to cross-pollinate cultures, values, and ethics and to cause changes in the social arena.[14]

Similar problems have befallen international financial institutions. For example, although the **International Monetary Fund** (http://www.imf.org) has functioned well so far, it is currently under severe challenge by new substantial financial requirements. So far, the IMF has been able to smooth over the most difficult problems, but has not found ways to solve them. For example, on September 6, 2002, the International Monetary Fund approved Brazil's request for a 15-month stand-by credit of $30.4 billion to support the country's economic and financial program through December 2003.[15] Yet, given the financial needs of many other nations such as South Korea, Malaysia, Indonesia, Thailand, and Russia, the nations of central Europe, and many countries in Latin America, the IMF simply does not have enough funds to satisfy such needs. In cases of multiple financial crises, it then is unable to provide its traditional function of calming financial markets in turmoil.

Apart from its ability to provide funds, the IMF must also rethink its traditional rules of operations. For example, it is quite unclear whether stringent economic rules and benchmark performance measures are equally applicable to all countries seeking IMF assistance. New economic conditions that have not been experienced to date may require different types of approaches. The link between economic and political stability also may require different considerations, possibly substantially changing the IMF's mission.

Similarly, the **World Bank** (http://www.worldbank.org) successfully met its goal of aiding the reconstruction of Europe but has been less successful in furthering the economic goals of the developing world and the newly emerging market economies in the former Soviet bloc. Some even claim that instead of alleviating poverty, misguided bank policies may have created poverty.[16] Therefore, at the same time when domestic policy measures have become less effective, international institutions that could help to develop substitute international policy measures have been weakened by new challenges to their traditional missions and insufficient resources to meet such challenges.

SHARPENING OF THE CONFLICT BETWEEN INDUSTRIALIZED AND DEVELOPING NATIONS

In the 1960s and 1970s it was hoped that the developmental gap between industrialized nations and many countries in the less-developed world could gradually be closed. This goal was to be achieved with the transfer of technology and the infusion of major funds. Even though the 1970s saw vast quantities of petrodollars available for recycling and major growth in borrowing by some developing nations, the results have not been as expected. Although several less-developed nations have gradually emerged as newly industrialized countries (NICs), even more nations are facing grim economic futures.

In Latin America, many nations are still saddled with enormous amounts of debt, political instability, and very fragile economies. The newly emerging democracies in central Europe and the former Soviet Union also face major debt and employment problems. In view of their shattered dreams, policymakers in these nations have become increasingly aggressive in their attempts to reshape the ground rules of the world trade and investment flows. Although many policymakers share the view that major changes are necessary to resolve the difficulties that exist, no clear-cut solutions have emerged.

Lately, an increase in environmental awareness has contributed to a further sharpening of the conflict. Developing countries may place different emphasis on environmental protection. If they are to take measures that will assist the industrialized nations in their environmental goals, they expect to be assisted and rewarded in these efforts. Yet, many in the industrialized world view environmental issues as a "global obligation," rather than as a matter of choice, and are reluctant to pay.

Policy Responses to Changing Conditions

The word *policy* conjures up an image of a well-coordinated set of governmental activities. Unfortunately, in the trade and investment sector, as in most of the domestic policy areas, this is rarely the case. Policymakers need to respond too often to short-term problems, need to worry too much about what is politically salable to multiple constituencies, and in some countries, are in office too short a time to formulate a guiding set of long-term strategies. All too often, because of public and media pressures, policymakers must be concerned with current events—such as monthly trade deficit numbers and investment flow figures—that may not be very meaningful in the larger picture. In such an environment, actions may lead to extraordinarily good tactical measures but fail to achieve long-term success.

RESTRICTIONS OF IMPORTS

In the United States, the Congress has increasingly focused on trade issues and provided the president with additional powers to affect trade. Unfortunately, apart from the consent to the NAFTA and WTO trade agreements, most of these new powers provide only for an increasing threat against foreign importers and investors, not for better conditions for U.S. exporters of goods, services, or capital. As a result, the power of the executive branch of government to improve international trade and

The Global Environment: A Source of Conflict between Developed and Less-Developed Nations

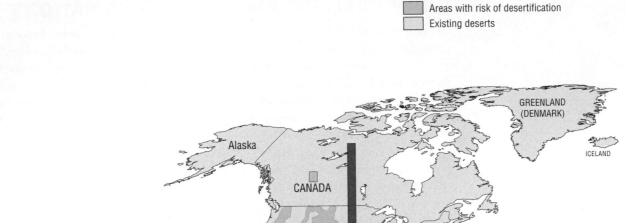

DESERTIFICATION

Areas with risk of desertification

Existing deserts

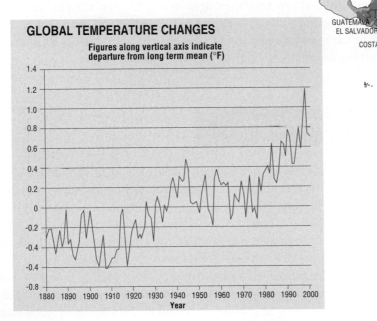

GLOBAL TEMPERATURE CHANGES

Figures along vertical axis indicate departure from long term mean (°F)

Sources: U.S. National Climatic Data Center, 2001; U.S. Department of Agriculture, 2001; National Geographic Society, Biodiversity map supplement, Feb. 1999; *AAAS Atlas of Population and Environment*, 2000; United Nations Environment Programme, 2001; World Resources Institute, World Resources , 1998–1999; Energy Information Administration, *International Energy Annual*, 1999.

RAINFOREST DESTRUCTION

Present distribution of forest area

Area originally forested

GREENHOUSE GAS EMISSIONS
Million metric tons of carbon equivalent

100–200

200–400

over 400

Color of bar indicates total emissions;
height of bar per capita level of emissions

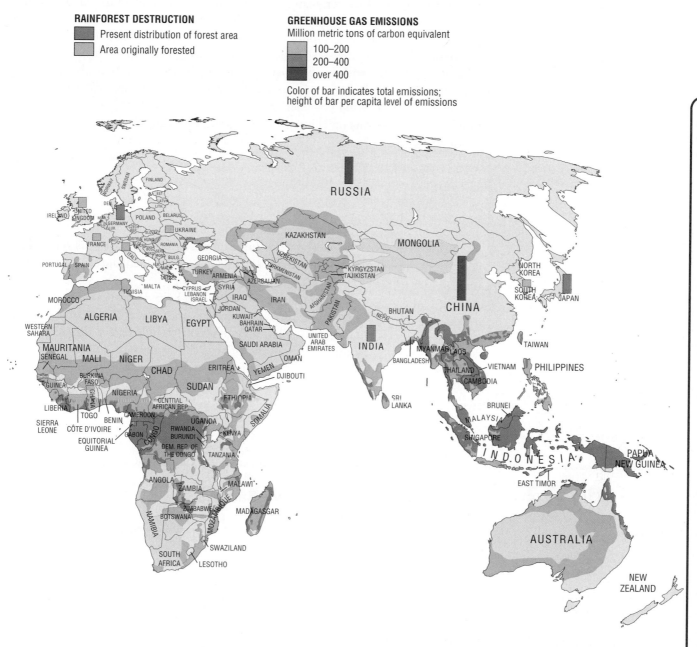

MAP

investment opportunities for U.S. firms through international negotiations and the relaxation of rules, regulations, and laws has become increasingly restricted over time.

Worldwide, most countries maintain at least a surface-level conformity with international principles. However, many exert substantial restraints on free trade through import controls and barriers. Some of the more frequently encountered barriers are listed in Table 3.2. They are found particularly in countries that suffer from major trade deficits or major infrastructure problems, causing them to enter into voluntary restraint agreements with trading partners or to selectively apply trade-restricting measures such as tariffs, quotas, or nontariff barriers against trading partners.

Tariffs are taxes based primarily on the value of imported goods and services. **Quotas** are restrictions on the number of foreign products that can be imported. **Nontariff barriers** consist of a variety of measures such as testing, certification, or simply bureaucratic hurdles that have the effect of restricting imports. All of these measures tend to raise the price of imported goods. They therefore constitute a transfer of funds from the buyers (or, if absorbed by them, the sellers) of imports to the government, and—if accompanied by price increases of competing domestic products—to the domestic producers of such products. Even though there has been a global drive toward decreasing tariffs and other trade barriers, Focus on Politics demonstrates how and why some countries are slow to implement agreed-upon reductions of barriers.

Voluntary restraint agreements are designed to help domestic industries reorganize, restructure, and recapture production prominence. Even though officially voluntary, these agreements are usually implemented through severe threats against trading partners. Due to their "voluntary" nature, the agreements are not subject to any previously negotiated bilateral or multilateral trade accords.

When nations do not resort to the subtle mechanism of voluntary agreements to affect trade flows, they often impose tariffs and quotas. Many countries use **anti-**

 TABLE 3.2   **Trade Barriers**

There are literally hundreds of ways to build a barrier. The following list provides just a few of the trade barriers that exporters face.

• Special Import authorization	• Country quotas
• Restrictions on data processing	• Testing, labeling
• Voluntary export restraints	• Seasonal prohibitions
• Advance import deposits	• Health and sanitary prohibitions
• Taxes on foreign exchange deals	• Certification
• Preferential licensing applications	• Foreign exchange licensing
• Excise duties	• Barter and countertrade requirements
• Licensing fees	• Customs surcharges
• Discretionary licensing	• Stamp taxes
• Trade restriction on e-commerce	• Consular invoice fees
• Anti-competitive practices	• Taxes on transport

Source: Adapted from Office of the United States Trade Representative, 2003 National Trade Estimate Report on Foreign Trade Barriers, Washington, DC, August 2003.

Focus On ⬇

Mexico and the United States Battle over NAFTA

A debate is raging between Mexico and the United States over tariff reductions on farm produce. Under the North American Free Trade Agreement (NAFTA), all tariffs will disappear completely by 2008. Since the process is gradual, every year more and more Mexican products are losing their protective tariffs and are losing market share to cheaper American goods. Mexico's concern is not the effect on its gross domestic product. Farming and agriculture contribute only 4 percent to the total economy, but nearly one quarter of the Mexican workforce lives off the land. Decreasing agricultural tariffs affects a much greater portion of the population than the same process in the United States, where only 2.5 percent of the population is engaged in farming.

The root of the disagreement comes from farm subsidies. Farmers in the United States are subsidized, on average, about $40 per acre, while farmers in Mexico receive about half that for the same amount of land. Making this disparity even worse is the fact that farms in Mexico are far smaller, averaging just 13 acres each, a result of land reforms set in place after the Mexican revolution. U.S. farms average 200 hectares (nearly 500 acres). Farmers in the United States average $20,000 a year in subidies, while farmers in Mexico average $260 a year. U.S. farmers argue that their subsidies still fall far short of those in Europe and Japan, and that Mexico has failed to fix the real problems of corrupt government officials and poor infrastructure within its agricultural system—barriers that add greatly to the cost of farming in Mexico.

Government officials in Sinaloa, a rural state in northwest Mexico, estimate that about 15 percent of farm subsidies are embezzled by cor-

rupt bureaucrats and never reach the farmers. Farmers in Mexico also face diesel fuel prices that are 40 percent higher than those in the United States, while electricity and credit are one third more expensive. These differences exist because many industries in the Mexican economy, particularly power and fuel, are public and private monopolies protected by the Mexican Constitution. These monopolies face no competition and so have no incentive to add infrastructure, improve service, or lower costs. Yields in Sinaloa average 8.5 tons of corn per hectare, nearly the same as in the United States, further evidence that the problem is not efficiency but rather the high cost of farming in Mexico. The Mexican farming industry is facing world competition when selling its products but must accept local cost conditions for their production.

Mexico's agricultural exports to the United States doubled between 1990 and 2000 to $6.3 billion. Mexico made significant export gains in labor-intensive crops like cucumbers and tomatoes, while U.S. producers with their larger, more capital-intensive farms increased exports of rice, cattle, dairy products, and apples nearly 15 percent during the same period. The Mexican government has been using antidumping duties and sanitary restrictions to bar the entry of U.S. agricultural products into its markets. However, as more and more tariffs are being lifted, Mexican politicians are calling for the delay of tariff reduction and in some cases the renegotiation of NAFTA. Mexican President Vicente Fox has warned that these tariff reductions would increase unemployment in the countryside, adding pressure on the border as more farmers would try to enter the United States illegally.

Sources: http://www.usda.gov/news/releases/2003/01/0023.htm, accessed February 4, 2003; http://www.businessweek.com/:/print/magazine/content/02_46/b3808083.htm?gb, accessed February 4, 2003; "Mexico's farmers floundering in a tariff-free landscape," *The Economist,* November 30, 2002, 31.

dumping laws to impose tariffs on imports. Antidumping laws are designed to help domestic industries that are injured by unfair competition from abroad due to products being "dumped" on them. Dumping may involve selling goods overseas at prices lower than those in the exporter's home market or at a price below the cost of production or both. The growing use of antidumping measures by governments around the world complicates the pricing decisions of exporters. Large domestic firms, on the other hand, can use the antidumping process to obtain strategic shelter from foreign competitors.[17]

For example, in 1983 the International Trade Commission imposed a five-year tariff on Japanese heavy motorcycles imported into the United States. The 49.4 percent duty was granted at the request of Harley-Davidson, which could no longer compete with the heavily discounted bikes being imported by companies such as Honda and Kawasaki. The gradually declining tariff gave Harley-Davidson the time to enact new management strategies. Within four years, Harley-Davidson was back on its feet and again had the highest market share in the heavyweight class of bikes. In 1987, Harley-Davidson officials requested that the tariff be lifted a year early. As a result, the policy was labeled a success. However, at no time were the costs of these measures to U.S. consumers even considered.

Imports are also restricted by nontariff barriers. These consist of buy-domestic campaigns, preferential treatment for domestic bidders compared with foreign bidders, national standards that are not comparable to international standards, and an emphasis on the design rather than the performance of products. Such nontariff barriers are often the most insidious obstacles to free trade, since they are difficult to detect, hard to quantify, and demands for their removal are often blocked by references to a nation's cultural and historic heritage.

Another way in which imports are reduced is by tightening market access and entry of foreign products through involved procedures and inspections. Probably the most famous are the measures implemented by France. In order to stop or at least reduce the importation of foreign video recorders, the French government ruled that all of them had to be sent to the customs station at Poitiers. This customhouse was located away from major transport routes, woefully understaffed, and open only a few days each week. In addition, the few customs agents at Poitiers insisted on opening each package separately to inspect the merchandise. Within a few weeks, imports of video recorders came to a halt. Members of the French government, however, were able to point to the fact that they had not restrained trade at all; rather, they had only made some insignificant changes in the procedures of domestic governmental actions.

The Effects of Import Restriction

Policymakers are faced with several problems when trying to administer import controls. First, most of the time such controls exact a huge price from domestic consumers. Import controls may mean that the most efficient sources of supply are not available. The result is either second-best products or higher costs for restricted supplies, which in turn cause customer service standards to drop and consumers to pay

China's agreement to lift the 20-year prohibition to the export of U.S. citrus, grain, beef and poultry could have significant benefits in terms of greatly expanded exports of these products. With this agreement, the United States and China will launch their agricultural partnership, based on sound science and the mutual benefits of the open market, into the 21st century.

© AFP/CORBIS

significantly higher prices. Even though these costs may be widely distributed among many consumers and are less obvious, the social cost of these controls may be damaging to the economy and subject to severe attack from individuals. However, these attacks are countered by pressure from protected groups that benefit from import restrictions. For example, while citizens of the European Union may be forced by import controls to pay an elevated price for all the agricultural products they consume, agricultural producers in the region benefit from higher incomes. Achieving a proper trade-off is often difficult, if not impossible, for the policymaker.

A second major problem resulting from import controls is the downstream change in the composition of imports that may result. For example, if the importation of copper ore is restricted, through either voluntary restraints or quotas, producing countries may opt to shift their production systems and produce copper wire instead, which they can export. As a result, initially narrowly defined protectionistic measures may snowball in order to protect one downstream industry after another.

Another major problem that confronts the policymaker is that of efficiency. Import controls designed to provide breathing room to a domestic industry so it can either grow or recapture its competitive position often do not work. Rather than improve the productivity of an industry, such controls may provide it with a level of safety and a cushion of increased income, subsequently causing it to lag behind in technological advancements.

One must also be aware of the corporate response to import restrictions. Corporations faced with such restrictions can encourage their governments to erect similar barriers to protect them at home. The result is a gradually escalating set of trade obstacles. In addition, corporations can make strategic use of such barriers by incorporating them into their business plans and exploiting them in order to gain market share. For example, some multinational corporations have pressed governments to initiate antidumping actions against their competitors when faced with low-priced imports. In such instances, corporations may substitute adroit handling of government relations for innovation and competitiveness.

Finally, corporations also can circumvent import restrictions by shifting their activities. For example, instead of conducting trade, corporations can shift to foreign direct investment. The result may be a drop in trade inflow, yet the domestic industry may still be under strong pressure from foreign firms. The investments of Japanese car producers in the United States serve as an example. However, due to the job-creation effects of such investment, such shifts may have been the driving desire on the part of the policymakers who implemented the import controls.

RESTRICTIONS OF EXPORTS

In addition to imposing restraints on imports, nations also control their exports. The reasons are short supply, national security and foreign policy purposes, or the desire to retain capital.

The United States, for example, regards trade as a privilege of the firm, granted by government, rather than a right or a necessity. U.S. legislation to control exports focuses on **national security** controls—that is, the control of weapons exports or high-technology exports that might adversely affect the safety of the nation. In addition, exports can be controlled for reasons of foreign policy and short supply. These controls restrict the international business opportunities of firms if a government believes that such a restriction would send a necessary foreign policy message to another country. Such action may be undertaken regardless of whether the message will have any impact or whether similar products can easily be supplied by companies in other nations. Although perhaps valuable as a tool of international relations, such policies may give a country's firms the reputation of being unreliable suppliers and may divert orders to firms in other nations.

EXPORT PROMOTION

The desire to increase participation in international trade and investment flows has led nations to implement export promotion programs. These programs are designed primarily to help domestic firms enter and maintain their position in international markets and to match or counteract similar export promotion efforts by other nations. Every day, new firms are beginning to learn about the international market and are running into barriers to international trade. For example, in any given year, 15 percent of U.S. exporters will stop exporting, while 10 percent of non-exporters will enter the global market.[18] The most critical juncture for firms is when they begin or cease exporting, which is where export promotion has its greatest impact.

Most governments supply some support to their firms participating or planning to participate in international trade. While such support is widespread and growing, its intensity varies by country. For example, the United States spends 3 cents per $1,000 of GDP on export promotion, compared with Germany's and Japan's expenditures of 5 cents, Great Britain's 7 cents, France's 18 cents, and Canada's 33 cents.[19]

Governments have developed various approaches toward export promotion. One focuses on knowledge transfer to enable greater competence within firms. Here, governments offer either export service programs or market development programs. Service programs typically consist of seminars for potential exporters, export counseling, and "how to export" handbooks. Market development programs provide sales leads to local firms, offer participation in foreign trade shows, preparation of market analyses, and export newsletters. Within each category, program efforts can provide informational knowledge (of the "how to" nature) or experiential knowledge, which provides hands-on exposure.

A second export-promotion approach deals with direct or indirect subsidization of export activities. For example, low-cost export financing can produce an attractive and competitive offer, particularly for large sales that are paid over time, such as airplanes or power plants. Exports are also supported by lower tax rates for export earnings and favorable insurance rates. The overall focus of these subsidized activities is to increase the profitability of exporting to the firm, either by reducing the risks or by increasing the rewards.

A third approach to export promotion consists of reducing governmental red tape for exporters. For instance, the requirements for multiple export licenses or permits issued by various government agencies and the imposition of technology export controls constitute impediments to exporting, which the government can remove, thus stimulating an increase in exports. Similarly, the reduction of antitrust concerns in the export arena has led to the formation of (export) trading firms, which are able to share facilities and expertise without the threat of government intervention.[20]

Given the deterioration of the U.S. trade balance, U.S. government trade policy is focusing on export programs to improve the international trade performance of U.S. firms. The Department of Commerce offers information services that provide data on foreign trade and market developments (http://www.export.gov/commercialservice/). The department's **Commercial Service** posts hundreds of professionals around the world to gather information and to assist business executives in their activities abroad.

In addition, a wide variety of federal and state agencies are now collaborating in order to coordinate their activities in support of exporters. As a result, a national network of export assistance centers has been created, capable of providing one-stop shops for exporters in search of export counseling and financial assistance. Also, an advocacy network helps U.S. companies win overseas contracts for large government purchases abroad.

Another area of activity by the U.S. government is export financing. The Export-Import Bank of the United States provides U.S. firms with long-term loans and loan guarantees so that they can bid on contracts where financing is a key issue. In response to actions by foreign competitors, the bank has, on occasion also resorted to offering **mixed aid credits.** The credits, which take the form of loans composed partially of commercial interest rates and partially of highly subsidized developmental aid interest rates, result in very low interest loans to exporters.

Tax legislation that inhibited the employment of Americans by U.S. firms abroad has also been altered. In the past, U.S. nationals living abroad were, with some minor exclusion, fully subject to U.S. federal taxation. The cost of living abroad can often be quite high—for example, rent for a small apartment can approach $5,000 per month— so this tax structure often imposed a significant burden on U.S. firms and citizens abroad. As a result, companies frequently were not able to send U.S. employees to their foreign subsidiaries. However, a revision of the tax code now allows a substantial amount of income (up to $80,000 in 2002) to remain tax-free.[21] More Americans can now be posted abroad. In their work they may specify the use of U.S. products, thus enhancing the competitive position of U.S. firms.

Any export promotion raises several questions. One concerns the justification of the expenditure of public funds for what is essentially an activity that should be driven by profits. It appears, however, that the start-up cost for international operations, particularly for smaller firms, may be sufficiently high to warrant some kind of government support.[22] A second question focuses on the capability of government to provide such support. Both for the selection and reach of firms as well as the distribution of support, government is not necessarily better equipped than the private sector to do a good job. A third issue concerns competitive export promotion. If countries provide such support to their firms, they may well distort the flow of trade. If other countries then increase their support of firms in order to counteract the effects, all that results is the same volume of trade activity, but at subsidized rates. It is therefore important to carefully evaluate export promotion activities as to their effectiveness and competitive impact. Perhaps such promotion is only beneficial when it addresses existing market gaps.

Overall, export promotion will only comprise a small fraction of any national budget and directly support only a minute portion of exports. It cannot be the role of export promotion to directly support all export activities. Rather, export promotion needs to initiate activities, to blaze trails with new approaches and experimentation, and highlight news ways of overcoming hurdles. Perhaps one should characcterize export promotion funds as the venture capital of international economic activity.

IMPORT PROMOTION

Some countries have also developed import promotion measures. The measures are implemented primarily by nations that have accumulated and maintained large balance-of-trade surpluses. They hope to allay other nations' fears of continued imbalances and to gradually redirect trade flows.

Japan, for example, has completely refurbished the operations of the Japan External Trade Organization (JETRO) (http://www.jetro.org). This organization, which initially was formed to encourage Japanese exports, has now begun to focus on the promotion of imports to Japan. It organizes trade missions of foreign firms coming to

Japan, hosts special exhibits and fairs within Japan, and provides assistance and encouragement to potential importers.

INVESTMENT POLICIES

The discussion of policy actions has focused thus far on merchandise trade. Similar actions are applicable to investment flows and, by extension, to international trade in services. In order to protect ownership, control, and development of domestic industries, many countries attempt to influence investment capital flows. Most frequently, investment-screening agencies decide on the merits of any particular foreign investment project. Canada, for example, has "Investment Canada," an agency that scrutinizes foreign investments.[23] So do most developing nations, where special government permission must be obtained for investment projects. This permission frequently carries with it certain conditions, such as levels of ownership permitted, levels of dividends that can be repatriated, numbers of jobs that must be created, or the extent to which management can be carried out by individuals from abroad. The United States restricts foreign investment in instances where national security or related concerns are at stake. Major foreign investments may be reviewed by the **Committee on Foreign Investments in the United States (CFIUS).**

THE HOST-COUNTRY PERSPECTIVE

The host government is caught in a love-hate relationship with foreign direct investment. On the one hand, the host country has to appreciate the various contributions, especially economic, that the foreign direct investment will make. On the other hand, fears of dominance, interference, and dependence are often voiced and acted on. The major positive and negative impacts are summarized in Table 3.3.

TABLE 3.3

Positive and Negative Impacts of Foreign Direct Investment on Host Countries

Positive Impact

1. Capital formation
2. Technology and management skills transfer
3. Regional and sectoral development
4. Internal competition and entrepreneurship
5. Favorable effect on balance of payments
6. Increased employment

Negative Impact

1. Industrial dominance
2. Technological dependence
3. Disturbance of economic plans
4. Cultural change
5. Interference by home government of multinational corporation

Sources: Jack N. Behrman, *National Interests and the Multinational Enterprise* (Englewood Cliffs. NJ: Prentice-Hall, 1970), Chapters 2 through 5; Jack N. Behrman, *Industrial Policies: International Restructuring and Transnationals* (Lexington, MA: Lexington Books, 1984), Chapter 5; and Christopher M. Korth, *International Business* (Englewood Cliffs, NJ: Prentice-Hall, 1985), Chapters 12 and 13.

The Positive Impact

Foreign direct investment has contributed greatly to world development in the past 40 years. Said Lord Lever, a British businessman who served in the cabinets of Harold Wilson and James Callaghan, "Europe got twenty times more out of American investment after the war than the multinationals did; every country gains by productive investment."[24]

Capital flows are especially beneficial to countries with limited domestic sources and restricted opportunities to raise funds in the world's capital markets. In addition, foreign direct investment may attract local capital to a project for which local capital alone would not have sufficed.

Foreign direct investment is closely linked to **technology transfer.** Technology transfer includes the introduction of not only new hardware to the market but also the techniques and skills to operate it. In industries where the role of intellectual property is substantial, such as pharmaceuticals or software development, access to parent companies' research and development provides benefits that may be far greater than those gained through infusion of capital. This explains the interest that many governments have expressed in having multinational corporations establish R&D facilities in their countries.

An integral part of technology transfer is managerial skills, which are the most significant labor component of foreign direct investment. With the growth of the service sector, many economies need skills rather than expatriate personnel to perform the tasks.

Foreign direct investment can be used effectively in developing a geographical region or a particular industry sector. Foreign direct investment is one of the most expedient ways in which unemployment can be reduced in chosen regions of a country. Furthermore, the costs of establishing an industry are often too prohibitive and the time needed too excessive for the domestic industry, even with governmental help, to try it on its own. In many developing countries, foreign direct investment may be a

Starbucks celebrated the September 2003 opening of its Bangkok store with free "Muan Jai" coffee blend to patrons. The "Muan Jai" uses beans grown by hill tribes in Northern Thailand and is one of Starbuck's "Commitment to Origins" blends. Starbuck's commitment to coffee producers, their families and communities, and the natural environment to help promote a sustainable social, ecological, and economic model for the production and trade of coffee is part of the company's guiding business mission.

© EPA PHOTO/EPA/VINAI DITHAJOHN

way to diversify the industrial base and thereby reduce the country's dependence on one or a few sectors.

At the company level, foreign direct investment may intensify competition and result in benefits to the economy as a whole as well as to consumers through increased productivity and possibly lower prices. Competition typically introduces new techniques, goods and services, and ideas to the markets. It may improve existing patterns of how business is done.

The major impact of foreign direct investment on the balance of payments is long term. Import substitution, export earnings, and subsidized imports of technology and management all assist the host nation on the trade account side of the balance of payments. Not only may a new production facility substantially decrease the need to import the type of products manufactured, but it may start earning export revenue as well. Several countries, such as Brazil, have imposed export requirements as a precondition for foreign direct investment. On the capital account side, foreign direct investment may have short-term impact in lowering a deficit as well as long-term impact in keeping capital at home that otherwise could have been invested or transferred abroad. However, measurement is difficult because significant portions of the flows may miss—or evade—the usual government reporting channels.

Jobs are often the most obvious reason to cheer about foreign direct investment. Foreign companies directly employ 6.4 million Americans, or about 7 percent of the private sector workforce, and indirectly create opportunities for millions more.[25] The benefits reach far beyond mere employment. Salaries paid by multinational corporations are usually higher than those paid by domestic firms. The creation of jobs translates also into the training and development of a skilled workforce. Consider, for example, the situation of many Caribbean states that are dependent on tourism for their well-being. In most cases, multinational hotel chains have been instrumental in establishing a pool of trained hospitality workers and managers.

All of the benefits discussed are indeed possible advantages of foreign direct investment. Their combined effect can lead to an overall enhancement in the standard of living in the market as well as an increase in the host country's access to the world market and its international competitiveness. It is equally possible, however, that the impact can be negative rather than positive.

The Negative Impact

Although some of the threats posed by multinational corporations and foreign direct investment in terms of stunted economic development, low levels of research and development, and poor treatment of local employees are exaggerated, in many countries some industrial sectors are dominated by foreign-owned entities.

Foreign direct investment most often is concentrated in technology-intensive industries. Therefore, research and development is another area of tension. Multinational corporations usually want to concentrate their R&D efforts, especially their basic research. With its technology transfer, the multinational corporation can assist the host country's economic development, but it may leave the host country dependent on flows of new and updated technology. Furthermore, the multinational firm may contribute to the **brain drain** by attracting scientists from host countries to its central research facility. Many countries have demanded and received research facilities on their soil, where they can better control results. Many countries are weary of the technological dominance of the United States and Japan and view it as a long-term threat. Western European nations, for example, are joining forces in basic research and development under the auspices of the EUREKA project, which is a pan-

European pooling of resources to develop new technologies with both governmental and private sector help.

The economic benefits of foreign direct investment are controversial as well. Capital inflows may be accompanied by outflows in a higher degree and over a longer term than is satisfactory to the host government. For example, hotels built in the Caribbean by multinational chains often were unable to find local suppliers and had to import supplies and thus spend much-needed foreign currency. Many officials also complain that the promised training of local personnel, especially for management positions, has never taken place. Rather than stimulate local competition and encourage entrepreneurship, multinationals with their often superior product offering and marketing skills have stifled competition. Many countries, including the United States, have found that multinational companies do not necessarily want to rely on local suppliers but rather bring along their own from their domestic market.

Governments also see multinationals as a disturbance to their economic planning. Decisions are made concerning their economy over which they have little or no control. Host countries do not look favorably on a multinational that may want to keep the import content of a product high, especially when local suppliers may be available.

Multinational companies are, by definition, change agents. They bring about change not only in the way business may be conducted but also, through the products and services they generate and the way they are marketed, causing change in the lifestyles of the consumers in the market. The extent to which this is welcomed or accepted varies by country. For example, the introduction of fast-food restaurants to Taiwan dramatically altered eating patterns, especially of teenagers, who made these outlets extremely popular and profitable. Concern has been expressed about the apparent change in eating patterns and the higher relative cost of eating in such establishments.

The multinational corporation will also have an impact on business practices. Although multinationals usually pay a higher salary, they may also engage in practices that are alien to the local workforce, such as greater flexibility in work rules. Older operators in Japan, for example, may be removed from production lines to make room for more productive employees. In another country where the Japanese firm establishes a plant, tradition and union rules may prevent this.[26]

Some host nations have expressed concern over the possibility of interference, economically and politically, by the home government of the multinational corporation; that is, they fear that the multinational may be used as an instrument of influence.[27] The United States has used U.S.-based corporations to extend its foreign policy in areas of capital flows, technology controls, and competition. Foreign direct investment regulations were introduced in the United States in the 1960s to diminish capital outflows from the country and thus to strengthen the country's balance-of-payment situation. If the actions of affiliates of U.S.-based companies are seen to have a negative impact on competition in the U.S. market, antitrust decrees may be used to change the situation.

Of course, the multinational firm is subject not only to the home government political and economic directions but also to those of the host government and other groups. Fixed investments by multinationals can be held hostage by a host country in trying to win concessions from other governments.

Countries engage in informal evaluation of foreign direct investment, both outbound and inbound. Canada, for example, uses the Foreign Investment Review Agency to determine whether foreign-owned companies are good corporate citizens. Sweden reviews outbound foreign direct investment in terms of its impact on the home country, especially employment.

THE HOME-COUNTRY PERSPECTIVE

Most of the aspects of foreign direct investment that concern host countries apply to the home country as well. Foreign direct investment means addition to the home country's gross domestic product from profits, royalties, and fees remitted by affiliates. Intracompany transfers bring about additional exports. Many countries, in promoting foreign direct investment, see it as a means to stimulate economic growth—an end that would expand export markets and serve other goals, such as political motives, as well. Some countries, such as Japan, have tried to gain preferential access to raw materials by purchasing firms that owned the deposits. Other factors of production can be obtained through foreign direct investment as well. Companies today may not have the luxury of establishing R&D facilities wherever they choose but must locate them where human power is available. This explains, for example, why Northern Telecom, the Canadian telecommunications giant, has more than 500 of its roughly 2,000 R&D people based in the United States, mostly in California.

The major negative issue centers on employment. Many unions point not only to outright job loss but also to the effect on imports and exports. The most controversial have been investments in plants in developing countries that export back to the home countries. Multinationals such as electronics manufacturers, who have moved plants to southeast Asia and Mexico, have justified this as a necessary cost-cutting competitive measure.

Another critical issue is that of technological advantage. Some critics state that, by establishing plants abroad or forming joint ventures with foreign entities, the country may be giving away its competitive position in the world marketplace. This is especially true when the recipients may be able to avoid the time and expense involved in developing new technologies.

RESTRICTIONS ON INVESTMENT

Many nations also restrict exports of capital, because **capital flight** is a major problem for them. Particularly in situations where countries lack necessary foreign exchange reserves, governments are likely to place restrictions on capital outflow. In essence, government claims to have higher priorities for capital than its citizens. They, in turn, often believe that the return on investment or the safety of the capital is not sufficiently ensured in their own countries. The reason may be governmental measures or domestic economic factors, such as inflation. These holders of capital want to invest abroad. By doing so, however, they deprive their domestic economy of much-needed investment funds.

Once governments impose restrictions on the export of funds, the desire to transfer capital abroad only increases. Because companies and individuals are ingenious in their efforts to achieve capital flight, governments, particularly in developing countries, continue to suffer. In addition, few new outside investors will enter the country because they fear that dividends and profits will not be remitted easily.

INVESTMENT PROMOTION

Many countries also implement policy measures to attract foreign direct investment. These policies can be the result of the needs of poorer countries to attract additional foreign capital to fuel economic growth without taking out more loans that call for fixed schedules of repayment.[28] Industrialized nations also participate in these efforts since governments are under pressure to provide jobs for their citizens and have come to recognize that foreign direct investment can serve as a major means to increase employment and income. Focus on Politics reports on some of the invest-

Focus On

Money Buys Investments

Once the hub of the U.S. textile industry, the southern states of Alabama, Tennessee, and Mississippi have reinvented their economies and are fast becoming the epicenter of the worldwide auto manufacturing industry. In the late 1970s, threatened changes in U.S. trade policy forced carmakers selling to American consumers to relocate manufacturing operations to the United States. Eager to attract foreign auto plants, the southern states offered millions of dollars in incentives packages that include massive tax breaks, new infrastructure, and extensive job-training programs. Mississippi approved a $295 million package to host Nissan, while Alabama offered incentives worth $158 million to Honda and $119 million to Mercedes-Benz. The reward? High-paying, skilled jobs and a thriving local economy.

Individual U.S. states have investment agencies in Europe that court foreign investors, offering cash incentives for job creation in the United States. For every job Mercedes-Benz created at its Alabama factory, it reaped around $165,000 in state subsidies; at its Spartanburg, South Carolina, plant, BMW received more than $100,000 per job. Honda received $158 million in incentives for a plant that will generate 1,500 jobs.

To control competition among European countries, the European Union maintains strict rules covering incentives. For example, Ireland's low corporate tax rate of 10 percent, which lured a number of firms, was seen as unfair by the rest of Europe, and Irish officials raised it to 12.5 percent.

In the European Union, the competition for foreign investors is fierce. Britain lured LG, a South Korean electronics firm, by paying $48,600 for each of 6,000 jobs created. France paid over $55,000 per job to get Mercedes-Benz's Swatch auto plant to locate in its eastern region of Lorraine.

American companies investing in Europe have also benefited from investment support. Ford received a $104 million grant for a new Jaguar plant in Birmingham, U.K. The auto maker later threatened to close its assembly plant in Liverpool unless it received a government grant toward the cost of restructuring the plant for building a new model there.

When countries such as China and Mexico offer low-cost locations for production, industrialized nations feel compelled to counter with other kinds of incentives. By offering incentive packages, Curitiba, 250 miles from Sao Paolo, has become Brazil's second largest auto center. Manufacturers who invest in eastern Germany can obtain cash worth up to 50 percent of their capital investment. Changwon, South Korea, offers cheap loans and tax rebates to foreign manufacturers.

Governments use subsidies to induce investment not only from auto firms but, at even greater cost, from high-tech computer and electronics companies. With countries engaged in a bidding war for multinational investment, smaller nations face the prospect of being outspent by bigger competitors. Despite the high cost of the handouts, no country wants to miss the opportunity to gain job growth and modernized industry, especially when plagued by high unemployment.

Sources: Sue Anne Pressley, "The South's New Car-Smell," *The Washington Post,* May 11, 2001; Weld Royal, "Money for Jobs," *Industry Week,* April 3, 2000; Bruce Barnard, "A Buyer's Job Market," *The Journal of Commerce* (February 12, 1997): 1C, 23C.

ment promotion efforts undertaken by governments. Increasingly, even state and local governments are participating in investment promotion. Some U.S. states, for example, are sending out "Invest in the USA" missions on a regular basis. Others have opened offices abroad to inform local businesses about the beneficial investment climate at home.

Incentives used by policymakers to facilitate such investments are mainly of three types: fiscal, financial, and nonfinancial. **Fiscal incentives** are specific tax measures designed to attract the foreign investor. They typically consist of special depreciation allowances, tax credits or rebates, special deductions for capital expenditures, tax holidays, and the reduction of tax burdens on the investor. **Financial incentives** offer special funding for the investor by providing, for example, land or building, loans, and loan guarantees. **Nonfinancial incentives** can consist of guaranteed government purchases; special protection from competition through tariffs, import quotas, and local content requirements; and investments in infrastructure facilities.

All of these incentives are designed primarily to attract more industry and therefore create more jobs. They may slightly alter the advantage of a region and therefore make it more palatable for the investor to choose to invest in that region. By themselves, they are unlikely to spur an investment decision if proper market conditions do not exist.

Investment promotion policies may succeed in luring new industries to a location and in creating new jobs, but they may also have several drawbacks. For example, when countries compete for foreign investment, several of them may offer more or less the same investment package. The slight advantage that the incentives of one country may have over another's package generally makes little difference in the investment site selected.[29] Moreover, investment policies aimed at attracting foreign direct investment may occasionally place established domestic firms at a disadvantage if they do not receive any support.

MANAGEMENT OF THE POLICY RELATIONSHIP

Arguments for and against foreign direct investment are endless. Costs and benefits must be weighed. Only the multinational corporation itself can assess expected gains against perceived risks in its overseas commitments. At the same time, only the host and home countries can assess benefits realized against costs in terms of their national priorities. If these entities cannot agree on objectives because their most basic interests are in conflict, they cannot agree on the means either. In most cases, the relationship between the parties is not necessarily based on logic, fairness, or equity, but on the relative bargaining power of each. Political changes may cause rapid changes in host government–MNC relations.

The bargaining positions of the multinational corporation and the host country change over time. The course of these changes is summarized in Figure 3.2. The

FIGURE 3.2

Bargaining Position of Multinational Corporation (MNC) and Host Country

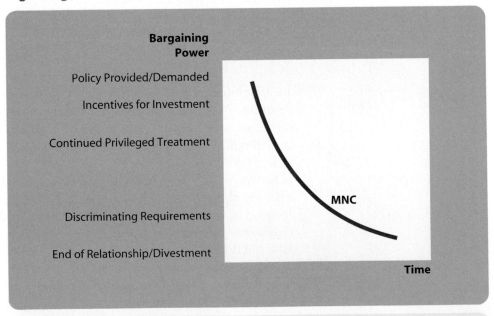

Sources: Thomas A. Poynter, "Managing Government Intervention: A Strategy for Defending the Subsidy," *Columbia Journal of World Business* 21 (winter 1986): 55–65; and Christopher M. Korth, *International Business,* (Englewood Cliffs, NJ: Prentice-Hall, 1985), 350.

multinational wields its greatest power before the investment is actually made; in the negotiation period, it can require a number of incentives over a period of time. Whether or not the full cycle of events takes place depends on developments in the market as well as the continued bargaining strength of the multinational.

The multinational corporation can maintain its bargaining strength by developing a local support system through local financing, procurement, and business contracts as well as by maintaining control over access to technology and markets. The first approach attempts to gain support from local market entities if discriminating actions by the government take place. The second approach aims to make the operation of the affiliate impossible without the contribution of the parent.

Host countries, on the other hand, try to enhance their role by instituting control policies and performance requirements. Governments attempt to prevent the integration of activities among affiliates and control by the parent. In this effort, they exclude or limit foreign participation in certain sectors of the economy and require local participation in the ownership and management of the entities established. The extent of this participation will vary by industry, depending on how much the investment is needed by the host economy. Performance requirements typically are programs aimed at established foreign investors in an economy. These often are such discriminatory policies as local content requirements, export requirements, limits on foreign payments (especially profit repatriation), and demands concerning the type of technology transferred or the sophistication and level of operation engaged in. In some cases, demands of this type have led to firms' packing their bags. For example, Coca-Cola left India when the government demanded access to what the firm considered to be confidential intellectual property. Only India's free-market reforms have brought Coca-Cola and many other investors back to the country. Cadbury Schweppes sold its plant in Kenya because price controls made its operation unprofitable.[30] On their part, governments can, as a last resort, expropriate the affiliate, especially if they believe that the benefits are greater than the cost.[31]

A Strategic Outlook for Trade and Investment Policies

All countries have international trade and investment policies. The importance and visibility of these policies have grown dramatically as international trade and investment flows have become more relevant to the well-being of most nations. Given the growing links among nations, it will be increasingly difficult to consider domestic policy without looking at international repercussions.

A U.S. PERSPECTIVE

The U.S. need is for a positive trade policy rather than reactive, ad hoc responses to specific situations. **Protectionistic legislation** can be helpful, provided it is not enacted. Proposals in Congress, for example, can be quite useful as bargaining chips in international negotiations. If passed and signed into law, however, protectionistic legislation can result in the destruction of the international trade and investment framework.

It has been suggested that a variety of regulatory agencies could become involved in administering U.S. trade policy. Although such agencies could be useful from the standpoint of addressing narrowly defined grievances, they carry the danger that commercial policy will be determined by a new chorus of discordant voices. Shifting the power of setting trade and investment policy from the executive branch to agencies or even states could give the term *New Federalism* a quite unexpected meaning and might cause progress at the international negotiation level to grind to a halt. No U.S. negotiator can expect to retain the goodwill of foreign counterparts if he or she cannot place issues on the table that can be negotiated without constantly having to check back with various authorities.

In light of continuing large U.S. trade deficits, there is much disenchantment with past trade policies. The disappointment with past policy measures, particularly trade negotiations, is mainly the result of overblown expectations. Too often, the public has mistakenly expected successful trade negotiations to affect the domestic economy in a major way, even though the issue addressed or resolved was only of minor economic importance. Yet, in light of global changes, U.S. trade policy does need to change. Rather than treating trade policy as a strictly "foreign" phenomenon, it must be recognized that it is mainly domestic economic performance that determines global competitiveness. Trade policy must become more domestically oriented at the same time that domestic policy must become more international in vision. Such a new approach should pursue at least five key goals. First, the nation must improve the quality and amount of information government and business share to facilitate competitiveness. Second, policy must encourage collaboration among companies in such areas as goods and process technologies. Third, U.S. industry collectively must overcome its export reluctance and its short-term financial orientation. Fourth, the United States must invest in its people, providing education and training suited to the competitive challenges of the next century.[32] Finally, the executive branch must be given authority by Congress to negotiate international agreements with a reasonable certainty that the negotiation outcome will not be subject to minute amendments. Therefore, the existence of **trade promotion authority**, which gives Congress the right to accept or reject trade treaties and agreements, but reduces the amendment procedures, is very important. Such authority is instrumental for new, large-scale trade accords such as the Doha Round to succeed. But, how to pay for the cost of policy adjustments? Currently, there is no link between governmental market openings and benefits obtained by an industry. Trade negotiations result in winners and losers, but winners have no incentive to share their bounty. The beneficiaries of protective measures do not show how they have used their revenues to help the transition of workers and communities. This must change. Private-sector winners must supplement the federal Trade Adjustment Assistance programs to help fund the cost of adjustment and become an essential engine for further trade liberalization. After all, even free trade has its price.[33]

AN INTERNATIONAL PERSPECTIVE

From an international perspective, trade and investment negotiations must continue. In doing so, trade and investment policy can take either a multilateral or bilateral approach. **Bilateral negotiations** are carried out mainly between two nations, while **multilateral negotiations** are carried out among a number of nations. The approach can also be broad, covering a wide variety of products, services, or investments, or it can be narrow in that it focuses on specific problems.

In order to address narrowly defined trade issues, bilateral negotiations and a specific approach seem quite appealing. Very specific problems can be discussed and resolved expediently. However, to be successful on a global scale, negotiations need to produce winners. Narrow-based bilateral negotiations require that there be, for each issue, a clearly identified winner and loser. Therefore, such negotiations have less chance for long-term success, because no one wants to be the loser. This points toward multilateral negotiations on a broad scale, where concessions can be traded off among countries, making it possible for all participants to emerge and declare themselves as winners. The difficulty lies in devising enough incentives to bring the appropriate and desirable partners to the bargaining table.

Policymakers must be willing to trade off short-term achievements for long-term goals. All too often, measures that would be beneficial in the long term are sacrificed to short-term expediency to avoid temporary pain and the resulting political cost. Given the increasing links among nations and their economies, however, such adjustments are inevitable. In the recent past, trade and investment volume continued to grow for everyone. Conflicts were minimized and adjustment possibilities were increased manyfold. As trade and investment policies must be implemented in an increasingly competitive environment, however, conflicts are likely to increase significantly. Thoughtful economic coordination will therefore be required among the leading trading nations. Such coordination will result to some degree in the loss of national sovereignty.

New mechanisms to evaluate restraint measure will also need to be designed. The beneficiaries of trade and investment restraints are usually clearly defined and have much to gain, whereas the losers are much less visible, which will make coalition building a key issue. The total cost of policy measures affecting trade and investment flows must be assessed, must be communicated, and must be taken into consideration before such measures are implemented.[34]

The affected parties need to be concerned and join forces. The voices of retailers, consumers, wholesalers, and manufacturers all need to be heard. Only then will policymakers be sufficiently responsive in setting policy objectives that increase opportunities for firms and choice for consumers.

Summary

Trade and investment policies historically have been a subset of domestic policies. Domestic policies in turn have aimed primarily at maintaining and improving the standard of living, the developmental level, and the employment level within a nation. Occasionally, foreign policy concerns also played a role. Increasingly, however, this view of trade and investment policies is undergoing change. While the view was appropriate for global developments that took place following World War II, changes in the current world environment require changes in policies.

Increasingly, the capability of policymakers simply to focus on domestic issues is reduced because of global links in trade and investment. In addition, traditional international institutions concerned with these policies have been weakened, and the developmental conflict among nations has been sharpened. As a result, there is a tendency by many nations to restrict imports either through tariff or nontariff barriers. Yet, all these actions have repercussions that negatively affect industries and consumers.

Nations also undertake efforts to promote exports through information and advice, production and marketing support, and financial assistance. While helpful to the individual firm, in the aggregate, such measures may only assist firms in efforts that the profit motive would encourage them to do anyway. Yet, for new entrants to the international market such assistance may be useful. Foreign direct investment restrictions are often debated in many countries. Frequently, nations become concerned about levels of foreign direct investment and the "selling out" of the patrimony. However, the bottom line is that although the restriction of investments may permit more domestic control over industries, it also denies access to foreign capital. This in turn can result in a tightening up of credit markets, higher interest rates, and less impetus for innovation. Governments also promote imports and foreign direct investment in order to receive needed products or to attract economic activity.

In the future, nations must cooperate closely. They must view domestic policymaking in the global context in order to maintain a viable and growing global trade and investment environment. Policies must be long term in order to ensure the well-being of nations and individuals.

Questions for Discussion

1. Discuss the role of voluntary import restraints in international business.
2. What is meant by multilateral negotiations?
3. Discuss the impact of import restrictions on consumers.
4. Why would policymakers sacrifice major international progress for minor domestic policy gains?
5. Discuss the varying inputs to trade and investment restrictions by beneficiaries and by losers.
6. Why are policymakers often oriented to the short term?
7. Discuss the effect of foreign direct investment on trade.

8. Do investment promotion programs of state (or provincial) governments make sense from a national perspective?
9. The Bureau of Economic Analysis (http://www.bea.gov) and Stat-USA (http://www.stat-usa.gov) provide a multitude of information about the current state of the U.S. economy. Go to the International Investment Tables (D-57) to find the current market value of direct investment abroad as well as the value of direct investment in the United States.

Internet Exercises

1. Go to the World Bank web site (http://www.worldbank.org) to obtain an overview of the bank's purpose and programs. Search for criticism of bank programs on other web sites and prepare a two-page report of the key issues accounting for the "World Bank Controversy."

2. Check the U.S. Department of Commerce web site (http://www.doc.gov) to determine the assistance available to exporters. Which programs do you find most helpful to firms?

Take a Stand

During the war in Iraq, antiwar French and Germans boycotted many American goods such as McDonalds, Marlboro, and Coca-Cola. At the same time, boycotts of French and German goods were common in the United States. A fast-food restaurant called Cubbie's in Beaufort, North Carolina, renamed its French fries "freedom fries" in protest of France's antiwar stance. United States Representative Bob Ney, the House Administrative Committee chairman whose committee is in charge of the eateries in the House of Representatives Cafeterias, officially changed the menu item names "French fries" and "French toast" to "freedom fries" and "freedom toast." Ney said the action was "a small but symbolic effort to show the strong displeasure of many on Capitol Hill with the actions of our so-called ally, France."

For Discussion

While these antics may seem trivial, boycotts can have significant effects on business and international trade. Those charged with promoting transatlantic trade have said that boycotting American brand products may often endanger German jobs. For example, "The Coca-Cola sold in Germany is manufactured in Germany by German employees," says Fred Irwin, head of the American Chamber of Commerce in Frankfurt. While boycotting may seem like a simple and productive way of expressing our concerns about important issues, in the end the outcomes are dubious. What would you suggest?

Sources: http://www.house.gov/ney/freedomfriespr.htm, accessed July 30, 2003; "Don't Buy American," *The Economist,* April 12, 2003.

The Home–
Country
Perspective

Host Country
Political and
Legal
Environment

International
Relations and
Laws

Politics
and Law

Learning Objectives

- To understand the importance of the political and legal environments in both the home and host countries to the international business executive

- To learn how governments affect business through legislation and regulations

- To see how the political actions of countries expose firms to international risks

- To examine the differing laws regulating international trade found in different countries

- To understand how international political relations, agreements, and treaties can affect international business

Corruption, Guns, and Terrorism

In a global economy, companies transact business in emerging nations where the political and legal climates are unfamiliar and often unstable. Productive trade relationships are under constant threat when corruption, lawlessness, and political turmoil reign, yet business often continues in the face of adversity.

Before the September 11 terrorist attacks on the United States, a brisk trade of contraband goods across borders played a critical role in the fragile economies of Afghanistan and Pakistan. Electronics from Dubai, televisions from Japan, and cosmetics from Iran all moved swiftly through Taliban-controlled checkpoints, selling in Pakistan at far lower prices than legally imported items. Millions of dollars in "Islamic levies" imposed by the Taliban, along with protection money paid to powerful people in Pakistan, also facilitated the trafficking of drugs across borders, headed for black-market bazaars in Pakistan. Together, drugs and illegal contraband were estimated to be worth $30 billion a year—half of Pakistan's official gross domestic product. Following the attacks, Afghan warlords quickly took control of border cities such as Herat on the Afghan-Iran border, sustaining the underground economy even in the face of political chaos.

Zimbabwe used to have one of the most vibrant economies in Africa. Recently, however, corruption, mismanagement, and the near complete disruption of commercial farming have led to a crisis that has seen unemployment rise to close to 70 percent and the inflation rate soar above 100 percent. Consequently, more than half of the country's 12 million citizens are thought to be at risk of famine.

This economic collapse is widely blamed on government incompetence and President Robert Mugabe's controversial seizure of white-owned farms. Of the 4500 white farmers, only 600 have stayed on their farms since the program commenced two years ago. The land was earmarked for "redistribution" to the country's poor but an audit by a ministerial committee ascertained that less than one third of the allocated plots had actually been worked. Critics say the new farmers lack the financial backing and infrastructure needed to restore Zimbabwe's agricultural sector. In truth, Mugabe's "land reform" has chiefly benefited idle party hacks and stalwarts, not landless peasants.

What's more, Mugabe's administration has been unwilling to devalue its currency and has been keeping its official exchange rate at just Zim$55 to the U.S. dollar, while its real worth (parallel rate) is about Zim$811 to the U.S. dollar. This exchange rate imbalance, economists say, makes economic management impossible. Businesses are paid for their exports at the official rate, but are obliged to buy imports from abroad at the parallel rate. As a result the Zimbabwean economy contracted by 12 percent in 2002.

Because of Mr. Mugabe's misrule many, both from inside and outside Africa, are calling for him to step down as president. Both Great Britain and the United States have instituted visa restrictions barring travel to their respective countries by members of Mr. Mugabe's inner circle. Also, prominent statesmen such as the U.S. Secretary of State Colin Powell have been vocal in their growing impatience with other African nations for not putting pressure on Zimbabwe to reform. In their minds it is becoming increasingly evident that Zimbabwe's implosion will continue to threaten the peace, stability, and prosperity of the region.

Sources: BBC News Service http://news.bbc.co.uk/2/hi/business/2476563.stm, accessed July 1, 2003; http://www.zwnews.com/issuefull.cfm?ArticleI=7421, accessed July 1, 2003; "If You Want a Mercedes, Try Heart," *The Economist,* January 24, 2002; www.economist.com; "Dark Days for a Black Market," *BusinessWeek Online,* October 15, 2001, www.businessweek.com.

Politics and laws play a critical role in international business. Even the best plans can go awry as a result of unexpected political or legal influences, and the failure to anticipate these factors can be the undoing of an otherwise successful business venture.

Of course, a single international political and legal environment does not exist. The business executive has to be aware of political and legal factors on a variety of levels. For example, while it is useful to understand the complexities of the host country's legal system, such knowledge may not protect against sanctions imposed by the home country. The firm, therefore, has to be aware of conflicting expectations and demands in the international arena.

This chapter will examine politics and laws from the manager's point of view. The two subjects are considered together because laws generally are the result of political decisions. The chapter discussion will break down the study of the international political and legal environment into three segments: the politics and laws of the home country; those of the host country; and the bilateral and multilateral agreements, treaties, and laws governing the relations among host and home countries.

The Home–Country Perspective

No manager can afford to ignore the rules and regulations of the country from which he or she conducts international business transactions. Many of the laws and regulations may not specifically address international business issues, yet they can have a major impact on a firm's opportunities abroad. Minimum-wage legislation, for example, has a bearing on the **international competitiveness** of a firm using production processes that are highly labor intensive. The cost of domestic safety regulations may significantly affect the pricing policies of firms. For example, U.S. legislation creating the Environmental Superfund requires payment by chemical firms based on their production volume, regardless of whether the production is sold domestically or exported. As a result, these firms are at a disadvantage internationally when exporting their commodity-type products. They are required to compete against firms that have a cost advantage because their home countries do not require payment into an environmental fund.

Other legal and regulatory measures, however, are clearly aimed at international business. Some may be designed to help firms in their international efforts. For example, governments may attempt to aid and protect the business efforts of domestic companies facing competition from abroad by setting standards for product content and quality.

The political environment in most countries tends to provide general support for the international business efforts of firms headquartered within the country. For example, a government may work to reduce trade barriers or to increase trade opportunities through bilateral and multilateral negotiations. Such actions will affect individual firms to the extent that they improve the international climate for free trade.

Often governments also have specific rules and regulations that restrict international business. Such regulations are frequently political in nature and are based on governmental objectives that override commercial concerns. The restrictions are particularly sensitive when they address activities outside the country. Such measures challenge the territorial sovereignty of other governments and raise the issue of **extraterritoriality**—meaning a nation's attempt to set policy outside its territorial limits. Yet actions implying such extraterritorial reach are common, because nations often argue that their citizens and products maintain their nationality wherever they may be, and they therefore continue to be subject to the rules and laws of their home country.

Three main areas of governmental activity are of major concern to the international business manager. They are embargoes or trade sanctions, export controls, and the regulation of international business behavior.

EMBARGOES AND SANCTIONS

The terms **sanction** and **embargo** as used here refer to governmental actions that distort free flows of trade in goods, services, or ideas for decidedly adversarial and political, rather than economic, purposes. Sanctions tend to consist of specific coercive trade measures such as the cancellation of trade financing or the prohibition of high-technology trade, while embargoes are usually much broader in that they prohibit trade entirely. For example, the United States imposed sanctions against some countries by prohibiting the export of weapons to them, but it initiated an embargo against Cuba when all but humanitarian trade was banned. To understand sanctions and embargoes better, it is useful to examine the auspices and legal justifications under which they are imposed.

Trade embargoes have been used quite frequently and successfully in times of war or to address specific grievances. For example, in 1284, the Hansa, an association of north German merchants, believed that its members were suffering from several injustices by Norway. On learning that one of its ships had been attacked and pillaged by the Norwegians, the Hansa called an assembly of its members and resolved an economic blockade of Norway. The export of grain, flour, vegetables, and beer was prohibited on pain of fines and confiscation of the goods. The blockade was a complete success. Deprived of grain from Germany, the Norwegians were unable to obtain it from England or elsewhere. As a contemporary chronicler reports: "Then there broke out a famine so great that they were forced to make atonement." Norway was forced to pay indemnities for the financial losses that had been caused and to grant the Hansa extensive trade privileges.[1]

Over time, economic sanctions and embargoes have become a principal tool of the foreign policy for many countries. Often, they are imposed unilaterally in the hope of changing a country's government or at least changing its policies. Reasons for the impositions have varied, ranging from the upholding of human rights to attempts to promote nuclear nonproliferation or antiterrorism.

After World War I, the League of Nations set a precedent for the legal justification of economic sanctions by subscribing to a covenant that contained penalties or sanctions for breaching its provisions. The members of the League of Nations did not intend to use military or economic measures separately, but the success of the blockades of World War I fostered the opinion that "the economic weapon, conceived not as an instrument of war but as a means of peaceful pressure, is the greatest discovery and most

Following the irregularities of Haiti's May 2000 legislative election, international donors—including the US and EU—instituted an economic embargo.

GETTY IMAGES

precious possession of the League."[2] The basic idea was that economic sanctions could force countries to behave peacefully in the international community.

The idea of multilateral use of economic sanctions was again incorporated into international law under the charter of the United Nations, but greater emphasis was placed on the enforcement process. Sanctions decided on are mandatory, even though each permanent member of the Security Council can veto efforts to impose them. The charter also allows for sanctions as enforcement actions by regional agencies, such as the Organization of American States, the Arab League, and the Organization of African Unity, but only with the Security Council's authorization.

The apparent strength of the United Nations' enforcement system was soon revealed to be flawed. Stalemates in the Security Council and vetoes by permanent members often led to a shift of discussions to the General Assembly, where sanctions are not enforceable. Also, concepts such as "peace" and "breach of peace" were seldom perceived in the same context by all members, and thus no systematic sanctioning policy developed under the United Nations.[3]

Another problem with sanctions is that frequently their unilateral imposition has not produced the desired result. Sanctions may make the obtaining of goods more difficult or expensive for the sanctioned country, yet their purported objective is almost never achieved. In order to work, sanctions need to be imposed multilaterally and affect goods that are vital to the sanctioned country—goals that are clear, yet difficult to implement.

Close multinational collaboration can strengthen the sanctioning mechanism of the United Nations greatly. Economic sanctions can extend political control over foreign companies operating abroad, with or without the support of their local government.[4] When one considers that sanctions may well be the middle ground between going to war or doing nothing, their effective functioning can represent a powerful arrow in the quiver of international policy measures.

Sanctions usually mean significant loss of business to firms. One estimate claims that the economic sanctions held in place by the United States annually cost the country some $20 billion in lost exports.[5] Due to these costs, the issue of compensating the domestic firms and industries affected by these sanctions needs to be considered. Yet, trying to impose sanctions slowly or making them less expensive to ease the burden on these firms undercuts their ultimate chance for success. The international business manager is often caught in this political web and loses business as a result. Frequently, firms try to anticipate sanctions based on their evaluations of the international political climate. Nevertheless, even when substantial precautions are taken, firms may still suffer substantial losses due to contract cancellations. However, the reputation of a supplier unable to fill a contractual obligation will be damaged much more seriously than that of an exporter who anticipates sanctions and realizes it cannot offer a transaction in the first place.[6]

EXPORT CONTROLS

Many nations have **export-control systems,** which are designed to deny or at least delay the acquisition of strategically important goods by adversaries. The legal basis for export controls varies in nations. For example, in Germany, armament exports are covered in the so-called War Weapons list which is a part of the War Weapons Control Law. The exports of other goods are covered by the German Export List. **Dual use items,** which are goods useful for both military and civilian purposes, are then controlled by the Joint List of the European Union.[7] In the United States, the export control system is based on the Export Administration Act and the Munitions

Control Act. These laws control all export of goods, services, and ideas from the United States. The determinants for controls are national security, foreign policy, short supply, and nuclear nonproliferation.

Export licenses are issued by the Department of Commerce, which administers the Export Administration Act.[8] In consultation with other government agencies—particularly the Departments of State, Defense, and Energy—the Commerce Department has drawn up a list of commodities whose export is considered particularly sensitive. In addition, a list of countries differentiates nations according to their political relationship with the United States. Finally, a list of individual firms that are considered to be unreliable trading partners because of past trade-diversion activities exists for each country.

After an export license application has been filed, specialists in the Department of Commerce match the commodity to be exported with the **critical commodities list,** a file containing information about products that are either particularly sensitive to national security or controlled for other purposes. The product is then matched with the country of destination and the recipient company. If no concerns regarding any of the three exist, an export license is issued. Control determinants and the steps in the decision process are summarized in Figure 4.1.

This process may sound overly cumbersome, but it does not apply in equal measure to all exports. Most international business activities can be carried out under NLR conditions, which stands for "no license required." NLR provides blanket permission to export to most trading partners, provided that neither the end-user nor the end-use is considered sensitive. It therefore pays to check out the denied persons list published by the U.S. government (http://www.bis.doc.gov) to ensure that one's trading partner is not a prohibited trading partner. However, the process becomes more complicated and cumbersome when products incorporating high-level technologies and countries not friendly to the United States are involved. The exporter must then apply for an export license, which consists of written authorization to send a product abroad. However, even in most of these cases, license applications can be submitted via the Internet and licensing forms can be downloaded from it.

FIGURE 4.1

U.S. Export Control System

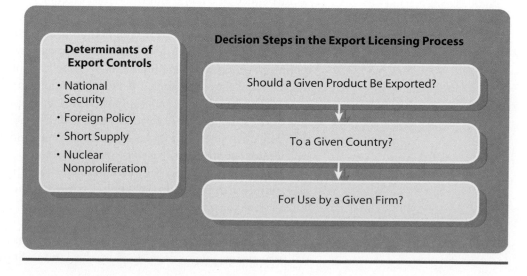

The international business repercussions of export controls are important. It is one thing to design an export control system that is effective and that restricts those international business activities subject to important national concerns. It is, however, quite another when controls lose their effectiveness and when one country's firms are placed at a competitive disadvantage with firms in other countries whose control systems are less extensive or even nonexistent.

A NEW ENVIRONMENT FOR EXPORT CONTROLS

Terrorist attacks have again highlighted the importance of export controls. Restricting the flow of materials can be crucial in avoiding the development of weapons of mass destruction; restricting technology can limit the ability to target missiles; restricting the flow of funds can inhibit the subsidization of terrorist training.

Nowadays, the principal focus of export controls must rest on the Third World. Quite a number of countries from this region want chemical and nuclear weapons and the technology to make use of them. For example, a country such as Libya can do little with its poison gas shells without a suitable delivery system.[9] As a result, export controls have moved from a "strategic balance" to a "tactical balance" approach. Nevertheless, even though the political hot spots addressed may be less broad in terms of their geographic expanse, the peril emanating from regional disintegration and local conflict may be just as dangerous to the world community as earlier strategic concerns with the Soviet Union.[10]

A third major change consists of the loosening of mutual bonds among allied nations. For many years the United States, Western Europe, and Japan, together with emerging industrialized nations, held a generally similar strategic outlook. This outlook was driven by the common desire to reduce, or at least contain, the influence of the Soviet Union. However, with the disintegration of the Soviet Union in 1991, individual national interests that had been subsumed by the overall strategic objective gained in importance. As a consequence, differences in perspectives, attitudes, and outlooks can now lead to ever-growing conflicts among the major players in the trade field.

Major change has also resulted from the increased **foreign availability** of high technology products. In the past decade, the number of participants in the international trade field has grown rapidly. High technology products are available worldwide from many sources. The broad availability makes any denial of such products more difficult to enforce. If a nation does control the exports of widely available products, it imposes a major competitive burden on its firms.

The speed of change and the rapid dissemination of information and innovation around the world also has shifted. For example, the current life cycle of computer chips is only 18 months. More than 70 percent of the data processing industry's sales resulted from the sale of devices that did not exist two years earlier.[11] This enormous technical progress is accompanied by a radical change in computer architecture. Instead of having to replace a personal computer or a workstation with a new computer, it is possible now to simply exchange microprocessors or motherboards with new, more efficient ones. Furthermore, today's machines can be connected to more than one microprocessor and users can customize and update configurations almost at will. Export controls that used to be based largely on capacity criteria have become almost irrelevant because they can no longer fulfill the function assigned to them. A user simply acquires additional chips, from whomever, and uses expansion slots to enhance the capacity of his or her computer.

The question arises as to how much of the latest technology is required for a country to engage in "dangerous" activity. For example, nuclear weapons and sophisticated delivery systems were developed by the United States and the Soviet Union long before supercomputers became available. Therefore, it is reasonable to assert that researchers in countries working with equipment that is less than state of the art, or even obsolete, may well be able to achieve a threat capability that can result in major destruction and affect world safety.

From a control perspective, there is also the issue of equipment size. Due to their size, supercomputers and high technology items used to be fairly difficult to hide and any movement of such products was easily detectable. Nowadays, state-of-the-art technology has been miniaturized. Much leading-edge technological equipment is so small that it can fit into a briefcase, and most equipment is no larger than the luggage compartment of a car. Given these circumstances, it has become difficult to closely supervise the transfer of such equipment.

There are several key export control problem areas for firms and policymakers. First is the continuing debate about what constitutes military-use products, civilian-use products, and dual use items. Increasingly, goods are of a dual-use nature, typically commercial products that have potential military applications. The classic example is a pesticide factory that, some years later, is revealed to be a poison gas factory.[12] It is difficult enough to clearly define weapons. It is even more problematic to achieve consensus among nations regarding dual-use goods. For example, what about quite harmless screws if they are to be installed in rockets or telecommunications equipment used by the military? The problem becomes even greater with attempts to classify and list subcomponents and regulate their exportation. Individual country lists will lead to a distortion of competition if they deviate markedly from each other. The very task of drawing up any list is itself fraught with difficulty when it comes to components that are assembled. For example, the Patriot missile consists, according to German law, only of simple parts whose individual export is permissible. Focus on Politics shows how slippery the slope can be.

Even if governments were to agree on lists and continuously updated them, the resulting control aspects would be difficult to implement. Controlling the transfer of components within and among companies across economic areas such as NAFTA or the European Union (EU) would significantly slow down business. Even more importantly, to subject only the export of physical goods to surveillance is insufficient. The transfer of knowledge and technology is of equal or greater importance. Weapons-relevant information easily can be exported via books, periodicals, and disks, therefore their content also would have to be controlled. Foreigners would need to be prevented from gaining access to such sources during visits or from making use of data networks across borders. Attendance at conferences and symposia would have to be regulated, the flow of data across national borders would have to be controlled, and today's communication systems and highways such as the Internet would have to be scrutinized. All these concerns have led to the emergence of controls of **deemed exports.** These controls address people rather than products in those instances where knowledge transfer could lead to a breach of export restrictions. More information is available under http://www.bis.doc.gov/.

Conflicts can also result from the desire of nations to safeguard their own economic interests. Due to different industrial structures, these interests vary between nations. For example, Germany, with a strong world market position in machine tools, motors, and chemical raw materials, will think differently about manufacturing equipment controls than a country such as the United States, which sees computers as an area of its competitive advantage.

The terrorist attacks on Washington DC and New York have led to a renewal of international collaboration in the export-control field. Policies are being scrutinized as to their sensibility in light of the dangers of proliferation and international terrorism.

Focus On ⬇

Space Secrets Sold!

The United States State Department has settled with Boeing Satellite Systems and Hughes Electronics, two of the world's largst aerospace companies, over charges that the pair was illegally transferring U.S. space technology to China. The companies could have faced fines of up to $60 million and been barred from selling controlled technology overseas for up to three years. The administrative charges stemmed initially from work Hughes did for the Chinese government beginning in 1995. Hughes Electronics' space launch division was helping China launch rockets that would put satellites into space. Boeing was charged in the case because it bought the space-launch division from Hughes Electronics in 2000. As part of the settlement the two companies issued a joint statement taking responsibility for the illegal technology transfer and acknowledged the potential harm the transfer could do to U.S. security and foreign-policy interests in the region. Boeing will also pay a $20 million fine over the next seven years and spend an additional $8 million on the further development of its internal export-control processes.

Hughes officials had given the Chinese military detailed information about rocketry to help ascertain why rockets were failing just after launch. The office of defense trade controls at the State Department claimed that these discussions breached the Arms Export Control Act and the International Traffic in Arms Regulations. Since 1988 U.S. firms have been allowed to launch their satellites via China's Long March rockets but U.S. firms are specifically barred from giving the Chinese

any help on the actual launch itself without U.S. licenses and the supervision of Pentagon inspectors. The U.S. government was concerned that technical advice given to the Chinese military to help with the launch of the Long March rockets would later be used by the Chinese to improve the performance of their nuclear-tipped missiles. Chinese space officials, however, became very aggressive in requiring "technology transfer" as a condition for U.S. corporations to enter its lucrative satellite market. The situation was exacerbated every time a rocket crashed because the international insurance companies covering the losses insisted on in-depth probes into the technical causes of the launch failure. As a result, U.S. corporations faced intensifying pressure from many sides to share technical information with the Chinese space program.

Loral Space & Communication Company was involved in similar activities in China at about the same time. The firm had also been investigated by the U.S. State Department and in early 2002 agreed to pay a $14 million fine and spend $6 million on internal reforms to stop this kind of overseas technology transfer. In exchange, the government did not bring similar administrative charges against Loral and has praised the company for facing up to prior transgressions and implementing corporate reforms aimed at preventing any recurrence. If Loral had been found liable it could have lost hundreds of millions of dollars in overseas sales of satellites and other foreign space business.

Sources: http://www.washingtonpost.com/wp-dyn/articles/A48407-2003Mar5.html, accessed March 18, 2003; http://abcnews.go.com/sections/world/cox_report/security1.html, accessed February 6, 2003; http://www.cnn.com/ALLPOLITICS/1998/05/22/china.money/, accessed February 6, 2003; Washington Post, "Firms Accused of Giving Space Technology to China," January 1, 2003, A7.

Closer collaboration among countries has resulted in an easing of export-control policies in the technology field.[13] Determined to bring U.S. economic as well as military power to bear in the fight against terrorism, the Bush Administration has also used policy both as a stick and as a carrot by deploying preferential trade measures, removing existing controls coupled with loans to reward allies, and imposing new sanctions to intimidate adversaries.[14] The role of export controls and their sophistication can therefore be expected to increase.

REGULATING INTERNATIONAL BUSINESS BEHAVIOR

Home countries may implement special laws and regulations to ensure that the international business behavior of firms headquartered in them is conducted within moral and ethical boundaries considered appropriate. The definition of appropriateness may vary from country to country and from government to government. Therefore, the content, enforcement, and impact of such regulations on firms may vary substantially among nations. As a result, the international manager must walk a careful line, balancing the expectations held in different countries.

One major area in which nations attempt to govern international business activities involves **boycotts.** As an example, Arab nations developed a blacklist of companies that deal with Israel. Further, Arab customers frequently demand assurance that products they purchase are not manufactured in Israel and that the supplier company does not do any business with Israel. The goal of these actions clearly is to impose a boycott on business with Israel. U.S. political ties to Israel caused the U.S. government to adopt antiboycott laws to prevent U.S. firms from complying with the boycott. The laws include a provision to deny foreign income tax benefits to companies that comply with the boycott. They also require notifying the U.S. government if boycott requests are received. U.S. firms that comply with the boycott are subject to heavy fines and to denial of export privileges. See http://www.bis.doc.gov/AntiboycottCompliance. Boycotts, however, may also spring from the reactions of disgruntled consumers or legislators. For example, Focus on Politics on the next page shows how the United States Congress, unhappy with the lack of French support in the campaign against Iraq, officially renamed foods with the word "French" in them and placed French foreign direct investment under scrutiny.

Caught in a web of governmental activity, firms may be forced either to lose business or to pay substantial fines. This is especially true if the firm's products are competitive yet not unique, so that the supplier can opt to purchase them elsewhere. The heightening of such conflict can sometimes force companies to search for new, and possibly risky, ways to circumvent the law or to totally withdraw operations from a country.

Another area of regulatory activity affecting the international business efforts of firms is **antitrust laws.** These laws often apply to international operations as well as to domestic business. In many countries, antitrust agencies watch closely when a firm buys a company, engages in a joint venture with a foreign firm, or makes an agreement abroad with a competing firm in order to ensure that the action does not result in restraint of competition.

Given the increase in worldwide cooperation among companies, however, the wisdom of extending antitrust legislation to international activities is being questioned. Some limitations to these tough antitrust provisions were already implemented decades ago. For example, in the United States the **Webb-Pomerene Act** of 1918 excludes from antitrust prosecution firms cooperating to develop foreign markets. This law was passed as part of an effort to aid export efforts in the face of strong foreign competition by oligopolies and monopolies. The exclusion of international activities from antitrust regulation was further enhanced by the Export Trading Company Act of 1982, which ensures that cooperating firms are not exposed to the threat of treble damages. Further steps to loosen the application of antitrust laws to international business are under consideration because of increased competition from strategic alliances and global megacorporations.

Firms operating abroad are also affected by laws against **bribery** and **corruption.** In many countries, payments or favors are a way of life, and "a greasing of the wheels" is expected in return for government services. As a result, many companies doing business internationally routinely are forced to pay bribes or do favors for foreign officials in order to gain contracts. Every year, businesses pay huge amounts of money in bribes to win friends, influence, and contracts. These bribes are conservatively estimated to run to $80 billion a year—roughly the amount that the UN believes is needed to eradicate global poverty. The U.S. Commerce Department reports that, annually, bribery is believed to be a factor in commercial contracts worth $145 billion.[15]

Focus On ⬇

Whaddaya Mean "French"?

Au revoir, French fries! Hello, Freedom fries! That's exactly what members of the U.S. Congress did when they announced, amid much fanfare, that French fries and French toast served in the Congressional dining facilities were being renamed "Freedom Fries" and "Freedom Toast" due to France's refusal to support the U.S.- and British-led Operation Iraqi Freedom. There were also proposals for a more tangible means of conveying American anger toward a so-called ally: cutting off U.S. military contracts with Sodexho, a French-owned catering firm.

In the midst of Operation Iraqi Freedom, a letter signed by 59 House members was sent to Defense Secretary Donald Rumsfeld, urging the cancellation of Sodexho's $881 million catering contract for 55 U.S. Marines facilities. As the letter's author, Representative Jack Kingston of Georgia, argued, "My colleagues and I abhor the idea of continuing to pour American dollars into a French-based firm."

It is true that Sodexho is a subsidiary of Sodexho Alliance SA, which is headquartered in Paris. What is being overlooked, however, is that the catering giant has U.S. subsidiaries and employs 110,000 Americans, including 4,000 in Rep. Kingston's home state.

In addition to causing the loss of U.S. jobs, the danger in canceling Sodexho's contract, which was won in fair and open bidding, is the consequence to future foreign investments in the United States. Clearly, foreign investment is both necessary and desirable. Sodexho is not responsible for French government policy and making official reprisals against private companies is not an advantageous precedent. The argument for trade becomes diluted if foreign companies feel their U.S. holdings are at risk of congressional irritability.

In today's global economy, efforts to use trade policies against other nations often runs afoul of deep international linkages. The danger of forbidding all French trade and investments is clear: French firms are the fifth-largest foreign investors in the United States, owning businesses that employ 649,000 Americans. As Brink Lindsey of the Cato Institute says, "There's no way, however rightfully upset we are with the French about their foreign policy, that it's going to be reflected in a sundering of commercial relations between our two countries, because that would be biting off our nose to spite our face."

In response to Congressional proposals and in an effort to distance itself from France's foreign policies, Sodexho's CEO Michel Landel issued a public statement: "The people of Sodexho are behind U.S. troops 100 percent, and we are especially proud that our efforts have enabled the U.S. Marine Corps to redeploy hundreds of troops in the fight against terrorism."

Sources: Blustein, Paul, "House Members Target Sodexho for French Ties," *The Washington Post,* March 29, 2003, E1; "No French Food for U.S. Marines," http://news.bbc.co.uk/1/hi/business/2894383.stm, accessed March 28, 2003.

Corruption is particularly widespread in nations where the administrative apparatus enjoys excessive and discretionary power and where there is a lack of transparency of laws and processes. Poverty, insufficient salaries of government servants, and income inequalities also tend to increase corruption.[16] Fighting corruption is therefore not only an issue of laws and ethics, but also of creating an environment that makes honesty possible and desirable.

In the 1970s, a major national debate erupted in the United States about these business practices, led by arguments that U.S. firms have an ethical and moral leadership obligation and that contracts won through bribes do not reflect competitive market activity. As a result, the **Foreign Corrupt Practices Act** was passed in 1977, making it a crime for U.S. executives of publicly traded firms to bribe a foreign official in order to obtain business.

A number of U.S. firms have complained about the act, arguing that it hinders their efforts to compete internationally against companies whose home countries have no such antibribery laws. The problem is one of ethics versus practical needs and, to some extent, of the amounts involved. For example, it may be hard to draw the line between providing a generous tip and paying a bribe in order to speed up a business transaction. Many business executives believe that the United States should not apply its moral principles to other societies and cultures in which bribery and corruption are endemic. To compete internationally, executives argue, they must be free to use the most common methods of competition in the host country.

On the other hand, applying different standards to executives and firms based on whether they do business abroad or domestically is difficult to do. Also, bribes may open the way for shoddy performance and loose moral standards among executives and employees and may result in a spreading of general unethical business practices. Unrestricted bribery could result in firms concentrating on how to bribe best rather than on how to best produce and market their products. Typically, international businesses that use bribery fall into three categories: those who bribe to counterbalance the poor quality of their products or their high price; those who bribe to create a market for their unneeded goods; and, in the bulk of cases, those who bribe to stay competitive with other firms that bribe.[17] In all three of these instances, the customer is served poorly, the prices increase, and the transaction does not reflect economic competitiveness.

The international manager must carefully distinguish between reasonable ways of doing business internationally—that is, complying with foreign expectations—and outright bribery and corruption. To assist the manager in this task, the 1988 Trade Act clarifies the applicability of the Foreign Corrupt Practices legislation. The revisions outline when a manager is expected to know about violation of the act, and they draw a distinction between the facilitation of routine governmental actions and governmental policy decisions. Routine actions concern issues such as the obtaining of permits and licenses, the processing of governmental papers (such as visas and work orders), the providing of mail and phone service, and the loading and unloading of cargo. Policy decisions refer mainly to situations in which the obtaining or retaining of a contract is at stake. While the facilitation of routine actions is not prohibited, the illegal influencing of policy decisions can result in the imposition of servere fines and penalties. The risks inherent in bribery have grown since 1999, when the Organization for Economic Cooperation and Development (OECD) adopted a treaty criminalizing the bribery of foreign public officials, moving well beyond its previous discussions, which only sought to outlaw the tax deductibility of improper payments. The Organization of American States (OAS) has also officially condemned bribery. Similarly, the World Trade Organization has decided to consider placing bribery rules on its agenda. In addition, nongovernmental organizations such as Transparency International are conducting widely publicized efforts to highlight corruption and bribery and even to rank countries on a Corruption Perceptions Index (http://www.transparency.de).

These issues place managers in the position of having to choose between home-country regulations and foreign business practices. This choice is made even more difficult because diverging standards of behavior are applied to businesses in different countries. However, the gradually emerging consensus among international organizations may eventually level the playing field.

A final, major issue that is critical for international business managers is that of general standards of behavior and ethics. Increasingly, public concerns are raised about such issues as environmental protection, global warming, pollution, and moral behavior. However, these issues are not of the same importance in every country. What may be frowned upon or even illegal in one nation may be customary or at least acceptable in others. For example, the cutting down of the Brazilian rain forest may be acceptable to the government of Brazil, but scientists and concerned consumers may object vehemently because of the effect on global warming and other climatic changes. The export of U.S. tobacco products may be legal but results in accusations of exporting death to developing nations. China may use prison labor in producing products for export, but U.S. law prohibits the importation of such products. Mexico may permit the use of low safety standards for workers, but the buyers of Mexican products may object to the resulting dangers.

International firms must understand the conflicts in standards and should assert leadership in implementing change. Not everything that is legally possible should be exploited for profit. By acting on existing, leading-edge knowledge and standards, firms will be able to benefit in the long term through consumer goodwill and the avoidance of later recriminations.

International executives are "selling" the world on two key issues: one is the benefit of market forces that result in the interplay of supply and demand. This interplay in turn uses price signals instead of government fiat to adjust activities, thrives on competition, and works within an environment of respect for profitability and private property. The second key proposition is that international marketers will do their best to identify market niches and bring their products and services to customers around the globe. Since these activities take up substantial financial resources, they provide individuals with the opportunity to invest their funds in the most productive and efficient manner.

Key underlying dimensions of both of these issues are managerial and corporate virtue, vision, and veracity. Unless the world can believe in what executives say and do, and trust their global activities, it will be hard, if not impossible, to forge a global commitment between those doing the marketing and the ones being marketed to. It is therefore of vital interest to executives to ensure that corruption, bribery, lack of transparency, and the misleading of consumers, investors, and employees are systematically relegated to the history books—where they belong. It will be the extent of openness, responsiveness, long-term thinking, and truthfulness that will determine the degrees of freedom of international business.[18]

Host Country Political and Legal Environment

Politics and laws of a host country affect international business operations in a variety of ways. The good manager will understand these dimensions of the countries in which the firm operates so that he or she can work within existing parameters and can anticipate and plan for changes that may occur.

POLITICAL ACTION AND RISK

Firms usually prefer to conduct business in a country with a stable and friendly government, but such governments are not always easy to find. Managers must therefore continually monitor the government, its policies, and its stability to determine the potential for political change that could adversely affect corporate operations.

There is **political risk** in every nation, but the range of risks varies widely from country to country. In general, political risk is lowest in countries that have a history of stability and consistency. Political risk tends to be highest in nations that do not have this sort of history. In a number of countries, however, consistency and stability that were apparent on the surface have been quickly swept away by major popular movements that drew on the bottled-up frustrations of the population. Three major types of political risk can be encountered: **ownership risk,** which exposes property and life; **operating risk,** which refers to interference with the ongoing operations of a firm; and **transfer risk,** which is mainly encountered when attempts are made to shift funds between countries. Firms can be exposed to political risk due to government actions or even actions outside the control of governments. The type of actions and their effects are classified in Figure 4.2.

A major political risk in many countries is that of conflict and violent change. A manager will want to think twice before conducting business in a country in which the likelihood of such change is high. To begin with, if conflict breaks out, violence directed toward the firm's property and employees is a strong possibility. Guerrilla warfare, civil disturbances, and **terrorism** often take an anti-industry bent, making companies and their employees potential targets. International corporations are often subject to major threats, even in countries that boast great political stability. Sometimes the sole fact that a firm is market oriented is sufficient to attract the wrath of terrorists. Following U.S. military strikes in Afghanistan, in the spring of 2002 a group of suspected Muslim militants in Pakistan kidnapped and murdered journalist Daniel Pearl, a reporter with *The Wall Street Journal*, the flagship of U.S. business journalism.

International terrorists frequently target U.S. facilities, operations, and personnel abroad. Since the September 11 attacks on the World Trade Center and the Pentagon, we know that such attacks can also take place within the United States. U.S. firms, by their nature, cannot have the elaborate security and restricted access of U.S. diplomatic

FIGURE 4.2

Exposure to Political Risk

Contingencies May Include:	**Loss May Be the Result of:**	
	The actions of legitimate government authorities	Events caused by factors outside the control of government
The involuntary loss of control over specific assets without adequate compensation	• Total or partial expropriation • Forced divestiture • Confiscation • Cancellation or unfair calling of performance bonds	• War • Revolution • Terrorism • Strikes • Extortion
A reduction in the value of a stream of benefits expected from the foreign-controlled affiliate	• Nonapplicability of "national treatment" • Restriction in access to financial, labor, or material markets • Controls on prices, outputs, or activities • Currency and remittance restrictions • Value-added and export performance requirements	• Nationalistic buyers or suppliers • Threats and disruption to operations by hostile groups • Externally induced financial constraints • Externally imposed limits on imports or exports

Source: José de la Torre and David H. Neckar, "Forecasting Political Risks for International Operations," in H. Vernon-Wortzel and L. Wortzel, *Global Strategic Management: The Essentials*," 2nd ed. (New York: John Wiley and Sons, 1990), 195.

MAP

Patterns of Global Terrorism Outside the United States, 2001

International Terrorist Incidents, 2001

- 191
- 45
- 6 to 8
- 3 to 5
- 1 or 2
- None or no data

Source: Based on *U.S. Department of State*, 2001; see also
http://www.state.gov/s/ct/rls/pgtrpt/2001/html/10273.htm.

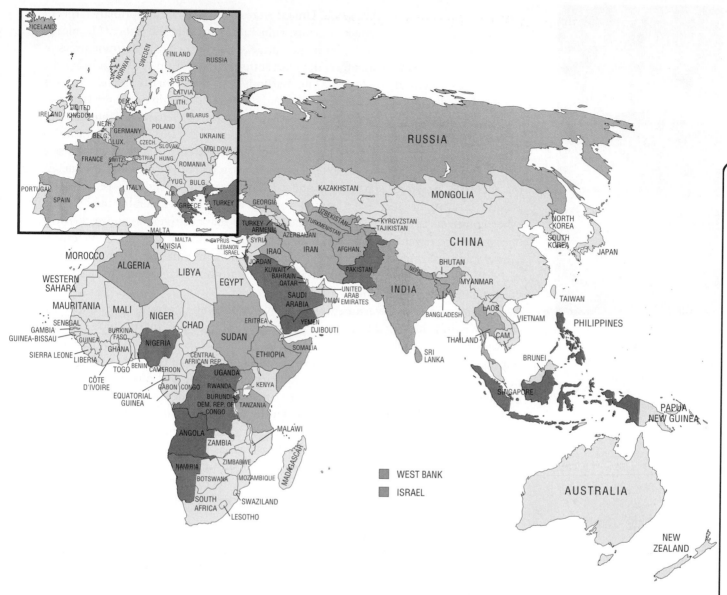

MAP

WEST BANK
ISRAEL

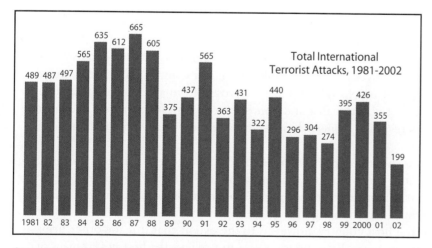

Total International
Terrorist Attacks, 1981-2002

Source: http://www.state.gov/documents/organization/20125.pdf,
accessed June 25, 2003.

© AP/WIDE WORLD PHOTOS/DAVID LONGSTREATH

McDonald's franchises, both within and outside the United States, have been the targets of international terrorists around the world, from Canada to France to Moscow to Seattle.

offices and military bases. As a result, United States businesses are the primary target of terrorists worldwide, and remain the most vulnerable targets in the future.[19] Ironically enough, in many instances, the businesses attacked or burned are the franchisees of U.S. business concepts. Therefore, the ones suffering most from such attacks are the local owners and local employees. The methods used by terrorists against business facilities include bombing, arson, hijacking, and sabotage. To obtain funds, the terrorists resort to kidnapping executives, armed robbery, and extortion.[20] To reduce international terrorism, recent experience has demonstrated that international collaboration is imperative to identify and track terrorist groups and to systematically reduce their safe havens and financial support. In spite of such efforts, terrorism is likely to continue. As former U.S. senators Hart and Rudman have written: "prudence requires we assume . . . adversaries . . . have learned from the attacks how vulnerable the U.S. and other countries are. They will also have observed that relatively low-cost terrorist operations . . . can inflict extensive damage and profound disruption. . . . As long as catastrophic attacks are likely to yield tangible results in undermining our economy and way of life, undertaking these attacks will be attractive to those who regard the U.S. and its allies as their enemy."[21]

As a consequence, governments are likely to continue imposing new regulations and restrictions intended to avert terrorist acts. For example, increasingly complex customs clearance and international logistical requirements, or specific requirements imposed to enhance security systems, all combine to increase the cost of doing business internationally. Moreover, these security measures will also tend to lessen the efficiency with which international business channels can function.[22]

In many countries, particularly in the developing world, **coups d'état** can result in drastic changes in government. The new government often will attack foreign firms as remnants of a Western-dominated colonial past, as has happened in Cuba, Nicaragua, and Iran. Even if such changes do not represent an immediate physical threat, they can lead to policy changes that may have drastic effect. The past decades have seen coups in Ghana, Ethiopia, Pakistan, and Ivory Coast, for example, that have seriously impeded the conduct of international business.

Less drastic, but still worrisome, are changes in government policies that are not caused by changes in the government itself. These occur when, for one reason or another, a government feels pressured to change its policies toward foreign businesses. The pressure may be the result of nationalist or religious factions or widespread anti-Western feeling.

A broad range of policy changes is possible as a result of political unrest. All of the changes can affect the company's international operations, but not all of them are equal in weight. Except for extreme cases, companies do not usually have to fear violence against their employees, although violence against company property is quite common. Also common are changes in policy that result from a new government or a strong new stance that is nationalist and opposed to foreign investment. The most drastic public steps resulting from such policy changes are usually expropriation and confiscation.

Expropriation is the transfer of ownership by the host government to a domestic entity with payment of compensation. Expropriation was an appealing action to many countries because it demonstrated their nationalism and transferred a certain amount of wealth and resources from foreign companies to the host country immediately. It did have costs to the host country, however, to the extent that it made other firms more hesitant to invest there. Expropriation does not relieve the host government of providing compensation to the former owners. However, these compensation negotiations are often protracted and frequently result in settlements that are unsatisfactory to the owners. For example, governments may offer compensation in the form of local, nontransferable currency or may base compensation on the book value of the firm. Even though firms that are expropriated may deplore the low levels of payment obtained, they frequently accept them in the absence of better alternatives.

The use of expropriation as a policy tool has sharply decreased over time. In the mid-1970s, more than 83 expropriations took place in a single year. By the turn of the century, the annual average had declined to fewer than 3. Apparently, governments have come to recognize that the damage they inflict on themselves through expropriation exceeds the benefits they receive.[23]

Confiscation is similar to expropriation in that it results in a transfer of ownership from the firm to the host country. It differs in that it does not involve compensation for the firm. Some industries are more vulnerable than others to confiscation and expropriation because of their importance to the host country's economy and their lack of ability to shift operations. For this reason, such sectors as mining, energy, public utilities, and banking have frequently been targets of such government actions.

Confiscation and expropriation constitute major political risk for foreign investors. Other government actions, however, are equally detrimental to foreign firms. Many countries are turning from confiscation and expropriation to more subtle forms of control, such as **domestication**. The goal of domestication is the same—that is, to gain control over foreign investment—but the method is different. Through domestication, the government demands transfer of ownership and management responsibility. It can impose **local content** regulations to ensure that a large share of the product is locally produced or demand that a larger share of the profit is retained in the country. Changes in labor laws, patent protection, and tax regulations are also used for purposes of domestication.

Domestication can have profound effects on an international business operation for a number of reasons. If a firm is forced to hire nationals as managers, poor cooperation and communication can result. If domestication is imposed within a very short time span, corporate operations overseas may have to be headed by poorly trained and inexperienced local managers. Domestic content requirements may force a firm to purchase its supplies and parts locally. This can result in increased costs, less efficiency, and lower-quality products. Export requirements imposed on companies may create havoc for their international distribution plans and force them to change or even shut down operations in third countries.

Finally, domestication usually will shield an industry within one country from foreign competition. As a result, inefficiencies will be allowed to thrive due to a lack of market discipline. This will affect the long-run international competitiveness of an operation abroad and may turn into a major problem when, years later, domestication is discontinued by the government.

If government action consists of weakening or not enforcing **intellectual property right** (IPR) protection, companies run the risk of losing their core competitive edge. Such steps may temporarily permit domestic firms to become quick imitators. Yet, in the longer term, they will not only discourage the ongoing transfer of technology and knowledge by multinational firms, but also reduce the incentive for local firms to invest in innovation and progress.

Poor IPR legislation and enforcement in the otherwise lucrative markets of Asia illustrate a clash between international business interests and developing nations' political and legal environments. Businesses attempting to enter the markets of China, Indonesia, Malaysia, Singapore, Taiwan, Thailand, and the Philippines face considerable risk in these countries, which have the world's worst records for copyright piracy and intellectual property infringements. But these newly industrialized countries argue that IPR laws discriminate against them because they impede the diffusion of technology and artificially inflate prices. They also point to the fact that industrialized nations such as the United States and Japan violated IPR laws during earlier stages of development. In fact, the United States became a signatory to the Berne Convention on copyrights only in 1989—around one hundred years after its introduction—and Japan disregarded IPR laws in adapting Western technologies during the 1950s. Furthermore, although newly industrialized nations are becoming increasingly aware that strong IPR protection will encourage technology transfer and foreign investment, the weak nature of these countries' court structures and the slow pace of legislation often fail to keep pace with the needs of their rapidly transforming economies.[24]

Due to successful international negotiations in the Uruguay Round, the World Trade Organization now has agreement on significant dimensions of the trade-related aspects of intellectual property rights (TRIPS) (http://www.wto.org). This agreement sets minimum standards of protection to be provided by each member country for copyrights, trademarks, geographical indications, industrial designs, patents, layout designs of integrated circuits, and undisclosed information such as trade secrets and test data.[25] While not all-encompassing, these standards provide substantial assurances of protection, which after an implementation delay for the poorest countries, will apply to virtually all parts of the world.

One might ask why companies would choose to do business in risky markets. However, as with anything international (or any business for that matter), the issue is not whether there is any risk but rather the degree of risk that exists. Key links to risk are the dimension of reward. With appropriate rewards, many risks become more tolerable. For example, between 1991 and 1997, the average return on foreign direct investment in Africa was higher than in any other region, according to the UN Conference on Trade and Development. This is partly because the perceived risk of doing business in very poor countries is so great that firms tend to invest only in projects that promise quick profits. But it is also because there are good opportunities. For brave businessfolk, there may be rich returns in unexpected places.[26]

ECONOMIC RISK

Most businesses operating abroad face a number of other risks that are less dangerous, but probably more common, than the drastic ones already described. A host government's political situation or desires may lead it to impose economic regulations or laws to restrict or control the international activities of firms.

Nations that face a shortage of foreign currency will sometimes impose controls on the movement of capital into and out of the country. Such controls may make it difficult for a firm to remove its profits or investments from the host country. Sometimes **exchange controls** are also levied selectively against certain products or companies in an effort to reduce the importation of goods that are considered to be luxuries or to be sufficiently available through domestic production. Such regulations often affect the importation of parts, components, or supplies that are vital to production operations in the country. They may force a firm either to alter its production program or, worse yet, to shut down its entire plant. Prolonged negotiations with government officials may be necessary to reach a compromise on what constitutes a "valid" expenditure of foreign currency resources. Because the goals of government officials and corporate managers are often quite different, such compromises, even when they can be reached, may result in substantial damage to the international operations of the firm.

Countries may also use **tax policy** toward foreign investors in an effort to control multinational corporations and their capital. Tax increases may raise much-needed revenue for the host country, but they can severely damage the operations of foreign investors. This damage, in turn, will frequently result in decreased income for the host country in the long run. The raising of tax rates needs to be carefully differentiated from increased tax scrutiny of foreign investors. Many governments believe that multinational firms may be tempted to shift tax burdens to lower-tax countries by using artificial pricing schemes between subsidiaries. In such instances, governments are likely to take measures to obtain their fair contribution from multinational operations. In the United States, for example, increased focus on the taxation of multinational firms has resulted in various back-tax payments by foreign firms and the development of new corporate pricing policies developed in collaboration with the Internal Revenue Service.[27]

The international executive also has to worry about **price controls.** In many countries, domestic political pressures can force governments to control the prices of imported products or services, particularly in sectors considered highly sensitive from a political perspective, such as food or health care. A foreign firm involved in these areas is vulnerable to price controls because the government can play on citizens' nationalistic tendencies to enforce the controls. Particularly in countries that suffer from high inflation, frequent devaluations, or sharply rising costs, the international executive may be forced to choose between shutting down the operation or continuing production at a loss in the hope of recouping profits when the government loosens or removes its price restrictions. Price controls can also be administered to prevent prices from being too low. As explained in more detail in Chapter 14, governments have enacted antidumping laws, which prevent foreign competitors from pricing their imports unfairly low in order to drive domestic competitors out of the market. Since dumping charges depend heavily on the definition of "fair" price, a firm can sometimes become the target of such accusations quite unexpectedly. Proving that no dumping took place can become quite onerous in terms of time, money, and information disclosure.

MANAGING THE RISK

Managers face the risk of confiscation, expropriation, domestication, or other government interference whenever they conduct business overseas, but ways exist to lessen the risk. Obviously, if a new government comes into power and is dedicated to the removal of all foreign influences, there is little a firm can do. In less extreme cases, however, managers can take actions that will reduce the risk, provided they understand the root causes of the host country's policies.

Adverse governmental actions are usually the result of nationalism, the deterioration of political relations between home and host country, the desire for independence, or opposition to colonial remnants. If a host country's citizens feel exploited by foreign investors, government officials are more likely to take antiforeign action. To reduce the risk of government intervention, the international firm needs to demonstrate that it is concerned with the host country's society and that it considers itself an integral part of the host country, rather than simply an exploitative foreign corporation. Ways of doing this include intensive local hiring and training practices, better pay, contributions to charity, and societally useful investments. In addition, the company can form joint ventures with local partners to demonstrate that it is willing to share its gains with nationals. Although such actions will not guarantee freedom from political risk, they will certainly lessen the exposure.

Another action that can be taken by corporations to protect against political risk is the close monitoring of political developments. Increasingly, private sector firms offer such monitoring assistance, permitting the overseas corporation to discover potential trouble spots as early as possible and to react quickly to prevent major losses.

Firms can also take out insurance to cover losses due to political and economic risk. Most industrialized countries offer insurance programs for their firms doing business abroad. In Germany, for example, Hermes Kreditanstalt (http://www.hermes.de) provides exporters with insurance. In the United States, the Overseas Private Investment Corporation (OPIC) (http://www.opic.gov) can cover three types of risk insurance: currency inconvertibility insurance, which covers the inability to convert profits, debt service, and other remittances from local currency into U.S. dollars; expropriation insurance, which covers the loss of an investment due to expropriation, nationalization, or confiscation by a foreign government; and political violence insurance, which covers the loss of assets or income due to war, revolution, insurrection, or politically motivated civil strife, terrorism, and sabotage. The cost of coverage varies by country and type of activity, but for manufacturers it averages $0.35 for $100 of coverage per year to protect against inconvertibility, $0.50 to protect against expropriation, and $0.45 to compensate for damage to business income and assets from political violence.[28] Usually the policies do not cover commercial risks and, in the event of a claim, cover only the actual loss—not lost profits. In the event of a major political upheaval, however, risk insurance can be critical to a firm's survival.

The discussion to this point has focused primarily on the political environment. Laws have been mentioned only as they appear to be the direct result of political change. However, the laws of host countries need to be considered on their own to some extent, for the basic system of law is important to the conduct of international business.

LEGAL DIFFERENCES AND RESTRAINTS

Countries differ in their laws as well as in their use of the law. For example, over the past decade the United States has become an increasingly litigious society in which institutions and individuals are quick to initiate lawsuits. Court battles are often protracted and costly, and even the threat of a court case can reduce business opportunities. In contrast, Japan's tradition tends to minimize the role of the law and of lawyers. On a per capita basis, Japan has only about 5 percent of the number of lawyers that the United States has.[29] Whether the number of lawyers is cause or effect, the Japanese tend not to litigate. Litigation in Japan means that the parties have failed to compromise, which is contrary to Japanese tradition and results in loss of face. A cultural predisposition therefore exists to settle conflicts outside the court system.

Over the millenia of civilization, many different laws and legal systems have emerged. King Hammurabi of Babylon codified a series of decisions by judges into a body of laws. Legal issues in many African tribes were settled through the verdicts of clansmen. A key legal perspective that survives today is that of **theocracy.** Examples are Hebrew law and Islamic law (the sharia) which are the result of the dictates of God, scripture, prophetic utterances and practices, and scholarly interpretations.[30] These legal systems have faith and belief as their key focus and are a mix of societal, legal, and spiritual guidelines.

While legal systems are important to society, from an international business perspective, the two major legal systems worldwide can be categorized into common law and code law. **Common law** is based on tradition and depends less on written statutes and codes than on precedent and custom. Common law originated in England and is the system of law in the United States. **Code law** on the other hand, is based on a comprehensive set of written statutes. Countries with code law try to spell out all possible legal rules explicitly. Code law is based on Roman law and is found in the majority of the nations of the world.

In general, countries with the code law system have much more rigid laws than those with the common law system. In the latter, courts adopt precedents and customs to fit cases, allowing a better idea of basic judgment likely to be rendered in new situations. The differences between code law and common law and their impact on international business, while wide in theory, are not as broad in practice. One reason is that many common-law countries, including the United States, have adopted commercial codes to govern the conduct of business.

Host countries may adopt a number of laws that affect the firm's ability to do business. Tariffs and quotas, for example, can affect the entry of goods. Special licenses for foreign goods may be required.

Other laws may restrict entrepreneurial activities. In Argentina, for example, pharmacies must be owned by the pharmacist. This legislation prevents an ambitious businessperson from hiring druggists and starting a pharmacy chain. Similarly, the law prevents the addition of a drug counter to an existing business such as a supermarket and thus the broadening of the product offering to consumers.

Specific legislation may also exist regulating what does and does not constitute deceptive advertising. Many countries prohibit specific claims that compare products to the competition, or they restrict the use of promotional devices. Even when no laws exist, regulations may hamper business operations. For example, in some countries, firms are required to join the local chamber of commerce or become a member of the national trade association. These institutions in turn may have internal sets of rules that specify standards for the conduct of business that may be quite confining.

Seemingly innocuous local regulations that may easily be overlooked can have a major impact on the international firm's success. For example, Japan had an intricate process regulating the building of new department stores or supermarkets. The government's desire to protect smaller merchants brought the opening of new, large stores to a virtual standstill. Since department stores and supermarkets serve as the major conduit for the sale of imported consumer products, the lack of new stores severely affected opportunities for market penetration of imported merchandise.[31] Only after intense pressure from the outside did the Japanese government decide to reconsider the regulations. Another example concerns the growing global controversy that surrounds the use of genetic technology. Governments increasingly devise new rules that affect trade in genetically modified products. Australia introduced a mandatory standard for foods produced using biotechnology, which prohibits the sale of such products unless the food has been assessed by the Australia New Zealand Food Authority.

Other laws may be designed to protect domestic industries and reduce imports. For example, while food stuffs and domestic goods are taxed at a 10 percent rate, Russia charges a 20 percent value-added tax on most imported goods, assesses high excise taxes on goods such as cigarettes, automobiles, and alcoholic beverages, and provides a burdensome import licensing regime for alcohol to depress Russian demand for imports.[32]

Finally, the interpretation and enforcement of laws and regulations may have a major effect on international business activities. For example, in deciding what product can be called a "Swiss" Army knife or "French" wine, the interpretation given by courts to the meaning of a name can affect consumer perceptions and sales of products.

THE INFLUENCING OF POLITICS AND LAWS

To succeed in a market, the international manager needs much more than business know-how. He or she must also deal with the intricacies of national politics and laws. Although to fully understand another country's legal political system will rarely be possible, the good manager will be aware of its importance and will work with people who do understand how to operate within the system. To do so is particularly important for multinational corporations. These firms work in many countries and must manage relationships with a large number of governments. Often, these governments have a variety of ideologies, which may require different corporate responses. To be strategically successful, the firm must therefore be able to formulate and implement political activities on a global scale.[33]

Many areas of politics and law are not immutable. Viewpoints can be modified or even reversed, and new laws can supersede old ones. Therefore, existing political and legal restraints do not always need to be accepted. To achieve change, however, some impetus for it—such as the clamors of a constituency—must occur. Otherwise, systemic inertia is likely to allow the status quo to prevail.

The international manager has various options. One is to simply ignore prevailing rules and expect to get away with it. Pursuing this option is a high-risk strategy because the possibility of objection and even prosecution exists. A second, traditional, option is to provide input to trade negotiators and expect any problem areas to be resolved in multilateral negotiations. The drawbacks to this option are, of course, the quite time-consuming process involved and the lack of control by the firm.

A third option involves the development of coalitions and constituencies that can motivate legislators and politicians to consider and ultimately implement change. This option can be pursued in various ways. One direction can be the recasting or redefinition of issues. Often, specific terminology leads to conditioned, though inappropriate, responses. For example, before China's accession to the World Trade Organization in 2001, the country's trade status with the United States was highly controversial for many years. The U.S. Congress had to decide annually whether or not to grant "Most Favored Nation" (MFN) status to China. The debate on this decision was always very contentious and acerbic, and often framed around the question as to why China deserved to be treated the "most favored way." Lost in the debate was often the fact that the term "most favored" was simply taken from WTO terminology, and only indicated that trade with China would be treated like that with any other country. Only in late 1999 was the terminology changed from MFN to NTR or "normal trade relations." Even though there was still considerable debate regarding China, at least the controversy about special treatment had been eliminated.[34]

Beyond terminology, firms can also highlight the direct links and their costs and benefits to legislators and politicians. For example, a manager can explain the employment and economic effects of certain laws and regulations and demonstrate the benefits of change. The picture can be enlarged by including indirect links. For example, suppliers, customers, and distributors can be asked to help explain to decision makers the benefit of change. In addition, the public at large can be involved through public statements or advertisements.

Developing such coalitions is not an easy task. Companies often seek assistance in effectively influencing the government decision-making process. Typical categories of firm-level political behavior are lobbying, public/government relations, industry alliances and associations, and political incentives.[35] Lobbying usually works best when narrow economic objectives or single-issue campaigns are involved. Typically, **lobbyists** provide this assistance. Usually, there are well-connected individuals and

Lobbyists from other countries have a strong presence in Washington, DC, where they work to influence legislation that will be favorable to their home countries.

firms that can provide access to policymakers and legislators in order to communicate new and pertinent information.

Many U.S. firms have representatives in Washington, DC, as well as in state capitals and are quite successful at influencing domestic policies. Often, however, they are less adept at ensuring proper representation abroad even though, for example, the European Commission in Brussels wields far-reaching economic power. For example, a survey of U.S. international marketing executives found that knowledge and information about foreign trade and government officials was ranked lowest among critical international business information needs. This low ranking appears to reflect the fact that many U.S. firms are far less successful in their interactions with governments abroad and far less intensive in their lobbying efforts than are foreign entities in the United States.[36]

Many countries and companies have been effective in their lobbying in the United States. As an example, Brazil has retained nearly a dozen U.S. firms to cover and influence trade issues. Brazilian citrus exporters and computer manufacturers have hired U.S. legal and public relations firms to provide them with information on relevant U.S. legislative activity. The Banco do Brasil also successfully lobbied for the restructuring of Brazilian debt and favorable U.S. banking regulations. The other forms of political behavior are more useful when it comes to general issues applicable to a wide variety of firms or industries, or when long-term policy directions are at stake. In such instances, the collaboration and power of many market actors can help sway the direction of policy.

Although representation of the firm's interests to government decision makers and legislators is entirely appropriate, the international manager must also consider any potential side effects. Major questions can be raised if such representation becomes very overt. Short-term gains may be far outweighed by long-term negative repercussions if the international firm is perceived as exerting too much political influence.

International Relations and Laws

In addition to understanding the politics and laws of both home and host countries, the international manager must also consider the overall international political and legal environment. This is important because policies and events occurring among countries can have a profound impact on firms trying to do business internationally.

INTERNATIONAL POLITICS

The effect of politics on international business is determined by both the bilateral political relations between home and host countries and by multilateral agreements governing the relations among groups of countries.

The government-to-government relationship can have a profound influence in a number of ways, particularly if it becomes hostile. President Bush's characterization in February 2002 of Iran, Iraq, and North Korea as an "axis of evil" aggravated already unstable political relationships and threatened to set back negotiations by U.S. companies to secure lucrative oil deals.[37] In another example, although the internal political changes in the aftermath of the Iranian revolution certainly would have affected any foreign firm doing business in Iran, the deterioration in U.S.–Iranian political relations that resulted had a significant additional impact on U.S. firms, which were injured not only by the physical damage caused by the violence, but also by the anti-American feelings of the Iranian people and their government. The resulting clashes between the two governments subsequently destroyed business relationships, regardless of corporate feelings or agreements on either side.

International political relations do not always have harmful effects. If bilateral political relations between countries improve, business can benefit. One example is the improvement in Western relations with Central Europe following the official end of the Cold War. The political warming opened the potentially lucrative former Eastern bloc markets to Western firms.

The overall international political environment has effects, whether good or bad, on international business. For this reason, the manager must strive to remain aware of political currents and relations worldwide and will attempt to anticipate changes in the international political environment so that his or her firm can plan for them.

INTERNATIONAL LAW

International law plays an important role in the conduct of international business. Although no enforceable body of international law exists, certain treaties and agreements are respected by a number of countries and profoundly influence international business operations. For example, the World Trade Organization (WTO) defines internationally acceptable economic practices for its member nations. Although it does not directly deal with individual firms, it does affect them indirectly by providing some predictability in the international environment.

The **Patent Cooperation Treaty (PCT)** provides procedures for filing one international application designating countries in which a patent is sought, which has the same effect as filing national applications in each of those countries. Similarly, the European Patent Office examines applications and issues national patents in any of its member countries. Other regional offices include the African Industrial Property Office (ARIPO), the French-speaking African Intellectual Property Organization (OAPI), and one in Saudi Arabia for six countries in the Gulf region.

International organizations such as the United Nations and the Organization for Economic Cooperation and Development have also undertaken efforts to develop codes and guidelines that affect international business. These include the Code on International Marketing of Breast-milk Substitutes, which was developed by the World Health Organization (WHO) (http://www.who.int/en), and the UN Code of Conduct for Transnational Corporations. Even though there are 34 such codes in existence, the lack of enforcement ability hampers their full implementation.

In addition to multilateral agreements, firms are affected by bilateral treaties and conventions between the countries in which they do business. For example, a number of countries have signed bilateral Treaties of Friendship, Commerce, and Navigation (FCN). The agreements generally define the rights of firms doing business in the host country. They normally guarantee that firms will be treated by the host country in the same manner in which domestic firms are treated. While these treaties provide for some sort of stability, they can also be canceled when relations worsen.

The international legal environment also affects the manager to the extent that firms must concern themselves with jurisdictional disputes. Because no single body of international law exists, firms usually are restricted by both home and host country laws. If a conflict occurs between contracting parties in two different countries, a question arises concerning which country's laws are to be used and in which court the dispute is to be settled. Sometimes the contract will contain a jurisdictional clause, which settles the matter with little problem. If the contract does not contain such a clause, however, the parties to the dispute have a few choices. They can settle the dispute by following the laws of the country in which the agreement was made, or they can resolve it by obeying the laws of the country in which the contract will have to be fulfilled. Which laws to use and in which location to settle the dispute are two different decisions. As a result, a dispute between a U.S. exporter and a French importer could be resolved in Paris but be based on New York State law. The importance of such provisions was highlighted by the lengthy jurisdictional disputes surrounding the Bhopal incident in India.

In cases of disagreement, the parties can choose either arbitration or litigation. Litigation is usually avoided for several reasons. It often involves extensive delays and is very costly. In addition, firms may fear discrimination in foreign countries. Therefore, companies tend to prefer conciliation and **arbitration,** because they result in much quicker decisions. Arbitration procedures are often spelled out in the original contract and usually provide for an intermediary who is judged to be impartial by both parties. Intermediaries can be representatives of chambers of commerce, trade associations, or third-country institutions. One key nongovernmental organization handling international commercial disputes is the International Court of Arbitration, founded in 1923 by the International Chamber of Commerce (http://www.iccwbo.org). Each year it handles arbitrations in some 48 different countries with arbitrators of some 57 different nationalities. Arbitration usually is faster and less expensive than litigation in the courts. In addition, the limited judicial recourse available against arbitral awards, as compared with court judgments, offers a clear advantage. Parties that use arbitration rather than litigation know that they will not have to face a prolonged and costly series of appeals. Finally, arbitration offers the parties the flexibility to set up a proceeding that can be conducted as quickly and economically as the circumstances allow. For example, a multimillion dollar ICC arbitration was completed in just over two months.[38]

Summary

The political and legal environment in the home and host countries and the laws and agreements governing relationships among nations are important to the international business executive. Compliance is mandatory in order to do business successfully abroad. To avoid the problems that can result from changes in the political and legal environment, it is essential to anticipate changes and to develop strategies for coping with them. Whenever possible, the manager must avoid being taken by surprise and letting events control business decisions.

Governments affect international business through legislation and regulations, which can support or hinder business transactions. An example is when export sanctions or embargoes are imposed to enhance foreign policy objectives. Similarly, export controls are used to preserve national security. Nations also regulate the international business behavior of firms by setting standards that relate to bribery and corruption, boycotts, and restraint of competition.

Through political actions such as expropriation, confiscation, or domestication, countries expose firms to international risk. Management therefore needs to be aware of the possibility of such risk and alert to new developments. Many private sector services are available to track international risk situations. In the event of a loss, firms may rely on insurance for political risk or they may seek redress in court. International legal action, however, may be quite slow and may compensate for only part of the loss.

Managers need to be aware that different countries have different laws. One clearly pronounced difference is between code law countries, where all possible legal rules are spelled out, and common law countries such as the United States, where the law is based on tradition, precedent, and custom.

Managers must also pay attention to international political relations, agreements, and treaties. Changes in relations or rules can mean major new opportunities and occasional threats to international business. Even though conflict in international business may sometimes lead to litigation, the manager needs to be aware of the alternative of arbitration, which may resolve the pending matter more quickly and at a lower cost.

Questions for Discussion

1. Discuss this potential dilemma: "High political risk requires companies to seek a quick payback on their investments. Striving for a quick payback, however, exposes firms to charges of exploitation and results in increased political risk."

2. Discuss this statement: "The national security that our export control laws seek to protect may be threatened by the resulting lack of international competitiveness of U.S. firms."

3. Discuss the advantages and disadvantages of common law and code law.

4. The United States has been described as a litigious society. How does frequent litigation affect international business?

5. After you hand your passport to the immigration officer in country X, he misplaces it. A small "donation" would certainly help him find it again. Should you give him the money? Is this a business expense to be charged to your company? Should it be tax deductible?

Internet Exercises

1. What are some of the countries suspected of nuclear proliferation by the United States? What types of exports might be barred from going to these countries? How would you go about obtaining a U.S. export license? What are some of the penalties that the U.S. government can impose on noncompliant exporters (see http://www.bis.doc.gov)?

2. According to the anticorruption monitoring organization Transparency International, which countries have the highest levels of corruption? Which have the lowest levels? (Use the Corruption Perception Index found at http://www.transparency.de.) What problems might an exporter have in doing business in a country with high levels of corruption?

Take a Stand

Peer to peer on-line sharing has become a lucrative business that allows on-line service providers like Kazaa to enable its users to swap music and videos without paying for them, and prevents artists from receiving royalties. Consequently, Kazaa and other file-sharing services have been the subject of blistering legal and public relations campaigns by the entertainment industry aimed at shutting down their businesses or at least undermining consumer confidence in them. Senator Orrin Hatch (R–Utah), a musician himself, said that if nothing else could stop people from stealing copyrighted works, he would support using programs to damage the computers of those who do.

For Discussion

Despite all of this, file sharing is thriving, and although Kazaa says it does not support piracy, companies usually cannot control how consumers use its software. Should the government intervene?

Source: *Beyond Kazaa, a Grand Plan: Executive Seeks Partnership with Showbiz.* The Washington Post, E01 6-19-03.

KEA, the world's largest home furnishings retail chain, was founded in Sweden in 1943 as a mail-order company and opened its first showroom ten years later. From its headquarters in Almhult, IKEA has since expanded to worldwide sales of $12 billion from 175 outlets in 32 countries (see Table 1). In fact, the second store that IKEA built was in Oslo, Norway. Today, IKEA operates large warehouse showrooms in Sweden, Norway, Denmark, Holland, France, Belgium, Germany, Switzerland, Austria, Finland, Italy, Canada, the United States, Saudi Arabia, Spain, and the United Kingdom. It has smaller stores in Kuwait, United Arab Emirates, Australia, Hong Kong, Singapore, Malaysia, Taiwan, the Canary Islands, and Iceland. A store near Budapest, Hungary, opened in 1990, followed by outlets in Poland and the Czech Republic in 1991 and Slovakia in 1992, followed by Taiwan in 1994, Finland and Malaysia in 1996, and mainland China in 1998. Plans call for opening two stores in Japan by 2006. IKEA first appeared on the Internet in 1997 with the World Wide Living Room Web site. The IKEA Group's new organization has three regions: Europe, North America, and Asia-Pacific.

The international expansion of IKEA has progressed in three phases, all of them continuing at the present time: Scandinavian expansion, begun in 1963; West European expansion, begun in 1973; and North American expansion, begun in 1976. Of the individual markets, Germany is the largest, accounting for 21.6, followed by the U.S. at 13 percent of company sales. The phases of expansion are detectable in the worldwide sales shares depicted in Figure 1. "We want to bring the IKEA concept to as many people as possible," IKEA officials have said. The company estimates that over 260 million people visit its showrooms annually.

The IKEA Concept

Ingvar Kamprad, the founder, formulated as IKEA's mission to "offer a wide variety of home furnishings of good design and function at prices so low that the majority of people can afford to buy them." The principal target market of IKEA, which is similar across countries and regions in which IKEA has a presence, is composed of people who are young, highly educated, liberal in their cultural values, white-collar workers, and not especially concerned with status symbols.

IKEA follows a standardized product strategy with a universally accepted assortment around the world. Today, IKEA carries an assortment of thousands of different home furnishings that range from plants to pots, sofas to soup spoons, and wine glasses to wallpaper. The smaller items are carried to complement the bigger ones. IKEA has very limited manufacturing of its own, but designs all of its furniture. The network of subcontracted manufacturers numbers 2,000 in 55 different countries. The top five purchasing countries are: China (14 percent), Sweden (14 percent), Poland (8 percent), Germany (6 percent), and Italy (6 percent).

IKEA's strategy is based on cost leadership secured by contract manufacturers, many of which are in low-labor-cost countries and close to raw materials, yet accessible to logistics links. High-volume production of standardized items allows for significant economies of scale. In exchange for long-term contracts, leased equipment, and technical support from IKEA, the suppliers manufacture exclusively at low prices for IKEA. IKEA's designers work with the suppliers to build savings-generating features into the production and products from the outset.

IKEA has some of its production as well, constituting 10 percent of its total sales. While new facilities were opened in 2000 in Latvia, Poland, and Romania to bring the total number to 30, IKEA plans to have its

Sources: This case prepared by Ilkka Ronkainen is based on "IKEA's Enormous Niche Market," BBC News Online, August 1, 2003; "How IKEA Designs Its Sexy Price Tags," Business 2.0, October 2002: 108; "Oma Tuotanto Vahvistuu," Kauppalehti, March 9, 2001, 5; "Furnishing the World," The Economist (November 19, 1994): 79; Richard Norman and Rafael Ramirez, "From Value Chain to Value Constellation: Designing Interactive Strategy," Harvard Business Review 71 (July/August 1993): 65–77; "IKEA's No-Frills Strategy Extends to Management Style," Business International (May 18, 1992): 149–150; Bill Saporito, "IKEA's Got 'Em Lining Up," Fortune (March 11, 1991): 72; Rita Martenson, "Is Standardization of Marketing Feasible in Culture-Bound Industries? A European Case Study," International Marketing Review 4 (Autumn 1987): 7–17; Eleanor Johnson Tracy, "Shopping Swedish Style Comes to the U.S.," Fortune, (January 27, 1986): 63–67; Mary Krienke, "IKEA—Simple Good Taste," Stores (April 1986): 58; Jennifer Lin, "IKEA's U.S. Translation," Stores (April 1986): 63; "Furniture Chain Has a Global View," Advertising Age (October 26, 1987): 58; Bill Kelley, "The New Wave from Europe," Sales & Marketing Management (November 1987): 46–48. Updated information available from http://www.ikea.com.

TABLE 1

IKEA's International Expansion

Year	Outlets[a]	Countries[a]	Coworkers	Catalog Circulation[b]	Turnover in Swedish Crowns[c]
1954	1	1	15	285,000	3,000,000
1964	2	2	250	1,200,000	79,000,000
1974	10	5	1,500	13,000,000	616,000,000
1984	66	17	8,300	45,000,000	6,770,000,000
1988	75	19	13,400	50,535,000	14,500,000,000
1990	95	23	16,850	n.a.	19,400,000,000
1995	131	27	30,500	n.a.	38,557,000,000
2000	159	30	61,700	n.a.	81,187,000,000
2002	175	32	65,000	110,000,000[b]	99,200,000,000

[a]Stores/countries being opened by 2002.
[b]Estimate.
[c]Corresponding to net sales of the IKEA group of companies.

Source: http://www.ikea.com.

own production not exceed 10 percent, mainly to secure flexibility.

Manufacturers are responsible for shipping the components to large distribution centers, for example, to the central one in Almhult. These twelve distribution centers then supply the various stores, which are in effect miniwarehouses.

IKEA consumers have to become "prosumers"—half producers, half consumers—because most products have to be assembled. The final distribution is the

FIGURE 1

IKEA's Worldwide Sales Expressed as Percentages of Turnover by Market Unit

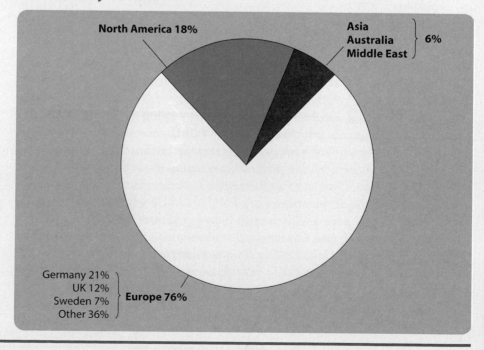

customer's responsibility as well. Although IKEA expects its customers to be active participants in the buy-sell process, they are not rigid about it. There is a "moving boundary" between what consumers do for themselves and what IKEA employees will do for them. Consumers save the most by driving to the warehouses themselves, putting the boxes on the trolley, loading them into their cars, driving home, and assembling the furniture. Yet IKEA can arrange to provide these services at an extra charge. For example, IKEA cooperates with car rental companies to offer vans and small trucks at reasonable rates for customers needing delivery service. Additional economies are reaped from the size of the IKEA outlets; for example, the Philadelphia store is 169,000 square feet (15,700 square meters). IKEA stores include babysitting areas and cafeterias and are therefore intended to provide the value-seeking, car-borne consumer with a complete shopping destination. IKEA managers state that their competitors are not other furniture outlets but all attractions vying for the consumers' free time. By not selling through dealers, the company hears directly from its customers.

Management believes that its designer-to-user relationship affords an unusual degree of adaptive fit. IKEA has "forced both customers and suppliers to think about value in a new way in which customers are also suppliers (of time, labor information, and transportation), suppliers are also customers (of IKEA's business and technical services), and IKEA itself is not so much a retailer as the central star in a constellation of services." Figure 2 provides a presentation of IKEA's value chain.

Although IKEA has concentrated on company-owned, larger-scale outlets, franchising has been used in areas in which the market is relatively small or where

uncertainty may exist as to the response to the IKEA concept. These markets include Hong Kong and the United Arab Emirates. IKEA uses mail order in Europe and Canada but has resisted expansion into the United States, mainly because of capacity constraints.

IKEA offers prices that are 30 to 50 percent lower than fully assembled competing products. This is a result of large-quantity purchasing, low-cost logistics, store location in suburban areas, and the do-it-yourself approach to marketing. IKEA's prices do vary from market to market, largely because of fluctuations in exchange rates and differences in taxation regimes, but price positioning is kept as standardized as possible.

IKEA's promotion is centered on the catalog. The IKEA catalog is printed in seventeen languages and has a worldwide circulation of well over 110 million copies. The catalogs are uniform in layout except for minor regional differences. The company's advertising goal is to generate word-of-mouth publicity through innovative approaches. The IKEA concept is summarized in Table 2.

IKEA in the Competitive Environment

IKEA's strategy positioning is unique. As Figure 3 illustrates, few furniture retailers anywhere have engaged in long-term planning or achieved scale economies in production. European furniture retailers, especially those in Sweden, Switzerland, Germany, and Austria, are much smaller than IKEA. Even when companies have joined forces as buying groups, their heterogeneous operations have made it difficult for them to achieve the same

FIGURE 2

IKEA's Value Chain

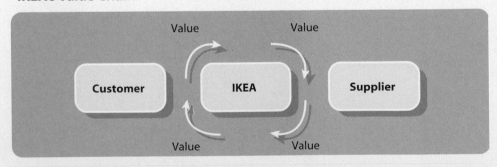

Source: Richard Norman and Rafael Ramirez, "From Value Chain to Value Constellation: Designing Interactive Strategy." *Harvard Business Review 71* (July/August 1993): 72.

TABLE 2

The IKEA Concept

Target market:	"Young people of all ages"
Product:	IKEA offers the same products worldwide. The number of active articles is 12,000. The countries of origin of these products are: Europe (66 percent), Asia (30 percent), and North America (4 percent). Most items have to be assembled by the customer. The furniture design is modern and light.
Distribution:	IKEA has built its own distribution network. Outlets are outside the city limits of major metropolitan areas. Products are not delivered, but IKEA cooperates with car rental companies that offer small trucks. IKEA offers mail order in Europe and Canada.
Pricing:	The IKEA concept is based on low price. The firm tries to keep its price-image constant.
Promotion:	IKEA's promotional efforts are mainly through its catalogs. IKEA has developed a prototype communications model that must be followed by all stores. Its advertising is attention-getting and provocative. Media choices vary by market.

degree of coordination and concentration as IKEA. Because customers are usually content to wait for the delivery of furniture, retailers have not been forced to take purchasing risks.

The value-added dimension differentiates IKEA from its competition. IKEA offers limited customer assistance but creates opportunities for consumers to choose (for example, through informational signage), transport, and assemble units of furniture. The best summary of the competitive situation was provided by a manager at another firm: "We can't do what IKEA does, and IKEA doesn't want to do what we do."

FIGURE 3

Competition in furniture Retailing

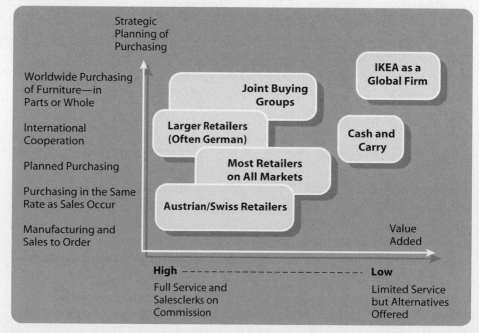

Source: Rita Martenson, "Is Standardization of Marketing Feasible in Culture-Bound Industries? A European Case Study," *International Marketing Review* 4 (Autumn 1987), 14.

IKEA in the United States

After careful study and assessment of its Canadian experience, IKEA decided to enter the U.S. market in 1985 by establishing outlets on the East Coast and, in 1990, one in Burbank, California. In 2003, a total of seventeen stores (eight in the Northeast, seven in California, one in Seattle, and one in Texas) generated sales of over $1.5 billion. (12 percent of worldwide). The stores employ over 6,000 workers. The overwhelming level of success in 1987 led the company to invest in a warehousing facility near Philadelphia that receives goods from Sweden as well as directly from suppliers around the world. Plans call for two to three additional stores annually over the next twenty-five years, concentrating on the northeastern United States and California.

Success today has not come without compromises. "If you are going to be the world's best furnishing company, you have to show you can succeed in America, because there is so much to learn here," said Goran Carstedt, head of North American operations. Whereas IKEA's universal approach had worked well in Europe, the U.S. market proved to be different. In some cases, European products conflicted with American tastes and preferences. For example, IKEA did not sell matching bedroom suites that consumers wanted. Kitchen cupboards were too narrow for the large dinner plates needed for pizza. Some Americans were buying IKEA's flower vases for glasses.

Adaptations were made. IKEA managers adjusted chest drawers to be an inch or two deeper because consumers wanted to store sweaters in them. Sales of chests increased immediately by 40 percent. In all, IKEA has redesigned approximately a fifth of its product range in North America. Today, 45 percent of the furniture in the stores in North America is produced locally, up from 15 percent in the early 1990s. In addition to not having to pay expensive freight costs from Europe, this has also helped in cut stock-outs. And because Americans hate standing in lines, store layouts have been changed to accommodate new cash registers. IKEA offers a more generous return policy in North America than in Europe, as well as next-day delivery service.

In hindsight, IKEA executives are saying they "behaved like exporters, which meant not really being in the country. . . . It took us time to learn this." IKEA's adaptation has not meant destroying its original formula. Their approach is still to market the streamlined and contemporary Scandinavian style to North America by carrying a universally accepted product range but with a mind on product lines and features that appeal to local preferences. The North American experience has caused the company to start remixing its formula elsewhere as well. Indeed, now that Europeans are adopting some American furnishing concepts (such as sleeper sofas), IKEA is transferring some American concepts to other markets such as Europe.

Questions for Discussion

1. What has allowed IKEA to be successful with a relatively standardized product and product line in a business with strong cultural influence? Did adaptations to this strategy in the North American market constitute a defeat to their approach?

2. Which features of the "young people of all ages" are universal and can be exploited by a global/regional strategy?

3. Is IKEA destined to succeed everywhere it cares to establish itself?

The U.S. Catfish Industry

The cultivation of water plants and animals for human use started thousands of years ago. Globally, aquaculture's growth has more than doubled in the 1990s (to more than 35 million tons a year). To meet the demand for imporved quality protein sources, scallops, oysters, salmon, and catfish are being raised in controlled environments. Farm-raised fish is of high quality and, unlike ocean-caught fish, is available all year long.

U.S. aquaculture production has grown more than 49 percent since 1991.[1] Aquaculture is the fastest growing segment of agriculture in the U.S. Farmed seafood makes up about one third of the seafood consumed in the United States. About two thirds of the shrimp and salmon and almost all of the catfish and trout consumed by Americans are raised in ponds.[2]

Thick-skinned, whiskered, wide-mouthed wild catfish can be found in the wild in channels and rivers of the southern United States. Wild catfish is typically described as pungent, bony, and muddy. However, as a result of acquaculture technology, catfish is now an economical farm-raised species with a mild flavor. Catfish are raised in clay-based ponds filled with fresh water pumped from underground wells. They are fed an enriched, high-protein, grain-based food. Their firm, white flesh can convey strong flavors and stands up to a variety of cooking techniques, which makes it suit virtually any ethnic cuisine.[3]

Americans consumed about 275 million kilograms (more than 600 million pounds) of catfish in 2000,[4] most of which came from 150,000 acres of catfish ponds in the United States, mainly located in Mississippi, Arkansas and Louisiana. The U.S. catfish industry is estimated to sell more than $4 billion worth of fish product each year. Catfish is especially popular in Southern dishes, but its use has been growing also in the Midwest. Filets are now available in New York supermarkets and fish stores. One recent poll placed catfish as the country's third favorite seafood, beaten only by shrimp and lobster.[5]

Sources: This case was written by Professor Michael R. Czinkota, Georgetown University McDonough School of Business, and graduate student Armen S. Hovhannisyan, Georgetown University School of Foreign Service.

The Issue

The United States is the leading market for Vietnamese catfish (followed by Hong Kong, the European Union, and Australia). In 2001, the United States produced 270.5 million kilograms (597 million pounds) and imported about 3.7 million kilograms (8.2 million pounds) of catfish out of which ninety percent, about 3.2 million kilograms (7 million pounds), came from Vietnam. By the end of 2001, prices for U.S. catfish had dropped to 50 cents a pound, about 15 cents below the cost of production and about 30 cents below the price in 2000. U.S. producers blamed the Vietnamese for the falling prices.[6]

Vietnamese catfish exporters and importers in turn blame U.S. producers for dragging prices down. They say that the Americans are mainly at fault for expanding inventories up to 30 percent, a figure obtained from the National Agricultural Statistics Service (http://www.usda.gov/nass). Vietnamese fish importers also claim that American catfish growers are to blame for their own difficulties because they sell the domestic fish in only a few states. "It is the failure to adequately marekt the product effectively throughout the U.S.," says Andrew Forman, president of Boston-based Infinity Seafood LLC. According to a report by Consulting Trends International, a California-based consulting firm, the price drop is "primarily the result of higher domestic catfish inventories in the U.S., which will depress prices through the end of 2001 and 2002."

The American catfish industry has almost tripled in size from 1985 to 2001. Hugh Warren, vice president of the Catfish Institute of America, says that this growth is strictly due to the industry's marketing effort of $50 million. He feels that as importers, the Vietnamese get a free ride.[7] The U.S. industry offers 15,000 jobs that earn $8 an hour in the poorest parts of America. These jobs are being "stolen" by cheap Vietnamese imports.[8]

In an attempt to change this situation, American catfish farmers, industry associations, and supporting organizations came to Washington, D.C. to call on officials at the State Department, the Commerce Department, the Food and Drug Administration, and Congress (which in July 2000 signed a bilateral agreement with Vietnam to foster free trade) for help. They waged an advertising campaign against their Vietnamese competitors in order to convince the public that Vietnamese catfish is of low quality and raised in dirty waters.[9]

Congressional Reaction

The support from Congress was swift. In December 2001 an amendment was added to an appropriations bill that barred the Food and Drug Adminstration (FDA) from spending money "to allow admission of fish or fish products labeled in whole or in part with the term 'catfish' unless the fish is from the Ictaluridae family." The senators from the South, who introduced the labeling bill, claimed Vietnamese fish to be as different scientifically from catfish "as cow from a yak."[10] Supporting a different view, Senator Phil Gramm (R-Tex.) characterized the Vietnamese catfish as follows: "Not only does it look like a catfish, but it acts like a catfish. And the people who make a living in fish science call it a catfish. Why do we want to call it anything other than a catfish?"[11] This meant that the FDA needed to identify different kinds of catfish.

In January 2002, under Congress' direction, the Food and Drug Administration (FDA) published "Guidance for Industry" regulations on how the imported catfish should be labeled. Under the regulation, Flat Whiskered Fish is an acceptable substitute for the Flat Whiskered Catfish; but Katfish or Cat Fish are not. Instead, importers, restaurants, and grocery stores will have to use a name such as "basa," which is one other name to call catfish from the Pangasius (Pangasiidae) family. U.S. producers were counting on such labels to discourage the sales of imported fish.

About 30 percent of U.S. seafood restaurants serve Vietnamese catfish, which is slightly milder and softer than the American variety. The amendment and the regulation were not a good news for them. As the owner of Piazza's Seafood World, a New Orleans-based importer, put it: "Nobody in the U.S. owns the word 'catfish.'"[12] However, Vietnam is still free to export catfish to the United States, as long as it's called something other than catfish.

When Is a Catfish a Catfish?

In order to identify different kinds of catfish, the FDA sought expert help on the catfish question. Before promulgating its regulation it consulted Dr. Carl J. Ferraris of the ichthyology department at the California Academy of Sciences. Dr. Ferraris's response was that there was no scientific justification to treat or rename catfish from Vietnam differently those from the United States.[13]

According to U.S. catfish farmers, the only true catfish belongs to the family with the Latin name Ictaluridae. The Vietnamese variety is in the family Panasiidae, which are "freshwater catfishes of Africa and southern Asia." Vietnamese catfish farmers claim that they have created a new agricultural industry, turning their rice and soybean fields into profitable fish farms in the poor regions of the country. By giving up crops, they gave up heavy use of chemical fertilizers and pesticides, which is good for the environment. They also gave up agriculture subsidies at a time when lawmakers wanted to get the government out of farming.[14]

U.S. catfish farmers say their catfish is raised in purified water ponds, which have to be tested by federal agencies and meet the standards of Catfish Institute. The U.S. catfish industry must go through inspections from 17 federal agencies (including Department of Commerce, Food and Drug Administration, and Environmental Protection Agency). By contrast, the Vietnamese imports have only to meet FDA approval.[15] The Vietnamese catfish are raised in cages that float in marshes in the Mekong river; some of the senators from the South talk about the possibility of toxins from Vietnam being in that "dirty" river.[16]

The Issue and the Free Trade

Vietnam's catfish industry provides a useful example of how global cooperation can enhance participation in global business. An Australian importer, for example, taught the Vietnamese how to slice catfish fillet, French researchers worked with a local university on low-cost breeding techniques, and Vietnam's leading catfish exporters depended on American industrial equipment from the United States.[17] However, a stumbling U.S. economy has made American farmers, along with many others in a number of industries, very sensitive to surging imports, and the catfish dispute represents a case of domestic politics alignment against free-market forces.[18] Critics in both Vietnam and the United States say that the catfish issue is an example of protectionism and hypocrisy, undermining the free-trade policies most recently espoused by the United States at the World Trade Organization talks in Doha.

"After spending years encouraging the Vietnamese that open trade is a win-win situation, it would be a shame if immediately after the trade agreement is signed the U.S. shifts to a protectionist 'we win, you lose' approach on catfish," says Virginia Foote, president of the U.S.–Vietnam Trade Council in Washington.[19]

In the ongoing dispute of how to manage global trade, agriculture and its cousin aquaculture are very sensitive issues. On the one side are industrial nations that use farm policy not only to promote their agribusiness overseas but also to protect their markets and farmers at home. European countries have used their agricultural subsidies to defend their countryside from the urban invasion, whereas developing countries try to raise their standard of living by breaking into those markets with less expensive products.

Questions for Discussion

1. Is it fair for the Vietnamese catfish importers to step in and capture market share while the market has been expanded due to the significant efforts and investments of the domestic industry? How should quality (if quality differences exist) considerations be reconciled?

2. The label ban would probably make consumers pay a higher price than they would have paid otherwise. Is this right?

3. Can any industry in the United States influence lawmakers to make decisions in their favor?

Endnotes

1. Catfish Institute, http://www.catfishinstitute.com.
2. Elizabeth Becker, "Delta Farmers Want Copyright on Catfish," *The New York Times*, January 16, 2002, A1.
3. Meredith Petran, "Catfish," *Restaurant Business*, New York, February 1, 2000.
4. Margot Cohen and Murray Hiebert, "Muddying the Waters," *Far Eastern Economic Review*, December 6, 2001.
5. *The Vietnamese invade: Catfish in the South*. See note 16.
6. Philip Brasher, "When is a Catfish Not a Catfish," *Washington Post*, December 27, 2001.
7. James Toedman, "Fighting Like Cats and Dogs Over Fish; It's U.S. vs. Vietnamese as trade battle goes global," *Newsday*, March 10, 2002, F2.
8. *The Vietnamese invade: Catfish in the South*. See note 16.
9. "One of these negative advertisements, which ran in the national trade weekly *Supermarket News*, tells us in shrill tones, 'Never trust a catfish with a foreign accent!' This ad characterizes Vietnamese catfish as dirty and goes on to say, 'They've grown up flapping around in Third World rivers and dining on whatever they can get their fins on. . . . Those other guys probably couldn't spell U.S. even if they tried.'"—quoted in Senator John McCain's December 18, 2001 Press Release, http://mccain.senate.gov/catfish.htm.
10. Philip Brasher, "When is a Catfish Not a Catfish."
11. Ibid.
12. Margot Cohen and Murray Heibert, "Mudding the Waters."
13. Elizabeth Becker, "Delta Farmers Want Copyright on Catfish."
14. Ibid.
15. Tim Brown, "South and Southeast, Vietnam Embroiled in Catfish Controversy," *Marketing News*, October 22, 2001.
16. "The Vietnamese Invade: Catfish in the South," *The Economist*, October 6, 2001.
17. Ibid.
18. James Toedman, "Fighting Like Cats and Dogs Over Fish; It's U.S. vs. Vietnamese as trade battle goes global."
19. Margot Cohen and Murray Hiebert, "Muddying the Waters."

PROTECTION OF THE STEEL INDUSTRY

THE WHITE HOUSE

A PRESIDENTIAL PROCLAMATION ON STEEL

For Immediate Release
The White House
Washington, D.C.
March 5, 2002

To Facilitate Positive Adjustment to Competition From Imports of Certain Steel Products by the President of the United States of America a Proclamation

1. On December 19, 2001, the United States International Trade Commission (ITC) transmitted to the President a report on its investigation . . . with respect to imports of certain steel products.
2. The ITC reached affirmative determinations under section 202(b) of the Trade Act that the following products are being imported into the United States in such increased quantities as to be a substantial cause of serious injury, or threat of serious injury, to the domestic industries producing like or directly competitive articles. . . .

. . .

6. The ITC commissioners voting in the affirmative under section 202(b) of the Trade Act also transmitted to the President their recommendations made pursuant to section 202(e) of the Trade Act (19 U.S.C. 2252(e)) with respect to the actions that, in their view, would address the serious injury, or threat thereof, to the domestic industries and be most effective in facilitating the efforts of those industries to make a positive adjustment to import competition.

. . .

9. Pursuant to section 203 of the Trade Act (19 U.S.C. 2253), the actions I have determined to take shall be safeguard measures in the form of:
   (a) a tariff rate quota on imports of slabs described in paragraph 7, imposed for a period of 3 years plus 1 day, with annual increases in the within-quota quantities and annual reductions in the rates of duty applicable to goods entered in excess of those quantities in the second and third years; and
   (b) an increase in duties on imports of certain flat steel, other than slabs (including plate, hot-rolled steel, cold-rolled steel and coated steel), hot-rolled bar, cold-finished bar, rebar, certain welded tubular products, carbon and alloy fittings, stainless steel bar, stainless steel rod, tin mill products, and stainless steel wire, as described in paragraph 7, imposed for a period of 3 years plus 1 day, with annual reductions in the rates of duty in the second and third years, as provided in the Annex to this proclamation.

. . .

11. These safeguard measures shall apply to imports from all countries, except for products of Canada, Israel, Jordan, and Mexico.
12. These safeguard measures shall not apply to imports of any product described in paragraph 7 of a developing country that is a member of the World Trade Organization (WTO), as long as that country's share of total imports of the product, based on imports during a recent representative period, does not exceed 3 percent. . . .

. . .

IN WITNESS WHEREOF, I have hereunto set my hand this fifth day of March, in the year of our Lord two thousand two, and of the Independence of the United States of America the two hundred and twenty-sixth.

GEORGE W. BUSH

Sources: This case was written byProfessor Michael R. Czinkota, Gerogetown University, and graduate student Armen S. Houhannisyan, Georgetown University.

Background

Steel has traditionally been a very important industry worldwide. On the strategic side, weapons, buildings, and ships require lots of steel. Among industrial products, cars are the major absorbers of steel production. Steel is therefore an important ingredient and symbol of an economy. As a result, governments around the world have tended to be highly protective of their steel industries.

Steel production quantity and location shift constantly. The use of steel (and hence production) tends to increase when economies are growing. Global consumption of steel rose from 28 million tons at the beginning of the twentieth century to 780 million tons at the end—an average increase of 3.4 percent per year. In 1900, the United States was producing 37 percent of the world's steel. One hundred years later, Asia accounted for almost 40 percent, Europe produces 36 percent, and North America 14.5 percent[1] (see Figures 1 and 2).

Since the late 1960s the rate of growth in steel production has leveled off, which is due to greater efficiency in the use of steel. In addition, the auto industry now uses plastics for many parts. Steel-making pro-

cesses have also shown significant progress, from the Bessemer Converter at the turn of the century to the introduction in the 1950s of oxygen conversion processes and continuous casting in the 1960s. Steel is one of the most recycled of all industrial materials. Even after decades of useful life, steel can be recycled. The recycling is processed in minimills that use steel scrap as a raw material. Generally these minimills, which use electrical power, are more productive than traditional steel casting in coal-heated furnaces.

The production costs of steel tend to differ greatly from one country to another. Steel-industry wages account for the major price differential. Until 1968, steel wages in the United States were in line with average wages in the manufacturing sector. Starting in the late 1960s and continuing through the mid-1980s, steel firms provided their workers with very generous wages and retirement benefits. In 1976, U.S. steel companies required import controls to get back on their feet. Twenty-six years later, the same steelmakers were in trouble again. Tens of billions of dollars worth of quotas, tariffs, subsidies, and the like that had been provided to the steel companies had obviously had little effect.

FIGURE 1

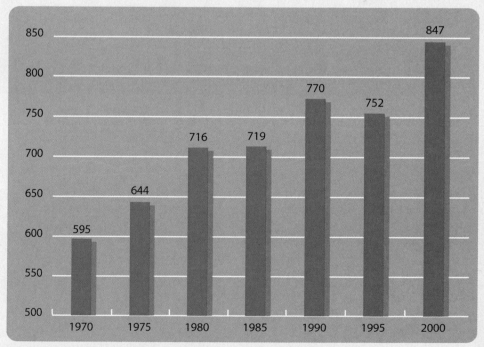

World Crude Steel Production, 1970 to 2000 (in millions of metric tons)

Source: International Iron and Steel Institute, http://www.worldsteel.org, October 1, 2002.

FIGURE 2

The Major Steel-Producing Countries, 2001 (blue column) and 2000 (plum column)

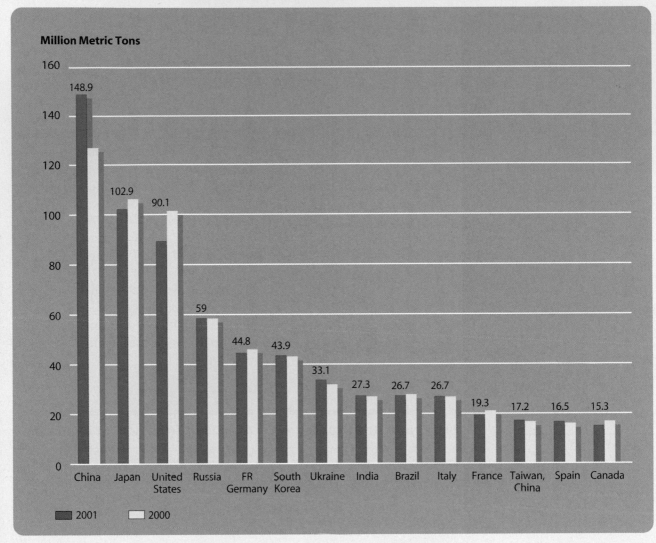

Million Metric Tons

China 148.9, Japan 102.9, United States 90.1, Russia 59, FR Germany 44.8, South Korea 43.9, Ukraine 33.1, India 27.3, Brazil 26.7, Italy 26.7, France 19.3, Taiwan, China 17.2, Spain 16.5, Canada 15.3

■ 2001   ☐ 2000

Source: International Iron and Steel Institute, http://www.worldsteel.org/media/wsif/wsif2003.pdf, October 1, 2002.

In the early 2000s the supply of steel in the world continued to outstrip the demand, pushing prices to their lowest level in 20 years. World steel demand was expected to decline from 741 million tons in 2001 to 736 million tons in 2002. Production was expected to fall from 838 million tons to 828 million tons, but likely to remain significantly ahead of consumption.[3]

The Asian financial crisis cut the demand for steel in Japan and other nations. That left the United States as one of the few places for foreign manufacturers to sell their steel. From the period between 1999 and 2002, 31 U.S. steel companies filed for bankruptcy protection— mostly the older, integrated steelmakers such as Bethlehem Steel Corporation and LTV Corp. that use huge, coal-fired blast furnaces to turn ore into metal.

The Evolution of the Issue

During the 2000 election presidential candidate George W. Bush campaigned energetically to gain votes from the steelworkers in swing states such as West Virginia, Ohio, and Pennsylvania. Vice-presidential candidate Dick Cheney promised West Virginia's steelworkers that the administration would not forget them; in August 2001, then-president George W. Bush told steelworkers in Pittsburgh that their product was "an important national security issue."[3] In light of the crisis in the world steel industry, President Bush had asked the U.S. International Trade Commission (ITC) in June 2002 to determine whether a surge in imports had seriously damaged the U.S. steel industry. At the same time, he ordered trade officials to launch negotiations with foreign governments aimed at cutting overproduction and government subsidies.

In November 2001 the ITC found that the U.S. industry had sustained serious injury from imports. It recommended that the president impose some combination of import quotas and tariffs ranging from 15 percent to 40 percent, depending on the type of steel. Substantial tariffs on steel imports would raise U.S. domestic steel prices and would give the industry the financial breathing room to consolidate into fewer, larger, and more modern producers.

The Major Argument for Tariffs[4]

America is the world's largest steel consumer and its demand is growing. America's steel producers claim that after years of massive investment, technological improvements, and reductions in its workforce, they are the most advanced and the most productive in the world. Yet, 31 American steel producers are in bankruptcy, partly because most of the steel imported into America today is selling at subsidized low prices.

These subsidized steel imports are a bargain for American consumers. However, in the long term, subsidized imports may destroy a vital American industry and high paying, high-quality U.S. jobs. America may become dependent upon Russia, Japan, China, Brazil, and developing countries for something as basic as steel. A century ago this issue was framed by Abraham Lincoln in the following terms: "If we purchase a ton of steel rails from England for $20, then we have the rails and England the money. But if we buy a ton of steel rails from an American for $25, then America has both the rails and the money."[5]

Legacy Costs

U.S. steel companies won numerous antidumping cases in previous decades. This could serve as evidence that the industry was not modernized or restructured sufficiently. Europe suffered similar problems in the early 1990s but through job cuts and industry consolidation Europe now has very large and highly efficient steel producers. However, there is an important difference with the United States: European steel manufacturers do not pay for their retirees' health benefits since that is the responsibility of the government. In the United States, the industry pays such "legacy costs" to its retired workers, who outnumber actively employed steel workers by four times (150,000 to 600,000).[6] The United Steelworkers Association puts the aggregate figure at about $1 billion annually (on average, $9 per ton of steel produced in the United States). Legacy costs over the actuarial lifetimes of workers and retirees are said to total $13 billion.[7]

One way of dealing with the problem might be the consolidation of the industry, into fewer but bigger producers. U.S. Steel Corp., the largest and most profitable of the surviving integrated steelmakers, proposed to buy Bethlehem Steel and as many as three other rivals, if the federal government agreed to assume some of the health care and pension obligations to the companies' retirees.

The Case for Free Trade

Without protection and support, nearly 60,000 U.S. steel workers may lose their jobs.[8] However, increasing tariffs to protect steel industry workers is costly. A 20 percent increase will cost consumers $7 billion over four years. Consumers would pay more than an average of $326,000 per worker.[9]

Steel consumers, such as automakers and construction companies, far outnumber steelmakers (9 million to 150,000).[10] Protection of steel manufacturers will increase prices and hurt businesses that rely on steel as an input. Facing the prospect of tariffs that could raise domestic steel prices by as much as 10 percent, steel-consuming industries—makers of tractors, washing machines, airplane fasteners, and auto parts argue that they would lose sales if they were forced to pay more than foreign competitors for a key raw material.

A bailout for the steel industry sets a dangerous precedent and may invite similar demands from other industries, such as textiles and wood products, that have also been hard hit by imports. There is also a question of the feasibility of "rewarding" the old-line unionized companies that got into trouble in the first place due to overly generous health and retirement plans.

Imposing tariffs on steel imports goes against U.S. initiatives for trade liberalization, and possibly leads to a trade war, as EU officials and companies warned. An agreement to cut global production levels by 100 million tons annually was reached by major steel producing nations in Paris late in 2001 and was conditional to the United States keeping its tariffs unchanged.[11]

The Decision

Tariffs on steel create winners and losers, shifting jobs and incomes among companies, industries, regions, and countries. The Prsident faced a difficult choice. If he did too little, he could trigger another round of steel company bankruptcies and layoffs, jeopardize passage of trade-liberalizing legislation, sacrifice control of the House of Representatives—and perhaps endanger prospects for his own reelection in 2004. On the other hand, if he did too much, it could cause a trade war with Europe, create new entitlements for American workers, set up problems for steel-using companies, and invite other industries to demand similar trade barriers and government bailouts.

On March 5, 2002, President Bush decided to impose tariffs of up to 30 percent on most imported steel. Under the plan, steel imported from Canada and Mexico would be exempt from custom duties (under NAFTA). Japan, China, South Korea, Russia, Ukraine, and Brazil would be among the nations subject to the tariffs. Developing countries such as Argentina, Thailand, and Turkey would be exempt because they account for less than 3 percent of total imports. Administration officials said the purpose of the tariffs was to encourage U.S. companies to shift, at least temporarily, from buying foreign steel to U.S. steel, and in the process raise prices in the U.S. market from their 20-year lows. The tariffs are set to decline in the second and third years, subject to a review by the president after 18 months.

This was the most aggressive action taken by a president to protect a domestic industry from imports since Ronald Reagan imposed steel import restraints in the mid-1980s. President Bush said it was an appropriate exception in the face of years of unfair trading practices by foreign countries that had "resulted in bankruptcies, serious dislocation, and job losses" in the United States.[13]

According to political observers, the pursuit of trade liberalization always involves striking a delicate balance between the demands of domestic constituencies on the one hand and trading partners on the other. They argue that whatever damage the temporary tariffs might inflict on the political cause of free trade, it is nothing compared with the damage that would have been caused if half of the U.S. steel industry were forced to shut down.[14] They calculate that as many as six house seats—

exactly the number it would take for Democrats to take control of the chamber—hinged on the fallout from the steel decision.

Private economists predicted that the tariff regime will increase domestic prices by 6 percent to 8 percent in the first year. If fully passed on to consumers—not a sure thing by any means—that would raise the price of a $30,000 car by about $50 or a washing machine by less than $5. Such increases are probably not enough to substantially affect sales.

The International Reaction

As expected, the introduction of the tariff was immediately criticized by leading steel-producing countries. World leaders took turns pointing out what they viewed as U.S. hypocrisy. America's largest trading partner, the EU, threatened to retaliate with its own tariffs. Japan, Australia, South Korea, and Brazil promised to take the United States to a WTO arbitration panel—despite protests from U.S. officials that the tariffs comply with rules allowing just such temporary "safeguards." "The international market isn't the Wild West where everyone acts as he pleases," said the EU's trade commissioner, Pascal Lamy. German Chancellor Gerhard Schroeder declared the Bush decision "against free world markets," while French President Jacques Chirac called the move "serious and unacceptable."[15]

China's Foreign Trade Ministry declared Beijing's "strong displeasure" at the U.S. action, while a top South Korean trade official called it a "tragedy" for that country's economy. Japan's trade minister Hiranuma condemned the U.S. move as "deeply regrettable" and warned it could well trigger "compound retaliations."[17]

Russians said the tariff would have a serious impact on the relations between the two countries. Russian officials claimed that it would not help with the war on terrorism if the United States hits a blow to one of Russia's major export industries. In early March 2002, Russia announced it would not issue import permits for U.S. poultry because of health concerns about the use of antibiotics in the animals. Russia's decision signaled the beginning of a low-level trade war.

Thomas Dawson, external relations director at the International Monetary Fund (IMF), said: "The fund clearly believes that lowering, not raising, trade barriers is the appropriate policy for our members, developed and developing, to follow." The IMF was concerned that the U.S. action could hamper its effort to persuade developing countries to reduce their trade barriers.[17] However, the United States targeted the steel tariffs in such a way that virtually all developing countries are exempt from the action.

Implications

EU companies account for a major share of the goods hit by the 30 percent import tariffs that took effect March 20, 2002. But those exports amount to only 2.5 percent of the EU's 160 million metric tons in annual steel production. The tariffs also aren't high enough to block all EU sales to the United States, partly because the strong dollar continues to give European companies a competitive advantage over their U.S. competitors. The biggest fear among European steelmakers isn't reduced exports to the United States, but a flood of cheap imports diverted into Europe by nations such as Japan, South Korea, and Russia, which are blocked by the new tariffs from selling as much steel to the United States as they used to.[18]

Expecting to face a surge in steel imports, Europe may adopt the same remedy of protective tariffs. The damage may possibly spread to other kinds of trade, and a good part of the cost will end up with developing-country producers, while the leaders of Europe and the United States preach liberal trade to the rulers of the developing world, and promise better access to their own markets.

Some claim that in a global world, local issues are important. When it comes to trade, expectations of a perfect track record may be the enemy of good achievements. Trade is only one component of the mosaic of mankind's activity. Policy needs to reflect the broad scope of human desires and needs. The steel decision needs to be seen in such a context. There is a political price tag associated with strong U.S. support of free trade. The rare and limited protection of a domestic industry with much leverage is such a price.[19]

Endnotes

1. International Iron and Steel Institute, http://www.world-steel.org.
2. Peter Marsh, "Outlook for steel 'highly adverse,'" *Financial Times*, January 21, 2002.
3. "Romancing Big Steel George Bush's Promise to help is coming back to haunt him," *Economist*, February 16, 2002.
4. For more on this, see: American Iron and Steel Institute, http://www.steel.org; International Iron and Steel Institute, http://www.iisi.org. See also: Gary Clyde Hufbauer and Ben Goodrich, *Time for a Grand Bargain in Steel?* Institute for International Economics, January 2002. http://www.iie.com/publications/pb/pb02=1.htm.
5. Frank Swoboda, "U.S. Steel Seeks to Team with Its Rivals Foreign Firms Would Still Outstrip Domestic Giant," *Washington Post*, December 5, 2001, E1.
6. Leslie Wayne, "Rivals and Others Criticize Steel Makers' Bid for U.S. Aid," *New York Times*, December 6, 2001.
7. Gary Clyde Hufbauer and Ben Goodrich, *Time for a Grand Bargain in Steel?* Policy Brief 02-01 Institute for International Economics, January 2002, http://www.iie.com/publications/pb/pb02=1.htm.
8. Number according to Thomas Usher, CEO of U.S. Steel Corporation, quoted by Leslie Wayne, "Parched, Big Steel Goes to Its Washington Well," *New York Times*, January 20, 2002, Section 3, Pagge 1.
9. Figures from Gary Clyde Hufbauer, 2002.
10. Leslie Wayne, "Rivals and Others Criticize Steel Makers' Bid for U.S. Aid," *New York Times*, December 6, 2001, Business/Financial Desk, C9.
11. Peter Marsh, "U.S. urges drop in steel production: Officials to embark on worldwide tour in effort to stave off financial crises in sector," *Financial Times*, November 23, 2001.
12. Mike Allen and Steven Pearlstein, "Bush Settles On Tariff for Steel Imports," *Washington Post*, March 5, 2002, A1.
13. Steven Pearlstein, "Bush Sets Tariffs on Steel Imports President Opts for Compromise on Free Trade," *Washington Post*, March 6, 2002, E1.
14. George F. Will, "Bending for Steel," *Washington Post*, March 7, 2002, A21.
15. Steven Pearlstein and Clay Chandler, "Reaction Abroad on Steel Is Harsh, Bush Decision to Impose Tariffs Called Setback to Free-Trade Effort," *Washington Post*, March 7, 2002, E1.
16. Ibid.
17. Edward Alden and Michael Mann, "EU hits at U.S. 'unilateralism' on steel: Trade dispute Pascal Lamy says tariffs contradict Bush administration's rhetoric on free trade," *Financial Times*, March 14, 2002.
18. Geoff Winestock and Philip Shishkin, "EU Tempers Anger at U.S. Steel Tariffs—While Spurring Threats, Levies Seem Unlikely to Bring Harsh Action," *Wall Street Journal*, March 8, 2002, A8.
19. Michael R. Czinkota, "Free trade carries a price," Special to *The Japan Times*, March 18, 2002.

H-1B VISAS: A HIGH-TECH DILEMMA

Images of immigration typically include border crossings and refugees trying to enter a country illegally. Jobs filled by immigrants are perceived to be low-paying menial ones that cannot find takers among the residents. However, the most heated debate on immigration is being waged in the world of high tech, where industry argues for more freedom to bring in people with "a body of highly specialized knowledge" and where opponents characterize the situation as the present-day version of indentured servitude.

The H-1B is a high-tech visa that allows foreign engineers, computer scientists, and other highly trained technical workers from a variety of countries to work in the United States on a temporary basis for a maximum of six years. The program began in the 1950s to attract individuals with mathematics, engineering, and technical backgrounds during the Cold War. However, the boom of the information-technology sector, which demands 1.6 million workers yearly, has made the H-1B visa a major subject of discussion. In 1999, the full allotment of 115,000 H-1B visas was exhausted by June, and in 2000, by April.

On October 3, 2000, the U.S. Congress overwhelmingly approved legislation in a vote of 96 to 1 that would increase the number of H-1B visas issued from 115,000 to 195,000 each year for the next three years, with the possibility for renewal for another three years. In 2001, despite the severe downturn in the economy, 163,200 applications were approved. The bill passed because high-tech lobbyists were successful in positioning the visas as protection for the U.S. competitive edge in technology. In the short term, the United States needs to fill key positions immediately so opportunities are not lost to foreign competitors. The supporters' argued

Sources: This case was written by Beverly Reusser and Ilkka Ronkainen. It is based on publicly available materials such as "65,000 H-1B Visas—Will Our Economy Benefit or Hurt When the Cap Goes Back Down?" The GT Immigration Observer, August/September 2003, 4–5; Patricj Thibodeau, "Jobless Push for Visa Reform," Computerworld, August 11, 2003, 1; "Skilled Workers or Indentured Servants?" Business Week, June 16, 2003, 54; "Overseas Workers Filling High-Tech Spots,": The Chicago Tribune, February 10, 2002; "A Special News Report about Life on the Job—And Trends Taking Shape There," The Wall Street Journal, February 19, 2001; "Visas Bill Brings Tech a Manpower Win," The Washington Post, October 7, 2000, E2; and "American Competitiveness in the Twenty-first Century Act of 2000," Congressional Record–Senate, Volume 146, No. 117, September 27, 2000.

that the survival of U.S. companies is at stake without foreign workers. This view was also taken by Federal Reserve Chief Alan Greenspan, who warned that labor shortages threatened the national economy and who proposed increased immigration as a way to ease labor shortages and reduce inflationary pressure.

Greenspan's comments were only one indication of dramatic changes taking place. Two years earlier, the same legislation had been opposed by anti-immigration Republicans and the labor unions. In 1996, the U.S. Congress focused on deportation, and the U.S. Commission on Immigration Reform (the Jordan Commission) proposed to cut legal immigration by at least a third and eliminate illegal immigration.

In October 2003, the annual cap fell to 65,000 as a reflection of the downturn in the economy and the bursting of the dot-com bubble. As shown in Table 1, the number of H-1Bs actually used each year reflect economic trends. The debate is whether lowering the cap will benefit jobless computer scientists and mathematicians (jobless rates for this group stood at 6 percent in 2003 versus 0.7 percent in 1998) or harmful to an economy when it is looking for an upturn.

The stagnant economy has led to accusations of more abuses of the H-1B system. The scarcity of jobs has left many skilled immigrants more dependent on their employers and less willing to quit. If employers discontinue their sponsorship of a visa holder, the immigrant may have to return home or find another sponsor.

Labor's Position

Organized labor has also started to change its traditional stance. While historically opposing immigration on the grounds that it displaces American workers and lowers wages, organized labor abandoned its opposition to the October bill—although they did support the stipulation that U.S. employers must pay the prevailing wage—and announced it would no longer oppose illegal immigration. Union leaders increasingly see immigrants as potential recruits.

While organized labor supported the provision to pay prevailing wages of what a recent college graduate entering the computer science field would typically command, the high-tech industry opposed that provision on the grounds of increased paperwork and administrative

TABLE 1 — H-1B Facts 2000–2002

Year	Total petitions filed	Petitions against cap	Initial employment	Continuing employment	Labor law violations
2000	299,046	***	164,814	134,232	51
2001	342,035	163,200	201,543	140,492	83
2002	215,190	79,100	109,576	105,614	113

costs involved to maintain these statistics. The industry point of view won and the provision that required employers to present tax forms showing how much H-1B holders were paid was dropped from the final version of the legislation.

There is opposition also from non-traditional workers' groups on the issues of wages. According to critics, foreign workers in Silicon Valley earn substantially less than a U.S. citizen with comparable education and experience. For example, newly graduated immigrants with H-1B visas are paid $35,000, while the national average for new computer science graduates is $45,000. Groups of technical workers, such as the Programmers Guild and the American Engineering Association, banded together to fight the bill. Their argument is that U.S. technology businesses rely too heavily on cheaper foreign labor at the expense of older and more expensive U.S. workers. The higher numbers create a market in which employers do not have to cultivate "home grown" talent because there is a constant flow of new people. While some employers may not save on the salaries of programmers of the same age and background, they still save on salaries of employees with H-1B visas whose median age is 28 and who may replace a U.S. citizen over the age of 40.

Other groups, such as the Urban League, have demanded that corporations train more U.S. citizens for the jobs that are going to foreign engineers, computer scientists, and other highly trained technicians. Colin Powell stressed the need for increased training of U.S. students at the Republican Convention in 2000. The H-1B visa's filing fee of $1,000 is supposed to go to programs to increase U.S. student and worker training in science and technology. Since establishing such a program in 1997, the Virginia High Tech Partnership program has placed 140 minority students at 75 firms, including AOL, IBM, and start-ups. However, it is clear that these initiatives will not have any immediate effect on the demand for H-1B visas.

Critics have also argued that, contrary to claims of programmer shortage, U.S. companies such as Cisco, Microsoft, and Qualcomm hire only a small percentage of applicants and reject most without even interviewing them. Cisco, for example, receives 20,000 applications per month but hires only 5 percent of them.

Industry View

The positive vote of the past on H-1B visas is seen as further evidence of the clout the high-tech industry has in the United States. In 1999, the U.S. Congress passed a bill that protected Silicon Valley against Y2K litigation. Recent legislation has also eased restrictions on export encryption rules, and high-tech companies are not required to maintain separate tax records on foreign workers. U.S. Congressman Tom Davis, a Republican from Virginia, stated, "This is not a popular bill with the public, it is popular with the CEOs. This is a very important issue for the high-tech executives who give the money."

The industry's argument is straightforward: information technology has dramatically changed the composition of the U.S. workforce by producing an incredible demand for workers. In many sectors, the positions have high complexity and a scarcity of qualified applicants. U.S. companies have been forced to slow their expansion or cancel projects due to the lack of technically qualified individuals. As a result, some have argued for the elimination of H-1B caps altogether.

According to a report by the General Accounting Office, the average H-1B worker is an Indian male between the ages of 25 and 29 who earns a salary of $45,000. As shown in Figure 1, Indians account for the majority of the new arrivals, with China and Canada as distant followers. In Silicon Valley, immigrants make up one third of IT workers, and more than 25 percent of

FIGURE 1

Percentages of U.S. Immigrants with H-1B Visas from Various Nations

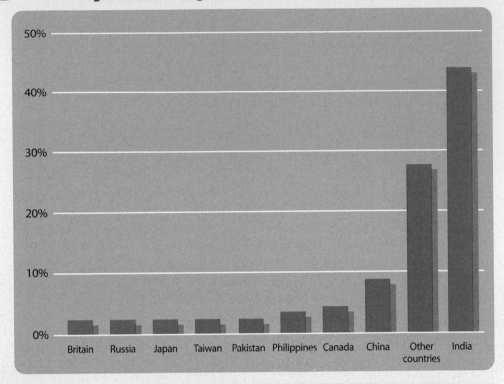

Source: "Alliance Fights Boost in Visas for Tech Workers," *Los Angeles Times,* August 5, 2000, A14.

them hold senior executive positions. More than 750 Silicon Valley companies worth $3.5 billion and employing 16,000 workers are owned by Indians.

View from India

The IT industry is growing rapidly in India. The area around Bangalore is known as the Silicon Valley of India. In the past decade, Indian software exports to the United States have grown from $150 million to $3.9 billion. The Indian software industry is expected to grow to $80 billion by 2008. India exports software to 91 countries, with 64 percent going to the United States. In 1998, Microsoft opened a research and development center in Hyderabad. Indian laws were recently liberalized for direct foreign investment and joint ventures. The passage of the visa bill is seen in some parts of Asia—but not all—as having the potential to inspire trading interest in India's frontline software industry.

Exactly one week after passage of the bill, the Indian press (*The Statesman*) issued a broadside that criticized the H-1B program as subsidizing Bill Gates. The argument was that the high-tech industries in Western countries are being fueled with workers trained at Indian institutions at Indian taxpayer expense. The replacement of Indian subsidies with grants and student loans as a way to stem "useless degrees in comparative literature" was urged. However, no mention was made of requiring Indian graduates to work at home, possibly because there are not enough employers in India. Interestingly enough, there is a sector-specific problem. So many technical professionals are leaving for foreign jobs in the United Kingdom, Germany, and Japan that there are already pockets of shortages in the Indian software industry, with projections for a widening and deepening shortage to continue for the foreseeable future.

Why is the Indian high-tech worker so prevalent or so sought after? The fact that there are not enough employers in India to employ qualified workers is only a part of the picture. Their government's educational system has given priority to computer training far longer than many other developing countries. The India Institute of Technology (IIT) was founded in the 1950s by Prime Minister Jawaharlal Nehru to train an elite that could build and manage massive industrial development projects. Today the government runs six institute campuses and accepts only 2 percent of more than 100,000 applicants annually. IIT graduates Vinod Khosla, cofounder of Sun Microsystems, Inc., and Rakesh Gangwal, president of USAirways, have parlayed H-IB visas into lucrative careers. The value added for U.S. companies is three-fold: (1) the pick of the top tier of an educated elite from (2) the largest pool of skilled English-speaking workers second only to the United States, who (3) possess the ability to more easily adapt products for foreign markets.

The Indian Visa Holder's Perspective

The young Indian male between the ages of 25 and 29 who is highly educated, ambitious, and eager to work but unable to find a job in India that will pay enough to attract a wife is happy to go to the United States and earn $45,000 a year, roughly four times what he would earn in India. The October bill offers longer-term attractions, having lifted restrictions that previously hampered career progression. Called the "portability provision," it is now easier for H-1B visa-holders to change jobs without having to wait for the Immigration and Naturalization Service to formally approve the immigrant's application with a new company. This provision facilitates movement up the career ladder, possibly to the level of an officer at an IT firm and the growing of equity in the company and accumulating wealth. In the past, foreign-born workers were often dissuaded from switching jobs because of the fear that they would run into problems in processing of their visa paperwork. Problems could mean that they would have to return home.

Immigrants who have been in the United States for three years on the H-1B visa may have a different perspective. In many cases, the renewal for another three years may come, but not without a lot of work and worry. The initial exhilaration to come to the United States is often followed by homesickness. The spouse, who may also be highly educated, is not necessarily permitted to work in the United States.

With approximately 90,000 Indians arriving every year, and with the strict quota imposed by the Immigration and Naturalization Service of 15,000 green cards per year per country, there is an additional dilemma. The October bill acknowledges this problem; the language in the bill directs the INS to make the unused green card allocations of other countries available to applicants from oversubscribed countries and to extend the amount of time H-1B workers can remain in the United States while waiting for green cards. However, many workers feel discarded at the end of the six years, leaving full of disappointment and delusion and holding much bitterness toward the United States.

The Balance

Many of the young workers who do head abroad will return home and plow their new wealth into ventures at home. In one well-publicized story, an IIT graduate founded Internet browser Junglee.com with three other Indians, and sold it to Amazon.com in 1998 for US$180 million. He gave $1 million to his alma mater and started another company in Mountain View, California, and Bangalore, India, as well as investing a 25 percent stake in a dot-com startup in India. The "brain drain" may reveal its silver lining as more and more successful Indian entrepreneurs are seeding ventures at home. The dot-com boom in India is seen as one of the mega markets of the future. Instead of sending workers to foreign markets, the Indian IT companies are sending their work to foreign markets via the Internet; "offshore development" is now a viable alternative to onsite workers.

The nascent IT industry in India is becoming more and more attractive to foreign investment. While Indian firms will lobby for more visas and investment, their U.S. counterparts are likely to seek reciprocal concessions. U.S. multinationals interested in establishing a business in India want some improvements in infrastucture, reduction in bureaucratic interference, and quicker responses from the government. New Delhi has taken the first steps aimed at accelerating telecom reform to free long-distance telephone service from their government monopoly and allowing 100 foreign direct investments in Internet service providers.

In the United States, the issue of equitable wages needs to be addressed; currently no reporting and auditing controls are in place to protect both foreign and U.S. workers. The lack of these controls both undercuts the domestic worker and takes advantage of the foreign worker. Many programs have been very successful in training new groups of workers and could work well as a regional model in the industry corridors in the United States. In the long term, the country needs to determine what can be done to make certain that there are sufficiently trained U.S citizens to fill the demand for high-tech jobs. Perhaps not enough time has passed to judge what effect the retraining of U.S. workers, often older or displaced, has had on the new technologies. Little published data are available at this time, and anecdotal data suggest the retraining may be too little, too late.

Questions for Discussion

1. Comment on the following statement: "The firms of the New Economy seem to be awfully fond of the Old Economy—of 200 years ago, when indentured servitude was in vogue."

2. Will a visa program like the H-1B result in an escalation of brain drain from developing or emerging countries?

3. Should the cap for H-1B visas be eliminated altogether? Should no such provision exist at all and efforts be directed at domestic supply?

Part 3 provides theoretical background for international trade and investment activities. Classical concepts such as absolute and comparative advantage are explained. Key emphasis rests with modern-day theoretical developments that are presented in light of the realities of international business. In addition, the international economic activity of nations and the balance of payments are discussed.

PART
Foundations

3

CHAPTER

5

The Theory of Trade and Investment

Learning Objectives

- To understand the traditional arguments of how and why international trade improves the welfare of all countries

- To review the history and compare the implications of trade theory from the original work of Adam Smith to the contemporary theories of Michael Porter

- To examine the criticisms of classical trade theory and examine alternative viewpoints of which business and economic forces determine trade patterns between countries

- To explore the similarities and distinctions between international trade and international investment

Global Outsourcing: Comparative Advantage Today

Comparative advantage is still a relevant theory to explain why particular countries are most suitable for exports of goods and services that support the global supply chain of both MNEs and domestic firms. The comparative advantage of the twenty-first century, however, is one which is based more on services, and their cross-border facilitation by telecommunications and the Internet. The source of a nation's comparative advantage, however, still is created from the mixture of its own labor skills, access to capital, and technology. The table below provides a sample of the many recent global outsourcing ventures.

For example, India has developed a highly efficient and low-cost software industry. This industry supplies not only the creation of custom software, but also call centers for customer support, and other information technology services. The Indian software industry is composed of both subsidiaries of MNEs and independent companies.

If you own a Compaq computer and call the customer support center number for help, you are likely to reach a call center in India. Answering your call will be a knowledgable Indian software engineer or programmer who will "walk" you through your problem. India has a large number of well-educated, English-speaking, technical experts

Country	Activity
Examples of Global Outsourcing of Comparative Advantage in Intellectual Skills	
China	Chemical, mechanical, and petroleum engineering services; business and product development centers for companies like GE
Costa Rica	Call centers for Spanish-speaking consumers in many industrial markets; Accenture has IT support and back-office operations call centers
Eastern Europe	American and IT service providers operate call centers for customer and business support in Hungary, Poland, and the Czech Republic; Romania and Bulgarian centers for German-speaking IT customers in Europe
India	Software engineering and support; call centers for all types of computer and telecom services; medical analysis and consultative services; Indian companies such as Tata, Infosys, and Wipro are already global leaders in IT design, implementation, and support
Mexico	Automotive engineering and electronic-sector services
Philippines	Financial and accounting services; architecture services; telemarketing and graphic arts
Russia	Software and engineering services; R&D centers for Boeing, Intel, Motorola, and Nortel
South Africa	Call- and user-support services for French, English, and German-speaking consumers throughout Europe

Source: Abstracted from "Is Your Job Next," *Business Week*, February 3, 2003.

who are paid only a fraction of the salary and overhead earned by their U.S. counterparts. The overcapacity and low cost of international telecommunication networks today further enhances the comparative advantage of an Indian location.

As illustrated by the table, the extent of global outsourcing is already reaching out to every corner of the globe. From financial back-offices in Manila, to information technology engineers in Hungary, modern telecommunications now take business activities to labor, rather than labor migrating to the places of business.

The debates, the costs, the benefits, and the dilemmas of international trade have in many ways not changed significantly from the time when Marco Polo crossed the barren wastelands of Eurasia to the time of the expansion of U.S. and Canadian firms across the Rio Grande into Mexico under the North American Free Trade Agreement. At the heart of the issue is what the gains—and the risks—are to the firm and the country as a result of a seller from one country servicing the needs of a buyer in a different country. If a Spanish firm wants to sell its product to the enormous market of mainland China, whether it produces at home and ships the product from Cadiz to Shanghai (international trade) or actually builds a factory in Shanghai (international investment), the goal is still the same: to sell a product for profit in the foreign market.

This chapter provides a directed path through centuries of thought on why and how trade and investment across borders occurs. Although theories and theorists come and go with time, a few basic questions have dominated this intellectual adventure:

- Why do countries trade?
- Do countries trade or do firms trade?
- Do the elements that give rise to the competitiveness of a firm, an industry, or a country as a whole, arise from some inherent endowment of the country itself, or do they change with time and circumstance?
- Once identified, can these sources of competitiveness be manipulated or managed by firms or governments to the benefit of the traders?

International trade is expected to improve the productivity of industry and the welfare of consumers. Let us learn how and why we still seek the exotic silks of the Far East and the telecommunication-linked call centers of Manila.

The Age of Mercantilism

The evolution of trade into the form we see today reflects three events: the collapse of feudal society, the emergence of the mercantilist philosophy, and the life cycle of the colonial systems of the European nation-states. Feudal society was a state of **autarky,** a society that did not trade because all of its needs were met internally. The feudal estate was self-sufficient, although hardly "sufficient" in more modern terms, given the limits of providing entirely for oneself. Needs literally were only those of food and shelter, and all available human labor was devoted to the task of fulfilling those basic needs. As merchants began meeting in the marketplace, as travelers began exchanging goods from faraway places at the water's edge, the attractiveness of trade became evident.

In the centuries leading up to the Industrial Revolution, international commerce was largely conducted under the authority of governments. The goals of trade were, therefore, the goals of governments. As early as 1500 the benefits of trade were clearly established in Europe, as nation-states expanded their influence across the globe in the creation of colonial systems. To maintain and expand their control over these colonial possessions, the European nations needed fleets, armies, food, and all other resources the nations could muster. They needed wealth. Trade was therefore conducted to fill the governments' treasuries, at minimum expense to themselves but to the detriment of their captive trade partners. Although colonialism normally is associated with the exploitation of those captive societies, it went hand in hand with the evolving exchange of goods among the European countries themselves, **mercantilism.**

Mercantilism mixed exchange through trade with accumulation of wealth. Since government controlled the patterns of commerce, it identified strength with the accumulation of **specie** (gold and silver) and maintained a general policy of exports dominating imports. Trade across borders—exports—was considered preferable to domestic trade because exports would earn gold. Import duties, tariffs, subsidization of exports, and outright restriction on the importation of many goods were used to maximize the gains from exports over the costs of imports. Laws were passed making it illegal to take gold or silver out of the country, even if such specie was needed to purchase imports to produce their own goods for sale. This was one-way trade, the trade of greed and power.

The demise of mercantilism was inevitable given class structure and the distribution of society's product. As the Industrial Revolution introduced the benefits of mass production, lowering prices and increasing the supplies of goods to all, the exploitation of colonies and trading partners came to an end. However, governments still exercise considerable power and influence on the conduct of trade.

Classical Trade Theory

The question of why countries trade has proven difficult to answer. Since the second half of the eighteenth century, academicians have tried to understand not only the motivations and benefits of international trade, but also why some countries grow faster and wealthier than others through trade. Figure 5.1 provides an overview of the evolutionary path of trade theory since the fall of mercantilism. Although somewhat simplified, it shows the line of development of the major theories put forward over the past two centuries. It also serves as an early indication of the path of modern theory: the shifting focus from the country to the firm, from cost of production to the market as a whole, and from the perfect to the imperfect.

THE THEORY OF ABSOLUTE ADVANTAGE

Generally considered the father of economics, Adam Smith published *The Wealth of Nations* in 1776 in London. In this book, Smith attempted to explain the process by which markets and production actually operate in society. Smith's two main areas of contribution, *absolute advantage* and the *division of labor* were fundamental to trade theory.

Production, the creation of a product for exchange, always requires the use of society's primary element of value, human labor. Smith noted that some countries, owing to the skills of their workers or the quality of their natural resources, could produce the same products as others with fewer labor-hours. He termed this efficiency **absolute advantage.**

Adam Smith observed the production processes of the early stages of the Industrial Revolution in England and recognized the fundamental changes that were occurring

FIGURE 5.1

The Evolution of Trade Theory

The Theory of Absolute Advantage
Adam Smith
Each country should specialize in the production and export of that good which it produces most efficiently, that is, with the fewest labor-hours.

The Theory of Comparative Advantage
David Ricardo
Even if one country was most efficient in the production of two products, it must be relatively more efficient in the production of one good. It should then specialize in the production and export of that good in exchange for the importation of the other good.

The Theory of Factor Proportions
Eli Heckscher and Bertil Ohlin
A country that is relatively labor abundant (capital abundant) should specialize in the production and export of that product which is relatively labor intensive (capital intensive).

The Leontief Paradox
Wassily Leontief
The test of the factor proportions theory which resulted in the unexpected finding that the United States was actually exporting products that were relatively labor intensive, rather than the capital intensive products that a relatively capital abundant country should, according to the theory.

Overlapping Product Ranges Theory
Staffan Burenstam Linder
The type, complexity, and diversity of product demands of a country increase as the country's income increases. International trade patterns would follow this principle, so that countries of similar income per capita levels will trade most intensively having overlapping product demands.

Product Cycle Theory
Raymond Vernon
The country that possesses comparative advantage in the production and export of an individual product changes over time as the technology of the product's manufacture matures.

Imperfect Markets and Strategic Trade
Paul Krugman
Theories that explain changing trade patterns, including intra-industry trade, based on the imperfection of both factor markets and product markets.

The Competitive Advantage of Nations
Michael Porter
A nation's competitiveness depends on the capacity of its industry to innovate and upgrade. Companies gain competitive advantage because of pressure and challenge. Companies benefit from having strong domestic rivals, aggressive home-based suppliers, and demanding local customers. Competitive advantage is also established through geographic "clusters" or concentrations of companies in different parts of the same industry.

in production. In previous states of society, a worker performed all stages of a production process, with resulting output that was little more than sufficient for the worker's own needs. The factories of the industrializing world were, however, separating the production process into distinct stages, in which each stage would be performed exclusively by one individual, the **division of labor.** This specialization increased the production of workers and industries. Smith's pin factory analogy has long been considered the recognition of one of the most significant principles of the industrial age.

> To take an example, therefore, from a very trifling manufacture; but one in which the division of labour has been very often taken notice of, the trade of the pin maker; a workman not educated to this business . . . could scarce, perhaps, with his utmost industry, make one pin in a day, and certainly could not make twenty. But in a way in which this business is now carried on, not only the whole work is a peculiar trade, but it is divided into a number of branches, of which the greater part are likewise peculiar trades. One man draws out the wire, another straights it, a third cuts it, a fourth points it, a fifth grinds it at the top for receiving the head: to make the head requires two or three distinct operations; to put it on is a peculiar business . . . I have seen a small manufactory of this kind where ten men only were employed, and where some of them consequently performed two or three distinct operations. But though they were very poor, and therefore but indifferently accommodated with the necessary machine, they could, when they exerted themselves, make among them about twelve pounds of pins in a day. There are in a pound upwards of four thousand pins of a middling size.[1]

Adam Smith then extended his division of labor in the production process to a division of labor and specialized product across countries. Each country would specialize in a product for which it was uniquely suited. More would be produced for less. Thus, by each country specializing in products for which it possessed absolute advantage, countries could produce more in total and exchange products—trade—for goods that were cheaper in price than those produced at home.

THE THEORY OF COMPARATIVE ADVANTAGE

Although Smith's work was instrumental in the development of economic theories about trade and production, it did not answer some fundamental questions about trade. First, Smith's trade relied on a country possessing absolute advantage in production, but did not explain what gave rise to the production advantages. Second, if a country did not possess absolute advantage in any product, could it (or would it) trade?

David Ricardo, in his 1819 work entitled *On the Principles of Political Economy and Taxation*, sought to take the basic ideas set down by Smith a few steps further. Ricardo noted that even if a country possessed absolute advantage in the production of two products, it still must be relatively more efficient than the other country in one good's production than the other. Ricardo termed this the **comparative advantage.** Each country would then possess comparative advantage in the production of one of the two products, and both countries would then benefit by specializing completely in one product and trading for the other.

A NUMERICAL EXAMPLE OF CLASSICAL TRADE

To fully understand the theories of absolute advantage and comparative advantage, consider the following example. Two countries, France and England, produce only two products, wheat and cloth (or beer and pizza, guns and butter, and so forth). The relative efficiency of each country in the production of the two products is measured

TABLE 5.1

Absolute Advantage and Comparative Advantage*

Country	Wheat	Cloth
England	2	4
France	4	2

- England has absolute advantage in the production of wheat. It requires fewer labor-hours (2 being less than 4) for England to produce one unit of wheat.
- France has absolute advantage in the production of cloth. It requires fewer labor-hours (2 being less than 4) for France to produce one unit of cloth.
- England has comparative advantage in the production of wheat. If England produces one unit of wheat, it is forgoing the production of 2/4 (0.50) of a unit of cloth. If France produces one unit of wheat, it is forgoing the production of 4/2 (2.00) of a unit of cloth. England therefore has the lower opportunity cost of producing wheat.
- France has comparative advantage in the production of cloth. If England produces one unit of cloth, it is forgoing the production of 4/2 (2.00) of a unit of wheat. If France produces one unit of cloth, it is forgoing the production of 2/4 (0.50) of a unit of wheat. France therefore has the lower opportunity cost of producing cloth.

* Labor-hours per unit of output.

by comparing the number of labor-hours needed to produce one unit of each product. Table 5.1 provides an efficiency comparison of the two countries.

England is obviously more efficient in the production of wheat. Whereas it takes France four labor-hours to produce one unit of wheat, it takes England only two hours to produce the same unit of wheat. France takes twice as many labor-hours to produce the same output. England has absolute advantage in the production of wheat. France needs two labor-hours to produce a unit of cloth that it takes England four labor-hours to produce. England therefore requires two more labor-hours than France to produce the same unit of cloth. France has absolute advantage in the production of cloth. The two countries are exactly opposite in relative efficiency of production.

David Ricardo took the logic of absolute advantages in production one step further to explain how countries could exploit their own advantages and gain from international trade. Comparative advantage, according to Ricardo, was based on what was given up or traded off in producing one product instead of the other. In this numerical example England needs only two-fourths as many labor-hours to produce a unit of wheat as France, while France needs only two-fourths as many labor-hours to produce a unit of cloth. England therefore has comparative advantage in the production of wheat, while France has comparative advantage in the production of cloth. A country cannot possess comparative advantage in the production of both products, so each country has an economic role to play in international trade.

NATIONAL PRODUCTION POSSIBILITIES

If the total labor-hours available for production within a nation were devoted to the full production of either product, wheat or cloth, the **production possibilities frontiers** of each country can be constructed. Assuming both countries possess the same number of labor-hours, for example 100, the production possibilities frontiers for each country can be graphed, as in Figure 5.2. If England devotes all labor-hours (100) to the production of wheat (which requires 2 labor-hours per unit produced), it can produce a maximum of 50 units of wheat. If England devotes all labor to the produc-

FIGURE 5.2

Production Possibility Frontiers, Specialization of Production, and the Benefits of Trade

England
1. Initially produces and consumes at point A.
2. England chooses to specialize in the production of wheat and shifts production from point A to point B.
3. England now exports the unwanted wheat (30 units) in exchange for imports of cloth (30 units) from France.
4. England is now consuming at point C, where it is consuming the same amount of wheat but 15 more units of cloth than at original point A.

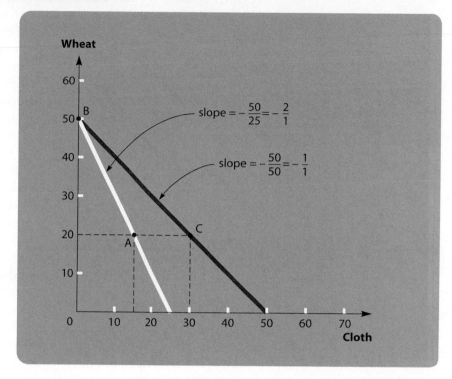

France
1. Initially produces and consumes at point D.
2. France chooses to specialize in the production of cloth and shifts production from point D to point E.
3. France now exports the unwanted cloth (30 units) in exchange for imports of wheat (30 units) from England.
4. France is now consuming at point F, where it is consuming the same amount of cloth but 15 more units of wheat than at original point D.

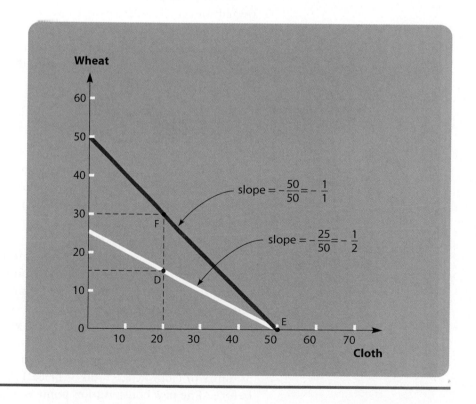

tion of cloth instead, the same 100 labor-hours can produce a maximum of 25 units of cloth (100 labor-hours/4 hours per unit of cloth). If England did not trade with any other country, it could only consume the products that it produced itself. England would therefore probably produce and consume some combination of wheat and cloth such as point A in Figure 5.2 (15 units of cloth, 20 units of wheat).

France's production possibilities frontier is constructed in the same way. If France devotes all 100 labor-hours to the production of wheat, it can produce a maximum of 25 units (100 labor-hours/4 hours per unit of wheat). If France devotes all 100 labor-hours to cloth, the same 100 labor-hours can produce a maximum of 50 units of cloth (100 labor-hours/2 hours per unit of cloth). If France did not trade with other countries, it would produce and consume at some point such as point D in Figure 5.2 (20 units of cloth, 15 units of wheat).

These frontiers depict what each country could produce in isolation—without trade (sometimes referred to as *autarky*). The slope of the production possibility frontier of a nation is a measure of how one product is traded off in production with the other (moving up the frontier, England is choosing to produce more wheat and less cloth). The slope of the frontier reflects the "trade-off" of producing one product over the other; the trade-offs represent prices, or **opportunity costs.** Opportunity cost is the forgone value of a factor of production in its next-best use. If England chooses to produce more units of wheat (in fact, produce only wheat), moving from point A to point B along the production possibilities frontier, it is giving up producing cloth to produce only wheat. The "cost" of the additional wheat is the loss of cloth. The slope of the production possibilities frontier is the ratio of product prices (opportunity costs). The slope of the production possibilities frontier for England is $-50/25$, or -2.00. The slope of the production possibilities frontier for France is flatter, $-25/50$, or -0.50.

The relative prices of products also provide an alternative way of seeing comparative advantage. The flatter slope of the French production possibilities frontier means that to produce more wheat (move up the frontier), France would have to give up the production of relatively more units of cloth than would England, with its steeper sloped production possibilities frontier. But, as the Focus on Ethics describes, prices don't always tell the whole story.

THE GAINS FROM INTERNATIONAL TRADE

Continuing with Figure 5.2, if England were originally not trading with France (the only other country) and it was producing at its own maximum possibilities (on the frontier and not inside the line), it would be producing at point A. Since it was not trading with another country, whatever it was producing it must also be consuming. So England could be said to be consuming at point A also. Therefore, without trade, you consume what you produce.

If, however, England recognized that it has comparative advantage in the production of wheat, it should move production from point A to point B. England should specialize completely in the product it produces best. It does not want to consume only wheat, however, so it would take the wheat it has produced and trade with France. For example, England may only want to consume 20 units of wheat, as it did at point A. It is now producing 50 units, and therefore has 30 units of wheat it can export to France. If England could export 30 units of wheat in exchange for imports of 30 units of cloth (a 1:1 ratio of prices), England would clearly be better off than before. The new consumption point would be point C, where it is consuming the same amount of wheat as point A, but is now consuming 30 units of cloth instead of just 15. More is better; England has benefited from international trade.

Focus On ⬇

Over- and Underinvoicing

A recent study raises questions about the legitimacy of the invoicing practices of many importers and exporters operating in the United States. The study estimated that MNEs avoided $45 billion in U.S. taxes in the year 2000. Import transactions were examined for over-invoicing, the use of a transfer price to pay more than what is typical for that product or service. Overinvoicing is one method of moving funds out of the United States and into the subject country. Export transactions were examined for underinvoicing, the use of a lower than normal export price to also reposition profits outside the United States.

The study examined approximately 15,000 import commodity-code categories and 8,000 export commodity codes to determine the average selling prices—import and export—to determine implied prices. The study first calculated the medium price, lower export quartile price, and upper import quartile price by bilateral transfers (between the United States and nearly 230 individual countries). The following is a sample of some of the more suspicious results.

Overpriced Imports

Item	From	Unit Price
Sunflower seeds	France	$5,519/kg
Toothbrushes	U.K.	$5,655/unit
Hacksaw blades	Germany	$5,485/unit
Razor blades	India	$461/unit
Vinegar	Canada	$5,430/ltr
Flashlights	Japan	$5,000/unit
Sawdust	U.K.	$642/kg
Iron/steel ladders	Slovenia	$15,852/unit
Inkjet printers	Colombia	$179,000/unit
Lard	Canada	$484/kg
Hypodermic syringes	Switzerland	$2,306/unit

Underpriced Imports

Item	To	Unit Price
Truck caps	Mexico	$4.09/unit
Turbojet engines	Romania	$10,000/unit
Cameras (SLRs)	Mexico	$3.30/unit
Soybeans	Netherlands	$1.58/ton
ATM machines	Salvador	$35.93/unit
Bulldozers	Mexico	$527.94/unit
Rocket launchers	Bolivia	$40.00/unit
Toilets, porcelain	Hong Kong	$1.08/unit
Prefabricated bldgs	St. Lucia	$0.82/unit
Video projectors	Malta	$28.71/unit
Radial tires (bus)	U.K.	$8.46/unit

Source: "U.S. Trade With The World: An Estimate of 2000 Lost U.S. Federal Income Tax Revenues Due to Over-Invoiced Imports and Under-Invoiced Exports," Simon Pak and John Zdanowicz, Florida International University, November 1, 2001, unpublished.

France, following the same principle of completely specializing in the product of its comparative production advantage, moves production from point D to point E, producing 50 units of cloth. If France now exported the unwanted cloth, for example 30 units, and exchanged the cloth with England for imports of 30 units of wheat (note that England's exports are France's imports), France too is better off as a result of international trade. Each country would do what it does best, exclusively, and then trade for the other product.

But at what prices will the two countries trade? Since each country's production possibilities frontier has a different slope (different relative product prices), the two countries can determine a set of prices between the two domestic prices. In the above example, England's price ratio was $-2:1$, while France's domestic price was $-1:2$. Trading 30 units of wheat for 30 units of cloth is a price ratio of $-1:1$, a slope or set of prices between the two domestic price ratios. The dashed line in Figure 5.2 illustrates this set of trade prices.

Are both countries better off as a result of trade? Yes. The final step to understanding the benefits of classical trade is to note that the point where a country produces (point B for England and point E for France in Figure 5.2) and the point where it consumes are now different. This allows each country to consume beyond their own production possibilities frontier. Society's welfare, which is normally measured in its ability to consume more wheat, cloth, or any other goods or services, is increased through trade.

MAP

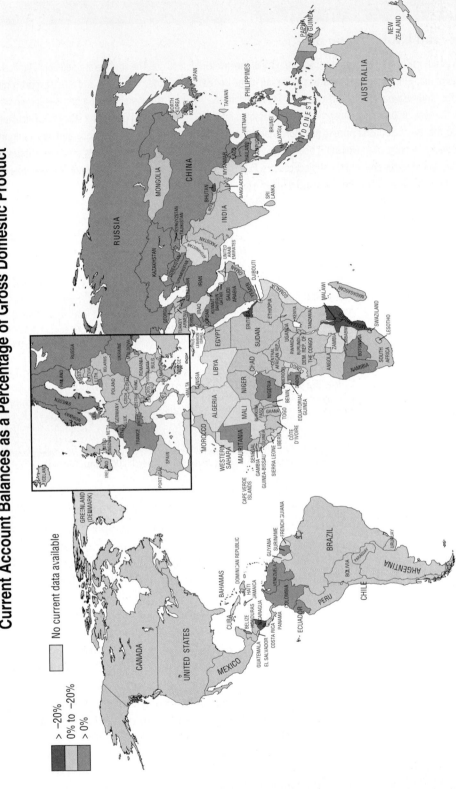

Current Account Balances as a Percentage of Gross Domestic Product

> 0%
0% to −20%
> −20%
No current data available

Source: *2002 World Development Indicators*, The World Bank.

CONCLUDING POINTS ABOUT CLASSICAL TRADE THEORY

Classical trade theory contributed much to the understanding of how production and trade operates in the world economy. Although like all economic theories they are often criticized for being unrealistic or out of date, the purpose of a theory is to simplify reality so that the basic elements of the logic can be seen. Several of these simplifications have continued to provide insight in understanding international business.

- **Division of Labor.** Adam Smith's explanation of how industrial societies can increase output using the same labor-hours as in preindustrial society is fundamental to our thinking even today. Smith extended this specialization of the efforts of a worker to the specialization of a nation.
- **Comparative Advantage.** David Ricardo's extension of Smith's work explained for the first time how countries that seemingly had no obvious reason for trade could individually specialize in producing what they did best and trade for products they did not produce.
- **Gains from Trade.** The theory of comparative advantage argued that nations could improve the welfare of their populations through international trade. A nation could actually achieve consumption levels beyond what it could produce by itself. To this day this is one of the fundamental principles underlying the arguments for all countries to strive to expand and "free" world trade.

Factor Proportions Trade Theory

Trade theory changed drastically in the first half of the twentieth century. The theory developed by the Swedish economist Eli Heckscher and later expanded by his former student Bertil Ohlin formed the theory of international trade that is still widely accepted today, **factor proportions theory.**

FACTOR INTENSITY IN PRODUCTION

The Heckscher-Ohlin theory considered two **factors of production,** labor and capital. Technology determines the way they combine to form a good. Different goods required different proportions of the two factors of production.

Figure 5.3 illustrates what it means to describe a good by its factor proportions. The production of one unit of good X requires 4 units of labor and 1 unit of capital. At the same time, to produce 1 unit of good Y requires 4 units of labor and 2 units of capital. Good X therefore requires more units of labor per unit of capital (4 to 1) relative to Y (4 to 2). X is therefore classified as a relatively labor-intensive product, and Y is relatively capital intensive. These **factor intensities,** or **proportions,** are truly relative and are determined only on the basis of what product X requires relative to product Y and not to the specific numbers of labor to capital.

It is easy to see how the factor proportions of production differ substantially across goods. For example, the manufacturing of leather footwear is still a relatively labor-intensive process, even with the most sophisticated leather treatment and patterning machinery. Other goods, such as computer memory chips, however, although requiring some highly skilled labor, require massive quantities of capital for production. These large capital requirements include the enormous sums needed for research and

FIGURE 5.3

Factor Proportions in Production

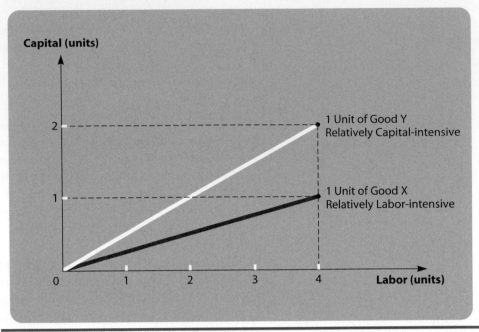

development and the manufacturing facilities needed for clean production to ensure the extremely high quality demanded in the industry.

According to factor proportions theory, factor intensities depend on the state of technology—the current method of manufacturing a good. The theory assumed that the same technology of production would be used for the same goods in all countries. It is not, therefore, differences in the efficiency of production that will determine trade between countries as it did in classical theory. Classical theory implicitly assumed that technology or the productivity of labor is different across countries. Otherwise, there would be no logical explanation why one country requires more units of labor to produce a unit of output than another country. Factor proportions theory assumes no such productivity differences.

FACTOR ENDOWMENTS, FACTOR PRICES, AND COMPARATIVE ADVANTAGE

If there is no difference in technology or productivity of factors across countries, what then determines comparative advantage in production and export? The answer is that factor prices determine cost differences. And these prices are determined by the endowments of labor and capital the country possesses. The theory assumes that labor and capital are immobile; factors cannot move across borders. Therefore, the country's endowment determines the relative costs of labor and capital as compared with other countries.

Using these assumptions, factor proportions theory stated that a country should specialize in the production and export of those products that use intensively its relatively abundant factor.

- A country that is relatively labor abundant should specialize in the production of relatively labor-intensive goods. It should then export those labor-intensive goods in exchange for capital-intensive goods.
- A country that is relatively capital abundant should specialize in the production of relatively capital-intensive goods. It should then export those capital-intensive goods in exchange for labor-intensive goods.

ASSUMPTIONS OF THE FACTOR PROPORTIONS THEORY

The increasing level of theoretical complexity of the factor proportions theory, as compared with the classical trade theory, increased the number of assumptions necessary for the theory to "hold." It is important to take a last look at the assumptions before proceeding further.

1. The theory assumes two countries, two products, and two factors of production, the so-called $2 \times 2 \times 2$ assumption. Note that if both countries were producing all of the output they could and trading only between themselves (only two countries), both countries would have to have balances in trade!

2. The markets for the inputs and the outputs are perfectly competitive. The factors of production, labor, and capital were exchanged in markets that paid them only what they were worth. Similarly, the trade of the outputs (the international trade between the two countries) was competitive so that one country had no market power over the other.

3. Increasing production of a product experiences diminishing returns. This meant that as a country increasingly specialized in the production of one of the two outputs, it eventually would require more and more inputs per unit of output. For example there would no longer be the constant "labor-hours per unit of output" as assumed under the classical theory. Production possibilities frontiers would no longer be straight lines but concave. The result was that complete specialization would no longer occur under factor proportions theory.

4. Both countries were using identical technologies. Each product was produced in the same way in both countries. This meant the only way that a good could be produced more cheaply in one country than in the other was if the factors of production used (labor and capital) were cheaper.

Although a number of additional technical assumptions were necessary, these four highlight the very specialized set of conditions needed to explain international trade with factor proportions theory. Much of the trade theory developed since has focused on how trade changes when one or more of these assumptions is not found in the real world.

THE LEONTIEF PARADOX

One of the most famous tests of any economic or business theory occurred in 1950, when economist Wassily Leontief tested whether the factor proportions theory could be used to explain the types of goods the United States imported and exported. Leontief's premise was the following.

A widely shared view on the nature of the trade between the United States and the rest of the world is derived from what appears to be a common sense assumption that this country has a comparative advantage in the production of commodities which require for their manufacture large quantities of capital and relatively small amounts of labor. Our economic relationships with other countries are supposed to be based mainly on the export of such "capital intensive" goods in exchange for forgoing products which—if we were to make them at home—would require little capital but large quantities of American labor. Since the United States possesses a relatively large amount of capital—so goes this oft-repeated argument—and a comparatively small amount of labor, direct domestic production of such "labor intensive" products would be uneconomical; we can much more advantageously obtain them from abroad in exchange for our capital intensive products.[2]

Leontief first had to devise a method to determine the relative amounts of labor and capital in a good. His solution, known as **input-output analysis,** was an accomplishment on its own. Input-output analysis is a technique of decomposing a good into the values and quantities of the labor, capital, and other potential factors employed in the good's manufacture. Leontief then used this methodology to analyze the labor and capital content of all U.S. merchandise imports and exports. The hypothesis was relatively straightforward: U.S. exports should be relatively capital intensive (use more units of capital relative to labor) than U.S. imports. Leontief's results were, however, a bit of a shock.

Leontief found that the products that U.S. firms exported were relatively more labor intensive than the products the United States imported.[3] It seemed that if the factor proportions theory was true, the United States is a relatively labor-abundant country! Alternatively, the theory could be wrong. Neither interpretation of the results was acceptable to many in the field of international trade.

A variety of explanations and continuing studies have attempted to solve what has become known as the **Leontief Paradox.** At first, it was thought to have been simply a result of the specific year (1947) of the data. However, the same results were found with different years and data sets. Second, it was noted that Leontief did not really analyze the labor and capital contents of imports but rather the labor and capital contents of the domestic equivalents of these imports. It was possible that the United States was actually producing the products in a more capital-intensive fashion than were the countries from which it also imported the manufactured goods.[4] Finally, the debate turned to the need to distinguish different types of labor and capital. For example, several studies attempted to separate labor factors into skilled labor and unskilled labor. These studies have continued to show results more consistent with what the factor proportions theory would predict for country trade patterns.

LINDER'S OVERLAPPING PRODUCT RANGES THEORY

The difficulties in empirically validating the factor proportions theory led many in the 1960s and 1970s to search for new explanations of the determinants of trade between countries. The work of Staffan Burenstam Linder focused, not on the production or supply side, but instead on the preferences of consumers—the demand side. Linder acknowledged that in the natural resource–based industries, trade was indeed determined by relative costs of production and factor endowments.

However, Linder argued, trade in manufactured goods was dictated not by cost concerns but rather by the similarity in product demands across countries. Linder's was a significant departure from previous theory and was based on two principles:

1. As income, or more precisely per-capita income, rises, the complexity and quality level of the products demanded by the country's residents also rises. The total

range of product sophistication demanded by a country's residents is largely determined by its level of income.

2. The entrepreneurs directing the firms that produce society's needs are more knowledgeable about their own domestic market than about foreign markets. An entrepreneur could not be expected to effectively serve a foreign market that is significantly different from the domestic market because competitiveness comes from experience. A logical pattern would be for an entrepreneur to gain success and market share at home first then expand to foreign markets that are similar in their demands or tastes.

International trade in manufactured goods would then be influenced by similarity of demands. The countries that would see the most intensive trade are those with similar per-capita income levels, for they would possess a greater likelihood of overlapping product demands.

So where does trade come in? According to Linder, the overlapping ranges of product sophistication represent the products that entrepreneurs would know well from their home markets and could therefore potentially export and compete with in foreign markets. For example, the United States and Canada have almost parallel sophistication ranges, implying they would have a lot of common ground, overlapping product ranges, for intensive international trade and competition. They are quite similar in their per-capita income levels. But Mexico and the United States, or Mexico and Canada, would not. Mexico has a significantly different product sophistication range as a result of a different per capita income level.

The overlapping product ranges described by Linder would today be termed **market segments.** Not only was Linder's work instrumental in extending trade theory beyond cost considerations, but it also found a place in the field of international marketing. As illustrated in the theories following the work of Linder, many of the questions that his work raised were the focus of considerable attention in the following decades.

International Investment and Product Cycle Theory

A very different path was taken by Raymond Vernon in 1966 concerning what is now termed **product cycle theory.** Diverging significantly from traditional approaches, Vernon focused on the product (rather than the country and the technology of its manufacture), not its factor proportions. Most striking was the appreciation of the role of information, knowledge, and the costs and power that go hand in hand with knowledge.

> . . . we abandon the powerful simplifying notion that knowledge is a universal free good, and introduce it as an independent variable in the decision to trade or to invest.

Using many of the same basic tools and assumptions of factor proportions theory, Vernon added two technology-based premises to the factor-cost emphasis of existing theory:

1. Technical innovations leading to new and profitable products require large quantities of capital and highly skilled labor. These factors of production are predominantly available in highly industrialized capital-intensive countries.

2. These same technical innovations, both the product itself and more importantly the methods for its manufacture, go through three stages of maturation as the product becomes increasingly commercialized. As the manufacturing process becomes more standardized and low-skill labor-intensive, the comparative advantage in its production and export shifts across countries. And as the Focus on Politics describes, even accurately tracking exports and imports is sometimes daunting.

THE STAGES OF THE PRODUCT CYCLE

Product cycle theory is both supply-side (cost of production) and demand-side (income levels of consumers) in its orientation. Each of these three stages that Vernon described combines differing elements of each.

Stage I: The New Product

Innovation requires highly skilled labor and large quantities of capital for research and development. The product will normally be most effectively designed and initially manufactured near the parent firm and therefore in a highly industrialized market due to the need for proximity to information and the need for communication among the many different skilled-labor components required.

In this development stage, the product is nonstandardized. The production process requires a high degree of flexibility (meaning continued use of highly skilled labor). Costs of production are therefore quite high. The innovator at this stage is a monopolist and therefore enjoys all of the benefits of monopoly power, including the high profit margins required to repay the high development costs and expensive production process. Price elasticity of demand at this stage is low; high-income consumers buy it regardless of cost.

Stage II: The Maturing Product

As production expands, its process becomes increasingly standardized. The need for flexibility in design and manufacturing declines, and therefore the demand for highly skilled labor declines. The innovating country increases its sales to other countries. Competitors with slight variations develop, putting downward pressure on prices and profit margins. Production costs are an increasing concern.

As competitors increase, as well as their pressures on price, the innovating firm faces critical decisions on how to maintain market share. Vernon argues that the firm faces a critical decision at this stage, either to lose market share to foreign-based manufacturers using lower-cost labor or to invest abroad to maintain its market share by exploiting the comparative advantages of factor costs in other countries. This is one of the first theoretical explanations of how trade and investment become increasingly intertwined.

Stage III: The Standardized Product

In this final stage, the product is completely standardized in its manufacture. Thus, with access to capital on world capital markets, the country of production is simply the one with the cheapest unskilled labor. Profit margins are thin, and competition is fierce. The product has largely run its course in terms of profitability for the innovating firm.

The country of comparative advantage has therefore shifted as the technology of the product's manufacture has matured. The same product shifts in its location of production. The country possessing the product during that stage enjoys the benefits of

POLITICS

When the Numbers Don't Add Up

The international trade statistics between countries, as reported by each, often do not match. As part of the continuing cooperation between the North American Free Trade Agreement (NAFTA) countries, the U.S. Department of Commerce recently concluded a study into the differences among the official trade statistics released by the United States, Mexico, and Canada in 1998 and 1999. The significance of these differences is compounded by the importance of trade among the three countries: 30 percent of all U.S. merchandise trade is with Canada and Mexico; 80 percent of Mexico's merchandise and service trade is with the United States and Canada.

The primary sources of the discrepancy in statistics include *geographic coverage, partner country attribution, nonfiling of U.S. exports,* and *low-value transactions*. An example of *geographic coverage* would be that the United States considers Puerto Rico and the U.S. Virgin Islands as part of the United States for reporting reasons, while Mexico regards them as separate trading partners. *Partner country attribution* occurs, for example, in Mexico, where the import entry form allows for the reporting of only a single country of origin. As a result, some imports are misattributed to the United States.

For more details on the study of trade statistics discrepancies see http://www.census.gov/foreign-trade/

net trade surpluses. But such advantages are fleeting, according to Vernon. As knowledge and technology continually change, so does the country of that product's comparative advantage.

TRADE IMPLICATIONS OF THE PRODUCT CYCLE

Product cycle theory shows how specific products were first produced and exported from one country but, through product and competitive evolution, shifted their location of production and export to other countries over time. Figure 5.4 illustrates the trade patterns that Vernon visualized as resulting from the maturing stages of a specific product cycle. As the product and the market for the product mature and change, the countries of its production and export shift.

The product is initially designed and manufactured in the United States. In its early stages (from time t_0 to t_1), the United States is the only country producing and consuming the product. Production is highly capital-intensive and skilled-labor intensive at this time. At time t_1 the United States begins exporting the product to Other Advanced Countries, as Vernon classified them. These countries possess the income to purchase the product in its still New Product Stage, in which it was relatively high priced. These Other Advanced Countries also commerce their own production at time t_1 but continue to be net importers. A few exports, however, do find their way to the Less Developed Countries at this time as well.

As the product moves into the second stage, the Maturing Product Stage, production capability expands rapidly in the Other Advanced Countries. Competitive variations begin to appear as the basic technology of the product becomes more widely known, and the need for skilled labor in its production declines. These countries eventually also become net exporters of the product near the end of the stage (time t_3). At time t_2 the Less Developed Countries begin their own production, although they continue to be net importers. Meanwhile, the lower cost of production from these growing competitors turns the United States into a net importer by time t_4. The competitive advantage for production and export is clearly shifting across countries at this time.

The third and final stage, the Standardized Product Stage, sees the comparative advantage of production and export now shifting to the Less Developed Countries.

FIGURE 5.4

Trade Patterns and Product Cycle Theory

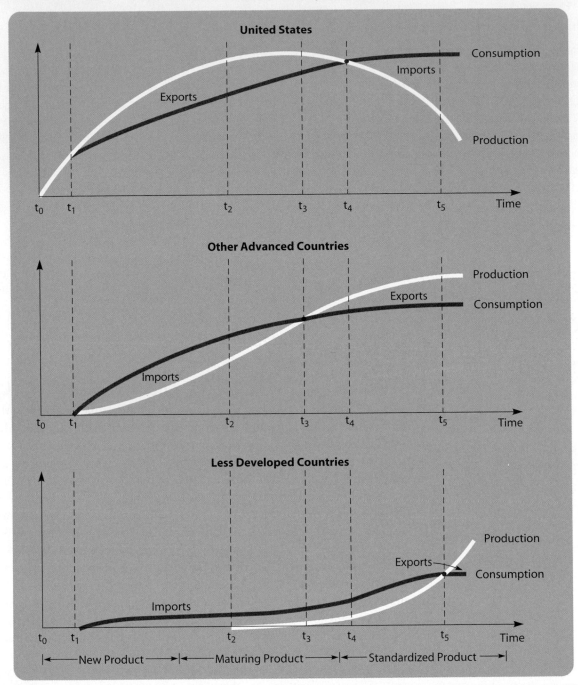

Source: Raymond Vernon, "International Investment and International Trade in the Product Cycle." Quarterly Journal of Economics (May 1966): 199.

The product is now a relatively mass-produced product that can be made with increasingly less-skilled labor. The United States continues to reduce domestic production and increase imports. The Other Advanced Countries continue to produce and export, although exports peak as the Less Developed Countries expand production and become net exporters themselves. The product has run its course or life cycle in reaching time t_5.

A final point: Note that throughout this product cycle, the countries of production, consumption, export, and import are identified by their labor and capital levels, not firms. Vernon noted that it could very well be the same firms that are moving production from the United States to Other Advanced Countries to Less Developed Countries. The shifting location of production was instrumental in the changing patterns of trade but not necessarily in the loss of market share, profitability, or competitiveness of the firms. The country of comparative advantage could change.

Although interesting in its own right for increasing emphasis on technology's impact on product costs, product cycle theory was most important because it explained international investment. Not only did the theory recognize the mobility of capital across countries (breaking the traditional assumption of factor immobility), it shifted the focus from the country to the product. This made it important to match the product by its maturity stage with its production location to examine competitiveness.

Product cycle theory has many limitations. It is obviously most appropriate for technology-based products. These are the products that are most likely to experience the changes in production process as they grow and mature. Other products, either resource-based (such as minerals and other commodities) or services (which employ capital but mostly in the form of human capital), are not so easily characterized by stages of maturity. And product cycle theory is most relevant to products that eventually fall victim to mass production and therefore cheap labor forces. But, all things considered, product cycle theory served to breach a wide gap between the trade theories of old and the intellectual challenges of a new, more globally competitive market in which capital, technology, information, and firms themselves were more mobile.

The New Trade Theory: Strategic Trade

Global trade developments in the 1980s and 1990s led to much criticism of the existing theories of trade. First, although there was rapid growth in trade, much of it was not explained by current theory. Secondly, the massive size of the merchandise trade deficit of the United States—and the associated decline of many U.S. firms in terms of international competitiveness—served as something of a country-sized lab experiment demonstrating what some critics termed the "bankruptcy of trade theory." Academics and policymakers alike looked for new explanations.

Two new contributions to trade theory were met with great interest. Paul Krugman, along with several colleagues, developed a theory of how trade is altered when markets are not perfectly competitive, or when production of specific products possesses economies of scale. A second and very influential development was the growing work of Michael Porter, who examined the competitiveness of industries on a global basis, rather than relying on country-specific factors to determine competitiveness.

ECONOMIES OF SCALE AND IMPERFECT COMPETITION

Paul Krugman's theoretical developments once again focused on cost of production and how cost and price drive international trade. Using theoretical developments from microeconomics and market structure analysis, Krugman focused on two types of economics of scale, *internal economies of scale* and *external economies of scale*.[5]

According to the government, Chinese cell phone usage reached 200 million subscribers in 2002. As domestic spending grows, China will be able to sustain its economic growth and as a result be less dependent upon exports. This growing Chinese economy also helps China's trade partners.

Internal Economies of Scale

When the cost per unit of output depends on the size of an individual firm, the larger the firm the greater the scale benefits, and the lower the cost per unit. A firm possessing internal economies of scale could potentially monopolize an industry (creating an *imperfect market*), both domestically and internationally. If it produces more, lowering the cost per unit, it can lower the market price and sell more products, because it *sets* market prices.

The link between dominating a domestic industry and influencing international trade comes from taking this assumption of imperfect markets back to the original concept of comparative advantage. For this firm to expand sufficiently to enjoy its economies of scale, it must take resources away from other domestic industries in order to expand. A country then sees its own range of products in which it specializes narrowing, providing an opportunity for other countries to specialize in these so-called **abandoned product ranges.** Countries again search out and exploit comparative advantage.

A particularly powerful implication of internal economies of scale is that it provides an explanation of intra-industry trade, one area in which traditional trade theory had indeed seemed bankrupt. **Intra-industry trade** is when a country seemingly imports and exports the same product, an idea that is obviously inconsistent with any of the trade theories put forward in the past three centuries. According to Krugman, internal economies of scale may lead a firm to specialize in a narrow product line (to produce the volume necessary for economies of scale cost benefits); other firms in other countries may produce products that are similarly narrow, yet extremely similar: **product differentiation.** If consumers in either country wish to buy both products, they will be importing and exporting products that are, for all intents and purposes, the same.[6]

Intra-industry trade has been studied in detail in the past decade. Intra-industry trade is measured with the Grubel-Lloyd Index, the ratio of imports and exports of the same product occurring between two trading nations. It is calculated as follows:

$$\text{Intra-Industry Trade Index}_i = \frac{|X_i - M_i|}{(X_i + M_i)}$$

where i is the product category and $|X - M|$ is the absolute value of net exports of that product (exports − imports). For example, if Sweden imports 100 heavy machines for its forest products industry from Finland, and at the same time exports to Finland 80 of the same type of equipment, the intra-industry trade (IIT) index would be:

$$\text{IIT} = \frac{|80 - 100|}{(80 + 100)} = 1 - .1111 = .89$$

The closer the index value to 1, the higher the level of intra-industry trade in that product category. The closer the index is to 0, the more one-way the trade between the countries exists, as traditional trade theory would predict.

Intra-industry trade is now thought to compose roughly 25 percent of global trade. And to its credit, intra-industry trade is increasingly viewed as having additive benefits to the fundamental benefits of comparative advantage. Intra-industry trade does allow some industrial segments in some countries to deepen their specialization while simultaneously allowing greater breadth of choices and commensurate benefits to consumers. Of course, one potentially disturbing characteristic of the growth in intra-industry trade is the potential for trade of all kinds to continue to expand in breadth and depth between the most industrialized countries (those producing the majority of the more complex manufactured goods) while those less industrialized nations do not see this added boost to trade growth.

External Economies of Scale

When the cost per unit of output depends on the size of an industry, not the size of the individual firm, the industry of that country may produce at lower costs than the same industry that is smaller in size in other countries. A country can potentially dominate world markets in a particular product, not because it has one massive firm producing enormous quantities (for example, Boeing), but rather because it has many small firms that interact to create a large, competitive, critical mass (for example, semiconductors in Penang, Malaysia). No one firm need be all that large, but several small firms in total may create such a competitive industry that firms in other countries cannot ever break into the industry on a competitive basis.[7]

Unlike internal economies of scale, external economies of scale may not necessarily lead to imperfect markets, but they may result in an industry maintaining its dominance in its field in world markets. This provides an explanation as to why all industries do not necessarily always move to the country with the lowest-cost energy, resources, or labor. What gives rise to this critical mass of small firms and their interrelationships is a much more complex question. The work of Michael Porter provides a partial explanation of how these critical masses are sustained.

STRATEGIC TRADE

Often criticized as being simplistic or naive, trade theory in recent years has, in the words of one critic, grown up. One fundamental assumption that both classical and modern trade theories have not been willing to stray far from is the inefficiencies introduced with governmental involvement in trade. Economic theory, however, has long recognized that government can play a beneficial role when markets are not purely competitive. This theory has now been expanded to government's role in international trade as well. This growing stream of thought is termed **strategic trade.** There are (at least) four specific circumstances involving imperfect competition in which strategic trade may apply, which we denote as *price, cost, repetition,* and *externalities.*

Price

A foreign firm that enjoys significant international market power—monopolistic power—has the ability to both restrict the quantity of consumption and demand higher prices. One method by which a domestic government may thwart that monopolistic power is to impose import duties or tariffs on the imported products. The monopolist, not wishing to allow the price of the product to rise too high in the target market, will often absorb some portion of the tariff. The result is roughly the same amount of product imported, and at relatively the same price to the customer, but the excessive profits (**economic rent** in economic theory) have been partly shifted from the monopolist to the domestic government. Governments have long fought the power of global petrochemical companies with these types of import duties.

Cost

Although much has been made in recent years about the benefits of "small and flexible," some industries still are dominated by the firms that can gain massive productive size—**scale economies.** As the firm's size increases, its per unit cost of production falls, allowing it a signficant cost advantage in competition. Governments wishing for specific firms to gain this stature may choose to protect the domestic market against foreign competition to provide a home market of size for the company's growth and maturity. This strategic trade theory is actually quite similar to the traditional arguments for the protection of infant industries, though this is a protection whose benefits accrue to firms in adolescence rather than childhood!

Repetition

Some firms in some industries have inherent competitive advantages, often efficiency based, from simply having produced repetitively for years. Sometimes referred to as "learning-by-doing," these firms may achieve competitive cost advantages from producing not only more units (as in the scale economies described above) but from producing more units *over time.* A goverment that wishes to promote these efficiency gains by domestic firms can help the firm move down the learning curve faster by protecting the domestic market from foreign competitors. Again similar in nature to the infant industry argument, the idea is not only to allow the firm to produce more, but to produce more cumulatively over time to gain competitive knowledge from the actual process itself.

Externalities

The fourth and final category of strategic trade involves those market failures in which the costs or benefits of the business process are not borne or captured by the firm itself. If, for example, the government believes that the future of business is in specific knowledge-based industries, it may be willing to subsidize the education of workers for that industry, protect that inudstry from foreign competition, or even aid the industry in overcoming the costs of environmental proection in order to promote the industry's development. This argument is similar to those used by governments in the 1970s and 1980s to support the development of certain industries in their countries (for example, microelectronics in Japan and steel in Korea) which was then referred to as **industrial policy.** In fact, this strategic trade argument could be used in support of Michael Porter's cluster theory, in which society and industry would reap benefits of reaching critical mass in experience and interactions through promotion and protection.

Although the arguments by proponents of strategic trade are often seductive, critics charge that these theories play more to emotion than rational thought. Industries do not often learn by doing or reduce costs through scale, and governments are infamous for their inability to effectively protect (and unprotect, when the time comes) in order to promote industrial development and growth. Protection and state-supported monopolists are often some of the world's least efficient rather than most efficient. And as always, there is no assurance that foreign governments themselves will not react and retaliate, again undermining the potentially rational policies put into place in isolation. A final note of caution about strategic trade goes back to the very origins of trade theory: Many of the benefits of international trade accrue to those who successfully divorce the politic from the economic.

THE COMPETITIVE ADVANTAGE OF NATIONS

The focus of early trade theory was on the country or nation and its inherent, natural, or endowment characteristics that might give rise to increasing competitiveness. As trade theory evolved, it shifted its focus to the industry and product level, leaving the national-level competitiveness question somewhat behind. Recently, many have turned their attention to the question of how countries, governments, and even private industry can alter the conditions within a country to aid the competitiveness of its firms.

The leader in this area of research has been Michael Porter of Harvard. As he states:

> National prosperity is created, not inherited. It does not grow out of a country's natural endowments, its labor pool, its interest rates, or its currency's values, as classical economics insists.
>
> A nation's competitiveness depends on the capacity of its industry to innovate and upgrade. Companies gain advantage against the world's best competitors because of pressure and challenge. They benefit from having strong domestic rivals, aggressive home-based suppliers, and demanding local customers.
>
> In a world of increasingly global competition, nations have become more, not less, important. As the basis of competition has shifted more and more to the creation and assimilation of knowledge, the role of the nation has grown. Competitive advantage is created and sustained through a highly localized process. Differences in national values, culture, economic structures, institutions, and histories all contribute to competitive success. There are striking differences in the patterns of competitiveness in every country; no nation can or will be competitive in every or even most industries. Ultimately, nations succeed in particular industries because their home environment is most forward-looking, dynamic, and challenging.[8]

Porter argued innovation is what drives and sustains competitiveness. A firm must avail itself of all dimensions of competition, which he categorized into four major components of "the diamond of national advantage":

1. **Factor Conditions:** The appropriateness of the nation's factors of production to compete successfully in a specific industry. Porter notes that although these factor conditions are very important in the determination of trade, they are not

the only source of competitiveness as suggested by the classical, or factor proportions, theories of trade. Most importantly for Porter, it is the ability of a nation to continually create, upgrade, and deploy its factors (such as skilled labor) that is important, not the initial endowment.

2. **Demand Conditions:** The degree of health and competition the firm must face in its original home market. Firms that can survive and flourish in highly competitive and demanding local markets are much more likely to gain the competitive edge. Porter notes that it is the character of the market, not its size, that is paramount in promoting the continual competitiveness of the firm. And Porter translates *character* as demanding customers.

3. **Related and Supporting Industries:** The competitiveness of all related industries and suppliers to the firm. A firm that is operating within a mass of related firms and industries gains and maintains advantages through close working relationships, proximity to suppliers, and timeliness of product and information flows. The constant and close interaction is successful if it occurs not only in terms of physical proximity but also through the willingness of firms to work at it.

4. **Firm Strategy, Structure, and Rivalry:** The conditions in the home-nation that either hinder or aid in the firm's creation and sustaining of international competitiveness. Porter notes that no one managerial, ownership, or operational strategy is universally appropriate. It depends on the fit and flexibility of what works for that industry in that country at that time.

These four points, as illustrated in Figure 5.5, constitute what nations and firms must strive to "create and sustain through a highly localized process" to ensure their success.

Porter's emphasis on innovation as the source of competitiveness reflects an increased focus on the industry and product that we have seen in the past three decades. The acknowledgment that the nation is "more, not less, important" is to many eyes a welcome return to a positive role for government and even national-level

FIGURE 5.5

Determinants of National Competitive Advantage: Porter's Diamond

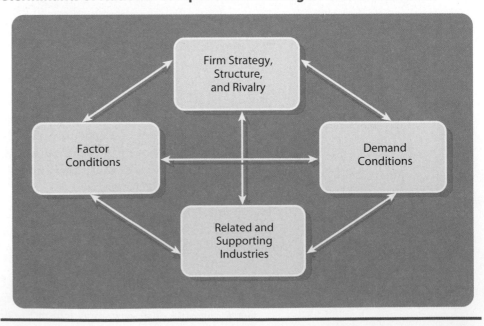

private industry in encouraging international competitiveness. Including factor conditions as a cost component, demand conditions as a motivator of firm actions, and competitiveness all combine to include the elements of classical, factor proportions, product cycle, and imperfect competition theories in a pragmatic approach to the challenges that the global markets of the twenty-first century present to the firms of today.

CLUSTERS AND THE NEW ECONOMICS

Michael Porter added an additional theoretical development to the concept of competitive advantage, that of **competitive clusters** (Porter, 1998). *Clusters*, according to Porter, are "critical masses—in one place—of unusual competitive success in particular fields." Examples often cited are leather fashion product manufacturing in northern Italy, textiles in the Carolinas and wine in California in the United States, or semiconductors on the Penang Peninsula in Malaysia. These geographic concentrations of competitive excellence seemingly fly in the face of modern thought on the mobility of capital and knowledge.

Porter's theoretical argument was based on his assertion that significant advantages accrue to companies from being in proximity to complementary products and services—within reach of all the suppliers and partners in the product value chain. The premise was quite simple: Competitive advantages are gained through interconnected companies and institutions locally, not through the scale and scope of the firms themselves. Cluster theory suggests that competition is altered in at least three ways when clusters form successfully: 1) by increasing the productivity of the companies based in the area; 2) by driving and supporting the momentum of innovation in the area; and 3) by stimulating the creation of new companies and new configurations of business in the area. In effect, the cluster itself acts as an extended family or single firm, but flexibly and efficiently. Interestingly, the cluster's competitive sustainability is assured by the second change—the momentum gains to innovation—which is consistent with Porter's earlier work on what drives competitive advantage of the individual firm through time.

The writing of Porter and others has continued to be instrumental in the thinking of both business and government when approaching trade policy. Many, although supporting much of the findings of Porter's theories, see the true insights as being related to the complex relationships between knowledge and how knowledge is developed, shared, and transmitted within industries over time.

The Theory of International Investment

Trade is the production of a good or service in one country and its sale to a buyer in another country. In fact, it is a firm (not a country) and a buyer (not a country) that are the subjects of trade, domestically or internationally. A firm is therefore attempting to access a market and its buyers. The producing firm wants to utilize its competitive advantage for growth and profit and can also reach this goal by international investment.[9]

Although this sounds easy enough, consider any of the following potholes on the road to investment success. Any of the following potholes may be avoided by producing within another country.

• Sales to some countries are difficult because of tariffs imposed on your good when it is entering. If you were producing within the country, your good would no longer be an import.

- Your good requires natural resources that are available only in certain areas of the world. It is therefore imperative that you have access to the natural resources. You can buy them from that country and bring them to your production process (import) or simply take the production to them.
- Competition is constantly pushing you to improve efficiency and decrease the costs of producing your good. You therefore may want to produce where it will be cheaper—cheaper capital, cheaper energy, cheaper natural resources, or cheaper labor. Many of these factors are still not mobile, and therefore you will go to them instead of bringing them to you.

There are thousands of reasons why a firm may want to produce in another country, and not necessarily in the country that is cheapest for production or the country where the final good is sold.

The subject of international investment arises from one basic idea: the mobility of capital. Although many of the traditional trade theories assumed the immobility of the factors of production, it is the movement of capital that has allowed **foreign direct investments** across the globe. If there is a competitive advantage to be gained, capital can and will get there.

THE FOREIGN DIRECT INVESTMENT DECISION

Consider a firm that wants to exploit its competitive advantage by accessing foreign markets as illustrated in the decision-sequence tree of Figure 5.6.

The first choice is whether to exploit the existing competitive advantage in new foreign markets or to concentrate its resources in the development of new competitive advantages in the domestic market. Although many firms may choose to do both as resources will allow, more and more firms are choosing to go international as at least part of their expansion strategies.

Second, should the firm produce at home and export to the foreign markets, or produce abroad? The firm will choose the path that will allow it to access the resources and markets it needs to exploit its existing competitive advantage. But it will also consider two additional dimensions of each foreign investment decision: (1) the degree of control over assets, technology, information, and operations and (2) the magnitude of capital that the firm must risk. Each decision increases the firm's control at the cost of increased capital outlays.

After choosing to produce abroad, the firm must decide how. The distinctions among different kinds of foreign direct investment (branch 3 and downward in Figure 5.6), licensing agreements to greenfield construction (building a new facility from the ground up), vary by degrees of ownership. The licensing management contract is by far the simplest and cheapest way to produce abroad. Another firm is licensed to produce the product, but with your firm's technology and know-how. The question is whether the reduced capital investment of simply licensing the product to another manufacturer is worth the risk of loss of control over the product and technology.

The firm that wants direct control over the foreign production process next determines the degree of equity control: to own the firm outright, or as a joint investment with another firm. Trade-offs with joint ventures continue the debate over control of assets and other sources of the firm's original competitive advantage. Many countries try to ensure the continued growth of local firms and investors by requiring that foreign firms operate jointly with local firms.

The final decision branch between a "greenfield investment"—building a firm from the ground up—and the purchase of an existing firm, is often a question of cost. A greenfield investment is the most expensive of all foreign investment alternatives.

FIGURE 5.6

The Direct Foreign Investment Decision Sequence

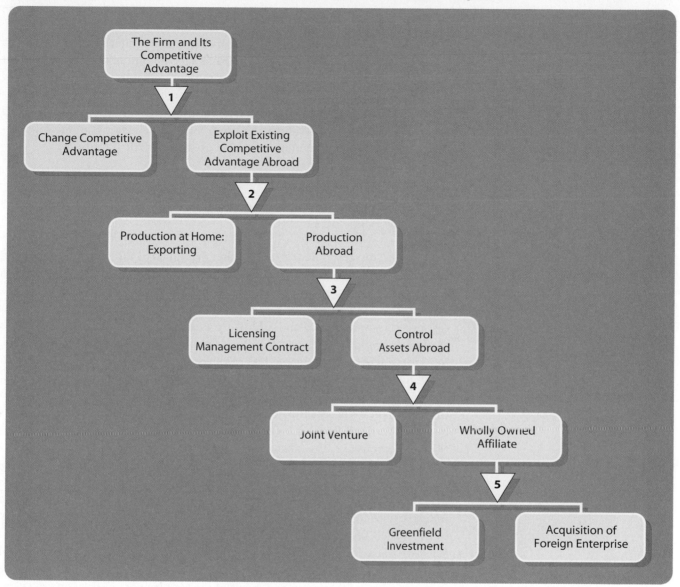

Source: Adapted from Gunter Dufey and R. Mirus, "Foreign Direct Investment: Theory and Strategic Considerations," unpublished, University of Michigan, May 1985.

The acquisition of an existing firm is often lower in initial cost but may also contain a number of customizing and adjustment costs that are not apparent at the initial purchase. The purchase of a going concern may also have substantial benefits if the existing business possesses substantial customer and supplier relationships that can be used by the new owner in the pursuit of its own business.

THE THEORY OF FOREIGN DIRECT INVESTMENT

What motivates a firm to go beyond exporting or licensing? What benefits does the multinational firm expect to achieve by establishing a physical presence in other countries? These are the questions that the theory of foreign direct investment has sought to answer. As with trade theory, the questions have remained largely the same over time, while the answers have continued to change. With hundreds of countries, thousands of firms, and millions of products and services, there is no question that the answer to such an enormous question will likely get messy.

The following overview of investment theory has many similarities to the preceding discussion of international trade. The theme is a global business environment that attempts to satisfy increasingly sophisticated consumer demands, while the means of production, resources, skills, and technology needed become more complex and competitive. The theory of foreign direct investment is indeed **eclectic,** representing a collection of forces and drivers. The man responsible for the majority of the theoretical development, John Dunning, termed the theory the **eclectic paradigm.**

FIRMS AS SEEKERS

A firm that expands across borders may be seeking any of a number of specific sources of profit or opportunity.

1. **Seeking Resources:** There is no question that much of the initial foreign direct investment of the eighteenth and nineteenth centuries was the result of firms seeking unique and valuable natural resources for their products. Whether it be the copper resources of Chile, the linseed oils of Indonesia, or the petroleum resources spanning the Middle East, firms establishing permanent presences around the world are seeking access to the resources at the core of their business.

2. **Seeking Factor Advantages:** The resources needed for production are often combined with other advantages that are inherent in the country of production. The same low-cost labor at the heart of classical trade theory provides incentives for firms to move production to countries possessing these factor advantages. As noted by Vernon's Product Cycle, the same firms may move their own production to locations of factor advantages as the products and markets mature.

3. **Seeking Knowledge:** Firms may attempt to acquire other firms in other countries for the technical or competitive skills they possess. Alternatively, companies may locate in and around centers of industrial enterprise unique to their specific industry, such as the footwear industry of Milan or the semiconductor industry of the Silicon Valley of California.

4. **Seeking Security:** Firms continue to move internationally as they seek political stability or security. For example, Mexico has experienced a significant increase in foreign direct investment as a result of the tacit support of the United States, Canada, and Mexico itself as reflected by the North American Free Trade Agreement.

5. **Seeking Markets:** Not the least of the motivations, the ability to gain and maintain access to markets is of paramount importance to multinational firms. Whether following the principles of Linder, in which firms learn from their domestic market and use that information to go international, or the principles of Porter, which emphasize the character of the domestic market as dictating international competitiveness, foreign market access is necessary.

FIRMS AS EXPLOITERS OF IMPERFECTIONS

Much of the investment theory developed in the past three decades has focused on the efforts of multinational firms to exploit the imperfections in factor and product markets created by governments. The work of Hymer, Kindleberger, and Caves noted that many of the policies of governments create imperfections. These market imperfections cover the entire range of supply and demand of the market: trade policy (tariffs and quotas), tax policies and incentives, preferential purchasing arrangements established by governments themselves, and financial restrictions on the access of foreign firms to domestic capital markets.

1. **Imperfections in Access:** Many of the world's developing countries have long sought to create domestic industry by restricting imports of competitive products in order to allow smaller, less competitive domestic firms to grow and prosper—so-called **import substitution** policies. Multinational firms have sought to maintain their access to these markets by establishing their own productive presence within the country, effectively bypassing the tariff restriction.

2. **Imperfections in Factor Mobility:** Other multinational firms have exploited the same sources of comparative advantage identified throughout this chapter— the low-cost resources or factors often located in less-developed countries or countries with restrictions on the mobility of labor and capital. However, combining the mobility of capital with the immobility of low-cost labor has characterized much of the foreign direct investment seen throughout the developing world over the past 50 years.

3. **Imperfections in Management:** The ability of multinational firms to successfully exploit or at least manage these imperfections still relies on their ability to gain an "advantage." Market advantages or powers are seen in international markets as in domestic markets: cost advantages, economies of scale and scope, product differentiation, managerial or marketing technique and knowledge, financial resources and strength.

All these imperfections are the things of which competitive dreams are made. The multinational firm needs to find these in some form or another to justify the added complexities and costs of international investments.

FIRMS AS INTERNALIZERS

The question that has plagued the field of foreign direct investment is, Why can't all of the advantages and imperfections mentioned be achieved through management contracts or licensing agreements (the choice available to the international investor at Step 3 in Figure 5.6)? Why is it necessary for *the firm itself* to establish a physical presence in the country? What pushes the multinational firm further down the investment decision tree?

The research of Buckley and Casson and Dunning has attempted to answer these questions by focusing on nontransferable sources of competitive advantage— proprietary information possessed by the firm and its people. Many advantages firms possess center around their hands-on knowledge of producing a good or providing a service. By establishing their own multinational operations they can internalize the production, thus keeping confidential the information that is at the core of the firm's competitiveness. **Internalization** is preferable to the use of arms-length arrangements such as management contracts or licensing agreements. They either do not allow the effective transmission of the knowledge or represent too serious a threat to the loss of the knowledge to allow the firm to successfully achieve the hoped-for benefits of international investment.

Summary

The theory of international trade has changed drastically from that first put forward by Adam Smith. The classical theories of Adam Smith and David Ricardo focused on the abilities of countries to produce goods more cheaply than other countries. The earliest production and trade theories saw labor as the major factor expense that went into any product. If a country could pay that labor less, and if that labor could produce more physically than labor in other countries, the country might obtain an absolute or comparative advantage in trade.

Subsequent theoretical development led to a more detailed understanding of production and its costs. Factors of production are now believed to include labor (skilled and unskilled), capital, natural resources, and other potentially significant commodities that are difficult to reproduce or replace, such as energy. Technology, once assumed to be the same across all countries, is now seen as one of the premier driving forces in determining who holds the competitive edge or advantage. International trade is now seen as a complex combination of thousands of products, technologies, and firms that are constantly innovating to either keep up with or get ahead of the competition.

Modern trade theory has looked beyond production cost to analyze how the demands of the marketplace alter who trades with whom and which firms survive domestically and internationally. The abilities of firms to adapt to foreign markets, both in the demands and the competitors that form the foreign markets, have required much of international trade and investment theory to search out new and innovative approaches to what determines success and failure.

Finally, as world economies grew and the magnitude of world trade increased, the simplistic ideas that guided international trade and investment theory have had to grow with them. The choices that many firms face today require them to directly move their capital, technology, and know-how to countries that possess other unique factors or market advantages that will help them keep pace with market demands. Even then, world business conditions constitute changing fortunes.

Questions for Discussion

1. According to the theory of comparative advantage as explained by Ricardo, why is trade always possible between two countries, even when one is absolutely inefficient compared to the other?

2. The factor proportions theory of international trade assumes that all countries produce the same product the same way. Would international competition cause or prevent this from happening?

3. What, in your opinion, were the constructive impacts on trade theory resulting from the empirical research of Wassily Leontief?

4. Product cycle theory has always been a very "attractive theory" to many students. Why do you think that is?

5. If the product cycle theory were accepted for the basis of policymaking in the United States, what should the U.S. government do to help U.S. firms exploit the principles of the theory?

6. Many trade theorists argue that the primary contribution of Michael Porter has been to repopularize old ideas, in new, more applicable ways. To what degree do you think Porter's ideas are new or old?

7. How would you analyze the statement that "international investment is simply a modern extension of classical trade"?

8. How can a crisis in Asia impact jobs and profits in the United States?

Internet Exercises

1. The differences across multinational firms is striking. Using a sample of firms such as those listed here, pull from their individual web pages the proportions of their incomes that are earned outside their country of incorporation.

Walt Disney	http://www.disney.com/
Nestlé S.A.	http://www.nestle.com/
Intel	http://www.intel.com/
Daimler-Chrysler	http://www.daimlerchrysler.com/
Mitsubishi Motors	http://www.mitsubishi-motors.com/

Also note the way in which international business is now conducted via the Internet. Several of the above home pages allow the user to choose the language of the presentation viewed. Others, like DaimlerChrysler, report financial results in two different accounting frameworks, those used in Germany and the Generally Accepted Accounting Practices (GAAP) used in the United States.

2. There is no hotter topic in business today than corporate governance, the way in which firms are controlled by management and ownership across countries. Use the following sites to view recent research, current events and news items, and other information related to the relationships between a business and its stakeholders.

| Corporate Governance Net | http://www.corpgov.net/ |
| Corporate Governance Research | http://www.irrc.org |

Take a Stand

Many multinational companies are now following a very similar strategy of moving their manufacturing facilities out of large, industrialized countries like the United States, Germany, and the United Kingdom, and relocating them to countries in which labor is much cheaper, such as mainland China. This is, however, very controversial given slow economic growth and growing unemployment in the industrial countries.

According to most theories of international trade, once the technology of an industry has matured and countries have deregulated their economies sufficiently to allow capital to flow across borders relatively freely, companies in industries that can use lower-cost labor—assuming sufficient skills are available—should move their manufacturing to those lower-labor-cost countries. The competitive strategy argument is that if one company does not, and another does, the first will be unable to compete in the future.

For Discussion

1. Multinationals should not continue to move their manufacturing out of industrial countries. They are contributing to rising unemployment, undermining the economies of countries like the United States and Germany, and are simply serving as devices to exploit cheap labor in developing countries.

2. Multinationals must continue to take whatever actions are necessary, including moving manufacturing to lower-cost countries, to remain competitive. The people, the workers, and the economies of countries like the United States and Germany cannot artifically protect their economies from global competition; it would only serve to create countries of lesser and lesser competitiveness in the coming years.

CHAPTER 6

The Balance of Payments

Learning Objectives

- To understand the fundamental principles of how countries measure international business activity, the balance of payments

- To examine the similarities of the current and capital accounts of the balance of payments

- To understand the critical differences between trade in merchandise and services, and why international investment activity has recently been controversial in the United States

- To review the mechanical steps of how exchange rate changes are transmitted into altered trade prices and eventually trade volumes

- To understand how countries with different government policies toward international trade and investment, or different levels of economic development, differ in their balance of payments

Ecuadorian Trade: A Tariff Here, A Bribe There

O r how about diverting your goods through this tunnel?

Soldiers, politicians, and priests have all had their chance to reform Ecuador's rotten customs service. They have failed to do the job so far, and some have not tried very hard. Take Carlos Flores, the former president's confessor, who, as head of the Quito customs district, helped importers evade more than $10 million in tariffs. Father Flores, having acquired four houses, four apartments, three cars, and $140,000, is now evading justice.

The customs system has three main problems: inefficiency, tax evasion, and outright corruption. Getting an imported container out of customs takes weeks or months, unless the process is greased with money or influence. Some importers use loopholes to place merchandise in lower tariff categories. Some imports are passed through a tunnel, where they bypass duties and enter the market as contraband. These and other skullduggeries, according to the Internal Revenue Service (SRI), cost the government from $600-$800 million each year—let alone the millions they cost business.

President Lucio Gutierrez, who took office in January, has made some effort to clean house—not just because it would bring in revenue, but also because it was one of the conditions of getting a $205 million deal from the IMF. Only a few days after taking office, Mr. Gutierrez ordered soldiers to take control of the customs area in the seaport of Guayaquil. He then sent a customs reform bill to Congress, in which the SRI would absorb the functions of the Ecuadorian Customs Corporation. Elsa de Mena, the SRI's director, had increased tax collection by 42% between 2000 and 2001, and the government hoped she could do the same for the customs service.

The IMF also said that customs administration should be moved from Guayaquil to Quito, the capital. But politicians on the coast complained that central government was taking their power away, so Congress vetoed the transfer. However, legislators have allowed Ms. de Mena to become president of the customs-service board of directors. This, as well as efforts to synchronize data between the tax service and the customs, is a small step in the right direction.

Straightening out customs would be the ultimate test of Mr. Gutierrez's self-declared war on corruption and bureaucracy. But corrupt officials, importers, and contraband-sellers will not give up without a fight. A complete reform of the system would take stronger action than the government has shown in years. A miracle, in fact.

International business transactions occur in many different forms over the course of a year. The measurement of all international economic transactions between the residents of a country and foreign residents is called the **balance of payments (BOP).**[1] Government policymakers need such measures of economic activity to evaluate the general competitiveness of domestic industry, to set exchange-rate or interest-rate policies or goals, and for many other purposes. Individuals and businesses use various BOP measures to gauge the growth and health of specific types of trade or financial transactions by country and regions of the world against the home country.

International transactions take many forms. Each of the following examples is an international economic transaction that is counted and captured in the U.S. balance of payments.

- U.S. imports of Honda automobiles, which are manufactured in Japan.
- A U.S.-based firm, Bechtel, is hired to manage the construction of a major water-treatment facility in the Middle East.
- The U.S. subsidiary of a French firm, Saint Gobain, pays profits (dividends) back to the parent firm in Paris.
- Daimler-Chrysler, the well-known German automobile manufacturer, purchases a small automotive parts manufacturer outside Chicago, Illinois.
- An American tourist purchases a hand-blown glass figurine in Venice, Italy.
- The U.S. government provides grant financing of military equipment for its NATO (North Atlantic Treaty Organization) military ally, Turkey.
- A Canadian dentist purchases a U.S. Treasury bill through an investment broker in Cleveland, Ohio.

These are just a small sample of the hundreds of thousands of international transactions that occur each year. The balance of payments provides a systematic method for the classification of all of these transactions. There is one rule of thumb that will always aid in the understanding of BOP accounting: Watch the direction of the movement of money.

The balance of payments is composed of a number of subaccounts that are watched quite closely by groups as diverse as investors on Wall Street, farmers in Iowa, politicians on Capitol Hill, and in boardrooms across America. These groups track and analyze the two major subaccounts, the **current account** and the **capital account,** on a continuing basis. Before describing these two subaccounts and the balance of payments as a whole, it is necessary to understand the rather unusual features of how balance of payments accounting is conducted.

Fundamentals of Balance of Payments Accounting

The balance of payments must balance. If it does not, something has either not been counted or counted properly. It is therefore improper to state that the BOP is in disequilibrium. It cannot be. The supply and demand for a country's currency may be imbalanced, but that is not the same thing. Subaccounts of the BOP, such as the merchandise trade balance, may be imbalanced, but the entire BOP of a single country is always balanced.

There are three main elements to the process of measuring international economic activity: (1) identifying what is and is not an international economic transaction; (2) understanding how the flow of goods, services, assets, and money creates debits and credits to the overall BOP; and (3) understanding the bookkeeping procedures for BOP accounting, called double entry.

DEFINING INTERNATIONAL ECONOMIC TRANSACTIONS

Identifying international transactions is ordinarily not difficult. The export of merchandise, goods such as trucks, machinery, computers, telecommunications equipment, and so forth, is obviously an international transaction. Imports such as French wine, Japanese cameras, and German automobiles are also clearly international transactions. But this merchandise trade is only a portion of the thousands of different international transactions that occur in the United States or any other country each year.

Many other international transactions are not so obvious. The purchase of a glass figure in Venice, Italy, by an American tourist is classified as a U.S. merchandise import. In fact, all expenditures made by American tourists around the globe that are for goods or services (meals, hotel accommodations, and so forth) are recorded in the U.S. balance of payments as imports of travel services in the current account. The purchase of a U.S. Treasury bill by a foreign resident is an international financial transaction and is dutifully recorded in the capital account of the U.S. balance of payments.

THE BOP AS A FLOW STATEMENT

The BOP is often misunderstood because many people believe it to be a balance sheet, rather than a cash flow statement. By recording all international transactions over a period of time, it is tracking the continuing flow of purchases and payments between a country and all other countries. It does not add up the value of all assets and liabilities of a country like a balance sheet does for an individual firm.

There are two types of business transactions that dominate the balance of payments:

1. **Real Assets:** The exchange of goods (for example, automobiles, computers, watches, textiles) and services (for example, banking services, consulting services, travel services) for other goods and services (barter) or for the more common type of payment, money.
2. **Financial Assets:** The exchange of financial claims (for example, stocks, bonds, loans, purchases or sales of companies) in exchange for other financial claims or money.

Although assets can be separated as to whether they are real or financial, it is often easier to simply think of all assets as being goods that can be bought and sold. An American tourist's purchase of a handwoven area rug in a shop in Bangkok is not all that different from a Wall Street banker buying a British government bond for investment purposes.

BOP ACCOUNTING: DOUBLE-ENTRY BOOKKEEPING

The balance of payments employs an accounting technique called **double-entry bookkeeping.** Double-entry bookkeeping is the age-old method of accounting in which every transaction produces a debit and a credit of the same amount. Simultaneously. It has to. A debit is created whenever an asset is increased, a liability is decreased, or an expense is increased. Similarly, a credit is created whenever an asset is decreased, a liability is increased, or an expense is decreased.

An example clarifies this process. A U.S. retail store imports from Japan $2 million worth of consumer electronics. A negative entry is made in the merchandise-import subcategory of the current account in the amount of $2 million. Simultaneously, a positive entry of the same $2 million is made in the capital account for the transfer of a $2 million bank account to the Japanese manufacturer. Obviously, the result of hundreds of thousands of such transactions and entries should theoretically result in a perfect balance.

That said, it is now a problem of application, and a problem it is. The measurement of all international transactions in and out of a country over a year is a daunting task. Mistakes, errors, and statistical discrepancies will occur. The primary problem is that although double-entry bookkeeping is employed in theory, the individual transactions are recorded independently. Current and capital account entries are recorded independent of one another, not together as double-entry bookkeeping would prescribe. It must then be recognized that there will be serious discrepancies (to use a nice term for it) between debits and credits, and the possibility in total that the balance of payments may not balance!

The following section describes the various balance of payment accounts, their meanings, and their relationships, using the United States as the example. The chapter then concludes with a discussion—and a number of examples—of how different countries with different policies or levels of economic development may differ markedly in their balance of payment accounts.

The Accounts of the Balance of Payments

The balance of payments is composed of two primary subaccounts, the *Current Account* and the *Financial/Capital Account*. In addition, the *Official Reserves Account* tracks government currency transactions, and a fourth statistical subaccount, the *Net Errors and Omissions Account*, is produced to preserve the balance in the BOP. The international economic relationships between countries do, however, continue to evolve, as the recent revision of the major accounts within the BOP discussed below indicates.[2]

THE CURRENT ACCOUNT

The *Current Account* includes all international economic transactions with income or payment flows occurring within the year, the *current* period. The *Current Account* consists of four subcategories:

1. **Goods Trade:** This is the export and import of goods. Merchandise trade is the oldest and most traditional form of international economic activity. Although many countries depend on imports of many goods (as they should according to the theory of comparative advantage), they also normally work to preserve either a balance of goods trade or even a surplus.

2. **Services Trade:** This is the export and import of services. Some common international services are financial services provided by banks to foreign importers and exporters, travel services of airlines, and construction services of domestic firms in other countries. For the major industrial countries, this subaccount has shown the fastest growth in the past decade.

3. **Income:** This category is predominantly *current income* associated with investments that were made in previous periods. If a U.S. firm created a subsidiary in South Korea to produce metal parts in a previous year, the proportion of net income that is paid back to the parent company in the current year (the divi-

dend) constitutes current investment income. Additionally, wages and salaries paid to nonresident workers is also included in this category.

4. **Current Transfers:** Transfers are the financial settlements associated with the change in ownership of real resources or financial items. Any transfer between countries that is one-way, a gift, or a grant, is termed a *current transfer*. A common example of a current transfer would be funds provided by the United States government to aid in the development of a less-developed nation. Transfers associated with the transfer of fixed assets are included in a new separate account, the Capital Account, which now follows the Current Account. The contents of what previously had been called the capital account are now included within the *Financial Account*.

All countries possess some amount of trade, most of which is merchandise. Many smaller and less-developed countries have little in the way of service trade, or items that fall under the income or transfers subaccounts.

The Current Account is typically dominated by the first component described—the export and import of merchandise. For this reason, the *Balance on Trade* (BOT), which is so widely quoted in the business press in most countries, refers specifically to the balance of exports and imports of goods trade only. For a larger industrialized country, however, the BOT is somewhat misleading because service trade is not included; it may be opposite in sign on net, and it may actually be fairly large as well.

Table 6.1 summarizes the Current Account and its components for the United States for the 1998–2001 period. As illustrated, the U.S. goods trade balance has

TABLE 6.1

The United States Current Account, 1998–2001 (billions of U.S. dollars)

	1998	1999	2000	2001
Goods exports	672	686	775	722
Goods imports	−917	−1030	−1224	−1146
Goods trade balance (BOT)	−245	−344	−450	−424
Services trade credits	260	271	290	276
Services trade debits	−183	−189	−219	−210
Services trade balance	78	81	71	66
Income receipts	259	291	353	284
Income payments	−252	−272	−331	−269
Income balance	8	18	22	14
Current transfers, credits	9	10	11	10
Current transfers, debits	−54	−58	−64	−60
Net transfers	45	−49	−53	−49
Current Account Balance	−204	−293	−410	−393

Source: Derived from International Monetary Fund's *Balance of Payments Statistics Yearbook, 2002.*

consistently been negative, but has been partially offset by the continuing surplus in services trade.

Goods Trade

Figure 6.1 places the Current Account values of Table 6.1 in perspective over time by dividing the Current Account into its two major components: (1) goods trade and (2) services trade and **investment income.** The first and most striking message is the magnitude of the goods trade deficit in 2000 and 2001 (a continuation of a position created in the early 1980s). The balance on services and income, although not large in comparison to net goods trade, has generally run a surplus over the past two decades.

The deficits in the BOT of the past decade have been an area of considerable concern for the United States. Merchandise trade is the original core of international trade. It has three major components: manufactured goods, agriculture, and fuels. The manufacturing of goods was the basis of the industrial revolution, and the focus of the theory of international trade described in the previous chapter. The U.S. goods trade deficit of the 1980s and 1990s was mainly caused by a decline in traditional manufacturing industries that have over history employed many of America's workers. Declines in the net trade balance in areas such as steel, automobiles, automotive parts, textiles, shoe manufacturing, and others caused massive economic and social disruption. The problems of dealing with these shifting trade balances will be discussed in detail in a later chapter.

FIGURE 6.1

U.S. Balance on Goods & Balance on Services & Income, 1985–2001 (billions of U.S. dollars)

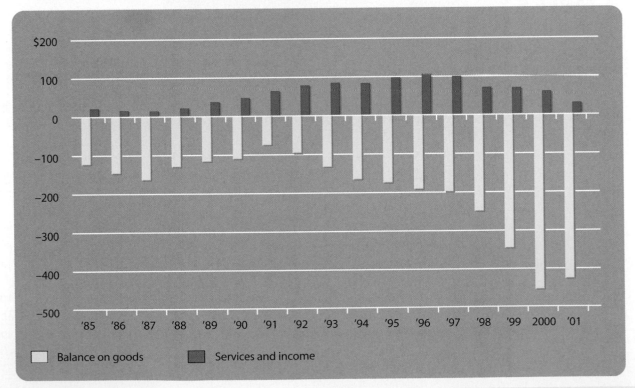

Source: International Monetary Fund, *Balance of Payments Statistics Yearbook, 2002.*

The most encouraging news for U.S. manufacturing trade is the growth of exports in recent years. A number of factors contributed to the growth of U.S. exports, such as the weaker dollar (which made U.S.-manufactured goods cheaper in terms of the currencies of other countries), more rapid economic growth in Europe, and a substantial increase in agricultural exports. Understanding merchandise import and export performance is much like understanding the market for any single product. The demand factors that drive both imports and exports are income, the economic growth rate of the buyer, and price (the price of the product in the eyes of the consumer after passing through an exchange rate). For example, U.S. merchandise imports reflect the income level and growth of American consumers and industry. As income rises, so does the demand for imports.

Exports follow the same principles but in the reversed position. U.S. merchandise exports depend not on the incomes of U.S. residents, but on the incomes of the buyers of U.S. products in all other countries around the world. When these economies are growing, the demand for U.S. products will also rise. However, the recent economic crises in Asia now raise questions regarding U.S. export growth in the immediate future. Focus on Politics illustrates how significant Asia is to U.S. export growth.

The service component of the U.S. Current Account is one of mystery to many. As illustrated in both Table 6.1 and Figure 6.1, the U.S. has consistently achieved a surplus in services trade income. The major categories of services include travel and passenger fares, transportation services, expenditures by U.S. students abroad and foreign students pursuing studies in the United States, telecommunications services, and financial services.

THE CAPITAL AND FINANCIAL ACCOUNT

The *Capital and Financial Account* of the balance of payments measures all international economic transactions of financial assets. It is divided into two major components, the *Capital Account* and the *Financial Account*.

Focus On

POLITICS

U.S. Exports to Asia and the Near East: How Important Are They?

The Asian economic crisis that began in the summer of 1997 had significant repercussions for all nations, both inside and outside the region. Yet Asia and the Near East still make up the largest developing market for U.S. merchandise imports and exports. In 1998, the region accounted for 22 percent of U.S. total trade (imports plus exports) and for 70 percent of trade with developing countries. The following table ranks the top ten countries in Asia and the Near East in 1998, according to U.S. exports.

Total Exports in U.S. Dollars to Asia and the Near East

	1998	Annual Growth (%) 1988–98	1997–98
Taiwan	18,157,132	4.3	−10.9
Singapore	15,673,479	10.7	−11.6
China	14,257,953	11.0	11.3
Hong Kong	12,923,479	8.6	−14.5
Saudi Arabia	10,524,898	11.1	24.5
Malaysia	8,952,869	15.4	−17.3
Israel	6,977,485	10.5	16.4
Philippines	6,736,172	13.9	−9.3
Thailand	5,233,361	12.0	−28.9
India	3,544,680	3.6	−2.0

Source: U.S. Merchandise Trade with Asia and the Near East, United States Agency for International Development, http://www.usaid.gov, accessed February 15, 2002.

- **The Capital Account.** The Capital Account is made up of transfers of financial assets and the acquisition and disposal of nonproduced/nonfinancial assets. The magnitude of capital transactions covered is of relatively minor amount, and will be included in principle in all of the following discussions of the financial account.

- **The Financial Account.** The financial account consists of three components: *direct investment, portfolio investment,* and *other asset investment.* Financial assets can be classified in a number of different ways including the length of the life of the asset (its maturity) and by the nature of the ownership (public or private). The Financial Account, however, uses a third way. It is classified by the degree of control over the assets or operations the claim represents: *portfolio investment,* where the investor has no control, or *direct investment,* where the investor exerts some explicit degree of control over the assets. (The contents of the Financial Account are for all intents and purposes the same as those of the Capital Account under the IMF's BOP accounting framework used prior to 1996. We will refer, from this point on, almost exclusively to the Financial Account.)

Table 6.2 shows the major subcategories of the U.S. capital account balance from 1998–2001, *direct investment, portfolio investment,* and *other long-term and short-term capital.*

1. **Direct Investment:** This is the net balance of capital dispersed out of and into the United States for the purpose of exerting control over assets. For example, if a U.S. firm either builds a new automotive parts facility in another country or actually purchases a company in another country, this would fall under *direct investment* in the U.S. balance of payments accounts. When the capital flows out

TABLE 6.2

The United States Financial Account and Components, 1998–2001 (billions of U.S. dollars)

	1998	1999	2000	2001
Direct Investment				
Direct investment abroad	−143	−189	−178	−128
Direct investment in the U.S.	179	289	308	131
Net direct investment	36	101	129	3
Portfolio Investment				
Assets, net	−136	−128	−128	−95
Liabilities, net	188	286	420	426
Net portfolio investment	51	157	292	331
Other Investment				
Other investment assets	−74	−169	−300	−144
Other investment liabilities	57	167	288	196
Net other investment	−17	−2	−12	52
Net Financial Account Balance	71	256	410	387

Source: Derived from International Monetary Fund's *Balance of Payments Statistics Yearbook, 2002.*

of the United States, it enters the balance of payments as a negative cash flow. If, however, foreign firms purchase firms in the United States (for example, Sony of Japan purchased Columbia Pictures in 1989) it is a capital inflow and enters the balance of payments positively. Whenever 10 percent or more of the voting shares in a U.S. company is held by foreign investors, the company is classified as the U.S. affiliate of a foreign company, and a *foreign direct investment*. Similarly, if U.S. investors hold 10 percent or more of the control in a company outside the United States, that company is considered the foreign affiliate of a U.S. company.

2. **Portfolio Investment:** This is net balance of capital that flows in and out of the United States, but does not reach the 10 percent ownership threshold of direct investment. If a U.S. resident purchases shares in a Japanese firm, but does not attain the 10 percent threshold, it is considered a *portfolio investment* (and in this case an outflow of capital). The purchase or sale of debt securities (like U.S. Treasury bills) across borders is also classified as *portfolio investment* because debt securities by definition do not provide the buyer with ownership or control.

3. **Other Investment Assets/Liabilities:** This final category consists of various short-term and long-term trade credits, cross-border loans from all types of financial institutions, currency deposits and bank deposits, and other accounts receivable and payable related to cross-border trade.

Direct Investment

Figure 6.2 shows how the major subaccounts of the U.S. capital account, *net direct investment*, *portfolio investment*, and *other investment* have changed since 1985.

The boom in foreign investment into the United States, or foreign resident purchases of assets in the United States, during the 1980s was extremely controversial. The source of concern over foreign investment in any country, including the United States, focuses on two topics—**control** and **profit.** Most countries possess restrictions on what foreigners may own in their country. This is based on the premise that domestic land, assets, and industry in general should be held by residents of the country. For example, up until 1990 it was not possible for a foreign firm to own more than 20 percent of any company in Finland. This rule is the norm, rather than the exception. The United States has traditionally had few restrictions on what foreign residents or firms can own or control in the United States; most restrictions that remain today are related to national security concerns. As opposed to many of the traditional debates over whether international trade should be free or not, there is not the same consensus that international investment should necessarily be free. This is a question that is still very much a domestic political concern first, and an international economic issue second.

The second major source of concern over foreign direct investment is who receives the profits from the enterprise. Foreign companies owning firms in the United States will ultimately profit from the activities of the firms, or put another way, from the efforts of American workers. In spite of evidence that foreign firms in the United States reinvest most of the profits in the United States (in fact at a higher rate than domestic firms), the debate has continued on possible profit drains. Regardless of the actual choices made, workers of any nation feel the profits of their work should remain in the hands of their own citizens. Once again, this is in many ways a political and emotional concern rather than an economic one.

The choice of words used to describe foreign investment can also influence public opinion. If these massive capital inflows are described as "capital investments from

FIGURE 6.2

**The United States Financial Account, 1985–2001
(billions of U.S. dollars)**

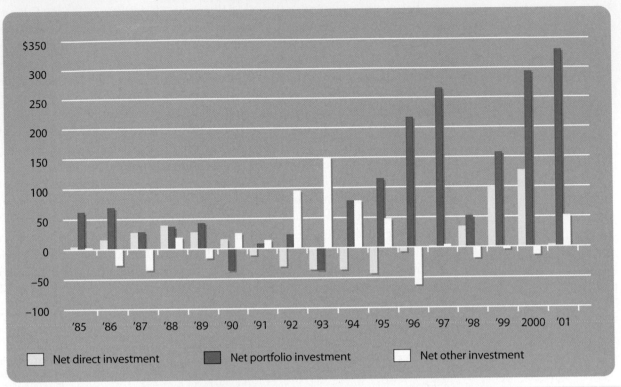

Net direct investment   Net portfolio investment   Net other investment

Source: International Monetary Fund, *Balance of Payments Statistics Yearbook, 2002.*

all over the world showing their faith in the future of American industry," the net capital surplus is represented as decidedly positive. If, however, the net capital surplus is described as resulting in "the United States as the world's largest debtor nation," the negative connotation is obvious. Both are essentially spins on the economic principles at work. Capital, whether short-term or long-term, flows to where it believes it can earn the greatest return for the level of risk. Although in an accounting sense that is "international debt," when the majority of the capital inflow is in the form of direct investment and a long-term commitment to jobs, production, services, technological, and other competitive investments, the impact on the competitiveness of American industry (an industry located within the United States) is increased. The "net debtor" label is misleading in that it inappropriately invites comparison with large debt crisis conditions suffered by many countries in the past, like Mexico and Brazil.

Portfolio Investment

Portfolio investment is capital invested in activities that are purely profit-motivated (return), rather than ones made in the prospect of controlling or managing the investment. Investments that are purchases of debit securities, bonds, interest-bearing bank accounts, and the like are only intended to earn a return. They provide no vote or control over the party issuing the debt. Purchases of debt issued by the U.S. government (U.S. Treasury bills, notes, and bonds) by foreign investors constitute net portfolio investment in the United States.

As illustrated in Figure 6.2, portfolio investment has shown a much more volatile behavior than net direct investment over the past decade. Many U.S. debt securities, such as U.S. Treasury securities and corporate bonds, were in high demand in the late 1980s, while surging emerging markets in both debt and equities caused a reversal in direction in the 1990s. The motivating forces for portfolio investment flows are always the same, *return* and *risk*. This theoretical fact, however, does not make them any the more predictable.

Current and Financial Account Balance Relationships

Figure 6.3 (A, B, and C) illustrates the current and financial account balances for Germany, Japan, and the United States over recent years. What the figure shows is one of the basic economic and accounting relationships of the balance of payments: *the inverse relationship between the Current and Financial accounts.* (The only exception is Germany in 1999, the year in which the euro was introduced.) This inverse relationship is not accidental. The methodology of the balance of payments, double-entry bookkeeping, requires that the current and financial accounts be offsetting. Countries experiencing large current account deficits "finance" these purchases through equally large surpluses in the financial account and vice versa.

FIGURE 6.3(A)

The U.S. Current and Financial Account Balances, 1993–2001 (billions of U.S. dollars)

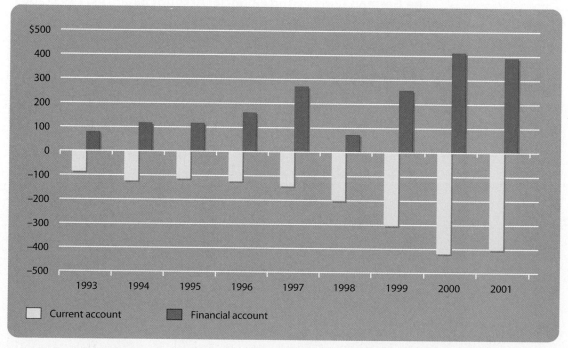

Source: International Monetary Fund, *Balance of Payments Statistics Yearbook, 2002.*

FIGURE 6.3(B)

The Japanese Current and Financial Account Balances, 1993–2001 (billions of U.S. dollars)

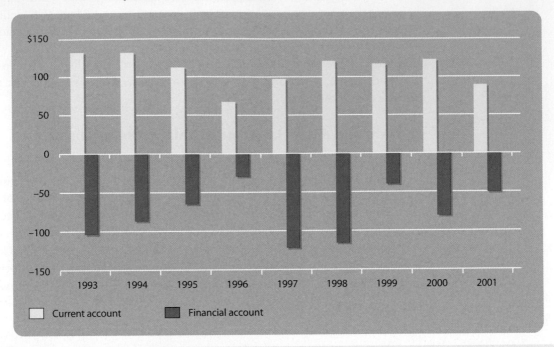

Source: International Monetary Fund, *Balance of Payments Statistics Yearbook, 2002.*

FIGURE 6.3(C)

The German Current and Financial Account Balances, 1993–2001 (billions of U.S. dollars)

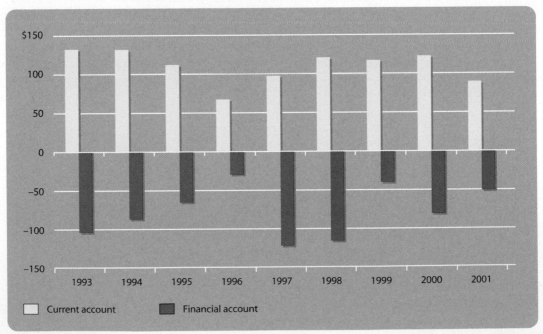

Source: International Monetary Fund, *Balance of Payments Statistics Yearbook, 2002.*

NET ERRORS AND OMISSIONS

As noted before, because Current Account and Financial Account entries are collected and recorded separately, errors or statistical discrepancies will occur. The **net errors and omissions account** (this is the title used by the International Monetary Fund) makes sure that the BOP actually balances.

OFFICIAL RESERVES ACCOUNT

The **official reserves account** is the total currency and metallic reserves held by official monetary authorities within the country. These reserves are normally composed of the major currencies used in international trade and financial transactions (so-called "hard currencies" like the U.S. dollar, German mark, and Japanese yen) and gold.

The significance of official reserves depends generally on whether the country is operating under a **fixed exchange rate** regime or a **floating exchange rate** system. If a country's currency is fixed, this means that the government of the country officially declares that the currency is convertible into a fixed amount of some other currency. For example, for many years the South Korean won was fixed to the U.S. dollar at 484 won equal to 1 U.S. dollar. It is the government's responsibility to maintain this fixed rate (also called *parity rate*). If for some reason there is an excess supply of Korean won on the currency market, to prevent the value of the won from falling, the South Korean government must support the won's value by purchasing won on the open market (by spending its hard currency reserves, its *official reserves*) until the excess supply is eliminated. Under a floating rate system, the government possesses no such responsibility and the role of official reserves is diminished.

The Balance of Payments in Total

The balance of payments is cross-border financial management of certain currencies balanced against other currencies.

Table 6.3 provides the official balance of payments for the United States as presented by the International Monetary Fund (IMF), the multinational organization that collects these statistics for over 160 different countries around the globe. Now that the individual accounts and the relationships among the accounts have been discussed, Table 6.3 gives a comprehensive overview of how the individual accounts are combined to create some of the most useful summary measures for multinational business managers.

The current account (line A in Table 6.3), the capital account (line B), and the financial account (line C) combine to form the *basic balance (Total, Groups A through C)*. This is one of the most frequently used summary measures of the BOP. It is used to describe the international economic activity of the nation as determined by market forces, not by government decisions (such as currency market intervention). The U.S. *basic balance* totaled a deficit of $5.77 billion in 2001. A second frequently used summary measure, the overall balance, also called the official settlements balance (*Total of Groups A through D* in Table 6.3), was at a surplus of $4.93 billion in 2001.

The meaning of the balance of payments has changed over the past 30 years. As long as most of the major industrial countries were still operating under fixed exchange rates, the interpretation of the BOP was relatively straightforward. A surplus in the BOP implied that the demand for the country's currency exceeded the supply, and that the government should then allow the currency value to increase (*revalue*) or to intervene and accumulate additional foreign currency reserves in the Official Reserves Account. This would occur as the government sold its own currency in exchange for other currencies, thus building up its stores of hard currencies. A deficit

TABLE 6.3   The United States Balance of Payments, 1996–2001 (billions of U.S. dollars)

	1996	1997	1998	1999	2000	2001
A. Current Account	**−117.84**	**−128.36**	**−203.85**	**−292.86**	**−410.30**	**−393.39**
Goods: exports fob	614.02	680.33	672.38	686.28	774.64	721.75
Goods: imports fob	−803.12	−876.51	−917.12	−1029.98	−1224.43	−1145.98
Balance on Goods	−189.10	−196.18	−244.74	−343.70	−449.79	−424.23
Services: credit	238.17	254.70	260.28	270.90	289.63	276.28
Services: debit	−150.91	−166.28	−182.53	−189.47	−218.52	−210.34
Balance on Goods and Services	−101.84	−107.76	−166.99	−262.27	−378.68	−358.29
Income: credit	225.86	260.58	259.40	290.56	353.03	283.76
Income: debit	−201.77	−240.39	−251.76	−272.39	−331.22	−269.39
Balance on Goods, Services, and Income	−77.75	−87.57	−159.35	−244.10	−356.87	−343.92
Current transfers: credit	8.89	8.49	9.19	9.57	10.65	10.47
Current transfers: debit	−48.98	−49.28	−53.69	−58.33	−64.08	−59.95
B. Capital Account	**0.69**	**0.35**	**0.70**	**−3.39**	**0.84**	**0.83**
Capital account: credit	0.69	0.35	0.70	0.60	0.84	0.83
Capital account: debit	0.00	0.00	0.00	−3.99	0.00	0.00
Total, Groups A Plus B	*−117.15*	*−128.01*	*−203.15*	*−296.25*	*−409.46*	*−392.56*
C. Financial Account	**130.52**	**220.16**	**70.60**	**256.11**	**409.81**	**386.79**
Direct investment	−5.36	0.77	36.39	100.53	129.45	2.96
Direct investment abroad	−91.88	−104.82	−142.64	−188.91	−178.29	−127.84
Direct investment in United States	86.52	105.59	179.03	289.44	307.74	130.80
Portfolio investment assets	−149.83	−118.98	−136.13	−128.44	−127.50	−94.66
Equity securities	−82.85	−57.58	−101.28	−114.31	−103.64	−106.81
Debt securities	−66.98	−61.40	−34.85	−14.13	−23.86	12.15
Portfolio investment liabilities	332.78	333.11	187.58	285.59	419.90	426.06
Equity securities	11.06	67.04	41.96	112.29	193.51	121.42
Debt securities	321.72	266.07	145.62	173.30	226.39	304.64
Other investment assets	−178.90	−262.83	−74.21	−169.00	−300.40	−143.54
Monetary authorities	0.00	0.00	0.00	0.00	0.00	0.00
General government	−1.00	0.06	−0.42	2.75	−0.94	−0.48
Banks	−91.56	−141.13	−35.58	−76.27	−148.66	−128.70
Other sectors	−86.34	−121.76	−38.21	−95.48	−150.80	−14.36
Other investment liabilities	131.83	268.09	56.97	167.43	288.36	195.97
Monetary authorities	56.88	−18.86	6.89	24.59	−6.70	35.10
General government	0.73	−2.7	−3.26	−0.85	−0.48	−4.35
Banks	22.19	171.32	30.27	67.19	122.72	80.39
Other sectors	52.03	118.33	23.07	76.50	172.82	84.83
Total, Groups A through C	*13.37*	*92.15*	*−132.55*	*−40.14*	*0.35*	*−5.77*
D. Net Errors and Omissions	**−20.04**	**−91.13**	**139.29**	**31.41**	**−0.05**	**10.70**
Total, Groups A through D	*−6.67*	*1.02*	*6.74*	*−8.73*	*0.30*	*4.93*
E. Reserves and Related Items	6.67	−1.02	−6.74	8.73	−0.30	−4.93

Note: Totals may not match original source due to rounding.

Source: International Monetary Fund, *Balance of Payments Statistics Yearbook, 2002,* p. 939.

in the BOP implied an excess supply of the country's currency on world markets, and the government would then either *devalue* the currency or expend its official reserves to support its value. But the transition to floating exchange rate regimes in the 1970s (described in the following chapter) changed the focus from the total BOP to its various subaccounts like the Current and Financial Account balances. These are the indicators of economic activities and currency repercussions to come. The recent crises in Mexico (1994), Asia (1997), Turkey (2001), and Argentina and Venezuela (2002) highlight the continuing changes in the role of the balance of payments. As the Focus on Politics in the Euro Area describes, even the changing definition of a country or group of countries has a balance of payments significance.

The Balance of Payments and Economic Crises

The sum of cross-border international economic activity—the balance of payments—can be used by international managers to forecast economic conditions and, in some cases, the likelihood of economic crises. The mechanics of international economic crisis often follow a similar path of development:

1. A country that experiences rapidly expanding current account deficits will simultaneously build financial account surpluses (the inverse relationship noted previously in this chapter).
2. The capital that flows into a country, giving rise to the financial account surplus, acts as the "financing" for the growing merchandise/services deficits—the constituent components of the current account deficit.
3. Some event, whether it be a report, a speech, an action by a government or business inside or outside the country, raises the question of the country's economic

Focus On

POLITICS

The Balance of Payments for the Euro Area

As the European Union continues down the path of political and economic integration, and following the introduction of the single currency—the euro—it is now meaningful to discuss the EU's consolidated balance of payments. The International Monetary Fund (IMF) now publishes, along with all of the individual member countries, the various balance of payments accounts for the 16-country Euro Area. The major balance of payments accounts, to date, are as follows:

	1999	*2000*	*2001*
Current Account	−19.31	−54.91	−2.15
Capital Account	13.65	8.90	7.64
Financial Account	0.49	73.00	−79.51
Net Errors and Omissions	−6.41	−43.14	57.13
Reserves and Related Items	11.58	16.14	16.89

The Euro Area experienced a major shift from a Current Account deficit–Financial Account surplus in 2000, to a Current Account surplus–Financial Account deficit in 2001.

Source: International Monetary Fund's *Balance of Payments Statistics Yearbook, 2002,* p. 301.

stability. Investors of many kinds, portfolio and direct investors in the country, fearing economic problems in the near future, withdraw capital from the country rapidly to avoid any exposure to this risk. This is prudent for the individual, but catastrophic for the whole if all individuals move similarly.

4. The rapid withdrawal of capital from the country, so-called "capital flight," results in the loss of the financial account surplus, creating a severe deficit in the country's overall balance of payments. This is typically accompanied by rapid currency depreciation (if a floating-rate currency) or currency devaluation (if a fixed-rate currency).

International debt and economic crises have occurred for as long as there have been international trade and commerce. And they will occur again. Each crisis has its own unique characteristics, but all follow some of the economic fundamentals described above (the one additional factor which differentiates many of the crises is whether inflation is a component). The recent Asian economic crisis was a devastating reminder of the tenuousness of international economic relationships. Focus on Politics describes India's recent initiative to solve a worsening balance of trade by attracting the offshore capital held by its own residents.

THE ASIAN CRISIS

The roots of the Asian currency crisis extended from a fundamental change in the economics of the region—the transition of many Asian nations from net exporters to net importers. Starting as early as 1990 in Thailand, the rapidly expanding economies of the Far East began importing more than they exported, requiring major net capital inflows to support their currencies. As long as the capital continued to flow in—for manufacturing plants, dam projects, infrastructure development, and even real estate speculation—the pegged exchange rates of the region could be maintained. When the investment capital inflows stopped, however, crisis was inevitable.

The most visible roots of the crisis were the excesses in capital flows into Thailand in 1996 and early 1997. With rapid economic growth and rising profits forming the backdrop, Thai firms, banks, and finance companies had ready access to capital on the international markets, finding cheap U.S. dollar loans offshore. Thai banks continued to raise capital internationally, extending credit to a variety of domestic investments

Focus On ⬇

POLITICS

India Tries to Borrow Its Way Out of Trouble

In October 2000, India hit on a not-so-novel idea to shield an economy made vulnerable by high international oil prices. The government floated a scheme for State Bank of India, the country's largest bank, to sell five-year foreign currency deposits to expatriate Indians to help tackle a worsening balance of payments situation. By October 2001, SBI, whose largest owner is the Indian central bank, had collected $5.5 billion from the sale of India Millennium Deposits (IMD).

India's oil import bill was also expected to double to about $18 billion. A widening trade deficit and a sell-off by foreign portfolio investors put the balance of payments in the red by about $1 billion in the quarter ended June 2000, as compared with a surplus of $3.32 billion in the previous quarter. The rupee had lost around 6 percent of its value against the dollar.

Sources: "An Incredible Shrinking Government," *The Economist*, February 7, 2002, http://www.economist.com; Niharika Bisaria, "Going on a Millenium Hunt," October 18, 2001, http://www.hometrade.com; Kala Rao, "India Tries to Borrow Its Way Out of Trouble," *Euromoney*, London, November 2000.

and enterprises beyond the level that the Thai economy could support. Capital flows into the Thai market hit record rates, pouring into investments of all kinds, including manufacturing, real estate, and even equity market margin-lending. As the investment "bubble" expanded, some participants raised questions about the economy's ability to repay the rising debt. The baht came under sudden and severe pressure.

Currency Collapse

The Thai government and central bank intervened in the foreign exchange markets directly (using up precious hard currency reserves) and indirectly (by raising interest rates to attempt to stop the continual out-flow). The Thai investment markets ground to a halt, causing massive currency losses and bank failures. On July 2, 1997, the Thai central bank, which had been expending massive amounts of its limited foreign exchange reserves to defend the baht's value, finally allowed the baht to float (or sink in this case). The baht fell 17 percent against the U.S. dollar and over 12 percent against the Japanese yen in a matter of hours. By November, the baht had fallen from Baht25/US$ to Baht40/US$, a fall of about 38 percent. As illustrated in Table 6.4, Thailand was not alone in creating massive current account deficits in the period leading up to 1997. In fact, with the rather special exceptions of China and Singapore, all of East Asia was in current account deficit beginning in 1994.

Within days, a number of neighboring Asian nations, some with and some without characteristics similar to Thailand, came under speculative attack by currency traders and capital markets. The Philippine peso, the Malaysian ringgit, and the Indonesian rupiah all fell within months, as shown in Figure 6.4. In late October, Taiwan caught the markets off balance with a surprise competitive devaluation of 15 percent. The Taiwanese devaluation seemed only to renew the momentum of the crisis. Although the Hong Kong dollar survived (at great expense to the central bank's foreign exchange reserves), the Korean won was not so lucky. In November the historically stable Korean won also fell victim, falling from Won900/US$ to more than Won1100/US$. By the end of November the Korean government was in the process of negotiating a US$50 billion bailout of its financial sector with the International Monetary Fund (IMF). The only currency which had not fallen besides the Hong Kong dollar was the Chinese renminbi, which was not freely convertible. Although the renminbi had not been devalued, there was rising speculation that the Chinese government would devalue it for competitive reasons. Figure 6.4 shows the change in exchange rates for four of these Asian economies.

Causal Complexities

The Asian economic crisis—for the crisis was more than just a currency collapse—had many roots besides the traditional balance of payments difficulties. The causes are different in each country, yet there are specific underlying similarities that allow comparison: corporate socialism, corporate governance, and banking stability and management.

Corporate Socialism   Although Western markets have long known the cold indifference of the free market, the countries of post–World War II Asia have largely known only the good. Because of the influence of government and politics in the business arena, even in the event of failure, government would not allow firms to fail, workers to lose their jobs, or banks to close. When the problems reached the size seen in 1997, the business liability exceeded the capacities of governments to bail business out. Practices that had persisted for decades without challenge, such as lifetime employment, were now no longer sustainable. The result was a painful lesson in the harshness of the marketplace.

TABLE 6.4 Current Account Balances of East Asian Countries, 1988–1999 (millions of U.S. dollars)

	1988	1989	1990	1991	1992	1993	1994	1995	1996	1997	1998	1999
Deficit Countries												
Indonesia	–1,397	–1,108	–2,988	–4,260	–2,780	–2,106	–2,792	–6,431	–7,663	–4,889	4,096	5,785
Korea	14,538	5,387	–1,745	–8,291	–3,944	990	–3,867	–8,507	–23,006	–8,167	40,365	24,477
Malaysia	1,867	315	–870	–4,183	–2,167	–2,991	–4,520	–8,644	–4,462	–5,935	9,529	12,606
Philippines	–390	–1,456	–2,695	–1,034	–1,000	–3,016	–2,950	–1,980	–3,953	–4,351	1,546	7,910
Thailand	–1,654	–2,498	–7,281	–7,571	–6,303	–6,364	–8,085	–13,554	–14,691	–3,021	14,243	12,428
Subtotal	**12,964**	**640**	**–15,579**	**–25,339**	**–16,194**	**–13,487**	**–22,214**	**–39,116**	**–53,775**	**–26,363**	**68,779**	**63,206**
Surplus Countries												
China	–3,802	–4,317	11,997	13,272	6,401	–11,609	6,908	1,618	7,243	36,963	31,472	15,667
Singapore	1,882	2,923	3,097	4,884	5,915	4,211	11,400	14,436	13,898	16,912	21,025	21,254
Subtotal	**–1,920**	**–1,394**	**15,094**	**18,156**	**12,316**	**–7,398**	**18,308**	**16,054**	**21,141**	**53,875**	**52,497**	**36,921**
										Asian	Crisis	

"Deficit Countries" are those with current account balances which were negative for the 1994 to 1997 period, leading up to the Asian Crisis. "Surplus Countries" are those with current account balances which were positive for the 1994 to 1997 period. Hong Kong and Taiwan are not listed, as they are not individually reported by the IMF. The Asian Crisis actually began with the devaluation of the Thai baht on July 1, 1997. However, given annual balance of payments statistics, it is shown here between the 1997 and 1998 calendar years.

Source: Data abstracted from the *Balance of Payments Statistics Yearbook 2000.* International Monetary Fund.

FIGURE 6.4

Dollar Index

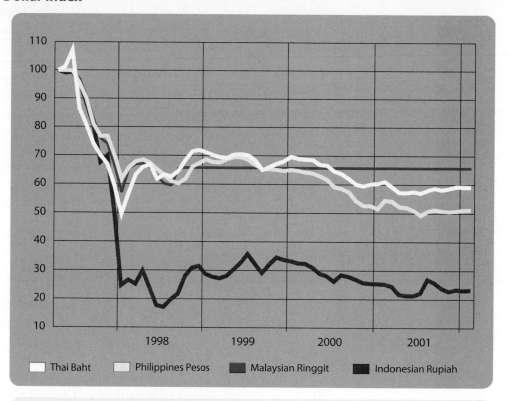

Thai Baht · Philippines Pesos · Malaysian Ringgit · Indonesian Rupiah

Source: Pacific Exchange Rate Service, http://fx.sauder.ubc.ca © 2002 by Prof. Werner Antweiler, University of British Columbia, Vancouver B.C., Canada. Time period shown in diagram: April 1, 1997 through February 1, 2002. Reproduced with permission.

Corporate Governance An expression largely unused until the 1990s, corporate governance refers to the complex process of how a firm is managed and operated, who it is accountable to, and how it reacts to changing business conditions. There is little doubt that many firms operating within the Far Eastern business environments were often largely controlled by either families or groups related to the governing party or body of the country. The interests of stockholders and creditors were often secondary at best to the primary motivations of corporate management. Without focusing on "the bottom line," the bottom line deteriorated.

Banking Liquidity and Management Banking is one of those sectors which has definitely fallen out of fashion in the past two decades. Bank regulatory structures and markets have been deregulated nearly without exception around the globe. The central role played by banks in the conduct of business, however, was largely ignored and underestimated. As firms across Asia collapsed, as government coffers were emptied, as speculative investments made by the banks themselves failed, banks closed. Without banks, the "plumbing" of business conduct was shut down. Firms could not obtain the necessary working capital financing they needed to manufacture their products or provide their services. This pivotal role of banking liquidity was the focus of the International Monetary Fund's bail-out efforts.

The Asian economic crisis had global impact. What started as a currency crisis quickly became a regionwide recession (or depression, depending on definitions).[3]

The slowed economies of the region quickly caused major reductions in world demand for many products, commodities especially. World oil markets, copper markets, and agricultural products all saw severe price falls as demand fell. These price falls were immediately noticeable in declining earnings and growth prospects for other emerging economies.

The post-1997 period has been one of dramatic reversal for the countries of East Asia. As Table 6.4 illustrates, beginning in 1998, every nation within East Asia listed has run a current account surplus as a result of massive recession (imports fell voluntarily, as well as being restricted by governments), significant domestic currency devaluation (resulting in significantly lower purchasing power, hence the countries could no longer afford to purchase imports), and rising exports (as currency devaluation made their merchandise relatively cheaper for countries in other parts of the world to purchase). Unfortunately, the adjustment period has been one of massive unemployment, social disruption, and economic reconstruction with high human cost.

Capital Mobility

As we have seen, the degree to which capital moves freely cross-border is critically important to a country's balance of payments. We have already seen how the United States, while experiencing a deficit in its Current Account balance over the past 20 years, has simultaneously enjoyed a Financial Account surplus. But the ability of capital to move involves both economic and political factors. The openness of the U.S. economy, the depth and breadth of its financial markets, and its relative political stability, have all contributed to making the United States an attractive nation for capital investment of all kinds. Other countries, however, depending on their economic prospects and their political openness, may not always attract capital.

Before leaving our discussion of the balance of payments we need to gain additional insights into the history of capital mobility and the contribution of capital inflows and capital outflows (so-called *capital flight*) to the balance of payments of selected countries in recent years.

Has capital always been free to move in and out of a country? Definitely not. The ability of foreign investors to own property, buy businesses, or purchase stocks and bonds in other countries has been controversial. Obstfeld and Taylor (2001) studied the globalization of capital markets and concluded that the pattern illustrated in Figure 6.5 is a fair representation of the "conventional wisdom" on the openness of global capital markets in recent history. Since 1860, the gold standard in use prior to the First World War and the post-1971 period of floating exchange rates have seen the greatest ability of capital to flow cross-border. Note that Obstfeld and Taylor use no specific quantitative measure of mobility. The diagram uses only a stylized distinction between "low" and "high," combining two primary factors, the exchange rate regimes and the state of international political and economic relations.

Obstfeld and Taylor argue that the post-1860 era can be subdivided into four distinct periods.

1. The first, 1860–1914, was a period characterized by continuously increasing capital openness as more and more countries adopted the gold standard and expanded international trade relations.
2. The second period, 1914–1945, was a period of global economic destruction. The combined destructive forces of two world wars and a worldwide depression

FIGURE 6.5

A Stylized View of Capital Mobility in Modern History

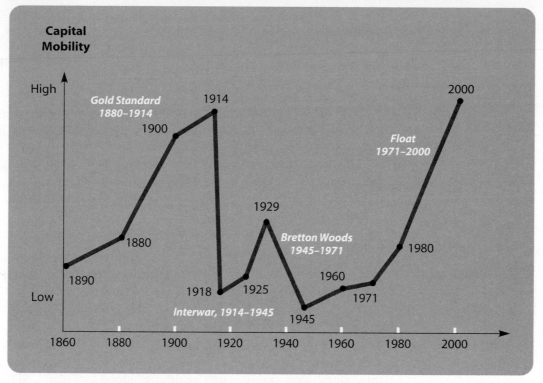

Source:"Globalization and Capital Markets," Maurice Obstfeld and Alan M. Taylor, NBER Conference Paper, May 4–5, 2001, p. 6.

led most nations to move toward highly nationalistic and isolationist political and economic policies, effectively eliminating any significant movement of capital between countries.

3. The third period, 1945–1971, the Bretton Woods era, saw a great expansion of international trade in goods and services. This time also saw the slow but steady recovery of capital markets. The fixed-exchange-rate regime of Bretton Woods may have failed because the sheer forces of global capital could no longer be held in check.

4. The fourth and current period, 1971–2000 [2002], is a period characterized by floating exchange rates and economic volatility, but rapidly expanding cross-border capital flows. The major industrial countries either no longer try, no longer need, or no longer can control the movement of capital. Because currency markets are free to reflect underlying economic fundamentals and investor sentiments about the future, capital movements increased in response to this openness.

Of course this is a stylized global view, and the situations of the individual countries always have their own characteristics. The currency crises of the latter half of the 1990s and of the early twenty-first century may result in the reversal of this freedom of cross-border capital movement; it is still too early to tell. It is clear, however, that the ability to move instantaneously and massively cross-border has been one of the major factors in the severity of recent currency crises.

CAPITAL FLIGHT

Many recent global and financial crises have been characterized by sudden and shocking outflows of capital from the national economy, *capital flight*. Although no single accepted definition of capital flight exists, the term is traditionally used to describe sudden capital withdrawals by investors from countries in which they perceive a political, economic, or currency crisis to be forthcoming. The capital is typically portfolio investments and bank deposits (a component of "other investment" within the Financial Accounts in the balance of payments), and may be owned or controlled by both domestic and foreign investors. Much like a bank run, it is typically characterized by nearly irrational or panic behavior, as no one wants to be the last one in line to try to take their money out of a falling economy.

The rapid and sometimes illegal transfer of capital out of a country poses significant economic and political problems. Many heavily indebted countries have suffered significant capital flight, which has compounded their problems of debt service.

Five primary mechanisms exist by which capital may be moved from one country to another.

1. Transfers via the usual international payments mechanisms, regular bank transfers, are obviously the easiest and lowest cost, and are legal. Most economically healthy countries allow free exchange of their currencies, but of course for such countries "capital flight" is not a problem.
2. Transfer of physical currency by bearer (the proverbial smuggling of cash in the false bottom of a suitcase) is more costly and, for transfers out of many countries, illegal. Such transfers may be deemed illegal for balance of payments reasons or to make difficult the movement of money from the drug trade or other illegal activities.
3. The transfer of cash into collectibles or precious metals, which are then transferred across borders.
4. *Money laundering*, the cross-border purchase of assets that are then managed in a way that hides the movement of money and its ownership.
5. False invoicing of international trade transactions. Capital is moved through the underinvoicing of exports or the overinvoicing of imports, where the difference between the invoiced amount and the actually agreed-upon payment is deposited in banking institutions in a country of choice.

The concern over capital movements—both in and out of a country—has led many countries to institute a variety of capital controls at different times in history. The following Focus on Politics provides a detailed illustration of how government policies may be used to restrict the movement of capital in the modern global economy.

Capital Inflows: The Case of China

The Chinese balance of payments serves as an interesting example of one country's ongoing efforts to manage its current and financial accounts. As illustrated in Figure 6.6, China was the recipient of massive capital inflows between 1993 and 1997. This reflected a return to political norms following the Tiananmen Square events of 1989, and the perceived growing promise of the Chinese marketplace. Simultaneously, the country enjoyed a small but positive current account surplus. Both accounts, however, were heavily managed through complex Chinese regulation and intervention. Capital inflows are through a permit process, with foreign investors being largely limited to joint venture investments within the country. At the same time, the Chinese govern-

Focus On ⬇

Malaysian Capital Controls

"All these countries have spent 40 years trying to build up their economies, and a moron like Soros comes along with a lot of money and undermines them. Currency trading is unnecessary, unproductive and immoral . . . it should be illegal."

—Malaysian Prime Minister Mahathir Mohammed on George Soros's purported role in the instigation of the Asian Crisis in July 1997

Following Prime Minister Mahathir's comments, Malaysia instituted significant restrictions and controls on the ability of investors of all kinds, from currency speculators to multinational corporations, to move capital both in and out of Malaysia. Malaysia required all investors to file documents stating the explicit reasons behind capital movements, particularly withdrawals from Malaysian banks and securities markets. After filing and consideration, the government would then either accept or deny the application for approval. The result was a growing reluctance on the part of international investors to put money into Malaysia as they feared the ability to pull the capital out if deemed necessary at a future date.

Capital controls are historically a double-edged sword for government use. While controls may effectively prevent capital flight, or what is sometimes referred to as *hot-money flows,* they also frequently act as a deterrent to new investment capital entering the national market. A policy intended to protect a nation's economic stability and balance of payments may have the unintended consequence of shrinking the country's balance of payments future.

ment has aggressively promoted exports of many products while exercising extreme control over imports, both in content and quantity.

The onslaught of the Asian Crisis in 1997, however, clearly brought the capital inflows to a halt (India suffered a similar fate as well). The Chinese financial account

FIGURE 6.6

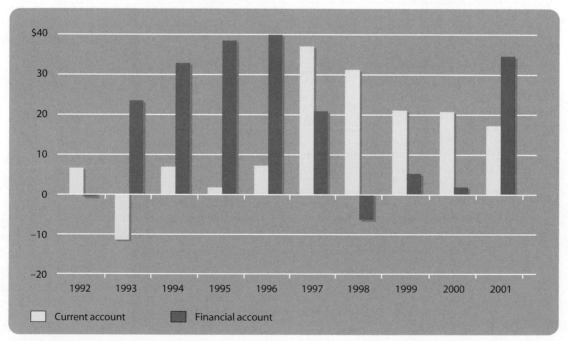

China's Current and Financial Account Balance, 1992–2001 (billions of U.S. dollars)

Source: International Monetary Fund, *Balance of Payments Statistics Yearbook, 2002,* p. 181.

balance fell back, suffering a deficit in 1998, and near zero balances in 1999 and 2000. But with the new millennium (remember, the official start of the new century was January 1, 2001, not 2000), China's attractiveness returned, as it was the recipient of more than $35 billion in capital inflows in 2001 alone. This massive capital injection by global investors—primarily multinational corporations—was indicative of the perceived attractiveness of the Chinese economy for future economic growth and the renewed comfort these investors felt with the current Chinese political regime.

Capital Outflows: The Case of Turkey

Turkey's economic and financial crisis of 2000–2001 serves as a prime example of how a country's balance of payments can deteriorate—or essentially collapse—in a very short period of time. Although there were a series of political, economic, and social ills that combined during the height of the crisis, a very large part of Turkey's crisis arose from capital flight. Figure 6.7 illustrates some of Turkey's financial accounts and how they deteriorated suddenly in 2001.

In the late 1990s many of Turkey's largest and most powerful banks borrowed large quantities of U.S. dollars on the international financial markets. The capital was not used for loans or development in Turkey, but rather on speculation related to Turkish government bonds. Bank funds and financing is listed in the "net other investment" subcategory of the balance of payments, and Turkey's net inflows 1997–2000 are obvious from Figure 6.7. However, a political crisis in February 2001 initiated a series of economic crises in Turkey, including the collapse of its currency. With this crisis, the capital that had so readily flowed into Turkey in the previous years now flew out. The

FIGURE 6.7

Turkey's Financial Accounts in Crisis, 1997–2001 (billions of U.S. dollars)

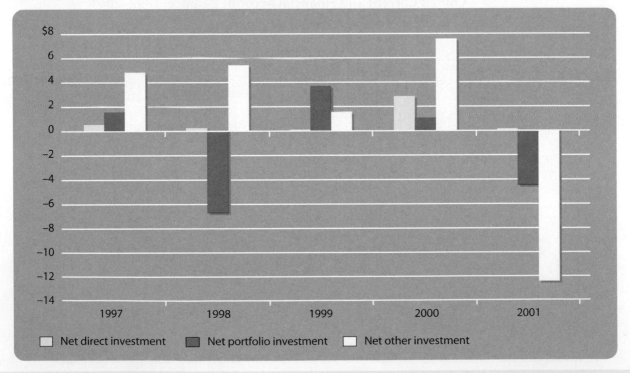

□ Net direct investment   ■ Net portfolio investment   □ Net other investment

Source: International Monetary Fund, *Balance of Payments Statistics Yearbook, 2002.*

devastating amount in 2001, over $12 billion, resulted in a structural collapse of the Turkish banking system.

Summary

The balance of payments is the summary statement of all international transactions between one country and all other countries. The balance of payments is a flow statement, summarizing all the international transactions that occur across the geographic boundaries of the nation over a period of time, typically a year. Because of its use of double-entry bookkeeping, the BOP must always balance in theory, though in practice there are substantial imbalances as a result of statistical errors and misreporting of current account and capital account flows.

The two major subaccounts of the balance of payments, the current account and the capital account, summarize the current trade and international capital flows of the country. Due to the double-entry bookkeeping method of accounting, the current account and capital account are always inverse on balance, one in surplus while the other experiences deficit. Although most nations strive for current account surpluses, it is not clear that a balance on current or capital account, or a surplus on current account, is either sustainable or desirable. The monitoring of the various subaccounts of a country's balance of payments activity is helpful to decision makers and policymakers at all levels of government and industry in detecting the underlying trends and movements of fundamental economic forces driving a country's international economic activity.

Questions for Discussion

1. Why must a country's balance of payments always be balanced in theory?
2. What is the difference between the merchandise trade balance (BOT) and the current account balance?
3. What is service trade?
4. Why is foreign direct investment so much more controversial than foreign portfolio investment? How did this relate to Mexico in the 1990s?
5. Should the fact that the United States may be the world's largest net debtor nation be a source of concern for government policymakers? Is the United States like Finland?
6. While the United States "suffered" a current account deficit and a capital account surplus in the 1980s, what were the respective balances of Japan doing?
7. What does it mean for the United States to be one of the world's largest indebted countries?
8. How do exchange rate changes alter trade so that the trade balance actually improves when the domestic currency depreciates?
9. How have trade balances in Asia contributed to the cause of the current Asian crisis?

Internet Exercises

1. The IMF, World Bank, and United Nations are only a few of the major world organizations that track, report, and aid international economic and financial development. Using these web sites and others that may be linked to them, briefly summarize the economic outlook for the developed and emerging nations of the world. For example, the full text of chapter 1 of the *World Economic Outlook* published annually by the World Bank is available through the IMF's web page.

International Monetary Fund	http://www.imf.org/
United Nations	http://www.unsystem.org/
The World Bank Group	http://www.worldbank.org/
Europa (EU) Homepage	http://www.europa.eu.int/
Bank for International Settlements	http://www.bis.org/

2. Current economic and financial statistics and commentaries are available via the IMF's web page under "What's New," "Fund Rates," and the "IMF Committee on Balance of Payments Statistics." For an in-depth examination of the IMF's ongoing initiative on the validity of these statistics, termed metadata, visit the IMF's Dissemination Standards Bulletin Board listed below.

International Monetary Fund	http://www.imf.org/
IMF's Dissemination Standards Bulletin Board	http://dsbb.imf.org/

3. Visit Moody's sovereign ceilings and foreign currency ratings service site on the web to evaluate what progress is being made in the nations of the Far East on recovering their perceived creditworthiness.

Moody's Sovereign Ceilings	http://www.moodys.com/

Take a Stand

For years, the International Monetary Fund (IMF) has been the object of significant criticism about the way it conducts its activities in emerging markets. The IMF's primary responsibility traditionally has been to provide additional financial resources to aid countries in the grip of balance of payments crises. The IMF has, on many occasions, done just that—providing enormous quantities of capital to cash-strapped economies in the throes of crisis—but at a price. The price has been that the country must often agree to specific changes in government policies and practices before the money is provided. These policy changes frequently include the elimination of government budget deficits, removal of restrictions on capital movements, new banking standards and regulations, elimination of specific trade tariffs and quotas, to name but a few.

Critics of the IMF have argued that its job is to help those in need, and not become an advocate of specific market philosophies. The IMF's increasingly dictatorial style has turned it into an institution that is essentially a new form of capitalist imperialist, dictating the conditions upon which much-needed funds may only be made available.

For Discussion

1. The IMF should cease imposing its restrictive requirements and philosophies on the countries that need these funds so drastically. This organization was created to

aid the people of the world during a time of crisis, not to take advantage of their plight to impose the IMF's increasingly right-wing philosophy on their countries and sovereignty. What the IMF so often refers to as "austerity measures" prove to be policies that place the greater burden of the bailout on the people who are already suffering.

2. The IMF is not attempting to impose its political viewpoints on countries applying for funds, but rather taking prudent measures to assure that the capital goes to good use, and does not end up being good money thrown after bad. Most countries in crisis did not get into this condition by accident, but typically as a result of significant government failure to make tough decisions regarding responsible economic management. The IMF simply wants to be assured that the right steps are being taken by government to "stop the bleeding" before providing this money that is so difficult to come by.

It was only when optimistic Turks started snapping up imports that investors began to doubt that foreign capital inflows would be sufficient to fund both spendthrift consumers and the perennially penurious government.

— "On the Brink Again," *The Economist,* February 24, 2001

In February 2001 Turkey's rapidly escalating economic *kriz*, or crisis, forced the devaluation of the Turkish lira. The Turkish government had successfully waged war on the inflationary forces embedded in the country's economy in early 2000, but just as the economy began to boom, pressures on the country's balance of payments and currency rose. The question asked by many analysts in the months following the crisis was whether the crisis had been predictable and what early signs should have been noted by the outside world.

Sources: Copyright ©2002 Thunderbird, The American Graduate School of International Management. All rights reserved. This case was prepared by Professor Michael H. Moffett for the purpose of classroom discussion only, and not to indicate either effective or ineffective management.

The Balance of Payments Accounts

Figure 1 presents the Turkish balance on current account and financial account between 1993 and 2000 (ending less than two months prior to the devaluation). Several issues are immediately evident:

- First, Turkey seemingly suffered significant volatility in the balances on these key international accounts. The financial account swung between surplus (1993) to deficit (1994), and back to surplus again (1995–1997). After plummeting in 1998, the financial surplus returned in 1999 and 2000.
- Second, as is typically the case, the current account behaved in a relatively inverse manner to the financial account, running deficits in most of the years shown. But significantly, the deficit on current account grew dramatically in 2000, to more than $9.8 billion, from a deficit in 1999 of only $1.4 billion.

Many analysts are quick to point out that the sizeable increase in the current account deficit should have been seen as a danger signal of imminent collapse. Others, however, point out quite correctly that most national

FIGURE 1

Turkey's Balance of Payments, 1993–2000

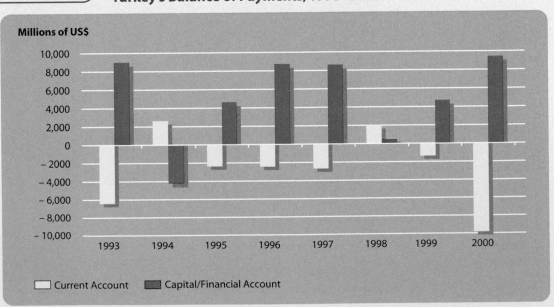

Millions of US$

Current Account / Capital/Financial Account

economies experience rapid increases in trade and current account deficits during rapid periods of economic growth. And to add weight to the argument, the net surplus on the financial account seemed to indicate a growing confidence in the Turkish economy's outlook by foreign investors.

An examination of the sub-components of these major account balances is helpful. As illustrated in Table 1, the rapid deterioration of the current account in 2000 was largely the result of a rapid jump in imported goods and merchandise. The goods import bill rose from $39.8 billion in 1999 to more than $54.0 billion in 2000, an increase of 36 percent in one year. At the same time, services trade and current income accounts, both credits and debits subcomponents, showed little change. Unfortunately, the statistics reported to the IMF provide little in additional detail as to the composition of these rapid imports, their industry or nature, and their financing.

A similar decomposition of the surplus on the Financial Account also allows us to identify where in the various inflows and outflows of capital in Turkey there was a significant change. Table 2 provides this Financial Account decomposition. According to Table 2, the doubling of the Turkish Financial Account surplus in 2000 was largely the result of a massive increase—more than $7 billion—in "net other investment." This was partly the result of significant Turkish bank borrowing on international financial markets—capital acquired outside of Turkey. This is recorded as a net capital inflow. The problem, however, is that eventually the debt will have to be repaid.

One very important determinant of these account balances was the telecommunications sector. Throughout 2000 TelSim, the national telecommunications provider in Turkey, imported billions of dollars worth of equipment from Nokia (Finland) and Motorola (United States). The equipment was purchased on trade credit, meaning that TelSim would repay Nokia and Motorola at a future date for the equipment, primarily from the proceeds of activating the equipment for telecommunications services. TelSim, however, defaulted on its payments, and Nokia and Motorola were left with billions of dollars in losses.

As illustrated in Figure 2, the Turkish lira's collapse in February 2001 was large and sudden. Although the balance of payments current and financial accounts recorded major swings in their relative values in the year prior to the crisis, the question remained as to the underlying causes of the crisis.

TABLE 1

Sub-Accounts of the Turkish Current Account, 1998–2000 (millions of US dollars)

	1998	1999	2000
Goods: exports	31,220	29,325	31,664
Goods: imports	−45,440	−39,768	−54,041
Balance on Goods	−14,220	−10,443	−22,377
Services: credit	23,321	16,398	19,484
Services: debit	−9,859	−8,953	−8,149
Balance on Services	13,462	7,445	11,335
Income: credit	2,481	2,350	2,836
Income: debit	−5,466	−5,887	−6,838
Balance on Income	−2,985	−3,537	−4,002
Current transfers: credit	5,860	5,294	5,317
Current transfers: debit	−133	−119	−92
Balance on Transfers	5,727	5,175	5,225
Balance on Current Account	1,984	−1,360	−9,819

Source: International Monetary Fund, *Balance of Payments Statistics Yearbook, 2001,* p. 913.

TABLE 2

Sub-Accounts of the Turkish Financial Account, 1998–2000 (millions of US dollars)

	1998	1999	2000
Net direct investment	573	138	112
Net portfolio investment	–6,711	3,429	1,022
Net other investment	6,586	1,103	8,311
Balance on Financial Account	448	4,670	9,445

Source: International Monetary Fund, *Balance of Payments Statistics Yearbook, 2001*, p. 913.

Turkish Banking

The Turkish banking system was notoriously corrupt in the latter part of the 1990s. Bank licenses, which gave the holder the right to open commercial and investment banking operations in Turkey, were given or sold as political favors by influential members of the Turkish government. These banks, once operational, were free to go to the international marketplace and represent themselves as established and creditable borrowers. And borrow they did.

The crisis was Turkey's worst in decades. Its banks had borrowed billions of dollars at low rates, con-

verted them to lira, and bought high-yielding Turkish government T-bills. The strategy worked until the lira lost 40 percent of its value in a few days. Interbank interest rates hit 7,000 percent. Unable to pay their dollar debts, most Turkish banks were technically insolvent. ("Crash Control for a Broken Economy," *Business Week*, August 27, 2001)

Throughout 1998, 1999, and the first half of 2000, many Turkish banks borrowed large quantities of dollars outside of Turkey. The banks then converted the dollar proceeds into Turkish lira and purchased Turkish government bonds as investments. The motivation was clear: borrow-

FIGURE 2

Turkish Inflation Rate and Exchange Rate (quarterly)

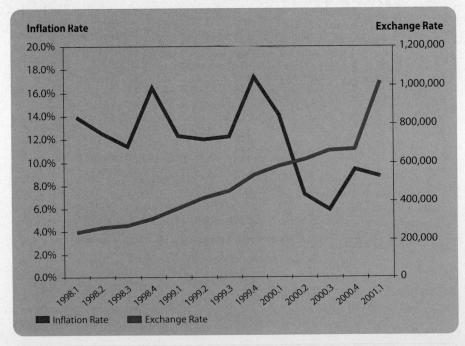

Source: International Monetary Fund, *International Financial Statistics*. October 2001, pp. 842–843.

ing at low dollar rates and reinvesting in much higher government bond rates created significant profits. These profits would persist as long as the Turkish lira held its value.

But the lira's value was heavily managed by the Turkish government. Because of the relatively high inflation rates suffered throughout 1998 and 1999 (see Figure 2), the Turkish government had pursued a gradual but continual devaluation policy. The managed devaluation, similar to Brazil's under the Real Plan between 1994 and 1999, was not sufficient. The lira was devalued at a rate significantly less than what the inflation differentials called for.

The activities of the banks added fuel to an economy already afire. This investment structure was none other than *uncovered interest arbitrage*. Uncovered interest arbitrage is when an investor borrows in a low-interest rate currency and reinvests in a high-interest rate currency, all the while assuming the exchange rate will not change significantly. If the exchange rate does not change, the investor reaps a sizeable speculative profit. If the exchange rate does change, and the high-interest rate currency falls in value (as most of international financial theory states it should), then the investor may suffer major losses.

This growing industry in interest arbitrage had a series of immediate and eventual impacts on the Turkish financial system:

- The dollar-to-lira conversion in the spot market aided in propping-up the value of the Turkish lira. As seen in Figure 3, the lira was managed in value against the U.S. dollar over time. Although Turkish inflation rates were substantially higher than U.S. dollar inflation, the large quantities of dollars converted into lira artificially boosted the demand for lira, raising its value (or preventing a further devaluation than what inflation would call for).
- The continuing demand for Turkish government bonds—government debt—allowed the government to fund increasing budget deficits at manageable costs. The strong demand by the banks for Turkish securities prevented the yields on government bonds from rising dramatically. It also prevented market forces from signaling to the government the dangers of its growing deficit spending and national debt.
- The growing external debt obligation of the Turkish banks, however, was an expanding threat to the stability of the banking system. Once the obligations

FIGURE 3

The Fall of the Turkish Lira

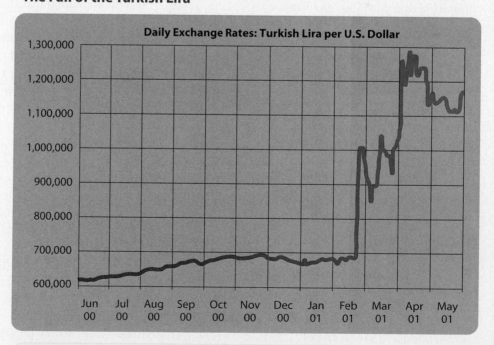

Source: Copyright © 2002 by Prof. Werner Antweiler: University of British Columbia, Vancouver BC, Canada. Time period shown in diagram: 1/Jun/2000–30/May/2001.

came due, and many of the bank debts were *callable*, in which the international banks could demand repayment overnight, the rush to exchange lira for dollars for debt service would drive the exchange rate down dramatically.

Turkey had, however, been quite successful in its fight against the ingrained inflationary forces. In the latter half of 2000 the inflation rate had dropped dramatically and interest rates had followed. The resulting economic boom immediately showed itself in a rapid increase in imports and the corresponding current account deficit for the year 2000. As a number of journalists noted, the country's disinflation program had been a "victim of its own success."

Economic Death Spiral

In the fall of 2000 the Turkish economy was booming, but the country's ability to service its growing international indebtedness was getting perilously close to the edge. In late October a major Turkish bank failed when it could not meet its foreign debt service obligations. As interest rates and inflation rates started spiraling upward once again, the Turkish government turned to the IMF for help. The banking system was saved—at least temporarily—by a $7.5 billion loan package from the IMF. (Between the fall of 1999 and the spring of 2001 the IMF committed over $11 billion to Turkey.) The IMF, as part of its loan conditions, required the government to reduce foreign indebtedness, reconstruct and clean up the Turkish banking system, and undertake a privatization program for many state-owned industries.

But these extensive measures were much easier said than done. As the economy now slowed, the various government and financial austerity measures were politically unpopular. Turk Telecom, the state-owned fixed-line telecommunications company, offered 33.5 percent ownership to any foreign or domestic investor. Not a single bid was received. An offer for controlling interest in Turkish Airlines was met by a similar lack of interest by international investors.

In December 2000 the European Union and Turkey engaged in a series of heated and public debates over political and trade relations. Turkey complained that the EU was placing unfair and discriminatory barriers in its way as it attempted to accede to EU membership. The EU responded that many of Turkey's current trade restrictions were not in the spirit of membership. Turkey explained that it was in the midst of an economic crisis,

and was only attempting to slow the rapidly growing current account deficit. Tensions escalated.

But in January 2001 there was some growing opinion, at least outside of Turkey, that the various reforms and initiatives could yet succeed.

The pending $7.5 billion IMF support package and stand-by arrangement are likely to ease market concerns about the credibility of Turkey's stabilization program, particularly in view of the revitalized privatization agenda and strengthened fiscal targets for 2001. The Turkish lira has strengthened on the back of IMF funding.

On a three-month view, however, expect the lira to return to track inflation performance suggesting a level below TL750,000 by the end of March. An outside probability of a full blown currency devaluation—similar to that in 1993—cannot be discounted, however. ("IMF Bailout of Turkey Appears Successful," *Corporate Finance*, January 2001.)

Turkish Kriz

On February 18, 2001, a public argument erupted between President Ahmet Necdet Sezer and the Prime Minister Bulent Ecevit, over the lack of progress in removing corrupt politicians from office. President Sezer complained that the Prime Minister's efforts had been "half-hearted." Although the Prime Minister quickly tried to quell international concerns by renewing his commitment to the Turkish disinflation program and the on-going initiatives to reduce political corruption, the damage was done.

The following day, February 19, international investors pulled more than $5 billion of capital out of the country. The Turkish central bank's total foreign exchange reserves, $20 billion, would be unable to sustain a defense at this rate of capital flight. On February 22 the Turkish government announced it was floating the lira. As illustrated in Figure 3, the lira's value immediately plummeted from TL685,000/$ to over TL1,000,000/$.

In the months that followed, the Turkish lira continued to fall, and many of the country's banks collapsed. Industrial production, which had grown 2 percent and 1 percent in the third and fourth quarters of 2000, respectively, fell 20 percent in the first quarter of 2001. The road to economic reform and prosperity appeared to extend far into the future for the people of Turkey.

Questions for Discussion

1. Where in the current account would the imported telecommunications equipment be listed? Would this correspond to the increase in magnitude and timing of the financial account?

2. Why do you think that TelSim defaulted on its payments for equipment imports from Nokia and Motorola?

3. Was the Turkish lira's collapse the result of a balance of payments crisis, an inflation crisis, a political crisis, or an economic crisis?

4. Describe precisely how the Turkish banks were performing uncovered interest arbitrage. Do you feel this was an inappropriate investment policy?

5. How could the Turkish banks be contributing to financial crisis if they were purchasing Turkish government bonds and helping finance and support their own government?

6. Which do you think is more critical to a country such as Turkey, fighting inflation or fighting a large trade and current account deficit?

7. The quote from *Corporate Finance* magazine, although noting the outside possibility of a devaluation, was largely positive regarding Turkey's future in January 2001. What would you have thought?

Operating internationally requires managers to be aware of a highly complex environment. Domestic and international environmental factors and their interaction have to be recognized and understood. In addition, ongoing changes in these environments have to be appreciated.

Part 4 delineates the macro factors and institutions affecting international business. It explains the workings of the international business. It explains the workings of the international monetary system and financial markets and highlights the increasing trend toward economic integration around the world. This section concludes with a chapter on doing business in emerging markets. Particular focus rests on the new market orientation of nations whose economies used to be centrally planned, such as those of the former Soviet Union.

PART
Markets

4

CHAPTER 7

Financial Markets

Learning Objectives

- To understand how currencies are traded and quoted on world financial markets

- To examine the links between interest rates and exchange rates

- To understand the similarities and differences between domestic sources of capital and international sources of capital

- To examine how the needs of individual borrowers have changed the nature of the instruments traded on world financial markets in the past decade

- To understand how the debt crises of the 1980s and 1990s are linked to the international financial markets and exchange rates

217

Asian Currencies and the Fear of Floating

After sinking for the first half of 2003, the dollar came up for air, regaining some of its value against the euro in the second half of the year. But it is quite likely to plunge again, pulled under by America's huge current-account deficit. So far the dollar's descent has been uneven. It has fallen by around one-quarter against the euro since the start of 2002. But it has lost only 10 percent or less against the yen and many other Asian currencies, and it is unchanged against the Chinese yuan, although most of the Asian economies have large balance-of-payments surpluses.

America's biggest bilateral trade deficit is with China ($103 billion in 2002). Asia as a whole accounts for half of America's total deficit. If these currencies cling to the dollar, then others such as the euro will have to rise disproportionately if America's deficit is to be trimmed.

And cling they do. The Chinese yuan and the Malaysian ringgit are pegged to the dollar and protected by capital controls. The Hong Kong dollar is also tied to the greenback through a currency board. Officially, other Asian currencies float, but central banks have been intervening on a grand scale in the foreign-exchange market to hold down their currencies as the dollar has weakened.

In a free market, China's currency would surely rise. But demands from foreigners are likely to fall on deaf ears. The Chinese government is worried about rising unemployment as jobs are lost in unprofitable state companies, and deflation remains an issue. And, so long as the yuan is pegged to the dollar, other Asian countries will have a big reason to resist appreciation too.

Source: Abstracted from "Fear of Floating," *The Economist.com,* July 10, 2003.

International financial markets serve as links between the financial markets of each individual country and as independent markets outside the jurisdiction of any one country. The market for currencies is the heart of this international financial market. International trade and investment are often denominated in a foreign currency, so the purchase of the currency precedes the purchase of goods, services, or assets.

This chapter provides a detailed guide to the structure and functions of the foreign currency markets, the international money markets, and the international securities markets. All firms striving to attain or preserve competitiveness will need to work with and within these international financial markets in the 2000s.

The Market for Currencies

The price of any one country's currency in terms of another country's currency is called a **foreign currency exchange rate**. For example, the exchange rate between the U.S. dollar ($ or USD) and the European euro (€ or EUR) may be "1.1478 dollars per euro," or simply abbreviated as $1.1478/€. This is the same exchange rate as when stated "EUR1.00 = USD 1.1478." Since most international business activities require at least one of the two parties to first purchase the country's currency before purchasing any good, service, or asset, a proper understanding of exchange rates and exchange rate markets is very important to the conduct of international business.

A word about currency symbols: As already noted, the letters USD and EUR are often used as the symbols for the U.S. dollar and the European Union's euro. These are the computer symbols (ISO-4217 codes). The field of international finance suffers, however, from a lack of agreement when it comes to currency abbreviations. This chapter uses the more common symbols used in the financial press—$ and € in this case. As a practitioner of international finance, however, stay on your toes. Every market, every country, and every firm, may have its own set of symbols. For example, the symbol for the British pound sterling can be £ (the pound symbol), GBP (Great Britain pound), STG (British pound sterling), ST£ (pound sterling), or UKL (United Kingdom pound).

EXCHANGE RATE QUOTATIONS AND TERMINOLOGY

The order in which the foreign exchange rate is stated is sometimes confusing to the uninitiated. For example, when the rate between the U.S. dollar and the European euro was stated above, $1.1478/€, a **direct quotation** on the U.S. dollar was used. This is simultaneously an **indirect quotation** on the European euro. The direct quote on any currency is when that currency is stated first; an indirect quotation refers to when the subject currency is stated second. Figure 7.1 illustrates both forms, direct and indirect quotations, for major world currencies for Wednesday, July 23, 2003.

Most of the quotations listed in Figure 7.1 are **spot rates**. A spot transaction is the exchange of currencies for immediate delivery. Although it is defined as immediate, in actual practice settlement actually occurs two business days following the agreed-upon exchange. The other time-related quotations listed in Figure 7.1 are the **forward rates.** Forward exchange rates are contracts that provide for two parties to exchange currencies on a future date at an agreed-upon exchange rate. Forwards are typically traded for the major volume currencies for maturities of 30, 90, 120, 180, and 360 days

Foreign exchange traders at banks can move millions of dollars, yen, or marks around the world with a few keystrokes on their networked computers. The deregulation of international capital flows contributes to faster, cheaper transactions in the currency markets.

FIGURE 7.1

Exchange Rate and Cross Rate Tables

EXCHANGE RATES

The foreign exchange mid-range rates below apply to trading among banks in amounts of $1 million and more, as quoted at 4 p.m. Eastern time by Reuters and other sources. Retail transactions provide fewer units of foreign currency per dollar.

Country	U.S. $ EQUIV.		CURRENCY PER U.S. $	
	Wed	Tue	Wed	Tue
Argentina (Peso)-y	.3600	.3594	2.7778	2.7824
Australia (Dollar)	.6595	.6515	1.5163	1.5349
Bahrain (Dinar)	2.6523	2.6522	.3770	.3770
Brazil (Real)	.3454	.3470	2.8952	2.8818
Canada (Dollar)	.7153	.7062	1.3980	1.4160
1-month forward	.7140	.7049	1.4006	1.4186
3-months forward	.7120	.7029	1.4045	1.4227
6-months forward	.7091	.7004	1.4102	1.4278
Chile (Peso)	.001421	.001420	703.73	704.23
China (Renminbi)	.1208	.1208	8.2781	8.2782
Colombia (Peso)	.0003467	.0003472	2884.34	2880.18
Czech. Rep. (Koruna)				
Commercial rate	.03569	.03509	28.019	28.498
Denmark (Krone)	.1544	.1524	6.4767	6.5617
Ecuador (US Dollar)	1.0000	1.0000	1.0000	1.0000
Egypt (Pound)-y	.1637	.1637	6.1099	6.1099
Hong Kong (Dollar)	.1282	.1282	7.8003	7.8003
Hungary (Forint)	.004311	.004244	231.96	235.63
India (Rupee)	.02169	.02169	46.104	46.104
Indonesia (Rupiah)	.0001162	.0001188	8606	8418
Israel (Shekel)	.2282	.2276	4.3821	4.3937
Japan (Yen)	.008411	.008394	118.89	119.13
1-month forward	.008419	.008403	118.78	119.01
3-months forward	.008436	.008418	118.54	118.79
6-months forward	.008460	.008443	118.20	118.44
Jordan (Dinar)	1.4104	1.4104	.7090	.7090
Kuwait (Dinar)	3.3371	3.3318	.2997	.3001
Lebanon (Pound)	.0006634	.0006634	1507.39	1507.39
Malaysia (Ringgit)-b	.2632	.2632	3.7994	3.7994
Mexico (Peso)				
Floating rate	.0946	.0958	10.5675	10.4341

Country	U.S. $ EQUIV.		CURRENCY PER U.S. $	
	Wed	Tue	Wed	Tue
New Zealand (Dollar)	.5801	.5755	1.7238	1.7376
Norway (Krone)	.1377	.1356	7.2622	7.3746
Pakistan (Rupee)	.01732	.01735	57.737	75.637
Peru (new Sol)	.2880	.2881	3.4722	3.4710
Phillippines (Peso)	.01853	.01860	53.967	53.763
Poland (Zloty)	.2598	.2560	3.8491	3.9063
Russia (Ruble)-a	.03295	.03296	30.349	30.340
Saudi Arabia (Riyal)	.2667	.2666	3.7495	3.7509
Singapore (Dollar)	.5696	.5692	1.7556	1.7569
Slovak Rep. (Koruna)	.02709	.02674	36.914	37.397
South Africa (Rand)	.1334	.1321	7.4963	7.5700
South Korea (Won)	.0008468	.0008454	1180.92	1182.87
Sweden (Krona)	.1245	.1222	8.0321	8.1833
Switzerland (Franc)	.7424	.7345	1.3470	1.3615
1-month forward	.7430	.7350	1.3459	1.3605
3-months forward	.7440	.7360	1.3441	1.3587
6-months forward	.7454	.7374	1.3416	1.3561
Taiwan (Dollar)	.02911	.02910	34.353	34.364
Thailand (Baht)	.02379	.02389	42.035	41.859
Turkey (Lira)	.00000071	.00000072	1408451	1388889
U.K. (Pound)	1.6083	1.5975	.6218	.6260
1-month forward	1.6052	1.5943	.6230	.6272
3-months forward	1.5990	1.5885	.6254	.6295
6-months forward	1.5903	1.5796	.6288	.6331
United Arab (Dirham)	.2723	.2722	3.6724	3.6738
Uruguay (Peso)				
Financial	.03720	.03720	26.882	26.882
Venezuela (Bolivar)	.000626	.000626	1597.44	1597.44
SDR	1.3951	1.3920	.7168	.7184
Euro	1.1478	1.1330	.8712	.8826

Special Drawing Rights (SDR) are based on exchange rates for the U.S., British, and Japanese currencies.

Source: International Monetary Fund

KEY CURRENCY CROSS RATES

Late New York Trading Wednesday, July 23, 2003

	Dollar	Euro	Pound	SFranc	Peso	Yen	CdnDlr
Canada	1.3980	1.6046	2.2484	1.0379	.13229	.01176	••••
Japan	118.89	136.46	191.21	88.265	11.251	••••	85.043
Mexico	10.5675	12.1293	16.996	7.8453	••••	.08888	7.5589
Switzerland	1.347	1.5461	2.1664	••••	.12746	.01133	.9635
U.K.	.62180	.7137	••••	.4616	.05884	.00523	.44476
Euro	.87120	••••	1.4012	.64680	.08244	.00733	.62319
U.S.	••••	1.1478	1.6083	.74240	.09463	.00841	.71530

Source: Reuters

(from the present date). The forward, like the basic spot exchange, can be for any amount of currency. Forward contracts serve a variety of purposes, but their primary purpose is to allow a firm to lock in a future rate of exchange. This is a valuable tool in a world of continually changing exchange rates.

The quotations listed will also occasionally indicate if the rate is applicable to business trade (the commercial rate) or for financial asset purchases or sales (the financial rate). Countries that have government regulations regarding the exchange of their currency may post official rates, while the markets operating outside their jurisdiction will list a floating rate. In this case, any exchange of currency that is not under the control of its government is interpreted as a better indication of the currency's true market value.

DIRECT AND INDIRECT QUOTATIONS

The Wall Street Journal quotations (Figure 7.1) list rates of exchange between major currencies, both in direct and indirect forms. The exchange rate for the Japanese yen (¥) versus the U.S. dollar in the third column is ¥118.89/$. This is a *direct quote* on the Japanese yen and an *indirect quote* on the U.S. dollar. The inverse of this spot exchange rate for the same day is listed in the first column, the indirect quote on the U.S. dollar, $.008411/¥. The two forms of the exchange rate are of course equal, one being the inverse of the other:[1]

$$\frac{1}{¥118.89/\$} = \$0.008411/¥.$$

Luckily, world currency markets do follow some conventions to minimize confusion. With only a few exceptions, most currencies are quoted in direct quotes versus the U.S. dollar (SF/$, Baht/$, Pesos/$), also known as **European terms.** The major exceptions are currencies at one time or another associated with the British Commonwealth (including the Australian dollar) and now the European euro. These currencies are customarily quoted as U.S. dollars per pound sterling or U.S. dollars per Australian dollar, known as **American terms.** Once again, it makes no real difference whether you quote U.S. dollars per Japanese yen or Japanese yen per U.S. dollar, as long as you know which is being used for the transaction.

Figure 7.2, the foreign currency quotations from the *Financial Times* of London, provides wider coverage of the world's currencies, including many of the lesser-known and traded. These quotes are for July 19, 2003.

CROSS RATES

Although it is common among exchange traders worldwide to quote currency values against the U.S. dollar, it is not necessary. Any currency's value can be stated in terms of any other currency. When the exchange rate of a currency is stated without using the U.S. dollar as a reference, it is referred to as a **cross rate.** For example, if the Japanese yen and European euro are both quoted versus the U.S. dollar, they would appear as ¥118.89/$ and $1.1478/€. But if the ¥/€ cross rate is needed, it is simply a matter of multiplication:

$$¥118.89/\$ \times \$1.1478/€ = ¥136.46/€$$

The yen per euro cross rate of 136.46 is the third leg of the triangle of currencies, which must be true if the first two exchange rates are known. If one of the exchange rates changes due to market forces, the others must adjust for the three exchange rates again to align. If they are out of alignment, it would be possible to make a profit simply by exchanging one currency for a second, the second for a third, and the third back to the first. This is known as *triangular arbitrage.* Besides the potential profitability of arbitrage that may occasionally occur, cross rates have become increasingly common in a world of rapidly expanding trade and investment.

PERCENTAGE CHANGE CALCULATIONS

The quotation form is important when calculating the percentage change in an exchange rate. For example, if the spot rate between the Japanese yen and the U.S. dollar changed from ¥125/$ to ¥150/$, the percentage change in the value of the Japanese yen is:

$$\frac{¥125/\$ - ¥150/\$}{¥150/\$} \times 100 = -16.67\%$$

FIGURE 7.2

Guide to World Currencies

CURRENCY RATES

Jul 18 Currency	DOLLAR Closing mid	Day's change	EURO Closing mid	Day's change	POUND Closing mid	Day's change
Argentina (Peso)	2.8050	+0.0200	3.1451	+0.0305	4.4429	+0.0138
Australia (A$)	1.5511	+0.0181	1.7392	+0.0247	2.4569	+0.0188
One Month	–	–	1.7431	+0.0248	2.4598	+0.0188
One Year	–	–	1.7837	+0.0253	2.4897	+0.0192
Bahrain (Dinar)	0.3770	–	0.4228	+0.0011	0.5972	–0.0024
Bolivia (Boliviano)	7.6792	–	8.6104	+0.0223	12.1636	–0.0491
Brazil (R$)	2.8750	+0.0135	3.2236	+0.0234	4.5539	+0.0031
Canada (C$)	1.4106	+0.0151	1.5817	+0.0211	2.2344	+0.0151
One Month	1.413	+0.0151	1.5829	+0.0211	2.2338	+0.0150
Three Month	1.4173	+0.0151	1.5848	+0.0209	2.232	+0.0147
One Year	1.4331	+0.0144	1.5922	+0.0201	2.2224	+0.0136
Chile (Peso)	701.050	+2.8000	786.052	+5.1640	1110.43	–0.0300
Colombia (Peso)	2883.60	–5.58	3233.12	+2.12	4567.32	–27.32
Costa Rica (Colon)	400.920	+0.1700	449.552	+1.3930	635.037	–2.2960
Czech Rep. (Koruna)	28.6064	+0.0755	32.0750	+0.1675	45.3113	–0.0628
One Month	28.6347	+0.0757	32.0777	+0.1679	45.2687	–0.0624
One Year	28.8974	+0.0770	32.1047	+0.1683	44.811	–0.6000
Denmark (DKr)	6.8304	–0.0182	7.4343	–0.0012	10.5022	–0.0715
One Month	6.6364	–0.0180	7.4342	–0.0011	10.4914	–0.0711
Three Month	6.6473	–0.0181	7.4333	–0.0010	10.4688	–0.0713
One Year	6.6929	–0.0171	7.4357	+0.0001	10.3786	–0.0685
Egypt (Egypt £)	6.1487	–	6.8943	+0.0178	9.7393	–0.0394
Estonia (Kroon)	13.9534	–0.0377	15.6453	–0.0017	22.1015	–0.1493
Hong Kong (HK$)	7.7992	–0.0001	8.7449	+0.0224	12.3536	–0.0501
One Month	7.7999	–0.0001	8.7378	+0.0226	12.3309	–0.0500
Three Month	7.8012	–	8.7238	+0.0227	12.2863	–0.0499
One Year	7.8154	–0.0004	8.6829	+0.0220	12.1193	–0.0494
Hungary (Forint)	236.955	+0.1200	265.686	+0.8220	375.325	–1.3260
One Month	238.79	+0.2300	267.5016	+0.9519	377.503	–1.1590
One Year	253.55	–0.8200	281.6909	–0.1814	393.177	–2.8570
India (Rs)	48.2400	–0.0200	51.8466	+0.1564	73.2418	–0.2641
One Month	46.3613	+0.0238	51.9356	+0.1614	73.2924	–0.2582
One Year	47.2825	+0.0325	52.5302	+0.1716	73.3203	–0.2441
Indonesia (Rupiah)	8330.00	+71.50	9340.01	+104.12	13194.30	+60.40
One Month	–	–	0331.60	+104.13	13168.88	+60.33
Une Year	–	–	9254.52	+103.12	12917.22	+59.40
Iran (Rial)	8230.00	–	9228.30	+24.69	13035.90	–52.70
Israel (Shk)	4.4350	+0.0050	4.9728	+0.0185	7.0248	0.0205
Japan (Y)	118.905	+0.1500	133.322	+0.5120	188.340	–0.5220
One Month	188.78	+0.1450	133.0615	+0.5034	187.78	–0.5320
Three Month	118.56	+0.1450	132.5816	+0.5097	186.725	–0.5220
One Year	117.495	+0.1700	130.5354	+0.5276	182.2	0.4620
Kenya (Shilling)	75.0500	+0.3000	84.1499	+0.5532	118.876	–0.0030
Kuwait (Dinar)	0.3004	+0.0002	0.3368	+0.0010	0.4758	–0.0016
One Month	0.3008	+0.0002	0.3369	+0.0011	0.4754	–0.0016
One Year	0.3036	+0.0005	0.3373	+0.0014	0.4708	–0.0010
Malaysia (M$)	3.8000	–	4.2608	+0.0110	6.0190	–0.0243
Mexico (New Peso)	10.3605	+0.0115	11.6167	+0.0429	16.4105	–0.0480
One Month	10.3949	+0.0111	11.6448	+0.0427	16.4333	–0.0487
Three Month	10.479	+0.0113	11.7182	+0.0432	16.5033	–0.0492
One Year	10.9438	–0.0002	12.1584	+0.0312	16.9704	–0.0684
New Zealand (NZ$)	1.7527	+0.0343	1.9652	+0.0435	2.7762	+0.0434
One Month	–	–	1.9703	+0.0437	2.7805	+0.0435
One Year	–	–	2.0231	+0.0459	2.8238	–0.0458
Nigeria (Naira)	129.750	–0.1000	145.482	+0.2640	205.518	–0.9890
Norway (NKr)	7.4198	–0.0580	8.3195	–0.0433	11.7526	–0.1397
One Month	7.4376	–0.0579	8.3318	–0.0431	11.758	–0.1395
Three Month	7.4635	–0.0577	8.3461	–0.0425	11.7542	–0.1390
One Year	7.5726	–0.0562	8.4131	–0.0405	11.7427	–0.1347
Pakistan (Rupee)	57.6900	–0.0600	64.6850	+0.1002	91.3781	–0.4646
Peru (New Sol)	3.4684	–0.0011	3.8890	+0.0088	5.4939	–0.0239
Phillipines (Peso)	53.7250	+0.1500	60.2392	+0.3236	85.0978	–0.1053
One Month	53.9835	+0.1460	60.4744	+0.3203	85.3425	–0.1129

Currency	DOLLAR Closing mid	Day's change	EURO Closing mid	Day's change	POUND Closing mid	Day's change
Three Month	54.5655	+0.1520	61.0180	+0.3282	85.9353	–0.1089
One Year	57.353	+0.1865	63.7185	+0.3712	88.9367	–0.0671
Poland (Zloty)	3.9824	–0.0226	4.4653	–0.0138	6.3080	–0.0615
One Month	3.9968	–0.0225	4.4773	–0.0136	6.3185	–0.0614
One Year	4.1321	–0.0229	4.5907	–0.0136	6.4076	–0.0615
Romania (Leu)	32764.00	+21.50	36736.60	+119.00	51896.50	–175.50
Russia (Rouble)	30.4252	–0.0198	34.1143	+0.0661	48.1920	–0.2262
Saudi Arabia (SR)	3.7502	–0.0001	4.2050	+0.0108	5.9402	–0.0241
One Month	3.7518	–0.0002	4.2029	+0.0107	5.9313	–0.0242
One Year	3.7668	–0.0005	4.1849	+0.0103	5.8412	–0.0241
Singapore (S$)	1.7632	+0.0019	1.9770	+0.0072	2.7929	–0.0081
One Month	1.7627	+0.0020	1.9746	+0.0073	2.7866	–0.0081
One Year	1.7566	+0.0021	1.9515	+0.0074	2.7239	–0.0076
Slovakia (Koruna)	37.6187	+0.2154	42.1800	+0.3500	59.5862	+0.1018
One Month	37.7852	+0.2154	42.3285	+0.3507	59.7346	+0.1007
One Year	39.3812	+0.2739	43.7521	+0.4166	61.068	+0.1810
Slovenia (Tolar)	109.160	–0.5050	234.521	+0.0420	331.299	–2.1420
South Africa (R)	7.6825	–0.0437	8.6140	–0.0266	12.1686	–0.1188
One Month	7.7548	–0.0439	8.6871	–0.0266	12.2594	–0.1194
Three Month	7.881	–0.0452	8.8129	–0.0276	12.4116	–0.1221
One Year	8.3415	–0.0472	9.2672	–0.0285	12.9349	–0.1256
South Korea (Won)	1182.55	+3.55	1325.93	+7.40	1873.10	–1.92
One Month	1185.70	+3.55	1328.27	+7.42	1874.47	–1.93
Three Month	1191.75	+3.50	1332.68	+7.37	1876.89	–2.09
One Year	1213.30	+2.55	1347.96	+6.30	1881.45	–3.59
Sweden (SKr)	8.2541	–0.0077	9.2550	–0.0154	13.0742	–0.0650
One Month	8.2668	–0.0075	9.2608	+0.0157	13.069	–0.0647
Three Month	8.2896	–0.0077	9.2700	+0.0157	13.0555	–0.0649
One Year	8.3896	–0.0057	9.3208	+0.0178	13.0097	–0.0612
Switzerland (SFr)	1.3707	–0.0041	1.5369	–0.0007	2.1711	–0.0154
One Month	1.3697	–0.0041	1.5344	–0.0006	2.1654	–0.0154
Three Month	1.3679	–0.0041	1.5296	–0.0007	2.1542	–0.154
One Year	1.3601	–0.0040	1.5111	–0.0005	2.1092	–0.148
Taiwan (T$)	34.1700	+0.0400	38.6495	+0.1447	54.5988	–0.1569
One Month	34.425	+0.0275	38.5642	+0.1309	54.4224	–0.1760
One Year	34.085	+0.0250	37.8680	+0.1255	52.8552	–0.1734
Thailand (Bt)	41.7500	+0.0700	46.8122	+0.1993	66.1299	–0.1559
One Month	41.752	+0.0700	46.7722	+0.1997	66.0057	–0.1554
One Year	41.825	+0.0700	46.4781	+0.1975	64.873	–0.1518
Tunisia (Dinar)	1.2979	–0.0015	1.4553	+0.0021	2.0559	–0.0106
Turkey (Lira)	1403500	+25500	1573675	+32588	2223074	+31572
UAE (Dirham)	3.6730	–0.0001	4.1184	+0.0106	5.8178	–0.0237
One Month	3.6731	–0.0001	4.1147	+0.0105	5.8178	–0.0236
One Year	3.6755	–0.0001	4.0834	+0.0104	5.6995	–0.0231
UK (0.6313)* (£)	1.5840	–0.0063	0.7079	+0.0047	–	–
One Month	1.581	–0.0062	0.7086	+0.0047	–	–
Three Month	1.575	–0.0063	0.7100	+0.0047	–	–
One Year	1.5508	–0.0061	0.7165	+0.0048		
Uruguay (Peso)	26.7650	+0.0500	30.0103	+0.1335	42.3944	–0.0918
USA ($)	–	–	1.1213	+0.0029	1.5840	–0.0063
One Month	–	–	1.1202	+0.0029	1.581	–0.0062
Three Month	–	–	1.1183	+0.0029	1.575	–0.0063
One Year	–	–	1.1110	+0.0029	1.5508	–0.0061
Venezuela (Bolivar)	1598.00	–	1791.76	+4.64	2531.15	–10.23
Vietnam (Dong)	15513.00	–2.00	17394.00	+42.80	24571.80	–102.50
Euro (0.8918)* (Euro)	1.1213	+0.0030	–	–	1.4126	–0.0094
One Month	1.1203	+0.0030	–	–	1.4112	–0.0093
Three Month	1.1183	+0.0030	–	–	1.4083	–0.0094
One Year	1.111	+0.0030	–	–	1.3957	–0.0092
SDR	–	0.72090	–	0.80835	+0.0019	1.141900	–

*The closing mid-point rates for the Euro and £ against the $ are shown in brackets. The other figures in the dollar column of both the Euro and Sterling rows are in the reciprocal form in line with market convention. †Floating rate now shown for Argentina. ‡Official rate set by Malaysian government. The WM/Reuters rate for the valuation of capital assets is 3.80 MYR/USD. Rates are derived from th WM/REUTERS 4pm (London time) CLOSING SPOT and FORWARD RATE services. Some values are rounded by the F.T. The exchange rates printed in this table are also available on the internet at http://www.FT.com.

Euro Locking Rates: Austrian Schilling 13.7603. Belgium/Luxembourg Franc 40.3399, Finnish Markha 5.94573, French Franc 6.55957, German Mark 1.95583, Greek Drachma 340.75, Irish Punt 0.787564, Italian Lira 1936.27, Netherlands Guilder 2.20371, Portuguese Escudo 200.482, Spanish Peseta 166.386.

Source: Financial Times, July 19/20, 2003, p. 16.

The Japanese yen has declined in value versus the U.S. dollar by 16.67 percent. This is consistent with the intuition that it now requires more yen (150) to buy a dollar than it used to (125).

The same percentage change result can be achieved by using the inverted forms of the same spot rates (indirect quotes on the Japanese yen), if care is taken to also "invert" the basic percentage change calculation. Using the inverse of ¥125/$ ($0.0080/¥) and the inverse of ¥150/$ ($0.0067/¥), the percentage change is still −16.67 percent:

$$\frac{\$0.0067/¥ - \$0.0080/\$}{\$0.0080/¥} \times 100 = -16.67\%$$

If the percentage changes calculated are not identical, it is normally the result of rounding errors introduced when inverting the spot rates. Both methods are identical, however, when calculated properly.

FOREIGN CURRENCY MARKET STRUCTURE

The market for foreign currencies is a worldwide market that is informal in structure. This means that it has no central place, pit, or floor like the floor of the New York Stock Exchange, where the trading takes place. The "market" is actually the thousands of telecommunications links among financial institutions around the globe, and it is open nearly 24 hours a day. Someone, somewhere, is nearly always open for business. Figure 7.3 illustrates how the trading day moves with the sun for the four largest

FIGURE 7.3

Global Currency Trading: The Trading Day

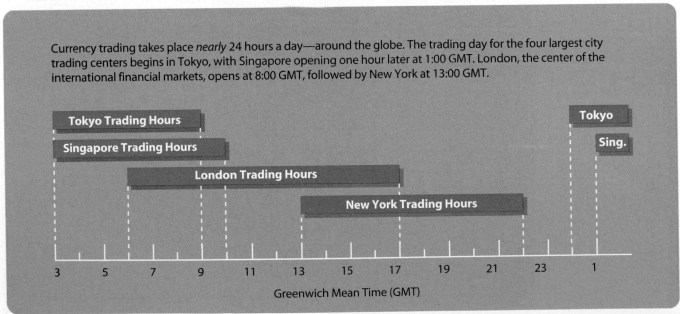

Currency trading takes place *nearly* 24 hours a day—around the globe. The trading day for the four largest city trading centers begins in Tokyo, with Singapore opening one hour later at 1:00 GMT. London, the center of the international financial markets, opens at 8:00 GMT, followed by New York at 13:00 GMT.

Source: Based on data found at http://www.currenex.com/efx/efx.shtml?efx&.

trading centers—Tokyo, Singapore, London, and New York. As described in Focus on e-Commerce, trading is also moving to the Internet.

For example, Table 7.1 reproduces a computer screen from one of the major international financial information news sources, Reuters. This is the spot exchange screen, called FXFX, which is available to all subscribers to the Reuters news network. The screen serves as a bulletin board, where all financial institutions wanting to buy or sell foreign currencies can post representative prices. Although the rates quoted on these computer screens are indicative of current prices, the buyer is still referred to the individual bank for the latest quotation due to the rapid movement of rates worldwide. There also are hundreds of banks operating in the markets at any moment that are not listed on the brief sample of Reuters FXFX page.[2] The speed with which this market moves, the multitude of players playing on a field that is open 24 hours a day, and the circumference of the earth with its time and day differences produce many different "single prices." Focus on Culture illustrates how trading occurs between traders themselves.

MARKET SIZE AND COMPOSITION

Until recently there was little data on the actual volume of trading on world foreign currency markets. Starting in the spring of 1986, however, the Federal Reserve Bank of New York, along with other major industrial countries' central banks through the auspices of the Bank for International Settlements (BIS), started surveying the activity of currency trading every three years. Some of the principal results are shown in Figure 7.4.

Growth in foreign currency trading has been nothing less than astronomical. The survey results for the month of April 1998 indicate that daily foreign currency trading on world markets exceeded $1,500,000,000,000 (a trillion with a *t*). In comparison, the annual (not daily) U.S. government budget deficit has never exceeded $300 billion, and the U.S. merchandise trade deficit has never topped $200 billion.

The majority of the world's trading in foreign currencies is still taking place in the cities where international financial activity is centered: London, New York, and Tokyo. A recent survey by the U.S. Federal Reserve of currency trading by financial institutions and independent brokers in New York reveals additional information of

Focus On ⬇

e-BUSINESS

Online Global Currency Exchange

Currenex, Inc. is the first independent and open online global currency exchange, linking institutional buyers and sellers worldwide. Operational today, Currenex's Internet-based service, Fxtrades, provides banks, corporate treasury departments, institutional funds/asset managers, government agencies, international organizations, and central banks instant access to the $1 trillion daily globe foreign exchange market through multiple price discovery mechanisms on an open, impartial exchange.

Fxtrades is a real-time FX marketplace that provides secure and comprehensive FX trading from initiation and execution to settlement and reporting. As members in the Currenex exchange, CFOs, treasurers, and fund managers can approach currency transactions knowing that they are able to secure the most competitive bid while improving operational efficiencies, increasing productivity, and providing tight integration with back office operations.

Currenex, founded in 1999, has major multinational members including MasterCard International and Intel Corporation, as well as more than 25 global market-making banks, among them ABN Amro, Barclays Capital, and Merrill Lynch.

Source: http://www.currenex.com

TABLE 7.1

Typical Foreign Currency Quotations on a Reuters Screen

13:07	CCY	Page	Name	*Reuters Spot Rates*	CCY	HI* Euro**	Lo FXFX
13.06	GBP	AIBN	AL IRISH	N.Y.	1.7653/63 * GBP	1.7710	1.7630
13.06	CHF	CITX	CITIBANK	ZUR	1.5749/56 * CHF	1.5750	1.5665
13.06	JPY	CHNY	CHEMICAL	N.Y.	128.53/58 * JPY	128.70	128.23
13.02	XEV	PRBX	PRIVAT	COP	1.1259/68 * XEV	1.1304	1.1255

Column 1: Time of entry of the latest quote to the nearest minute (British Standard time).

Column 2: Currency of quotation (bilateral with the U.S. dollar); quotes are currency per USD, except for the British pound sterling (dollars per unit of pound) and the European Currency Unit (dollars per unit of XEV). The currency symbols are as follows: GBP—British pound sterling; CFH—Swiss franc; JPY—Japanese yen; XEV—European Currency Unit.

Column 3: Mnemonic of inputting bank. Allows the individual trader to dial up the correct page (by this mnemonic) where the trader could see the full set of spot and forward quotes for this and other currencies being offered by this bank.

Column 4: Name of the inputting bank.

Column 5: Branch location of that bank from which the quote has emanated (so that an inquiring trader can telephone the correct branch); N.Y.—New York; ZUR—Zurich; LDN—London.

Column 6: Spot exchange rate quotation, bid quote, then offer quote.

Column 7: Recent high price for this specific quote.

Column 8: Recent low price for this specific quote.

Source: Adapted from C. A. E. Goodhart and L. Figliuoli, "Every Minute Counts in Financial Markets," *Journal of International Money and Finance,* 10, 1991, pp. 23–52.

Focus On ⬇

CULTURE

The Linguistics of Currency Trading

"Yoshi, it's Maria in New York. May I have a price on twenty cable?"

"Yoshi, it's Maria in New York. I am interested in either buying or selling 20 million British pounds."

"Sure, One seventy-five, twenty-thirty."

"Sure. I will buy them from you at 1.7520 dollars to each pound or sell them to you at 1.7530 dollars to each pound."

"Mine twenty."

"I'd like to buy them from you at 1.7530 dollars to each pound."

"All right. At 1.7530, I sell you twenty million pounds."

"All right. I sell you 20 million pounds at 1.7530 dollars per pound."

"Done."

"The deal is confirmed at 1.7530."

"What do you think about the Swiss franc? It's up 100 pips."

"Is there any information you can share with me about the fact that the Swiss franc has risen one-one hundredth of a franc against the U.S. dollar in the past hour?"

"I saw that. A few German banks have been buying steadily all day. . . ."

"Yes, German banks have been buying Swiss francs all day, causing the price to rise a little. . . ."

Source: Adapted from *The Basics of Foreign Trade and Exchange,* by Adam Gonelli, The Federal Reserve Bank of New York, Public Information Department, 1993.

FIGURE 7.4

**Global Foreign Exchange Market Turnover
(daily averages in April, billions of U.S. dollars)**

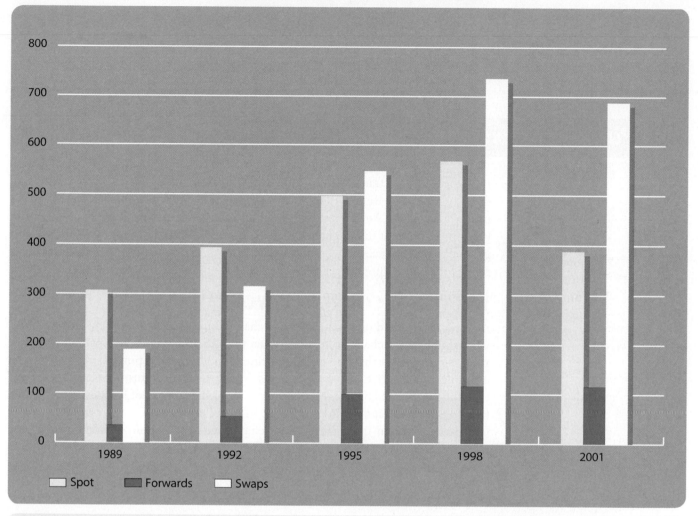

Spot   Forwards   Swaps

Source: Bank for International Settlements, "Central Bank Survey of Foreign Exchange and Derivatives Market Activity in April 2001," October 2001, http://www.bis.org.

interest. Approximately 66 percent of currency trading occurs in the morning hours (Eastern Standard Time), with 29 percent between noon and 4 P.M., and the remaining 5 percent between 4 P.M. and 8 A.M. the next day.

Three reasons typically given for the enormous growth in foreign currency trading are:

1. **Deregulation of International Capital Flows:** It is easier than ever to move currencies and capital around the world without major governmental restrictions. Much of the deregulation that has characterized government policy over the past 10 to 15 years in the United States, Japan, and the now European Union has focused on financial deregulation.

2. **Gains in Technology and Transaction Cost Efficiency:** It is faster, easier, and cheaper to move millions of dollars, yen, or marks around the world than ever

before. Technological advancements not only in the dissemination of information, but also in the conduct of exchange or trading, have added greatly to the ability of individuals working in these markets to conduct instantaneous arbitrage (some would say speculation).

3. **The World Is a Risky Place:** Many argue that the financial markets have become increasingly volatile over recent years, with larger and faster swings in financial variables such as stock values and interest rates adding to the motivations for moving more capital at faster rates.

The Purpose of Exchange Rates

If countries are to trade, they must be able to exchange currencies. To buy wheat, or corn, or videocassette recorders, the buyer must first have the currency in which the product is sold. An American firm purchasing consumer electronic products manufactured in Japan must first exchange its U.S. dollars for Japanese yen, then purchase the products. And each country has its own currency.[3] The exchange of one country's currency for another should be a relatively simple transaction, but it's not.

WHAT IS A CURRENCY WORTH?

At what rate should one currency be exchanged for another currency? For example, what should the exchange rate be between the U.S. dollar and the Japanese yen? The simplest answer is that the exchange rate should equalize purchasing power. For example, if the price of a movie ticket in the United States is $6, the "correct" exchange rate would be one that exchanges $6 for the amount of Japanese yen it would take to purchase a movie ticket in Japan. If ticket prices are ¥540 (a common symbol for the yen is ¥) in Japan, then the exchange rate that would equalize purchasing power would be:

$$\frac{¥540}{\$6} = ¥90/\$.$$

Therefore, if the exchange rate between the two currencies is ¥90/$, she or he can purchase a ticket regardless of which country the moviegoer is in. This is the theory of **purchasing power parity (PPP),** generally considered the definition of what exchange rates ideally should be. The purchasing power parity exchange rate is simply the rate that equalizes the price of the identical product or service in two different currencies:

$$\text{Price in Japan} = \text{Exchange rate} \times \text{Price in U.S.}$$

If the price of the same product in each currency is $P^¥$ and $P^\$$, and the spot exchange rate between the Japanese yen and the U.S. dollar is $S^{¥/\$}$, the price in yen is simply the price in dollars multiplied by the spot exchange rate:

$$P^¥ = S^{¥/\$} \times P^\$.$$

If this is rearranged (dividing both sides by P$^\$$), the spot exchange rate between the Japanese yen and the U.S. dollar is the ratio of the two product prices:

$$\frac{P^¥}{S^{¥/\$}} = P^\$.$$

These prices could be the price of just one good or service, such as the movie ticket mentioned previously, or they could be price indices for each country that cover many different goods and services. Either form is an attempt to find comparable products in different countries (and currencies) in order to determine an exchange rate based on purchasing power parity. The question then is whether this logical approach to exchange rates actually works in practice.

THE LAW OF ONE PRICE

The version of purchasing power parity that estimates the exchange rate between two currencies using just one good or service as a measure of the proper exchange for all goods and services is called the **Law of One Price.** To apply the theory to actual prices across countries, we need to select a product that is identical in quality and content in every country. To be truly theoretically correct, we would want such a product to be produced entirely domestically, so that there are no import factors in its construction.

Where would one find such a perfect product? McDonald's. Table 7.2 presents what *The Economist* magazine calls "the golden-arches standard." What it provides is a product that is essentially the same the world over and is produced and consumed entirely domestically.

The Big Mac Index compares the actual exchange rate with the exchange rate implied by the purchasing power parity measurement of comparing Big Mac prices across countries. For example, using the Big Mac prices quoted in Table 7.2, the average price of a Big Mac in the United States on a specific date was $2.71. On that same date, the price of a Big Mac in Mexico, in pesos, was Peso23.00. These relative Big Mac prices are then used to calculate the implied purchasing power parity exchange rate between the two currencies:

$$\frac{\text{Peso}23.00}{\$2.71} = \text{Peso}8.4871/\$.$$

The exchange rate between the Mexican peso and the U.S. dollar should be—according to purchasing power parity theory—Peso8.4871/$ (or Peso8.49/$ rounded to two decimal places as they did in Table 7.2). The actual exchange rate in the marketplace on that date was Peso10.53/$. This means that the *market* valued a dollar at 10.53 pesos, when the *theory* valued the dollar at 8.49 pesos. Therefore, if one is to believe the Big Mac Index, the Mexican peso was undervalued by 19 percent.

TABLE 7.2   The Hamburger Standard

	BIG MAC PRICES				
	In Local Currency	In Dollars	Implied PPP* of the Dollar	Actual Dollar Exchange Rate April 22nd	Under(–)/Over (+) Valuation Against the Dollar, %
United States†	$2.71	2.71			
Argentina	Peso 4.10	1.43	1.51	2.88	−47
Australia	A$3.00	1.86	1.11	1.61	−31
Brazil	Real 4.55	1.48	1.68	3.07	−45
Britain	£ 1.99	3.14	1.36‡	1.58‡	+16
Canada	C$3.20	2.21	1.18	1.45	−18
Chile	Peso 1,400	1.95	517	716	−28
China	Yuan 9.90	1.20	3.65	8.28	−56
Czech Rep	Koruna 56.57	1.96	20.9	28.9	−28
Denmark	DKr27.75	4.10	10.2	6.78	+51
Egypt	Pound 8.00	1.35	2.95	5.92	−50
Euro area	€ 2.71	2.97	1.00§	1.10§	+10
Hong Kong	HK$11.50	1.47	4.24	7.80	−46
Hungary	Forint 490	2.18	181	224	−19
Indonesia	Rupiah 16,100	1.84	5,941	8,740	−32
Japan	¥262	2.19	96.7	120	−19
Malaysia	M$5.04	1.33	1.86	3.80	−51
Mexico	Peso 23.00	2.18	8.49	10.53	−19
New Zealand	NZ$3.95	2.21	1.46	1.78	−18
Peru	New Sol 7.90	2.29	2.92	3.46	−16
Philippines	Peso 65.00	1.24	24.0	52.5	−54
Poland	Zloty 6.30	1.62	2.32	3.89	−40
Russia	Rouble 41.00	1.32	15.1	31.1	−51
Singapore	S$3.30	1.86	1.22	1.78	−31
South Africa	Rand 13.95	1.84	5.15	7.56	−32
South Korea	Won 3,300	2.71	1,218	1,220	nil
Sweden	SKr30.00	3.60	11.1	8.34	+33
Switzerland	SFr6.30	4.59	2.32	1.37	+69
Taiwan	NT$70.00	2.01	25.8	34.8	−26
Thailand	Baht 59.00	1.38	21.8	42.7	−49
Turkey	Lira 3,750,000	2.34	1,383,764	1,600,500	−14
Venezuela	Bolivar 3,700	2.32	1,365	1,598	−15

*Purchasing power parity: local price divided by price in United States
†Average of New York, Chicago, San Francisco, and Atlanta
‡Dollars per pound
§Dollars per euro

Monetary Systems of the Twentieth Century

The mixed fixed/floating exchange rate system operating today is only the latest stage of a continuing process of change. The systems that have preceded the present system varied between gold-based standards **(The Gold Standard)** and complex systems in which the U.S. dollar largely took the place of gold **(The Bretton Woods Agreement).** To understand why the dollar, the mark, and the yen are floating today, it is necessary to return to the (pardon the pun) *golden oldies.*

THE GOLD STANDARD

Although there is no recognized starting date, the gold standard as we call it today began sometime in the 1880s and extended up through the outbreak of the First World War. The gold standard was premised on three basic ideas:

1. A system of fixed rates of exchange existed between participating countries;
2. "Money" issued by member countries had to be backed by reserves of gold; and
3. Gold would act as an automatic adjustment, flowing in and out of countries, and automatically altering the gold reserves of that country if imbalances in trade or investment did occur.

Under the gold standard, each country's currency would be set in value per ounce of gold. For example, the U.S. dollar was defined as $20.67 per ounce, while the British pound sterling was defined as £4.2474 per ounce. Once each currency was defined versus gold, the determination of the exchange rate between the two currencies (or any two currencies) was simple:

$$\frac{\$20.57/\text{ounce of gold}}{£4.2474/\text{ounce of gold}} = \$4.8665/£.$$

The use of gold as the pillar of the system was a result of historical tradition, and not anything inherently unique to the metal gold itself. It was shiny, soft, rare, and generally acceptable for payment in all countries.

THE INTERWAR YEARS, 1919–1939

The 1920s and 1930s were a tumultuous period for the international monetary system. The British pound sterling, the dominant currency prior to World War I, survived the war but was greatly weakened. The U.S. dollar returned to the gold standard in 1919, but gold convertibility was largely untested across countries throughout the 1920s, as world trade took a long time to recover from the destruction of the war. With the economic collapse and bank runs of the 1930s, the U.S. was forced to once again abandon gold convertibility.

The economic depression of the 1930s was worldwide. As all countries came under increasingly desperate economic conditions, many countries (including the United States) resorted to isolationist policies and protectionism. World trade slowed to a trickle, and with it the general need for currency exchange. It was not until the latter stages of the Second World War that international trade and commerce once again demanded a system for currency convertibility and stability.

THE BRETTON WOODS AGREEMENT, 1944–1971

The governments of 44 of the Allied Powers gathered together in Bretton Woods, New Hampshire, in 1944 to plan for the postwar international monetary system. The British delegation, headed by Lord John Maynard Keynes, the famous economist, and the U.S. delegation, headed by Secretary of the Treasury Henry Morgenthau, Jr., and director of the Treasury's monetary research department, Harry D. White, labored long and hard to reach an agreement. In the end, all parties agreed that a postwar system would be stable and sustainable only if it was able to provide sufficient liquidity to countries during periods of crisis. Any new system had to have facilities for the extension of credit for countries to defend their currency values.

After weeks of debate, the Bretton Woods Agreement was reached. The plan called for the following:

1. Fixed exchange rates between member countries, termed an "adjustable peg";
2. The establishment of a fund of gold and currencies available to members for stabilization of their respective currencies (the **International Monetary Fund**); and
3. The establishment of a bank that would provide funding for long-term development projects (the **World Bank**).

Like the gold standard at the turn of the century, all participants were to establish par values of their currencies in terms of gold. Unlike the prior system, however, there was little if any convertibility of currencies for gold expected; convertibility was versus the U.S. dollar ("good as gold"). In fact, the only currency officially convertible to gold was the U.S. dollar (pegged at $35/ounce). It was this reliance on the value of the dollar and the reliance on the economic stability of the U.S. economy, in fact, which led to 25 years of relatively stable currency and to the system's eventual collapse.

TIMES OF CRISIS, 1971–1973

On August 15, 1971, President Richard M. Nixon of the United States announced that "I have instructed [Treasury] Secretary [John B.] Connally to suspend temporarily the convertibility of the dollar into gold or other assets." With this simple statement, President Nixon effectively ended the fixed exchange rates established at Bretton Woods, New Hampshire, more than 25 years earlier.

In the weeks and months following the August announcement, world currency markets devalued the dollar, although the United States had only ended gold convertibility, not officially declared the dollar's value to be less. In late 1971, the Group of Ten finance ministers met at the Smithsonian Institution in Washington, DC, to try to piece together a system to keep world markets operational. First, the dollar was officially devalued to $38/ounce of gold (as if anyone had access to gold convertibility). Second, all other major world currencies were revalued against the dollar (the dollar was relatively devalued), and all would now be allowed to vary from their fixed parity rates by plus/minus 2.25 percent from the previous 1.00 percent.

Without convertibility of at least one of the member currencies to gold, the system was doomed from the start. Within weeks, currencies were surpassing their allowed deviation limits; revaluations were occurring more frequently; and the international monetary system was not a "system," it was chaos. Finally, world currency trading nearly ground to a halt in March 1973. The world's currency markets closed for two weeks. When they reopened, major currencies (particularly the U.S. dollar) were simply allowed to float in value. In January 1976, the Group of Ten once again met, this time in Jamaica, and the Jamaica Agreement officially recognized what the markets had known for years—the world's currencies were no longer fixed in value.

FLOATING EXCHANGE RATES, 1973–PRESENT

Since March 1973, the world's major currencies have floated in value versus each other. This flotation poses many problems for the conduct of international trade and commerce, problems that are themselves the subject of entire courses of study (*currency risk management* for one). The inability of a country, a country's government to be specific, to control the value of its currency on world markets has been a harsh reality for most.

Throughout the 1970s, if a government wished to alter the current value of its currency, or even slow or alter a trending change in the currency's value, the government would simply buy or sell its own currency in the market using its reserves of other major currencies. This process of **direct intervention** was effective as long as the depth of the government's reserve pockets kept up with the volume of trading on currency markets. For these countries—both then and today—the primary problem is maintaining adequate foreign exchange reserves.

By the 1980s, however, the world's currency markets were so large that the ability of a few governments (the United States, Japan, and Germany to name three) to move a market simply through direct intervention was over. The major tool now left was for government (at least when operating alone) to alter economic variables such as interest rates—to alter the *motivations* and *expectations* of market participants for capital movements and currency exchange. During periods of relative low inflation (a critical assumption), a country that wishes to strengthen its currency versus others might raise domestic interest rates to attract capital from abroad. Although relatively effective in many cases, the downside of this policy is that it raises interest rates for domestic consumers and investors alike, possibly slowing the domestic economy. The result is that governments today must often choose between an external economic policy action (raising interest rates to strengthen the currency) and a domestic economic policy action (lowering interest rates to stimulate economic activity).

There is, however, one other method of currency value management that has been selectively employed in the past 15 years, termed **coordinated intervention.** After the U.S. dollar had risen in value dramatically over the 1980 to 1985 period, the Group of Five, or G5, nations (France, Japan, West Germany, United States, and United Kingdom) met at the Plaza Hotel in New York in September 1985 and agreed to a set of goals and policies, the **Plaza Agreement.** These goals were to be accomplished through coordinated intervention among the central banks of the major nations. By the Bank of Japan (Japan), the Bundesbank (Germany), and the Federal Reserve (United States) all simultaneously intervening in the currency markets, they hoped to reach the combined strength level necessary to push the dollar's value down. Their actions were met with some success in that instance, but there have been few occasions since then of coordinated intervention.

The European Monetary System and the Euro

In the week following the suspension of dollar convertibility to gold in 1971, the finance ministers of a number of the major countries of western Europe discussed how they might maintain the fixed parities of their currencies independent of the U.S. dollar. By April 1972, they had concluded an agreement that was termed the "snake within the tunnel." The member countries agreed to fix parity rates between currencies with allowable trading bands of 2.25 percent variance. As a group they would allow themselves to vary by 4.5 percent versus the U.S. dollar. Although the effort was well intentioned, the various pressures and crises that rocked international economic order in the 1970s, such as the OPEC price shock of 1974, resulted in a relatively short life for the "snake."

In 1979 a much more formalized structure was put in place among many of the major members of the European Community. The **European Monetary System (EMS)** officially began operation in March 1979 and once again established a grid of fixed parity rates among member currencies. The EMS was a much more elaborate system for the management of exchange rates than its predecessor "snake." The EMS consisted of three different components that would work in concert to preserve fixed parities (also termed central rates).

First, all countries that were committing their currencies and their efforts to the preservation of fixed exchange rates entered the **Exchange-Rate Mechanism (ERM).** Although all the currencies of the countries of the European Union would be used in the calculation of important indices for management purposes, several countries chose not to be ERM participants. Participation in the ERM technically required that countries accept bilateral responsibility of maintaining the fixed rates.

The second element of the European Monetary System was the actual grid of bilateral exchange rates with their specified band limits. As under the Smithsonian Agreement and the former snake, member currencies were allowed to deviate ±2.25 percent from their parity rate. Some currencies, however, such as the Italian lira, were originally allowed larger bands (610 percent variance) due to their more characteristic volatility.

The third and final element of the European Monetary System was the creation of the European Currency Unit (ECU). The ECU was a weighted average index of the currencies that are part of the EMS. Each currency was weighted by a value reflecting the relative size of that country's trade and gross domestic product. This allowed each currency to be defined in units per ECU.

The need for fixed exchange rates within Europe was clear. The countries of western Europe trade among themselves to a degree approaching interstate commerce in the United States. It was therefore critical to the economics and businesses of Europe that exchange rates be as stable as possible. Although it had its critics, the EMS generally was successful in providing exchange rate stability.

THE MAASTRICHT TREATY

In an attempt to maintain the momentum of European integration, the members of the European Union concluded the **Maastricht Treaty** in December 1991. The treaty, besides laying out long-term goals of harmonized social and welfare policies in the Union, specified a timetable for the adoption of a single currency to replace all individual currencies. This was a very ambitious move. The Maastricht Treaty called for the integration and coordination of economic and monetary policy so that few financial differences would exist by the time of currency unification in 1997. For a single currency to work, there could be only one monetary policy across all countries. Otherwise, different monetary policies would lead to different interest rates. Differences in interest rates often lead to large capital flows.

The first major hurdle for the single currency was the acceptance of the treaty. Denmark had been successful in gaining the right to conduct a popular vote of its citizens to determine whether the degree of integration described by Maastricht was indeed desirable. In May 1992, the Danes voted "nej" (no). The Irish and French immediately scheduled popular votes in their own countries. The Irish vote resulted in a relatively strong show of support, while the French vote conducted on September 20 was an extremely narrow yes vote. The French result was immediately dubbed "le petit oui."

THE EURO

On December 31, 1998, the final fixed rates between the eleven participating currencies and the euro were put into place. On January 1, 1999, the **euro** was officially launched as a single currency for the European Union. This new currency will eventually replace all the individual currencies of the participating member states, resulting in a single, simple, efficient medium of exchange for all trade and investment activities.

"Why" Monetary Unification

According to the European Union, "Economic and Monetary Union (EMU) is a single currency area within the European Union single market in which people, goods, services, and capital move without restrictions." Beginning with the Treaty of Rome in 1957 and continuing with the Single European Act of 1987, the Maastricht Treaty of 1992, and the Treaty of Amsterdam of 1997 (draft), a core set of European countries has been working steadily toward integrating their individual countries into one larger, more efficient, domestic market. Even after the launch of the 1992 Single Europe program, however, a number of barriers to true openness remained. The use of different currencies was thought to still require both consumers and companies to treat the individual markets separately. And currency risk of cross-border commerce still persisted. The creation of a single currency is to move beyond these last vestiges of separated markets.

The growth of global markets and the increasing competitiveness of the Americas and Asia drove the members of the European Union in the 1980s and 1990s to take actions which would allow their people and their firms to compete globally. The reduction of barriers across all member countries to allow economies of scale (size and cost per unit) and scope (horizontal and vertical integration) was thought to be Europe's only hope to not be left behind in the new millennium. The economic potential of the EU is substantial. The successful implementation of a single, strong, and dependable currency for the conduct of "life" could well alter the traditional dominance of the U.S. dollar as the world's currency.

Fiscal Policy and Monetary Policy

The monetary policy for the EMU will be conducted by the newly formed European Central Bank (ECB), which according to its founding principles in the Maastricht Treaty will have one singular responsibility: to safeguard the stability of the euro. Following the basic structures that were used in the establishment of the Federal Reserve System in the United States and the Bundesbank in Germany, the ECB is free of political pressures that historically have caused monetary authorities to yield to employment pressures by inflating economies. The ECB's independence will allow it to focus simply on the stability of the currency without falling victim to history's trap.

The ECB is headquartered in Frankfurt, and became operational in June 1998. It became responsible for the entire monetary policy of the eleven participating states on January 1, 1999. It consists of a president whose term is eight years, assisted by a vice president and four executives from member states. The ECB's governing council sets interest rates in conjunction with the directors of the individual national central banks. These national central banks now—in conjunction with the ECB—form the European System of Central Banks (ESCB). The ECB will for the most part establish policy and the ESCB will be responsible for implementation, regulation, and enforcement. All things considered, however, the ECB will now set only one interest rate for the whole of the EU 11.

Fixing the Value of the Euro

The December 31, 1998, fixing of the rates of exchange between national currencies and the euro resulted in the conversion rates shown in Table 7.3. These are permanent fixes for these currencies. As illustrated, there are 11 EU member participants in the EMU. The British, as has been the case since the passage of the Maastricht Treaty, are skeptical of increasing EU infringement on their sovereignty, including the euro itself. Sweden, which has failed to see significant benefits from EU membership (although it is one of the newest members), is also skeptical of EMU participation. Sweden rejected euro membership in September 2003, as noted in the accompanying Focus on Politics. Denmark, like Britain and Sweden, has a strong political element that is highly nationalistic, and has opted for now not to participate. The Greeks, however, were very much in favor of participation but could not currently qualify because of the size of their fiscal deficits and national debt, as well as inflation. It is believed, however, they will be able to reach the qualifying numbers relatively soon.

The European Union has been very careful to differentiate the euro from its predecessor the ECU (the European Currency Unit). The euro is actually money, whereas the ecu was an index of money. The ecu was never legal tender under European law, whereas the euro is legal tender. The ecu's value was based on the composition currencies of the European Union's participants in the European Monetary System, whereas the euro is a completely independent currency or money that is exchangeable into other currencies, but not dependent on them for its value. The primary purpose for the ecu's existence was the construction of the exchange rate bands for the conduct of the Exchange Rate Mechanism (ERM) of the EMS. The euro replaced all individual currencies.

On January 4, 1999, the euro began trading on world currency markets. Its introduction was a smooth one, with trading heavy and relatively stable. The euro's value

TABLE 7.3

The Fixing of the Exchange Rates to the Euro (€)

Previous Currency	Symbol	Per Euro	
Belgian or Luxembourg francs	BEF/LUF	40.3399	1 euro = 40.3399 BEF or LUF
Deutschemarks	DEM	1.95583	1 euro = 1.95583 DEM
Spanish peseta	ESP	166.386	1 euro = 166.386 ESP
French francs	FRF	6.55957	1 euro = 6.55957 FRF
Irish punts	IEP	0.787564	1 euro = 0.787564 IEP
Italian lira	ITL	1936.27	1 euro = 1936.27 ITL
Netherlands guilders	NLG	2.20371	1 euro = 2.20371 NLG
Austrian shillings	ATS	13.7603	1 euro = 13.7603 ATS
Portuguese escudo	PTE	200.482	1 euro = 200.482 PTE
Finnish marks	FIM	5.94573	1 euro = 5.94573 FIM

Focus On ⬇

POLITICS

Sweden Says No to the Euro

Europe's common currency, the euro—introduced four and one half years ago as a global competitor to the dollar and the most visible symbol of the continent's postwar unity—is facing its most serious crisis since its inception. France and Germany, which have the biggest economies of the 12 countries that use the euro, are breaking the strict budget rules governing the currency by running huge public-spending deficits. Growth continues to sputter in the euro zone, while the United States is showing initial signs of recovery. Unemployment has risen to 12.5 million. And the near-record-high value of the currency is hurting competitiveness by dampening exports.

Last week voters in Sweden overwhelmingly rejected adopting the euro in favor of keeping their national currency, the krona. Sweden's entry would have expanded the euro zone's economy just 3.6 percent, but the rejection, based in part on voters' concerns about problems they see in the euro zone, could strengthen resistance in the other two holdouts in the 15-country European Union, Britain and Denmark.

"The outcome of the Swedish referendum was no surprise," said Dominique Barbet, senior economist for the French bank BNP Paribas. "The euro zone is definitely not looking attractive right now." He added, "We knew from the beginning that the euro zone was not a perfect monetary zone."

The euro's current troubles are highlighting the enormous difficulties of melding a dozen disparate economies into a single monetary union. It shows that despite statements of integration and European unity, many countries are willing to break ranks when they feel their national interests are being subordinated to a common goal. "I don't see any threat" to the euro zone as a whole, said Lars Calmfors, a Stockholm University economist. "But what is happening now is serious, and it's a bad situation in some countries."

Source: Abstracted from "Euro Facing a Major Test: Zone Nations Show Willingness to Break Ranks," by Keith B. Richburg, *The Washington Post,* September 24, 2003, p. E1.

has first fallen substantially, then risen substantially, against the dollar since its inception. In both 2000 and 2001 its value neared \$0.85/€, but in 2003 surged to nearly \$1.18/€. Figure 7.5 illustrates the euro's value versus the U.S. dollar since its inception.

Beginning on January 1, 2002, the individual coins and notes of the national currencies were gradually withdrawn from circulation and replaced with euro notes and coins. This constituted the last stage of monetary unification and was completed with few problems of any significance.

The official abbreviation of the euro is EUR, and has been registered with the International Standards Organization (ISO), and is similar to the three-letter computer symbols used for the United States dollar, USD, and the British pound sterling, GBP. The official symbol of the euro is €, an E with two horizontal parallel lines across it. According to the European Commission, the symbol was inspired by the Greek letter epsilon, simultaneously referring to Greece's ancient role as the source of European civilization, as well as being the first letter in the word Europe.

Where the euro's value will go in the coming months and years is now a matter of markets. The fundamental factors that affect the supply and demand for any currency—inflation, monetary and fiscal policy, balance of payments—all will now drive the value of the euro. Many pundits believe the inherent strength and structure of the ECB will continue to provide a sound footing for the growth of EU business, and therefore the continued health of the euro's value on world currency markets. It is important to note, however, that the long-term goal of most exchange rate policies is stability, not *strength* or *weakness*.

FIGURE 7.5

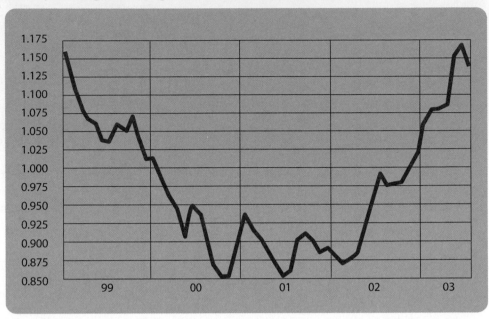

Monthly Average Exchange Rates: U.S. Dollars per Euro

Source: © 2003 by Prof. Werner Antweiler, University of British Columbia, Vancouver, BC, Canada. Permission is granted to reproduce the above image provided that the source and copyright are acknowledged. Time period shown in diagram: 1/Jan/1999–23/Jul/2003.

International Money Markets

A money market traditionally is defined as a market for deposits, accounts, or securities that have maturities of one year or less. The international money markets, often termed the Eurocurrency markets, constitute an enormous financial market that is in many ways outside the jurisdiction and supervision of world financial and governmental authorities.

EUROCURRENCY MARKETS

A **Eurocurrency** is any foreign currency-denominated deposit or account at a financial institution outside the country of the currency's issuance. For example, U.S. dollars that are held on account in a bank in London are termed **Eurodollars.** Similarly, Japanese yen held on account in a Parisian financial institution would be classified as Euroyen. The *Euro* prefix does not mean these currencies or accounts are only European, as German marks on account in Singapore would also be classified as a Eurocurrency, a Euromark account.

EUROCURRENCY INTEREST RATES

What is the significance of these foreign currency-denominated accounts? Simply put, it is the purity of value that comes from no governmental interference or restrictions with their use. Eurocurrency accounts are not controlled or managed by governments (for example, the Bank of England has no control over Eurodollar accounts), therefore, the financial institutions pay no deposit insurance, hold no reserve requirements, and normally are not subject to any interest rate restrictions with respect to such accounts. Eurocurrencies are one of the purest indicators of what these currencies should yield in terms of interest. Sample Eurocurrency interest rates are shown in Table 7.4.

There are hundreds of different major interest rates around the globe, but the international financial markets focus on a very few, the **interbank interest rates.** Interbank rates charged by banks to banks in the major international financial centers such as London, Frankfurt, Paris, New York, Tokyo, Singapore, and Hong Kong are generally regarded as "the interest rate" in the respective market. The interest rate that is used most often in international loan agreements is the Eurocurrency interest rate on U.S. dollars (Eurodollars) in London between banks: the London Interbank Offer Rate (LIBOR). Because it is a Eurocurrency rate, it floats freely without regard to governmental restrictions on reserves or deposit insurance or any other regulation or restriction that would add expense to transactions using this capital. The interbank rates for other currencies in other markets are often named similarly, PIBOR (Paris Interbank Offer Rate), MIBOR (Madrid Interbank Offer Rate), HIBOR (either Hong Kong or Helsinki Interbank Offer Rate), SIBOR (Singapore Interbank Offer Rate). While **LIBOR** is the offer rate—the cost of funds "offered" to those acquiring a loan—the equivalent deposit rate in the **Euromarkets** is LIBID, the London Interbank Bid Rate, the rate of interest other banks can earn on Eurocurrency deposits.

How do these international Eurocurrency and interbank interest rates differ from domestic rates? Answer: not by much. They generally move up and down in unison, by currency, but often differ by the percentage by which the restrictions alter the rates of interest in the domestic markets. For example, because the Euromarkets have no restrictions, the spread between the offer rate and the bid rate (the loan rate and the deposit rate) is substantially smaller than in domestic markets. This means the loan rates in international markets are a bit lower than domestic market loan rates, and deposit rates are a bit higher in the international markets than in domestic markets.

TABLE 7.4

Exchange Rates and Eurocurrency Interest Rates

Interest Rate/Exchange Rate	Maturity	Eurodollar Interest Rates	Euro-Pound Interest Rates
	1 month	1.900%	3.850%
	3 months	1.920%	4.040%
	6 months	2.200%	4.260%
	12 months	2.500%	4.650%
Exchange rates:			
Spot rate		$1.4178/£	
Forward rates	1 month	$1.4155/£	
	3 months	$1.4104/£	
	6 months	$1.4035/£	
	12 months	$1.3887/£	

This is, however, only a big-player market. Only well-known international firms, financial or nonfinancial, have access to the quantities of capital necessary to operate in the Euromarkets. But as described in the following sections on international debt and equity markets, more and more firms are gaining access to the Euromarkets to take advantage of deregulated capital flows.

LINKING EUROCURRENCY INTEREST RATES AND EXCHANGE RATES

Eurocurrency interest rates also play a large role in the foreign exchange markets themselves. They are, in fact, the interest rates used in the calculation of the forward rates we noted earlier. Recall that a forward rate is a contract for a specific amount of currency to be exchanged for another currency at a future date, usually 30, 60, 90, 180, or even 360 days in the future. Forward rates are calculated from the spot rate in effect on the day the contract is written along with the respective Eurocurrency interest rates for the two currencies.

For example, to calculate the 90-day forward rate for the U.S. dollar–British pound cross rate, the spot exchange rate is multiplied by the ratio of the two Eurocurrency interest rates—the eurodollar and the euro-pound rates. Note that it is important to adjust the interest rates for the actual period of time needed, 90 days (3 months) of a 360-day financial year:

$$\text{90-Day Forward Rate} = \text{Spot} \times \frac{1 + \left(i_{90}^{\$} \times \frac{90}{360}\right)}{1 + \left(i_{90}^{\pounds} \times \frac{90}{360}\right)}$$

Now, plugging in the spot exchange rate of \$1.4178/£ and the two 90-day (3-month) Eurocurrency interest rates from Table 7.4 (1.92 percent for the dollar and 4.04 percent for the pound), the 90-day forward exchange rate is:

$$\text{90-Day Forward Rate} = \$1.4178/\pounds \times \frac{1 + \left(.0192 \times \frac{90}{360}\right)}{1 + \left(.0404 \times \frac{90}{360}\right)} = \$1.4104/\pounds$$

The forward rate of 1.4104/£ is a "weaker rate" for the British pound than the current spot rate. This is because one British pound will yield \$1.4178 in the spot market, but only \$1.4104 in the forward market (at 90 days). The British pound would be said to be "selling forward at a discount," while the dollar would be described as "selling forward at a premium" because its value is stronger at the 90-day forward rate.

Why is this the case? The reason is that the 90-day Eurocurrency interest rate on the U.S. dollar is lower than the corresponding Eurocurrency interest rate on the British pound. If it were the other way around—if the U.S. dollar interest rate were higher than the British pound interest rate—the British pound would be selling forward at a premium. The forward exchange rates quoted in the markets, and used so frequently in international business, simply reflect the difference in interest rates between currencies.

Businesses frequently use forward exchange rate contracts to manage their exposure to currency risk. As Chapter 18 will detail, corporations use many other financial instruments and techniques beyond forward contracts to manage currency risk, but forwards are still the mainstay of industry.

International Capital Markets

Just as with the money markets, the international capital markets serve as links among the capital markets of individual countries, as well as constituting a separate market of their own—the capital that flows into the Euromarkets. Firms can now raise capital, debit or equity, fixed or floating interest rates, in any of a dozen currencies, for maturities ranging from one month to thirty years, in the international capital markets. Although the international capital markets traditionally have been dominated by debt instruments, international equity markets have shown considerable growth in recent years.

The international financial markets can be subdivided in a number of ways. The following sections describe the international debt and equity markets for securitized and nonsecuritized capital. This is capital that is separable and tradable, like a bond or a stock. *Nonsecuritized*, a fancy term for bank loans, was really the original source of international capital (as well as the international debt crisis).

DEFINING INTERNATIONAL FINANCING

The definition of what constitutes an international financial transaction is dependent on two fundamental characteristics: (1) whether the borrower is domestic or foreign, and (2) whether the borrower is raising capital denominated in the domestic currency or a foreign currency. These two characteristics form four categories of financial transactions, as illustrated in Figure 7.6

- **Category 1: Domestic Borrower/Domestic Currency.** This is a traditional domestic financial market activity. A borrower who is resident within the country raises capital from domestic financial institutions denominated in local currency. All countries with basic market economies have their own domestic financial markets, some large and some quite small. This is still by far the most common type of financial transaction.

- **Category 2: Foreign Borrower/Domestic Currency.** This is when a foreign borrower enters another country's financial market and raises capital denominated in the local currency. The international dimension of this transaction is based only on who the borrower is. Many borrowers, both public and private, increasingly go to the world's largest financial markets to raise capital for their enterprises. The ability of a foreign firm to raise capital in another country's financial market is sometimes limited by that government's restrictions on who can borrow, as well as the market's willingness to lend to foreign governments and companies that it may not know as well as domestic borrowers.

- **Category 3: Domestic Borrower/Foreign Currency.** Many borrowers in today's international markets need capital denominated in a foreign currency. A domestic firm may actually issue a bond to raise capital in its local market where it is known quite well, but raise the capital in the form of a foreign currency. This type of financial transaction occurs less often than the previous two types because it requires a local market in foreign currencies, a Eurocurrency market. A number of countries, such as the United States, highly restrict the amount and types of financial transactions in foreign currency. International financial centers such as London and Zurich have been the traditional centers of these types of transactions.

- **Category 4: Foreign Borrower/Foreign Currency.** This is the strictest form of the traditional Eurocurrency financial transaction, a foreign firm borrowing foreign currency. Once again, this type of activity may be restricted by which

FIGURE 7.6

**Categorizing International Financial Transactions:
Issuing Bonds in London**

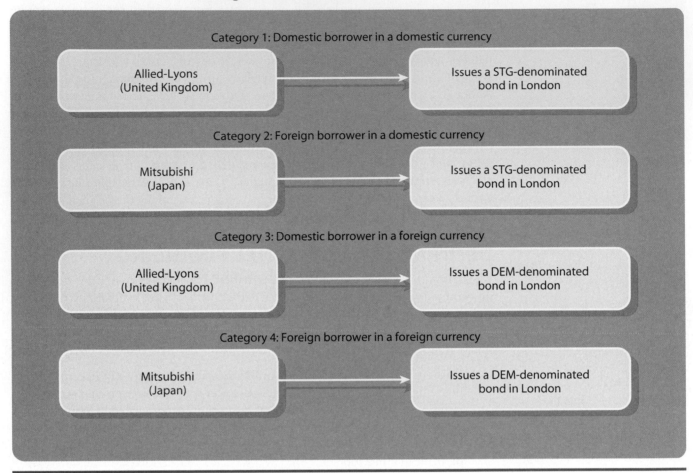

Category 1: Domestic borrower in a domestic currency

Allied-Lyons
(United Kingdom) → Issues a STG-denominated
bond in London

Category 2: Foreign borrower in a domestic currency

Mitsubishi
(Japan) → Issues a STG-denominated
bond in London

Category 3: Domestic borrower in a foreign currency

Allied-Lyons
(United Kingdom) → Issues a DEM-denominated
bond in London

Category 4: Foreign borrower in a foreign currency

Mitsubishi
(Japan) → Issues a DEM-denominated
bond in London

borrowers are allowed into a country's financial markets and which currencies are available. This type of financing dominates the activities of many banking institutions in the **offshore banking** market.

Using this classification system, it is possible to categorize any individual international financial transaction. For example, the distinction between an international bond and a Eurobond is simply that of a Category 2 transaction (foreign borrower in a domestic currency market) and a Category 3 or 4 transaction (foreign currency denominated in a single local market or many markets).

International Banking and Bank Lending

Banks have existed in different forms and roles since the Middle Ages. Bank loans have provided nearly all of the debt capital needed by industry since the start of the Industrial Revolution. Even in this age in which securitized debt instruments (bonds, notes, and other types of tradable paper) are growing as sources of capital for firms

The Locations of the World's International Financial Centers (IFCs) and International Offshore Financial Centers (IOFCs)

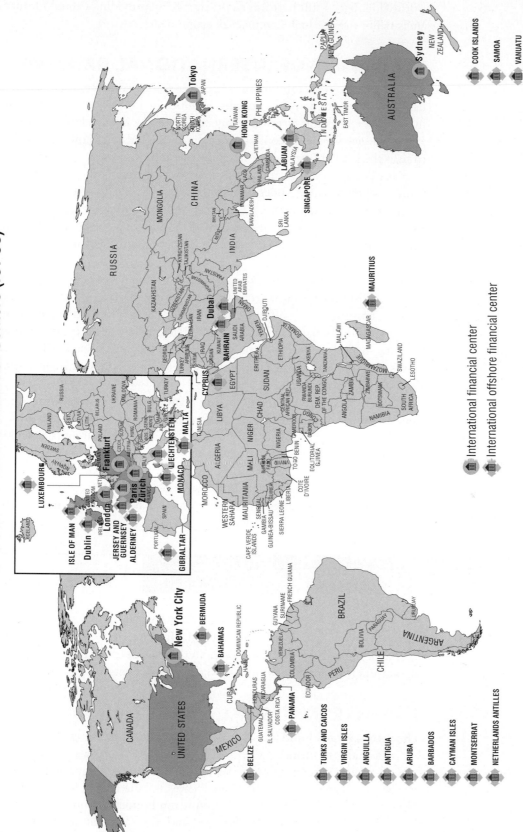

Note: *International Financial Centers (IFCs)* are the traditional centers of international financial activity, and normally include the conduct of both domestic and international financial transactions. *International Offshore Financial Centers (IOFCs)* are centers of offshore financial activities only (no interaction is allowed with the domestic financial or business community), and normally exist because of specific tax laws and provisions which encourage their establishment and allow them special treatment.

International financial center

International offshore financial center

MAP

Source: *Multinational Business Finance*, 7th Ed., Eiteman, Stonehill, and Moffett.

worldwide, banks still perform a critical role by providing capital for medium-sized and smaller firms, which dominate all economies.

STRUCTURE OF INTERNATIONAL BANKING

Similar to the direct foreign investment decision sequence discussed in Chapter 5, banks can expand their cross-border activities in a variety of ways. Like all decisions involving exports and direct investment, increasing the level of international activity and capability normally requires placing more capital and knowledge at risk to be able to reap the greater benefits of expanding markets.

A bank that wants to conduct business with clients in other countries but does not want to open a banking operation in that country can do so through correspondent banks or representative offices. A **correspondent bank** is an unrelated bank (by ownership) based in the foreign country. By the nature of its business, it has knowledge of the local market and access to clients, capital, and information, which a foreign bank does not.

A second way that banks may gain access to foreign markets without actually opening a banking operation there is through representative offices. A **representative office** is basically a sales office for a bank. It provides information regarding the financial services of the bank, but cannot deliver the services itself. It cannot accept deposits or make loans. The foreign representative office of a U.S. bank will typically sell the bank's services to local firms that may need banking services for trade or other transactions in the United States.

If a bank wants to conduct banking business within the foreign country, it may open a branch banking office, a banking affiliate, or even a wholly owned banking subsidiary. A branch banking office is an extension of the parent bank and is not independently financed from the parent. The branch office is not independently incorporated, and therefore is commonly restricted in the types of banking activities that it may conduct. Branch banking is by far the most common form of international banking structure used by banks, particularly by banks based in the United States.

International Security Markets

Although banks continue to provide a large portion of the international financial needs of government and business, it is the international debt securities markets that have experienced the greatest growth in the past decade. The international security markets include bonds, equities, and private placements.

THE INTERNATIONAL BOND MARKET

The **international bond** market provides the bulk of financing. The four categories of international debt financing discussed previously particularly apply to the international bond markets. Foreign borrowers have been using the large, well-developed capital markets of countries such as the United States and the United Kingdom for many years. These issues are classified generally as **foreign bonds** as opposed to Eurobonds. Each has gained its own pet name for foreign bonds issued in that market. For example, foreign bond issues in the United States are called Yankee bonds, in the United Kingdom Bulldogs, in the Netherlands Rembrandt bonds, and in Japan they are called Samurai bonds. When bonds are issued by foreign borrowers in these markets, they are subject to the same restrictions that apply to all domestic borrowers. If a Japanese firm issues a bond in the United States, it still must comply with all rules of the U.S. Securities and Exchange Commission, including the fact that they must be dollar-denominated.

Bonds that fall into Categories 3 and 4 are termed **Eurobonds.** The primary characteristic of these instruments is that they are denominated in a currency other than that of the country where they are sold. For example, many U.S. firms may issue Euro-yen bonds on world markets. These bonds are sold in international financial centers such as London or Frankfurt, but they are denominated in Japanese yen. Because these Eurobonds are scattered about the global markets, most are a type of bond known as a **bearer bond.** A bearer bond is owned officially by whoever is holding it, with no master registration list being held by government authorities who then track who is earning interest income from bond investments.[4] Bearer bonds have a series of small coupons that border the bond itself. On an annual basis, one of the coupons is cut or "clipped" from the bond and taken to a banking institution that is one of the listed paying agents. The bank will pay the holder of the coupon the interest payment due, and usually no official records of payment are kept.

INTERNATIONAL EQUITY MARKETS

Firms are financed with both debt and equity. Although the debt markets have been the center of activity in the international financial markets over the past three decades, there are signs that international equity capital is becoming more popular. As more and more firms raise capital in the international equity markets, they also may find themselves more vulnerable to market reactions to war and terrorism, as described in the following Focus on Culture.

Again using the same categories of international financial activities, the Category 2 transaction of a foreign borrower in a domestic market in local currency is the predominant international equity activity. Foreign firms often issue new shares in foreign markets and list their stock on major stock exchanges such as those in New York, Tokyo, or London. The purpose of foreign issues and listings is to expand the investor base in the hope of gaining access to capital markets in which the demand for shares of equity ownership is strong.

Focus On ⬇

CULTURE

Equity Market Crises in the Twentieth Century

The largest equity market losses in the past century were primarily related to war and terrorism, and their associated economic devastation.

Country	Event	Equity Market Losses (real returns, %)
US	Terrorist attacks, September 11, 2001	−14%
US	October 1987 stock market crash	−23%
US	Bear market, 2000–2001	−37%
US	Wall Street crash of 1929	−60%
UK	Bear market, 1973–1974	−71%
Germany	World War II, 1945–1948	−91%
Japan	World War II, 1944–1947	−97%

Source: Adapted from Elroy Dimson, Paul Marsh, and Mike Staunton, *Triumph of the Optimists, 101 Years of Global Investment Returns,* Princeton: Princeton University Press, 2002, p. 58.

A foreign firm that wants to list its shares on an exchange in the United States does so through American Depository Receipts. These are the receipts to bank accounts that hold shares of the foreign firm's stock in that firm's country. The equities are actually in a foreign currency, so by holding them in a bank account and listing the receipt on the account on the American exchange, the shares can be revalued in dollars and redivided so that the price per share is more typical of that of the U.S. equity markets ($20 to $60 per share frequently being the desired range).

There was considerable growth in recent years in the Euro-equity markets. A Euro-equity issue is the simultaneous sale of a firm's shares in several different countries, with or without listing the shares on an exchange in that country. The sales take place through investment banks. Once issued, most Euro-equities are listed at least on the computer screen quoting system of the International Stock Exchange (ISE) in London, the SEAQ. As of late 1994, the Frankfurt stock exchange was the most globalized of major equity exchanges, with more than 45 percent of the firms listed on the exchange being foreign. At the same time, 18.8 percent of the firms on the London exchange were foreign, New York was a distant third with 7.6 percent foreign firms, with Tokyo fourth with less than 6 percent.

PRIVATE PLACEMENTS

One of the largest and largely unpublicized capital markets is the **private placement** market. A private placement is the sale of debt or equity to a large investor. The sale is normally a one-time-only transaction in which the buyer of the bond or stock purchases the investment and intends to hold it until maturity (if debt) or until repurchased by the firm (if equity). How does this differ from normal bond and stock sales? The answer is that the securities are not resold on a secondary market such as the domestic bond market or the New York or London stock exchanges. If the security was intended to be publicly traded, the issuing firm would have to meet a number of disclosure and registration requirements with the regulatory authorities. In the United States, this would be the Securities and Exchange Commission.

Historically, much of the volume of private placements of securities occurred in Europe, with a large volume being placed with large Swiss financial institutions and large private investors. But in recent years the market has grown substantially across all countries as the world's financial markets have grown and as large institutional investors (particularly pension funds and insurance firms) have gained control over increasing shares of investment capital.

GAINING ACCESS TO INTERNATIONAL FINANCIAL MARKETS

Although the international markets are large and growing, this does not mean they are for everyone. For many years, only the largest of the world's multinational firms could enter another country's capital markets and find acceptance. The reasons are information and reputation.

Financial markets are by definition risk-averse. This means they are very reluctant to make loans to or buy debt issued by firms that they know little about. Therefore, the ability to gain access to the international markets is dependent on a firm's reputation, its ability to educate the markets about what it does, how successful it has been, and its patience. The firm must in the end be willing to expend the resources and effort required to build a credit reputation in the international markets. If successful, the firm may enjoy the benefits of new, larger, and more diversified sources of the capital it needs.

The individual firm, whether it be a chili dog stand serving the international tastes of office workers at the United Nations Plaza or a major multinational firm such as Honda of Japan, is affected by exchange rates and international financial markets. Although the owner of the chili dog stand probably has more important and immediate problems than exchange rates to deal with, it is clear that firms such as Honda see the movements in these markets as critically important to their long-term competitiveness.

Summary

This chapter has spanned the breadth of the international financial markets from currencies to capital markets. The world's currency markets expanded threefold in only six years, and there is no reason to believe this growth will end. It is estimated that more than $1 trillion worth of currencies change hands daily, and the majority of it is either U.S. dollars, German marks, or Japanese yen. These are the world's major floating currencies.

But the world's financial markets are much more than currency exchanges. The rapid growth in the international financial markets—both on their own and as links between domestic markets—has resulted in the creation of a large and legitimate source of finance for the world's multinational firms. The recent expansion of market economics to more and more of the world's countries and economies sets the stage for further growth for the world's currency and capital markets, but also poses the potential for new external debt crises.

Questions for Discussion

1. What is the purpose of an exchange rate?
2. Who trades currencies? Why?
3. What is a forward exchange rate?
4. What is a currency worth?
5. Why is the Big Mac a good indicator of purchasing power parity?
6. Why would a gold standard probably not work today?
7. What is a "eurocurrency"?
8. Why was the euro created to replace the individual currencies of the European Union member rates?
9. How are exchange rates and interest rates combined to form forward exchange rates?
10. What are the major sources of debt and equity for multinational firms trying to raise capital in the international markets?

Internet Exercises

1. The IMF, World Bank, and United Nations are only a few of the major world organizations that track, report, and aid international economic and financial development. Using these web sites and others that may be linked to them, briefly summarize the economic outlook for the developed and emerging nations of the world. For example, the full text of Chapter 1 of the *World Economic Outlook*, published annually by the World Bank, is available through the IMF's web page.

International Monetary Fund	http://www.imf.org/
United Nations	http://www.unsystem.org/
The World Bank Group	http://www.worldbank.org/
Europa (EU) Homepage	http://europa.eu.int/
Bank for International Settlements	http://www.bis.org/

2. Current economic and financial statistics and commentaries are available via the IMF's web page under "What's New," "Fund Rates," and the "IMF Committee on Balance of Payments Statistics." For an in-depth examination of the IMF's ongoing initiative on the validity of these statistics, termed metadata, visit the IMF's Dissemination Standards Bulletin Board listed below.

International Monetary Fund	http://www.imf.org/
IMF's Dissemination Standards Bulletin Board	http://dsbb.imf.org/

3. Visit Moody's sovereign ceilings and foreign currency ratings service site on the web to evaluate what progress is being made in the nations of the Far East on recovering their perceived creditworthiness.

Moody's Sovereign Ceilings	http://www.moodys.com

4. American Depository Receipts (ADRs) now make up more than 10 percent of all equity trading on U.S. stock exchanges. As more companies based outside of the United States list on U.S. markets, the need to understand the principal forces that drive ADR values increases with each trading day. Beginning with JP Morgan's detailed description of the ADR process and current ADR trading activity, prepare a briefing for senior management in your firm encouraging them to consider internationally diversifying the firm's liquid assets portfolio with ADRs.

JP Morgan	http://www.JPMorgan.com

Take a Stand

More and more companies from emerging markets are listing their shares on the world's largest equity markets—such as London, Paris, New York, and Tokyo. By listing their shares they are opening the door to investors, and their capital, from around the world, allowing the firms to gain access to larger quantities of capital at cheaper rates sooner. But they are also giving up their exclusive ownership. No longer are investors limited to the citizens of one country; after listing, the companies are owned by the "citizens of the world." Companies like Nokia, once owned and operated by the citizens of Finland, or Cemex of Mexico, are now largely owned by large groups of institutional investors out of New York and London.

For Discussion

1. In order for companies to compete in the twenty-first century, they need global access to capital, meaning the ability to raise large quantities at the lowest possible

internationally available price. A company that wishes to remain largely domestic in ownership is doomed to slower growth versus global multinationals, and in the end, may simply be doomed altogether.

2. The ability to restrict ownership of firms to the residents of their own home country is the prerogative of all companies, and one that should not be given up lightly. What defines culture, society, and the economic context of nationalism is at the heart of the globalization debate. Not only should the concept of shareholder value maximization be tempered, but the very definition of who the shareholders should be.

CHAPTER

8

Economic Integration

Learning Objectives

- To review types of economic integration among countries

- To examine the costs and benefits of integrative arrangements

- To understand the structure of the European Union and its implications for firms within and outside Europe

- To explore the emergence of other integration agreements, especially in the Americas and Asia

- To suggest corporate response to advancing economic integration

Building Blocs Toward Worldwide Free Trade

Regional groupings based on economics became increasingly important in the last ten years. Thirty-two such groupings are estimated to be in existence: three in Europe, four in the Middle East, five in Asia, and ten each in Africa and the Americas. Trade within the three major blocs, the American, European, and Asian, has grown rapidly, while trading among these blocs or with outsiders is either declining or growing far more moderately.

Some of these groupings around the world have the superstructure of nation-states (such as the European Union), some (such as the ASEAN Free Trade Area) are multinational agreements that may be more political arrangements than cohesive trading blocs at present. Increasingly, new blocs are made up of several independent blocs; for example, the

European Economic Area is composed of the EU member nations and the nations belonging to the European Free Trade Area. Some arrangements are not trading blocs per se, but work to further them. The Free Trade Area of the Americas is a foreign policy initiative designed to further democracy in the region through incentives to capitalistic development and trade liberalization. The Andean Common Market and MERCOSUR have both indicated an intention to negotiate with the parties of the North American Free Trade Agreement (NAFTA) to create a hemispheric market. Regional economic integration in Asia has been driven more by market forces than by treaties and by a need to maintain balance in negotiations with Europe and North America. Broader formal agreements are in formative stages; for example, the Asia Pacific Economic

NAFTA
North American Free Trade Agreement

Canada, Mexico, United States
GNP: $10.8 trillion; 406 million people

EEA
European Economic Area

Total of 29 European nations

GNP: $10.8 trillion; 461 million people

APEC
21 countries
GNP: $18 trillion
2.5 billion people

FTAA
Free Trade Area of the Americas
34 countries
GNP: $14.4 trillion
800 million people

MERCOSUR
Southern Cone Common Market
Argentina, Brazil, Paraguay, Uruguay
GNP: $1.3 trillion; 220 million people

APEC

AFTA ASEAN Free Trade Area

Brunei, Cambodia, Indonesia, Laos, Malaysia, Myanmar, Philippines, Singapore, Thailand, Vietnam
GNP: $546 billion; 512 million people

Cooperation (APEC) initiated in 1989 would bring together partners from multiple continents and blocs. AFTA members are joined by such economic powerhouses as China, South Korea, Taiwan, and the United States.

Regional groupings are constantly being developed in multiple ways either internally, by adding new dimensions to the existing ones, or by creating new blocs. In 1995, informal proposals were made to create a new bloc between NAFTA and EU members called TAFTA, the Transatlantic Free Trade Area. Since the elimination of the Soviet Union in 1991, 12 former republics have tried to forge common economic policies, but thus far only Belarus, Kazakhstan, and Russia are signatories. In 2002, 12 EU countries adopted the euro as a common currency and eliminated their respective national currencies, and in 2004, the EU expanded to 25 nations, accepting eight

Central European and two Mediterranean countries to the Union.

Companies are facing ever-intensifying competition within these blocs but, at the same time, can take advantage of emerging opportunities. As new countries join blocs, fears that these blocs are nothing but protectionism on a grander scale are allayed. As governments liberalize their industrial sectors and allow for competition, they give birth to companies that are not only competitive regionally but globally as well.

Sources: "A Nervous New Arrival on the European Union's Bloc," *The Economist,* August 30, 2003, 16–18; "Mega Europe 25 states, 450 million Citizens," *Business Week,* November 25, 2002, 62; *The World Factbook 2003* available at http://www.cia.gov/; "The Euro: What You Need to Know," *The Wall Street Journal,* January 4, 1999, A5: A6; "World Trade Growth Slower in 1998 after Unusually Strong Growth in 1997," World Trade Organization press release, April 16, 1999, http://www.wto.org; "American Politics, Global Trade," *The Economist,* September 27, 1997, 23–26; and Ilkka A. Ronkainen, "Trading Blocs: Opportunity or Demise for International Trade?" *Multinational Business Review* 1 (Spring 1993): 1–9.

The benefits of free trade and stable exchange rates are available only if nation-states are willing to give up some measure of independence and autonomy. This has resulted in increased economic integration around the world with agreements among countries to establish links through movement of goods, services, capital, and labor across borders. Some predict, however, that the regional **trading blocs** of the new economic world order will divide into a handful of protectionist superstates that, although liberalizing trade among members, may raise barriers to external trade.

Economic integration is best viewed as a spectrum. At one extreme we might envision a truly global economy in which all countries share a common currency and agree to a free flow of goods, services, and factors of production. At the other extreme would be a number of closed economies, each independent and self-sufficient. The various integrative agreements in effect today lie along the middle of this spectrum. The most striking example of successful integration is the historic economic unification that is taking place around the world today. These developments were discussed in the chapter's opening vignette. Some countries, however, give priority to maintaining economic self-sufficiency and independence. Their ranks have thinned considerably with countries such as Vietnam becoming heavily involved in international trade and investment as well as regional economic integration through membership in two blocs. Even North Korea is now considered as a possible future market by companies such as Coca-Cola.

This chapter will begin with an explanation of the various levels of economic integration. The level of integration defines the nature and degree of economic links among countries. The major arguments both for and against economic integration will be reviewed. Next, the European Union, the North American Free Trade Agreement, Asia Pacific Economic Cooperation, and other economic alliances will be discussed. Finally, possible strategic moves by international managers in response to integration are outlined.

Levels of Economic Integration

A trading bloc is a preferential economic arrangement among a group of countries. The forms it may take are shown in Table 8.1. From least to most integrative, they are the free trade area, the customs union, the common market, and the economic union.[1] It should be noted that countries (or groups of countries) may give preferential treatment to other countries on the basis of historic ties or due to political motivations. Examples include the European Union's granting preferential access for selected products from their former colonies under the Lomé Convention, or similar treatment by the United States of Caribbean nations (the Caribbean Basin Initiative). Since the benefits are unidirectional, these arrangements are not considered to be part of economic integration.

THE FREE TRADE AREA

The **free trade area** is the least restrictive and loosest form of economic integration among countries. In a free trade area, all barriers to trade among member countries are removed. Therefore, goods and services are freely traded among member countries in much the same way that they flow freely between, for example, South Carolina and New York. No discriminatory taxes, quotas, tariffs, or other trade barriers are allowed. Sometimes a free trade area is formed only for certain classes of goods and services. An agricultural free trade area, for example, implies the absence of restrictions on the trade of agricultural products only. The most notable feature of a free trade area is that each country continues to set its own policies in relation to nonmembers. In other words, each member is free to set any tariffs, quotas, or other restrictions that it chooses on trade with countries outside the free trade area. Among such free trade areas the most notable are the European Free Trade Area (EFTA) and the North American Free Trade Agreement (NAFTA). As an example of the freedom members have in terms of their policies toward nonmembers, Mexico has signed a number of bilateral free trade agreements with other blocs (the European Union) and nations (Chile) to both improve trade and to attract foreign direct investment.

TABLE 8.1   **Forms of International Economic Integration**

Stage of Integration	Abolition of Tariffs and Quotas Among Members	Common Tariff and Quota System	Abolition of Restrictions on Factor Movements	Harmonization and Unification of Economic Policies and Institutions
Free trade area	Yes	No	No	No
Customs union	Yes	Yes	No	No
Common market	Yes	Yes	Yes	No
Economic union	Yes	Yes	Yes	Yes

Source: Franklin R. Root, *International Trade and Investment*, Cincinnati, Ohio: South-Western Publishing Company, 1992, 254.

Similarly, the United States has free trade agreements with Israel, Jordan, Chile, Singapore, and is in negotiations with the five Central American countries that form the Central American Common Market. Future discussions on free trade may involve such diverse countries as Morocco, Australia, and selected southern African nations.[2]

THE CUSTOMS UNION

The **customs union** is one step further along the spectrum of economic integration. Like the members of a free trade area, members of a customs union dismantle barriers to trade in goods and services among themselves. In addition, however, the customs union establishes a common trade policy with respect to nonmembers. Typically, this takes the form of a common external tariff, where imports from nonmembers are subject to the same tariff when sold to any member country. Tariff revenues are then shared among members according to a prespecified formula. The Southern African Customs Union is the oldest and most successful example of economic integration in Africa.

THE COMMON MARKET

Further still along the spectrum of economic integrations is the **common market.** Like the customs union, a common market has no barriers to trade among members and has a common external trade policy. In addition, however, factors of production are also mobile among members. Factors of production include labor, capital, and technology. Thus restrictions on immigration, emigration, and cross-border investment are abolished. The importance of **factor mobility** for economic growth cannot be overstated. When factors of production are freely mobile, then capital, labor, and technology may be employed in their most productive uses. To see the importance of factor mobility, imagine the state of the U.S. economy if unemployed steelworkers in Pittsburgh were prevented from migrating to the growing Sunbelt in search of better opportunities. Alternatively, imagine that savings in New York banks could not be invested in profitable opportunities in Chicago.

Despite the obvious benefits, members of a common market must be prepared to cooperate closely in monetary, fiscal, and employment policies. Furthermore, while a common market will enhance the productivity of members in the aggregate, it is by no means clear that individual member countries will always benefit. Because of these difficulties, the goals of common markets have proved to be elusive in many areas of the world, notably Central America and Asia. However, the objective of the **Single European Act** was to have a full common market in effect within the EU at the end of 1992. While many of the directives aimed at opening borders and markets were implemented on schedule, some sectors, such as automobiles and telecommunications, took longer to be liberalized.

THE ECONOMIC UNION

The creation of a true **economic union** requires integration of economic policies in addition to the free movement of goods, services, and factors of production across borders. Under an economic union, members would harmonize monetary policies, taxation, and government spending. In addition, a common currency would be used by all members. This could be accomplished de facto, or in effect, by a system of fixed exchange rates. Clearly, the formation of an economic union requires nations to surrender a large measure of their national sovereignty to supranational authorities in communitywide institutions such as the European Parliament. The ratification of the Maastricht Treaty by all of the then 12 member countries created the European

Union, effective January 1, 1994. The treaty (jointly with the Treaty of Amsterdam, which took effect in 1999) set the foundation for economic and monetary union (EMU) with the establishment of the euro (€) as a common currency by January 1, 1999. A total of 12 of the EU countries are currently part of "Euroland" (Austria, Belgium, Finland, France, Germany, Greece, Holland, Ireland, Italy, Luxembourg, Portugal, and Spain). In addition, moves would be made toward a **political union** with common foreign and security policy, as well as judicial cooperation.[3]

Arguments Surrounding Economic Integration

A number of arguments surround economic integration. They center on (1) trade creation and diversion; (2) the effects of integration on import prices, competition, economies of scale, and factor productivity; and (3) the benefits of regionalism versus nationalism.

TRADE CREATION AND TRADE DIVERSION

Economist Jacob Viner first formalized the economic costs and benefits of economic integration.[4] Chapter 5 illustrated that the classical theory of trade predicts a win-win result for countries participating in free trade. The question is whether similar benefits accrue when free trade is limited to one group of countries. The case examined by Viner was the customs union. The conclusion of Viner's analysis was that either negative or positive effects may result when a group of countries trade freely among themselves but maintain common barriers to trade with nonmembers.

Viner's arguments can be highlighted with a simple illustration. In 1986, Spain formally entered the European Union (EU) as a member. Prior to membership, Spain—like all nonmembers such as the United States, Canada, and Japan—traded with the EU and suffered the common external tariff. Imports of agricultural products from Spain or the United States had the same tariff applied to their products, for example, 20 percent. During this period, the United States was a lower-cost producer of wheat compared to Spain. U.S. exports to EU members may have cost $3.00 per bushel, plus a 20 percent tariff of $0.60, for a total of $3.60 per bushel. If Spain at the same time produced wheat at $3.20 per bushel, plus a 20 percent tariff of $0.64 for a total cost to EU customers of $3.84 per bushel, its wheat was more expensive and therefore less competitive.

But when Spain joined the EU as a member, its products were no longer subject to the common external tariffs; Spain had become a member of the "club" and therefore enjoyed its benefits. Spain was now the low-cost producer of wheat at $3.20 per bushel, compared to the price of $3.60 from the United States. Trade flows changed as a result. The increased export of wheat and other products by Spain to the EU as a result of its membership is termed **trade creation.** The elimination of the tariff literally created more trade between Spain and the EU. At the same time, because the United States was still outside of the EU, its products suffered the higher price as a result of tariff application. U.S. exports to the EU fell. When the source of trading competitiveness is shifted in this manner from one country to another, it is termed **trade diversion.**

Whereas trade creation is distinctly positive in moving toward freer trade, and therefore lower prices for consumers within the EU, the impact of trade diversion is negative. Trade diversion is inherently negative because the competitive advantage has shifted away from the lower-cost producer to the higher-cost producer. The benefits of Spain's membership are enjoyed by Spanish farmers (greater export sales) and EU consumers (lower prices). The two major costs are reduced tariff revenues collected and costs borne by the United States and its exports as a result of lost sales. In such cases, the injured party may seek compensation based on global trade rules. As a result of the European Union's expansion in 2004, the Japanese government argued that its exporters would lose sales of $22 million in the new member countries in product categories such as autos and consumer electronics. The EU argued that the Union's expansion would benefit Japanese companies in the long term.[5]

From the perspective of nonmembers such as the United States, the formation or expansion of a customs union is obviously negative. Most damaged will naturally be countries that may need to have trade to build their economies, such as the countries of the Third World. From the perspective of members of the customs union, the formation or expansion is only beneficial if the trade creation benefits exceed trade diversion costs. When Finland and Sweden joined the EU, the cost of an average food basket decreased by 10 percent. The only major item with a significant price increase was bananas due to the quota and tariff regime that the EU maintained in favor of its former colonies and against the major banana-producing nations in Latin America.

REDUCED IMPORT PRICES

When a small country imposes a tariff on imports, the price of the goods will typically rise because sellers will increase prices to cover the cost of the tariff. This increase in price, in turn, will result in lower demand for the imported goods. If a bloc of countries imposes the tariff, however, the fall in demand for the imported goods will be substantial. The exporting country may then be forced to reduce the price of the goods. The possibility of lower prices for imports results from the greater market power of the bloc relative to that of a single country. The result may then be an improvement in the trade position of the bloc countries. Any gain in the trade position of bloc members, however, is offset by a deteriorating trade position for the exporting country. Again, unlike the win-win situation resulting from free trade, the scenario involving a trade bloc is instead win-lose.

INCREASED COMPETITION AND ECONOMIES OF SCALE

Integration increases market size and therefore may result in a lower degree of monopoly in the production of certain goods and services.[6] This is because a larger market will tend to increase the number of competing firms, resulting in greater efficiency and lower prices for consumers. Moreover, less energetic and productive economies may be spurred into action by competition from the more industrious bloc members.

Many industries, such as steel and automobiles, require large-scale production in order to obtain economies of scale in production. Therefore, certain industries may simply not be economically viable in smaller, trade-protected countries. However, the formation of a trading bloc enlarges the market so that large-scale production is justified. The lower per-unit costs resulting from scale economies may then be obtained. These lower production costs resulting from greater production for an enlarged market are called **internal economies of scale.** This is evident if the region adopts common standards, thus allowing not only for bigger markets for the companies but enabling them to become global powerhouses. Ericsson and Nokia both benefited from the EU adopting the GSM standard for wireless communication to build scale beyond their small domestic markets.

In a common market, **external economies of scale** may also be present. Because a common market allows factors of production to flow freely across borders, the firm may now have access to cheaper capital, more highly skilled labor, or superior technology. These factors will improve the quality of the firm's good or service or will lower costs or both.

HIGHER FACTOR PRODUCTIVITY

When factors of production are freely mobile, the wealth of the common market countries, in aggregate, will likely increase. The theory behind this contention is straightforward: factor mobility will lead to the movement of labor and capital from areas of low productivity to areas of high productivity. In addition to the economic gains from factor mobility, there are other benefits not so easily quantified. The free movement of labor fosters a higher level of communication across cultures. This, in turn, leads to a higher degree of cross-cultural understanding; as people move, their ideas, skills, and ethnicity move with them.

Again, however, factor mobility will not necessarily benefit each country in the common market. A poorer country, for example, may lose badly needed investment capital to a richer country, where opportunities are perceived to be more profitable. Another disadvantage of factor mobility that is often cited is the brain-drain phenomenon. A poorer country may lose its most talented workers when they are free to search out better opportunities. More-developed member countries worry that companies may leave for other member countries where costs of operation, such as social costs, are lower. Many multinationals, such as Philips and Goodyear, have shifted their MERCOSUR production to Brazil from Argentina to take advantage of lower costs and incentives provided by the Brazilian government.[7]

REGIONALISM VERSUS NATIONALISM

Economists have composed elegant and compelling arguments in favor of the various levels of economic integration. It is difficult, however, to turn these arguments into reality in the face of intense nationalism. The biggest impediment to economic integration remains the reluctance of nations to surrender a measure of their autonomy. Integration, by its very nature, requires the surrender of national power and self-determinism. An example of this can be seen in Focus on Ethics.

European Integration

ECONOMIC INTEGRATION IN EUROPE FROM 1948 TO THE MID-1980S

The period of the Great Depression from the late 1920s through World War II was characterized by isolationism, protectionism, and fierce nationalism. The economic chaos and political difficulties of the period resulted in no serious attempts at economic integration until the end of the war. From the devastation of the war, however, a spirit of cooperation gradually emerged in Europe.

The first step in this regional cooperative effort was the establishment of the Organization for European Economic Cooperation (OEEC) in 1948 to administer Marshall Plan aid from the United States. Although the objective of the OEEC was

Focus On ⬇

Integration Pains

Economic integration will not make everyone happy, despite promises of great benefits from the free flow of people, goods, services, and money. More developed countries, such as the United States and France, fear a hemorrhage of jobs as companies shift their operations to less prosperous regions with lower wages or fewer governmental controls.

Approximately 85 percent of the over–$250 billion in U.S.–Mexican trade moves on trucks. More than 4 million commercial vehicles enter the United States from Mexico each year through 25 border crossings in Arizona, California, New Mexico, and Texas. Currently, all but a fraction are limited to a narrow strip along the border where freight is transferred to U.S.-based truckers for delivery to final destinations. Under NAFTA, cross-border controls on trucking were to be eliminated by the end of 1995, allowing commercial vehicles to move freely in four U.S. and six Mexican border states. But U.S. truckers, backed by the Teamsters Union, would have none of this, arguing that Mexican trucks were dangerous and exceeded weight limits. The union also worried that opening of the border would depress wages, because it would allow U.S. trucking companies to team up with lower-cost counterparts in Mexico. In early 2001, the NAFTA Arbitration Panel ruled that Mexican trucks must be allowed to cross U.S. borders, and in December the Senate finally approved a measure that permitted Mexican truckers to haul cargo on U.S. roads as long as they are subject to strict safety and inspection rules. The Bush administration, initially opposed to the bill on the grounds that it singled out Mexico for tougher inspections

and therefore violated NAFTA, withdrew its opposition after the September 11th terrorist attacks, accepting that safety standards on truck traffic, especially hazardous cargo, are a top priority.

In Europe, politicians blame other member countries for the loss of investment opportunities and the jobs they represent. France missed out to the United Kingdom when U.S. vacuum-cleaner firm Hoover shifted European production to Scotland, where a flexible workforce agreed to limits on strike actions, lower wages, and economies of scale, allowing the company to cut costs. France accused Britain of "social dumping"—eroding workers' rights in a bid to attract foreign direct investment. In France, firm labor laws protect wages and pensions and make redundancy decisions costly for employers. In May 2002, in response to a bill that would make it even tougher to lay off employees, Italian-owned Moulinex-Brandt and British retailer Marks & Spencer decided to pull back operations in France. Moulinex-Brandt announced plans to close three factories, laying off 2,900 workers. Medef, a French employers' organization, insists that unless France reforms its legal and fiscal business environment, it will continue to lose jobs and wealth-creating enterprises to its competitors in Europe. France's law reducing the work week from 39 hours to 35 has not helped matters, either. PSA Peugeot Citroën has diverted jobs outside of its home base. Its workforce outside of France has doubled to 68,000 over the last decade, while the domestic workforce has dwindled to 4,000. The expansion of the EU to cheaper-labor Central European countries may erode that base further.

Sources: "Mexican Trucks May Get Full Access," *The Washington Post,* November 28, 2002, A4; "Clocking Out," *The Wall Street Journal,* August 8, 2002, A1; "Hogtied," *The Economist,* January 17, 2002; Lyzette Alvarez, "Senate Votes to Let Mexican Trucks in U.S.," *The New York Times,* December 5, 2001; "Business Not As Usual," *The Economist,* April 26, 2001; "U.S. Is Told to Let Mexican Trucks Enter," *The Wall Street Journal,* February 7, 2001, A2; Ben Fox, "Border Nations Near Deal on Trucking," *The Associated Press,* June 3, 1999; "The Trucks That Hold Back NAFTA," *The Economist,* December 13, 1997: 23–24; "French Say United Europe Promotes 'Job Poaching,'" *The Washington Post,* February 10, 1993.

limited to economic reconstruction following the war, its success set the stage for more ambitious integration programs.

In 1952, six European countries (West Germany, France, Italy, Belgium, the Netherlands, and Luxembourg) joined in establishing the European Coal and Steel Community (ECSC). The objective of the ECSC was the formation of a common market in coal, steel, and iron ore for member countries. These basic industries were rapidly revitalized into competitive and efficient producers. The stage was again set for further cooperative efforts.

In 1957, the European Economic Community (EEC) was formally established by the **Treaty of Rome.** In 1967, ECSC and EEC as well as the European Atomic Energy Community (EURATOM) were merged to form the European Community (EC). Table 8.2 shows the founding members of the community in 1957, members who have joined since, as well as those invited to join early in the twenty-first century. The Treaty of Rome is a monumental document, composed of more than 200 articles.

TABLE 8.2   Membership of the European Union

1957	1993	1995	2004		2007+
France	+ Great Britain (1973)	+ Austria (1995)	+ Czech Republic	Latvia	Bulgaria
West Germany	Ireland (1973)	Finland (1995)	Cyprus	Lithuania	Romania
Italy	Denmark (1973)	Sweden (1995)	Estonia	Malta	
Belgium	Greece (1981)		Hungary	Slovakia	
Netherlands	Spain (1986)		Poland		
Luxembourg	Portugal (1986)		Slovenia		

The main provisions of the treaty are summarized in Table 8.3. The document was (and is) quite ambitious. The cooperative spirit apparent throughout the treaty was based on the premise that the mobility of goods, services, labor, and capital—the "four freedoms"—was of paramount importance for the economic prosperity of the region. Founding members envisioned that the successful integration of the European economies would result in an economic power to rival that of the United States.

Some countries, however, were reluctant to embrace the ambitious integrative effort of the treaty. In 1960, a looser, less integrated philosophy was endorsed with the formation of the European Free Trade Association (EFTA) by eight countries: United Kingdom, Norway, Denmark, Sweden, Austria, Finland, Portugal, and Switzerland. Barriers to trade among member countries were dismantled, although each country maintained its own policies with nonmember states. Since that time EFTA has lost much of its original significance due to its members joining the European Union (Denmark and the United Kingdom in 1973, Portugal in 1986, and Austria, Finland, and Sweden in 1995). EFTA countries have cooperated with the EU through bilateral free trade agreements, and, since 1994, through the European Economic Area (EEA) arrangement, which allows for free movement of people, goods, services, and capital within the combined area of the EU and EFTA. Of the EFTA countries, Iceland and Liechtenstein (which joined the EEA only in May 1995) have decided not to apply for membership in the EU. Norway was to have joined in 1995, but after a referendum

TABLE 8.3   Main Provisions of the Treaty of Rome

1. Formation of a free trade area: the gradual elimination of tariffs, and other barriers to trade among members
2. Formation of a customs union: the creation of a uniform tariff schedule applicable to imports from the rest of the world
3. Formation of a common market: the removal of barriers to the movement of labor, capital, and business enterprises
4. The adoption of common agricultural policies
5. The creation of an investment fund to channel capital from the more advanced to the less developed regions of the community

declined membership, as it did in 1973. Switzerland's decision to stay out of the EEA (mainly to keep the heaviest EU truck traffic from its roads) has hampered its negotiations for membership in the EU. In 2000, however, it entered into a series of bilateral agreements to liberalize its trading relations with the EU.[8]

A conflict that intensified throughout the 1980s was between the richer and more industrialized countries and the poorer countries of the Mediterranean region. The power of the bloc of poorer countries was strengthened in the 1980s when Greece, Spain, and Portugal became EU members. Many argue that the dismantling of barriers between the richer and poorer countries will benefit the poorer countries by spurring them to become competitive. However, it may also be argued that the richer countries have an unfair advantage and therefore should accord protection to the poorer members before all barriers are dismantled.

Another source of difficulty that intensified in the 1980s was the administration of the community's **common agricultural policy (CAP).** Most industrialized countries, including the United States, Canada, and Japan, have adopted wide-scale government intervention and subsidization schemes for the agriculture industry. In the case of the EU, however, these policies have been implemented on a communitywide, rather than national, level. The CAP includes: (1) a price-support system whereby EU agriculture officials intervene in the market to keep farm product prices within a specified range; (2) direct subsidies to farmers; and (3) rebates to farmers who export or agree to store farm products rather than sell them within the community. The implementation of these policies absorbs about two-thirds of the annual EU budget.

The CAP has caused problems both within the EU and in relationships with nonmembers. Within the EU, the richer, more industrialized countries resent the extensive subsidization of the more agrarian economies, including new member countries, such as Poland. Outside trading partners, especially the United States, have repeatedly charged the EU with unfair trade practices in agriculture. Developing countries complain about the EU's average 20 percent tariffs against their agricultural exports to the bloc and their $100 billion subsidies to their own farmers.[9]

THE EUROPEAN UNION SINCE THE MID-1980S

By the mid-1980s, a sense of "Europessimism" permeated most discussions of European integration. Although the members remained committed in principle to the "four freedoms," literally hundreds of obstacles to the free movement of goods, services, people, and capital remained. For example, there were cumbersome border restrictions on trade in many goods, and although labor was theoretically mobile, the professional certifications granted in one country were often not recognized in others.

Growing dissatisfaction with the progress of integration, as well as threats of global competition from Japan and the United States, prompted the Europeans to take action. A policy paper published in 1985 (now known as the **1992 White Paper**) exhaustively identified the remaining barriers to the four freedoms and proposed means of dismantling them.[10] It listed 282 specific measures designed to make the four freedoms a reality.

The implementation of the White Paper proposals began formally in 1987 with the passage of the Single European Act, which stated that "the community shall adopt measures with the aim of progressively establishing the internal market over a period expiring on 31 December 1992." The Single European Act envisaged a true common market where goods, people, and money could move between Germany and France with the same ease that they move between Wisconsin and Illinois.

Progress toward the goal of free movement of goods has been achieved largely due to the move from a "common standards approach" to a "mutual recognition approach." Under the common standards approach, EU members were forced to negotiate the specifications for literally thousands of products, often unsuccessfully. For example, because of differences in tastes, agreement was never reached on specifications for beer, sausage, or mayonnaise. Under the mutual recognition approach, the laborious quest for common standards is in most cases no longer necessary. Instead, as long as a product meets legal and specification requirements in one member country, it may be freely exported to any other, and customers serve as final arbiters of success.

Less progress toward free movement of people in Europe has been made than toward free movement of goods. The primary difficulty is that EU members have been unable to agree on a common immigration policy. As long as this disagreement persists, travelers between countries must pass through border checkpoints. Some countries—notably Germany—have relatively lax immigration policies, while others—especially those with higher unemployment rates—favor strict controls on immigration. A second issue concerning the free movement of people is the acceptability of professional certifications across countries. In 1993, the largest EU member countries passed all of the professional worker directives. This means that workers' professional qualifications will be recognized throughout the EU, guaranteeing them equal treatment in terms of employment, working conditions, and social protection in the host country.

Attaining free movement of capital within the EU entails several measures. First, citizens will be free to trade in EU currencies without restrictions. Second, the regulations governing banks and other financial institutions will be harmonized. In addition, mergers and acquisitions will be regulated by the EU rather than by national governments. Finally, securities will be freely tradable across countries.

A key aspect of free trade in services is the right to compete fairly to obtain government contracts. Under the 1992 guidelines, a government should not give preference to its own citizens in awarding government contracts. However, little progress has been made in this regard. Open competition in public procurement has been calculated to save $10 billion a year. Yet the nonnational share of contracts has been 5 percent since 1992. Worse still, few unsuccessful bidders complain, for fear that they would be ignored in future bids.[11]

Project 1992 was always a part of a larger plan and a process more so than a deadline.[12] Many in the EU bureaucracy argued that the 1992 campaign required a commitment to **economic and monetary union (EMU)** and subsequently to political union. These sentiments were confirmed at the Maastricht summit in December 1991, which produced various recommendations to that effect. The ratification of the Maastricht Treaty in late 1993 by all of the 12 member countries of the EC created the **European Union** starting January 1, 1994. The treaty calls for a commitment to economic and monetary union and a move toward political union with common foreign and security policy. (The European Monetary System, its history, and future are discussed in detail in Chapter 7.)

Despite the uncertainties about the future of the EU, new countries want to join. Most EFTA countries have joined or are EU applicants in spite of the fact that the EEA treaty gives them most of the benefits of a single market. They also want to have a say in the making of EU laws and regulations. Access to the EU is essential for the growth of the Baltic and Central European countries. At the same time, the EU hopes to underpin democracy and free markets in the once centrally planned dictatorships and create a zone of stability at the EU's eastern flank.[13] The enlargement will create investment opportunities for firms and ensure cheaper goods for consumers in the EU. Before investment occurs, however, productivity in the new member countries has to improve significantly. Turkey's application has been hindered by its poor human rights record, its unresolved dispute with Greece over Cyprus, and internal problems with Kurdish separatists. In the meantime, it will enjoy preferential trade rights through association memberships with the EU. In the long term, countries such as Belarus, Moldova, and Ukraine may become membership candidates.

ORGANIZATION OF THE EU

The executive body of the EU is the European Commission, headquartered in Brussels. The commission may be likened to the executive branch of the U.S. government. It is composed of 20 commissioners (two from each larger member country and one from each smaller member) and headed by a president. The commissioners oversee more than 30 directorates-general (or departments), such as agriculture, transportation, and external relations. The commissioners are appointed by the member states, but according to the Treaty of Rome, their allegiance is to the community, not to their home country. The commission's staff in Brussels numbers over 24,000. Since the EU has 11 official languages (9 more after 2004), 20 percent of the staff are interpreters and translators.

The Council of Ministers has the final power to decide EU actions. The votes are allocated to the representatives of member countries on the basis of country size. With the reweighting of votes to accommodate new members, the U.K. has 29 votes, while Finland has seven. Some of the most important provisions of the Single European Act expanded the ability of the council to pass legislation. The number of matters requiring unanimity was reduced, and countries' ability to veto legislation was weakened substantially. Most decisions are taken by qualified majority vote. The presidency of the Council rotates among the member states every six months.

The Court of Justice is somewhat analogous to the judicial branch of the U.S. government. The court is composed of 15 judges and is based in Luxembourg. The court adjudicates matters related to the European Constitution, especially trade and business disputes. Judicial proceedings may be initiated by member countries, as well as by firms and individuals.

The European Parliament is composed of 626 members elected by popular vote in member countries for a five-year term. The Parliament started essentially as an advisory body with relatively little power. The fact that the only elected body of the EU had little policymaking power led many to charge that the EU suffered from a "democratic deficit." In other words, decisions are made bureaucratically rather than democratically. However, the Single European Act empowered the Parliament to veto EU membership applications as well as trade agreements with non-EU countries. The Maastricht and Amsterdam Treaties empowered the Parliament to veto legislation in certain policy areas and confer with the Council to settle differences in their respective drafts of legislation. Furthermore, the Parliament can question the Commission and Council, amend and reject the budget, and dismiss the entire Commission.[14] The entities and the process of decision making are summarized in Figure 8.1. Not shown are the Court of Auditors (who are to ensure the sound financial management of the EU) and the European Central Bank, which is responsible for monetary policy and the euro.

The future expansion of the EU will cause changes in the decision-making processes. The five big members will give up their second commissioner in 2005, and new members will be able to name a commissioner until the EU reaches 27 members.

© ZEFA VISUAL MEDIA—GERMANY

The European Union has several governing bodies, one of which is the EU Parliament. The Parliament has 626 members (732 after 2004) elected by popular vote in their home nations. The Parliament has power to veto membership applications and trade agreements with non-EU countries. The Commission must enjoy the confidence of the Parliament.

FIGURE 8.1

Organization and Decision Making of the EU

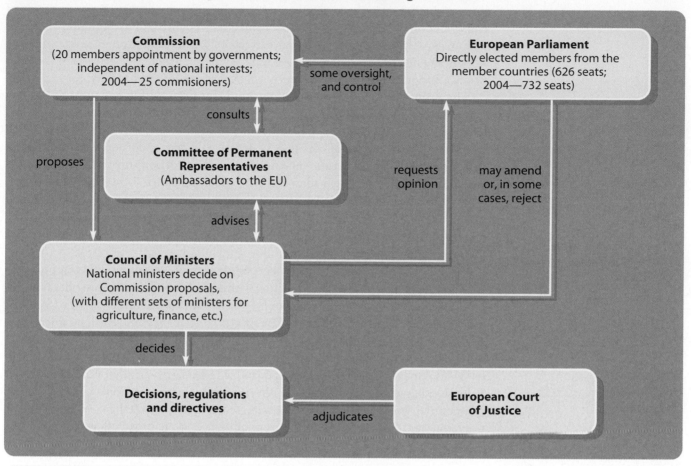

Sources: "EU Perustuslaki Voi Tuoda Suomeen Uuden Superministerin," *Helsingin Sanomat,* August 1, 2003, A6; schematic adapted from "My, How You've Grown," *The Economist,* January 25, 1992, 31–32.

At that stage, a rotational system will take over. The European Parliament will be enlarged to 732 members.[15] The EU's Constitutional Convention has proposed that a president would head the European Council (which brings together the heads of state and the president of the Commission at least twice a year to discuss the broader vision for the EU, while the Council of Ministers would continue as the decision-making body on legislation). The Council's presidency would, therefore, no longer rotate among member countries.[16]

IMPLICATIONS OF THE INTEGRATED EUROPEAN MARKET

Perhaps the most important implication of the four freedoms for Europe is the economic growth that is expected to result.[17] Several specific sources of increased growth have been identified. First, there will be gains from eliminating the transaction costs associated with border patrols, customs procedures, and so forth. Second, economic growth will be spurred by the economies of scale that will be achieved when production facilities become more concentrated. Third, there will be gains from more intense competition among EU companies. Firms that were monopolists in one country will now be subject to competition from firms in other EU countries. The introduction of the euro is expected to add to the efficiencies, especially in terms of consolidation of firms across industries and across countries. Furthermore, countries in Euroland will enjoy cheaper transaction costs, reduced currency risks, and consumers and businesses will enjoy price transparency and increased price-based competition. Corporate reactions to the euro will be discussed further in Chapter 14.

The proposals have important implications for firms within and outside Europe. There will be substantial benefits for those firms already operating in Europe. Those firms will gain because their operations in one country can now be freely expanded into others, and their products may be freely sold across borders. In a borderless Europe, firms will have access to many more millions of consumers. In addition, the free movement of capital will allow the firms to sell securities, raise capital, and recruit labor throughout Europe. Substantial economies of scale in production and marketing will also result. The extent of these economies of scale will depend on the ability of the managers to find panregional segments or to homogenize tastes across borders through their promotional activity.

For firms from nonmember countries, European integration presents various possibilities depending on the firm's position within the EU.[18] Table 8.4 provides four different scenarios with proposed courses of action. Well-established U.S.-based multinational marketers such as H.J. Heinz and Colgate-Palmolive will be able to take advantage of the new economies of scale. For example, 3M plants earlier turned out different versions of the company's products for various markets. Now, the 3M plant in Wales, for example, makes videotapes and videocassettes for all of Europe. Colgate-Palmolive has to watch out for competitors, such as Germany's Henkel, in the brutally competitive detergent market. At the same time, large-scale retailers, such as France's Carrefour and Germany's Aldi group, are undertaking their own efforts to exploit the

---

TABLE 8.4   Proposed Company Responses to European Markets

Company Status	Challenges	Response
Established multinational in one market/multiple markets	Exploit opportunities from improved productivity	Pan-European strategy
	Meet challenge of competitors	
	Cater to customers/intermediaries doing same	
Firm with one European subsidiary	Competition	Expansion
	Loss of niche	Strategic alliances
		Rationalization
		Divestment
Exporter to Europe	Competition	European branch
	Access	Selective acquisition
		Strategic alliance
No interest in Europe	Competition at home	Entry
	Lost opportunity	

Source: Material drawn from John F. Magee, "1992 Moves Americans Must Make." Harvard Business Review 67 (May–June 1989): 78–84.

situation with hypermarkets supplied by central warehouses with computerized inventories. Their procurement policies have to be met by companies such as Heinz. Many multinationals are developing pan-European strategies to exploit the emerging situation; that is, they are standardizing their products and processes to the greatest extent possible without compromising local input and implementation.

A company with a foothold in only one European market is faced with the danger of competitors who can use the strength of multiple markets. Furthermore, the elimination of barriers may do away with the company's competitive advantage. For example, more than half of the 45 major European food companies are in just one or two of the individual European markets and seriously lag behind broader-based U.S. and Swiss firms. Similarly, automakers PSA and Fiat are nowhere close to the cross-manufacturing presence of Ford and GM. The courses of action include expansion through acquisitions or mergers, formation of strategic alliances (for example, AT&T's joint venture with Spain's Telfónica to produce state-of-the-art microchips), rationalization by concentrating only on business segments in which the company can be a pan-European leader, and finally, divestment.

Exporters will need to worry about maintaining their competitive position and continued access to the market. Small and mid-sized U.S. companies account for more than 60 percent of U.S. exports to the EU. Their success, despite the high value of the dollar, which makes exports more expensive, is based on the relationships they have developed with their customers, especially in hi-tech.[19] Companies with a physical presence may be in a better position to assess and to take advantage of the developments. Internet-systems provider WatchGuard Technologies has almost doubled its staff in Europe, from 12 to 20 in 2002 in the wake of September 11, 2001, and despite increasing concern about viruses. In some industries, marketers do not see a reason either to be in Europe at all or to change from exporting to more involved modes of entry. Machinery and machine tools, for example, are in great demand in Europe, and marketers in these companies say they have little reason to manufacture there.

The term **Fortress Europe** has been used to describe the fears of many U.S. firms about a unified Europe. The concern is that while Europe dismantles internal barriers, it will raise external ones, making access to the European market difficult for U.S. and other non-EU firms. In a move designed to protect European farmers, for example, the EU has occasionally banned the import of certain agricultural goods from the United States. The EU has also called on members to limit the number of U.S. television programs broadcast in Europe. Finally, many U.S. firms are concerned about the relatively strict domestic content rules, such as geographic indications, recently passed by the EU. These rules require certain products sold in Europe to be manufactured with European inputs. One effect of the perceived threat of Fortress Europe has been an increased direct investment in Europe by U.S. firms. Fears that the EU will erect barriers to U.S. exports and of the domestic content rules governing many goods have led many U.S. firms to initiate or expand European direct investment.

North American Economic Integration

Although the EU is undoubtedly the most successful and well-known integrative effort, integration efforts in North America, although only a few years old, have gained momentum and attention. What started as a trading pact between two close and economically well-developed allies has already been expanded conceptually to include Mexico, and long-term plans call for further additions. However, in North American integration the interest is purely economic; there are no constituencies for political integration.

U.S.–CANADA FREE TRADE AGREEMENT

After three failed tries this century, the United States and Canada signed a free trade agreement that went into effect January 1, 1989. The agreement created a $5 trillion continental economy. The two countries had already had sectoral free trade arrangements; for example, one for automotive products had existed for over 20 years. Even before the agreement, however, the United States and Canada were already the world's largest trading partners, and there were relatively few trade barriers. The new arrangement eliminated duties selectively in three stages over the 1989–1999 period.[20] For example, the first round eliminated a 3.9 percent tariff on U.S. computers shipped to Canada as well as 4.9–22 percent duties on trade in whiskey, skates, furs, and unprocessed fish. The sensitive sectors, such as textiles, steel, and agricultural products, were not liberalized until the latter part of the transitionary period. Both countries see the free trade agreement as an important path to world competitiveness. Although there have been some dislocations, due to production consolidation, for example, the pact has created 750,000 jobs in the United States and 150,000 in Canada. It has also added as much as 1 percent in growth to both countries' economies. Trade between the United States and Canada exceeded $440 billion in 2002.

NORTH AMERICAN FREE TRADE AGREEMENT

Negotiations on a North American Free Trade Agreement (NAFTA) began in 1991 to create the world's largest free market, with currently over 400 million consumers and a total output of nearly 11 trillion.[21] The pact marked a bold departure: never before had industrialized countries created such a massive free trade area with a developing country neighbor.

Since Canada stands to gain very little from NAFTA (its trade with Mexico is 1 percent of its trade with the United States), much of the controversy has centered on the gains and losses for the United States and Mexico. Proponents have argued that the agreement will give U.S. firms access to a huge pool of relatively low-cost Mexican labor at a time when demographic trends are indicating labor shortages in many parts of the United States. At the same time, many new jobs will be created in Mexico. The agreement will give firms in both countries access to millions of additional consumers, and the liberalized trade flows will result in faster economic growth in both countries. The top 20 exports and imports between Mexico and the United States are in virtually the same industries, indicating intra-industry specialization and building of economies of scale for global competitiveness.[22] Overall, the corporate view toward NAFTA is overwhelmingly positive.

Opposition to NAFTA has been on issues relating to labor and the environment. Unions in particular worried about job loss to Mexico given lower wages and work standards, some estimating that six million U.S. workers were vulnerable to job loss. A distinctive feature of NAFTA is the two side agreements that were worked out to correct perceived abuses in labor and in the environment in Mexico. The North American Agreement on Labor Cooperation (NAALC) was set up to hear complaints about worker abuse. Similarly, the Commission on Environmental Compliance was established to act as a public advocate on the environment. The side agreements have, how-

Trucks from Mexico cross the border into the United States. In defiance of veto threats from the White House and warnings from Mexico, the Senate approved a $60.1 billion bill that subjects Mexican truckers to increased inspections, insurance, and other requirements before entering the U.S.

ever, had little impact, mainly because the mechanisms they created have almost no enforcement power.[23]

After a remarkable start in increased trade and investment, NAFTA suffered a serious setback due to significant devaluation of the Mexican peso in early 1995 and the subsequent impact on trade. Critics of NAFTA argued that too much was expected too fast of a country whose political system and economy were not ready for open markets. In response, advocates of NAFTA argued that there was nothing wrong with the Mexican real economy and that the peso crisis was a political one that would be overcome with time. As a matter of fact, with the help of the United States and the IMF, Mexico's economy started a strong recovery in 1996.

Trade between Canada, Mexico, and the United States has increased dramatically since NAFTA took effect, with total trade exceeding $602 billion in 2002.[24] Reforms have turned Mexico into an attractive market in its own right. Mexico's gross domestic product has been expanding by more than 3 percent every year since 1989, and exports to the United States have risen 20 percent a year to $134 billion in 2002. By institutionalizing the nation's turn to open markets, the free trade agreement has attracted considerable new foreign investment. The United States has benefited from Mexico's success. U.S. exports to Mexico are nearly double those to Japan at $97 billion in 2002. While the surplus of $1.3 billion in 1994 has turned to a deficit of $37 billion in 2002, these imports have helped in Mexico's growth and will, therefore, strengthen NAFTA in the long term. Furthermore, U.S. imports from Mexico have been shown to have much higher U.S. content than imports from other countries.[25] At present, cooperation between Mexico and the United States is taking new forms beyond trade and investment; for example, binational bodies have been established to tackle issues such as migration, border control, and drug trafficking.[26]

Among the U.S. industries to benefit are computers, autos, petrochemicals, financial services, and aerospace. Aerospace companies such as Boeing, Honeywell, Airbus Industrie, and GE Aircraft Engines have recently made Mexico a center for both parts manufacture and assembly. Aerospace is now one of Mexico's largest industries, second only to electronics, with 10,000 workers employed.[27] In Mexico's growth toward a more advanced society, manufacturers of consumer goods will also stand to benefit. NAFTA has already had a major impact in the emergence of new retail chains, many established to handle new products from abroad.[28] Not only have U.S. retailers, such as Wal-Mart, expanded to and in Mexico, but Mexican retailers, such as Grupo Gigante, have entered the U.S. market.[29] Wal-Mart's use of lower tariffs, physical proximity, and buying power is changing the Mexican retail landscape as shown in the Focus on Entrepreneurship.

Focus On ⬇

NAFTA: Reshaping the Retail Market in Mexico and Beyond

Wal-Mart saw the promise of the Mexican market in 1991 when it stepped outside of the United States for the first time by launching Sam's Clubs in 50-50 partnership with Cifra, Mexico's largest retailer. The local partner was needed to provide operational expertise in a market of significant culture and income differences from Wal-Mart's domestic one. Within months the first outlet—a bare-bones unit that sold bulk items at just above wholesale prices—was breaking all Wal-Mart records in sales. While tariffs still made imported goods pricey, "Made in the USA" merchandise also started appearing on the shelves.

After NAFTA took effect in 1994, tariffs tumbled, unleashing pent-up demand in Mexico for U.S.-made goods. The trade treaty also helped eliminate some of the transportation headaches and government red tape that had kept Wal-Mart from fully realizing its competitive advantage. NAFTA resulted in many European and Asian manufacturers setting up plants in Mexico, giving the retailer cheaper access to more foreign brands.

Wal-Mart's enormous buying power has kept it ahead of its Mexican competitors who are making similar moves. Because Wal-Mart consolidates its orders for all goods it sells outside of the United States, it can wring deeper discounts from suppliers than its local competitors. Wal-Mart Mexico has repeatedly exploited NAFTA and other economic forces to trigger price wars. For example, rather than pocket the windfall that resulted when tariffs on Lasko brand floor fans fell

from 20 percent to 2 percent, price cuts took place equal to the tariff reductions.

Behind Wal-Mart's success are increasingly price-conscious consumers. The greater economic security of NAFTA has helped tame Mexico's once fierce inflation. The resulting price stability has made it easier for Mexican consumers to spot bargains. In addition, Wal-Mart's clean, brightly lit interiors, orderly and well-stocked aisles, and consistent pricing policies are a relief from the chaotic atmosphere that still prevails in many local stores.

Wal-Mart's aggressive tactics have resulted in complaints as well. In 2002, Mexico's Competition Commission was asked to probe into reports that Wal-Mart exerts undue pressure on suppliers to lower their prices. Local retailers, such as Comerci, Gigante, and Soriana, have seen their profits plummet but are forced to provide prices competitive to Wal-Mart's. In addition, they have engaged in aggressive rehauls of their operations. Soriana, for example, invested $250 million in new stores in 2002. Soriana took out ads in local newspapers warning about "foreign supermarkets" when regulators fined a Wal-Mart in Monterrey because a shelf price did not match the price on the checkout receipt.

Wal-Mart's success continues and it is Mexico's top retailer. It already has 579 grocery stores, wholesale-club outlets, and restaurants in Mexico, and has budgeted $600 million to open 63 new Mexican units by mid-2003. Sales are expected to top $10 billion in 2002.

Customers leaving the WalMart in Mexico City. WalMart has stores across the U.S. and recently opened operations in Canada, Puerto Rico, Brazil, Germany and Asia.

Albertson's brand as seen competing against Bimbo, Mexican-brand bread, on a shelf of a California Super Savers market. Super Savers, owned by Albertson's, are focused toward the growing Hispanic market. Mexico-based Gigante has opened five Southern California stores in an effort to attract that same demographic.

Source: "War of the Superstores," *Business Week,* September 23, 2002, 60; "How Well Does Wal-Mart Travel?" *Business Week,* September 3, 2001, 82–84; "How NAFTA Helped Wal-Mart Reshape the Mexican Market," *The Wall Street Journal,* August 31, 2001, A1–A2; and Vijay Govindarajan and Anil K. Gupta, "Taking Wal-Mart Global: Lessons from Retailing's Giant," *Strategy and Business* (Fourth Quarter, 1999): 45–56.

Free trade does produce both winners and losers. Although opponents concede that the agreement is likely to spur economic growth, they point out that segments of the U.S. economy will be harmed by the agreement. Overall wages and employment for unskilled workers in the United States will fall because of Mexico's low-cost labor pool. U.S. companies have been moving operations to Mexico since the 1960s. The door was opened when Mexico liberalized export restrictions to allow for more so-called **maquiladoras,** over 3,600 plants that make goods and parts or process food for export back to the United States. The supply of labor is plentiful, the pay and benefits are low, and the work regulations are lax by U.S. standards. In the last two decades, maquiladoras evolved from low-end garment or small-appliance assembly outfits to higher-end manufacturing of big-screen TVs, computers, and auto parts. The factories shipped $76.8 billion worth of goods (half of all Mexican exports), almost all of it to the United States. But the arrangement is in trouble. The NAFTA treaty required Mexico to strip maquiladoras of their duty-free status by 2001. Tariff breaks formerly given to all imported parts, supplies, equipment, and machinery used by foreign factories in Mexico now apply only to imports from Canada, Mexico, and the United States. This effect is felt most by Asian factories since they still import a large amount of components from across the Pacific (for example, 97 percent of components for TVs assembled in Tijuana are imported, mostly from Asia). Europeans are less affected because of Mexico's free-trade agreement with the EU, which will eliminate tariffs gradually by 2007.[30] Wages have also been rising to $3.52 an hour (up from $2.29 in 1997) resulting in some low-end manufacturers of apparel and toys moving production to Asia.[31] While the Mexican government is eager to attract maquiladora investment, it is also keen to move away from using cheap labor as a central element of competitiveness.

Despite U.S. fears of rapid job loss if companies send business south of the border, recent studies have put job gain or loss as almost a washout. The good news is that free trade has created higher-skilled and better-paying jobs in the United States as a result of growth in exports. As a matter of fact, jobs in exporting firms tend to pay 10 to 15 percent more than the jobs they replace. Losers have been U.S. manufacturers of auto parts, furniture, and household glass; sugar, peanut, and citrus growers; and seafood and vegetable producers. The U.S. Labor Department has certified 316,000 jobs as threatened or lost due to trade with Mexico and Canada. At the same time, the U.S. economy has added some 20 million jobs in the years since NAFTA. The fact that job losses have been in more heavily unionized sectors has made these losses politically charged. In most cases, high Mexican shipping and inventory costs will continue to make it more efficient for many U.S. industries to serve their home market from U.S. plants. Outsourcing of lower-skilled jobs is an unstoppable trend for developed economies such as the United States. However, NAFTA has given U.S. firms a way of taking advantage of cheaper labor while still keeping close links to U.S. suppliers. Mexican assembly plants get 82 percent of their parts from U.S. suppliers, while factories in Asia are using only a fraction of that.[32] Without NAFTA, entire industries might be lost to Asia rather than just the labor-intensive portions.

Countries dependent on trade with NAFTA countries are concerned that the agreement will divert trade and impose significant losses on their economies. Asia's continuing economic success depends largely on easy access to the North American markets, which account for more than 25 percent of annual export revenue for many Asian countries. Lower-cost producers in Asia are likely to lose some exports to the United States if they are subject to tariffs while Mexican firms are not and may, therefore, have to invest in NAFTA[33] Similarly, many in the Caribbean and Central

America fear that the apparel industries of their regions will be threatened, as would much-needed investments.

NAFTA may be the first step toward a hemispheric bloc, but nobody expects it to happen any time soon. It took more than three years of tough bargaining to reach an agreement between the United States and Canada, two countries with parallel economic, industrial, and social systems. The challenges of expanding free trade throughout Latin America will be significant. However, many of Latin America's groupings are making provisions to join NAFTA and create a hemispheric trade regime.[34] For this to happen, for example, many Latin nations will demand trade concessions in citrus, sugar, steel, apparel, and other industries that the United States may, for political reasons, find extremely difficult to grant.[35] Overall, many U.S. companies fear that Latin Americans will move closer to the Europeans if free trade discussions do not progress. For example, both MERCOSUR and Mexico have signed free trade agreements with the EU.[36]

Other Economic Alliances

The world's developing countries have perhaps the most to gain from successful integrative efforts. Because many of these countries are also quite small, economic growth is difficult to generate internally. Many of these countries have adopted policies of **import substitution** to foster economic growth. With an import substitution policy, new domestic industries produce goods that were formerly imported. Many of these industries, however, can be efficient producers only with a higher level of production than can be consumed by the domestic economy. Their success, therefore, depends on accessible export markets made possible by integrative efforts.

INTEGRATION IN LATIN AMERICA

Before the signing of the U.S.–Canada Free Trade Agreement, all of the major trading bloc activity in the Americas had taken place in Latin America. One of the longest-lived integrative efforts among developing countries was the Latin America Free Trade Association (LAFTA), formed in 1961. As the name suggests, the primary objective of LAFTA was the elimination of trade barriers. The 1961 agreement called for trade barriers to be gradually dismantled, leading to completely free trade by 1973. By 1969, however, it was clear that a pervasive protectionist ideology would keep LAFTA from meeting this objective, and the target date was extended to 1980. In the meantime, however, the global debt crisis, the energy crisis, and the collapse of the Bretton Woods system prevented the achievement of LAFTA objectives. Dissatisfied with LAFTA, the group made a new start as the Latin American Integration Association (LAIA) in 1980. The objective is a higher level of integration than that envisioned by LAFTA; however, the dismantling of trade barriers remains a necessary and elusive first step.

The Central American Common Market (CACM) was formed by the Treaty of Managua in 1960. The CACM has often been cited as a model integrative effort for other developing countries. By the end of the 1960s, the CACM had succeeded in eliminating restrictions on 80 percent of trade among members. A continuing source of difficulty, however, is that the benefits of integration have fallen disproportionately to the richer and more developed members. Political difficulties in the area have also hampered progress. However, the member countries renewed their commitment to integration by negotiating free trade agreements with its trading partners. For example, a free trade agreement with the United States is considered desirable due to the complementary nature of trade flows, which exceed $20 billion each year.

Integration efforts in the Caribbean have focused on the Caribbean Community and Common Market formed in 1968. Caribbean nations (as well as Central American nations) have benefited from the **Caribbean Basin Initiative (CBI),** which, since 1983, has extended trade preferences and granted access to the markets of the United States. Under NAFTA the preferences were lost, which meant that the Caribbean countries had to cooperate more closely with each other. They have argued that their small size entitles them to special concessions, especially in their fight against growing and trafficking in drugs.[37] Legislation by the United States to extend unilaterally NAFTA benefits to CBI countries to protect them from investment and trade diversion was passed in 2000.[38]

None of the activity in Latin America has been hemispheric; the Central Americans have had their structures, the Caribbean nations theirs, and the South Americans had their own different forms. However, in a dramatic transformation, these nations are now looking for free trade as a salvation from stagnation, inflation, and debt. In response to the recent developments, Brazil, Argentina, Uruguay, and Paraguay set up a common market with completion by the end of 1994 called MERCOSUR (Mercado Comun del Sur).[39] Despite their own economic challenges and disagreements over trade policy, the MERCOSUR members and the three associate members, Bolivia, Chile, and Peru have agreed to economic-convergence targets similar to those of the EU. These are in areas of inflation, public debt, and fiscal deficits. Bolivia, Colombia, Ecuador, Peru, and Venezuela have formed the Andean Common Market (ANCOM). Since two ANCOM members already have free trade agreements with MERCOSUR, the others have indicated their interest in establishing similar ties.[40] Latin nations are realizing that if they do not unite, they will become increasingly marginal in the global market. In approaching the EU with a free trade agreement, for example, MERCOSUR members want to diversify their trade relationships and reduce their dependence on U.S. trade.

The ultimate goal is a hemispheric free trade zone from Point Barrow, Alaska, to Patagonia. The first step to such a zone was taken in December 1994, when leaders of 34 countries in the Americas agreed to work toward the **Free Trade Area of the Americas (FTAA)** by 2005. Ministerials held since have established working groups to gather data and make recommendations in preparation for the FTAA negotiations. The larger countries have agreed to consider giving smaller and less-developed countries more time to reduce tariffs, to open their economies to foreign investment, and to adopt effective laws in areas such as anti-trust, intellectual property rights, bank regulation, and prohibitions on corrupt business practices. At the same time, the less-developed countries have agreed to include labor and environmental standards in the negotiations.[41]

Changes in corporate behavior have been swift. Free market reforms and economic revival have had companies ready to export and to invest in Latin America. For example, Brazil's opening of its computer market resulted in Hewlett-Packard establishing a joint venture to produce PCs. Companies are also changing their approaches with respect to Latin America. In the past, Kodak dealt with Latin America through 11 separate country organizations. It has since streamlined its operations to five "boundariless" companies organized along product lines and, taking advantage of trade openings, created centralized distribution, thereby making deliveries more efficient and decreasing inventory-carrying costs.[42]

INTEGRATION IN ASIA

The development in Asia has been quite different from that in Europe and in the Americas. While European and North American arrangements have been driven by political will, market forces may compel politicians in Asia to move toward formal integration. While Japan is the dominant force in the area and might seem the choice to take leadership in such an endeavor, neither the Japanese themselves nor the other nations want Japan to do it. The concept of a "Co-Prosperity Sphere" of 50 years ago has made nations wary of Japan's influence.[43] Also, in terms of economic and political distance, the potential member countries are far from each other, especially compared to the EU. However, Asian interest in regional integration is increasing for pragmatic reasons. First, European and American markets are significant for the Asian producers, and some type of organization or bloc may be needed to maintain leverage and balance against the two other blocs. Second, given that much of the growth in trade for the nations in the region is from intra-Asian trade, having a common understanding and policies will become necessary. A future arrangement will most likely use the frame of the most established arrangement in the region, the Association of Southeast Asian Nations (ASEAN). Before 1991, ASEAN had no real structures, and consensus was reached through information consultations. In October 1991, ASEAN members (Brunei, Indonesia, Malaysia, Philippines, Singapore, Thailand, Vietnam and, since 1997, Cambodia, Myanmar, and Laos) announced the formation of a customs union called ASEAN Free Trade Area (AFTA). The ten member countries have agreed to reduce tariffs to a maximum level of 5 percent by 2003 and to create a customs union by 2010.

The Malaysians have pushed for the formation of the East Asia Economic Group (EAEG), which would add Hong Kong, Japan, South Korea, and Taiwan to the list. This proposal makes sense; without Japan and the rapidly industrializing countries of the region such as South Korea and Taiwan, the effect of the arrangement would be small. Japan's reaction has been generally negative toward all types of regionalization efforts, mainly because it has had the most to gain from free trade efforts. However, part of what has been driving regionalization has been Japan's reluctance to foster some of the elements that promote free trade, such as reciprocity.[44] Should the other trading blocs turn against Japan, its only resort may be to work toward a more formal trade arrangement in Pacific Asia.

Another formal proposal for cooperation would start building bridges between two emerging trade blocs. Some individuals have publicly called for a U.S.–Japan common market. Given the differences on all fronts between the two, the proposal may be quite unrealistic at this time. Negotiated trade liberalization will not open Japanese markets due to major institutional differences, as seen in many rounds of successful negotiations but totally unsatisfactory results. The only solution for the U.S. government is to forge better cooperation between the government and the private sector to improve competitiveness.[45]

In 1989, Australia proposed the Asia Pacific Economic Cooperation (APEC) as an annual forum. The proposal called for ASEAN members to be joined by Australia, New Zealand, Japan, China, Hong Kong, Taiwan, South Korea, Canada, and the United States. It was initially modeled after the Organization for Economic Cooperation and Development (OECD), which is a center for research and high-level discussion. Since then, APEC's goals have become more ambitious. At present, APEC has 21 members with a combined GNP of $18 trillion, nearly 44 percent of global trade, and is the third largest economy of the world. The key objectives of APEC are to liberalize trade by 2020, to facilitate trade by harmonizing standards, and to build human capacities for realizing the region's ambitions. The trade-driven economies of the region have the world's largest pool of savings, the most advanced technologies, and fastest growing markets. Therefore, companies with interests in the region are observing and supporting APEC-related developments closely as shown in Focus on Politics.

However, the future actions of the other two blocs will determine how quickly and in what manner the Asian bloc, whatever it is, will respond. Also, the stakes are the highest for the Asian nations since their traditional export markets have been in Europe and in North America and, in this sense, very dependent on free access.

Focus On ⬇

POLITICS

In Support of Free Trade in Asia

General Motors—and all the major car makers—are driving into Asia. In the period of 2001–2010, vehicle sales in Asia are expected to grow by more than that of Europe and North America combined, making Asia the second largest automotive market with sales approaching 20 million per year. The world's largest industrial company has found the environmental challenges considerable despite the lure of substantial market potential made possible by the growing middle class. In addition to distribution challenges and aggressive competition from other manufacturers, both local and foreign, the most daunting ones are barriers to free trade. For example, in Indonesia, GM faces competition from a local model, the Timor, which costs substantially less due to government supports (that is, lower duties on imported components). Before President Suharto's resignation, the company was run by one of his sons.

To work around the trade barriers and get on solid footing in Asian markets, GM has invested heavily to build up local manufacturing and distribution. The company's buildup in Asia started in 1990 with the establishment of a regional office in Hong Kong and representative offices in Bangkok, Beijing, Jakarta, and Kuala Lumpur. In 1994, GM's Asia headquarters were moved from Detroit to Singapore. Singapore not only provides coordination and support, but allows GM to tailor manufacturing, distribution, and sales to local requirements. In Japan, GM now owns a 49 percent equity stake in Isuzu, while in China, the company established GM China as a separate entity. GM has two factories there and is planning further expansion. For example, through a

$100 million joint venture with Chinese state-owned car manufacturers, GM is making headway in the minivan sector, one of the fastest growing segments in the market. Another investment, a $251 million stake in ailing automaker Daewoo Motor Company, gives GM a foothold in South Korea, Asia's second largest auto market. To highlight its presence in Asia, GM is investing $450 million in a regional manufacturing facility in Thailand's Rayong Province to build the specially designed and engineered Opel "Car for Asia."

To combat protectionism and further the cause of free trade, GM has developed a three-pronged strategy. The first approach focuses on executives working with government representatives from the United States, European Union, and Japan to dismantle what GM regards as the largest flaws. The company uses its clout as a major investor, but it can also call on support from industries that follow it into a new market, such as component manufacturers. On the second level, GM works within existing frameworks to balance the effects of nationalistic policies. In countries such as Indonesia and Malaysia, it develops company-specific plans to preserve avenues of sales even under challenging circumstances. Finally, GM is also pursuing its business strategy in Asia's free trade areas. Since it will be a long time before barriers are taken down in the Asia Pacific Economic Cooperation Forum (APEC), its immediate focus is on the ASEAN Free Trade Area (AFTA). GM is hopeful that the automotive sector will be a beneficiary of tariff reductions—provided that member governments can be persuaded that such cuts are in their best interests.

Sources: Robyn Meredith, "Crazy Like a Fox," *Forbes,* July 8, 2002, 74; Peter Wonacott, "GM's Chinese Unit, Two Partners, Join Up to Make Minivehicles," *The Wall Street Journal,* June 4, 2002; "U.S. Auto Makers Demonstrate Commitment to Thailand," U.S.–ASEAN Business Council press release, May 12, 1999, http://www.us–asean.org; "GM Delays Plans to Open Big Thai Plant," *The Wall Street Journal,* January 6, 1998, A2; and "GM Presses for Free Trade in Asia," *Crossborder Monitor,* January 15, 1997, 1, 9. See also: http://www.GMBuyPower.com and http://www.gmautoworld.com.tw.

Economic integration has also taken place on the Indian subcontinent. In 1985, seven nations of the region (India, Pakistan, Bangladesh, Sri Lanka, Nepal, Bhutan, and the Maldives) launched the South Asian Association for Regional Cooperation (SAARC). Cooperation is limited to relatively noncontroversial areas, such as agriculture and regional development. Elements such as the formation of a common market have not been included.

INTEGRATION IN AFRICA AND THE MIDDLE EAST

Africa's economic groupings range from currency unions among European nations and their former colonies to customs unions among neighboring states. In addition to wanting to liberalize trade among members, African countries want to gain better access to European and North American markets for farm and textile products. Given that most of the countries are too small to negotiate with the other blocs, alliances have been the solution. In 1975, 16 West African nations attempted to create a mega-market large enough to interest investors from the industrialized world and reduce hardship through economic integration. The objective of the Economic Community of West African States (ECOWAS) was to form a customs union and eventual common market. Although many of its objectives have not been reached, its combined population of 160 million represents the largest economic entity in sub-Saharan Africa. Other entities in Africa include the Common Market for Eastern and Southern Africa (COMESA), the Economic Community of Central African States (CEEAC), the Southern African Customs Union, the Southern African Development Community (SADC), and some smaller, less globally oriented blocs such as the Economic Community of the Great Lakes Countries, the Mano River Union, and the East African Community (EAC). Most member countries are part of more than one block (for example, Tanzania is a member in both the EAC and SADC). The blocs, for the most part, have not been successful due to the small size of the members and lack of economic infrastructure to produce goods to be traded inside the blocs. Moreover, some of the blocs have been relatively inactive for substantial periods of time while their members endure internal political turmoil or even warfare amongst each other.[46] In 2002, African nations established the African Union (AU) for regional cooperation. Eventually, plans call for a pan-African parliament, a court of justice, a central bank, and a shared currency.[47]

Countries in the Arab world have made some progress in economic integration. The Arab Maghreb Union ties together Algeria, Libya, Mauritania, Morocco, and Tunisia in northern Africa. The Gulf Cooperation Council (GCC) is one of the most powerful, economically speaking, of any trade groups. The per-capita income of its six member states (Bahrain, Kuwait, Oman, Qatar, Saudi Arabia, and the United Arab Emirates) is in the nineteenth percentile in the world. The GCC was formed in 1980 mainly as a defensive measure due to the perceived threat from the Iran–Iraq war. Its aim is to achieve free trade arrangements with the EU and EFTA as well as bilateral trade agreements with western European nations. A proposal among GCC members calls for the creation of a common currency by 2010. A strong regional currency would help the GCC become a viable trading bloc, able to compete in the new global environment. Two key elements required to create a common currency are underway: the dismantling of trade barriers among members and the creation of a GCC member bank.[48]

A listing of the major regional trade agreements is provided in Table 8.5.

TABLE 8.5

Major Regional Trade Agreements

AFTA **ASEAN Free Trade Area**
Brunei, Cambodia, Indonesia, Laos, Malaysia, Myanmar, Philippines, Singapore, Thailand, Vietnam

ANCOM **Andean Common Market**
Bolivia, Colombia, Ecuador, Peru, Venezuela

APEC **Asia Pacific Economic Cooperation**
Australia, Brunei, Canada, Chile, China, Hong Kong, Indonesia, Japan, Malaysia, Mexico, New Zealand, Papua New Guinea, Peru, Philippines, Russia, Singapore, South Korea, Taiwan, Thailand, United States, Vietnam

CACM **Central American Common Market**
Costa Rica, El Salvador, Guatemala, Honduras, Nicaragua, Panama

CARICOM **Caribbean Community**
Antigua and Barbuda, Bahamas, Barbados, Belize, Dominica, Grenada, Guyana, Jamaica, Montserrat, St. Kitts-Nevis, St. Lucia, St. Vincent and the Grenadines, Suriname, Trinidad-Tobago

ECOWAS **Economic Community of West African States**
Benin, Berkina Faso, Cape Verde, Gambia, Ghana, Guinea, Guinea-Bissau, Ivory Coast, Liberia, Mali, Mauritania, Niger, Nigeria, Senegal, Sierra Leone, Togo

EU **European Union**
Austria, Belgium, Cyprus, Czech Republic, Denmark, Estonia, Finland, France, Germany, Greece, Hungary, Ireland, Italy, Latvia, Lithuania, Luxembourg, Malta, Netherlands, Poland, Portugal, Slovakia, Slovenia, Spain, Sweden, United Kingdom

EFTA **European Free Trade Association**
Iceland, Liechtenstein, Norway, Switzerland

GCC **Gulf Cooperation Council**
Bahrain, Kuwait, Oman, Qatar, Saudi Arabia, United Arab Emirates

LAIA **Latin American Integration Association**
Argentina, Bolivia, Brazil, Chile, Colombia, Cuba, Ecuador, Mexico, Paraguay, Peru, Uruguay, Venezuela

MERCOSUR **Southern Common Market**
Argentina, Brazil, Paraguay, Uruguay

NAFTA **North American Free Trade Agreement**
Canada, Mexico, United States

SAARC **South Asian Association for Regional Cooperation**
Bangladesh, Bhutan, India, Maldives, Nepal, Pakistan, Sri Lanka

SACU **Southern African Customs Union**
Botswana, Lesotho, Namibia, South Africa, Swaziland

For information see http://www.aseansec.org; http://www.apec.org; http://www.caricom.org; http://www.eurounion.org; http://www.nafta-customs.org.

Economic Integration and the International Manager

Regional economic integration creates opportunities and challenges for the international manager. Economic integration may have an impact on a company's entry mode by favoring direct investment, since one of the basic rationales for integration is to generate favorable conditions for local production and inter-regional trade. By design, larger

MAP

International Groupings

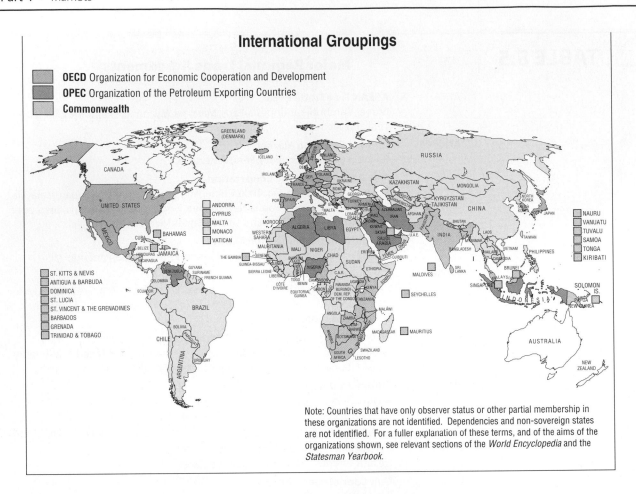

OECD Organization for Economic Cooperation and Development
OPEC Organization of the Petroleum Exporting Countries
Commonwealth

Note: Countries that have only observer status or other partial membership in these organizations are not identified. Dependencies and non-sovereign states are not identified. For a fuller explanation of these terms, and of the aims of the organizations shown, see relevant sections of the *World Encyclopedia* and the *Statesman Yearbook*.

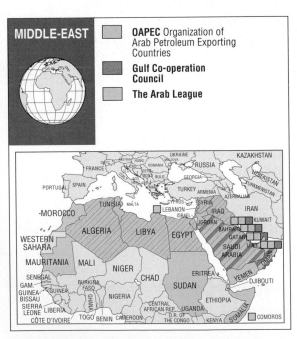

MIDDLE-EAST

OAPEC Organization of Arab Petroleum Exporting Countries

Gulf Co-operation Council

The Arab League

EUROPE

EU European Union

Countries with **EU** membership applications

EU membership in 2004

Sources: Statesman Yearbook ; The European Union: A Guide for Americans, 2000, http://www.eurunion.org/infores/euguide/euguide.html; "Afrabet Soup," http://www.oapecorg.org; http://www.arab.de/arabinfo/league; http://www.europa.eu.int; *The Economist,* February 10, 2001, p. 77, http://www.economist.com

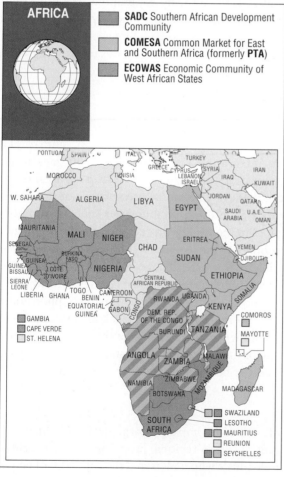

MAP

markets are created with potentially more opportunity. Harmonization efforts may result in standardized regulations, which can positively affect production and marketing efforts.

Decisions regarding integrating markets must be assessed from four different perspectives: the range and impact of changes resulting from integration, development of strategies to relate to these chanages, organizational changes needed to exploit these changes, and strategies to influence change in a more favorable direction.[49]

EFFECTS OF CHANGE

The first task is to create a vision of the outcome of the change. Change in the competitive landscape can be dramatic if scale opportunities can be exploited in relatively homogeneous demand conditions. This could be the case, for example, for industrial goods and consumer durables, such as cameras and watches, as well as for professional services. The international manager will have to take into consideration varying degrees of change readiness within the markets themselves; that is, governments and other stakeholders, such as labor unions, may oppose the liberalization of competition, especially when national champions such as airlines, automobiles, energy, and telecommunications are concerned. However, with deregulation monopolies have had to transform into competitive industries. In Germany, for example, the price of long-distance calls has fallen 40 percent forcing the former monopolist, Deutsche Telekom, to streamline its operations and seek new business abroad. By fostering a single market for capital, the euro is pushing Europe closer to a homogeneous market in goods and services, thereby exerting additional pressure on prices.[50]

STRATEGIC PLANNING

The international manager will have to develop a strategic response to the new environment to maintain a sustainable long-term competitive advantage. Those companies already present in an integrating market should fill in gaps in goods and market portfolios through acquisitions or alliances to create a regional or global company. It is increasingly evident that even a regional presence is not sufficient and sights need to be set on a presence beyond that. In industries such as automobiles, mobile telephony, and retailing, blocs in the twenty-first century may be dominated by two or three giants leaving room only for niche players. Those with currently weak positions, or no presence at all, will have to create alliances for market entry and development with established firms. General Mills created Cereal Partners Worldwide with Nestlé to establish itself in Europe and to jointly develop new market opportunities in Asia. An additional option for the international manager is leaving the market altogether in response to the new competitive conditions or the level of investment needed to remain competitive. Bank of America sold its operations in Italy to Deutsche Bank once it determined the high cost of becoming a pan-European player.

REORGANIZATION

Whatever the changes, they will call for company reorganization.[51] Structurally, authority will have to be more centralized so regional programs can be executed. In staffing, focus will have to be on individuals who understand the subtleties of consumer behavior across markets and therefore are able to evaluate the similarities and differences among cultures and markets. In developing systems for the planning and implementation of regional programs, adjustments will have to be made to incorporate views throughout the organization. If, for example, decisions on regional advertising campaigns are made at headquarters without consultation with country operations, resentment by the local staff will lead to less-than-optimal execution. The introduction of the euro will mean increased coordination in pricing as compared to the relative autonomy in price setting enjoyed by country organizations in the past. Companies may move corporate or divisional headquarters from the domestic market to be closer to the customer or centers of innovation. For example, after Procter & Gamble's reorganization, the fabric and home care business unit was headquartered in Brussels, Belgium.

LOBBYING

The international manager, as a change agent, must constantly seek ways to influence the regulatory environment in which they must operate. Economic integration will involve various powers and procedures, such as the EU's Commission and its directives. The international manager is not powerless to influence both of them; a passive approach may result in competitors gaining an advantage or a disadvantageous situation emerging for the company. For example, it was very important for the U.S. pharmaceutical industry to obtain tight patent protection as part of the NAFTA agreement and substantial time and money was spent on lobbying both the executive and legislative branches of the U.S. government in the effort to meet its goal. Often policymakers rely heavily on the knowledge and experience of the private sector in carrying out its own work. Influencing change will therefore mean providing policymakers with industry information such as test results. Lobbying will usually have to take place at multiple levels simultaneously; within the EU, this means the European Commission in Brussels, the European Parliament in Strasbourg, or the national governments within the EU. Managers with substantial resources have established their own lobbying offices in Brussels, while smaller companies get their voices heard through joint offices or their industry associations. In terms of lobbying, U.S. firms have been at an advantage given their experience in their home market; however, for many non-U.S. firms, lobbying is a new, yet necessary, skill to be acquired. At the same time, managers in two or more blocs can work together to produce more efficient trade through, for example, mutual recognition agreements (MRAs) on standards.[52]

Cartels and Commodity Price Agreements

An important characteristic that distinguishes developing countries from industrialized countries is the nature of their export earnings. While industrialized countries rely heavily on the export of manufactured goods, technology, and services, the developing countries rely chiefly on the export of primary products and raw materials—for example, copper, iron ore, and agricultural products. This distinction is important for several reasons. First, the level of price competition is higher among sellers of primary goods, because of the typically larger number of sellers and also because primary goods are homogeneous. This can be seen by comparing the sale of computers with, for example, copper. Only three of four countries are competitive forces in the computer market, whereas at least a dozen compete in the sale of copper. Furthermore, while goods differentiation and therefore brand loyalty are likely to exist in the market for computers, buyers of copper are likely to purchase on the basis of price alone. A second distinguishing factor is that supply variability will be greater in the market for primary goods because production often depends on uncontrollable factors such as weather. For these reasons, market prices of primary goods—and therefore developing country export earnings—are highly volatile.

Responses to this problem have included cartels and commodity price agreements. A **cartel** is an association of producers of a particular good. While a cartel may consist of an association of private firms, our interest is in the cartels formed by nations. The objective of a cartel is to suppress the market forces affecting its good in order to gain greater control over sales revenues. A cartel may accomplish this objective in several ways. First, members may engage in price fixing. This entails an agreement by producers to sell at a certain price, eliminating price competition among sellers. Second, the cartel may allocate sales territories among its members, again suppressing competition. A third tactic calls for members to agree to restrict production, and therefore supplies, resulting in artificially higher prices.

The most widely known cartel is the Organization of Petroleum Exporting Countries (OPEC). It consists of 11 oil-producing and exporting countries (Algeria, Indonesia, Iran, Iraq, Kuwait, Libya, Nigeria, Qatar, Saudi Arabia, United Arab Emirates, and Venezuela). OPEC became a significant force in the world economy in the 1970s. In 1973, the Arab members of OPEC were angered by U.S. support for Israel in the war in the Mideast. In response, the Arab members declared an embargo on the shipment of oil to the United States and quadrupled the price of oil—from approximately $3 to $12 per barrel. OPEC tactics included both price fixing and production quotas. Continued price increases brought the average price per barrel to nearly $35 by 1981. The cartel has experienced severe problems since, however. First, the demand for OPEC oil declined considerably as the result of conservation, efficiency (for example, while U.S. output has increased by 20 percent in the past years, oil consumption has increased only by 9 percent), the use of alternative sources, and increased oil production by nonmembers. Furthermore, the Asian financial crisis resulted in a downturn for oil for the last years of the twentieth century. OPEC's market share has declined from its 55 percent peak in 1974 to 40 percent at present.[53] All of these factors also contributed to sharp declines in the price of oil. Second, the cohesiveness among members diminished. Sales often occurred at less than the agreed-upon price, and production quotas were repeatedly violated. However, when low prices made it less profitable to explore for new reserves and resources, OPEC decided to cut back production in 1999 to coincide with Asia's economic rebound and increasing demand. To avoid damage to the global economy that a $40 per barrel price might bring, cooperation from OPEC in terms of production amounts is necessary.[54] As a result of the oil embargo of 1974, the United States spearheaded the development of the International Energy Agency (IEA), the task of which was to gather stockpiles of oil to offset any supply shortage. Rather than acting as adversaries, the IEA and OPEC have agreed that the IEA will use its emergency stocks only as a last resort, while OPEC has promised to keep the world well-supplied with oil.[55]

International **commodity price agreements** involve both buyers and sellers in an agreement to manage the price of a certain commodity. Often, the free market is allowed to determine the price of the commodity over a certain range. However, if demand and supply pressures cause the commodity's price to move outside that range, an elected or appointed manager will enter the market to buy or sell the commodity to bring the price back into the range. The manager controls the **buffer stock** of the commodity. If prices float downward, the manager purchases the commodity and adds to the buffer stock. Under upward pressure, the manager sells the commodity from the buffer stock. This system is somewhat analogous to a managed exchange rate system, in which authorities buy and sell to influence exchange rates.

International commodity agreements are currently in effect for sugar, tin, rubber, cocoa, and coffee.

Summary

Economic integration involves agreements among countries to establish links through the movements of goods, services, and factors of production across borders. These links may be weak or strong depending on the level of integration. Levels of integration include the free trade area, customs union, common market, and full economic union.

The benefits derived from economic integration include trade creation, economies of scale, improved terms of trade, the reduction of monopoly power, and improved cross-cultural communication. However, a number of disadvantages may also exist. Most important, economic integration may work to the detriment of nonmembers by causing deteriorating terms of trade and trade diversion. In addition, no guarantee exists that all members will share the gains from integration. The biggest impediment to economic integration is nationalism. There is strong resistance to surrendering autonomy and self-determinism to cooperative agreements.

The most successful example of economic integration is the European Union. The EU has succeeded in eliminating most barriers to the free flow of goods, services, and factors of production. In addition, the EU has made progress toward the evolution of a common currency and central bank, which are fundamental requirements of an economic union. In the Americas, NAFTA is paving the way for a hemispheric trade bloc.

A number of regional economic alliances exist in Africa, Latin America, and Asia, but they have achieved only low levels of integration. Political difficulties, low levels of development, and problems with cohesiveness have impeded integrative progress among many developing countries. However, many nations in these areas are seeing economic integration as the only way to prosperity in the future.

International commodity price agreements and cartels represent attempts by producers of primary products to control sales revenues and export earnings. The former involves an agreement to buy or sell a commodity to influence prices. The latter is an agreement by suppliers to fix prices, set production quotas, or allocate sales territories. OPEC for example, has had inestimable influence on the global economy during the past 40 years.

Questions for Discussion

1. Explain the difference between a free-trade area and a customs union. Speculate why negotiations were held for a North American Free Trade Agreement rather than for a North American Common Market.

2. What problems might a member country of a common market be concerned about?

3. Construct an example of a customs union arrangement resulting in both trade creation and trade diversion.

4. Distinguish between external and internal economies of scale resulting from economic integration.

5. Are economic blocs (such as the EU and NAFTA) building blocs or stumbling blocs as far as worldwide free trade is concerned?

6. Suppose that you work for a medium-sized manufacturing firm in the Midwest. Approximately 20 percent of your sales are to European customers. What threats and opportunities does your firm face as a result of an integrated European market?

Internet Exercises

1. Compare and contrast two different points of view on expanding free trade by accessing the Web site of The Business Roundtable, an industry coalition promoting increased access to world markets (http://www.brtable.org), and the AFL-CIO, American Federation of Labor–Congress of Industrial Organizations (http://www.aflcio.org).

2. The euro will be either a source of competitive advantage or disadvantage for managers. Using "Euro case study: Siemens," available at http://news.bbc.co.uk/hi/english/events/the_launch_of_emu, assess the validity of the two points of view.

Take a Stand

The European Union is the most significant market in the world for bananas, consuming over 37 percent of the world's output. That is why a decision by the EU Farm Council attracted attention among both banana-growing nations and those consuming them. The decision was made to favor imports coming from EU countries' (mainly British, French, and Spanish) former colonies in Africa, Caribbean, and the Pacific under a preferential trading agreement called the Lomé Convention. Other producing countries would be subject to a quota of 2.2 million tons with a 20 percent tariff. All imports beyond that amount would be subject to a 170 percent tariff.

The EU's stated reason for the decision was to protect the former colonies in what, for some of them, is the main source of revenue. For example, in the case of St. Lucia, more than 60 percent of its export revenue is from bananas. One of the other (hidden agenda) reasons was to attempt to curb U.S. influence in the banana trade. The United States is home to three of the major companies in the business: Chiquita, Del Monte, and Dole.

The Caribbean nations have favored the decision as a consideration of smaller nations' right to exist with a decent standard of living, self-determination, and independence. Their main concern is that free trade would soon put their growers out of business due to the inherent inefficiencies of smaller farms. In Latin America, the view was quite the opposite. For countries such as Equador, Costa Rica, Colombia, and Honduras, the restrictions resulted in losses of $1 billion and 170,000 jobs. The unit-costs of production in Latin America are typically 2.5 times less than in the Caribbean.

Initially, the United States acted as an interested observer given that it is not a banana-growing nation (except for small amounts grown in Hawaii). However, at the request of Chiquita, the United States filed a complaint with the World Trade Organization. The main driver was the dangerous precedent of inaction if the EU banana regime went unchallenged. Unless deterred, the EU could possibly enjoy similar measures in other sectors of agriculture.

For Discussion
1. Is the involvement of the United States in the "banana wars" justified?
2. Are there any other ways the EU countries could support their former colonies apart from erecting trade barriers?

CHAPTER 9

Emerging Markets

Learning Objectives

- To understand the special concerns that must be considered by the international manager when dealing with emerging market economies

- To survey the vast opportunities for trade offered by emerging market economies

- To understand why economic change is difficult and requires much adjustment

- To become aware that privatization offers new opportunities for international trade and investment

High-Tech Teaching in China

Blackboard Inc. is a Washington, DC-based e-learning firm that was created in 1994. The Blackboard system gives students and faculty members an individualized Internet-based file space that is a part of a central system. This allows students and teachers to collect, share, discover, and manage important materials from articles, research papers, presentations, and multimedia files. Blackboard includes Web applications to help instructors manage student submissions, maintain grade records, and permit e-mail communication among class participants.

The technology is appealing to users because it is not particularly complex, and allows professors and students alike to quickly incorporate it into coursework. Blackboard's software is currently being used in 60 countries by more than 3,000 universities, 600 of which are located outside of the United States. Blackboard produces the software in twelve languages and the software is able to accommodate a large number of users—95,000 at one Mexican university alone.

The company has entered into a joint venture with Cernet Corp., a Chinese education company established by the Ministry of Education, to provide e-learning capabilities for Chinese universities. Blackboard will provide an online platform where professors can post class assignments and announcements, conduct tests or quizzes, and initiate online discussions. Blackboard will also be used to provide preparation services for college entrance exams, the GRE, and TOEFL. Blackboard's current expansion into China represents a huge opportunity for the company. In its first years the Blackboard system will be available to six universities in China and up to one hundred thousand students are expected to use it!

The potential for growth is high. Estimates are that within five years, 5–10 million Chinese students will be using Blackboard. In ten years, more than 20 million users could be served. China has tremendous market potential with more than 230 million students, and the Chinese government plans to wire all schools, elementary through university level, by 2010. Blackboard facilitates the Chinese educational reform initiatives, by offering more modern teaching methods that emphasize student involvement and creativity. First year revenue from the venture is expected to be between $3 and $5 million.

There are, however, some risks associated with expansion into China. Many education analysts point out that China's per capita education spending is low when compared to Western education systems. For Western systems, buying a product like Blackboard is a fairly minor outlay; for Chinese universities it is an expensive proposition. It may therefore be difficult for the company to convince universities to spend their limited resources on the Blackboard system.

Another issue of contention is intellectual property rights. By uploading articles and other content onto Blackboard, faculty and students could inadvertently be violating various copyright laws. Were such a violation to be prosecuted, the situation could be embarrassing and expensive for the university and instructor involved. The past poor record of China's payments for intellectual property is making Blackboard cautious.

Sources: http://www.washingtonpost.com/wp-dyn/articles/A17254-2003Sep2.html, accessed September 5, 2003; http://www.iht.com/articles/108305.html, accessed September 5, 2003; and http://www.blackboard.com/b3/guest/news/pressdetail.asp?tid=254, accessed September 5, 2003.

This chapter addresses major societal, economic, and ideological shifts that take place in the global economy. The focus is on the transition economies of central and eastern Europe and the new nations that were part of the former Soviet Union. These nations are called transition economies, since their economic thinking is undergoing a process of shifting from central planning to market orientation. In addition, economic changes in large markets such as China, Southeast Asia, Latin America, and Africa are presented and the role of privatization is discussed. These nations are called emerging economies, since they are only gradually becoming integrated into the global economy.[1]

The rise of new players in world trade has important implications for the international business manager both in terms of opportunities and of risks, as this chapter's opening vignette has shown. Privatization is addressed because the increasing transition of economic activity from government ownership into private hands presents a substantial shift in market orientation and offers new opportunities for trade and investment. Developmental issues are presented to reflect the special needs of large regions of the world and the resulting special responsibilities of international business.

Doing Business with Transition Economies

The major market economies emerging out of formerly centrally planned economies are Russia and the now independent states of the former Soviet Union, East Germany (now unified with West Germany), and the eastern and central European nations (Albania, Bulgaria, the Czech and Slovak Republics, Hungary, Poland, and Romania). For information regarding the population and GDP of the transition economies, consult this chapter's map. Shown also are the population levels and migration flows of countries around the world. It is evident that insufficient economic opportunity results in migration from developing nations into industrialized ones. Successful economic transition is a key tool to reduce such migration. If people have a reasonable chance for economic prosperity at home they are less likely to leave.

It is a common belief that business ties between the Western world and these nations are a recent phenomenon. That is not the case. In the 1920s, for example, General Electric and RCA helped develop the Soviet electrical and communications industries. Ford constructed a huge facility in Nizhni Novgorod to build Model A cars and buses. DuPont introduced its technology to Russia's chemical industry. However, due to the political divide between communism and capitalism in the late 1940s, former centrally planned economies and Western corporations had rather limited international business contact.[2]

Socialist countries perceived international corporations as "aggressive business organizations developed to further the imperialistic aims of Western, especially American, capitalists the world over."[3] Furthermore, many aspects of capitalism, such as the private ownership of the means of production, were seen as exploitative and antithetical to communist ideology. Western managers, in turn, often saw socialism as a threat to the market system and the Western world in general.

A BRIEF HISTORICAL REVIEW

Due to differing politics and ideology, the trade history of socialist countries is quite different from that of the United States and the West. The former Soviet system of foreign trade dates to a decree signed by Lenin on April 22, 1918. It established that the state would have a monopoly on foreign trade and that all foreign trade operations were to be

Migration Flow and Population

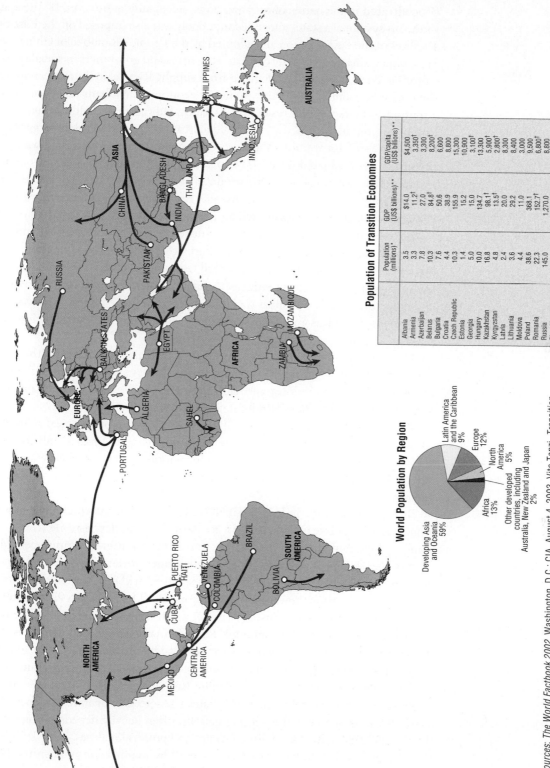

Population of Transition Economies

	Population (millions)*	GDP (US$ billions)**	GDP/capita (US$ billions)**
Albania	3.5	$14.0	$4,500
Armenia	3.3	11.2†	3,350†
Azerbaijan	7.8	27.0	3,300
Belarus	10.3	84.8†	8,200†
Bulgaria	7.6	50.6	6,600
Croatia	4.4	38.9	8,800
Czech Republic	10.3	155.9	15,300
Estonia	1.4	15.2	10,900
Georgia	5.0	15.0	3,100†
Hungary	10.0	134.7	13,300
Kazakhstan	16.8	98.1†	5,900†
Kyrgyzstan	4.8	13.5†	2,800†
Latvia	2.4	20.0	8,300
Lithuania	3.6	29.2	8,400
Moldova	4.4	11.0	3,000
Poland	38.6	368.1	9,500
Romania	22.3	152.7†	6,800†
Russia	145.0	1,270.0	8,800
Slovakia	5.4	66.0	12,200
Tajikistan	6.7	7.5†	1,140†
Turkmenistan	4.7	21.5†	4,700†
Ukraine	48.4	205.0†	4,200†
Uzbekistan	25.6	62.0†	2,500†

* July 2002 estimate.
** 2002 estimate, except where noted.
† 2001 estimate.

World Population by Region

Developing Asia and Oceania 59%

Africa 13%

Other developed countries, including Australia, New Zealand and Japan 2%

North America 5%

Europe 12%

Latin America and the Caribbean 9%

Sources: The World Factbook 2002, Washington, D.C.: CIA, August 4, 2003. Vito Tanzi, Transition and the Changing Role of Government, Finance, and Development, Washington, D.C.: June 1999, pp. 20–23; http://www.un.org/esa/population/; http://www.odci.gov/cia/publications/factbook, Feb. 22, 2001; 2001 World Development Indicators, The World Bank, April 2001.

MAP

concentrated in the hands of organizations specifically authorized by the state. Over time, this system of a state-controlled monopoly was also imposed on the East European satellites of the Soviet Union and adopted by the People's Republic of China.

In effect, this trade structure isolated the firms and consumers in socialist economies from the West and unlinked demand from supply. Rigid state bureaucracies regulated the entire economy. Eventually, domestic economic problems emerged. The lack of attention to market forces resulted in misallocated resources, and the lack of competition promoted inefficiency. Centralized allocation prevented the emergence of effective channels of distribution. Managers of plants were more concerned with producing the quantities stipulated by a rigid **central plan** (often five-year plans, one following another) than with producing the products and the quality desired. Entrepreneurship was disdained, innovation risky. Consequently, socialist economies achieved only lackluster growth, and their citizens fell far behind the West in their standard of living.

In the mid-1980s, the Soviet Union developed two new political and economic programs: **perestroika** and **glasnost.** Perestroika was to fundamentally reform the Soviet economy by improving the overall technological and industrial base as well as the quality of life for Soviet citizens through increased availability of food, housing, and consumer goods. Glasnost was to complement those efforts by encouraging the free exchange of ideas and discussion of problems, pluralistic participation in decision making, and increased availability of information.[4]

These domestic steps were followed shortly by legislative measures that thoroughly reformed the Soviet foreign-trade apparatus. In a major move away from previous trade centralization, national agencies, large enterprises, and research institutes were authorized to handle their own foreign transactions directly.

Concurrent with the steps taken in the Soviet Union, other socialist countries also initiated major reforms affecting international business. Virtually all socialist countries began to invite foreign investors to form joint ventures in their countries to help satisfy both domestic and international demand and started to privatize state enterprises.

By late 1989, all the individual small shifts resulted in the emergence of a new economic and geopolitical picture. With an unexpected suddenness, the Iron Curtain disappeared, and, within less than three years, the Communist empire ceased to exist. Virtually overnight, Eastern Europe and the former Soviet Union, with their total population of 400 million and a combined GNP of $3 trillion,[5] shifted their political and economic orientations toward a market economy. The former socialist satellites shed their communist governments. Newly elected democratic governments decided to let market forces shape their economies. East Germany was unified with West Germany. Former Eastern European nations such as Hungary, Poland, the Czech and the Slovak Republics, Lithuania, Latvia, and Estonia became integrated into the European Union in 2004. By 1992 the entire Soviet Union had disappeared. Individual regions within the Commonwealth of Independent States reasserted their independence and autonomy, resulting in a host of emerging nations, often heavily dependent on one another, but now separated by nationalistic feelings and political realities.

The political changes were accompanied by major economic shifts. Externally, trade flows were completely redirected. Up to 1987, due to the plan, most Soviet-bloc trade took place within the political organization. That meant, for example, that more than 35 percent of Czech trade took place with the Soviet Union, and only 20 percent with Western Europe. Once governments and firms were free to trade with trading partners of their choice, the picture shifted radically. By 2000, more than 70 percent of Czech trade took place within the European Union, while trade with the Soviet Union had declined to less than 5 percent.[6]

Internally, austerity programs were introduced and prices of subsidized products were adjusted upward to avoid distorted trade flows due to distorted prices. Wages were kept in check to reduce inflation and governmental reforms aimed to stimulate productivity by emulating the capitalist practice of pay-for-performance.[7] Entire industries were either privatized or closed down. These steps led to a significant decrease in the standard of living of the population. The support for the internal economic transformation continued, demonstrating the great desire on the part of individuals and governments to become market oriented. However, increasing economic difficulties precipitated large levels of discontent and, by some, a desire for a return to the old days. As a result, some countries have experienced civil and political strife, and the reemergence of political hard-liners. Economic progress will be a crucial component of democratic political stability.

From a Western perspective, all these changes ended the Cold War. After the ebbing of initial euphoria, it was learned that the shouts for democracy were, to a large degree, driven not only by political but also by economic desires. Freedom meant not only the right to free elections but also the expectation of an increased standard of living in the form of color televisions, cars, and the many benefits of a consumer society. To sustain the drive toward democracy, these economic desires had to appear attainable. Therefore, it was in the interest of the Western world as a whole to contribute to the democratization of the former Communist nations by searching for ways to bring them "the good life."

THE REALITIES OF ECONOMIC CHANGE

For Western firms, the political and economic shifts converted a latent but closed market into a market offering very real and vast opportunities. Yet the shifts are only the beginning of a process. The announcement of an intention to change does not automatically result in change itself. For example, the abolition of a centrally planned economy does not create a market economy. Laws permitting the emergence of private sector entrepreneurs do not create entrepreneurship. The reduction of price controls does not immediately make goods available or affordable. Deeply ingrained systemic differences between the transition economies and Western firms continue. Highly prized, fully accepted fundamentals of the market economy, such as the reliance on competition, support of the profit motive, and the willingness to live with risk on a corporate and personal level, are not yet fully accepted. Major changes still need to take place. The evaluation of risk is therefore especially precarious because the established models of risk assessment do not seem to apply.[8] It is therefore useful to review the major economic and structural dimensions of the changes taking place in order to identify major shortcomings and opportunities for international business.

Many transition economies face major **infrastructure shortages.** Transportation systems, particularly those leading to the West, require vast improvement. Long-haul trucking is an extremely expensive and difficult mode of transportation. Warehousing facilities are either lacking or very poor outside the major cities. A lack of refrigeration facilities places severe handicaps on transshipments of perishable products.[9] The housing stock is in need of major overhaul. Market intermediaries often do not exist. Payments and funds-transfer systems are inadequate. These infrastructure shortcomings will inhibit economic growth for years to come.

Capital shortages are also a major constraint. Catching up with the West in virtually all industrial areas requires major capital infusions. Even though major programs have been designed to attract hidden personal savings into the economy, transition economies must rely to a large degree on attracting capital from abroad. Continued domestic uncertainties and high demand for capital around the world make this difficult. In light of existing inefficiencies, corruption[10] and domestic uncertainties, it is

Wendy's International operates four restaurants in Hungary.

© ILONA CZINKOTA

also a major task to ensure that the capital remains in the country . Often, capital flight more than compensates for any incoming foreign investment, thus leaving the domestic capital markets in a precarious position.

Firms doing business with transition economies often encounter interesting demand conditions. Buyers' preferences are frequently vague and undefined. Available market information is inaccurate. For example, knowledge about pricing, advertising, research, and trading is very limited, and few institutions are able to accurately research demand and channel supply. As a result, even if they want to, it is quite difficult for corporations to respond to demand. In emerging markets, consumption patterns can change rapidly. Companies that can anticipate these discontinuities can exploit them. When the Chinese government decided to develop an affordable housing program nationwide, supplemented by a new mortgage system, it meant that thousands of households would be moving to new dwellings in the next several years. Research among Chinese consumers showed that these families would then also be willing to spend money to keep their homes in good condition (as compared to their previous homes where kitchens and bathroom facilities were shared). A surge in the demand for household cleaning products was to be expected and companies such as Procter & Gamble readied themselves for it.[11]

Investors find that these countries have substantial knowledge resources to offer. For example, it is claimed that Russia and Central Europe possess about 35 to 40 percent of all researchers and engineers in the world.[12] At the same time, however, these nations suffer from the disadvantages imposed by a lack of management skills. In the past, management mainly consisted of skillful maneuvering within the allocation process. Central planning, for example, required firms to request tools seven years in advance; material requirements needed to be submitted two years in advance. Ordering was done haphazardly, since requested quantities were always reduced, and surplus allocations could always be traded with other firms. The driving mechanism for management was therefore not responsiveness to existing needs, but rather plan fulfillment through the development of a finely honed **allocation mentality,** which waited for instructions from above.

Commitment by managers and employees to their work is difficult to find. Many employees are still caught up in old work habits, which consisted of never having to work a full shift due to other commitments and obligations. The notion that "they pretend to pay us, and we pretend to work" is still strong. The dismantling of the past policy of the "Iron Rice Bowl," which made layoffs virtually impossible, reduces rather than increases such commitment.

The new environment also complicates managerial decision making. Even simple changes often require an almost unimaginable array of adjustments of licenses, taxes, definitions, and government rules. The challenges to managers in emerging markets is not restricted to the governmental front. The success of operations frequently rests on managers' ability to compete effectively with unconventional competition such as product counterfeiters, product diverters, and informal competitors who ignore local labor and tax laws.[13]

To cope with all these challenges, transition economies need trained managers. Since no large supply of such individuals exists, much of the training must be newly developed. Simply applying established Western guidelines to such training is inappropriate due to the differences in the people to be trained and the society in which they live. Business learning in transition economies must focus on key business issues such as marketing, strategic planning, international business, and financial analysis. However, it must not just focus on the transmission of knowledge, but also aim to achieve behavioral change. Given the lack of market orientation in the previous business environment, managers must adapt their behavior in areas such as problem solving, decision making, the development of customer orientation, and team building. In addition, the attitudes held by managers toward business and Western teaching approaches must be taken into consideration. One often finds substantial reluctance to accept new business knowledge and practice.

Adjusting to Global Change

Both institutions and individuals tend to display some resistance to change. The resistance grows as the speed of change increases. It does not necessarily indicate a preference for the earlier conditions but rather a concern about the effects of adjustment and a fear of the unknown. Major shifts have occurred both politically and economically in central Europe and the former Soviet Union, accompanied by substantial dislocations. Therefore, resistance should be expected. Deeply entrenched interests and traditions are not easily supplanted by the tender and shallow root of market-oriented thinking. The understanding of links and interactions cannot be expected to grow overnight. For example, greater financial latitude for firms also requires that inefficient firms be permitted to go into bankruptcy—a concept not cherished by many. The need for increased efficiency and productivity causes sharp reductions in employment—a painful step for the workers affected. The growing ranks of unemployed are swelled by the members of the military who have been brought home or demobilized. Concurrently, wage reforms threaten to relegate blue-collar workers, who were traditionally favored by the socialist system, to second-class status, while permitting the emergence of a new entrepreneurial class of the rich, an undesirable result for those not participating in the upswing. Retail price reforms endanger the safety net of larger population segments, and widespread price changes introduce inflation. It is difficult to accept a system where there are winners and losers, particularly for those on the losing side. As a result, an increase in ambivalence and uncertainty may well produce rapid shifts in economic and political thinking.

But it is not just in the emerging democracies that major changes have come about. The shifts experienced there also have major impact on the established market economies of the West. Take the reorientation of trade flows. With traditional and "forced" trade relationships vanishing, many more countries exert major efforts to become new partners in global trade. They attempt to export much more of their domestic production. Many of the exports are in product categories such as agriculture, basic manufacturing, steel, aluminum, and textiles, which are precisely the economic sectors in which the industrialized nations are already experiencing surpluses. As a result, the threat of displacement is high for traditional producers in industrialized nations.

Job shifts have led to decreasing employment in the manufacturing sector of industrialized nations. U.S. manufacturing employment in 2002, at 14.8 percent of total, had decreased below the levels of when it was first officially measured in 1867. For a global context, Figure 9.1 compares employment changes in manufacturing in the United States, Germany, and Japan. German manufacturing employment dropped by more than 13 percentage points from 1970–2001. In Japan, manufacturing employment dropped by 6.5 percentage points during the same time.

All of these declines in employment reflected a transfer of manufacturing away from the industrialized nations toward the emerging economies. Figure 9.2 shows how the proportion of manufacturing has grown rapidly in nations such as Malaysia, South Korea, Thailand, and Indonesia.[14]

Due to domestic economic dislocations, the pressure is on Western governments to restrict the inflow of trade from the East. Giving in to such pressure, however, would be

FIGURE 9.1

Manufacturing in Germany, Japan, and the US, 1970–2000

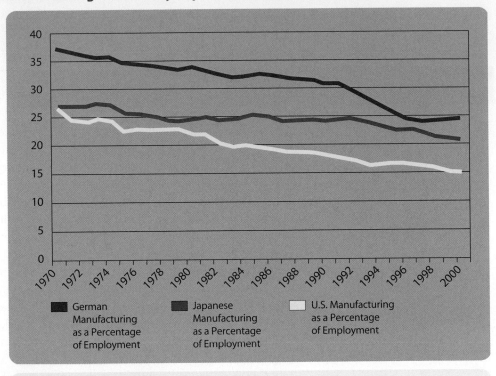

Source: SourceOECD online database.

highly detrimental to the further development of these new market economies. The countries in transition need assistance in their journey. Providing them with open markets is the best form of assistance, much more valuable than the occasional transfer of aid funds. Rapid changes and substantial economic dislocation have caused many individuals and policymakers in the East to become suspicious and wary of Western business approaches. Unless Western governments and businesses are able to convincingly demonstrate how competition, variety, trade, and freedom of choice can improve the quality of life, the opportunity to transform postsocialist societies may be jeopardized. The West shares the burden of global economic adjustment—a responsibility which has grown over the years. Particularly in light of the continued global upheavals since the 2001 attacks on the United States, it is important to heed the words of Robert Zoellick, the United States Trade Representative: "Erecting new barriers and closing old borders will not help the impoverished. It will not feed hundreds of millions struggling for subsistence. It will not liberate the persecuted. It will not improve the environment in developing countries or reverse the spread of AIDS. It will not help the railway orphans I visited in India. It will not improve the livelihoods of the union members I met in Latin American. It will not aid the committed Indonesians I visited who are trying to build a functioning, tolerant democracy in the largest Muslim nation in the world."[15]

INTERNATIONAL BUSINESS CHALLENGES AND OPPORTUNITIES

The pressure of change also presents vast opportunities for the expansion of international business activities. Large populations offer new potential consumer demand

FIGURE 9.2

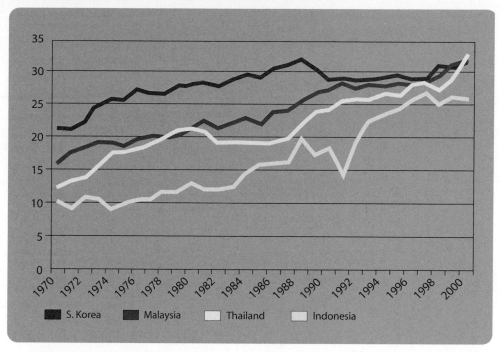

Manufacturing as a Percentage of GDP 1970–2000

Source: World Bank World Development Indicators Database.

and production capability. Many opportunities arise out of the enthusiasm with which a market orientation is embraced in some nations. Companies that are able to tap into the desire for an improved standard of living can develop new demand on a large scale.

One major difficulty encountered is the frequent unavailability of convertible currency. Products, however necessary, often cannot be purchased by emerging market economies because no funds are available to pay for them. As a result, many countries resort to barter and countertrade. This places an additional burden on the international manager, who must not only market products to the clients but must also market the products received in return to other consumers and institutions.

Problems also have arisen from the lack of protection some of the countries afford to intellectual property rights. Firms have complained about frequent illegal copying of films, books, and software, and about the counterfeiting of brand-name products. Unless importers can be assured that government safeguards will protect their property, trade and technology transfer will be severely inhibited.

Problems can be encountered when attempting to source products from emerging market economies. Many firms have found that selling is not part of the economic culture in some countries. The few available descriptive materials are often poorly written and devoid of useful information. Obtaining additional information about a product may be difficult and time-consuming.

The quality of the products obtained can be a major problem. In spite of their great desire to participate in the global marketplace, many producers still tend to place primary emphasis on product performance. They often neglect issues of style and product presentation. Therefore, the international manager must require manufacturers to improve quality and offer prompt delivery using advanced information technology.

Nevertheless, many international business opportunities exist. Some transition economies have products that are unique in performance. While they could not be traded during a time of ideological conflict, they are becoming successful global products in an era of new trade relations. For example, research shows that Russian tractors can be sold successfully in the United States. A study found that many of the previously held negative attitudes about imports from transition economies have been modified by the changed political climate.[16] These nations can offer consumers in industrialized nations a variety of products at low costs once their labor force can perform at an international level.

Currently, most sourcing opportunities from Eastern Europe and the Commonwealth of Independent States are for industrial products, which reflects the past orientation of research and development expenditures. Over time, however, consumer products may play a larger role, sometimes even a surprising one. For example, both Hungary and China are rapidly becoming major competitors in the production and export of *foie gras*, the famed delicacy made from goose or duck livers. Derided for decades as France's contribution to capitalist greed and decadence, this product is increasingly supplied at more competitive prices by emerging market economies.[17] There are also substantial opportunities for technology transfer. For example, the former Soviet training program for cosmonauts, which prepared space travelers for long periods of weightlessness, actually provides quite useful information for U.S. manufacturers of exercise equipment. Therefore, even if not interested in entering the transition economies, the international business executive would be wise to maintain relationships with them in order not to lose a potentially valuable source of supply.

State Enterprises and Privatization

One other area where the international business executive must deal with a period of transition is that of **state-owned enterprises.** These firms represent a formidable pool of international suppliers, customers, and competitors. Many of them are located in emerging market economies and are currently being converted into privately owned enterprises. This transition also presents new opportunities.

REASONS FOR STATE-OWNED ENTERPRISES

A variety of economic and noneconomic factors has contributed to the existence of state-owned enterprises. Two primary ones are national security and economic security. Many countries believe that, for national security purposes, certain industrial sectors must be under state control. Typically, these sectors include telecommunications, airlines, banking, and energy.

Economic security reasons are primarily cited in countries that are heavily dependent on specific industries for their economic performance. This may be the case when countries are heavily commodity dependent. Governments frequently believe that, given such heavy national dependence on a particular sector, government control is necessary to ensure national economic health.

Other reasons also contributed to the development of state-owned enterprises. On occasion, the sizable investment required for the development of an industry is too large to come from the private sector. Therefore, governments close the gap between national needs and private sector resources by developing these industries themselves.

In addition, governments often decide to rescue failing private enterprises by placing them in government ownership. In doing so, they fulfill important policy objectives, such as the maintenance of employment, the development of depressed areas, or the increase of exports.

Some governments also maintain that state-owned firms may be better for the country than privately held companies because they may be more societally oriented and therefore contribute more to the greater good. This was particularly the case in areas such as telecommunications and transportation, where profit maximization, at least from a governmental perspective, was not always seen as the appropriate primary objective. Rather, social goals such as employment may be valued much higher than profits or rates of return.[18]

THE EFFECT OF STATE-OWNED ENTERPRISES ON INTERNATIONAL BUSINESS

There are three types of activities where the international manager is likely to encounter state-owned enterprises: Market entry, the sourcing or marketing process, and international competition. On occasion, the very existence of a state-owned enterprise may inhibit or prohibit foreign market entry. For reasons of development and growth, governments frequently make market entry from the outside quite difficult so that the state-owned enterprise can perform according to plan. Even if market entry is permitted, the conditions under which a foreign firm can conduct business are often substantially less favorable than the conditions under which state-owned enterprises operate. Therefore, the international firm may be placed at a competitive disadvantage and may not be able to perform successfully even though economic factors would indicate success.

The international manager also faces a unique situation when sourcing from or marketing to state owned enterprises. Even though the state-owned firm may appear to be simply another business partner, it is ultimately an extension of the government and its activities. This may mean that the state-owned enterprise conducts its transactions according to the overall foreign policy of the country rather than according to economic rationale. For example, political considerations can play a decisive role in purchasing decisions. Contracts may be concluded for noneconomic reasons rather than be based on product offering and performance. Contract conditions may depend on foreign policy outlook, prices may be altered to reflect government displeasure, and delivery performance may change to "send a signal." Exports and imports may be delayed or encouraged depending on the current needs of government.

Finally, the international firm also may encounter international competition from state-owned enterprises. Very often, the concentration of such firms is not in areas of comparative advantage, but rather in areas that are most beneficial for the government owning the firm. Policy objectives often are much more important than input costs. Sometimes, state-owned enterprises may not even know the value of the products they buy and sell because price levels have such a low priority. As a result, the international manager may be confronted with competition that is very tough to beat.

PRIVATIZATION

Governments and citizens have increasingly recognized the drawbacks of government control of enterprises. Competition is restrained, which results in lower quality of goods and reduced innovation. Citizens are deprived of lower prices and of choice. The international competitiveness of state-controlled enterprises typically declines, often resulting in the need for growing government subsidies. In addition, rather than focusing on business, many government-controlled corporations have become grazing grounds for political appointees or vote winners through job allocations. As a result, many government-owned enterprises excel only at losing money.[19]

It is possible to reduce the cost of governing by changing government's role and involvement in the economy. Through **privatization,** budgets can be reduced and more efficient—not fewer—services can be provided. Privatized goods and services are often more competitive and more innovative. Two decades of experience with privatization indicate that private enterprises almost invariably outperform state-run companies.[20] The conversion of government monopolies into market-driven activities also tends to attract foreign investment capital, bringing additional know-how and financing to enterprises. Finally, governments can use proceeds from privatization to fund other pressing domestic needs.

The methods of privatization vary from country to country. Some nations come up with a master plan for privatization, whereas others deal with it on a case-by-case basis. The Treuhandanstalt of Germany, for example, which was charged with disposing of most East German state property, aimed to sell firms but also to maximize the number of jobs retained. In other countries, ownership shares are distributed to citizens and employees. Some nations simply sell to the highest bidder in order to maximize the proceeds. For example, Mexico has used most of its privatization proceeds to amortize its internal debt, resulting in savings of nearly $1 billion a year in interest payments. As Figure 9.3 shows, governments have raised substantial amounts through privatization. Focus on Politics shows that, in spite of its many advantages, the support for privatization is not unanimous. Too often, the process itself and the distribution of the funds obtained appear to be corrupt or at least not very transparent.

The purpose of most privatization programs is to improve productivity, profitability, and product quality and to shrink the size of government. As companies are exposed to market forces and competition, they are expected to produce better goods and services at lower costs. Privatization also intends to attract new capital for these firms so that they can carry out necessary adjustments and improvements. Since local

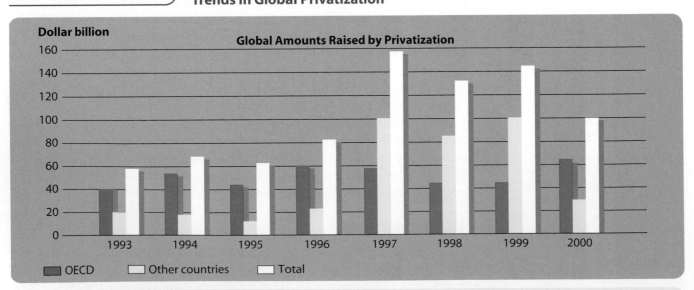

FIGURE 9.3

Trends in Global Privatization

Source: Organization for Economic Cooperation and Development, *Financial Market Trends,* 79 (June 2001), http://www.oecd.org.

Focus On ⬇

"For Sale" Signs Up in Russia

Nearly ten years after the fall of communism, Russia has finally allowed the sale of real estate property. Advocates for the measure say that the move is needed to convert Russia into a market economy. Andrei Neschadin, executive director of the Expert Institute, an independent Moscow-based think tank explains that "the expansion of commercial activity, the growth of towns and cities, has long hinged upon this question. A normal market in land will eventually make us a normal country at last." He argues that with a stable set of laws supporting the ownership rights over land and property, wealthy Russians and foreign investors will begin to sink money into the Russian real estate markets. Anatoly Manillia, deputy director of the Center for Political Research, adds, "the lack of private property in land has been the major logjam in all our efforts to attract investment, fight corruption, and build a dynamic market economy."

As it stands now there is a black market to exchange property, but because law does not govern these transactions, the process usually involves bribing government officials—which makes many international companies nervous. Bribery and corruption are illegal in most Western nations and the Organization for Economic Cooperation and

Development (OECD) in 1999 adopted a treaty criminalizing the bribery of foreign public officials. The Foreign Corrupt Practices Act also makes it a crime for companies publicly traded in the United States to bribe a foreign official in order to obtain business.

Opponents of private land ownership, the communist party among others, see it as another opportunity for the rich to rob the majority of the Russian people. The privatization efforts in Russia over the last decade have been disorderly and were tainted by allegations of corruption that nearly always proved to be true. Ordinary Russians are skeptical after such an ill-fated transition to capitalism and are willing to listen to communist claims that "another mass robbery of their national heritage is afoot." Yeygeny Kozlov is in charge of the municipal land department for the city of Kolomna. Even he concedes that people "are suspicious now that changes will only work against them. People remember how a few people became rich through privatization and the rest were impoverished, and they worry." This is an issue of contention within Russia and shows one of the country's major dilemmas. How can Russia become a market economy and attract foreign capital without disenfranchising its people?

Sources: Peter Baker, "Russia Allows 'For Sale' Signs on Urban Property," *Washington Post,* October 27, 2001, A24; Fred Weir, "Russia: Tough Capitalist Frontier Opens Up," *Christian Science Monitor,* http://www.csmonitorarchive.com, accessed September 3, 2002.

capital is often scarce, privatization efforts increasingly aim to attract foreign capital investment. Privatization, however, is no magic wand. Its key benefits come from corporate adjustments, which are often quite painful.

The trend toward privatization offers unique opportunities for international managers. Existing firms, both large and small, can be acquired at low cost, often with governmental support through tax exemptions, investment grants, special depreciation allowances, and low-interest-rate credits. The purchase of such firms enables the international firm to expand operations without having to start from scratch. In addition, since wages are often low in the countries where privatization takes place, there is a major opportunity to build low-cost manufacturing and sourcing bases. Furthermore, the international firm can also act as a catalyst by accelerating the pace of transferring business skills and technology and by boosting trade prospects. In short, the very process of change offers new opportunities to the adept manager.

THE LESS-DEVELOPED MARKETS[21]

The time may have come to look at the four billion people in the world who live in poverty, subsisting on less than $1,500 a year (see Figure 9.4). Despite intitial skepticism, companies are finding that they can make profits while at the same time having a positive effect on the sustainable livelihoods of people not normally considered potential customers.[22] However, it will require radical departures from the traditional business models: e.g., new partnerships (ranging from local governments to nonprofits) and new pricing structures (allowing customers to rent or lease, rather than buy).

FIGURE 9.4

The World Economic Pyramid

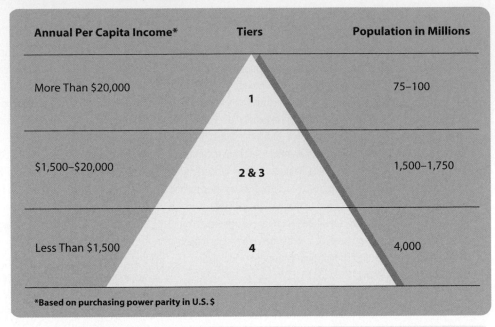

Annual Per Capita Income*	Tiers	Population in Millions
More Than $20,000	1	75–100
$1,500–$20,000	2 & 3	1,500–1,750
Less Than $1,500	4	4,000

*Based on purchasing power parity in U.S. $

Source: UN World Development Reports.

The first order of business is to learn about the needs, aspirations, and habits of targeted populations for which traditional intelligence gathering may not be the most effective. Hewlett-Packard has an initiative called World e-Inclusion which, working with a range of global and local partners, aims to sell, lease, or donate a billion dollars worth of satellite-powered computer products and services to markets in Africa, Asia, Eastern Europe, Latin America, and the Middle East. To engage with communities in Senegal, Hewlett-Packard partnered with Joko, Inc., a company founded by revered Senegalese pop star Youssou n'Dour.

In the product area, companies must combine advanced technology with local insights. Hindustan Lever (part of Unilever) learned that low-income Indians, usually forced to settle for low-quality products, wanted to buy high-end detergents and personal care products, but could not afford them in quantities available. In response, the company developed extremely low-cost packaging material and other innovations that allowed for a product priced in pennies instead of the $4 to $15 price of the regular containers. The same brand is on all of the product forms, regardless of packaging. Given that these consumers do not shop at supermarkets, Lever employs local residents with pushcarts who take small quantities of the sachets to kiosks.

Due to economic and physical isolation of poor communities, providing access can lead to a thriving business. In Bangladesh (with income levels of $200 per year), GrameenPhone Ltd. leases access to wireless phones to villagers. Every phone is used by an average of 100 people and generates $900 in revenue a month—two to three times the revenue generated by wealthier users who own their phones in urban areas. Similarly, the Jhai Foundation, an American-Lao foundation, is helping villagers in Laos obtain Internet access. The first step, however, was to develop an inexpensive and robust computer. The computer has no moving, and very few delicate, parts. Instead of a hard disk, it relies on flash-memory chips, and instead of an energy-guzzling glass cathode ray tube, its screen is a liquid-crystal display.

The emergence of these markets presents a great opportunity for companies. It also creates a chance for business, government, and civil society to join together in a common cause to help the poor aspiring to join the world market economy. Lifting billions of people from poverty may help avert social decay, political chaos, terrorism, and enviromental deterioration that is certain to continue if the gap between rich and poor countries continues to widen.

The Role of the Multinational Firm*

All problems aside, the market potential of transition and emerging economies is enormous. It is this promise that is paramount to understanding the developing role of multinational firms in transition economies. They enter because they see substantial profit potential. This potential, however, may not be attained quickly, and firms must time their entry and activity to pace themselves for the long race.

The experience to date in many transition economies has been mixed in terms of business success. Many of the newly formed purely domestic businesses have experienced relatively short life spans often characterized by rapid growth and significant profitability, albeit short lived in duration. The causes of failure typically are problems in general business management, the institution of new government regulations or taxes, or regulatory failures.

Multinational firms, however, have experienced higher rates of success in transition economies for a variety of reasons. First, foreign firms have had a tendency to enter—at least initially—service sectors that allowed high profit potential with minimal capital investments. This permits a first-stage entry of little capital at risk. Many of these service-sector market niches, such as insurance, Internet-based telecommunication services, security sales and brokerage services, and management consulting, to name a few, are "markets" that simply did not exist under the prior economic system.

As multinational firms gain experience and knowledge of the local markets, they may then increase the size of their capital investments, for example in the form of acquisitions or greenfield investments. The local market is then used as an export base to neighboring and other transition and emerging economies, taking advantage of long-standing links across countries for trade and commerce. At this point, the domestic market is not the focus of the firm's activity. With few exceptions, the profit potential is seen as cost-based access to other external markets.

This export orientation of the multinational firm is quite consistent with the economic policy goals of many economies. They are often sorely in need of export earnings. Having a multinational firm use their economic system as "base camp" for export-led development adds employment and infrastructure support. This is also one of the factors contributing to the special privileges accorded foreign multinationals by host governments such as preferential import duties, corporate tax breaks, and subsidized labor. In fact, many multinationals quickly find their access to local capital through the rapidly developing domestic financial sector to be easier than that of

*The authors gratefully acknowledge the valuable input of Professor Viktoria Dalko to this section.

other domestic borrowers, since many domestic companies are effectively excluded from accessing necessary capital. This is in many ways an unfortunate result of the lower-risk profile of the multinational firm compared to recently established domestic enterprises. If not balanced by encouragement for domestic firms, this disadvantage may result in growing criticism of multinational firms and their impact on vulnerable economies. It can also lead to renewed nationalist pressures on governments and reduce the ability of multinational firms to expand their activities globally.

Finally, as multinational firms mature in transition or emerging economies, many find that the domestic market itself represents a legitimate market opportunity on a stand-alone basis. Although this is the commonly assumed goal of privatization, it is not always achieved. For example, as global firms expand their presence in an economy, thereby expanding their offerings in industrial and retail products and services, they may quickly become net importers of capital equipment and other necessary inputs for providing the high level of economic goods demanded by the populace. Due to simultaneous investments by many firms, they may also find many more competitors in this new market than they had expected.

Many economies now recognize that if they are to develop businesses that are **world-class competitors** and not just poor domestic copies of foreign firms, they must somehow tap the knowledge base already thriving within successful global firms. Frequently, multinational firms are invited to begin joint ventures only with domestic parties. This in itself is often difficult, given that these domestic businesses or entities rarely have significant capital to contribute, but rather bring to the table nonquantifiable contributions such as market savvy and emerging business networks.

For example, in the global telecommunications industry, access to capital is only one of the many needs for industrial development. The technical know-how of the world's key global players is also needed for the development of a first-class industry. Countries like Hungary, Indonesia, and Brazil have invited foreign companies in conjunction with domestic parties to form international joint ventures to bid for the rights to develop large segments or geographic areas within their borders. This requirement is intended to serve as a way of tapping the enormous technical and market knowledge base and commitment of established multinational firms. Without their cooperation, the ability to close the gap with the leading global competitors may be impossible.

Often the multinational firm is invited into an economy to bring capital and technical and market know-how to help improve existing second-class companies. For example, in the early 1990s, General Motors negotiated extensively with the Polish government on the establishment of a joint venture with one of the government-owned automobile manufacturers. GM would contribute capital and technology, while the Polish automobile manufacturer contributed its own existing asset base, workers already in place, and access to a potentially large market. The problem confronted by GM and so many other multinational firms in similar circumstances is that they view the contributions of their domestic partner to be less significant than the potential loss of technical and intellectual property, and the risks associated with maintaining the multinational firm's own reputation and quality standards. In addition, it is frequently more expensive to retool an existing manufacturing facility than it is to simply start fresh with a greenfield facility. These are difficult partnerships, and each and every one requires extended discussion, negotiation, and special "chemistry" for success.

Multinational corporations are very often the only ones that can realistically make a difference in solving some of the problems in developing markets, as shown in

Focus On ⬇

Meeting Need and Opportunity in Developing Markets

Micronutrient deficiencies, or a lack of vitamins and minerals such as vitamin A, iron, and zinc, are believed to afflict about two billion children around the world. The impact on the learning capabilities of these children and their overall health and mortality is high. With vitamin pills costly to distribute and pill-taking hard to enforce, fortification of foods offers the most promising prospects for combating these deficiencies.

Developing a fortified drink that is cheap, effective, and does not have an aftertaste is a challenge for any company. Attempts in the past failed either because technology was not advanced enough for the idea to work or because development efforts resulted in drinks that were priced too high for customers most in need. For some companies the idea of dealing with the poorest markets in the world has not been appealing due to the lack of immediate growth prospects.

Coca-Cola has introduced "Project Mission" in Botswana to launch a drink to combat anemia, blindness, and other afflictions common in poorer parts of the world. The drink, called Vitango, is like the company's Hi-C orange-flavored drink, but it contains 12 vitamins and minerals chronically lacking in the diets of people in developing countries. Vitango will put the company in head-to-head competition with Procter & Gamble, which has a similar drink called Nutristar. Nutristar is sold in Venezuela in most food stores in flavors such as mango and passion fruit and promises "taller, stronger, and smarter kids."

The project satisfies multiple objectives for the Coca-Cola Company. First, it could help boost sales at a time when global sales of carbonated drinks are slowing, and, second, it will help in establishing relationships with governments and other local constituents that will serve as a positive platform for the Coca-Cola brand. The market for such nutritional drinks may be limited, but entering the markets offers both Coca-Cola and Procter & Gamble the chance to play the role of good corporate citizen at a time when being perceived as such is increasingly important for multinational corporations. "It is the right thing to do," says Steven Heyer, Coca-Cola's president and chief operating officer for noncarbonated beverages. "The marginal cost is low, and the return to society is high."

Aiming their products at the developing world, the companies have to tread carefully (remembering Nestlé's debacle with infant formula). To succeed they will have to win the support of nutrition and health experts. No claims are being made that these drinks are a one-stop shop for health but merely a supplement to a healthy diet.

Sources: C. K. Prahalad and Stuart L. Hart, "The Fortune at the Bottom of the Pyramid," *Strategy and Business* (first quarter, 2002): 35–47; "Drinks for Developing Countries," *Wall Street Journal,* November 27, 2001, B1, B6; and Dana James, "B2-4B Spells Profits," *Marketing News,* November 5, 2001, 1, 11–12.

Focus on Entrepreneurship. Developing new technologies or products is a resource-intensive task and requires knowledge transfer from one market to another. Without multinationals as catalysts, nongovernmental organizations, local governments, and communities will continue to flounder in their attempts to bring development to the poorest nations in the world.[23]

Summary

Special concerns must be considered by the international manager when dealing with former centrally planned economies in transition. Although the emerging market economies offer vast opportunities for trade, business practices may be significantly different from those to which the executive is accustomed.

In the emerging market economies, the key to international business success will be an understanding of the fact that societies in transition require special adaptation of business skills and time to complete the transformation. Due to their growing degree of industrialization, other economies are also becoming part of the world trade and investment picture. It must be recognized that these global changes will, in turn, precipitate adjustments in industrialized nations, particularly in the manufacturing and trade sectors. Adapting early to these changes can offer new opportunities to the international firm.

Often the international manager is also faced with state-owned enterprises that have been formed in noncommunist nations for reasons of national or economic security. These firms may inhibit foreign market entry, and they frequently reflect in their transactions the overall domestic and foreign policy of the country rather than any economic rationale. The current global trend toward privatization offers new opportunities to the international firm, either through investment or by offering business skills and knowledge to assist in the success of privatization.

Questions for Discussion

1. Planning is necessary, yet central planning is inefficient. Why?
2. Discuss the observation that "Russian products do what they are supposed to do—but only that."
3. How can and should the West help eastern European countries?
4. How can central European managers be trained to be market oriented?
5. Where do you see the greatest potential in future trade between emerging market economies and industrialized nations?
6. What are the benefits of privatization?
7. Why do most transition economy governments require foreign multinationals to enter business via joint ventures with existing domestic firms?
8. Why do foreign multinationals often have advantaged access to capital in emerging economies over purely domestic companies?

Internet Exercises

1. Identify the key programs and information services offered to exporters operating in the former Soviet Union through the U.S. Department of Commerce. (Refer to Commerce's Business Information Service for the Newly Independent States, BISNIS, http://www.ita.doc.gov.)
2. What role does the European Bank for Reconstruction and Development play in transforming the formerly communist economies of Eastern Europe and the Soviet Union? (Refer to the Web site, http://www.ebrd.com.)

Take a Stand

With the demise of the communist economies of Eastern Europe and the former Soviet Union, as well as the advances in international communication and information technologies, globalization is an accomplished fact. While many countries grow to unprecedented levels of wealth and economic security, others continue to experience permanent debt and instability. Activists are warning of the dangers of "savage capitalism," where social safety nets are dismantled and the greedy are ensured a constant supply of exploitable cheap labor from the world's poorest countries.

For Discussion

Pope John Paul II has urged adapting to new needs, modifying the rules of the marketplace, and developing new models of sharing between rich and poor countries. How do you evaluate the risk of the greediness of a few, leaving many on the margin of survival?

CAR FINANCING IN CHINA

"In China, car financing is a lot like the unification of North and South Korea. Just about everyone wants it to happen. But before that can happen, first you need to sweep away the land mines."
— Mike Dunne, *Automotive News*, 2000.

China and the WTO

After 15 years of negotiations, China formally became a member of the World Trade Organization (WTO) on December 11, 2001. During the negotiations, China had been gradually liberalizing most of its trade and investment policies, making the official admission largely symbolic. More than anything, WTO membership signals China's commitment to establish clear and enforceable nondisriminatory rules to conduct business in and with the country. For example, China's trademark and copyright laws were brought in line with international standards in October, 2001. Many companies had established their strategies in the 1990s based on the assumption that China would gain entry into the WTO and now are ready to execute those plans.

Given China's unwillingness to show progress on political reform, the commitment to structural economic reforms has been particularly noteworthy. The constitutional amendment in 1999 that legitimized private capital and granted private firms the same legal rights as state-owned enterprises laid a foundation for sustained, market-based growth. The private sector has grown to 40 percent of the GDP and employs more than 30 percent of Chinese workers. New jobs created

in the private sector account for 38 percent of all new formal employment, 56 percent in urban areas. The significance of this is more pronounced given the layoffs in the state-owned-enterprises sector.

China has been the fastest growing economy in the last ten years, with annual real GDP growth averaging 10.8 percent. While average national GDP per capital is under $1,000, urban populations (such as those in Shanghai and Guangzhou) enjoy incomes of more than $3,000 (a point where consumption increases dramatically). This has meant that urban households can afford color TVs (96 percent have them), phones (76 percent), and mobile phones (28 percent). Similar wealth is gradually (albeit slowly) spreading to rural areas as well. Furthermore, an attitude change is occurring among the young urban consumers: they now accept purchasing on credit.

China's integration into the world economy has resulted in spectacular numbers both in trade and in investment. China's trade with the world quadrupled in the 1990s to $474 billion, with more than $100 billion of that with the United States. (In 2001, China retained its spot as the country with the largest trade imbalance with the United States, at $83 billion.) While the lowering of trade barriers may permit more sales of foreign goods in China in the future, the rush by many companies from the Americas and Europe to manufacture in China for exports may maintain China's trade imbalance with these trading partners. With Asian countries, however, China has been running a trade deficit since 2000 and will continue to be a source of demand as markets liberalize.

China received more foreign direct investment (FDI) in the 1990s than any country in the world except for the United States. The inflows have amounted to more than $60 billion per year in the last five years, as shown in Figure 1. China's FDI has come at the expense of the rest of Asia, however. FDI inflows go to areas (within a region and a country) with comparative advantages—some to areas with abundant labor, some to areas with technological skills. With China leading in terms of inward investment flows, it may emerge as a hub for interregional demand for goods and services. Countries such as Japan will have to reorient themselves to focus on research and development, design, software, and high-precision manufactured goods.

Of economic significance is China's effort to stabilize its currency in the last five years. While officially

Sources: This case was compiled by Ilkka A. Ronkainen using publicly available materials, including: "Motor Nation," *Business Week*, June 17, 2002: 44–45; Gong Zhenzheng, "Auto Price Wars Start to Rev Up," *China Daily*, January 22, 2002: 5; Joe Studwell, *The China Dream* (New York: Atlantic Monthly Press, 2002): chapter 7, note 29; "China's Carmakers Flattened by Falling Tariffs," *Business Week*, December 3, 2001; Mike Dunne, "Car Loans: Ready, Set, Go?" *Automotive News International*, September 1, 2000: 33; "Why Auto Financing is Difficult in China," *Access Asia*, November 24, 2001; "Shanghai Leads in Efforts to Build Personal Credit for Chinese," *Xinhua News Agency*, July 20, 2000; "First Auto-Finance Firms to be Launched in Early 2002," *Access Asia*, December 6, 2001; "China's Carmakers: Flattened by Falling Tariffs," *Business Week*, December 3, 2001: 51; and Danny Hakim, "All that Easy Credit Haunts Detroit Now," *New York Times*, January 6, 2002, section 3, page 1. For further information, see http://www.gmacfs.com and http://www.fordcredit.com.

FIGURE 1

Foreign Direct Investment Inflows to Asia and China

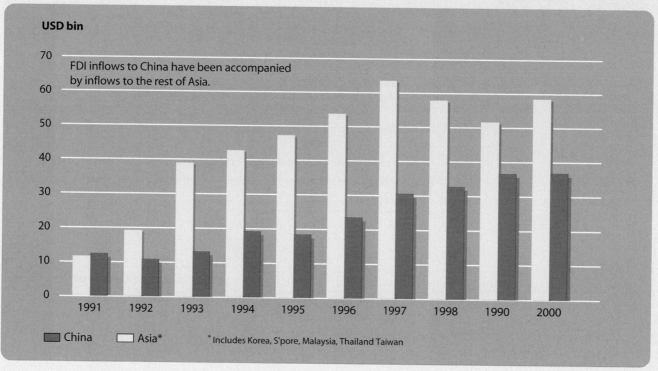

USD bin

FDI inflows to China have been accompanied by inflows to the rest of Asia.

☐ China   ☐ Asia*   * Includes Korea, S'pore, Malaysia, Thailand Taiwan

Source: Chi Lo, "Asia's Competitiveness Endgame: Life After China's WTO Entry," *The China Business Review,* January–February 2002: 22–26.

described as a managed float, the currency (yuan renminbi) is effectively pegged to the U.S. dollar. This has resulted in China being immune to currency fluctuations that have wreaked havoc among emerging markets such as Mexico, Indonesia, Russia, Brazil, and Argentina. However, due to China's increasing foreign exchange reserves, strong capital inflows, and current account surplus, as well as pressure from Asian countries, (especially Japan), the currency has come under substantial appreciating pressure. However, with the trade liberalization due to the WTO, the higher value of the renminbi would aggravate the shock on domestic companies that compete with imports, as well as on exporters who have to compete in the global market (often on the basis of price). The Chinese authorities have acknowledged the need for financial and currency liberalization but the damaging impact of the rising currency in the short term will most likely keep the currency regime unchanged. This will naturally result in low currency risk for investors.

It has been widely assumed that large corporations from around the world would benefit from the liberalization measures undertaken and committed to (see Table 1.) For example, the Motion Picture Association estimated that lifting the barriers to film distribution would result in $80 million in revenues, in addition to $120 million from sales and rentals of videos that would no longer be plagued by rampant piracy. Some sectors, such as banking and insurance, are expected to make especially strong moves as markets open up. Foreign insurers can now operate beyond the two cities they have been limited to and expect nationwide access by 2005. Majority ownership in Chinese companies is possible, as is the choice of joint venture partners.

As many imports now face no tariff barriers (and the remaining ones will be eliminated by 2010) or nontariff barriers (many quotas were eliminated on accession and the rest will be by 2005, and as trading and distribution rights are to be expected, the primary question is about the timetable for change. Most business leaders have been quite realistic in not expecting substantive changes immediately and have therefore built long-term game plans. In some sectors, competition has already heated up, given the expectations of consumers for more—and less expensive—choices.

TABLE 1   China's WTO Obligations

2001:	After membership, China will open new cities to foreign banks for local currency business.
2002:	China will eliminate restrictions on where foreign law firms may operate and the number of offices that can be opened.
2004:	Foreign companies are permitted to provide health and group insurance to the Chinese.
2005:	U.S. to eliminate Chinese textile quotas but adopt measures to prevent import surges.
2006:	China to reduce auto tariffs to 25 percent from current 80 to 100 percent.
2007:	Foreign companies can hold 49 percent in telecom services (voice) joint ventures.

Source: "China Begins Career as a WTO Member," *The Washington Post,* December 11, 2001, A14.

The transformation will have to be seen in the context of political change, which is slow in countries such as China. Many adverse effects of the WTO membership are expected in terms of output and employment in sectors such as agriculture, financial services, and, in general, "less-competitive industries," which are typically dominated by state-owned enterprises. For example, agricultural employment is forecast to fall by 11 million, and a substantial share of the 1.7 million workers in the four largest state-owned banks are in jeopardy. These factors have led the government to move with caution in allowing for change in the post-WTO environment. Furthermore, any dramatic change usually faces opposition from regional or local levels of government that may see themselves as protectors of local interests.

There are already examples of the challenges to be faced as the WTO agreement is implemented at the industry and regional level. Companies wanting to exploit the world's largest mobile telecommunications market were promised a 49 percent stake in domestic operators. To do so, companies have found that waiting periods for official approval would be between 270 to 310 days and that any local partner would have to put up 75 percent of 1 billion renminbi before permission will be granted. This will mean that the number of joint-venture partners is considerably smaller than expected, possibly limited to state-owned entities. In a similar fashion, banks have found their aspirations dampened. Under the WTO agreement, foreign banks were to be able to offer renminbi banking services to Chinese corporate clients in 2004 and to Chinese consumers starting in 2007. New regulations stipulate that foreign banks can only open one branch per year which, given that many are starting from scratch, (only 158 branches of foreign banks existed in 2001) and given the tens of thousands of branches currently held by local entities (for example, Bank of China has 15,200), the task is daunting. Foreign branches are required to have 1 billion renminbi in operating capital in order to conduct a full range of services, an amount considered discriminatory by those hoping to develop the sector. Exporters have found delays in certifications that would allow their products to enter the China market, especially in areas that are sensitive, such as agriculture.

The expectation is that disputes and problems will emerge but will be taken care over time. A parallel can be drawn between the United States and its trading partners (such as the European Union and Canada), which continue to have disagreements within the WTO framework. The extent of the challenges will depend to a large extent on the economic health of China and its ability to absorb the competitive shocks of the WTO membership. Of concern for the politicians will be that the growing gap between the haves and the have-nots (especially the urban and the rural) and the costs of reforming the state sector will cause social unrest challenging the legitimacy of the political structures.

The Western world has had a commercial fascination with China for the last 2000 years. The latest wave of interest started in 1979 with the official opening of China, culminating with the official acceptance of China as the 143rd member of the WTO. Companies will continue to speculate on what sales might be achieved if only a fraction of the Chinese population buys its products or services.

China's economic stature will undoubtedly continue to grow. Increased investment will make China a production base for the world as global companies put their best practices to work in the largest emerging market in the world. For the United States, this may mean losses of more than 600,000 jobs and a widening trade deficit with China which, in turn, may result in growing tensions between two world superpowers. At the corporate level, the huge investments have meant that while the efforts in China may be profitable, they are not earning their cost of capital (which many multinationals calculate at 15 percent).

Those companies interested in entering China primarily to exploit its domestic market may have more freedoms to do so (such as having control of its own distribution or the ability to provide financing) but will continue to face the same challenges as before the WTO agreement. It is no longer enough to extend products and services (however famous their brand names, for example, may be) without adjusting to local market conditions. While foreign players are dominant in sectors such as beverages, film, and personal care, local companies still dominate in televisions, refrigerators, and washing machines despite multinational company presence. Multinationals may bring their best practices to China but local firms are quick to copy those practices and with their inherent advantages are able to compete effectively. While some doubt these Chinese companies will be competitive in the global markets due to the lack of success factors such as global brands, some companies are already dominant in commodity-based sectors. Qingdao-based appliance maker Haier already has a 40 percent market share in small refrigerators and is planning to expand its base in the United States to, among other things, learn to be more effective at home.

Changes in the Car Market in China

A full-scale price war between car makers in China broke in the first months of 2002. The phenomenon was a result of Chinese consumers' delays in buying cars throughout 2001, as well as increased imports following China's tariff cuts as part of the WTO agreement. The slashing of tariffs in the car sector were the biggest in any sector (from 80 percent to 50 percent now, and down to 25 percent by 2006).

Consumers had been waiting for cheaper cars for years and this dream became a reality through the effects of the WTO agreement. For example, the Buick

Sail's pre-WTO price was $13,855, but after the WTO it dropped to $12,040—with further decreases possible as domestic makers lower their prices to maintain a competitive advantage. The war was ignited on January 12, 2000, when Tianjin Automotive Industry Group slashed prices of all of its Xiali compact cars by 9,000–23,000 yuan ($1,084–2,771). More than 3,600 are reported to have been sold during four days after the price cut. Chang'an Suzuki, a joint venture between Chongqing-based Chang'an Motor and Japan's Suzuki Motors cut its prices by 20 percent. Analysts estimated that domestic carmakers of vehicles priced at less than 150,000 yuan ($18,070) would have to reduce prices, although carmakers such as Shanghai General Motors and Shanghai Volkswagen would try to hold on and let dealers engage in price promotions. Even with the price decreases, comparable cars cost far less in Europe, a fact not lost on the Chinese consumer.

Carmakers already producing in China are bracing for intense competition. As the Chinese government phases out regulations as to what models to produce, GM, VW, Ford, Honda, and Toyota all plan to launch models aimed at quality- and cost-conscious consumers. For example, Ford will launch a compact in 2003 based on its Ikon model, now made in India at a price below $12,000. With new freedoms, carmakers will have to focus on the customer desires more than ever before.

Eventually, lower prices and wider choice should create a thriving auto industry. Experts predict car sales to increase to 900,000 units in 2002, and hit the 2-million-unit mark by 2005. It should be noted that planned capacity as early as 1999 exceeded 2.75 million units (with actual sales only reaching 565,000 units).

Current Market Structure for Car Financing in China

In calendar year 2000, approximately 600,000 cars were sold in China. Only 16 percent were financed. Two thirds of that 16 percent were business-to-business loans between banks and taxi companies. That leaves 25,000 units financed by individuals and private enterprises. In comparison, GM and Ford—by themselves—provided auto financing to approximately the same number of individuals and private enterprises in the state of Maryland in 2000. U.S. auto purchasers finance between 65 and 93 percent of all units purchased, depending on make.

China is currently a very small market for auto financing, and for consumer credit in general. There are a number of reasons behind the small market size. Auto financing was not permitted by the Chinese government before 1998. Currently, only four state-owned and two private banks are authorized by the Chinese government to provide loans with interest rates regulated by the government. These include Bank of China, China's oldest bank, as well as China Construction Bank. These institutions have onerous requirements to gain approval for a loan, including: (1) collateral other than the car (home, deposits at the bank) valued at 100 to 120 percent of the amount of the loan, (2) a guarantor, (3) proof of income and tax payments (not onerous in and of itself, but many Chinese underreport income and taxes to an extent that verifiable income is insufficient for loan repayment), (4) a marriage certificate, (5) an official estimate of the value of the vehicle; and (6) the bank will mandate vehicle purchase through an "approved" retailer. This has meant that nearly one third of car buyers have opted to quit the process rather than complete it. Even with the onerous requirements, initial results have not been promising: default rates in 1998 ranged from 10 to 30 percent.

In addition, the infrastructure is not yet developed for car financing. Most vehicle regulatory agencies do not allow liens or security interests in autos that are registered for personal use. Laws and regulations that protect insurance companies when investing in loans or underwriting loan risks are not consistently in place. Repossession procedures are not generally codified. Where rules exist, the Public Security Bureau must effect repossession and will decide the resale value on repossessed vehicles.

Regional differences are significant. While the industry is still in its infancy, Shanghai is the most advanced both in terms of amounts of consumer credit and the systems in place. The urban populations of the east will play a major role in the change process with their increasing wealth and nontraditional attitudes toward buying on credit. Foreign interest in the market for car-financing is predicated on the long-term potential of the market influenced by China's membership in the WTO: possibility to operate and demand for car financing. While government rules made market entry possible prior to January 2002, setting up operations is still challenging. For example, government rules going forward mandate loans denominated in renminbi (the local currency, "people's money"). Renminbi funding sources are scarce and foreign banks do not have access to funding in renminbi. Furthermore, foreign entities can count on local competition from existing and new government-owned institutions as well as private entities. The State Development Planning Commission (SDPC) has dis-

closed that China will launch its first auto financing company in early 2002. Yafei Auto Chain General Store—with default rates at less than 2 percent and 90 percent regional market share—is a chain of auto dealerships that gets preferential treatment from the Beijing government and enjoys exclusive underwriting support from the China People's Life Insurance Company.

The WTO agreement will cause a drop in the tariffs of imported cars from a range of 70 to 80 percent of the list price to 50–60 percent. In 2002, sedan imports are expected to leap 50 percent, to 120,000 units. By 2006, duties are to sink another 25 percent—enough to put cars within the reach of China's middle class.

Expected Market Changes in Car Financing in China

All indications are that auto financing in China in the twenty-first century will be a lucrative business both at the macro level and the micro level. Only 1 percent of China's total consumption was made through consumer credit in 1999. In an effort to fuel economic growth, Chinese officials have stated that they are working toward percentages of consumption from credit that are more in line with the Western world. Most of the Western economies average between 20–25 percent of consumption through consumer credit.

Average household income in China's 35 largest cities is in excess of $2172 USD, with GDP per capita in those cities in excess of $1100. GDP per capita in Shanghai, Beijing, and Guangzhou exceeds $2000. Most experts agree that automotive purchases generally, and automotive finance specifically, expand rapidly after crossing the $2000 per capita GDP threshold.

Consensus estimates for the car financing market—both personal and business use—in 2002 are 20 percent of the 830,000 expected unit sales (166,000 units). This number is expected to increase by 40 to 60 percent over a five-year period, resulting in a $3.25 billion market. While this is not large by Western standards, it does provide sufficient scale to mirror other world market characteristics (such as those in Brazil) and allow for a fairly precise prediction of the costs to develop the market.

All indications are that Chinese consumers' aversion to debt is waning—at least in the cities of the south and east. Estimates for consumer lending in general can be extrapolated from analogous evidence. In 1995, 15,000 individuals in Shanghai borrowed 570 million yuan worth of mortgages and in 1999, 680,000 individuals in Shanghai borrowed 54 billion yuan worth of mortgages.

The industry is dependent on accurate and timely information as well as a transparent system of operation. Shanghai Credit Information Services is maturing as a reliable source of credit information for more than 1 million Chinese. Rules for recordation of liens and repossession and remarketing of vehicles are now in place in Shanghai and Beijing (albeit in their infancy and open to local interpretation).

Options for Market Entry and Development

There are four ways that auto finance companies can be set up in China:

- Automakers can launch an auto-financing services subsidiary;
- (Chinese) banks can set up special auto financing institutions;
- Nonbanking financial institutions owned by enterprise groups can form an auto financing company; or
- Existing lending consortiums can provide financing services for auto companies' sales divisions

Draft rules for foreign investment are currently being circulated. The foreign firms that have submitted an application for license to do business include VW Credit, Ford Motor Credit, Peugeot/Citroen Credit, and GMAC. Of the firms listed above, those that have traditionally undertaken diversified lending activities outside the area of auto financing have been the most aggressive in terms of new market entry and pricing once they have entered a market.

GMAC's Competitive Position

GMAC and the other financing arms of carmakers are at an obvious disadvantage in relation to home-country institutions because the market was reserved for Chinese institutions until January 2002. GMAC previously acted in an advisory capacity to GM's Shanghai JV manufacturing facility, which, in turn, has set up relationships with official government lending institutions (such as China Construction Bank, Bank of Shanghai). Currently, GMAC has one person in Shanghai with the task of market investigation and support of GM activities.

GMAC's competitive position vis-à-vis the other foreign companies applying for entry appears to be solid for a number of reasons:

- GM is the largest corporate FDI contributor to China in the world and has a substantial partnership with the government;
- GMAC has numerous manufacturing partners to leverage—SGM, Jinbei GM (which produces the Chevrolet S-10 pickup and Blazer SUV), Wuling (GM has an equity stake in the largest producer of minicars for the Chinese market). These partners deliver the second most FDI autos in the market—just behind VW and far ahead of Ford Motor Credit and Peugeot; and
- GMAC has numerous GM-network partners to leverage (Isuzu, Suzuki, Fiat, Fuji Heavy Industries).

GMAC's expertise in auto lending generally and in the following ancillary areas critical to doing business in China should allow for the business to get up and running. It has extensive experience in auto lending in developing markets without efficient infrastructure (e.g., India with no credit bureaus and state involvement in repossession and remarketing). Partnering with other private and quasi-state-run institutions such as Fannie Mae, GMAC subsidiaries (GMAC Mortgage, GMAC Commercial Mortgage and Residential Funding Corporation) have developed expertise in profitable loan securitization, (mortgage) loan servicing, and receivables purchase and sale have given it the necessary skills to work together with third parties and governmental units. Finally, market presence in many other countries in the Asia Pacific region gives it the human resources necessary for China expansion. These offices are staffed with a broad array of third country expatriates from China and other cultures that have better insight to the Chinese market than do GMAC's U.S.-based staff.

Despite the overwhelming external and internal opportunities, challenges exist as well. Ford's and GM's credit ratings were downgraded by Moody's and Standard & Poor's in 2001, forcing the automakers out of commercial paper and into other, more expensive forms of funding. The no- or low-interest loans and cheap leases to pump up sales in 2001 have threatened the financial health of the carmakers' credit arms. For example, GMAC North America's huge success with 0 percent financing during 2001 Q4's "Keep America Rolling" campaign ate up significant resources. Effectively, GMAC may be out of cash for big market-entry investments and equity investment from the parent company, when GM as a whole faces an unfunded pension liability and reduced cash flow that is critical for reinvestment into future product programs. Ford

Motor Credit is facing even bigger problems given its more aggressive lending practices of the recent past.

Implications for Global Operations

A carmaker's captive financing arm exists for two reasons: to assist in delivering additional cars and trucks to consumers, and to provide a superior return on investment and cash flow to its sole stockholder. While still extremely risky and lacking in short-term profit, the China market is still valued by the carmakers because of the market potential it displays for sales and because of the potential it displays for the financing arm in term of auto finance and mortgages. The questions is now, how to deliver on the promise and the mandate. For example, Ford Motor Company has adopted a wait-and-see attitude at this time.

Questions for Discussion

1. Suggest reasons for GMAC to enter or not to enter the Chinese market for auto financing.
2. What is the most prudent mode of entry and market development for GMAC should it choose to enter the market?
3. If it enters, where should GMAC make its moves and with what type of products?
4. What should GMAC do to influence the positive change in China in its favor?

C ountries and governments have been raising capital in the international financial markets for centuries. The Russian government of Czar Nicholas IV issued a 100-year bearer bond in 1894 (the bond itself is reproduced in Figure 1).

A **bearer bond** is a security sold to an investor in which the *bearer* of the bond, the holder, is entitled to receive an interest payment at regularly scheduled dates as listed on the bond. There is no record kept by any authority on who the owner of the bond is, allowing the investor to earn the interest payments without tax authorities knowing the investor's identity. This allowed the bond issuer, in this case the Czar, to raise capital at lower interest rates because investors would most likely be able to avoid paying taxes on the interest income they received.

In order for the investor to receive their interest payments, the bond contained a sheet of coupons which were numbered and dated. These individual coupons were clipped from the sheet and taken to one of the listed banks around the world to receive their interest payment. This bond listed the cities and the amount of the interest payment in local currency terms. The 118th coupon in the series is reproduced in Figure 2.

This 118th coupon, which the bearer can present for payment beginning June 18, 1923, indicates what payment the bearer can receive depending on which currency the bearer is receiving payment. This obviously

FIGURE 1

Bearer Bond Issued by Czar Nicholas IV

BOND   R. 125.

of one hundred and twenty five Gold Roubles
= 500 Francs = 404 German Marks = 19 Pounds Sterling 15 shill. 6 pence
= 239 Dutch Flor. = $96_{,25}$ United States Gold Dollars,
inscribed into the Great Book of the Public Debt at the Office of the Imperial Commission of the Sinking Fund

to Bearer.

The Bear of this Bond is entitled to the amount of one hundred and twenty five Gold Roubles bearing interest at FOUR per cent per annum until its redemption of drawing.
This Bond is for ever exempt from every present and future Russian Tax whatever.

The interest will be paid against the coupons every three months viz: on the 20th March/1st April, 19th June/1st July, 19th September/1st October, 20th December/1st January of each year, at the choice of the Bearer:

in ST.-PETERSBURG:	at the State Bank, in Gold Roubles or Credit Roubles, at the rate of exchange of the day;
in PARIS:	at the Banque de Paris et des Pays-Bas, at the Crédit Lyonnais, at the Comptoir National d'Escompte de Paris, at the office of the Russian Bank of Foreign Trade and at Messrs Hottingeur & Cº, in Francs;
in LONDON:	at the Russian Ban for Foreign Trade (London-branch), in Pounds Sterling;
in BERLIN:	at Messrs Mendelssohn & Cº, in German Marks
in AMSTERDAM:	At Messrs Lippmann, Rosenthal & Cº, in Dutch Florins;
in NEW-YORK:	at Messrs Baring, Magoun & Cº, in Gold Dollars.

(continued)

FIGURE 1

Bearer Bond Issued by Czar Nicholas IV *(continued)*

These Bonds will be redeemed at par, within 81 years by drawings by lot, which will take place at the Imperial Commission of the Sinking Fund half yearly, the 20th March/1st April and 19th September/1st October, beginning from 19th September/1st October 1894. To the redemption of this Loan will be applied every half year 0,084281% of the nominal amount of the original issue together with 2% on the amount of the Bonds previously drawn.

Up to the 19th December/1st January 1904, the amount allotted for the amortization of this Loan, mentioned at the previous article, shall not be increased, not shall up to the said date be admitted reimbursement or conversion of the whole Loan. The payment of the drawn Bonds will take place on the date of payment of the next following coupon, at the same places and in the same currencies as the coupons. Coupons due after the date of payment of the drawn bonds must remain attached thereto, otherwise the amount of missing coupons will be deducted from the capital upon payment of the Bond. The drawn Bonds of this Loan not presented for payment within 30 years, from the date fixed for their reimbursement falling under prescription, shall be void; coupons not presented within 10 years after their due date will likewise be void through prescription.

The Bonds of this Loan bear coupons up to the 19th December 1903/1st January 1904 and a Talon, on presentation of which after the said date new coupon sheets will be delivered, free of charge, for the undrawn Bonds, at the places designated for the payment of the coupons. The Bonds of this Loan are issued either nominative or on Bearer. The rules for the nominative Bonds, their exchange for Bonds on Bearer and vice-versa are to be approved by the Minister of Finance.

WE ORDER:
1) to issue 4% Bonds for a nominal amount of one hundred and thirteen millions six hundred thousand (113,600,000) Gold Roubles and to inscribe this issue in the Great Book of the Public Debt under the denomination of Russian Four per cent Gold Loan, 6th issue, 1894;
2) the interest on these bonds to run from the 20th December 1893/1st January 1894 and their amortization to take place within 81 years from the 20th December 1894/1st January 1895;
3) to fix all other conditions of this issue in conformity with the ones established by Art. IV of Our Imperial Ukase of the 9th/21st August 1893 for the Russian Four per cent Gold Loan, 5th issue, 1893;
4) to determine simultaneously with the issue of these Bonds the right and privilege concerning their acceptance as security for State-contracts and as guarantee for due payment of accise-duties.

implies a set of fixed exchange rates in effect on the date of issuance (1894). Use the coupon in Figure 2 and the bond in Figure 1 to answer the following questions.

Questions for Discussion

1. What is the value of the total bond as originally issued in French francs, German marks, British pounds, Dutch florins, and U.S. dollars?

2. Create a chart that shows the fixed rate implied by the coupon for the six different currencies.

3. Create a second chart that compares these exchange rates with these same exchange rates today (use either the *Wall Street Journal* or *Financial Times* to find current exchange rates.

FIGURE 2

Coupon for Redemption of Bearer Bond

RUSSIAN 4% GOLD LOAN, SIXTH ISSUE, 1894

Talon of the Bond of 187 Rouble 50 Cop. (1/Rouble = 1/15 Imper.)

118th Coupon of the Bond, due 18 June/1 July 1923:

in Paris 5 Francs, in Berlin 4 Mark 4 Pf.,
in London 3 Schill. 11 1/2 P., in Amsterdam 2 Flor. 39C.,
In New York 96 1/4 Cents.

Valid for 10 years.

In order to operate successfully abroad, firms must prepare for their market entry. Key in the preparation is the conduct of research to build a knowledge base of country-specific issues and market-specific opportunities and concerns.

Once such a base is established, the company can enter international markets, initially through exporting and international intermediaries. Over time, expansion can occur through foreign direct investment and lead to the formation of the multinational corporation.

Concurrent to the entry and expansion, the firm must engage in substantial strategic planning. Such planning and the subsequent steps necessary for organization, implementation, and control round out this section.

PART
Strategy

5

CHAPTER 10

Building the Knowledge Base

Learning Objectives

- To gain an understanding of the need for research

- To explore the differences between domestic and international research

- To learn where to find and how to use sources of secondary information

- To gain insight into the gathering of primary data

- To examine the need for international management information systems

Cool Hunters: Finding Tomorrow's Trends Today

Armed with a digital camera and a notebook, a special breed of market researcher is prowling the malls, skate parks, teahouses, and pizza parlors from Los Angeles to Antwerp. The job title? Cool hunter. Charged with the task of identifying the "next big thing" for young people, these cultural anthropologists turned detectives serve as consultants to some of the top retailers, movie studios, car companies, and apparel and cosmetics manufacturers in the world.

Cool hunting sounds like fun, but it's no easy task. Consider the nature of "cool" itself. As soon as too many people start wearing, carrying, or doing something that is "cool," it ceases to be cool. However, for a brief instant, the market for that cool new product or service is huge. Combine that with the fact that the youth segment in the United States currently includes more than 100 million consumers with more than $300 billion in spending power. It's easy to see why competition is fierce for young consumers' attention.

Toyota employed an independent cool hunter, David Wales, to gain insight on how teenagers use technology as it designed the Scion xB—a new automobile within the company's youth-oriented subbrand called "Scion." As part of his research he actually analyzed the contents of messenger bags, backpacks, and purses of New Yorkers. Sony drew upon street

© TAXI/ANDREAS POLLOK

intelligence to design a Walkman with a heavy-duty clip resembling the chains young athletes wear. Converse's One Star sneaker sandal was inspired by the "cholo" look of Mexican girl gangs.

However, not all of cool hunters' predictions result in successful product introductions. In fact, most of them don't. In 2001, Lauren Holden, the former director of design inspiration at Nike, predicted that mainstream American teenagers would soon be wearing organic love beads. Around the same time, trend watchers forecasted that tight, calf-clutching trousers would replace baggy pants in the wardrobes of urban youth. Yet these trends never seemed to catch on.

One major challenge that trend forecasters face is determining whether or not a trend identified in one geographical area can and will translate across cultural and geographical borders. For example, since cell phone text messaging and gaming have such higher penetration rates in Europe and Asia, applications developers in the United States can, to some extent, look to other countries for creative inspiration. Today, mobile messaging is booming in Europe, where Forrester Research expects to see 17 billion messages a month by 2007. But will this popularity come to the United States? Perhaps not. As Greg Clayman, cofounder and VP of business development for Upoc, a mobile messaging developing company, reasoned, "In Japan they eat squid on their pizza. I don't think that's coming here any time soon." Schuyler Brown, Associate Director of Euro RSCG Worldwide's Strategic Trendspotting and Research team, explains that the lifestyle of American teens is a huge factor working against expanded use of mobile-phone technologies: "American teens drive to and from school and work, reducing the amount of time they spend on hands-free commuting. In Europe and Asia, commuting via bus or train is a prime time for services like SMS [Short Message Service] and gaming."

Sources: "Y RN'T WE N2 SMS?" *PR Newswire,* "February 12, 2003; Gotting, Peter, "Cool Hunters," *Sydney Morning Herald,* January 10, 2003; La Ferla, Ruth, "Once Hot, Now Not, Cool Hunters Are in a Deep Freeze," *The New York Times,* July 7, 2002, 6; Gubbins, Ed, "The Definition of Cool Is Not in Your Dictionary," *Wireless Review,* June 2002, 6.

The single most important cause of failure in international business is insufficient preparation and information. The failure of managers to comprehend cultural disparities, the failure to remember that customers differ from country to country, and the lack of investigation into whether or not a market exists prior to market entry has made international business a high-risk activity.[1] International business research is therefore instrumental to international business success since it permits the firm to take into account different environments, attitudes, and market conditions. Fortunately, such research has become less complicated. As the opening vignette shows, information from around the globe can be obtained quite easily.

This chapter discusses data collection and provides a comprehensive overview of how to obtain general screening information on international markets, to evaluate business potential, and to assess current or potential opportunities and problems. Data sources that are low cost and that take little time to accumulate—in short, secondary data—are considered first. The balance of the chapter is devoted to more sophisticated forms of international research, including primary data collection and the development of an information system.

International and Domestic Research

The tools and techniques of international research are the same as those of domestic research. The difference is in the environment to which the tools are applied. The environment determines how well the tools, techniques, and concepts work. Although the objectives of research may be the same, the execution of international research may differ substantially from that of domestic research. The four primary reasons for this difference are new parameters, new environmental factors, an increase in the number of factors involved, and a broader definition of competition.

NEW PARAMETERS

In crossing national borders, a firm encounters parameters not found in domestic business. Examples include duties, foreign currencies and changes in their value, different modes of transportation, and international documentation. New parameters also emerge because of differing modes of operating internationally. For example, the firm can export, license its products, engage in a joint venture, or carry out foreign direct investment. The firm that has done business only domestically will have had little or no experience with the requirements and conditions of these types of operations. Managers must therefore obtain information in order to make good business decisions.

NEW ENVIRONMENTAL FACTORS

When going international, a firm is exposed to an unfamiliar environment. Many of the domestic assumptions on which the firm and its activities were founded may not hold true internationally. Management needs to learn the culture of the host country, understand its political systems and level of stability, and comprehend the existing differences in societal structures and language. In addition, it must understand pertinent legal issues in order to avoid violating local laws. The technological level of the society must also be incorporated in the business plan. In short, all the assumptions that were formulated over the years based on domestic business activities must now be reevaluated. This crucial point is often neglected because most managers are born in the environment of their domestic operations and only subconsciously learn to understand the constraints and opportunities of their business activities. The situation is analogous to learning one's native language. Being born to a language makes speaking it seem easy. Only when attempting to learn a foreign language does one begin to appreciate the structure of language and the need for grammatical rules.

THE NUMBER OF FACTORS INVOLVED

Environmental relationships need to be relearned whenever a firm enters a new international market. The number of changing dimensions increases geometrically. Coordination of the interaction among the dimensions becomes increasingly difficult because of their sheer number. Such coordination, however, is crucial to the international success of the firm for two reasons. First, in order to exercise some central control over its international operations, a firm must be able to compare results and activities across countries. Otherwise, any plans made by headquarters may be inappropriate. Second, the firm must be able to learn from its international operations and must find ways to apply the new lessons learned to different markets. Without coordination, such learning cannot take place in a systematic way. The international research process can help in this undertaking.

BROADER DEFINITION OF COMPETITION

The international market exposes the firm to a much greater variety of competition than that found in the home market. For example, a firm may find that ketchup competes against soy sauce. Similarly, firms that offer labor-saving devices domestically may encounter competition abroad from cheap manual labor. Therefore, firms must determine the breadth of the competition, track competitive activities, and evaluate their actual and potential impact on company operations on an ongoing basis.

Recognizing the Need for International Research

Many firms do little research before they enter a foreign market. Often, decisions concerning entry and expansion in overseas markets and selection and appointment of distributors are made after a cursory, subjective assessment of the situation. The research done is often less rigorous, less formal, and less quantitative than for domestic activities.

A major reason why managers are reluctant to engage in international research is their lack of sensitivity to differences in culture, consumer tastes, and market demands. Often managers assume that their methods are both best and acceptable to all others. Fortunately, this is not true. What a boring place the world would be if it were!

A second reason is a limited appreciation for the different environments abroad. Often managers are insufficiently informed about the effect of geographic boundaries and do not understand that even national boundaries need not always coincide with culturally homogenous societies.[2] In addition, they are not prepared to accept that labor rules, distribution systems, the availability of media, or advertising regulations may be entirely different from those in the home market. Due to pressure to satisfy short-term financial goals, managers are unwilling to spend money to find out about the differences.

A third reason is lack of familiarity with national and international data sources and inability to use international data once they are obtained. As a result, the cost of conducting international research is perceived to be prohibitively high and therefore not a worthwhile investment relative to the benefits to be gained.[3] However, the Internet makes international research much easier and much less expensive. Data which are hard to find now become accessible at a click of a mouse, as the opening vignette has shown. As the availability of the Internet grows around the world, so does the availability of research information.

Finally, firms often build their international business activities gradually, frequently based on unsolicited orders. Over time, actual business experience in a country or with a specific firm may then be used as a substitute for organized research.

Despite the reservations firms have, research is as important internationally as it is domestically. Firms must learn where the opportunities are, what customers want, why they want it, and how they satisfy their needs and wants so that the firm can serve them efficiently. Firms must obtain information about the local infrastructure, labor market, and tax rules before making a plant location decision. Doing business abroad without the benefit of research places firms, their assets, and their entire international future at risk.

Research allows management to identify and develop international strategies. The task includes the identification, evaluation, and comparison of potential foreign business opportunities and the subsequent target market selection. In addition, research is necessary for the development of a business plan that identifies all the requirements necessary for market entry, market penetration, and expansion. On a continuing basis, research provides the feedback needed to fine-tune various business activities. Finally, research can provide management with the intelligence to help anticipate events, take appropriate action, and adequately prepare for global changes.

Determining Research Objectives

As a starting point for research, research objectives must be determined. They will vary depending on the views of management, the corporate mission of the firm, the firm's level of internationalization, and its competitive situation. These objectives must be embedded in a firm's internal level of readiness to participate in the global market. A review of corporate capabilities such as personnel resources and the degree of financial exposure and risk that the firm is willing and able to tolerate also needs to be conducted. Existing diagnostic tools can be used to compare a firm's current preparedness on a broad-based level.[4] Knowing its internal readiness, the firm can then pursue its objectives with more confidence.

GOING INTERNATIONAL—EXPORTING

A frequent objective of international research is that of **foreign market opportunity analysis.** When a firm launches its international activities, it will usually find the world to be uncharted territory. Fortunately, information can be accumulated to provide basic guidelines. The aim is not to conduct a painstaking and detailed analysis of the world on a market-by-market basis, but instead to utilize a broad-brush approach. Accomplished quickly and at low cost, this approach will narrow the possibilities for international business activities.

Such an approach should begin with a cursory analysis of general variables of a country, including total and per capita GDP, mortality rates, and population figures. Although these factors in themselves will not provide any detailed information, they will enable the researcher to determine whether corporate objectives might be met in the market. For example, high-priced consumer products are unlikely to be successful in the People's Republic of China, as their price may be equal to a significant proportion of the customer's annual salary, the customer benefit may be minimal, and the government is likely to prohibit their importation. Similarly, the offering of computer software services may be of little value in a country where there is very limited use of computers. Such a cursory evaluation will help reduce the number of markets to be considered to a more manageable number—for example, from 225 to 25.

As a next step, the researcher will require information on each individual country for a preliminary evaluation. Information typically desired will highlight the fastest growing markets, the largest markets for a particular category of product or service, demand trends, and business restrictions. Although precise and detailed information on individual products may not be obtainable, information is available for general product categories or service industries. Again, this overview will be cursory but will serve to quickly evaluate markets and further reduce their number.

At this stage, the researcher must select appropriate markets for in-depth evaluation. The focus will now be on opportunities for a specific type of service, product, or brand, and will include an assessment as to whether demand already exists or can be stimulated. Even though aggregate industry data may have been obtained previously, this general information is insufficient to make company-specific decisions. For example, the demand for sports equipment should not be confused with the potential demand for a specific brand. The research now should identify demand and supply patterns and evaluate any regulations and standards. Finally, a **competitive assessment** needs to be made, matching markets to corporate strengths and providing an analysis of the best potential for specific offerings. A summary of the various stages in the determination of market potential is provided in Figure 10.1.

GOING INTERNATIONAL—IMPORTING

When importing, the major focus shifts from supplying to sourcing. Management must identify markets that produce supplies or materials desired or that have the potential to do so. Foreign firms must be evaluated in terms of their capabilities and competitive standing.

Just as management would want to have some details on a domestic supplier, the importer needs to know, for example, about the reliability of a foreign supplier, the consistency of its product or service quality, and the length of delivery time. Information obtained through the subsidiary office of a bank or an embassy can prove very helpful. Information from business rating services and recommendations from current customers are also very useful in evaluating the potential business partner.

FIGURE 10.1

A Sequential Process of Researching Foreign Market Potentials

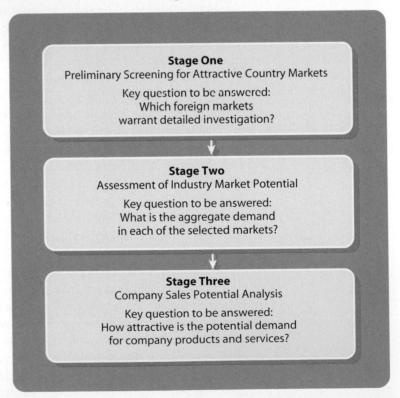

Stage One
Preliminary Screening for Attractive Country Markets

Key question to be answered:
Which foreign markets
warrant detailed investigation?

↓

Stage Two
Assessment of Industry Market Potential

Key question to be answered:
What is the aggregate demand
in each of the selected markets?

↓

Stage Three
Company Sales Potential Analysis

Key question to be answered:
How attractive is the potential demand
for company products and services?

Source: S. Tamer Cavusgil, "Guidelines for Export Market Research," *Business Horizons* 28 (November–December 1985): 29. Copyright 1985 by the Foundation for the School of Business at Indiana University. Reprinted by permission.

In addition, foreign government rules must be scrutinized as to whether exportation from the source country is possible. As examples, India may set limits on the cobra handbags it allows to be exported, and laws protecting a nations's cultural heritage may prevent the exportation of pre-Columbian artifacts from Latin American countries.

The international manager must also analyze domestic restrictions and legislation that may prohibit the importation of certain goods into the home country. Even though a market may exist at home for foreign umbrella handles, for example, quotas may restrict their importation to protect domestic industries. Similarly, even though domestic demand may exist for ivory, its importation may be illegal because of legislation enacted to protect wildlife worldwide.

MARKET EXPANSION

Research objectives include obtaining more detailed information for business expansion or monitoring the political climate so that the firm successfully can maintain its international operation. Information may be needed to enable the international manager to evaluate new business partners or assess the impact of a technological breakthrough on future business operations. The better defined the research objective is, the better the researcher will be able to determine information requirements and thus conserve the time and financial resources of the firm.

Conducting Secondary Research

IDENTIFYING SOURCES OF DATA

Typically, the information requirements of firms will cover both macro information about countries and trade, as well as micro information specific to the firm's activities. Table 10.1 provides an overview of the types of information that are most crucial for international business executives. If each firm had to go out and collect all the information needed on-site in the country under scrutiny, the task would be unwieldy and far too expensive. On many occasions, however, firms can make use of **secondary data,** that is, information that already has been collected by some other organization. A wide variety of sources present secondary data. The principal ones are governments, international institutions, service organizations, trade associations, directories, and other firms. This section provides a brief review of major data sources. Details on selected monitors of international issues are presented in Appendix 10A at the end of the chapter.

 TABLE 10.1

Critical International Information

Macro Data	Micro Data
• Tariff information	• Local laws and regulatons
• U.S. export/import data	• Size of market
• Nontariff measures	• Local standards and specifications
• Foreign export/import data	• Distribution system
• Data on government trade policy	• Competitive activity

Governments

Most countries have a wide array of national and international trade data available. Typically, the information provided by governments addresses either macro and micro issues or offers specific data services. Macro information includes data on population trends, general trade flows among countries, and world agriculture production. Micro information includes materials on specific industries in a country, their growth prospects, and the extent and direction to which they are traded.

Unfortunately, the data are often published only in their home countries and in their native languages. The publications mainly present numerical data, however, and so the translation task is relatively easy. In addition, the information sources are often available at embassies and consulates, whose missions include the enhancement of trade activities. The commercial counselor or commercial attaché can provide the information as can government-sponsored web sites. The user should be cautioned that the printed information is often dated and that the industry categories used abroad may not be compatible with industry categories used at home. Increasingly, government data are available on the Internet—often well before they are released in printed form. Closer collaboration between governmental statistical agencies also makes the data more accurate and reliable, since it is now much easier to compare data such as bilateral exports and imports to each other.

While many of the current data are available at no charge, governments often charge a fee for the use of data libraries. Given the depth of information such data can provide, the cost usually is a worthwhile expenditure for firms in light of the insights into trade patterns and reduction in risk they can achieve.

International Organizations

International organizations often provide useful data for the researcher. The *Statistical Yearbook* produced by the United Nations (UN) contains international trade data on products and provides information on exports and imports by country. However, because of the time needed for worldwide data collection, the information is often dated. Additional information is compiled and made available by specialized substructures of the United Nations. Some of these are the United Nations Conference on Trade and Development (http://www.unctad.org), which concentrates primarily on international issues surrounding developing nations, such as debt and market access, and the United Nations Center on Transnational Corporations and the International Trade Centre (http://www.intracen.org). The *World Atlas* published by the World Bank (http://www.worldbank.org) provides useful general data on population, growth trends, and GNP figures. The World Trade Organization (http://www.wto.org) and the Organization for Economic Cooperation and Development (OECD) (http://www.oecd.org) also publish quarterly and annual trade data on its member countries. Organizations such as the International Monetary Fund (http://www.imf.org) and the World Bank publish summary economic data and occasional staff papers that evaluate region- or country-specific issues in depth.

Service Organizations

A wide variety of service organizations that provide information include banks, accounting firms, freight forwarders, airlines, international trade consultants, research firms, and publishing houses located around the world. Frequently they are able to provide information on business practices, legislative or regulatory requirements, and political stability, as well as trade and financial data.

Trade Associations

Associations such as world trade clubs and domestic and international chambers of commerce (such as the American Chamber of Commerce abroad) can provide good information on local markets. Often files are maintained on international trade flows and trends affecting international managers. Valuable information can also be obtained from industry associations. These groups, formed to represent entire industry segments, often collect a wide variety of data from their members that are then published in an aggregate form. Most of these associations represent the viewpoints of their member firms to the government, so they usually have one or more publicly listed representatives in the capital. The information provided is often quite general, however, because of the wide variety of clientele served.

Directories and Newsletters

A large number of industry directories are available on local, national, and international levels. The directories primarily serve to identify firms and to provide very general background information, such as the name of the chief executive officer, the level of capitalization of the firm, the location, the address and telephone number, and some description of the firm's products. A host of newsletters discuss specific international business issues, such as international trade finance, legislative activities, countertrade, international payment flows, and customs news. Usually these newsletters cater to narrow audiences but can provide important information to the firm interested in a specific area.

Electronic Information Services

When information is needed, managers often cannot spend a lot of time, energy, or money finding, sifting through, and categorizing existing materials. Consider laboring through every copy of a trade publication to find out the latest news on how environmental concerns are affecting marketing decisions in Mexico. With electronic information services, search results can be obtained almost immediately. International online computer database services, numbering in the thousands, can be purchased to supply information external to the firm, such as exchange rates, international news, and import restrictions. Most database hosts do not charge any sign-up fee and request payment only for actual use. The selection of initial database hosts depends on the choice of relevant databases, taking into account their product and market limitations, language used, and geographical location. A large number of databases, developed by analysts who systematically sift through a wide range of periodicals, reports, and books in different languages, provide information on given products and markets. Many of the main news agencies now have information available through online databases, providing information on events that affect certain markets. Some databases cover extensive lists of companies in given countries and the products they buy and sell. Figure 10.2 provides an example.

Compact Disk/Read-Only Memory (CD-ROM) technology allows for massive amounts of information (the equivalent of 300 books of 1,000 pages each, or 1,500 floppy disks) to be stored on a single 12-centimeter plastic disk. Increasingly, the technology is used for storing and distributing large volumes of information, such as statistical databases. Typically, the user pays no user fees but instead invests in a CD-ROM "reader" and purchases the actual CDs.

An online service widely used in the United States is the National Trade Data Bank (NTDB), offered by the U.S. Department of Commerce's Economics and Statistics

FIGURE 10.2

An Advertisement for International Information Services

Source: http://www.eiu.com

Administration (http://www.Stat-USA.gov). The NTDB includes more than 170,000 documents, including full-text market research reports, domestic and foreign economic data, import and export statistics, trade information and country studies, all compiled from 20 government agencies.[5] Another example of valuable online information is the Country Commercial Guides, an example of which is shown in Appendix 10B of this chapter.

Using data services for research means that professionals do not have to leave their offices, going from library to library to locate the facts they need. Many online services have late-breaking information available within 24 hours to the user. These techniques of research are cost-effective as well. Stocking a company's library with all the books needed to have the same amount of data that is available online or with CD-ROM would be too expensive and space-consuming.

In spite of the ease of access to data on the Internet, it must be remembered that search engines only cover a portion of international publications. Also, they are heavily biased towards English-language publications. As a result, sole reliance on electronic information may let the researcher lose out on valuable input.[6] Electronic databases should therefore be seen as only one important dimension of research scrutiny. A listing of selected databases useful for international business is presented in Appendix 10A of this chapter.

SELECTION OF SECONDARY DATA

Just because secondary information has been found to exist does not mean that it must be used. Even though one key advantage of secondary data over primary research is that they are available relatively quickly and inexpensively, the researcher should still assess the effort and benefit of using them. Secondary data should be evaluated regarding the quality of their source, their recency, and their relevance to the task at hand. Clearly, since the information was collected without the current research requirements in mind, there may well be difficulties in coverage, categorization, and comparability. For example, an "engineer" in one country may differ substantially in terms of training and responsibilities from a person in another country holding the same title. It is therefore important to be careful when getting ready to interpret and analyze data.

The ease of access to information through online searches has raised concerns about information usage. As Focus on Ethics shows, governments and private-sector organizations are analyzing the effects of declassification programs that may place sensitive information into the hands of dangerous people.

INTERPRETATION AND ANALYSIS OF SECONDARY DATA

Once secondary data have been obtained, the researcher must creatively convert them into information. Secondary data were originally collected to serve another purpose than the one in which the researcher is currently interested. Therefore, they can often be used only as **proxy information** in order to arrive at conclusions that address the research objectives. For example, the market penetration of video recorders may be used as a proxy variable for the potential demand for DVD-players. Similarly, in an industrial setting, information about plans for new port facilities may be useful in determining future container requirements.

The researcher must often use creative inferences, and such creativity brings risks. Therefore, once interpretation and analysis have taken place, a consistency check must be conducted. The researcher should always cross-check the results with other possible sources of information or with experts. Yet, if properly implemented, such creativity can open up one's eyes to new market potential.

DATA PRIVACY

The attitude of society toward obtaining and using both secondary and primary data must be taken into account. Many societies are increasingly sensitive to the issue of **data privacy,** and the concern has grown exponentially as a result of e-business. Readily accessible databases may contain information valuable to marketers, but they may also be considered privileged by individuals who have provided the data.

ETHICS

To Share Research or Not to Share Research?

Concern over terrorist activity in the United States has led to a reevaluation of the current open system of international information sharing. While the free exchange of research is viewed as vital by academics, policymakers see sensitive information falling into the wrong hands. Of key concern is information on chemical and biological weapons.

Unlike with nuclear arms, where the key task is to gain access to material, the development of chemical and biological arms depends mostly on the acquisition of knowledge. The know-how for the development of such arms is available with alarming ease. For example, anyone can buy a 57-page government report entitled "Selection of Process for Freeze-Drying, Particle Size Reduction and Filling of Selected BW Agents," a manuscript on germs for biological warfare, for a mere $15. Although the available documents are decades old, they provide detailed descriptions of deadly biological agents such as anthrax. At the very least, the documents can accelerate the process of acquiring lethal biological arms by acting as a solid research base upon which to start a program.

Hundreds of similar documents have been released by the U.S. government as part of an effort to make the inner workings of the government more public. Federal agencies have routinely sold these documents to historians and other researchers, mostly by Internet and telephone. In an interview, a military expert expressed alarm over the availability of information after evaluating 3,500 documents open to the public. Policymakers and experts in germ warfare are now working toward the reclassification of the most sensitive documents.

A global organization of nearly 500 germ banks, the World Federation of Culture Collections (WFCC), has also reevaluated the information it makes available and has removed some details on anthrax from its Internet database. However, it has added information on how to deal with dangerous agents. Thus, the public has access to facts pertaining to public health, but not on how to terrorize a nation.

While there is certainly cause for concern in monitoring the flow of research, policies focused on limiting free academic exchange can also be harmful. In response to the September 11 attacks, the U.S. government has decreased the number of visas issued to foreign students. The Massachusetts Intitute of Technology even walked away from a $404,000 grant in response to the government's condition that foreign students be barred from research.

The recent recall of available information brings into question the costs versus the benefits of unfettered information exchange. The free flow of research has been viewed by academics as an accelerant to any field. But shouldn't this flow be stopped, or at the very least dampened, for the sake of national security? Where does one draw the line between free academic exchange and security? Is it fair to block foreign students' access to education and hinder the progress of U.S. students and institutions?

Sources: Piller, James, "Biodefense Lab on the Defensive," *Los Angeles Times,* February 12, 2003; Broad, William J., "US Selling Papers Showing How to Make Germ Weapons," *New York Times,"* January 13, 2002; Geitner, Paul, "Precaution Taken Vs. Bioterrorism," *Associated Press,* October 23, 2001.

The European Union requires member states to block transmission of data to non-EU countries if these countries do not have domestic legislation that provides for a level of protection judged as adequate by the European Union. These laws restrict access to lifestyle information and its use for segmentation purposes. It is particularly difficult for direct marketers to obtain international access to voter rolls, birth records, or mortgage information.[7] There are key differences between the European and the U.S. perspective on data privacy. The EU law permits companies to collect personal data only if the individuals consent to the collection, know how the data will be used, and have access to databases to correct or erase their information. The U.S. approach strictly safeguards data collected by banks and government agencies. However, it also recognizes that most personal data, such as age or zip code, are collected because someone is trying to sell something. Consumers who are annoyed by such data requests or sales pitches can only refuse to provide the information, throw out the junk mail, or hang up on telemarketers.

Increasingly, however, the desire for personal privacy, particularly in the context of business contacts, is growing in value in the United States. Firms must inform their customers of privacy policies and inform them of the right to deny the use of their personal information. Therefore, the gap in policies is likely to shrink.

Conducting Primary Research

Even though secondary data are useful to the researcher, on many occasions primary information will be required. **Primary data** are obtained by a firm to fill specific information needs. Although the research may not be conducted by the company with the need, the work must be carried out for a specific research purpose in order to qualify as primary research. Typically, primary research intends to answer such clear-cut questions as:

- What is the sales potential for our measuring equipment in Malaysia?
- How much does the typical Greek consumer spend on fast food?
- What effect will our new type of packaging have on our green consumers in Norway?
- What service standards do industrial customers expect in Japan?

The researcher must have a clear idea of what the population under study should be and where it is located before deciding on the country or region to investigate. Conducting research in an entire country may not be necessary if, for example, only urban centers are to be penetrated. Multiple regions of a country need to be investigated, however, if a lack of homogeneity exists because of different economic, geographic, or behavioral factors. One source reports of the failure of a firm in Indonesia due to insufficient geographic dispersion of its research. The firm conducted its study only in large Indonesian cities during the height of tourism season, but projected the results to the entire population. When the company set up large production and distribution facilities to meet the expected demand, it realized only limited sales to city tourists.[8]

The discussion presented here will focus mainly on the research-specific issues. Application dimensions such as market choice and market analysis will be covered in Chapter 14.

INDUSTRIAL VERSUS CONSUMER SOURCES OF DATA

The researcher must decide whether research is to be conducted in the consumer or the industrial product area, which in turn determines the size of the universe and respondent accessibility. Consumers usually are a very large group, whereas the total population of industrial users may be limited. Cooperation by respondents may also vary. In the industrial setting, differentiation between users and decision makers may be important because their personalities, their outlooks, and their evaluative criteria may differ widely. Determining the proper focus of the research is therefore of major importance to its successful completion.

DETERMINING THE RESEARCH TECHNIQUE

Selection of the research technique depends on a variety of factors. First, the objectivity of the data sought must be determined. Standardized techniques are more useful in the collection of objective data than of subjective data. **Unstructured data** will require more open-ended questions and more time than structured data. Whether the data are to be collected in the real world or in a controlled environment must be determined. Finally, it must be decided whether to collect historical facts or information about future developments. This is particularly important for consumer research, because firms frequently want to determine the future intentions of consumers about buying a certain product.

Once the desired data structure is determined, the researcher must choose a research technique. As in domestic research, the types available are interviews, focus groups, observation, surveys, and the use of web technology. Each one provides a different depth of information and has its own unique strengths and weaknesses.

Interviews

Interviews with knowledgeable people can be of great value for the corporation that wants international information. Bias from the individual may slant the findings, so the intent should be to obtain not a wide variety of data, but rather in-depth information. When specific answers are sought to very narrow questions, interviews can be particularly useful.

Focus Groups

Focus groups are a useful research tool resulting in interactive interviews. A group of knowledgeable people is gathered for a limited period of time (two to four hours). Usually, seven to ten participants is the ideal size for a focus group. A specific topic is introduced and thoroughly discussed by all group members. Because of the interaction, hidden issues are sometimes raised that would not have been detected in an individual interview. The skill of the group leader in stimulating discussion is crucial to the success of a focus group. Like in-depth interviews, focus groups do not provide statistically significant information; however, they can be helpful in providing information about perceptions, emotions, and attitudinal factors. In addition, once individuals have been gathered, focus groups are a highly efficient means of rapidly accumulating a substantial amount of information.

When planning international research using focus groups, the researcher must be aware of the importance of language and culture in the interaction process. Major differences may exist already in preparing for the focus group. In some countries, participants can simply be asked to show up at a later date at a location where they will join the focus group. In other countries, participants have to be brought into the group immediately because commitments made for a future date have little meaning. In some nations, providing a payment to participants is sufficient motivation for them to open up in discussion. In other countries, one first needs to host a luncheon or dinner for the group so that members get to know each other and are willing to interact.

Once the focus group is started, the researcher must remember that not all societies encourage frank and open exchange and disagreement among individuals. Status consciousness may result in the opinion of one participant being reflected by all others. Disagreement may be seen as impolite, or certain topics may be taboo. Unless a native focus group leader is used, it also is possible to completely misread the interactions among group participants and to miss out on nuances and constraints participants feel when commenting in the group situation. One of this book's authors, for example, used the term *group discussion* in a focus group with Russian executives, only to learn that the translated meaning of the term was *political indoctrination session.*[9] As Focus on Culture explains, the use of different languages in research makes it necessary to check one's translations very carefully.

Observation

Observation requires the researcher to play the role of a nonparticipating observer of activity and behavior. In an international setting, observation can be extremely useful

Focus On ⬇

Check Your Translations!

All sorts of things can go wrong when a company translates its advertising into foreign languages. Kentucky Fried Chicken's slogan "Finger-lickin' good" was translated into the less appetizing "Eat your fingers off" in Chinese. Chevrolet launched the Nova in South America not knowing that "no va" means "it won't go" in Spanish. Schweppes Tonic Water didn't sell so well in Italy where it was translated to Schweppes Toilet Water. Advertising mistakes receive a fair amount of attention in the media and the international business world when they occur, but many people never stop to think about what would happen if a company unknowingly committed translation errors much earlier—in the research phase.

The possibility of disaster due to such errors is in many ways even greater than in the advertising stage because research findings are often used to determine a firm's strategy or for new product development. A translation blunder that goes undiscovered at this stage could set a company on the wrong track entirely. Imagine spending millions of dollars to develop a new product or to enter a new market only to find that your company's surveys had asked the wrong questions!

Researchers at the Pew Research Center for the People and the Press in Washington, DC, are not new to international research. They have been conducting public opinion research around the globe for more than a decade. Their findings related to attitudes toward the press, politics, and public policy issues are regularly cited in the media. However, the company received an unwelcome surprise when it translated one of its worldwide polls into 63 languages and then back into English. As it turns out, the ride to the foreign languages and back again was a bit bumpier than they had imagined.

For example, in Ghana, the original phrase "married or living with a partner" was first translated into one of the country's tribal languages as, "married but have a girlfriend," and the category "separated" became, "There's a misunderstanding between me and my spouse." The original version of a questionnaire to be used in Nigeria had similar problems: "American ideas and customs" came out, "the ideology of America and border guards" (get it, customs? border guards?) and the phrase "success in life is pretty much determined by forces outside our control" initially read, "Goodness in life starts with blessings from one's personal god." In the original Nigerian Yoruba version, "Fast food" had been translated to "microwave food" and "the military" became "Herbalist/medicine man." Not quite the same thing, is it?

Fortunately, the meanings were corrected in the final translations of the questionnaire, said the Center's director Andrew Kohut. The lesson? Multinational researchers, check your translations!

Sources: Richard Morin, "Words Matter," The Washington Post, January 19, 2003, B5; Ian Dow, "Your ad is a tad mad," The Scottish Daily Record, October 5, 2002, 8; Global Attitudes Report, "What the World Thinks in 2002," December 4, 2002 (from the Pew Research Center for the People and the Press).

in shedding light on practices not previously encountered or understood. This aspect is especially valuable to the researcher who has no knowledge of a particular market or market situation. It can help in understanding phenomena that would have been difficult to assess with other techniques. For example, Toyota sent a group of its engineers and designers to southern California to nonchalantly observe how women get into and operate their cars. They found that women with long fingernails have trouble opening the door and operating various knobs on the dashboard. Toyota engineers and designers were able to comprehend the women's plight and redesign some of their automobile exteriors and interiors, producing more desirable cars.[10]

All the research instruments discussed so far are useful primarily for the gathering of **qualitative information.** The intent is not to amass data or to search for statistical significance, but rather to obtain a better understanding of given situations, behavioral patterns, or underlying dimensions. The researcher using these instruments must be cautioned that even frequent repetition of the measurements will not lead to a statistically valid result. However, statistical validity often may not be the major focus of corporate research. Rather, it may be the better understanding, description, and prediction of events that have an impact on decision making. When **quantitative data** are desired, surveys and experimentation are more appropriate research instruments.

Surveys

Survey research is useful in quantifying concepts. **Surveys** are usually conducted via questionnaires that are administered personally, by mail, or by telephone. Use of the survey technique presupposes that the population under study is accessible and able to comprehend and respond to the question posed through the chosen medium. Particularly for mail and telephone surveys, a major precondition is the feasibility of using the postal system or the widespread availability of telephones. Obviously, this is not a given in all countries. In many nations only limited records about dwellings, their location, and their occupants are available. In Venezuela, for example, most houses are not numbered but rather are given individual names such as Casa Rosa or El Retiro. In some countries, street maps are not even available. As a result, reaching respondents by mail is virtually impossible. In other countries, obtaining a correct address may be easy, but the postal system may not function well.

Telephone surveys may also be inappropriate if telephone ownership is rare. In such instances, any information obtained would be highly biased even if the researcher randomized the calls. In some cases, inadequate telephone networks and systems, frequent line congestion, and a lack of telephone directories may also prevent the researcher from conducting surveys.

Since surveys deal with people who in an international setting display major differences in culture, preference, education, and attitude, just to mention a few factors, the use of the survey technique must be carefully examined. For example, in some regions of the world, recipients of letters may be illiterate. Others may be very literate, but totally unaccustomed to some of the standard research scaling techniques used in the United States and therefore may be unable to respond to the instrument. Survey respondents in different countries may have different extreme response styles. If members of one culture are much more likely than those of another culture to agree very much or very little with a question, for example, then the researcher must adjust the findings in order to make them comparable to each other.[11] Other recipients of a

Conducting surveys can ensure population representation, and assist in interpreting the results by better understanding your respondents.

survey may be reluctant to respond in writing, particularly when sensitive questions are asked. This sensitivity, of course, also varies by country. In some nations, any questions about income, even in categorical form, are considered highly proprietary; in others the purchasing behavior of individuals is not readily divulged.

The researcher needs to understand such constraints and prepare a survey that is responsive to them. For example, surveys can incorporate drawings or even cartoons to communicate better. Personal administration or collaboration with locally accepted intermediaries may improve the response rate. Indirect questions may need to substitute for direct ones in sensitive areas. Questions may have to be reworded to ensure proper communication. Figure 10.3 provides an example of a rating scale developed by researchers to work with a diverse population with relatively little education. In its use, however, it was found that the same scale aroused negative reactions among better-educated respondents, who considered the scale childish and insulting to their intelligence.

In spite of all the potential difficulties, the survey technique remains a useful one because it allows the researcher to rapidly accumulate a large quantity of data amenable to statistical analysis. With constantly expanding technological capabilities, international researchers will be able to use this technique even more in the future.

Web Technology

The growing use of technology has given rise to new marketing research approaches that allow consumers to be heard much more and permit firms to work much harder at their listening skills. Two primary research approaches are rapidly growing in their use: web-based research and e-mail-based surveys.

The increasing degree to which the World Wide Web truly lives up to its name is making it possible for international marketers to use this medium in their research efforts. The technology can reach out in a low-cost fashion and provide innovative ways to present stimuli and collect data. For example, on a web site, product details, pictures of products, brands, and the shopping environment can be portrayed with intergrated graphics and sound—thus bringing the issues to be researched much closer to the respondent. In addition, the behavior of visitors to a site can be traced and interpreted regarding the interest in product, services, or information.[12]

Surveys can be administered either through a web site or through e-mail. If they are posted on a site, surveys can be of the pop-up nature, where visitors can be specifically

FIGURE 10.3

The Funny Faces Scale

Very Happy   Happy   Not Happy But Also Not Unhappy   Unhappy   Very Unhappy

Source: C. K. Corder, "Problems and Pitfalls in Conducting Marketing Research in Africa," *Marketing Expansion in a Shrinking World*, ed. Betsy Gelb. Proceedings of American Marketing Association Business Conference (Chicago: AMA, 1978), pp. 86–90.

targeted. An e-mail survey eliminates the need for postage and printing. As a result, larger and geographically diverse audiences can be the focus of an inquiry. Research indicates that there is a higher and faster response rate to such electronic inquiries. In addition, the process of data entry can be automated so that responses are automatically fed into data-analysis software.[13]

However, it would be too simplistic to assume that the digitalization of survey content is all that it takes to go global on the web. There are cultural differences that must be taken into account by the researcher. Global visitors to a site should encounter research that matches their own cultural values, rituals, and symbols, and testimonials or encouragement should be delivered by culture-specific heroes. For example, a web site might first offer a visitor from Korea the opportunity to become part of a product-user community. A low-context visitor from the United States may in turn be exposed to product features immediately.[14]

In addition, such electronic research suffers from a lack of confidentiality of the participants since e-mails disclose the identity of the sender. This issue, in turn, triggers concerns and rules of data privacy, which may limit the use of these tools in some nations or regions. Also, the opportunity to overuse a tool may result in the gradual disenchantment of its audience. Therefore, current high response rates may well decline over time.

Nonetheless, the new technology offers international marketers an entire array of new opportunities that will grow rather than diminish. As stated by a leading marketing research expert, in the not-too-distant future, web-based survey research will become the norm, not the exception.[15]

The International Information System

Many organizations have data needs that go beyond specific international research projects. Most of the time, daily decisions must be made for which there is neither time nor money for special research. An **information system** can provide the decision maker with basic data for most ongoing decisions. Defined as "the systematic and continuous gathering, analysis, and reporting of data for decision-making purposes,"[16] such a system serves as a mechanism to coordinate the flow of information to corporate managers.

To be useful to the decision maker, the system must have certain attributes. First of all, the information must be *relevant*. The data gathered must have meaning for the manager's decision-making process. Only rarely can corporations afford to spend large amounts of money on information that is simply "nice to know." Any information system will have to continuously address the balance to be struck between the expense of the research design and process and the value of the information to ongoing business activities. Second, the information must be *timely*. Managers derive little benefit if decision information needed today does not become available until a month from now. To be of use to the international decision maker, the system must therefore feed from a variety of international sources and be updated frequently. For multinational corporations, this means a real-time link between international subsidiaries and a broad-based ongoing data input operation. Third, information must be *flexible*—that is, it must be available in the form needed by management. An information system must therefore permit manipulation of the format and combination of the data. Fourth, information contained in the system must be *accurate*. This is especially important in international research because information quickly becomes outdated as a result of major environmental changes. Fifth, the system's information bank must be reasonably *exhaustive.* Factors that may influence a particular decision must be appropriately represented in the information system because of the interrelationships among variables. This means that the information system must be based on a wide variety of factors. Sixth, the collection and processing of data must be *consistent.* This is to hold down project cost and turnaround time, while ensuring that data can be compared regionally. This can be achieved by centralizing the management under one manager who oversees the system's design, processing, and analysis.[17] Finally, to be useful to managers, the system must be *convenient* to use. Systems that are cumbersome and time-consuming to reach and to use will not be used enough to justify corporate expenditures to build and maintain them.

One area where international firms are gradually increasing the use of information system technology is in the export field. In order to stay close to their customers, proactive firms are developing **export complaint systems.** These systems allow customers to contact the original supplier of a product in order to inquire about products, to make suggestions, or to present complaints. Firms are finding that about 5 percent of their customers abroad are dissatisfied with the product. By establishing direct contact via e-mail, a toll-free telephone number, or a web site, firms do not need to rely on the filtered feedback from channel intermediaries abroad and can learn directly about product failures, channel problems, or other causes of customer dissatisfaction. The development of such an export complaint system requires substantial resources, intensive planning, and a high degree of cultural sensitivity. Customers abroad must be informed of how to complain, and their cost of complaining must be minimized, for example, by offering an interactive web site. The response to complaints must also be tailored to the culture of the complainant. For example, to some customers, the speed of reply matters most, while to others the thoughtfulness of the reply is of key concern. As a result, substantial resources must be invested into personnel training so the system works in harmony with customer expectations. Most important, however, is a firm's ability to aggregate and analyze complaints and to make use of them internally. Complaints are often the symptom for underlying structural problems of a product or a process. If used properly, an export complaint system can become a rich source of information for product improvement and innovation.

Increasingly, the Internet enables customers to provide feedback on their experiences with a firm. On-line reputation can have an important effect on a firm's prospects and can even preclude individuals from participating in business transactions. A symposium sponsored by the National Science Foundation and MIT highlighted the increased use of reputational measures and the need for firms to work with such evaluations.[18]

To build an information system, corporations use the internal data that are available from divisions such as accounting and finance and also from various subsidiaries. In addition, many organizations put mechanisms in place to enrich the basic data flow to information systems. Three such mechanisms are environmental scanning, Delphi studies, and scenario building.

Environmental Scanning

Any changes in the business environment, whether domestic or foreign, may have serious repercussions on the activities of the firm. Corporations therefore understand the necessity for tracking new developments. Although this can be done implicitly in the domestic environment, the remoteness of international markets requires a continuous information flow. For this purpose, some large multinational organizations have formed environmental scanning groups.

Environmental scanning activities provide continuous information on political, social, and economic affairs internationally; on changes of attitudes of public institutions and private citizens; and on possible upcoming alterations. Environmental scanning models can be used for a variety of purposes, such as the development of long-term strategies, getting managers to broaden their horizons, or structuring action plans. Obviously, the precision required for environmental scanning varies with its purpose. The more immediate and precise the application will be within the corporation, the greater the need for detailed information. On the other hand, heightened precision may reduce the usefulness of environmental scanning in strategic planning, which is long term.

Environmental scanning can be performed in various ways. One consists of obtaining factual input on a wide variety of demographic, social, and economic characteristics of foreign countries. Frequently, managers believe that factual data alone are insufficient for their information needs. Particularly when forecasting future developments, other methods are used to capture underlying dimensions of social change. One significant method is that of **content analysis.** A wide array of newspapers, magazines, and other publications are scanned worldwide in order to pinpoint over time the gradual evolution of new views or trends. Corporations also use the technique of media analysis to pinpoint upcoming changes in their line of business. For example, the Alaskan oil spill by the Exxon *Valdez* and the rash of oil spills that followed resulted in entirely new international concern about environmental protection and safety, reaching far beyond the actual incidents and participants.

With the current heightened awareness of environmental and ethical issues such as pollution, preservation of natural resources, and animal testing, firms are increasingly looking for new opportunities to expand their operations while remaining within changing moral and environmental boundaries.

Environmental scanning is conducted by a variety of groups within and outside the corporation. Quite frequently, small corporate staffs are created at headquarters to coordinate the information flow. In addition, subsidiary staff can be used to provide occasional intelligence reports. Groups of volunteers are also formed to gather and analyze information worldwide and feed their individual analyses back to corporate headquarters, where the "big picture" can then be constructed. Rapidly growing use of the Internet also allows firms to find out about new developments in their fields of interest and permits them to gather information through bulletin boards and discussion groups. For example, some firms use search engines to comb through thousands of newsgroups for any mention of a particular product or application. If they find frequent references, they can investigate further to see what customers are saying.[19]

Finally, it should be kept in mind that internationally there may be a fine line between tracking and obtaining information and the misappropriation of corporate secrets. With growing frequency, governments and firms claim that their trade secrets are being obtained and abused by foreign competitors. The perceived threat from economic espionage has led to legislation[20] and accusations of government spying networks trying to undermine the commercial interests of companies.[21] Information gatherers must be sensitive to these issues in order to avoid conflict.

Delphi Studies

To enrich the information obtained from factual data, corporations and governments frequently resort to the use of creative and highly qualitative data-gathering methods.

One approach is through **Delphi studies.** These studies are particularly useful in the international environment because they are "a means for aggregating the judgments of a number of . . . experts . . . who cannot come together physically."[22] This type of research clearly aims at qualitative measures by seeking a consensus from those who know, rather than average responses from many people with only limited knowledge.

Typically, Delphi studies are carried out with groups of about 30 well-chosen participants who possess expertise in an area of concern, such as future developments of the international trade environment. The participants are asked to identify the major issues in the given area of concern. They are also requested to rank order their statements according to importance and explain the rationale behind the order. The aggregated information and comments are then sent to all participants in the Delphi group. Group members are encouraged to agree or disagree with the various rank orders and the comments. This allows statements to be challenged. In another round, the participants respond to the challenges. Several rounds of challenges and responses result in a reasonably coherent consensus.

The Delphi technique is particularly valuable because it uses mail, facsimile, or electronic communication to bridge large distances and therefore makes experts quite accessible at a reasonable cost. It avoids the drawback of ordinary mail investigations, which lack interaction among participants. Several rounds may be required, however, so substantial time may elapse before the information is obtained. Also, a major effort must be expended in selecting the appropriate participants and in motivating them to participate in the exercise with enthusiasm and continuity. When carried out on a regular basis, Delphi studies can provide crucial augmentation of the factual data available for the information system. For example, a large portion of this book's last chapter was written based on an extensive Delphi study carried out by the authors.

Scenario Building

The information obtained through environmental scanning or Delphi studies can then be used to conduct a scenario analysis. One approach involves the development of a series of plausible scenarios that are constructed from trends observed in the environment. Another method consists of formally reviewing assumptions built into existing business plans and positions.[23] Subsequently, some of these key assumptions such as economic growth rates, import penetration, population growth, and political stability, can be varied. By projecting variations for medium- to long-term periods, completely new environmental conditions can emerge. The conditions can then be analyzed for their potential domestic and international impact on corporate strategy.

The identification of crucial variables and the degree of variation are of major importance in **scenario building.** Scenario builders also need to recognize the non-linearity of factors. To simply extrapolate from currently existing situations is insufficient, since extraneous factors often enter the picture with significant impact. The possibility of **joint occurrences** must be recognized as well, because changes may not come about in isolated fashion but instead may spread over wide regions. For example, given large technological advances, the possibility of wholesale obsolescence of current technology must be considered. Quantum leaps in computer development and new generations of computers may render obsolete the entire technological investment of a corporation.

For scenarios to be useful, management must analyze and respond to them by formulating contingency plans. Such planning will broaden horizons and may prepare managers for unexpected situations. Through the anticipation of possible problems, managers hone their response capability and in turn shorten response times to actual problems.

The development of an international information system is of major importance to the multinational corporation. It aids the ongoing decision process and becomes a vital tool in performing the strategic planning task. Only by observing global trends and changes will the firm be able to maintain and improve its competitive position. Much of the data available are quantitative in nature, but researchers must also pay attention to qualitative dimensions. Quantitative analysis will continue to improve as the ability to collect, store, analyze, and retrieve data increases as a result of computer development. Nevertheless, the qualitative dimension will remain a major component for corporate research and planning activities.

Summary

Constraints of time, resources, and expertise are the major inhibitors to international research. Nevertheless, firms need to carry out planned and organized research in order to explore foreign market opportunities and challenges successfully. Such research must be linked closely to the decision-making process.

International research differs from domestic research in that the environment—which determines how well tools, techniques, and concepts apply—is different abroad. In addition, the international manager must deal with duties, exchange rates, and international documentation; a greater number of interacting factors; and a much broader definition of the concept of competition.

When the firm is uninformed about international differences in consumer tastes and preferences or about foreign market environments, the need for international research is particularly great. Research objectives need to be determined based on the corporate mission, the level of international expertise, and the business plan. These objectives will enable the research to identify the information requirements.

Given the scarcity of resources, companies beginning their international effort must rely on data that have already been collected. These secondary data are available from sources such as governments, international organizations, or electronic information services. It is important to respect privacy laws and preferences when making use of secondary data.

To fulfill specific information requirements, the researcher may need to collect primary data. An appropriate research technique must be selected to collect the information. Sensitivity to different international environments and cultures will aid the researcher in deciding whether to use interviews, focus groups, observation, surveys, or web technology as data-collection techniques.

To provide ongoing information to management, an information system is useful. Such a system will provide for the continuous gathering, analysis, and reporting of data for decision-making purposes. Data gathered through environmental scanning, Delphi studies, or scenario building enable management to prepare for the future and hone its decision-making abilities.

Questions for Discussion

1. What is the difference between domestic and international research?
2. You are employed by National Engineering, a firm that designs subways. Because you have had a course in international business, your boss asks you to spend the next week exploring international possibilities for the company. How will you go about this task?
3. Discuss the possible shortcomings of secondary data.
4. Why should a firm collect primary data in its international research?
5. Of all the OECD countries, which one(s) derives the largest share of its GDP from the services sector? from agriculture? from industry? (these figures can be downloaded from the OECD in Figures on the site http://www.oecd.org).

6. What are the top ten trading partners for the United States? What was the U.S.'s top commodity import from France? What was the U.S.'s top commodity export to Japan (use the U.S. Foreign Trade Highlights tables on the Department of Commerce's International Trade Administration site, http://www.ita.doc.gov)?
7. What are some of the products and services the World Bank offers to firms doing business in the developing world (refer to the World Bank's web page "Doing Business with the Bank," through http://www.worldbank.org)?
8. To which group of countries are NAFTA members most likely to export (use the Inter-American Development Bank's exports tables under the "Research and Statistics" database section of its web page, http://www.iadb.org)?

Internet Exercise

1. Show macro, aggregate changes in international markets by listing the total value of three commodities exported from your country to five other countries for the last four years. For each of the countries, provide a one paragraph statement in which you identify positive or negative trends. Give your opinion on whether or not these trends are relevant or reflect the reality of today's international business environment. What are the dangers of relying on perceived trends? You are encouraged to conduct research on products from your hometown or region.

Take a Stand

Business research by its very nature is intrusive. The researcher tries to find out something which is not obvious, and often not readily available. Business research is usually conducted with an expected end goal in mind—there has to be some pay-off.

For Discussion

In light of these two facts, some say that international business research should only be conducted with the permission of the people to be researched. This should also include the use of secondary data. Others claim that it is through research that companies can make life easier for their customers—we need more of it. Finally, some argue that not enough research is done on poor markets and marginal customers—they deserve to be heard too.

Chapter Appendix 10A

Monitors of International Issues

European Union

- **EUROPA**
  The umbrella server for all institutions
  http://www.europa.eu.int

- **ISPO (Information Society Project Office)**
  Information on telecommunications and
    information market developments
  Information Society
  European Commission
  Directorate General Information Society
  BU 24 O/74
  Rue de la Loi 200
  B-1049 Brussels
  http://europa.eu.int/information_society

- **CORDIS**
  Information on EU research programs
  http://www.cordis.lu

- **EUROPARL**
  Information on the European Parliament's
    activities
  http://www.europarl.eu.int

- **Delegation of the European Commission
  to the U.S.**
  Press releases, EURECOM:
    Economic and Financial News, EU-US
      relations, information on EU policies and
      Delegation programs
  European Union
  Delegation of the European Commission to the
    United States
  2300 M Street, NW
  Washington, DC 20037
  http://www.eurunion.org

- **Citizens Europe**
  Covers rights of citizens of EU member states
  citizens.eu.int

- **EURLEX (European Union Law)**
  Bibliographic database
  http://europa.eu.int/eur_lex/

- **Euro**
  The Single Currency
  http://www.euro.ecb.int

- **European Agency for the Evaluation of
  Medicinal Products**
  Information on drug approval procedures
    and documents of the Committee for
    Proprietary Medicinal Products and the
    Committee for Veterinary Medicinal
    Products
  http://www.emea.eu.int

- **European Central Bank**
  Kaiserstrasse 29
  D-60311 Frankfurt am Main
  Germany
  Postal:
  Postfach 160319
  D-60066 Frankfurt am Main
  Germany
  http://www.ecb.int

- **European Centre for the Development of
  Vocational Training**
  Under construction with information
    on the Centre and contact information
  Cedefop
  Europe 123
  GR-57001 Thessaloniki
  (Pylea)
  Mailing Address:
  PO Box 22427
  Thessaloniki
  GR-55102 Thessaloniki
  http://www.cedefop.gr

- **European Environment Agency**
  Information on the mission, products and
    services, and organizations and staff of
    the EEA
  http://www.eea.eu.int

- **European Investment Bank**
  Press releases and information on
  borrowing and loan operations, staff,
  and publications
  100, boulevard Konrad Adenauer
  L-2950 Luxembourg
  http://www.eib.org

- **European Union Internet Resources**
  Main Library, 2nd Floor
  The Library
  University of California
  Berkeley, CA 94720-6000
  http://www.lib.berkeley.edu/doemoff/
  gov_eu.html

- **Office for Harmonization in the
  Internal Market**
  Guidelines, application forms and other
  information to registering an
  EU trademark
  http://oami.eu.int

- **Council of the European Union**
  Information and news from the Council with
  sections covering Common Foreign and
  Security Policy (CFSP) and Justice and
  Home Affairs Under Construction
  http://ue.eu.int

- **Court of Justice**
  Overview, press releases, publications, and
  full-text proceedings of the court
  http://www.curia.eu.int/en/index.htm

- **Court of Auditors**
  Information notes, annual reports, and other
  publications
  http://www.eca.eu.int/en/menu.htm

- **European Community Information Service**
  200 Rue de la Loi
  1049 Brussels, Belgium
  and
  2100 M Street NW, 7th Floor
  Washington, DC 20037

- **European Bank for Reconstruction and
  Development**
  One Exchange Square
  London EC2A 2JN
  United Kingdom
  http://www.ebrd.com

- **European Union**
  200 Rue de la Loi
  1049 Brussels, Belgium
  and
  2100 M Street NW 7th Floor
  Washington, DC 20037
  http://www.eurunion.org

United Nations

http://www.un.org

- **Conference of Trade and Development**
  Palais des Nations
  1211 Geneva 10
  Switzerland
  http://www.unctad.org

- **Department of Economic and Social Affairs**
  1 United Nations Plaza
  New York, NY 10017
  http://www.un.org/esa

- **Industrial Development Organization**
  1660 L Street NW
  Washington, DC 20036
  and
  Post Office Box 300
  Vienna International Center
  A-1400 Vienna, Austria
  http://www.unido.org

- **International Trade Centre**
  UNCTAD/WTO
  54–56 Rue de Mountbrillant
  CH-1202 Geneva
  Switzerland
  http://www.intracen.org

- **UN Publications**
  Room 1194
  1 United Nations Plaza
  New York, NY 10017
  http://www.un.org/Pubs/

- **Statistical Yearbook**
  1 United Nations Plaza
  New York, NY 10017
  http://www.un.org/Pubs/

- **Yearbook of International Trade Statistics**
  United Nations Publishing Division
  1 United Nations Plaza
  Room DC2-0853
  New York, NY 10017
  http://www.un.org/Pubs/

U.S. Government

- **Agency for International Development**
  Office of Business Relations
  Washington, DC 20523
  http://www.info.usaid.gov

- **Customs and Border Protection**
  1300 Pennsylvania Ave. NW
  Room 6.3D
  Washington, DC 20229
  http://www.customs.ustreas.gov

- **Department of Agriculture**
  12th Street and Jefferson Drive SW
  Washington, DC 20250
  http://www.usda.gov

- **Department of Commerce**
  Herbert C. Hoover Building
  14th Street and Constitution Avenue NW
  Washington, DC 20230
  http://www.commerce.gov

- **Department of Homeland Security**
  http://www.whitehouse.gov/homeland

- **Department of State**
  2201 C Street NW
  Washington, DC 20520
  http://www.state.gov

- **Department of the Treasury**
  15th Street and Pennsylvania Avenue NW
  Washington, DC 20220
  http://www.ustreas.gov

- **Federal Trade Commission**
  6th Street and Pennsylvania Avenue NW
  Washington, DC 20580
  http://www.ftc.gov

- **International Trade Commission**
  500 E Street NW
  Washington, DC 20436
  http://www.usitc.gov

- **Small Business Administration**
  409 Third Street SW
  Washington, DC 20416
  http://www.sbaonline.sba.gov

- **Trade Information Center**
  International Trade Administration
  U.S. Department of Commerce
  Washington, D.C. 20230
  http://www.ita.doc.gov/td/tic/

- **U.S. Trade and Development Agency**
  1621 North Kent Street
  Rosslyn, VA 22209
  http://www.tda.gov

- **World Trade Centers Association**
  60 East 42nd Street, Suite 1901
  New York, NY 10169
  http://www.iserve.wtca.org

- **Council of Economic Advisers—**
  http://www.whitehouse.gov/cea

- **Department of Defense—**
  http://www.dod.gov

- **Department of Energy—**
  http://www.osti.gov

- **Department of Interior—**
  http://www.doi.gov

- **Department of Labor—**
  http://www.dol.gov

- **Department of Transportation—**
  http://www.dot.gov

- **Environmental Protection Agency—**
  http://www.epa.gov

- **National Trade Data Bank—**
  http://www.stat-usa.gov

- **National Economic Council—**
  http://www.whitehouse.gov/nec

- **Office of the U.S. Trade Representative—**
  http://www.ustr.gov

- **Office of Management and Budget—**
  http://www.whitehouse.gov/omb

- **Overseas Private Investment Corporation—**
  http://www.opic.gov

Selected Organizations

- **American Bankers Association**
  1120 Connecticut Avenue NW
  Washington, DC 20036
  http://www.aba.com

- **American Bar Association**
  750 N. Lake Shore Drive
  Chicago, IL 60611
  and
  1800 M Street NW
  Washington, DC 20036
  http://www.abanet.org/intlaw/home.html

- **American Management Association**
  440 First Street NW
  Washington, DC 20001
  http://www.amanet.org

- **American Marketing Association**
  311 S. Wacker Drive, Suite 5800
  Chicago, IL 60606
  http://www.marketingpower.com

- **American Petroleum Institute**
  1220 L Street NW
  Washington, DC 20005
  http://www.api.org

- **Asia-Pacific Economic Cooperation Secretariat**
  438 Alexandra Road
  #41-00, Alexandra Road
  Singapore 119958
  http://www.apecsec.org.sg

- **Asian Development Bank**
  2330 Roxas Boulevard
  Pasay City, Philippines
  http://www.adb.org

- **Association of Southeast Asian Nations (ASEAN)**
  Publication Office
  c/o The ASEAN Secretariat
  70A, Jalan Sisingamangaraja
  Jakarta 11210
  Indonesia
  http://www.asean.or.id

- **Canadian Market Data**
  http://www.strategis.ic.gc.ca

- **Chamber of Commerce of the United States**
  1615 H Street NW
  Washington, DC 20062
  http://www.uschamber.org

- **Commission of the European Communities to the United States**
  2100 M Street NW
  Suite 707
  Washington, DC 20037
  http://www.eurunion.org

- **Conference Board**
  845 Third Avenue
  New York, NY 10022
  and
  1755 Massachusetts Avenue
  NW Suite 312
  Washington, DC 20036
  http://www.conference-board.org

- **Deutsche Bundesbank**
  Wilhelm-Epstein-Str. 14
  P.O.B. 10 06 02
  D-60006 Frankfurt am Main
  http://www.bundesbank.de

- **Electronic Industries Alliance**
  2001 Pennsylvania Avenue NW
  Washington, DC 20004
  http://www.eia.org

- **The Emerging Markets Directory**
  http://www.emdirectory.com

- **Export-Import Bank of the United States**
  811 Vermont Avenue NW
  Washington, DC 20571
  http://www.exim.gov

- **Federal Reserve Bank of New York**
  33 Liberty Street
  New York, NY 10045
  http://www.ny.frb.org

- **The Federation of International Trade Associations**
  11800 Sunrise Valley Drive, Suite 210
  Reston, VA 20191
  http://www.fita.org

- **Inter-American Development Bank**
  1300 New York Avenue NW
  Washington, DC 20577
  http://www.iadb.org

- **International Bank for Reconstruction and Development (World Bank)**
  1818 H Street NW
  Washington, DC 20433
  http://www.worldbank.org

- **International Monetary Fund**
  700 19th Street NW
  Washington, DC 20431
  http://www.imf.org

- **International Chamber of Commerce**
  38, Cours Albert ler
  7800 Paris, France
  http://www.iccwbo.org

- **International Telecommunication Union**
  Place des Nations
  Ch-1211 Geneva 20
  Switzerland
  http://www.itu.int

- **International Trade Law Monitor**
  http://lexmercatoria.org

- **Michigan State University Center for International Business Education and Research**
  http://www.globaledge.msu.edu

- **Marketing Research Society**
  111 E. Wacker Drive, Suite 600
  Chicago, IL 60601

- **National Association of Manufacturers**
  1331 Pennsylvania Avenue
  Suite 1500
  Washington, DC 20004
  http://www.nam.org

- **National Federation of Indepedent Business**
  600 Maryland Avenue SW
  Suite 700
  Washington, DC 20024
  http://www.nfib.org

- **Organization for Economic Cooperation and Development**
  2 rue Andre Pascal
  75775 Paris Cedex Ko, France
  and
  2001 L Street NW, Suite 700
  Washington, DC 20036
  http://www.oecd.org

- **Organization of American States**
  17th and Constitution Avenue NW
  Washington, DC 20006
  http://www.oas.org

- **Society for International Development**
  1401 New York Avenue NW
  Suite 1100
  Washington, DC 20005
  http://www.sidint.org

- **Transparency International**
  Otto-Suhr-Allee 97-99
  D-10585 Berlin
  Germany
  http://www.transparency.de

Indexes to Literature

- **Business Periodical Index**
  H.W. Wilson Co.
  950 University Avenue
  Bronx, NY 10452

- **New York Times Index**
  University Microfilms International
  300 N. Zeeb Road
  Ann Arbor, MI 48106
  http://www.nytimes.com

- **Public Affairs Information Service Bulletin**
  11 W. 40th Street
  New York, NY 10018
  http://www.pais.org

- **Reader's Guide to Periodical Literature**
  H.W. Wilson Co.
  950 University Avenue
  Bronx, NY 10452
  http://www.tulane.edu/~horn/rdg.html

- **Wall Street Journal Index**
  University Microfilms International
  300 N. Zeeb Road
  Ann Arbor, MI 48106
  http://www.wsj.com

Directories

- **American Register of Exporters and Importers**
  38 Park Row
  New York, NY 10038

- **Arabian Year Book**
  Dar Al-Seuassam Est. Box 42480
  Shuwahk, Kuwait

- **Directories of American Firms Operating in Foreign Countries**
  World Trade Academy Press
  Uniworld Business Publications Inc.
  50 E. 42nd Street
  New York, NY 10017

- **The Directory of International Sources of Business Information**
  Pitman
  128 Long Acre
  London WC2E 9AN, England

- **Encyclopedia of Associations**
  Gale Research Co.
  Book Tower
  Detroit, MI 48226

- **Polk's World Bank Directory**
  R.C. Polk & Co.
  2001 Elm Hill Pike
  P.O. Box 1340
  Nashville, TN 37202

- **Verified Directory of Manufacturer's Representatives**
  MacRae's Blue Book Inc.
  817 Broadway
  New York, NY 10003

- **World Guide to Trade Associations**
  K.G. Saur & Co.
  175 Fifth Avenue
  New York, NY 10010

Encyclopedias, Handbooks, and Miscellaneous

- **A Basic Guide to Exporting**
  U.S. Government Printing Office
  Superintendent of Documents
  Washington, DC 20402

- **Doing Business In . . . Series**
  Price Waterhouse
  1251 Avenue of the Americas
  New York, NY 10020

- **Economic Survey of Europe**
  United Nations Publishing Division
  1 United Nations Plaza
  Room DC2-0853
  New York, NY 10017

- **Economic Survey of Latin America**
  United Nations Publishing Division
  1 United Nations Plaza
  Room DC2-0853
  New York, NY 10017

- **Encyclopedia Americana, International Edition**
  Grolier Inc.
  Danbury, CT 06816

- **Encyclopedia of Business Information Sources**
  Gale Research Co.
  Book Tower
  Detroit, MI 48226

- **Europa Year Book**
  Europa Publications Ltd.
  18 Bedford Square
  London WCIB 3JN, England

- **Export Administration Regulations**
  U.S. Government Printing Office
  Superintendent of Documents
  Washington, DC 20402

- **Exporters' Encyclopedia—World Marketing Guide**
  Dun's Marketing Services
  49 Old Bloomfield Rd.
  Mountain Lake, NJ 07046

- **Export-Import Bank of the United States Annual Report**
  U.S. Government Printing Office
  Superintendent of Documents
  Washington, DC 20402

- **Exporting for the Small Business**
  U.S. Government Printing Office
  Superintendent of Documents
  Washington, DC 20402

- **Exporting to the United States**
  U.S. Government Printing Office
  Superintendent of Documents
  Washington, DC 20402

- **Export Shipping Manual**
  U.S. Government Printing Office
  Superintendent of Documents
  Washington, DC 20402

- **Foreign Business Practices: Materials on Practical Aspects of Exporting, International Licensing, and Investing**
  U.S. Government Printing Office
  Superintendent of Documents
  Washington, DC 20402

- **A Guide to Financing Exports**
  U.S. Government Printing Office
  Superintendent of Documents
  Washington, DC 20402

- **Handbook of Marketing Research**
  McGraw-Hill Book Co.
  1221 Avenue of the Americas
  New York, NY 10020

Periodic Reports, Newspapers, Magazines

- **Advertising Age**
  Crain Communications Inc.
  740 N. Rush Street
  Chicago, IL 60611
  http://www.adage.com

- **Advertising World**
  Directories International Inc.
  150 Fifth Avenue, Suite 610
  New York, NY 10011
  http://advertising.utexas.edu/world/

- **Agricultural Outlook**
  U.S. Department of Agriculture
  Economic Research Service
  http://www.ers.usda.gov/
  publications/AgOutlook/Archives/

- **Arab Report and Record**
  84 Chancery Lane
  London WC2A 1DL, England

- **Barron's**
  University Microfilms International
  300 N. Zeeb Road
  Ann Arbor, MI 48106
  http://www.barrons.com

- **Business America**
  U.S. Department of Commerce
  14th Street and Constitution Avenue NW
  Washington, DC 20230
  http://www.doc.gov

- **Business International**
  Business International Corp.
  One Dag Hammarskjold Plaza
  New York, NY 10017

- **Business Week**
  McGraw-Hill Publications Co.
  1221 Avenue of the Americas
  New York, NY 10020
  http://www.businessweek.com

- **Commodity Trade Statistics**
  United Nations Publications
  1 United Nations Plaza
  Room DC2-0853
  New York, NY 10017

- **Conference Board Record**
  Conference Board Inc.
  845 Third Avenue
  New York, NY 10022
  http://www.conference-board.org

- **Customs Bulletin**
  U.S. Customs Service
  1301 Constitution Avenue NW
  Washington, DC 20229

- **The Economist**
  Economist Newspaper Ltd.
  25 St. James Street
  London SWIA 1HG, England
  http://www.economist.com

- **Europe Magazine**
  2100 M Street NW Suite 707
  Washington, DC 20037
  http://www.eurunion.org/magazine/home.htm

- **The Financial Times**
  Bracken House
  10 Cannon Street
  London EC4P 4BY, England
  http://www.news.ft.com/home/us

- **Forbes**
  Forbes, Inc.
  60 Fifth Avenue
  New York, NY 10011
  http://www.forbes.com

- **Fortune**
  Time, Inc.
  Time & Life Building
  1271 Avenue of the Americas
  New York, NY 10020
  http://www.fortune.com

- **International Financial Statistics**
  International Monetary Fund
  Publications Unit
  700 19th Street NW
  Washington, DC 20431
  http://www.imf.com

- **Investor's Business Daily**
  Box 25970
  Los Angeles, CA 90025
  Journal of Commerce
  110 Wall Street
  New York, NY 10005
  http://www.investors.com

- **Journal of Commerce**
  100 Wall Street
  New York, NY 10005
  http://www.joc.com

- **Sales and Marketing Management**
  Bill Communications Inc.
  633 Third Avenue
  New York, NY 10017

- **Wall Street Journal**
  Dow Jones & Company
  200 Liberty Street
  New York, NY 10281
  http://www.wsj.com

- **Pergamon Press Inc.**
  Journals Division
  Maxwell House
  Fairview Park
  Elmsford, NY 10523

- **World Trade Center Association (WTCA) Directory**
  World Trade Centers Association
  60 East 42nd Street, Suite 1901
  New York, NY 10169

- **International Encyclopedia of the Social Sciences**
  Macmillan and the Free Press
  866 Third Avenue
  New York, NY 10022

- **Marketing and Communications Media Dictionary**
  Media Horizons Inc.
  50 W. 25th Street
  New York, NY 10010

- **Market Share Reports**
  U.S. Government Printing Office
  Superintendent of Documents
  Washington, DC 20402
  http://www.access.gpo.gov

- **Media Guide International: Business/Professional Publications**
  Directories International Inc.
  150 Fifth Avenue, Suite 610
  New York, NY 10011

- **Overseas Business Reports**
  U.S Government Printing Office
  Superintendent of Documents
  Washington, DC 20402
  http://www.access.gpo.gov

- **Sales and Marketing Management**
  http://www.salesandmarketing.com/smmnew/

- **Trade Finance**
  U.S. Department of Commerce
  International Trade Administration
  Washington, DC 20230
  http://www.doc.gov

- **World Economic Conditions in Relation to Agricultural Trade**
  U.S. Government Printing Office
  Superintendent of Documents
  Washington, DC 20402
  http://www.access.gpo.gov

Chapter Appendix 10B

The Structure of a Country Commercial Guide

Country Commercial Guide for Austria
Table of Contents

F. U.S.-Based Multipliers

G. Washington-Based U.S. Government Contacts

Chapter 12 Market Research

A. Foreign Agriculture Service
Commodity Reports/Market Briefs

B. Department of Commerce Industry Subsector Analyses

Chapter 13 Trade Event Schedule

A. Scheduled Agricultural/Food Trade Events

B. Scheduled Trade Events—U.S. Commercial Service Vienna

Source: U.S. Department of Commerce, The Commercial Service, Washington, DC, 2002.
http://www.buyusa.gov/europe

CHAPTER

11

Entry and Expansion

Learning Objectives

- To learn how firms gradually progress through an internationalization process

- To understand the strategic effects of internationalization on the firm

- To study the various modes of entering international markets

- To understand the role and functions of international intermediaries

- To learn about the opportunities and challenges of cooperative market development

An Accidental Exporter

Maynard Sauder, chairman of ready-to-assemble furniture maker Sauder Woodworking Company of Archbold, Ohio, thought for the longest while that exporting was not for him. The do-it-yourself household furnishings market in the United States had been gathering steam in the late 1980s. Sauder Woodworking was a supplier to national general merchandisers such as Wal-Mart, Kmart, Sears, and J.C. Penney. It was supplying retailers with products in the $19 to $399 range and had just reached a sales volume of $200 million. Annual growth was humming at 12 to 15 percent. Exports at this time were negligible and occurred almost by accident. For instance, the firm started to sell products in the Caribbean because a salesman vacationed there.

How times have changed. Today, Sauder Woodworking does business in more than 70 countries worldwide, with corporate revenues of over $500 million annually. Domestic volume has gone flat, while international accounts have posted an average annual increase of 30 percent. It wasn't until Jerry Paterson, a former export manager for Owens-Corning Fiberglass Corp., caught Sauder's attention that the company became serious about exporting. "I questioned our ability to compete in foreign markets," Sauder says today. "I wasn't sure we could make it on price, and then I wondered if customers outside the United States would accept our designs." But the cost-benefit analysis, plus Paterson's presence, made it worth a try. "If Jerry Paterson can bring our export sales up to $2 million a year, it will more than pay his expenses," Sauder recalls. "It took us three to four years to reach a critical mass in exporting, but I knew after a year or so that we were going to give our program full support, and that we were in it for the long pull, not casually and not lukewarm."

Paterson quickly went to work, and allayed Sauder's initial fears about jumping into exporting. Soon he realized that the company's proximity to particleboard suppliers in central Ohio would help keep prices competitive worldwide. Concerns over decor preferences also evaporated. "Our styles and colors have proved very acceptable, especially in France, where our penetration has been remarkable. But we're doing very well in Turkey, too." Add to this a positive outlook for sales in India and plans to ship to China via Hong Kong.

"We proved in a very short time that we can compete anywhere in the world," Sauder says. Many U.S. exporters are discovering that American labor can compete with workers anywhere in the world, thanks to increased efficiency and the higher quality of the finished product. "[Our made-in-the-U.S.A. products] are a great sales booster for us the world over."

Sources: Daniel McConville, "An Accidental Exporter Turns Serious," *World Trade,* March 1996, 28; and Sauder Company Web site, http://www.sauder.com, accessed August 19, 2003.

International business holds out the promise of large new market areas, yet firms cannot simply jump into the international marketplace and expect to be successful. They must adjust to needs and opportunities abroad, have quality products, understand their customers, and do their homework to understand the vagaries of international markets. The rapid globalization of markets, however, reduces the time available to adjust to new market realities.

This chapter is concerned with firms preparing to enter international markets and companies expanding their current international activities. Initial emphasis is placed on export activities with a focus on the role of management in starting up international operations and a description of the basic stimuli for international activities. Entry modes for the international arena are highlighted, and the problems and benefits of each mode are discussed. The role of facilitators and intermediaries in international business is described. Finally, alternatives that involve a local presence by the firm are presented.

The Role of Management

Management dynamism and commitment are crucial to a firm's first steps toward international operations. Managers of firms with a strong international performance typically are active, aggressive, and display a high degree of international orientation.[1] Such an orientation is indicated by substantial global awareness and cultural sensitivity.[2] Conversely, the managers of firms that are unsuccessful or inactive internationally usually exhibit a lack of determination or devotion to international business. The issue of **managerial commitment** is a critical one because foreign market penetration requires a vast amount of market development activity, sensitivity toward foreign environments, research, and innovation. Regardless of what the firm produces or where it does business internationally, managerial commitment is crucial for enduring stagnation and sometimes even setbacks and failure. After all, it is top management that determines the willingness to take risk, to introduce new products, to seek new solutions to problems, and to continuously strive to succeed abroad.[3] To achieve such a commitment, it is important to involve all levels of management early on in the international planning process and to impress on all players that the effort will only succeed with a commitment that is companywide.[4]

Initiating international business activities takes the firm in an entirely new direction, quite different from adding a product line or hiring a few more people. Going international means that a fundamental strategic change is taking place. Companies that initiate international expansion efforts and succeed with them, typically begin to enjoy operational improvements—such as positioning strengths in competition—long before financial improvements appear.[5]

The decision to export usually comes from the highest levels of management, typically the owner, president, chairman, or vice president of marketing.[6] The carrying out of the decision—that is, the implementation of international business transactions—is then the primary responsibility of marketing personnel. It is important to establish an organizational structure in which someone has the specific responsibility for international activities. Without such a responsibility center, the focus necessary for success can easily be lost. Such a center need not be large. For example, just one person assigned part time to international activities can begin exploring and entering international markets.

The first step in developing international commitment is to become aware of international business opportunities. Management must then determine the degree and timing of the firm's internationalization. For instance, a German corporation that expands its operation into Austria, Switzerland, Belgium, and the Netherlands is less international than a German corporation that launches operations in Japan and Brazil. Moreover, if a German-based corporation already has activities in the United States, setting up a business in Canada does not increase its degree of internationalization as much as if Canada was the first "bridgehead" in North America.[7] Management must decide the timing of when to start the internationalization process and how quickly it should progress. For example, market entry might be desirable as soon as possible because clients are waiting for the product or because competitors are expected to enter the market shortly. In addition, it may be desirable to either enter a market abroad selectively or to achieve full market coverage from the outset. Decisions on these timing issues will determine the speed with which management must mobilize and motivate the people involved in the process.[8] It must be kept in mind that a firmwide international orientation does not develop overnight, but rather needs time to grow. Internationalization is a matter of learning, of acquiring experiential knowledge. A firm must learn about foreign markets and institutions, but also about its own internal resources in order to know what it is capable of when exposed to new and unfamiliar conditions.[9] Planning and execution of an export venture must be incorporated into the firm's strategic management process. A firm that sets no strategic goals for its export venture is less likely to make the venture a long-term success.[10] As markets around the world become more linked and more competitive, the importance of developing and following a strategy becomes increasingly key to making things better.[11]

Management is often much too preoccupied with short-term, immediate problems to engage in sophisticated long-run planning. As a result, many firms are simply not interested in international business. Yet certain situations may lead a manager to discover and understand the value of going international and to decide to pursue international business activities. One trigger factor can be international travel, during which new business opportunities are discovered. Alternatively, the receipt of information can lead management to believe that international business opportunities exist. **Unsolicited orders** from abroad are an example. Research in Scotland has shown that two thirds of small exporting firms started to do so because of unsolicited approaches from buyers or third parties. Management's entrepreneurial spirit manifested itself by following through on the lead.[12] Nonetheless, while such management by serendipity may be useful in a start-up phase, it is no substitute for effective planning when it comes to setting the long-term strategic corporate direction.

Managers who have lived abroad and have learned foreign languages or are particularly interested in foreign cultures are more likely to investigate whether international business opportunities would be appropriate for their firms. Countries or regions with high levels of immigration may, over time, benefit from greater export success due to more ties, better information, and greater international business sensitivity by their new residents.

New management or new employees can also introduce an international orientation. For example, managers entering a firm may already have had some international business experience and may use this experience to further the business activities of their new employer.

Motivations to Go Abroad

Normally, management will consider international activities only when stimulated to do so. A variety of motivations can push and pull individuals and firms along the international path. An overview of the major motivations that have been found to make firms go international is provided in Table 11.1. Proactive motivations represent stimuli for firm-initiated strategic change. Reactive motivations describe stimuli that result in a firm's response and adaptation to changes imposed by the outside environment. In other words, firms with proactive motivations go international because they want to; those with reactive motivations go international because they have to.

PROACTIVE MOTIVATIONS

Profits are the major proactive motivation for international business. Management may perceive international sales as a potential source of higher profit margins or of more added-on profits. Of course, the profitability expected when planning to go international is often quite different from the profitability actually obtained. Profitability is often linked with international growth—yet many corporate international entry decisions are made based on expectations of market growth rather than on actual market growth.[13] Particularly in start-up operations, initial profitability may be quite low due to the cost of getting ready for going international, and the losses resulting from early mistakes.[14] The gap between expectation and reality may be especially large when the firm has not previously engaged in international business. Even with thorough planning, unexpected influences can change the profit picture substantially. Shifts in exchange rates, for example, may drastically affect profit forecasts.

Unique products or a technological advantage can be another major stimulus. A firm may produce goods or services that are not widely available from international competitors. Again, real and perceived advantages must be differentiated. Many firms believe that they offer unique products or services, even though this may not be the case internationally. If products or technologies are unique, however, they certainly can provide a competitive edge. What needs to be considered is how long such an advantage will last. The length of time is a function of the product, its technology, and the creativity of competitors. In the past, a firm with a competitive edge could often count on being the sole supplier to foreign markets for years to come. This type of advantage has shrunk dramatically because of competing technologies and the frequent lack of international patent protection.

© JOHN MCDERMOTT

Nike's international success is a result of the company's efforts to connect the brand to consumers emotionally, culturally, and with local relevance. In June 2000, Nike joined "Globel Compact," a UN project that supports human rights and environmental standards in business. Nike's involvement lends credence to the project, since its annual sales in Asia are more than $1.2 billion.

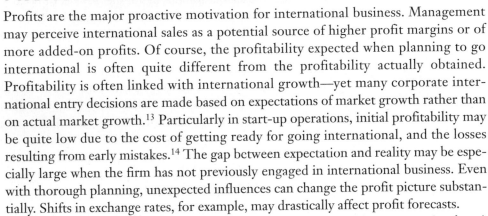

❈ TABLE 11.1

Major Motivations to Firms

Proactive Motivations	Reactive Motivations
Profit advantage	Competitive pressures
Unique products	Overproduction
Technological advantage	Declining domestic sales
Exclusive information	Excess capacity
Tax benefit	Saturated domestic markets
Economies of scale	Proximity to customers and ports

Special knowledge about foreign customers or market situations may be another proactive stimulus. Such knowledge may result from particular insights by a firm, special contacts an individual may have, in-depth research, or simply from being in the right place at the right time (for example, recognizing a good business situation during a vacation trip). Although such exclusivity can serve well as an initial stimulus for international business, it will rarely provide prolonged motivation because competitors can be expected to catch up with the information advantage. Only if firms build up international information advantage as an ongoing process, through, for example, broad market scanning or special analytical capabilities, can prolonged corporate strategy be based on this motivation.

Tax benefits can also play a major motivating role. Many governments use preferential tax treatment to encourage exports. As a result of such tax benefits, firms either can offer their product at a lower cost in foreign markets or can accumulate a higher profit. However, international trade rules make it increasingly difficult for governments to use tax subsidies to encourage exports. For example, to counteract the value-added tax refund provided to exporters by the European Union, the United States has provided for tax deferment for its exporters. This deferment, originally called the Domestic International Sales Corporation (DISC) and now known as the Extraterritorial Income Tax Exclusion (ETI) has repeatedly been found to be in violation of World Trade Organization (WTO) rules and subject to abolishment or retaliatory tariffs by trading partners.

A final major proactive motivation involves economies of scale. International activities may enable the firm to increase its output and therefore rise more rapidly on the learning curve. The Boston Consulting Group has shown that the doubling of output can reduce production costs up to 30 percent. Increased production for international markets can therefore help to reduce the cost of production for domestic sales and make the firm more competitive domestically as well.[15]

REACTIVE MOTIVATIONS

Reactive motivations influence firms to respond to environmental changes and pressures rather than blaze new trails. Competitive pressures are one example. A company may worry about losing domestic market share to competing firms that have benefited from the economies of scale gained through international business activities. Further, it may fear losing foreign markets permanently to competitors that have decided to focus on these markets. Since market share usually is most easily retained by firms that initially obtain it, some companies may enter the international market head over heels. Quick entry, however, may result in equally quick withdrawal once the firm recognizes that its preparation has been inadequate.

Similarly, overproduction may represent a reactive motivation. During downturns in the domestic business cycle, foreign markets can provide an ideal outlet for excess inventories. International business expansion motivated by overproduction usually does not represent full commitment by management, but rather a temporary safety valve. As soon as domestic demand returns to previous levels, international business activities are curtailed or even terminated. Firms that have used such a strategy once may encounter difficulties when trying to employ it again because many international customers are not interested in temporary or sporadic business relationships.

Declining domestic sales, whether measured in sales volume or market share, have a similar motivating effect. Goods marketed domestically may be at the declining stage of their product life cycle. Instead of attempting to push back the life cycle process domestically, or in addition to such an effort, firms may opt to prolong the product life cycle by expanding the market. Such efforts often meet with success, particularly with high-technology products that are outmoded by the latest innovation. Such "just-dated" technology may enable vast progress in manufacturing or services industries and, most importantly, may make such progress affordable. For example, a hospital without any imaging equipment may be much better off acquiring a "just-dated" MRI machine, rather than waiting for enough funding to purchase the latest state-of-the-art equipment.

Excess capacity can also be a powerful motivator. If equipment for production is not fully utilized, firms may see expansion abroad as an ideal way to achieve broader distribution of fixed costs. Alternatively, if all fixed costs are assigned to domestic production, the firm can penetrate foreign markets with a pricing scheme that focuses mainly on variable cost. Yet such a view is feasible only for market entry. A market-penetration strategy based on variable cost alone is unrealistic because, in the long run, fixed costs have to be recovered to replace production equipment.

The reactive motivation of a saturated domestic market has similar results to that of declining domestic sales. Again, firms in this situation can use the international market to prolong the life of their good and even of their organization.

A final major reactive motivation is that of proximity to customers and ports. Physical and psychological closeness to the international market can often play a major role in the international business activities of the firm. For example, a firm established near a border may not even perceive itself as going abroad if it does business in the neighboring country. Except for some firms close to the Canadian or Mexican border, however, this factor is much less prevalent in the United States than in many other nations. Most European firms automatically go abroad simply because their neighbors are so close.

In this context, the concept of psychic or **psychological distance** needs to be understood. Geographic closeness to foreign markets may not necessarily translate into real or perceived closeness to the foreign customer. Sometimes cultural variables, legal factors, and other societal norms make a foreign market that is geographically close seem psychologically distant. For example, research has shown that U.S. firms perceive Canada to be much closer psychologically than Mexico. Even England, mainly because of the similarity in language, is perceived by many U.S. firms to be much closer than Mexico or other Latin American countries, despite the geographic distances. However, in light of the reduction of trade barriers as a result of the North American Free Trade Agreement (NAFTA), and a growing proportion of the U.S. population with Hispanic backgrounds, this long-standing perception may be changing rapidly.

It is important to remember two major issues in the context of psychological distance. First off, some of the distance seen by firms is based on perception rather than reality. For example, many U.S. firms may see the United Kingdom as psychologically very close due to the similarity in language. However, the attitudes and values of managers and customers may vary substantially between markets. Too much of a focus on the similarities may let the firm lose sight of the differences. Many Canadian firms have incurred high costs in learning this lesson when entering the United States. At the same time, closer psychological proximity does make it easier for firms to enter markets. Therefore, for firms new to international business it may be advantageous to begin this new activity by entering the psychologically closer markets first in order to gather experience before venturing into markets that are farther away.

In general, firms that are most successful in international business are usually motivated by proactive—that is, firm internal—factors. Proactive firms are also frequently more service oriented than reactive firms. Further, proactive firms tend to be more marketing and strategy oriented than reactive firms, which have as their major concern operational issues. Focus on Entrepreneurship describes the proactive efforts of

Focus On

An International Bug

How did a small Phoenix-based environmental cleanup company boost international sales from zero to 25 percent of annual revenues? By proactively going for the world!

First, Dan Kelley, CEO of Tierra Dynamic Company, and his 30 employees had to discover a very special "bug." Tierra Dynamic patented a discovery called the *bio sparge*, a naturally occurring bacteria that Tierra cultivates, then induces to eat spilled hydrocarbons at an accelerated rate. According to Kelley, "this technique remediates soil three times faster than other methods now on the market, a significant advantage when you're concerned about carcinogens that can cause cancers and other health problems."

Second, Kelley discovered a gaping hole in the international market for his product—and leaped to fill that hole. Kelley comments, "The environmental industry is new to many developing countries and we can compete better over there than we can in more developed countries. . . . There's a big void in the market and we're happy to fill it."

Third came the identification of locations that required environmental cleanup. Kelley focused on Brazil and Argentina, as well as Indonesia, Malaysia, and Singapore. His market analysis was based primarily on the environmental regulation enforcement priorities of a given country.

Next came the practical issue of setting up shop on foreign soil. Kelley prefers working with a local partner, one who has the necessary local contacts, but who lacks the requisite technology.

After five years, Tierra found a match, then another, and eventually secured an international reputation for environmental cleanup within emerging markets. Tierra created a joint venture company called Mileto-Innovative Remediation Technologies in its target country of Argentina. Despite the current economic crisis affecting both Argentina and Brazil that has caused a drastic devaluation of their currency, Kelley is optimistic: "Others are pulling out, but we're in for the long haul." By combining emerging market opportunities with support from the Inter-American Development Bank, Tierra Dynamic seems prepared to weather the Latin American crisis.

Tierra Dynamic is currently negotiating the rights to another patented technology that can destroy not only hydrocarbons, but also PCBs, a lethal source of carcinogens that can be found in soil and water. As for the future of environmental cleanup, Kelley hopes new technologies will continue to protect the health of families worldwide.

Sources: Doug Barry, "Have Microbes, Will Travel: Small Sun Belt Company Finds Niche in Cleaning Up After Others," *Export America,* Vol. 3, No. 2, February 2002.

an exporter. The clearest differentiation between the two types of firms can probably be made after the fact by determining how they initially entered international markets. Proactive firms are more likely to have solicited their first international order, whereas reactive firms frequently begin international activities after receiving an unsolicited order from abroad.

Strategic Effects of Going International

Going international presents the firm with new environments, entirely new ways of doing business, and a host of new problems. The problems have a wide range. They can consist of strategic considerations, such as service delivery and compliance with government regulations. In addition, the firm has to focus on start-up issues, such as how to find and effectively communicate with customers and operational matters, such as information flows and the mechanics of carrying out an international business transaction. This involves a variety of new documents, including commercial invoices, bills of lading, consular invoices, inspection certificates, and shipper's export declarations. The paperwork is necessary to comply with various domestic, international, or foreign regulations. The regulations may be designed to control international business activities, to streamline the individual transaction, or, as in the case of the shipper's export declaration, to compile trade statistics.

The firm needs to determine its preparedness for internationalization by assessing its internal strengths and weaknesses. This preparedness has to be evaluated in the context of the globalization of the industry within which the firm operates, since this context will affect the competitive position and strategic options available to the firm.[16] Unusual things can happen to both risk and profit. Management's perception of risk exposure grows in light of the gradual development of expertise, the many concerns about engaging in a new activity, and uncertainty about the new environment it is about to enter. Domestically, the firm has gradually learned about the market and therefore managed to decrease its risk. In the course of international expansion, the firm now encounters new and unfamiliar factors, exposing it to increased risk. At the same time, because of the investment needs required by a serious international effort, immediate profit performance may slip. In the longer term, increasing familiarity with international markets and the diversification benefits of serving multiple markets will decrease the firm's risk below the previous "domestic only" level and increase profitability as well. In the short term, however, managers may face an unusual, and perhaps unacceptable, situation: rising risk accompanied by decreasing profitability. In light of this reality, which is depicted in Figure 11.1, many executives are tempted to either not initiate international activities or to discontinue them.[17]

Understanding the changes in risk and profitability can help management overcome the seemingly prohibitive cost of going international, since the negative developments may only be short-term. Yet, success does require the firm to be a risk taker, and firms must realize that satisfactory international performance will take time.[18] Satisfactory performance can be achieved in three ways: effectiveness, efficiency, and competitive strength. Effectiveness is characterized by the acquisition of market share abroad and by increased sales. Efficiency is manifested later by rising profitability.

FIGURE 11.1

Profit and Risk During Early Internationalization

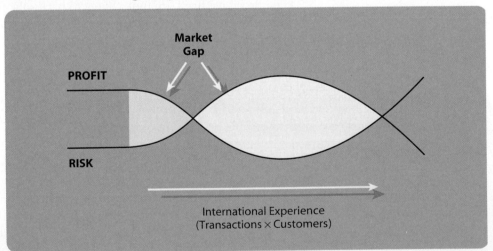

Source: Michael R. Czinkota, "A National Export Development Policy for New and Growing Businesses," in *Best Practices in International Business* (M. Czinkota and I. Ronkainen, eds.), Cincinnati: South-Western, 2001: 35–45.

Competitive strength refers to the firm's position compared to other firms in the industry, and, due to the benefits of international experience, is likely to grow. The international executive must appreciate the time and performance dimensions associated with going abroad in order to overcome short-term setbacks for the sake of long-term success.

Entry and Development Strategies

Here we will present the most typical international entry and expansion strategies. These are exporting and importing, licensing, and franchising. Another key way to expand is through a local presence, either via interfirm cooperation or foreign direct investment. These can take on many forms such as contractual agreements, equity participation and joint ventures, or direct investment conducted by the firms alone.

EXPORTING AND IMPORTING

Firms can be involved in exporting and importing in an indirect or direct way. **Indirect involvement** means that the firm participates in international business through an intermediary and does not deal with foreign customers or firms. **Direct involvement** means that the firm works with foreign customers or markets with the opportunity to develop a relationship. Firms typically opt for direct involvement based on cost decisions. **Transaction cost theory** postulates that firms will evaluate and compare the costs of integrating an operation internally, as compared to the cost of using an external party to act for the firm abroad.[19] Once it becomes easier and more efficient for a firm to conduct all the research, negotiations, shipping, and monitoring itself, rather than paying someone else to do it, the firm is likely to become a direct exporter or importer.

The end result of exporting and importing is similar whether the activities are direct or indirect. In both cases, goods and services either go abroad or come to the domestic market from abroad, and goods may have to be adapted to suit the targeted market. However, the different approaches have varying degrees of impact on the knowledge and experience levels of firms. The less direct the involvement of the firm, the less likely is the internal development of a storehouse of information and expertise on how to do business abroad, information that the firm can draw on later for further international expansion. Therefore, while indirect activities represent a form of international market entry, they may not result in growing management commitment to international markets or increased capabilities in serving them.

Many firms are indirect exporters and importers, often without their knowledge. As an example, merchandise can be sold to a domestic firm that in turn sells it abroad. This is most frequently the case when smaller suppliers deliver products to large multinational corporations, which use them as input to their foreign sales. Foreign buyers may also purchase products locally and then send them immediately to their home country. While indirect exports may be the result of unwitting participation, some firms also choose this method of international entry as a strategic alternative that conserves effort and resources while still taking advantage of foreign opportunities.

At the same time, many firms that perceive themselves as buying domestically may in reality buy imported products. They may have long-standing relations with a domestic supplier who, because of cost and competitive pressures, has begun to source products from abroad rather than to produce them domestically. In this case, the buyer firm has become an indirect importer.

Firms that opt to export or import directly have more opportunities ahead of them. They learn more quickly the competitive advantages of their products and can therefore expand more rapidly. They also have the ability to control their international activities better and can forge relationships with their trading partners, which can lead to further international growth and success.

However, the firms also are faced with obstacles. These hurdles include indentifying and targeting foreign suppliers and/or customers and finding retail space, all of which are processes that can be very costly and time-consuming. Some firms are overcoming such barriers through the use of mail-order catalogs or electronic commerce ("storeless" distribution) networks. In Japan, for example, "high-cost rents, crowded shelves, and an intricate distribution system have made launching new products via conventional methods an increasingly difficult and expensive proposition. Direct marketing via e-commerce eliminates the need for high-priced shop space."[20] In addition, particularly in industry sectors characterized by very thin profit margins, survival is determined by sales volume. Under such conditions, a large market size is essential for success—pointing many firms in the direction of international markets reached through electronic business.[21]

As a firm and its managers gather experience with exporting, they move through different levels of commitment, ranging from awareness, interest, trial, evaluation, and finally, adaptation of an international outlook as part of corporate strategy. Of course, not all firms will progress with equal speed through all these levels. Some will do so very rapidly, perhaps encouraged by success with an electronic commerce approach, and move on to other forms of international involvement such as foreign direct investment. Others may withdraw from exporting, due to disappointing experiences or as part of a strategic resource allocation decision.[22]

Increasingly, there are many new firms that either start out with an international orientation or develop one shortly after their establishment. Such **born global** firms emerge particularly in industries that require large numbers of customers, and in countries that only offer small internal markets. They tend to be small and young[23] and often make heavy use of electronic commerce in reaching out to the world. In some countries more than one third of new companies have been reported to export within two years.[24] Firms, managers, and governments therefore will need to be much quicker than they have been in the past, when it comes to introducing firms to and preparing them for the international market.

International Intermediaries

Both direct and indirect importers and exporters frequently make use of intermediaries who can assist with troublesome yet important details such as documentation, financing, and transportation. The intermediaries also can identify foreign suppliers and customers and help the firm with long- or short-term market penetration efforts. Major types of international intermediaries are export management companies and trading companies. Together with export facilitators, the intermediaries can bring the global market to the domestic firm's doorstep and help overcome financial and time constraints. Table 11.2 shows those areas in which intermediaries have been found to be particularly helpful.

TABLE 11.2   How a Trade Intermediary Can Offer Assistance

1. Knows foreign market competitive conditions
2. Has personal contacts with potential foreign buyers
3. Evaluates credit risk associated with foreign buyers
4. Has sales staff to call on current foreign customers in person
5. Assumes responsibility for physical delivery of product to foreign buyer

Source: Richard M. Castaldi, Alex F. De Noble, and Jeffrey Kantor, "The Intermediary Service Requirements of Canadian and American Exporters," *International Marketing Review* 9, 2 (1992): 21–40.

It is the responsibility of the firm's management to decide how to use the intermediaries. Options range from using their help for initial market entry to developing a long-term strategic collaboration. It is the degree of corporate involvement in and control of the international effort that determines whether the firm operates as an indirect or direct internationalist.

EXPORT MANAGEMENT COMPANIES

Firms that specialize in performing international business services as commission representatives or as distributors are known as **export management companies (EMCs).** Most EMCs are quite small. Many were formed by one or two principals with experience in international business or in a particular geographic area. Their expertise enables them to offer specialized services to domestic corporations.

EMCs have two primary forms of operation: they take title to goods and distribute internationally on their own account, or they perform services as agents. They often serve a variety of clients, thus their mode of operation may vary from client to client and from transaction to transaction. An EMC may act as an agent for one client and as a distributor for another. It may even act as both for the same client on different occasions.

When working as an **agent,** the EMC is primarily responsible for developing foreign business and sales strategies and establishing contacts abroad. Because the EMC does not share in the profits from a sale, it depends heavily on a high sales volume, on which it charges commission. The EMC may therefore be tempted to take on as many products and as many clients as possible to obtain a high sales volume. As a result, the EMC may spread itself too thin and may be unable to adequately represent all the clients and products it carries. The risk is particularly great with small EMCs.

EMCs that have specific expertise in selecting markets because of language capabilities, previous exposure, or specialized contacts appear to be the ones most successful and useful in aiding client firms in their international business efforts. For example, they can cooperate with firms that are already successful in international business but have been unable to penetrate a specific region. By sticking to their area of expertise and representing only a limited number of clients, such agents can provide quite valuable services.

When operating as a **distributor,** the EMC purchases products from the domestic firm, takes title, and assumes the trading risk. Selling in its own name, it has the opportunity to reap greater profits than when acting as an agent. The potential for greater profit is appropriate, because the EMC has drastically reduced the risk for the domestic firm while increasing its own risk. The burden of the merchandise acquired provides a major motivation to complete an international sale successfully. The domestic firm selling to the EMC is in the comfortable position of having sold its merchandise and received its money without having to deal with the complexities of the international market. On the other hand, it is less likely to gather much international business expertise.

Compensation of EMCs

The mechanism of an EMC may be very useful to the domestic firm if such activities produce additional sales abroad. However, certain activities must take place and must be paid for. As an example, a firm must incur market development expenses to enter foreign markets. At the very least, product availability must be communicated, goods must be shown abroad, visits must be arranged, or contacts must be established. These activities must be funded.

One possibility is a fee charged to the manufacturer by the EMC for market development, sometimes in the form of a retainer and often on an annual basis. The retainers vary and are dependent on the number of products represented and the difficulty of foreign market penetration. Frequently, manufacturers are also expected to pay all or part of the direct expenses associated with foreign market penetration. These expenses may involve the production and translation of promotional product brochures, the cost of attending trade shows, the provision of product samples, or trade advertising.

Alternatively, the EMC may demand a price break for international sales. In one way or another, the firm that uses an EMC must pay the EMC for the international business effort. Otherwise, despite promises, the EMC may simply add the firm and product in name only to its product offering and do nothing to achieve international success.

Power Conflicts Between EMCs and Clients

The EMC faces the continuous problem of retaining a client once foreign market penetration is achieved. Many firms use an EMC's services mainly to test the international arena, with the clear desire to become a direct participant once successful operations have been established. Of course, this is particularly true if foreign demand turns out to be strong and profit levels are high. The conflict between the EMC and its clients, with one side wanting to retain market power by not sharing too much international business information, and the other side wanting to obtain that power, often results in short-term relationships and a lack of cooperation. Since international business development is based on long-term efforts, this conflict frequently leads to a lack of success.

For the concept of an export management company to work, both parties must fully recognize the delegation of responsibilities, the costs associated with those activities, and the need for information sharing, cooperation, and mutual reliance. Use of an EMC should be viewed just like a domestic channel commitment, requiring a thorough investigation of the intermediary and the advisability of relying on its efforts, a willingness to cooperate on a relationship rather than on a transaction basis, and a willingness to properly reward its efforts. The EMC in turn must adopt a flexible approach to managing the export relationship. As access to the Internet is making customers increasingly sophisticated and world-wise, export management companies must ensure that they continue to deliver true value added. They must acquire, develop, and deploy resources such as new knowledge about foreign markets or about export processes in order to lower their client firm's export-related transaction costs and therefore remain a useful intermediary.[25] By doing so, the EMC lets the client know that the cost is worth the service and thereby reduces the desire for circumvention.

TRADING COMPANIES

Another major intermediary is the trading company. The concept was originated by the European trading houses such as the Fuggers of Augsburg, Germany. Later on, monarchs chartered traders to form corporate bodies that enjoyed exclusive trading rights and protection by the naval forces in exchange for tax payments. Examples of such early trading companies are the Oost-Indische Compagnie of the Netherlands, formed in 1602, followed shortly by the British East India Company and La Compagnie des Indes chartered by France.[26] Today, the most famous trading companies are the **sogoshosha** of Japan. Names such as Mitsubishi, Mitsui, and C. Itoh have become household words around the world. The nine trading company giants of Japan act as intermediaries for about one third of the country's exports and two fifths of its imports.[27] The general trading companies play a unique role in world commerce by importing, exporting, countertrading, investing, and manufacturing. Their vast size allows them to benefit from economies of scale and perform their operations at high rates of return, even though their profit margins are less than 2 percent.

Four major reasons have been given for the success of the Japanese sogoshosha. First, by concentrating on obtaining and disseminating information about market opportunities and by investing huge funds in the development of information systems, the firms have the mechanisms and organizations in place to gather, evaluate, and translate market information into business opportunities. Second, economies of scale permit the firms to take advantage of their vast transaction volume to obtain preferential treatment by, for example, negotiating transportation rates or even opening up new transportation routes and distribution systems. Third, the firms serve large internal markets, not only in Japan but also around the world, and can benefit from opportunities for countertrade. Finally, sogoshosha have access to vast quantities of capital, both within Japan and in the international capital markets. They can therefore carry out transactions that are too large or risky to be palatable or feasible for other firms.[28] In spite of changing trading patterns, these giants continue to succeed by shifting their strategy to expand their domestic activities in Japan, entering more newly developing markets, increasing their trading activities among third countries, and forming joint ventures with non-Japanese firms.

Expansion of Trading Companies

For many decades, the emergence of trading companies was commonly believed to be a Japan-specific phenomenon. Japanese cultural factors were cited as the reason that such intermediaries could operate successfully only from that country. In the last few decades, however, many other governments have established trading companies. In countries as diverse as Korea, Brazil, and Turkey, trading companies handle large portions of national exports.[29] The reason these firms have become so large is due, in good measure, to special and preferential government incentives, rather than market forces alone. Therefore, they may be vulnerable to changes in government policies.

In the United States, trading companies in which firms could cooperate internationally were initially permitted through the Webb-Pomerene associations established in 1918. While in the 1930s these collaborative ventures accounted for about 12 percent of U.S. exports, their share had dropped to less than 1 percent by 2002. Another governmental approach to export trade facilitation was **export trading company (ETC)** legislation designed to improve the export performance of small and medium-sized firms. Bank participation in trading companies was permitted, and the antitrust threat to joint export efforts was reduced through precertification of planned activities by the U.S. Department of Commerce. Businesses were encouraged to join together to export or offer export services.

Permitting banks to participate in ETCs was intended to allow ETCs better access to capital and therefore permit more trading transactions and easier receipt of title to goods. The relaxation of antitrust provisions in turn was meant to enable firms to form joint ventures more easily. The cost of developing and penetrating international markets would then be shared, with the proportional share being, for many small and medium-sized firms, much easier to bear. As an example, in case a warehouse is needed in order to secure foreign market penetration, one firm alone does not have to bear all the costs. A consortium of firms can jointly rent a foreign warehouse. Similarly, each firm need not station a service technician abroad at substantial cost. Joint funding of a service center by several firms makes the cost less prohibitive for each one. The trading company concept also offers a one-stop shopping center for both the firm and its foreign customers. The firm can be assured that all international functions will be performed efficiently by the trading company, and at the same time, the foreign customer will have to deal with few individual firms.

Although ETCs seem to offer major benefits to U.S. firms that want to go abroad, they have not been very extensively used. By 2003 only 190 individual ETC certificates had been issued by the U.S. Department of Commerce. Since some of the certificates covered all the members of trade associations, more than 5,000 companies were part of an ETC.[30]

PRIVATE SECTOR FACILITATORS

Facilitators are entities outside the firm that assist in the process of going international. They supply knowledge and information but do not participate in the transaction. Such facilitators can come both from the private and the public sector.

Major encouragement and assistance can result from the statements and actions of other firms in the same industry. Information that would be considered proprietary if it involved domestic operations is often freely shared by competing firms when it concerns international business. The information not only has source credibility but is viewed with a certain amount of fear, because a too-successful competitor may eventually infringe on the firm's domestic business.

A second influential group of private sector facilitators is distributors. Often a firm's distributors are engaged, through some of their business activities, in international business. To increase their international distribution volume, they encourage purely domestic firms to participate in the international market. This is true not only for exports but also for imports. For example, a major customer of a manufacturing firm may find that materials available from abroad, if used in the domestic production process, would make the product available at lower cost. In such instances, the customer may approach the supplier and strongly encourage foreign sourcing.

Banks and other service firms, such as accounting and consulting firms, can serve as major facilitators by alerting their clients to international opportunities. While these service providers historically follow their major multinational clients abroad, increasingly they are establishing a foreign presence on their own. Frequently, they work with domestic clients on expanding market reach in the hope that their service will be used for any international transaction that results. Given the extensive information network of many service providers—banks, for example, often have a wide variety of correspondence relationships—the role of these facilitators can be major. Like a mother hen, they can take firms under their wings and be pathfinders in foreign markets.

Chambers of commerce and other business associations that interact with firms can frequently heighten their interest in international business. Yet, in most instances, such organizations function mainly as secondary intermediaries, because true change is brought about by the presence and encouragement of other managers.

PUBLIC SECTOR FACILITATORS

Government efforts can also facilitate the international efforts of firms. In the United States, for example, the Department of Commerce provides major export assistance, as do other federal organizations such as the Small Business Administration and the Export-Import Bank. Most countries maintain similar export support organizations. Table 11.3 provides the names of selected export promotion agencies from around the globe, together with their web addresses. Employees of these organizations typically visit firms and attempt to analyze their international business opportunities. Through rapid access to government resources, these individuals can provide data, research reports, counseling, and financing information to firms. Government organizations can also sponsor meetings that bring interested parties together and alert them to new business opportunities abroad. Key governmental support is also provided when firms are abroad. By receiving information and assistance from their embassies, many business ventures abroad can be made easier.

Increasingly, organizations at the state and local level also are active in encouraging firms to participate in international business. Many states and provinces have formed agencies for economic development that provide information, display products abroad, conduct trade missions, and sometimes even offer financing. Similar services can also be offered by state and local port authorities and by some of the larger cities. State and local authorities can be a major factor in facilitating international activities because of their closeness to firms.

Educational institutions such as universities and community colleges can also be major international business facilitators. They can act as trade information clearinghouses, facilitate networking

TABLE 11.3 **Selected Export Promotion Agencies around the Globe**

Australia: Australian Trade Commission
http://www.austrade.gov.au
Canada: Export Development Corporation
http://www.edc.ca/
France: Centre Français du Commerce Extérieur
http://www.cfce.fr/
Germany: Federal Office of Foreign Trade Information (BfAI)
http://www.bfai.com
India: India Trade Promotion Organisation (ITPO)
http://www.indiatradepromotion.org
Japan: Japan External Trade Organization (JETRO)
http://www.jetro.go.jp
Singapore: International Enterprise Singapore
http://www.iesingapore.gov.sg
South Korea: Trade-Investment Promotion Agency (KOTRA)
http://www.kotra.or.kr/
United Kingdom: Overseas Trade Services
http://www.dti.gov.uk
United Nations/World Trade Organization: International Trade Centre
http://www.intracen.org
United States: Export-Import Bank
http://www.exim.gov
International Trade Administration
http://www.ita.doc.gov
Foreign Agricultural Service
http://www.fas.usda.gov

opportunities, provide client counseling and technical assistance, and develop trade education programs.[31] They can also develop course projects that are useful to firms interested in international business. For example, students may visit a firm and examine its potential in the international market as a course requirement. With the skill and supervision of faculty members to help the students develop the final report, such projects can be useful to firms with scarce resources, while they expose students to real-world problems.

LICENSING

Under a **licensing agreement,** one firm permits another to use its intellectual property for compensation designated as **royalty.** The recipient firm is the licensee. The property licensed might include patents, trademarks, copyrights, technology, technical know-how, or specific business skills. For example, a firm that has developed a bag-in-the-box packaging process for milk can permit other firms abroad to use the same process. Licensing therefore can also be called the export of intangibles.

Licensing has intuitive appeal to many would-be international managers. As an entry strategy, it requires neither capital investment nor detailed involvement with foreign customers. By generating royalty income, licensing provides an opportunity to exploit research and development already conducted. After initial costs, the licensor can reap benefits until the end of the license contract period. Licensing also reduces the risk of expropriation because the licensee is a local company that can provide leverage against government action.

Licensing may help to avoid host-country regulations applicable to equity ventures. It also may provide a means by which foreign markets can be tested without major involvement of capital or management time. Similarly, licensing can be used as a strategy to preempt a market before the entry of competition, especially if the licensor's resources permit full-scale involvement only in selected markets. Licensing also relieves the originating company from having to come up with culturally responsive changes in every market. As Focus on Culture shows, the local licensees can worry about that part.

A special form of licensing is **trademark licensing,** which has become a substantial source of worldwide revenue for companies that can trade on well-known names and characters. Trademark licensing permits the names or logos of designers, literary characters, sports teams, or movie stars to appear on clothing, games, foods and beverages, gifts and novelties, toys, and home furnishings. Licensors can make millions of dollars with little effort, while licensees can produce a brand or product that

Focus On ⬇

CULTURE

TV Program Licenses Are International

For most of the history of television, American programming has dominated the airwaves in the United States and abroad. The most popular shows in any given country were likely to be American concepts produced by American firms. The cop show, the sitcom, and the western are all television concepts developed in the United States.

The privatization of many state-run television enterprises during the 1980s created more competition and increased demand for American programming. The new commercial stations lacked the expertise needed to produce hit shows in a cost-effective way, so they filled their many open hours of airtime by purchasing programming from the United States.

American companies took advantage of high demand and prices skyrocketed. The trend continued through the 1990s as prices increased fivefold. During a bidding war in Britain, for example, the price of each episode of "The Simpsons" went up to $1.5 million. American companies also bundled their offerings and forced television stations to buy less popular programming along with popular shows.

Over time, the situation abroad has changed. Local stations have become more adept at developing and producing their own programming. Tastes also changed as consumers demanded television shows more reflective of their own cultural values and preferences. All this means that stations no longer rely on American programming to win prime-time ratings battles.

In addition to claiming a larger share of their domestic markets, European production companies have turned the tables with licensing agreements. Now they develop winning television shows and license the idea to other companies for production in their own country.

Some very successful U.S. reality series were pioneered overseas. One example is the Dutch hit show "Big Brother." New concepts are being developed, tested in foreign markets, and exported all the time. The British television hit "Pop Idol" gave rise to licensed versions in Poland, South Africa, and the United States. In the new international television market, winning ideas can come from any country.

Sources: http://www.endemol.com, accessed May 14, 2003; Bill Brioux, "Excuse Me, Is that a Canadian Idol?" *Edmonton Sun,* October 23, 2002.

consumers will recognize immediately. Trademark licensing is possible, however, only if the trademark name conveys instant recognition.

Licensing is not without disadvantages. It is a very limited form of foreign market participation and does not in any way guarantee a basis for future expansion. As a matter of fact, quite the opposite may take place. In exchange for the royalty, the licensor may create its own competitor not only in the market for which the agreement was made but for third-country markets as well.

Licensing has also come under criticism from many governments and supranational organizations. They have alleged that licensing provides a mechanism for corporations in industrialized countries to capitalize on older technology. These accusations have been made even though licensing offers a foreign entity the opportunity for immediate market entry with a proven concept. It therefore eliminates the risk of R&D failure, the cost of designing around the licensor's patents, or the fear of patent-infringement litigation.

FRANCHISING

Franchising is the granting of the right by a parent company (the franchisor) to another, independent entity (the franchisee) to do business in a prescribed manner. The right can take the form of selling the franchisor's products, using its name, production, and marketing techniques, or using its general business approach.[32] Usually franchising involves a combination of many of those elements. The major forms of franchising are manufacturer-retailer systems (such as car dealerships), manufacturer-wholesaler systems (such as soft drink companies), and service-firm retailer systems (such as lodging services and fast-food outlets). In 2002, global franchise sales increased by almost 16,000 franchisors and more than 1 million franchisees were estimated to be close to $1.5 trillion.[33]

Typically, to be successful in international franchising, the firm must be able to offer unique products or unique selling propositions. A franchise must also offer a high degree of standardization, which does not require 100 percent uniformity, but rather,

Gulf Arab tourists eat at a KFC franchise in the Lebanese mountain resort town of Bhamdoun, Lebanon. Tourists visiting Lebanon are mainly Arabs who see the country as a safer haven from potential harassment or travel inconveniences than Europe or the U.S. would be. Lebanon is seeking to regain its former position as a regional tourism hot spot.

GETTY IMAGES

international recognizability. Concurrent with this recognizability, the franchisor can and should adapt to local circumstances. Food franchisors, for example, will vary the products and product lines offered depending on local market conditions and tastes.

Key reasons for the international expansion of franchise systems are market potential, financial gain, and saturated domestic markets. From a franchisee's perspective, the franchise is beneficial because it reduces risk by implementing a proven concept. There are also major benefits from a governmental perspective. The source country does not see a replacement of exports or an export of jobs. The recipient country sees franchising as requiring little outflow of foreign exchange, since the bulk of the profits generated remains within the country.[34]

Franchising has been growing rapidly, but government intervention is a major problem. In the Philippines, for example, government restrictions on franchising and royalties hindered ComputerLand's Manila store from offering a broader range of services, leading to a separation between the company and its franchisee. Selection and training of franchisees represents another problem area. Many franchise systems have run into difficulty by expanding too quickly and granting franchises to unqualified entities. Although the local franchisee knows the market best, the franchisor still needs to understand the market for product adaptation and operational purposes. The franchisor, in order to remain viable in the long term, needs to coordinate the efforts of individual franchisees—for example, to share ideas and engage in joint undertakings, such as cooperative advertising.

Local Presence

INTERFIRM COOPERATION

The world is too large and the competition too strong for even the largest companies to do everything independently. Technologies are converging and markets are becoming integrated, thus making the costs and risks of both goods and market development ever greater. Partly as a reaction to and partly to exploit the developments, management in multinational corporations has become more pragmatic about what it takes to be successful in global markets. The result has been the formation of **strategic alliances** with suppliers, customers, competitors, and companies in other industries to achieve multiple goals.

A strategic alliance (or partnership) is an informal or formal arrangement between two or more companies with a common business objective. It is something more than the traditional customer-vendor relationship but something less than an outright acquisition. The alliances can take forms ranging from informal cooperation to joint ownership of worldwide operations. For example, Texas Instruments has reported agreements with companies such as IBM, Hyundai, Fujitsu, Alcatel, and L. M. Ericsson using such terms as "joint development agreement," "cooperative technical effort," "joint program for development," "alternative sourcing agreement," and "design/exchange agreement for cooperative product development and exchange of technical data."[35]

Reasons for Interfirm Cooperation

Strategic alliances are used for many different purposes by the partners involved. Market development is one common focus. Penetrating foreign markets is a primary objective of many companies. In Japan, Motorola is sharing chip designs and manufacturing facilities with Toshiba to gain greater access to the Japanese market. Some alliances aim to defend home markets. With no orders coming in for nuclear power plants, Bechtel Group has teamed up with Germany's Siemens to service existing U.S. plants. Another key focus is to either share the risk of engaging in a particular activity in a particular market, or to share the resource requirements of an activity.[36] The costs of developing new jet engines are so vast that they force aerospace companies into collaboration. One such consortium was formed by United Technologies' Pratt & Whitney division, Britain's Rolls-Royce, Motoren-und-Turbinen Union from Germany, Fiat of Italy, and Japanese Aero Engines (made up of Ishikawajima Heavy Industries and Kawasaki Heavy Industries).[37] Some alliances are formed to block and co-opt competitors.[38] For example, Caterpillar formed a heavy equipment joint venture with Mitsubishi in Japan to strike back at its main global rival, Komatsu, in its home market.

The most successful alliances are those that match the complementary strengths of partners to satisfy a joint objective. Often the partners have different product, geographic, or functional strengths that the partners build on, rather than use to fill gaps.[39] Some of the major alliances created on this basis are provided in Figure 11.2.

Types of Interfirm Cooperation

Each form of alliance is distinct in terms of the amount of commitment required and the degree of control each partner has. The equity alliances—minority ownership,

FIGURE 11.2

Complementary Strengths Create Value

Partner *Strength...*	+ Partner *Strength...*	= Joint Objective
Pepsico *marketing clout for canned beverages*	**Lipton** *recognized tea brand and customer franchise*	*To sell canned iced tea beverages jointly*
Philips *consumer electronics innovation and leadership*	**Levi Strauss** *fashion design and distribution*	*Outdoor wear with integrated electronic equipment for fashion-conscious consumers*
KFC *established brand and store format, and operations skills*	**Mitsubishi** *real estate and site-selection skills in Japan*	*To establish a KFC chain in Japan*
Siemens *presence in range of telecommunications markets worldwide and cable-manufacturing technology*	**Corning** *technological strength in optical fibers and glass*	*To create a fiber-optic-cable business*
Ericsson *technological strength in public telecommunications networks*	**Hewlett-Packard** *computers, software, and access to electronics-channels*	*To create and market network management systems*

Sources: "Portable Technology Takes the Next Step: Electronics You Can Wear," *Wall Street Journal,* August 22, 2000, B1, B4; Joel Bleeke and David Ernst, "Is Your Strategic Alliance Really a Sale?" *Harvard Business Review* 73 (January–February 1995): 97–105. See also 97–105: and Melanie Wells, "Coca-Cola Proclaims Nestea Time for CAA," *Advertising Age,* January 30, 1995, 2. See also http://www.pepsico.com; http://www.lipton.com; http://www.kfc.com; http://www.siecor.com; http://www.ericsson.com; and http://www.hp.com.

joint ventures, and consortia—feature the most extensive commitment and shared control. The types of strategic alliances are summarized in Figure 11.3, using the extent of equity involved and the number of partners in the endeavor as defining characteristics.

Informal Cooperation   In informal cooperative deals, partners work together without a binding agreement. This arrangement often takes the form of visits to exchange information about new products, processes, and technologies or may take the more formal form of the exchange of personnel for limited amounts of time. Often such partners are of no real threat in each other's markets and are of modest size in comparison to the competition, making collaboration necessary.[40] The relationships are based on mutual trust and friendship, and may lead to more formal arrangements, such as contractual agreements or joint projects.

Contractual Agreements   Strategic alliance partners may join forces for joint R&D, joint marketing, or joint production. Similarly, their joint efforts might include **licensing**, cross-licensing, or **cross-marketing activities**. Nestlé and General Mills

FIGURE 11.3

Forms of Interfirm Cooperation

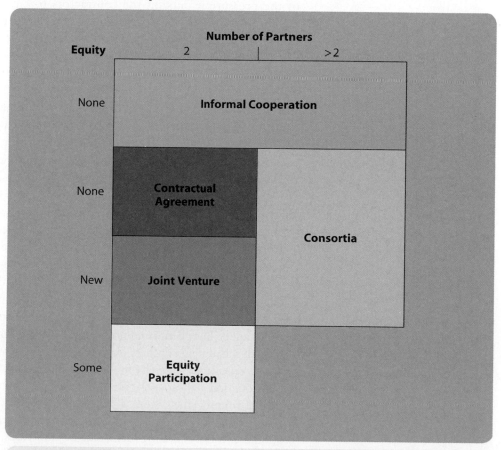

Source: Adapted with permission from Bernard L. Simonin, *Transfer of Knowledge of International Strategic Alliances: A Structural Approach,* unpublished dissertation, the University of Michigan, Ann Arbor: 1991.

had an agreement whereby Honey Nut Cheerios and Golden Grahams were made in General Mills's U.S. plants and shipped in bulk to Europe for packaging by Nestlé. Such an arrangement—complementary marketing (also known as piggybacking)—allows firms to reach objectives that they cannot reach efficiently by themselves.[41] The alliance between General Mills and Nestlé evolved into a joint venture, Cereal Partners Worldwide, which markets both companies' products in Europe and Asia. Firms also can have a reciprocal arrangement whereby each partner provides the other access to its market. The New York Yankees and Manchester United sell each others' licensed products and develop joint sponsorship programs. International airlines share hubs, coordinate schedules, and simplify ticketing. Alliances such as Star (joining United and Lufthansa), Oneworld (British Airways and American Airlines), and Sky Team (Delta and Air France) provide worldwide coverage for their customers both in the travel and shipping communities.

Contractual agreements also exist for outsourcing. For example, General Motors buys cars and components from South Korea's Daewoo, and Siemens buys computers from Fujitsu. As corporations look for ways to simultaneously grow and maintain their competitive advantage, outsourcing has become a powerful new tool for achieving those goals. **Contract manufacturing** allows the corporation to separate the physical production of goods from the research and development and marketing stages, especially if the latter are the core competencies of the firm. Benefits of such contracting are to improve company focus on higher value-added activities, to gain access to world-class capabilities, and to reduce operating costs. Contract manufacturing has been criticized because of the pressure it puts on the contractors to cut prices and, thereby, labor costs. However, such work does provide many companies, especially in developing countries, the opportunity to gain the necessary experience in product design and manufacturing technology to allow them to function in world markets. Some have even voiced concerns that the experience eventually may make future competitors of current partners.

In some parts of the world and in certain industries, governments insist on complete or majority ownership of firms. There, multinational companies offer **management contracts,** selling their expertise in running a company while avoiding the risk or benefit of ownership. Depending on the contract, doing so may even permit some measure of control. As an example, the manufacturing process may have to be relinquished to local firms, yet international distribution may be required for the product. A management contract could maintain a strong hold on the operation by ensuring that all distribution channels remain firmly controlled.

A management contract may be the critical element in the success of a project. For example, financial institutions may gain confidence in a project because of the existence of a management contract and may even make it a precondition for funding.[42]

One specialized form of management contract is the **turnkey operation.** Here, the arrangement permits a client to acquire a complete international system, together with skills sufficient to allow unassisted maintenance and operation of the system following its completion.[43] The client need not search for individual contractors or subcontractors or deal with scheduling conflicts or with difficulties in assigning responsibilities or blame. Instead, a package arrangement focuses responsibility on one entity, thus greatly easing the negotiation and supervision requirements and subsequent accountability. When the project is running, the system will be totally owned, controlled, and operated by the customer. Companies such as AES are part of consortia building electric power facilities around the world, operating them, and, in some cases, even owning parts of them.

Management contracts have clear benefits for the client. They provide organizational skills not available locally, expertise that is immediately available, and management assistance in the form of support services that would be difficult and costly to replicate locally. For example, hotels managed by the Sheraton Corporation have access to Sheraton's worldwide reservation system. Management contracts today typically involve training locals to take over the operation after a given period.

Similar advantages exist for the supplier. The risk of participating in an international venture is substantially lowered, while significant amounts of control are still exercised. Existing know-how that has been built up through substantial investment can be commercialized, and frequently the impact of fluctuations in business volume can be reduced by making use of experienced personnel who otherwise would have to be laid off. Accumulated service knowledge should be used internationally. Management contracts permit firms to do so.

Equity Participation   Many multinational corporations have acquired minority ownerships in companies that have strategic importance for them to ensure supplier ability and build formal and informal working relationships. An example of this is Ford Motor Company's 33.4 percent share of Mazda. The partners continue operating as distinctly separate entities, but each enjoys the strengths the other partner provides. For example, thanks to Mazda, Ford has excellent support in the design and manufacture of subcompact cars, while Mazda has improved access to the global marketplace. Equity ownership in an innovator may also give the investing company first access to any new technology developed.

Another significant reason for equity ownership is market entry and support of global operations. Telefonica de Espana has acquired varying stakes in Latin American telecommunications systems—a market that is the fastest-growing region of the world after Asia.

Joint Ventures   A joint venture can be defined as the participation of two or more companies in an enterprise in which each party contributes assets, has some equity, and shares risk.[44] The venture is also considered long term. The reasons for establishing a joint venture can be divided into three groups: (1) government policy or legislation; (2) one partner's needs for other partners' skills; and (3) one partner's needs for other partners' attributes or assets.[45] Equality of the partners or of their contribution is not necessary. In some joint ventures, each partners' contributions—typically consisting of funds, technology, plant, or labor—also vary.

The key to a joint venture is the sharing of a common business objective, which makes the arrangement more than a customer-vendor relationship but less than an outright acquisition. The partners' rationales for entering into the arrangement may vary. An example is New United Motor Manufacturing Inc. (NUMMI), the joint venture between Toyota and GM. Toyota needed direct access to the U.S. market, while GM benefited from the technology and management approaches provided by its Japanese partner.

Joint ventures may be the only way in which a firm can profitably participate in a particular market since many governments restrict equity participation in local operations by foreigners. Other entry modes may be limited; for example, exports may be restricted because of tariff barriers. Joint ventures are valuable when the pooling of resources results in a better outcome for each partner than if each were to conduct its activities individually. This is particularly true when each partner has a specialized advantage in areas that benefit the venture. For example, a firm may have new technology yet lack sufficient capital to carry out foreign direct investment on its own. Through a joint venture, the technology can be used more quickly and market penetration achieved more easily. Similarly, one of the partners may have a distribution system already established or have better access to local suppliers, either of which permits a greater volume of sales in a shorter period of time.

Joint ventures also permit better relationships with local government and other organizations such as labor unions. Government-related reasons are the main rationale for joint ventures to take place in less-developed countries. If the local partner is politically influential, the new venture may be eligible for tax incentives, grants, and government support. Negotiations for certifications or licenses may be easier because authorities may not perceive themselves as dealing with a foreign firm. Relationships between the local partner and the local financial establishment may enable the joint venture to tap local capital markets. The greater experience (and therefore greater familiarity) with the local culture and environment of the local partner may enable the joint venture to benefit from greater insights into changing market conditions and needs.

Many joint ventures fall short of expectations and/or are disbanded. The reasons typically relate to conflicts of interest, problems with disclosure of sensitive information, and disagreements over how profits are to be shared. There is also often a lack of communication before, during, and after formation of the venture. In some cases, managers have been more interested in the launching of the venture than the actual running of the enterprise. Many of the problems stem from a lack of careful consideration in advance of how to manage the new endeavor. A partnership works on the basis of trust and commitment or not at all.

Typical disagreements cover the whole range of business decisions, including strategy, management style, accounting and control, marketing policies and strategies, research and development, and personnel. The joint venture may, for example, identify a particular market as a target only to find that one of the partners already has individual plans for it. U.S. partners have frequently complained that their Japanese counterparts do not send their most competent personnel to the joint venture; instead, because of their lifetime employment practice, they get rid of less competent managers by sending them to the new entities.

Similarly, the issue of profit accumulation and distribution may cause discontent. If one partner supplies the joint venture with a good, the partner will prefer that any profits accumulate at headquarters and accrue 100 percent to one firm rather than at the joint venture, where profits are divided according to equity participation. Such a decision may not be greeted with enthusiasm by the other partner. Once profits are accumulated, their distribution may lead to dispute. For example, one partner may insist on a high payout of dividends because of financial needs, whereas the other may prefer the reinvestment of profits into a growing operation.

Consortia A new drug can cost $500 million to develop and bring to market; a mainframe computer or a telecommunications switch can require $1 billion. Some $7 billion goes into creating a new generation of computer chips. To combat the high costs and risks of research and development, research consortia have emerged in the United States, Japan, and Europe. For example, Ericsson, Panasonic, Samsung, Siemens, Sony, Motorola, Nokia, and Psion have formed Symbian to develop technologies for wireless communication. Headquartered in the U.K., the firm also has offices in Japan, Sweden, and the United States. Since the passage of the **Joint Research and Development Act** of 1984 (which allows both domestic and foreign firms to participate in joint basic research efforts without the fear of antitrust action), well over 100 consortia have been registered in the United States. The consortia pool their resources for research into technologies ranging from artificial intelligence to semiconductor manufacturing. (The major consortia in those fields are MCC and Sematech.) The European Union has five megaprojects to develop new technologies registered under the names EUREKA, ESPRIT, BRITE, RACE, and COMET. Japanese consortia have worked on producing the world's highest-capacity memory chip and advanced computer technologies. On the manufacturing side, the formation of Airbus Industries secured European production of commercial jets. The consortium, now backed by the European Aeronautic Defence and Space Company (EADS), which emerged from the link-up of the German DaimlerChrysler Aerospace AG, the French Aerospatiale Matra, and CASA of Spain,[46] has become a prime global competitor especially in the development of megaliners.

Managerial Considerations   The first requirement of interfirm cooperation is to find the right partner. Partners should have an orientation and goals in common and should bring complementary and relevant benefits to the endeavor. The venture makes little sense if the expertise of both partners is in the same area; for example, if both have production expertise but neither has distribution know-how. Patience should be exercised; a deal should not be rushed into, nor should the partners expect immediate results. Learning should be paramount in the endeavor while at the same time, partners must try not to give away core secrets to each other.[47]

Second, the more formal the arrangement, the greater the care that needs to be taken in negotiating the agreement. In joint venture negotiations, for example, extensive provisions must be made for contingencies. The points to be explored should include: (1) clear definition of the venture and its duration; (2) ownership, control, and management; (3) financial structure and policies; (4) taxation and fiscal obligation; (5) employment and training; (6) production; (7) government assistance; (8) transfer of technology; (9) marketing arrangements; (10) environmental protection; (11) record keeping and inspection; and (12) settlement of disputes.[48] These issues have to be addressed before the formation of the venture; otherwise, they eventually will surface as points of contention. A joint venture agreement, although comparable to a marriage agreement, should contain the elements of a divorce contract. In case the joint venture cannot be maintained to the satisfaction of partners, plans must exist for the dissolution of the agreement and for the allocation of profits and costs. Typically, however, one of the partners buys out the other partner(s) when partners decide to part ways.

A strategic alliance, by definition, also means a joining of two corporate cultures, which can often be quite different. To meet this challenge, partners must have frequent communication and interaction at three levels of the organization: the top management, operational leaders, and workforce levels. Trust and relinquishing control are difficult not only at the top but also at levels where the future of the venture is determined. A dominant partner may determine the corporate culture, but even then the other partners should be consulted. The development of specific alliance managers may be advised to forge the net of relationships both within and between alliance partners and, therefore, to support the formal alliance structure.[49]

Strategic alliances operate in a dynamic business environment and must therefore adjust to changing market conditions. The agreement between partners should provide for changes in the original concept so that the venture can flourish and grow. The trick is to have a prior understanding as to which party will take care of which pains and problems so that a common goal is reached.

Government attitudes and policies have to be part of the environmental considerations of corporate decision makers. While some alliances may be seen as a threat to the long-term economic security of a nation, in general, links with foreign operators should be encouraged. For example, the U.S. government urged major U.S. airlines to form alliances with foreign carriers to gain access to emerging world markets, partly in response to the failure to achieve free access to all markets through the negotiation of so-called "open-skies" agreements.[50]

FULL OWNERSHIP

For some firms, foreign direct investment requires, initially at least, 100 percent ownership. The reason may have an ethnocentric basis; that is, management may believe that no outside entity should have an impact on corporate decision making. Alternatively, it may be based on financial concerns. For example, the management of IBM held the belief in the early 1990s that by relinquishing a portion of its ownership abroad, it would be setting a precedent for shared control with local partners that would cost more than any possible gains.[51] In some cases, IBM withdrew operations from countries rather than agree to government demands for local ownership.

In order to make a rational decision about the extent of ownership, management must evaluate the extent to which total control is important to the success of its international marketing activities. Often full ownership may be a desirable, but not a necessary, prerequisite for international success. At other times it may be essential, particularly when strong links exist within the corporation. Interdependencies between and among local operations and headquarters may be so strong that nothing short of total coordination will result in an acceptable benefit to the firm as a whole.[52]

Increasingly, however, the international environment is hostile to full ownership by multinational firms. Government action through outright legal restrictions or discriminatory actions is making the option less attractive. There seems to be a distinct "liability of foreignness" to which multinational firms are exposed. Such disadvantages can result from government resentment of greater opportunities by multinational firms. But they can also be the consequence of corporate actions such as the decision to have many expatriates rotate in top management positions, which may weaken the standing of a subsidiary and its local employees.[53]

To overcome market barriers abroad, firms can either build competitive capabilities from scratch or acquire them from local owners.[54] The choice is often to accept a reduction in control or to lose the opportunity to operate efficiently in a country. In addition to formal action by the government, the general conditions in the market may make it advisable for the firm to join forces with local entities.

A Comprehensive View of International Expansion

The central driver of internationalization is the level of managerial commitment. This commitment will grow gradually from an awareness of international potential to the adaptation of international business as a strategic business direction. It will be influenced by the information, experience, and perception of management, which in turn is shaped by motivations, concerns, and the activities of change agents.

Management's commitment and its view of the capabilities of the firm will then trigger various international business activities, which can range from indirect exporting and importing to more direct involvement in the global market. Eventually, the firm may then expand further through measures such as joint ventures, strategic alliances, or foreign direct investment.

All of the developments, processes, and factors involved in the overall process of going international are linked to each other. A comprehensive view of these links is presented schematically in Figure 11.4.

FIGURE 11.4

A Comprehensive Model of International Market Entry and Development

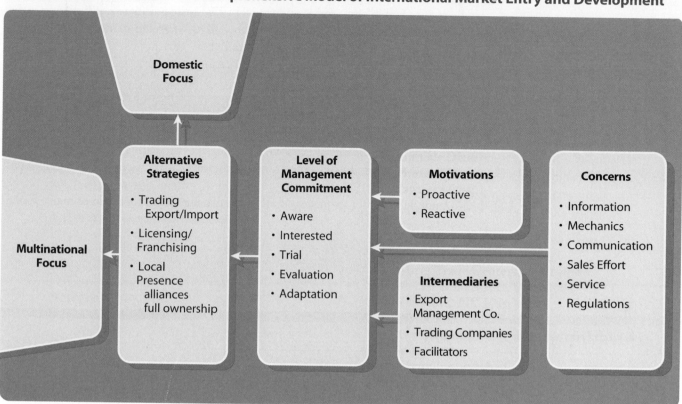

Summary

Firms do not become experienced in international business overnight, but rather progress gradually through an internationalization process. The process is triggered by different motivations to go abroad. The motivations can be proactive or reactive. Proactive motivations are initiated by aggressive management, whereas reactive motivations are the defensive response of management to environmental changes and pressures. Firms that are primarily stimulated by proactive motivations are more likely to enter international business and succeed.

In going abroad, firms encounter multiple problems and challenges, which range from a lack of information to mechanics and documentation. In order to gain assistance in its initial international experience, the firm can make use of either intermediaries or facilitators. Intermediaries are outside companies that actively participate in an international transaction. They are export management companies or trading companies. In order for these intermediaries to perform international business functions properly, however, they must be compensated. This will result in a reduction of profits.

International facilitators do not participate in international business transactions, but they contribute knowledge and information. Increasingly, facilitating roles are played by private sector groups, such as industry associations, banks, accountants, or consultants, and by universities and federal, state, and local government authorities.

Apart from exporting and importing, alternatives for international business entry are licensing, franchising, and local presence. The basic advantage of licensing is that it does not involve capital investment or knowledge of foreign markets. Its major disadvantage is that licensing agreements typically have time limits, are often proscribed by foreign governments, and may result in creating a competitor. The use of franchising as a means of expansion into foreign markets has increased dramatically. Franchisors must learn to strike a balance between adapting to local environments and standardizing to the degree necessary to maintain international recognizability.

Full ownership is becoming more unlikely in many markets as well as industries, and the firm has to look at alternative approaches. The main alternative is interfirm cooperation, in which the firm joins forces with other business entities, possibly even a foreign government. In some cases, when the firm may not want to make a direct investment, it will offer its management expertise for sale in the form of management contracts.

Questions for Discussion

1. Why is management commitment so important to export success?
2. Explain the benefits that international sales can have for domestic business activities.
3. Comment on the stance that "licensing is really not a form of international involvement because it requires no substantial additional effort on the part of the licensor."
4. What is the purpose of export intermediaries?
5. How can an export intermediary avoid circumvention by a client or customer?
6. The rate of expropriation has been ten times greater for a joint venture with the host government than for a 100 percent U.S.-owned subsidiary, according to a study on expropriation since 1960. Is this not contrary to logic?
7. Comment on the observation that "a joint venture may be a combination of Leonardo da Vinci's brain and Carl Lewis's legs; one wants to fly, the other insists on running."
8. Why would an internationalizing company opt for a management contract over other modes of operation? Relate your answer especially to the case of hospitality companies such as Hyatt, Marriott, and Sheraton.

Internet Exercises

1. What forms of export assistance are offered by the Small Business Administration and the Export-Import Bank (consult their web sites at http://www.sba.gov and http://www.exim.gov.)?
2. Prepare a one-page memo to a foreign company introducing your product or service. Include a contact listing of ten businesses in foreign countries looking to import your particular product. Include the company name, address, and other contact information along with special requirements of the company you note from their posting of an offer to buy. Cite the sources from which you prepared your list.

Sample sources of trade leads:

http://www.business-europa.co.uk
http://www.tradenet.gov
http://mnileads.com

3. Working conditions in subcontract factories have come under criticism for wages and working conditions. Using Nike's response (see http://www.nike.com/nikebiz/nikebiz.shtml?page=25), assess the type of criticisms heard and the ability of a company to address them.

Take a Stand

China's trade and investment activities have grown substantially since the 1980s. Yet there are many who question the ethics of supporting a regime that has systematically ignored important rights. Many organizations have called for global customers to boycott goods made in China. These groups cite basic human rights violations including China's lack of employment standards and rights, its oppressive policy toward Tibet, and its forced abortion and sterilization programs as reasons why Chinese goods should be boycotted.

For Discussion

Conversely, others believe the best way to improve human rights in China and bring about democracy is through trade and investment. Foreign direct investment and multinational corporations operating in China are portrayed as important engines for change that will generate reformation of the government and improve Chinese peoples' lives. Nevertheless, does this stance ultimately send the message that economic priorities trump ethical concerns, or can they coexist?

Globalization

*The Strategic
Planning Process*

Strategic
Planning

Learning Objectives

- To outline the process of strategic planning in the context of the global marketplace

- To examine both the external and internal factors that determine the conditions for development of strategy and resource allocation

- To illustrate how best to utilize the environmental conditions within the competitive challenges and resources of the firm to develop effective programs

- To suggest how to achieve a balance between local and regional/global priorities and concerns in the implementation of strategy

The Changing Landscape of Global Markets

Global markets for everything from cars to telecommunications have witnessed major consolidations in the last five years. Not only are companies playing the global game by being in all major, and even minor, markets of the world, but they are doing so by acquiring local players.

The beer industry has become the latest global battleground. The business has been more fragmented than most: the top four brewing companies have had less than one third of the global market (whereas the top four spirits makers easily control more than half of their markets). That is changing rapidly and dramatically as companies are pushing to acquire strong local brands and their distribution networks to push their already established global brands.

A major change occurred in 2002, when Anheuser-Busch lost its position as the number one company in the world for the first time in 50 years. The new leader is South African Breweries, which acquired Miller Brewing Company and a 21 percent market share in the United States. Anheuser-Busch is still in control of nearly half of U.S. sales but it has identified the need to expand globally as well. For example, in China (which boasts the second largest beer market in the world), Anheuser-Busch has increased its share to 9.9 percent in Tsingtao, China's largest brewery. In Mexico, Anheuser-Busch owns 50 percent of Grupo Modelo, and in Argentina and Chile, it has a share of the CCU brewery. Increasingly, however, its expansion has been challenged by its competitors. In Italy, SAB Miller beat Anheuser-Busch by acquiring its former licensee Birra Peron to make its first major Western European move.

After years of standing on the sidelines, Dutch Heinekin has been active in acquiring companies around the world. In Egypt, it

World's Largest Breweries		
Production (billions of liters)	1998	2002
SAB Miller (South Africa)	46.8	132.5
Anheuser-Busch (United States)	117.2	128.8
Heineken (Holland)	58.2	91.7
Interbrew (Belgium)	34.2	84.4
American Beverage (Brazil)	42.4	72.9
Carlsberg (Denmark)	35.3	55.6
Scottish & Newcastle (United Kingdom)	18.3	45.6
Coors (United States)	26.0	39.6
Grupo Modelo (Mexico)	32.2	38.4
Kirin (Japan)	40.0	36.7

bought a majority stake in Al Ahram Beverages to use the company's fruit-flavored, nonalcoholic beverages as an entry to other Muslim markets. The next major battleground for Heineken and its competitors will be Central and Eastern Europe, where Heineken acquired Karlovacka Pivovar in Croatia, and Austrian BBAG, which has breweries in the Czech Republic, Hungary, Poland, and Romania.

With the recent changes, the ten largest companies now control 51 percent of the world markets, with the top 40 in charge of 79 percent. With the five largest companies increasing their production at a much faster rate than those following them, further consolidation of power is to be expected.

Heineken's World*

Holland: Heineken, Amstel, Kylian, Lingen's Blond, Murphy's Irish Red

United States: Heineken, Amstel, Paulaner, Moretti
China: Tiger, Reeb
Singapore: Heineken, Tiger
France: Heineken, Amstel, Buckler, Desperados
Italy: Heineken, Amstel, Birra Moretti
Poland: Heineken, Zywiec
Kazakhstan: Tian Shan, Amstel
Panama: Soberana, Panama
Egypt: Fayrouz
Israel: Maccabee, Gold Star
Nigeria: Amstel Malta, Maltina

*Heineken operates in 170 countries and this presentation is a sampling of that presence.

Sources: "Waking Up Heineken," *Business Week,* September 8, 2003, 68–72; "In Search of Froth: Beer in Europe," *The Economist,* June 28, 2003, 89; "Anheuser-Busch Raises Its Stake in Chinese Brewer," *Wall Street Journal,* June 30, 2003, A24; "Panimoiden Keskittyminen on Kiivaassa Vauhdissa," *Kauppalehti,* June 10, 2003, 14–15; and "Heineken Brews Comeback Plans for U.S. Market," *Wall Street Journal,* May 27, 2003, B1.

Globalization

The transformations in the world marketplace have been extensive and, in many cases, rapid. Local industries operating in protected national economies are challenged by integrated global markets contested by global players. National borders are becoming increasingly irrelevant as liberalization and privatization take place. This has then led to such phenomena as the growing scale and mobility of the world's capital markets and many companies' ability to leverage knowledge and talent across borders.[1] Even the biggest companies in the biggest home markets cannot survive by taking their situation as a given if they are in global industries such as automobiles, banking, consumer electronics, entertainment, pharmaceuticals, publishing, travel services, home appliances, or beer as shown in the opening vignette for the chapter. Rather than seeking to maximize their share of the pie in home markets, they have to seek to maximize the size of the pie by having a presence in all of the major markets of the world. Companies from emerging markets, such as China, have entered the megamarkets of North America and Europe not only to gain necessary size but also to gain experience in competing against global players in their home markets.[2]

Globalization reflects a business orientation based on the belief that the world is becoming more homogeneous and that distinctions between national markets are not only fading but, for some products, will eventually disappear. As a result, companies need to globalize their international strategy by formulating it across markets to take advantage of underlying market, cost, environmental, and competitive factors.

As shown in Figure 12.1, globalization can be seen as the culmination of a process of international market entry and expansion. Before globalization, companies utilize to a great extent a country-by-country **multidomestic strategy** with each country organization operated as a profit center. Each national entity markets a range of dif-

FIGURE 12.1

Evolution of Global Strategy

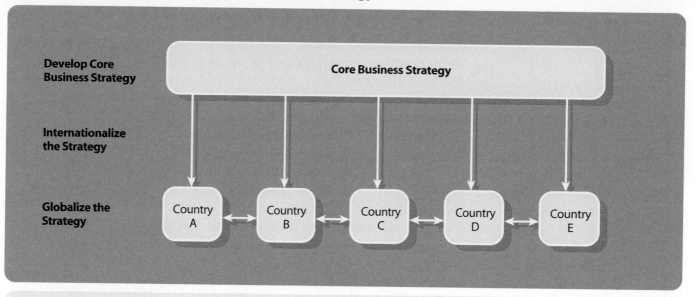

Source: George S. Yip, *Total Global Strategy II* (Upper Saddle River, NJ: Prentice Hall, 2002), 4.

ferent products and services targeted to different customer segments, utilizing different strategies with little or no coordination of operations between countries.

However, as national markets become increasingly similar and scale economies become increasingly important, the inefficiencies of duplicating product and program development and manufacture in each country become more apparent and the pressure to leverage resources and coordinate activities across borders gains urgency. Similarly, the number of customers operating globally, as well as the same or similar competitors faced throughout the major markets, add to the need for strategy coordination and integration.

GLOBALIZATION DRIVERS[3]

Both external and internal factors will create the favorable conditions for development of strategy and resource allocation on a global basis. These factors can be divided into market, cost, environmental, and competitive factors.

Market Factors

The world customer identified by Ernst Dichter more than 30 years ago has gained new meaning today.[4] For example, Kenichi Ohmae has identified a new group of consumers emerging in the triad of North America, Europe, and the Far East whom marketers can treat as a single market with the same spending habits.[5] Approximately 600 million in number, these consumers have similar educational backgrounds, income levels, lifestyles, use of leisure time, and aspirations. One reason given for the similarities in their demand is a level of purchasing power (ten times greater than that of LDCs or NICs) that translates into higher diffusion rates for certain products. Another reason is that developed infrastructures—diffusion of telecommunications and an abundance of paved roads—lead to attractive markets for other products.

Similarities in demand conditions throughout the triad facilitates product design and the transferability of other program elements.

At the same time, channels of distribution are becoming more global; that is, a growing number of retailers are now showing great flexibility in their strategies for entering new geographic markets.[6] Some are already world powers (e.g., Benetton and McDonald's), whereas others are pursuing aggressive growth (e.g., ALDI, Toys 'Я' Us, and IKEA). Also noteworthy are cross-border retail alliances, which expand the presence of retailers to new markets quite rapidly.

Technology is changing the landscape of markets as well. In the area of personal financial services, for instance, 95 percent of the $300 billion market is currently captured by nationally based competitors. By 2005, this market is likely to double and will be accessible to global competitors via transplants or electronic distribution.

Cost Factors

Avoiding cost inefficiencies and duplication of effort are two of the most powerful globalization drivers. A single-country approach may not be large enough for the local business to achieve all possible economies of scale and scope as well as synergies, especially given the dramatic changes in the marketplace. Take, for example, pharmaceuticals. In the 1970s, developing a new drug cost about $16 million and took four years. The drug could be produced in Britain or the United States and eventually exported. Now, developing a drug costs from $500 million to $1 billion and takes as long as 12 years, with competitive efforts close behind. For the leading companies, annual R&D budgets can run to $5 billion. Only a global product for a global market can support that much risk.[7] Size has become a major asset, which partly explains the many mergers and acquisitions in industries such as aerospace, pharmaceuticals, and telecommunications. The paper industry underwent major regional consolidation between 1998 and 2000, as shown in Table 12.1. International Paper Company won Champion International in a tense bidding contest with Finland's UPM-Kymmene to protect its home market position. As a result, UPM immediately targeted Sappi Ltd., a South African magazine-paper maker with significant North American operations and two U.S.-based paper makers, Mead and Bowater.[8] In the heavily contested consumer goods sectors, launching a new brand may cost as much as $100 million, meaning that companies such as Unilever and Procter & Gamble are not necessarily going to spend precious resources on one-country projects.

In many cases, expanded market participation and activity concentration can accelerate the accumulation of learning and experience. General Electric's philosophy is to be first or second in the world in a business or to get out. This can be seen, for example, in its global effort to develop premium computed tomography (CT), a diagnostic scanning system. GE swapped its consumer electronics business with the French Thomson for Thomson's diagnostic imaging business. At the same time, GE established GE Medical Systems Asia in Tokyo, anchored on Yokogawa Medical Systems, which is 75 percent owned by GE.

Environmental Factors

As shown earlier in this text, government barriers have fallen dramatically in the last years to further facilitate the globalization of markets and the activities of companies within them. For example, the forces pushing toward a pan-European market are very powerful: The increasing wealth and mobility of European consumers (favored by the relaxed immigration controls), the accelerating flow of information across borders, the introduction of new products where local preferences are not well established, and

TABLE 12.1 Consolidation in the Paper Industry 1998–2002

Acquirer	Target	Value	Date Announced
Weyerhaeuser (United States)	**Willamette Industries**	$6.2 billion	1/28/02
MeadWestvaco (United States)	**Mead** (United States)	$3.2 billion	8/29/01
Norske Skogindustrier (Norway)	**Fletcher Challenge Paper** (New Zealand)	$2.5 billion	4/03/00
Smurfir-Stone (United States)	**St. Laurent Paperboard** (Canada)	$1.0 billion	2/23/00
Stora Enso (Finland)	**Consolidated Papers** (United States)	$3.9 billion	2/22/00
Int'l Paper (United States)	**Champion Int'l** (United States)	$7.3 billion	5/12/00
Abitibi-Consol. (Canada)	**Donohue** (Canada)	$4.0 billion	2/11/00
Int'l Paper (United States)	**Union Camp** (United States)	$5.9 billion	11/24/98
Stora (Sweden)*	**Enso** (Finland)*	Undisclosed	6/2/98

*Merger of equals

Sources: "Weyerhauser Company and Willamette Industries Sign Definitive Merger Agreement," Willamette Industries, Inc., press release, January 28, 2002, http://www.wii.com; "Paper Merger Attains Size Without Adding Huge Debt," Wall Street Journal, August 30, 2001, B4; "International Paper Has Its Work Cut Out For It," Wall Street Journal, May 15, 2000, A4; and "Stora Enso to Buy Consolidated Papers," Wall Street Journal, February 23, 2000, A3, A8. See also, http://storaenso.com; http://www.internationalpaper.com; http://www.upm-kymmene.com; http://www.abicon.com and http://www.weyerhaeuser.com.

the publicity surrounding the integration process itself all promote globalization.[9] Also, the resulting removal of physical, fiscal, and technical barriers is indicative of the changes that are taking place around the world on a greater scale.

At the same time, rapid technological evolution is contributing to the process. For example, Ford Motor Company is able to accomplish its globalization efforts by using new communications methods, such as teleconferencing intranet and CAD/CAM links, as well as travel, to manage the complex task of meshing car companies on different continents.[10] Newly emerging markets will benefit from advanced communications by being able to leapfrog stages of economic development. Places that until recently were incommunicado in China, Vietnam, Hungary, or Brazil are rapidly acquiring state-of-the-art telecommunications that will let them foster both internal and external development.[11]

A new group of global players is taking advantage of today's more open trading regions and newer technologies. **Mininationals,** or **born globals** (newer companies with sales between $200 million and $1 billion), are able to serve the world from a handful of manufacturing bases, compared with having to build a plant in every country as the established multinational corporations once had to do. Their smaller bureaucracies have also allowed these mininationals to move swiftly to seize new markets and develop new products—a key to global success.[12] This phenomenon is highlighted in Focus on Entrepreneurship.

Competitive Factors

Many industries are already dominated by global competitors that are trying to take advantage of the three sets of factors mentioned earlier. To remain competitive, a company may have to be the first to do something or to be able to match or preempt competitors' moves. Products are now introduced, upgraded, and distributed at rates unimaginable a decade ago. Without a global network, carefully researched ideas may

Focus On ⬇

Mininationals Leap into Global Markets

"We were nobody—too small for people to pay attention to us," recalls Hong Lu of his first attempts to take his fledgling California-based company, Unitech Telecom, into Beijing in 1993. China, with its population of 1.3 billion and extremely low teledensity, seemed the optimal market for Unitech's telecommunications-access equipment. Locked out by towering multinationals Motorola, Lucent, and Siemens, Lu quickly shifted his attention to Hangzhou, a midcoastal university city. With its population of 1 million, Hangzhou offered a solid customer base, an educated workforce, and easier access to government-owned phone companies. Within a year, Unitech posted sales of almost $4 million into China. Following a merger with Starcom, a telecommunications software company with manufacturing facilities in China, revenues skyrocketed. Today, UTStarcom generates sales in excess of $165 million a year and has expanded into Taiwan, the Philippines, South Korea, and Japan.

UTStarcom is a prime example of the small- to medium-sized firms that are reinventing the global corporation. Termed *mininationals,* their success proves that sheer size is no longer a buffer against competition, especially in markets that demand specialized or customized products. Electronic process technology allows mininationals to compete on price and quality—often with greater flexibility than larger rivals. In today's open trading regions, they are able to serve the world from a handful of manufacturing bases. Less red tape means that they are able to move swiftly in seizing new markets and developing new products, typically in focused markets. In many cases, these new markets were developed by the mininationals themselves. For example, Symbol Technologies, Inc., of Holtsville, New York, invented handheld laser scanners and now dominates this field. In a sector that did not exist in 1988, Cisco Systems Inc, of San Jose, California, grew from a mininational into a multinational corporation with 36,786 employees in more than 430 offices in 60 countries. Through its partnerships, Cisco sells its computer networking systems into a total of 115 countries. Other mininationals continue to focus on their core products and services, growing and excelling at what they do best. An empirical study of exporting firms established in the last ten years found that more than half could be classified as born globals.

The lessons from these new generation global players are to: (1) keep focused and concentrate on being number one or number two in a technology niche; (2) stay lean by having small headquarters to save on costs and to accelerate decision making; (3) take ideas and technologies to and from wherever they can be found; (4) take advantage of employees regardless of nationality to globalize thinking; and (5) solve customers' problems by involving them rather than pushing standardized solutions on them. As a result of being flexible, they are able to weather storms, such as the Asian crisis, better by changing emphases in the geographical operations.

Sources: China Success Story at http://www.utstar.com, accessed September 25, 2003; Øystein Moen and Per Servais, "Born Global or Gradual Global? Examining the Export Behavior of Small and Medium-Sized Enterprises," *Journal of International Marketing* 10, 3 (2002): 49–72; Øystein Moen, "The Born Globals: A New Generation of Small European Exporters," *International Marketing Review* 19, 2 (2002): 156–175; Gary Knight, "Entrepreneurship and Marketing Strategy: The SME Under Globalization," *Journal of International Marketing* 8, 2 (2000): 12–32; "Corporate Profile," *Cisco Systems 2000 Annual Report* at http://www.cisco.com; Grossman, "Great Leap into China," *Inc. Magazine,* October 15, 1999; "Turning Small into an Advantage," *Business Week,* July 13, 1998, 42–44; Michael W. Rennie, "Born Global," *The McKinsey Quarterly* (number 4, 1993): 45–52; "Mininationals Are Making Maximum Impact," *Business Week,* September 6, 1993, 66–69.

be picked off by other global players. This is what Procter & Gamble and Unilever did to Kao's Attack concentrated detergent, which they mimicked and introduced into the United States and Europe before Kao could react.

With the triad markets often both flat in terms of growth and fiercely competitive, many global marketers are looking for new markets and for new product categories for growth. Nestlé, for example, is setting its sights on consumer markets in fast-growing Asia, especially China, and has diversified into pharmaceuticals by acquiring Alcon and by becoming a major shareholder in the world's number one cosmetics company, France's L'Oreal.[13] Between 1985 and 2000, Nestlé spent $26 billion on acquisitions, and another $18 billion from 2001 to 2002.[13]

Market presence may be necessary to execute global strategies and to prevent others from having undue advantage in unchallenged markets. Caterpillar faced mounting global competition from Komatsu but found out that strengthening its products and operations was not enough to meet the challenge. Although Japan was a small part of the world market, as a secure home base (no serious competitors), it generated 80 percent of Komatsu's cash flow. To put a check on its major global competitor's market share and cash flow, Caterpillar formed a heavy-equipment joint venture with Matsushita to serve the Japanese market.[14] Similarly, when Unilever tried to acquire Richardson-Vicks in the United States, Procter & Gamble saw this as a threat to its home market position and outbid its archrival for the company.

The Outcome

The four globalization drivers have affected countries and sectors differently. While some industries are truly globally contested, such as paper and pulp and soft drinks, some sectors, such as government services, are still quite closed and will open up as a decades-long evolution. Commodities and manufactured goods are already in a globalized state, while many consumer goods are accelerating toward more globalization. Similarly, the leading trading nations of the world display far more openness than low-income countries, thus advancing the state of globalization in general. The expansion of the global trade arena is summarized in Figure 12.2. The size of markets estimated to be global by the turn of the century is well over $21 billion, boosted by new sectors and markets becoming available. For example, while financially unattractive in the short- to medium term, low-income markets may be attractive for learning the business climate, developing relationships, and building brands for the future. Hewlett-Packard, through its e-Inclusion initiative, is looking at speech interfaces for the Internet, solar applications, and cheap devices that connect with the Web.[15]

FIGURE 12.2

The Global Landscape by Industry and Market

Country	Industry: Commodities and scale-driven goods	Consumer goods and locally delivered goods and services	Government services	
Triad*	Old arena Globalized in 1980s			More globalized
Emerging countries†	Growing arena Globally contestable today			
Low-income countries‡	Closed arena Still blocked or lacking significant opportunity			Less globalized

Global ←——————————————————————————————→ Local

* 30 OECD countries from North America, Western Europe, and Asia; Japan and Australia included
† 70 countries with middle income per capita, plus China and India
‡ 100 Countries of small absolute size and low income per capita

Source: Adapted and updated from Jagdish N. Sheth and Atul Parkatiyar, "The Antecedents and Consequences of Integrated Global Marketing," *International Marketing Review* 18, 1 (2001): 16–29; and Jane Fraser and Jeremy Oppenheim, "What's New About Globalization?" *The McKinsey Quarterly* 2 (1997), 173.

Leading companies by their very actions drive the globalization process. There is no structural reason why soft drinks should be at a more advanced stage of globalization while beer and spirits remain more local except for the opportunistic behavior of Coca-Cola. Similarly, Nike and Reebok have driven their business in a global direction by creating global brands, a global customer segment, and a global supply chain. By creating a single online trading exchange for all of their parts and suppliers, General Motors, Ford, and DaimlerChrysler created a worldwide market of $240 billion in automotive components.[16]

The Strategic Planning Process

Given the opportunities and challenges provided by the new realities of the marketplace, decision makers have to engage in strategic planning to match markets with products and other corporate resources more effectively and efficiently to strengthen the company's long-term competitive advantage. While the process has been summarized as a sequence of steps in Figure 12.3, many of the stages can occur in parallel. Furthermore, feedback as a result of evaluation and control may restart the process at any stage.

It has been shown that for globally committed marketers, formal strategic planning contributes to both financial performance and nonfinancial objectives.[17] These benefits include raising the efficacy of new-product launches, cost-reduction efforts, and improving product quality and market-share performance. Internally, these efforts increase cohesion and improve understanding of different units' points of view.

UNDERSTANDING AND ADJUSTING THE CORE STRATEGY

The planning process has to start with a clear definition of the business for which strategy is to be developed. Generally, the strategic business unit (SBU) is the unit around which decisions are based. In practice, SBUs represent groupings with product-market similarities based on: (1) needs or wants to be met; (2) end-user customers to be targeted; or (3) the good or service used to meet the needs of specific customers. For a global company such as Black & Decker, the options may be to define the business to be analyzed as the home improvement business, the do-it-yourself business, or the power tool business. Ideally, each of these SBUs should have primary responsibility and authority in managing its basic business functions.

This phase of the planning process requires the participation of executives from different functions, especially marketing, production, finance, logistics, and procurement. Geographic representation should be from the major markets or regions as well as from the smaller, yet emerging, markets. With appropriate members, the committee can focus on product and markets as well as competitors whom they face in different markets, whether they are global, regional, or purely local. Heading this effort should be an executive with highest-level experience in regional or global markets. For example, one global firm called on the president of its European operations to come back to headquarters to head the global planning effort. This effort calls for commitment by the company itself both in calling on the best talent to participate in the planning effort and later in implementing their proposals.

FIGURE 12.3

Global Strategy Formulation

The authors appreciate the contributions of Robert M. Grant in the preparation of this figure.

It should be noted that this assessment against environmental realities may mean a dramatic change in direction and approach. For example, the once-separate sectors of computing and mobile telephony will be colliding and the direction of future products is still uncertain. The computer industry believes in miniaturizing the general-purpose computer, while the mobile-phone industry believes in adding new features (such as photo-messaging, gaming, and location-based information) to its existing products.[18] The joint venture between Ericsson and Sony aims at taking advantage of this trend, something that neither party can do on its own.

Market and Competitive Analysis

Planning on a country-by-country basis can result in spotty worldwide market performance. The starting point for global strategic planning is to understand the underlying forces that determine business success are common to the different countries in which the firm competes. Planning processes that focus simultaneously across a broad range of markets provide global marketers with tools to help balance risks, resource requirements, competitive economies of scale, and profitability to gain stronger long-term positions.[19] On the demand side this requires an understanding of the common features of customer requirements and choice factors. In terms of competition, the key is to understand the structure of the global industry in order to identify the forces that will drive competition and determine profitability.[20]

For Ford Motor Company, strategy begins not with individual national markets, but with understanding trends and sources of profit in the global automobile market. What are the trends in world demand? What are the underlying trends in lifestyles and transportation patterns that will shape customer expectations and preferences with respect to safety, economy, design, and performance? What is the emerging structure of the industry, especially with regard to consolidation among both auto makers and their suppliers? What will determine the intensity of competition among the different auto makers? The level of excess capacity (currently about 40 percent in the worldwide auto industry) is likely to be a key influence.[21] If competition is likely to intensify, which companies will emerge the winners? An understanding of scale economies, state of technology, and the other factors that determine cost efficiency is likely to be critically important.

Internal Analysis

Organizational resources have to be used as a reality check for any strategic choice in that they determine a company's capacity for establishing and sustaining competitive advantage within global markets. Industrial giants with deep pockets may be able to establish a presence in any market they wish, while more thinly capitalized companies may have to move cautiously. Human resources may also present a challenge for market expansion. A survey of multinational corporations revealed that good marketing managers, skilled technicians, and production managers were especially difficult to find. This difficulty is further compounded when the search is for people with cross-cultural experience to run future regional operations.[22]

At this stage it is imperative that the company assess its own readiness for the moves necessary. This means a rigorous assessment of organizational commitment to global or regional expansion, as well as an assessment of the good's readiness to face the competitive environment. In many cases this has meant painful decisions to focus on certain industries and to leave others. For example, Nokia, one of the world's largest manufacturer of cellular phones, started its rise in the industry when a decision was made at the company in 1992 to focus on digital cellular phones and to sell off dozens of other product lines (such as PCs, automotive tires, and toilet tissue). By focusing its efforts on this line, the company was able to bring new products to market quickly, build scale economies into its manufacturing, and concentrate on its customers, thereby communicating a commitment to their needs. Nokia's current 40 percent share allows it the best global visibility of and by the market.[23]

FORMULATING GLOBAL MARKETING STRATEGY

The first step in the formulation of global strategy is the choice of competitive strategy to be employed followed by the choice of country markets to be entered or to be penetrated further.

Choice of Competitive Strategy

In dealing with the global markets, the manager has three general choices of strategies, as shown in Figure 12.4: (1) cost leadership; (2) differentiation, and (3) focus.[24] A focus strategy is defined by its emphasis on a single industry segment within which the orientation may be either toward low cost or differentiation. Any one of these strategies can be pursued on a global or regional basis, or the manager may decide to mix and match strategies as a function of market or product dimensions.

FIGURE 12.4

Competitive Strategies

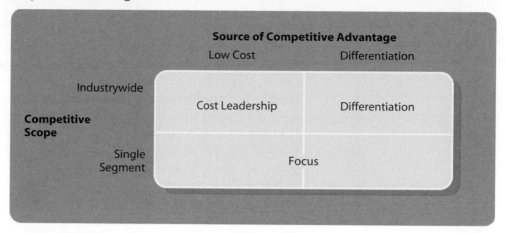

Source: Michael Porter, *Competitive Advantage* (New York: The Free Press, 1987), ch. 1.

In pursuing **cost leadership,** the company offers an identical product or service at a lower cost than competition. This often means investment in scale economies and strict control of costs, such as overheads, research and development, and logistics. **Differentiation,** whether it is industrywide or focused on a single segment, takes advantage of the manager's real or perceived uniqueness on elements such as design or after-sales service. It should be noted, however, that a low-price, low-cost strategy does not imply a commodity situation.[25] Although Japanese, U.S., and European technical standards differ, mobile phone manufacturers like Motorola and Nokia design their phones to be as similar as possible to hold down manufacturing costs. As a result, they can all be made on the same production line, allowing the manufacturers to shift rapidly from one model to another to meet changes in demand and customer requirements. In the case of IKEA, the low-price approach is associated with clear positioning and a unique brand image focused on a clearly defined target audience of "young people of all ages." Similarly, companies that opt for high differentiation cannot forget the monitoring of costs. One common denominator of consumers around the world is their quest for value for their money. With the availability of information increasing and levels of education improving, customers are poised to demand even more of their suppliers.

Most global companies combine high differentiation with cost containment to enter markets and to expand their market shares. Flexible manufacturing systems using mostly standard components and total quality management, reducing the occurrence of defects, are allowing companies to customize an increasing amount of their production, while at the same time saving on costs. Global activities will in themselves permit the exploitation of scale economies not only in production but also in marketing activities, such as promotion.

Country-Market Choice

A global strategy does not imply that a company should serve the entire globe. Critical choices relate to the allocation of a company's resources among different countries and segments. The usual approach is first to start with regions and further split the analysis by country. Many managers use multiple levels of regional groupings to follow the organizational structure of the company, e.g., splitting Europe into northern, central, and southern regions, which display similarities in demographic and behavioral traits. An important consideration is that data may be more readily available if existing structures and frameworks are used.[26]

Various **portfolio models** have been proposed as tools for this analysis. They typically involve two measures—internal strength and external attractiveness.[27] As indicators of internal strength, the following variables have been used: relative market share, product fit, contribution margin, and market presence, which would incorporate the level of support by constituents as well as resources allocated by the company itself. Country attractiveness has been measured using market size, market growth rate, number and type of competitors, governmental regulation, as well as economic and political stability. An example of such a matrix is provided in Figure 12.5.

The 3 × 3 matrix on country attractiveness and company strength is applied to the European markets. Markets in the invest/grow position will require continued commitment by management in research and development, investment in facilities, and the training of personnel at the country level. In cases of relative weakness in growing markets, the company's position may have to be strengthened (through acquisitions or strategic alliances) or a decision to divest may be necessary.[28] For example, Procter & Gamble decided to pull out of the disposable diaper markets in Australia and New Zealand due to well-entrenched competition, international currency fluctuations, and importation of products from distant production facilities into the markets.[29]

FIGURE 12.5

Example of a Market-Portfolio Matrix

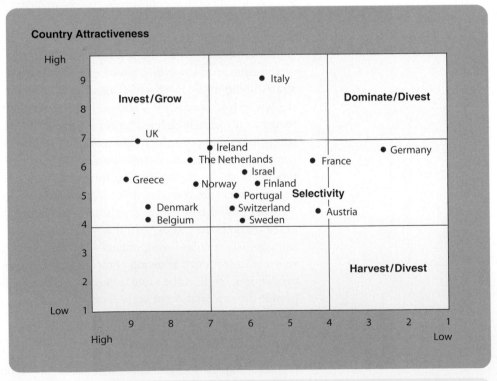

Source: Adapted from Gilbert D. Harrell and Richard O. Kiefer, "Multinational Market Portfolios in Global Strategy Development," *International Marketing Review* 10 (1993): 60–72.

It is critical that those involved in the planning endeavor consider potential competitors and their impact on the markets should they enter. For example, rather than license software for their next-generation mobile phones from Microsoft, the largest makers (with a combined market share of 80 percent of the mobile handset market) established a software consortium called Symbian to produce software of their own. This will allow the participants to try out many different designs without having to start from scratch every time or to be dependent on a potential competitor.[30]

Portfolios should also be used to assess market, product, and business interlinkages. This effort should utilize increasing market similarities through corporate adjustments by setting up appropriate strategic business units and the coordination of programs. The presentation in Figure 12.6 shows a market-product-business portfolio for a global food company, such as Nestlé. The interconnections are formed by common target markets served, sharing of research and development objectives, use of similar technologies, and the benefits that can be drawn from sharing common marketing experience. The example suggests possibilities within regions and between regions: frozen food both in Europe and the United States, and ice cream throughout the three megamarkets.

Finally, the portfolio assessment also needs to be put into a larger context. The Korean market and the Korean automakers may not independently warrant urgent action on the part of the leading companies. However, as a part of the global strategic

FIGURE 12.6

Example of Strategic Interconnectedness Matrix

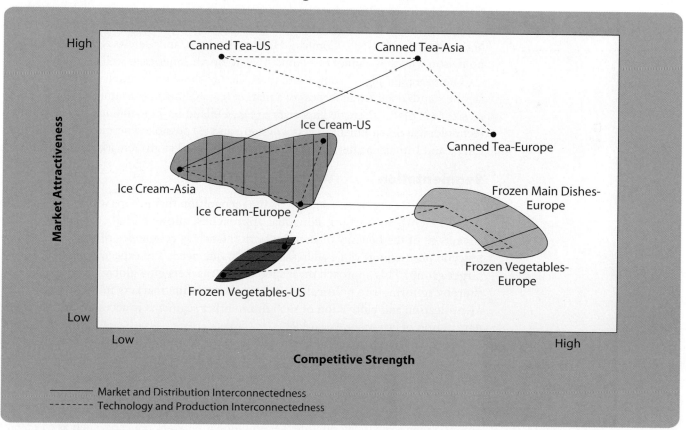

Source: Adapted from Susan P. Douglas and C. Samual Craig, "Global Portfolio Planning and Market Interconnectedness," *Journal of International Marketing* 4, 1 (1996): 93–110.

setting in the auto industry, both the market and its companies become critically important. Asia is expected to account for 70 percent of the growth in the world auto market between 2000 and 2004. Korea, along with China and Japan, is one of the three most important vehicle markets in Asia and can be considered an ideal platform for exporting to other parts of the continent. While Korean automakers, such as Daewoo Motor Company and Samsung Motors are heavily in debt, acquiring them would bring about the aforementioned benefits. Both Ford and GM want to acquire Daewoo to attain the top-producer position in the world. Renault, which wants to acquire Samsung, sees synergistic benefits in that Samsung relies heavily on technology from Nissan, acquired by Renault earlier. There are also other indirect benefits; whoever acquires Daewoo will gain the number one spot in Poland, long deemed crucial for tapping growth in Eastern Europe.[31] In choosing country markets, a company must make decisions beyond those relating to market attractiveness and company position. A market expansion policy will determine the allocation of resources among various markets. The basic alternatives are concentration on a small number of markets and diversification, which is characterized by growth in a relatively large number of markets.

The conventional wisdom of globalization requires a presence in all of the major triad markets of the world. In some cases, markets may not be attractive in their own right but may have some other significance, such as being the home market of the most demanding customers, thereby aiding in product development, or being the home market of a significant competitor (a preemptive rationale). For example, Procter & Gamble "rolled" its Charmin bath tissue into European markets in 2000 to counter an upsurge in European paper products sales by its global rival Kimberly-Clark.[32] European PC makers, such as Germany's Maxdata and Britain's Tiny both are taking aim at the U.S. market based on the premise that if they can compete with the big multinationals (Dell, Compaq, Hewlett-Packard, and Gateway) at home, there is no reason why they cannot be competitive in North America as well.[33]

Therefore, for global companies, three factors should determine country selection: (1) the stand-alone attractiveness of a market (e.g., China in consumer products due to its size); (2) global strategic importance (e.g., Finland in shipbuilding due to its lead in technological development in vessel design); and (3) possible synergies (e.g., entry into Latvia and Lithuania after success in the Estonian market given market similarities).

Segmentation

Effective use of segmentation, that is, the recognition that groups within markets differ sufficiently to warrant individual approaches, allows global companies to take advantage of the benefits of standardization (such as economies of scale and consistency in positioning) while addressing the unique needs and expectations of a specific target group. This approach means looking at markets on a global or regional basis, thereby ignoring the political boundaries that define markets in many cases. The identification and cultivation of such intermarket segments is necessary for any standardization of programs to work.[34]

The emergence of segments that span across markets is already evident in the world marketplace. Global companies have successfully targeted the teenage segment, which is converging as a result of common tastes in sports and music fueled by their computer literacy, travels abroad, and, in many countries, financial independence.[35] Furthermore, a media revolution is creating a common fabric of attitudes and tastes among teenagers. Today satellite TV and global network concepts such as MTV are both helping create this segment and providing global companies an access to the teen audience around the world. For example, Reebok used a global ad campaign to launch its Instapump line of sneakers in the United States, Germany, Japan, and 137 other countries. Given that teenagers around the world are concerned with social issues, particularly environmentalism, Reebok has introduced a new ecological climbing shoe made from recycled and environmentally sensitive materials. Similarly, two other distinct segments have been detected to be ready for a panregional approach, especially in Europe. One includes trendsetters who are wealthier and better educated and tend to value independence, refuse consumer stereotypes, and appreciate exclusive products. The second one includes Europe's businesspeople who are well-to-do, regularly travel abroad, and have a taste for luxury goods.

The greatest challenge for the global company is the choice of an appropriate base for the segmentation effort. The objective is to arrive at a grouping or groupings that are substantial enough to merit the segmentation effort (for example, there are nearly 230 million teenagers in the Americas, Europe, and the Asia-Pacific, with the teenagers of the Americas spending nearly $60 billion of their own money yearly) and are reachable as well by the marketing effort (for example, the majority of MTV's audience consists of teenagers).

The possible bases for segmentation are summarized in Figure 12.7. Managers have traditionally used environmental bases for segmentation. However, using geographic proximity, political system characteristics, economic standing, or cultural

FIGURE 12.7

Bases for Global Market Segmentation

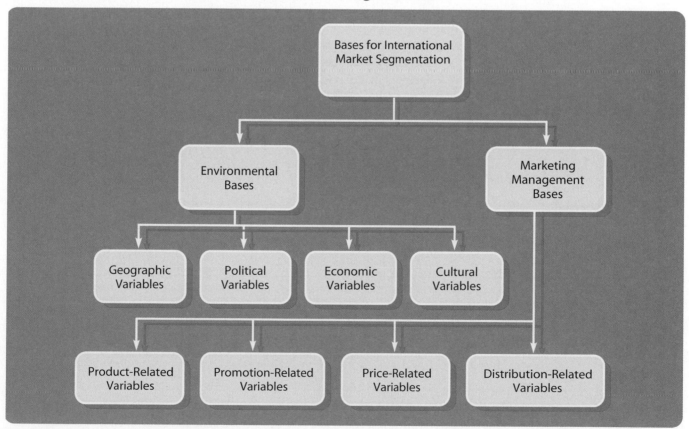

Source: Imad B. Baalbaki and Naresh K. Malhotra, "Marketing Management Bases for International Market Segmentation: An Alternate Look at the Standardization/Customization Debate," *International Marketing Review* 10, 1 (1993): 19–44.

traits as stand-alone bases may not provide relevant data for decision making. Using a combination of them, however, may produce more meaningful results. One of the segments pursued by global companies around the world is the middle-class family. Defining the composition of this global middle class is tricky, given the varying levels of development among nations in Latin America and Asia. However, some experts estimate that 23 percent of the world population enjoy middle-class lives, some 250 million in India alone.[36] Using household income alone may be quite a poor gauge of class. Income figures ignore vast differences in international purchasing power. Chinese consumers, for example, spend less than 5 percent of their total outlays on rent, transportation, and health, while a typical U.S. household spends 45 to 50 percent. Additionally, income distinctions do not reflect education or values—two increasingly important barometers of middle-class status. A global segmentation effort using cultural values is presented in Table 12.2.

It has also been proposed that markets that reflect a high degree of homogeneity with respect to marketing mix variables could be grouped into segments and thereby targeted with a largely standardized strategy.[37] Whether bases related to product, promotion, pricing, or distribution are used, their influence should be related to environmentally based variables. Product-related bases include the degree to which products are culture-based, which stage of the life cycle they occupy, consumption patterns, attitudes toward product attributes (such as country of origin), as well as consumption infrastructure (for example, telephone lines for modems). The growth of microwave sales, for example, has been surprising in low-income countries; however, microwaves have become status symbols and buying them more of an emotional issue. Many consumers in these markets also want to make sure they get the same product as available in developed markets, thereby eliminating the need in many cases to develop market-specific products. Adjustments will have to be made, however. Noticing that for reasons of status and space, many Asian consumers put their refrigerators in their living rooms, Whirlpool makes refrigerators available in striking colors such as red and blue.

With promotional variables, the consumers' values and norms may necessitate local solutions rather than opting for a regional approach. Similar influences may be exerted by the availability, or lack, of media vehicles or government regulations affecting

---

TABLE 12.2   **Global Segments Based on Cultural Values**

Segment	Characteristics	Geographics
Strivers	More likely to be men; place more emphasis on material and professional goals	One third of people in developing Asia; one quarter in Russia and developed Asia
Devouts	22 percent of adults; women more than men; tradition and duty are paramount	Africa, Asia, Middle East; least common in Europe
Altruists	18 percent of adults; larger portion of females; interested in social issues and welfare of society; older	Latin America and Russia
Intimates	15 percent of population; personal relationships and family	Europeans and North Americans
Fun Seekers	12 percent of population; youngest group	Developed Asia
Creatives	10 percent worldwide; strong interest in education, knowledge, and technology	Europe and Latin America

Source: Tom Miller, "Global Segments from 'Strivers' to 'Creatives,'" *Marketing News*, July 20, 1998, 11. See also http://www.ropercenter.uconn.edu.

promotional campaigns. On the pricing side, dimensions such as customers' price sensitivity may lead the manager to go after segments that insist on high quality despite high price in markets where overall purchasing power may be low to ensure global or regional uniformity in the marketing approach. Affordability is a major issue for customers, whose buying power may fall short for at least the time being. Offering only one option may exclude potential customers of the future who are not yet part of a targeted segment. Companies like Procter & Gamble and Gillette offer an array of products at different price points to attract customers and to keep them as they move up the income scale.[38] As distribution systems converge, for example, with the increase of global chains, markets can also be segmented by outlet types that reach environmentally defined groups. For example, toy manufacturers may look at markets not only in terms of numbers of children but by how effectively and efficiently they can be reached by global chains such as Toys 'Я' Us, as opposed to purely local outlets.

GLOBAL PROGRAM DEVELOPMENT

Decisions need to be made regarding how best to utilize the conditions set by globalization drivers within the framework of competitive challenges and the resources of the firm. Decisions will have to be made in four areas: (1) the degree of standardization in the product offering; (2) the marketing program beyond the product variable; (3) location and extent of value-adding activities; and (4) competitive moves to be made.

Product Offering

Globalization is not equal to standardization except in the case of the core product or the technology used to produce the product. The components used in a personal computer may to a large extent be standard, with the localization needed only in terms of the peripherals; for example, IBM produces 20 different keyboards for Europe alone. Product standardization may result in significant cost savings upstream. For example, Stanley Works' compromise between French preferences for handsaws with plastic handles and "soft teeth" and British preferences for wooden handles and "hard teeth"—to produce a plastic-handled saw with "hard teeth"—allowed consolidation for production and resulted in substantial economies of scale. At Whirlpool, use of common platforms allow European and American appliances to share technology and suppliers to lower cost and to streamline production. Many of the same components are used for products that eventually are marketed to segments looking for top-of-the-line or no-frills versions.[39] Similar differences in customer expectations have Bestfoods selling 15 versions of minestrone soup in Europe. Shania Twain's double CD *Up!* is an example of catering to multiple segments at the same time: both discs contain the same 19 tracks, but one with the effects pop fans appreciate, the other with country dimensions. A third disc with "an Asian Indian vibe" replaces the country disc in Europe.[40]

Marketing Approach

Nowhere is the need for the local touch as critical as in the execution of the marketing program. Uniformity is sought especially in elements that are strategic (e.g., positioning) in nature, whereas care is taken to localize necessary tactical elements (e.g., distribution). This approach has been called **glocalization.** For example, Unilever achieved great success with a fabric softener that used a common positioning, advertising theme, and symbol (a teddy bear) but differing brand names (e.g., Snuggle, Cajoline, Kuschel-weich, Mimosin, and Yumos) and bottle sizes. Gillette Co. scored a huge success with its Sensor shaver when it was rolled out in the United States, Europe, and

Japan with a common approach based on the premise that men everywhere want the same thing in a shave. Although the language of its TV commercials varied, the theme ("the best a man can get") and most of the footage were the same. A comparison of the marketing mix elements of two global marketers is given in Table 12.3. Notice that adaptation is present even at Coca-Cola, which is acknowledged to be one of the world's most global companies.

Location of Value-Added Activities

Globalization strives at cost reductions by pooling production or other activities or exploiting factor costs or capabilities within a system. Rather than duplicating activities in multiple, or even all, country organizations, a firm concentrates its activities. For example, Texas Instruments has designated a single design center and manufacturing organization for each type of memory chip. To reduce high costs and to be close to markets, it placed two of its four new $250-million memory chip plants in Taiwan and Japan. To reduce high R&D costs, it has entered into a strategic alliance with Hitachi. Many global companies have established R&D centers next to key production facilities so that concurrent engineering can take place every day on the factory floor. To enhance the global exchange of ideas, the centers have joint projects and are in real-time contact with each other.

The quest for cost savings and improved transportation methods has allowed some companies to concentrate customer service activities rather than having them present in all country markets. For example, Sony used to have repair centers in all of the Scandinavian countries and Finland; today, all service and maintenance activities are actually performed in a regional center in Stockholm, Sweden. Similarly, MasterCard has teamed up with Mascon Global in Chennai, India, where MasterCard's core processing functions—authorization, clearing, and settlement—for worldwide operations are handled.[41]

TABLE 12.3　　　　　**Globalization of the Marketing Mix**

Marketing Mix Elements	ADAPTATION		STANDARDIZATION	
	Full	Partial	Partial	Full
Product			N	C
Brand name			N	C
Product positioning		N		C
Packaging			C/N	
Advertising theme		N		C
Pricing		N	C	
Advertising copy	N			C
Distribution	N	C		
Sales promotion	N	C		
Customer service	N	C		

Key: C = Coca-Cola; N = Nestlé.

Source: John A. Quelch and Edward J. Hoff, "Customizing Global Marketing," *Harvard Business Review,* May–June 1986 (Boston: Harvard Business School Publishing Division), 61. Reprinted by permission of Harvard Business Review. Copyright © 1986 by the President and Fellows of Harvard College; all rights reserved.

To show commitment to a given market, both economically and politically, centers may be established in these markets. Philips Electronics has chosen China as their Asian center for global product research and development.[42]

Competitive Moves

A company with regional or global presence will not have to respond to competitive moves only in the market where it is being attacked. A competitor may be attacked in its profit sanctuary to drain its resources, or its position in its home market may be challenged.[43] When Fuji began cutting into Kodak's market share in the United States, Kodak responded by drastically increasing its penetration in Japan and created a new subsidiary to deal strictly with that market. In addition, Kodak solicited the support of the U.S. government to gain more access to Japanese distribution systems that Kodak felt were unfairly blocked from them.

Cross-subsidization, or the use of resources accumulated in one part of the world to fight a competitive battle in another, may be the competitive advantage needed for the long term.[44] One major market lost may mean losses in others, resulting in a domino effect. Jockeying for overall global leadership may result in competitive action in any part of the world. This has manifested itself in the form of "wars" between major global players in industries such as soft drinks, automotive tires, computers, and wireless phones. The opening of new markets often signals a new battle, as happened in the 1990s in Russia, in Mexico after the signing of the North American Free Trade Agreement, and in Vietnam after the normalization of relations with the United States. Given their multiple bases of operation, global companies may defend against a competitive attack in one country by countering in another country or, if the competitors operate in multiple businesses, countering in a different product category altogether. In the wireless phone category, the winners in the future will be those who can better attack less-mature markets with cheaper phones, while providing Internet-based devices elsewhere.[45]

In a study of how automakers develop strategies that balance the conflicting pressures of local responsiveness and regional integration in Europe, Japanese marketers were found to practice standardization in model offerings but selectively respond to differences in market conditions by manipulating prices and advertising levels.[46]

IMPLEMENTING GLOBAL PROGRAMS

The successful global companies of the future will be those that can achieve a balance between the local and the regional/global concerns. Companies that have tried the global concept have often run into problems with local differences. Especially early on, global programs were seen as standardized efforts dictated to the country organizations by headquarters. For example, when Coca-Cola reentered the Indian market in 1993, it invested most heavily in its Coke brand, using its typical global positioning, and had its market leadership slip to Pepsi. Recognizing the mistake, Coke reemphasized a popular local cola brand (Thums Up) and refocused the Coke brand advertising to be more relevant to the local Indian consumer.[47] In the past ten years, Coca-Cola has been acquiring local soft-drink brands (such as Inca Cola in Peru), which now account for 10 percent of company sales.[48]

Challenges

Pitfalls that handicap global programs and contribute to their suboptimal performance include market-related reasons, such as insufficient research and a tendency to overstandardize, as well as internal reasons, such as inflexibility in planning and implementation.

If a product is to be launched on a broader scale without formal research as to regional or local differences, the result may be failure. An example of this is Lego A/S, the Danish toy manufacturer, which decided to transfer sales promotional tactics successful in the U.S. market unaltered to other markets, such as Japan. This promotion included approaches such as "bonus packs" and gift promotions. However, Japanese consumers considered these promotions wasteful, expensive, and not very appealing.[49] Going too local has its drawbacks as well. With too much customization or with local production, the marketer may lose its import positioning. For example, when Miller Brewing Company started brewing Löwenbräu under license, the brand lost its prestigious import image. Often, the necessary research is conducted only after a program has failed to meet set objectives.

Globalization by design requires a balance between sensitivity to local needs and deployment of technologies and concepts globally. This means that neither headquarters nor independent country managers can alone call the shots. If country organizations are not part of the planning process, or if adoption is forced on them by headquarters, local resistance in the form of the **not-invented-here syndrome (NIH)** may lead to the demise of the global program or, worse still, to an overall decline in morale. Subsidiary resistance may stem from resistance to any idea originating from the outside or from valid concerns about the applicability of a concept to that particular market. Without local commitment, no global program will survive.

LOCALIZING GLOBAL MOVES

The successful global companies of the twenty-first century will be those that can achieve a balance between country managers and global product managers at headquarters. This balance may be achieved by a series of actions to improve a company's ability to develop and implement global strategy. These actions relate to management processes, organization structures, and overall corporate culture, all of which should ensure cross-fertilization within the firm.[50]

Management Processes

In the multidomestic approach, country organizations had very little need to exchange ideas. Globalization, however, requires transfer of information not only between headquarters and country organizations but also between the country organizations themselves. By facilitating the flow of information, ideas are exchanged and organizational values strengthened. Information exchange can be achieved through periodic meetings of marketing managers or through worldwide conferences to allow employees to discuss their issues and local approaches to solving them. IBM, for example, has a Worldwide Opportunity Council that sponsors fellowships for employees to listen to business cases from around the world and develop global platforms or solutions. IBM has found that some country organizations find it easier to accept input of other country organizations than that coming directly from headquarters.

Part of the preparation for becoming global has to be personnel interchange. Many companies encourage (or even require) mid-level managers to gain experience abroad during the early or middle stages of their careers. The more experience people have in working with others from different nationalities—getting to know other markets and surroundings—the better a company's global philosophy, strategy, and actions will be integrated locally.

The role of headquarters staff should be that of coordination and leveraging the resources of the corporation. For example, this may mean activities focused on combining good ideas that come from different parts of the company to be fed into global planning. Many global companies also employ world-class staffs whose role should be to consult subsidiaries by upgrading their technical skills and to focus their attention not only on local issues but also on those with global impact.

Globalization calls for the centralization of decision-making authority far beyond that of the multidomestic approach. Once a strategy has been jointly developed, headquarters may want to permit local managers to develop their own programs within specified parameters and subject to approval rather than forcing them to adhere strictly to the formulated strategy. For example, Colgate Palmolive allows local units to use their own approaches, but only if they can prove they can beat the global "benchmark" version. With a properly managed approval process, effective control can be exerted without unduly dampening a country manager's creativity.

Overall, the best approach against the emergence of the NIH syndrome is utilizing various motivational policies such as: (1) ensuring that local managers participate in the development of strategies and programs; (2) encouraging local managers to generate ideas for possible regional or global use; (3) maintaining a product portfolio that includes local as well as regional and global brands; and (4) allowing local managers control over their budgets so that they can respond to local customer needs and counter global competition (rather than depleting budgets by forcing them to participate only in uniform campaigns). Acknowledging this local potential, global companies can pick up successful brands in one country and make them cross-border stars. Since Nestlé acquired British candy maker Rowntree Mackintosh, it has increased its exports by 60 percent and made formerly local brands, such as After Eight Dinner mints, pan-European hits. When an innovation or a product is deemed to have global potential, rolling it out in other regions or worldwide becomes an important consideration.

Organization Structures

Various organization structures have emerged to support the globalization effort. Some companies have established global or regional product managers and their support groups at headquarters. Their task is to develop long-term strategies for product categories on a worldwide basis and to act as the support system for the country organizations. This matrix structure focused on customers, which has replaced the traditional country-by-country approach, is considered more effective in today's global marketplace according to companies that have adopted it.

Whenever a product group has global potential, firms such as Procter & Gamble, 3M, and Henkel create strategic-planning units to work on the programs. These units, such as 3M's EMATs (European Marketing Action Teams) consist of members from the country organizations that market the products, managers from both global and regional headquarters, as well as technical specialists.

To deal with the globalization of customers, companies such as Hewlett-Packard and DHL are extending national account management programs across countries, typically for the most important customers.[51] In a study of 165 multinational companies, 13 percent of their revenue came from global customers (revenue from all international customers was 46 percent). While relatively small, these 13 percent come from the most important customers, who cannot be ignored.[52] AT&T, for example, distinguishes between international and global customers and provides the global customers with special services including a single point of contact for domestic and international operations and consistent worldwide service. Executing **global account management** programs builds relationships not only with important customers but also allows for the development of internal systems and interaction.

Technology has allowed companies to take unique advantage of strengths that are present in different parts of the world. A powerful new business model for organizations may be emerging, as shown in Focus on e-Business.

Focus On ⬇

Taking Globalism to the Extremes

A new breed of high-tech companies is defying conventional wisdom about how corporations ought to operate. While most large companies have extensive worldwide operations, these new players aim to transcend nationality altogether. Some leading examples are included below:

Trend Micro

Having a computer-virus response center in low-cost Manila and six smaller centers scattered around the globe allows this American/Japanese/Taiwanese company to guarantee delivery of inoculations against major viruses in less than two hours. No rival has comparable reach.

Logitech International

With dual headquarters in Switzerland and Silicon Valley, Logitech competes effectively with Microsoft in computer peripherals. Its advantage is that the main manufacturing decisions are made in Taiwan, enabling the company to make quick decisions about whether to manufacture products in Chinese facilities or to farm them out.

Wipro

The company's vice-chairman is in the United States so he can work the client base in the largest market for technology services, but 17,000 out of 20,000 engineers and consultants are in India, where annual cost per employee is less than one fifth that of Silicon Valley.

Cognos

The Canadian/American company's international orientation has changed the way it makes software. In the past, it released different versions for each country. Currently, it ships business software, designed for multinational customers, that includes all the major languages, plus data on local currencies and tax regulations.

What is unique about these entities is that many operations are virtual. Top executives and core corporate functions are placed in different countries to gain a competitive edge through the availability of talent and capital, low cost, or proximity to their most important customers. To deal with the gaps between time zones and cultures, these companies operate like virtual computer networks. Thanks to the Internet, they can communicate in real time via e-mail, instant messaging, or videoconferencing.

However, the model is not without its challenges. Executives are separated by oceans and time zones, making it difficult to maintain basic communications and routines that traditional companies take for granted.

Sources: "Borders Are so 20th Century," *Business Week,* September 22, 2003, 68–73; Julian Birkinshaw and Tony Sheehan, "Managing the Knowledge Lifecycle," *Sloan Managment Review* 44 (Fall 2002): 75–83; and "The Stateless Corporation," *Business Week,* May 14, 1990, 98–106.

Corporate Culture

Whirlpool's corporate profile states the following: "Beyond selling products around the world, being a global home-appliance company means identifying and respecting genuine national and regional differences in customer expectations, but also recognizing and responding to similarities in product development, engineering, purchasing, manufacturing, marketing and sales, distribution, and other areas. Companies which exploit the efficiencies from these similarities will outperform others in terms of market share, cost, quality, productivity, innovation, and return to shareholders."[53] In truly global companies, very little decision making occurs that does not support the goal of treating the world as a single market. Planning for and execution of programs take place on a worldwide basis.

An example of a manifestation of the global commitment is a global identity that favors no specific country (especially the "home country" of the company). The management features several nationalities, and whenever teams are assembled, people from various country organizations get represented. The management development system has to be transparent, allowing nonnational executives an equal chance for the fast track to top management.[54]

In determining the optimal combination of products and product lines to be marketed, a firm should consider choices for individual markets as well as transfer of products and brands from one region or market to another. This will often result in a particular country organization marketing product lines and goods that are a combination of global, regional, and national brands.

Decisions on specific targeting may result in the choice of a narrowly defined segment in the countries chosen. This is a likely strategy of specialized products to clearly definable markets, for example, ocean-capable sailing boats. Catering to multiple segments in various markets is typical of consumer-oriented companies that have sufficient resources for broad coverage.

Summary

Globalization has become one of the most important strategy issues for managers in the past ten years. Many forces, both external and internal, are driving companies to globalize by expanding and coordinating their participation in foreign markets. The approach is not standardization, however. Managers may indeed occasionally be able to take identical concepts and approaches around the world, but most often, they must be customized to local tastes. Internally, companies must make sure that country organizations around the world are ready to launch global products and programs as if they had been developed only for their markets. Firms that are able to exploit commonalities across borders and to do so with competent marketing managers in country organizations are able to see the benefits in their overall performance.[55]

Managers need to engage in strategic planning to better adjust to the realities of the new marketplace. Understanding the firm's core strategy (i.e., what business they are really in) starts the process, and this assessment may lead to adjustments in what business the company may want to be in. In formulating global strategy for the chosen business, the decision makers have to assess and make choices about markets and competitive strategy to be used in penetrating them. This may result in the choice of one particular segment across markets or the exploitation of multiple segments in which the company has a competitive advantage. In manipulating and implementing programs for maximum effect in the chosen markets, the old adage, "think globally, act locally," becomes a critical guiding principle both as far as customers are concerned and in terms of country organization motivation.

Questions for Discussion

1. What is the danger in oversimplifying the globalization approach? Would you agree with the statement that "if something is working in a big way in one market, you better assume it will work in all markets"?

2. What are the critical ways in which globalization and standardization differ?

3. In addition to teenagers as a global segment, are there possibly other groups with similar traits and behaviors that have emerged worldwide?

4. Why is the assessment of internal resources critical as early as possible in developing a global strategic plan?

5. Outline the basic reasons why a company does not necessarily have to be large and have years of experience to succeed in the global marketplace.

6. What are the basic reasons why country operations would not embrace a new regional or global plan (i.e., why the not-invented-here syndrome might emerge)?

Internet Exercises

1. Using the material available at their web site (http://www.unilever.com), suggest ways in which Unilever's business groups can take advantage of global and regional strategies due to interconnections in production and marketing.

2. Bestfoods is one of the largest food companies in the world with operations in more than 60 countries and products sold in 110 countries in the world. Based on the brand information given (http://www.bestfoods.com/about.asp), what benefits does a company derive from having a global presence?

Take a Stand

Asian autos, once scorned by European consumers, are now in high demand in Western Europe. Sales of Japanese brands rose 7.4 percent in 2003, while the overall market shrank by 2.2 percent. Steady gains over the past two years have helped boost Japanese market share to 12.4 percent. Korean makers, such as Hyundai, have been able to gain a foothold, and have a 1.7 percent share. By contrast every European maker (except for Citroën) lost ground in 2003.

During the 1990s, Japanese automakers' top priority was winning in the U.S. market. In Europe, they maintained low-key operations, and invested little. Market share hovered around 10 percent for a decade. Now, boosted by their success in the United States (where they have a 29.1 share), they are ready to repeat their success in Europe, the world's most competitive market. All restrictions on Japanese auto imports were removed in 2000, giving them free access throughout the 19 member countries of the EEA. (Japan had "voluntarily restricted" its exports to Europe to 993,000 cars before that.)

The Japanese success is not just based on price. Asian makers are mastering the art of European automobile allure as well. They are building local design centers and tapping into the best talent pools on the continent: i.e., cars with Japanese DNA in line with tastes of European consumers. In addition, they are using technological finesse. Knowing the Europeans' preference for diesel engines, Honda's and Nissan's new models all feature diesel engines. In the last five years, Toyota has redesigned its European models' interiors, added manual transmissions, tailored engines and handling to more rigorous driving habits, and boosted sales by 48 percent.

For Discussion

1. Are the Japanese likely to conquer the European market to the same degree as they did in the United States?

2. Should the European Union have continued its restrictions on Japanese auto imports to protect its own companies?

CHAPTER 13

Organization, Implementation, and Control

Learning Objectives

- ■ To describe alternative organizational structures for international operations

- ■ To highlight factors affecting decisions about the structure of international organizations

- ■ To indicate roles for country organizations in the development of strategy and implementation of programs

- ■ To outline the need for and challenges of controls in international operations

Organizing to Think Globally and Act Locally

There is a big difference between selling products in 140 different countries around the world and planning and managing lines of business on a global basis. These two divergent yet complementary perspectives led Procter & Gamble (P&G) to embark on a reorganization program named "Organization 2005." The commitments to global and local considerations allow the company to build major global brands through strong programs based on local understanding. Global Business Units (GBU) are charged with strategy on a global basis, while Market Development Organizations (MDO) will tailor programs to local markets. At the same time, the P&G vision for growth is further supported by a commitment to minimize administrative costs and a constant striving to be the smartest and the best. Through Global Business Services (GBS), operations are consolidated and streamlined, while Corporate Functions (CF) work to maintain P&G's place on the vanguard of our industries.

How this new organization works can be highlighted with an example. The GBUs define the equity, or what a brand stands for. The Pantene brand gives a customer healthy, shiny

	Global Business Units (GBU)	Market Development Organizations (MDO)	Global Business Services (GBS)	Corporate Functions (CF)
Philosophy:	Think Globally	Act Locally	Minimize Administrative Costs	Be the Smartest/Best
General Role:	Create strong brand equities, robust strategies, and ongoing innovation in product and marketing to build major global brands.	Interface with customers to ensure marketing plans fully capitalize on local understanding, to seek synergy across programs to leverage corporate scale, and to develop strong programs that change the game in our favor at point of purchase.	Bring together transactional activities such as accounting and order management in a single organization to provide services to all P&G Units at best-in-class quality, cost, and speed.	Ensure that the functional capability integrated into the rest of the company remains on the cutting edge of the industry. We want to be the thought leader within each CF.
There Are:	**Five GBUs:** • Baby, Feminine & Family Care; • Fabric & Home Care; • Food and Beverage; • Health Care; • Beauty Care	**Seven MDO Regions:** • North America; • ASEAN/India/Australia; • North East Asia; • Greater China; • Central-Eastern Europe/Middle East/Africa; • Western Europe; • Latin America	**Three GBS Centers:** • GBS Americas located in Costa Rica; • GBS Asia located in Manila; • GBS Europe, Middle East & Africa located in Newcastle	**Ten CFs:** • Customer Business Development; • Finance & Acct.; • Human Resources; • Information Technology; • Legal; • Marketing; • Consumer & Market Knowledge; • Product Supply; • Research & Development

hair, and a Pantene Team within the Health & Beauty Care GBU is charged with building on this. It starts with product initiatives or upgrades, which ideally would be launched simultaneously around the world. It includes a marketing campaign that communicates the same fundamental benefit around the world, and it includes manufacturing the product against global formula and package specifications. The MDOs then ensure Pantene excels in their region. In the United States, this could mean focusing on Club Stores, which might entail partnering with the GBU to develop large-size packaging the outlet demands in order to maximize value for their shoppers. Conversely, the focus in Latin America might be to develop the smallest possible package like a sachet, as consumers in that region want to minimize their out-of-pocket costs. The outcome should be the same overall brand equity, but very different executions by region. The GBS Center in Costa Rica would provide support for both the U.S. and Latin America MDOs in this example (and for any other brand business team from these regions). Some of the services would include accounting, employee benefits and payroll, order management and product logicstics, and systems operations. Those working directly on the business teams would likely determine the amount of Corporate Function support. Each function would want to ensure that they are capitalizing on the latest thinking or methodologies for each discipline. In this capacity, think of CF's as a consulting group ready to provide service if called upon.

As with any change of consequence, P&G's reorganization presented challenges as well. The projected $2 billion in savings also resulted in 9,600 layoffs. Furthermore, many positions had new reporting structures and even new locations. More than half of the executives at various levels are now in new jobs. Physical transfers were significant as well; e.g., about 1,000 people were moved to Geneva from around Europe and another 200 to Singapore from different Asian locations. Furthermore, the changed reporting structures raised concerns as well. Food and beverages managers, who are mostly in Cincinnati, report to a president in Caracas, Venezuela, while everyone in laundry and household cleaners reports to

Brussels. Personnel transferred from MDOs suddenly had no brands to manage and had to think across borders. The change from a U.S.-centric company to a globally thinking one was a substantial demand in a short period of time and has required adjustments by those affected and in the timetables set.

Sources: "Think Globally, Act Locally," available at http://www.pg.com, accessed May 5, 2003; Jack Neff, "Does P&G Still Matter?" *Advertising Age,* September 25, 2000, 48–56; "Rallying the Troops at P&G," *The Wall Street Journal,* August 31, 2000, B1, B4; "P&G Jump-Starts Corporate Change," *Internetweek,* November 1, 1999, 30; "All Around the World," *Traffic World,* October 11, 1999, 22–24; "Organization 2005 Drive for Accelerated Growth Enters Next Phase," P&G News Releases, June 9, 1999, 1–5; and "Procter & Gamble Moves Forward with Reorganization," *Chemical Market Reporter,* February 1, 1999, 12.

As companies evolve from purely domestic to multinational, their organizational structure and control systems must change to reflect new strategies. With growth comes diversity in terms of products and services, geographic markets, and people in the company itself, bringing along a set of challenges for the company. Two critical issues are basic to all of these challenges: (1) the type of organization that provides the best framework for developing worldwide strategies while at the same time maintaining flexibility in implementation with respect to individual markets and operations, and (2) the type and degree of control to be exercised from headquarters to maximize total effort. Organizational structures, organizations' abilities to implement strategies, and control systems have to be adjusted as market conditions change, as seen in the chapter's opening vignette. While some units are charged with the development of global strategies, others are charged with local adaptation and creating synergies across programs.

This chapter will focus on the advantages and disadvantages of various organizational structures, as well as their appropriateness at different stages of internationalization. A determining factor is where decision-making authority within the organizational structure will be placed. The roles of the different entities that make up the organization need to be defined, including how to achieve collaboration among the units for the benefit of the entire network. The chapter will also outline the need for devising a control system to oversee the international operations of the company, emphasizing the additional control instruments needed beyond those used in domestic business and the control strategies of multinational corporations. The appropriateness and eventual cost of the various control approaches will vary as the firm expands its international operations. The overall objective of the chapter is to study the intraorganizational relationships critical to the firm's attempt to optimize its competitiveness.

Organizational Structure

The basic functions of an organization are to provide: (1) a route and locus of decision making and coordination, and (2) a system for reporting and communications. Increasingly, the coordination and communication dimensions have to include learning from the global marketplace through the company's different units.[1] These networks are typically depicted in the organizational chart.

ORGANIZATIONAL DESIGNS

The basic configurations of international organizations correspond to those of purely domestic ones; the greater the degree of internalization, the more complex the structures can become. The types of structures that companies use to manage foreign activities can be divided into three categories, based on the degree of internationalization:

1. Little or no formal organizational recognition of international activities of the firm. This category ranges from domestic operations handling an occasional international transaction on an ad hoc basis to firms with separate export departments.
2. International division. Firms in this category recognize the ever-growing importance of the international involvement.
3. Global organizations. These can be structured by product, area, function, process, or customer, but ignore the traditional domestic-international split.

Hybrid structures may exist as well, in which one market may be structured by product, another by areas. Matrix organizations have merged in large multinational corporations to combine product-specific, regional, and functional expertise. As worldwide competition has increased dramatically in many industries, the latest organizational response is networked global organizations in which heavy flows of hardware, software, and personnel take place between strategically interdependent units to establish greater global integration. The ability to identify and disseminate best practices throughout the organization is an important competitive advantage for global companies. For example, a U.S. automaker found that in the face of distinctive challenges presented by the local environment, Brazilian engineers developed superior seals, which the company then incorporated in all its models worldwide.[2]

Little or No Formal Organization

In the very early stages of international involvement, domestic operations assume responsibility for international activities. The role of international activities in the sales and profits of the corporation is initially so minor that no organizational adjustment takes place. No consolidation of information or authority over international sales is undertaken or is necessary. Transactions are conducted on a case-by-case basis, either by the resident expert or quite often with the help of facilitating agents, such as freight forwarders.

As demand from the international marketplace grows and interest within the firm expands, the organizational structure will reflect it. As shown in Figure 13.1, an export department appears as a separate entity. This may be an outside export management company—that is, an independent company that becomes the de facto export department of the firm. This is an indirect approach to international involvement in that very little experience is accumulated within the firm itself. Alternatively, a firm may establish its own export department, hiring a few seasoned individuals to take responsibility for international activities. Organizationally, the department may be a sub-department of marketing (as shown in Figure 13.1) or may have equal ranking with the various functional departments. The choice will depend on the importance assigned to overseas activities by the firm. The export department is the first real step

FIGURE 13.1

The Export Department Structure

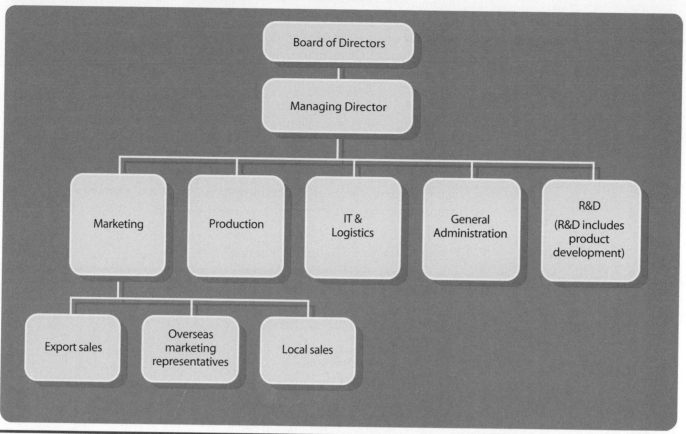

toward internationalizing the organizational structures. It should be a full-fledged marketing organization and not merely a sales organization; i.e., it should have the resources for market research and market-development activities (such as trade show participation).

Licensing as an international entry mode may be assigned to the R&D function despite its importance to the overall international strategy of the firm. A formal liaison among the export, marketing, production, and R&D functions has to be formed for the maximum utilization of licensing.[3] If licensing indeed becomes a major activity for the firm, a separate manager should be appointed.

The more the firm becomes involved in foreign markets, the more quickly the export department structure will become obsolete. For example, the firm may undertake joint ventures or direct foreign investment, which require those involved to have functional experience. The firm therefore typically establishes an international division.

Some firms that acquire foreign production facilities pass through an additional stage in which foreign subsidiaries report directly to the president or to a manager specifically assigned the duty. However, the amount of coordination and control that are required quickly establish the need for a more formal international organization in the firm.

The International Division

The international division centralizes in one entity, with or without separate incorporation, all of the responsibility for international activities, as illustrated in Figure 13.2. The approach aims to eliminate a possible bias against international operations that may exist if domestic divisions are allowed to serve international customers independently. In some cases, international markets have been treated as secondary to domestic markets. The international division concentrates international expertise, information flows concerning foreign market opportunities, and authority over international activities. However, manufacturing and other related functions remain with the domestic divisions to take advantage of economies of scale.

To avoid putting the international division at a disadvantage in competing for products, personnel, and corporate services, coordination between domestic and international operations is necessary. Coordination can be achieved through a joint staff or by requiring domestic and international divisions to interact in strategic planning and

FIGURE 13.2

The International Division Structure

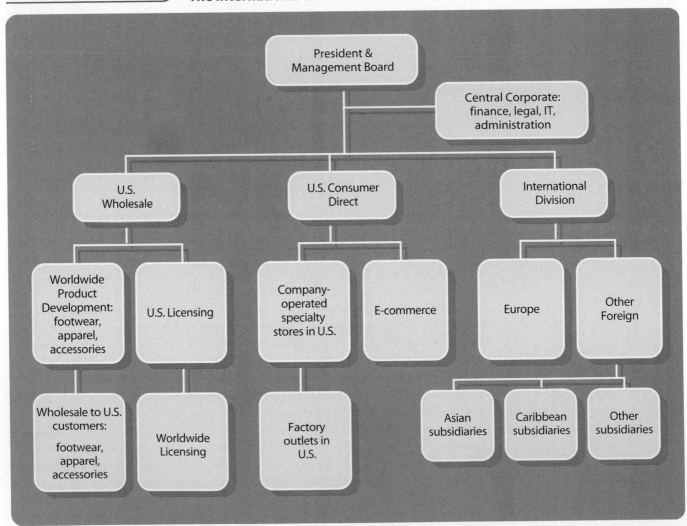

to submit the plans to headquarters. Further, many corporations require and encourage frequent interaction between domestic and international personnel to discuss common problems in areas such as product planning. Coordination is also important because domestic operations are typically organized along product or functional lines, whereas international divisions are geographically oriented.

International divisions best serve firms with few products that do not vary significantly in terms of their environmental sensitivity and with international sales and profits that are still quite insignificant compared with those of the domestic divisions.[4] Companies may outgrow their international divisions as their sales outside of the domestic market grow in significance, diversity, and complexity. European companies have traditionally used international divisions far less than their U.S. counterparts due to the relatively small size of their domestic markets. Philips, Nestlé, or Nokia, for example, would have never grown to their current prominence by relying on their home markets alone. While international divisions were popular among U.S. companies in the 1980s and 1990s, globalization of markets and the increased share of overseas sales have made international divisions less suitable in favor of global structures.[5] For example, Loctite, a leading marketer of sealants, adhesives, and coatings, moved from an international division to a global structure by which the company is managed by market channel (e.g., industrial automotive and electronics industry) to enable Loctite employees to synergize efforts and expertise worldwide.[6]

Global Organizational Structures

Global structures have grown out of competitive necessity. In many industries, competition is on a global basis, with a result that companies must have a high degree of reactive capability.

Six basic types of global structures are available:

1. Global product structure, in which product divisions are responsible for all manufacture and marketing worldwide
2. Global area structure, in which geographic divisions are responsible for all manufacture and marketing in their respective areas
3. Global functional structures, in which functional areas (such as production, marketing, finance, and personnel) are responsible for the worldwide operations of their own functional area
4. Global customer structures, in which operations are structured based on distinct worldwide customer groups
5. Mixed—or hybrid—structures, which may combine the other alternatives
6. Matrix structures, in which operations have reporting responsibility to more than one group (typically, product, functions, or area)

Product Structure The **product structure** is the form most often used by multinational corporations.[7] The approach gives worldwide responsibility to strategic business units for the marketing of their product lines, as shown in Figure 13.3. Most consumer-product firms use some form of this approach, mainly because of the diversity of their products. One of the major benefits of the approach is improved cost efficiency through centralization of manufacturing facilities. This is crucial in industries in which competitive position is determined by world market share, which in turn is often determined by the degree to which manufacturing is rationalized.[8] Adaptation to this approach may cause problems because it is usually accompanied by consolidation of operations and plant closings. A good example is Black & Decker,

FIGURE 13.3

The Global Product Structure (Kodak)

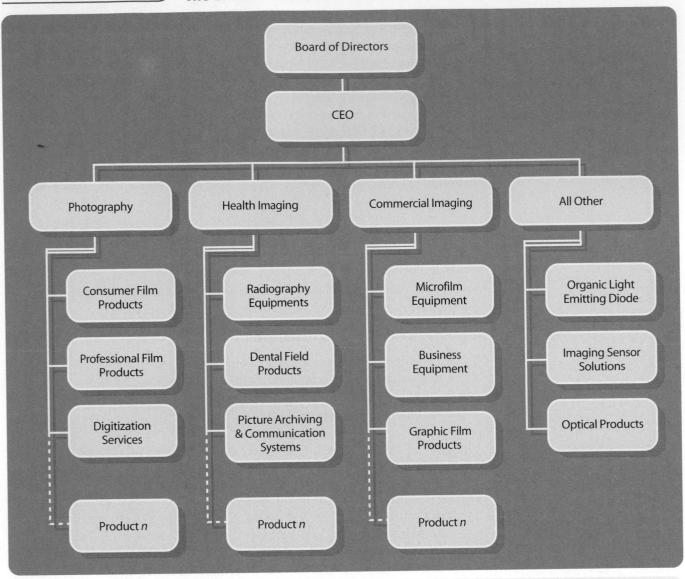

Source: http://www.kodak.com/US/en/corp/aboutKodak/bu.shtml. Courtesy © Eastman Kodak Company.

which rationalized many of its operations in its worldwide competitive effort against Makita, the Japanese power-tool manufacturer. Similarly, Goodyear reorganized itself into a single global organization with a complete business-team approach for tires and general products. The move was largely prompted by tightening worldwide competition.[9] In a similar move, Ford merged its large and culturally distinct European and North American auto operations by vehicle platform type to make more efficient use of its engineering and product development resources against rapidly globalizing rivals.[10] The Ford Focus, Ford's compact car introduced in 1999, was designed by one team of engineers for worldwide markets.

Other benefits of the product structure are the ability to balance the functional inputs needed for a product and the ability to react quickly to product-specific problems in the marketplace. Even smaller brands receive individual attention. Product-specific attention is important because products vary in terms of the adaptation they need for different foreign markets. All in all, the product approach is ideally suited to the development of a global strategic focus in response to global competition.

At the same time, the product structure fragments international expertise within the firm because a central pool of international experience no longer exists. The structure assumes that managers will have adequate regional experience or advice to allow them to make balanced decisions. Coordination of activities among the various product groups operating in the same markets is crucial to avoid unnecessary duplication of basic tasks. For some of these tasks, such as market research, special staff functions may be created and then filled by the product divisions when needed. If they lack an appreciation for the international dimension, product managers may focus their attention only on the larger markets or only on the domestic, and fail to take the long-term view.

Area Structure   The second most used approach is the **area structure,** illustrated in Figure 13.4. Such firms are organized on the basis of geographical areas; for example,

FIGURE 13.4

The Global Area Structure

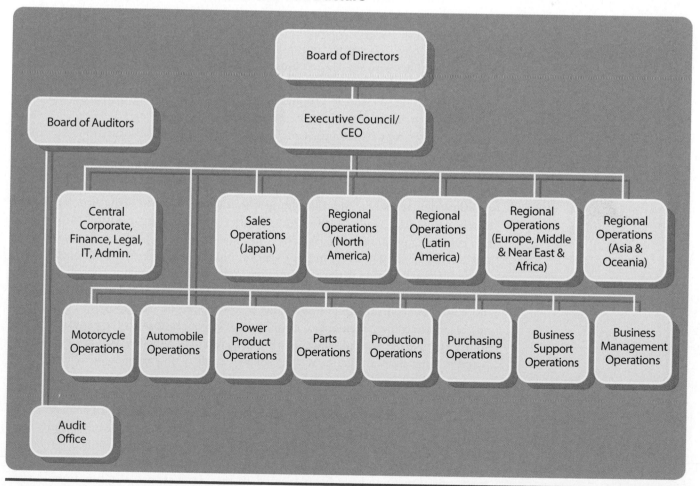

operations may be divided into those dealing with Asia-Pacific, North America, Latin America, and Europe. Ideally, no special preference is given to the region in which the headquarters is located—for example, North America or Europe. Central staffs are responsible for providing coordination support for worldwide planning and control activities performed at headquarters.

Regional integration is playing a major role in area structuring; for example, many multinational corporations have located their European headquarters in Brussels, where the EU has its headquarters. In some U.S. companies, North American integration led to the development of a North American division, which replaced the U.S. operation as the power center of the company. Organizational changes were made at 3M as a result of NAFTA, with the focus on three concepts: simplification, linkage, and empowerment. As an example, this means that new-product launches are coordinated throughout North America, with standardizing of as many elements as feasible and prudent.[11] The driver of structural choices may also be cultural similarity, such as in the case of Asia, or historic connections between countries, such as in the case of combining Europe with the Middle East and Africa. As new markets emerge, they may be first delegated to an established country organization for guidance with the ultimate objective of having them be equal partners with others in the organization. When Estonia regained its independence and started its transformation to a market economy, many companies assigned the responsibility of the Estonian unit's development to their country organization in Finland. In Latvia's case, the Swedish country organization got the job.

The area approach follows the marketing concept most closely because individual areas and markets are given concentrated attention. If market conditions with respect to product acceptance and operating conditions vary dramatically, the area approach is the one to choose. Companies opting for this alternative typically have relatively narrow product lines with similar end uses and end users. However, expertise is needed in adapting the product and its marketing to local market conditions. Once again, to avoid duplication of effort in product management and in functional areas, staff specialists—for product categories, for example—may be used.

Without appropriate coordination from the staff, essential information and experience may not be transferred from one regional entity to another. Also, if the company expands its product lines and if end markets begin to diversify, the area structure may become inappropriate.

Some managers may feel that going into a global product structure may be too much, too quickly, and opt, therefore, to have a regional organization for planning and reporting purposes. The objective may also be to keep profit or sales centers of similar size at similar levels in the corporate hierarchy. If a group of countries has small sales as compared with other country operations, they may be consolidated into a region. The benefit of a regional operation and regional headquarters would be the more efficient coordination of programs across the region (as opposed to globally), a more sensitized management to country-market operations in the region, and the ability to have the region's voice heard more clearly at global headquarters (as compared to what an individual, especially smaller, country operation could achieve).[12]

Functional Structure Of all the approaches, the **functional structure** is the simplest from the administrative viewpoint because it emphasizes the basic tasks of the firm—for example, manufacturing, sales, and research and development. The approach, illustrated in Figure 13.5, works best when both products and customers are relatively few and similar in nature. Coordination is typically the key problem, therefore, staff functions have been created to interact between the functional areas.

FIGURE 13.5

The Global Functional Structure

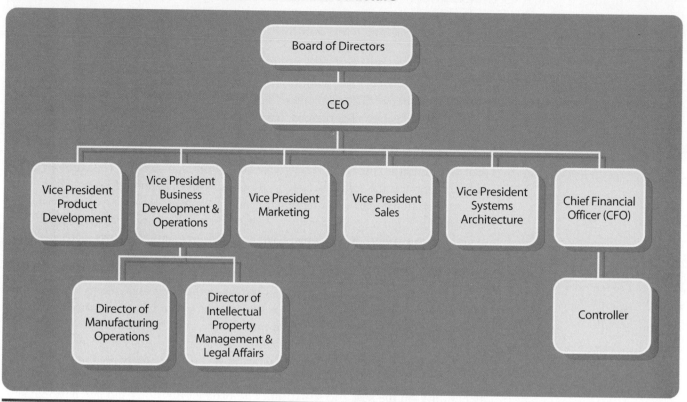

Otherwise, the company's operational and regional expertise may not be exploited to the fullest extent possible.

A variation of the functional approach is one that uses processes as a basis for structure. The **process structure** is common in the energy and mining industries, where one corporate entity may be in charge of exploration worldwide and another may be responsible for the actual mining operations.

Customer Structure   Firms may also organize their operations using the **customer structure,** especially if the customer groups they serve are dramatically different—for example, consumers and businesses and governments. Catering to such diverse groups may require concentrating specialists in particular divisions. The product may be the same, but the buying processes of the various customer groups may differ. Governmental buying is characterized by bidding, in which price plays a larger role than when businesses are the buyers.

Mixed Structure   In some cases, mixed, or hybrid, organizations exist. A **mixed structure** combines two or more organizational dimensions simultaneously. It permits adequate attention to product, area, or functional needs as is needed by the company. The approach may only be a result of a transitional period after a merger or an acquisition, or it may come about due to unique market characteristics or product line. It may also provide a useful structure before the implementation of a worldwide matrix structure.[13]

Naturally, organizational structures are never as clear-cut and simple as presented here. Whatever the basic format, product, functional, and area inputs are needed. Alternatives could include an initial product structure that would subsequently have regional groupings or an initial regional structure with subsequent product groupings. However, in the long term, coordination and control across such structures become tedious.

Matrix Structure   Many multinational corporations, in an attempt to facilitate planning for, organizing, and controlling interdependent businesses, critical resources, strategies, and geographic regions, have adopted the **matrix structure.**[14] Business is driven by a worldwide business unit (for example, photographic products or commercial and information systems) and implemented by a geographic unit (for example, Europe or Latin America). The geographical units, as well as their country subsidiaries, serve as the "glue" between autonomous product operations.

Organizational matrices integrate the various approaches already discussed, as the example in Figure 13.6 illustrates. The seven product divisions (which are then divided into sixty product groups) have rationalized manufacturing to provide products for continentwide markets rather than lines of products for individual markets.[15] These product groups adjust to changing market conditions; e.g., the Components division has been slated to be merged into the other divisions due to lack of standalone profitability.[16] In "key" markets, such as the United States, France, and Japan, product divisions manage their own marketing as well as manufacturing. In "local business" countries, such as Nigeria and Peru, the organizations function as importers from product divisions, and if manufacturing occurs, it is purely for the local market. In "large" markets, such as Brazil, Spain, and Taiwan, a hybrid arrangement is used, depending on the size and situation. The product divisions and the national subsidiaries interact in a matrixlike configuration, with the product divisions responsible for the globalization dimension and the national subsidiaries responsible for local representation and coordination of common areas of interest, such as recruiting.

Matrices vary in terms of their number of dimensions. For example, Dow Chemical's three-dimensional matrix consists of five geographic areas, three major functions (marketing, manufacturing, and research), and more than 70 products. The matrix approach helps cut through enormous organizational complexities in making business managers, functional managers, and strategy managers cooperate. However, the matrix requires sensitive, well-trained middle managers who can cope with problems that arise from reporting to two bosses—for example, a product-line manager and an area manager. For example, every management unit may have a multidimensional reporting relationship, which may cross functional, regional, or operational lines. On a regional basis, group managers in Europe, for example, report administratively to a vice president of operations for Europe, but report functionally to group vice presidents at global headquarters.

Most companies have found the matrix arrangement problematic.[17] The dual reporting channel easily causes conflict, complex issues are forced into a two-dimensional decision framework, and even minor issues may have to be solved through committee discussion. Ideally, managers should solve the problems themselves through formal and informal communication; however, physical and psychic distance often make that impossible. The matrix structure, with its inherent complexity, may actually increase the reaction time of a company, a potentially serious problem when competitive conditions require quick responses. As a result, the authority has started to shift in many organizations from area to product, although the matrix still may officially be used.

FIGURE 13.6

Global Matrix Structure

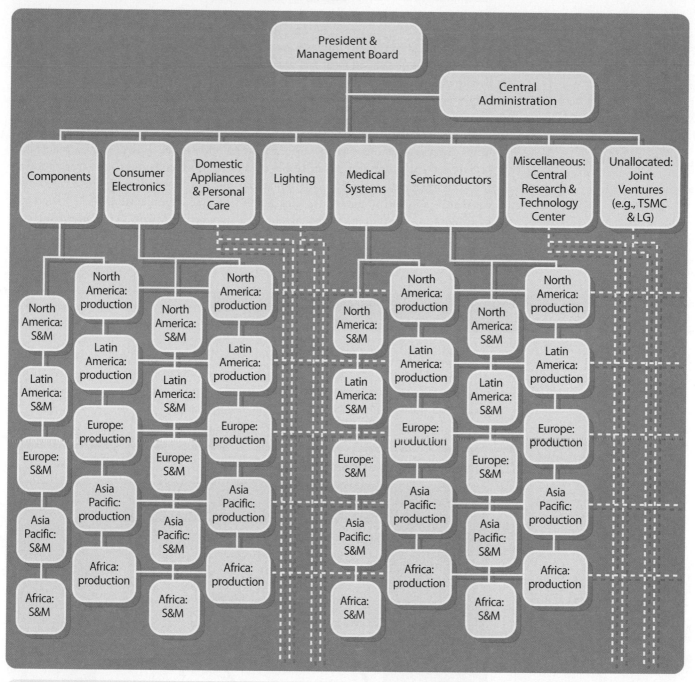

Note: S&M stands for Sales and Marketing.

Evolution of Organizational Structures

Companies have been shown to develop new structures in a pattern of stages as their products diversify and share of foreign sales increases.[18] At the first stage of autonomous subsidiaries reporting directly to top management, the establishment of an international division follows. As product diversity and the importance of the foreign marketplace increase, companies develop global structures to coordinate subsidiary operations and to rationalize worldwide production. As multinational corporations have been faced with simultaneous pressures to adapt to local market conditions and to rationalize production and globalize competitive reactions, many have opted for the matrix structure. The matrix structure probably allows a corporation to best meet the challenges of global markets (to be global and local, big and small, decentralized with centralized reporting) by allowing the optimizing of businesses globally and maximizing performance in every country of operation.[19] The evolutionary process is summarized in Figure 13.7.

Whatever the organizational arrangement may be, the challenge of employees working in "silos" remains. Employee knowledge tends to be fragmented, with one unit's experience and know-how inaccessible to other units. Therefore, the wheel gets reinvented each time—at considerable cost to the company and to the frustration to those charged with tasks. Information technology can be used to synchronize knowledge across even the most complicated and diverse organizations.[20] At Procter & Gamble, for example, brand managers use a standardized, worldwide ad-testing system that allows them to access every ad the company has ever run, providing examples of how to meet particular needs.

Implementation

Organizational structures provide the frameworks for carrying out decision-making processes. However, for that decision making to be effective, a series of organizational initiatives are needed to develop strategy to its full potential, that is, to secure implementation both at the national level and across markets.[21]

FIGURE 13.7

Evolution of International Structures

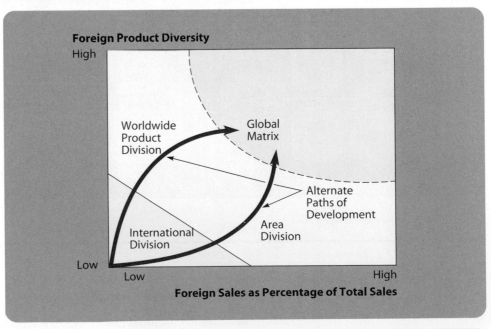

Source: From Christopher A. Bartlett, "Building and Managing the Transnational: The New Organizational Challenge," in *Competition in Global Industries,* ed. Michael E. Porter (Boston: Harvard Business School Press, 1986), 368.

LOCUS OF DECISION MAKING

Organizational structures themselves do not indicate where the authority for decision making and control rests within the organization nor will it reveal the level of coordination between the units. The different levels of coordination between country units are summarized in Table 13.1. Once a suitable structure is found, it has to be made to work by finding a balance between the center and country organizations.

If subsidiaries are granted a high degree of autonomy, the system is called **decentralization.** In decentralized systems, controls are relatively loose and simple, and the flows between headquarters and subsidiaries are mainly financial; that is, each subsidiary operates as a profit center. On the other hand, if controls are tight and the strategic decision making is concentrated at headquarters, the system is described as **centralization.** Firms are typically neither completely centralized nor decentralized; for example, some functions of the firm—such as finance—lend themselves to more centralized decision making; others—such as promotional decisions—do so far less. Research and development in organizations is typically centralized, especially in cases of basic research work. Some companies have, partly due to governmental pressures, added R&D functions on a regional or local basis. In many cases, however, variations are product and market based; for example, Corning Incorporated's TV tube strategy requires global decision making for pricing and local decision making for service and delivery.

The basic advantage of allowing maximum flexibility at the country-market level is that subsidiary management knows its market and can react to changes more quickly. Problems of motivation and acceptance are avoided when decision makers are also the implementors of the strategy. On the other hand, many multinationals faced with global competitive threats and opportunities have adopted global strategy formulation, which by definition requires a higher degree of centralization. What has emerged as a result can be called **coordinated decentralization.** This means that overall corporate strategy is provided from headquarters, while subsidiaries are free to implement it within the range agreed on in consultation between headquarters and the subsidiaries.

However, companies moving into this new mode may face significant challenges. Among these systemic difficulties are a lack of widespread commitment to dismantling traditional national structures, driven by an inadequate understanding of the larger,

TABLE 13.1

Levels of Coordination

Level	Description
5. Central control	No national structures
4. Central direction	Central functional heads have line authority over national functions
3. Central coordination	Central staff functions in coordinating role
2. Coordinating mechanisms	Formal committees and systems
1. Informal cooperation	Functional meetings: exchange of information
0. National autonomy	No coordination between decentralized units, which may even compete in export markets

Level 5 = highest; Level 0 = lowest. Most commonly found levels are 1–4.

Source: Norman Blackwell, Jean-Pierre Bizet, Peter Child, and David Hensley, "Creating European Organizations That Work," Michael R. Czinkota and Ilkka A. Ronkainen, eds., *Readings in Global Marketing* (London: The Dryden Press, 1995): 376–385.

global forces at work. Power barriers from perceived threats to the personal roles of national managers, especially if their tasks are under the threat of being consolidated into regional organizations, can lead to proposals being challenged without valid reason. Finally, some organizational initiatives (such as multicultural teams or corporate chat rooms) may be jeopardized by the fact the people do not have the necessary skills (e.g., language ability) or that an infrastructure (e.g., intranet) may not exist in an appropriate format.[22]

One particular case is of special interest. Organizationally, the forces of globalization are changing the country manager's role significantly. With profit-and-loss responsibility, oversight of multiple functions, and the benefit of distance from headquarters, country managers enjoyed considerable decision-making autonomy as well as entrepreneurial initiative when country operations were largely stand-alone. Today, however, many companies have to emphasize global and regional priorities, which means that the power has to shift at least to some extent from the country manager to worldwide strategic business unit and product-line managers. Many of the local decisions are now subordinated to global strategic moves. However, regional and local programs still require an effective local management component. Therefore, the future country manager will have to wear many hats in balancing the needs of the operation for which the manager is directly responsible with those of the entire region or strategic business unit.[23] To emphasize the importance of the global/regional dimension in the country manager's portfolio, many companies have tied the country manager's compensation to how the company performs globally or regionally, not just in the market for which the manager is responsible.

FACTORS AFFECTING STRUCTURE AND DECISION MAKING

The organizational structure and locus of decision making in a multinational corporation are determined by a number of factors, such as: (1) its degree of involvement in international operations; (2) the products the firm markets; (3) the size and importance of the firm's markets; and (4) the human resource capability of the firm.[24]

The effect of the degree of involvement on structure and decision making was discussed earlier in the chapter. With low degrees of involvement, subsidiaries can enjoy high degrees of autonomy as long as they meet their profit targets. The same situation can occur even with the most globally oriented companies, but within a different framework. Consider, for example, Philips USA, which generates 20 percent of the company's worldwide sales. Even more important, it serves as a market that is on the leading edge of digital media development. Therefore, it enjoys independent status in terms of local policy setting and managerial practices but is still, nevertheless, within the parent company's planning and control system.

The firm's country of origin and the political history of the area can also affect organizational structure and decision making. For example, Swiss-based Nestlé, with only 3 to 4 percent of its sales from its small domestic market, has traditionally had a highly decentralized organization. Moreover, European history for the past 80 years—particularly the two world wars—has often forced subsidiaries of European-based companies to act independently to survive.

The type and variety of products marketed will affect organizational decisions. Companies that market consumer products typically have product organizations with high degrees of decentralization, allowing for maximum local flexibility. On the other hand, companies that market technologically sophisticated products—such as GE, which markets turbines—display centralized organizations with worldwide product responsibilities.

Going global has recently meant transferring world headquarters of important business units abroad. For example, Philips has moved headquarters of several of its global business units to the United States, including its Digital Video Group, Optimal Storage, and Flat Panel Display activities to Silicon Valley.

Apart from situations that require the development of an area structure, the unique characteristics of particular markets or regions may require separate and specific considerations for the firm. For example, when it was set up, AT&T's China division was the only one of twenty divisions in the world based on geography rather than on product or service line. Furthermore, it was the only one to report directly to the CEO.[25]

The human factor in any organization is critical. Managers at both headquarters and the country organizations must bridge the physical and cultural distances separating them. If country organizations have competent managers who rarely need to consult headquarters about their challenges, they may be granted high degrees of autonomy. In the case of global organizations, local management must understand overall corporate goals in that decisions that meet the long-term objectives may not be optimal for the individual local market.

THE NETWORKED GLOBAL ORGANIZATION

No international structure is ideal and some have challenged the wisdom of even looking for one. They have recommended attention to new processes that would, in a given structure, help to develop new perspectives and attitudes that reflect and respond to the complex, opposing demands of global integration and local responsiveness. The question thus changes from which structural alternative is best to how the different perspectives of various corporate entities can better be taken into account when making decisions. In structural terms, nothing may change. As a matter of fact, Philips has not changed its basic matrix structure, yet major changes have occurred in internal relations. The basic change was from a decentralized federation model to a networked global organization, the effects of which are depicted in Figure 13.8. The term **glocal** has been coined to describe this approach.[26]

Companies that have adopted the approach have incorporated the following three dimensions into their organizations: (1) the development and communication of a clear corporate vision; (2) the effective management of human resource tools to broaden individual perspectives and develop identification with corporate goals; and (3) the integration of individual thinking and activities into the broad corporate agenda.[27] The first dimension relates to a clear and consistent long-term corporate mission that guides individuals wherever they work in the organization. Examples of this are Johnson & Johnson's corporate credo of customer focus and NEC's C&C (computers and communications). The second relates both to the development of global managers who can find opportunities in spite of environmental challenges as well as creating a global perspective among country managers. The last dimension relates to the development of a cooperative mind-set among country organizations to ensure effective implementation of global strategies. Managers may believe that global strategies are intrusions on their operations if they do not have an understanding of the corporate vision, if they have not contributed to the global corporate agenda, or if they are not given direct responsibility for its implementation. Defensive, territorial attitudes can lead to the emergence of the "not-invented-here" syndrome, that is, country organizations objecting to or rejecting an otherwise sound strategy.

FIGURE 13.8

The Networked Global Organization

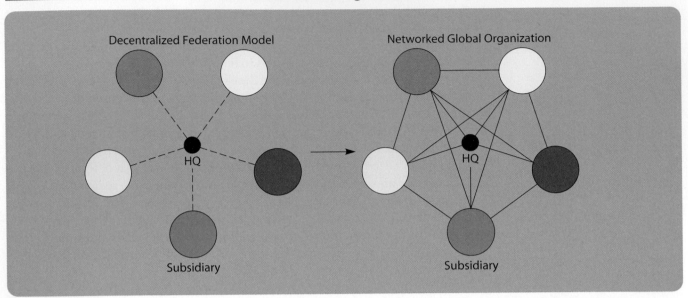

Source: Thomas Gross, Ernie Turner, and Lars Cederholm, "Building Teams for Global Operations," *Management Review,* June 1987 (New York: American Management Association), 34.

For example, in an area structure, units (such as Europe and North America) may operate quite independently, sharing little expertise and information with the other units. While they are supposed to build links to headquarters and other units, they may actually be building walls. To tackle this problem, Nissan established four management committees that meet once a month to supervise regional operations. Each committee includes representatives of the major functions (e.g., manufacturing, marketing, and finance) and the committees (for Japan, Europe, the United States, and general overseas markets) are chaired by Nissan executive vice presidents based in Japan. The CEO attends the committee meetings periodically but regularly.[28]

The network avoids the problems of effort duplication, inefficiency and resistance to ideas developed elsewhere by giving subsidiaries the latitude, encouragement, and tools to pursue local business development within the framework of the global strategy. Headquarters considers each unit a source of ideas, skills, capabilities, and knowledge that can be utilized for the benefit of the entire organization. This means that subsidiaries must be upgraded from mere implementors and adaptors to contributors and partners in the development and execution of worldwide strategies. Efficient plants may be converted into international production centers, innovative R&D units converted into centers of excellence (and thus role models), and leading subsidiary groups given the leadership role in developing new strategies for the entire corporation. These centers of excellence are discussed in the chapter's Focus on Entrepreneurship.

PROMOTING INTERNAL COOPERATION

The global business entity in today's environment can only be successful if is able to move intellectual capital within the organization; i.e., take ideas and move them around faster and faster.[29]

Focus On ⬇

Centers of Excellence

Country-market operations are gaining more significant roles as companies scan the world for ideas that can cross borders. The consensus among managers is that many more countries can be the birthplaces and incubators for solutions that can be applied on a worldwide basis. This realization has given rise to centers of excellence both in global manufacturing and service firms.

Centers of excellence have common themes. First, they are established in areas that top management considers to be of strategic importance to the firm. Given the increasing importance of emerging and developing markets, many companies are convinced that an intimate understanding of these new markets can only be achieved through proximity. Consequently, Unilever has installed innovation centers in 19 countries to develop unique solutions for these markets. Second, the heart of each center of excellence is the leading-edge knowledge of a small number of indidivuals responsible for the continual maintenance and upgrading of the knowledge in question. Within ABB, for example, ABB Strömberg in Finland has worldwide responsibility for the electric drives, a category for which it is the recognized world leader. Third, centers of excellence typically have a dual role: to leverage and/or transfer the current leading-edge capabilities, and to continually fine-tune and enchance those capabilities so that they remain state of the art. For example, Corning has established a Center for Marketing Excellence where sales and marketing staff from all of Corning's businesses—from glass to television components—will be able to find help with marketing intelligence, strategies, new product lines, and e-business.

Centers of excellence can emerge in three formats: charismatic, focused, or virtual. Charismatic centers of excellence are individuals who are internationally recognized for their expertise in a function or an area. These individuals are called upon to build, through mentoring relationships, a capability in the firm that has been lacking. The most common type are focused centers of excellence, which are based on a single area of expertise, be it technological or product-based. The center has an identifiable location from which the members provide advice and leadership. In virtual centers of excellence, the core individuals live and work around the world and keep in touch through electronic means and meetings. The knowledge of dispersed individuals is brought together, integrated into a coherent whole, and disseminated throughout the firm.

An increasingly important determinant of competitive advantage is the ability to make proprietary knowledge available and usable on a global scale. Centers of excellence are a way for companies to exploit their geographically dispersed expertise more effectively.

Sources: Julian Birkinshaw and Tony Sheehan, "Managing the Knowledge Life Cycle," *Sloan Management Review* 44 (Fall 2002): 75–83; Erin Strout, "Reinventing a Company," *Sales and Marketing Management* 152 (February 2000): 86–92; and Karl Moore and Julian Birkinshaw, "Managing Knowledge in Global Service Firms," *Academy of Management Executive* 12 (number 4, 1998): 81–92.

One of the tools is teaching. For example, at Ford Motor Company, teaching takes three distinct forms as shown in Table 13.2. Ford's approach is similarly undertaken at many leading global companies. The focus is on teachable points of view; i.e., is an explanation of what a person knows and believes about what it takes to succeed in his or her business.[30] For example, GE's Jack Welch coined the term "boundarylessness" to describe to which means that people can act without regard to status or functional loyalty and can look for better ideas from anywhere. Top leadership of GE spends considerable time at GE training centers interacting with up-and-comers from all over the company. Each training class is given a real, current company problem to solve, and the reports can be career makers (or breakers). A number of benefits arise from this approach. A powerful teachable point of view can reach the entire company within a reasonable period by having students become teachers themselves. At PepsiCo, the CEO passed his teachable point to 110 executives who then passed it to 20,000 people within 18 months. Secondly, participants in teaching situations are encouraged to maintain the international networks they develop during the sessions. It should be noted that teachers do not necessarily need to be only top managers. When General Electric launched a massive effort to embrace e-commerce, many managers found that they knew little about the Internet. Following a London-based manager's idea to have an Internet mentor, GE encourages all managers to have one for a period of time for training each week.[31]

TABLE 13.2   Teaching Programs at Ford Motor Co.

Program	Participants	Teachers	Components
Capstone	24 senior executives at a time	The leaderhip team	• About 20 days training annually • Six-month team projects • 360-degree feedback • Community service
Business Leadership	All Ford salaried employees—100,000	The participants' managers	• Three days training annually • 100-day team projects • 360-degree feedback • Community service • Exercises contrasting old and new Ford
Executive Partnering	Promising young managers	The leaderhip team	• Eight weeks shadowing senior executives
Let's Chat about the Business	Everyone who receives e-mail at Ford—about 100,000 employees	CEO	• Weekly e-mails describing Ford's new approach to business
Customer-Driven Six Sigma	1900 full-time employees awarded "Black Belt" in 2001	The leadership team	• Five days of intensive instruction • "Learn-by-doing" learning model • Teams assigned multiple problem-solving projects

Sources: Ford Motor Company Annual Report 2000 and 2001 Corporate Citizenship Report, http://www.ford.com, accessed March 14, 2002; Suzy Wetlaufer, "Driving Change: An Interview with Ford Motor Company's Jacques Nasser," *Harvard Business Review* 77 (March–April 1999): 76–88.

Another method to promote internal cooperation for global strategy implementation is the use of international teams or councils. In the case of a new product or program an international team of managers may be assembled to develop strategy. While final direction may come from headquarters, it has been informed of local conditions, and implementation of the strategy is enhanced since local-country managers were involved in its development. The approach has worked even in cases involving seemingly impossible market differences. Both Procter & Gamble and Henkel have successfully introduced pan-European brands for which strategy was developed by European teams. These teams consisted of country managers and staff personnel to smooth eventual implementation and to avoid unnecessarily long and disruptive discussions about the fit of a new product to individual markets.

On a broader and longer-term basis, companies use councils to share **best practice;** e.g., an idea that may have saved money or time, or a process that is more efficient than existing ones. Most professionals at the leading global companies are members of multiple councils. In some cases, it is important to bring in members of other constituencies (e.g., suppliers, intermediaries, service providers) to such meetings to share their views and experiences and make available their own best practice for benchmarking.

While technology has made such teamwork possible wherever the individual participants may be, relying only on technology may not bring about the desired results;

"high-tech" approaches inherently mean "low touch," at the expense of results. Human relationships are still paramount.[32] A common purpose is what binds team members to a particular task, which can only be achieved through trust, achievable through face-to-face meetings. At the start of its 777 project, Boeing brought members of the design team from a dozen different countries to Everett, Washington, giving them the opportunity to work together for up to 18 months. Beyond learning to function effectively within the company's project management system, they also shared experiences which, in turn, engendered a level of trust between individuals that later enabled them to overcome obstacles raised by physical separation. The result was a design and launch in 40 percent faster time than with comparable projects.

The term *network* also implies two-way communications between headquarters and subsidiaries and between subsidiaries themselves. This translates into intercultural communication efforts focused on developing relationships.[33] While this communication can take the form of newsletters or regular and periodic meetings of appropriate personnel, new technologies are allowing businesses to link far-flung entities and eliminate the traditional barriers of time and distance. **Intranets** integrate a company's information assets into a single accessible system using Internet-based technologies such as e-mail, news groups, and the World Wide Web. In effect, the formation of **virtual teams** becomes a reality. For example, employees at Levi Strauss & Co. can join an electronic discussion group with colleagues around the world, watch the latest Levi's commercials, or comment on latest business programs or plans.[34] "Let's Chat About the Business" e-mails go out at Ford every Friday at 5 P.M. to about 100,000 employees to share information throughout the company and encourage dialogue. In many companies, the annual videotaped greeting from management has been replaced by regular and frequent e-mails (called e-briefs at GE). The benefits of intranet are: (1) increased productivity in that there is no longer a time lag between an idea and the information needed to assess and implement it; (2) enhanced knowledge capital, which is constantly updated and upgraded; (3) facilitated teamwork enabling online communication at insignificant expense; and (4) incorporation of best practice at a moment's notice by allowing managers and functional-area personnel to make to-the-minute decisions anywhere in the world.

As can be seen from the discussion, the networked approach is not a structural adaptation but a procedural one, calling for a change in management mentality. It requires adjustment mainly in the coordination and control functions of the firm. And while there is still considerable disagreement as to which of the approaches work, some measures have been shown to correlate with success. Of the many initiatives developed to enhance the workings of a networked global organization, such as cross-border task forces and establishment of centers of excellence, the most significant was the use of electronic networking capabilities.[35]

Further adjustment in organizational approaches is required as businesses face new challenges such as emerging markets, global accounts, and the digitization of business.[36] Emerging markets present the company with unique challenges such as product counterfeiters and informal competitors who ignore local labor and tax laws. How these issues are addressed may require organizational rethinking. Colgate-Palmolive, for example, grouped its geographies under two different organizations: one responsible for mature, developed economies and the other for high-growth, emerging markets.[37] Global account managers need to have skills and the empowerment to work across functional areas and borders to deliver quality service to the company's largest clients. Finally, digital business, such as business-to-business and business-to-consumer Internet-based activities, needs to be brought into the mainstay of the businesses' activities and structures and not seen as a separate activity.

THE ROLE OF COUNTRY ORGANIZATIONS

Country organizations should be treated as a source of supply as much as a source of demand. Quite often, however, headquarters managers see their role as the coordinators of key decisions and controllers of resources and perceive subsidiaries as implementors and adaptors of global strategy in their respective local markets. Furthermore, they may see all country organizations as the same. This view severely limits utilization of the firm's resources and deprives country managers of the opportunity to exercise their creativity.[38]

The role that a particular country organization can play naturally depends on that market's overall strategic importance as well as its organizational competence. Using these criteria, four different roles emerge, as shown in Figure 13.9.

The role of a **strategic leader** can be played by a highly competent national subsidiary located in a strategically critical market. Such a country organization serves as a partner of headquarters in developing and implementing strategy. Procter & Gamble's Eurobrand teams, which analyze opportunities for greater product and marketing program standardization, are chaired by a brand manager from a "lead country." For example, a strategic leader market may have products designed specifically with it in mind. Nissan's Z-cars have always been designated primarily for the U.S. market, starting with the 240Z in the 1970s to the 350Z introduced in 2002.[39] The new model was designed by the company's La Jolla, California, studio.

FIGURE 13.9

Roles for Country Organizations

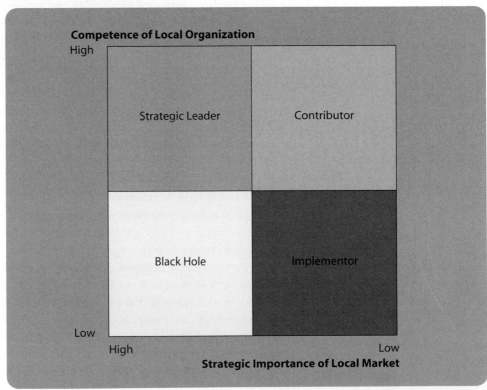

Source: Christopher Bartlett and Sumantra Ghoshal, "Tap Your Subsidiaries for Global Reach," *Harvard Business Review* 64, November–December 1986 (Boston: Harvard Business School Publishing Division), 87–94.

A **contributor** is a country organization with a distinctive competence, such as product development. Increasingly, country organizations are the source of new products. These range from IBM's recent breakthrough in superconductivity research, generated in its Zurich lab, to low-end innovations such as Procter & Gamble's liquid Tide, made with a fabric-softening compound developed in Europe.[40] A contributor designation may be a function of geography as well. Companies such as Carrier, IBM, and Hewlett-Packard use their units in Finland to penetrate the Russian market.[41] For products or technologies with multiple applications, leadership may be divided among different country operations. For example, DuPont delegates responsibility for each different application of Lycra to managers in a country where the application is strongest; i.e., Brazil for swimwear and France for fashion. The global brand manager for Lycra ensures that those applications come together in an overall strategy.[42]

Implementors provide the critical mass for the global effort. These country organizations may exist in smaller, less-developed countries in which there is less corporate commitment for market development, and exist mostly for sales purposes. Although most entities are given this role, it should not be slighted, since the implementors provide the opportunity to capture economies of scale and scope that are the basis of a global strategy.

The **black hole** situation is one in which the international company has a low-competence country organization—or no organization at all—in a highly strategic market. A company may be in a "black hole" situation because it has read the market incorrectly (for example, penetration of the beverage market in Japan may require a local partner) or because government may restrict its activites (for example, foreign banks are restricted in terms of activities and geography in China). If possible, the marketer can use strategic alliances or acquisitions to change its competitive position. Whirlpool established itself in the European Union by acquiring Philips' white goods operation and has used joint ventures to penetrate the Chinese market. If governmental regulations hinder the scale of operations, the firm may use its presence in a major market as an observation post to keep up with developments before a major thrust for entry is executed (for example, with China's WTO membership, the banking sector should start opening up).

Depending on the role of the country organization, its relationship with headquarters will vary from loose control based mostly on support to tighter control to ensure that strategies get implemented appropriately. Yet, in each of these cases, it is imperative that country organizations have enough operating independence to cater to local needs and to provide motivation to country managers. For example, an implementor's ideas concerning the development of a regional or global strategy or program should be heard. Country organization initiative is the principal means by which global companies can tap into new opportunities in markets around the world.[43] For example, customers' unmet demands in a given market may result not only in the launch of a local product but subsequently in its roll-out regionally or even globally. This may mean that subsidiaries are allowed to experiment with projects that would not be seen as feasible by headquarters. For example, developing products for small-scale power generation using renewable resources may not generate interest in Honeywell's major markets and subsidiaries but may well be something that one of its developing-country subsidiaries should investigate. In executing global strategies, country-specific buy-in is best secured through involvement of these organizations at the critical points in strategy development. Strategy formulators should make sure that appropriate implementation can be achieved at the country level.

Controls

The function of the organizational structure is to provide a framework in which objectives can be met. A set of instruments and processes is needed, however, to influence the performance of organizational members so as to meet the goals. Controls focus on means to verify and correct actions that differ from established plans. Compliance needs to be secured from subordinates through different means of coordinating specialized and interdependent parts of the organization.[44] Within an organization, control serves as an integrating mechanism. Controls are designed to reduce uncertainty, increase predictability, and ensure that behaviors originating in separate parts of the organization are compatible and in support of common organizational goals despite physical, psychic, and temporal distances.

The critical issue here is the same as with organizational structure: What is the ideal amount of control? On the one hand, headquarters needs controls to ensure that international activities contribute the greatest benefit to the overall organization. On the other hand, they should not be construed as a code of laws and subsequently allowed to stifle local initiative.

This section will focus on the design and functions of control instruments available for international business operations, along with an assessment of their appropriateness. Emphasis will be placed on the degree of formality of controls used by firms.

TYPES OF CONTROLS

Most organizations display some administrative flexibility, as demonstrated by variations in how they apply management directives, corporate objectives, or measurement systems. A distinction should be made, however, between variations that have emerged by design and those that are the result of autonomy. The first are the result of a management decision, whereas the second typically have grown without central direction and are based on emerging practices. In both instances, some type of control will be exercised. Controls that result from headquarters initiative rather than those that are the consequences of tolerated practices will be discussed here. Firms that wait for self-emerging controls often experience rapid international growth but subsequent problems in product-line performance, program coordination, and strategic planning.[45]

Whatever the system, it is important in today's competitive environment to have internal benchmarking. This relates to organizational learning and sharing of best practices throughout the corporate system to avoid the costs of reinventing solutions that have already been discovered. A description of the knowledge transfer is provided in the Focus on e-business. Three critical features are necessary in sharing best practice. First, there needs to be a device for organizational memory. For example, at Xerox, contributors to solutions can send their ideas to an electronic library where they are indexed and provided to potential adopters in the corporate family. Second, best practice must be updated and adjusted to new situations. For example, best practice adopted by a company's China office will be modified and customized, and this learning should then become part of the database. Finally, best practice must be legitimized. This calls for a shared understanding that exchanging knowledge across units is organizationally valued and that these systems are important mechanisms for knowledge exchange. Use can be encouraged by including an assessment in employee performance evaluations of how effectively employees share information with colleagues and utilize the databases.

In the design of the control systems, a major decision concerns the object of control. Two major objects are typically identified: output and behavior.[46] Output con-

Focus On ⬇

Knowledge across Boundaries

Spurred by competitive pressures, global knowledge networks allow multinationals to share information and best practices across geographically dispersed units and time zones. Corporations save millions of dollars each year as a result of the up-to-the-minute knowledge transfer and feedback that such networks allow. In addition, the bonds that develop between employees in locations scattered around the globe are instrumental in achieving global objectives. Whether the goal is customer loyalty, increased production efficiency, or retention of skilled employees, a knowledge-sharing network focused on improvement of operational practices worldwide helps multinationals meet the challenge of building a cohesive, global, corporate culture.

Ford Motor Company has established 25 "communities of practice" organized around functions. For example, painters in every assembly plant around the world belong to the same community. If local employees find a better way of conducting any of the 60-plus steps involved in painting, a template for that improvement is disseminated to all plants where the process can be replicated. From 1995 to 2000, Ford has discovered a total of 8,000 better ways of doing business through its Best Practices Replication Plan, saving more than $886 million in operating efficiencies.

Eureka, a knowledge-sharing system at Xerox Corp., saves the company between $25 million and $125 million a year, depending on how the numbers are tallied. The system connects service technicians around the world who provide information and, more importantly, feedback intended to improve Xerox's electronic product documentation. Eureka has evolved into an easy-access problem-solving database, with more than 30,000 tips submitted by technicians in every country in which Xerox operates. The success of Eureka inspired Xerox to create knowledge-sharing systems to benefit other operational functions. Focus 500 allows the companies' top 500 executives to share information on their interactions with customers and industry partners. Project Library details costs, resources, and cycle times of more than 2,000 projects. It is a vital resource in improving Six Sigma quality in project management. PROFIT allows salespeople to submit hot selling tips—with cash incentives for doing so.

The 2001 merger of energy giants Texaco and Chevron represented an opportunity to integrate global knowledge networks. Active in nearly 180 countries, ChevronTexaco expects to leverage its knowledge systems into millions of dollars in cost savings. The company's information technology–enabled infrastructure allows scientists across the globe to work in virtual teams. More than 50,000 employees share platforms for every business process and communication, allowing real-time interactions among global workforces.

Sources: Louise Lee, "The Other Instant Powerhouse in Energy Trading," *Business Week,* November 26, 2001; Kristine Ellis, "Sharing Best Practices Globally," *Training,* July 2001; http://www.chevrontexaco.com.

trols include balance sheets, sales data, production data, product-line growth, and performance reviews of personnel. Measures of output are accumulated at regular intervals and forwarded from the foreign locale to headquarters, where they are evaluated and critiqued based on comparisons to the plan or budget. Behavioral controls require the exertion of influence over behavior after—or, ideally, before—it leads to action. Behavioral controls can be achieved through the preparation of manuals on such topics as sales techniques to be made available to subsidiary personnel or through efforts to fit new employees into the corporate culture.

To institute either of these measures, instruments of control have to be decided upon. The general alternatives are either bureaucratic/formalized control or cultural control. Bureaucratic controls consist of a limited and explicit set of regulations and rules that outline the desired levels of performance. Cultural controls, on the other hand, are much less formal and are the result of shared beliefs and expectations among the members of an organization. Table 13.3 provides a schematic explanation of the types of controls and their objectives.

Bureaucratic/Formalized Control

The elements of a bureaucratic/formalized control system are: (1) an international budget and planning system; (2) the functional reporting system; and (3) policy manuals used to direct functional performance.

TABLE 13.3 Comparison of Bureaucratic and Cultural Control Mechanisms

Object of Control	TYPE OF CONTROL		Characteristics of Control
	Pure Bureaucratic/ Formalized Control	**Pure Cultural Control**	
Output	Formal performance reports	Shared norms of performance	HQ sets short-term performance target and requires frequent reports from subsidiaries
Behavior	Company policies, manuals	Shared philosophy of management	Active participation of HQ in strategy formulation of subsidiaries

Sources: Peter J. Kidger, "Management Structure in Multinational Enterprises: Responding to Globalization," *Employee Relations,* August 2001, 69–85; and B. R. Baliga and Alfred M. Jaeger, "Multinational Corporations: Control Systems and Delegation Issues," *Journal of International Business Studies* 15 (Fall 1984): 25–40.

Budgets refers to shorter-term guidelines regarding investment, cash, and personnel policies, while *plans* refers to formalized plans with more than a one-year horizon. The budget and planning process is the major control instrument in headquarters-subsidiary relationships. Although systems and their execution vary, the objective is to achieve as good a fit as possible with the objectives and characteristics of the firm and its environment.

The budgetary period is typically one year, since it is tied to the accounting systems of the multinational. The budget system is used for four main purposes: (1) allocation of funds among subsidiaries; (2) planning and coordination of global production capacity and supplies; (3) evaluation of subsidiary performance; and (4) communication and information exchange among subsidiaries, product organizations, and corporate headquarters.[47] Long-range plans vary dramatically, ranging from two years to ten years in length, and are more qualitative and judgmental in nature. However, shorter periods such as two years are the norm, considering the added uncertainty of diverse foreign environments.

Although firms strive for uniformity, achieving it may be as difficult as trying to design a suit to fit the average person. The processes themselves are very formalized in terms of the schedules to be followed.

Control can also be seen as a mechanism to secure cooperation of local units. For example, while a company may grant substantial autonomy to a country organization in terms of strategies, headquarters may use allocation of production volume as a powerful tool to ensure compliance. Some of the ways for headquarters to gain cooperation of country organizations are summarized in Figure 13.10. Some of the methods used are formal, such as approval of strategic plans and personnel selection, while some are more informal, including personal contact and relationships, as well as international networking.[48]

Since the frequency of reports required from subsidiaries is likely to increase due to globalization, it is essential that subsidiaries see the rationale for the often time-consuming exercise. Two approaches, used in tandem, can facilitate the process: participation and feedback. The first refers to avoiding the perception at subsidiary levels that reports are "art for art's sake" by involving the preparers in the actual use of the reports. When this is not possible, feedback about their consequences is warranted. Through this process, communication is enhanced as well.

On the behavioral front, headquarters may want to guide the way in which subsidiaries make decisions and implement agreed-upon strategies. U.S.-based multinationals tend to

FIGURE 13.10

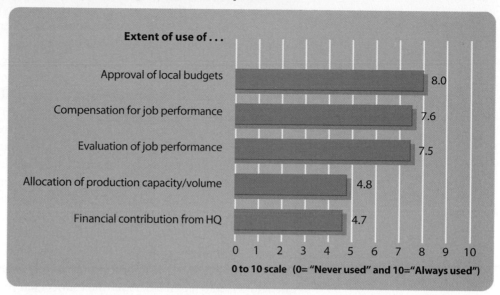

Securing Country-Organization Cooperation

Extent of use of . . .

Approval of local budgets	8.0
Compensation for job performance	7.6
Evaluation of job performance	7.5
Allocation of production capacity/volume	4.8
Financial contribution from HQ	4.7

0 1 2 3 4 5 6 7 8 9 10

0 to 10 scale   (0= "Never used" and 10="Always used")

Source: Henry P. Conn and George S. Yip, "Global Transfer of Critical Capabilities," in Michael R. Czinkota and Ilkka A. Ronkainen, eds., *Best Practices in International Business* (Mason, OH: South-Western, 2001): 256–274.

be far more formalized than their Japanese and European counterparts, with a heavy reliance on manuals for all major functions.[49] The manuals discuss such items as recruitment, training, motivation, and dismissal policies. The use of manuals is in direct correlation with the required level of reports from subsidiaries, discussed in the previous section.

Cultural Control

As seen from the country comparisons, less emphasis is placed outside the United States on formal controls, as they are viewed as too rigid and too quantitatively oriented. Rather, MNCs in other countries emphasize corporate values and culture, and evaluations are based on the extent to which an individual or entity fits in with the norms. Cultural controls require an extensive socialization process to which informal, personal interaction is central. Substantial resources have to be spent to train the individual to share the corporate cultures, or "the way things are done at the company."[50] To build common vision and values, managers spend a substantial share of their first months at Matsushita in what the company calls "cultural and spiritual training." They study the company credo, the "Seven Spirits of Matsushita," and the philosophy of the founder, Konosuke Matsushita and learn how to translate the internalized lessons into daily behavior and operational decisions. Although more prevalent in Japanese organizations, many Western entities have similar programs, such as Philips's "organization cohesion training" and Unilever's "indoctrination." This corporate acculturation will be critical to achieve the acceptance of possible transfers of best practice within the organization.[51]

The primary instruments of cultural control are the careful selection and training of corporate personnel and the institution of self-control. The choice of cultural controls can be justified if the company enjoys a low turnover rate; they are thus applied when companies can offer and expect lifetime or long-term employment, as many firms do in Japan.

In selecting home-country nationals and, to some extent, third-country nationals, MNCs are exercising cultural control. The assumption is that the managers have already internalized the norms and values of the company and they tend to run a country organization with a more global view. In some cases, the use of headquarters personnel to ensure uniformity in decision making may be advisable; for example, Volvo uses a home-country national for the position of chief financial officer. Expatriates are used in subsidiaries not only for control purposes but also to effect change processes. Companies control the efforts of management specifically through compensation and promotion policies, as well as through policies concerning replacement.

When the expatriate corps is small, headquarters can still exercise its control through other means. Management training programs for overseas managers as well as time at headquarters will indoctrinate individuals to the company's ways of doing things. Similarly, formal visits by headquarters teams (for example, for a strategy audit) or informal visits (perhaps to launch a new product) will enhance the feeling of belonging to the same corporate family. Some of the innovative global companies assemble temporary teams of their best talent to build local skills. IBM, for example, drafted 50 engineers from its facilities in Italy, Japan, New York, and North Carolina to run three-week to six-month training courses on all operations carried on at its Shenzhen facility in China. After the trainers left the country, they stayed in touch by e-mail, so whenever the Chinese managers have a problem, they know they can reach someone for help. The continuation of the support has been as important as the training itself.[52]

Corporations rarely use one pure control mechanism. Rather, most use both quantitative and qualitative measures. Corporations are likely, however, to place different levels of emphasis on different types of performance measures and on how they are derived.

EXERCISING CONTROLS

Within most corporations, different functional areas are subject to different guidelines because they are subject to different constraints. For example, the marketing function has traditionally been seen as incorporating many more behavioral dimensions than manufacturing or finance. As a result, many multinational corporations employ control systems that are responsive to the needs of the function. Yet such differentiation is sometimes based less on appropriateness than on personalities. It has been hypothesized that manufacturing subsidiaries are controlled more intensively than sales subsidiaries because production more readily lends itself to centralized direction, and technicians and engineers adhere more firmly to standards and regulations than do salespeople.[53]

Similarly, the degree of control imposed will vary by subsidiary characteristics, including location. For example, since Malaysia is an emerging economy in which managerial talent is in short supply, headquarters may want to participate more in all facets of decision making. If a country-market witnesses economic or political turmoil, controls may also be tightened to ensure the management of risk.[54]

In their international operations, U.S.-based multinationals place major emphasis on obtaining quantitative data. Although this allows for good centralized comparisons against standards and benchmarks or cross-comparisons among different corporate units, it entails several drawbacks. In the international environment, new dimensions—such as inflation, differing rates of taxation, and exchange rate fluctuations— may distort the performance evaluation of any given individual or organizational unit.

For the global corporation, measurement of whether a business unit in a particular country is earning a superior return on investment relative to risk may be irrelevant to the contribution an investment may make worldwide or to the long-term results of the firm. In the short term, the return may even be negative.[55] Therefore, the control mechanism may quite inappropriately indicate reward or punishment. Standardizing the information received may be difficult if the various environments involved fluctuate and require frequent and major adaptations. Further complicating the issue is the fact that although quantitative information may be collected monthly, or at least quarterly, environmental data may be acquired annually or "now and then," especially when a crisis seems to loom on the horizon. To design a control system that is acceptable not only to headquarters but also to the organization and individuals abroad, great care must be taken to use only relevant data. Major concerns, therefore, are the data collection process and the analysis and utilization of data. Evaluators need management information systems that provide for greater comparability and equity in administering controls. The more behaviorally based and culture-oriented controls are, the more care needs to be taken.

In designing a control system, management must consider the costs of establishing and maintaining it versus the benefits to be gained. Any control system will require investment in a management structure and in systems design. Consider, for example, costs associated with cultural controls: personal interaction, use of expatriates, and training programs are all quite expensive. Yet these expenses may be justified by cost savings through lower employee turnover, an extensive worldwide information system, and an improved control system.[56] Moreover, the impact goes beyond the administrative component. If controls are misguided or too time-consuming, they can slow or undermine the strategy implementation process and thus the overall capability of the firm. The result will be lost opportunities or, worse yet, increased threats. In addition, time spent on reporting takes time from everything else, and if the exercise is seen as mundane, it results in lowered motivation. A parsimonious design is therefore imperative. The control system should collect all the information required and trigger all the intervention necessary; however, it should not lead to the pulling of strings by a puppeteer.

The impact of the environment has to be taken into account, as well, in two ways. First, the control system must measure only those dimensions over which the organization has actual control. Rewards or sanctions make little sense if they are based on dimensions that may be relevant to overall corporate performance but over which no influence can be exerted, such as price controls. Neglecting the factor of individual performance capability would send wrong signals and severely harm motivation. Second, control systems have to be in harmony with local regulations and customs. In some cases, however, corporate behavioral controls have to be exercised against local customs even though overall operations may be affected negatively. This type of situation occurs, for example, when a subsidiary operates in markets in which unauthorized facilitating payments are a common business practice.

Corporations are faced with major challenges in appropriate and adequate control systems in today's business environment. Given increased local government demands for a share in companies established, controls can become tedious, especially if the MNC is a minority partner. Even if the new entity is a result of two companies' joining forces through a merger—such as the one between Ciba and Sandoz to create Novartis—or two companies joining forces to form a new entity—such as Siecor established by Siemens AG and Corning Incorporated—the backgrounds of the partners may be different enough to cause problems in devising the required controls.

Summary

This chapter discussed the structures and control mechanisms needed to operate in the international business field. The elements define relationships between the entities of the firm and provide the channels through which the relationships develop. The fundamental tests of organizational design are whether there is a fit with the company's overall marketing strategy and whether it reflects the strengths of the entities within the organization.[57]

International firms can choose from a variety of organizational structures, ranging from a domestic organization that handles ad hoc export orders to a full-fledged global organization. The choice will depend heavily on the degree of internationalization of the firm, the diversity of international activities, and the relative importance of product, area, function, and customer variables in the process. A determining factor is also the degree to which headquarters wants to decide important issues concerning the whole corporation and the individual subsidiaries. Organizations that function effectively still need to be revisited periodically to ensure that they remain responsive to a changing environment. Some of the responsiveness is showing up not as structural changes, but rather in how the entities conduct their internal business.

In addition to organization, the control function takes on major importance for multinationals, due to the high variability in performance resulting from divergent local environments and the need to reconcile local objectives with the corporate goal of synergism. While it is important to grant autonomy to country organizations so that they can be responsive to local market needs, it is of equal importance to ensure close cooperation among units to optimize corporate effectiveness.

Control can be exercised through bureaucratic means, which emphasize formal reporting and evaluation of benchmark data or through cultural means, in which norms and values are understood by the individuals and entities that make up the corporation. U.S. firms typically rely more on bureaucratic controls, while MNCs from other countries frequently run operations abroad through informal means and rely less on stringent measures.

The implementation of controls requires great sensitivity to behavioral dimensions and the environment. The measurements used must be appropriate and reflective of actual performance rather than marketplace vagaries. Similarly, entities should be judged only on factors over which they have some degree of control.

Questions for Discussion

1. Firms differ, often substantially, in their organizational structures even within the same industry. What accounts for the differences in their approaches?

2. Discuss the benefits gained by adopting a matrix form of organizational structure.

3. What changes in the firm and/or in the environment might cause a firm to abandon the functional approach?

4. Is there more to the not-invented-here syndrome than simply hurt feelings on the part of those who believe they are being dictated to by headquarters?

5. "Implementors are the most important country organizations in terms of buy-in for a global strategy." Comment.

6. How can systems that are built for global knowledge transfer be used as control tools?

Internet Exercises

1. Improving internal communications is an objective for networked global organizations. Using the web site of the Lotus Development Corporation (http://www.lotus.com) and their section on solutions and success stories, outline how companies have used Lotus Notes to help companies interactively share information.

2. Using company and product information available on their web sites, determine why Dow (http://www.dow.com) and Siemens (http://www.siemens.com) have opted for global product/business structures for their organizations.

Take a Stand

A new executive team at Parker Pen had been impressed with the overall success many companies had had with globalization. As a result, these new managers wanted to make Parker Pen the writing instrument equivalent of the Marlboro man.

Up to that point, Parker Pen's subsidiaries had enjoyed a high degree of autonomy, which, in turn, had resulted in diverse product lines, and there were 40 different advertising agencies handling the Parker Pen account worldwide. The new team wanted to streamline and rid the company of replicated efforts. The goal was to have "one look, one voice," with all the planning taking place at headquarters.

The idea of selling pens the same way around the world did not sit well with many Parker Pen units. Pens were indeed the same, but markets, they believed, were different. France and Italy fancied expensive fountain pens, while northern Europe was a ballpoint market. In some markets, Parker could assume an above-the-fray stance; in others it would have to get into the trenches and compete on price.

Headquarters initially stated that directives were to be used only as starting points and that they allowed for ample local flexibility. The subsidiaries saw it differently and some fought the scheme all the way. Conflict arose, with one of the new executive team members shouting at one of the meetings, "Yours is not to reason why; yours is to implement."

For Discussion
1. Could this situation have been avoided altogether?
2. What should companies do if headquarters–subsidiary conflicts emerge?

S tan Otis was in a contemplative mood. He had just hung up the phone after talking with Roger Morey, vice president of Citicorp. Morey had made him an offer in the investment banking sector of the firm. The interview had gone well, and Citicorp management was impressed with Stan's credentials from a major northeastern private university. "I think you can do well here, Stan. Let us know within a week whether you accept the job," Morey had said.

The three-month search had paid off well, Stan thought. Yet an alternative plan complicated the decision to accept the position.

Stan had returned several months before from an extended trip throughout Europe, a delayed graduation present from his parents. Among other places, he had visited Reykjavik, Iceland. Even though he could not communicate well, he found the island enchanting. What particularly fascinated him was the lack of industry and the purity of the natural landscape. In particular, he felt the water tasted extremely good. Returning home, he began to consider making this water available in the United States.

The Water Market in the United States

In order to consider the possibilities of importing Icelandic water, Stan knew that he first had to learn more about the general water market in the United States. Fortunately, some former college friends were working in a market research firm. Owing Stan some favors, these friends furnished him with a consulting report on the water market.

The Consulting Report

Bottled water has more than a 16 percent share of total beverage consumption in the United States. The overall distribution of market share is shown in Figure 1 and Table 1. Primary types of water available for human consumption in the United States are treated or processed water, mineral water, sparkling or effervescent water, and spring well water.

Treated or processed water comes from a well stream or central reservoir supply. This water usually flows as tap water and has been purified and fluoridated.

Mineral water is spring water that contains a substantial amount of minerals, which may be injected or occur naturally. Natural mineral water is obtained from underground water strata or a natural spring. The composition of the water at its source is constant, and the source discharge and temperature remain stable. The natural content of the water at the source is not modified by an artificial process.

Sparkling or effervescent water is water with natural or artificial carbonation. Some mineral waters come to the surface naturally carbonated through underground gases but lose their fizz on the surface with normal pressure. Many of these waters are injected with carbon dioxide later on.

Minerals are important to the taste and quality of water. The type and variety of minerals present in the water can make it a very healthy and enjoyable drink. The combination of minerals present in the water determines its relative degree of acidity. The level of acidity is measured by the pH factor. A pH 7 rating indicates a neutral water. A higher rating indicates that the water contains more solids, such as manganese calcium, and is said to be "hard." Conversely, water with a lower rating is classified as "soft." Most tap water is soft, whereas the majority of commercially sold waters tend to be hard.

Water Consumption in the United States

Tap water has generally been inexpensive, relatively pure, and plentiful in the United States. Traditionally, bottled water has been consumed in the United States by the very wealthy. In the past several years, however, bottled water has begun to appeal to a wider market. The four main reasons for this change are:

1. An increasing awareness among consumers of the impurity of city water supplies
2. Increasing dissatisfaction with the taste and odor of city tap water
3. Rising affluence in society
4. An increasing desire to avoid excess consumption of caffeine, sugar, and other substances in coffee and soft drinks.

Sources: This study was prepared by Michael R. Czinkota, using the following background material: International Bottled Water Association, Beverage Marketing Corporation, Beverage Aisle, 2002. The author is grateful for the input from Prof. Ingjaldur Hannibalsson and the students at the University of Iceland.

FIGURE 1

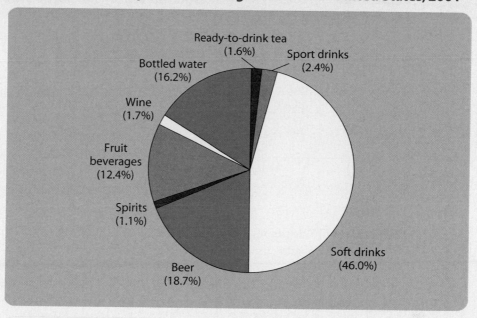

Per Capita Consumption of Beverage Products in United States, 2001

- Ready-to-drink tea (1.6%)
- Sport drinks (2.4%)
- Bottled water (16.2%)
- Wine (1.7%)
- Fruit beverages (12.4%)
- Spirits (1.1%)
- Beer (18.7%)
- Soft drinks (46.0%)

Source: Beverage Aisle.

Bottled water consumers are found chiefly in the states of California, Texas, Florida, New York, and Arizona. Consumers in California, Texas, Florida, New York, and Arizona account for 70 percent of the bottled water consumption in the United States, with California consuming the most. Nationwide, per capita consumption is estimated to be nearly 20 gallons (19.5). As Table 2 shows, the volume of bottled water sold rose from only 354.3 million gallons in 1976 to nearly 5.5 billion gallons in 2001, more than a fifteen-fold increase. Since 1995, there has been growth of nearly 74 percent, gaining market share on soft drinks, tea, beer, and spirits. Volume is expected to increase to 7.2 billion gallons in 2005, a 43 percent increase from 2000 levels.

In 2001, the industry's receipts totaled $6.5 billion on wholesale and $7.7 billion retail (see Figure 2), a 30

TABLE 1

U.S. Beverage Consumption, 2001

	Retail Receipts (in Billions of Dollars)	Per Capita Consumption (in Gallons)
Soft drinks	55.9	55.4
Beer	58.1	22.5
Spirits	38.1	1.3
Fruit beverages	19.5	15.0
Wine	18.9	2.0
Bottled water	7.7	19.5
Sports drinks	3.7	2.9
Ready-to-drink tea	2.8	1.9

Source: Beverage Aisle, Table and graph data taken from *Beverage Aisle,* 11 (no 8): 38. August 15, 2002. Figures are determined based upon industry contracts with the help of Adams Business Media.

TABLE 2

U.S. Bottled Water Market Volume, 1976–2005

Year	Millions of Gallons	Year	Millions of Gallons
1976	354	1995	3,167
1980	605	2002	5,033
1985	1,214	2005*	7,200
1990	2,237		

*Projected.

Source: Beverage Aisle, Table and graph data taken from *Beverage Aisle,* 11 (no 8): 38. August 15, 2002. Figures are determined based upon industry contracts with the help of Adams Business Media.

percent increase in retail sales from 1999. While the volume of total bottled water more than doubled between 1990 and 2000, consumption of nonsparkling bottled water increased 90 percent as consumption of sparkling water declined by 20 percent. Overall, domestic nonsparkling water held the lion's share of the market, as Figure 3 shows.

Though between 1998 and 2000 the volume of imported bottled water decreased 16 percent, imports have almost doubled since 1990 (see Table 3). The lead-

FIGURE 2

U.S. Bottled Water Market, 1990–2001

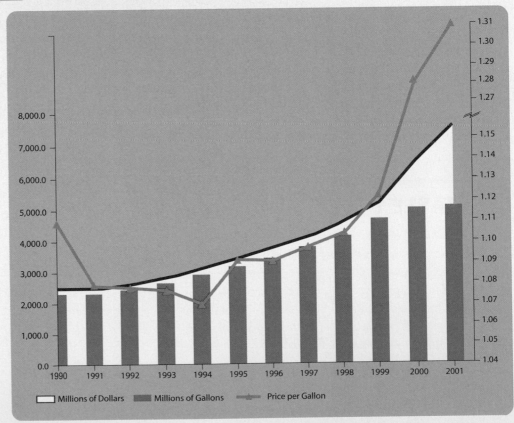

Source: Beverage Marketing Corporation.

FIGURE 3

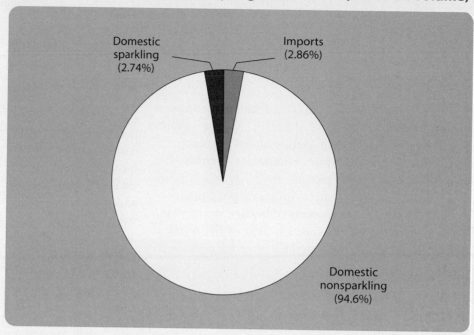

Market Share of Bottled Water by Segment in 2001 (Based on Volume)

Domestic sparkling (2.74%)

Imports (2.86%)

Domestic nonsparkling (94.6%)

Source: Beverage Marketing Corporation.

TABLE 3

U.S. Bottled Water Market by Segments, 1990–2000

Year	Non-Sparkling Volume*	Change	Sparkling Volume*	Change	Imports Volume*	Change	Total Volume*	Change
1990	1,987.7	8.2%	176.0	28.4%	73.9	32.9%	2,237.6	10.3%
1991	2,042.8	2.8%	172.3	−2.1%	71.4	−3.4%	2,286.5	2.2%
1992	2,163.4	5.9%	172.3	0.0%	86.3	20.9%	2,422.0	5.9%
1993	2,356.7	8.9%	174.7	1.4%	92.5	7.2%	2,623.9	8.3%
1994	2,623.1	11.3%	174.8	0.1%	104.0	12.4%	2,901.9	10.6%
1995	2,906.2	10.8%	164.2	−6.1%	97.1	−6.7%	3,167.5	9.2%
1996	3,178.5	9.4%	159.0	−3.2%	111.8	15.2%	3,449.3	8.9%
1997	3,472.9	9.3%	153.8	−3.3%	149.1	33.4%	3,775.8	9.5%
1998	3,839.1	10.5%	146.1	−5.0%	160.8	7.9%	4,146.0	9.8%
1999	4,349.0	13.3%	146.0	−0.1%	151.1	−6.1%	4,646.1	12.1%
2000	4,751.1	9.2%	144.2	−1.2%	137.8	−8.8%	5,033.2	8.3%

*Millions of gallons.

Source: Beverage Marketing Corporation, 2002.

ing country importing water to the United States is France, with a 53.1 percent share of total bottled water imports. Canada is second with 20.8 percent market share. Ranked ninth, bottled water from Iceland holds 0.05 percent market share (see Figure 4).

Among producers, Perrier is a strong leader with a 30.5 percent market share. The Perrier Group's top four selling bottled water brands are Arrowhead, Poland Spring, Ozarka, and Zephrhills—all among the top-ten selling brands in the United States. Suntory Water Group has 9.7 percent and McKesson has 8.0 percent of the market share, with both companies comprised of many relatively small brands.

Overall, a cursory analysis indicates good potential for success for a new importer of bottled water in the United States. This is especially true if the water is exceptionally pure and can be classified as mineral water.

Additional Research

Further exploring his import idea, Stan Otis gathered information on various other marketing facets. One of his main concerns was government regulations.

Bottled Water Regulations in the United States

The bottled water industry in the United States is regulated and controlled at two levels—by the federal government and by various state governments. Some states, such as California and Florida, impose even stricter regulations on bottled water than they are required to follow under the federal regulations. Others, such as Arizona, do not regulate the bottled water industry beyond the federal requirements. About 75 percent of bottled water is obtained from springs, artesian wells, and drilled wells. The other 25 percent comes from municipal water systems, which are regulated by the Environmental Protection Agency (EPA). All bottled water is considered food and is thus regulated by the Food and Drug Administration (FDA). Under the 1974 Safe Drinking Water Act, the FDA adopted bottled water standards compatible with EPA's standards for water from public water systems. As the EPA revises its drinking water regulations, the FDA revises its drinking water regulations, the FDA is required to revise its standards for bottled water to explain in the Federal Register why it decided not to do so. The FDA requires bottled water products to be clean and safe for human consumption, processed and distributed under sanitary conditions, and produced in

FIGURE 4

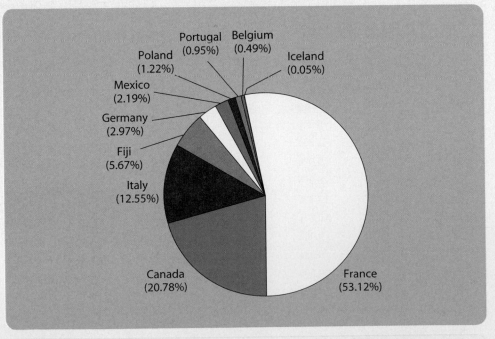

2001 Bottled Water Imports by Country (by Volume)

Portugal (0.95%)
Belgium (0.49%)
Poland (1.22%)
Iceland (0.05%)
Mexico (2.19%)
Germany (2.97%)
Fiji (5.67%)
Italy (12.55%)
Canada (20.78%)
France (53.12%)

Source: U.S. Census Bureau.

compliance with FDA good manufacturing practices. In addition, domestic bottled water producers engaged in interstate commerce are subject to periodic, unannounced FDA inspections.

In 1991, an investigation by the U.S. House Energy and Commerce Committee found that 25 percent of the higher-priced bottled water comes from the same sources as ordinary tap water, another 25 percent of producers were unable to document their sources of water, and 31 percent exceeded limits of microbiological contamination. The Committee faulted the FDA with negligent oversight. In response, the FDA established, in November 1995, definitions for artesian water, groundwater, mineral water, purified water, sparkling bottled water, sterile water, and well water in order to ensure fair advertising by the industry. These results went into effect in May 1996. They include specification of the mineral content of water that can be sold as mineral water. Previously, mineral water was not regulated by the FDA, which resulted in varying standards for mineral water across states. In addition, under these rules, if bottled water comes from a municipal source, it must be labeled to indicate its origin.

The Icelandic Scenario

Iceland is highly import-dependent. In terms of products exported, it has little diversity and is dangerously dependent on its fish crop and world fish prices. The government, troubled by high inflation rates and low financial reserves, is very interested in diversifying its export base. An Icelandic Export Board has been created and charged with developing new products for export and aggressively promoting them abroad.

The Ministry of Commerce, after consulting the Central Bank, has the ultimate responsibility in matters concerning import and export licensing. The Central Bank is responsible for the regulation of foreign exchange transactions and exchange controls, including capital controls. It is also responsible for ensuring that all foreign exchange due to residents is surrendered to authorized banks. All commercial exports require licenses. The shipping documents must be lodged with an authorized bank. Receipts exchanged for exports must be surrendered to the Central Bank.

All investments by nonresidents in Iceland are subject to individual approval. The participation of nonresidents in Icelandic joint venture companies may not exceed 49 percent. Nonresident-owned foreign capital entering in the form of foreign exchange must be surrendered.

Iceland is a member of the United Nations, the European Free Trade Association, and the World Trade Organization. Iceland enjoys "most favored nation" status with the United States. Under this designation, mineral and carbonated water from Iceland is subject to a tariff of 0.33 cents per liter, and natural (still) water is tariff-free.

Questions for Discussion

1. Is there sufficient information to determine whether importing water from Iceland would be a profitable business? If not, what additional information is needed to make a determination?
2. Is the market climate in the United States conducive to water imports from Iceland?
3. What are some possible reasons for the fluctuation in the market share held by imports over the past ten years?
4. Should the U.S. government be involved in regulating bottled water products?

To compete on technology, you have to spend on it, but we have nothing to spend. Were there a normal economic situation in the country, people wouldn't be buying these cars.

—Vladimir Kadannikov,
Chairman, AvtoVAZ of Russia

There are 42 defects in the average new car from AvtoVAZ, Russia's biggest car marker. And that counts as the good news. When the firm introduced a new model last year, a compact saloon called the VAZ-2110, each car came with 92 defects—all the fun of the space station Mir, as it were, without leaving the ground.

—"Mir On Earth," The Economist,
August 21, 1997

In June 2001, David Herman, President of General Motors (GM) Russia, and his team arrived in Togliatti, Russia, for joint venture negotiations between GM and OAO AvtoVAZ, the largest automobile producer in Russia. GM and AvtoVAZ had originally signed a memorandum of understanding (MOU)—a non-binding commitment—on March 3, 1999, to pursue a joint venture in Russia. Now, nearly two years later, Herman had finally received GM's approval to negotiate the detailed structure of the joint venture (JV) with AvtoVAZ to produce and sell Chevrolets in the Russian market.

The Russian car market was expected to account for a significant share of global growth over the next decade. Herman was increasingly convinced that if GM did not move decisively and soon, the market opportunity would be lost to other automakers. Ford, for example, was proceeding with a substantial JV in Russia and was scheduled to begin producing the Ford Focus in late 2002 (it was already importing car kits). Fiat of Italy was already in the construction phases of a plant to build 15,000 Fiat Palios per year beginning in late 2002. Daewoo of Korea had started assembly of compact sedan "kits" in 1998 and was currently selling 15,000 cars a year.

However, Herman also knew that doing business in Russia presented many challenges. The Russian economy,

although recovering from the 1998 collapse, remained weak, uncertain, and subject to confusing tax laws and government rules. The Russian car industry seemed to reel from one crisis to another. The second largest automobile producer, GAZ, had been the victim of an unexpected hostile takeover only three months previous. GAZ's troubles had contributed to GM's fears over the actual ownership of AvtoVAZ itself. In addition, AvtoVAZ had been the subject of an aggressive income tax evasion case by Russian tax authorities in the summer of 2000. Finally, from a manufacturing point of view, AvtoVAZ was far from world class. AvtoVAZ averaged 320 manhours to build a car, a stark comparison against the 28 hours typical of Western Europe and 17 hours in Japan.

Further complicating the situation was a lack of consensus within different parts of GM about the Russian JV. GM headquarters in Detroit had told Herman to find a third party to share the risk and the investment of a Russian JV. Within Adam Opel, GM's European division, there were questions about the scope and timing of Opel's role. Prior to becoming GM's vice president for the former Soviet Union, Herman had been chairman of Adam Opel. He had been forced out of Opel after growing disagreements with Lou Hughes, vice president of GM's international operations, the unit that oversaw Opel. Hughes wanted Opel to lead the development of three global auto platforms, whereas Herman wished to keep Opel focused on recovering its once dominant position in Germany and Western Europe. Now, Herman needed Opel's support for the Russian JV and had to convince his former colleagues that the time was right to enter Russia. As he prepared for the upcoming negotiations, Herman knew there were many more battles to be fought both within GM and in Russia.

General Motors Corporation

General Motors Corporation (United States), founded in 1908, was the largest automobile manufacturer in the world. GM employed more than 388,000 people, operated 260 subsidiaries, affiliates, and joint ventures, managed operations in more than 50 countries, and closed the year 2000 with $160 billion in sales and $4.4 billion in profits.

John F. "Jack" Smith had been appointed chairman of GM's Board of Directors in January 1996, after spending the previous five years as president and chief executive officer. Taking Jack Smith's place as president and CEO was G. Richard "Rick" Wagoner, Jr., previously the director of strategic and operational leadership within GM. GM's international operations were divided into GM Europe, GM Asia Pacific, and GM Latin America, Africa, Middle-East. GM Europe, headquartered in Zurich, Switzerland, provided oversight for GM's various European operations including Opel of Germany and the new initiatives in Russia.

Although the largest automobile manufacturer in the world, GM's market share had been shrinking. By the end of 2000, GM's global market share (in units) was 13.6 percent, with the Ford group closing quickly with a 11.9 percent share, and Volkswagen a close third at 11.5 percent. Emerging markets, like that of Russia, represented so-called "white territories" which were still unclaimed and uncertain markets for the traditional Western automakers.

The Russian Automobile Industry

The Russian auto industry lagged far behind that of the Western European, North American, or Japanese industries. Although the Russian government had made it a clear priority to aid in the industry's modernization and development, inadequate capital, poor infrastructure, and deep-seated mismanagement and corruption resulted in out-dated, unreliable, and unsafe automobiles.

Nevertheless, the industry was considered promising because of the continuing gap between Russian market demand and supply and because of expected future growth in demand. As illustrated in Table 1, between

TABLE 1   The Russian Automobile Industry, 1991–1999 (units)

Russian Production	1991	1992	1993	1994	1995	1996	1997	1998	1999
AvtoVAZ	677,280	676,857	660,275	530,876	609,025	684,241	748,826	605,728	717,660
GAZ	69,000	69,001	105,654	118,159	118,673	124,284	124,339	125,398	125,486
AvtoUAZ	52,491	54,317	57,604	53,178	44,880	33,701	51,411	37,932	38,686
Moskovich	104,801	101,870	95,801	67,868	40,600	2,929	20,599	38,320	30,112
KamAZ	3,114	4,483	5,190	6,118	8,638	8,935	19,933	19,102	28,004
IzhMash	123,100	56,500	31,314	21,718	12,778	9,146	5,544	5,079	4,756
DonInvest	0	0	0	0	321	4,062	13,225	4,988	9,395
Other	14	14	6	7	1	41	3,932	3,061	1,307
Total	1,029,800	963,042	955,844	797,924	834,916	867,339	985,809	839,608	955,406
Percent change	−6.6%	−6.5%	−0.7%	−16.5%	4.6%	3.9%	13.7%	−14.8%	13.8%
Russian Exports	411,172	248,032	533,452	143,814	181,487	144,774	120,551	67,913	107,701
Percent of production	39.9%	25.8%	55.8%	18.0%	21.7%	16.7%	12.2%	8.1%	11.3%
Imports into Russia	26,649	43,477	405,061	97,400	69,214	54,625	42,974	62,718	55,701
Percent of sales	4.1%	5.7%	49.0%	13.0%	9.6%	7.0%	4.7%	7.5%	6.2%
Auto Sales in Russia	645,277	758,487	827,453	751,510	722,643	777,190	908,232	834,413	903,406
Percent growth		17.5%	9.1%	−9.2%	−3.8%	7.5%	16.9%	−8.1%	8.3%

Source: http://www.just-auto.com. December 2000.

1991 and 1993 purchases of cars in Russia had grown dramatically. But this growth had been at the expense of domestic producers, as imports had garnered most of the increase in sales, largely because of a reduction in automobile import duties. With the reduction of import duties in 1993, imports surged to 49 percent of sales and Russian production hit the lowest level of the decade. Domestic producers reacted by increasing their focus on export sales, largely to former CIS countries. Exports ranged between 18 percent and 56 percent of all production during the 1991–95 period.

With the reimposition of import duties in 1994, the import share of the Russian marketplace returned to a level of about 7 to 10 percent. Domestic production began growing again and fewer Russian-made cars were exported. Unfortunately, just as domestic producers were nearly back to early-1990s production levels, the 1998 financial crisis sent the Russian economy and auto industry into a tailspin. Domestic production of automobiles fell nearly 15 percent in 1998. Auto sales in Russia as a whole fell 8 percent. The industry, however, experienced a strong resurgence in 1999 and 2000.

Russian auto manufacturing was highly concentrated, with AvtoVAZ holding a 65 percent market share in 2000, followed by GAZ with 13 percent, and an assorted collection of what could be called "boutique-producers."[1] Although foreign producers accounted for less than 2 percent of all auto manufacturing in Russia in 2000, estimates of the influx of used foreign-made cars were upwards of 350,000 units in 2000 alone.

Although much had changed in Russia in the 1990s, much had also remained the same. In the Russian automobile market, demand greatly exceeded supply. Russians without the right political connections had to wait years for their cars. Cars were still rare, spare parts still difficult to find, and crime still rampant. It was still not unusual to remove windshield wipers from cars for safekeeping parked on major city streets. Cars had to be paid for in cash, as dealer financing was essentially unheard of as a result of the inability of the Russian financial and banking sector to perform adequate credit checks on individuals or institutions. And once paid for, most Russian-made new cars were full of defects to the point that "repair" was often required before driving a new car.

AvtoVAZ

It's mind-blowingly huge. The assembly line goes on for a mile and a quarter. Workstation after workstation. No modules being slapped in. It's piece by piece. The hammering is incessant. Hammering the gaskets in, hammering the doors down, hammering the bumpers. On the engine line a man seems to be screwing in pistons by hand and whopping them with a hammer. If there's a robot on the line, we didn't see it. Forget statistical process control.

—"Would You Want to Drive a Lada?," *Forbes*, August 26, 1996

AvtoVAZ, originally called "VAZ" for Volzhsky Avtomobilny Zavod (Volga Auto Factory), was headquartered approximately 1,000 kilometers southeast of Moscow in Togliatti, a town named after an Italian communist. The original auto manufacturing facility was a JV (in effect, a pure turn-key operation) with Fiat SpA of Italy. The original contract, signed in 1966, resulted in the first cars produced in 1970. The cars produced at the factory were distributed under the Lada and Zhiguli brands and for the next 20 years became virtually the only car the average Russian could purchase.

AvtoVAZ employed more than 250,000 people in 1999 (who were paid an average of $333 per month), and produced 677,700 cars, $1.9 billion in sales, and $458 million in gross profits. However, the company had a pre-tax loss of $123 million. AvtoVAZ was publicly listed on the Moscow Stock Exchange. The Togliatti auto plant, with an estimated capacity of 750,000 vehicles per year, was the largest single automobile assembly facility in the world. It had reached full capacity in 2000. But the company developed only one new car in the 1990s and had spent an estimated $2 billion doing so.

In the early 1990s, following the era of Perestroika and the introduction of economic reforms, AvtoVAZ began upgrading its technology and increasing its prices. As prices skyrocketed, Russians quickly switched to comparably priced imports of higher quality. As a result, AvtoVAZ suffered continual decreases in market share throughout the 1990s (see Table 1), although it still dominated all other Russian manufacturers.

The financial crisis of August 1998 had actually bolstered AvtoVAZ's market position, with the fall of the Russian rouble from Rbl 11/$ to over Rbl 25/$. Imports were now prohibitively expensive for most Russians.

It's cynical to say, but in the case of a devaluation, the situation at AvtoVAZ would be better. There would be a different effectiveness of export sales, and demand would be different. Seeing that money is losing value, people would buy durable goods in the hopes of saving at least something.

—Vladimir Kadannikov, Chairman
of the Board, AvtoVAZ, May 1998

AvtoVAZ also suffered from tax problems and was called a "tax deadbeat" by the Russian press. In July 2000 the Russian Tax Police accused AvtoVAZ of tax fraud. The accusations centered on alleged under-reporting of automobile production by falsifying vehicle identification numbers (VINs). The opening of the criminal case coincided with warnings from the Kremlin that the new administration of President Vladimir Putin would not tolerate continued industry profiteering and manipulation from the country's oligarchs, individuals who had profited greatly from Russia's difficult transition to market capitalism. AvtoVAZ denied the charges and less than one month later, the case was thrown out by the chief prosecutor for tax evasion. A spokesman for the prosecutor's office stated that investigators had found no basis for the allegations against AvtoVAZ executives.

AvtoVAZ Ownership

One of the primary deterrents to foreign investment in Russia had been the relatively lax legal and regulatory structure for corporate governance. Identifying the owners of most major Russian companies was extremely difficult.

Although much about the ownership of AvtoVAZ remained unclear, it was believed that two different management groups controlled the majority of Avto-VAZ shares. One group was led by the current Chairman, Vladimir Kadannikov, and held 33.2 percent of total shares through an organization he controlled, the All-Russian Automobile Alliance (AVVA). A second group, represented by a Mr. Yuri Zukster, controlled 19.2 percent through a different organization, the Automobile Finance Corporation (AFC). A Russian investment fund, Russ-Invest, held 5 percent, with the remaining 42.6 percent under "undisclosed" ownership.

AvtoVAZ itself held an 80.8 percent interest in Kadannikov's AVVA Group, an investment fund. AVVA, in turn, held a 33.2 percent interest in AvtoVAZ (see Figure 1 for an overview of the complex relationships surrounding AvtoVAZ). AVVA itself was in some way influenced, controlled, or owned in part, by one of the most high-profile oligarchs in Russia, Boris Berezovsky.

In 1989, prior to the implementation of President Boris Yelstin's economic reforms, Boris Berezovsky, a mathematician and management-systems consultant to AvtoVAZ, persuaded Vladimir Kadannikov to cooperate in a new car distribution system. Berezovsky formed an automobile dealer network, LogoVAZ that was supplied with AvtoVAZ vehicles on consignment. Logo-VAZ did not pay for the cars it distributed (termed "re-export" by Berezovsky) until a date significantly after his dealer network sold the cars and received payment themselves. The arrangement proved disastrous for AvtoVAZ and incredibly profitable for Berezovsky. In the years that followed, hyperinflation raged in Russia, and Berezovsky was able to run his expanding network of businesses with AvtoVAZ's cash flow. (Mr. Berezovsky has admitted to the arrangement, and its financial benefits to him. He has also pointed out, correctly, that under Russian law he has not broken any laws.) LogoVAZ was also one of the largest auto importers in Russia.

In 1994, the Russian government began privatizing many state-owned companies, including AvtoVAZ. Boris Berezovsky, Vladimir Kadannikov, and Alexander Voloshin, recently appointed chief of staff for Russian President Vladimir Putin, then formed AVVA. The stated purpose of AVVA was to begin building a strong dealer network for the automobile industry in Russia. AVVA quickly acquired its 33.2 percent interest in AvtoVAZ, in addition to many other enterprises. AVVA frequently represented AvtoVAZ's significant international interests around the world.

By 2000 Berezovsky purportedly no longer had formal relations with AVVA, but many observers believed he continued to have a number of informal lines of influence. In December 2000, AVVA surprised many analysts by announcing that it was amending its charter to change its status from an investment fund to a holding company. Auto analysts speculated that AVVA was positioning itself to run AvtoVAZ, which had reorganized into divisions (car production, marketing and sales, research and development).

Share ownership anxiety had intensified in November 2000 when the second largest automobile manufacturer in Russia, GAZ, had been the victim of a hostile takeover. Beginning in August 2000, Sibirsky Alyuminiy (SibAl) started accumulating shares in GAZ until reaching the 25 percent plus one share threshold necessary for veto power under Russian law. The exact amount of SibAl ownership in GAZ, however, was unknown, even to GAZ. Current regulations required

FIGURE 1

AvtoVAZ's Web of Influence and Ownership

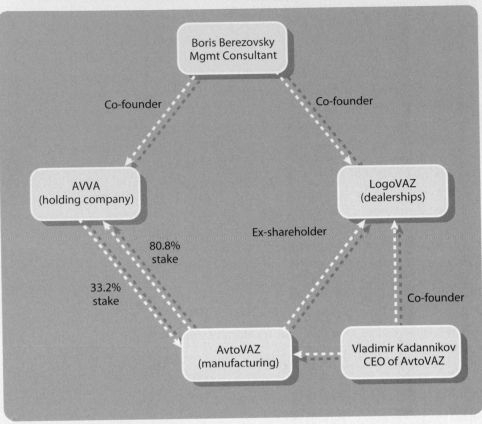

Source: Adapted from http://www.just-auto.com.

---

only the disclosure of the identity and stake of stock-holders of 5 percent equity stake or more. Only direct investors were actually named, and those named were frequently only agents operating on behalf of the true owners. Adding to the confusion was the fact that frequently the "nominees" named represent multiple groups of ultimate owners. The inadequacy of information about ownership in Russia was demonstrated by GAZ's inability to actually confirm whether SibAl did indeed have a 25 percent ownership position.

Rumors surfaced immediately that AvtoVAZ could be next, and the threat could arise from SOK, Avto-VAZ' largest single supplier. Many industry players, however, viewed this as highly unlikely.

"Besides Kadannikov, the brass at AvtoVAZ tend to keep a low profile, but they still rank among Russia's elite executives, and they are independent," said an official of a foreign supplier in Russia. "SOK may be powerful with AvtoVAZ,

and AvtoVAZ may find SOK highly useful, but I doubt SOK ever could impact AvtoVAZ strategy, and I think SOK ultimately plays by rules set by AvtoVAZ."

—"Domino Theory: AvtoVAZ following GAZ falling to new owner?," http://www. just-auto.com, December 12, 2000

Management of AvtoVAZ also felt they had an additional takeover defense, which strangely enough, arose from their history of not paying corporate taxes. In 1997, as part of a settlement with Russian tax authorities on $2.4 billion in back-taxes, AvtoVAZ gave the Russian tax authorities the right to 50 percent plus one share of AvtoVAZ if the firm failed—in the future—to make its tax payments. AvtoVAZ management now viewed this as their own version of a "poison pill." If the target of a hostile takeover, management could stop paying taxes and the Russian government would take management control, defeating the hostile takeover.[2]

AvtoVAZ Suppliers

Unlike many former Communist enterprises, AvtoVAZ was not vertically integrated. The company depended on a variety of suppliers for components and subassemblies and an assortment of retail distributors. It had little control over its suppliers, and was prohibited by law from retail distribution. In recent years, AvtoVAZ's supplier base had been continually consolidated. The three biggest suppliers to AvtoVAZ were DAAZ, Plastik, and Avtopribor (see Table 2 below), all of which had been purchased by the Samara Window Company (abbreviated as "SOK" from the Russian name) in the preceding years.[3]

Starting from a relatively small base, SOK had grown from a small glass window factory to a diversified enterprise of roughly $2 billion sales in 1999, with businesses that included bottled water, building construction, medical equipment, plastic parts, and windows, and most recently, AvtoVAZ's largest supplier and retailer. Although SOK officially purchased only 8,000 cars per year for distribution from AvtoVAZ, it was purportedly selling over 40,000 cars per year. The difference was rumored to be cars assembled by SOK from kits purchased or "exchanged" with AvtoVAZ. AvtoVAZ, often short of cash, frequently paid taxes, suppliers, and management in cars.

Dealerships and Distribution

In the early 1990s hundreds of trading companies were formed around the company. Most trading companies would exchange parts and inputs for cars, straight from the factory, at prices 20 percent to 30 percent below market value. The trading companies then sold the cars themselves, capturing significant profit, while AvtoVAZ waited months for payment of any kind from the trad-

ing companies. The practice continued unabated in 1996 and 1997 because most of the trading companies were owned and operated by AvtoVAZ managers. Russian law did not prevent management from pursuing private interests related to their own enterprises.

Crime was also prevalent on the factory floor. Mobsters purportedly would enter the AvtoVAZ factory and take cars directly from the production lines at gun point. Buyers or distributors were charged $100 for "protection" at the AvtoVAZ factory gates. To quote one automobile distributor, "They were bandits. Nevertheless, they provided a service." By the fall of 1997 the intrusion of organized crime became so rampant within AvtoVAZ that Vladimir Kadannikov used Russian troops to clear the plant of thugs.

International Activities

AvtoVAZ was actually a multinational company, with significant international operations in addition to significant export sales.

As illustrated in Table 3, in 1991 AvtoVAZ was exporting more than 125,000 cars per year to the countries of the Soviet state. With the deconstruction of the old Soviet Union, sales plummeted to the now-CIS countries as a result of the proliferation of weak currencies from country to country, as well as the imposition of new import duties at every border to Russia of 30 percent or more.[4] In the late 1990s, sales were essentially zero. Similarly, sales in the Baltic countries of Latvia, Lithuania, and Estonia had also essentially disappeared.

Brazil has been the site of substantial AvtoVAZ activity in the past decade, with starts and stops. AvtoVAZ had originally flooded the Brazilian market in 1990 with imports when the government of Brazil had opened its

TABLE 2   AvtoVAZ Suppliers Owned or Controlled by SOK

Supplier	Location	Parts
Avtopribor	Vladimir	clusters for instrument panels, gauges, speedometers
Avtosvet	Kirzhach	connectors, exterior and interior lights, reflectors, signals
DAAZ	Dimitrovgrad	electronics, lights, moldings, wheels
Osvar	Vyazniki	exterior and interior lights, reflectors, signals, warning lights
Plastik	Syzran	foam, plastics, sealants
Syzranselmash	Syzran	chemicals, headliners, sun visors, window lifters

Source: http://www.just-auto.com. December 2000.

TABLE 3   AvtoVAZ Exports

	1991	1992	1993	1994	1995	1996	1997	1998	1999
Baltic countries	8,392	3,895	3,325	590	8,832	2,648	1,101	716	487
CIS countries	126,440	42,900	19,644	4,491	1,601	1,074	962	108	331
Elsewhere	269,936	271,763	280,593	196,696	175,161	129,957	94,303	68,689	49,957
Total exports	404,768	318,558	303,562	201,777	185,594	133,679	96,366	69,513	50,775
Total Sales	674,884	673,821	656,403	528,845	607,279	680,965	736,000	599,829	677,669
Export percentage	60%	47%	46%	38%	31%	20%	13%	12%	7%

Source: http://www.just-auto.com. December 2000.

borders to imports. Despite 85 percent import duties, deeply discounted Ladas and Nivas sold well. However, in 1995, the Brazilian government excluded AvtoVAZ from a list of select international manufacturers which would be allowed much lower import duties. AvtoVAZ then withdrew from the Brazilian market. In November of 2000, AvtoVAZ concluded the negotiation of an agreement with a Brazilian entrepreneur, Carlos de Moraes, for his company, Abeiva Car Imports, to begin assembly of Nivas in 2001. The target price, 17,000 Brazilian reais, (about US$8,900), would hopefully make them affordable for Brazilian farmers.

In the past decade, AvtoVAZ has exported to a variety of European countries as well, including Germany, Portugal, Spain, the United Kingdom, and Greece. These sales have typically been small special-order models of the Niva (diesel engines, Peugeot gas engines, etc.). Continued issues surrounding quality and reliability, however, had pushed the company toward an emerging market strategy. It was hoped that low-income markets such as Egypt, Ecuador, and Uruguay would reignite the export potential of the company. GM's strategy was based on extreme low prices to successfully penetrate local markets.

Foreign Entry into Russia

GM interest in Russia extended back to the 1970s when Opel had proposed shipping car kits to Moscow for assembly. The plan foundered because of GM concerns about quality control. In 1991 GM renewed its interest in Russia, once again opening talks with a number of potential JV partners. But after more than a decade, few deals had materialized.

In December 1996 GM opened a plant in Elabuga, Tatarstan, in a JV with Yelaz to assemble Chevrolet Blazers from imported kits (complete knockdown kits, or CKDs). The original plan had been to ramp up production volumes rapidly to 50,000 units a year. But the operation struggled. One problem was the product; the Blazers were two-wheel drive with 2.2 liter engines. The Russian consumer wanted the four-wheel driver version widely sold in the United States, typically powered by a 3-liter engine. A second problem was the origin of the kits. The CKDs were imported from Brazil and most Russians did not have a high degree of respect for Brazilian products.

In September 1998 operations were suspended as a result of the Russian financial crisis. Only 3,600 units had been assembled. An attempt was made to restart assembly operations in 1999, this time assembling Opel Vectras, but when it became apparent that the market for a vehicle costing $20,000 would not succeed in the needed volumes, the JV's assembly operations were closed. GM still had more than 200 Blazers in inventory in January 2001 and was attempting to close out the last vestiges of the operation.

From 1998 to 2002, there were a number of foreign automobile producers in various stages of entry into the Russian marketplace, as summarized in Table 4. Daewoo of Korea, which had made major volume achievements in a number of former Eastern Bloc countries such as Poland, had begun assembly of compact sedan kits in 1998, and had quickly reached a sales level in Russia of 15,000 units in 1999. Similarly, Renault of France had followed the kit assembly entry strategy with the Renault Megane in 1998, but had only assembled and sold 1,100 units by end of year 1999.

Others, like Ford Motor Company of the United States, had announced JVs with Russian manufacturers to actually build automobiles in Russia. The Ford Focus, priced on the relatively high side at $13,000 to $15,000,

TABLE 4 — Foreign Auto Producers in Russia

Foreign Manufacturer	Russian Partner	Auto Model	Target Price Range	Capacity per Year	Expected Startup
Daewoo (Korea)	Doninvest	Compact	$6,000–$8,000	20,000	1998
BMW (Germany)	Avtotor	523, 528	$36,000–$53,000	10,000	2000
Renault (France)	City of Moscow	Megane	$8,500–$13,500	100,000	1998
Ford (USA)	Bankirsky	Dom Focus	$13,000–$15,000	25,000	2002
Fiat (Italy)	GAZ	Palio, Siena	$7,000–$10,000	15,000	2002
GM (USA)	AvtoVAZ	Niva, T3000	$7,500–$10,000	75,000	2002

was planned for a production launch in late 2002. The facility planned was to produce 25,000 cars per year. The Russian government had given its blessing to the venture by allowing the elimination of import duties on imported inputs as long as the local content of the Focus reached 50 percent within five years of startup (2007 under current plans). Ford was already importing the Focus to begin building a market, but in the early months of 2001, sales were sluggish.

Fiat of Italy was potentially the most formidable competitor. Fiat planned to introduce the Fiat Palio and Fiat Siena into the Russian marketplace through a JV with GAZ in 2002. Although the planned capacity of the plant was only 15,000 cars per year, the Fiat Palio was considered by many auto experts as the right product for the market. The critical question was whether Fiat could deliver the Palio to the market at a low enough price. In its negotiations with the Russian gov-

ernment, Fiat announced its intentions to make the Palio a true "Russian-made" automobile which would quickly rise to over 70 percent in local content. If Fiat could indeed achieve this, and there were many who believed that if anyone could it was Fiat, then this would be the true competitive benchmark.

Renewed Interest

For most Russians, price was paramount. The average income levels in Russia prevented automobile pricing at Western levels. As seen in Table 5, prices over the past few years had dropped as a result of the 1998 financial crisis. For 2001, analysts estimated that almost the entire market in Russia was for cars priced below $10,000. Given that the average Russian's salary was about $100 per month, cars remained out of reach for the average Russian.

TABLE 5 — Russian Auto Market Shares by Price

Price Range	1998		1999	
	Seg	Cum	Seg	Cum
Below $5,000	3%	3%	85%	85%
$5,001–$10,000	65%	68%	12%	97%
$10,001–$15,000	15%	83%	1%	98%
Above $15,000	17%	100%	2%	100%

Seg=segment
Cum=cumulative.

Source: General Motors.

In a September 2000 interview, David Herman summarized GM's viewpoint on pricing and positioning:

> We could not make an interesting volume with a base price above $10,000. Such a vehicle would feature few specifications—ABS and airbags plus a 1.6-liter 16-valve engine. But, if the car costs $12,000, it is only $2,000 less than certain foreign imports, and this gap may be too small to generate enough sales to justify a factory. We knew we could make a vehicle cheaper with AvtoVAZ, but we need to ensure the price advantage of T3000 imports over competitive models is closer to $7,000 than $2,000.[5]

GM had originally considered the traditional emerging market approach of building complete cars in existing plants and then disassembling them by removing bumpers, wheels, and other separable parts, shipping the disassembled "kit" into Russia, and reassembling with local labor. The disassembly/assembly process allowed the automobile to be considered domestically produced by Russian authorities, thereby avoiding prohibitive import duties. The market assessment group at GM, however, believed that Russian buyers (as opposed to customs officials) would see through the "ruse" and consider the cars high-quality imports. But marketing research indicated the opposite: Russians did not want to buy cars reassembled by Russians. The only way they would purchase a Russian-made automobile was if it was extremely cheap, like the majority of the existing AvtoVAZ and GAZ product lines, which retailed for as little as $3,000 per car. GM, realizing that it could not deliver the reassembled Opel to the Russian marketplace for less than $15,000 per car, dropped the kit proposal.

GM's marketing research unveiled an additional critical element. Russians would gladly pay an additional $1,000 to $1,500 per car if it had a *Chevrolet* label or badge on it. This piece of research resulted in the original proposal that David Herman and his staff had been pursuing since early 1999: a two-stage JV investment with AvtoVAZ that would allow GM to both reach price targets and position the firm for expected market growth. In the first stage, GM would co-produce a four-wheel-drive SUV named the Lada Niva II (VAZ-2123). The target price was $7500 and plant capacity was to be 90,000 cars. The Niva II would be largely Russian-engineered and, therefore GM would avoid many of the development costs associated with the introduction of a totally new vehicle. The Lada Niva I had originally been introduced in 1977 and updated in new models in 1990 and again in 1996. It had been a successful line for AvtoVAZ, averaging 70,000 units per year throughout the 1990s.[6] Since the Niva II was largely Russian-engineered, GM would bring capital and name to the venture.

The second stage of the project would be the construction of a new factory to produce 30,000 Opel Astras (T3000) for the Russian market. Herman's proposal was for AvtoVAZ to use a basic Opel AG vehicle platform as a pre-engineering starting point. Pre-engineering represented about 30 percent of the development cost of a vehicle. The remaining 70 percent would be developed by AvtoVAZ's 10,000 engineers and technicians who worked at a much lower cost than Opel's engineers in Germany. Herman's Russian Group estimated that even if GM and AvtoVAZ used AvtoVAZ's factory to build the existing Opel Astra from mostly imported parts and kits from Germany, the resulting price tag would have to fall to between $12,500 and $14,000 per car. This was still considered too expensive for substantial economic volumes. Using the Russian engineering approach, the car would be cheaper, but still fall at the higher end of the spectrum, retailing at about $10,000 per car. As seen in Exhibit 3, this would still put the higher-priced Chevrolet in the lower end of the foreign-made market.

By no means was there consensus within GM and Opel about the viability of the proposed JV. One concern was that as a result of the cash shortage at AvtoVAZ and the slow rate of negotiation progress, in order to build test-models of the new Niva, AvtoVAZ had to use 60 percent of the old Niva's parts. Although many of the consumers that tested the Niva II ranked it above all other Russian-built cars, the car was rough riding and noisy by Western standards. One Opel engineer from Germany who safety-tested the Niva II and evaluated its performance declared it "a real car, if primitive." Heidi McCormack, General Director for GM's Russian operations believed that with some minor engineering adjustments, better materials for the interior construction, and a new factory built and operated by GM, the quality of the Niva II would be "acceptable."

GM management was pleased AvtoVAZ appeared willing to contribute the rejuvenated Niva to the JV. "That's their brand-new baby," said McCormack. "It's been shown in autoshows. And here's GM, typical big multinational, saying, 'Just give us your best product.'"[7] But in the end, AvtoVAZ's limited access to capital was the driver. Without GM, AvtoVAZ would probably take five years to get the Niva II to market; with GM the time could be cut in half.

Negotiations

Negotiations between AvtoVAZ and GM had taken a number of twists and turns over the years, involving every possible dimension of the project. The JV's market strategy, scope, timing, financing, and structure were all under continual debate. GM's team was led by David Herman.

Herman had been appointed V.P. of General Motors Corporation for the former Soviet Union in 1998. Starting with General Motors Treasury as an attorney in 1973, Herman had extensive international experience, including three years as GM's manager of sales development in the USSR (1976–1979), and other managing director positions in Spain (1979–1982), Chile (1982–1984), and Belgium (1986–1988). These were followed by chief executive positions for GM (Europe) in Switzerland and Saab Automobile. From 1992 to 1998, Herman had been chairman and managing director of Adam Opel AG in Germany. Herman's departure from Opel in Germany was purportedly the result of losing a highly publicized internal battle over the future strategic direction of Opel. Herman had argued that Opel should focus on developing product for the domestic market, while others in the organization argued that Opel should focus on "filling the pipeline for GM's ambitions in emerging markets." Many have characterized his new appointment as head of GM's market initiatives in Russia as a Siberian exile. Herman's parents were Belorussian and he had studied Russian at Harvard. In addition to Russian and English, he was also fluent in German and Spanish.

Market Strategy

Back in Detroit, the JV proposal continued to run into significant opposition. GM President Rick Wagoner continued to question whether the Russian market could actually afford the Opel-based second car, the Opel T3000. Wagoner wondered whether the second phase of the project should not be cut, making the Niva the single product which the JV would produce. This could potentially reduce GM's investment to $100 million.

A further point of debate concerned export sales. As a result of the 1998 financial crisis in Russia, a number of people inside both GM and AvtoVAZ pushed for a JV which would produce a car designed for both Russian sales and export sales. After 1998 the weaker Russian rouble meant that Russian exports were more competitive. If the product quality was competitive for the targeted markets, there was a belief that Russian cars could be profitably exported. As a result, Herman expanded his activities to include export market development. The working proposal now assumed that one third of all the Chevrolet Nivas produced would be exported. The domestic market continued to be protected with a 30 percent import duty against foreign-made automobiles, both new and used.

Herman brought AvtoVAZ senior management to the Detroit auto show in the spring of 2000 to meet with GM President Rick Wagoner and Vice Chairman Harry Pearce. The meetings went well. In March 2000, however, GM announced an alliance with Fiat. A key element of the alliance involved GM acquiring 20 percent of Fiat's automotive business. GM paid $2.4 billion using GM common stock for the 20 percent stake, which resulted in Fiat owning 5.1 percent of GM. In June 2000, GM and Fiat submitted a joint bid for Daewoo, which was part of the bankrupt Daewoo chaebol. The bid was rejected. Herman returned to Russia, once again slowing negotiations until any possible overlap between GM and Fiat ambitions in Russia were resolved.

Timing

In the summer of 1999, AvtoVAZ had formally announced the creation of a JV with General Motors to produce Opel Astras and the Chevrolet Niva. However, this announcement was not confirmed by GM. Later in 1999, GM's European management, primarily via the Opel division, lobbied heavily within GM to postpone the proposed Chevrolet Niva launch until 2004 to allow a longer period of economic recovery in Russia. Upon learning of this, Kadannikov reportedly told GM to "keep its money," that AvtoVAZ would launch the new Niva on its own. The two sides were able to agree on a tentative 2003 launch date.

Financing

In May 2000 Herman's presentation of the JV proposal to Wagoner and Pearce in Detroit hit another roadblock: The proposed $250 million investment was considered "too large and too risky for a market as risky as Russia—with a partner as slippery as AvtoVAZ."[8] Wagoner instructed Herman to find a third party to share the capital investment and the risk, as GM would not risk more than $100 million itself. Within three months Herman found a third party—the European Bank for Reconstruction and Development (EBRD). EBRD was willing to provide debt and equity. It would lend $93 million to the venture and invest an additional $40 million for an equity stake of 17 percent.[9]

The European Bank for Reconstruction and Development was established in 1991 with the express purpose of fostering the transition to open market-oriented economies and promoting private and entrepreneurial ventures in Eastern Europe and the Commonwealth of Independent States (CIS). As a catalyst of change the bank seeks to co-finance with firms that are providing foreign direct investment (FDI) in these countries in order to help mobilize domestic capital and reduce the risks associated with FDI. Recent economic reforms and the perceived stability of President Putin's government had convinced the EBRD's senior management that conditions were right.

GM management knew that $332 million would be insufficient to build a state-of-the-art manufacturing facility. However, given that AvtoVAZ contributions would include the design, land, and production equipment, $332 million was believed to be sufficient to launch the new Niva. The planned facility would include a car body paint shop, assembly facilities, and testing areas. AvtoVAZ would supply the JV with the car-body, engine and transmission, chassis units, interior components, and electrical system.

Structure

A continuing point of contention was where the profits of the JV would be created. For example, AvtoVAZ had consistently quoted a price for cement for the proposed plant which was thought to be about 10 times what GM would customarily pay in Germany. Then, just prior to the venture's going before the GM Board for preliminary approval for continued negotiations, AvtoVAZ made a new and surprising demand that GM increase the price the JV would pay AvtoVAZ for Niva parts by 25 percent. (Vladimir Kadannikov demanded to know where the profits would be, "in the price of the parts each side supplied to the joint venture or in the venture itself?").[10] When Herman warned them this would scuttle the deal, AvtoVAZ backed off. After heated debate, the two parties now agreed that they would not try to profit from the sale of components to the JV.

The structure for the management team and specific allocation of managerial responsibilities had yet to be determined. Although both sides expected to be actively involved in day-to-day management, GM had already made it clear that management control of the JV was a priority for going forward. GM also wanted to minimize the number of expatriate managers assigned to the venture. AvtoVAZ saw the JV as an opportunity for its managers to gain valuable experience and expected to have significant purchasing, assembly, and marketing responsibilities. AvtoVAZ expected GM to develop and support an organizational structure that ensured technology transfer to the JV. AvtoVAZ knew that in China

GM had created a technical design center as a separate JV with its Chinese partner. The specific details as to how GM might be compensated for technology transfer to Russia remained unclear. Finally, the issue of who would control the final documentation for the JV agreement had yet to be agreed.

The JV would be located on the edge of the massive AvtoVAZ complex in Togliatti. It would utilize one factory building which was partially finished and previously abandoned. The building already housed much equipment in various operational states, including expensive plastic molding and cutting tools imported from Germany in the early 1990s which AvtoVAZ had been unable to operate effectively but could not resell.

Progress

Again, primarily out of frustration with the pace of negotiations, AvtoVAZ announced in January 2001 that it would begin small-scale production of a SUV under its own Lada brand. Herman once again was able to intervene. Herman promised GM's Board that AvtoVAZ would actually build no more than a few dozen of the SUVs "for show." The two sides also continued to debate whether AvtoVAZ would be allowed to sell the prototypes of the new Niva that AvtoVAZ planned to build (approximately 500). GM was adamant, according to long-standing policy, that these should not find their way to the marketplace. AvtoVAZ countered that this was routine for Russian manufacturers and served as a type of "test fleet."

Finally, on February 6, 2001, Herman presented the current proposal to GM's board in Detroit. After heated debate, the board approved the proposal. The possibility of entering a large and developing market, with shared risk and investment, was a rare opportunity to get in early and develop a new local market. According to Rick Wagoner, "Russia's going to be a very big market."

"We'll sell it in former Soviet Union, and eventually export it and because of the cost of material and labor in Russia, we should reach a price point which gives us a decent volume. That will give us a chance to get a network and get started with suppliers and other partners in Russia in a way which I hope will make us amongst the leaders."[11]

David Herman had gained the approval of the General Motors Board to pursue and complete negotiations with AvtoVAZ. The negotiations themselves, however, represented an enormous undertaking, and both GM and AvtoVAZ had many issues yet to be resolved. The two sides at the negotiating table in June included David Herman and Heidi McCormack of GM Russia and Vladimir Kadannikov and Alexei Nikolaev representing AvtoVAZ.

Questions for Discussion

1. What are the specific pros and cons of the proposed joint venture from the AvtoVAZ perspective?

2. What are the specific pros and cons of the proposed joint venture from the General Motors perspective?

3. If you were negotiating on the part of AvtoVAZ, what specific issues would have to be resolved (so-called "walk-away points") before the joint venture would be acceptable?

4. If you were negotiating on the part of General Motors, what specific issues would have to be resolved before the joint venture would be acceptable?

Endnotes

1. Other significant Russian automobile manufacturers included AutoUAX, AZLK, KAMAZ, Roslada, SeAZ, IzhMash, and Doninvest.

2. The Russian government was not, however, anxious for this series of events to unfold. It would also mean that AvtoVAZ would be entering an 18-month period in which it paid no taxes whatever to the government if the option were exercised by the Tax Police.

3. *Sok* means "juice" in Russian, but in the auto sector in Russia, the English-language joke was that SOK was SOKing-up the supplier industry.

4. AvtoVAZ did attempt to restart CIS sales in 1997 with the introduction of hard-currency contracts. The governments of Uzbekistan, Byelorussia, and Ukraine, however, forbid residents from converting local currency into hard currency for the purpose of purchasing automobiles (in two cases, specifically the product of AvtoVAZ). AvtoVAZ has accused the authorities in these countries of working in conjunction with Daewoo of Korea, which has production facilities in Uzbekistan and the Ukraine, of working to shut them out.

5. "Exclusive Interview: David Herman on GM's Strategy for Russia," http://www.just-auto.com, September 2000.

6. One of the primary reasons for the success of the Niva was the poor state of Russian roads. The four-wheel-drive Niva handled the pot-holed road infrastructure with relative ease.

7. Gregory L. White, "off Road: How the Chevy Name Landed on SUV Using Russian Technology," *Wall Street Journal*, February 20, 2001.

8. *Wall Street Journal*, February 20, 2001.

9. The willingness of EBRD to invest was a bit surprising given that two of its previous investments with Russian automakers, GAZ and KamAZ, had resulted in defaults on EBRD credits. A third venture in which EBRD was still a partner (20 percent equity), Nizhegorod Motors, a JV between Fiat and GAZ, had delayed its car launch from late 1998 to the first half of 2002.

10. *Wall Street Journal*, February 21, 2001.

11. "David Herman on GM's Strategy for Russia," http://www.just-auto.com, September 2000.

APPENDIX 1

OAO AvtoVAZ Profit and Loss Statement, 1996–1999

(Thousands of roubles)	1996	1997	1998	Jan–Oct 1999
Net sales less VAT	23,697,167	26,255,183	9,533,172	33,834,987
Less cost of goods sold	(18,557,369)	(21,552,999)	(7,650,161)	(25,998,011)
Gross profits	5,139,798	4,702,184	1,883,011	7,836,976
Gross margin	21.7%	17.9%	19.8%	23.2%
Less sales & marketing expenses	(638,739)	(497,540)	(168,381)	(603,170)
Operating income	4,501,059	4,204,644	1,714,630	7,233,806
Operating margin	19.0%	16.0%	18.0%	21.4%
Interest	—	—	—	—
Dividend income	3,366	3,392	159	8,749
Income on asset disposal	3,084,203	23,052,035	2,516,466	4,115,346
Loss on asset disposal	(3,935,990)	(21,718,864)	(3,430,751)	(5,716,732)
Income from core business	3,652,638	5,541,207	800,504	5,641,169
Non-operating income	400,185	372,340	69,415	252,713
Non-operating expenses	(1,136,225)	(1,033,305)	(299,123)	(1,124,448)
Income for period	2,916,598	4,880,242	570,796	4,769,434
Less income tax	(682,556)	(1,166,911)	77,268	(1,112,039)
Disallowable expenses	(409,906)	(7,069,333)	(251,574)	(1,674,947)
Net income	1,824,136	(3,356,002)	396,490	1,982,448
Return on sales (ROS)	7.7%	−12.8%	4.2%	5.9%
In U.S. dollars				
Exchange rate (roubles/US$)	5.6	6.0	9.7	24.6
Net sales	$4,231,636,964	$ 4,375,863,833	$982,801,237	$1,375,405,976
Gross profits	917,821,071	783,697,333	194,124,845	318,576,260
Income from core business	652,256,786	923,534,500	82,526,186	229,315,813
Income for period	520,821,071	813,373,667	58,844,948	193,879,431
Net income	325,738,571	(559,333,667)	40,875,258	80,587,317

Source: AvtoVAZ

APPENDIX 2   AvtoVAZ Product Prices by City
(February 2001, in Russian roubles)

Code	Model	Type	Tolyatti	Moscow	St. Petersburg
21060	Lada Classic	1976 sedan	84,100	86,500	90,100
2107	Lada Classic	1982 sedan	86,700	91,700	94,400
21083	Lada Samara	1985 3-door hatch	111,900	117,500	115,800
21093	Lada Samara	1987 5-door hatch	112,200	119,700	115,800
21099	Lada Samara	1990 sedan	122,500	132,000	132,600
21102	Lada 2110	1996 sedan	146,500	150,700	151,700
21103	Lada 2110	1997 station wagon	161,100	164,800	162,300
21110	Lada 2110	1999 5-door hatch	157,200	161,900	168,900
2112	Lada Samara II	2001 3-door hatch	167,300	168,600	168,300
2115	Lada Samara II	1997 sedan	143,000	153,700	149,600
21213	Lada Niva	1997 SUV	103,500	111,300	111,100
Average (roubles)			126,909	132,582	123,582
Exchange rate (roubles/US$)			30.00	30.00	30.00
Average (US$)			$4,230	$4,419	$4,111

Source: AvtoVAZ

APPENDIX 3   Russian Demographics and Economics, 1993–2005

	Actual						
Indicator	1993	1994	1995	1996	1997	1998	1999
Real GDP growth (%)	−8.7%	−12.7%	−4.1%	−3.5%	−0.8%	−4.9%	3.2%
GDP per capita (US$)	1,135	1,868	2,348	2,910	3,056	1,900	1,260
Consumer price index (% chg)	875%	308%	198%	48%	15%	28%	86%
External debt (bill US$)	112.7	119.9	120.4	125.0	123.5	183.6	174.3
Foreign direct investment (bill US$)	na	0.5	0.7	0.7	3.8	1.7	0.8
Population (millions)	148.2	148.0	148.1	147.7	147.1	146.5	146.0
Unemployment rate (%)	5.3%	7.0%	8.3%	9.3%	10.8%	11.9%	12.5%
Wages (US$/hour)						0.63	0.36
Exchange rate (roubles/US$)	1.2	3.6	4.6	5.6	6.0	9.7	24.6

	Estimates					
Indicator	2000	2001	2002	2003	2004	2005
Real GDP growth (%)	5.8%	3.5%	4.0%	4.0%	4.5%	4.2%
GDP per capita (US$)	1,560	1,760	1,970	2,170	2,390	2,610
Consumer price index (% chg)	21%	17%	14%	12%	11%	8%
External debt (bill US$)	160.6	171.2	176.8	182.8	186.2	188.8
Foreign direct investment (bill US$)	2.0	4.0	5.7	6.5	6.5	6.5
Population (millions)	145.4	145.1	144.8	144.5	144.2	143.2
Unemployment rate (%)	10.8%	10.1%	10.1%	9.8%	9.2%	9.1%
Wages (US$/hour)	0.44	0.52	0.60	0.70	0.80	0.90
Exchange rate (roubles/US$)	28.4	30.5	32.0	33.5	35.0	36.0

Source: Economist Intelligence Unit, February 2001.

APPENDIX 4 **Foreign Automobile Manufacturers and Russian Partners in Russia**

Manufacturer/ Partner	Model	Price Range		Capacity per year	Startup
		Low	High		
Daewoo Doninvest	Compact sedan	$6,000	$8,000	20,000	1998 Assembly
BMW Group ZAO Avtotor	523 & 528 models	$36,450	$53,010	10,000	2000 Assembly
Renault City of Moscow	Clio Symbol	$8,500	$9,000	100,000	1998 Assembly
	Megane	$13,500	$16,000	3,000	2002 Assembly
Ford Motor Co ZAO Bankirsky Dom	Focus	$13,000	$15,000	25,000	2002 Staged to >50% local in 5 yrs
Fiat SpA OAO Gaz	Palio	$9,000	$10,000	10,000	2002 Production
	Siena	$10,000	$11,000	5,000	
General Motors OAO AvtoVAZ	New Niva	$7,500	$10,000	75,000	2002 Production
	Astra T3000	$10,000	$12,000		

Source: Economist Intelligence Unit, February 2001.

 APPENDIX 5 **Russian Automobile Sales Forecasts by Scenario, 2000–2008 (millions)**

Scenario	2000	2001	2002	2003	2004	2005	2006	2007	2008
Optimistic	1.317	1.387	1.439	1.498	1.538	1.560	1.615	1.650	1.710
Moderate	1.045	1.131	1.232	1.288	1.315	1.368	1.483	1.500	1.570
Pessimistic	1.017	1.090	1.099	1.125	1.145	1.153	1.174	1.191	1.135

Source: http://www.just-auto.com, September 2000. Average annual growth rates by scenario: 3.3 percent, 5.2 percent, and 1.4 percent, respectively.

APPENDIX 6

EBRD's Commitment to the GM-VAZ Joint Venture, Russia

The EBRD proposes to provide financing for the construction and operation of a factory to manufacture and assemble up to 75,000 Niva vehicles in Togliatti, Russia.

Operation Status: Signed

Board Review Date: 28 March 2000

Business Sector: Motor vehicle manufacturing

Portfolio Classification: Private sector

The Client: General Motors—AvtoVAZ Joint Venture is a closed joint-stock company to be created under Russian law specifically for the purpose of carrying out the project. Once the investment is complete, AvtoVAZ (VAZ) and General Motors (GM) will hold an equal share in the venture. GM is currently the world's top automotive manufacturer with production facilities in 50 countries and 388,000 employees worldwide. VAZ is the largest producer of vehicles in Russia, having sold approximately 705,500 (over 70 percent of the Russian new car market) in 2000.

Proposed EBRD Finance: The EBRD proposes to provide up to 41 percent of the financing of the venture in a combination of a loan of US$100 million (€ 108 million) and an equity investment of US$40 million (€ 43 million). The loan includes interest during the construction phase. Up to US$38 million of the loan may be syndicated after signing to reduce EBRD exposure.

Total Project Cost: US$338 million (€ 365 million)

Project Objectives: The construction and operation of a factory to manufacture and assemble up to 75,000 Niva vehicles per annum in Togliatti, Russia.

Expected Transition Impact: The transition impact potential of this transaction stems primarily from the demonstration effects associated with the entrance of a major Western strategic investor into the Russian automotive market. The fact that this investment has two well-known partners who are investing equally in the joint venture adds both to the visibility and the potential of the project. This complex project is one of the largest examples of foreign direct investment in post-crisis Russia in a period when many foreign investors are still adopting a wait and see approach. The use of Russian design and engineering skills together with the introduction of Western technologies, methods and processes and the related development of skills are further key sources of positive demonstration effect, especially given the huge modernization needs of the Russian automotive sector. Other suppliers and client companies will also benefit from technological links or training programs with the joint venture.

Environmental Impact: The project was screened B/1, requiring an audit of the existing facility and an analysis of the impact associated with the joint venture (JV). While typical environmental issues associated with heavy manufacturing are present at the main AvtoVAZ facility, there have been no prior operations at the site of the proposed JV. Potential liabilities arising from historic soil and ground water pollution were addressed as part of the due diligence, and no significant levels of contamination have been identified. The engine for the new Niva will meet Euro II (Russian market) and Euro IV (European market) standards for vehicle emissions. All vehicles will be fitted with catalytic converters. Safety standards for all vehicles will meet EU and GM standards in full. On formation, the JV will adopt GM management and operations systems and GM corporate practices for all aspects of environment, health and safety and will be in compliance with all applicable EU and best international environmental standards.

Source: http://www.ebd.com/english/opera/psd/psd2002001/483gm.htm, accessed September 2001.

Mismanagement, poor regulation or simple inertia had left more than half of state-owned enterprises "unhealthy." State-appointed managers ran companies like fiefdoms; bloated, failing industries were kept alive more from national pride than economic sense. As 1997 came to a close, 164 state firms were reporting a combined pre-tax profit of just $1.2 billion. Yet state enterprises employed more than 700,000 Indonesians and were worth some $60 billion. They were overseen by touchy ministers and entrenched managers. They were wrapped in a mythology of development. Slimming down or selling off these sacred cows meant playing with fire.

—*"Anatomy of a Deal," by Jose Manuel Tesoro,*
Asia Week, January 22, 1999

On July 6, 1998, the Indonesian government announced that Cementos Mexicanos (Cemex) was the preferred bidder for the largest government-owned cement company—PT Semen Gresik. The first round of bidding had pitted Cemex against Holderbank of Switzerland and Heidelberger of Germany, two of the largest cement manufacturing firms in the world. A mere seven weeks had passed since the resignation of President Suharto, a turning point in Indonesia's political and economic future.

The privatization program for Indonesia had moved quickly and efficiently in the spring and early summer of 1998. The government's desire to move Indonesia toward a more open, market-based economy, and to get government out of its ownership and control positions in many industries, created a fast-track privatization process that Cemex was keenly interested in. But all had not proceeded according to plan.

Indonesia Privatization

The Indonesian privatization drive was the direct result of the economic crisis in which Indonesia was currently mired, and the subsequent promises made by President Suharto to the International Monetary Fund (IMF) in

order to obtain economic and financial assistance. The structural reform program agreement signed with the IMF required Indonesia and President Suharto to open the Indonesian economy to outside investors and market forces. Under the terms of the agreement, Indonesia would sell stakes in four firms by the end of 1998, and 12 companies by the end of 1999.

The World Bank would supervise the privatization process implemented by the government. In stage one, each bidder—upon the completion of due diligence—would submit a binding offer for shares in the company based on directives given by the government (typically, on how much of the government's share was actually up for sale). The winning bid would combine financial, social (employment guarantees), and environmental dimensions. Third parties were then allowed to submit bids in a second stage to improve upon the winning bidder's offer. The winning bidder of stage one was then given the right to match the better offer, if it wished, in order to win the bid.

Many of these state-owned enterprises were already publicly traded—minority shares, to that market values did exist for these firms. However, these market capitalizations had been severely degraded following the onslaught of the Asian economic crisis. In addition to the individual equities traded, markets had fallen across Asia. Indonesia's gross domestic product was expected to fall 10 percent in 1998.

Cementos de Mexicanos

Founded in 1906, Cemex was the largest cement manufacturer in the Americas and the third largest cement producer in the world, just behind Holderbank of Switzerland and Lafarge of France. Based in Monterey, Mexico, Cemex had operations in 22 countries and trade relations with more than 60 countries worldwide. Cemex was the market leader in Mexico, Spain, Venezuela, Panama, and the Dominican Republic. It had a rapidly expanding presence in Colombia, the Caribbean, the southwestern portion of the United States, and most recently, the Philippines.

Cemex had little experience in Asia, but it did possess significant experience of its own in surviving an economic crisis. Cemex had survived the 1994 devaluation of the Mexican peso and had gained experience in surviving crises. It now hoped to use these capabilities in Asia. Asian cement stocks were trading at significant discounts to what were their likely true values.

"This is most definitely the right time to buy in Asia. The current crisis in Asia has resulted in a fall in value per tonne of capacity for cement companies to US$100 per tonne from US$500 per tonne."

—Lorenzo Zambrano, Chairman,
Cemex, *Financial Times*, November 7, 1997

The Asian currency crisis had led to a significant differentiation—some would say distortion—of relative costs and prices across the Asian cement industry. As illustrated in Table 1, cash costs ranged from a low of $10/tonne in Indonesia to $30/tonne in Taiwan. At the same time, prices were also the lowest in Indonesia, currently falling to $16/tonne, while Pakistan and Taiwan sold at $55 and $54/tonne, respectively. The result was an Indonesian industry which was both low cost and low margin.

The large discrepancies in costs and prices had led many of the world's largest cement producers to consider something lone forgotten—large-scale low-cost production and international distribution through exports. For example, the Taiwanese cement market may be quite vulnerable to Indonesian exports.

Assuming cash production costs in Indonesia of $10/tonne, loading costs (on both ends) of $2/tonne, and shipping costs to Kaohsiung (Taiwan) from East Java (Indonesia) of $10/tonne, Indonesian exports could severely undercut domestic Taiwanese producers. Several analysts argued that even the United States cement markets may be vulnerable to indonesian exports if shipping costs between Indonesia and and United States could be kept at $35 to $40/tonne. Current cement prices in the United States hovered just below $75/tonne. Semen Gresik was currently in the process of a significant upgrading of its port facilities to increase its export capabilities.

We believe that Gresik would be on the top of the list of acquisition targets for foreign cement players. The partial sell-down of the government's 65 percent stake will represent a unique opportunity for the foreign players to take a meaningful stake in the Indonesian cement industry (previously closed). however, in our view this foreign interest is dependent on, at a minimum, gaining management control.

Indosuex W.I. Carr Securities Ltd., June 22, 1998

Tumultuous Summer

For months rumors had been circulating in West Sumatra that the new owners of Semen Gresik would lay off nearly half the 3,000 employees of Semen Gresik's operations. During the due diligence process in which the Cemex team had direct contact with present Gresik management and labor, cemex's acquisition team had guaranteed that no one would be laid off before the year 2000. Demonstrations intensified in West Sumatra

TABLE 1

Bagged Cement Prices and Cash Costs Across Asia, June 1998

Country	Ex-Factory Price (US$/tonne)	Cash Costs (US$/tonne)	Margin (US$/tonne)	Gross Margin (per tonne)
Pakistan	55	29	26	47%
Malaysia	40	26	14	35%
India	46	27	19	41%
Philippines	39	23	16	41%
Korea	39	28	11	28%
Taiwan	54	30	24	44%
Thailand	38	20	18	47%
Indonesia	16	10	6	38%
Average	41	24	17	40%

Source: Indosuez W.I. Carr Securities, June 12, 1998.

and Jakarta, however, after the first round of bidding. Protests in Jakarta grew in size and fervor, and by late July were occurring nearly daily. Rumors that management of Semen Gresik paid demonstrators in both West Sumatra and Jakarta were denied by employees.

The governor of West Sumatra now threatened to remove certain land rights and concessions provided to the company if control of Semen Gresik was allowed to pass to foreign investors. The final tide turned when a former army general and West Sumatra governor took the unofficial lead in opposing the privatization. Cemex was informed that the sale of Semen Gresik would have to be restructured and the second round of bidding would be postponed.

Cemex's Final Bid

On August 20, 1998, the Indonesian government announced that it would entertain bids for only 14 percent of Semen Gresik, rather than the original 35 percent offered, assuring that the government would remain the controlling shareholder after the sale. Cemex was informed that its stage-one bid would have to be restructured. It would keep its preferred bidder status, but the second-round bids would be accepted. It was now up to Cemex to determine what it wished to do in its restructured stage-one bid. Competitor bids were due no later than September 28.

Questions for Discussion

1. What was the bias of the bidding process as structured? Did it benefit the seller over the buyer?
2. Why did Cemex want Semen Gresik? Why did the Indonesian government want to sell Semen Gresik?
3. Do you think Cemex should have anticipated the political opposition to the privatization of Semen Gresik? Should that have affected its bidding?
4. Should Cemex bid the second time around, or walk away? If it did win the second round bidding and gain the 14 percent ownership share, how would it actually implement its strategy in Asia using Semen Gresik?

Over 200,000 pieces of stainless steel flatware are just sitting in a Pier 1 Imports warehouse. Where did these come from? Most recently they were stocked in Pier 1 stores—that is until a couple of customers informed store managers that the stainless steel pieces rusted. The company response? After a very rapid testing process that confirmed the customers' observations, the offending product was pulled from all stores and sent to its "resting place"—all within a two-week period.

The people in merchandising at company headquarters in Forth Worth, Texas, and the local Pier 1 agent in China now have ascertained that while there are 47 different types of stainless steel, only one—referred to as 18-8—can be used to make serviceable flatware that won't rust. This newly recognized quality specification has been quickly communicated to all other company agents who purchase flatware assuring that this product quality issue will not arise again.

It is John Baker's responsibility to oversee the network of corporate buyers and on-site agents who are directly responsible for finding, choosing, and assuring the quality of merchandise imported from around the world. Baker, the Senior Manager of Merchandise Compliance, accepted a position at Pier 1 Imports more than twenty years ago after working for various department stores purchasing tabletop and kitchen wares. When he first came on board as a buyer, he spent nearly six months of the year on the road, working with the agent network and finding new vendors for Pier 1 merchandise. Today, Baker also handles the increasingly complex area of government regulations of merchandise.

Because such a high percentage of Pier 1 Imports' merchandise is imported (more than 85 percent), it is especially critical that U.S. government regulations regarding various product categories be studied and communicated to the manufacturers in other countries. These government regulations form one of the two measures of quality assurance for Pier 1 products. The second is that the products must conform to aesthetic standards that guarantee that the product fits the Pier 1 image and Pier 1 customer desires. It is in large part the buyer's expertise that assures that these standards are met.

What is the process for finding and selecting vendors in countries other than the United States? First of all, Pier 1 depends upon a well- and long-established network of agents in every country from which they import. In some lesser-developed regions, Pier 1 agents work with governments to help locate professional exporters. Some exporters are found at international trade fairs as well. The bulk of Pier 1 agents are native to the country in which they work, and some have been in place for as long as thirty years with their children now taking over the local positions.

The agents' jobs include finding local producers of handcrafted items that fit the Pier 1 customer needs. Buyers look for new sources of products at local craft fairs and even flea markets. Right now, for example, local agents in several countries are looking for sources of wooden furniture—primarily chests and tables—because Pier 1 would like to add to this in-story category. Based upon the location of raw materials, in this case in Italy, South America, Indonesia, and Thailand, agents are searching for just the right manufacturers to be brought to the buyers' attention.

Because it is the agents based within the various exporting countries who must enforce quality requirements, it is critical that John Baker and his colleagues carefully communicate both governmental and aesthetic product requirements to the agents. The agents can then "sit down at the table" with the manufacturers and work out the quality issues. If misunderstandings occur, Pier 1 is always ready to accept some of the responsibility because they view their manufacturers and agents as their partners in this business.

Because Pier 1 Imports has carefully carved out a unique niche in the speciality retail store industry, buyers are hard to hire from outside the company. As Baker noted, "The bulk of our staff has come out of our stores. It is easy for a buyer to move from Macy's to Hudson's—the products are the same as are most of the vendors. The Pier 1 buyer, however, must understand the Pier 1 store in order to be able to effectively and efficiently buy for it." These Pier 1 buyers, along with their agents onsite around the globe, serve as the company's primary link to product quality.

Questions for Discussion

1. What are the implications for sales, customer satisfaction, and profits for companies like Pier 1 (http://www.pier1.com) when low quality merchandise is not identified early in the purchasing process?
2. Do you think that Pier 1 might have avoided this problem if it had a very aggressive quality assurance program, i.e., ISO 9000, in place?

Within a few months after becoming CEO of Whirlpool Corp. in 1987, David Whitwam met with his senior managers to plot a strategy for securing future company growth. At the time, Whirlpool was the market leader among U.S. appliance makers, but it generated only weak sales outside North America. Operating in a mature market, it faced the same low profit margins as major competitors like General Electric and Maytag. In addition to price wars, especially in mature markets, the industry had started to consolidate, and consumers were demanding more environmentally friendly products.

Whirlpool and Its Options

Whitwam and his management team explored several growth options, including diversifying into other industries experiencing more rapid growth, such as furniture or garden products; restructuring the company financially; and expanding vertically and horizontally. The group sharpened its focus to consider opportunities for expanding the appliance business beyond North American markets. After all, the basics of managing the appliance business and the product technologies are similar in Europe, North America, Asia, and Latin America. As Whitwam put it, "We were very good at what we did. What we needed was to enter appliance markets in other parts of the world and learn how to satisfy different kinds of customers."

Whirlpool industry data predicted that, over time, appliance manufacturing would become a global industry. As Whitwam saw it, his company had three options: "We could ignore the inevitable—a decision that would have condemned Whirlpool to a slow death. We could

Sources: Portions of this case were researched from material available at http://www.whirlpool.com. The Global Success Factors section is derived from a report on the global appliance industry by John Bonds, German Estrada, Peter Jacobs, Jorge Harb-Kallab, Paul Kunzer, and Karin Toth at Georgetown Unviersity, March 2000. See also Ilkka A. Ronkainen and Ivan Menezes, "Implementing Global Marketing Strategy," *International Marketing Review* 13 (Number 3, 1996): 56–63; "The Right Way to Go Global: An Interview with Whirlpool CEO David Whitwam," *Harvard Business Review* 72 (March–April 1994): 134–145; and "Chinese Industry Races to Make a Global Name for Itself," *Washington Post*, April 23, 2000, H1, H5.

wait for globalization to begin and then try to react, which would have put us in a catch-up mode, technologically and organizationally. Or we could control our own destiny and try to shape the very nature of globalization in our industry. In short, we could force our competitors to respond to us."

Whitwam and his team chose the third option and set out on a mission to make Whirlpool "one company worldwide." They aimed much higher than simply marketing products or operating around the globe. For decades, Whirlpool had sold some appliances in other countries to buyers who could afford them. Whitwam wanted to expand this reach by establishing a vision of a company that could leverage global resources to gain a long-term competitive advantage. In his words, this effort meant "having the best technologies and processes for designing, manufacturing, selling, and servicing your products at the lowest possible costs. Our vision at Whirlpool is to integrate our geographical businesses wherever possible, so that our most advanced expertise in any given area—whether it's refrigeration technology or distribution strategy—isn't confined to one location or one division. We want to be able to take the best capabilities we have and leverage them in all of our operations worldwide."

As its first step in transforming a largely domestic operation into a global powerhouse, Whirlpool purchased the European appliance business of Dutch consumer goods giant, Philips Electronics. Philips had been losing market share for years, running its European operations as independent regional companies that made different appliances for individual markets. "When we bought this business," Whitwam recalls, "we had two automatic washer designs, one built in Italy and one built in Germany. If you as a consumer looked at them, they were basically the same machines. But there wasn't anything common about those two machines. There wasn't even a common screw."

The Whirlpool strategy called for reversing the decline in European market share and improving profitability by changing product designs and manufacturing processes and by switching to centralized purchasing. The change reorganized the national design and research staffs inherited from Philips into European product teams that worked closely with Whirlpool's U.S. designers. Redesigned models shared more parts, and inventory costs fell when Whirlpool consolidated warehouses from 36 to 8. The transformation trimmed Philips's list of 1,600 suppliers by 50 percent, and it converted the national operations to regional companies.

Whitwam believed that the drive to become one company worldwide required making Whirlpool a global brand—a formidable task in Europe, where the name was not well-known. The company rebranded the Philips product lines, supported by a $135 million pan-European advertising campaign that initially presented both the Philips and Whirlpool names and eventually converted to Whirlpool alone.

Another important component of the Whirlpool global strategy—product innovation—sought to develop superior products based on consumer needs and wants. "We have to provide a compelling reason other than price for consumers to buy Whirlpool-built products," says Whitwam. "We can do that only by understanding the consumer better than anyone else does and then translating our understanding into clearly superior product designs, features, and after-sales support. Our goal is for consumers to prefer the Whirlpool brand because it offers greater overall value than competing products."

One successful product innovation led to the Whirlpool Crispwave microwave oven. Extensive research with European consumers revealed a desire for a microwave that could brown and crisp food. In response, Whirlpool engineers designed the VIP Crispwave, which can fry crispy bacon and cook a pizza with a crisp crust. The new microwave proved successful in Europe, and Whirlpool later introduced it in the United States.

Whirlpool's global strategy includes a goal to become the market leader in Asia, which will be the world's largest appliance market in the twenty-first century. In 1988, it began setting up sales and distribution systems in Asia to help it serve Asian markets and to make the firm more familiar with those markets and potential customers. The company established three regional offices: one in Singapore to serve Southeast Asia, a second in Hong Kong to handle the Chinese market, and a Tokyo office for Japan. Through careful analysis, Whirlpool marketers sought to match specific current products with Asian consumers. They studied existing and emerging trade channels and assessed the relative strengths and weaknesses of competitors in the Asian markets. The company set up joint ventures with five Asian manufacturers for four appliance lines with the highest market potential: refrigerators, washers, air conditioners, and microwave ovens. With a controlling interest in each of the joint ventures, the newly global company confidently expects to excel in the world's fastest-growing market.

Whirlpool has come a long way since embarking on its global strategy. By 2003, revenues had doubled to more than $10.3 billion. The company now reaches markets in more than 170 countries, leading the markets in both North America and Latin America. Whirlpool is number three in Europe and the largest Western appliance company in Asia. For building its integrated global network, "Whirlpool gets very high marks," says an industry analyst. "They are outpacing the industry dramatically."

Global Success Factors

The global appliance market of $70 billion (expected to grow to $120 billion by 2010) is undergoing major consolidation and globalization. While U.S. markets are mature and price wars common, economic integration in Europe has fueled market growth. Despite the financial crises of 1997–2002, markets in Asia and Latin America are expanding and global companies developing their presence to exploit the opportunities.

From a global perspective, there are three success factors that affect all of the different geographic regions. The first key success factor on a global scale is successful branding. Each of the large global manufacturers has been very successful in developing a branding strategy. Most of these players sell a variety of brands, where each is targeted to certain quality and price levels. In addition, the strong brand reputation has been necessary for the major manufacturers either to expand operations into new regions or to launch new product lines. For example, Maytag did not have a line of products in the dishwasher category but had a large brand presence in the washer/dryer category. To expand its product line, Maytag decided to launch a new line of products in the dishwasher segment. Through a successful branding campaign, in less than two years Maytag captured the second largest market share in the segment. It leveraged its successful brand image in one segment to quickly steal share from less successful competitors.

The second key success factor on a global scale is price sensitivity. Given the large cost of these goods, large-scale manufacturers have been able to lower prices to meet the demand of customers. While there is little price elasticity, some manufacturers have been able to raise prices on their high-end goods, but for the most part, most manufacturers have lowered prices, and thus margins, to stay competitive with other brands. With razor-thin margins across each segment, only manufacturers that have the size to realize economies of scale have been able to remain competitive and lower prices to meet demands of their customers. This price sensitivity and the need to continually lower prices made up one of the major forces driving the consolidation within the industry. Many smaller brands were not able to compete and therefore were sold to the larger appliance brands.

The third success factor is presence in the major markets of the world. Not only does this provide the necessary scale to compete but also the opportunity to learn and cross-subsidize resources across borders. Chinese appliance makers, such as Haier and Kelon, are both expanding globally. Beyond the goal of expanded sales, one of the most significant drivers in establishing operations in India, Malaysia, and the United States, is to remain competitive at home. Joining the WTO means that China's trade barriers will fall, bringing the best foreign products to China.

China and Asia

Aside from the global key success factors, two key success factors within China and Asia are very important. First, appliance manufacturers must have access to distribution channels and therefore the ability to provide the products across several different Chinese regions. The access to Chinese distribution channels can be very limiting for international corporations whereas China-based companies, such as Kelon and Haier, have a definite competitive advantage.

Second, large appliance manufacturers must have a large scope of products for success. Specifically, it is the number of different segments in which a company sells products that will lead to success in China, not the scope of products within a given segment. Kelon manufactures 112 different types of air conditioners, but it is not a full-line supplier of appliances to its customers. Contrarily, Haier is a full-line supplier that manufactures products in each product segment and so provides its customers with a variety of appliances under one brand name. Haier's global market share is still small (2.8 percent) compared to Whirlpool's (11.3 percent) and Electrolux's (8.2 percent), but the company is on an ambitious growth trajectory, having opened its first plant in the United States.

The Japanese market has a different set of criteria for success than China and the rest of Asia. Instead, the Japanese market closely resembles certain aspects of the European and U.S. markets. Aside from the global success factors, success in the Japanese market is based on two key factors. First, due to the size of dwellings in Japan, innovation with regard to product size is very important. Japanese customers are looking for product innovations that will fit into smaller spaces while providing the most use of cabinet space. Second, to be successful in Japan, a manufacturer must sell a product that is very high in quality. Japanese customers are very demanding in regard to product quality, and they expect their products to last decades. Therefore, manufacturers selling products that are very high in quality will have a competitive advantage.

United States

Within the United States, two key success factors outside of the global factors are necessary for a company's success. First, a company must develop innovative products that incorporate new features while still operating efficiently. U.S. customers are very aware that energy consumption of a product will have a long-term effect on their utility bills, so they look for products that operate more efficiently. In addition, customers are willing to pay a premium for innovative features on a high-end product. Many manufacturers were surprised that Maytag was able to raise its prices for its front-loading washer not once, but twice. Customers were not as concerned with the price as they were concerned with the convenience of the product.

The second key success factor within the U.S. market is product quality, in respect to durability. U.S. consumers are willing to pay more for a product, but they expect it to operate for well over a decade with little to no maintenance. Therefore, for an appliance manufacturer to succeed in the United States, it must deliver products that are of high quality and of innovative design.

Europe

Outside of the two global success factors, the European market has two distinct factors that are required for success. First, to succeed in Europe, manufacturers must develop innovative products. In this context, innovative products are defined as products that are efficient and environmentally friendly. The "green" movement within Europe is very strong, and therefore a manufacturer that does not sell "eco-products" will not succeed when compared to a company that offers that type of product.

Second, quality is a key success factor for Europe. Similar to other markets, in this context quality refers to durability. European consumers are looking for products that are durable and will last over a long period of time. In this regard, the European market is very similar to the U.S., Japanese, and Latin American markets.

Latin America

Within Latin America, there are two additional success factors for a manufacturer to consider outside the global success factors. First, Latin American companies that provide excellent service to customers will have an advantage over the competition. The amount of time that the average consumer owns an appliance in Latin America is somewhat longer than in other global regions, so consumers are looking for excellent service. The economy in Latin America has had several challenges in recent history, and so consumers would much rather repair an existing product than buy a new appliance.

Second, quality is another success factor for Latin America. This key success factor ties directly into the service success factor. Initially, Latin Americans are looking for a durable product that will last for more than a decade; then through customer service, the product will be repaired to extend its life for several more years.

Questions for Discussion

1. Whirlpool's marketing goal is to leverage resources across borders. How is this evident in its marketing approach? Consult http://www.whirlpool.com for additional information.
2. The challenge facing Whirlpool is not only external in catering to local customers' needs worldwide, but also internal—all the regional and local units have to "buy in" to the global vision. What types of particular issues (such as product or technology transfers) may arise, and how should they be dealt with?
3. Visit the Web site of the Association of Home Appliance Manufacturers, http://www.aham.org, and suggest some of the global trends among the major manufacturers of household appliances.

Now that the firm has entered and established itself in international markets, it is important to devise and implement strategies that will help provide a competitively advantageous position. Part 6 focuses on important overarching dimensions such as services and supply-chain management, as well as on the traditional functional areas of marketing, finance, accounting, taxation, and human resources management.

Each one of the chapters in Part 6 is structured to differentiate between smaller firms and multinational corporations (MNCs). Low cost and low resource approaches are presented for firms with little international experience. Subsequently, a globally oriented perspective with a major focus on MNCs is offered.

PART

Operations

6

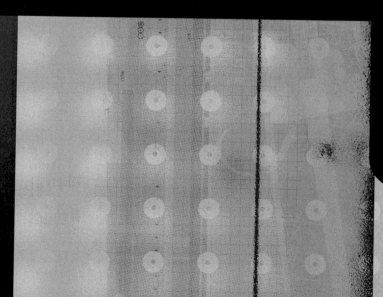

Target Market Selection

Marketing Management

Marketing

Learning Objectives

- To suggest how markets for international expansion can be selected, their demand assessed, and appropriate strategies for their development devised

- To describe how environmental differences generate new challenges for the international marketing manager

- To compare and contrast the merits of standardization versus localization strategies for country markets and of regional versus global marketing efforts

- To discuss market-specific and global challenges facing the marketing functions: product, price, distribution, and promotion within both the traditional and e-business dimensions

Being a Good Sport Globally

In any given country, the majority of corporate sponsorship goes to sports. Of the nearly $25 billion spent worldwide in 2002, two thirds was allocated to sports. Within sports, the two flagship events are the World Cup in soccer and the Olympic Games (both summer and winter). Sponsors want to align themselves with—and create—meaningful sport-related moments for consumers. At the same time, consumers associate sponsors of sporting events with leadership, teamwork, pursuit of excellence, as well as friendship.

Sponsorships have been a cornerstone of the Coca-Cola Company's marketing efforts for 100 years, starting with their use of sports stars such as world champion cyclist Bobby Walthour in ads in 1903. Presently, the company is the world's biggest sports sponsor with total sponsorship-related expenses at $1 billion annually. These activities span different types of sports and various geographies (as shown below).

Coca-Cola spent $26 million for its sponsorship of the World Cup in 2002, which gave it the right to use the World Cup logo/trademarks, exclusive positioning and branding around the event, as well as premium perimeter advertising positions at every game. Sponsorships include a guarantee that no rival brands can be officially linked to the tournament or use the logo or trademarks. To assure exclusivity, FIFA (soccer's governing body) bought all key billboard advertising space around the main stadia for the tournament, and this space was offered to the sponsors first. In addition, every main sponsor got 250 tickets for each game of the tournament for promotional purposes or corporate entertainment (of key constituents, such as intermediaries or customers).

Each country organization within Coca-Cola decides which programs it wants to use during sponsorship depending on its goals, which are jointly set by local managers and headquarters. For example, in Rio de Janeiro, the company erected huge TV screens on which people could watch the games. Given that Ecuador qualified for the tournament for the first time in its history, this fact was played up in local advertising. In Japan, the company used I-mode phones, in addition to traditional media, to create meaningful and relevant connections with the World Cup. Naturally, there is always substantial overlap in programs between markets, with headquarters' 20-person team in charge of the coordination effort. One example of this was an online World Cup game that headquarters created in conjunction with Yahoo! and then helped each interested country localize. Another global program was Coca-Cola Go! Stadium Art, which allowed consumers and artists to compete to create ads that ran in the various stadia throughout the tournament. The company also joined forces with other sponsors for cross-promotional efforts; e.g., with Adidas to give away the Official Match Ball, with McDonald's for consumer promotions, and with Toshiba on a cyber-cup tournament.

Although marketers have become far more demanding in terms of their sponsorships, the World Cup is one of the few global events available. Pulling out would mean allowing a competitor to step in. (For example, when Vauxhall left in 1998, Hyundai took its place.)

While measuring the return on such investment is challenging, Coca-Cola evaluates dimensions such as the number of new corporate customers that sell Coke in their stores, the incremental amount of promotional/display activity, and new vending placement. The influence on the brand is the most difficult to establish; World Cup sponsorship has been suggested to have boosted its presence especially in the emerging and developing markets.

Coca-Cola's Sports Sponsorships
- Olympics (since 1928)
  - Supports athletes and teams in nearly 200 countries in exchange for exclusive rights in nonalcoholic beverage category through 2008
  - Official soft/sports drink (Coca-Cola, PowerAde)
  - Runs marketing programs in over 130 countries
- Soccer
  - FIFA partner since 1974—signed landmark eight-year agreement through 2006 to be official soft/sports drink at Men's World Cup 2002/2006, Women's World Cup 1999/2003, Confederation Cup competitions, under 20/ under 17 World Youth Championships
  - Also sponsors Copa America, Asian Football Confederation, over 40 national teams
- Basketball
  - Signed 100-year agreement in 1998 for Sprite to be official soft drink of NBA/WNBA
  - Advertising in over 200 countries
- Others
  - Coca-Cola Classic: official soft drink of National Football League
  - Surge/PowerAde: official soft drink of National Hockey League
  - Coca-Cola Classic/PowerAde: official soft drink/sports drink of Rugby World Cup
  - Sponsor of International Paralympics/Special Olympics

Sources: "Still Waiting for that Winning Kick," *Business Week*, October 21, 2002, 116–118; "The Best Global Brands," *Business Week*, August 5, 2002, 92–94; "World Cup: Sponsors Need to Get in the Game," *Business Week*, June 17, 2002, 52; "World Cup Marketing," *Advertising Age Global*, March 2002, 17–30; and "Too Many Players on the Field," *Advertising Age*, December 10, 2001, 3.

Marketing is the process of planning and executing the conception, pricing, promotion, and distribution of ideas, goods, and services to create exchanges that satisfy individual and organizational objectives.[1] The concepts of satisfaction and exchange are at the core of marketing. For an exchange to take place, two or more parties have to come together physically or electronically and they must communicate and deliver things of perceived value. Customers should be perceived as information seekers who evaluate marketers' offerings in terms of their own drives and needs. When the offering is consistent with their needs, they tend to choose the good or service; if it is not, other alternatives are chosen. A key task of the marketer is to recognize the ever-changing nature of needs and wants. Marketing techniques apply not only to goods but to ideas and services as well. Further, well over 50 percent of all marketing activities are business marketing—directed at other businesses, governmental entities, and various types of institutions.

The marketing manager's task is to plan and execute programs that will ensure a long-term competitive advantage for the company. This task has two integral parts: (1) the determining of specific target markets and (2) marketing management, which consists of manipulating marketing mix elements to best satisfy the needs of the individual target markets. Regardless of geographic markets, the basic tasks do not vary; they have been called the technical universals of marketing.[2]

This chapter will focus on the formulation of marketing strategy for international operations. The first section describes target market selection and how to identify pertinent characteristics of the various markets. The balance of the chapter is devoted to adjusting the elements of the marketing program to a particular market for maximum effectiveness and efficiency, while attempting to exploit global and regional similarities, as highlighted in the opening vignette.

Target Market Selection

The process of target market selection involves narrowing down potential country markets to a feasible number of countries and market segments within them. Rather than try to appeal to everyone, firms best utilize their resources by: (1) identifying potential markets for entry and (2) expanding selectively over time to those deemed attractive.

IDENTIFICATION AND SCREENING

A four-stage process for screening and analyzing foreign markets is presented in Figure 14.1. It begins with very general criteria and ends with product-specific market analyses. The data and the methods needed for decision making change from secondary to primary as the steps are taken in sequence. Although presented here as a screening process for choosing target markets, the process is also applicable to change of entry mode or even divestment.

If markets were similar in their characteristics, the international marketer could enter any one of the potential markets. However, differences among markets exist in three dimensions: physical, psychic, and economic.[3] Physical distance is the geographic distance between home and target countries; its impact has decreased as a result of recent technological developments. Psychic, or cultural, distance refers to differences in language, tradition, and customs between two countries. Economic distance translates into the target's ability to pay. Generally, the greater the overall distance—or difference—between the two countries, the less knowledge the marketer has about the target market. The amount of information that is available varies dramatically. For example, although the marketer can easily learn about the economic environment from secondary sources, invaluable interpretive information may not be available until the firm actually operates in the market. In the early stages of the assessment, international marketers can be assisted by numerous online and CD-ROM-based data sources as shown in Chapter 10.

The four stages in the screening process are: preliminary screening, estimation of market potential, estimation of sales potential, and identification of segments. Each stage should be given careful attention. The first stage, for example, should not merely reduce the number of alternatives to a manageable few for the sake of reduction, even though the expense of analyzing markets in depth is great. Unless care is taken, attractive alternatives may be eliminated.

Preliminary Screening

The preliminary screening process must rely chiefly on secondary data for country-specific factors as well as product- and industry-specific factors. Country-specific factors typically include those that would indicate the market's overall buying power; for example, population, gross national product in total and per capita, total exports and imports, and production of cement, electricity, and steel.[4] Product-specific factors narrow the analysis to the firm's specific areas of operation. A company such as Motorola, manufacturing for the automotive aftermarket, is interested in the number

FIGURE 14.1

The Screening Process in Target Market Choice

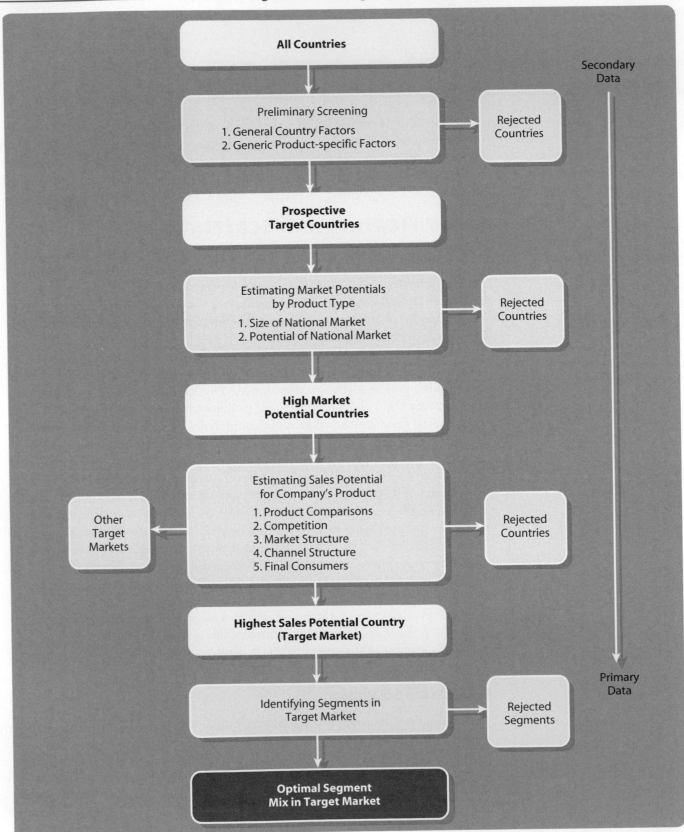

Source: Adapted from *Entry Strategies for International Markets,* p. 56, by Franklin R. Root (Lexington, MA: Lexington Books, D.C. Heath & Co. Copyright 1994, D. C. Heath & Co.)

of passenger cars, trucks, and buses in use. The statistical analyses must be accompanied by qualitative assessments of the impact of cultural elements and the overall climate for foreign firms and products. A market that satisfies the levels set becomes a prospective target country.

Estimating Market Potential

Total market potential is the sales, in physical or monetary units, that might be available to all firms in an industry during a given period under a given level of industry marketing effort and given environmental conditions.[5] The international marketer needs to assess the size of existing markets and forecast the size of future markets. A number of techniques, both quantitative and qualitative, are available for this task.

Income elasticity of demand is the relationship between demand and economic progress. The share of income spent on necessities reflects the level of development of the market as well as monies left for other purchases. When consumption per capita of a product category is mapped against GNP per capita, it reflects a diminishing rate in consumption as incomes rise. For the majority of goods, consumption rises most quickly between $3,000 and $10,000 per capita, bringing in new consumers to the market while those who are already in the market may be trading into higher-value substitutes.[6] This points out the attractiveness of emerging markets in spite of their volatility.

If the data are available for product-specific analysis, the simplest way to establish a market-size estimate is to conduct a **market audit,** which adds together local production and imports with exports deducted from the total. However, in many cases, data may not exist, be current, or be appropriate. In such cases, market potentials may have to be estimated by methods such as **analogy.** This approach is based on the use of proxy variables that have been shown (either through research or intuition) to correlate with the demand for the product in question. The market size for a product (such as video games) in country A is estimated by comparing a ratio for an available indicator (e.g., PC ownership) for country A and country B, and using this ratio in conjunction with market data available on videogames for country B. In some cases, a time lag in demand patterns may be seen, thus requiring a **longitudinal analysis.** For example, the use of wireless communication in Southern Europe is suggested to lag Northern Europe by two years and that wireless telephony use overall is tied to the state of the economy (for example, GNP per capita). Therefore, to estimate wireless use in Southern Europe, the following formula could be used:

$$WC_{SE}^{2005} = GNP_{SE}^{2005} * (WC_{NE}^{2003}/GNP_{NE}^{2003})$$

In similar fashion, a country or a group of countries may be used as a proxy for an entire region. For example, Coca-Cola Company launched Georgia, a ready-to-drink coffee brand developed in Japan, in Northern Europe as a test for wider international rollout.[7] The choice was based on the fact that Northern Europe leads the world in per capita consumption of coffee in general.

Despite the valuable insight generated through these techniques, caution should be used in interpreting the results. All of the quantitative techniques are based on historical data that may be obsolete or inapplicable because of differences in cultural and geographic traits of the market. Further, with today's technological developments, lags between markets are no longer at a level that would make all of the measurements valid. Moreover, the measurements look at a market as an aggregate; that is, no regional differences are taken into account. In industrialized countries, the richest 10 percent of the population consumes 20 percent of all goods and services, whereas the respective figure for the developing countries may be as high as 50 percent.[8]

Income Distribution: A Factor in Evaluating Market Potential

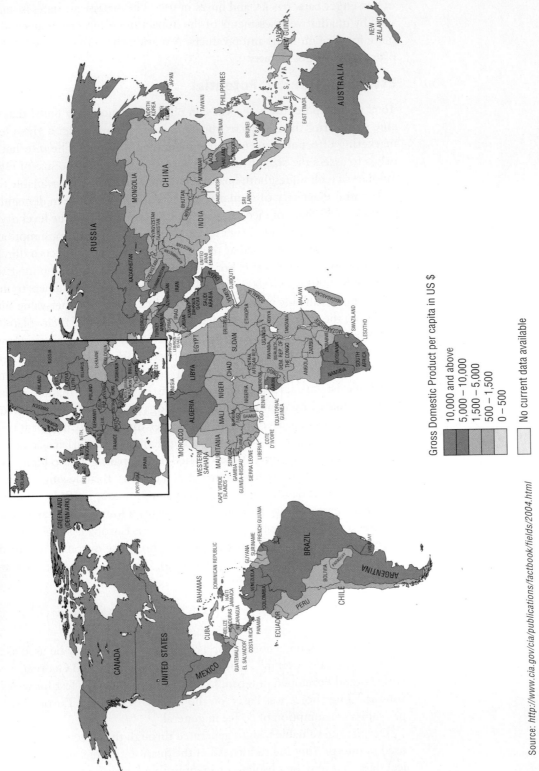

Gross Domestic Product per capita in US $

- 10,000 and above
- 5,000 – 10,000
- 1,500 – 5,000
- 500 – 1,500
- 0 – 500
- No current data available

Source: *http://www.cia.gov/cia/publications/factbook/fields/2004.html*

Therefore, even in the developing countries with low GNP figures, segments exist with buying power rivaled only in the richest developed countries.

In addition to these quantitative techniques that rely on secondary data, international marketers can use various survey techniques. They are especially useful when marketing new technologies. A survey of end-user interest and responses may provide a relatively clear picture of the possibilities in a new market. Surveys can also be administered through a web site or through e-mail.[9]

Comparing figures for market potential with actual sales will provide the international marketer with further understanding of his or her firm's chances in the market. If the difference between potential and reality is substantial, the reasons can be evaluated using **gap analysis.** The differences can be the result of usage, distribution, or product line gaps.[10] If the firm is already in the market, part of the difference between its sales and the market potential can be explained through the competitive gap. Usage gaps indicate that not all potential users are using the product or that those using it are not using as much as they could, which suggests mainly a promotional task. Distribution gaps indicate coverage problems, which may be vertical (concentrating only on urban markets) or horizontal (if the product is only available at large-scale international retailers and not local ones). Product line gaps typically suggest latent demand. An emerging trend in which Japanese consumers want to acquire an American look will help drive sales for companies like Ralph Lauren, L. L. Bean, and Northeastern Log Homes.

Estimating Sales Potential

Even when the international marketer has gained an understanding of markets with the greatest overall promise, the firm's own possibilities in those markets are still not known. Sales potential is the share of the market potential that the firm can reasonably expect to get over the longer term. To arrive at an estimate, the marketer needs to collect product- and market-specific data. The data will have to do with:

1. Competition—strength, likely reaction to entry
2. Market—strength of barriers
3. Consumers—ability and willingness to buy
4. Product—degree of relative advantage, compatibility, complexity, trialability, and communicability
5. Channel structure—access to retail level

In studying the Russian market for entry, GM found that it would have to charge at least $15,000 for cars assembled there. The fact that nine out of ten new cars sold in Russia cost under $10,000 made the plan not feasible. However, the same research found that consumers would be willing to pay $1,000 to $1,500 more for a locally made car if it was called a Chevrolet. GM signed an agreement to put its logo on a vehicle developed by Russian automaker AvtoVAZ and to sell it for only about $7,500.[11] The marketer's questions can never be fully answered until the firm has made a commitment to enter the market and is operational. The mode of entry has special significance in determining the firm's sales potential.

Identifying Segments

Within the markets selected, individuals and organizations will vary in their wants, resources, geographical locations, buying attitudes, and buying practices. Initially, the firm may cater to one or only a few segments and later expand to others, especially if the product is innovative. Segmentation is indicated when segments are indeed different enough to warrant individualized attention, are large enough for profit potential, and can be reached through the methods that the international marketer wants to use. For example, a European or U.S. entity in China may choose to offer the same product in China as it does at home and do so only through the western retailers such as Wal-Mart. This will mean that it focuses only on the urban consumers who are well-to-do.

Once the process is complete for a market or group of markets, the international marketer may begin it again for another one. When growth potential is no longer in market development, the firm may opt for market penetration.

CONCENTRATION VERSUS DIVERSIFICATION

Choosing a market expansion policy involves the allocation of effort among various markets. The major alternatives are **concentration** on a small number of markets or **diversification,** which is characterized by growth in a relatively large number of markets in the early stages of international market expansion.[12]

Expansion Alternatives

Either concentration or diversification is applicable to market segments or to total markets, depending on the resource commitment the international marketer is willing and able to make. One option is a dual-concentration strategy, in which efforts are focused on a few segments in a limited number of countries. Another is a dual-diversification strategy, in which entry is to most segments in most available markets. The first is a likely strategy for small firms or firms that market specialized products to clearly definable markets, for example, ocean-capable sailing boats. The second is typical for large consumer-oriented companies that have sufficient resources for broad coverage. Market concentration/segment diversification opts for a limited number of markets but for wide coverage within them, putting emphasis on company acceptance. Market diversification/segment concentration usually involves the identification of a segment, possibly worldwide, to which the company can market without major changes in its marketing mix.

Factors Affecting Expansion Strategy

Expansion strategy is determined by the factors relating to market, mix, and company that are listed in Table 14.1. In most cases, the factors are interrelated.

Market-Related Factors These factors are the ones that were influential in determining the attractiveness of the market in the first place. In the choice of expansion strategy, demand for the firm's products is a critical factor. With high and stable growth rates in certain markets, the firm will most likely opt for a concentration strategy. If the demand is strong worldwide, diversification may be attractive.

A forecast of the sales response function can be used to predict sales at various levels of marketing expenditure. Two general response functions exist: concave and S curve. When the function is concave, sales will increase at a decreasing rate because of competition and a lowering adoption rate. The function might involve a unique, innovative product or marketing program. An S-curve function assumes that a viable market share can be achieved only through sizable marketing efforts. This is typical for new entrants to well-established markets.

The uniqueness of the firm's offering with respect to competition is also a factor in the expansion strategy. If lead time over competition is considerable, the decision to

TABLE 14.1

Factors Affecting the Choice Between Concentration and Diversification Strategies

Factor	Diversification	Concentration
Market growth rate	Low	High
Sales stability	Low	High
Sales response function	Concave	S curve
Competitive lead time/response	Short	Long
Spillover effects	High	Low
Need for product adaptation	Low	High
Need for communication adaptation	Low	High
Economies of scale in distribution	Low	High
Extent of constraints	Low	High
Program control requirements	Low	High

Source: Adapted from Igal Ayal and Jehiel Zif, "Marketing Expansion Strategies in Multinational Marketing," *Journal of Marketing* 43 (Spring 1979): 89.

diversify may not seem urgent. However, complacency can be a mistake in today's competitive environment; competitors can rush new products into the market in a matter of days. Competition may present other challenges as well. In their expansion abroad, U.S.-based Internet portals, such as AOL, have been branded by local competitors as "digital colonialists." In Brazil, AOL's slogan, "We're the biggest because we're the best," brought charges of misleading advertising from local companies.[13]

In many product categories marketers, knowingly or unknowingly, will be affected by spillover effects. Consider, for example, the impact that satellite channels have had on advertising in Europe or Asia, where ads for a product now reach most of the markets. Where geographic (and psychic) distances are short, spillover is likely, and marketers are most likely to diversify.

Government constraints—or the threat of them—can be a powerful motivator in a firm's expansion. While government barriers may naturally prevent new-market entry, marketers may seek access through using new entry modes, adjusting marketing programs, or getting into a market before entry barriers are erected.

Mix-Related Factors   These factors relate to the degree to which marketing mix elements—primarily product, promotion, and distribution—can be standardized. The more that standardization is possible, the more diversification is indicated. Overall savings through economies of scale can then be utilized in marketing efforts.

Depending on the product, each market will have its own challenges. Whether constraints are apparent (such as tariffs) or hidden (such as tests or standards), they will complicate all of the other factors. Nevertheless, regional integration has allowed many marketers to diversify their efforts.

Company-Related Factors   These include the objectives set by the company for its international operations and the policies it adopts in those markets. As an example, the firm may require—either by stated policy or because of its goods—extensive interaction with intermediaries and clients. When this is the case, the firm's efforts will likely be concentrated because of resource constraints.

The opportunity to take advantage of diversification is available for all types of companies, not only the large ones. The identification of unique worldwide segments for which a customized marketing mix is provided has proven to be successful for many small and medium-sized companies. For example, Symbol Technologies invented the handheld laser scanner and now dominates the field worldwide. Cisco Systems claims 50 percent of the world market for gear that connects networks of computers, a field not in existence ten years ago.[14]

Marketing Management

After target markets are selected, the next step is the determination of marketing efforts at appropriate levels. A key question in international marketing concerns the extent to which the elements of the marketing mix—product, price, place, and distribution—should be standardized. The marketer also faces the specific challenges of adjusting each of the mix elements in the international marketplace.

STANDARDIZATION VERSUS ADAPTATION

The international marketer must first decide what modifications in the mix policy are needed or warranted. Three basic alternatives in approaching international markets are available:

1. Make no special provisions for the international marketplace but, rather, identify potential target markets and then choose products that can easily be marketed with little or no modification.
2. Adapt to local conditions in each and every target market (the multidomestic approach).
3. Incorporate differences into a regional or global strategy that will allow for local differences in implementation (globalization approach).

In today's environment, standardization usually means cross-national strategies rather than a policy of viewing foreign markets as secondary and therefore not important enough to have products adapted for them. Ideally, the international marketer should think globally and act locally, focusing on neither extreme: full standardization or full localization. Global thinking requires flexibility in exploiting good ideas and products on a worldwide basis regardless of their origin. Factors that encourage standardization or adaptation are summarized in Table 14.2.

TABLE 14.2

Standardization versus Adaptation

Factors Encouraging Standardization	Factors Encouraging Adaptation
• Economies in product R & D	• Differing use conditions
• Economies of scale in production	• Government and regulatory influences
• Economies in marketing	• Differing buyer behavior patterns
• Control of marketing programs	• Local initiative and motivation in implementation
• "Shrinking" of the world marketplace	• Adherence to the marketing concept

The adaptation decision will also have to be assessed as a function of time and market involvement. The more companies learn about local market characteristics in individual markets, the more they are able to establish similarities and, as a result, standardize their approach. This market insight will give them legitimacy with local constituents in developing a common understanding of the extent of standardization versus adaptation.[15] For example, for years Mattel marketed Barbie dolls around the world that featured local characteristics. Recently, however, Mattel's research has found that the original Barbie (with its yellow hair and blue eyes) plays equally well around the world.[16]

Factors Affecting Adaptation

Even when marketing programs are based on highly standardized ideas and strategies, they depend on three sets of variables: (1) the market(s) targeted; (2) the product and its characteristics; and (3) company characteristics, including factors such as resources and policy.

Questions of adaptation have no easy answers. Marketers in many firms rely on decision-support systems to aid in program adaptation, while others consider every situation independently. All goods must, of course, conform to environmental conditions over which the marketer has no control. Further, the international marketer may use adaptation to enhance its competitiveness in the marketplace.

PRODUCT POLICY

Goods or services form the core of the firm's international operations. Its success depends on how well goods satisfy needs and wants and how well they are differentiated from those of the competition. This section focuses on product and product-line adaptation to foreign markets as well as product counterfeiting as a current problem facing international marketers.

Factors in Product Adaptation

Factors affecting product adaptation to foreign market conditions are summarized in Figure 14.2. The changes vary from minor ones, such as translation of a user's manual, to major ones, such as a more economical version of the product. Many of the factors have an impact on product selection as well as product adaptation for a given market.

Studies of product adaptation show that the majority of products have to be modified for the international marketplace one way or another. Changes typically affect packaging, measurement units, labeling, product constituents and features, usage instructions, and, to a lesser extent, logos and brand names.[17]

Regional, Country, or Local Characteristics Typically, the market environment mandates the majority of product modifications. However, the most stringent requirements often result from government regulations. Some of the requirements may serve no purpose other than a political one (such as protection of domestic industry or response to political pressures). Because of the sovereignty of nations, individual firms must comply, but they can influence the situation either by lobbying directly or through industry associations to have the issue raised during trade negotiations. Government regulations may be spelled out, but firms need to be ever vigilant for changes and exceptions. The member countries of the European Economic Area are imposing standards in more than 10,000 product categories ranging from toys to tractor seats. While companies such as Murray Manufacturing have had to change their products to comply with the standards (in Murray's case, making its lawnmowers

FIGURE 14.2

Factors Affecting Product Adaptation Decisions

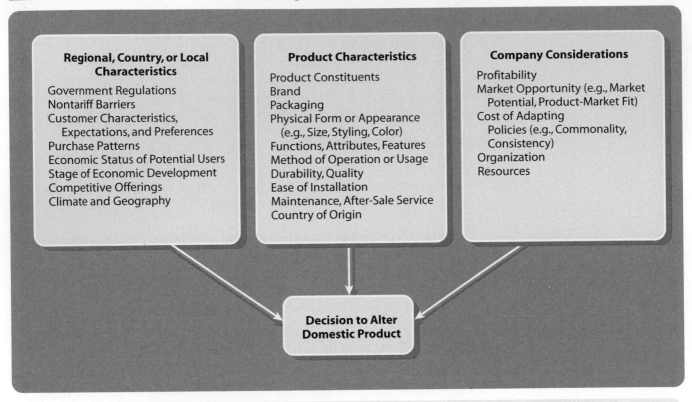

Regional, Country, or Local Characteristics

Government Regulations
Nontariff Barriers
Customer Characteristics, Expectations, and Preferences
Purchase Patterns
Economic Status of Potential Users
Stage of Economic Development
Competitive Offerings
Climate and Geography

Product Characteristics

Product Constituents
Brand
Packaging
Physical Form or Appearance (e.g., Size, Styling, Color)
Functions, Attributes, Features
Method of Operation or Usage
Durability, Quality
Ease of Installation
Maintenance, After-Sale Service
Country of Origin

Company Considerations

Profitability
Market Opportunity (e.g., Market Potential, Product-Market Fit)
Cost of Adapting
    Policies (e.g., Commonality, Consistency)
Organization
Resources

Decision to Alter Domestic Product

Source: Adapted from V. Yorio, *Adapting Products for Export* (New York: The Conference Board, 1983), 7.

quieter), they will be able to produce one European product in the future. Overall, U.S. producers may be forced to improve quality of all their products because some product rules require adoption of an overall system approved by the International Standards Organization (ISO).[18] By December 2002, more than 561,747 ISO 9000 certificates (relating to product and process quality) had been issued in 146 countries worldwide.[19]

Product decisions made by marketers of consumer products are especially affected by local behavior, tastes, attitudes, and traditions—all reflecting the marketer's need to gain the customer's approval. A knowledge of cultural and psychological differences may be the key to success. For example, Brazilians rarely eat breakfast or they eat it at home; therefore, Dunkin' Donuts markets doughnuts as snacks, as dessert, and for parties. To further appeal to Brazilians, doughnuts are made with local fruit fillings such as papaya and guava.[20] Chinese and Western consumers share similar standards when it comes to evaluating brand names. Both appreciate a brand name that is catchy, memorable, distinct, and says something indicative of the product. But, because of cultural and linguistic factors, Chinese consumers expect more in terms of how the names are spelled, written, and styled, and whether they are considered lucky. PepsiCo, Inc., introduced Cheetos in the Chinese market under a Chinese name, *qi duo*, roughly pronounced "chee-do," that translates as "many surprises."[21]

Often no concrete product changes are needed, only a change in the product's **positioning.** Positioning is the perception by consumers of the firm's brand in relation to competitors' brands; that is, the mental image a brand, or the company as a whole, evokes. Coca-Cola took a risk in marketing Diet Coke in Japan because the population is not overweight by Western standards. Further, Japanese women do not like to drink anything clearly labeled as a diet product. The company changed the name to Coke Light and subtly shifted the promotional theme from "weight loss" to "figure maintenance."

Nontariff barriers include product standards, testing or approval procedures, subsidies for local products, and bureaucratic red tape. The nontariff barriers affecting product adjustments usually concern elements outside the core product. The U.S. Department of Commerce estimates that a typical machine manufacturer can expect to spend between $50,000 and $100,000 a year complying with foreign standards. For certain exports to the European Union, that figure can reach as high as $200,000.[22] Because nontariff barriers are usually in place to keep foreign products out or to protect domestic producers, getting around them may be the single toughest problem for the international marketer.

The monitoring of competitors' product features, as well as determining what has to be done to meet and beat them, is critical to product-adaptation decisions. Competitive offerings may provide a baseline against which resources can be measured—for example, they may help to determine what it takes to reach a critical market share in a given competitive situation. American Hospital Supply, a Chicago-based producer of medical equipment, adjusts its product in a preemptive way by making products that are hard to duplicate. As a result, the firm increased sales and earnings in Japan about 40 percent a year over a ten-year period.

Management must take into account the stage of economic development of the overseas market. As a country's economy advances, buyers are in a better position to buy and to demand more sophisticated products and product versions. On the other hand, the situation in some developing markets may require **backward innovation;** that is, the market may require a drastically simplified version of the firm's product because of lack of purchasing power or of usage conditions. Economic conditions may shift rapidly, thus warranting change in the product or the product line. During the Asian currency crisis, McDonald's replaced French fries with rice in its Indonesian restaurants due to cost considerations. With the collapse of the local rupiah, potatoes, the only ingredient McDonald's imports to Indonesia, quintupled in price. In addition, a new rice and egg dish was introduced to maintain as many customers as possible.[23]

Product Characteristics   Product characteristics are the inherent features of the product offering, whether actual or perceived. The inherent characteristics of products, and the benefits they provide to consumers in the various markets in which they are marketed, make certain products good candidates for standardization—and others not.

The international marketer has to make sure that products do not contain ingredients that might violate legal requirements or religious or social customs. DEP Corporation, a Los Angeles manufacturer with $19 million in annual sales of hair and skin products, takes particular pains to make sure that no Japan-bound products contain formaldehyde, an ingredient commonly used in the United States, but illegal in Japan. Where religion or custom determines consumption, ingredients may have to be replaced for the product to be acceptable. In Islamic countries, for example, vegetable shortening has to be substituted for animal fats. In deference to Hindu and Muslim beliefs, McDonald's "Maharaja Mac" is made with mutton in India.

Packaging is an area where firms generally do make modifications. Due to the longer time that products spend in channels of distribution, international companies, especially those marketing food products, have used more expensive packaging materials and/or more expensive transportation modes for export shipments. Food processors have solved the problem by using airtight, reclosable containers that seal out moisture and other contaminants.

The promotional aspect of packaging relates primarily to labeling. The major adjustments concern legally required bilinguality, as in Canada (French and English), Belgium (French and Flemish), and Finland (Finnish and Swedish). Other governmental requirements include more informative labeling of products for consumer protection and education. Inadequate identification, failure to use the required languages, or inadequate or incorrect descriptions printed on the labels may all cause problems. Increasingly, environmental concerns are having an impact on packaging decisions. On the one hand, governments want to reduce the amount of packaging waste by encouraging marketers to adopt the four environmentally correct Rs: redesign, reduce, reuse, and recycle.[24] On the other hand, many markets have sizable segments of consumers who are concerned enough about protecting the environment to change their consumption patterns, which has resulted in product modifications such as the introduction of recyclable yogurt containers from marketers such as Dany and Danone in Europe.

Brand names convey the image of the good or service. Offhand, brands may seem to be one of the most standardizable items in the product offering. However, the establishment of worldwide brands is difficult; how can a marketer establish world brands when the firm sells 800 products in more than 200 countries, most of them under different names? This is the situation of Gillette. A typical example is Silkience hair conditioner, which is sold as Soyance in France, Sientel in Italy, and Silkience in Germany. Standardizing the name to reap promotional benefits is difficult because names have become established in each market, and the action would lead to objections from local managers or even government. In response, marketers have standardized all other possible elements of brand aesthetics, such as color, symbols, and packaging.[25]

Brand aesthetics have to take market-specific realities, such as culture, into account. A Finnish exporter of bottled water had to adjust its traditional logo (featuring a mermaid) to a more neutral one for its shipments for Saudi Arabia, as shown in Figure 14.3.

The product offered in the dometic market may not be operable in the foreign market. One of the major differences faced by appliance manufacturers is electrical power systems. In some cases, variations may exist within a country, such as Brazil. Some companies have adjusted their products to operate in different systems; for example, video equipment can be adjusted to record and play back on different color systems.

When a product that is sold internationally requires repairs, parts, or service, the problems of obtaining, training, and holding a sophisticated engineering or repair staff are not easy to solve. If the product breaks down and the repair arrangements are not up to standard, the product image will suffer. In some cases, products abroad may not even be used for their intended purpose and thus may require not only modifications in product configuration but also in service frequency. For instance, snowplows exported from the United States are used to remove sand from driveways in Saudi Arabia.

The country of origin of a product, typically communicated by the phrase "made in (country)," has considerable influence on quality perceptions. The perception of products manufactured in certain countries is affected by a built-in positive or negative assumption about quality. One study of machine tool buyers found that the United States and Germany were rated higher than Japan, with Brazil rated below all three of them.[26] These types of findings indicate that steps must be taken by the inter-

FIGURE 14.3

Adjusting Brand Aesthetics to International Market Requirements

On top is the Vellamo label as it appears in its native market of Finand, and below is the same label as adjusted for the Arabic market.

Source: Courtesy of Heinolan Viqua Oy.

national marketer to overcome or at least neutralize biases. The issue is especially important to developing countries that need to increase exports, and for importers who source products from countries different from where they are sold.[27] Some countries have started promotional campaigns to improve their overall images in support of exports and investment.[28]

Company Considerations   Company policy will often determine the presence and degree of adaptation. Discussions of product adaptation often end with the question, "Is it worth it?" The answer depends on the company's ability to control costs, to correctly estimate market potential, and, finally, to secure profitability. The decision to adapt should be preceded by a thorough analysis of the market. Formal market research with primary data collection and/or testing is warranted. From the financial standpoint, some companies have specific return-on-investment levels (for example, 25 percent) to be satisfied before adaptation. Others let the requirement vary as a function of the market considered and also the time in the market—that is, profitability may be initially compromised for proper market entry.

Most companies aim for consistency in their market efforts. This means that all products must fit in terms of quality, price, and user perceptions. Consistency may be difficult to attain, for example, in the area of warranties. Warranties can be uniform only if use conditions do not vary drastically and if the company is able to deliver equally on its promise anywhere it has a presence.

Product Line Management

International marketers' product lines consist of local, regional, and global brands. In a given market, an exporter's product line, typically shorter than domestically, concentrates on the most profitable products. Product lines may vary dramatically from one market to another depending on the extent of the firm's operations. Some firms at first cater only to a particular market segment, then eventually expand to cover an entire market. For example, Japanese auto manufacturers moved into the highly profitable luxury car segment after establishing a strong position in the world small-car segment.

The domestic market is not the only source of new-product ideas for the international marketer, nor is it the only place where they are developed.[29] Some products may be developed elsewhere for worldwide consumption because of an advantage in skills. Colgate-Palmolive has set up **centers of excellence** around the world; in hair care, they are located in Paris, France, and Bangkok, Thailand. Ford Europe was assigned the task to develop the Ford Focus, which was then introduced to North America a year later.

Sensitivity to local requirements and tastes also has to be reflected in the company's product line. In Brazil, Levi Strauss developed a line of jeans exclusively for women there, who prefer ultratight jeans. However, what is learned in one market can often be adopted in another. Levi's line of chino pants and casual wear originated in the company's Argentine unit and was applied to loosely cut pants by its Japanese subsidiary. The company's U.S. operation adopted both in 1986, and the line became global in the 1990s.[30] This sensitivity also has to exist in how products are developed. With the Ford Focus, the Europeans maintained an overall leadership role but key responsibilities were divided. The U.S. side took over automatic transmissions, with Europe handling the manual version.[31]

Product Counterfeiting

About $350 billion in domestic and export sales are estimated to be lost by companies worldwide annually because of product counterfeiting and trademark patent infringement of consumer and industrial products.[32] The hardest hit are software, entertainment, and pharmaceutical sectors. Counterfeit goods are any goods bearing an unauthorized representation of a trademark, patented invention, or copyrighted work that is legally protected in the country where it is marketed.

The practice of product counterfeiting has spread to high technology and services from the traditionally counterfeited products: high-visibility, strong brand-name consumer goods. In addition, a new dimension has emerged to complicate the situation. Previously, the only concern was whether a firm's product was being counterfeited; now, management has to worry about whether raw materials and components purchased for production are themselves real.[33]

Four types of action that can be taken against counterfeiting are legislative action, bilateral and multilateral negotiations, joint private sector action, and measures taken by individual firms. Governments have enacted special legislation and set country-specific negotiation objectives for reciprocity and retaliatory options for intellectual property protection.

In today's environment, firms are taking more aggressive steps to protect themselves. Victimized firms are not only losing sales but also goodwill in the longer term if customers, believing they are getting the real product, unknowingly end up with a copy of inferior quality. In addition to the normal measures of registering trademarks and copyrights, firms are taking steps in product development to prevent the copying of trademarked goods. For example, new authentication materials in labeling are virtually impossible to duplicate. Jointly, companies have formed organizations to lobby for legislation and to act as information clearinghouses.

PRICING POLICY

Pricing is the only element in the marketing mix that is revenue generating; all of the others are costs. It should therefore be used as an active instrument of strategy in the major areas of marketing decision making. Pricing in the international environment is more complicated than in the domestic market, however, because of such factors as government influence, different currencies, and additional costs. International pricing situations can be divided into four general categories: export pricing, foreign market pricing, price coordination, and intracompany, or transfer, pricing.

Export Pricing

Three general price-setting strategies in international marketing are a standard worldwide price; dual pricing, which differentiates between domestic and export prices; and market-differentiated pricing.[34] The first two are cost-oriented pricing methods that are relatively simple to establish, are easy to understand, and cover all of the necessary costs. **Standard worldwide pricing** is based on average unit costs of fixed, variable, and export-related costs.

In **dual pricing**, domestic and export prices are differentiated, and two approaches are available: the **cost-plus method** and the **marginal cost method.** The cost-plus strategy involves the actual costs, that is, a full allocation of domestic and foreign costs to the product. Although this type of pricing ensures margins, the final price may put the product beyond the reach of the customer. As a result, some exporters resort to flexible cost-plus strategy, wherein discounts are provided when necessary as a result of customer type, intensity of competition, or size of order. The marginal cost method considers the direct costs of producing and selling for export as the floor beneath which prices cannot be set. Fixed costs for plants, R&D, domestic overhead, and domestic marketing costs are disregarded. An exporter can thus lower export prices to be competitive in markets that otherwise might have been considered beyond access.

On the other hand, **market-differentiated pricing** is based on a demand-oriented strategy and is thus more consistent with the marketing concept. This method also allows consideration of competitive forces in setting export price. The major problem is the exporter's perennial dilemma: lack of information. Therefore, in most cases, marginal costs provide a basis for competitive comparisons, on which the export price is set.

In preparing a quotation, the exporter must be careful to take into account unique export-related costs and, if possible, include them. They are in addition to the normal costs shared with the domestic side. They include:

1. The cost incurred in modifying the good for foreign markets.
2. Operational costs of the export operation. Examples are personnel, market research, additional shipping and insurance costs, communications costs with foreign customers, and overseas promotional costs.

3. Costs incurred in entering foreign markets. These include tariffs and taxes; risks associated with a buyer in a different market (mainly commercial credit risks and political risks); and dealing in other than the exporter's domestic currency—that is, foreign exchange risk.

The combined effect of both clear-cut and hidden costs results in export prices far in excess of domestic prices. This is called **price escalation.** Dollar-based prices may also become expensive to local buyers in the case of currency devaluation. For example, during the Asian currency turmoil, many companies in Indonesia, Malaysia, South Korea, and Thailand scaled down their buying. The exporter has many alternatives under these circumstances, such as stretching out payment terms, cutting prices, or bringing scaled-down, more affordable products to the affected markets.[35]

Inexpensive imports often trigger accusations of **dumping**—that is, selling goods overseas for less than in the exporter's home market, at a price below the cost of production, or both. Dumping ranges from predatory to unintentional. Predatory dumping is the tactic of a foreign firm that intentionally sells at a loss in another country to increase its market share at the expense of domestic producers. This amounts to an international price war. Unintentional dumping is the result of time lags between the date of sales transactions, shipment, and arrival. Prices, including exchange rates, can change in such a way that the final sales price is below the cost of production or below the price prevailing in the exporter's home market.

In the United States, domestic producers may petition the government to impose antidumping duties on imports alleged to be dumped. The remedy is a duty equal to the dumping margin. International agreements and U.S. law provide for countervailing duties. They may be imposed on imports that are found to be subsidized by foreign governments. They are designed to offset the advantages imports would otherwise receive from the subsidy.

Foreign Market Pricing

Pricing within the individual markets in which the firm operates is determined by: (1) corporate objectives; (2) costs; (3) customer behavior and market conditions; (4) market structure; and (5) environmental constraints. All of these factors vary from country to country, and pricing policies of the multinational corporation must vary as well. Despite arguments in favor of uniform pricing in multinational markets, price discrimination is an essential characteristic of the pricing policies of firms conducting business in differing markets. In a study of 42 U.S.-based multinational corporations, the major problem areas they reported in making pricing decisions were meeting competition, cost, lack of competitive information, distribution and channel factors, and governmental barriers.[36]

Studies have shown that non-U.S. based companies allow their U.S. subsidiaries considerable freedom in pricing due to the size and unique features of the market. Further, it has been argued that these subsidiaries control the North American market and that distances create a natural barrier against arbitrage practices (i.e., customers going for the lowest price) that would be more likely to emerge in Europe. However, many argue that price coordination has to be worldwide as a result of increasing levels of economic integration efforts around the world.

Price Coordination

The issue of standard worldwide pricing may be mostly a theoretical one because of the influence of environments, but if standardization is sought, it relates more to price levels and the use of pricing as a positioning tool.

Calls for price coordination have increased, especially after the introduction of the euro in 12 EU countries. The single currency will make prices completely transparent for all buyers. If discrepancies are not justifiable due to market differences such as consumption preferences, competition, or government interference, cross-border purchases will occur. The simplest solution would be to have one euro-based price throughout the market. However, given significant differences up to 500 percent, that solution would lead to significant losses in sales and/or profits, as a single price would likely to be closer to the lower-priced countries' level. The recommended approach is a pricing corridor that considers existing country-specific prices while optimizing the profits at a pan-European level.[37] Such a corridor defines the maximum and minimum prices that a country organization can charge—enough to allow flexibility as a result of differences in price elasticities and competition, but not enough to attract people to engage in cross-border shopping that starts at price differences of 20 percent or higher.[38] This approach moves pricing authority away from country managers to regional management and requires changes in management systems and incentive structures.

Significant price gaps lead to the emergence of **gray markets**/parallel importation. The term refers to brand-name imports that enter a country legally but outside regular, authorized distribution channels. The gray market is fueled by companies that sell goods in foreign markets at prices that are far lower than prices charged to, for example, U.S. distributors, and by one strong currency, such as the dollar or the yen. The gray market in the United States has flourished in cars, watches, and even baby powder, cameras, and chewing gum. The retail value of gray markets in the United States has been estimated at $6 billion to $10 billion. This phenomenon not only harms the company financially but also may harm its reputation, because authorized distributors often refuse to honor warranties on items bought through the gray market. Cars bought through the gray market in the United States, for example, may not pass EPA inspections and thus may cause major expense to the unsuspecting buyer.[39]

The proponents of gray marketing argue for their right to "free trade" by pointing to manufacturers who are both overproducing and overpricing in some markets. The main beneficiaries are consumers, who benefit from lower prices, and discount distributors, who now have access to the good. Companies can combat gray marketing through strategic interference. For example, companies can make sure authorized dealers do not engage in transshipments. Companies can also promote the deficiencies in gray-marketed goods, which may not carry a full warranties or after-sales service.

Transfer Pricing

Transfer, or intracompany, pricing is the pricing of sales to members of the corporate family. The overall competitive and financial position of the firm forms the basis of any pricing policy. In this, transfer pricing plays a key role. Intracorporate sales can easily change consolidated global results because they often are one of the most important ongoing decision areas in a company.

Four main transfer-pricing possibilities have merged over time: (1) transfer at direct cost; (2) transfer at direct cost plus additional expenses; (3) transfer at a price derived from end-market prices; and (4) transfer at an **arm's length price,** or the price that unrelated parties would have reached on the same transaction. Doing business overseas requires coping with complexities of environmental peculiarities, the effect of which can be alleviated by manipulating transfer prices. Factors that call for adjustments include taxes, import duties, inflationary tendencies, unstable governments, and other regulations.[40] For example, high transfer prices on goods shipped to a subsidiary and low ones on goods imported from it will result in minimizing the tax liability of a subsidiary operating in a country with a high income tax. Tax liability thus results not only from the absolute tax rate but also from differences in how income is computed. On the other hand, a higher transfer price may have an effect on the import duty, especially if it is assessed on an ad valorem basis. Exceeding a certain threshold may boost the duty substantially and thus have a negative impact on the subsidiary's posture.

Quite often the multinational corporation is put in a difficult position. U.S. authorities may think the transfer price is too low, whereas the foreign entity (especially a less-developed country) may perceive it to be too high. In a survey of 400 multinational companies, respondents facing transfer pricing disputes were able to defend their profit to local tax authorities in only half of the inquiries.[41]

In the host environments, the concern of the multinational corporation is to maintain its status as a good corporate citizen. Many corporations, in drafting multinational codes of conduct, have specified that intracorporate pricing will follow the arm's length principle. Multinationals have also been found to closely abide by tax regulations governing transfer pricing.[42] The OECD has issued transfer pricing guidelines including methodology and documentation scenarios to assist in the compliance process.

DISTRIBUTION POLICY

Channels of distribution provide the essential links that connect producers and customers. The channel decision is the longest term of the marketing mix decisions in that it cannot be readily changed. In addition, it involves relinquishing some of the control the firm has over the marketing of its products. The two factors make choosing the right channel structure a crucial decision. Properly structured and staffed, the distribution system will function more as one rather than as a collection of often quite different units.

Channel Design

The term *channel design* refers to the length and width of the channel employed. **Channel design** is determined by factors that can be summarized as the 11 Cs: customer, culture, competition, company, character, capital, cost, coverage, control, continuity, and communication. While there are no standard answers to channel design, the international marketer can use the 11 Cs as a checklist to determine the proper approach to reach target audiences before selecting channel members to fill the roles. The first three factors are givens in that the company must adjust its approach to the existing structures. The other eight are controllable to a certain extent by the marketer.

1. **Customers** The demographic and psychographic characteristics of targeted *customers* will form the basis for channel-design decisions. Answers to questions such as what customers need as well as why, when, and how they buy are used to determine ways in which products should be made available to generate a competitive advantage. Customer characteristics may cause one product to be distributed through two different types of channels. All sales of Caterpillar's earthmoving equipment are handled by independent dealers, except for sales to the U.S. government and the People's Republic of China, which are direct.

2. **Culture** The marketer must analyze existing channel structures, or what might be called the distribution *culture* of a market. For example, the general nature of the Japanese distribution system presents one of the major reasons for the apparent failure of foreign companies to penetrate the market.[43] In most cases, the international

marketer must adjust to existing structures. Foreign legislation affecting distributors and agents is an essential part of the distribution culture of a market. For example, legislation may require foreign companies to be represented only by firms that are 100 percent locally owned. Some countries have prohibited the use of dealers so as to protect consumers from abuses in which intermediaries have engaged.

3. Competition   Channels used by *competitors* may make up the only distribution system that is accepted both by the trade and by consumers. In this case, the international marketer's task is to use the structure more effectively and efficiently, as Wal-Mart has been able to do in Europe. An alternate strategy is to use a totally different distribution approach from the competition and hope to develop a competitive advantage in that manner as IKEA has been able to do with its use of supermarketing concepts in furniture retail.

4. Company Objectives   Sometimes, management goals may conflict with the best possible channel design. Fast-food chains have typically rushed into newly opened markets to capitalize on the development. The companies have attempted to establish mass sales as soon as possible by opening numerous restaurants in the busiest sections of several cities. Unfortunately, control has proven to be quite difficult because of the sheer number of openings over a relatively short period of time.

5. Character   The type or *character* of the good will have an impact on the design of the channel. Generally, the more specialized, expensive, bulky, or perishable the product and the more it may require after-sale service, the more likely the channel is to be relatively short. Staple items, such as soap, tend to have longer channels, while services have short channels. The type of channel chosen has to match the overall positioning of the product in the market. Changes in overall market conditions, such as currency fluctuations, may require changes in distribution as well. An increase in the value of the dollar may cause a repositioning of the marketed product as a luxury item, necessitating an appropriate channel (such as an upscale department store) for its distribution.

6. Capital   The term *capital* is used to describe the financial requirements in setting up a channel system. The international marketer's financial strength will determine the type of channel and the basis on which channel relationships will be built. The stronger the marketer's finances, the more able the firm is to establish channels it either owns or controls. Intermediaries' requirements for beginning inventories, selling on a consignment basis, preferential loans, and need for training will all have an impact on the type of approach chosen by the international marketer.

7. Cost   Closely related to the capital dimension is *cost*—that is, the expenditure incurred in maintaining a channel once it is established. Costs will naturally vary over the life cycle of the relationship as well as over the life cycle of the product marketed. An example of the costs involved is promotional monies spent by a distributor for the marketer's product. Costs may also be incurred in protecting the company's distributors against adverse market conditions. A number of U.S. manufacturers helped their distributors maintain competitive prices through subsidies when the high rate for the U.S. dollar caused pricing problems.

8. Coverage   The term *coverage* is used to describe both the number of areas in which the marketer's products are represented and the quality of that representation.

Coverage, therefore, is two-dimensional in that both horizontal and vertical coverage need to be considered in channel design. The number of areas to be covered depends on the dispersion of demand in the market and also the time elapsed since the product's introduction to the market. A company typically enters a market with one local distributor, but, as volume expands, the distribution base often has to be adjusted.

9. Control   The use of intermediaries will automatically lead to loss of some *control* over the marketing of the firm's products. The looser the relationship is between the marketer and the intermediaries, the less control can be exerted. The longer the channel, the more difficult it becomes for the marketer to have a final say over pricing, promotion, and the types of outlets in which the product will be made available.

10. Continuity   Nurturing *continuity* rests heavily on the marketer because foreign distributors may have a more short-term view of the relationship. For example, Japanese wholesalers believe that it is important for manufacturers to follow up initial success with continuous improvement of the product. If such improvements are not forthcoming, competitors are likely to enter the market with similar, but lower-priced, products and the wholesalers of the imported product will turn to the Japanese suppliers.[44]

11. Communication   Proper communication will perform important roles for the international marketer. It will help convey the marketer's goals to the distributors, help solve conflict situations, and aid in the overall marketing of the product. Communication is a two-way process that does not permit the marketer to dictate to intermediaries. Sometimes the planned program may not work because of a lack of communication. Prices may not be competitive; promotional materials may be obsolete or inaccurate and not well received overall.

Selection and Screening of Intermediaries

Once the basic design of the channel has been determined, the international marketer must begin a search to fill the defined roles with the best available candidates. Choices will have to be made within the framework of the company's overall philosophy on distributors versus agents, as well as whether the company will use an indirect or direct approach to foreign markets.

Firms that have successful international distribution attest to the importance of finding top representatives. For companies such as Loctite, whose adhesives require high levels of technical selling skills, only the best distributors in a given market will do. The undertaking should be held in the same regard as recruiting and hiring within the company because an ineffective foreign distributor can set you back years; it is almost better to have no distributor than a bad one in a major market.

Various sources exist to assist the marketer in locating intermediary candidates. One of the easiest and most economical ways is to use the service of governmental agencies. The U.S. Department of Commerce has various services that can assist firms in identifying suitable representatives abroad; some have been designed specifically for that purpose. A number of private sources are also available to the international marketer. Trade directories, such as those by Dun & Bradstreet, usually list foreign representatives geographically and by product classification. Telephone directories, especially the yellow page sections or editions, can provide distributor lists. Although not detailed, the listings will give addresses and an indication of the products sold. The firm can solicit the support of some of its facilitating agencies, such as banks, advertising agencies, shipping lines, and airlines. The marketer can take an even more direct approach by buying advertising space to solicit representation. The advertisements typically indicate the type of support the marketer will be able to give to its distributor.

Intermediaries can be screened on their performance and professionalism. An intermediary's performance can be evaluated on the basis of financial standing and sales as well as the likely fit it would provide in terms of its existing product lines and coverage. Professionalism can be assessed through reputation and overall standing in the business community. Information on these dimensions can be secured either from governmental or private-sector sources as shown in Figure 14.4

Managing the Channel Relationship

A channel relationship can be likened to a marriage in that it brings together two independent entities that have shared goals. For the relationship to work, each party has to be open about its expectations and openly communicate changes perceived in the other's behavior that might be contrary to the agreement. A framework for managing channel relationships is provided in Table 14.3.

The complicating factors that separate the two parties fall into three categories: ownership, geographic and cultural distance, and different rules of law. Rather than lament their existence, both parties must take strong action to remedy them. Often the first major step is for both parties to acknowledge that differences exist.

FIGURE 14.4

Providers of International Intermediary Information

Source: Courtesy of the U.S. Commercial Service (http://www.usatrade.gov). Copyright Dun & Bradstreet and the Guild Group.

TABLE 14.3   Managing Relations with Overseas Distributors

High Export Performance Inhibitors →	Bring	Remedy Lies In
Separate ownership	• Divided loyalties • Seller-buyer atmosphere • Unclear future intentions	Offering good incentives, helpful support schemes, discussing plans frankly, and interacting in a mutually beneficial way
Geographic and cultural separation	• Communication blocks • Negative attitudes toward foreigners • Physical distribution strains	Making judicious use of two-way visits, establishing a well-managed communication program
Different rules of law	• Vertical trading restrictions • Dismissal difficulties	Complying fully with the law, drafting a strong distributor agreement

Source: Adapted from Philip J. Rosson, "Source Factors in Manufacture–Overseas Distributor Relationships in International Marketing," in *International Marketing Management,* ed. Erdener Kaynak (New York: Praeger, 1984), 95.

E-Commerce

E-commerce, the ability to offer goods and services over the Web, is forecast to grow at a compound annual rate of 50+ percent within five years. While the United States has accounted for the majority of e-commerce activity, Western Europe is identified as the area with most significant growth, as shown in Table 14.4. A survey by Taylor Nelson Sofres shows that 90 percent of companies in the United States and 86 percent of companies in Britain are currently using the Internet for such activities as customer relationship marketing, order fulfillment, and sales, compared to only 60 percent of organizations in Japan and 36 percent in France.[45]

Many companies willing to enter e-commerce will not have to do it on their own. Hub sites (also known as virtual malls or digital intermediaries) will bring together buyers, sellers, distributors, and transaction payment processors in one single marketplace, making convenience the key attraction. With 1,400 of them in place, entities such as Compare.net (http://www.compare.net), Priceline.com (http://www.priceline.com), eBay (http://www. ebay. com), and VerticalNet (http://www.verticalnet.com) leading the way.[46]

As soon as customers have the ability to access a company through the Internet, the company itself must be prepared to provide 24-hour order taking and customer

TABLE 14.4   Worldwide E-Commerce Revenue by Region (in $ billions)

Region	2001	2006	Compound Annual Growth
United States	255.8	1,917.8	49.6%
Western Europe	153.7	1,985.3	66.8%
Japan	99.0	602.5	43.5%
Asia/Pacific	37.4	892.7	88.6%
Rest of world	52.0	335.6	45.2%
Share of B2B	81.8%	89.3%	

Source: From IDC Internet Commerce Market Model, Version 8.3; http://www.idc.com.

service, have the regulatory and customs-handling expertise to deliver internationally, and have an in-depth understanding of marketing environments for the further development of the business relationship. The instantaneous interactivity users experience will also be translated into an expectation of expedient delivery of answers and products ordered. Many people living outside the United States who purchase online expect U.S.-style service. However, in many cases, these shoppers may find that shipping is not even available outside of the United States.

The challenges faced in terms of response and delivery capabilities can be overcome through outsourcing services or by building international distribution networks. Air express carriers such as DHL, FedEX, and UPS offer full-service packages that leverage their own Internet infrastructure with customs clearance and e-mail shipment notification. If a company needs help in order fulfillment and customer support, logistics centers offer warehousing and inventory management services as well as same-day delivery from in-country stocks. DHL, for example, has 7 express logistics centers and 45 strategic parts centers worldwide, with key centers in Bahrain for the Middle East, Brussels for Europe, and Singapore for Asia-Pacific. Some companies elect to build their own international distribution networks. Both QVC, a televised shopping service, and Amazon.com, an online retailer of books, have distribution centers in Britain and Germany to take advantage of the European Internet audience and to fulfill more quickly and cheaply the orders generated by their Web sites.

Transactions and the information they provide about the buyer allow for more customization and service by region, market, or even by individual customer. One of the largest online sellers, Dell Computer, builds for its corporate customers with more than 400 employees a Premier Page that is linked to the customer's intranet, allowing approved employees to configure PCs, pay for them, and track their delivery status. Premier Pages also provide access to instant technical support and Dell sales representatives. Presently there are 5,000 companies with such service and $5 million of Dell PCs are ordered every day.[47]

Although English has long been perceived as the *lingua franca* of the Web, the share of non-English speakers worldwide increased to 65 percent of all the users in 2002. It has also been shown that Web users are three times more likely to buy when the offering is made in their own language.[48] However, not even the largest of firms can serve all markets with a full line of their products. Getting a Web site translated and running is an expensive proposition, and, if done correctly, time-consuming as well. If the site is well developed, it will naturally lead to expectations that order fulfillment will be of equal caliber. Therefore, any World Wide Web strategy has to be tied closely to the company's overall growth strategy in world markets.

A number of hurdles and uncertainties are keeping companies out of global markets or from exploiting them to their full potential. Some argue that the World Wide Web does not live up to its name, since it is mostly a tool for the United States and Europe. Yet, as Internet penetration levels increase in the near future due to technological advances, improvements in many countries' Web infrastructures, and customer acceptance, e-business will become truly global. As a matter of fact, in some cases, emerging markets may provide a chance to try out new approaches because the markets and the marketers in them are not burdened by history as seen in Focus on e-Business.

The marketer has to be sensitive to the governmental role in e-commerce. No real consensus exists on the taxation of e-commerce, especially in the case of cross-border transactions. While the United States and the EU have agreed not to impose new taxes on sales through the Internet, there is no uniformity in the international taxation of transactions.[49] Other governments believe, however, that they have something to gain

Focus On ⬇

Testing Channels of the Future

Consumers today are increasingly interested in using the Internet to make car shopping and ownership easier and more convenient. A total of eight to ten million consumers surf the Internet for information to help them buy new cars. Expanding the use beyond providing information (e.g., owner handbooks, recall announcements, and maintenance) has proved to be challenging, however.

Although the United States has the greatest potential for online buying due to large customer base, channel culture reasons prevent its automakers from realizing it. The U.S. retail system consists of 20,000 dealers protected in many cases by state franchise laws that stand in the way of Internet sales. Additionally, automakers' production facilities cannot accommodate real-time Internet orders. As a result, GM and Ford are focusing more on the supplier side of their e-operations.

General Motors is testing electronic commerce strategies in overseas markets such as Taiwan, where it already sells 10 percent of its vehicles through the Internet and began to build cars to order starting in 2000. "Emerging markets are a lab for us," said Mark Hogan, who heads the new E-GM unit. "We do not have a lot of bricks and mortar in these markets, so they provide perfect conditions for us to learn from." The company hopes to sell about 30 percent of units in the next several years.

However, in many of the emerging markets, especially in Asia and Latin America, both GM and Ford have factories that are more flexible and will allow for build-to-order programs at a much faster pace. Furthermore, and more important, automakers do not have existing retail systems that would need to be overhauled. In some cases, as with GM in Taiwan, GM owns a significant share of the retail operations. Ford is experimenting with its Internet ideas in markets such as the Philippines where it has set up an e-commerce system that links consumers, dealers, the manufacturer, and suppliers to create a seamless e-business.

In addition to being able to buy cars online, Taiwanese customers can make service appointments through the GM web site. The company will come to the owner's house or office, pick up the car and return it within hours or overnight after completing the service.

Retailers are also getting on the bandwagon. Internet malls are mushrooming in Korea, for example. To gain access to products, Web retailer Libero teamed up with 100 traditional car dealers. Profits for the cyber dealers are slim—as little as $180 on each car. In addition, car makers and dealers have threatened to sue their Web competitors for selling vehicles at low prices, which disrupts the traditional way of doing business.

Source: "Car Makers Rev Up to New E-Commerce Initiatives," *Network World,* September 2, 2002, 1, 16; "Follow-Through," *Forbes,* December 24, 2001, 48; " Ford and GM Unveil E-Commerce Alliances," *E-Commerce Times,* January 10, 2000, at http://www.ecommercetimes.com/perl/printer/2169/; "Asia Awakes to E-Commerce," *IndustryWeek.com,* January 5, 2000, at http://www.industryweek.com/CurrentArticles/asp/articles.asp?ArticleID= 808; and "GM Tests E-Commerce Plans in Emerging Markets," *Wall Street Journal,* October 25, 1999, B6. See also http://www.gm.com, http://www. GMBuyPower.com, http://www.gmautoworld.com.tw, and http://www.libero.co.kr.

by levying new e-taxes. Until more firm legal precedents are established, international marketers should be aware of their potential tax liabilities and prepare for their imposition, especially if they are considering substantial e-commerce investments. One of the likely scenarios is an e-commerce tax system that closely resembles sales taxes at physical retail outlets. Vendors will be made responsible for the collection of sales taxes and forwarding them to the governments concerned, most likely digitally. Another proposal involves the bit-tax—a variation of the Internet access tax.[50]

In addition, any product traded will still be subject to government regulations. For example, Virtual Vineyards has to worry about country-specific alcohol regulations, while software makers such as Softwareland.com Inc. have to comply with U.S. software export regulations. Dell Computer was fined $50,000 by the U.S. Department of Commerce for shipping computers online to Iran, a country on the sanctions list due to its sponsorship of terrorism.

Governments will also have to come to terms with issues related to security, privacy, and access to the Internet.[51] The private sector argues for the highest possible ability to safeguard its databases, to protect cross-border transmission of confidential information, and to conduct secure financial transactions using global networks. This would require an unrestricted market for encryption products that interoperate globally. However, some governments, and especially the United States, fear that too good of an encryption will enable criminals and terrorist organizations to avoid detection and tracking. Therefore, a strong argument is made in favor of limiting the extent of encryption.

Privacy issues have grown exponentially as a result of e-business. In 1998, the European Union passed a directive that introduced high standards of data privacy to ensure the free flow of data throughout the 15 member states. Each individual has the right to review personal data, correct them, and limit their use. But, and more important, the directive also requires member states to block transmission of data to countries, including the United States, if those countries' domestic legislation does not provide an adequate level of protection. The issue between the United States and the EU will most likely be settled by companies, such as IBM, adopting global privacy policies for managing information online and getting certified by groups such as the Better Business Bureau or Trust-E that are implementing privacy labeling systems that tell users when a site adheres to their privacy guidelines.[52] A 2001 study conducted by Consumers International found that Internet users' privacy was better protected in the United States than in Europe.[53]

For industries such as music and motion pictures, the Internet is both an opportunity and a threat. The Web provides a new efficient method of distribution and customization of products. At the same time, it can be a channel for intellectual property violation through unauthorized posting on web sites where they can be downloaded.[54] In addition, the music industry is concerned about a shift in the balance of economic power: if artists can deliver their works directly to customers via technologies such as MP3, what will be the role of labels and distributors?

PROMOTIONAL POLICY

The international marketer must choose a proper combination of the various promotional tools—advertising, personal selling, sales promotion, and publicity—to create images among the intended target audience. The choice will depend on the target audience, company objectives, the product or service marketed, the resources available for the endeavor, and the availability of promotional tools in a particular market. The focus may not only be on a product or service but the company's overall image.

Advertising

The key decision-making areas in advertising are: (1) media strategy; (2) the promotional message; and (3) the organization of the promotional program.

Media strategy is applied to the selection of media vehicles and the development of a media schedule. Worldwide media spending, which totaled $312 billion in 2002, varies dramatically around the world. In absolute terms, the United States spends the most, followed by Japan, the United Kingdom, Germany, France, and Brazil. The mature U.S. market anticipates slower growth in the future, but European integration and the development of the Pacific Rim's consumer markets are likely to fuel major growth.[55] The major spenders in 2002 were Procter & Gamble ($3.8 billion), General Motors ($3.0 billion), Uniliver ($3.0 billion), Ford ($2.3 billion), and Toyota ($2.2 billion). While General Motors spent 74 percent of its budget in the United States, Unilevers's spending there was only 19 percent. P&G spent 45 percent in the United States.[56]

Media spending varies also by market. Countries devoting the highest percentage to television were Peru (84 percent) and Mexico (73 percent). In some countries, the highest percentage is devoted to print: Kuwait (91) and Norway (77). Radio accounts for more than 20 percent in only a few countries, such as Trinidad and Tobago, and

Nepal. Outdoor advertising accounted for 48 percent of Bolivia's media spending but only 3 percent of Germany's. Cinema advertising is important in India and Nigeria.[57]

Media regulations will also vary. Some regulations include limits on the amount of time available for advertisements; in Italy, for example, the state channels allow a maximum of 12 percent of advertising per hour and 4 percent over a week, and commercial stations allow 18 percent per hour and 15 percent per week. Furthermore, the leading Italian stations do not guarantee audience delivery when spots are bought. Strict separation between programs and commercials is almost a universal requirement, preventing U.S.-style sponsored programs. Restrictions on items such as comparative claims and gender stereotypes are prevalent; for example, Germany prohibits the use of superlatives such as "best."

Global media vehicles have been developed that have target audiences on at least three continents and for which the media buying takes place through a centralized office. These media have traditionally been publications that, in addition to the worldwide edition, have provided advertisers the option of using regional editions. For example, *Time* provides 133 editions, enabling advertising to reach a particular country, a continent, or the world. Other global publications include The *International Herald Tribune*, The *Wall Street Journal*, and *National Geographic*. The Internet provides the international marketer with an additional global medium. U.S. marketers have been slow to react to its potential because their domestic market is so dominant. They have also been reluctant to adapt their Web sites but are willing to repeat what happened in the United States in these regions. One simple way of getting started is to choose a few key languages for the Web site. For example, Gillette decided to add German and Japanese to its Mach3 Web site after studying the number of Internet users in the countries.[58] If the marketer elects to have a global site and region-specific sites (e.g., organized by country), the look should be similar, especially in terms of the level of sophistication of the global site. Another method is to join forces with Internet service providers. For example, Unilever has expanded its sponsorship of the Microsoft online network in the United States to France, Germany, and the United Kingdom.[59] With the agreement, Unilever will provide banner ads, links, and sponsorship to MSN sites, particularly Women Central. Premier sponsorship on the MSN sites will include logo placement at the top right corner of the Web pages. The projection is that the Internet may have a 10 percent market share by 2005, with ad spending reaching nearly $28 billion ($16.9 in North America, $5.2 in Europe, and $3.8 in the Asia-Pacific).[60] The level may reach $33 billion by 2004 as other markets increase their volume as well. In addition to PCs, wireless phones and interactive TV will become delivery mechanisms.

In broadcast media, panregional radio stations have been joined in Europe by television as a result of satellite technology. Approximately half of the households in Europe have access to additional television broadcasts either through cable or direct satellite, and television is no longer restricted by national boundaries. As a result, marketers need to make sure that advertising works not only within markets but across countries as well. The launch of STAR TV has increased the use of regional advertising in Asia (see Figure 14.5).

Developing the **promotional message** is referred to as creative strategy. The marketer must determine what the consumer is really buying—that is, the consumer's motivations. They will vary, depending on:

1. The diffusion of the product, service, or concept into the market. For example, to enter China with online sales may be difficult with only 1 percent of the population and 10 percent of the urban population having a PC.

FIGURE 14.5

Example of a Panregional Medium

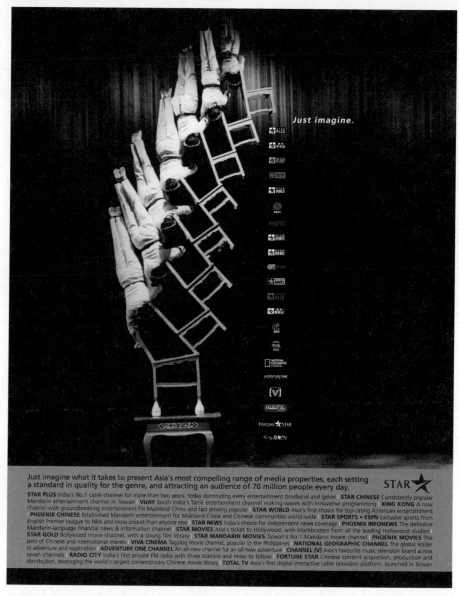

Source: Star Group Limited 2003 http://www.Startv.com

2. The criteria on which the consumer will evaluate the product. For example, in traditional societies, the time-saving qualities of a product may not be the best ones to feature, as Campbell Soup learned in Italy, Brazil, and Poland, where preparers felt inadequate if they did not make soups from scratch.

3. The product's positioning. For example, Parker Pen's upscale image around the world may not be profitable enough in a market that is more or less a commodity business. The solution is to create an image for a commodity product and make the public pay for it—for example, the positioning of Perrier in the United States as a premium mineral water.

The ideal situation in developing message strategy is to have a world brand—a product that is manufactured, packaged, and positioned the same around the world. However, a number of factors will force companies to abandon identical campaigns in favor of recognizable campaigns. The factors are culture, of which language is the main manifestation, economic development, and lifestyles. Consider, for example, the campaign for Marriott International presented in Figure 14.6. International marketers customized the advertising copy to appeal to the local market. While retaining similar graphic elements, these Marriott ads were uniquely designed and written to appeal to the different cultures of Japan, Latin America, and Portugal.

Many multinational corporations are staffed and equipped to perform the full range of promotional activities. In most cases, however, they rely on the outside expertise of advertising agencies and other promotions-related companies such as media-buying companies and specialty marketing firms. In a study of 40 multinational marketers, 32.5 percent are using a single agency worldwide, 20 percent are using two, 5 percent are using three, 10 percent are using four, and 32.5 percent are using more than four agencies. Of the marketers using only one or two agencies, McCann-Erickson was the most popular with 17 percent of the companies.[61] Local agencies will survive, however, because of governmental regulations. In Peru, for example, a law mandates that any commercial aired on Peruvian television must be 100 percent nationally produced. Local agencies tend to forge ties with foreign ad agencies for better coverage and customer service, and thus become part of the general globalization effort. Marketers are choosing specialized interactive shops over full-service agencies for Internet advertising. However, a major weakness with the interactive agencies is their lack of international experience.

Personal Selling

Although advertising is often equated with the promotional effort, in many cases promotional efforts consist of personal selling. In the early stages of internationalization, exporters rely heavily on personal contact. The marketing of industrial goods, especially of high-priced items, requires strong personal selling efforts. In some cases, personal selling may be truly international; for example, Boeing or Northrop Grumman salespeople engage in sales efforts around the world. However, in most cases, personal selling takes place at the local level. The best interests of any company in the industrial area lie in establishing a solid base of dealerships staffed by local people. Personal selling efforts can be developed in the same fashion as advertising. For the multinational company, the primary goal again is the enhancement and standardization of personal selling efforts, especially if the product offering is standardized.

As an example, Eastman Kodak has developed a line-of-business approach to allow for standardized strategy throughout a region.[62] In Europe, one person is placed in charge of the entire copier-duplicator program in each country. That person is responsible for all sales and service teams within the country. Typically, each customer is served by three representatives, each with a different responsibility. Sales representatives maintain ultimate responsibility for the account; they conduct demonstrations, analyze customer requirements, determine the right type of equipment for each installation, and obtain orders. Service representatives install and maintain the equipment and retrofit new-product improvements to existing equipment. Customer service representatives are the liaison between sales and service. They provide operator training on a continuing basis and handle routine questions and complaints. Each team is positioned to respond to any European customer within four hours.

FIGURE 14.6

Global Advertising Campaign Approaches

Sales Promotion

Sales promotion has been used as the catchall term for promotion that is not advertising, personal selling, or publicity. Sales promotion directed at consumers involves such activities as couponing, sampling, premiums, consumer education and demonstration activities, cents-off packages, point-of-purchase materials, and direct mail. The success in Latin America of Tang, General Foods's presweetened powder juice substitute, is for the most part traceable to successful sales promotion efforts. One promotion involved trading Tang pouches for free popsicles from Kibon (General Foods's Brazilian subsidiary). Kibon also placed coupons for free groceries in Tang pouches. In Puerto Rico, General Foods ran Tang sweepstakes. In Argentina, in-store sampling featured Tang poured from Tang pitchers by girls in orange Tang dresses. Decorative Tang pitchers were a hit throughout Latin America.

For sales promotion to work, the campaigns planned by manufacturers or their agencies have to gain the support of the local retailer population. As an example, retailers must redeem coupons presented by consumers and forward them to the manufacturer or to the company handling the promotion. A. C. Nielsen tried to introduce cents-off coupons in Chile and ran into trouble with the nation's supermarket union, which notified its members that it opposed the project and recommended that coupons not be accepted. The main complaint was that an intermediary, such as Nielsen, would unnecessarily raise costs and thus the prices to be charged to consumers. Also, some critics felt that coupons would limit individual negotiations, because Chileans often bargain for their purchases.

Sales promotion directed at intermediaries, also known as trade promotion, includes activities such as trade shows and exhibits, trade discounts, and cooperative advertising. For example, attendance at an appropriate trade show is one of the best ways to make contacts with government officials and decision makers, work with present intermediaries, or attract new ones.

Public Relations

Public relations is the marketing communications function charged with executing programs to earn public understanding and acceptance, which means both internal and external communication. Internal communication is important, especially in multinational companies, to create an appropriate corporate culture. External campaigns can be achieved through the use of corporate symbols, corporate advertising, customer relations programs, the generation of publicity, as well as getting a company's view to the public via the Internet. Some material on the firm is produced for special audiences to assist in personal selling.

A significant part of public relations activity focuses on portraying multinational corporations as good citizens of their host markets. IBM's policies of good corporate citizenship are summarized in the Focus on Ethics. Cisco Systems' Networking Academy is an example of how a marketer can link philanthropic strategy, its competitive advantage, and broader social good. To address a chronic deficit in IT job applicants, the company created The Network Academy concept, whereby it contributes networking equipment to schools. Cisco now operates 9,000 academies in secondary schools, community colleges, and community-based organizations in 147 countries. As the leading player in the field, Cisco stands to benefit the most from this improved labor pool. At the same time, Cisco has attracted worldwide recognition for this program, boosted its employee morale and partner goodwill, and has generated a reputation for leadership in philanthropy.[63]

Focus On ⬇

Global Corporate Philanthropy

A recent Rope survey found that 92 percent of the respondents feel that it is important for companies to seek out ways to become good corporate citizens, and they are most interested in those who get involved in environmental, educational, and health issues. Many respondents are worried that globalization has brought about a decline in corporate conduct and responsibility. However, many companies have seen it as completely the opposite. Community relations is, as one chief executive put it, "food for the soul of the organization." It has become a strategic aspect of business and a fundamental ingredient for the long-term health of the enterprise. As a global company, IBM has a network of staff who are accountable for corporate responsibility throughout the 152 countries where it operates. Major initiatives that address environmental concerns, support programs for the disabled, and boost education reform have been pioneered by IBM around the world.

IBM's policy of good corporate citizenship means accepting responsibility as a participant in community and national affairs and striving to be among the most-admired companies in its various host countries. IBM sponsors Worldwide Intitiatives in Volunteerism, a $1 million-plus program to fund projects worldwide and promote employee volunteerism. In Thailand, for example, IBM provides equipment and personnel to universities and donates money to the nation's wildlife fund and environmental protection. It is one of the very few companies with a U.S.-based parent to have won the Garuda Award, which recognizes significant contributions to Thailand's social and economic development.

As a part of its long-term strategy for growth in Latin America, IBM has invested millions of dollars in an initiative that brings the latest technology to local schools. IBM does not donate the computers (they are bought by governments, institutions, and other private donors), but it does provide the needed instruction and technological support. This initiative is a creative combination of marketing, social responsibility, and long-term relationship building that fits with the company's goal of becoming a "national asset."

Increased privatization and cutbacks in public spending in many countries offer numerous opportunities for companies to make substantive contributions to solving serious global, regional, or local problems. Conservative governments in Europe are welcoming private-sector programs to provide job training for inner-city youth, to meet the needs of immigrants, and to solve massive pollution problems. IBM Germany provided computer equipment and executive support to clean the heavily polluted River Elbe, which runs through the Czech Republic and Germany into the North Sea.

There are considerable company-internal reasons for this activity as well. Employees do not want to work for companies that have no social conscience, suppliers and customers do not want to do business with companies that pollute the environment or are notorious for shoddy products and practices, and communities do not welcome companies that are not good citizens. Increasingly, many shareholder issues are socially driven.

Sources: Michael E. Porter and Mark R. Kramer, "The Competitive Advantage of Corporate Philanthropy," *Harvard Business Review* 80 (December 2002): 56–68; Roger L. Martin, "The Virtue Matrix: Calculating the Return on Corporate Responsibility," *Harvard Business Review* 80 (March 2002): 68–75; and Bradley K. Googins, "Why Community Relations Is a Strategic Imperative," *Strategy and Business* (third quarter, 1997): 64–67.

Increasingly, the United Nations is promoting programs to partner multinationals and NGOs to tackle issues such as healthcare, energy, and biodiversity. For example Merck and GlaxoSmithKline have partnered with UNICEF and the World Bank to improve access to AIDS care in the hardest hit regions of the world.[64]

Public relations activity includes anticipating and countering criticism. The criticisms range from general ones against all multinational corporations to specific complaints. They may be based on a market: for example, a company's presence in China. They may concern a product: for example, Nestlé's practices in advertising and promoting infant formula in developing countries where infant mortality is unacceptably high. They may center on the company's conduct in a given situation: for example, Union Carbide's perceived lack of response in the Bhopal industrial diaster. If not addressed, such criticisms can lead to more significant problems, such as an internationally orchestrated boycott of products. The six-year boycott of Nestlé over its marketing of infant formula did not so much harm earnings as it harmed image and employee morale.

Summary

The task of the international marketer is to seek new opportunities in the world marketplace and satisfy emerging needs through creative management of the firm's good, pricing, distribution, and promotional policies. By its very nature, marketing is the most sensitive of business functions to environmental effects and influences.

The analysis of target markets is the first of the international marketer's challenges. Potential and existing markets need to be evaluated and priorities established for each, ranging from rejection to a temporary holding position to entry. Decisions at the level of the overall marketing effort must be made with respect to the selected markets, and a plan for future expansion must be formulated. The closer that potential target markets are in terms of their geographical, cultural, and economic distance, the more attractive they typically are to the international marketer.

A critical decision in international marketing concerns the degree to which the overall marketing program should be standardized or localized. The ideal is to standardize as much as possible without compromising the basic task of marketing: satisfying the needs and wants of the target market. Many multinational marketers are adopting globalization strategies that involve the standardization of good ideas, while leaving the implementation to local entities.

The technical side of marketing management is universal, but environments require adaptation within all of the mix elements. The degree of adaptation will vary by market, good, or service marketed, and overall company objectives.

Questions for Discussion

1. Many rational reasons exist for rejecting a particular market in the early stages of screening. Such decisions are made by humans, thus some irrational reasons must exist as well. Suggest some.

2. If, indeed, the three dimensions of distance are valid, to which countries would U.S. companies initially expand? Consider the interrelationships of the distance concepts.

3. Is globalization ever a serious possibility, or is the regional approach the closest the international marketer can ever hope to get to standardization?

4. What are the possible exporter reactions to extreme foreign exchange rate fluctuations?

5. Argue for and against gray marketing.

6. What courses of action are open to an international marketer who finds all attractive intermediaries already under contract to competitors?

Internet Exercises

1. The software industry is the hardest hit by piracy. Using the Web site of the Business Software Alliance (http://www.bsa.org), assess how this problem is being tackled.
2. Many traditionalists do not foresee that virtual trade shows will become a major threat to the actual shows themselves. Their view is that nothing can replace the actual seeing and touching of a product in person. Visit the E-Expo USA site (http://www.e-expousa.doc.gov) and develop arguments for and/or against this view.

Take a Stand

Ferrari is among the best-known names in high-performance automobiles. Many factors contribute to this, including the fact that only a select number of Ferraris are made annually and the amount sold in the United States, for example, is limited to about 1,000. Usually, anyone placing an order would have to wait over two years for delivery of a car that costs $200,000 to $300,000, depending on the model.

As a result of this shortage in supply, some importers and buyers have started importing these cars outside of the authorized channels (known as parallel importation or gray marketing). Due to the differences in government regulations in car features between, for example, the European Union and the United States, the U.S government requires that these nonconforming cars are reported to the Office of Vehicle Safety Compliance. The importer will have to explain how they will replace foreign parts with U.S. parts and adjust the engineering to conform with U.S. regulations. The bumpers, for example, are thicker in U.S. versions; seat belt warning systems have to be added, and speedometers must be adjusted from kilometers to miles. This practice had been going on for years with automakers mostly looking the other way. However, when the high value of the dollar started making vehicle purchases directly from Europe 30 to 40 percent cheaper and the volume of these imports shot up, Ferrari felt it had to do something.

In late June 2001, Ferrari asked the U.S. government to halt the importation of Ferrari Modenas and 550 Maranellos until the company had time to prepare its objections to gray-market imports. Ferrari's formal brief released later that summer stated that gray-market imports differed from their authorized (and specially manufactured) U.S. counterparts in "hundreds" of ways and could not be readily modified to meet U.S. requirements. Ferrari countered criticism of its actions by stating that they were not doing so for business, but for safety reasons.

For Discussion
1. Should distribution be reserved only for intermediaries authorized by the originator?
2. Why is it that in most cases governments allow gray-market flows to exist? When should they take exception to this practice?

CHAPTER

15

Services

Learning Objectives

- To examine the important role of services in international business

- To understand why trade in services is more complex than trade in goods

- To appreciate the heightened sensitivity required for international service success

- To learn that stand-alone services are becoming more important to world trade

- To examine the competitive advantage of firms in the service sector

Help Wanted: The Global Job Shift

Globalization's next wave is under way. The new job shift is the biggest trend in reshaping the global economy. The first wave in the global job market began two decades ago with the shift of U.S. manufactures of shoes, cheap electronics, and toys to developing nations such as China and Cambodia. The next wave came with the exodus of simple service work like credit-card receipt processing and software code writing. Today, globalization is shifting upscale jobs abroad.

Large and small businesses alike are dipping into the new global job market of "knowledge workers." Cities like Manila, Shanghai, Budapest, and San Jose, Costa Rica, have become major supporting offices for American, European, and Asian firms. Take SGV & Co., for example. The name may not mean much to you, but this Manila firm's accountants are the major support staff for Ernst & Young International. And while million-dollar home buyers in San Francisco demand the creativity of architect David Marlatt, his blueprints and three-dimensional computer models are actually refined by the architects of Zimay, a Hungarian firm. Even in healthcare, a field where physical proximity to patients is usually thought of as being a necessity, jobs are going abroad: Near Bangalore's airport, the Indian firm Wipro Ltd. has five radiologists who interpret CT scans daily for Massachusetts General Hospital.

Three major factors account for this world-wide job shift. First, the forces of technology—digitalization, the Internet, and high-speed data networks—make design, analysis, and research easy to perform abroad. Secondly, a global pool of college-educated men and women is readily available and increasing, especially in low-wage countries. With a population of 75 million, the Philippines graduates 380,000 college students trained in U.S. accounting standards *per year*. Clearly, a major impetus for shifting "knowledge jobs" abroad is the cost of production factor—cheaper labor. Bank of America, for example, now hires information-technology specialists in India, where the labor costs $20 an hour versus the U.S.'s rate of $100. Other sectors such as insurance and accounting can obtain workers abroad at 40 percent of the U.S.'s cost.

Outsourcing by hiring from abroad isn't new, though. For years, American Express, Dell Computers, and Eastman Kodak have hired across national boundaries to maintain 24-hour customer care services. What's different now is that outsourced workers spearhead crucial R&D projects: GE Electrical employs 6,000 scientists and engineers in 10 different countries while Microsoft invests $400 million in India, in addition to the $750 million already dedicated to China.

While there are dissenting voices, the new global job shift is certain to continue. Analysts from Forrester Research predict that 3.3 million white-collar jobs, which amounts to $136 billion in wages, will shift from the United States to lower-cost countries by 2015. European firms from England, France, and Germany are joining the trend by hiring in Russia, the Baltics, Eastern Europe, China, and India. From the developing nations' perspective, a decrease in participation in the global job market is unlikely. McKinsey & Co. studies note that by 2008, India's IT and service exports will generate $57 billion in revenue and employ 7 million.

Sources: Pete Enfardio, Aaron Bernstein, and Manjeet Kripalani, "The New Global Job Shift," *BusinessWeekOnline*, February 3, 2003, accessed February 5, 2002, http://www.businessweek.com/magazine/content/03_05/b3818001.htm; Diane Lewis, "Shift of Tech Jobs Abroad Speeding Up," *Boston Globe*, December 25, 2002, E1.

Services are a major component of world trade. This chapter will highlight international business dimensions that are specific to services. A definition of services will be provided, and trade in services and in goods will be differentiated. The role of services in the world economy will then be explained. The chapter will discuss the opportunities and new problems that have arisen because of increasing service trade, with particular focus on the worldwide transformations of industries as a result of profound changes in the environment and in technology. The strategic responses to the transformations by both governments and firms will be explained. Finally, the chapter will outline the initial steps that firms need to undertake to offer services internationally and will look at the future of service trade.

Differences between Services and Goods

We rarely contemplate or analyze the precise role of services in our lives. Services often accompany goods, but they are also, by themselves, an increasingly important part of the economy. One author has contrasted services and products by stating that "a good is an object, a device, a thing; a service is a deed, a performance, an effort."[1] That definition, although quite general, captures the essence of the difference between goods and services. Services tend to be more intangible, personalized, and custom-made than goods. Services also are typically using a different approach to customer satisfaction. It has been stated that "service firms do not have products in the form of preproduced solutions to customer's problems; they have processes as solutions to such problems."[2] Services are the fastest growing sector in world trade and as this chapter's opening vignette shows, employment in the services sector is becoming increasingly global. These major differences add dimensions to services that are not present in goods.

LINK BETWEEN SERVICES AND GOODS

Services may complement goods; at other times, goods may complement services. The offering of goods that are in need of substantial technological support and maintenance may be useless if no proper assurance for service can be provided. For this reason, the initial contract of sale often includes important service dimensions. This practice is frequent in aircraft sales. When an aircraft is purchased, the buyer contracts not only for the physical good—namely, the plane—but often for the training of personnel, maintenance service, and the promise of continuous technological updates. Similarly, the sale of computer hardware depends on the availability of proper servicing and software. In an international setting, the proper service support can often be crucial. Particularly for newly opening markets or for goods new to market, providing the good alone may be insufficient. The buyer wants to be convinced that proper service backup will be offered for the good before making a commitment.

The link between goods and services often brings a new dimension to international business efforts. A foreign buyer, for example, may want to purchase helicopters and contract for service support over a period of ten years. If the sale involves a U.S. firm, both the helicopter and the service sale will require an export license. Such licenses, however, are issued only for an immediate sale. Therefore, over the ten years, the seller will have to apply for an export license each time service is to be provided. The issuance of a license is often dependent on the political climate; therefore, the buyer and the seller are haunted by uncertainty. As a result, sales may go to firms in countries that can unconditionally guarantee the long-term supply of support services.

Services can be just as dependent on goods. For example, an airline that prides itself on providing an efficient reservation system and excellent linkups with rental cars and hotel reservations could not survive if it were not for its airplanes. As a result, many offerings in the marketplace consist of a combination of goods and services. Figure 15.1 illustrates tangible and intangible elements in the market offering of an airline. Following the terrorist attacks of September 11, 2001, improved airline security is another possible intangible element.

The knowledge that services and goods interact, however, is not enough. Successful managers must recognize that different customer groups will frequently view the service-good combination differently. The type of use and the usage conditions will affect evaluations of the market offering. For example, the intangible dimension of "on-time arrival" by airlines may be valued differently by college students than by business executives. Similarly, a twenty-minute delay will be judged differently by a passenger arriving at his or her final destination than by one who has just missed an overseas connection. As a result, adjustment possibilities in both the service and the goods areas emerge that can be used as a strategic tool to stimulate demand and increase profitability. As Figure 15.2 shows, service and goods elements may vary substantially in any market offering. The manager must identify the role of each and

FIGURE 15.1

Tangible and Intangible Offerings of Airlines

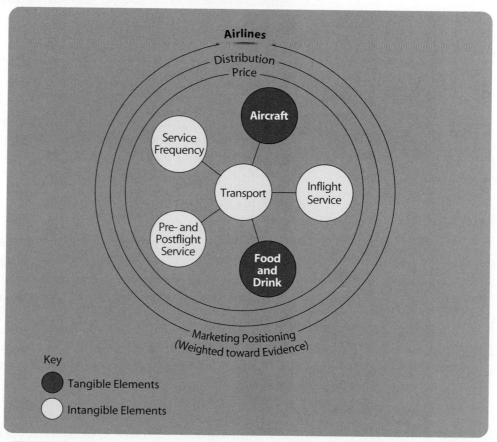

Source: G. Lynn Shostack, "Breaking Free from Product Marketing," in *Services Marketing: Text, Cases, and Readings,* ed. Christopher H. Lovelock (Englewood Cliffs, NJ: Prentice-Hall, Inc., 1984), 40.

FIGURE 15.2

Scale of Dominance between Goods and Services

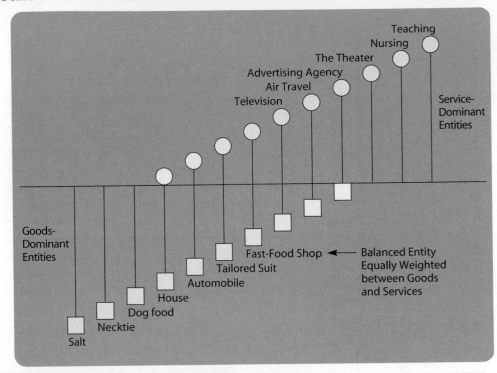

Source: Reprinted with permission from *Marketing of Services*, eds. J. Donnelly and W. George; G. Lynn Shostack, "How to Design a Service," 1981, p. 222, published by the American Marketing Association, Chicago, IL 60606.

adjust all of them to meet the desires of the target customer group. By rating the offerings on their dominant (in)tangibility, the manager can compare offerings and also generate information for subsequent market positioning strategies.

STAND-ALONE SERVICES

Services do not have to come in unison with goods. They can compete against goods and become an alternative offering. For example, rather than buy an in-house computer, the business executive can contract computing work to a local or foreign service firm. Similarly, the purchase of a car (a good) can be converted into the purchase of a service by leasing the car from an agency. Services therefore can transform the ownership of a good into its possession or use. This transformation can greatly affect business issues such as distribution, payment structure and flows, and even recycling.

Services by themselves can satisfy needs and wants of customers. Entertainment services such as movies or music offer leisure time enjoyment. Insurance services can protect people from financial ruin in case of a calamity.

Services may also compete against one another. As an example, a store may have the option of offering full service to customers or of converting to the self-service format. With automated checkout services, customers may have to be self-sufficient with other activities such as selection, transportation, packaging, and pricing.

Services differ from goods most strongly in their **intangibility:** They are frequently consumed rather than possessed. Though the intangibility of services is a primary differentiating criterion, it is not always present. For example, publishing services ultimately result in a tangible good—namely, a book or a computer disk. Similarly, construction services eventually result in a building, a subway, or a bridge. Even in those instances, however, the intangible component that leads to the final good is of major concern to both the producer of the service and the recipient of the ultimate output, because it brings with it major considerations that are non-traditional to goods.

Another major difference concerns the storing of services. Due to their nature, services are difficult to inventory. If they are not used, the "brown around the edges" syndrome tends to result in high **perishability.** Unused capacity in the form of an empty seat on an airplane, for example, becomes nonsalable quickly. Once the plane has taken off, selling an empty seat is virtually impossible—except for an in-flight upgrade from coach to first class—and the capacity cannot be stored for future use. The difficulty of keeping services in inventory makes it troublesome to provide service back-up for peak demand. To maintain **service capacity** constantly at levels necessary to satisfy peak demand would be very expensive. The business manager must therefore attempt to smooth out demand levels through pricing or promotional tools in order to optimize overall use of capacity.

For the services offering, the time of production is usually very close to or even simultaneous with the time of consumption. This often means close **customer involvement** in the production of services. Customers frequently either service themselves or cooperate in the delivery of services. As a result, the service provider may need to be physically present when the service is delivered. This physical presence creates both problems and opportunities, and introduces a new constraint that is seldom present in the marketing of goods. For example, close interaction with the customer requires a much greater understanding of and emphasis on the cultural dimension of each market. A good service delivered in a culturally unacceptable fashion is doomed to failure. Even in a domestic setting, international exposure can make a service culturally controversial, as Table 15.1 shows. A common pattern of internationalization for service businesses is therefore to develop stand-alone business systems in each country.[3]

TABLE 15.1

Examples of Cultural Service Gaps

Manifestations of the Service Provider Performance Gap	Example: Japanese Guests in a German Restaurant
Provider's physical environment gap	Customers cannot read the menu or they mix up the restrooms because they cannot read the signs
Provider's personnel gap	Customers feel uneasy because waiter maintains eye contact while taking the order
Provider's system gap	Customers are irritated because they are neither greeted at the door nor seated
Provider's co-customer gap	Customer feels uneasy because other guests greet them with a handshake when joining their table

Source: Bernd Stauss and Paul Mang, "'Culture Shocks' in Inter-cultural Service Encounters?" *Journal of Services Marketing,*" 13, 4/5, 1999, 329–346.

The close interaction with customers also points to the fact that services often are custom-made. This contradicts the desire of the firm to standardize its offering; yet at the same time, it offers the service provider an opportunity to differentiate the service. The concomitant problem is that, in order to fulfill customer expectations, **service consistency** is required. For anything offered online, however, consistency is difficult to maintain over the long run. Therefore, the human element in the service offering takes on a much greater role than in the offering of goods. Errors may enter the system, and unpredictable individual influences may affect the outcome of the service delivery. The issue of quality control affects the provider as well as the recipient of services. Efforts to increase control through service uniformity may sometimes be perceived by customers as the limiting of options. Since research has shown that the relative importance of the serviced quality dimensions varies from one culture to another,[4] one single approach to service quality may therefore have a negative market effect.

Buyers have more difficulty observing and evaluating services than goods. This is particularly true when the shopper tries to choose intelligently among service providers. Even when sellers of services are willing and able to provide more **market transparency,** the buyer's problem is complicated: Customers receiving the same service may use it differently. Since production lines cannot be established to deliver an identical service each time, and the quality of a service cannot be tightly controlled, the problem of **service heterogeneity** emerges,[5] meaning that services may never be the same from one delivery to another. For example, the counseling by a teacher, even if it is provided on the same day by the same person, may vary substantially depending on the student. But over time, even for the same student, the counseling may change. As a result, service offerings are not directly comparable, which makes quality measurements quite challenging. Therefore, service quality may vary for each delivery. Nonetheless, maintaining service quality is vitally important, since the reputation of the service provider plays an overwhelming role in the customer's choice process.

Services often require entirely new forms of distribution. Traditional channels frequently are multitiered and long and therefore slow. They often cannot be used at all because of the perishability of services. A weather news service, for example, either reaches its audience quickly or rapidly loses value. As a result, direct delivery and short distribution channels are required for international services. When they do not exist, service providers need to be distribution innovators to reach their market.

Increasingly, many services are "footloose," in that they are not tied to any specific location. Advances in technology make it possible for firms to separate production and consumption of services. As a result, labor-intensive service performance can be moved anywhere around the world where qualified, low-cost labor is plentiful. As communication technology further improves, services such as teaching, medical diagnosis, or bank account management can originate from any point in the world and reach customers around the globe.

The unique dimensions of services exist in both international and domestic settings, but their impact has greater importance for the international manager. For example, the perishability of a service, which may be a mere obstacle in domestic business, may become a major barrier internationally because of the longer distances involved. Similarly, quality control for international services may be much more difficult because of different service uses, changing expectations, and varying national regulations.

Services are delivered directly to the user and are therefore frequently much more sensitive to cultural factors than are products. Their influence on the individual abroad may be welcomed or greeted with hostility. For example, countries that place a strong emphasis on cultural identity have set barriers inhibiting market penetration by foreign films. France is leading a major effort within the European Union, for instance, to cap the volume of U.S.-produced films to obtain more playing time for French movies.

The Role of Services in the U.S. Economy

Since the Industrial Revolution, the United States has seen itself as a primary international competitor in the production of goods. In the past decades, however, the U.S. economy has increasingly become a service economy, as Figure 15.3 shows. Transformations in society, such as increased specialization, employment by family members, scarcity of time, and a constantly growing desire for convenience are some of the factors which have led to the rapid growth in services.[6] The service sector now produces 81 percent of the private sector GDP and employs 82 percent of the workforce.[7] The major segments that comprise the service sector are communications, transportation, public utilities, finance, insurance and real estate, wholesale and retail businesses, government, and "services" (a diverse category including business services, personal services, and professional and health services). The service sector accounts for all of the growth in total nonfarm employment.

FIGURE 15.3

Employment in Industrial Sectors as a Percentage of the Total Labor Force

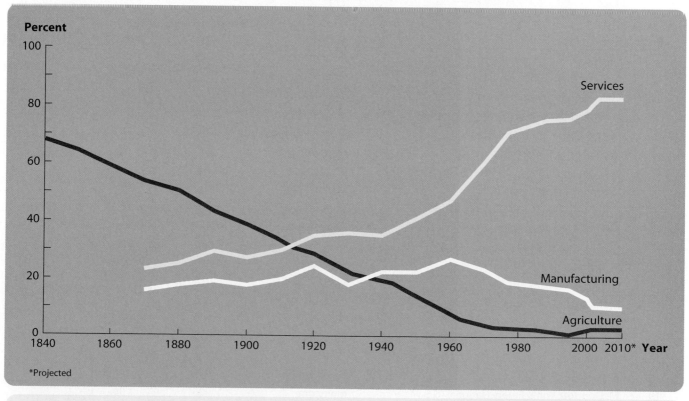

*Projected

Sources: "Employment Situation: Historical Data for the A Series," Bureau of Labor Statistics, http://www.bls.gov/rofod/3915.pdf (accessed July 16, 2003), *Services Industries*, Coalition of Service Industries, and Office of Service Industries, U.S. Department of Commerce, Washington, D.C., July 2002; J. B. Quinn, "The Impacts of Technology on the Service Sector," *Technology and Global Industry: Companies and Nations in the World Economy* (Washington, DC: National Academy of Sciences, 1987).

Only a limited segment of the total range of U.S. services is sold internationally. Federal, state, and local government employees, for example, sell few of their services to foreigners. U.S. laundries and restaurants only occasionally service foreign tourists. Many service industries that do sell abroad often have at their disposal large organizations, specialized technology, or advanced professional expertise. Strength in these characteristics has enabled the United States to become the world's largest exporter of services. Total U.S. services exported grew from $15 billion in 1970 to almost $289 billion in 2002.[8]

Global service trade has had very beneficial results for many U.S. firms. Most of the large management consulting firms derive more than half of their revenue from international sources. The largest advertising agencies serve customers around the globe, some of them in 107 countries. As Table 15.2 shows, 10 of the largest 20 law firms in the world are headquartered in the United States, but up to 80 percent of their lawyers reside outside their home country. These facts demonstrate that many service firms and industries have become truly international and formidable in size. Focus on Politics explains the growth of international education, and posits some of the key policy issues faced by this industry.

However, dramatic global growth is not confined to U.S. firms. The import of services into the United States is also increasing dramatically. In 2002, the United

TABLE 15.2   World's Largest Law Firms

Rank	Firm	Web Site	Number of Lawyers/Fee Earners	Lawyers Outside Home Country	Countries in Which Firm Has Offices
1	Baker & McKenzie International (U.S.)	bakerinfo.com	2,923	80%	31
2	Andersen Legal International (U.K.)	andersenlegal.com	2,880	n/a	36
3.	Clifford Chance International (U.K.)	cliffordchance.com	2,868	80%	14
4	Freshfields Bruckhaus Deringer International (U.K.)	freshfields.com	2,030	56%	15
5	Allen & Overy International (U.K.)	allenovery.com	1,912	61%	15
6	Eversheds National (U.K.)	eversheds.com	1,864	2%	7
7	Skadden, Arps, Slate, Meagher & Flom New York	skadden.com	1,504	8%	11
8	Linklaters International (U.K.)	linklaters.com	1,400	48%	12
9	Jones, Day, Reavis & Pogue National (U.S.)	jonesday.com	1,330	13%	11
10	White & Case International (U.S.)	whitecase.com	1,150	56%	24
11	Lovells International (U.K.)	lovells.com	1,130	52%	13
12	Holland & Knight Tampa	hlaw.com	1,035	2%	4
13	Latham & Watkins Los Angeles	lw.com	1,034	6%	7
14	Morgan, Lewis & Bockius National (U.S.)	morganlewis.com	1,005	4%	5
15	DLA National (U.K.)	dia.com	996	4%	3
16	Mallesons Stephen Jaques National (Australia)	msj.com.au	987	2%	3
17	Akin, Gump, Strauss, Hauer & Feld National (U.S.)	akingump.com	943	3%	4
18	Herbert Smith London	herbertsmith.com	918	34%	9
19	McDermott, Will & Emery National (U.S.)	mwe.com	906	0%	1
20	Shearman & Sterling New York	sherman.com	887	32%	9

Source: http://www.law.com, accessed July 8, 2003

Focus On ⬇

Serving Up Education

International student enrollment in the United States grew by 6.4 percent to 582,996 in the 2001–2002 academic year, marking the highest growth since 1980. During the same time, the number of U.S. students studying abroad increased 7.4 percent to 154,168. These increases took place despite predictions that enrollment would drop due to increases in security concerns and the suffering economy. Although total enrollment has grown, the U.S. share of the international student market has dropped from 40 percent to 30 percent in the past 20 years. Other English-speaking countries, such as Britain and Australia, have increased in popularily amongst students studying abroad.

Education constitutes the fifth largest service-sector export in the United States. Tuition and school-related costs of international students contributed $12 billion to the U.S. economy. International students also contribute to the economy further by consuming goods and services during their stay. U.S. students aborad likewise contribute to their host economies through enrollment in international education programs. The benefits of international education go far beyond economic gains; enrollment in universities abroad provides a chance for students to gain new experiences and insights. Furthermore, students enrolled in foreign institutions diversify the college atmosphere and expose local students to different ideas and cultures.

Education abroad also forges international bonds. Today's students are tomorrow's leaders in business and government. Their interpersonal relationships are a crucial step in ensuring open doorways in the future. Terry Hartle, Senior Vice President of the American Council on Education, testified before the House Judiciary Committee that international students offer many native-born studetns a first chance for sustained friendships with someone from another country. "As the world grows ever smaller, meaningful exposure to international students will better prepare American students to live and compete in the global economy." But these are major policy concerns. In an era where governments are becoming increasingly wary of global terrorism, international students are under scrutiny. Will education be yet another sector in which trade is restricted? Are the security concerns great enough to justify losing out on adding billions of dollars to the domestic economy? Can we afford to lose out on the human linkages?

Sources: http://opendoors.iienetwork.org, accessed February 4, 2003; Terry W. Hartle, Testimony on Foreign Students Tracking Program to the Immigration and Claims Subcommittee of the House Judiciary Committee, September 18, 2002, retrieved from the Federal Document Clearing House February 4, 2003.

States imported more than $240 billion worth of services. Competition in global services is rising rapidly at all levels. Hong Kong, Singapore, and Western Europe are increasingly active in service industries such as banking, insurance, and advertising. Years ago, U.S. construction firms could count on a virtual monopoly on large-scale construction projects. Today, firms from South Korea, Italy, and other countries are taking a major share of the international construction business.

The Role of Global Services in the World Economy

The rise of the service sector is a global phenomenon. Services account for 70 percent of GDP in Jordan, 65 percent in Uruguay, 52 percent in Zambia, and 50 percent in India and Pakistan.[9] Even in the least developed countries, services typically contribute at least 45 percent of GDP. With growth rates higher than other sectors, such as agriculture and manufacturing, services are instrumental in job creation in these countries.[10] In addition, service exports are very important to developing and transitional economies. On average, 20 percent of developing and transitional economy exports are service exports, accounting for more than 29 percent of the world's total services exports.

The economies of developing countries have traditionally first established a strong agricultural and then a manufacturing sector to meet basic needs such as food and shelter before venturing into the services sector. Some countries, such as Mexico, Singapore, Hong Kong, Bermuda, and the Bahamas, are steering away from the traditional economic development pattern and are concentrating on developing strong service sectors.[11] The reasons vary from a lack of natural resources with which to develop agricultural and/or manufacturing sectors to recognition of the strong demand for services and the ability to provide them through tourism and a willing, skilled, and inexpensive labor force. As a result, it is anticipated that services trade will continue to grow. However, as more countries enter the sector, the global services business will become more competitive.

Global Transformations in the Services Sector

Major changes in the environment and technology account for the dramatic rise in services trade. One key environmental change has been the reduction of **government regulation** of service industries. In the early 1980s, many governments adopted the view that reduced government interference in the marketplace would enhance competition. As a result, new players have entered the marketplace. Some service sectors have benefited and others have suffered from this withdrawal of government intervention. Regulatory changes were initially thought to have primarily domestic effects, but they have rapidly spread internationally. For example, the 1984 **deregulation** of the U.S. telecommunication giant AT&T gave rise to the deregulation of Japan's telecommunication monopoly NT&T in 1985. European deregulation followed in the mid-1990s.

Similarly, deregulatory efforts in the transportation sector have had international repercussions. New air carriers have entered the market to compete against established trunk carriers and have done so successfully by pricing their services differently, both nationally and internationally. Obviously, a Dutch airline can count only to a limited extent on government support to remain competitive with new, low-priced fares offered by other carriers from abroad also serving the Dutch market. The deregulatory movement has fostered new competition and new competitive practices. Many of these changes resulted in lower prices, stimulating demand and leading to a rise in the volume of international services trade.

There also has been decreased regulation of service industries by their service groups. For example, business practices in fields such as health care, law, and accounting are becoming increasingly competitive and aggressive. New economic realities require firms in these industries to search for new ways to attract market share and expand their markets. International markets are one frequently untapped possibility for market expansion and have therefore become a prime target for such firms.

Technological advancement is a second major change that has taken place. Technology offers new ways of doing business and permits businesses to expand their horizons internationally. Through computerization, for instance, service exchanges that previously would have been prohibitively expensive are now feasible. As an example, Ford Motor Company uses one major computer system to carry out new car designs simultaneously in the United States and in Europe. This practice not only lowers expenditures on hardware and permits better utilization of existing equipment but also allows design teams based in different countries to interact closely and produce a car that can be successful in multiple markets. Of course, this development could take place only after advances in data transmission procedures. Technology has also sharply reduced the **cost of communication.** Fiberoptic cables have made the cost of international links trivial. A minute on a transatlantic cable laid 40 years ago cost $2.44, but now the same amount of time costs barely more than one cent.

The Internet and web technology have improved the transaction economics of services and succeeded in making many formerly location-bound services tradable.[12] At the same time, the increased use of outsourcing by firms has led to a greater need for global

The developing and industrialized world meet at a crossroad in Vietnam. New trade agreements have opened the Vietnamese market to U.S. service providers.

service performance. For example, more use of just-in-time inventory systems has created the need to better coordinate the supply-chain function and has resulted in the creation of more service intermediaries.[13]

Service industry expansion is not confined to those services that are labor intensive and therefore better performed in areas of the world where labor possesses a comparative advantage. Technology-intensive services are becoming the sunrise industries of the next century. Increasingly, firms in a variety of industries can use technology to offer a presence without having to be there physically. Banks, for example, can offer their services through automatic teller machines or telephone and Internet banking. Consultants can advise via videoconferences and teachers can teach the world through multimedia classrooms. Physicians can advise and even perform operations in a distant country if proper computer links can drive roboticized medical equipment.

Due to the growth of corporate web sites, some firms—particularly in the service sector—can quickly become unplanned participants in the international market. For example, potential customers from abroad can visit a web site and require the firm to deliver internationally as well. Of course the firm can choose to ignore foreign interests and lose out on new markets. Alternatively, it can find itself unexpectedly an international service provider. Specialty retailing such as book stores and fitness equipment are examples of services that in this way have become international.[14]

Many service providers have the opportunity to become truly global players. To them, the traditional international market barrier of distance no longer matters. Knowledge, the core of many service activities, can offer a global reach without requiring a local presence. Service providers therefore may have only a minor need for local establishment, since they can operate without premises. You don't have to be there to do business! The effect of such a shift in service activities will be major. Insurance and bank palaces in the downtowns of the world may soon become obsolete. Talented service providers will see the demand for their performance increase, while less capable ones will suffer from increased competition. Most importantly, consumers and society will have a much broader range and quality of service choices available, often at a lower cost.

Problems in Service Trade

Together with the increase in the importance of service trade, new problems have emerged in the service sector. Many of these problems have been characterized as affecting mainly the negotiations between nations, but they are of sufficient importance to firms engaged in international activities to merit a brief review.

DATA COLLECTION PROBLEMS

The data collected on service trade are sketchy. Service transactions are often invisible statistically as well as physically. For example, the trip abroad of a consultant for business purposes may be hard to track and measure. The interaction of variables such as citizenship, residency, location of the transaction, and who or what (if anything) crosses national boundaries further contributes to the complexity of services transactions. Imagine that an Irish citizen working for a Canadian financial consulting firm headquartered in Sweden advises an Israeli citizen living in India on the management of funds deposited in a Swiss bank. Determining the export and import dimensions of such a services transaction is not easy.[15]

The fact that governments have precise data on the number of trucks exported down to the last bolt but little information on reinsurance flows reflects past

MAP

Services as a Portion of Gross Domestic Product

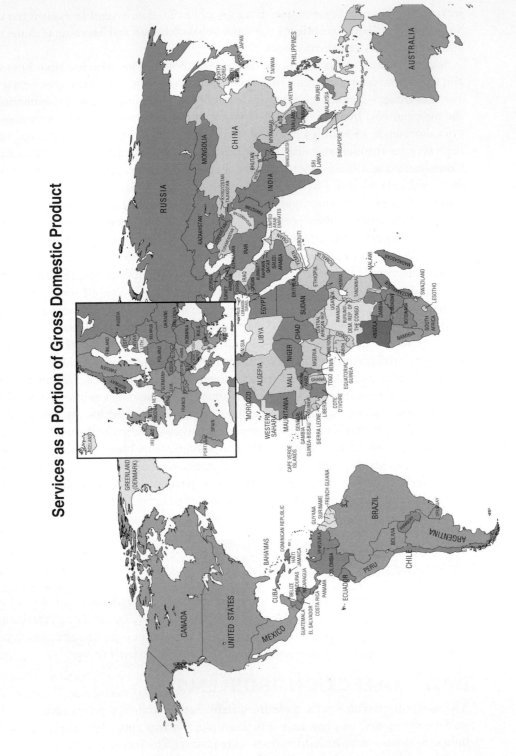

Services as a percent of GDP

- 61% to 85%
- 41% to 60%
- 21% to 40%
- 0% to 20%
- No current data available

Source: 2002 World Development Indicators, The World Bank.

governmental inattention to services. Consequently, estimates of services trade vary. Total actual volume of services trade is likely to be larger than the amount shown by official statistics.

Consider the problem of services data collection in industrialized countries, with their sophisticated data gathering and information systems. Now imagine how many more problems are encountered in countries lacking such elaborate systems and unwilling to allocate funds for them. Insufficient knowledge and information have led to a lack of transparency, which makes it difficult for nations either to gauge or to influence services trade. As a result, regulations are often put into place without precise information as to their repercussions on actual trade performance.

GLOBAL REGULATIONS OF SERVICES

Global obstacles to service trade can be categorized into two major types: barriers to entry and problems in performing services abroad.

Barriers to entry are often explained by reference to **"national security"** and **"economic security."** For example, the impact of banking on domestic economic activity is given as a reason why banking should be carried out only by nationals or indeed should be operated entirely under government control. Sometimes the protection of service users is cited, particularly of bank depositors and insurance policyholders. Another justification used for barriers is the **infant-industry** argument: "With sufficient time to develop on our own, we can compete in world markets." Often, however, this argument is used simply to prolong the ample licensing profits generated by restricted entry. Yet, defining a barrier to services is not always easy. For example, Taiwan gives an extensive written examination to prospective accountants (as do most countries) to ensure that licensed accountants are qualified to practice. The examination is given in Chinese. The fact that few German accountants, for example, read and write Chinese and hence are unable to pass the examination does not necessarily constitute a barrier to trade in accountancy services.

Service companies also encounter difficulties once they have achieved access to the local market. One reason is that rules and regulations based on tradition may inhibit innovation. A more important reason is that governments pursue social objectives through national regulations. The distinction between **discriminatory** and **nondiscriminatory regulations** is of primary importance here. Regulations that impose larger operating costs on foreign service providers than on the local competitors, that provide subsidies to local firms only, or that deny competitive opportunities to foreign suppliers are a proper cause for international concern. The problem of discrimination becomes even more acute when foreign firms face competition from government-owned or government-controlled enterprises. On the other hand, nondiscriminatory regulations may be inconvenient and may hamper business operations, but they offer less cause for international criticism. Yet, such national regulations can be key inhibitors for service innovations. For example, in Japan, pharmaceuticals cannot be sold outside of a licensed pharmacy. Similarly, travel arrangements can only be made within a registered travel office and banking can only be done during banking hours. As a result, innovations offered by today's communications technology cannot be brought to bear in these industries.[16]

All of these regulations make it difficult for international services to penetrate world markets. At the governmental level, services frequently are not recognized as a major facet of world trade or are viewed with suspicion because of a lack of understanding, and barriers to entry often result. To make progress in tearing them down, much educational work needs to be done.

In a major breakthrough in the Uruguay Round, the major GATT participants agreed to conduct services trade negotiations parallel with goods negotiations. The negotiations resulted in 1995 in the forging of a **General Agreement on Trade in Services (GATS)** as part of the World Trade Organization, the first multilateral, legally enforceable agreement covering trade and investment in the services sector. Similar to earlier agreements in the goods sector, GATS provides for most-favored-nation treatment, national treatment, transparency in rule making, and the free flow of payments and transfers. Market-access provisions restrict the ability of governments to limit competition and new-market entry. In addition, sectoral agreements were made for the movement of personnel, telecommunications, and aviation. However, in several sectors, such as entertainment, no agreement was obtained. In addition, many provisions, due to their newness, are very narrow. Therefore, future negotiations have been agreed upon, which will attempt to improve free trade in services.

Corporations and Services Trade

SERVICES AND E-COMMERCE

Electronic commerce has opened up new horizons for global services reach, and has drastically reduced the meaning of distance. For example, when geographic obstacles make the establishment of retail outlets cumbersome and expensive, firms can approach their customers via the World Wide Web. Government regulations which might be prohibitive to a transfer of goods may not have any effect on the international marketing of services. Also, regardless of size, companies are finding it increasingly easy to appeal to a global marketplace. The Internet can help service firms in developing and transitional economies overcome two of the biggest barriers they face: gaining credibility in international markets and saving on travel costs. Little-known firms can become instantly "visible" on the Internet. Even a small firm can develop a polished and sophisticated web presence and promotion strategy. Customers are less concerned about geographic location if they feel the firm is electronically accessible. An increasing number of service providers have never met their foreign customers except "virtually" online.[17] A quantitative assessment conducted by the World Trade Organization indicated that the share of value added that potentially lends itself to electronic commerce represents about 30 percent of GDP, most importantly distribution, finance, and business services.[18]

Nonetheless, several notes of caution must be kept in mind. First, the introduction of the Internet has occurred at different rates in different countries. There are still many businesses and consumers who do not have access to electronic business media. Unless they are to be excluded from a company's focus, more traditional ways of reaching them must be considered. Also, firms need to prepare their Internet presence for global visitors. For example, the language of the Internet is English—at least as far as large corporations are concerned. Yet, many of the visitors coming to web sites either may not have English as their first language or may not speak English at all. Companies respond differently to such visitor language capabilities. For example, one study determined that 70 percent of non-American companies with a web site offered more than their local language on their sites, while only 14 percent of American companies offered non-English language content.[19] Many companies do not permit any interaction on their web sites, thus missing out on feedback or even order placement from visitors. Some web sites are so culture bound that they often leave their visitors bewildered and disappointed due to the cultural assumptions made. However, over time, increasing understanding of doing business in the global marketplace will enable companies to be more refined in their approach to their customers.

TYPICAL INTERNATIONAL SERVICES

Although many firms are active in the international service arena, others do not perceive their existing competitive advantage. Numerous services that are efficiently performed in the home market may have great potential for internationalization.

Financial institutions can offer some functions very competitively internationally in the field of banking services. U.S. banks possess advantages in fields such as mergers and acquisitions, securities sales, credit cards, and asset management. Banks in Europe and Japan are boosting their leadership through large assets and capital bases.

Construction, design, and **engineering services** also have great international potential. Providers of these services can achieve economies of scale not only for machinery and material but also in areas such as personnel management and the overall management of projects. Particularly for international projects that are large scale and long term, the experience advantage weighs heavily in favor of international firms.

Insurance services can be sold internationally by firms knowledgeable about underwriting, risk evaluation, and operations. Firms offering legal and accounting services can aid their clients abroad through support activities; they can also help firms and countries improve business and governmental operations. Knowledge of computer operations, data manipulations, data transmission, and data analysis is insufficiently exploited internationally by many small and medium-sized firms.

Similarly, **communication services** have substantial future international opportunities. For example, firms experienced in the areas of videotext, home banking, and home shopping can find international success, particularly where geographic obstacles make the establishment of retail outlets cumbersome and expensive. In addition, global communication services can lead to collaboration, which greatly expands the capability of corporations as shown in Figure 15.4.

Many institutions in the educational and corporate sectors have developed expertise in **teaching services.** They are very knowledgeable in training and motivation as well as in the teaching of operational, managerial, and theoretical issues, yet have largely concentrated their work in their domestic markets. It is time to take education global! Too much good and important knowledge is not made available to broad audiences. More knowledge must be communicated, be it through distance learning, study and teaching abroad, or attracting foreign students into the domestic market. The latter option can spur a service industry in itself.

Management **consulting services** can be provided by firms and individuals to the many countries and corporations in need of them. Of particular value is management expertise in areas where many developing economies need most help, such as transportation and logistics. Major opportunities also exist for industries that deal with societal problems. For example, firms that develop environmentally safe products or produce pollution-control equipment can find new markets, as nations around the world increase their awareness of and concern about the environment and tighten their laws. Similarly, advances in health care or new knowledge in combating AIDS offer major opportunities for global service success.

Tourism also represents a major service export. Every time foreign citizens come to a country and spend their funds, the Current Account effect is that of an export.

FIGURE 15.4

Global Cooperation

Only through global cooperation of service providers—Dutch environmental experts, U.S. maritime consultants, and Brazilian oil rig managers—was it possible to avoid the sinking of this rig.

Source: ©AFP/CORBIS

World travel and tourism are projected to generate US$463 billion of economic activity in 2003, which will account for 3.7 percent of total world GDP.[20] This volume makes tourism one of the most important services in the world. However, this growing exchange of people has also led to greater interdependence and dependence between nations. As Focus on Policy shows, the widespread outbreak of illnesses can now have quicker and deeper repercussions than ever before.

An attractive international service mix can also be achieved by pairing the strengths of different partners. For example, information technology from one country can be combined with the financial resources of other countries. The strengths of the partners can then be used to offer maximum benefits to the international community.

Combining international advantages in services may ultimately result in the development of an even more drastic comparative lead. For example, if a firm has an international head start in such areas as high technology, information gathering, information processing, information analysis, and teaching, the major thrust of its international services might not be to provide these service components individually but rather to enable clients, based on a combination of competitive resources, to make better decisions.

For many firms, participation in the Internet will offer the most attractive starting point in marketing their services internationally. The set up of a web site will allow visitors from any place in the globe to come see the offering. Of course, the most important problem will be how to communicate the existence of one's site and how to entice visitors to come. For that, often very traditional advertising and communication approaches need to be used. In some countries, for example, one can find rolling billboards announcing web sites and their benefits. Overall, however, one needs to keep in mind that not everywhere do firms and individuals have access to or make use of the new e-commerce opportunities.

Focus On ⊽

SARS Scars Global Tourism Industry

Still reeling from security fears sparked by September 11th and the Iraq war, the global tourism industry, which accounts for over 200 million jobs and 10 percent of global output, was dealt another blow with the outbreak of the deadly Severe Acute Respiratory Syndrome (SARS). China was the country most affected by SARS, with more than 5,000 of the approximately 7,500 probable cases worldwide and 257 of 588 reported deaths. In addition to the human toll, there was a substantial economic price to pay.

The World Travel and Tourism Council (WTTC) noted that China, Hong Kong, Singapore, and Vietnam—the countries most affected by the flu-like disease—lost more than 2.9 million jobs, or 30 percent of their tourism industry. Neighboring countries in the Asian-Pacific region, such as Australia, Fiji, Indonesia, and Thailand lost 15 percent of their tourism labor force. In China alone, economists expect a 1 percentage point decrease in 2003 economic growth, which translates to a loss of nearly $11 billion. As aptly noted by WTTC Vice President Richard Miller, "The impact of SARS on these countries is over five times the impact of the September 11 attacks in the United States."

Ripple effects were experienced in Toronto, Canada, where the worst non-Asian outbreak of SARS occurred, with 264 infections and 21 deaths. Statistics Canada reports that SARS cost the Canadian economy more than $1.5 billion and 12,000 jobs in April of 2003 alone. At the height of the epidemic in Toronto, Air Canada reported a loss of $3.5 million per day and was forced to ground 40 percent of its aircraft. Retail sales were down by nearly 30 percent, and many conventions scheduled for Toronto were cancelled.

After being blacklisted by the World Health Organization, the SARS crisis shattered Canada's image as a safe place to visit and gave the nation's policymakers the daunting challenge of winning back the trust of travelers. "Toronto, Vancouver, they're all the same to many tourists," said Alex Rose, a West Coast consultant who noted that the Vancouver cruise ship season faced damage from SARS.

In an urgent attempt to contain Canada's damaged reputation, Toronto devised a $176 million international publicity campaign with celebrity spokespeople such as Austin Power's Mike Myers to lure travelers back to the city. As Pamela Groberman, a Canadian media and public relations consultant notes, "The Number One thing for rebuilding reputation is to make sure the public health effort has all the resources it needs, so that a month from now, it will be Toronto, the city that beat SARS. Toronto the Good. Toronto the Clean. Toronto the Healthy."

© AP PHOTO/NG HAN GUAN

Sources: Clifford Krauss, "Toronto Is Stricken from Warning List by WHO," *The New York Times,* May 15, 2003, A18; Jonathan Fowler, "UN Labor Agency: SARS Fears Could Cause 5 Million Tourism Job Losses," *Associated Press Worldstream,* May 14, 2003; "Toronto Unveils Publicity Plan to Woo Back Tourists After SARS Scare," *Associated Press Worldstream,* May 16, 2003.

STARTING TO OFFER SERVICES INTERNATIONALLY

For services that are delivered mainly in support of or in conjunction with goods, the most sensible approach for the international novice is to follow the path of the good. For years, many large accounting and banking firms have done this by determining where their major multinational clients have set up new operations and then following them. Smaller service providers who supply manufacturing firms can determine where the manufacturing firms are operating internationally. Ideally, of course, it would be possible to follow clusters of manufacturers abroad to obtain economies of scale internationally while simultaneously looking for entirely new client groups.

Service providers whose activities are independent from goods need a different strategy. These individuals and firms must search for market situations abroad that are similar to the domestic market. Such a search should be concentrated in their area of expertise. For example, a design firm learning about construction projects abroad can investigate the possibility of rendering its design services. Similarly, a management consultant learning about the plans of a country or firm to computerize its operations can explore the possibility of overseeing a smooth transition from manual to computerized activities. What is required is the understanding that similar problems are likely to occur in similar situations.

Another opportunity consists of identifying and understanding points of transition abroad. If, for example, new transportation services are introduced in a country, an expert in containerization may wish to consider whether to offer his or her service to improve the efficiency of the new system.

Leads for international service opportunities can also be gained by staying informed about international projects sponsored by domestic organizations such as the U.S. Agency for International Development or the Trade and Development Agency, as well as international organizations such as the United Nations, the International Finance Corporation, or the World Bank. Frequently, such projects are in need of support through services. Overall, the international service provider needs to search for similar situations, similar problems, or scenarios requiring similar solutions to formulate an effective international expansion strategy.

STRATEGIC INDICATIONS

To be successful in the international service offering, the manager must first determine the nature and the aim of the services-offering core—that is, whether the service will be aimed at people or at things and whether the service act in itself will result in tangible or intangible actions. Figure 15.5 provides examples of such a classification strategy that will help the manager to better determine the position of the services effort.

During this determination, the manager must consider other tactical variables that have an impact on the preparation of the service offering. For example, in conducting research for services, the measurement of capacity and delivery efficiency often remains highly qualitative rather than quantitative. In communication and promotional efforts, the intangibility of the service reduces the manager's ability to provide samples. This makes communicating the service offered much more difficult than communicating an offer for a good. Brochures or catalogs explaining services often must show a proxy for the service to provide the prospective customer with tangible clues. A cleaning service, for instance, can show a picture of an individual removing trash or cleaning a window. However, the picture will not fully communicate the performance of the service. Service exporters have three ways to gain credibility abroad: (1) providing objective verification of their capabilities—perhaps through focusing on the company's professional license or certification by international organizations; (2) providing personal

FIGURE 15.5

Understanding the Service Act

	Who or What Is the Direct Recipient of the Service?	
What Is the Nature of the Service Act?	**People**	**Possessions**
Tangible Actions	*People processing* (services directed at people's bodies): Passenger transportation Healthcare Lodging Beauty salons Physical therapy Fitness center Restaurant/bars Barbers Funeral services	*Possession processing* (services directed at physical possessions): Freight transportation Repair and maintenance Warehousing/storage Office cleaning services Retail distribution Laundry and dry cleaning Refueling Landscaping/gardening Disposal/recycling
Intangible Actions	*Mental stimulus processing* (services directed at people's minds): Advertising/PR Arts and entertainment Broadcasting/cable Management consulting Education Information services Music concerts Psychotherapy Religion Voice telephone	*Information processing* (services directed at intangible assets): Accounting Banking Data processing Data transmission Insurance Legal services Programming Research Securities investment Software consulting

Source: Christopher H. Lovelock, *Services Marketing: People, Technology, Strategy,* 4th ed., 38. © 2001. Reprinted by permission of Pearson Education, Inc., Upper Saddle River, NJ.

guarantees of performance, including referrals and testimonials by satisfied customers; and (3) cultivating a professional image through public appearances at international trade events or conferences and promotional materials such as a web site.[21] Due to the different needs and requirements of individual consumers, the manager must also pay attention to the two-way flow of communication. In the service area, mass communication often must be supported by intimate one-on-one follow-up.

The role of personnel deserves special consideration in international service delivery. The customer interface is intense, therefore, proper provisions need to be made for training of personnel both domestically and internationally. Major emphasis must be placed on appearance. Most of the time the person delivering the service—rather than the service itself—will communicate the spirit, value, and attitudes of the service corporation. Since the service person is both the producer as well as the marketer of the service, recruitment and training techniques must focus on dimensions such as customer relationship management and image projection as well as competence in the design and delivery of the service.[22]

This close interaction with the consumer will also have organizational implications. While tight control over personnel may be desired, the individual interaction that is required points toward the need for an international decentralization of service delivery. This, in turn, requires delegation of large amounts of responsibility to individuals and service "subsidiaries" and requires a great deal of trust in all organizational units. This trust, of course, can be greatly enhanced through proper methods of training and supervision. Sole ownership also helps strengthen this trust. Research has shown that service firms, in their international expansion, tend to greatly prefer the establishment of full-control ventures. Only when costs escalate and the company-specific advantage diminishes will service firms seek out shared-control ventures.[23]

The areas of pricing and financing require special attention. Because services cannot be stored, much greater responsiveness to demand fluctuation must exist, and therefore greater pricing flexibility must be maintained. At the same time, flexibility is countered by the desire to provide transparency for both the seller and the buyer of services in order to foster an ongoing relationship. The intangibility of services also makes financing more difficult. Frequently, even financial institutions with large amounts of international experience are less willing to provide financial support for international services than for products. The reasons are that the value of services is more difficult to assess, service performance is more difficult to monitor, and services are difficult to repossess. Therefore, customer complaints and difficulties in receiving payments are much more troublesome for a lender to evaluate in the area of services than for goods.

Finally, the distribution implications of international services must be considered. Usually, short and direct channels are required. Within these channels, closeness to the customer is of overriding importance to understand what the customer really wants, to trace the use of the service, and to aid the customer in obtaining a truly tailor-made service.

Summary

Services are taking on an increasing importance in international trade. They need to be considered separately from trade in merchandise because they no longer simply complement goods. Often, goods complement services or are in competition with them. Service attributes such as their intangibility, their perishability, their custom design, and their cultural sensitivity frequently make international trade in services more complex than trade in goods.

Services play a growing role in the global economy. International growth and competition in this sector have begun to outstrip that of merchandise trade and are likely to intensify in the future. Even though services are unlikely to replace production, the sector will account for the shaping of new competitive advantages internationally, particularly in light of new facilitating technologies which encourage electronic commerce.

The many service firms now operating only domestically need to investigate the possibility of going global. Historical patterns of service providers following manufacturers abroad have become partially obsolete as stand-alone services become more important to world trade. Management must therefore assess its vulnerability to service competition from abroad and explore opportunities to provide its services internationally.

Questions for Discussion

1. How has the Internet affected your services purchases? Have any of your purchases been international?
2. Discuss the major reasons for the growth of international services.
3. How does the international sale of services differ from the sale of goods?
4. What are some of the international business implications of service intangibility?

5. What are some ways for a firm to expand its services internationally?
6. How can a firm in a developing country participate in the international services boom?
7. Which services would you expect to migrate abroad in the next decade? Why?

Internet Exercises

1. Find the most current data on the five leading export and import countries for commercial services. The information is available on the World Trade Organization site http://www.wto.org—click the statistics button.

2. What are the key U.S. services exports and imports? What is the current services trade balance? (http://www.bea.gov)

Take a Stand

Service functions are increasingly being outsourced internationally because costs are lower. Although this is advantageous for the companies, it raises imporant questions for consumers. Some argue that critical and extremely time-sensitive functions should be barred from international outsourcing because of the high risks associated with a disruption of services. For example, if hospital workers are having difficulty with their MRI machine and cannot get through to the service center in the Pacific due to a typhoon, patients may be at risk. Or, a breakdown in back-office operations abroad could disrupt the workings of electronic systems such as gas station credit card readers, leaving motorists stranded. Others argue that domestic disasters can disrupt service as well.

For Discussion
1. Should there be legislation in place to bar critical services from going abroad?
2. Who should determine which services are critical?

CHAPTER 16

Logistics and Supply-Chain Management

Learning Objectives

- To understand the escalating importance of logistics and supply-chain management as crucial tools for competitiveness

- To learn about materials management and physical distribution

- To learn why international logistics is more complex than domestic logistics

- To see how the transportation infrastructure in host countries often dictates the options open to the manager

- To learn why international inventory management is crucial for success

Distribution and Supply-Chain Management Logistics in China

On a midsummer day in Shanghai, a dozen workers load cases of brand-name imported wine onto a small, uncovered, and unrefrigerated truck, which will spend hours on poor roads to the central city. Martin Tong, a manager for a computer-peripherals maker, waits impatiently for seven days for computer parts to come from Shanghai to Sichuan, China's most populous province. Stacks of DVD players and cases of Hennessy XO cognac stand idle at Shanghai's loading docks, quickly losing value while waiting for truckers to return from previous deliveries.

To compete globally, China tries to adopt international best practices: Firms in the technology, telecommunications, insurance, and petroleum industries have rapidly closed the performance gap with their global competitors. Yet, best practices in logistics have yet to proliferate in China. The cost for its inadequate logistical infrastructure is enormous: $230 billion, or 20 percent of GDP, is dedicated to logistics each year.

China's transportation bottleneck costs can easily outweigh its gains from trade, a McKinsey and Co. study asserts. Poor infrastructure, continued restrictions for foreign entrance in logistics and transportation, inefficient freight operators, and corruption are only some of the barriers separating multinational companies from the 1.3 billion potential Chinese consumers. Total shipping costs in China are 40 to 50 percent more expensive than in the United States. Of 673 Shanghai trucking firms surveyed, 400 are cottage operators with less than two vehicles and only four have fleets of more than 100. In addition, only 20 percent of China's freight trucks are containerized, leaving most transported merchandise bouncing about in open-back vehicles.

While 70 percent of Fortune 500's global firms leverage their competitive advantage by outsourcing to third-party logistics (3PL) providers, China has yet to catch on, with only 2 percent of its companies employing 3PLs. Outsourcing to 3PLs allows manufacturers to minimize costs and focus on the core competency of creating better products. Since 3PL providers represent many firms, they have greater leverage with freight carriers and can demand lower transportation prices and better service. Moreover, 3PL companies are better equipped and experienced at integrating logistics functions into a firm's existing supply chain.

A major block for foreign 3PL firms planning to enter the Chinese market is the Ministry of Foreign Trade and Economic Co-operation. This government office heavily regulates the logistics industry with complicated approval processes for logistics joint ventures, limitations on required licenses, and cumbersome and inefficient customs clearance procedures.

With the expected increase in the volume of cargo shipped between China and the rest of the world due to WTO accession, Chinese authorities plan to improve their logistics operations. Spending billions of dollars to modernize its rail and road systems, China is also updating its Shanghai port, the fifth largest in the world, to perform on the same level as the Hong Kong and Singapore ports. While enormous potential exists in the Chinese consumer market, logistical challenges sharply limit that potential.

Sources: Ben Dolven, "The Perils of Delivering the Goods," *Far Eastern Economic Review,* September 25, 2002; Diana Huang, and Mark Kadar, "Third-Party Logistics in China: Still a Tough Market," *Mercer Report on Travel and Transport* Winter 2003, http://www.mercermc.com, accessed February 2003; "Moving Goods in China," McKinsey & Co., February 2002, http://www.mckinsey.de, accessed February 2003.

For the international firm, customer locations and sourcing opportunities are widely dispersed. The firm can attain a strategically advantageous position only if it is able to successfully manage complex international networks consisting of its vendors, suppliers, other third parties, and its customers. Neglect of links within and outside of the firm brings not only higher costs but also the risk of eventual noncompetitiveness, due to diminished market share, more expensive supplies, or lower profits. As discussed in the opening vignette, effective international logistics and supply-chain management can produce higher earnings and greater corporate efficiency, which are the cornerstones of corporate competitiveness.

This chapter will focus on international logistics and supply-chain management. Primary areas of concentration will be the links between the firm, its suppliers, and its customers, as well as transportation, inventory, packaging, and storage issues. The logistics management problems and opportunities that are peculiar to international business will also be highlighted.

International Logistics Defined

International logistics is the design and management of a system that controls the forward and reverse flow of materials, services, and information into, through, and out of the international corporation. It encompasses the total movement concept by covering the entire range of operations concerned with movement, including therefore both exports and imports. By taking a systems approach, the firm explicitly recognizes the links among the traditionally separate logistics components within and outside of a corporation. By incorporating the interaction with outside organizations and individuals such as suppliers and customers, the firm is able to build on jointness of purpose by all partners in the areas of performance, quality, and timing. As a result of implementing these systems considerations successfully, the firm can develop just-in-time (JIT) delivery for lower inventory cost, electronic data interchange (EDI) for more efficient order processing, and early supplier involvement (ESI) for better planning of goods development and movement. In addition, the use of such a systems approach allows a firm to concentrate on its core competencies and to form outsourcing alliances with other companies. For example, a firm can choose to focus on manufacturing and leave all aspects of order filling and delivery to an outside provider. By working closely with customers such as retailers, firms can also develop efficient customer response (ECR) systems, which can track sales activity on the retail level. As a result, manufacturers can precisely coordinate production in response to actual shelf replenishment needs, rather than based on forecasts.

Two major phases in the movement of materials are of logistical importance. The first phase is **materials management,** or the timely movement of raw materials, parts, and supplies into and through the firm. The second phase is **physical distribution,** which involves the movement of the firm's finished product to its customers. In both phases, movement is seen within the context of the entire process. Stationary periods (storage and inventory) are therefore included. The basic goal of logistics management is the effective coordination of both phases and their various components to result in maximum cost effectiveness while maintaining service goals and requirements.

Key to business logistics are three major concepts: (1) the systems concept; (2) the total cost concept; and (3) the trade-off concept. The **systems concept** is based on the notion that materials-flow activities within and outside of the firm are so extensive and complex that they can be considered only in the context of their interaction. Instead of each corporate function, supplier, and customer operating with the goal of individual optimization, the systems concept stipulates that some components may have to work suboptimally to maximize the benefits of the system as a whole. The systems concept intends to provide the firm, its suppliers, and its customers, both domestic and foreign, with the benefits of synergism expected from the coordinated application of size.

In order for the systems concept to work, information flows and partnership trust are instrumental. Logistics capability is highly information dependent, since information availability is key to planning and to process implementation. Long-term partnership and trust are required in order to forge closer links between firms and managers.

A logical outgrowth of the systems concept is the development of the **total cost concept.** To evaluate and optimize logistical activities, cost is used as a basis for measurement. The purpose of the total cost concept is to minimize the firm's overall logistics cost by implementing the systems concept appropriately.

Implementation of the total cost concept requires that the members of the system understand the sources of costs. To develop such understanding, a system of activity-based costing has been developed, which is a technique designed to more accurately assign the indirect and direct resources of an organization to the activities performed based on consumption.[1] In the international arena, the total cost concept must also incorporate the consideration of total after-tax profit, by taking the impact of national tax policies on the logistics function into account. The objective is to maximize after-tax profits rather than minimizing total cost.

The **trade-off concept,** finally, recognizes the links within logistics systems that result from the interaction of their components. For example, locating a warehouse near the customer may reduce the cost of transportation. However, additional costs are associated with new warehouses. Similarly, a reduction of inventories will save money but may increase the need for costly emergency shipments. Managers can maximize performance of logistics systems only by formulating decisions based on the recognition and analysis of such trade-offs. A trade-off of costs may go against one's immediate interests. Consider a manufacturer building several different goods. The goods all use one or both of two parts, A and B, which the manufacturer buys in roughly equal amounts. Most of the goods produced use both parts. The unit cost of part A is $7, of part B, $10. Part B has more capabilities than part A; in fact, B can replace A. If the manufacturer doubles its purchases of part B, it qualifies for a discounted $8 unit price. For products that incorporate both parts, substituting B for A makes sense to qualify for the discount, since the total parts cost is $17 using A and B, but only $16 using Bs only. Part B should therefore become a standard part for the manufacturer. But departments building products that only use part A may be reluctant to accept the substitute part B because, even discounted, the cost of B exceeds that of A. Use of the trade-off concept will solve the problem.[2]

Supply-Chain Management

The integration of these three concepts has resulted in the new paradigm of **supply-chain management,** where a series of value-adding activities connects a company's supply side with its demand side. It has been defined by the Ohio State University Global SMC forum as "the integration of business processes from end user through original suppliers, that provide products, services, and information that add value for customers."[3] This approach views the supply chain of the entire extended enterprise, beginning with the supplier's suppliers and ending with consumers or end users. The perspective encompasses the entire flow of funds, products and information that form one cohesive link to acquire, purchase, convert/manufacture, assemble, and distribute goods and services to the ultimate consumers. The implementation effects of such supply-chain management systems can be major.

Export supply-chain management skills facilitate the identification of attractive sources of supply and help firms develop a low-cost competitive supply position in export markets. They also help develop good relationships with suppliers, and ensure quality inputs at reasonable prices delivered on a timely basis.[4] For example, it has permitted Wal-Mart, the largest U.S. retailer, to reduce inventories by 90 percent, has saved the company hundreds of millions of dollars in inventory holding costs, and allows it to offer low prices to its customers.[5] Advances in information technology have been crucial to progress in supply-chain management. For example, companies such as GE and Pitney Bowes have implemented web-based sourcing and payables systems. GE's Trading Process Network (http://www.gxs.com) allows GE Lighting's 25 production facilities and other buying facilities around the world to quickly find and purchase products from approved suppliers electronically. The electronic catalog information reflects the pricing and contract terms GE has negotiated with each of the suppliers and also ties in with GE's inventory and accounts payable systems. The result has been the virtual elimination of paper and mailing costs, a reduction in cycle time from 14 days to 1 day, 50 percent staff reduction, and 20 percent overall savings in the procurement process. Pitney Bowes' suppliers need only Internet access and a standard web browser to be electronically linked to the manufacturer's supply system to see how many of their products are on hand and to indicate how many will be needed in the future. The site, VendorSite (http://www.eventra.com/solutions/vendorsite) even includes data that small suppliers can use for production planning.

These developments open up supplier relationships for companies outside of the buyer's domestic market; however, the supplier's capability of providing satisfying goods and services will play the most critical role in securing long-term contracts. In addition, the physical delivery of goods often can be old-fashioned and slow. Nevertheless, the use of such strategic tools will be crucial for international managers to develop and maintain key competitive advantages. An overview of the international supply chain is shown in Figure 16.1.

THE IMPACT OF INTERNATIONAL LOGISTICS

Logistics costs comprise between 10 and 30 percent of the total landed cost of an international order.[6] International firms already have achieved many of the cost reductions that are possible in financing and production, and are now using international logistics as a competitive tool. The environment facing logistics managers in the next ten years will be dynamic and explosive. Technological advances and progress in communication systems and information-processing capabilities are particularly significant in the design and management of logistics systems.

For example, close collaboration with suppliers is required to develop a just-in-time inventory system, which in turn may be crucial to maintaining manufacturing costs at globally competitive levels. Yet, without electronic data interchange, such collaborations or alliances are severely handicapped. While most industrialized countries can offer the technological infrastructure for such computer-to-computer exchange of business information, the application of such a system in the global environment may be severely restricted. It may not be just the lack of technology that forms the key obstacle to modern logistics management, but rather the entire business infrastruc-

FIGURE 16.1

The International Supply Chain

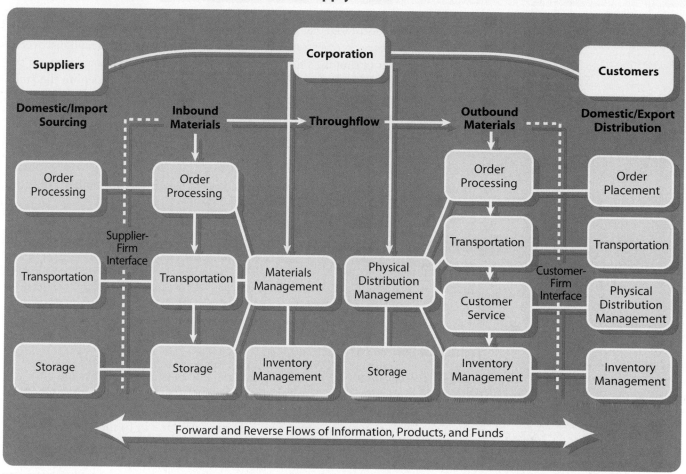

Forward and Reverse Flows of Information, Products, and Funds

ture, ranging from ways of doing business in fields such as accounting and inventory tracking, to the willingness of businesses to collaborate with each other. A contrast between the United States and Russia is useful here.

In the United States more than 40 percent of shipments are under a just-in-time/ quick response regime. For the U.S. economy, the total cost of distribution is close to 9 percent of GNP.[7] By contrast, Russia only now is beginning to work on the rhythm of demand and the need to bring supply in line. The country is battling space constraints, poor lines of supply, nonexistent distribution and service centers, limited rolling stock, and inadequate transportation systems. Producers are uninformed about issues such as inventory carrying costs, store assortment efficiencies, and replenishment techniques. The need for information development and exchange systems, for integrated supplier–distributor alliances, and for efficient communication systems is only poorly understood. As a result, distribution costs remain at well above 30 percent of GNP, holding back the domestic economy and severely restricting its international competitiveness. Unless substantial improvements are made, major participation by Russian producers in world trade will be severely handicapped,[8] since the high logistics and transaction costs make any transaction expensive and slow. Logistics and supply-chain management increasingly are the key dimensions by which firms distinguish themselves internationally.

The New Dimensions of International Logistics

In domestic operations, logistics decisions are guided by the experience of the manager, possible industry comparisons, an intimate knowledge of trends, and discovered heuristics—or rules of thumb. The logistics manager in the international firm, on the other hand, frequently has to depend on educated guesses to determine the steps required to obtain a desired service level. Variations in locale mean variations in environment. Lack of familiarity with such variations leads to uncertainty in the decision-making process. By applying decision rules based only on the environment encountered at home, the firm will be unable to adapt well to new circumstances, and the result will be inadequate profit performance. The long-term survival of international activities depends on an understanding of the differences inherent in the international logistics field.

INTERNATIONAL TRANSPORTATION ISSUES

Transportation determines how and when goods will be received. Focus on Entrepreneurship details some of the problems that can be encountered in the transportation process. The transportation issue can be divided into three components: infrastructure, the availability of modes, and the choice of modes among the given alternatives.

Transportation Infrastructure

In industrialized countries, firms can count on an established transportation network. Around the globe, however, major infrastructural variations will be encountered. Some countries may have excellent inbound and outbound transportation systems but weak internal transportation links. This is particularly true in former colonies, where the original transportation systems were designed to maximize the extractive potential of the countries. In such instances, shipping to the market may be easy, but distribution within the market may represent a very difficult and time-consuming task. Infrastructure problems can also be found in countries where most transportation networks were established between major ports and cities in past centuries. The areas lying outside the major transportation networks will encounter problems in bringing their goods to market.

New routes of commerce have also opened up, particularly between the former East and West political blocs. Yet, without the proper infrastructure, the opening of markets is mainly accompanied by major new bottlenecks. On the part of the firm, it is crucial to have wide market access to be able to appeal to sufficient customers. The firm's **logistics platform,** which is determined by a location's ease and convenience of market reach under favorable cost circumstances, is a key component of a firm's competitive position. Since different countries and regions may offer alternative logistics platforms, the firm must recognize that such alternatives can be the difference between success and failure. Policymakers in turn must recognize the impact they have on the quality of infrastructure. It is governmental planning that enables supply-chain capabilities and substantially affects logistics performance on the corporate level. In an era of foreign direct investment flexibility, the public sector's investment priorities, safety regulations, tax incentives, and transport policies can have major effects on the logistics decisions of firms.[9] For example, whether or not a country has a strong navy can become very meaningful for the logistician in light of the fact that piracy against the world's shipping keeps rising rapidly. In the first half of 2003 alone, there were 234 attacks against ocean carriers.[10]

Focus On ⬇

Late, Lost, and Damaged Goods

No shipper would want to win Roberts Express "Shipments from Hell" contest. "Winners" have nightmare tales of late, lost, broken, or even burned shipments, demonstrating just about everything that could possibly go wrong in transit. Judges from *Industry Week* and *Transportation and Distribution* magazines gave the top award to a shipment of auto parts that needed to be at an assembly plant in a few hours, since the factory operated on a just-in-time basis. But a misunderstanding over the chartered plane's arrival time and the time the parts needed to arrive kept the freight on the ground for hours. The entire production line was forced to shut down, costing thousands of dollars a minute. Then a thunderstorm delayed the plane's take-off by another half-hour, adding more dollars to the cost of the late shipment.

In another "Shipment from Hell," attention to detail could have averted a sticky disaster. A Danish company arranged to send a shipment by rail from New York to Washington State, but forgot to mention that the cargo needed refrigeration. After a week's journey in a railcar, the shipment of imported margarine was a gooey yellow mess. Instances of damaged or destroyed goods abound in the contest. One "winner" found its custom-made products at the bottom of Houston Harbor. Another company's million-dollar computer system was smashed as it rolled off the delivery truck. In an ironic twist on the damaged goods problem, one shipment was found burned and melted inside a forty-foot ocean container. It turned out the goods were firefighting equipment, sprinklers, and valves.

One contest "winner" had to bring in the police to retrieve a lost shipment. A medical supply house handed over a $90,000 surgical kit to a courier who signed for it and then lost it. The company eventually reported the kit stolen so that police could search the courier's offices. They found that the kit had been there all along.

The stories behind the "Shipments from Hell" illustrate that a host of bizarre circumstances can turn an ordinary shipment into a comedy of errors. Other notable shipping calamities included a shipment held hostage, another sent with stowaway black widow spiders, and several that were frozen or melted along the way.

While strange shipments continue, the contest has not. Roberts Express's parent company, Caliber System Inc., was acquired by FedEx in 1998, which renamed Roberts Express as FedEx Custom Critical in 2000.

Source: http://customcritical.fedex.com; Gregory S. Johnson, "Damaged Goods: Hard-luck Tales of '97," *The Journal of Commerce,* January 9, 1998, 1A, accessed July 23, 2003.

The logistics manager must therefore learn about existing and planned infrastructures abroad and at home and factor them into the firm's strategy. In some countries, for example, railroads may be an excellent transportation mode, far surpassing the performance of trucking, while in others the use of railroads for freight distribution may be a gamble at best. The future routing of pipelines must be determined before any major commitments are made to a particular location if the product is amenable to pipeline transportation. The transportation methods used to carry cargo to seaports or airports must be investigated. Mistakes in the evaluation of transportation options can prove to be very costly. One researcher reported the case of a food processing firm that built a pineapple cannery at the delta of a river in Mexico. Since the pineapple plantation was located upstream, the company planned to float the ripe fruit down to the cannery on barges. To its dismay, however, the firm soon discovered that at harvest time the river current was far too strong for barge traffic. Since no other feasible alternative method of transportation existed, the plant was closed and the new equipment was sold for a fraction of its original cost.[11]

Extreme variations also exist in the frequency of transportation services. For example, a particular port may not be visited by a ship for weeks or even months. Sometimes only carriers with particular characteristics, such as small size, will serve a given location.

All of these infrastructural concerns must be taken into account in the planning of the firm's location and transportation framework. The opportunity of a highly competitive logistics platform may be decisive for the firm's investment decision, since it forms a key component of the cost advantages sought by multinational corporations.

If a location loses its logistics benefits, due to, for example, a deterioration of the railroad system, a firm may well decide to move on to another, more favorable locale. Business strategist Michael Porter addressed the importance of infrastructure as a determinant of national competitive advantage and highlighted the capability of governmental efforts to influence this critical issue.[12] Governments must keep the transportation dimension in mind when attempting to attract new industries or trying to retain existing firms.

Availability of Modes

International transportation frequently requires ocean or airfreight modes, which many corporations only rarely use domestically. In addition, combinations such as **land bridges** or **sea bridges** may permit the transfer of freight among various modes of transportation, resulting in **intermodal movements.** The international logistics manager must understand the specific properties of the different modes to be able to use them intelligently.

Ocean Shipping   Water transportation is a key mode for international freight movement. Three types of vessels operating in **ocean shipping** can be distinguished by their service: liner service, bulk service, and tramp or charter service. **Liner service** offers regularly scheduled passage on established routes. **Bulk service** mainly provides contractual services for individual voyages or for prolonged periods of time. **Tramp service** is available for irregular routes and scheduled only on demand.

In addition to the services offered by ocean carriers, the type of cargo a vessel can carry is also important. Most common are conventional (break bulk) cargo vessels, container ships, and roll-on-roll-off vessels. Conventional cargo vessels are useful for oversized and unusual cargoes but may be less efficient in their port operations. **Container ships** carry standardized containers that greatly facilitate the loading and unloading of cargo and intermodal transfers. As a result, the time the ship has to spend in port is reduced as are the port charges. **Roll-on-roll-off (RORO)** vessels are essentially oceangoing ferries. Trucks can drive onto built-in ramps and roll off at the destination. Another vessel similar to the RORO vessel is the LASH (lighter aboard ship) vessel. LASH vessels consist of barges stored on the ship and lowered at the point of destination. The individual barges can then operate on inland waterways, a feature that is particularly useful in shallow water.

The availability of a certain type of vessel, however, does not automatically mean that it

can be used. The greatest constraint in international ocean shipping is the lack of ports and port services. For example, modern container ships cannot serve some ports because the local equipment cannot handle the resulting traffic. The problem is often found in developing countries, where local authorities lack the funds to develop facilities. In some instances, governments may purposely limit the development of **ports** to impede the inflow of imports. Increasingly, however, governments have begun to recognize the importance of an appropriate port facility structure and are developing such facilities in spite of the large investments necessary.

Air Shipping   **Airfreight** is available to and from most countries. This includes the developing world, where it is often a matter of national prestige to operate a national airline. The tremendous growth in international airfreight is shown in Figure 16.2. The total volume of airfreight in relation to total shipping volume in international business remains quite small. However, 40 percent of the world's manufactured exports (by value) travel by air.[13] Clearly, high-value items are more likely to be shipped by air, particularly if they have a high **density,** that is, a high weight-to-volume ratio.

Over the years, airlines have made major efforts to increase the volume of airfreight. Many of these activities have concentrated on developing better, more efficient ground facilities, automating air waybills, introducing airfreight containers, and providing and marketing a wide variety of special services to shippers. In addition, some airfreight companies and ports have specialized and become partners in the international logistics effort.

Changes have also taken place within the aircraft. As an example, 40 years ago, the holds of large propeller aircraft could take only about 10 tons of cargo. Today's jumbo jets can load up to 120 metric tons of cargo with an available space of 636 cubic meters,[14] hold more than 92 tons, and can therefore transport bulky products, such as locomotives, as shown in Figure 16.3. In addition, aircraft manufacturers have responded to industry demands by developing both jumbo cargo planes and combination passenger and cargo aircraft. The latter carry passengers in one section of the main deck and freight in another. These hybrids can be used by carriers on routes that would be uneconomical for passengers or freight alone.

From the shipper's perspective, the products involved must be appropriate for air shipment in terms of their size. In addition, the market situation for any given product must be evaluated. Airfreight may be needed if a product is perishable or if, for other reasons, it requires a short transit time. The level of customer service needs and expectations can also play a decisive role. For example, the shipment of an industrial product that is vital to the ongoing operations of a customer may be much more urgent than the shipment of packaged consumer products.

SELECTING A MODE OF TRANSPORT

The international logistics manager must make the appropriate selection from the available modes of transportation. The decision will be heavily influenced by the needs of the firm and its customers. The manager must consider the performance of each mode on four dimensions: transit time, predictability, cost, and noneconomic factors.

Transit Time

The period between departure and arrival of the carrier varies significantly between ocean freight and airfreight. For example, the 45-day **transit time** of an ocean shipment can be reduced to 24 hours if the firm chooses airfreight. The length of transit

FIGURE 16.2

International Airfreight, 1960–2005

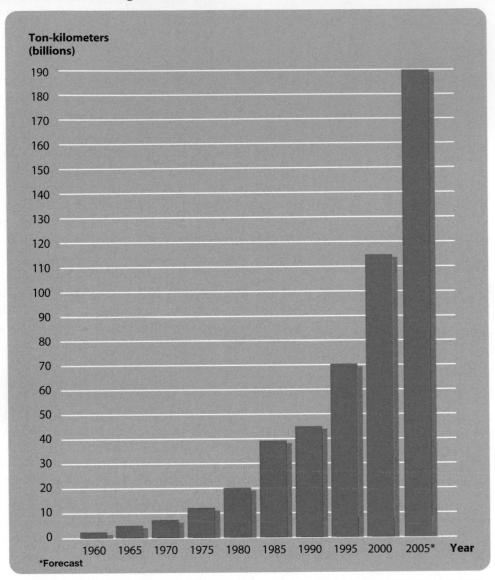

Based on data supplied by member states of the International Civil Aviation Organization (ICAO). As the number of member states increased from 116 in 1970 to 150 in 1983, there is some upward bias in the data, particularly from 1970 on, when data for the USSR were included for the first time.

Sources: Civil Aviation Statistics of the World (Montreal: ICAO), (http://www.icao.org.) Industries Global Market Forecast 2001–2015, http://www.airbus.com, accessed July 22, 2003.

time can have a major impact on the overall operations of the firm. As an example, a short transit time may reduce or even eliminate the need for an overseas depot. Also, inventories can be significantly reduced if they are replenished frequently. As a result, capital can be freed up and used to finance other corporate opportunities. Transit time can also play a major role in emergency situations. For example, if the shipper is about to miss an important delivery date because of production delays, a shipment normally made by ocean freight can be made by air. Overall, it has been estimated that each day

FIGURE 16.3

Shipping by airfreight has really taken off in the past 20 years. Even large and heavy items, such as this locomotive, are shipped to their destination by air.

Loading a Train on a Plane

Source: Printed in the *Journal of Commerce,* August 29, 1994.

that goods are in transit adds about 0.8 percent to the cost of the goods. Therefore, an extra twenty-day period spent at sea adds the equivalent of a 16 percent tariff on those goods, drastically reducing their competitiveness.[15]

Perishable products require shorter transit times. Transporting them rapidly prolongs the shelf life in the foreign market. Air delivery may be the only way to enter foreign markets successfully with products that have a short life span. International sales of cut flowers have reached their current volume only as a result of airfreight.

The interaction among selling price, market distance, and form of transportation is not new. Centuries ago, Johann von Thünen, a noted German economist, developed models for the market reach of agricultural products that incorporated these factors. These models informed farmers as to what product could be raised profitably at different distances from its market. Yet, given the forms of transportation available today, the factors no longer pose the rigid constraints experienced by von Thünen, but rather offer new opportunities in international business.

At all times, the logistics manager must understand the interactions between different components of the logistics process and their effect on transit times. Unless a smooth flow throughout the supply chain can be assured, bottlenecks will deny any timing benefits from specific improvements. For example, Levi Strauss, the blue jeans manufacturer, offers customers in some of its stores the chance to be measured by a body scanner. Less than an hour after such measurement, a Levi factory has begun to cut the jeans of their choice. Unfortunately, it then takes ten days to get the finished jean to the customer.[16]

Predictability

Providers of both ocean freight and airfreight service wrestle with the issue of reliability. Both modes are subject to the vagaries of nature, which may impose delays. Yet, because **reliability** is a relative measure, the delay of one day for airfreight tends to be seen as much more severe and "unreliable" than the same delay for ocean freight. However, delays tend to be shorter in absolute time for air shipments. As a result, arrival time via air is more predictable. This attribute has a major influence on corporate strategy. For example, because of the higher predictability of airfreight, inventory safety stock can be kept at lower levels. Greater predictability also can serve as a useful sales tool, since it permits more precise delivery promises to customers. If inadequate port facilities exist, airfreight may again be the better alternative. Unloading operations for oceangoing vessels are more cumbersome and time-consuming than for planes. Merchandise shipped via air is likely to suffer less loss and damage from exposure of the cargo to movement. Therefore, once the merchandise arrives, it is more likely to be ready for immediate delivery—a fact that also enhances predictability.

An important aspect of predictability is also the capability of a shipper to track goods at any point during the shipment. **Tracking** becomes particularly important as corporations increasingly obtain products from and send them to multiple locations around the world. Being able to coordinate the smooth flow of a multitude of interdependent shipments can make a vast difference in a corporation's performance.[17] Tracking allows the shipper to check on the functioning of the supply chain and to take remedial action if problems occur. Cargo also can be redirected if sudden demand surges so require. However, such enhanced corporate response to the predictability issue is only possible if an appropriate information system is developed by the shipper and the carrier, and easily accessible to the user. Due to rapid advances in information technology, the ability to know where a shipment is has increased dramatically, while the cost of this critical knowledge has declined. Focus on e-Business explains this further.

Cost of Transportation   International transportation services are usually priced on the basis of both cost of the service provided and value of the service to the shipper. Due to the high value of the products shipped by air, airfreight is often priced according to the value of the service. In this instance, of course, price becomes a function of market demand and the monopolistic power of the carrier.

The manager must decide whether the clearly higher cost of airfreight can be justified. In part, this will depend on the cargo's properties. The physical density and the value of the cargo will affect the decision. Bulky products may be too expensive to ship by air, whereas very compact products may be more appropriate for airfreight transportation. High-priced items can absorb transportation costs more easily than low-priced goods because the cost of transportation as a percentage of total product cost will be lower. As a result, sending diamonds by airfreight is easier to justify than sending coal. Alternatively, a shipper can decide to mix modes of transportation in order to reduce overall cost and time delays. For example, part of the shipment route can be covered by air, while another portion can be covered by truck or ship.

Most important, however, are the supply-chain considerations of the firm. The manager must determine how important it is for merchandise to arrive on time, which, for example, will be different for standard garments versus high fashion dresses. The effect of transportation cost on price and the need for product availability abroad must also be considered. Simply comparing transportation modes on the basis of price alone is insufficient. The manager must factor in all corporate, supplier, and customer activities that are affected by the modal choice and explore the full implications of each alternative. For example, some firms may want to use airfreight as a new tool for aggressive market expansion. Airfreight may also be considered a good way to begin operations in new markets without making sizable investments for warehouses

Focus On ⬇

Product Tracking: "The Best Thing Since the Barcode!"

Radio Frequency Identification (RFID) tags are revolutionizing the tracking of goods from the factory to the shelf. This tracking technology is not new but through recent advancements in processing has become relatively inexpensive, plunging from $2 a tag in 1998 to 20 cents a tag in 2003. The price is expected to drop to five cents or less per tag by 2005. RFID systems are made up of the tag, a microchip processor with an antenna, and the reader. When the tag nears the reader, it broadcasts the information contained in the chip.

For supermarket chains like the United Kingdom's Sainsbury it has meant that the time spent on receiving at the warehouse has been cut from 2½ hours to 15 minutes. Instead of an employee checking the bar code on each product in a crate individually, an entire pallet can be sent through an RFID portal and up to 65 RFID tags can be read at once. Portals are located at critical points in the supply chain and forward the information to a central computer controlling the distribution process. For Sainsbury this near-perfect information means that all the products in the supply chain can be tracked in real time. When an individual store orders food for delivery, the computer automatically tells the warehouse manager which crates to pick, based on expiration date and other factors, helping to ensure the best possible product rotation. Tracking goods helps reduce inventory shrinkage, automates the verification of stock movement, and provides full visibility of stock.

Gillette is also using RFID smart tags in its business in two different ways. The first is to put smart tagged products onto smart shelves, which are fitted with readers. Gillette estimates that retailers in America lose upward of $30 billion a year in sales because stores run out of products and the shelves are empty. Under the new Gillette system the tagged razors let the shelf know at what rate the product is being sold and the shelf keeps count. If the shelf become empty the shelf sends a signal to the store employees alerting them to the situation. The tags can also function as security against theft; if a large number of razors leave the shelf at the same time, the staff is alerted. Gillette also uses the tags in much the same way as Sainsbury. It tracks the product from factory to supermarket using the smart tags, replacing the labor-intensive, error-prone barcode process. Consultants at IBM have estimated that the smart tag could reduce inventories by between 5 and 25 percent because manufacturers can be certain that they are shipping the right quantity of goods to the right place at the right time, reducing the need for the inventories they maintain in case of error.

In the future, this technology will simplify life for consumers as well. Customers won't have to wait for someone to ring up each item in a shopping cart one at a time; instead, the RFID tags on each product can communicate with an electronic reader that detects each product in the cart and can even send the bill to the bank, which will deduct the corresponding amount from the customer's account. The product manufacturers know that customers have bought their products and the store's computers know exactly how many of each product need to be reordered. Once the products reach the home they can be put into a smart refrigerator equipped with a tag reader that can let the customer know exactly what they have and its expiration date. When the item is close to depleted, it can be added to an automatically generated shopping list. For those who feel that the smart tags are too much of an invasion of privacy, several companies have included a "kill command" in their chip specification, which permanently disables the tag after checkout.

Sources: "The Best Thing since the Bar-code," *The Economist,* February 8, 2003, 57–58; http://electronics.howstuffworks.com/smart-label.htm/printable, accessed April 3, 2003; http://www.packagingdigest.com/articles/200011/82.html, accessed April 3, 2003.

and distribution centers. The final selection of a mode will be the result of the importance of different modal dimensions to the markets under consideration. A useful overall comparison of different modes of transportation is provided in Table 16.1.

Noneconomic Factors   The transportation sector, nationally and internationally, both benefits and suffers from government involvement. Even though transportation carriers are one prime target in the sweep of privatization around the globe, many carriers are still owned or heavily subsidized by governments. As a result, governmental pressure is exerted on shippers to use national carriers, even if more economical alternatives exist. Such **preferential policies** are most often enforced when government cargo is being transported. Restrictions are not limited to developing

TABLE 16.1

Evaluating Transportation Choices

Characteristics of Mode	MODE OF TRANSPORTATION				
	Air	Pipeline	Highway	Rail	Water
Speed (1=fastest)	1	4	2	3	5
Cost (1=highest)	1	4	2	3	5
Loss and Damage (1=least)	3	1	4	5	2
Frequency[1] (1=best)	3	1	2	4	5
Dependability (1=best)	5	1	2	3	4
Capacity[2] (1=best)	4	5	3	2	1
Availablity (1=best)	3	5	1	2	4

[1]Frequency: number of times mode is available during a given time period.
[2]Capacity: ability of mode to handle large or heavy goods.

Source: Ronald H. Ballou, *Business Logistics Management,* 4th ed. (Upper Saddle River, NJ: Prentice-Hall, 1998), p. 146.

countries. For example, in the United States, the federal government requires that all travelers on government business use national flag carriers when available.

For balance of payments reasons, international quota systems of transportation have been proposed. The United Nations Conference on Trade and Development (UNCTAD), for example, has recommended that 40 percent of the traffic between two nations be allocated to vessels of the exporting country, 40 percent to vessels of the importing country, and 20 percent to third-country vessels. However, stiff international competition among carriers and the price sensitivity of customers frequently render such proposals ineffective, particularly for trade between industrialized countries.

EXPORT DOCUMENTATION

A firm must deal with numerous forms and documents when exporting to ensure that all goods meet local and foreign laws and regulations.

A **bill of lading** is a contract between the exporter and the carrier indicating that the carrier has accepted responsibility for the goods and will provide transportation in return for payment. The bill of lading can also be used as a receipt and to prove ownership of the merchandise. There are two types of bills, negotiable and nonnegotiable. **Straight bills of lading** are nonnegotiable and are typically used in prepaid transactions. The goods are delivered to a specific individual or company. **Shipper's order** bills of lading are negotiable; they can be bought, sold, or traded while the goods are still in transit and are used for letter of credit transactions. The customer usually needs the original or a copy of the bill of lading as proof of ownership to take possession of the goods.

A **commercial invoice** is a bill for the goods stating basic information about the transaction, including a description of the merchandise, total cost of the goods sold, addresses of the shipper and seller, and delivery and payment terms. The buyer needs the invoice to prove ownership and to arrange payment. Some governments use the commercial invoice to assess customs duties.

Other export documents that may be required include export licenses, consular invoices (used to control and identify goods, they are obtained from the country to which the goods are being shipped), certificates of origin, inspection certification, dock and/or warehouse receipts, destination control statements (serve to notify the carrier and all foreign parties that the item may only be exported to certain destinations), insurance certificates, shipper's export declarations (used to control exports and compile trade statistics), and export packaging lists.[18]

The documentation required depends on the merchandise in the shipment and its destination. The number of documents required can be quite cumbersome and costly, creating a deterrent to trade. For example, before the introduction of document simplification, it was estimated that the border-related red tape and controls within the then-European Community cost European companies $9.2 billion in extra administrative costs and delays annually. [19] To eliminate the barriers posed by all this required documentation, Europe introduced the Single Administrative Document (SAD), which led to the elimination of nearly 200 customs forms required of truckers when traveling from one member country to another.

To ensure that all documentation required is accurately completed and to minimize potential problems, firms just entering the international market should consider using **freight forwarders,** who specialize in handling export documentation. Freight forwarders increasingly choose to differentiate themselves through the development of sophisticated information management systems, particularly with electronic data interchange (EDI).

TERMS OF SHIPMENT AND SALE

The responsibilities of the buyer and the seller should be spelled out as they relate to what is and what is not included in the price quotation and when ownership of goods passes from seller to buyer. **Incoterms** are the internationally accepted standard definitions for terms of sale set by the International Chamber of Commerce (ICC) since 1936.[20] The Incoterms 2000 went into effect on January 1, 2000, with significant revisions to better reflect changing transportation technologies and the increased use of electronic communications.[21] Although the same terms may be used in domestic transactions, they gain new meaning in the international arena. The terms are grouped into four categories, starting with the term whereby the seller makes the goods available to the buyer only at the seller's own premises (the "E"-terms), followed by the group whereby the seller is called upon to deliver the goods to a carrier appointed by the buyer (the "F"-terms). Next are the "C"-terms, whereby the seller has to contract for carriage but without assuming the risk of loss or damage to the goods or additional costs after the dispatch, and finally the "D"-terms, whereby the seller has to bear all costs and risks to bring the goods to the destination determined by the buyer. The most common of the Incoterms used in international marketing are summarized in Figure 16.4.

Prices quoted **ex-works (EXW)** apply only at the point of origin, and the seller agrees to place the goods at the disposal of the buyer at the specified place on the date or within the fixed period. All other charges are for the account of the buyer.

One of the new Incoterms is **free carrier (FCA),** which replaced a variety of FOB terms for all modes of transportation except vessel. FCA (named inland point) applies only at a designated inland shipping point. The seller is responsible for loading goods into the means of transportation; the buyer is responsible for all subsequent expenses. If a port of exportation is named, the costs of transporting the goods to the named port are included in the price.

Free alongside ship (FAS) at a named U.S. port of export means that the exporter quotes a price for the goods, including charges for delivery of the goods alongside a

FIGURE 16.4

Selected Trade Terms

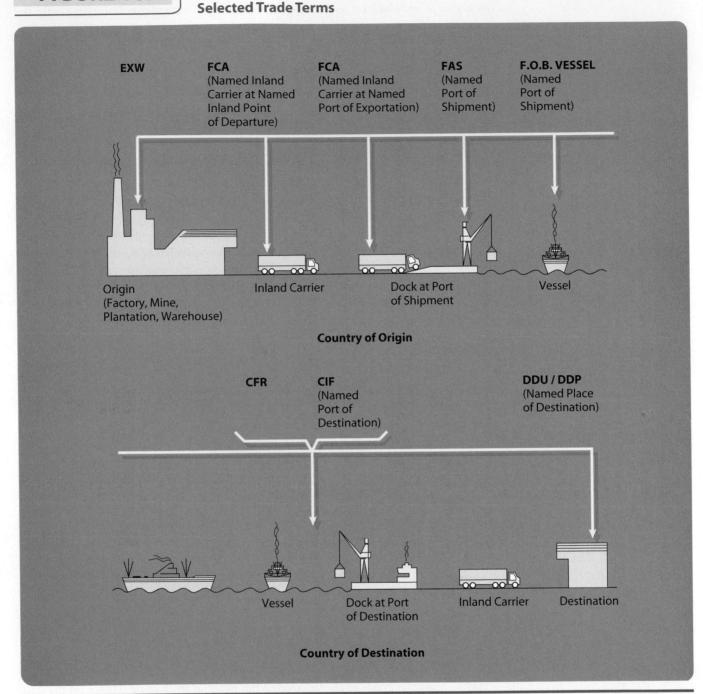

vessel at the port. The seller handles the cost of unloading and wharfage; loading, ocean transportation, and insurance are left to the buyer.

Free on board (FOB) applies only to vessel shipments. The seller quotes a price covering all expenses up to, and including, delivery of goods on an overseas vessel provided by or for the buyer.

Under **cost and freight (CFR)** to a named overseas port of import, the seller quotes a price for the goods, including the cost of transportation to the named port of debarkation. The cost of insurance and the choice of insurer are left to the buyer.

With **cost, insurance, and freight (CIF)** to a named overseas port of import, the seller quotes a price including insurance, all transportation, and miscellaneous charges to the point of debarkation from the vessel. If other than waterway transport is used, the terms are **CPT** (carriage paid to) or **CIP** (carriage and insurance paid to).

With **delivered duty paid (DDP),** the seller delivers the goods, with import duties paid, including inland transportation from import point to the buyer's premises. With **delivered duty unpaid (DDU),** only the destination customs duty and taxes are paid by the consignee. Ex-works signifies the maximum obligation for the buyer; delivered duty paid puts the maximum burden on the seller.

Careful determination and clear understanding of terms used, and their acceptance by the parties involved, are vital to avoid misunderstandings and disputes. These terms are also powerful competitive tools. The exporter should therefore learn what importers usually prefer in the particular market and what the specific transaction may require. An inexperienced importer may be discouraged by a quote such as "ex-plant Jessup, Maryland," whereas "CIF Helsinki" will assure the Finnish importer that many additional costs will only be in the familiar home environment.

Increasingly, exporters are quoting more inclusive terms. The benefits of taking charge of the transportation on either a CIF or DDP basis include the following: (1) exporters can offer foreign buyers an easy-to-understand "delivered cost" for the deal; (2) by getting discounts on volume purchases for transportation services, exporters cut shipping costs and can offer lower overall prices to prospective buyers; (3) control of product quality and service is extended to transport, enabling the exporter to ensure that goods arrive to the buyer in good condition; and (4) administrative procedures are cut for both the exporter and the buyer.[22]

When taking control of transportation costs, however, the exporter must know well in advance what impact the additional costs will have on the bottom line. If the approach is implemented incorrectly, exporters can be faced with volatile shipping rates, unexpected import duties, and restive customers. Most exporters do not want to go beyond the CIF quotation because of uncontrollables and unknowns in the destination country. Whatever terms are chosen, the program should be agreed to by the exporter and the buyer(s) rather than imposed solely by the exporter.

International Inventory Issues

Inventories tie up a major portion of corporate funds. Capital used for inventory is not available for other corporate opportunities. Annual **inventory carrying costs** (the expense of maintaining inventories) though heavily influenced by the cost of capital and industry-specific conditions, can account for 15 percent or more of the value of the inventories themselves.[23] Therefore, proper inventory policies should be of major concern to the international logistician. In addition, **just-in-time inventory** policies, which minimize the volume of inventory by making it available only when it is needed, are increasingly required by multinational manufacturers and distributors engaging in supply-chain management. They choose suppliers on the basis of their delivery and inventory performance and their ability to integrate themselves into the supply chain. Proper inventory management may therefore become a determining variable in obtaining a sale.

The purpose of establishing **inventory** systems—to maintain product movement in the delivery pipeline and to have a cushion to absorb demand fluctuations—is the same for domestic and international operations. The international environment, however, includes unique factors such as currency exchange rates, greater distances, and duties. At the same time, international operations provide the corporation with an opportunity to explore alternatives not available in a domestic setting, such as new sourcing or location alternatives. In international operations, the firm can make use of currency fluctuation by placing varying degrees of emphasis on inventory operations, depending on the stability of the currency of a specific country. Entire operations can be shifted to different nations to take advantage of new opportunities. International inventory management can therefore be much more flexible in its response to environmental changes.

In deciding the level of inventory to be maintained, the international manager must consider three factors: the order cycle time, desired customer service levels, and use of inventories as a strategic tool.

ORDER CYCLE TIME

The total time that passes between the placement of an order and the receipt of the merchandise is referred to as **order cycle time.** Two dimensions are of major importance to inventory management: the length of the total order cycle and its consistency. In international business, the order cycle is frequently longer than in domestic business. It comprises the time involved in order transmission, order filling, packing and preparation for shipment, and transportation. Order transmission time varies greatly internationally depending on the method of communication. Supply-chain driven firms use electronic data interchange (EDI) rather than facsimile, telex, telephone, or mail.

EDI is the direct transfer of information technology between computers of trading partners.[24] The usual paperwork the partners send each other, such as purchase orders and confirmations, bills of lading, invoices, and shipment notices, are formatted into standard messages and transmitted via a direct link network or a third-party network. EDI can streamline processing and administration and reduce the costs of exchanging information.

The order-filling time may also increase because lack of familiarity with a foreign market makes the anticipation of new orders more difficult. Packing and shipment preparation require more detailed attention. Finally, of course, transportation time increases with the distances involved. Larger inventories may have to be maintained both domestically and internationally to bridge the time gaps.

Consistency, the second dimension of order cycle time, is also more difficult to maintain in international business. Depending on the choice of transportation mode, delivery times may vary considerably from shipment to shipment. The variation may require the maintenance of larger safety stocks to be able to fill demand in periods when delays occur.

CUSTOMER SERVICE LEVELS

The level of **customer service** denotes the responsiveness that inventory policies permit for any given situation. A customer service level of 100 percent would be defined as the ability to fill all orders within a set time—for example, three days. If, within the same three days, only 70 percent of the orders can be filled, the customer service level is 70 percent. The choice of customer service level for the firm has a major impact on the inventories needed. In highly industrialized nations, firms frequently are expected to adhere to very high levels of customer service. Corporations are often tempted to design international customer service standards to similar levels.

Yet, service levels should not be oriented primarily around cost or customary home-country standards. Rather, the international service level should be based on expectations encountered in each market. These expectations are dependent on past performance, product desirability, customer sophistication, and the competitive status of the firm.

Because high customer service levels are costly, the goal should not be the highest customer service level possible, but rather an acceptable level. Different customers have different priorities. Some will be prepared to pay a premium for speed, some may put a higher value on flexibility, and another group may see low cost as the most important issue. Flexibility and speed are expensive, so it is wasteful to supply them to customers who do not value them highly.[25] If, for example, foreign customers expect to receive their merchandise within 30 days, it does not make sense for the international corporation to promise delivery within 10 or 15 days. Indeed, such delivery may result in storage problems. In addition, the higher prices associated with higher customer service levels may reduce the competitiveness of a firm's product. By contrast, in a business-to-business setting, sometimes even a few-hour delay in the delivery of a crucial component may be unacceptable, since the result may be a shutdown of the production process.

In such instances, strategically placed depots in a region must ensure that near instantaneous response becomes possible. For example, Storage Technologies, a maker of storage devices for mainframe computers, keeps parts at seven of its European subsidiary offices so that in an emergency it can reach any continental customer within four hours.[26]

INVENTORY AS A STRATEGIC TOOL

Inventories can be used by the international corporation as a strategic tool in dealing with currency valuation changes or to hedge against inflation. By increasing inventories before an imminent devaluation of a currency instead of holding cash, the corporation may reduce its exposure to devaluation losses. Similarly, in the case of high inflation, large inventories can provide an important inflation hedge. In such circumstances, the international inventory manager must balance the cost of maintaining high levels of inventories with the benefits accruing from hedging against inflation or devaluation. Many countries, for example, charge a property tax on stored goods. If the increase in tax payments outweighs the hedging benefits to the corporation, it would be unwise to increase inventories before a devaluation.

International Packaging Issues

Packaging is instrumental in getting the merchandise to the ultimate destination in a safe, maintainable, and presentable condition. Packaging that is adequate for domestic shipping may be inadequate for international transportation because the shipment will be subject to the motions of the vessel on which it is carried. Added stress in international shipping also arises from the transfer of goods among different modes of transportation. Figure 16.5 provides examples of some sources of stress in intermodal movement that are most frequently found in international transportation.

The responsibility for appropriate packaging rests with the shipper of goods. The U.S. Carriage of Goods by Sea Act of 1936 states: "Neither the carrier nor the ship shall be responsible for loss or damage arising or resulting from insufficiency of packing." The shipper must therefore ensure that the goods are prepared appropriately for international shipping. This is important because it has been found that "the losses

FIGURE 16.5

Stresses in Intermodal Movement

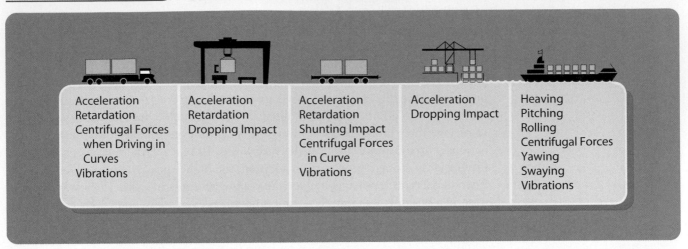

Acceleration Retardation Centrifugal Forces when Driving in Curves Vibrations	Acceleration Retardation Dropping Impact	Acceleration Retardation Shunting Impact Centrifugal Forces in Curve Vibrations	Acceleration Dropping Impact	Heaving Pitching Rolling Centrifugal Forces Yawing Swaying Vibrations

Note: Each transportation mode exerts a different set of stresses and strains on containerized cargoes. The most commonly overlooked are those associated with ocean transport.

Source: David Greenfield, "Perfect Packing for Export," from *Handling and Shipping Management,* September 1980 (Cleveland, Ohio: Penton Publishing), 47.

that occur as a result of breakage, pilferage, and theft exceed the losses caused by major maritime casualties, which include fires, sinkings, and collision of vessels. Thus the largest of these losses is a preventable loss."[27]

Packaging decisions must also take into account differences in environmental conditions—for example, climate. When the ultimate destination is very humid or particularly cold, special provisions must be made to prevent damage to the product. The task becomes even more challenging when one considers that, in the course of long-distance transportation, dramatic changes in climate can take place. Still famous is the case of a firm in Taiwan that shipped drinking glasses to the Middle East. The company used wooden crates and padded the glasses with hay. Most of the glasses, however, were broken by the time they reached their destination. As the crates traveled into the dry Middle East, the moisture content of the hay dropped. By the time the crates were delivered, the thin straw offered almost no protection.[28]

The weight of packaging must also be considered, particularly when airfreight is used, as the cost of shipping is often based on weight. At the same time, packaging material must be sufficiently strong to permit stacking in international transportation. Another consideration is that, in some countries, duties are assessed according to the gross weight of shipments, which includes the weight of packaging. Obviously, the heavier the packaging, the higher the duty will be.

The shipper must pay sufficient attention to instructions provided by the customer for packaging. For example, requests by the customer that the weight of any one package should not exceed a certain limit or that specific package dimensions should be adhered to, usually are made for a reason. Often they reflect limitations in transportation or handling facilities at the point of destination.

Although the packaging of a product is often used as a form of display abroad, international packaging can rarely serve the dual purpose of protection and display. Therefore double packaging may be necessary. The display package is for future use at the point of destination; another package surrounds it for protective purposes.

© DON MASON/CORBIS

A ship loaded with containers arrives in port. It is a reflection of the premium assigned to speed and ease of handling that has caused a decline in the use of general cargo vessels and a sharp increase in the growth of container ships, which carry standardized containers that greatly facilitate the loading and unloading of cargo and intermodal transfers.

One solution to the packaging problem in international logistics has been the development of intermodal containers—large metal boxes that fit on trucks, ships, railroad cars, and airplanes and ease the frequent transfer of goods in international shipments. Developed in different forms for both sea and air transportation, containers also offer better utilization of carrier space because of standardization of size. The shipper therefore may benefit from lower transportation rates. In addition, containers can offer greater safety from pilferage and damage. Of course, at the same time, the use of containers allows thieves to abscond with an entire shipment rather than just parts of it. On some routes in Russia, for example, theft and pilferage of cargo are so common that liability insurers will not insure container haulers in the region.[29]

Container traffic is heavily dependent on the existence of appropriate handling facilities, both domestically and internationally. In addition, the quality of inland transportation must be considered. If transportation for containers is not available and the merchandise must be unpacked and reloaded the expected cost reductions may not materialize.

In some countries, rules for the handling of containers may be designed to maintain employment. For example, U.S. union rules obligate shippers to withhold containers from firms that do not employ members of the International Longshoremen's Association for the loading or unloading of containers within a fifty-mile radius of Atlantic or Gulf ports. Such restrictions can result in an onerous cost burden.

Overall, cost attention must be paid to international packaging. The customer who ordered and paid for the merchandise expects it to arrive on time and in good condition. Even with replacements and insurance, the customer will not be satisfied if there are delays. Dissatisfaction will usually translate directly into lost sales.

International Storage Issues

Although international logistics is discussed as a movement or flow of goods, a stationary period is involved when merchandise becomes inventory stored in warehouses. Heated arguments can arise within a firm over the need for and utility of warehousing internationally. On the one hand, customers expect quick responses to orders and rapid delivery. Accommodating the customer's expectations would require locating many distribution centers around the world. On the other hand, warehouse

MAP

Trade and Travel Networks

Civilization depends on trade for growth and travel makes this possible. Shipping is the most important method of world transport but economic progress and mobility are constantly being improved by the development of new routes and new methods of transport.

Road and Rail

Integrated road and rail networks are the basis of industrial society. Containerization and the extension of modern highway systems have increased flexibility and reduced the emphasis on railways transporting freight.

Roads

Bar length equals the total road network in log scale.
Number next to country name is the total road network in thousands of kilometers.

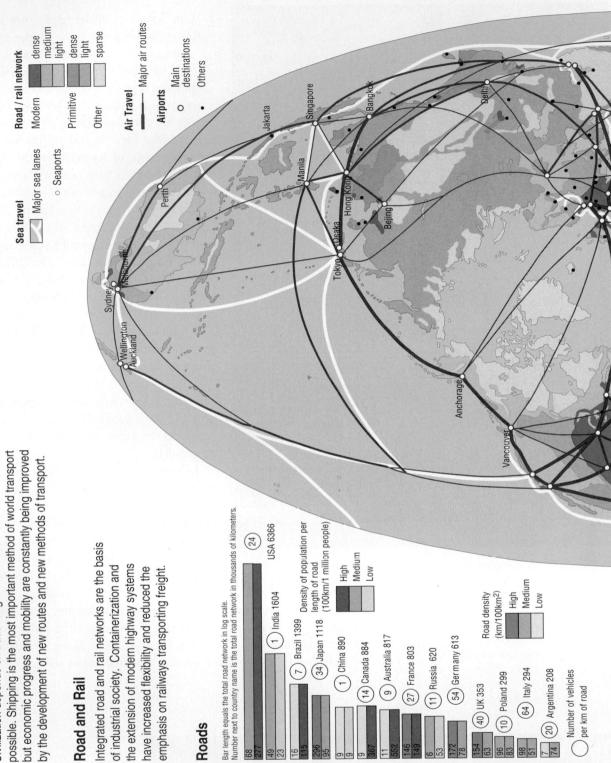

Sea travel
▨ Major sea lanes
○ Seaports

Road / rail network

Modern — dense / medium / light

Primitive — dense / light

Other — sparse

Air Travel
— Major air routes

Airports
○ Main destinations
• Others

Density of population per length of road (100km/1 million people)
High / Medium / Low

Road density (km/100km²)
High / Medium / Low

○ Number of vehicles per km of road

(24) USA 6366 — 68 / 277
(1) India 1604 — 49 / 23
(7) Brazil 1399 — 16 / 115
(34) Japan 1118 — 296 / 95
(1) China 890 — 9 / 9
(14) Canada 884 — 9 / 367
(9) Australia 817 — 11 / 552
(27) France 803 — 146 / 149
(11) Russia 620 — 6 / 53
(54) Germany 613 — 172 / 78
(40) UK 353 — 154 / 63
(10) Poland 299 — 96 / 83
(64) Italy 294 — 98 / 51
(20) Argentina 208 — 7 / 74

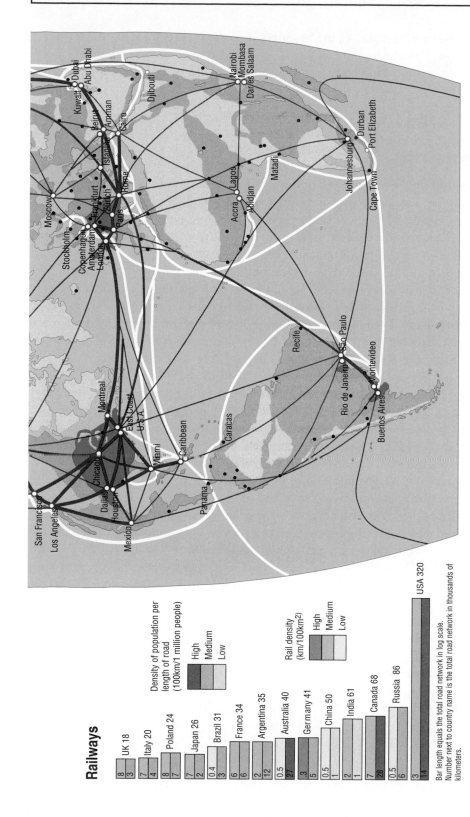

Railways

UK 18 `8` `3`
Italy 20 `7` `4`
Poland 24 `8` `7`
Japan 26 `7` `2`
Brazil 31 `0.4` `3`
France 34 `6` `6`
Argentina 35 `2` `12`
Australia 40 `0.5` `27`
Germany 41 `.3` `5`
China 50 `0.5` `1`
India 61 `2` `1`
Canada 68 `7` `28`
Russia 86 `0.5` `6`
USA 320 `3` `14`

Bar length equals the total road network in log scale.
Number next to country name is the total road network in thousands of kilometers.

Density of population per length of road (100km/1 million people)

■ High
▨ Medium
□ Low

Rail density (km/100km²)

■ High
▨ Medium
□ Low

Air and Sea Routes

A complex network of primary air routes centered on the Northern Hemisphere provides rapid transit across the world for mass travel, mail, and urgent freight.

Ships also follow these principal routes, plying the oceans between major ports and transporting the commodities of world trade in bulk.

Journey Time

The Suez Canal cuts 3600 nautical miles off the London-Singapore route.

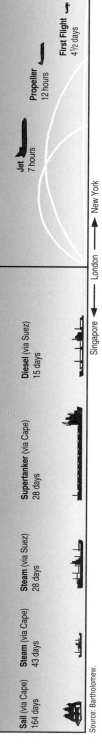

Sail (via Cape) 164 days

Steam (via Cape) 43 days

Steam (via Suez) 28 days

Supertanker (via Cape) 28 days

Diesel (via Suez) 15 days

Singapore —— London —— New York

Jet 7 hours

Propeller 12 hours

First Flight 4½ days

MAP

Source: Bartholomew.

space is expensive. In addition, the larger volume of inventory increases the inventory carrying cost. Fewer warehouses allow for consolidation of transportation and therefore lower transportation rates to the warehouse. However, if the warehouses are located far from customers, the cost of outgoing transportation increases. The international logistician must consider the tradeoffs between service and cost to the supply chain in order to determine the appropriate levels of warehousing.

STORAGE FACILITIES

The **location decision** addresses how many distribution centers to have and where to locate them. The availability of facilities abroad will differ from the domestic situation. For example, while public storage is widely available in some countries, such facilities may be scarce or entirely lacking in others. Also, the standards and quality of facilities can vary widely. As a result, the storage decision of the firm is often accompanied by the need for large-scale, long-term investments. Despite the high cost, international storage facilities should be established if they support the overall logistics effort. In many markets, adequate storage facilities are imperative to satisfy customer demands and to compete successfully. For example, since the establishment of a warehouse connotes a visible presence, in doing so a firm can convince local distributors and customers of its commitment to remain in the market for the long term.

Once the decision is made to use storage facilities abroad, the warehouse conditions must be carefully analyzed. As an example, in some countries warehouses have low ceilings. Packaging developed for the high stacking of products is therefore unnecessary or even counterproductive. In other countries, automated warehousing is available. Proper bar coding of products and the use of package dimensions acceptable to the warehousing system are basic requirements. In contrast, in warehouses still stocked manually, weight limitations will be of major concern. And, if no forklift trucks are available, palletized delivery is of little use.

To optimize the logistics system, the logistician should analyze international product sales and then rank order products according to warehousing needs. Products that are most sensitive to delivery time might be classified as "A" products. "A" products would be stocked in all distribution centers, and safety stock levels would be kept high. Alternatively, the storage of products can be more selective, if quick delivery by air can be guaranteed. Products for which immediate delivery is not urgent could be classified as "B" products. They would be stored only at selected distribution centers around the world. Finally, products for which there is little demand would be stocked only at headquarters. Should an urgent need for delivery arise, airfreight could again assure rapid shipment. Classifying products enables the international logistician to substantially reduce total international warehousing requirements and still maintain acceptable service levels.

SPECIAL TRADE ZONES

Areas where foreign goods may be held or processed and then reexported without incurring duties are called **foreign trade zones.** The zones can be found at major ports of entry and also at inland locations near major production facilities. For example, Kansas City, Missouri, has one of the largest foreign trade zones in the United States.

The existence of trade zones can be quite useful to the international firm. For example, in some countries, the benefits derived from lower labor costs may be offset by high duties and tariffs. As a result, location of manufacturing and storage facilities in these countries may prove uneconomical. Foreign trade zones are designed to exclude the impact of duties from the location decision. This is done by exempting merchandise in the foreign trade zone from duty payment. The international firm can therefore import merchandise; store it in the foreign trade zone; and process, alter, test, or demonstrate it—all without paying duties. If the merchandise is subsequently shipped abroad (that is, reexported), no duty payments are ever due. Duty payments become due only if the merchandise is shipped into the country from the foreign trade zone.

Trade zones can also be useful as transshipment points to reduce logistics cost and redesign marketing approaches. For example, Audiovox was shipping small quantities of car alarms from a Taiwanese contract manufacturer directly to distributors in Chile. The shipments were costly and the marketing strategy of requiring high minimum orders stopped distributors from buying. The firm resolved the dilemma by using a Miami trade zone to ship the alarms from Taiwan and consolidate the goods with other shipments to Chile. The savings in freight costs allowed the Chilean distributors to order whatever quantity they wanted and allowed the company to quote lower prices. As a result, sales improved markedly.[30]

All parties to the arrangement benefit from foreign trade zones. The government maintaining the trade zone achieves increased employment and investment. The firm using the trade zone obtains a spearhead in the foreign market without incurring all of the costs customarily associated with such an activity. As a result, goods can be reassembled, and large shipments can be broken down into smaller units. Also, goods can be repackaged when packaging weight becomes part of the duty assessment. Finally, goods can be given domestic "made-in" status if assembled in the foreign trade zone. Thus, duties may be payable only on the imported materials and component parts rather than on the labor that is used to finish the product.

In addition to foreign trade zones, governments also have established export processing zones and special economic areas. The common dimensions for all the zones are that special rules apply to them when compared with other regions of the country, and that the purpose of these special rules lies in the government's desire to stimulate the economy, particularly the export side of international trade.

Export processing zones usually provide tax- and duty-free treatment for production facilities whose output is destined abroad. The **maquiladoras** of Mexico are one example of a program that permits firms to take advantage of sharp differentials in labor costs. Firms can carry out the labor-intensive part of their operations in Mexico, while sourcing raw materials or component parts from other nations.

One country that has used trade zones very successfully for its own economic development is China. Through the creation of **special economic zones,** in which there are no tariffs, substantial tax incentives, and low prices for land and labor, the government has attracted many foreign investors bringing in billions of dollars. The investors have brought new equipment, technology, and managerial know-how and have increased local economic prosperity substantially. The job generation effect has been so strong that the central Chinese government has expressed concern about the overheating of the economy and the inequities between regions with and without trade zones.[31]

For the logistician, the decision whether to use such zones mainly is framed by the overall benefit for the supply-chain system. Clearly, additional transport and retransport are required, warehousing facilities need to be constructed, and material handling frequency will increase. However, the costs may well be balanced by the preferential government treatment or by lower labor costs.

Management of International Logistics

The very purpose of a multinational firm is to benefit from system synergism and a persuasive argument can be made for the coordination of international logistics at corporate headquarters. Without coordination, subsidiaries will tend to optimize their individual efficiency but jeopardize the efficiency of the overall performance of the supply chain.

CENTRALIZED LOGISTICS MANAGEMENT

A significant characteristic of the centralized approach to international logistics is the existence of headquarters staff that retains decision-making power over logistics activities affecting international subsidiaries. If headquarters exerts control, it must also take the primary responsibility for its decisions. Clearly, ill will may arise if local managers are appraised and rewarded on the basis of a performance they do not control. This may be particularly problematic if headquarters staff suffers from a lack of information or expertise.

To avoid internal problems, both headquarters staff and local management should report to one person. This person, whether the vice president for international logistics or the president of the firm, can then become the final arbiter to decide the firm's priorities. Of course, the individual should also be in charge of determining appropriate rewards for managers, both at headquarters and abroad, so that corporate decisions that alter a manager's performance level will not affect the manager's appraisal and evaluation. Further, the individual can contribute an objective view when inevitable conflicts arise in international logistics coordination. The internationally centralized decision-making process leads to an overall supply-chain management perspective that can dramatically improve profitability.

DECENTRALIZED LOGISTICS MANAGEMENT

When a firm serves many international markets that are diverse in nature, total centralization might leave the firm unresponsive to local adaptation needs. If each subsidiary is made a profit center in itself, each one carries the full responsibility for its performance, which can lead to greater local management satisfaction and to better adaptation to local market conditions. Yet often such decentralization deprives the logistics function of the benefits of coordination. For example, while headquarters, referring to its large volume of overall international shipments, may be able to extract bottom rates from transportation firms, individual subsidiaries by themselves may not have similar bargaining power. The same argument applies also to the sourcing situation, where the coordination of shipments by the purchasing firm may be much more cost-effective than individual shipments from many small suppliers around the world.

Once products are within a specific market, however, increased input from local logistics operations should be expected and encouraged. At the very least, local managers should be able to provide input into the logistics decisions generated by headquarters. Ideally, within a frequent planning cycle, local managers can identify the logistics benefits and constraints existing in their particular market and communicate them to headquarters. Headquarters can then either adjust its international logistics strategy accordingly or explain to the manager why system optimization requires actions different from the ones recommended. Such a justification process will help greatly in reducing the potential for animosity between local and headquarters operations.

OUTSOURCING LOGISTICS SERVICES

A third option, used by some corporations, is the systematic outsourcing of logistics capabilities. By collaborating with transportation firms, private warehouses, or other specialists, corporate resources can be concentrated on the firm's core product.

Many firms whose core competency does not include logistics find it more efficient to use the services of companies specializing in international shipping. This is usually true for smaller shipping volumes, for example in cases when smaller import-export firms or smaller shipments are involved. Such firms prefer to outsource at least some of the international logistics functions, rather than detracting from staff resources and time. Some logistical services providers carve specific niches in the transnational shipping market, specializing for example in consumer goods forwarding. The resulting lower costs and better service make such third parties the preferred choice for many firms. On the other hand, when hazardous or other strictly regulated materials are involved, some firms may choose to retain control over handling and storing activities, in view of possible liability issues.[32]

Going even further, **one-stop logistics** allows shippers to buy all the transportation modes and functional services from a single carrier, instead of going through the pain of choosing different third parties for each service. One-stop logistics ensures a more efficient global movement of goods via different transportation modes. Specialized companies provide EDI tracking services and take care of cumbersome customs procedures; they also offer distribution services, such as warehousing and inventory management. Finally, third parties may even take some of the international shipper's logistical functions. This rapidly growing trend provides benefits to both carriers and shippers.[33] The latter enjoy better service and simplified control procedures, and claims settlement. On the other hand, one-stop logistics can help carriers achieve economies of scale and remain competitive in a very dynamic market. The proliferation of one-stop logistics practices is facilitated by the wider acceptance of EDI and the growing importance of quality criteria versus cost criteria in shipping decisions.

While the cost savings and specialization benefits of such a strategy seem clear, one must also consider the loss of control for the firm, its suppliers, and its customers that may result from such outsourcing. Yet, contract logistics does not and should not require the handing over of control. Rather, it offers concentration on one's specialization—a division of labor. The control and responsibility toward the supply chain remain with the firm, even though operations may move to a highly trained outside organization.

The Supply Chain and the Internet

The internet has been instrumental in transforming supply-chain management. Firms are now able to conduct many more global comparisons among suppliers and select from a wide variety of choices. At the same time, firms can be much more informed in the structure of their supplier network. In consequence, the supply base of many firms has become much broader, but includes fewer participants.

Many firms still use their Web sites as a marketing and advertising tool without expanding them to order-taking capabilities. That is changing rapidly. Net e-commerce revenue in Europe alone reached $87.4 billion in 2000 out of a global total of $657 billion.[34]

Companies wishing to enter e-commerce will not have to do so on their own. Hub sites (also known as virtual malls or digital intermediaries) bring together buyers, sellers, distributors, and transaction payment processors in a single marketplace, making convenience the key attraction. Forrester Research estimates that B2B (business-to-business) e-commerce will surge past $1.6 *trillion* by 2004. The future is also growing brighter for hubs in the consumer-to-consumer market, where companies like eBay are setting high standards of profitability.[35]

When customers have the ability to access a company through the Internet, a company itself has to be prepared for 24-hour order-taking and customer service, and to have the regulatory and customs-handling expertise for international delivery. The instantaneous interactivity that users experience will also be translated into an expectation of expedient delivery of answers and products ordered. Firms must remember that web sites should encourage business, not preclude it. If prospective customers cannot easily and rapidly find what they are looking for on a Web site, they are likely to move on and find another site that makes its information and interactivity more apparent.[36]

Some companies elect to build their own international distribution networks. Both QVC, a televised shopping service, and amazon.com, an online retailer of books, have distribution centers in Britain and Germany to take advantage of the European Internet audience and to fulfill more quickly and cheaply the orders generated by their Web sites. Transactions and the information they provide about the buyers will also allow for more customization and service by region, market, or even individual customer.

For industries such as music and motion pictures, the Internet is both an opportunity and a threat. The Web provides a new, efficient method of distribution and customization of products. At the same time, it can be a channel for intellectual property violation through unauthorized posting on other Web sites where these products can be downloaded. For example, the music industry is very concerned about a shift in the balance of economic power: If artists can deliver their works directly to customers via technologies such as MP3, what will be the role of labels and distributors?

A number of hurdles and uncertainties may keep companies out of global markets or from exploiting them to their full potential. Some argue that the World Wide Web does not yet live up to its name, since it is mostly a tool for the United States and Europe. For all countries, but particularly developing nations, the issue of universal access to the Internet is crucial. Such access depends on the speed with which governments end their monopolistic structures in telecommunication and open their markets to competition. The 1997 World Trade Organization agreement on telecommunication accelerated the process of liberalization, while access to the Internet is undergoing major expansion through new technologies such as NetTV and Web phones. As Internet penetration levels increase in the near future due to technological advances, improvements in many countries' Web infrastructures, and customer acceptance, e-business will become truly global.

Logistics and Security

The entire field of supply-chain management and logistics has been thoroughly affected by newly emerging security concerns. After the terrorist attacks of 2001, companies have had to learn that the pace of international transactions has slowed down and that formerly routine steps will now take longer. While in decades past many governmental efforts were devoted to speeding up transactions across borders, national security reasons are now forcing governments to erect new barriers and conduct new inspections. Logistics is one of the business activities most affected,[37] as Focus on Politics shows.

Focus On ⊽

Logistics and National Security

The Department of Homeland Security is a cabinet-level agency designed to coordinate U.S. efforts in the war against terror. Twenty-two federal agencies are united in this new department. Some of the agencies in the new department affect international shippers, including the Customs Service, Coast Guard, the Transportation Security Administration, and the import inspection services of the Food and Drug Administration.

Importers to the United States and the customs brokers who serve them are feeling the pressure to help secure U.S. borders. The Bureau of Customs and Border Protection has introduced measures that call for the international trade community to increase advance reporting of cargo data and to do more self-policing. Many importers are concerned about how Customs will carry out its duties now that it is integrated in the Department of Homeland Security. "We're already detecting a decline in the attention given to regulatory matters by Customs," says John Simpson, president of the American Association of Exporters and Importers (AAEI) in Washington, DC. In addition, shippers may find themselves caught in a struggle between the Transportation Security Administration and Customs over which agency makes the final decisions regarding cargo security.

Ed Balderas, import manager with Robert F. Barnes Customs Brokers, says more of his customers are getting their cargo inspected by the federal government's Customs agency. His company's San Antonio office handles imports coming from Japan, Germany, and China. When inspections are demanded, he has to arrange for the cargo to be stored and unloaded for inspections at a local freight station.

Since February 2003, Customs enforces the requirement that carriers and freight forwarders electronically report certain information on cargo before it's loaded for import or export. The new 24-hour rule requires sea carriers and nonvessel operating common carriers (NVOCCs) to give Customs detailed descriptions of the contents of U.S.-bound sea containers 24 hours before a container is loaded on a vessel. Such a task has added more time and cost to the trade process. Is the cost worth the price? Can there be absolute security?

Sources: Lisa Taylor, "Shipping Security," *The Business Journal,* March 10, 2003, http://www.bizjournals.com/sanantonio/stories/2003/03/10/smallb4.html, accessed July 17, 2003; "Shipper groups worry about impact of Homeland Security Department," *Logistics Management,* (2003): 32–36.

Modern transportation systems have proved to be critical to terrorist activities. They provide the means for the perpetrators to quickly arrive at, and depart from, the sites of attacks. On occasion, terrorists have even used transportation systems themselves to carry out their crimes.

Logistics systems are often the targets of attacks. Consider the vulnerability of pipelines used for carrying oil, natural gas, and other energy sources. Logistics systems also serve as the conduit for the weapons or people who are planning to carry out attacks. These systems are the true soft spots of vulnerability for both nations and firms. Take the issue of sea ports: Some 95 percent of all international trade shipments to the United States arrive by sea at 361 ports around the nation. Thousands of additional shipments arrive by truck and rail. In most instances, the containers are secured by nothing more than a ten-cent seal that easily can be broken.

The need to institute new safeguards for international shipments will affect the ability of firms to efficiently plan their international shipments. There is now more uncertainty and less control over the timing of arrivals and departures. There is also a much greater need for internal control and supervision of shipments. Cargo security will increasingly need not only to ensure that nothing goes missing, but also that nothing has been added to a shipment.

Firms with a just-in-time regimen are exploring alternative management strategies. Planning includes the shift of international shipments from air carriage to sea. Some U.S. firms are thinking about replacing international shipments with domestic ones, where transportation via truck would replace transborder movement altogether and eliminate the use of vulnerable ports. Further down the horizon are planning scenarios in which firms consider the effects of substantial and long-term interruptions of supplies or operations. Still, any actual move away from existing JIT systems is likely to be minor unless new large-scale interruptions occur.

Logistics and the Environment

The logistician plays an increasingly important role in allowing the firm to operate in an environmentally conscious way. Environmental laws, expectations, and self-imposed goals set by firms are difficult to adhere to without a logistics orientation that systematically takes such concerns into account. Since laws and regulations differ across the world, the firm's efforts need to be responsive to a wide variety of requirements. One logistics orientation that has grown in importance due to environmental concerns is the development of **reverse distribution** systems. Such systems are instrumental in ensuring that the firm not only delivers the product to the market, but also can retrieve it from the market for subsequent use, recycling, or disposal. To a growing degree the ability to develop such reverse logistics is a key determinant for market acceptance and profitability.

Society also recognizes that retrieval should not be restricted to short-term consumer goods, such as bottles. Rather, it may be even more important to devise systems that enable the retrieval and disposal of long-term capital goods, such as cars, refrigerators, air conditioners, and industrial goods, with the least possible burden on the environment. In Germany, for example, car manufacturers are required to take back their used vehicles for dismantling and recycling purposes. Focus on e-Business presents some of the major issues connected to the design of a reverse logistics system.

Managers are often faced with the trade-offs between environmental concerns and logistical efficiency. Companies increasingly need to learn how to simultaneously achieve environmental and economic goals. Esprit, the apparel maker, and The Body Shop, the well-known British cosmetics producer, screen their suppliers for environmental and social responsibility practices. The significance of this trend is reaffirmed in the new set of rules issued by the International Organization of Standardization. ISO-14000 specifically targets international environmental practices by evaluating companies both at the organization level (management systems, environmental performance, and environmental auditing) and product level (life-cycle assessment, labeling, and product standards).[38]

From the perspective of materials management and physical distribution, environmental practices are those that bring about fewer shipments, less handling, and more direct movement. Such practices are to be weighted against optimal efficiency routines, including just-in-time inventory and quantity discount purchasing.

On the transportation side, logistics managers will need to expand their involvement in carrier and routing selection. For example, shippers of oil or other potentially hazardous materials increasingly will need to ensure that the carriers used have excellent safety records and use only double-hulled ships. Society may even expect corporate involvement in choosing the route that the shipment will travel, preferring routes that are far from ecologically important and sensitive zones. Firms will need to assert leadership in such consideration of the environment to provide society with a better quality of life.

e-BUSINESS

Reverse Logistics in Action

Reverse logistics concerns the handling and disposition of returned products and use of related materials and information. U.S. companies pay more than an estimated $35 billion annually for handling, transportation, and processing of returned products—and this figure does not include the costs of disposing or recycling of unwanted items. Nor does it factor in lost administrative time. Managing the reverse flow of goods is particularly important for firms in the e-tail business. They ship products that their customers have selected but often encounter the need to accommodate product returns.

Reverse logistics planning involves better gatekeeping of returns and their quick disposition; sound financial, warehouse, and transportation management; and well-defined strategies for recycling, refurbishment, or reuse of returned items. Since each product has its own life-cycle and may require special treatment depending upon whether it is defective, damaged, or repackageable, only a comprehensive returns system can deliver increased efficiency.

New York–based Estee Lauder is a champion of return management. Its proprietary software system has enabled the cosmetics company to reduce production and inventory levels, shave $500,000 from annual labor costs, and write off far fewer destroyed products. The system automates the time-intensive process of sorting through returns. When Lauder receives returns, it scans each barcode to determine expiration date and condition. This makes it easier to consolidate items and scrap damaged or expired ones.

Through its RISE (returns, irregulars, samples, exit strategy returns) system, Levi Strauss has reduced the processing time for returned prod-

ucts from weeks to days—and has done away with mountains of paperwork. All off-price merchandise is returned to a single location, where customized software runs a system that scans, sorts, then out picks items, ready to load them onto pallets bound for particular destinations.

While other e-tailers are reporting returns rates as high as 50 percent, Office Depot Online has kept its returns under 10 percent. Believing that prevention is better than cure, Office Depot takes care to ensure that customers don't request the wrong item by mistake. When shoppers order laser-printer toner cartridges, for example, they're automatically asked for their printer's brand name to prevent mix-ups. At any time during the transaction, they can review their purchases, thus reducing unnecessary duplication.

Ingram-Micro—a wholesale provider of technology parts—has a centralized, fully automated reverse logistics center that collects, processes, and recycles products and product parts. The result is reduced disposal costs and improved supply-chain efficiencies. Ingram also services BestBuy.com, allowing the e-tailer to opt out of inventory management altogether, because Ingram stores, distributes, and handles returns for all goods.

In addition to trimmed costs, enhanced revenues, and happier customers, improved reverse logistics systems offer another valuable benefit—information on *why* products fail to satisfy customers. Shared with the company's design and production teams, these data contribute to improving every new product—and thereby reduce the likelihood of future returns.

Sources: "Levi Strauss Gets a Leg Up on Reverse Logistics," *IIE Solutions,* Institute of Industrial Engineers, September 2001; "Ingram Enhances Services, Partners with BestBuy.com," *This Week in Electronic Commerce,* June 11, 2001; Harvey Meyer, "Many Happy Returns," *Journal of Business Strategy* 20, July–August 1999, 27–31; http://www.officedepot.com; http://www.esteelauder.com.

Summary

As competitiveness is becoming increasingly dependent on efficiency, international logistics and supply-chain management are becoming of major importance.

International logistics is concerned with the flow of materials into, through, and out of the international corporation and therefore includes materials management as well as physical distribution. The logistician must recognize the total systems demands on the firm, its suppliers, and customers to develop trade-offs between various logistics components. By taking a supply-chain perspective, the manager can develop logistics systems that are supplier- and customer-focused and highly efficient.

Implementation of such a system requires close collaboration between all members of the supply chain.

International logistics differs from domestic activities in that it deals with greater distances, new variables, and greater complexity because of national differences. One major factor to consider is transportation. The international manager needs to understand transportation infrastructures in other countries and modes of transportation such as ocean shipping and airfreight. The choice among these modes will depend on the customer's demands and the firm's transit time, predictability, and cost requirements. In addition, noneconomic factors such as government regulations weigh heavily in this decision.

Inventory management is another major consideration. Inventories abroad are expensive to maintain yet often crucial for international success. The logistician must evaluate requirements for order cycle times and customer service levels to develop an international inventory policy that can also serve as a strategic management tool.

International packaging is important because it ensures arrival of the merchandise at the ultimate destination in safe condition. In developing packaging, environmental conditions such as climate and handling conditions must be considered.

The logistics manager must also deal with international storage issues and determine where to locate inventories. International warehouse space will have to be leased or purchased and decisions will have to be made about utilizing foreign trade zones.

International logistics management is increasing in importance. Implementing the logistics function with an overall supply-chain perspective that is responsive to environmental demands will increasingly be a requirement for successful global competitiveness.

Questions for Discussion

1. Explain the key aspects of supply-chain management.
2. Contrast the use of ocean shipping and airfreight.
3. Explain the meaning and impact of transit time in international logistics.
4. How and why do governments interfere in "rational" freight carrier selection?
5. How can an international firm reduce its order cycle time?
6. What role can the international logistician play in improving the environmental friendliness of the firm?

Internet Exercises

1. What types of information are available to the exporter on The Transport Web? Go to http://www.transportweb.com, and give examples of transportation links that an exporter would find helpful and explain why.
2. Use an online database to select a freight forwarder. (Refer to http://www.freightnet.com or http://forwarders.com, directories of freight forwarders.)

Take a Stand

All customers like to choose from a wide variety of products and follow-up service for improvements or if things go wrong. Companies in turn are willing to provide the selection and service, as long as they are making money, either directly or indirectly, by growing markets or retaining customers. In most instances, managers who desire to improve specific service levels in any region have to justify the ensuing benefits to the firm. Since the population of developing nations is mostly poor, it is difficult to justify high service levels. Therefore, even if people in these countries can afford to purchase a good, they may not receive the follow-up service that is available in industrialized nations. In other words, they pay more and get less.

For Discussion

1. Should logistics cost differentials be determined on a market-by-market basis?
2. Should service delivery be cost-blind in order to delight customers?

Financial Management

Learning Objectives

- To understand how value is measured and managed across the multiple units of the multinational firm

- To understand how international business and investment activity alters and adds to the traditional financial management activities of the firm

- To understand the three primary currency exposures that confront the multinational firm

- To examine how exchange rate changes alter the value of the firm, and how management can manage or hedge these exposures

Plowed-Under: The Financial Challenges of Schering-Plough

Fred Hassan had something of a reputation for turning troubled companies around. But when he committed to move from Pharmacia to Schering-Plough, taking over as chairman and CEO in April 2003, he most likely was not really ready for what awaited him. Hassan had engineered a solution to Pharmacia's woes by arranging a merger with Monsanto to gain possession of the painkiller Celebrex. But given the problems of Schering-Plough, it may be some time before the company is in any condition to be the object of anyone's eye.

Schering-Plough's major allergy drug, Claritin, lost patent protection in November 2002, and Schering had moved it to the over-the-counter market quickly. Claritin's declines, combined with declining sales of nearly every major product in Schering's portfolio, sent sales and profits reeling in the first quarter of 2003. And it did not stop there. In the second quarter of 2003 Schering agreed to pay $500 million in fines to the Food and Drug Administration related to what was termed "sloppy manufacturing" and related problems in 2001 and 2002. And to add insult to injury, in September 2003 the Securities and Exchange Commission fined the company's previous chief executive, Richard Kogan, along with another senior executive, for passing on information about disappointing earnings to some investors privately before making the information public.

In August 2003 Schering-Plough acknowledged that it may not have enough cash in the United States to fund operations for the rest of the year if it maintained both its current spending levels and its dividends to stockholders. Although the company noted that it had significant cash reserves, a large portion of the company's $3.6 billion in cash resides in overseas accounts. The company noted that it was not anxious to repatriate the cash from overseas, being unwilling to take on the heavy taxes associated with repatriating the money. After an extensive review of the company's failing financial health, in September 2003 Schering-Plough slashed its dividend by 68% (from 17 cents per share per quarter to 5.5 cents) and slated at least 1,000 employees to leave under an early retirement program.

Many of the firm's critics, however, do not see how the firm's actions are in the best interests of anyone. Avoiding tax ordinarily may ultimately benefit stockholders, but not if the firm simultaneously slashes their returns in dividends. And the higher costs of early retirement are not a bargain for anyone involved either, except perhaps the retirees themselves.

Source: Based on "Schering-Plough Reiterates Warnings About Cash Shortage," *Wall Street Journal,* August 13, 2003; and "Schering-Plough Corp. Cuts Its Dividends 68%," *Wall Street Journal,* August 22, 2003, B5.

What exactly is the leadership of the multinational firm attempting to achieve? *Profit maximization*—the first words that leap from the lips—is the simplest answer. But as is the case with much of global business, it is not quite that simple. Should leadership be maximizing the profits in the short run, the long run, for stockholders alone, or for all of the stakeholders of the multinational organization?

What Is the Goal of Management?

The Anglo-American markets, primarily the United States and the United Kingdom, are characterized by many publicly traded companies that seek to maximize shareholder wealth—so-called *stockholder wealth maximization*. Stockholder wealth maximization dictates that the management of the company should actively seek to maximize the returns to stockholders by working to push share prices up and to continually grow the dividends paid out to those same shareholders. This implies in the extreme, however, that management is not seeking to build value or wealth for the other stakeholders in the multinational enterprise: the creditors, management itself, employees, suppliers, the communities in which these firms reside, and even government itself. Clearly the modern concept of free market capitalism is a near sole focus on building wealth for stockholders alone, and has been frequently interpreted as extremely short-run in focus.

But this is not an accepted universal truth in global business. Continental European and Japanese firms have long pursued a wider definition of wealth maximization—*corporate wealth maximization*—that directs management to consider the financial and social health of all stakeholders, and not to focus exclusively on the financial returns of the multinational firm alone. This is not to say that the firm is not driven to maximize its profitability, but it does direct the firm to consider and balance short-term financial goals against long-term societal goals of continued employment, community citizenship, and public welfare needs—an extremely difficult task, at best.

These two different philosophies are not necessarily exclusive, and many firms—in all markets—attempt to find some balance between the two. The stockholder wealth maximization is in many ways much simpler and easier to pursue, having a single objective and in many ways a single client. Although simplistic, and sometimes leading to the abuses that have been so widely reported in recent years (Enron, Worldcom, and Tyco, to name but a few), it has led to the development of the relatively more competitive global business. The Focus on Ethics that follows, highlighting the story of Enron, is but one example of how a lack of ethical balance may lead to ruin.

Although in many ways a kinder and gentler philosophy, corporate wealth maximization has the unenviable charge of attempting to meet the desires of multiple stakeholders. Decision making becomes slower, less decisive, and frequently results in organizations that cannot meet the constantly growing pressures of a global marketplace that rewards innovation, speed, and lower costs. The concerns of social impacts, environmental responsibility, and sustainable development—while sounding good on the public relations releases—impose heavy burdens on organizations trying to compete in a wireless, Internet-based marketplace. The financial objectives of the multinational enterprise of the coming century will be those that find the unique balance that works for them and their own corporate culture.

Focus On ⬇

Stockholder Wealth Maximization and Corporate Culture: The Enron Debacle

Enron may be the classic tale of how the singular pursuit of one philosophy, in the absence of consideration of other interests or beliefs, can lead to ruin.

The company's origins were humble: a simple natural gas pipeline operator that saw considerable growth in the 1980s. As the 1980s drew to a close, however, the company's new management team saw new opportunities to build additional shareholder value in making markets in natural gas using the information that flowed naturally to the firm from its existing operations. The Enron story was the subject of countless business school case studies, news stories, and Wall Street admiration.

Although now a global player, building and operating pipelines and power plants all over the world, the firm now found itself creating enormous profits through market-making, primarily in North America. As the firm hired more and more of the young best and brightest—paying premium salaries and signing bonuses to the new graduates of the best MBA programs—it built a corporate culture that was singularly focused on profits and greed. Without the healthy balance of wisdom and experience from a time-tested corporate culture, it in many ways became a naive and blind pursuer of stockholder wealth maximization.

By the late 1990s it became increasingly clear to many at the top of Enron that the story itself was losing steam, and profits could not be sustained. Many believe that it was the company's own corporate culture, one based on nothing other than earnings-per-share growth, that led to many of the questionable ethical decisions and ultimately to its demise.

GLOBAL FINANCIAL GOALS

The multinational firm, because it is a conglomeration of many firms operating in a multitude of economic environments, must determine for itself the proper balance between three primary financial objectives:

1. Maximization of consolidated, after-tax, income
2. Minimization of the firm's effective global tax burden
3. Correct positioning of the firm's income, cash flows, and available funds

These goals are frequently inconsistent, in that the pursuit of one goal may result in a less desirable outcome in regard to another goal. Management must make decisions about the proper trade-offs between goals about the future (which is why people are employed as managers, not computers).

GENUS CORPORATION

A sample firm aids in illustrating how the various components of the multinational firm fit together, and how financial management must make decisions regarding trade-offs. Genus Corporation is a U.S.-based manufacturer and distributor of extremity-stimulus medical supplies.[1] The firm's corporate headquarters and original manufacturing plant are in New Orleans, Louisiana.

Genus currently has three wholly owned foreign subsidiaries located in Brazil, Germany, and China. In addition to the parent company selling goods in the domestic (U.S.) market and exporting goods to Mexico and Canada, each of the foreign subsidiaries purchases subassemblies (transfers) from the parent company. The subsidiaries then add value in the form of specific attributes and requirements for the local-country market, and distribute and sell the goods in the local market (Brazil, Germany, and China).

The three countries where Genus has incorporated subsidiaries pose very different challenges for the financial management of the firm. These challenges are outlined in Figure 17.1.

FIGURE 17.1

Genus Corporation and Foreign Subsidiaries

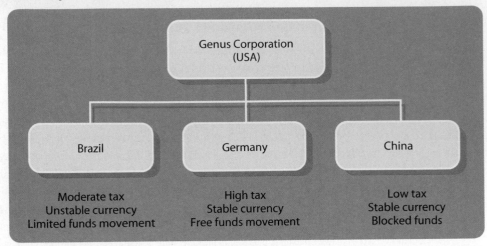

Tax Management

Genus, like all firms in all countries, would prefer to pay less taxes rather than more. Whereas profits are taxed at relatively low to moderate rates in China and Brazil, Germany's income tax rate is relatively high (though currently equal to that in the United States). If Genus could "rearrange" its profits among its units, it would prefer to make more of its profits in China and Brazil, given the lower tax burden placed on profits in those countries.

Currency Management

Ultimately, for valuation purposes, the most important attribute of any of the three country currencies is its ability to maintain its value versus the U.S. dollar, the reporting currency of the parent company. In 2001, the euro replaced the German mark and eleven other European currencies. Although the value of the euro has fluctuated, it is one of the world's primary currencies and is expected to maintain its value well over time. The Chinese renminbi (or yuan as it is sometimes called) is not freely convertible into other currencies without governmental approval, and its value is therefore highly controlled and maintained. The Brazilian real, however, is of particular worry. In previous years the value of the Brazilian currency has been known to fall dramatically, wiping out the value of profits generated in Brazil when converted to any other currency, like the dollar. As opposed to what tax management would recommend, Genus would prefer to "rearrange" its profits into Germany and euros for currency management purposes.

Funds Flow Management

The ability to move funds with relative ease and timeliness in a multinational firm is extremely important. For Genus, the German subsidiary experiences no problems with funds movements, as the German financial system is highly developed and open. Although Brazil possesses a number of bureaucratic requirements for justifying the movement of funds in and out of the country, it is still relatively open for moving funds cross-border. Genus's problems lie in China. The Chinese government makes it nearly impossible for foreign corporations to move funds out of China with any frequency, although bringing capital into China is not a problem. For funds management purposes, Genus would like to "rearrange" its profits and cash flows to minimize having funds blocked up in China.

The challenge to financial management of the global firm is management's ability to find the right trade-off between these often conflicting goals and risks.

MULTINATIONAL MANAGEMENT

A number of helpful reminders about multinational companies aid in describing the financial management issues confronting Genus:

- The primary goal of the firm, domestic or multinational, is the maximization of consolidated profits, after tax.
- *Consolidated profits* are the profits of all the individual units of the firm originating in many different currencies as expressed in the currency of the parent company, in this case, the U.S. dollar. Consolidated profits are *not* limited to those earnings that have been brought back to the parent company (repatriated), and in fact these profits may never be removed from the country in which they were earned.
- Each of the incorporated units of the firm (the U.S. parent company and the three foreign subsidiaries) has its own set of traditional financial statements: statement of income, balance sheet, and statement of cash flows. These financial statements are expressed in the local currency of the unit for tax and reporting purposes to the local government.

Table 17.1 provides an overview of the current year's profits before and after tax on both the individual unit level and on the consolidated level, in both local currency and U.S. dollar value.

TABLE 17.1

Genus Corporation's Consolidated Gross Profits (in 000s)

Unit (currency)	Profit (local currency)	Income Tax Rate (percent)	Taxes Payable (local currency)	Profit After Tax (local currency)	Exchange Rate (currency/US$)	Profit (US$)
U.S. parent company (dollar)	4,500	35%	1,575	2,925	1.0000	$2,925.00
Brazilian subsidiary (real)	6,250	25%	1,563	4,688	2.5000	$1,875.00
German subsidiary (euro)	3,000	35%	1,050	1,950	1.1600	$2,262.00
Chinese subsidiary (Rmb)	2,500	30%	750	1,750	8.500	$205.88

Consolidated

Profits after tax (000s of US$)	$7,267.88
Shares outstanding (000s)	10,000
Earnings per share (US$)	$0.73

Notes:
1. Each individual unit of the company maintains its books in local currency as required by host governments.
2. The Brazilian real and Chinese renminbi are expressed as local currency per U.S. dollar. The euro, however, as is common practice, is quoted in U.S. dollars per euro.
3. Each individual unit's profits are translated into U.S. dollars using the average exchange rate for the period (year).
4. U.S. parent company's sales are derived from both sales to unrelated parties in the United States, Mexico (exporting), and Canada (exporting), as well as intrafirm sales (transfers) to the three individual foreign subsidiaries.
5. Tax calculations assume all profits are derived from the active conduct of merchandise trade and all profits are retained in the individual foreign subsidiaries (no dividend distribution from the foreign subsidiary back to the U.S. parent company).

- The owners of Genus, its shareholders, track the firm's financial performance on the basis of its earnings per share (EPS). EPS is simply the consolidated profits of the firm, in U.S. dollars, divided by the total number of shares outstanding:

$$\text{EPS} = \frac{\text{Consolidated profits after tax}}{\text{Shares outstanding}} = \frac{\$7,267,880}{10,000,000} = \$0.73/\text{share}$$

- Each affiliate is located within a country's borders and is therefore subject to all laws and regulations applying to business activities within that country. These laws and regulations include specific practices as they apply to corporate income and tax rates, currency of denomination of operating and financial cash flows, and conditions under which capital and cash flows may move into and out of the country.

Multinational financial management is not a separate set of issues from domestic or traditional financial management, but the additional levels of risk and complexity introduced by the conduct of business across borders. Business across borders introduces different laws, different methods, different markets, different interest rates, and most of all, different currencies.

The many dimensions of multinational financial management are most easily explained in the context of a firm's financial decision-making process in evaluating a potential foreign investment. Such an evaluation includes:

- Capital budgeting, which is the process of evaluating the financial feasibility of an individual investment, whether it be the purchase of a stock, real estate, or a firm
- Capital structure, which is the determination of the relative quantities of debt capital and equity capital that will constitute the funding of the investment
- Working capital and cash flow management, which is the management of operating and financial cash flows passing in and out of a specific investment project

Multinational financial management means that all the above financial activities will be complicated by the differences in markets, laws, and especially currencies. This is the field of financial risk management. Firms may intentionally borrow foreign currencies, buy forward contracts, or price their products in different currencies to manage their cash flows that are denominated in foreign currencies.

Changes in interest and exchange rates will affect each of the above steps in the international investment process. All firms, no matter how "domestic" they may seem in structure, are influenced by exchange rate changes. The financial managers of a firm that has any dimension of international activity, imports or exports, foreign subsidiaries or affiliates, must pay special attention to these issues if the firm is to succeed in its international endeavors. The discussion begins with the difficulties of simply getting paid for international sales, import/export financing.

Import/Export Trade Financing

Unlike most domestic business, international business often occurs between two parties that do not know each other very well. Yet, in order to conduct business, a large degree of financial trust must exist. This financial trust is basically the trust that the buyer of a product will actually pay for it on or after delivery. For example, if a furniture manufacturer in South Carolina receives an order from a distributor located in Cleveland, Ohio, the furniture maker will ordinarily fill the order, ship the furniture, and await payment. Payment terms are usually 30 to 60 days. This is trade on an "open account basis." The furniture manufacturer has placed a considerable amount of financial trust in the buyer but normally is paid with little problem.

Internationally, however, financial trust is pushed to its limit. An order from a foreign buyer may constitute a degree of credit risk (the risk of not being repaid) that the producer (the exporter) cannot afford to take. The exporter needs some guarantee that the importer will pay for the goods. Other factors that tend to intensify this problem include the increased lag times necessary for international shipments and the potential risks of payments in different currencies. For this reason, arrangements that provide guarantees for exports are important to countries and companies wanting to expand international sales. This can be accomplished through a sequence of documents surrounding the letter of credit.

TRADE FINANCING USING A LETTER OF CREDIT (L/C)

A lumber manufacturer in the Pacific Northwest of the United States, Vanport, receives a large order from a Japanese construction company, Endaka, for a shipment of old-growth pine lumber. Vanport has not worked with Endaka before and therefore seeks some assurance that payment for the lumber will actually be made. Vanport ordinarily does not require any assurance of the buyer's ability to pay (sometimes a small down payment or deposit is made as a sign of good faith), but an international sale of this size is too large a risk. If Endaka could not or would not pay, the cost of returning the lumber products to the United States would be prohibitive. Figure 17.2 illustrates the following sequence of events that will complete the transaction.

1. Endaka Construction (JAP) requests a letter of credit (L/C) to be issued by its bank, Yokohama Bank.
2. Yokohama Bank will determine whether Endaka is financially sound and capable of making the payments as required. This is a very important step because Yokohama Bank simply wants to guarantee the payment, not make the payment.
3. Yokohama Bank, once satisfied with Endaka's application, issues the L/C to a representative in the United States or to the exporter's bank, Pacific First Bank. The L/C guarantees payment for the merchandise if the goods are shipped as stipulated in accompanying documents. Customary documents include the

FIGURE 17.2

Trade Financing with a Letter of Credit (L/C)

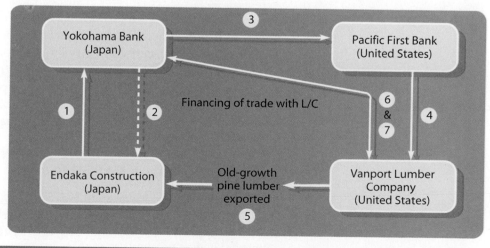

commercial invoice, customs clearance and invoice, the packing list, certification of insurance, and a bill of lading.

4. The exporter's bank, Pacific First, assures Vanport that payment will be made after evaluating the letter of credit. At this point the credit standing of Yokohama Bank has been substituted for the credit standing of the importer itself, Endaka Construction.

5. When the lumber order is ready, it is loaded onboard the shipper (called a common carrier). When the exporter signs a contract with a shipper, the signed contract serves as the receipt that the common carrier has received the goods, and it is termed the **bill of lading.**

6. Vanport draws a **draft** against Yokohama Bank for payment. The draft is the document used in international trade to effect payment and explicitly requests payment for the merchandise, which is now shown to be shipped and insured consistent with all requirements of the previously issued L/C. (If the draft is issued to the bank issuing the L/C, Yokohama Bank, it is termed a **bank draft.** If the draft is issued against the importer, Endaka Construction, it is a **trade draft.**) The draft, L/C, and other appropriate documents are presented to Pacific First Bank for payment.

7. If Pacific First Bank (US) had **confirmed** the letter of credit from Yokohama Bank, it would immediately pay Vanport for the lumber and then collect from the issuing bank, Yokohama. If Pacific First Bank had not confirmed the letter of credit, it only passes the documents to Yokohama Bank for payment (to Vanport). The confirmed, as opposed to unconfirmed, letter of credit obviously speeds up payment to the exporter.

Regardless, with the letter of credit as the financial assurance, the exporter or the exporter's bank is collecting payment from the importer's bank, not from the importer itself. It is up to the specific arrangements between the importer (Endaka) and the importer's bank (Yokohama) to arrange the final settlement at that end of the purchase.

If the trade relationship continues over time, both parties will gain faith and confidence in the other. With this strengthening of financial trust, the trade financing relationship will loosen. Sustained buyer-seller relations across borders eventually end up operating on an open account basis similar to domestic commerce.

Multinational Investing

Any investment, whether it be the purchase of stock, the acquisition of real estate, or the construction of a manufacturing facility in another country, is financially justified if the present value of expected cash inflows is greater than the present value of expected cash outflows; in other words, if it has a positive **net present value (NPV).** The construction of a **capital budget** is the process of projecting the net operating cash flows of the potential investment to determine if it is indeed a good investment.

CAPITAL BUDGET COMPONENTS AND DECISION CRITERIA

All capital budgets are only as good as the accuracy of the cost and revenue assumptions. Adequately anticipating all of the incremental expenses that the individual project imposes on the firm is critical to a proper analysis.

A capital budget is composed of three primary cash flow components:

1. **Initial Expenses and Capital Outlays:** The initial capital outlays are normally the largest net cash outflow occurring over the life of a proposed investment. Because the cash flows occur up front, they have a substantial impact on the net present value of the project.
2. **Operating Cash Flows:** The operating cash flows are the net cash flows the project is expected to yield once production is underway. The primary positive net cash flows of the project are realized in this stage; net operating cash flows will determine the success or failure of the proposed investment.
3. **Terminal Cash Flows:** The final component of the capital budget is composed of the salvage value or resale value of the project at its end. The terminal value will include whatever working capital balances can be recaptured once the project is no longer in operation (at least by this owner).

The financial decision criterion for an individual investment is whether the net present value of the project is positive or negative.[2] The net cash flows in the future are discounted by the average cost of capital for the firm (the average of debt and equity costs). The purpose of discounting is to capture the fact that the firm has acquired investment capital at a cost (interest). The same capital could have been used for other projects of other investments. It is therefore necessary to discount the future cash flows to account for this foregone income of the capital, its opportunity cost. If NPV is positive, then the project is an acceptable investment. If the project's NPV is negative, then the cash flows expected to result from the investment are insufficient to provide an acceptable rate of return, and the project should be rejected.

A PROPOSED PROJECT EVALUATION

The capital budget for a manufacturing plant in Singapore serves as a basic example. ACME, a U.S. manufacturer of household consumer products, is considering the construction of a plant in Singapore in 2003. It would cost US$1,660,000 to build and would be ready for operation on January 1, 2004. ACME would operate the plant for three years and then would sell the plant to the Singapore government.

To analyze the proposed investment, ACME must estimate what the sales revenues would be per year, the costs of production, the overhead expenses of operating the plant per year, the depreciation allowances for the new plant and equipment, and the Singapore tax rate on corporate income. The estimation of all net operating cash flows is very important to the analysis of the project. Often the entire acceptability of a foreign investment may depend on the sales forecast for the foreign project.

But ACME needs U.S. dollars, not Singapore dollars. The only way the stockholders of ACME would be willing to undertake the investment is if it would be profitable in terms of their own currency, the U.S. dollar. This is the primary theoretical distinction between a domestic capital budget and a multinational capital budget. The evaluation of the project in the viewpoint of the parent will focus on whatever cash flows, either operational or financial, will find their way back to the parent firm in U.S. dollars.

ACME must therefore forecast the movement of the Singapore dollar (S$) over the four-year period as well. The spot rate on January 1, 2003 is S$1.6600/US$. ACME concludes that the rate of inflation will be roughly 5 percent higher per year in Singapore than in the United States. If the theory of purchasing power parity holds, as described in Chapter 7, it should take roughly 5 percent more Singapore dollars to buy a U.S. dollar per year. Using this assumption, ACME forecasts the exchange rate from 2003 to 2006.

After considerable study and analysis, ACME estimates that the net cash flows of the Singapore project, in Singapore dollars, would be those on line 1 in Table 17.2.

Telecom's titan, AT&T Corporation, launched China's first foreign telecom venture with Telecom's Shanghai branch after seven years of negotiation.

Line 2 lists the expected exchange rate between Singapore dollars and U.S. dollars over the four-year period, assuming it takes 5 percent more Singapore dollars per U.S. dollar each year (the Singapore dollar is therefore expected to depreciate versus the U.S. dollar). Combining the net cash flow forecast in Singapore dollars with the expected exchange rates, ACME can now calculate the net cash flow per year in U.S. dollars. ACME notes that although the initial expense is sizable, S$1,660,000 or US$1,000,000, the project produces positive net cash flows in its very first year of operations (2004) of US$172,117, and remains positive every year after.

ACME estimates that its cost of capital, both debt and equity combined (the weighted average cost of capital), is about 16 percent per year. Using this as the rate of discount, the discount factor for each of the future years is found. Finally, the net cash flow in U.S. dollars multiplied by the present value factor yields the present values of each net cash flow. The net present value of the Singapore project is a negative US$107,919; ACME may now decide not to proceed with the project since it is financially unacceptable.

RISKS IN INTERNATIONAL INVESTMENTS

How is the ACME capital budget different from a similar project constructed in Bangor, Maine? It is riskier, at least from the standpoint of cross-border risk. The higher risk of an international investment arises from the different countries, their laws, regulations, potential for interference with the normal operations of the investment project, and obviously currencies, all of which are unique to international investment.

The risk of international investment is considered greater because the proposed investment will be within the jurisdiction of a different government. Governments have the ability to pass new laws, including the potential nationalization of the entire project. The typical problems that may arise from operating in a different country are changes in foreign tax laws, restrictions placed on when or how much in profits may be repatriated to the parent company, and other types of restrictions that hinder the free movement of merchandise and capital among the proposed project, the parent, and any other country relevant to its material inputs or sales.

 TABLE 17.2

Multinational Capital Budget: Singapore Manufacturing Facility

Line #	Description	2003	2004	2005	2006
1	Net cash flow in S$	(1,660,000)	300,000	600,000	1,500,000
2	Exchange rate, S$/US$	1.6600	1.7430	1.8302	1.9217
3	Net cash flow in US$	(1,000,000)	172,117	327,833	780,559
4	Present value factor	1.0000	0.8621	0.7432	0.6407
5	Present value in US$	(1,000,000)	148,377	243,633	500,071
6	Net present value in US$	(107,919)			
7	Net present value in S$	5,505			

Notes:
a. The spot exchange rate of S$1.6600/US$ is assumed to change by 5 percent per year, 1.6600 × 1.05 = 1.7430.
b. The present value factor assumes a weighted average cost of capital, the discount rate, of 16 percent. The present value factor then is found using the standard formula of $1/(1 + .16)^t$, where t is the number of years in the future (1, 2, or 3).

Inflation Rates and Interest Rates around the World

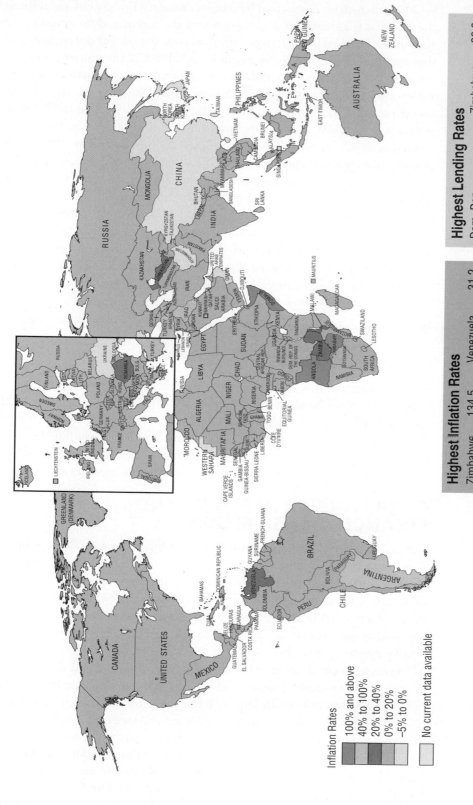

Highest Inflation Rates

Zimbabwe	134.5	Venezuela	31.2
Angola	106.0	Malawi	27.4
Somalia	Over 100	Uzbekistan	26.0
Iraq	70.0	Romania	22.5
Myanmar	53.7	Zambia	21.0
Turkey	45.2	Serb. & Mont.	19.0
Belarus	42.8	Suriname	17.0
Argentina	41.0		

Highest Lending Rates

Dem. Rep.		Zimbabwe	38.0
of Congo	165.0	Kyrgyzstan	37.3
Angola	96.0	Ukraine	32.3
Brazil	57.6	Mongolia	30.2
Malawi	56.2	Moldova	28.7
Uruguay	51.7	Haiti	28.6
Belarus	47.0	Paraguay	28.3
Zambia	46.2	Argentina	27.7

Inflation Rates

- 100% and above
- 40% to 100%
- 20% to 40%
- 0% to 20%
- −5% to 0%
- No current data available

Sources: 2003 World Development Indicators, The World Bank;
http://www.cia.gov/cia/publications/factbook/fields/2092.html

MAP

The other major distinction between a domestic investment and a foreign investment is that the viewpoint or perspective of the parent and the project are no longer the same. The two perspectives differ because the parent only values cash flows it derives from the project. So, for example, in Table 17.2 the project generates sufficient net cash flows in Singapore dollars that the project is acceptable from the project's viewpoint, but not from the parent's viewpoint. Assuming the same 16 percent discount rate, the NPV in Singapore dollars is +S$5,505, while the NPV to the U.S. parent was −US$107,919 as noted previously. But what if the exchange rate were not to change at all—remain *fixed* for the 2003–2006 period? The NPV would then be positive from both viewpoints (project NPV remains +S$5,505, parent's NPV is now US$3,316). Or what if the Singapore government were to restrict the payment of dividends back to the U.S. parent firm, or somehow prohibit the Singapore subsidiary from exchanging Singapore dollars for U.S. dollars (capital controls)? Without cash flows in U.S. dollars, the parent would have no way of justifying the investment. And all of this could occur while the project itself is sufficiently profitable when measured in local currency (Singapore dollars). This split between project and parent viewpoint is a critical difference in international investment analysis.

International Cash Flow Management

Cash management is the financing of short-term or current assets, but the term is used here to describe all short-term financing and financial management of the firm. Even a small multinational firm will have a number of different cash flows moving throughout its system at one time. The maintenance of proper liquidity, the monitoring of payments, and the acquisition of additional capital when needed—all of these require a great degree of organization and planning in international operations.

OPERATING CASH FLOWS AND FINANCING CASH FLOWS

Firms possess both operating cash flows and financing cash flows. **Operating cash flows** arise from the everyday business activities of the firm such as paying for materials or resources (accounts payable) or receiving payments for items sold (accounts receivable). In addition to the direct cost and revenue cash flows from operations, there are a number of indirect cash flows. The indirect cash flows are primarily license fees paid to the owners of particular technological processes and royalties to the holders of patents of copyrights.

Financing cash flows arise from the funding activities of the firm. The servicing of existing funding sources, interest on existing debt, and dividend payments to shareholders constitute potentially large and frequent cash flows. Periodic additions to debt or equity through new bank loans, new bond issuances, or supplemental stock sales may also add to the volume of financing cash flows in the multinational firm.

Figure 17.3 provides an overview of how operational and financial cash flows may appear for a U.S.-based multinational firm. In addition to having some export sales in Canada, it may import some materials from Mexico. The firm has gained access to several different European markets by first selling its product to its German subsidiary, which then provides the final touches necessary for sales in Germany, France, and Switzerland. Sales and purchases by the parent with Canada and Mexico give rise to a continuing series of accounts receivables and accounts payable, which may be denominated in Canadian dollars, Mexican pesos, or U.S. dollars.

FIGURE 17.3

Operating and Financing Cash Flows of a U.S.-Based Multinational Firm

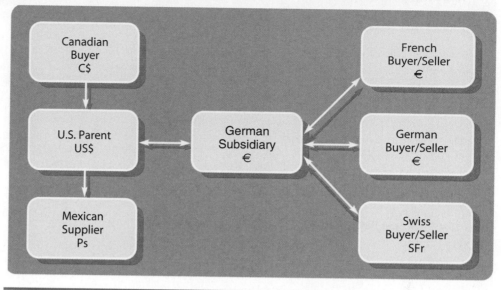

INTRAFIRM CASH FLOWS AND TRANSFER PRICES

Cash flows between the U.S. parent and the German subsidiary will be both operational and financial in nature. The sale of the major product line to the German subsidiary creates intrafirm account receivables and payables. The payments may be denominated in either U.S. dollars or euros. The intrafirm sales may, in fact, be two-way if the German subsidiary is actually producing a form of the product not made in the United States but needed there.

One of the most difficult pricing decisions many multinational firms must make concerns the price at which they sell their products to their own subsidiaries and affiliates. These prices, called **transfer prices,** theoretically are equivalent to what the same product would cost if purchased on the open market. However, it is often impossible to find such a product on the open market; it may be unique to the firm and its product line. The result is a price that is set internally and may result in the subsidiary being more or less profitable. This, in turn, has impacts on taxes paid in host countries. The following Focus on Politics illustrates what happens when governments and firms do not agree on transfer prices. (See Chapter 14 for a more detailed discussion of transfer pricing.)

The foreign subsidiary may also be using techniques, machinery, or processes that are owned or patented by the parent firm and so must pay royalties and license fees. The cash flows are usually calculated as a percentage of the sales price in Germany. Many multinational firms also spread the overhead and management expenses incurred at the parent over their foreign affiliates and subsidiaries that are using the parent's administrative services.

There are also a number of financing cash flows between the U.S. parent and the German subsidiary. If the subsidiary is partially financed by loans extended by the parent, the subsidiary needs to make regular payments to the parent. If the German subsidiary is successful in its operations and generates a profit, then dividends will be paid back to the parent. If, at some point, the German subsidiary needs more capital than what it can retain from its own profits, it may need additional debt or equity capital. These obviously would add to the potential financial cash flow volume.

Focus On ⬇

POLITICS

Swiss Unit Pays Penalty for Transfer Pricing Abuse

Tax authorities believe that Nippon Roche K.K. failed to declare taxable income totaling ¥14 billion between 1992 and 1995, according to sources familiar with the case. The income in question was allegedly transferred to the company's Swiss parent firm, Roche Holding Ltd., through a practice known as transfer pricing, in which a subsidiary pays artificially inflated prices for goods purchased from its overseas parent to cut taxable income in the host country, they said.

The sources said Nippon Roche allegedly manipulated prices of raw materials for cancer drugs and other medicine purchased from

F. Hoffman-La Roche Ltd., a drug company under Roche Holding. Nippon Roche could be ordered to pay an additional ¥3.8. billion in taxes for failing to declare ¥4.5 billion in taxable income between 1989 and 1991. Under an agreement with Swiss tax authorities earlier this year, Japanese tax authorities settled on a figure of some ¥5.5 billion for the amount of undeclared income transferred to the parent firm to avoid double taxation.

Source: "Swiss Unit Faces Hefty Penalty for Tax Evasion," *Japan Times,* November 10, 1996.

The subsidiary, in turn, is dependent on its sales in Germany (euro revenues), France (euro revenues), and Switzerland (Swiss franc revenues) to generate the needed cash flows for paying everyone else. This "map" of operating and financing cash flows does not even attempt to describe the frequency of the various foreign currency cash flows, or to assign the responsibility for managing the currency risks. The management of cash flows in a larger multinational firm, one with possibly 10 or 20 subsidiaries, is obviously complex. The proper management of the cash flows is, however, critical to the success of the multinational business.

CASH MANAGEMENT

The structure of the firm dictates how cash flows and financial resources can be managed. The trend in the past decade has been for the increasing centralization of most financial and treasury operations. The centralized treasury often is responsible for both funding operations and cash flow management. The centralized treasury often may enjoy significant economies of scale, offering more services and expertise to the various units of the firm worldwide than the individual units themselves could support. However, regardless of whether the firm follows a centralized or decentralized approach, there are a number of operating structures that help the multinational firm manage its cash flows.

Netting

Figure 17.4 expands our firm to two European subsidiaries, one in Germany and one in France. The figure illustrates how many of the cash flows between units of a multinational firm are two-way and may result in unneeded transfer costs and transaction expenses. Coordination between units simply requires planning and budgeting of intrafirm cash flows so that two-way flows are "netted" against one another, with only one smaller cash flow as opposed to two having to be undertaken.

Netting can occur between each subsidiary and the parent, and between the subsidiaries themselves (it is often forgotten that many of the activities in a multinational firm occur between subsidiaries, and not just between individual subsidiaries and the parent). Netting is particularly helpful if the two-way flow is in two

FIGURE 17.4

Netting and Cash Pooling of Cash Flows in the Multinational Firm

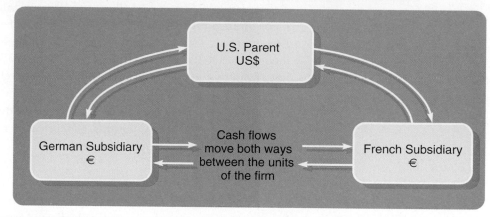

different currencies, as each would be suffering currency exchange charges for intrafirm transfers.

Cash Pooling

A large firm with a number of units operating both within an individual country and across countries may be able to economize on the amount of firm assets needed in cash if one central pool is used for **cash pooling.** With one pool of capital and up-to-date information on the cash flows in and out of the various units, the firm spends much less in terms of foregone interest on cash balances, which are held in safekeeping against unforeseen cash flow shortfalls.

For example, for the firm described in Figure 17.4, the parent and German and French subsidiaries may be able to consolidate all cash management and resources in one place—for example, New York (associated with the U.S. parent). One cash manager for all units would be in a better position for planning intercompany payments, including controlling the currency exposures of the individual units. A single large pool also may allow the firm to negotiate better financial service rates with banking institutions for cash-clearing purposes. In the event that the cash manager would need to be closer to the individual units (both proximity and time zone), the two European units could combine to run cash from one or the other for both.

Leads and Lags

The timing of payments between units of a multinational is somewhat flexible. Again, this allows the management of payments between the French and German subsidiaries and between the parent and the subsidiaries to be much more flexible, allowing the firm not only to position cash flows where they are needed most, but also to help manage currency risk. A foreign subsidiary that is expecting its local currency to fall in value relative to the U.S. dollar may try to speed up or **lead** its payments to the parent. Similarly, if the local currency is expected to rise versus the dollar, the subsidiary may want to wait, or **lag,** payments until exchange rates are more favorable.

Reinvoicing

Multinational firms with a variety of manufacturing and distribution subsidiaries scattered over a number of countries within a region may often find it more economical to have one office or subsidiary taking ownership of all invoices and payments between units.

For example, Figure 17.5 illustrates how our sample firm could be restructured to incorporate a **reinvoicing** center. The site for the reinvoicing center in this case is Luxembourg, a country that is known to have low taxes and few restrictions on income earned from international business operations. The Luxembourg subsidiary buys from one unit and sells to a second unit, therefore taking ownership of the goods and reinvoicing the sale to the next unit. Once ownership is taken, the sale/purchase can be redenominated in a different currency, netted against other payments, hedged against specific currency exposures, or repriced in accordance with potential tax benefits of the reinvoicing center's host country.

Internal Banks

Some multinational firms have found that their financial resources and needs are becoming either too large or too sophisticated for the financial services that are available in many of their local subsidiary markets. One solution to this has been the establishment of an **internal bank** within the firm. The internal bank actually buys and sells payables and receivables from the various units, which frees the units of the firm from struggling for continual working capital financing and lets them focus on their primary business activities.

All of these structures and management techniques often are combined in different ways to fit the needs of the individual multinational firm. Some techniques are encouraged or prohibited by laws and regulations (for example, many countries limit the ability to lead and lag payments), depending on the host country's government and stage of capital market liberalization. Multinational cash flow management requires flexibility in thinking—artistry in some cases—as much as technique on the part of managers.

FIGURE 17.5

Establishing a Reinvoicing Center in the Multinational Firm

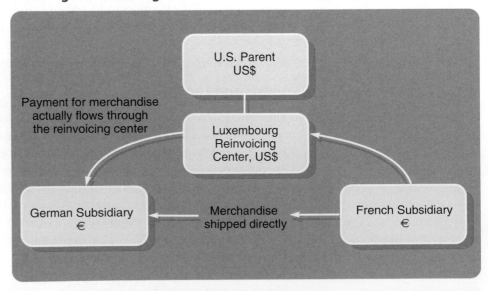

Foreign Exchange Exposure

Companies today know the risks of international operations. They are aware of the substantial risks to balance sheet values and annual earnings that interest rates and exchange rates may inflict on any firm at any time. Financial managers, international treasurers, and financial officers of all kinds are expected to protect the firm from such risks. Firms have, in varying degrees, three types of foreign currency exposure:

1. **Transaction exposure:** This is the risk associated with a contractual payment of foreign currency. For example, a U.S. firm that exports products to France will receive a guaranteed (by contract) payment in French francs in the future. Firms that buy or sell internationally have **transaction exposure** if any of the cash flows are denominated in foreign currency.
2. **Economic exposure:** This is the risk to the firm that its long-term cash flows will be affected, positively or negatively, by unexpected future exchange rate changes. Although many firms that consider themselves to be purely domestic may not realize it, all firms have some degree of **economic exposure.**
3. **Translation exposure:** This risk arises from the legal requirement that all firms consolidate their financial statements (balance sheets and income statements) of all worldwide operations annually. Therefore, any firm with operations outside its home country, operations that will be either earning foreign currency or valued in foreign currency, has **translation exposure.**

Transaction exposure and economic exposure are "true exposures" in the financial sense. This means they both present potential threats to the value of a firm's cash flows over time. The third exposure, translation, is a problem that arises from accounting, and will be discussed in Chapter 18. As illustrated by the Focus on Culture, hedging the currency risks of a multinational company is a controversial issue for management today.

TRANSACTION EXPOSURE

Transaction exposure is the most commonly observed type of exchange rate risk. Only two conditions are necessary for a transaction exposure to exist: (1) a cash flow that is denominated in a foreign currency and (2) the cash flow will occur at a future date. Any contract, agreement, purchase, or sale that is denominated in a foreign currency that will be settled in the future constitutes a transaction exposure.

The risk of a transaction exposure is that the exchange rate might change between the present date and the settlement date. The change may be for the better or for the worse. For example, suppose that an American firm signs a contract to purchase heavy rolled-steel pipe from a South Korean steel producer for 21,000,000 Korean won. The payment is due in 30 days upon delivery. The 30-day account payable, so typical of international trade and commerce, is a transaction exposure for the U.S. firm. If the spot exchange rate on the date the contract is signed is Won 700/$, the U.S. firm would expect to pay

$$\frac{\text{Won } 21,000,000}{\text{Won } 700/\$} = \$30,000$$

But the firm is not assured of what the exchange rate will be in 30 days. If the spot rate at the end of 30 days is Won 720/$, the U.S. firm would actually pay less. The

Focus On ↓

To Hedge or Not to Hedge?

If Coca-Cola (nyse: KO-news-people) wanted international business, it sure got it. But now that 75 percent of its operating profit is generated outside the United States, the company may want to rethink its wish—especially since the strength of the dollar is expected to come back to bite the company's profits. It's concerning indeed: J.P. Morgan analyst John Faucher downgraded the company to market perform and predicted the firm will likely lower fiscal guidance when it announces fourth-quarter earnings at the end of the month. Caroline Levy, an analyst at UBS, also recently lowered earnings-per-share expectations for 2002 and 2003, from $1.85 and $2.06 to $1.80 and $2.00, respectively.

"I see the stock languishing," Levy says. "There's not much downside, but I don't see any catalysts for upside until there are signs of a global economic recovery."

The timing couldn't be worse. Almost two years into his reign as Coca-Cola chief executive, Douglas Daft has, by most accounts, made decent progress improving the business. Now some Wall Street analysts accuse Daft of moving too slowly and some wonder how long he'll last in the position. Under Daft's direction, the company entered into an agreement with its bottling company, which had been a troubled relationship that hung over the stock. The company rolled out some new product lines including "Diet Coke with Lemon."

If it weren't for the little matter of currency, that might be true. Like most multinationals, Coca-Cola protects itself against foreign currency fluctuations by hedging, but the results lately have been mixed. For 1999, the company gained $87 million on its dealings, but for 2000 it lost $12 million. For 2002, Levy expects exposure to foreign currencies to shave off 5% of annual earnings (cutting earnings-per-share estimates by 5 cents), largely due to the Argentine peso and the South African rand. Further, Levy is concerned that if the Japanese yen remains depressed it could take a further bite out of 2003 earnings.

Sources: Betsy Schiffman, "Still Want to Teach the World to Sing?" January 16, 2002. Reprinted by permission of Forbes Magazine © 2004 Forbes, Inc., http://www.forbes.com.

payment would then be $29,167. If, however, the exchange rate changed in the opposite direction, for example to Won 650/$, the payment could just as easily increase to $32,308. This type of price risk, transaction exposure, is a major problem for international commerce.

TRANSACTION EXPOSURE MANAGEMENT

Management of transaction exposures usually is accomplished by either **natural hedging** or **contractual hedging.** Natural hedging is the term used to describe how a firm might arrange to have foreign currency cash flows coming in and going out at roughly the same times and same amounts. This is referred to as natural hedging because the management or hedging of the exposure is accomplished by matching offsetting foreign currency cash flows and, therefore, does not require the firm to undertake unusual financial contracts or activities to manage the exposure. For example, a Canadian firm that generates a significant portion of its total sales in U.S. dollars may acquire U.S. dollar debt. The U.S. dollar earnings from sales could then be used to service the dollar debt as needed. In this way, regardless of whether the C$/US$ exchange rate goes up or down, the firm would be naturally hedged against the movement. If the U.S. dollar went up in value against the Canadian dollar, the U.S. dollars needed for debt service would be generated automatically by the export sales to the United States. U.S. dollar inflows would match U.S. dollar cash outflows.

Contractual hedging is when the firm uses financial contracts to hedge the transaction exposure. The most common foreign currency contractual hedge is the **forward contract,** although other financial instruments and derivatives, such as currency futures and options, are also used. The forward contract (see Chapter 7) would allow the firm to be assured a fixed rate of exchange between the desired two currencies at the precise future date. The forward contract would also be for the exact amount of the exposure.

A **hedge** is an asset or a position whose value moves in the equal but opposite direction of the exposure. This means that if an exposure experienced a loss in value of $50, the hedge asset would offset the loss with a gain in value of $50. The total value of the position would not change. This would be termed a perfect hedge.

But perfect hedges are hard to find, and many people would not use them if they were readily available. Why? The presence of a perfect hedge eliminates all downside risk, but also eliminates all upside potential. Many businesses accept this two-sided risk as part of doing business. However, it is generally best to accept risk in the line of business, not in the cash-payment process of settling the business. As illustrated by the Focus on Ethics of Amazon.com, it is indeed possible to reap dramatic foreign currency gains.

RISK MANAGEMENT VERSUS SPECULATION

The distinction between managing currency cash flows and speculating with currency cash flows is sometimes lost among those responsible for the safekeeping of the firm's treasury. If the previous description of currency hedging is followed closely (the selection of assets or positions only to counteract potential losses on existing exposures), few problems should arise. Problems arise when currency positions or financial instruments are purchased (or sold) with the expectation that a specific currency movement will result in a profit, termed speculation.

There are a number of major multinational firms that treat their international treasury centers as "service centers," but rarely do they consider financial management a "profit center." One of the most visible examples of what can go wrong when currency speculation is undertaken for corporate profit occurred in Great Britain in 1991. A large British food conglomerate, Allied-Lyons, suffered losses of £158 million ($268 million) on currency speculation after members of its international treasury staff suffered losses on currency positions at the start of the Persian Gulf War and then doubled-up on their positions in the following weeks in an attempt to recover previous losses. They lost even more.[3]

TRANSACTION EXPOSURE CASE: LUFTHANSA

In January 1985, the German airline Lufthansa purchased 20 Boeing 737 jet aircraft. The jets would be delivered to Lufthansa in one year, in January 1986. Upon delivery of the aircraft, Lufthansa would pay Boeing (U.S.) $500 million. This constituted a huge transaction exposure for Lufthansa. (Note that the exposure falls on Lufthansa

Focus On ↓

ETHICS

The Role of Currency Gains in Amazon.com's Quest for Profits

Jeff Bezos, the CEO of Amazon.com, had promised that Amazon would turn a profit sometime in 2001. Although most analysts and investors did not believe him, he proved them wrong as Amazon.com reported a positive operating profit of $59 million and a net income of $5 million for the fourth quarter of 2001. He had indeed delivered on his promise.

But one issue primary to all investors is the quality of earnings. Although there are a number of technical components to earnings quality, one of the fundamental questions about reported earnings is whether they are sustainable. Did the earnings arise from operations, or from one-time asset sales, investment gains, or other nonsustainable transactions? In the case of Amazon.com, there was just one dimension to its quarterly profit return: the $5 million in net income was, at least in part, the result of a one-time foreign currency gain in the quarter of $16 million!

not Boeing. If the purchase agreement had been stated in deutschemarks, the transaction exposure would have been transferred to Boeing.)

The Exposure

The spot exchange rate in January 1985, when Lufthansa signed the agreement, was DM 3.2/$. The expected cost of the aircraft to Lufthansa was then

$$\$500,000,000 \times DM3.2/\$ = DM1,600,000,000.$$

Figure 17.6 illustrates how the expected total cost of $500 million changes to Lufthansa with the spot exchange rate. If the deutschemark continued to fall against the U.S. dollar as it had been doing for more than four years, the cost to Lufthansa of the Boeing jets could skyrocket easily to more than DM 2 billion.

But the most important word here is expected. There was no guarantee that the spot exchange rate in effect in January of the following year would be DM 3.2/$. The U.S. dollar had been appreciating against the deutschemark for more than four years at this point. Senior management of Lufthansa was afraid the appreciating dollar trend might continue. For example, if the U.S. dollar appreciated over the coming year from DM 3.2/$ to DM 3.4/$, the cost of the aircraft purchased from Boeing would rise by DM 100 million. Figure 17.7 shows how the DM/$ exchange rate had continued to trend upward for several years. By looking at graphics such as this, it was hard to believe that the U.S. dollar would do anything but continue to rise. It takes the truly brave to buck the trend.

But at the same time many senior members of Lufthansa's management believed that the U.S. dollar had risen as far as it would go. They argued that the dollar would fall over the coming year against the deutschemark (see Figure 17.7). If, for example, the spot rate fell to DM 3.0/$ by January 1986, Lufthansa would pay only DM 1,500 million, a savings of DM 100 million. This was true currency risk in every sense of the word.

FIGURE 17.6

Lufthansa's Transaction Exposure: Alternatives for Managing the Purchase of $500 Million in Boeing 737s

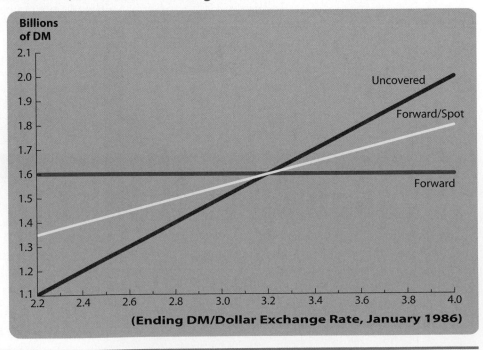

FIGURE 17.7

The DM/$ Spot Exchange Rate: Where Was It Headed?

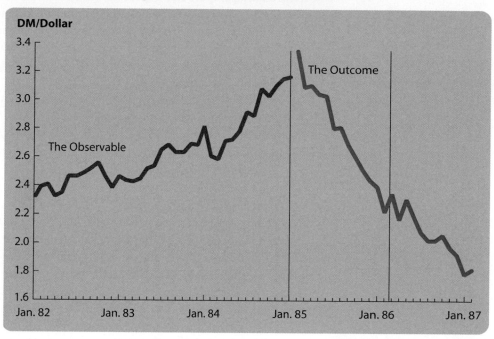

The Management Strategy

After much debate, Lufthansa's management decided to use forward contracts to hedge one half of the $500 million exposure. This was obviously a compromise. First, because the exposure was a single large foreign currency payment, to occur one time only, natural hedging was not a realistic alternative. Second, although management believed the dollar would fall, the risk was too large to ignore. It was thought that by covering one half of the exposure, Lufthansa would be protected against the U.S. dollar appreciating, yet still allow Lufthansa some opportunity to benefit from a fall in the dollar. Lufthansa signed a one-year forward contract (sold $250 million forward) at a forward rate of DM 3.2/$. The remaining $250 million owed Boeing was left unhedged.

The Outcome

By January 1986, the U.S. dollar not only fell, it plummeted versus the deutschemark. The spot rate fell from DM 3.2/$ in January 1985 to DM 2.3/$ in January 1986. Lufthansa had therefore benefited from leaving half the transaction exposure uncovered. But this meant that the half that was covered with forward contracts "cost" the firm DM 225 million!

The total cost to Lufthansa of delivering $250 million at the forward rate of DM 3.2/$ and $250 million at the ending spot rate of DM 2.3/$ was

$$[\$250{,}000{,}000 \times DM3.2/\$] + [\$250{,}000{,}000 \times DM2.3/\$] = DM\ 1{,}375{,}000{,}000.$$

Although this was DM 225 million less than the expected purchase price when the contract was signed in January 1985, Lufthansa's management was heavily criticized for covering any of the exposure. If the entire transaction exposure had been left uncovered, the final cost would have been only DM 1,150 million. The critics, of course, had perfect hindsight.

CURRENCY RISK SHARING

Firms that import and export on a continuing basis have constant transaction exposures. If a firm is interested in maintaining a good business relationship with one of its suppliers, it must work with that supplier to assure it that it will not force all currency risk or exposure off on the other party on a continual basis. Exchange rate movements are inherently random; therefore some type of risk-sharing arrangement may prove useful.

If Ford (U.S.) imports automotive parts from Mazda (Japan) every month, year after year, major swings in exchange rates can benefit one party at the expense of the other. One solution would be for Ford and Mazda to agree that all purchases by Ford will be made in Japanese yen as long as the spot rate on the payment date is between ¥120/$ and ¥130/$. If the exchange rate is between these values on the payment dates, Ford agrees to accept whatever transaction exposure exists (because it is paying in a foreign currency). If, however, the exchange rate falls outside of this range on the payment date, Ford and Mazda will "share" the difference. If the spot rate on settlement date is ¥110/$, the Japanese yen would have appreciated versus the dollar, causing Ford's costs of purchasing automotive parts to rise. Since this rate falls outside the contractual range, Mazda would agree to accept a total payment in Japanese yen that would result from a "shared" difference of ¥10. Thus, Ford's total payment in Japanese yen would be calculated using an exchange rate of ¥115/$.

Risk-sharing agreements like these have been in use for nearly 50 years on world markets. They became something of a rarity during the 1950s and 1960s, when exchange rates were relatively stable (under the Bretton Woods Agreement). But with the return to floating exchange rates in the 1970s, firms with long-term customer-supplier relationships across borders returned to some old ways of keeping old friends. And sometimes old ways work very well.

Economic Exposure

Economic exposure, also called operating exposure, is the change in the value of a firm arising from unexpected changes in exchange rates. Economic exposure emphasizes that there is a limit to a firm's ability to predict either cash flows or exchange rate changes in the medium to long term. All firms, either directly or indirectly, have economic exposure.

It is customary to think of only firms that actively trade internationally as having any type of currency exposure (such as Lufthansa described previously). But actually all firms that operate in economies affected by international financial events, such as exchange rate changes, are affected. A barber in Ottumwa, Iowa, seemingly isolated from exchange rate chaos, still is affected when the dollar rises as it did in the early 1980s. If U.S. products become increasingly expensive to foreign buyers, American manufacturers such as John Deere & Co. in Iowa are forced to cut back production and lay off workers, and businesses of all types decline—even the business of barbers. The impacts are real, and they affect all firms, domestic and international alike.

How exposed is an individual firm in terms of economic exposure? It is impossible to say. Measuring economic exposure is subjective, and for the most part it is dependent on the degree of internationalization present in the firm's cost and revenue structure, as well as potential changes over the long run. But simply because it is difficult to measure does not mean that management cannot take some steps to prepare the firm for the unexpected.

Companies are establishing manufacturing operations in countries around the world. As part of its global strategy, Corning Incorporated aims to be insulated against market fluctuations in any one particular country. This is a Japanese worker at the Corning Japan K.K. plant in Shizuoka, Japan.

COURTESY OF CORNING, INC.

IMPACT OF ECONOMIC EXPOSURE

The impacts of economic exposure are as diverse as are firms in their international structure. Take the case of a U.S. corporation with a successful British subsidiary. The British subsidiary manufactured and then distributed the firm's products in Great Britain, Germany, and France. The profits of the British subsidiary are paid out annually to the American parent corporation. What would be the impact on the profitability of the British subsidiary and the entire U.S. firm if the British pound suddenly fell in value against all other major currencies (as it did in September and October 1992)?

If the British firm had been facing competition in Germany, France, and its own home market from firms from those other two continental countries, it would now be more competitive. If the British pound is cheaper, so are the products sold internationally by British-based firms. The British subsidiary of the American firm would, in all likelihood, see rising profits from increased sales.

But what of the value of the British subsidiary to the U.S. parent corporations? The same fall in the British pound that allowed the British subsidiary to gain profits would also result in substantially fewer U.S. dollars when the British pound earnings are converted to U.S. dollars at the end of the year. It seems that it is nearly impossible to win in this situation. Actually, from the perspective of economic exposure management, the fact that the firm's total value, subsidiary and parent together, is roughly a wash as a result of the exchange rate change is desirable. Sound financial management assumes that a firm will profit and bear risk in its line of business, not in the process of settling payments on business already completed.

ECONOMIC EXPOSURE MANAGEMENT

Management of economic exposure is being prepared for the unexpected. A firm such as Hewlett-Packard (HP), which is highly dependent on its ability to remain cost competitive in markets both at home and abroad, may choose to take actions now that would allow it to passively withstand any sudden unexpected rise of the dollar. This could be accomplished through diversification: diversification of operations and diversification of financing.

Diversification of operations would allow the firm to be desensitized to the impacts of any one pair of exchange rate changes. For example, a multinational firm such as Hewlett-Packard may produce the same product in manufacturing facilities in Singapore, the United States, Puerto Rico, and Europe. If a sudden and prolonged rise in the dollar made production in the United States prohibitively expensive and uncompetitive, HP is already positioned to shift production to a relatively cheaper currency environment. Although firms rarely diversify production location for the sole purpose of currency diversification, it is a substantial additional benefit from such global expansion.

Diversification of financing serves to hedge economic exposure much in the same way as it did with transaction exposures. A firm with debt denominated in many different currencies is sensitive to many different interest rates. If one country or currency experiences rapidly rising inflation rates and interest rates, a firm with diversified debt will not be subject to the full impact of such movements. Purely domestic firms, however, are actually somewhat captive to the local conditions and are unable to ride out such interest rate storms as easily.

It should be noted that, in both cases, diversification is a passive solution to the exposure problem. This means that without knowing when or where or what the problem may be, the firm that simply spreads its operations and financial structure out over a variety of countries and currencies is prepared.

Countertrade

General Motors exchanged automobiles for a trainload of strawberries. Control Data swapped a computer for a package of Polish furniture, Hungarian carpet backing, and Russian greeting cards. Uzbekistan, one of the new countries of the former Soviet Union, is offering crude venom of vipers, toads, scorpions, black widows, and tarantulas, as well as growth-controlling substances from snakes and lizards, in countertrade.[4] These are all examples of countertrade activities carried out around the world. As noted in Focus on Politics, countertrade is growing in volume as well as in complexity.

A DEFINITION OF COUNTERTRADE

Countertrade is a sale that encompasses more than an exchange of goods, services, or ideas for money. In the international market, countertrade transactions "are those transactions that have as a basic characteristic a linkage, legal or otherwise, between exports and imports of goods or services in addition to, or in place of, financial settlements."[5] Historically, countertrade was mainly conducted in the form of **barter,** which is a direct exchange of goods of approximately equal value between parties, with no money involved. Such transactions were the very essence of business at times during which no money—that is, no common medium of exchange—existed or was available. Over time, money emerged as a convenient medium that unlinked transactions from individual parties and their joint timing and therefore permitted greater flexibility in trading activities. Repeatedly, however, we can see returns to the barter system as a result of environmental circumstances. For example, because of the tight financial constraints of both students and the institution, Georgetown University during its initial years of operation

Focus On ⬇

The Booming Business of Countertrade

As the global economy continues its downward spiral, many *Fortune 500* companies are turning to barter or countertrade arrangements to clear their warehouses of unsold stock, whether it be roller blades, sauerkraut, boxer shorts, or corporate jets.

Barter allows companies to become more flexible and quicker in the face of international competition. Rather than selling old inventory for only 20 cents on the dollar in cash, firms can gain 80 cents or more by bartering. Big deals are increasingly found in corporate barter. In fact, in 2001, barter companies traded $7.9 billion in goods and services worldwide. According to the International Reciprocal Trade Association (IRTA), the global recession will boost that figure by more than 20 percent in 2002, as companies dump stock surpluses and close-outs.

Barter companies deal in combination of cash and trade credits, which companies can exchange for business services, such as air travel and advertising. The deals have become increasingly complex and geographically dispersed, as the following examples illustrate:

- IBM's Mexico subsidiary exchanged 2,600 outmoded computers worth $1.7 million for $1 million worth of Volkswagen vehicles, plus $250,000 in trucking services and a quarter million worth of express-mail shipments.
- A cruise line used a barter company to trade $1 million worth of empty cabins for $1 million in trade credits. The cruise company used the credits, along with $3 million in cash, for a $4 million advertising campaign.
- A dental-care manufacturer exchanged 200,000 extra toothbrushes packaged in bulk for advertising worth twice the amount of the toothbrushes. A barter company repackaged the toothbrushes to be sold as a travel kit through a regional chain store.
- Volvo Cars of North America sold autos to the Siberian police force when it had no currency for the deal. A barter company accepted oil as payment for the vehicles, and used the gains from its sale to provide Volvo with advertising credits equal to the value of the cars.

Sources: "Juicy Stuff," *The Economist,* February 7, 2002; Paula L. Green, "The Booming Barter Business," *Journal of Commerce* (April 1, 1997), 1A, 5A.

after 1789 charged part of its tuition in foodstuffs and required students to participate in the construction of university buildings. During periods of high inflation in Europe in the 1920s, goods such as bread, meat, and gold were seen as much more useful and secure than paper money, which decreased in real value by the minute. In the late 1940s, American cigarettes were an acceptable medium of exchange in most European countries, much more so than any particular currency except for the dollar.

Countertrade transactions have therefore always arisen when economic circumstances made it more acceptable to exchange goods directly rather than to use money as an intermediary. Conditions that encourage such business activities are lack of money, lack of value of or faith in money, lack of acceptability of money as an exchange medium, or greater ease of transaction by using goods.

Increasingly, countries and companies are deciding that, sometimes, countertrade transactions are more beneficial to them than transactions based on financial exchange alone. One reason is that the world debt crisis has made ordinary trade financing very risky. Many countries, particularly in the developing world, simply cannot obtain the trade credit or financial assistance necessary to pay for desired imports. Heavily indebted countries, faced with the possibility of not being able to afford imports at all, hasten to use countertrade to maintain at least some product inflow. However, it should be recognized that countertrade does not reduce commercial risk. Countertrade transactions will therefore be encouraged by stability and economic progress. Research has shown that countertrade appears to increase with a country's creditworthiness, since good credit encourages traders to participate in unconventional trading practices.[6]

The use of countertrade permits the covert reduction of prices and therefore allows the circumvention of price and exchange controls.[7] Particularly in commodity markets with cartel arrangements, such as oil or agriculture, this benefit may be very useful to a producer. For example, by using oil as a countertraded product for industrial equipment, a surreptitious discount (by using a higher price for the acquired products) may expand market share.

Another reason for the increase in countertrade is that many countries are again responding favorably to the notion of bilateralism. Thinking along the lines of "you scratch my back and I'll scratch yours," they prefer to exchange goods with countries that are their major business partners.

Countertrade is also often viewed by firms and nations alike as an excellent mechanism to gain entry into new markets. When a producer believes that marketing is not its strong suit, the producer often hopes that the party receiving the goods will serve as a new distributor, opening up new international marketing channels and ultimately expanding the original market. For example, countertrade transactions agreed to between the Japanese firm NEC and the government of Egypt have resulted in a major increase of Japanese tourism to Egypt.[8]

Because countertrade is highly sought after in many large markets such as China, the former Eastern bloc countries, as well as South America, engaging in such transactions can provide major growth opportunities for firms. In increasingly competitive world markets, countertrade can be a good way to attract new buyers. By providing countertrade services, the seller is in effect differentiating its product from those of its competitors.[9]

Countertrade also can provide stability for long-term sales. For example, if a firm is tied to a countertrade agreement, it will need to source the product from a particular supplier, whether or not it wants to do so. This stability is often valued very highly because it eliminates, or at least reduces, vast swings in demand and thus allows for better planning. Countertrade, therefore, can serve as a major mechanism to shift risk from the producer to another party. In that sense, one can argue that countertrade offers a substitute for missing forward markets.[10] Finally, under certain conditions, countertrade can ensure the quality of an international transaction. In instances where the seller of technology is paid in output produced by the technology delivered, the seller's revenue depends on the success of the technology transfer and maintenance services in production. Therefore, the seller is more likely to be concerned about providing services, maintenance, and general technology transfer.[11]

In spite of all the apparent benefits of countertrade, there are strong economic arguments against the activity. The arguments are based mainly on efficiency grounds. As Samuelson stated, "Instead of there being a double coincidence of wants, there is likely to be a want of coincidence; so that, unless a hungry tailor happens to find an undraped farmer, who has both food and a desire for a pair of pants, neither can make a trade."[12] Clearly, countertrade ensures that instead of balances being settled on a multilateral basis, with surpluses from one country being balanced by deficits with another, accounts must now be settled on a country-by-country or even transaction-by-transaction basis. Trade then results only from the ability of two parties or countries to purchase specified goods from one another rather than from competition. As a result, uncompetitive goods may be traded. In consequence, the ability of countries and their industries to adjust structurally to more efficient production may be restricted. Countertrade can therefore be seen as eroding the quality and efficiency of production and as lowering world consumption.

These economic arguments notwithstanding, however, countries and companies increasingly see countertrade as an alternative that may be flawed but worthwhile to undertake, since some trade is preferable to no trade. As the accompanying map shows, both industrialized and developing countries exchange a wide variety of goods via countertrade. And as Table 17.3 shows, countertrade knows few limits across goods.

TABLE 17.3   A Sample of Barter Agreements

COUNTRY A	COUNTRY B	EXPORTED COMMODITY A	EXPORTED COMMODITY B
Hungary	Ukraine	• Foodstuffs • Canned foods • Pharmaceuticals	• Timber
Austria	Ukraine	• Power station emissions control equipment	• 800 megakilowatts/year for 15 years
U.S. (Chrysler)	Jamaica	• 200 pickup trucks	• Equivalent value in iron ore
Ukraine	Czech Republic	• Iron ore	• Mining equipment
U.S. (Pierre Cardin)	China	• Technical advice	• Silks and cashmeres
U.K. (Raleigh Bicycle)	CIS	• Training CIS scientists in mountain bike production	• Titanium for 30,000 bike frames per year
Indonesia	Uzbekistan	• Indian tea • Vietnamese rice • Miscellaneous Indonesian products	• 50,000 tons of cotton/year for three years
Zaire	Italy	• Scrap iron	• 12 locomotives
China	Russia	• 212 railway trucks of mango juice	• Passenger jet
Morocco	Romania	• Citrus products	• Several large ports/small harbors

Sources: American Countertrade Association, December 1996; Aspy P. Palia and Oded Shenkar, "Countertrade Practices in China." *Industrial Marketing Management*, 1991: 58. http://www.i-trade.com

Preferred Items for Export in Countertrade Transactions

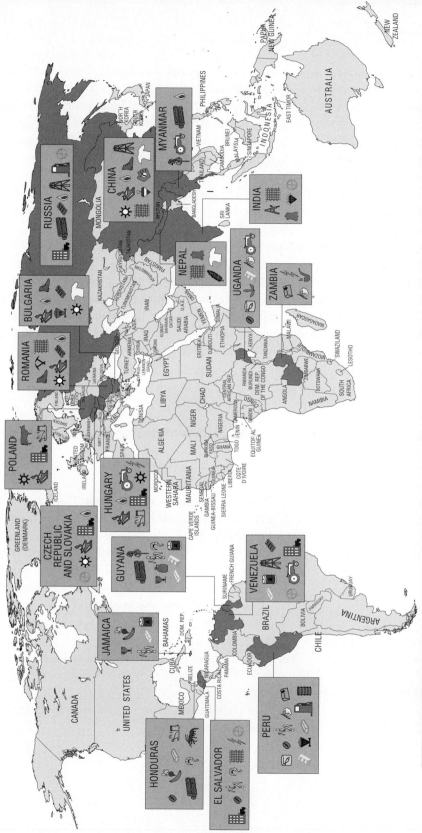

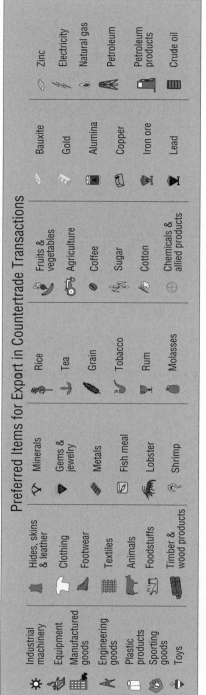

Source: http://www.cia.gov/cia/publications/factbook/fields/2049.html

MAP

Summary

Multinational financial management is both complex and critical to the multinational firm. Beginning with the very objective of management, stockholder wealth maximization or corporate wealth maximization, all traditional functional areas of financial management are affected by the internationalization of the firm. Capital budgeting, firm financing, capital structure, and working capital and cash flow management, all traditional functions, are made more difficult by business activities that cross borders and oceans, not to mention currencies and markets.

In addition to the traditional areas of financial management, international financial management must deal with the three types of currency exposure: (1) transaction exposure; (2) economic exposure; and (3) translation exposure. Each type of currency risk confronts a firm with serious choices regarding its exposure analysis and its degree of willingness to manage the inherent risks.

This chapter described not only the basic types of risk, but also outlined a number of the basic strategies employed in the management of the exposures. Some of the solutions available today have only arisen with the development of new types of international financial markets and instruments, such as the currency swap. Others, such as currency risk-sharing agreements, are as old as exchange rates themselves.

Questions for Discussion

1. What are the pros and cons of the two different theories of wealth maximization?
2. Why is it important to identify the cash flows of a foreign investment from the perspective of the parent rather than from just the project?
3. Is currency risk unique to international firms? Is currency risk good or bad for the potential profitability of the multinational?
4. Which type of currency risk is the least important to the multinational firm? Should resources be spent to manage this risk?
5. Are firms with no direct international business (imports and exports) subject to economic exposure?
6. What would you have recommended that Lufthansa do to manage its transaction exposure if you had been the airline's chief financial officer in January 1985?
7. Why do you think Lufthansa and Boeing did not use some form of "currency risk sharing" in their 1985–1986 transaction?
8. Which type of firm do you believe is more "naturally hedged" against exchange rate exposure, the purely domestic firm (the barber) or the multinational firm (subsidiaries all over the world)?
9. What are some of the causes for the resurgence of countertrade?
10. What forms of countertrade exist and how do they differ? What are their relative advantages and drawbacks?
11. How consistent is countertrade with the international trade framework?

Internet Exercises

1. Although major currencies like the U.S. dollar and the Japanese yen dominate the headlines, there are nearly as many currencies as countries in the world. Many of these currencies are traded in extremely thin and highly regulated markets, making their convertibility suspect. Finding quotations for these currencies is sometimes very difficult. Using some of the Web pages listed below, see how many African currency quotes you can find. See Emerging Markets at http://emgmkts.com/.

2. Use the *Economist*'s Web site to find the latest version of the Big Max Index of Currency over- and under-valuation. See http://www.economist.com.

3. The single unobservable variable in currency option pricing is the volatility, since volatility inputs are expected standard deviation of the daily spot rate for the coming period of the option's maturity. Using the following Web sites, pick one currency volatility and research how its value has changed in recent periods over historical periods. See Philadelphia Stock Exchange at http://www.phlx.com/.

4. Using the following major periodicals as starting points, find a current example of a firm with a substantial operating exposure problem. To aid in your search, you might focus on businesses having major operations in countries with recent currency crises, either through devaluation or major home currency appreciation. Sources are *Financial Times* at http://www.ft.com/; *The Economist* at http://www.economist.com/; *Wall Street Journal* at http://www.wsj.com/.

5. In the World Trade Organization's Agreement on Government Procurement, how are *offsets* defined and what stance is taken toward them (refer to the government procurement page on the Web site http://www. wto.org)?

Take a Stand

Many multinational companies believe that *hedging* is really nothing other than formalized *speculation*. Since many firms use the same complex financial instruments and derivatives that arbitragers and speculators use, they argue that companies are endangering their own future by allowing individuals within the organization to gamble with the company's own funds—for profit. And the profit only arises from the ability of the individual to "beat the market."

For Discussion

1. Multinationals should accept foreign currency risks as part of doing business internationally, and therefore should not spend precious resources and take unnecessary risks related to the use of financial derivatives for hedging. The cure is more harmful than the disease.

2. Multinationals must protect all of their stakeholders—stockholders, creditors, employees, and community—from the risks associated with conducting business in a global marketplace using currencies that bounce up and down in value. Although some hedging techniques may introduce new types of risks for the firm, it is in the entire firm's interest that it hedge significant cash flow risks and add certainty to the conduct of the firm's total business.

Corporate Governance, Accounting, and Taxation

Learning Objectives

- To explore the purpose and structure of corporate governance as it is practiced globally

- To examine the failures in corporate governance in recent years, and how authorities are responding to these changes

- To understand how accounting practices differ across countries, and how these differences may alter the competitiveness of firms in international markets

- To isolate which accounting practices are likely to constitute much of the competitiveness debate in the coming decade

- To examine the primary differences in international taxation across countries, and in turn how governments deal with both domestic and foreign firms operating in their markets

- To understand the problems faced by many U.S.-based multinational firms in paying taxes both in foreign countries and in the United States

Corporate Inversion and Stanley Works

This strategic initiative will strengthen our company over the long-term. An important portion of our revenues and earnings are derived from outside the United States, where nearly 50% of our people reside. Moreover, an increasing proportion of our materials are being purchased from global sources. This change will create greater operational flexibility, better position us to manage international cash flows and help us to deal with our complex international tax structure. As a result, our competitiveness, one of the three legs of our vision to become a Great Brand, will be enhanced. The business, regulatory and tax environments in Bermuda are expected to create considerable value for share owners. In addition to operational flexibility, improved worldwide cash management and competitive advantages, the new corporate structure will enhance our ability to access international capital markets, which is favorable for organic growth, future strategic alliances and acquisitions. Finally, enhanced flexibility to manage worldwide tax liabilities should reduce our global effective tax rate from its current 32% to within the range of 23%–25%.

Stanley Works, Form 14A, Securities and Exchange Commission, February 8, 2002

Over and over again courts have said there is nothing sinister in so arranging one's affairs as to keep taxes as low as possible. Everybody does so, rich and poor, and all do right, for nobody owes any public duty to pay more than the law demands: taxes are enforced extractions, not voluntary contributions. To demand more in the name of morals is mere cant.

Judge Learned Hand, Commissioner v. Newman, 159 F.2d 848 (CA-2, 1947)

A 37-year employee of Stanley, machinist Stan Piorkowski, said the deal "is going to cost me my retirement." He holds 3,500 shares of Stanley and said taxes on capital gains resulting from the move would cost him between $30,000 and $50,000.

"Stanley Approves Tax Move to Bermuda," *Washington Post,* May 10, 2002

On February 8, 2002, Stanley Works (USA) announced that it would enter into a **corporate inversion**, whereby the company would reincorporate itself as a Bermuda-based corporation. This was termed an **outbound inversion**, as the reincorporation was to move the company's incorporation out of the United States to a foreign country. Currently a U.S.-based corporation with head offices in New Britain, Connecticut, Stanley would make all U.S. operations a wholly owned subsidiary of a new parent company based in Bermuda—Stanley Tools, Ltd. Corporate headquarters, in fact all company offices and operational centers, would remain in Connecticut. The reasoning was simple: Stanley expected to save close to $30 million annually in corporate income taxes by changing its citizenship. On the date of the announcement the market value of Stanley increased by $199 million.

However, the announcement was met with heated opposition from employees, stockholders, and local, state, and federal authorities. After months of controversy, Stanley found itself a lightning rod for public debate on the responsibilities of a corporate citizen and the ethics of tax reduction and patriotism. Many regulators were now accusing the company of treaty shopping. In the end, the company gave up. It would remain a U.S.-based company, with all of its tax rights and responsibilities unchanged.

The structure and conduct of corporate governance, and the methods used in the measurement of company operations, accounting, principles, and practices, vary dramatically across countries. Corporate governance, as a result of the recent failures of Enron, Tyco, Worldcom, and Health South to name but a few, has raised what was once an obscure topic of interest to regulators only to the front page of the daily paper. Key elements of corporate governance, the transparency of the firm's operations, and financial results has stoked significant debate about both the accounting and tax practices of global companies. This chapter provides an overview of these issues and also presents current trends in both corporate practices and international regulatory approaches.

Taxation and accounting are fundamentally related. The principles by which a firm measures its sales and expenses, its assets and liabilities, all go into the formulation of profits, which are subject to taxation. The tax policies of more and more governments, in conjunction with accounting principles, are also becoming increasingly similar. Many of the tax issues of specific interest to officials, such as the avoidance of taxes in high-tax countries or the shielding of income from taxation by holding profits in so-called *tax havens*, are slowly being eliminated by increasing cooperation between governments. Like the old expression "death and taxes," they are today, more than ever, inevitable. Although the average business manager cannot be expected to have a detailed understanding (or recall) of the multitudes of tax laws and accounting principles across countries, a basic understanding of many of these issues aids in the understanding of how firms may structure and operate their businesses globally with the perpetual commitment to create value. We begin with the debate raging over corporate governance of the modern corporation.

Corporate Governance

The relationship among stakeholders used to determine and control the strategic direction and performance of an organization is termed *corporate governance*. The corporate governance of the organization is therefore the way in which order and process is established to ensure that decisions are made and interests are represented properly—for all stakeholders.

Although the governance structure of any company—domestic, international, or multinational—is fundamental to its very existence, this subject has become the lightning rod of political and business debate in the past few years as failures in governance in a variety of forms have led to corporate fraud and failure. Abuses and failures in corporate governance have dominated global business news in recent years. Beginning with the accounting fraud and questionable ethics of business conduct at Enron, culminating in its bankruptcy in the fall of 2001, to the retirement pay package of Richard Grasso, the chairman of the New York Stock Exchange, in September 2003, failures in corporate governance have raised issues about the ethics and culture of the conduct of business.

THE GOAL OF CORPORATE GOVERNANCE

The single overriding objective of corporate governance is the optimization over time of the returns to shareholders. In order to achieve this, good governance practices should focus the attention of the board of directors of the corporation on this objective by developing and implementing a strategy for the corporation that ensures corporate growth and improvement in the value of the corporation's equity. At the same time, it should ensure an effective relationship with stakeholders.[1]

The most widely accepted statement of good corporate governance practices are those established by the Organization for Economic Cooperation and Development (OECD) in 1999:[2]

- **The Rights of Shareholders:** The corporate governance framework should protect shareholders' rights.
- **The Equitable Treatment of Shareholders:** The corporate governance framework should ensure the equitable treatment of all shareholders, including minority and foreign shareholders. All shareholders should have the opportunity to obtain effective redress for violation of their rights.
- **The Role of Stakeholders in Corporate Governance:** The corporate governance framework should recognize the rights of stakeholders as established by law and encourage active cooperation between corporations and stakeholders in creating wealth, jobs, and the sustainability of financially sound enterprises.
- **Disclosure and Transparency:** The corporate governance framework should ensure that timely and accurate disclosure is made on all material matters regarding the corporation, including the financial situation, performance, ownership, and governance of the company.
- **The Responsibilities of the Board:** The corporate governance framework should ensure the strategic guidance of the company, the effective monitoring of management by the board, and the board's accountability to the company and the shareholders.

These principles obviously focus on several key areas—shareholder rights and roles, disclosure and transparency, and the responsibilities of boards—which we will discuss in more detail below.

THE STRUCTURE OF CORPORATE GOVERNANCE

Our first challenge is to try and capture what people mean when they use the expression "corporate governance." Figure 18.1 provides an overview of the various parties and their responsibilities associated with the governance of the modern corporation. The modern corporation is a complex organism living in a complex environment. Its actions and behaviors are directed and controlled by both internal forces and external forces.

The **internal forces**, the officers of the corporation (such as the Chief Executive Officer, or CEO) and the Board of Directors of the corporation (including the Chairman of the Board), are those directly responsible for determining both the strategic direction and the execution of the company's future. But they are not acting within a vacuum; they are subject to the constant prying eyes of the **external forces** in the marketplace that question the validity and soundness of their decisions and performance. These include the equity markets in which the shares are traded, the analysts who critique their investment prospects, the creditors and credit agencies who lend them money, the auditors who testify to the fairness of their reporting, and the multitude of regulators who oversee their actions in order to protect the public's investment.

The Board of Directors

The legal body that is accountable for the governance of the corporation is its Board of Directors. The board is composed of both employees of the organization (inside members) and senior and influential nonemployees (outside members). Areas of

FIGURE 18.1

The Structure of Corporate Governance

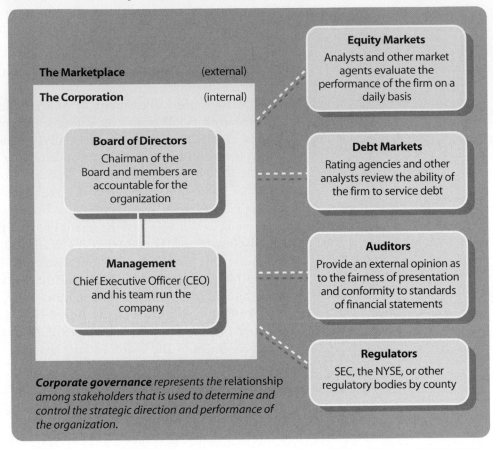

The Marketplace (external)

The Corporation (internal)

Board of Directors
Chairman of the Board and members are accountable for the organization

Management
Chief Executive Officer (CEO) and his team run the company

Equity Markets
Analysts and other market agents evaluate the performance of the firm on a daily basis

Debt Markets
Rating agencies and other analysts review the ability of the firm to service debt

Auditors
Provide an external opinion as to the fairness of presentation and conformity to standards of financial statements

Regulators
SEC, the NYSE, or other regulatory bodies by county

Corporate governance represents the relationship among stakeholders that is used to determine and control the strategic direction and performance of the organization.

debate surrounding boards include the following: 1) the proper balance between inside and outside members; 2) the means by which board members are compensated for their service; and 3) the actual ability of a board to adequately monitor and manage a corporation when board members are spending sometimes fewer than five days a year in board activities. Outside members, very often the current or retired chief executives of other major companies, may bring with them a healthy sense of distance and impartiality, which, although refreshing, may also result in limited understanding of the true issues and events within the company.

Officers and Management

The senior officers of the corporation, the Chief Executive Officer (CEO), the Chief Financial Officer (CFO), and the Chief Operating Officer (COO), are not only the most knowledgeable about the business, but are also the creators and directors of its strategic and operational direction. The management of the firm is, according to theory, acting as a contractor—as an *agent*—of stockholders to pursue value creation. They are motivated by salary, bonuses, and stock options (positively) or by the risk of losing their jobs (negatively). They may, however, have biases of self-enrichment or personal agendas that the board and other corporate stakeholders must oversee and police. Interestingly enough, in more than 80 percent of the companies in the Fortune

500, the CEO is also the Chairman of the Board. This is, in the opinion of many, a conflict of interest and not in the best interest of the company and its shareholders.

Equity Markets

The publicly traded company, regardless of country of residence, is highly susceptible to the changing opinion of the marketplace. The equity markets themselves, whether they be the New York Stock Exchange, London Stock Exchange, or Mexico City Bolsa, should mirror the market's constant reflections on the promise and performance of the individual company. The analysts are those self-described experts employed by the many investment banking firms who also trade in these company shares. They are expected (sometimes naively) to evaluate the strategies, plans for execution of the strategies, and financial performance of the firms on a real-time basis. Analysts depend on the financial statements and other public disclosures of the firm for their information.

Debt Markets

Although the debt markets (banks that provide loans and various forms of securitized debt like corporate bonds) are not specifically interested in building shareholder value, they are indeed interested in the financial health of the company. Their interest, specifically, is in the company's ability to repay its debt in a timely and efficient manner. These markets, like the equity markets, must rely on the financial statements and other disclosures (public and private in this case) of the companies with which they work.

Auditors

Auditors are responsible for providing an external professional opinion as to the fairness and accuracy of corporate financial statements. In this process, they attempt to determine whether the firm's financial records and practices follow what in the United States is termed **generally accepted accounting principles** in regard to accounting procedures. But auditors are hired by the firms they are auditing, leading to a rather unique practice of policing their employers. The additional difficulty that has arisen in recent years is that the major accounting firms pursued the development of large consulting practices, often leading to a conflict of interest. An auditor not giving a clean bill of health to a client could not expect to gain many lucrative consulting contracts from that same firm in the near future.

Regulators

Publicly traded firms in the United States are subject to the regulatory oversight of both governmental organizations and nongovernmental organizations. The Securities and Exchange Commission (SEC) is a careful watchdog of the publicly traded equity markets, both in the behavior of the companies themselves and of the various investors participating in those markets. The SEC and other authorities like it outside of the United States require a regular and orderly disclosure process of corporate performance in order that all investors may evaluate the company's investment value with adequate, accurate, and fairly distributed information. This regulatory oversight is often focused on when and what information is released by the company, to whom.

A publicly traded firm in the United States is also subject to the rules and regulations of the exchange in which they are traded (New York Stock Exchange, American Stock Exchange, and NASDAQ are the largest). These organizations, typically categorized as "self-regulatory" in nature, construct and enforce standards of conduct for both their member companies and themselves in the practice of share trading.

Unfortunately, as the recent case of Richard Grasso and his retirement package of $148 million illustrated, it often appears that the "fox is in charge of the henhouse."

COMPARATIVE CORPORATE GOVERNANCE

The origins of the need for a corporate governance process arise from the separation of ownership from management, and from the views (which vary by culture) of who the stakeholders are and of what significance they hold. As a result, corporate governance practices differ across countries, economies, and cultures. As described in Table 18.1, though, the various corporate governance structures may be classified by regime, the regimes in turn reflect the evolution of business ownership and direction within the countries over time.

Market-based regimes, like that of the United States and the United Kingdom, are characterized by relatively efficient capital markets in which the ownership of publicly traded companies is widely dispersed. **Family-based systems**, like those in many of the emerging markets, Asian markets, and Latin American markets, not only started with strong concentrations of family ownership (as opposed to partnerships or small investment groups, which are not family-based), but have continued to be largely controlled by families even after going public. **Bank-based** and **government-based regimes** are those in which government ownership of property and industry has been the constant force over time, resulting in only marginal "public ownership" of enterprise, and even then, subject to significant restrictions on business practices.

These regimes are therefore a function of at least three major factors in the evolution of global corporate governance principles and practices: financial market development, the degree of separation between management and ownership, and the concept of disclosure and transparency.

Financial Market Development

The depth and breadth of capital markets is critical to the evolution of corporate governance practices. Country markets that have had relatively slow growth, as in the emerging markets, or have industrialized rapidly, utilizing neighboring capital markets (as in the case of Western Europe), may not form large public equity market systems. Without significant public trading of ownership shares, high concentrations of ownership are preserved and few disciplined processes of governance are developed.

TABLE 18.1   Comparative Corporate Governance Regimes

Regime Basis	Characteristics	Examples
Market-based	Efficient equity markets; Dispersed ownership	United States, United Kingdom, Canada, Australia
Family-based	Management & ownership is combined; Family/majority and minority shareholders	Hong Kong, Indonesia, Malaysia, Singapore, Taiwan, France
Bank-based	Government influence in bank lending; Lack of transparency; Family control	Korea, Germany
Government affiliated	State ownership of enterprise; Lack of transparency; No minority influence	China, Russia

Source: Based on J. Tsui and T. Shieh, "Corporate Governance in Emerging Markets: An Asian Perspective," in *International Finance and Accounting Handbook,* Third Edition, Frederick D.S. Choi, ed., Hoboken, NJ: Wiley, 2004 (pp. 24.4–24.6).

For businesses, the first criterion of corporate social responsibility is *economic* responsibility. Recently, companies such as Enron, Lucent, and Nortel have failed to carry out their economic responsibility, especially when the value of the company stock plummeted. Not only have Enron employees such as those in the photo lost their jobs, but some lost most of their 401(k) retirement plans. One 61-year-old administrative assistant, who had dutifully placed 15 percent of her salary into a 401(k) plan, invested the entire amount in the company's rapidly climbing stock. She amassed close to $500,000, only to be forced out of work with a 401(k) worth only $22,000 when Enron collapsed.

Separation of Management and Ownership

In countries and cultures in which the ownership of the firm has continued to be an integral part of management, agency issues and failures have been less of a problem. In countries such as the United States, in which ownership has become largely separated from management (and widely dispersed), aligning the goals of management and ownership is much more difficult.

Disclosure and Transparency

The extent of disclosure regarding the operations and financial results of a company vary dramatically across countries. Disclosure practices reflect a wide range of cultural and social forces, including the degree of ownership that is public, the degree to which government feels the need to protect investors' rights versus ownership rights, and the extent to which family-based and government-based business remains central to the culture. Transparency, a parallel concept to disclosure, reflects the visibility of decision-making processes within the business organization.

Note that the word "ethics" has not been used. All of the principles and practices described so far have assumed that the individuals in roles of responsibility and leadership pursue them truly and fairly. That, however, has not always been the case.

THE CASE OF ENRON

Many of the issues related to corporate governance—and its failures—are best described by the case of Enron. Enron Corporation declared bankruptcy in November 2001 as a result of a complex combination of business and governance failures. As noted in its own board report as excerpted in the following Focus on Ethics, the failures involved organizations and individuals both inside and outside of Enron.

As it turns out, much of what Enron reported as "earnings" were not. Much of the debt raised by the company via a number of partnerships was not disclosed in corporate financial statements as it should have been. Simultaneous to the overreporting of profits and the underreporting of debt was the massive compensation packages and bonuses earned by corporate officers. How did this happen?

- It appears that the executive officers of the firm were successful in managing the board of directors toward their own goals. Management had moved the company into a number of new markets in which the firm suffered substantial losses, resulting in redoubled attempts on their part to somehow generate the earnings needed to meet Wall Street's unquenchable thirst for profitable growth.

Focus On ⬇

ETHICS

Enron's Board on What Happened at Enron

"The tragic consequences of the related-party transactions and accounting errors were the result of failures at many levels and by many people: a flawed idea, self-enrichment by employees, inadequately designed controls, poor implementation, inattentive oversight, simple (and not so simple) accounting mistakes, and overreaching in a culture that appears to have encouraged pushing the limits. Our review indicates that many of these consequences could and should have been avoided."

Source: "Report of Investigation: Special Investigative Committee of the Board of Directors of Enron Corporation," Board of Directors, Enron, February 1, 2002, 27–28.

- The board failed in its duties to protect shareholder interests by lack of due diligence, and most likely by putting faith in the officers that proved undeserved. It is also important to note that Enron's legal advisors, some of whom reported to the board, also failed to provide leadership on a number of glaring instances of malfeasance.
- Enron's auditors, Arthur Andersen, committed serious errors in judgment regarding accounting treatment for many Enron activities, including the above partnerships. Andersen was reported to have had serious conflicts of interest, earning $5 million in auditing fees from Enron in 2001, and more than $50 million in consulting fees in the same year.
- Enron's analysts were, in a few cases, blinded by the sheer euphoria over Enron's latent successes in the mid- to late-1990s, or working within investment banks that were earning substantial investment banking fees related to the complex partnerships. Although a few analysts continued to note that the company's earnings seemed strangely large relative to the falling cash flows reported, Enron's management was generally successful in arguing their point.

The rise and fall of Enron is a story that is far from complete. It may be that in the end, however, the true moral of the story is not in the failure of any specific process in place within the American system of corporate governance, nor in the mistaken focus on fair-value accounting, nor in the lack of diligence of the board's own audit committee, but simply the failure of people in a wide variety of positions of leadership.

Good Governance and Reputation

Does good governance matter? This is actually a difficult question, and the realistic answer has been, historically, largely dependent on outcomes. For example, as long as Enron's share price continued to rise dramatically throughout the 1990s, questions over transparency, accounting propriety, and even financial facts were largely overlooked by all of the stakeholders of the corporation. Yet, eventually, the fraud and deceit and failure of the multitude of corporate governance practices resulted in the bankruptcy of the firm, destroying not only the wealth of investors, but the careers, incomes, and savings of so many of its basic stakeholders—its own employees. Ultimately, yes, good governance does matter. A lot.

A second way of valuing good governance is by measuring the attitudes and tendencies of the large global institutional investors who make the biggest decisions about where capital may go. A recent McKinsey study surveyed more than 200 institutional investors as to the value they placed on good governance. The survey results presented in Figure 18.2 quantify good governance in the premium that institutional investors would be willing to pay for companies with good governance within specific country markets. Although this is not exactly equivalent to saying who has "good" and "bad" corporate governance globally, it does provide some insight as to which countries' institutional investors see good governance as scarce. It is again important to note that most of the emerging market nations have relatively few publicly traded companies, even today.

This is not a surprise to the "sell-side," the companies themselves. Corporate leadership globally is increasingly concerned with the nature of its reputation, and corporate governance failures are high on the list of issues that affect corporate reputation. Figure 18.3 presents survey results from 2003 in which CEOs were asked what external forces threatened their corporate reputation. Unethical behavior and product or service problems tied for the most frequently cited causes for destruction of corporate reputation.

FIGURE 18.2

The Value of Good Governance

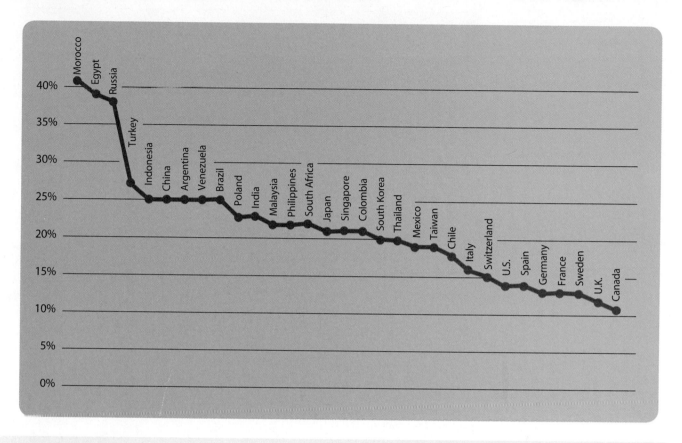

Source: Data compiled from "McKinsey Global Investor Opinion Survey on Corporate Governance, 2002," McKinsey & Company, July 2002.

CORPORATE GOVERNANCE REFORM

The debate regarding what needs to be done about corporate governance reform depends on which systems and regimes are deemed superior. To date, reform in the United States has been largely regulatory.

Sarbanes–Oxley

The U.S. Congress passed the Sarbanes–Oxley Act in July 2002. It had three major requirements: 1) CEOs of publicly traded firms must vouch for the veracity of the firm's published financial statements; 2) corporate boards must have audit committees drawn from independent (outside) directors; and 3) companies are prohibited from making loans to corporate officers and directors. The first provision—the so-called signature clause—has already had significant impact on the way in which companies prepare their financial statements. Although the provision was intended to instill a sense of responsibility and accountability in senior management (and therefore fewer explanations of "the auditors signed-off on it"), the companies themselves have pushed the same procedure downward in their organizations, often requiring business unit managers and directors at lower levels to sign their financial statements.

FIGURE 18.3

What Threatens Corporate Reputation?

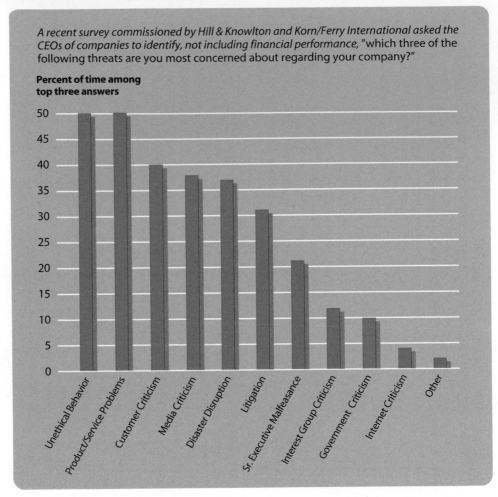

A recent survey commissioned by Hill & Knowlton and Korn/Ferry International asked the CEOs of companies to identify, not including financial performance, "which three of the following threats are you most concerned about regarding your company?"

Percent of time among top three answers

Source: "2003 Corporate Reputation Watch Survey," Hill & Knowlton and Korn/Ferry International, 2003.

Sarbanes–Oxley has been quite controversial internationally, as it is in conflict with a number of the existing corporate governance practices already in place in markets that view themselves as having better governance records than the United States. A foreign firm wishing to list or continue listing their shares on a U.S. exchange must comply with the law. Some companies, such as Porsche, withdrew plans for a U.S. listing specifically in opposition to Sarbanes–Oxley. Other companies, however, many of the largest foreign companies traded on U.S. exchanges, such as Unilever, Siemens, and ST Microelectronics, have stated their willingness to comply—if they can find acceptable compromises between U.S. law and the governance requirements and principles in their own countries.[3]

Board Structure and Compensation

Many critics have argued that the United States should move toward structural reforms more consistent with European standards. For example, prohibiting CEOs from also being Chairmen. Although this is increasingly common, there is no regulatory or other legal requirement to force the issue. Second, and more radically, would be to move toward the two-tiered structure of countries like Germany, in which there is a supervisory board (largely outsiders, and typically large—Siemens has 18 members) and a management board (predominantly insiders, and smaller—Siemens has 8 members). As illustrated by Table 18.2, it is not clear the composition of boards is truly the problem.

Also under considerable debate is the amount and form of board compensation. In the past, the United States was characterized by boards in which compensation was a combination of an annual stipend, and the award of significant stock options. The stock option incentive, although intended to align the goals and objectives of boards and executive directors with the interests of stockholders, seemingly resulted in a mind-set more akin to the gift of lotto tickets—encouraging aggressive growth and accounting in the interest of earnings growth and share price appreciation.

Transparency, Accounting, and Auditing

The concept of **transparency** is also one that has been raised in a variety of different markets and contexts. Transparency is a rather common term used to describe the degree to which an investor—either existing or potential—can discern the true activities and value drivers of a company from the disclosures and financial results reported. For example, Enron was often considered a "black box" when it came to what the actual operational and financial results and risks were for its multitude of business lines. The consensus of corporate governance experts is that all firms, globally, should work toward increasing the transparency of the firm's risk-return proposition.

The accounting process itself, the way in which we record the financial results and status of all firms, has now come under debate. The U.S. system is characterized as strictly rule-based, rather than conceptually based, as is common in Western Europe. Many critics of U.S. corporate governance practices point to this as a fundamental flaw, in which ever more clever accountants find ways to follow the rules, yet not meet the underlying purpose for which the rules were intended. An extension of the accounting process debate is that of the role and remuneration associated with auditing, the process of using third parties, paid by the firm, to vet their reporting practices as being consistent with accepted accounting principles and practices. As the collapse of Arthur Andersen illustrated following the Enron debacle, there are serious questions as to the faith investors can place in the results of this current practice.

TABLE 18.2

Board Composition and Compensation, Fortune 100

Size of Company (sales)	Total Directors	Outside Directors	Avg. Annual Retainer
Less than $3 billion	9	7	$33,792
$3–$4.9 billion	10	8	$37,567
$5–$9.9 billion	12	10	$42,264
$10–19.9 billion	12	10	$47,589
$20 billion and over	13	11	$ 6,587

Minority Shareholder Rights

Finally, the issue of minority shareholder rights continues to rage in many of the world's largest markets. Many of the emerging markets are still characterized by the family-based corporate governance regime, where the family remains in control even after the firm has gone public. But what of the interests and voices of the other stockholders? How are their interests preserved in organizations in which families or private investors control all true decisions, including those made by the boards? And as the following Focus on Ethics on Conrad Black of Hollinger International points out, minority shareholder rights are threatened in all markets, industrialized or emerging.

Accounting Diversity

The fact that accounting principles differ across countries is not, by itself, a problem. The primary problem is that real economic decisions by lenders, investors, or government policymakers may be distorted by the differences. Table 18.3 provides a simple example of the potential problems that may arise if two identical firms were operating in similar or dissimilar economic and accounting environments.

First, if two identical firms (in terms of structure, products, and strategies) are operating in similar economic situations and are subject to similar accounting treatment (cell A), a comparison of their performance will be logical in practice and easily interpreted. The results of a competitive comparison or even an accounting audit (measurement and monitoring of their accounting practices) will lead to results that make sense. The two same firms operating in dissimilar economic situations will, when subject to the same accounting treatment, potentially look very different. And it may be that they should appear different if they are operating in totally different environments.

For example, one airline may depreciate its aircraft over five years, while another airline may depreciate over ten years. Is this justified? It is if the two identical air carriers are in fundamentally different economic situations. If the first airline flies predominantly short commuter routes, which require thousands of takeoffs and landings, and the second airline flies only long intercontinental flights, which require far fewer takeoffs and landings, the first may be justified in depreciating its fixed assets much faster. The airline with more frequent takeoffs and landings will wear out its aircraft more quickly, which is what the accounting principle of depreciation is attempting to capture.[4] The economic situations are different.

Focus On ⬇

ETHICS

Conrad Black and Minority Shareholder Rights

Conrad Black is CEO of Hollinger International, a Canadian corporation listed on the New York Stock Excahnge. Black controls the company via a complex management agreement and through a holding company that he controls, which holds a majority of Hollinger's voting shares. He is known to have little patience for shareholder questions, particularly when they are about how he is managing the firm. In a recent stockholder meeting he responded to continued questions with the following: "You have a right to say whatever it is that is on your mind, all of you," he informed his investors. "You don't know what you are talking about, but you are still welcome as shareholders."

Source: Adapted from David Leonard, "Hollinger Black & Blue," *Fortune,* September 29, 2003.

TABLE 18.3

Accounting Diversity and Economic Environments

	ECONOMIC SITUATION OF TWO IDENTICAL FIRMS	
Accounting Treatment	**Similar**	**Dissimilar**
Similar	Logical practice A	May/may not be logical B
	Results are comparable	Results may/may not be comparable
Dissimilar	Illogical practice C	Logical practice D
	Results are not comparable	Results may not be comparable

Source: "International Accounting Diversity and Capital Market Decisions," Frederick D.S. Choi and Richard Levich, in *The Handbook of International Accounting,* Frederick D.S. Choi, ed., 1992.

The most blatantly obvious mismatch of economic environments and accounting treatments is probably that of cell C. Two identical firms operating within the same economic environment that receive different accounting treatment are not comparable. The same firms, if placed in the same environment, would appear differently, with one potentially gaining competitive advantage over the other simply because of accounting treatment.

Finally, cell D offers the mismatch of different environments and different accounting treatments. Although logical in premise, the results are most likely incomparable in outcome. Identical firms in differing economic environments require differing approaches to financial measurement. But the fact that the results of financial comparison may not be usable is not an error; it is simply a fact of the differing markets in which the firms operate. As firms expand internationally, as markets expand across borders, as businesses diversify across currencies, cultures, and economies, the movement toward cell A continues from market forces rather than from government intention.

Principal Accounting Differences Across Countries

International **accounting diversity** can lead to any of the following problems in international business conducted with the use of financial statements: (1) poor or improper business decision making; (2) hindering the ability of a firm or enterprise to raise capital in different or foreign markets; and (3) hindering or preventing a firm from monitoring competitive factors across firms, industries, and countries.

ORIGINS OF DIFFERENCES

Accounting standards and practices are in many ways no different from any other legislative or regulatory statutes in their origins. Laws reflect the people, places, and events of their time (see Focus on Culture). Most accounting practices and laws are linked to the objectives of the parties who will use the financial information, including investors, lenders, and governments.

Focus On ⬇

The Father of Accounting: Luca Pacioli Who?

Doctors have Hippocrates and philosophers have Plato. But who is the father of accounting? Knowing that accountants have long had inferiority complexes, two Seattle University professors have decided that the profession should have a father and that he should be Luca Pacioli.

But their anointing of the Renaissance scholar occasions an identity crisis. Hardly anyone—accountants included—has ever heard of Pacioli (pronounced pot-CHEE-oh-lee).

Five centuries ago, Pacioli published *Summa de Arithmetica, Geometria, Proportioni et Proportionalita*. It contained a slender tract for merchants on double-entry bookkeeping, which had been in wide use in Venice for years. Due to that, some accounting historians, including Professors Weis and Tinius, credit Pacioli with codifying accounting principles for the first time. That would seem to establish paternity.

Professor Vangermeersch, of the University of Rhode Island, says the origins of double-entry bookkeeping are open to question. "If you're crediting people of past centuries for contributions to accounting, you should include Leonardo of Pisa, who brought Arabic numerals to the West; James Pelle, who initiated journal-entry systems; and Emile Garcke and J.M. Fells, who applied accounting to factory use," he said. All the men have another thing in common, he added: They are just as obscure as Luca Pacioli.

Even in literature, says Vangermeersch, the only famous accountant was Daniel Defoe, who wrote *Robinson Crusoe*. Unfortunately, Defoe was a terrible businessman and failed in a series of ventures, the professor observed. "Even as a dissenter and pamphleteer, he was tarred and feathered by the public."

Source: Abstracted from "Father of Accounting Is a Bit of a Stranger to His Own Progeny," *Wall Street Journal,* January 29, 1993, A1, A6. Reprinted by permission of The Wall Street Journal, © 1993 Dow Jones & Company, Inc. All Rights Reserved Worldwide.

CLASSIFICATION SYSTEMS

There are several ways to classify and group national accounting systems and practices. Figure 18.4 illustrates one such classification based on a statistically based clustering of practices across countries by C.W. Nobes. The systems are first subdivided into micro-based (characteristics of the firms and industries) and macro-uniform (following fundamental government or economic factors per country). The micro-based national accounting systems are then broken down into those that follow a theoretical principle or pragmatic concerns. The latter category includes the national accounting systems of countries as diverse as the United States, Canada, Japan, the United Kingdom, and Mexico.

The macro-uniform systems, according to Nobes, are primarily used in European countries. The continental Europeans are typified by accounting systems that are formulated in secondary importance to legal organizational forms (Germany), for the apportionment and application of national tax laws (France, Spain, Italy), or the more pure forms of government and economic models (Sweden). An alternative approach to those in the European classification would be those used in Sweden and Germany, which have pushed their firms to adopt more widespread uniform standards. However, as with all classification systems, the subtle differences across countries can quickly make such classifications useless in practice. As the following sections will illustrate, slight differences can also yield significant competitive advantages or disadvantages to companies organized and measured under different financial reporting systems.

PRINCIPAL DIFFERENCES: THE ISSUES

The resulting impact of accounting differences is to separate or segment international markets for investors and firms alike. Communicating the financial results of a foreign company operating in a foreign country and foreign currency is often a task that must

FIGURE 18.4

Nobes Classification of National Accounting Systems

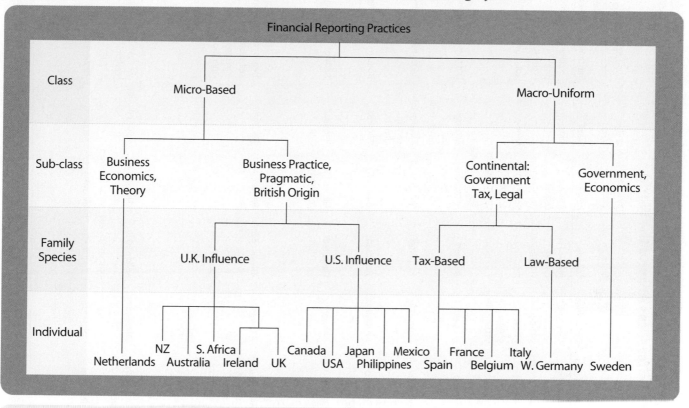

Source: C.W. Nobes, "International Classification of Accounting Systems," unpublished paper: April 1980. Table C. as cited in *International Accounting*, 2d ed. Frederick D.S. Choi and Gerhard G. Mueller: Englewood Cliffs, NJ: Prentice-Hall, 1992, p. 34.

be undertaken completely separately from the accounting duties of the firm. As long as significant accounting practices differ across countries, markets will continue to be segmented (and accountants may be required to be interpreters and marketers as much as bookkeepers).

Table 18.4 provides an overview of nine major areas of significant differences in accounting practices across countries.[5] There are, of course, many more hundreds of differences, but the nine serve to highlight some of the fundamental philosophical differences across countries. Accounting differences are real and persistent, and there is still substantial question of competitive advantages and informational deficiencies that may result from these continuing differences across countries.

Accounting for Research and Development Expenses

Are research and development expenses capitalized or expensed as costs are incurred? Those who argue that there is no certainty that the R&D expenditures will lead to benefits in future periods would require immediate recognition of all expenses as in typical conservative practice. Alternatively, if R&D expenditures do lead to future benefits and revenues, the matching of expenses and revenues would be better served if the R&D expenditures were capitalized, and expenses therefore spread out over the future benefit periods.

TABLE 18.4 Summary of Principal Accounting Differences Around the World

	United States	Japan	United Kingdom	France	Germany	The Netherlands	Switzerland	Canada	Italy	Brazil	INTERNATIONAL Benchmark	INTERNATIONAL Allowed Alternative
Capitalization of research and development	Not allowed	Allowed in certain circumstances	Allowed in certain circumstances	Allowed in certain circumstances	Not allowed	Allowed in certain circumstances	Allowed in certain circumstances	Allowed in certain circumstances	Allowed in certain circumstances	Allowed	Required in certain circumstances	None
Fixed asset revaluation stated at amount in excess of cost	Not allowed	Not allowed	Allowed	Allowed	Not allowed	Allowed in certain circumstances	Allowed in certain circumstances	Not allowed	Required in certain circumstances	Allowed	Not allowed	Allowed
Inventory valuation using LIFO	Allowed	Allowed	Allowed but rarely done	Allowed	Allowed in certain circumstances	Allowed	Allowed	Allowed	Allowed	Allowed but rarely done	Not allowed	Allowed
Finance leases capitalized	Required	Allowed in certain circumstances	Required	Allowed	Allowed in certain circumstances	Required	Allowed	Required	Not allowed	Allowed in certain circumstances	Required	None
Pension expense accrued during period of service	Required	Allowed	Required	Allowed	Required	Required	Allowed	Required	Allowed	Allowed	Required	None
Book and tax timing differences presented on the balance sheet as deferred tax	Required	Allowed in certain circumstances	Required in certain circumstances	Required	Allowed in certain circumstances	Required	Allowed	Required	Generally required	Required	Allowed	None
Current rate method used by foreign currency translation	Required for foreign operations whose functional currency is other than the reporting currency	Generally required	Required	Required for self-sustaining foreign operations	Allowed	Required for self-sustaining foreign operations	Allowed	Required for self-sustaining foreign operations	Required	Required	Required for self-sustaining foreign operations	None
Pooling method used for mergers	Required in certain circumstances	Allowed	Required in certain circumstances	Not allowed	Allowed in certain circumstances	Allowed but rarely done	Allowed but rarely done	Allowed in rare circumstances	Allowed in rare circumstances	Allowed but rarely done	Required in certain circumstances	None
Equity method used for 20–50% ownership	Required	Required	Required	Required	Required	Required	Allowed in certain circumstances	Required	Allowed	Required	Required	None

Source: William E. Decker, Jr., and Paul Brunner, "Summary of Accounting Principle Differences Around the World," in International Finance and Accounting Handbook, Third Edition, Frederick D. S. Choi, ed., p. 12.6. Hoboken, NJ: Wiley, 2003.

Differences in depreciation methods used in accounting for fixed assets result in different expensing schedules across countries. The issue is quite complex for the many international firms participating in the Three Gorges project, which proposes to build the largest hydroelectric project in the history of the world on China's Yangtze River.

Accounting for Fixed Assets

How are fixed assets (land, buildings, machinery, equipment) to be expensed and carried? The assets constitute large outlays of capital, result in assets that are held by the firm for many years, and yield benefits for many future years. All countries require companies to capitalize these fixed assets, so that they are depreciated over their future economic lives (once again spreading the costs out over periods roughly matching the revenue-earning useful life). There are, however, significant differences in depreciation methods used (straight-line, sum-of-years-digits, accelerated methods of cost recovery, and so forth), resulting in very different expensing schedules across countries.

The primary issue related to the accounting of fixed assets is whether they are to be carried on company financial statements at historical cost or current value. The conservative approach, used for example, in the United States, is to carry the fixed assets at historical cost and to allow analysts to use their own methods and additional financial statement notes to ascertain current values of individual fixed assets. The alternative is to allow the values of fixed assets to be periodically revalued up or down, depending on the latest appraised value. Countries such as the Netherlands argue that this is more appropriate, given that the balance sheet of a firm should present the present fair market value of all assets.

Inventory Accounting Treatment

How are inventories to be valued? For many companies inventories are their single largest asset. Therefore, the reconciliation of how goods are valued as sold (on the income statement) and valued as carried in inventory unsold (on the balance sheet) is important. The three typical inventory-valuation principles are last-in-first-out, **LIFO,** the **average cost method,** and first-in-first-out, **FIFO.**

The LIFO method assumes that the last goods purchased by the firm (last-in) are the first ones sold (first-out). This is considered conservative by accounting standards in that the remaining inventory goods were the first ones purchased. The resulting expenses of cost of goods sold is therefore higher. The use of FIFO is thought to be more consistent theoretically with the matching of costs and revenues of actual inventory flows. The use of FIFO is generally regarded as creating a more accurately measured balance sheet, as inventory is stated at the most recent prices.

Capitalizing or Expensing Leases

Are financing leases to be capitalized? The recent growth in popularity of leasing for its financial and tax flexibility has created a substantial amount of accounting discussion across countries. The primary question is whether a leased item should actually be carried on the balance sheet of the firm at all, since a lease is essentially the purchase of an asset only for a specified period of time. If not carried on the books, should the lease payments be expenses paid as if they were a rent payment?

Some argue that the lease results in the transfer of all risks and benefits of ownership to the firm (from the lessor to the lessee) and the lease contract should be accounted for as the purchase of an asset. This would be a capital lease, and if the lessee borrowed money in order to acquire the asset, the lease payments of principal and interest should be accounted for in the same manner as the purchase of any other capital asset.

The alternative is that the lessee has simply acquired the rental use of the services of the asset for a specified period of time, and payments on this **operating lease** should be treated only as rent. In this case the asset would remain on the books of the lessor.

Pension Plan Accounting

A private pension plan is the promise by an employer to provide a continuing income stream to employees after their retirement from the firm. The critical accounting question is whether the pension promise should be expensed and carried at the time the employee is working for the firm (providing a service to the firm that will not be fully paid for by the firm until all pension payments are completed) or expensed only as pension payments are made after retirement.

The primary problem with expensing the pension as the services are provided is that the firm does not know the exact amount or timing of the eventual pension payments. If it is assumed that these eventual pension payments can be reasonably approximated, the conservative approach is to account for the expenses as employee services are provided and to carry the **pension liabilities** on the books of the firm. In some countries, if it is believed that these pension liabilities cannot be accurately estimated, they will be expensed only as they are incurred on payment.

Accounting for Income Taxes

All countries require the payment of income taxes on earnings. However, the definition and timing of earnings can constitute a problem. In many countries, the definition of earnings for financial accounting purposes differs from earnings for tax purposes. The question then focuses on whether the tax effect should be recognized during the period in which the item appears on the income statement or during the period in which the item appears on the tax return.

If the expense is recognized during the period in which the item appears on the income statement, the tax gives rise to an associated asset or liability referred to as deferred tax. Some countries do not suffer the debate of whether the deferred tax should actually appear on the balance sheet of the firm by having all financial reporting follow tax rules.

Foreign Currency Translation

As introduced in Chapter 17, corporations that operate in more than one country and one currency must periodically *translate* and *consolidate* all financial statements for home-country reporting purposes. The primary issues in foreign currency translation are which exchange rates should be used in the translation of currencies (historical or current rates) and how gains or losses resulting from the translation should be handled in the consolidation. The critical handling issue is whether the gains or losses are recognized in current income or carried on the consolidated balance sheet as an item under equity capital.

Figure 18.5 provides a simple decision-tree approach to translation of foreign affiliates for U.S. corporations.

Accounting for Mergers and Acquisitions

This is a relatively new issue in international accounting, given the sudden and rapid growth of merger and acquisition activity beginning in the United States and the United Kingdom in the 1980s. The primary accounting question is whether the assets and liabilities acquired should be carried at their original historic value or at the value at acquisition. In certain cases, however, it is believed that the shareholders of the acquired company end up owning shares of the acquirer, and accountants argue that their assets and liabilities should not be revalued, but simply merged or pooled.

A second accounting issue of some concern is that often in the case of acquisitions, the price paid exceeds the fair value of the assets acquired. This is termed "goodwill"

FIGURE 18.5

United States Translation Procedure Flow Chart

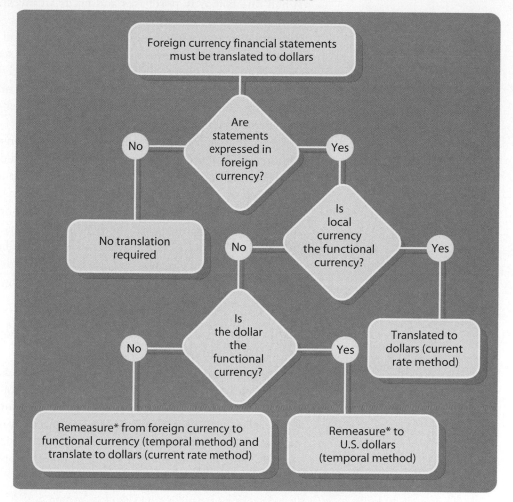

*The term *remeasure* means to translate so as to change the unit of measure from a foreign currency to the functional currency.
Source: Frederick D.S. Choi and Gerhard G. Mueller, *International Accounting,* 2d ed. (Englewood Cliffs, NJ: Prentice-Hall, 1992) p. 169

and constitutes a significant accounting problem. Many accountants argue that this is a true value that is purchased, and would not have been paid for if it did not exist. Even if goodwill is accepted as a legitimate economic value, the question remains as to how it is to be carried on the firm's balance sheet.

In other countries, accountants do not believe that goodwill is a real asset and therefore should not be carried on the books of the firm. In this case, such as in the United Kingdom, the firm is allowed to write off the entire amount against equity in the year of acquisition. It is also argued that this gives British firms a distinct advantage in their ability to make acquisitions and not suffer income statement dilution impacts in the years following as the asset is amortized in the countries that capitalize goodwill. This is a classic example of the potential competitive benefits of a similar activity receiving dissimilar accounting treatment discussed at the beginning of this chapter and presented in Table 18.3.

Consolidation of Equity Securities Holdings

When one company purchases and holds an investment in another company, the question arises as to how to account for the holdings. There are two major methods of consolidation of equity holdings, the equity method and the consolidation method. The equity method requires that the holder list the security holdings as a line item on the firm's balance sheet. This is generally required when the firm holds substantial interest in the other firm, typically 20 to 50 percent of outstanding voting shares, such that it can exert substantial influence over the other firm but not necessarily dictate management or policy.

The second method of equity holdings, the consolidation method, requires the addition of all of the investee's individual assets and liabilities to the company's assets and liabilities. A minority interest is then subtracted out for all assets for the percentage of the net asset not owned. When an investor has controlling interest in the other firm, most countries require the use of the consolidation method. The remaining accounting debates focus on whether the individual assets and liabilities should be consolidated when the subsidiaries are very dissimilar, even if controlling interest is held. Countries such as Italy and the United Kingdom believe that consolidation of dissimilar firms results in misleading information regarding the true financial status of the firms.

THE PROCESS OF ACCOUNTING STANDARDIZATION

One of the best indications as to the degree of success that has been achieved in international accounting standards is that there is still some conflict over the terminology of harmonization, standardization, or promulgation of uniform standards. For example, the Focus on Culture and Russia's accounting rules highlights the differing purposes for accounting in different countries. At the same time, the Focus on Ethics that discusses corporate social responsibility at Starbucks provides insight into how

Focus On ⬇

CULTURE

Russia's Taxing Accounting Rules

CEOs don't like uncertainty. Moreover, boards of directors don't have much patience with financial statements that don't clearly present the financial health of an enterprise. All of which makes doing business in Russia a unique challenge, where the traditional focus has not been on profit, but on control.

This focus is well stated in Pulitzer Prize winner Thomas L. Friedman's recent book, *The Lexus and the Olive Tree*. He writes: "The purpose of the Soviet economy was not to meet the demand of consumers, but to reinforce the control of the central government. . . . At a Soviet company that made bed frames, the managers were paid by the central government not according to how many bed frames they sold, but on the basis of how much steel they consumed. The number of bed frames sold is a measure of consumer satisfaction.

The amount of steel produced and used is a measure of state power. In the Cold War, the Soviet Union was only interested in the latter."

As a result, reports BISNIS, the section at the U.S. Department of Commerce that is the primary resource center for U.S. companies exploring business opportunities in Russia, "Russian accounting regulations (RARs) were drafted and used for tax calculation and bookkeeping purposes and not designed for use by potential investors as measurement of a company's financial performance. With the increased interest of Western investment, however, the need for understandable, comparable, transparent, detailed, and reliable financial statements has become apparent and the Government of the Russian Federation has taken steps to promote accounting reforms."

Source: Adapted from "Russia's Taxing Accounting Rules," *World Trade,* October 2000, by Scott T. Robertson.

companies are altering their performance reporting beyond traditional financial accounting.

As early as 1966, an Accountants International Study Group was formed by professional institutes in Canada, the United States, and the United Kingdom to begin the study of significant accounting differences across countries. They were primarily only to aid in the understanding of foreign practices, not to form guidelines for more consistent or harmonious policies.

The establishment of the International Accounting Standards Committee (IASC) in 1973 was the first strong movement toward the establishment of international accounting standards. In the latter half of the 1970s, other international institutions such as the United Nations, the Organization for Economic Co-operation and Development (OECD), and the European Union also began forming study groups and analyzing specific issues of confusion, such as corporate organization and varying degrees of disclosure required across countries.[6] The efforts of the European Union to harmonize standards between countries, not to standardize, is particularly important in understanding how accounting principles and practices may be reformed to allow individual country differences but at the same time minimize the economic distortions. Finally, in September 2003, the European Commission approved legislation requiring publicly traded companies to comply with IAS (International Accounting Standards) by 2005.

Two other recent developments concerning international standardization merit special note. In 1985, the General Electric Company became the first major U.S. corporation to acknowledge that the accounting principles underlying its 1984 financial statements "are generally accepted in the United States and are consistent with standards issued by the International Accounting Standards Committee."[7] Second, the Financial Accounting Standards Board (FASB), the organization in the United States

Focus On ⬇

ETHICS

Corporate Social Responsibility and Starbucks

Starbucks defines corporate social responsibility as conducting our business in ways that produce social, environmental, and economic benefits to the communities in which we operate. In the end, it means being responsible to our stakeholders.

There is growing recognition of the need for corporate accountability. Consumers are demanding more than "product" from their favorite brands. Employees are choosing to work for companies with strong values. Shareholders are more inclined to invest in businesses with outstanding corporate reputations. Quite simply, being socially responsible is not only the right thing to do; it can distinguish a company from its industry peers.

*Corporate Social Responsibility Annual Report
Starbucks Coffee, Fiscal 2001, p. 3.*

Starbucks found itself, somewhat to its surprise, an early target of the antiglobalist movement. Like McDonalds before it, it appeared to be yet another American cultural imperialist, bringing a chain-store sameness to all countries everywhere. Like McDonalds, Starbucks found that its uniquely defined brand and experience did not have to conform to local cultural norms, but could exist alongside traditional practices, creating its own market and successfully altering some consumer behaviors.

Unlike McDonalds, however, Starbucks was the purveyor of a commodity, coffee, which was priced and sold on global markets. Coffee was sourced from hundreds of thousands of small growers in Central and South America, many of which were severely impoverished by all global income and purchasing power standards. As coffee prices plummeted in the late 1990s, companies like Starbucks were criticized for both benefitting from lower cost sourcing and for their willingness to help improve the economic conditions of the coffee growers themselves.

Starbucks has implemented a multitude of programs to pursue its program for corporate social responsibility (CSR) and pursue sustainable economic development for the people in its supply chain. Although not wishing to own the supply chain, Starbucks strategy was a complex combination of altered business practices in procurement, direct support to the coffee growers and the formation of brands that would provide conduits for consumers wishing to support CSR initiatives. Starbucks has also been very clear as to why it is doing these things—because they are the right things to do.

charged with setting most standards for corporate accounting practices, committed itself to the full consideration of "an international perspective" to all its work in the future.

International Taxation

Governments alone have the power to tax. Each government wants to tax all companies within its jurisdiction without placing burdens on domestic or foreign companies that would restrain trade. Each country will state its jurisdictional approach formally in the tax treaties that it signs with other countries. One of the primary purposes of tax treaties is to establish the bounds of each country's jurisdiction to prevent double taxation of international income. Focus on Ethics shows the effect of taxes on one firm by its own government.

TAX JURISDICTIONS

Nations usually follow one of two basic approaches to international taxation: a residential approach or a territorial or source approach. The residential approach to international taxation taxes the international income of its residents without regard to where the income is earned. The territorial approach to transnational income taxes all parties, regardless of country of residency, within its territorial jurisdiction.

Most countries in practice must combine the two approaches to tax foreign and domestic firms equally. For example, the United States and Japan both apply the residential approach to their own resident corporations and the territorial approach to income earned by nonresidents within their territorial jurisdictions. Other countries, such as Germany, apply the territorial approach to dividends paid to domestic firms from their foreign subsidiaries; such dividends are assumed taxed abroad and are exempt from further taxation.

Within the territorial jurisdiction of tax authorities, a foreign corporation is typically defined as any business that earns income within the host country's borders but is incorporated under the laws of another country. The foreign corporation usually must surpass some minimum level of activity (gross income) before the host country assumes primary tax jurisdiction. However, if the foreign corporation owns income-producing assets or a permanent establishment, the threshold is automatically surpassed. As illustrated by Focus on Ethics, it is not always easy to capture income.

TAX TYPES

Taxes are generally classified as direct and indirect. **Direct taxes** are calculated on actual income, either individual or firm income. **Indirect taxes,** such as sales taxes, severance taxes, tariffs, and value-added taxes, are applied to purchase prices, material costs, quantities of natural resources mined, and so forth. Although most countries still rely on income taxes as the primary method of raising revenue, tax structures vary widely across countries.

The **value-added tax (VAT)** is the primary revenue source for the European Union. A value-added tax is applied to the amount of product value added by the production process. The tax is calculated as a percentage of the product price less the cost of materials and inputs used in its manufacture, which have been taxed previously. Through this process, tax revenues are collected literally on the value added by that specific stage of the production process. Under the existing General Agreement on

Accounting practices for the costs of environmental contamination treatment and restoration, such as BP's reclamation of the dunes of Coatham Sands, Great Britain, is an evolving issue in international business.

Focus On ⬇

Offshore Centers Under Fire

The European Commission has long criticized so-called "tax havens" such as the Channel Islands and the Isle of Man as having lax regulations, even by offshore standards. Illegal entry of goods into the EU costs member countries' treasuries from 5 billion to 6 billion euros per year in lost revenues. For example, a smuggler's potential profit per truck- or container-load of merchandise ranges from 100,000 euros for agricultural produce to 1 million euros for cigarettes. The Commission also suspects high levels of fraud in the public sector.

Illegal money-sheltering is not exclusive to the European Community. From the Cook Islands, a protectorate of New Zealand, to Switzerland, famed for the secrecy of its bank accounts, money acquired through criminal or fraudulent means is hidden in phantom entities in offshore centers around the globe. A campaign by the Organization for Economic Cooperation and Development (OECD) seeks to crack down on tax havens in the Caribbean, as part of a wider effort to fight money laundering and financial crimes worldwide. U.S. government officials claim that offshore money centers, long suspected of protecting the financial interests of the global drug-trafficking industry and of international mafia organizations, are also providing shelter for the assets of illegal terrorist groups and their supporters. Such charges can have a disastrous effect on the fragile economies that fall prey to them. Blacklisted by OECD, tiny island states like Barbados fear that undue scrutiny of their financial institutions will irreparably damage their fledgling financial services industries, leading to economic collapse.

Offshore centers frequently come under attack as harbors for organizations that seek to evade corporate taxes. An increasing number of U.S. companies, encouraged by their financial advisors, have incorporated in Bermuda as a means of lowering taxes without giving up the benefits of doing business in the United States. Tyco International, under investigation for corrupt accounting practices, saved $400 million in taxes during 2001 by incorporating in Bermuda via a paper transaction. The company continued to operate in the United States.

Sources: "Bermuda Havens to Be Reviewed," March 1, 2002, David Cay Johnston; "U.S. Corporations Are Using Bermuda to Slash Tax Bills," February 18, 2002, and "Caribbean Tax Havens in Spotlight," January 14, 2001, *New York Times;* "Offshore Centres' Regulations under Fire," *Financial Times,* December 4, 1996.

Tariffs and Trade (GATT), the legal framework under which international trade operates, value-added taxes may be levied on imports into a country or group of countries (such as the European Union) in order to treat foreign producers entering the domestic markets equally with firms within the country paying the VAT. Similarly, the VAT may be refunded on export sales or sales to tourists who purchase products for consumption outside the country or community. For example, an American tourist leaving London may collect a refund on all value-added taxes paid on goods purchased within the United Kingdom. The refunding usually requires documentation of the actual purchase price and the amount of tax paid.

INCOME CATEGORIES AND TAXATION

There are three primary methods used for the transfer of funds across tax jurisdictions: royalties, interest, and dividends. Royalties are under license for the use of intangible assets such as patents, designs, trademarks, techniques, or copyrights. Interest is the payment for the use of capital lent for the financing of normal business activity. Dividends are income paid or deemed paid to the shareholders of the corporation from the residual earnings of operations. When a corporation declares the percentage of residual earnings that is to go to shareholders, the dividend is declared and distributed.

Taxation of corporate income differs substantially across countries. Table 18.5 provides a summary comparison for Japan, Germany, and the United States. In some countries, for example the United States and Japan, there is one **corporate income tax** rate applied to all residual earnings, regardless of what is retained versus what is distributed as dividends. In other countries, for example Germany, separate tax rates apply to

TABLE 18.5

Comparison of Corporate Tax Rates: Japan, Germany, and the United States

Taxable Income Category	Japan	Germany	United States
Corporate income tax rates:			
Profits distributed to stockholders	37.5%	30%	35%
Undistributed profits	37.5%	45%	35%
Branches of foreign corporations	37.5%	42%	35%
Withholding taxes on dividends (portfolio):			
with Japan	—	15%	15%
with Germany	15%	—	15%
with United States	15%	5%	—
Withholding taxes on dividends (substantial holdings):[a]			
with Japan	—	25%	10%
with Germany	10%	—	5%
with United States	10%	10%	—
Withholding taxes on interest:			
with Japan	—	10%	10%
with Germany	10%	—	0%
with United States	10%	0%	—
Withholding taxes on royalties:			
with Japan	—	10%	10%
with Germany	10%	—	0%
with United States	10%	0%	—

[a]"Substantial holdings" for the United States apply only to intercorporate dividends. In Germany and Japan, "substantial holdings" apply to corporate shareholders of greater than 25 percent.

Source: *Corporate Taxes: A Worldwide Summary*, Price Waterhouse Coopers, 2003.

distributed and **undistributed earnings.** (Note that Germany lists a specific corporate income tax rate for the branches of foreign corporations operating within Germany.)

Royalty and interest payments to nonresidents are normally subject to **withholding taxes.** Corporate profits are typically double taxed in most countries, through corporate and personal taxes. Corporate income is first taxed at the business level with corporate taxes, then a second time when the income of distributed earnings is taxed through personal income taxes. Withholding tax rates also differ by the degree of ownership that the corporation possesses in the foreign corporation. Minor ownership is termed portfolio, while major or controlling influence is categorized as substantial holdings. In the case of dividends, interest, or royalties paid to nonresidents, governments routinely apply withholding taxes to their payment in the reasonable expectation that the nonresidents will not report and declare such income with the host-country tax authorities. Withholding taxes are specified by income category in all bilateral tax treaties. Notice in Table 18.5 the differentials in withholding taxes across countries by bilateral tax treaties. The U.S. tax treaty with Germany results in a 0 percent withholding of interest or royalty payments earned by German corporations operating in the United States.

U.S. Taxation of Foreign Operations

The United States exercises its rights to tax U.S. residents' incomes regardless of where the income is earned. The two major categories for U.S. taxation of foreign-source income are foreign branches of U.S. corporations and foreign subsidiaries of U.S. corporations.

TAXATION OF FOREIGN BRANCHES OF U.S. CORPORATIONS

The income of a foreign branch of a U.S. corporation is treated the same as if the income was derived from sources within the United States. Since a foreign branch is an extension of the U.S. corporation and not independently capitalized and established, its profits are taxed with those of the parent whether actually remitted to the parent or not. Similarly, losses suffered by foreign branches of U.S. corporations are also fully and immediately deductible against U.S. taxable income.

As always, however, the U.S. tax authorities want to prevent double taxation. The United States grants primary tax authority to the country in which the income is derived. If taxes are paid by the foreign branch to host-country tax authorities, the tax payments may be claimed as a tax credit toward U.S. tax liabilities on the same income.

TAXATION OF FOREIGN SUBSIDIARIES OF U.S. CORPORATIONS

Just as the United States taxes corporations from other countries operating within its borders, foreign countries tax the operations of U.S. corporations within their jurisdictions. Corporations operating in more than one country are therefore subject to double taxation. Double taxation could hinder the ability of U.S. corporations to operate and compete effectively abroad. The U.S. tax code removes the burden by reducing the U.S. taxes due on the foreign-source income by the amount of foreign taxes deemed paid.

The calculation of the foreign income taxes deemed paid and the additional U.S. taxes due, if any, involves the interaction of the following four components.

- **Degree of Ownership and Control.** The degree of ownership and control of the foreign corporation has a significant impact on the calculation of U.S. taxes payable on the foreign-source income. There are three basic ownership ranges applicable to taxation: (1) less than 10 percent; (2) 10 to 50 percent; and (3) more than 50 percent. Figure 18.6 illustrates the three ownership classes under U.S. tax law. If the U.S. corporation owns more than 50 percent of the voting shares in the foreign corporation, the foreign corporation is classified as a Controlled Foreign Corporation (CFC).[8]
- **Proportion of Income Distributed.** The proportion of after-tax income that is distributed as profits to stockholders as dividends is also important to the calculation of U.S. tax liability. Income that is retained by the foreign corporation and not distributed to shareholders, U.S. or other, will have the result, in certain cases, of reducing the U.S. tax liability on the foreign corporation's income.
- **Active versus Passive Income.** If a foreign subsidiary generates income through its own actions or activities (e.g., producing a product, selling a product,

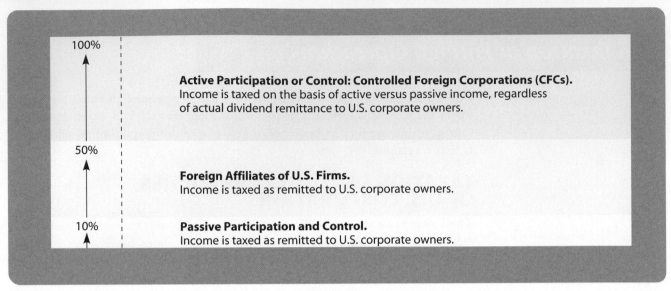

FIGURE 18.6

Classification of U.S. Ownership of Foreign Corporations for Tax Uses

100%

Active Participation or Control: Controlled Foreign Corporations (CFCs).
Income is taxed on the basis of active versus passive income, regardless
of actual dividend remittance to U.S. corporate owners.

50%

Foreign Affiliates of U.S. Firms.
Income is taxed as remitted to U.S. corporate owners.

10%

Passive Participation and Control.
Income is taxed as remitted to U.S. corporate owners.

providing a service), the income is classified as *active*. If, however, the foreign subsidiary or affiliate earns income through its ownership in another firm, or by acting as a creditor to another firm and earning interest income, the income is classified as *passive*. It is quite common for a foreign subsidiary to have both active and passive income. Each is then treated separately for tax purposes.

• **Relative Corporate Income Taxes.** Whether foreign corporate income taxes are higher or lower than similar U.S. corporate income taxes will largely determine whether the U.S. shareholders will owe additional taxes in the United States on the foreign-source income, or whether the foreign tax credit will completely cover U.S. tax liabilities. If withholding taxes were applied to dividends paid to nonresidents (the U.S. corporation owner), this also would affect the U.S. tax liability.

CALCULATION OF U.S. TAXES ON FOREIGN-SOURCE EARNINGS

Table 18.6 illustrates the complete calculation of foreign taxes, U.S. tax credits, additional U.S. taxes due on foreign income, and total worldwide tax burdens for four different potential cases. Each of the four cases is structured to highlight the different combinations of the three components, relative corporate income taxes (lines a, b, and c), degree of control or ownership of the U.S. corporation in the foreign corporation (line d), and the proportion of available income distributed to stockholders as dividends (line e).

Case 1: Foreign Affiliate of a U.S. Corporation in a High-Tax Environment

This is a very common case. A U.S. corporation earns income in the form of distributed earnings (100 percent payout of available earnings to stockholders) from a foreign corporation in which it holds substantial interest (more than 10 percent) but does not control (less than 50 percent). The foreign corporate income tax rate (40 percent) is higher than the U.S. rate (35 percent). The foreign corporation has total taxable

TABLE 18.6   U.S. Taxation of Foreign-Source Income
(thousands of U.S. dollars)

	Case 1	Case 2	Case 3	Case 4
Baseline Values				
a. Foreign corporate income tax rate	40%	20%	20%	20%
b. U.S. corporate income tax rate	35%	35%	35%	35%
c. Foreign dividend withholding tax rate	10%	10%	10%	10%
d. Proportional ownership held by U.S. corporation in foreign corporation	30%	30%	30%	100%
e. Payout rate (proportion of after-tax income declared as dividends)	100%	100%	50%	100%
Foreign Affiliate Tax Computation				
1. Taxable income of foreign affiliate	$2,000	$2,000	$2,000	$2,000
2. Foreign corporate income taxes (@ rate a above)	(800)	(400)	(400)	(400)
3. Net income available for profit distribution	$1,200	$1,600	$1,600	$1,600
4. Retained earnings (1 − rate e above × line 3)	—	—	800	—
5. Distributed earnings (rate e above × line 3)	$1,200	$1,600	$800	$1,600
6. Distributed earnings to U.S. corporation (rate d × line 5)	$360	$480	$240	$1,600
7. Withholding taxes on dividends to nonresidents (rate c × line 6)	(36)	(48)	(24)	(160)
8. Remittance of foreign income to U.S. corporation	$324	$432	$216	$1,440
U.S. Corporate Tax Computation on Foreign-Source Income				
9. Grossed-up U.S. income (rate d × rate e × line 1)	$600	$600	$300	$2,000
10. Tentative (theoretical) U.S. tax liability (rate b × line 9)	−210	−210	−105	−700
11. Foreign tax credit (rate d × rate e × line 2 + line 7)	276	168	84	560
12. Additional U.S. taxes due on foreign-source income				
(line 10 + line 11; if 11 > 10, U.S. tax liability is 0)	0	−42	−21	−140
13. After-tax dividends received by U.S. corporation (line 8 + line 12)	$324	$390	$195	$1,300
Worldwide Tax Burden				
14. Total worldwide taxes paid (line 10 or line 11, whichever is greater)	276	210	105	700
15. Effective tax rate on foreign income (line 14/line 9)	46.0%	35.0%	35.0%	35.0%

Note: When proportional ownership of the foreign corporation exceeds 50 percent, U.S. tax authorities classify it as a Controlled Foreign Corporation (CFC) and all passive income earned is taxed regardless of the payout rate or actual remittance to the U.S. corporation.

income of $2,000 (thousands of dollars), pays a 40 percent corporate income tax in the host country of $800, and distributes the entire after-tax income to stockholders. Total distributed earnings are therefore $1,200.

The foreign country imposes a 10 percent withholding tax on dividends paid to nonresidents. The U.S. corporation therefore receives its proportion of earnings (its 30 percent ownership entitles it to 30 percent of all dividends paid out) less the amount of the withholding taxes, $360 − $36, or $324. This is the net cash remittance actually received by the U.S. corporation on foreign earnings.

The calculation of U.S. taxes on foreign-source income requires first that the income be "grossed up," or reinflated to the amount of income the U.S. corporation has rights to prior to taxation by the foreign government. This is simply the percentage of ownership (30 percent) times the payout rate (100 percent) times the gross taxable income of the foreign affiliate ($2,000), or $600. A theoretical or **"tentative U.S.**

Corporate Tax Rates Around the World

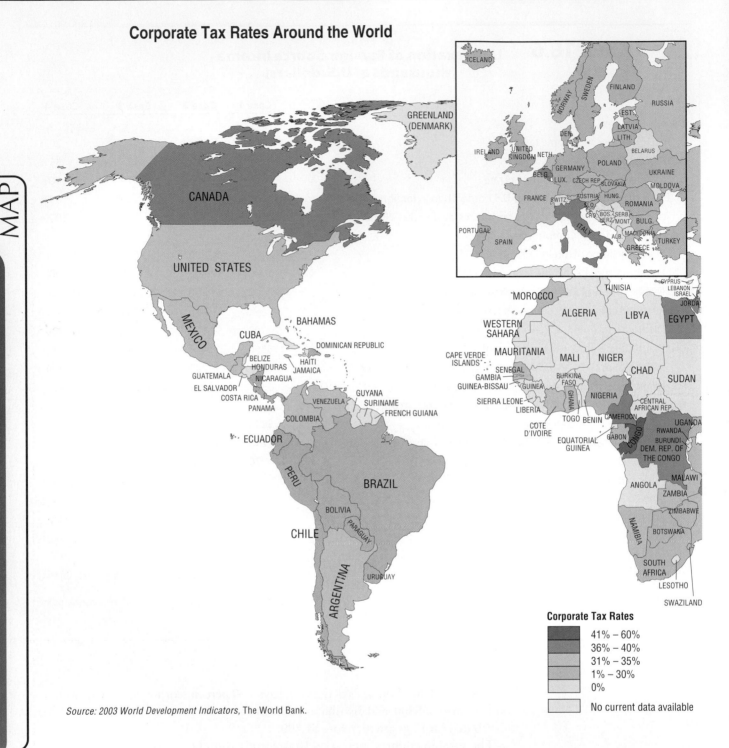

Corporate Tax Rates

- 41% – 60%
- 36% – 40%
- 31% – 35%
- 1% – 30%
- 0%
- No current data available

Source: 2003 World Development Indicators, The World Bank.

tax" is calculated on this income to estimate U.S. tax payments that would be due on this income if it had been earned in the United States (or simply not taxed at all in the foreign country). U.S. taxes of 35 percent yield a tentative tax liability of $210.

Since taxes were paid abroad, however, U.S. tax law allows U.S. tax liabilities to be reduced by the amount of the **foreign tax credit.** The foreign tax credit is the proportion of foreign taxes deemed paid attributable to its ownership (30 percent ownership times the 100 percent payout rate of the foreign taxes paid, $800, plus the amount of withholding taxes imposed on the distributed dividends to the U.S. corporation, $36). The total foreign tax credit is then $240 + $36, or $276. Since the foreign tax credit exceeds the total tentative U.S. tax liability, no additional taxes are due the U.S. tax authorities on this foreign-source income. Special note should be made that the foreign tax credit may exceed the U.S. tax liabilities, but any excess cannot be applied toward other U.S. tax liabilities in the current period (it can be carried forward or back against this foreign-source income, however).

Finally, an additional calculation allows the estimation of the total taxes paid, both abroad and in the United States, on this income. In this first case, the $276 of total tax on gross income of $600 is an **effective tax rate** of 46 percent.

Case 2: Foreign Affiliate of a U.S. Corporation in a Low-Tax Environment

This case is exactly the same as the previous example, with the sole exception that the foreign tax rate (20 percent) is lower than the U.S. corporate tax rate (35 percent). All earnings, tax calculations, and dividends distributions are the same as before.

With lower foreign corporate income taxes, there is obviously more profit to be distributed, more income to the U.S. corporation's 30 percent share, and more withholding taxes to be paid on the larger dividends distributed. Yet the grossed-up income of the foreign-source income is the same as in the previous case, because grossed-up income is proportional ownership and distribution in the absence of taxes.

With lower foreign taxes, the foreign tax credit is significantly lower and is no longer sufficient to cover fully the tentative U.S. tax liability. The U.S. corporation will have an additional $42 due in taxes on the foreign-source income. After-tax dividends in total are still higher, however, rising to $390 from $324. Total worldwide taxes paid are now significantly less, $210 rather than $276.

Cases 1 and 2 point out the single most significant feature of the U.S. tax code's impact on foreign operations of U.S. corporations: The effective tax rate may be higher on foreign-source income but will never drop lower than the basic corporate income tax rate in effect in the United States (35 percent).

Case 3: Foreign Affiliate of a U.S. Corporation in a Low-Tax Environment, 50 Percent Payout

The third case changes only one of the baseline values of the previous case, the proportion of income available for dividends that is paid out to stockholders. All distributed earnings and withholding taxes are therefore half what they were previously, as is grossed-up income and the additional U.S. tax liability (because the foreign tax credit has also been cut in half).

This third case illustrates that a reduced income distribution by the foreign subsidiary does reduce income received and taxes due in the United States on the foreign income. The effective tax rate is again at the minimum achievable, the rate of taxation that would be in effect if the income had been earned within the United States. As will be shown in the fourth and final case, this third case's results rely partially on the fact that the foreign corporation is only an affiliate (less than 50 percent ownership) of the U.S. corporation and is not controlled by the U.S. corporation.

Case 4: Foreign Subsidiary of a U.S. Corporation Is a CFC in a Low-Tax Environment

This final case highlights one of the critical components of U.S. taxation of foreign subsidiary earnings: If the foreign corporation is effectively controlled by the U.S. corporation, as indicated by its greater than 50 percent ownership, and all income is passive income, U.S. tax authorities calculate U.S. tax liabilities on the foreign income as if the entire income available for distribution to shareholders were remitted to the U.S. parent, regardless of what the actual payout rate is.

This tax policy, a result of the 1962 tax reform act, is referred to as Subpart F income. Subpart F income taxation is a reflection of the control component; it is assumed that the U.S. corporation exercises sufficient control over the management of the foreign subsidiary to determine the payout rate. If the subsidiary has chosen not to pay out all passive earnings, it is taken as a choice of the U.S. corporation and is deemed to be an effort at postponing U.S. tax liabilities on the income.

The 1962 tax act was largely aimed at eliminating the abuses of foreign affiliates of U.S. corporations paying dividends and other passive income flows out to subsidiaries in various tax havens (such as Bermuda, the Bahamas, Panama, Luxembourg, and the Cayman Islands), and not remitting the income back to the U.S. corporation. By placing the passive income in the tax havens, they effectively were postponing and evading taxation by the U.S. government.

CONCLUDING REMARKS REGARDING U.S. TAXATION OF FOREIGN INCOME

The previous series of sample tax calculations highlights the interplay of ownership, distribution, and relative tax rates between countries in determining the tax liabilities of income earned by U.S. interests abroad. In many ways, the case with the most long-term strategic significance was the first, the high-tax foreign environment. U.S. corporate income tax rates are among the lowest in the world. The usual result is the accumulation of substantial foreign tax credits by U.S. corporate interests, credits that increasingly cannot be applied to U.S. tax liabilities. The result is, as in Case 1, an effective tax rate that is significantly higher than if the income had been generated in the United States.

Recent accounting and tax rule changes may actually result in worsening this effective tax rate and excess foreign tax credit problem for U.S. corporations. Recent rule changes now require U.S. corporations to spread increasing amounts of parent-supplied overhead expenses to their foreign affiliates and subsidiaries, charging them for services provided. This results in increased costs for the foreign subsidiaries, reducing their profitability, reducing their taxable gross income, and subsequently reducing the foreign taxes, and tax credits, deemed paid. This is likely to increase the proportion of total taxes that are paid in the United States on the foreign-source income. Unfortunately, many of the overhead distributions are not recognized as a legitimate expense by many other governments (differing accounting practices in action), and the foreign units are paying a charge to the U.S. corporation that they are unable to expense against their local earnings. Recent concerns over the use of intrafirm sales (so-called transfer prices; see Chapter 16) to manipulate the profitability of foreign firms operating in the United States also has added fuel to the fires of governments and their individual shares of the world "tax pie." With that, the subject of accounting and taxation of international operations has completed a full circle.

Summary

Corporate government and accounting practices differ substantially across countries. The efforts of a number of international associates and agencies in the past two decades have, however, led to increasing cooperation and agreement among national accounting authorities. Real accounting differences remain, and many of these differences still contribute to the advantaged competitive position of some countries' firms over international competitors.

International taxation is a subject close to the pocketbook of every multinational firm. Although the tax policies of most countries are theoretically designed to not change or influence financial and business decision making by firms, they often do.

The taxation of the foreign operations of U.S. multinational firms involves the elaborate process of crediting U.S. corporations for taxes paid to foreign governments. The combined influence of different corporate tax rates across countries, the degree of ownership and control a multinational may have or exercise in a foreign affiliate, and the proportion of profits distributed to stockholders at home and abroad combine to determine the size of the parent's tax bill. As governments worldwide search for new ways to close their fiscal deficits and tax shortfalls, the pressures on international taxation and the reporting of foreign-source income will only increase.

Questions for Discussion

1. What entities have what roles in corporate governance?
2. What are the major corporate governance regimes in the world today?
3. Why is there so much focus on boards in corporate governance reform?
4. Do you think all firms, in all economic environments, should operate under the same set of accounting principles?
5. What is the nature of the purported benefit that accounting principles provide British firms over American firms in the competition for mergers and acquisitions?
6. Why do most U.S. corporations prefer the current rate method of translation over the temporal method? How does each method affect reported earnings per share per period?
7. Name two major indications that progress is being made toward standardizing accounting principles across countries.
8. What is the distinction between harmonizing accounting rules and standardizing accounting procedures and practices across countries?
9. Why are foreign subsidiaries in which U.S. corporations hold more than 50 percent voting power classified and treated differently for U.S. tax purposes?
10. Why do the U.S. tax authorities want U.S. corporations to charge their foreign subsidiaries for general and administrative services? What does this mean for the creation of excess foreign tax credits by U.S. corporations with foreign operations?
11. What would be the tax implications of combining Cases 1 and 4 in the U.S. taxation of foreign-source income, a U.S. Controlled Foreign Corporation (CFC) that is operating in a high-tax environment?
12. Why does countertrade pose special problems for accountants?

Internet Exercises

1. In order to analyze an individual firm's operating exposure more carefully, it is necessary to have more detailed information available than is in the normal annual report. Choose a specific firm with substantial international operations, for example Coca-Cola or PepsiCo, and search the Security and Exchange Commission's Edgar Files for more detailed financial reports of their international operations. Search SEC EDGAR Archives at http://www.edgar-online.com.

2. The Financial Accounting Standards Board promulgates standard practices for the reporting of financial results by companies in the United States. It also, however, often leads the way in the development of new practices and emerging issues around the world. One such major issue today is the valuation and reporting of financial derivatives and derivative agreements by firms. Use the FASB's home page and the Web pages of several of the major accounting firms and other interest groups around the world to see current proposed accounting standards and the current state of reaction to the proposed standards. Use the FASB home page at http://www.fasb.org.

3. Using Nestlé's Web page, check Current Press Releases for more recent financial results, including what the company reports as the primary currencies and average exchange rates used for translation of international financial results during the most recent period. See Nestlé: The World Food Company at http://www.ir.nestle.com.

Take a Stand

This chapter opened with a short article describing the failed initiative by Stanley Works to undergo a *corporate inversion*—to re-incorporate outside of the United States in order to reduce its overall tax burden. The Chief Executive Officer of Stanley, John Trani, only initiated such a controversial plan in order to try and reduce what he considered to be a globally uncompetitive tax burden suffered by U.S.-based companies compared to their foreign competitors. (Ingersoll-Rand, U.S.-based competitor to Stanley, successfully completed a corporate inversion offshore during the public debate about Stanley!)

The change in incorporation would not have altered anything about the company's operations, including jobs, wages, technology transfer, etc. It would, however, have reduced the taxes the company paid to the various units of the United States and individual state governments. In the end, Stanley withdrew the proposal after coming under extreme public attack by unions, federal, state, and local government officials, and even the business press. Most of the criticism was based on the assertion that a corporate inversion was un-American and unpatriotic, not that it was in any way illegal.

For Discussion

1. Multinational companies should undertake any and all actions needed to maintain and grow their global competitiveness, including the reduction of tax burdens in whatever legal ways possible. Anything less than this results in an uncompetitive firm that is not acting in the best interest of stockholders.

2. Multinational companies have an obligation to all their stakeholders, their employees, their creditors, their communities, their governments, in addition to their stockholders. They have responsibilities to support the social and political ideals that have afforded them the comfort and convenience of growing and profiting from their national origins.

*Managing
Managers*

*Managing Labor
Personnel*

Human
Resource
Management*

Learning Objectives

- To describe the challenges of managing managers and labor personnel both in individual international markets and in worldwide operations

- To examine the sources, qualifications, and compensation of international managers

- To assess the effects of culture on managers and management policies

- To illustrate the different roles of labor in international markets, especially that of labor participation in management

*This chapter was contributed by Susan C. Ronkainen.

Searching for Global Execs

Many corporate decision makers have realized that human resources play at least as significant a role as advanced technology and economies of scale do when it comes to competing successfully in the new global world order. A full 29 percent of *Fortune 500* firms surveyed had nowhere near enough global leaders; 56 percent said they had fewer than needed; and two thirds said that the global leaders in their companies had less capability than was needed. These global leaders are sought in three specific roles: running global business units or global functions, and as country managers.

According to a survey of 1,200 midsize U.S. multinationals with annual sales of $1 billion or less conducted by *International Business* magazine, senior executives seek managers who are culturally diverse but responsive to the direction of headquarters. Most U.S.-based companies try to fill senior positions abroad with locals (see accompanying chart), using expatriates only for such specific projects as technology transfer. However, the same companies send their U.S. middle managers the clear message that overseas operations are so important to corporate welfare that solid international experience is needed for advancement.

While major markets in Europe and Asia possess deeper pools of managerial talent than ever before, many of these nationals prefer to work for domestic rather than foreign firms. In particularly short supply are marketing managers—49 percent of the surveyed companies say marketing is the hardest slot to fill (see accompanying chart). It is especially hard to find people who have the cross-cultural experience to make good regional managers.

Very few global leaders are born that way, that is, with an international childhood, a command of several languages, and an education from an institution with an international focus. In most cases, they have to be trained and nurtured carefully. To make a business global, its leaders have to be able to: (1) see the world's challenges and opportunities; (2) think with an international mindset; (3) act with fresh, global-centric behaviors; and (4) mobilize a world-class team and company. A strong focus on Finland for a Nokia employee makes no sense. Three out of every five Nokia employees work outside of the company's home country, and one out of three outside of Europe.

To achieve this, companies are using various approaches. For example, Molex, a manufacturer based in Illinois with 54 manufacturing plants in 19 countries, concentrates on filling its human resource management positions with host-country nationals. Malou Roth, vice president of human resources, training, and development, explains that the company follows this practice not only so the managers can speak to employees in their own language and understand local legal requirements but also so the managers will know which current U.S. human resource practices will—and won't—work in their cultures.

Colgate-Palmolive promotes global leadership by hiring entry-level marketing candidates who have lived or worked abroad, speak more than one language, or can demonstrate an existing aptitude for global business. Black & Decker has a team-based performance appraisal and feedback system, with members from around the world. Korea's Sunkyong uses both classroom and action-learning projects that emphasize exposure to people throughout the company. NetFRAME Systems Inc., a maker of networking computers, gathers its expatriate and non-U.S. managers at its California headquarters every quarter to encourage joint planning and problem solving on a global basis. Nortel manages each phase of its international transfers through candidate pools, informed self-selection, predeparture training, support mechanisms, repatriation debefriefing for employees and families, and disseminating repatriates' international skills and knowledge throughout the company.

Companies that spend time and money creating and training global talent naturally want to retain it as long as possible. Loctite Corp., maker of industrial adhesives, offers global opportunity, professional challenge, and a competitive compensation package to keep its rising stars. Of the three approaches, claims the company, compensation is the least important to the managers.

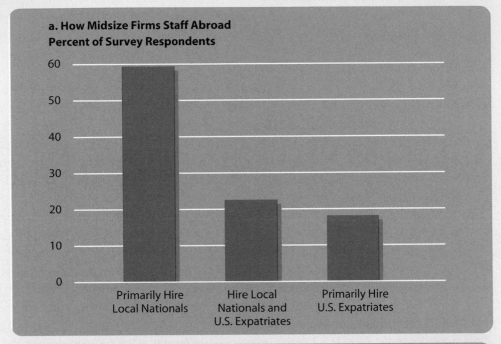

a. How Midsize Firms Staff Abroad
Percent of Survey Respondents

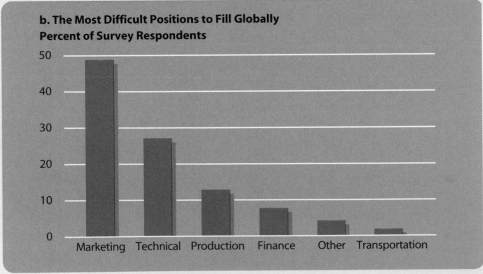

b. The Most Difficult Positions to Fill Globally
Percent of Survey Respondents

Sources: Christopher Bartlett and Sumantra Ghoshal, "What is a Global Manager?" *Harvard Business Review* 81 (August 2003): 99–107; Karl Moore, "Great Global Managers," *Across the Board*, 40 (May/June 2003): 38–42; "Distractions Make Global Manager a Difficult Role," *Wall Street Journal*, November 21, 2000, B1, B18; "Whither Global Leaders?" *HR Magazine*, May 2000, 83–88; Hal B. Gregersen, Allen J. Morrison, and J. Stewart Black, "Developing Global Leaders for the Global Frontier," *Sloan Management Review* 40, fall 1998, 31–40; Shari Caudron, "World-Class Execs," *Industry Week*, December 1, 1997, http://www.Industryweek.com; "Globe Trotter: If It's 5:30, This Must Be Tel-Aviv," *Business Week*, October 17, 1994; Lori Ioannou, "It's a Small World After All," *International Business*, February 1994, 82–88; Shawn Tully, "The Hunt for the Global Manager," *Fortune*, May 21, 1990, 140–144. http://www.netframe.com; http://www.loctite.com; http://www.molex.com; http://www.blackanddecker.com; http://www.colgate.com; http://www.nortelnetworks.com; http://www.sk.co.kr.

Organizations have two general human resource objectives. The first is the recruitment and retention of a workforce made up of the best people available for the jobs to be done. The recruiter in international operations will need to keep in mind both cross-cultural and cross-national differences in productivity and expectations when selecting employees. Once they are hired, the firm's best interest lies in maintaining a stable and experienced workforce.

The second objective is to increase the effectiveness of the workforce. This depends to a great extent on achieving the first objective. Competent managers or workers are likely to perform at a more effective level if proper attention is given to factors that motivate them.

To attain the two major objectives, the activities and skills needed include:

1. Personnel planning and staffing, the assessment of personnel needs, and recruitment
2. Personnel training to achieve a perfect fit between the employee and the assignment
3. Compensation of employees according to their effectiveness
4. An understanding of labor-management relations in terms of how the two groups view each other and how their respective power positions are established

All of this means that human resource management must become a basic element of a company's expansion strategy. In a study of 76 European and U.S. firms, a full 98 percent of the respondents had developed or were in the process of developing global human resource strategy. However, the majority reported that they had only moderate involvement in their company's overall business strategy. The task is, therefore, to establish human resources as not only a tactical element to fill needed positions but one whose programs affect overall business results.[1]

This chapter will examine the management of human resources in international business from two points of view, first that of manager and then that of labor.

Managing Managers

The importance of the quality of the workforce in international business cannot be overemphasized, regardless of the stage of internationalization of the firm. Those in early stages of internationalization focus on understanding cultural differences, while those more advanced are determined to manage and balance cultural diversity and eventually to integrate differences within the overall corporate culture. As seen in the chapter's opening vignette, international business systems are complex and dynamic and require competent people to develop and direct them.

EARLY STAGES OF INTERNATIONALIZATION

The marketing or sales manager of the firm typically is responsible for beginning export activities. As foreign sales increase, an export manager will be appointed and given the responsibility for developing and maintaining customers, interacting with the firm's intermediaries, and planning for overall market expansion. The export manager also must champion the international effort within the company because the general attitude among employees may be to view the domestic market as more important. Another critical function is the supervision of export transactions, particularly documentation. The requirements are quite different for international transactions than for domestic ones, and sales or profits may be lost if documentation is not properly handled. The first task of the new export manager, in fact, often is to hire a staff to handle paperwork that typically had previously been done by a facilitating agent, such as a freight forwarder.

The firm starting international operations will usually hire an export manager from outside rather than promote from within. The reason is that knowledge of the product or industry is less important than international experience. The cost of learning through experience to manage an export department is simply too great from the firm's standpoint. Further, the inexperienced manager would be put in the position of having to demonstrate his or her effectiveness almost at once.

The manager who is hired will have obtained experience through Foreign Service duty or with another corporation. In the early stages, a highly entrepreneurial spirit with a heavy dose of trader mentality is required. Even then, management should not expect the new export department to earn a profit for the first few years.

ADVANCED STAGES OF INTERNATIONALIZATION

As the firm progresses from exporting to an international division to foreign direct involvement, human resources-planning activities will initially focus on need vis-à-vis various markets and functions. Existing personnel can be assessed and plans made to recruit, select, and train employees for positions that cannot be filled internally. The four major categories of overseas assignments are: (1) CEO, to oversee and direct the entire operation; (2) functional head, to establish and maintain departments and ensure their proper performance; (3) troubleshooters, who are utilized for their special expertise in analyzing, and thereby preventing or solving, particular problems; and (4) white- or blue-collar workers.[2] Many technology companies have had to respond to shortages in skilled employees by globalized recruitment using Web sites or by hiring headhunters in places such as China and India. For example, 60 percent of Nokia's worldwide workforce are non-Finns while that share was only half in the late 1990s.[3]

One of the major sources of competitive advantage of global corporations is their ability to attract talent around the world. The corporations need systematic management-development systems, with the objective of creating and carefully allocating management personnel. An example of this is provided in Figure 19.1. Increasingly, plans call for international experience as a prerequisite for advancement; for example, at Ford, the goal is to have 100 percent of the top managers with international work experience with the company.[4]

In global corporations, there is no such thing as a universal global manager, but a network of global specialists in four general groups of managers has to work together.[5] Global business (product) managers have the task to further the company's global-scale efficiency and competitiveness. Country managers have to be sensitive and responsive to local market needs and demands but, at the same time, be aware of global implications. Functional managers have to make sure that the corporation's capabilities in technical, manufacturing, marketing, human resource, and financial expertise are linked and can benefit from each other. Corporate executives at headquarters have to manage interactions among the three groups of managers as well as identify and develop the talent to fill the positions.

As an example of this planning, a management review of human resources is conducted twice a year with each general manager of Heineken operating companies, which are located in such countries as Canada, France, Ireland, and Spain. The meet-

FIGURE 19.1

International Management Development

| Worldwide recruiting for talent | International experience (through short-term assignments)/ cross-cultural training | Company-wide screening for talent identification and promotion across countries and business units | Opportunities for international experience (through long-term assignments) in managing business units | International experience as a precondition for promotion to top management |

| 0 | 1 | 2 | 3 | 4 | 5 | 6 | 7 | 8 | 9 | 10 |

Years

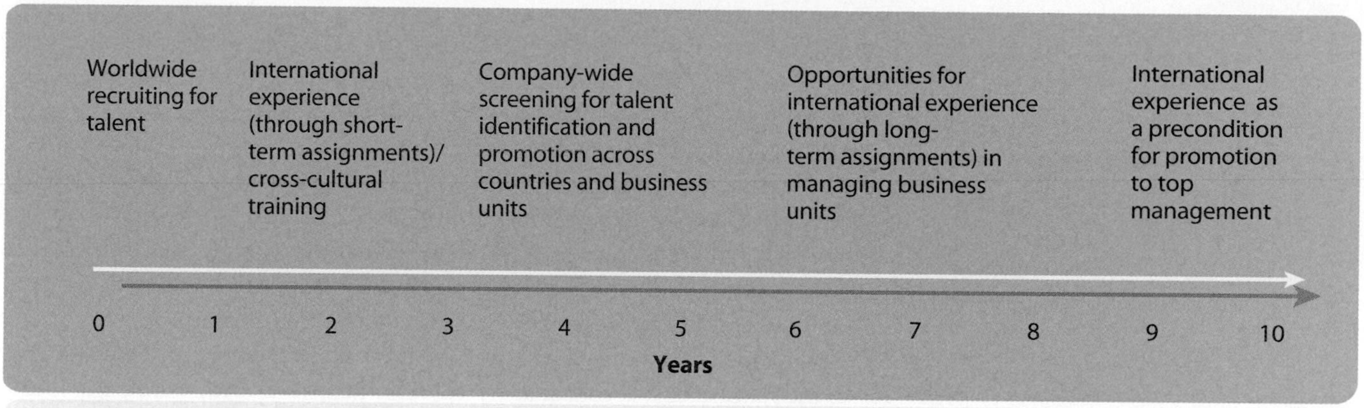

Source: Adapted from Ingo Theuerkauf, "Reshaping the Global Organization," *McKinsey Quarterly* 3, 1991, 104; and Paul Evans, Vladimir Pucik, and Jean-Louis Barsoux, *The Global Challenge: Frameworks for International Human Resource Management* (New York: McGraw-Hill/Irwin, 2002), Chapters 2–4.

ing is attended by the general manager, the personnel manager, the regional coordinating director in whose region the operating company is located, and the corporate director of management development. Special attention is given to managers "in the fast lane," the extent to which they are mobile, what might be done to foster their development, and where they fit into succession planning.[6] Of course, any gaps must be filled by recruitment efforts.

Companies should show clear career paths for managers assigned overseas and develop the systems and the organization for promotion.[7] This approach serves to eliminate many of the perceived problems and thus motivates managers to seek out foreign assignments. Furthermore, when jobs open up, the company can quickly determine who is able and willing to take them. Foreign assignments can occur at various stages of the manager's tenure. In the early stages, assignments may be short-term, such as a membership in an international task force or six to twelve months at headquarters in a staff function. Later, an individual may serve as a business-unit manager overseas. Many companies use cross-postings to other countries or across product lines to further an individual's acculturation to the corporation.[8] A period in a head office department or a subsidiary will not only provide an understanding of different national cultures and attitudes but also improve an individual's "know-who" and therefore establish unity and common sense of purpose necessary for the proper implementation of global programs.

At the most advanced stages of globalization, companies need to coordinate and leverage resources across borders. One of the most effective tools in achieving this is cross-border teams consisting of members of multiple nationalities.[9] For these teams to work, members need to have had the necessary experience to appreciate both global synergies and national/regional differences. Without assignments abroad, this is impossible.

INTERFIRM COOPERATIVE VENTURES

Global competition is forging new cooperative ties between firms from different countries, thereby adding a new management challenge for the firms involved. Although many of the reasons cited for these alliances (described in Chapter 11) are competitive and strategic, the human resource function is critical to their implementation. As a matter of fact, some of the basic reasons so many of these ventures fail relate to human resource management; for example, managers from disparate venture partners cannot work together, or managers within the venture cannot work with the owners' managers.[10] As more ventures are created in newly emerging markets, the challenge of finding skilled local managers is paramount. If such talent is not secured, developing loyalty to the company may be difficult.[11]

While the ingredients for success of the human resource function will differ with the type of cooperative venture, two basic types of tasks are needed.[12] The first task is to assign and motivate people in appropriate ways so that the venture will fulfill its set strategic tasks. This requires particular attention to such issues as job skills and compatibility of communication and other work styles. For example, some cooperative ventures have failed due to one of the partners' assigning relatively weak management resources to the venture or due to managers' finding themselves with conflicting loyalties to the parent organization and the cooperative venture organization. The second task is the strategic management of the human resources, that is, the appropriate use of managerial capabilities not only in the cooperative venture but in other later contexts, possibly back in the parent organization. An individual manager needs to see that an assignment in a cooperative venture is part of his or her overall career development.

SOURCES FOR MANAGEMENT RECRUITMENT

The location and the nationality of candidates for a particular job are the key issues in recruitment. A decision will have to be made to recruit from within the company or, in the case of larger corporations, within other product or regional groups, or to rely on external talent. Similarly, decisions will have to be made whether to hire or promote locally or use **expatriates;** that is, home-country nationals or third-country nationals (citizens of countries other than the home or host country). Typically, 65 percent of expatriates are posted in subsidiaries, while the remaining 35 percent have assignments in their company's headquarter's country (i.e., they are inpatriates).[13] The major advantages and disadvantages of expatriates are summarized in Table 19.1. In general, the choice process between expatriates and locals is driven by: (1) the availability and quality of the talent pool; (2) corporate policies and their cost; as well as (3) environmental constraints on the legal, cultural, or economic front. Many countries still resist letting jobs go to foreigners, but under pressure from employers in areas such as engineering and programming, the resistance is fading.[14] In the new economy in which the physical location of work may not matter, the choice of becoming an expatriate may be the employee's. A new breed of telecommuters live countries or even continents apart from their companies' home offices.[15]

The recruitment approach changes over the internationalization process of the firm. During the export stage, outside expertise is sought at first, but the firm then begins to develop its own personnel for international operations. With expanded and more involved foreign operations, the firm's reliance on home-country personnel will be reduced as host-country nationals are prepared for management positions. The use of home-country and third-country nationals may be directed at special assignments, such as transfer of technology or expertise. The use of expatriates will continue as a matter of corporate policy to internationalize management and to foster the infusion of particular corporate culture into operations around the world.

When international operations are expanded, a management development dilemma may result. Through internal recruitment, young managers will be offered interesting new opportunities. However, some senior managers may object to the constant drain of

© AFP/CORBIS

Jeffrey Bezos, founder and CEO of online retailer Amazon.com, with Japanese home-country manager Junichi Hasegawa.

TABLE 19.1

The Major Advantages and Disadvantages of Expatriates

The advantages of appointing a national of the headquarters country in an overseas post are that the expat:

1. Knows the company's products and culture.

2. Relates easily and efficiently to corporate headquarters; speaks the verbal and cultural language.

3. Has technical or business skills not available locally.

4. May have special transferable capabilities, for example, opening operations in emerging markets.

5. Will protect and promote the interests of headquarters in international joint ventures and acquisitions and other situations requiring tight financial control.

6. Is unlikely to steal proprietary knowledge and set up competing businesses.

7. Does not put the country ahead of the company (unless he or she "goes native").

8. Fits the company's need to develop future leaders and general managers with international experience.

The disadvantages of appointing an expat include:

1. High costs—covering relocation, housing, education, hardship allowance—often exceeding 200 percent of the home-country base.

2. Black-outs; 25 percent of expats have to be called home early.

3. Brown-outs: another 30 percent to 50 percent stay but underperform, leading to lost sales, low staff morale, and a decline in local goodwill.

4. Prolonged start-up and wind-down time: in a typical three-year assignment the first year is spent unpacking and the third year is spent packing and positioning for the next move.

5. A shortsighted focus: expats with a three-year assignment tend to focus on the next career rather than on building the local company.

6. Difficulty in finding experienced managers willing to move because of spouse's career, child's schooling or life-style and security concerns (for example, in Middle Eastern countries).

7. Expat's concern about negative out-of-sight, out-of-mind impact on career development.

8. Re-entry problems: a high percentage of expats leave their companies after overseas assignments because jobs with similar breadth of responsibility are either not available or not offered.

9. Division of senior managers to overseas markets is difficult especially for smaller companies that do not yet have a lock on their domestic markets.

Source: John A. Quelch and Helen Bloom, "Ten Steps to a Global Human Resources Strategy," *Strategy and Business* (First Quarter, 1999): 18–29.

young talent from their units. Selective recruitment from the outside will help to maintain a desirable combination of inside talent and fresh blood. Furthermore, with dynamic market changes or new markets and new business development, outside recruitment may be the only available approach. Even in Japan, the taboo against hiring executives from other companies is breaking down. The practice of hiring from the top universities can no longer be depended on to provide the right people in all circumstances.[16]

Currently, most managers in subsidiaries are host-country nationals. The reasons include an increase in availability of local talent, corporate relations in the particular market, and the economies realized by not having to maintain a corps of managers overseas. Local managers are generally more familiar with environmental conditions and how they should be interpreted. By employing local management, the multinational is responding to host-country demands for increased localization and providing advancement as an incentive to local managers. In this respect, however, localization can be carried too far. If the firm does not subscribe to a global philosophy, the manager's development is tied to the local operation or to a particular level of management in that operation. This has been an issue of contention, especially with Japanese employers in the United States. As a result, managers who outgrow the local operation may have nowhere to go except to another company.[17] Although the Japanese continue to express frustration in what they perceive to be disloyalty and opportunism on the part of U.S. employees, they are starting to change their practices so that they can retain talented U.S. nationals.[18]

Local managers, if not properly trained and indoctrinated, may see things differently from the way they are viewed at headquarters. As a result, both control and the overall coordination of programs may be jeopardized. For the corporation to work effectively, of course, employees must first of all understand each other. Most corporations have adopted a common corporate language, with English as the **lingua franca;** that is, the language habitually used among people of diverse speech to facilitate communication. At most global companies, all top-level meetings are conducted in English. In some companies, two languages are officially in use; for example, at Nestlé both English and French are corporate languages. However, corporate training should focus on a broad spectrum of international communication skills rather than just a systematic knowledge of any one or two langauges, and should include such areas as cultural appreciation.[19]

A second goal is to avoid overemphasis on localization, which would prevent the development of an internationalized group of managers with a proper understanding of the impact of the environment on operations. To develop language skills and promote an international outlook in their management pools, multinational corporations are increasingly recruiting among foreign students at business schools in the United States, western Europe, and the Far East. When these young managers return home, following an initial assignment at corporate headquarters, they will have a command of the basic philosophies of multinational operations.

Cultural differences that shape managerial attitudes must be considered when developing multinational management programs. For example, British managers place more emphasis than most other nationals on individual achievement and autonomy. French managers, however, value competent supervision, sound company policies, fringe benefits, security, and comfortable working conditions.[20]

The decision as to whether to use home-country nationals in a particular operation depends on such factors as the type of industry, the life-cycle stage of the product, the availability of managers from other sources, and the functional areas involved. The number of home-country managers is typically higher in the service sector than in the industrial sector, and overseas assignments may be quite short term. For example, many international hotel chains have established management contracts in the People's Republic of China with the understanding that home-country managers will train local successors within three to five years. In the start-up phase of an endeavor, headquarters involvement is generally substantial. This applies to all functions, including personnel. Especially if no significant pool of local managers is available or their competence levels are not satisfactory, home-country nationals may be used. For control and communication reasons, some companies always maintain a home-country national as manager in certain functional areas, such as accounting or finance. On occasion, the need to control may be more specific. For example, expatriates may be used in joint ventures to ascertain the proper use of funds or technologies by the local partner.[21]

The number of home-country nationals in an overseas operation rarely rises above 10 percent of the work force and is typically only 1 percent. The reasons are both internal and external. In addition to the substantial cost of transfer, a manager may not fully adjust to foreign working and living conditions. Good corporate citizenship today requires multinational companies to develop the host country's workforce at the management level. Legal impediments to manager transfers may exist, or other difficulties may be encountered. Many U.S.-based hotel corporations, for example, have complained about delays in obtaining visas to the United States not only for managers but also for management trainees.

The use of third-country nationals is most often seen in large multinational companies that have adopted a global philosophy. The practice of some companies, such as Philips, is to employ third-country nationals as managing directors in subsidiaries. An advantage is that third-country nationals may contribute to the firm's overall international expertise. However, many third-country nationals are career international managers, and they may become targets for raids by competitors looking for high levels of talent. They may be a considerable asset in regional expansion; for example, established subsidiary managers in Singapore might be used to start up a subsidiary in Malaysia. On the other hand, some transfers may be inadvisable for cultural or historical reasons, with transfers between Turkey and Greece as an example.

The ability to recruit for international assignments is determined by the value an individual company places on international operations and the experience gained in working in them. Based on a survey of 1,500 senior executives around the world, U.S. executives still place less emphasis on international dimensions than their Japanese, western European, and Latin American counterparts. While most executives agree that an international outlook is essential for future executives, 70 percent of foreign executives think that experience outside one's home country is important, compared with only 35 percent of U.S. executives, and foreign language capability was seen as important by only 19 percent of U.S. respondents, compared with 64 percent of non-U.S. executives.[22]

In an era of regional integration, many companies are facing a severe shortage of managers who can think and operate regionally or even globally. Very few companies—even those characterizing themselves as global—have systematically developed international managers by rotating young executives through a series of assignments in different parts of the world.[23] To help find the best cross-border talent, executive search firms such as A. T. Kearney and Heidrick & Struggles can be used.

SELECTION CRITERIA FOR OVERSEAS ASSIGNMENTS

The traits that have been suggested as necessary for the international manager range from the ideal to the real. One characterization describes "a flexible personality, with broad intellectual horizons, attitudinal values of cultural empathy, general friendliness, patience and prudence, impeccable educational and professional (or technical) credentials—all topped off with immaculate health, creative resourcefulness, and respect of peers. If the family is equally well endowed, all the better."[24] In addition to flexibility and adaptability, they have to be able to take action where there is no precedent. Traits typically mentioned in the choosing of managers for overseas assignments are listed in Table 19.2. Their relative importance may vary dramatically, of course, depending on the firm situation, as well as where the choice is being made. The United States is particularly good at business literacy, while Latin Americans have developed the ability to cope with complex social relations.[25]

TABLE 19.2   Criteria for Selecting Managers for Overseas Assignment

Competence	Adaptability	Personal Characteristics
Technical knowledge	Interest in overseas work	Age
Leadership ability	Relational abilities	Education
Experience, past performance	Cultural empathy	Sex
Area expertise	Appreciation of new	Health
Language	management styles	Marital relations
	Appreciation of environmental	Social acceptability
	constraints	
	Adaptability of family	

Competence Factors

An expatriate manager usually has far more responsibility than a manager in a comparable domestic position and must be far more self-sufficient in making decisions and conducting daily business. To be selected in the first place, the manager's technical competence level has to be superior to that of local candidates'; otherwise, the firm would in most cases have chosen a local person. The manager's ability to do the job in the technical sense is one of the main determinants of ultimate success or failure in an overseas assignment.[26] However, management skills will not transfer from one culture to another without some degree of adaptation. This means that, regardless of the level of technical skills, the new environment still requires the ability to adapt the skills to local conditions. Technical competence must also be accompanied by the ability to lead subordinates in any situation or under any conditions.

Especially in global-minded enterprises, managers are selected for overseas assignments on the basis of solid experience and past performance. Many firms use the foreign tour as a step toward top management. By sending abroad internally recruited, experienced managers, the firm also ensures the continuation of corporate culture—a set of shared values, norms, and beliefs and an emphasis on a particular facet of performance. Two examples are IBM's concern with customer service and 3M's concentration on innovation.

The role of **factual cultural knowledge** in the selection process has been widely debated. **Area expertise** includes a knowledge of the basic systems in the region or market for which the manager will be responsible—such as the roles of various ministries in international business, the significance of holidays, and the general way of doing business. None of these variables is as important as language, although language skill is not always highly ranked by firms themselves.[27] A manager who does not know the language of the country may get by with the help of associates and interpreters but is not in a position to assess the situation fully. Of the Japanese representing their companies in the United States, for example, almost all speak English. As a matter of fact, some Japanese companies, such as Honda, have deployed some of their most talented executives to U.S. operations.[28] Of the Americans representing U.S. companies in China, Japan, or Korea, however, few speak the local language well. Some companies place language skills or aptitude in a larger context; they see a strong correlation between language skill and adaptability. Another reason to look for language competence in managers considered for assignments overseas is that all managers spend most of their time communicating.

Adaptability Factors

The manager's own motivation to a great extent determines the viability of an overseas assignment and consequently its success. The manager's interest in the foreign culture must go well beyond that of the average tourist if he or she is to understand what an assignment abroad involves. In most cases, the manager will need counseling and training to comprehend the true nature of the undertaking.

Adaptability means a positive and flexible attitude toward change. The manager assigned overseas must progress from factual knowledge of culture to **interpretive cultural knowledge,** trying as much as possible to become part of the new scene, which may be quite different from the one at home. The work habits of middle-level managers may be more lax, productivity and attention to detail less, and overall environmental restrictions far greater. The manager on a foreign assignment is part of a multicultural team, in which both internal and external interactions determine the future of the firm's operations. For example, a manager from the United States may be used to an informal, democratic type of leadership that may not be applicable in countries such as Mexico or Japan, where employees expect more authoritarian leadership.[29]

Adaptability does not depend solely on the manager. Firms look carefully at the family situation because a foreign assignment often puts more strain on other family members than on the manager. As an example, a U.S. engineering firm had problems in Italy that were traced to the inability of one executive's wife to adapt. She complained to other wives, who began to feel that they too suffered hardships and then complained to their husbands. Morale became so low that the company, after missing important deadlines, replaced most of the Americans on the job.[30] As a response, networks intended for expatriate spouses have been developed on corporate intranets to allow for exchange of advice and ideas.[31]

The characteristics of the family as a whole are important. Screeners look for family cohesiveness and check for marital instability or for behavioral difficulties in children. Abroad, the need to work together as a family often makes strong marriages stronger and causes the downfall of weak ones. Further, commitments or interests beyond the nuclear family affect the adjustment of family members to a new environment. Some firms use earlier transfers within the home country as an indicator of how a family will handle transfer abroad. With the dramatic increase in two-career households, foreign assignments may call for one of the spouses to sacrifice a career or, at best, to put it on hold. Increasingly transferees are requesting for spouse reemployment assistance.[32] As a result, corporations are forming a consortia to try to tackle this problem. Members of the group interview accompanying spouses and try to find them positions with other member companies.[33] Increasingly, this means also male expatriate spouses who accompany their partners abroad.[34]

Personal Characteristics

Despite all of the efforts made by multinational companies to recruit the best person available, demographics still play a role in the selection process. Due to either a minimum age requirement or the level of experience needed, many foreign assignments go to managers in their mid-30s or older. Normally, companies do not recruit candidates from graduating classes for immediate assignment overseas. They want their international people first to become experienced and familiar with the corporate culture, and this can best be done at the headquarter's location.

Although the number of women in overseas assignments is only 18 percent according to one count, women are as interested as men are in the assignments.[35] Corporate hiring practices may be based on the myth that women will not be accepted in the host countries. Many of the relatively few women managers report being treated as foreign business people and not singled out as women. These issues are highlighted in Focus on Culture.

In the selection process, firms are concerned about the health of the people they may send abroad. Some assignments are in host countries with dramatically different environmental conditions from the home country, and they may aggravate existing health problems. Moreover, if the candidate selected is not properly prepared, foreign assignments may increase stress levels and contribute to the development of peptic ulcers, colitis, or other problems.

When candidates are screened, being married is usually considered a plus. Marriage brings stability and an inherent support system, provided family relations are in order. It may also facilitate adaptation to the local culture by increasing the number of social functions to which the manager is invited.

Social acceptability varies from one culture to another and can be a function of any of the other personal characteristics. Background, religion, race, and sex usually become critical only in extreme cases in which a host environment would clearly reject a candidate based on one or more of these variables. The Arab boycott of the state of Israel, for example, puts constraints on the use of managers of Jewish and Arab origin.

Focus On ⬇

CULTURE

Women and the Global Corporate Ladder

There is growing evidence to suggest that women are making greater strides on the international front than ever before. The 2002 Global Relocation Survey, conducted by Windham International and the National Foreign Trade Council, provides various measures of this trend. A full 18 percent of American corporate expatriates are women, up from 10 percent in 1993.

Some argue that the numbers are relatively small due to commonly held myths about women in international business. The first is that women do not want to be international managers, and the second is that foreigners' prejudice against them renders them ineffective, whether they are nationals or not.

In a study of more than 1,000 graduating MBAs from schools in North America and Europe, females and males displayed equal interest in pursuing international careers. They also agreed that firms offer fewer opportunities to women pursuing international careers than to

those pursuing domestic ones. Women expatriate managers agree that convincing superiors to let them go called for patience and persistence.

Expatriate women have generally reported numerous professional advantages to being female. Being highly visible (both internally and externally) has often been quoted as an advantage given that many women expatriates are "firsts" for their companies. Foreign clients are curious about them, want to meet them, and remember them after the first encounter. Emanuel Monogenis, a managing partner at the international search firm of Heidrick & Struggles, observed, "My clients now see women as equals in top global searches. In fact, more and more executives are saying they prefer women because they feel they are willing to work harder and take less for granted than male counterparts. Many also believe women have more of a sensibility and insight into human behavior and relationships than their male counterparts, and this is highly valued in culturally diverse workforces."

Sources: 2002 Global Relocation Trends Survey Report, Warren, NJ: GMAC Relocation Services, 2003, available at http://www.gmacglobalrelocation.com; Virginia E. Schein, "A Global Look at Psychological Barriers to Women's Progress in Management," *Journal of Social Issues* 57 (winter 2001): 675–689; "Stay-at-Home Careers?" *Global Business,* January 2001, 62; Lori Ioannou, "Women's Global Career Ladder," *International Business,* December 1994, 57–60; Nancy J. Adler and Dafna N. Izraeli, eds., *Competitive Frontiers: Women Managers in a Global Economy* (Cambridge, MA: Blackwell Business, 1994): Chapters 1 and 2; Diana Kunde, "Management Opportunities for Women Brighten," *Washington Post,* December 19, 1993, H2; and Anne B. Fisher, "When Will Women Get to the Top?" *Fortune,* September 21, 1992, 44–56; http://www.heidrick.com.

Women cannot negotiate contracts in many Middle Eastern countries. This would hold true even if the woman were president of the company.

The Selection and Orientation Challenge

Due to the cost of transferring a manager overseas, many firms go beyond standard selection procedures and use **adaptability screening** as an integral part of the process. During the screening phase, the method most often used involves interviewing the candidate and the family. The interviews are conducted by senior executives, human relations specialists within the firm, or outside firms. Interviewers ask the candidate and the family to consider the personal issues involved in the transfer; for example, what each will miss the most. In some cases, candidates themselves will refuse an assignment. In others, the firm will withhold the assignment on the basis of interviews that clearly show a degree of risk.

The candidate selected will participate in an **orientation program** on internal and external aspects of the assignment. Internal aspects include issues such as compensation and reporting. External aspects are concerned with what to expect at the destination in terms of customs and culture. The extent and level of the programs will vary; for example, in a survey of 120 U.S. companies, 42 percent reported having no cultural preparation training for their executives. As shown in Figure 19.2, most programs offered extend the orientation to the spouse or the entire family. If the company is still in the export stage, the emphasis in this training will be on interpersonal skills and local culture. With expatriates, the focus will be on both training and interacting with host-country nationals. Actual methods vary from area studies to sensitivity training. For a discussion of these methods, see Chapter 2.

FIGURE 19.2

Companies Offering Cultural Training

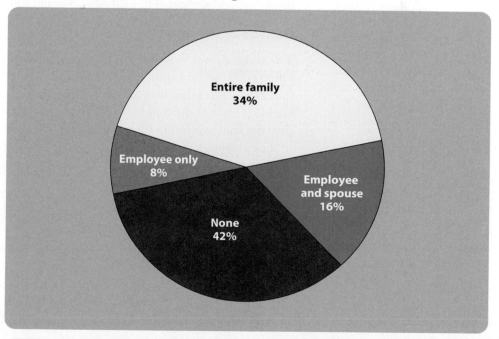

Source: Lori Ioannou, "Cultivating the New Expatriate Executive," *International Business* (July 1994): 46.

The attrition rate in overseas assignments averages 40 percent among companies with neither adaptability screening nor orientation programs, 25 percent among companies with cultural orientation programs, and 5 to 10 percent among companies that use both kinds of programs. Considering the cost of a transfer, catching even one potentially disastrous situation pays for the program for a full year. Most companies have no program at all, however, and others provide them for higher level management positions only. Companies that have the lowest failure rates typically employ a four-tiered approach to expatriate use: (1) clearly stated criteria; (2) rigorous procedures to determine the suitability of an individual across the criteria; (3) appropriate orientation; and (4) constant evaluation of the effectiveness of the procedures.[36]

In this context, it is also important to make the length of the overseas appointment make sense for the individual, the family, and the company. Three-year assignments are typical; however, in some cases when culture gaps are significant (as is in the case of Western and Eastern countries), it may be prudent to have longer tours.

It is important that the expatriate and his or her family feel the support continuing during their tour. A significant share of the dissatisfaction expressed pertains to perceived lack of support during the international experience, especially in cases of dual-career households.[37]

CULTURE SHOCK

The effectiveness of orientation procedures can be measured only after managers are overseas and exposed to security and socio-political tensions, health, housing, education, social network and leisure activities, language, availability of products and services, and climate. **Culture shock** is the term used for the pronounced reactions to the psychological disorientation that is experienced in varying degrees when spending an extended period of time in a new environment.[38]

Of the locations around the world, those perceived to be the most pleasant have included Hong Kong, Rome, Buenos Aires, Dubai, and Prague. The most difficult to live in include Karachi, Tiranë, Lagos, Saigon, and Moscow.[39]

Causes and Remedies

The culture shock cycle for an overseas assignment may last about fourteen months. Often goals set for a subsidiary or a project may be unrealistic or the means by which they are to be reached may be totally inadequate. All of these lead to external manifestations of culture shock, such as bitterness and even physical illness. In extreme cases, they can lead to hostility toward anything in the host environment.

The culture-shock cycle for an overseas assignment is presented in Figure 19.3. Four distinct stages of adjustment exist during a foreign assignment. The length of the stages is highly individual. The four stages are:

1. **Initial Euphoria:** Enjoying the novelty, largely from the perspective of a spectator
2. **Irritation and Hostility:** Experiencing cultural differences, such as the concept of time, through increased participation
3. **Adjustment:** Adapting to the situation, which in some cases leads to biculturalism and even accusations from corporate headquarters of "going native"
4. **Reentry:** Returning home to face a possibly changed home environment

The manager may fare better at the second stage than other members of the family, especially if their opportunities for work and other activities are severely restricted.

FIGURE 19.3

Culture Shock Cycle for an Overseas Assignment

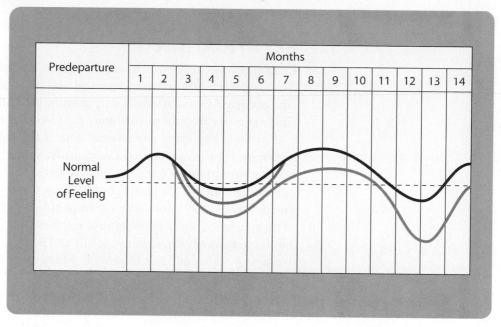

Note: Lines indicate the extreme severity with which culture shock may attack.
Source: L. Robert Kohls, *Survival Kits for Overseas Living* (Yarmouth, ME: Intercultural Press, 1984), 68.

The fourth stage may actually cause a reverse culture shock when the adjustment phase has been highly successful and the return home is not desired. The home environment that has been idealized during the tour abroad may not be perfect after all, and the loss of status and benefits enjoyed abroad may generate feelings of frustration.[40]

Firms themselves must take responsibility for easing one of the causes of culture shock: isolation. By maintaining contact with the manager beyond business-related communication, some of the shock may be alleviated. Exxon/Mobil, for example, assigns each expatriate a contact person at headquarters to share general information. This helps top management to keep tabs on the manager's progress especially in terms of management succession.

Terrorism: Tangible Culture Shock

International terrorists have frequently targeted corporate facilities, operations, and personnel for attack. Corporate reactions have ranged from letting terrorism have little effect on operations to abandoning certain markets. Some companies try to protect their managers in various ways by fortifying their homes and using local-sounding names to do business in troubled parts of the world.[41] Of course, insurance is available to cover key executives; the cost ranges from a few thousand dollars to hundreds of thousands a year depending on the extent and location of the company's operations. Leading insurers include American International Underwriters, Chubb & Son, and Lloyd's of London.[42] The threat of terrorist activity may have an effect on the company's operations beyond the immediate geographic area of concern. Travel may be banned or restricted in times or areas threatened. An array of organizations have emerged to service companies with employees in the world's hot spots. For example,

Rapid Air Support provides in-depth, up-to-the-minute information on government, security, and military situations in various countries and are ready to pull out clients' employees when emergencies arise.[43]

REPATRIATION

Returning home may evoke mixed feelings on the part of the expatriate and the family. Their concerns are both professional and personal. Even in two years, dramatic changes may have occurred not only at home but also in the way the individual and the family perceive the foreign environment. At worst, reverse culture shock may emerge.

The most important professional issue is finding a proper place in the corporate hierarchy. If no provisions have been made, a returning manager may be caught in a holding pattern for an intolerable length of time. For this reason, Dow Chemical, for example, provides each manager embarking on an overseas assignment with a letter that promises a job at least equal in responsibility upon return. Furthermore, because of their isolation, assignments abroad mean greater autonomy and authority than similar domestic positions. Both financially and psychologically, many expatriates find the overseas position difficult to give up. Many executive perks, such as club memberships, will not be funded at home.

The family, too, may be reluctant to give up their special status. In India, for example, expatriate families have servants for most of the tasks they perform themselves at home. Many longer-term expatriates are shocked by increases in the prices of housing and education at home. For the many managers who want to stay abroad, this may mean a change of company or even career—from employee to independent business person. According to one survey, as many as 25 percent of returnees may leave their companies within two years of coming home (many of them taking expatriate assignments with new employers).[44]

This alternative is not an attractive one for the company, which stands to lose valuable individuals who could become members of an international corps of managers. Therefore, planning for repatriation is necessary.[45] A four-step process can be used for this purpose. The first step involves an assessment of foreign assignments in terms of environmental constraints and corporate objectives, making sure that the latter are realistically defined. The second stage is preparation of the individual for an overseas assignment, which should include a clear understanding of when and how repatriation takes place. During the actual tour, the manager should be kept abreast of developments at headquarters, especially in terms of career paths. Finally, during the actual reentry, the manager should receive intensive organizational reorientation, reasonable professional adjustment time, and counseling for the entire family on matters of, for example, finance. A program of this type allows the expatriate to feel a close bond with headquarters regardless of geographical distance.

COMPENSATION

A Japanese executive's salary in cash is quite modest by U.S. standards, but he is comfortable in the knowledge that the company will take care of him. Compensation is paternalistic; for example, a manager with two children in college and a sizable mortgage would be paid more than a childless manager in a comparable job. As this example suggests, Japanese compensation issues go beyond salary comparisons. They include exchange rates, local taxes, and what the money will buy in different countries. Many compensation packages include elements other than cash.

A firm's expatriate compensation program has to be effective in: (1) providing an incentive to leave the home country on a foreign assignment; (2) maintaining a given standard of living; (3) taking into consideration career and family needs; and (4) facilitating reentry into the home country.[46] To achieve these objectives, firms pay a high premium beyond base salaries to induce managers to accept overseas assignments. The costs to the firm are 2 to 2.5 times the cost of maintaining a manager in a comparable position at home. For example, the average compensation package of a U.S. manager in Hong Kong is $225,500 (base salary is 47 percent of this figure) and for the British manager $170,500 (57 percent). U.S. firms traditionally offer their employees more high-value perks, such as bigger apartments.[47]

The compensation of the manager overseas can be divided into two general categories: (1) base salary and salary-related allowances and (2) nonsalary-related allowances. Although incentives to leave home are justifiable in both categories, they create administrative complications for the personnel department in tying them to packages at home and elsewhere. As the number of transfers increases, firms develop general policies for compensating the manager rather than negotiating individually on every aspect of the arrangement.

Base Salary and Salary-Related Allowances

A manager's **base salary** depends on qualifications, responsibilities, and duties, just as it would for a domestic position. Furthermore, criteria applying to merit increases, promotions, and other increases are administered as they are domestically. Equity and comparability with domestic positions are important, especially in ensuring that repatriation will not cause cuts in base pay. For administrative and control purposes, the compensation and benefits function in multinational corporations is most often centralized.

The cost of living varies considerably around the world, as can be seen in Table 19.3. The purpose of the **cost of living allowance (COLA)** is to enable the manager to maintain as closely as possible the same standard of living that he or she would have at home. COLA is calculated by determining a percentage of base salary that would be spent on goods and services at the foreign location. (Figures around 50 percent are typical.) The ratios will naturally vary as a function of income and family size. COLA tables for various U.S. cities (of which Washington, DC, is the most often used) and locations worldwide are available through the U.S. State Department Allowances Staff and various consulting firms, such as Business International Corporation. Fluctuating exchange rates will of course have an effect on the COLA as well, and changes will call for reviews of the allowance. As an example, assume that living in Helsinki costs the manager 49 percent more than living in Washington, DC. The manager's monthly pay is $10,000, and for his family of four, the disposable income is $5,375 (53.75 percent). Further assume that the dollar weakens from €1.08 to €1.00. The COLA would be:

$$\$5,375 \times 149/100 \times 1.08/1.00 = \$8,649$$

Similarly, if the local currency depreciated, the COLA would be less. When the cost of living is less than in the United States, no COLA is determined.

The **foreign service premium** is actually a bribe to encourage a manager to leave familiar conditions and adapt to new surroundings. Although the methods of paying the premium vary, as do its percentages, most firms pay it as a percentage of the base salary. The percentages range from 10 to 25 percent of base salary. One variation of the straightforward percentage is a sliding scale by amount—15 percent of the first $20,000, then 10 percent, and sometimes a ceiling beyond which a premium is not paid. Another variation is by duration, with the percentages decreasing with every year the manager spends abroad. Despite the controversial nature of foreign service premiums paid at some locations, they are a generally accepted competitive practice.

TABLE 19.3   International Cost Comparisons

Living cost comparisons for Americans residing in foreign areas are developed four times a year by the U.S. Department of State Allowances Staff. For each post, two measures are computed: (I) a government index to establish post allowances for U.S. government employees and (2) a local index for use by private organizations. The government index takes into consideration prices of goods imported to posts and price advantages available only to U.S. government employees.

The local index is used by many business firms and private organizations to determine the cost of living allowance for their American employees assigned abroad. Local index measures for 12 key areas around the world are shown in the accompanying table. Maximum housing allowances, calculated separately, are also given.

The reports are issued four times annually under the title *U.S. Department of State Indexes of Living Costs Abroad, Quarters Allowances, and Hardship Differentials* by the U.S. Department of Labor.

Location	COST OF LIVING INDEX[a] (WASHINGTON, DC = 100)		MAXIMUM ANNUAL HOUSING ALLOWANCE[b]		
	Survey Date	Index	Effective Date	Family of 2	Family of 3–4
Buenos Aires, Argentina	Dec. 2002	83	NA	NA	NA
Canberra, Australia	Jun. 2002	105	Oct. 1998	$17,600	$19,360
Brussels, Belgium	Mar. 2002	120	Nov. 2002	$30,700	$33,770
Brasilia, Brazil	Oct. 2001	94	NA	NA	NA
Paris, France	Feb. 2001	125	Feb. 2003	$63,500	$69,850
Frankfurt, Germany	Jan. 2002	117	May 2002	$25,700	$28,270
Hong Kong	Oct. 2001	163	NA	NA	NA
Toyko, Japan	Feb. 2002	175	Mar. 2002	$80,000	$88,000
Mexico City	Mar. 2001	124	Jun. 1995	$37,500	$41,250
The Hague, Netherlands	Apr. 2002	114	May 2002	$33,600	$36,960
Geneva, Switzerland	Apr. 2002	163	Jul. 2002	$53,600	$58,960
London, U.K.	Mar. 2001	138	Feb. 2003	$64,300	$70,730

[a]Excluding housing and education.

[b]For a family of three to four members with an annual income of $68,000 and over. Allowances are computed and paid in U.S. dollars.

NA = not available.

Source: http://www.state.gov.

The environments in which a manager will work and the family will live vary dramatically. For example, consider being assigned to London or Brisbane versus Dar es Salaam or Port Moresby or even Bogota or Buenos Aires. Some locations may require little, if any, adjustment. Some call for major adaptation because of climatic differences; political instability; inadequacies in housing, education, shopping, or recreation; or overall isolation. For example, a family assigned to Beijing may find that schooling is difficult to arrange, with the result that younger children go to school in Tokyo and the older ones in the United States. To compensate for this type of expense and adjustment, firms pay **hardship allowances.** The allowances are based on U.S. State Department Foreign Post Differentials. The percentages vary from zero (for example, the manager in Helsinki) to 50 percent (as in Monrovia). The higher allowances typically include a danger pay extra added to any hardship allowance.[48]

Housing costs and related expenses are typically the largest expenditure in the expatriate manager's budget. Firms usually provide a **housing allowance** commensurate with the manager's salary level and position. When the expatriate is the country manager for the firm, the housing allowance will provide for suitable quarters in which to receive business associates. In most cases, firms set a range within which the manager must find housing. For common utilities, firms either provide an allowance or pay the costs outright.

One of the major determinants of the manager's lifestyle abroad is taxes. A U.S. manager earning $100,000 in Canada would pay nearly $40,000 in taxes—in excess of $10,000 more than in the United States. For this reason, 90 percent of U.S. multinational corporations have **tax-equalization** plans. When a manager's overseas taxes are higher than at home, the firm will make up the difference. However, in countries with a lower rate of taxation, the company simply keeps the difference. The firms' rationalization is that it does not make any sense for the manager in Hong Kong to make more money than the person who happened to land in Singapore. Tax equalization is usually handled by accounting firms that make the needed calculations and prepare the proper forms. Managers can exclude a portion of their expatriate salary from U.S. tax; in 2001 the amount was $78,000, with the figure increasing annually by $2,000.[49] Starting in 2008, the exclusion will be indexed for inflation.

Nonsalary-Related Allowances

Other types of allowances are made available to ease the transition into the period of service abroad. Typical allowances during the transition stage include: (1) a relocation allowance to compensate for the additional expense of a move, such as purchase of electric converters; (2) a mobility allowance as an incentive to managers to go overseas, usually paid in a lump sum and as a substitute for the foreign service premium (some companies pay 50 percent at transfer, 50 percent at repatriation); (3) allowances related to housing, such as home sale or rental protection, shipment and storage of household goods, or provision of household furnishings in overseas locations; (4) automobile protection in terms of covering possible losses on the sale of a car or cars at transfer and having to buy others overseas, usually at a higher cost; (5) travel expenses, using economy-class transportation except for long flights (for example, from Washington to Taipei); and (6) temporary living expenses, which may become substantial if housing is not immediately available—as for the expatriate family that had to spend a year at a hotel in Beijing, for example. Companies are also increasingly providing support to make up for income lost by the accompanying spouse.

Education for children is one of the major concerns of expatriate families. Free public schooling may not be available and the private alternatives expensive. In many cases, children may have to go to school in a different country. Firms will typically reimburse for such expenses in the form of an **education allowance.** In the case of college education, firms reimburse for one round-trip airfare every year, leaving tuition expenses to the family.

Finally, firms provide support for medical expenses, especially to provide medical services at a level comparable to the expatriate's home country. In some cases, this means traveling to another country for care; for example, from Malaysia to Singapore, where the medical system is the most advanced in southeast Asia. Other health-related allowances are in place to allow the expatriate to leave the challenging location periodically for rest and relaxation. Some expatriates in Mexico City get $300 to $500 per family member each month to cover a getaway from the pollution of the city.[50] Leaves from hardship posts such as Port Moresby are routine.

Other issues should be covered by a clearly stated policy. Home leave is provided every year, typically after 11 months overseas, although some companies require a longer period. Home leaves are usually accompanied by consultation and training sessions at headquarters. At some posts, club memberships are necessary because: (1) the status of the manager requires them and (2) they provide family members with access to the type of recreation they are used to in the home environment. Because they are extremely expensive—for example, a "mandatory" golf club membership in Tokyo might cost thousands of dollars—the firm's assistance is needed. Benefits and allowances are extended to "significant others" in 24 percent of the companies. Of these, 85 percent recognize nonmarried opposite-sex partners, 84 percent recognize same-sex partners.

Method of Payment

The method of payment, especially in terms of currency, is determined by a number of factors. The most common method is to pay part of the salary in the local currency and part in the currency of the manager's home country. Host-country regulations, ranging from taxation to the availability of foreign currency, will influence the decision. Firms themselves look at the situation from the accounting and administrative point of view and would like, in most cases, to pay in local currencies to avoid burdening the subsidiary. The expatriate naturally will want to have some of the compensation in his or her own currency for various reasons; for example, if exchange controls are in effect, to get savings out of the country upon repatriation may be very difficult.

Compensation of Host-Country Nationals

The compensation packages paid to local managers—cash, benefits, and privileges—are largely determined as a function of internal equity and external competitiveness. Internal equity may be complicated because of cultural differences in compensation; for example, in Japan a year-end bonus of an additional month's salary is common. On the other hand, some incentive programs to increase productivity may be unknown to some nationals. Furthermore, in many countries, the state provides benefits that may be provided by the firm elsewhere. Since the firm and its employees contribute to the programs by law, the services need not be duplicated.

External competitiveness depends on the market price of trained individuals and their attraction to the firm. External competitiveness is best assessed through surveys of compensation and benefits levels for a particular market. The firm must keep its local managers informed of the survey results to help them realize the value of their compensation packages.

Managing Labor Personnel

None of the firm's objectives can be realized without a labor force, which can become one of the firm's major assets or one of its major problems depending on the relationship that is established. Because of local patterns and legislation, headquarters' role in shaping the relations is mainly advisory, limited to setting the overall tone for the interaction. However, many of the practices adopted in one market or region may easily come under discussion in another, making it necessary for multinational corporations to set general policies concerning labor relations. Often multinational corporations have been instrumental in bringing about changes in the overall work environment in a country. And as decisions are made where to locate and how to

UPS, the world's largest package distribution company, transports more than 3.1 billion parcels and documents annually. To transport packages most efficiently, UPS has developed an elaborate network of "hubs" or central sorting facilities located throughout the world.

streamline operations, education and training become important criteria for both countries and companies.

At many companies, educational programs are a means of leveraging valuable company resources. Eastman Kodak has established eight training centers of excellence with functional specializations (for example, technical training and general business education). In China, AT&T has provided customized technical training to the government workers who will run the AT&T-supplied telecommunications networks.[51]

Labor strategy can be viewed from three perspectives: (1) the participation of labor in the affairs of the firm, especially as it affects performance and well-being; (2) the role and impact of unions in the relationship; and (3) specific human resource policies in terms of recruitment, training, and compensation.

LABOR PARTICIPATION IN MANAGEMENT

Over the past quarter century, many changes have occurred in the traditional labor-management relationship as a result of dramatic changes in the economic environment and the actions of both firms and the labor force. The role of the worker is changing both at the level of the job performed and in terms of participation in the decision-making process. To enhance workers' role in decision making, various techniques have emerged: self-management, codetermination, minority board membership, and works councils. In striving for improvements in quality of work life, programs that have been initiated include flextime, quality circles, and work-flow reorganization. Furthermore, employee ownership has moved into the mainstream.

Labor Participation in Decision Making

The degree to which workers around the world can participate in corporate decision making varies considerably. Rights of information, consultation, and codetermination develop on three levels:

1. The shop-floor level, or direct involvement; for example, the right to be consulted in advance concerning transfers.
2. The management level, or through representative bodies; for example, works council participation in setting of new policies or changing of existing ones.
3. The board level: for example, labor membership on the board of directors.[52]

The extent of worker participation in decision making in 11 countries is summarized in Table 19.4. Yugoslavia, before its breakup, had the highest amount of worker participation in any country; **self-management** was standard through workers' councils, which decided all major issues including the choice of managing director and supervisory board. Currently, the greatest amount of cooperation between labor and capital in participative leadership exists in the Germanic group of European countries (Austria, Germany, Holland, and Switzerland).[53]

In some countries, employees are represented on the supervisory boards to facilitate communication between management and labor by giving labor a clearer picture of the financial limits of management and by providing management with a new awareness of labor's point of view. The process is called **codetermination**. In Germany, companies have a two-tiered management system with a supervisory board and the board of managers, which actually runs the firm. In a firm with 20,000 employees, for example, labor would have ten of the twenty supervisory board slots divided in the following way: three places for union officials and the balance to be elected from the workforce. At

TABLE 19.4   Degree of Worker Involvement in Decision Making of Firms

	Direct Involvement of Workers[a]	Involvement of Representative Bodies[a]	Board Representation Standing[b]	Overall Standing[c]
Germany	3	1	1	A
Sweden	4	2	1	A
Norway	1	10	1	B
Netherlands	9	4	2	C
France	7	3	2	C
Belgium	5	6	3	D
Finland	2	9	3	D
Denmark	8	7	1	D
Israel	11	5	3	D
Italy	6	8	3	E
Great Britain	10	11	3	E

[a]Involvement is rated on an 11-point scale, where 1 stands for the greatest degree of involvement and 11 for almost no involvement.
[b]All cases without any kind of board participation are coded 3; the right to appoint two or more members, 1; the in-between category, 2.
[c]Rankings are from high (A) to low (E).

Source: Adapted from Industrial Democracy in Europe International Research Group, *Industrial Democracy in Europe* (Oxford, England: Clarendon Press, 1981), 291; and Industrial Democracy in Europe International Research Group, *Industrial Democracy in Europe Revisited* (Oxford, England: Oxford University Press, 1993), chapter 3.

least one member must be a white-collar employee and one a managerial employee.[54] The supervisory board is legally responsible for the managing board. In some countries, labor has **minority participation.** In the Netherlands, for example, works councils can nominate (not appoint) board members and can veto the appointment of new members appointed by others. In other countries, such as the United States, codetermination has been opposed by unions as an undesirable means of cooperation, especially when management–labor relations are confrontational.

A tradition in labor relations, especially in Britain, is **works councils.** They provide labor a say in corporate decision making through a representative body, which may consist entirely of workers or of a combination of managers and workers. The councils participate in decisions on overall working conditions, training, transfers, work allocation, and compensation. In some countries, such as Finland and Belgium, workers' rights to direct involvement, especially as it involves their positions, are quite strong. The European Union's works council directive will ultimately require over 1,000 multinational companies, both European and non-European, to negotiate works council agreements. The agreements will provide for at least one meeting per year to improving dialogue between workers and management.[55]

The countries described are unique in the world. In many countries and regions, workers have few, if any, of these rights. The result is long-term potential for labor strife in those countries and possible negative publicity elsewhere. Over a ten-year period from 1989 to 1998, the most working days lost occurred in Iceland, followed by Spain, Greece, Canada, Turkey, and Italy. In 1998, the most strike-prone country was Denmark, where workers sought a sixth week of paid holiday through strikes.[56]

Primary Labor Force Occupation

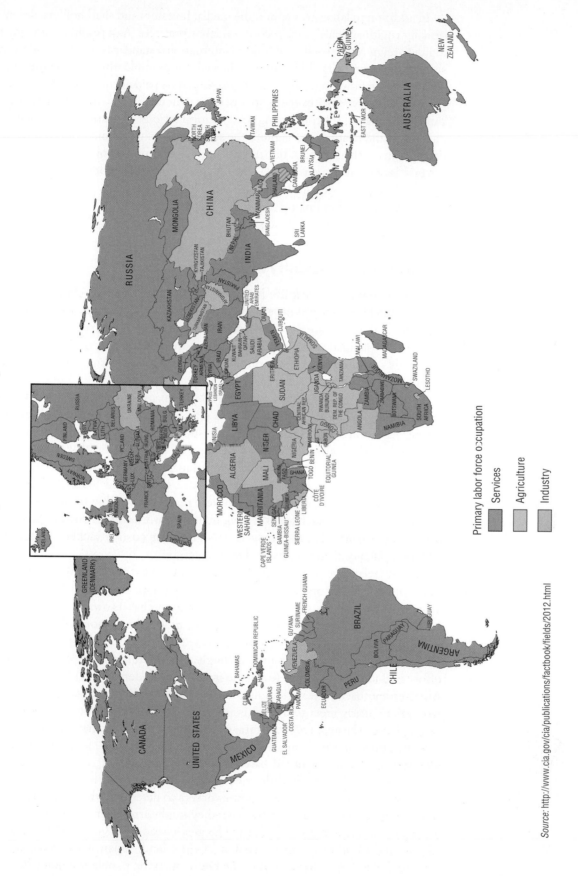

Primary labor force occupation

- Services
- Agriculture
- Industry

Source: http://www.cia.gov/cia/publications/factbook/fields/2012.html

MAP

In addition to labor groups and the media, investors and shareholders also are scrutinizing multinationals' track records on labor practices. As a result, a company investing in foreign countries should hold to international standards of safety and health, not simply local standards. This can be achieved, for example, through the use of modern equipment and training. Local labor also should be paid adequately. This increases the price of labor, yet ensures the best available talent and helps avoid charges of exploitation.[57] Companies subcontracting work to local or joint-venture factories need to evaluate industrial relations throughout the system not only to avoid lost production due to disruptions such as strikes, but to ensure that no exploitation exists at the facilities. Several large firms, such as Nike and Reebok, require subcontractors to sign agreements saying they will abide by minimum wage standards.[58] While companies have been long opposed to linking free trade to labor standards, the business community is rethinking its strategy mainly to get trade negotiations moving.[59]

Improvement of Quality of Work Life

The term **quality of work life** has come to encompass various efforts in the areas of personal and professional development. Its two clear objectives are to increase productivity and to increase the satisfaction of employees. Of course, programs leading to increased participation in corporate decision making are part of the programs; however, this section concentrates on individual job-related programs: work redesign, team building, and work scheduling.[60]

By adding both horizontal and vertical dimensions to the work, **work redesign programs** attack undesirable features of jobs. Horizontally, task complexity is added by incorporating work stages normally done before and after the stage being redesigned. Vertically, each employee is given more responsibility for making the decisions that affect how the work is done. Japanese car manufacturers have changed some of the work routines in their plants in the United States. For example, at Honda's unit in Marysville, Ohio, workers reacted favorably to the responsibilities they had been given, such as inspecting their own work and instructing others. On the other hand, work redesign may have significant costs attached, including wage increases, facility change costs, and training costs.

Closely related to work redesign are efforts aimed at **team building.** For example, in car plants, work is organized so that groups are responsible for a particular, identifiable portion of the car, such as interiors. Each group has its own areas in which to pace itself and to organize the work. The group must take responsibility for the work, including inspections, whether it is performed individually or in groups. The group is informed about its performance through a computer system. The team-building effort includes job rotation to enable workers to understand all facets of their jobs. Another approach to team building makes use of **quality circles,** in which groups of workers regularly meet to discuss issues relating to their productivity. Team building efforts have to be adapted to cultural differences. In cultures that are more individualistic, incentive structures may have to be kept at the individual level and discussions on quality issues should be broad-based rather than precise.[61]

Flexibility in **work scheduling** has led to changes in when and how long workers are at the workplace. **Flextime** allows workers to determine their starting and ending hours in a given workday; for example, they might arrive between 7:00 and 9:30 A.M. and leave between 3:00 and 5:30 P.M. The idea spread from Germany, to the European Union and to other countries such as Switzerland, Japan, New Zealand, and the United States. Some 40 percent of the Dutch working population holds flex- or part-time positions.[62] Despite its advantages in reducing absenteeism, flextime is not applicable to industries using assembly lines. Flexible work scheduling has also led to compressed workweeks—for example, the four-day week—and job sharing, which allows a position to be filled by more than one person.

Firms around the world also have other programs for personal and professional development, such as career counseling and health counseling. All of them are dependent on various factors external and internal to the firm. Of the external factors, the most important are the overall characteristics of the economy and the labor force. Internally, either the programs must fit into existing organizational structures or management must be inclined toward change. In many cases, labor unions have been one of the major resisting forces. Their view is that firms are trying to prevent workers from organizing by allowing them to participate in decision making and management.

THE ROLE OF LABOR UNIONS

When two of the world's largest producers of electrotechnology, Swedish Asea and Switzerland's Brown Boveri, merged to remain internationally competitive in a market dominated by a few companies such as General Electric, Siemens, Hitachi, and Toshiba, not everyone reacted positively to the alliance. For tax reasons, headquarters would not be located in Sweden, and this caused the four main Swedish labor unions to oppose the merger. They demanded that the Swedish government exercise its right to veto the undertaking because Swedish workers would no longer have a say in their company's affairs if it were headquartered elsewhere.

The incident is an example of the role labor unions play in the operation of a multinational corporation. It also points up the concerns of local labor unions when they must deal with organizations directed from outside their national borders.

The role of labor unions varies from country to country, often because of local traditions in management-labor relations. The variations include the extent of union power in negotiations and the activities of unions in general. In Europe, especially in the northern European countries, collective bargaining takes place between an employers' association and an umbrella organization of unions, on either a national or a regional basis, establishing the conditions for an entire industry. On the other end of the spectrum, negotiations in Japan are on the company level, and the role of larger-scale unions is usually consultative. Another striking difference emerges in terms of the objectives of unions and the means by which they attempt to attain them. In the United Kingdom, for example, union activity tends to be politically motivated and identified with political ideology. In the United States, the emphasis has always been on improving workers' overall quality of life.

Internationalization of business has created a number of challenges for labor unions. The main concerns that have been voiced are: (1) the power of the firm to move production from one country to another if attractive terms are not reached in a particular market; (2) the availability of data, especially financial information, to support unions' bargaining positions; (3) insufficient attention to local issues and problems while focusing on global optimization; and (4) difficulty in being heard by those who eventually make the decisions.[63] This has been countered by new activism to secure core labor standards as fundamental human rights, including freedom of association and the right to organize and bargain collectively.[64]

Although the concerns are valid, all of the problems anticipated may not develop. For example, transferring production from one country to another in the short term may be impossible, and labor strife in the long term may well influence such moves. To maintain participation in corporate decision making, unions are taking action individually and across national boundaries as seen in Focus on Ethics. Individual unions refer to contracts signed elsewhere when setting the agenda for their own negotiations.

Focus On ⬇

ETHICS

Global Unions versus Global Companies

The United States is perceived by European companies from the labor point of view as more flexible and less costly. However, when these companies attempt to challenge U.S. unions by downsizing the workforce to increase profitability, they meet resistance not only from the U.S. unions but from the international federations of trade unions. Conflict arises when there are different understandings of the role of labor unions.

Trelleborg, a Swedish metal and mining conglomerate with operations in eight European countries, expanded into the United States with the purchase of a plant in Copperhill, Tennessee, in 1991 after the owner went bankrupt. The plant was managed under Trelleborg's subsidiary, Boliden Intertrade Inc. The unions at Copperhill deferred over $5 million in wages to help keep the plant alive in the early 1990s. But labor-management relations deteriorated during contract negotiations in 1996, when Trelleborg insisted on sweeping changes in work rules. Boliden executives recognized that there would be a considerable loss of jobs, but saw no other way to regain competitiveness.

The workers saw the changes as a direct assault on their seniority system and a threat to worker safety, and went on strike after their contract expired. The company responded by hiring replacement workers and a squad of security guards. Two weeks later, the company said it had received a petition from its new employees indicating they did not want a union. Unions, on their part, demanded that Boliden withdraw its letter of derecognition and remove the replacement workers.

U.S. unions represent 16 percent of the public- and private-sector workforce, but in Sweden the unionization rate is over 80 percent. Although strikes are relatively rare in Sweden, replacing workers during a walkout is virtually unheard of. Swedish workers also have the right to shut down a company during a strike by stopping delivery trucks and other services, all actions that are banned in the United States.

Union activity was not limited to local moves in Tennessee. Metal, the powerful Swedish labor union representing Swedish workers in the industry, was recruited to pressure the parent company in Sweden. The International Federation of Chemical, Energy, Mine, and General Workers' Unions launched a campaign to pressure Trelleborg to rehire the Copperhill strikers. U.S. and Canadian unions warned institutional investors and pension fund managers that an investment in Boliden could be risky. They made their warnings as Trelleborg executives were visiting North America to raise $900 million in an initial public offering on the Toronto Stock Exchange.

Two months into the crisis, Trelleborg announced it would sell its U.S. subsidiary.

Source: Jay Mazur, "Labor's New Internationalism," *Foreign Affairs* 79 (January/February 2000): 79–93; Tim Schorrock, "Firm to Sell U.S. Unit at Center of Labor Flap," *The Journal of Commerce* (June 3, 1997); 3A: Joan Campbell, *The European Labor Unions* (Greenwood, CT: Greenwood Press, 1994), 429; and Tom DeVos, *U.S. Multinationals and Worker Participation in Management* (Westport, CT: Quorum Books, 1981), 195; http://www.trellgroup.se.

Supranational organizations such as the International Trade Secretariats and industry-specific organizations such as the International Metal Workers' Federation exchange information and discuss bargaining tactics. The goal is also to coordinate bargaining with multinational corporations across national boundaries. The International Labor Organization, a specialized agency of the United Nations, has an information bank on multinational corporations' policies concerning wage structures, benefits packages, and overall working conditions.

The relations between companies and unions can be cooperative as well. Alliances between labor and management have emerged to continue providing well-paying factory jobs in the United States in face of global competition. For example, the Amalgamated Clothing and Textile Workers Union of America and Xerox worked jointly to boost quality and cut costs to keep their jobs from going to Mexico, where wage rates were a fraction of U.S. costs.[65]

HUMAN RESOURCE POLICIES

The objectives of a human resource policy pertaining to workers are the same as for management: to anticipate the demand for various skills and to have in place programs that will ensure the availability of employees when needed. For workers, however, the firm faces the problem on a larger scale and does not have, in most cases, an expatriate alternative. This means that, among other things, when technology is transfe plant, it has to be adapted to the local workforce.

Although most countries have legislation and restrictions concerning the hiring of expatriates, many of them—for example some of the EU countries and some oil-rich Middle Eastern countries—have offset labor shortages by importing large numbers of workers from countries such as Turkey and Jordan. The EU by design allows free movement of labor. A mixture of backgrounds in the available labor pool can put a strain on personnel development. As an example, the firm may incur considerable expense to provide language training to employees. In Sweden, a certain minimum amount of language training must be provided for all "guest workers" at the firm's expense.

Bringing a local labor force to the level of competency desired by the firm may also call for changes. As an example, managers at Honda's plant in Ohio encountered a number of problems: Labor costs were originally 50 percent higher and productivity 10 percent lower than in Japan. Automobiles produced there cost $500 more than the same models made in Japan and then delivered to the United States. Before Honda began to produce the Accord in the United States, it flew 200 workers representing all areas of the factory to Japan to learn to build Hondas the Sayama way and then to teach their coworkers the skills.

Compensation of the work force is a controversial issue. Payroll expenses must be controlled for the firm to remain competitive; on the other hand, the firm must attract in appropriate numbers the type of workers it needs. The compensation packages of U.S.-based multinational companies have come under criticism, especially when their level of compensation is lower in developing countries than in the United States. Criticism has occurred even when the salaries or wages paid were substantially higher than the local average.

Comparisons of compensation packages are difficult because of differences in the packages that are shaped by culture, legislation, collective bargaining, taxation, and individual characteristics of the job. In northern Europe, for example, new fathers can accompany their wives on a two-week paternity leave at the employer's expense.

These differences in compensation and benefits may come to a head in merger and acquisition situations. When Ford Motor acquired Volvo, planned changes included moving to a three-shift, round-the-clock production schedule just like in the United States as compared to the two shifts in Sweden. Some of the differences may not be changeable, however. Night-shift workers get paid the same as day-shift workers although they work only 30 hours a week because of a government-mandated allocation. Some benefits, such as a fitness center which costs the company annually over $600,000 to maintain, may come under scrutiny by the new owners.[66]

Summary

A business organization is the sum of its human resources. To recruit and retain a pool of effective people for each of its operations requires: (1) personnel planning and staffing; (2) training activities; (3) compensation decisions; and (4) attention to labor-management relations.

Firms attract international managers from a number of sources, both internal and external. In the earlier stages of internationalization, recruitment must be external. Later, an internal pool often provides candidates for transfer. The decision then becomes whether to use home-country, host-country, or third-country nationals. If expatriate managers are used, selection policies should focus on competence, adaptability, and personal traits. Policies should also be set for the compensation and career progression of candidates selected for out-of-country assignments. At the same time, the firm must be attentive to the needs of local managers for training and development.

Labor can no longer be considered as simply services to be bought. Increasingly, workers are taking an active role in the decision making of the firm and in issues related to their own welfare. Various programs are causing dramatic organizational change, not only by enhancing the position of workers but by increasing the productivity of the work force as well. Workers employed by the firm usually are local, as are the unions that represent them. Their primary concerns in working for a multinational firm are job security and benefits. Unions therefore are cooperating across national boundaries to equalize benefits for workers employed by the same firm in different countries.

Questions for Discussion

1. Is a "supranational executive corps," consisting of cosmopolitan individuals of multiple nationalities who would be an asset wherever utilized, a possibility for any corporation?

2. Comment on this statement by Lee Iacocca: "If a guy wants to be a chief executive 25 or 50 years from now, he will have to be well rounded. There will be no more of 'Is he a good lawyer, is he a good marketing guy, is he a good finance guy?' His education and his experience will make him a total entrepreneur in a world that has really turned into one huge market. He better speak Japanese or German, he better understand the history of both of those countries and how they got to where they are, and he better know their economics pretty cold."

3. What additional benefit is brought into the expatriate selection and training process by adaptability screening?

4. A manager with a current base salary of $100,000 is being assigned to Lagos, Nigeria. Assuming that you are that manager, develop a compensation and benefits package for yourself in terms of both salary-related and nonsalary-related items.

5. What accounts for the success of Japanese companies with both American unions and the more ferocious British unions? In terms of the changes that have come about, are there winners or losers among management and workers? Could both have gained?

6. Develop general policies that the multinational corporation should follow in dealing (or choosing not to deal) with a local labor union.

Internet Exercises

1. Paguro.net (available at http://www.paguro.net) is a network that puts expatriates, and especially their family members, in touch with each other. What benefits can be gained from an individual or corporate membership to such a service?

2. Using a Web site such as monster.com (http://workabroad.monster.com/articles/cost/) compare the cost of living in your home city versus Vienna, Austria; Brussels, Belgium; Shanghai, China; Bogota, Colombia; and New Delhi, India. What accounts for the differences present?

Take a Stand

U.S.-based multinational corporations are increasingly debating whether they should establish grievance procedures for their nonunion, nonmanagerial professional and technical employees. Firms such as IBM, Marriott, Bechtel, and GE Power Systems have already installed procedures in an attempt to ensure organizational due process under such titles as "Employee Dispute Resolution Program" and "Dispute Resolution Process: Employee Handbook."

The rise of organizational due process in the private sector, both domestically and internationally, may be attributed to the void left by the declining institutional and economic power of unions in recent years. With industrial and trade unions retreating from the stage, multinational corporations are feeling more, not less, pressure to do what union leaders might have been pushing for in terms of employee rights. This results partly from a changing sense of employee relations and partly from a push to prevent unionization. For example, non-U.S. automakers have been able to keep unions out in their U.S. facilities by offering attractive packages and working environments to their employees.

The biggest challenge may be that a nonunion grievance procedure in which employees have complete confidence may be very difficult to create. The key tactical issues that need to be addressed for alternative dispute resolution and employee voice include the composition and nature of open-door policies and procedures and peer-review systems, as well as the operation of nonunion grievance arbitration systems.

For Discussion

1. Is providing a formal nonunion grievance procedure merely an incidental feature in the operation of a multinational corporation, or is it an ethical obligation for top management to fulfill?
2. Although there is no legal requirement that a corporation implement a system of due process in the workplace, how can such a procedure be viewed as a sound business decision?

Source: Courtesy of Dr. Douglas M. McCabe.

Ford Motor Company's Asian Pacific regional headquarters was located in Hiroshima, Japan. The Asian Pacific unit had shown only marginal profitability in recent years. The unit's sales within Asia had suffered significantly as a result of the Asian Crisis that began in July of 1997, and many of the major Asian retail markets had still not recovered by early 2001. In addition to sales within the region, the business unit also manufactured vehicles for export sales all over the world. One of the most important vehicle lines exported globally was the Ford Ranger. The problem was that Ford's current transfer pricing practice made it nearly impossible for Ford Asia Pacific to tell whether the Ford Ranger line was actually making a profit or not.

Organizational Structure

The Ranger was manufactured in Thailand by Auto Alliance Thailand (AAT), a joint venture between Ford and Mazda. ATT was responsible for all material procurement, manufacturing, and finished vehicle assembly. AAT then sold the Ranger to Ford Trading Company (FTC), the global sales unit of Ford, which served as the link between manufacturing and local distributors. FTC in turn sold the Ranger to multitudes of distributors in dozens of countries. Ford's problem was how to set prices between the three units.

Ford's transfer pricing took the three units in the Ranger supply chain and worked toward the middle. Ford set retail prices for local distributors twice a year. These prices were to be held. In turn, this price less a guaranteed margin for local distributors was then pushed back down to FTC. On the production end of the supply chain, at AAT, the costs plus margins for Rangers produced in Thailand were set four times a year. The price calculated was then used as the transfer price at which AAT sold the Ranger to FTC. FTC's profits were the residual spread between the price at which it bought from AAT and the price at which it sold to local distributors. This is shown in Figure 1.

Performance Pressure

All was well until sales slowed. Retailers began discounting prices in an effort to move inventory. These price cuts were then "validated" by Ford by affixing the standard distributor margin to the vehicle even after the price was discounted. The revenue recognized by FTC's profitability was reduced, if not eliminated. Given the role FTC played within the Ford value chain—as a buffer against cost or price pressures—this seemed appropriate.

However, it wasn't that simple. FTC in Asia was part of the general business unit of Ford Asia Pacific. As Ford Asia Pacific came under increasing pressure from Detroit to return to profitability, pressure increased on FTC to increase its profitability. Although the structure had been designed to have FTC serve as the locus of profit or loss in the value chain, the "loss" alternative was no longer accepted. Given the multitude of discounted prices now arising from local distributors all over the world, it was no longer really possible to tell if the Ford Ranger itself was a profitable vehicle or not. The question was "by whose price?"

Questions for Discussion

1. What possible advantages would Ford gain by positioning all profits and losses within the FTC business unit?
2. What types of incentives or disincentives does the transfer pricing structure described create with manufacturers like AAT and local distributors?
3. What would you suggest Ford do to improve the workings of their transfer pricing structure within the Ford Ranger value chain?

Sources: Copyright © 2003 Thunderbird, The American Graduate School of International Management. All rights reserved. This case was prepared by Professor Michael H. Moffett for the purpose of classroom discussion only, and not to indicate either effective or ineffective management.

FIGURE 1

The Ford Ranger: Transfer Pricing in Ford Asia Pacific

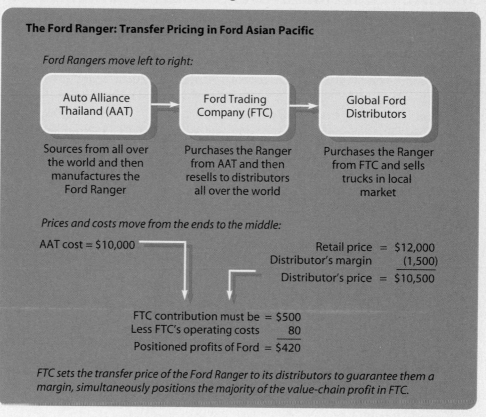

The Ford Ranger: Transfer Pricing in Ford Asian Pacific

Ford Rangers move left to right:

Auto Alliance Thailand (AAT) → Ford Trading Company (FTC) → Global Ford Distributors

Auto Alliance Thailand (AAT)	Ford Trading Company (FTC)	Global Ford Distributors
Sources from all over the world and then manufactures the Ford Ranger	Purchases the Ranger from AAT and then resells to distributors all over the world	Purchases the Ranger from FTC and sells trucks in local market

Prices and costs move from the ends to the middle:

AAT cost = $10,000

Retail price =	$12,000
Distributor's margin	(1,500)
Distributor's price =	$10,500

FTC contribution must be =	$500
Less FTC's operating costs	80
Positioned profits of Ford =	$420

FTC sets the transfer price of the Ford Ranger to its distributors to guarantee them a margin, simultaneously positions the majority of the value-chain profit in FTC.

The mood was jubilant when Motorola announced in September 2000 that it had lent an additional $700 million to TelSim, a Turkish-based Global System for Mobile Communication (GMS) operator, in support of its efforts to dominate the booming mobile telephone market in this emerging country. The overall agreement was potentially worth $2 billion for the deployment of a mobile network by vendor financing, and it was considered to be the largest financing deal in telecommunications. Motorola viewed entering Turkey's burgeoning cellular market as an important business objective.

Simultaneously, as the last act of its relationship with TelSim since 1994, Nokia of Espoo, Finland won a three-year deal worth $900 million in June 2000 with TelSim of Turkey to deliver a full GSM network expansion. After the announcement, Pertti Melamies, Area Vice President, Nokia Networks, confidently stated:

> This deal, the largest to date for Nokia Networks, illustrates our clear leadership in GSM equipment. By 2001, we estimate the number of mobile subscribers in Turkey will be in excess of 15 million. . . . This provides TelSim the flexibility to be ideally positioned to meet the voice and data capacity, quality of service and cost challenges of continued strong growth in the Turkish market.[1]

These happy days seemed quite distant later in 2001. A somber looking Christopher Galvin, CEO of Motorola of Schaumburg, Illinois, announced the third straight quarterly loss in 2001: $1.4 billion—one of the biggest quarterly losses in the history of the company. The stock price fell to $16.72 in October, from a 52-week high of $29.81. As disclosed by Motorola, the major cause of the loss was attributed to TelSim with the unpaid $728 million as the first installment of its debt.[2] Similarly, Nokia of Finland was unable to collect $240 million due from TelSim.

The press provided global, intensive coverage of the problem experienced by Motorola and Nokia, and the problem was also brought to the attention of the respec-

tive governments. Consequently, the two telecom giants jointly filed a lawsuit on January 28, 2002 in a New York federal court,[3] driven by fears that TelSim never intended to repay its loans.

In January 2002, Turkish Prime Minister Bulent Ecevit and U.S. President George Bush met in Washington, D.C. to discuss the legal battle going on between Turkish TelSim and American Motorola.

Importance of the Turkish Market as an Emerging Economy

Advances in wireless technology and a worldwide push toward privatization provided double-digit growth opportunities in the telecommunication sector. The demand was particularly strong in an emerging market. Strategically, Motorola and Nokia were able to position themselves to become the leading suppliers to startup telecom service companies. One of the emerging markets that drew the attention of the equipment manufacturers was Turkey.

Turkey, straddling Europe and Asia, is one of the leading emerging markets. With a population of more than 65 million, and a liberalized and booming economy and stock market, Turkey had started appearing on everybody's radar screen as a promising market for both trade and investment. Even though privatization was well under way, the state-owned enterprises, along with family-owned conglomerates, had played an important role in the economy.

Turkey signed a customs union agreement with the European Union in the late 1990s and liberalized the regulation of foreign direct investment. Accordingly, the leading major family conglomerates such as Koc and Sabanci established numerous joint ventures with foreign companies. Turkey was also one of the countries that encouraged and attracted foreign involvement in the Built-Operate-Transfer (BOT) scheme. Turkey's long established relationship with the Commonwealth of Independent States (CIS) was of particular interest for the international business community. Additionally, Turkey applied for membership in the European Union and the Turkish government was being careful not to jeopardize its standing with the IMF and the European Union member countries.

Sources: This case has been developed by Professor S. Tamer Cavusgil and Professor Emin Civi, Celal Bayar University, Turkey, with the assistance of Can Ceylanoglu and Can Karadogan, for classroom purposes.

Although three quarters of the population resides in urban areas, agriculture still plays a significant role in the country. It contributes 16 percent of GDP and employs around 40 percent of the workforce. Turkey, an upper-middle-income economy, had a per capita GDP (PPP) of $6,700 in 2002.

Inflation has been a problem for the Turkish economy for the last 20 years. In the last of a series of financial crises, in February 2001, the local currency was devalued by about 40 percent, which immediately hit Turkish firms hard. External shocks such as the devastating 1999 earthquakes and aftershock of September 11, 2001, have also affected the economy. GDP contracted by 8.5 percent in 2001. To support the efforts to lower the inflation rate and ease the economy, the IMF provided a $15.7 billion loan wrapped in a rescue.

The Uzan Conglomerate

TelSim is Turkey's second largest GSM operator and is privately managed by the Uzan family, as an affiliate of Rumeli Holding, with a 66 percent stake. The Uzans launched Telsim in 1994 in order to reap the benefits of the opportunities in the very promising, yet infant, Turkish telecom industry. TelSim announced that it had two million subscribers by the end of 1999 and its plan for 2000 involved 5.5 million. Even though it failed to meet its targets, TelSim had spectacular growth, with slightly less than five million users by 2000. It was the second private sector company to receive a GSM license, which will expire in 2023, from the Turkish government. TelSim tried to remain at the forefront of wireless communications and was first to embark on leading-edge new technologies and services. TelSim's investments in infrastructure, technology, and marketing reached $3 billion by 2001.

The Uzan family appeared as a significant player in the Turkish economy in the late 1980s. As is common in emerging markets, the Uzans' extensive operations in various sectors reported to and were controlled by a family-owned holding company, Rumeli Holding. Rumeli Holding operates in many sectors, from cement manufacturing to banking, including broadcasting and print media. The Uzan empire controls at least 137 entities in nine countries[4] and the Uzans' wealth is believed to exceed $1.6 billion.

The Uzans are one of Turkey's richest, most powerful clans. The Uzans are descended from farmers who immigrated to Turkey from Sarajevo around 1910. Family patriarch Kemal Uzan, 70, a civil engineer, was the first to make a mark in business, founding a construction company in 1956. He landed lucrative contracts for soccer stadiums in the 1960s, dams and hydroelectric power plants in the 1970s and 1980s, thanks in part to a cozy relationship with the Turkish prime minister (and later president) Turgut Ozal. He expanded the business into a banking and media empire. In 1984, Kemal Uzan bought Imar Bank for $21 million. A year later he founded Adabank, which was managed by his sons, Cem Cengiz, and Murat Hakan. Incidentally, Cem Uzan is also Bill Gates' neighbor at the top of the Trump World Tower in New York[5].

In the past two decades the Uzans have built a small family construction business into a giant private holding company with interests in everything from energy to "pay TV." The Uzan family ranked fifth in a published list of Turkish billionaires.

The banks provided Cem Uzan with an entrée into the family enterprises at age 24, after graduating with a degree in business from Pepperdine University. By the time he was 30, he proved his prowess by slyly overcoming Turkish laws preventing private transmission of TV signals: Working with Turgut Ozal's son, he rented studios in Germany and beamed the signal via satellite. Cem called it Star TV, which was the first-ever private TV channel in Turkey. It operated illegally for several years, and Ozal's administration not only turned a blind eye but actually encouraged it to operate freely and end the state monopoly on TV broadcasts. Then the Uzans pushed Ahmet Ozal out of the partnership and seized power[6] and a year later introduced radio stations; earlier in the year the Star group started a tabloid-style newspaper and called it the *Star Daily*. When the paper was launched, people began to wonder when and if the newspaper would be used like the TV station to extract favors for the Uzan Empire.

Motorola and Nokia are not the only business partners to receive a raw deal as a result of their involvement with the Uzan family. The Uzans have committed similar acts of fraud and deceit against other major domestic and international corporations, including Siemens, Ericsson, Italstrade/Fintecna, and many others.

Siemens provided vendor financing to TelSim until early 2000, when TelSim failed to pay a number of outstanding invoices issued by Siemens. The total debt owed to Siemens is in excess of $25 million. In March 2000, the Uzans demanded that Nokia increase the cash portion of a new loan facility by $25 million to permit TelSim to pay its debts to Siemens, which Nokia did. The Uzans, however, did not use this money to repay the Siemens debt. Siemens severed its ties with TelSim and filed an enforcement proceeding and a bankruptcy action against TelSim to collect the amounts owed. TelSim countersued on Siemens' collection action, asserting that Siemens had installed faulty equipment and alleging that the company owed TelSim $50 million.[7] In an act of extortion in connection with the commercial disputes, the Uzans used their Star newspaper companies to launch a series of libelous attacks against Siemens and its current and former chief executive officers, Zafer Incecik and Arnold Hornfeld.

Erikson Telekomunikasyon A.S. (Ericsson) had entered into a business arrangement with TelSim's chief rival in the Turkish cell phone industry, Turkcell. In an apparent act of retaliation aimed at Turkcell and Ericsson, Cem Uzan's Star TV twice aired a false "news" item during a nationally televised football match claiming that Ericsson funneled money to a terrorist organization.[8]

The Uzan family seemed to be more charitable abroad than it is at home. In return for attendance at a lavish dinner in Buckingham Palace, Cem Uzan gave generously to the Prince of Wales Foundation, a charity set up by the heir to the British throne.

Among other ventures, the Uzans formed a political party, The Youth Party, and participated in Turkey's most recent national elections. The Youth Party collected some seven percent of the votes cast, a major success for an organization that was formed only five months earlier. Critics commented that Cem Uzan was seeking to enter the Parliament in order to gain immunity from potential prosecution from questionable business matters. The Uzans were not only being prosecuted by U.S. and Finnish courts for fraud against Nokia and Motorola but also by the Turkish courts. It was claimed that he founded the party in order to transfer some of his assets. Cem Uzan has been likened by some to Italy's Prime Minister Silvio Berlusconi, or a younger version of the former U.S. presidential candidate Ross Perot. Italian media mogul Silvio Berlusconi became prime minister only three months after founding his Forza Italia party amid a similar disillusionment in Italian politics. The Uzan empire, like Berlusconi's, also embraces banking and finance enterprises, a soccer team, television and radio stations, and newspapers with a sharp tongue.

Motorola and Nokia: The Western Partners

Motorola is a U.S.-based high-tech company. Founded in 1928, Motorola has always been a manufacturer of consumer electronics products. By 1960, Motorola started expanding globally and by the mid-1970s, its focus shifted to high technology markets in commercial, industrial, and government fields.[9] Motorola was the second-largest manufacturer of mobile handsets and a leader in telecom infrastructure equipment. It reported $26,679 million in net sales, $2,485 million in net earnings (loss) and 97,000[10] employees in the year 2002.[11]

Motorola was the leader in the cell phones business with a 33 percent market share; however, its share eroded to 15 percent between 1999 and 2002. (Nokia became the market leader.) During that time, the company made a series of strategic mistakes. It was late in making the switch from old analog systems to more reliable digital technology. Then Motorola pushed expensive phones that could access the wireless Web instead of the cheaper phones that consumers wanted, a stumble that more nimble and style-conscious competitors such as Nokia used to race ahead. Also, its semiconductors division faced a substantial decline with the economic slowdown during the year 2000–2001. (It laid off 4000 workers in the semiconductor division in February 2001.) The telecommunications infrastructure division saw its fortunes diminish as well.[11] Consequently, in the first five months of 2001, more than 26,000 jobs were cut and a total of 39,000 were targeted to be cut in 2001.

Nokia

With a culture nearly 140 years old, Finland-based Nokia is the world's largest mobile phone producer and a global leader in mobile communications. Nokia grew its market share in mobile phones from 19 percent in 1997 to close to 40 percent in 2002. Its net sales reached $30.1 billion in 2002, of which Nokia Mobile Phones group made up around 76 percent.[12]

During the 1980s and 1990s, Nokia became a major player in telecommunications and consumer electronics in Europe. Nokia acquired companies in Sweden, Germany, France, and Switzerland. In the 1980s, Nokia advanced in information technologies, cable, and telecommunications fields.

Nokia redefined its corporate goals and focus in the early 1990s and decided to intensify its efforts in business and telecommunications. At the time, Ericsson of Sweden was the biggest competitor in the region and the world. Nokia became very competitive under the administration of CEO Jorma Ollila. Nokia's market share increased dramatically around the globe while Motorola of U.S.A and Ericsson of Switzerland lost market share

FIGURE 1

Motorola: By the Numbers

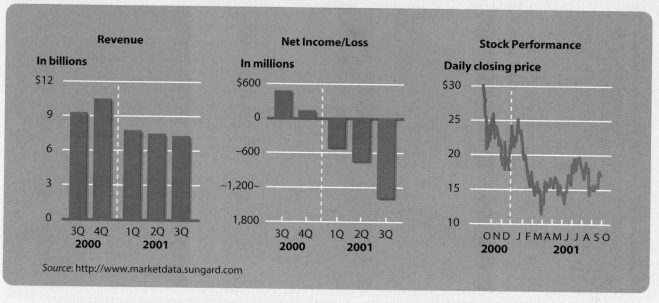

Revenue — In billions

Net Income/Loss — In millions

Stock Performance — Daily closing price

Source: http://www.marketdata.sungard.com

Source: http://www.marketdata.sungard.com.

steadily. Nokia eventually became the number one supplier of mobile phones in the world. Experts agree that Nokia's better understanding of the consumer market gave them the edge to be more competitive. The phone designs and operating costs were lower at Nokia, which helped their competitiveness at the global scale. The use of mobile phones skyrocketed between 1991 and 2000. The number of phones in use increased from 6 million to 400 million. Overall, in the wireless communications market, Nokia was perceived by the experts to be leaner

FIGURE 2

Motorola Performance 1999–2003

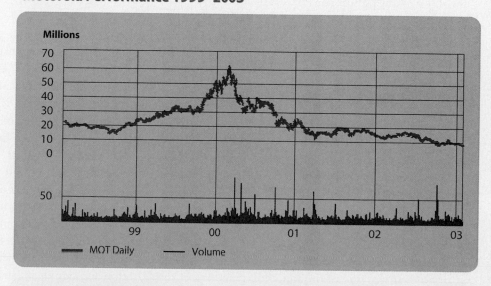

Source: http://www.motorola.com

FIGURE 3

Motorola Net Income/Loss 1999–2002

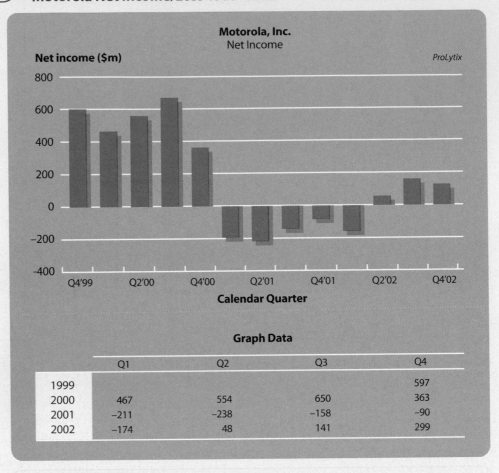

Motorola, Inc.
Net Income

Graph Data

	Q1	Q2	Q3	Q4
1999				597
2000	467	554	650	363
2001	−211	−238	−158	−90
2002	−174	48	141	299

Source: http://www.motorola.com

and more efficient. Today, it is the global sales leader in wireless communications.

The Turkish Telecom Market

Historically, telecom companies were state-owned firms with a monopoly position. Foreign ownership was not allowed. With the advent in wireless technology, an accelerated trend toward privatization and liberalization began to open up the national markets to competition from within and elsewhere. The Turkish telecom industry was one of the first to take advantage of these evolutions in the wireless sector.

Turkey's telecommunication industry is more than a century old. It was one of the founding members of the predecessor organization of the ITU in 1865. A telegraph line was installed in 1847 and the first automatic telephone exchange in the Balkans was installed in Ankara in 1926. At first, the phone service provided by the state-owned PTT was very bad; you could wait half a day for an international call to come through and 15 years for a telephone to be installed in your home. However, by the end of 2001, there were some 18.9 million fixed telephone lines in service, for a teledensity of 28. As of 1998, all of Turkey's 36,000 villages had a telephone.[13] Household telephone penetration is estimated at 87 percent and the digitalization ratio is 88 percent in switchboards and 97 percent in transmission.

TurkTelekom now ranks among the biggest telecom providers in emerging Europe. It stands out among developing telecom operators for its high rate of digitalization and significant strength in satellite capacity. This enables it to cover Turkey's remote areas and become an important transit venue for international traffic.

FIGURE 4

Motorola Revenues 1999–2002

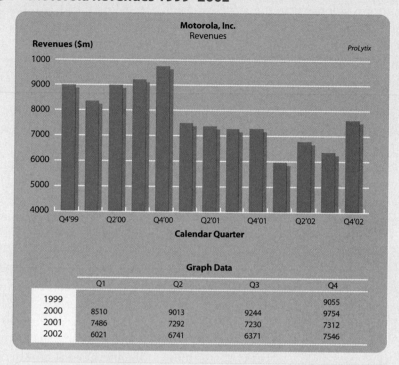

Graph Data

	Q1	Q2	Q3	Q4
1999				9055
2000	8510	9013	9244	9754
2001	7486	7292	7230	7312
2002	6021	6741	6371	7546

Source: http://www.motorola.com

FIGURE 5

**Telephone Subscribers (Fixed and Mobile)
per 100 Inhabitants in Turkey**

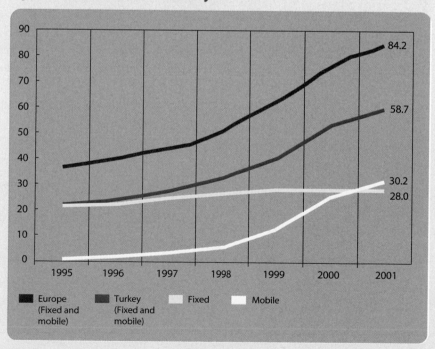

Source: Michael Minges, Turkey ICT Profile, http://www.itu.int/ITU-D/ict/cs/letters/turkey.html.

Turkey invested heavily in the 1980s in order to modernize and expand its telecom system. TurkTelekom, a state-owned company, still has the monopoly over land lines. A government plan calls for 2.5 million additional lines to be built between 2000 and 2005. A recently passed law required TurkTelekom to be privatized by spring 2003. A regulator, the Telecommunications Authority, was recently created.[14] On and off plans to privatize TurkTelekom, the incumbent telecommunication operator, finally look set to proceed as called for in Turkey's Letter of Intent with the IMF. It foresees selling at least 49 percent, including a stake to a strategic foreign investor. Furthermore, the expiration of TurkTelekom's fixed telephone line, domestic long distance, and international telephone monopoly has been brought forward to December 31, 2003. The Ministry of Transport is responsible for telecommunication policy including issuing licenses.

Turkey missed out in the 1990s when telecommunications witnessed a record number of mergers, acquisitions, and privatizations. In 1992 Morgan Stanley had valued TurkTelecom at between $18 billion and $20 billion. Lack of investment, loss of market share to the aggressive cellular companies, and unpopularity of emerging-market stocks have subsequently almost halved TT's market value. At the end of 1997 the government attached a price tag of $10 billion. In 1990s, there were many international telecom companies interested in the Turkish telecommunications market. These included Telefonica (Spain), SBC Communications (US), Vodafone Airtouch (UK), Mannesmann (Germany), Orange, British Telecom, Telecom Italia, Bezeq (Israel), France Telecom and Deutsche Telekom.

TurkTelekom represents a potentially profitable strategic chance for entry into the Turkish market. The foreign investor that purchases a stake in TurkTelekom will be granted access to a growing market not only for land-line telephony, but also for high-speed internet access, cellular communication, satellite services, cable television, paging, and video conferencing. TurkTelekom will remain an asset as new companies enter the land-line market starting in 2004. The privatization of TurkTelekom and the subsequent liberalization of the telecom market in Turkey will be a crucial barometer of the government's progress towards the goals set by the IMF and World Bank.

For the wireless communication sector, privatization has long been underway. With two private sector companies already in operation, Turkcell and TelSim, two more companies started operating in the second half of 2001. The market was expanding fast. The number of subscribers was 2.5 million in 1998 and reached 11 million in 2001. Despite this high growth, the penetration rate was a low 13 percent, compared to the penetration rates in U.K. of 23 percent, France at 29 percent, and Germany at 23 percent. The number of subscribers was projected to increase to 32 million by 2008, making Turkey as one of the five fastest growing wireless markets in Europe.

Turkey's mobile market has grown tremendously. TurkTelekom launched an analogue NMT network in 1986. In 1994, two digital GSM operators, Turkcell and TelSim, launched services in a revenue-sharing arrangement with Turk Telekom. The market leader is Turkcell, with 12 million subscribers. Turkcell shares are traded in IMKB (Istanbul Stock Exchange) and NYSE (New York Stock Exchange); however, a vast majority belong to Turkish Cukurova Holding, the third largest industrial conglomerate, which also manages the company, and Finnish Sonera, Finland's largest mobile operator. The others in the market, in descend-

TABLE 1   Wireless Markets in Europe

	GSM Penetration Rate	Number of Operators	Population (million)
UK	23%	4	59
France	29%	3	58
Germany	23%	4	82
Turkey	13%	4	65

Source: http://www.tradepartners.gov.uk/text/telecom/turkey/profile/overview.shtml.

ing order of number of subscribers, are TelSim, Aria (jointly owned by Turkish Is Bank and TelecomItalia) and Aycell of TurkTelekom. TelSim is owned by the Uzan family. The mobile market was further opened in 2001 when two new GSM 1800 operators introduced service. Aria, owned by TelecomItalia Mobile and Turkish Is Bank, launched in March 2001. In December, TurkTelekom's Aycell began operations.

Estimates of the size of Turkey's Internet market vary. An average of different estimates suggest that Turkey had some three million Internet users in 2001, for a penetration of 4.5 percent of the population. There are some 65 ISPs, of which the largest is Super-online, partly owned by Turkcell. TurkTelekom is also active in the market through its national backbone (Turnet), international gateway, and dial-up service (Ttnet, which features a IP Dial Tone service allowing nationwide Internet access).[16]

There is no Turkish provider of equipment and infrastructure for mobile services. Therefore, Turkish telecom service operators had to rely on external sources. The major equipment and infrastructure suppliers included Alcatel (France), Ericsson (Sweden), Motorola (US), Nokia (Finland) and Siemens (Germany). Existing equipment and infrastructure provider companies tend to have price and logistics advantages over new entrants. Their long-established relations with the key decision makers and influencers raise the barriers further against entries into the market. What's more, the costs of switching suppliers are high for the service operators. These factors make it quite difficult for latecomers to break into the market as a supplier. Such first-to-market advantages become especially important in the fast growing telecom sector, where the need for new equipment is inevitable.

TelSim's Foreign Partners and the Default

Motorola and TelSim signed an agreement for the supply and deployment of a third generation (3G) mobile network capable of providing advanced multimedia services, which was worth a total of $1.9 billion. For Motorola, Turkey was a very promising market. The number of mobile subscribers increased from 1.5 million in 1997 to 8.2 million in 1999. In many countries in Europe, more than half the population owned a mobile phone, while fewer than 10 percent of Turks did. The Turkish market was also a duopoly. That made the privately held TelSim seem to be a very attractive target for a foreign buyer. To Motorola, TelSim started to look less like a customer and more like a very smart investment bet.

Motorola committed to providing a vendor-financing loan (supplier's credit) to TelSim, to be paid back in installments. In vendor financing, the supplier company provides the buyer company with loans specifically issued to enable the procurement of its own products/services. There is a rising trend toward vendor financing in order to boost growth and increase market share; however, some consider it quite risky because the borrowers are usually startups or growing companies. In the presence of credit-worthy partners, vendor financing is a very wise tactic that can increase sales and help acquire loyal customers. The peak year for vendor financing came in 2000, with $25 billion to $30 billion in loans, many of them offered to the fourth or fifth largest carrier in a market.

The promise of a big payday, with a multinational swooping in to drop billions on TelSim, lured Motorola and Nokia into an increasingly tangled relationship with the Uzans. When TelSim asked for more money in

---

TABLE 2

Turkish Mobile Market Leaders

Operator	Major Owners
Turkcell[15]	Cukurova Holding 61%, Sonera (Finnish) 39%
TelSim	Rumeli Holding (controlled by the Uzan family)
Aria	Is-Tim (Is Bank of Turkey and TelecomItalia Mobil)
Aycell	TurkTelekom

September 1999 Motorola executives bit. They agreed to an additional $215 million loan for equipment and marketing, on the condition that TelSim repay swiftly with new financing guaranteed by a British export–import bank. However, when bankers came to review the company finances, a TelSim employee accused one of stealing documents. According to Motorola executives, an irate Hakan Uzan showed up at an Istanbul restaurant where they were dining and refused further access to the company books.[17]

The first installment, $728 million, to be paid back to Motorola, was due on April 30, 2001. To secure the loan, the deal gave Motorola the option to sell 66 percent of TelSim shares, which were put up as collateral. Under the original terms of the loan, TelSim would technically default if it failed to pay $728 million within 30 days of the original payment date.

As part of its ongoing business relations, TelSim signed a similar agreement with Nokia. The deal was worth around $700 million and the first repayment installment was $240 million, in April 2001. The collateral behind the debt was 7.5 percent of TelSim shares.

When the first payment date arrived, the two telecom giants did not receive any payments. In May 2001, the Uzans claimed that they had liquidity problems after the devaluation of Lira three months previously.[18] The Uzans argued that the conflict reflects their suppliers' unwillingness to face up to the losses stemming from the global crash in the telecommunications markets, recession in Turkey, and a substantial devaluation of the Turkish lira.

In January 2002, Motorola and Nokia jointly sued the family under the RICO Act (Racketeer Influenced and Corrupt Organizations Act, a law often used to indict mobsters) claiming that the Uzans never intended to repay the loans. Their claims were based on the dilution of the collateral: 66 percent stake of Motorola and 7.5% of Nokia were diluted to 22.5 percent and 2.5 percent with a capital increase. The suit was filed in New York because the Uzans had assets in the United States and were listed as residents of the city.[19] It is interesting to note that, in order to win their damages claim under U.S. racketeering legislation, plaintiffs must prove that they were victims of a pattern of behavior rather than of a simple breach of contract. The Uzans obtained a Turkish court order saying the New York lawsuit must be halted. None of the defendants or their lawyers attended the trial in New York. The family has similarly ignored orders entered by a British court, leading to 15-month jail terms being imposed on Kemal Uzan, the family patriarch, and Murat Hakan Uzan and Cem Cengiz Uzan, his two sons. The court also imposed a

four-month sentence on Aysegul Akay, their sister. The Uzans have also countered the attack in American and British courts with lawsuits filed in Turkey. They have arranged for criminal charges to be filed against Motorola and Nokia executives, who they say threatened to injure them physically. In a statement printed in the Uzan family-owned *Daily Star* newspaper, TelSim said it would seek compensation from both companies for "unfounded and hurtful" accusations made against it, and would sue Motorola for not fulfilling contracts.

In New York, a judge issued two temporary restraining orders freezing the Uzans' nine residences in New York and $8 million in funds the family is alleged to have in the United States. He also barred the Uzans from transferring any TelSim assets, took into a depository the stake in the company issued to Standart Telekom, and prohibited the family from exercising their voting rights on shares created at a meeting on January 4, 2002. The same judge then revoked the ruling on the 73.5 percent stake on February 15, allowing TelSim to remain in Turkish hands for the moment. A similar freezing of Uzan assets occurred in London a few days later.[20]

Following the suit, TelSim denied that the allegations made had any basis, either in law or in fact, and found the suit to be unethical. TelSim said it made numerous attempts to resolve the dispute, which was caused by economic difficulties in Turkey.[21]

Good partnerships are seen as keys to success by foreign investors, especially in nationalistic countries such as Turkey.[22] There are arguments that Motorola chose the wrong partner since the Uzans have been involved in more than 100 criminal and civil cases.[23] Moreover, Turkey's business elite has been virtually united in shunning the Uzans. TUSIAD, the premier businessman's group, refuses to invite any of them to be members.[24] However, Motorola disclosed in early 2002 that the two companies began their relationship in 1994 and there had been no defaults or signs of trouble for about six years. Similarly, Nokia said that TelSim had met its obligations early on.[25]

The Aftermath of the Conflict

The missed first installments triggered a series of events with significant implications for TelSim, its suppliers, the international business community, and the respective governments. The issue became a hot topic between top politicians of the United States, and Turkey and was even discussed by the presidents of each country. The most critical problem is probably the loss of credibility by Turkey and Turkish firms. As stated in *The Economist*: "Foreigners who want to do business in Turkey will be thinking twice."[26]

Another impact is expected on global vendor financing. It is expected that such decisions now will be made after deeper investigations and stricter requirements. As a result, growing firms in emerging markets may find fewer finance options.

Motorola and Nokia were blamed for their own wrongdoings. Authorities blamed the two telecom giants for choosing a poor or questionable partner. In recent years, the Uzans have been involved in many disputes ranging from a Polish prosecutor's investigation into losses at their cement works in Nowa Huta, to Turkish stock market regulators' long-running battle against irregularities at two publicly traded electricity plants that the Uzans control.

Regardless of Uzans' questionable business deals in and outside of Turkey, Nokia commented that there was no hint earlier in the dealings with TelSim that difficulties would emerge, while Motorola characterized its pre-default relations with TelSim as on the whole a good one. Another likely error on the part of Motorola and Nokia was the failure to anticipate loopholes in the Turkish legal system. The two companies filed their unusual joint civil action after Rumeli instigated a capital increase diluting TelSim shares held in an escrow account as their collateral for separate loans to Turkey's second cellular operator. During the hearing of the case in New York, Hakan Uan, the younger brother, said the capital increase was carried out to comply with Turkish company laws.

Motorola and Nokia were also criticized for not taking into account the political and economic risks of doing business in Turkey. Despite the booming economy and an explosive telecommunications market, instability, high inflation, two decades of frequent devaluations and financial crises, uneven income distribution, political failures, and distrust for politicians were some of the indicators of a troubled economy.

Questions for Discussion

1. What should Motorola and Nokia have done prior to partnership with the Uzan conglomerate in order to potentially avoid a disastrous relationship? How well informed were they about the Uzans? What criteria should been considered for partner selection? Would better-established conglomerates like Koc and Sabanci make better partners?

2. Did Motorola and Nokia choose the most appropriate form of partnership with the Uzan family? What should they have done to safeguard their interests?

3. How appropriate was it for Nokia and Motorola to resort to a legal resolution right at the outset? Could they have chosen a different strategy to dispute resolution that would have been more effective in an emerging market situation?

4. What do the plaintiffs aim to gain in court: The money, the prestige, or Wall Street's trust? How would the Motorola and Nokia shareholders react?

5. How did the recession in the global economy affect the chain of events? Would the lawsuit still take place during better economic times?

6. How should Western businesspeople better prepare themselves for conducting business in high-growth, yet high-risk, emerging markets? What strategies and guidelines should they follow?

Endnotes

1. http://www.nokia.com.
2. "Beware of Turks Bearing Phones: A Salutary Tale Of Byzantine Borrowing," *The Economist*, January 31, 2002.
3. Ibid.
4. The World Billionaires: Dial 'D' For Dummies, by Matthew Swibel, *Forbes*, 03.18.2002.
5. "Beware Turks Bearing Cell Phone: Motorola and Nokia Sue Turkey's TelSim," Christopher Bowe, *Financial Times*, February 2, 2002.
6. http://www.turkishdailynews.com/old_editions/10_07_99/comment.htm.
7. http://www.techlawjournal.com/courts2002/motorola/20020128.asp.
8. Ibid.
9. http://www.motorola.com/content/0,1037,115-280,00.html.
10. http://premium.hoovers.com/subscribe/co/factsnet.xhtml?COID-11023. http://www.hoovers.com/co/capsule/3/0,2163,11023,00.html.
11. "Motorola Has Third Straight Quarterly Loss," by Andrea Petersen, *The Wall Street Journal*, October 10, 200??.
12. http://www.nokia.com/nokia/0,8764, 72,00.html.
13. Michael Minges, Turkey ICT Profile, http://www.itu.int/ITU-D/ict/cs/letters/turkey.html.
14. http://www.tk.gov.tr/indexeng.html.
15. Turkcell iletisim Hizmetleri A.S.
16. Michael Minges, Turkey ICT Profile, http://www.itu.int/ITU-D/ict/cs/letters/turkey.html.
17. "The Stupid Loan Bubble: The story of how Motorola and Nokia lost nearly $3 billion in Turkey opens a window on excesses that still threaten big telecoms," by Karen Lowry Miller, *Newsweek International*, October 28, 2002.

18. "Beware Turks Bearing Phones: A Salutary Tale Of Byzantine Borrowing," *The Economist*, January 31, 2002.

19. "Beware Turks Bearing Cell Phone: Motorola and Nokia Sue Turkey's TelSim," by Christopher Bowe, *Financial Times*, February 2, 2002.

20. Ibid.

21. "Judge's Order Prevents Turkey's Uzan Family From Selling Apartments," *Wall Street Journal*, January 30, 2002.

22. "Investment Problems," by Leyla Boulton, *The Financial Times*, March 26, 2002.

23. Ibid.

24. Ibid.

25. Motorola And Nokia Allege Fraud, Sue Turkish Mobile-Phone Family, By Shawn Young and Hugh Pope, The Wall Street Journal, 01/29/2002.

26. "Beware Turks Bearing Phones: A Salutory Tale of Byzantine Borrowing," *The Economist*, January 31, 2002.

Many polls conducted abroad have shocked U.S. policymakers, corporate executives, and ordinary citizens alike. In many countries the United States is considered "ruthless, arrogant, aggressive, and biased" against certain groups and ideas (e.g., Islamic values and the Palestinian people). Moreover, many believe that U.S. culture and values are a corrupting influence on their societies (see Table 1).

The need for the United States to get its message out to foreign public audiences has become increasingly obvious. In articulating this need, the International Relations Committee of the U.S. House of Representatives stated that United States should "pursue a foreign policy along two separate tracks: the first with the governments of the world, the second with their peoples." To achieve this task, public diplomacy needed to adopt professional marketing practices, especially in building a brand. In the case of the United States, the question would be how to manage and market the brand more effectively.

Sources: This case was written by Ilkka A. Ronkainen based on publicly available materials such as "Washington's Sour Sales Pitch," *The New York Times*, October 4, 2003, A13; "Branding the USA: The Jungle Ad Challenge," Jungle, September 2003; 38–49; Tim Love, "Old Ideas Fail Brand America," *Advertising Age*, July 7, 2003; 12; Ann Joachim, "Country as a Whole Shapes U.S. Brand," *Marketing News*, April 28, 2003; 38; "Living with America," *The Economist*, January 4, 2003, 18–20; and Charles Skuba, "Branding America®," *Georgetown Journal of International Affairs*, Summer/Fall 2002; 105–113.

The Brand Promise

The United States stands for individual freedom and prosperity and works to convince other nations of that same wisdom. For this to work as a brand proposition, the message has to be seen as a promise and it has to be consistent over time. The State Department spent $15 million on an advertising campaign called "Shared Values" intended for Muslim countries. The focus was religious tolerance in the United States and it profiled thriving Muslims in various professions. However, many in the Muslim world are more interested in even-handed U.S. policy toward them, promotion of democratic choice in their countries against the repressive regimes they live under (which are often supported by the U.S. government), and a chance to escape the poverty they live in. For the core message to work, policy initiatives that are substantial and consistent with the target's expectations are called for. Whether the policy community is then willing to make needed changes is debatable.

Targets and Priorities

With any brand-management effort, the most valuable targets are those with positive dispositions to begin with, such as young, well-educated Arab men. Further segmentation by demographics and/or psychographics is also called for. Targeting the Muslim world at large (1.2 billion people living in 60 countries), as "Shared Values"

TABLE 1

What They Think

	Spread of American ideas is bad (% of respondents who agree)	Dislike American ideas about democracy (% of respondents who agree)
Britian	50	42
France	71	53
Germany	67	45
Poland	55	30
Russia	68	46
Egypt	84	Question not allowed
Jordan	82	69
Pakistan	81	60

Source: Pew Research Center, "What the World Thinks in 2002," Washington, DC, December 4, 2002, questions 67 and 68.

did, is a waste of resources. Recognizing regional differences in language and overall attitude toward the United States are critical in developing the message. It may also be prudent to go to the sources of negative feelings against the United States. In this regard, materials could be sent to educators, communication with their U.S. counterparts could be opened, and they could be encouraged to participate in exchange programs.

Marketing Communication Toolbox

Brand management means that the target gets the message at all possible points of contact; i.e., the marketing communication is integrated and all tools work in unison. Sophisticated messages may not get to the intended audience because of the lack of infrastructure, such as internet access. Governments may step in to curtail or ban communication efforts. For example, many Muslim countries did not allow the airing of the "Shared Values" ads, which are considered propaganda from another sovereign nation. Some of the other efforts have met with mixed reviews.

- The White House created an Office of Global Communications to counter hostile depictions of America in the foreign news media. The approach was to have officials rebut inaccuracies on Al Jazeera and other satellite networks.
- The State Department spent $6 million to start a youth magazine called *Hi*, with a cover price of $2 (in countries where per-capita income may be as low as $1,000).
- The military put up posters with Saddam Hussein's face superimposed over the bodies of Western idols such as Elvis Presley and Rita Hayworth. In Afghanistan, leaflets featured a clean-shaven Osama Bin-Laden in Western garb with the headline "The murderer and coward has abandoned you."

Brand Integration

All parties, but especially the party communicating a message, have to understand where common ground can be found. Many Americans have little first-hand experience in how others see the United States (for example, only 18 percent of the U.S. population hold valid passports, and 86 percent of travelers abroad visit Canada or Mexico). Most Americans would need more information on U.S. involvement in Iraq, for example, to understand the sentiments held there. Information on covert actions, arms deals, and betrayals would help Americans understand the cynicism and hostility with which the media there portray the United States.

Globalization's advancement throughout the entire world means that American ideas, products, and companies will be even more exposed in the future. U.S. policymakers and executives have to be increasingly sensitive to others' needs, wants, and desires to avoid an escalation of ill will.

Questions for Discussion

1. One U.S. State Department official has proposed that the ultimate goal should be to build a level of understanding so that despite policy differences people will not want to come to the United States "to kill us." Government should get out of the advertising business and instead help the Americans with something to offer play a bigger role. Comment on this view.
2. What type of communications campaign, and by whom, should be used to combat negative perceptions of the United States around the world?
3. What is the role of U.S. corporations, such as Coca-Cola and McDonald's in this effort?

December 10, 1998: The Job Offer

John and Joanna Lafferty had just opened a bottle of wine to share with friends who had come to see their new apartment in Toronto when the telephone rang. John, a lanky, easygoing development economist, excused himself to answer the phone in the kitchen.

Recently married, John and Joanna were excited to be building a life together in the same city at last. As a development economist specializing in Latin America, John Lafferty's work had taken him to Peru, Bolivia, and Guatemala on a series of three- to four-month assignments over the previous three years. While he loved the challenge and adventure of this fieldwork and had come to love the people and culture, he also wanted a home base and steady presence in Toronto, where Joanna worked as a human resource management consultant. Just before their wedding six months earlier, John accepted a position with a Toronto-based NGO (nongovernmental organization) focused on research, fund-raising and government lobbying on issues related to Central American political refugees. Throughout the 1980s, tens of thousands of refugees had fled political persecution and human rights abuse in war-torn Central America to seek political asylum in Canada; John's field experience in Guatemala and his natural diplomacy were invaluable to the Canadian organization. He was passionate about his work and quickly gained a reputation for being a savvy and politically astute advocate of refugees' cases.

As Joanna went to get some wine glasses from the kitchen, she could overhear her husband speaking in Spanish on the phone. Joanna had studied Spanish in college but had difficulty following the rapid, one-sided conversation. However, one phrase, "Me allegre mucho" and John's broad grin as he said it, was impossible to misinterpret. Joanna returned to her guests in the living room:

"It sounds like good news."

Sources: This case was written by Susan Bartholomew based on personal interviews. Names, dates, and details of situations have been modified for illustrative purposes. The various economic, political, and cultural conditions described are presented as perceptions of the individuals in the case; they do not necessarily reflect the actual conditions in the region. The events described are presented as a basis for classroom discussion rather than to illustrate effective or ineffective handling of a cross-cultureal situation. For more information on El Salvador, see http://www.yahoo.com/Regional/Countries/El_Salvador.

John's work with refugees in the Canadian NGO had caught the attention of the United Nations High Commission for Refugees, headquartered in Geneva, and he had recently returned from a one-week visit and series of interviews. While John had not been searching for a new job opportunity, the Geneva invitation had been too exciting to resist. John walked back into the living room with a huge smile:

"Forget the wine, I think we should open some champagne. The U.N. has just offered me the most incredible job."

"In Geneva?" Joanna asked excitedly.

John's smile grew even broader. "No. In El Salvador."

December 17, 1998: The Decision

The El Salvador assignment would be for two years, as a Program Officer responsible for organizing the repatriation of Salvadoran refugees from various refugee camps back to El Salvador and developing programs to ensure the protection and well-being of such refugees in their return to Salvadoran communities. The position would report to the Charge de Mission of the El Salvador office. While this office was based in the capital city, San Salvador, the job would also require frequent travel to various field offices and refugee camps throughout El Salvador, Nicaragua, Guatemala, and Honduras. The challenge of the assignment excited John tremendously; he also believed that this was an exceptional opportunity for him to make a real difference in the lives of the refugees of Central America. He certainly wanted to accept the job; however, he would only go if Joanna would be willing and happy to go with him.

Two questions would weigh heavily on Joanna's mind:

1. *"What about the political instability of the area?"*

The politics of El Salvador were complicated and difficult to understand, and the story seemed to vary depending on the source. As Joanna gathered, the civil war in El Salvador had come to an end in 1992 with a U.N.–brokered peace treaty between the conservative government of the Republican Nationalist Alliance (Arena) and the Marxist-led Farabundo Marti National Liberation Front (FMLN). Throughout the war, the U.S. had apparently spent more than $4 billion to support the government and military, while the Soviet Bloc supported the FMLN. Human-rights groups alleged that right-wing death squads had murdered 40,000 of the 70,000 people killed during the twelve-year war. However, the peace agreement had significantly reduced the size of the army, disbanded corrupt police forces, purged the country of the most notorious human-rights abusers, and disarmed the FMLN, allowing it to become a legal political party. The country appeared to have made substantial progress toward peace and democracy. The information and briefings they received from Salvadorans and other expatriates who had recently returned from the country suggested that life in the capital San Salvador was quite safe. Economically, the country was becoming more internationally open, with establishment of large export factories, increasing privatization, and reforms aimed at stimulating foreign investment. While certain precautions were required, and the area was still heavily patrolled by armed forces, Joanna was told she could expect a relatively normal lifestyle. They would live in a highly secure part of the city, in the area populated by all the foreign embassies. They would also be living and traveling on a U.N. diplomatic passport ("Laissez-passer"), which would afford them excellent protection.

2. *"What about my career?"*

Moving to El Salvador was the last thing Joanna had imagined when she married John Lafferty six months earlier. Joanna had worked in Toronto for three years as a human resource consultant after graduating with an MBA. She was bright and ambitious, and her career was advancing well. While she was very happy to be married, she also enjoyed her professional and financial independence. Besides, Toronto was not only professionally rewarding, it was also home, friends, and family. However, Joanna was also ready for a change; secretly, she had always envied John the sense of adventure that accompanied his work. Maybe this was an opportunity for her to develop her human resource consulting skills in an international context.

After much discussion, they decided that John would accept the assignment.

January–March, 1999: Predeparture Arrangements

When John confirmed with the Geneva office that he would take the assignment, it was arranged for him to move to San Salvador at the end of March and for Joanna

to follow one month later. It was often recommended in assignments of this kind to send married staff ahead of time to get settled into the job before their spouse and/or family arrived. This option made sense to the Laffertys and had several advantages. First, it would give Joanna more time to finish off her current consulting projects in Toronto and make a graceful exit from her present firm. She had a strong professional reputation and wanted to ensure she was remembered favorably by her corporate clients when she returned to Toronto two years later.

Second, John would be able to get the housing arrangements settled before Joanna's arrival. John's employer would provide ample financial and logistical support to staff in finding housing; however, John also knew from past experience that dealing with local realtors and utility companies in Central America could be highly frustrating. Tasks that were quite simple in Toronto, such as having a lease drawn up and getting a telephone installed, just didn't seem to follow any system or set of procedures. "Tomorrow" could mean next week or even next month. Patience, flexibility, and a good deal of charm were usually required; getting angry rarely helped. While John was used to the inconvenience and unpredictability of local services in Central America, he was uncertain how Joanna would react initially. John held a deep affection for the Central American people and felt hopeful that Joanna would develop an affinity for the culture as well. However, he hoped to at least have the majority of the living arrangements worked out before she arrived to make her transition to El Salvador as smooth as possible.

Finally, the extra time gave Joanna more opportunity to prepare herself for the transition. Joanna had taken a course on International Human Resource Management as an MBA and was familiar with the phenomenon of culture shock in international assignments. She recalled from her course that predeparture preparation and cultural orientation made a significant difference in helping employees and their families adapt to the foreign environment. Joanna was determined to read and learn as much about Salvadoran history and politics as she could. She was also keen to improve her Spanish before she arrived, and as soon as the decision was made that they would be going to El Salvador, she enrolled in night courses for six hours a week.

As Joanna walked home from her Spanish class one evening, pleased with her results on her comprehension test, she recalled with amusement a conversation she had had with Joan Taylor. Joan was the wife of a senior executive with Altron, a Canadian firm with offices throughout Latin America. The Taylors had just returned from a two-year assignment in Guatemala City, and Joanna had contacted Joan to get some insight on the practicalities of living in the region.

"My dear Joanna," Joan began, *"you will have a very fine life in Central America, or in most developing countries your husband will be sent to, for that matter. You will live better than you ever could anywhere else."* Joan gave Joanna a playful nudge *"Just watch out for the 'gilded cage syndrome'."*

"The what?" Joanna had asked.

"As corporate executives or diplomats in third-world postings, we live a pretty high life, certainly a standard of living far beyond what we could have in our own countries. Everything is there for you and everything is done for you. It's like living in a gilded cage. Some people love it, and get pretty spoiled; after a while you can't imagine even making a sandwich for yourself. . . ."

Humph, Joanna thought to herself at the time. *That would certainly never happen to me. I am a professional. This is an incredible learning opportunity, and I am going to make the most of it!*

May, 1999: Joanna's Arrival in El Salvador

Joanna arrived on a balmy afternoon, grateful for the warm breeze after a cold Toronto winter. She was excited to see John and only slightly disappointed that their first drive into San Salvador would not be alone, but accompanied by a young Salvadoran named Julio Cesar, who had been assigned as their driver. On the drive from the airport, Joanna tried hard to follow his rapid banter as he pointed out the sights to her. She had felt confident in her Spanish in the classroom in Toronto, but now she could barely understand a word Julio Cesar said. John, sensing her frustration, began to translate, and by the time they reached the house, Joanna was exhausted and discouraged.

John was proud of the house he had found, next door to the Mexican embassy and only a block from a tennis club where most of the members were expatriates. He thought this might provide a good social base for Joanna if she got homesick for North American lifestyle. The large twelve-room house was certainly impressive, with its shining terazzo floors and two large gardens. Joanna wondered what to do with all the space. It was also quite secure, with metal bars on all the windows, and surrounded by twelve-foot walls.

"This isn't a house, John, it's a fortress," Joanna said in amazement.

"Yeah . . . I know it's a bit much," said John. *"But this is the one area of the city we are strongly advised to live in, for security reasons. Smaller homes or apartments just don't exist. Most of the families living here are either expats or very wealthy Salvadorans. Most have live-in help and need the space."*

"But I don't want anyone else living with us. . . ."

"Come . . . I want you to meet Maria." Joanna followed John out to the back of the house, and was introduced to a small, brown woman, vigorously scrubbing clothes. *"Maria worked for the family who lived here before; it only seemed right that she should stay. She only lives a few blocks away, though, so she will go home each evening."*

After a week, Joanna soon learned Maria's work patterns. Maria would hand wash all their clothes in the cement tub and hang them to dry outside, a chore that would take all day long, as Maria would often wash things three times. The following day she would return to do the ironing, which would take another full day. As Joanna sat in her study upstairs, reading her books and newspapers, she felt an overwhelming sense of guilt thinking of Maria, hand washing every last item of their clothing in the cement tub. Some days Joanna longed to just walk into an empty house and put her own clothes in a washing machine. Then, when Joanna found out that John paid Maria $6.00 per day, she was furious. John explained to Joanna that this was the customary wage for the women from the "barrios marginales" who worked as domestic help for wealthy Salvadorans and expatriates. These "marginal communities" were small groupings of tin shacks located in the ravines that surrounded the city. A few had electricity, but many of the communities, including Maria's, still cooked their meals over fires and lit their homes with candles. Joanna began to slip more money into Maria's pay envelope.

Joanna hoped to make a friend of Maria and looked forward to having lunch each day with her and learning more of the local way of speaking. Joanna realized now that the formal Spanish she had learned in school was vastly different from the language she heard each day on the streets of San Salvador. However, Maria refused to eat at the same table as Joanna and insisted on serving Joanna first in the dining room, and then eating her own lunch on the stone steps in the back room. Joanna was deeply uncomfortable with this and began to eat lunch at the restaurant in her nearby tennis club instead.

Other things began to irritate Joanna as well. For example, one day, she started to wash the car in the driveway. Suddenly, Maria's son appeared and insisted that he do the job for her, horrified that "la Senora" would undertake such a task herself. Another time, Joanna began to dig up some of the plants in the garden for replanting; the following morning, a gardener appeared at the door, saying that he was a cousin of Maria's and would be pleased to take on additional gardening work.

Joanna resented this intrusion into her daily life. If she was going to be spending so much time at home, she wanted privacy to read and study. It was going to be a while, she realized, before she found a job. Joanna was disappointed with the job prospects among local and even international companies. Most available positions were clerical, for which she was vastly overqualified. *"I didn't get an MBA to work as a file clerk!"* she would think to herself angrily. Then, she would think sadly, *"My Spanish probably isn't even good enough to get a job as a file clerk."*

One day, in frustration, Joanna called her two closest friends in Toronto, colleagues from her old firm.

"I can't win!" Joanna complained. *"I feel guilty all the time. I feel guilty because I don't do anything myself. And I feel guilty if I don't hire local people to do the housework. They need the money so much. Then I feel guilty that we pay them six dollars a day. We can afford so much more. I feel guilty that I have a maid, and she lives in a tin shack in a ravine two blocks from my house. But John says we can't pay her more than the going rate because it would upset the whole balance of her community. He says they have their own economic structure and norms and we have to respect that. My*

Salvadoran neighbors tell me that if I pay Maria or the gardener more they won't respect me. But I do anyway, and then I feel guilty because I don't tell John. And then our driver, Julio Cesar...."

The sarcastic response was the same from both. *"Gee, Joanna, sounds tough. Beautiful house, a maid, gardener, and driver, afternoons at the tennis club ... no wonder you're so miserable?"*

Joanna got off the phone, feeling worse than ever. Had accepting this assignment been a big mistake? She knew how much this job meant to John, and it was a great step forward for his career. But what about her career and her own happiness? This had been a mutual decision. Something was going to have to change or they would be on a plane back to Toronto very soon. The question was ... what?

Questions for Discussion

1. Should Joanna have done anything differently in terms of her preparation for moving to El Salvador? What do you think she should do now?

2. If you were John, would you have taken the job in El Salvador? If you were Joanna, would you have agreed to go?

3. What can companies and organizations do to make foreign assignments more successful for couples and families? Is the happiness of the employee's spouse the responsibility of the company?

Gabriel Benguela had just walked into his office from attending an operations review when the telephone rang. Gabriel guessed that a call late in the day must be from one of his marketing managers based in the Far East. It was indeed; Peter Mai was calling from Avicular's Singapore office. Peter was the lead negotiator on a deal under negotiation with Pakistan International Airlines (PIA). It was July 6, 1997.

Peter: Gabriel, we have a problem with the PIA proposal. Although our local agent keeps assuring me that we have won this competition and we will get the deal, I'm not so sure. Pakistan's negotiations with the International Monetary Fund (IMF) to secure yet another loan to finance their current account deficit are causing more problems for this deal. Recent economic data for the country is also not very good, with low economic growth and continuing employment problems. There have been more demonstrations in Lahore because of the European Union's recent antidumping ruling imposing high tariffs against several cotton exporting countries, including Pakistan. The export of cotton is not only a major source of employment but also a source of badly needed hard currency. All this on the heels of the IMF's austerity program.

Gabriel: What does PIA want now? How long have we been trying to finalize this deal?

Peter: Seven months. PIA has asked that we accept local currency.

Gabriel: "That's just great! Peter, you know our division never accepts payment in local currency. Although nearly 50 percent of our business is international, we are just not set up to accept the risk that denominating sales in other currencies would bring. In fact, the whole aerospace business is conducted in U.S. dollars."

Peter: Hey, blame the IMF. They should be charged for inciting riots and billed for our expenses.

Gabriel: We need this program badly. These large cockpit retrofit opportunities are hard to find, and it seems that our division's management has already com-

mitted this $23.7 million sale to corporate on our latest stretch goal.

Peter: There is an alternative. Our agent, Makran, advised me that PIA can buy the receivable from us at a 5 percent discount and take all of the currency risk. Their Los Angeles subsidiary would pay us 30 days after our invoice.

Gabriel: But we can't take another hit to the return on sales on this deal. As the deal stands, we had to go to Group Level for approval on this one. This isn't good. I'll speak with the finance people and call you back within 24 hours.

Avicular Controls

Avicular Controls, Inc. (ACI), based in Chicago, had dominated the field of automatic controls since its founding in 1903. Beginning with furnace controls for the steel and power industries in 1903, it continued to grow for more than 90 years. By 1996, Avicular employed 13,000 people and conducted business in 52 countries. ACI was composed of two major business units: Industrial Process Controls (AvIPC, with 1996 sales of $1.75 billion), and Aviation Control (AvAC, with 1996 sales of $1.21 billion). In the summer of 1997 ACI was positioned to achieve its sales growth goal of $4 billion by the year 2000.

AvAC was once again on a growth path after several tough years. Avicular was recognized as the dominant force in the avionics market; market share had grown to a hefty 53 percent by 1996. But the industry had suffered a severe downturn beginning in 1992, and was only now reaching the sales levels last achieved in 1991. In fact, AvAC sales had been $1.6 billion in 1991, and would hopefully once again break $1.5 billion in 1997. The commercial aircraft industry returned to a healthy growth path in 1996 and early 1997, and growth was expected to stay robust through the year 2000.

ACI, specifically the Air Transport Systems division of the Space and Aviation Control business unit, had recorded a number of major wins in 1996. These wins included the contract for the cockpit retrofits for a major overnight package delivery firm's fleet of DC-10s, and numerous orders for the firm's new enhanced airborne collision avoidance system. Although U.S. government spending for electronic components was leveling off, international opportunities for military avionics retrofits and space systems were on the rise. Commercial space programs were also projected to grow rapidly, and ACI had landed key initial contracts with NASA and Lockheed Martin.

ACI was not new to international business, establishing its first foreign subsidiaries in 1936. Global treasury was headquartered (along with corporate) near O'Hare International Airport outside Chicago. Corporate treasury was a profit center, and charged 1 percent commission on all sales. Treasury, however, passed on the currency risk to the business unit. If a local affiliate, joint venture, or subsidiary required local currency, then treasury would try and match those requirements by accepting the A/R in the local currency. For many developing countries where ACI had little or no activities (such as Pakistan), this was only done on an exception basis. Treasury did agree that Aviation Controls could use their local affiliates to manage the sale of aviation products, but would have to pay between 3 percent and 8 percent for currency cover (the final fee would have to be negotiated between treasury and Aviation Controls). This was something that the division had an unwritten policy of not doing; the standard transfer charge imposed by treasury cut into sales margins.

Pakistan International Airlines (PIA)

Pakistan International Airlines Corporation (PIA) was the national carrier of the Islamic Republic of Pakistan. Founded in 1954, PIA operated both scheduled passenger and cargo services. The firm was 57 percent state-owned, with the remaining 43 percent held by private investors internal to Pakistan. PIA had been Pakistan's only airline for over 40 years, but in 1993 Aero Asia International Ltd. was born. By 1996, however, it had captured little of the domestic or Pakistan international market (only 5 percent of Aero Asia's sales were international). Two other recent entrants into the domestic market, Bhoja Airlines Pvt. LTD and Shaheen Air, had captured little of the market.

The latest projections of the International Air Transport Association (IATA) indicated that passenger and cargo traffic would double in Asia by the year 2010. Asia was expected to surpass Europe and North America in both size of fleets and passenger/cargo hauled. PIA was experiencing some of this growth, but its aging fleet was resulting in losses. Increasing numbers of flights were either delayed or canceled as a result of maintenance problems. Although a larger and larger proportion of the population was traveling by air, given the choice of taking a PIA or foreign carrier, passenger traffic was opting for the latter. It was imperative that PIA modernize its fleet.

In addition to PIA's traditional passenger and cargo services, a growing proportion of sales was arising from the yearly Islamic Haj (pilgrimage) traffic to Mecca and Medina in Saudia Arabia. Demand had always been strong, but increasing numbers of Pakistani citizens were obtaining visas for the pilgrimage, as Saudi Arabia had recently shuffled the allocation of Haj visas among nations and Pakistan had benefited. PIA was a direct beneficiary of the increased visa allocation.

PIA had originally planned to purchase new commercial aircraft to replace and add to their existing fleet. The fleet modernization program, however, was put on hold due to higher priorities within the Pakistan government in Islamabad. These priorities were established after a review by the IMF of the government's spending plan. Much to PIA's discomfort, the austerity plan proposed by the IMF did not include funds for modernization. PIA had been counting on this fleet modernization and had postponed the incorporation of some Federal Aviation Administration (FAA) safety directives. With the cancellation of the fleet modernization program, PIA now had to move fast to ensure compliance with FAA safety mandates, or face being locked out of some of its most profitable gates. If PIA did not have some of these safety systems and quieter engines installed on their aircraft by June 30, 1998, they would be barred from U.S. airspace.

PIA was in a predicament. It knew exactly what should be done, but government control—especially in these times of crisis—left it no choice. Once PIA agreed to putting the fleet *modernization program* on hold, the managing board decided to pursue a fleet *renovation program* which would require much less hard currency. This plan called for extensively refurbishing PIA's existing aircraft at their new heavy maintenance facility in Karachi. For example, instead of the new quieter engines which new aircraft possessed, PIA would have to make do with the use of *hush kits* for the older engines. It would also require completely new cockpit avionics to take advantage of not only FAA mandates, but recent improvements in the Air Traffic Network (ATN) infrastructure. The first aircraft to be modified would be those utilized on their long-haul flights to the United States, primarily the *B747 classics* (Boeing). Aircraft engine suppliers were approached first and negotiations concluded.

What remained on the table was the cockpit avionics integration supplier. A cockpit retrofit program would require contracts both with the appropriate original equipment manufacturer (OEM), in this case Boeing, and a systems integrator, such as Avicular. Prior to the adoption of the economic austerity plan, Karachi had been the sight of an intense competition between the largest OEMs, Boeing, McDonnell Douglas, and Airbus, for new aircraft sales. It was only after the adoption of the austerity plan that Boeing was willing to discuss cockpit retrofits instead. Due to ACI's extensive experience with a variety of control systems for Boeing, its history with PIA, and its recent work on cockpit retrofit for McDonnell Douglas aircraft, ACI felt it was truly the preferred supplier for PIA. ACI believed that if any other vendor were selected, the added regulatory certification costs and delays would be prohibitively expensive. However, ACI had not undertaken Boeing cockpit retrofits to date (no one had), and looked to the PIA deal as an opportunity to build a new competitive base. But ACI's best and final bid had been too high. PIA's insistence on payment in local currency terms was now thought to be a tactic to extract better concessions from ACI and their agent, Makran.

The Pakistani Economy

Pakistan was divided from India in 1947 as a homeland for Muslims. Pakistan's relationship with India had, however, been under continuous strain since that time for a variety of reasons. The sources of friction included overlapping claims to Kashmir, India's involvement in the demise of East Pakistan, and the birth of Bangladesh in 1971, to name but a few. Because of these conflicts the military had always loomed large over politics in Pakistan. The country's persistence in continuing a nuclear rivalry with India, when neither nation was thought to be able to afford such a *luxury*, was one indication of this. The United States is frequently at odds with Pakistan regarding its nuclear weapons program and had suspended military aid on several occasions, including a large F16 purchase in the early 1990s. However, Pakistan's proximity to Afghanistan and India make it strategically important to U.S. interests.

Pakistan practices Islamic Banking, which is based on the *shariah*. This code prohibits the payment of interest, and the suppliers of funds find themselves becoming investors, rather than creditors. Although financial profit in most forms was looked down upon under Islamic rule, there were 28 publicly traded equities in Pakistan in 1996. The trading of equity shares for profit was also somewhat inconsistent with the *shariah*.

Pakistan has relied upon the World Bank (WB), the IMF, and other multinational lenders (in addition to specific national foreign aid and investment providers) for much of its capital. The country's deteriorating trade gap in the mid-1990s had caused a sudden and significant drop in foreign currency reserves, from US$3 billion to less than US$1.5 billion in September of 1996. The IMF immediately interceded in the economy, imposing an austerity program in October. The government submitted to this austerity plan as a precondition of receiving a $600 million standby loan extended to cover balance of payments shortfalls. The political repercussions were swift and severe: the fall of the Benazir Bhutto administration.[1]

A central part of the IMF's austerity program was a devaluation of the Pakistan rupee by 7.86 percent against the U.S. dollar on October 22, 1996. Roughly six months later, there was renewed speculation that another devaluation was imminent in order to limit imports and help the export sector earn badly needed hard currency. Another recent economic setback had been the ruling by the European Union that Pakistan was guilty of dumping cotton, and had imposed antidumping fines of between 13.0 percent and 22.9 percent on Pakistani cotton. It was a painful blow to the export sector. The current exchange rate of 40.4795 Pakistan rupee (Rp) per dollar was maintained by the Pakistani Central Bank; all currency transactions were controlled by the Pakistani government, and were conducted at the official rate. The *black market rate* was approaching Rp50/US$, and as the spread between the black market rate and official rate increased, the probability of devaluation increased. There was no forward market for the Pakistani rupee.[2] Figure 1 illustrates the recent travails of the rupee.

The Avicular/PIA Relationship

ACI had been the preferred avionics supplier to PIA for many years, and the retrofit segment of the business was thought to fit well with the overall strategy of the division. The group president was personally involved with the PIA proposal since this new retrofit market niche was central to the division's growth plan.

The avionics business was divided into two segments: Standard Furnished Equipment (SFE) and Buyer Furnished Equipment (BFE). OEMs such as Boeing, McDonnell Douglas, and Airbus purchased avionics equipment to be installed on new aircraft as SFE. The

FIGURE 1

Daily Exchange Rates: Pakistani Rupees per U.S. dollar

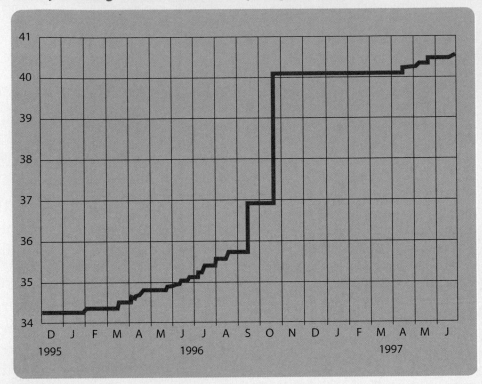

Source: © 1999 by Prof. Werner Antweiler, University of British Columbia, Vancouver, BC, Canada. Time period shown in diagram: 1/Dec/1995–30/Jun/1997. http://www.pacific.commerce.ubc.ca/xr.

margins in selling to this segment were traditionally very low due to the competitive necessity of keeping competitors "off the aircraft." The low margins on OEM sales, however, were made up by higher margins in the sales of spare avionics packages to the same airlines. The purchase of BFE (also called *freedom of choice*) by the airlines is optional, and usually bid among three suppliers. BFE was purchased directly by the airline and installed by either the airline itself or the OEM. Each time an airline made a new aircraft purchase, a BFE proposal would be presented to the airline. The PIA B747 classic fleet retrofit fell into this category.

The major players in the global avionics business in 1996, in addition to Avicular (U.S.), were Honeywell Incorporated (U.S.), Rockwell Collins (U.S.), Allied-Signal (U.S.), and Sextant Avionique (France). To a lesser extent, Litton Industries (U.S.) and Smiths Industries (UK) competed in small specialized segments. Of this competition, however, only Rockwell Collins and Honeywell had the capability to take on such a large cockpit retrofit job. Rockwell Collins was

considered very competitive, and had extensive experience in dealing with the Pakistani government on several large military contracts completed under the U.S. Foreign Military Assistance program.

The global aerospace industry was historically a U.S. dollar business; a dollar-denominated industry. The large airframe manufacturers like Boeing had long taken the lead with the sheer size of their purchase deals. Recently, however, cracks were appearing in this business practice. Competition now focused on more than price. Other competitive elements included credit terms, credit risk, as well as currency of contract denomination.

Ibrahim Makran Pvt. LTD

In countries like Pakistan, the use of an agent is often considered a necessary evil. The agent can oftentimes help to bridge the two business cultures and provide invaluable information—at a cost. ACI's agent, Ibrahim Makran Pvt. LTD., based in Hyderabad, was considered one of the most reliable and well connected in Pakistan.

Makran was also one of the largest import/export trading houses in Pakistan, giving it access to hard currency. It was 100 percent family-owned and managed.

Standard practice in the avionics business was to provide the agent with a 10 percent commission (10 percent of the total final sales price paid after payment is received). Typically, it was the agent who identified the business opportunity and submitted a Business Opportunity Request (BOR) to ACI Marketing. Sometimes this commission was negotiated, but due to the size and importance of this proposal, the commission was accepted without debate.

After PIA contacted ACI and Makran with their latest demand, Makran knew that ACI would want to maintain the deal in U.S. dollars. Makran had immediately inquired as to the availability of dollar funds from its own finance department for a deal of this size. The finance department confirmed that they had the necessary U.S. dollar funds to pay ACI, but noted that the standard fee was 5 percent of the invoiced amount.

Makran then advised ACI that it would be willing to purchase the receivable for the additional 5 percent (in addition to the 10 percent commission). The company's U.S. subsidiary based in Los Angeles would credit ACI within 30 days of ACI invoicing Makran. PIA advised Makran that if ACI accepted payment in Pakistan rupees, then local (Pakistan) payment terms would apply. This meant 180 days in principle, but often was much longer in practice. The agent also advised ACI that the Pakistan rupee was due for another devaluation soon. When pressed for more information, Makran simply replied that the company president, the elder Ibrahim Makran, had "good connections."

The ATS Finance Department

Philip Costa, the finance director for AvAC, had always wanted to be an engineer. His passion for exactness and numbers had, however, included the dollar sign, and he had moved up through the ranks at ACI quickly. The finance department he led was now in the midst of redesigning most of their processes and systems to reduce net working capital (NWC). One of these initiatives included a thorough review of existing payment terms and worldwide days sales receivable (DSR) rates. The department had a goal of reducing the worldwide DSR rate from 55 to 45 days in the current fiscal year. The Pay for Performance target for the current year (the annual performance bonus system at ACI) included NWC goals, and there was concern in the organization that the NWC goal might prove the obstacle to achieving a payout bonus

despite excellent sales growth. And all cash flows, in and out, were to be evaluated in present value terms using a 12 percent discount rate. Philip started his assessment by reviewing the latest DSR report shown in Table 1.

ACI payment terms were net 30 from date of invoice. However, payment terms and practices varied dramatically across country and region. ACI had not in the past enforced stringent credit terms on many customers; for example, neither contracts nor invoices stated any penalties for late payment. Many airlines did pay on time, but others availed themselves of ACI's low-cost financing.

A review of PIA's accounts receivable history indicated they consistently paid their invoices late. The current average DSR was 264 days. PIA had been repeatedly put on hold by the collections department, forcing marketing staff representatives to press the agent who in turn pressed PIA for payment. Philip's concern over the collection had driven him to search for guarantees of prompt payment. In the end, he had required the inclusion of a 20 percent advance payment clause in the contract as a means of self-insuring. Although marketing took the high DSR rate up with PIA and the agent, this deal was expected to be the same if not worse. One positive attribute of the contract was the fact that deliveries would not commence until one year after project start. If the expected improvements to the DSR were made in the meantime, maybe the high DSR rate on the PIA deal could be averaged with the rest of Asia. The 20 percent advance payment would be used to fund the front-end engineering work. Philip also insisted that it was the responsibility of his department to assess credit risk for the project. This typically required a detailed review of the buyer's financials. Unfortunately, the most recent published financial data for PIA was extremely sparse, and out of date (1990).

Meeting with Finance

Gabriel: Good morning, Philip. I am sorry to trouble you yet again with this PIA deal, but we have a problem. Peter called me last night and advised me that PIA wanted to pay in local currency. If we don't agree, we risk losing the deal. I think it's fallout from the 20 percent advance payment clause. Our agent, Makran, said they could accept the risk and net 30 payment terms for 5 percent of the sales price. Although we're confident that we are the only competing company that can meet PIA's requirements, should this requirement be real and we refuse, it could derail the whole PIA project.

Philip: Five percent is too steep! We simply cannot accept that. This is already one of the riskiest projects

TABLE 1

Average Days Sales Receivables by Region and OEM, Avaiation Systems Division

Region	Actual	Target	Amount
North America	44	40	$31 million
South America	129	70	$2.1 million
Europe	55	45	$5.7 million
Middle East	93	60	$3.2 million
Asia	75	55	$11 million
Firm			
PIA	264	180	$0.7 million
Boeing	39	30	$41 million
McDonnell Douglas	35	30	$18 million
Airbus Industrie	70	45	$13 million
Worldwide	55	45	

1. Many foreign carriers make purchases through U.S.-based trading companies, distorting the actual DSR practices by country.
2. The spread between individual customers within regions can be extremely large.
3. Disputed invoices are included. Amount is for all products, services, and exchanges.
4. Firms consistently meeting ACI's net 30-day terms were eligible for participation in ACI's preferred supplier program which entitled them to a 10 percent discount on future purchases. Only the largest customers had, to date, taken advantage of this discount.

we have undertaken. The 20 percent advance payment is to help with the DSR since it is one of our primary goals. The DSR is being watched on a daily basis by division management. We already had to secure Group Level approval for this deal because it fell below our minimum 20 percent ROS [return on sales] target. Whose side is this agent on?

Gabriel: Why don't we accept the forex risk? After all, the rupee is fixed by the government.

Philip: Gabriel, fixed exchanged rates are actually less stable than floating rates. If you consider the IMF and World Bank part of the Pakistani government, then you are right. However, the IMF and World Bank have far more influence over Pakistan's exchange rate than the Pakistani government. The recent currency devaluations in many emerging markets could keep spreading. In the last few days the Thai baht and Philippine peso were devalued, and this is likely to spill over to other Asian export-based countries. The Pakistan rupee was devalued late last year, and I would expect another late this year or early next year.

Gabriel: I agree we would prefer not to accept this risk, but we need to make the sale so we don't create a hole in our strategic plan. If PIA certifies our latest B777

cockpit technology in their B747 classics, we have a tremendous opportunity worldwide with that workhorse jumbo. What about our other unit, the local Industrial Process Controls (AvIPC) unit in Pakistan? Didn't they recently score a big contract with the national Pakistani petrochemical company? Don't they need rupees?

Philip: True, they must. Unfortunately, the CMS system charges 1 percent transaction cost but still passes on the currency risk to us. Unless we pay substantially more. If we were to receive the rupee receivable in the next few weeks, I might be willing to pay the 1 percent and take the risk, but that's not the case here. The dollar is continuing to climb, and it looks like a lot of Asia is starting to fall.

Gabriel: I need to get back to Peter. What should we do?

Questions for Discussion

1. Estimate the cash flows by currency which the proposal(s) would probably yield. What is the expected U.S. dollar value that would, in the end, be received?
2. Do you think the services that Makran is offering are worth the costs?
3. What would you do if you were heading the Honeywell SAC group negotiating the deal?

It was January 2002, and Toyota Motor Europe Manufacturing (TMEM) had a problem. More specifically, Mr. Toyoda Shuhei, the new President of TMEM, had a problem. He was on his way to Toyota Motor Company's (Japan) corporate offices outside Tokyo to explain the continuing losses of European manufacturing and sales operations. The CEO of Toyota Motor Company, Mr. Hiroshi Okuda, was expecting a proposal from Mr. Shuhei to reduce and eventually eliminate the European losses. The situation was intense given that TMEM was the only major Toyota subsidiary suffering losses.

Toyota Motor Company was the number one automobile manufacturer in Japan, the third largest manufacturer in the world by unit sales (5.5 million units or one auto every six seconds), but number eight in sales in Continental Europe. The global automobile manufacturing industry had been experiencing, like many industries, continued consolidation in recent years as margins were squeezed, economies of scale and scope pursued, and global sales slowed.

Toyota was no different. It had continued to rationalize its manufacturing along regional lines. Toyota had continued to increase the amount of local manufacturing in North America. In 2001, more than 60 percent of Toyota's North American sales were locally manufactured. But Toyota's European sales were nowhere close to this. Most of Toyota's automobile and truck manufacturing for Europe was still done in Japan. In 2001 only 24 percent of the autos sold in Europe were manufactured in Europe (including the U.K.), the remainder being imported from Japan (see Figure 1).

Toyota Motor Europe sold 634,000 automobiles in 2000. This was the second largest foreign market for Toyota, second only to North America. TMEM expected significant growth in European sales, and was planning to expand European manufacturing and sales to 800,000 units by 2005. But for fiscal 2001, the unit reported operating losses of ¥9.897 billion ($82.5 million at ¥120/$). TMEM had three assembly plants in the United Kingdom, one plant in Turkey, and one plant in

Portugal. In November 2000, Toyota Motor Europe announced that it would not generate positive profits for the next two years due to the weakness of the euro.

Toyota had recently introduced a new model to the European market, the Yaris, which was proving very successful. The Yaris, a super-small vehicle with a 1,000cc engine, had sold more than 180,000 units in 2000. Although the Yaris had been specifically designed for the European market, the decision had been made early on to manufacture it in Japan.

Currency Exposure

The primary source of the continuing operating losses suffered by TMEM was the falling value of the euro. Over the recent two year period the euro had fallen in value against both the Japanese yen and the British pound. As demonstrated in Figure 1, the cost base for most of the autos sold within the Continental European market was the Japanese yen. Figure 2 illustrates the slide of the euro against the Japanese yen.

As the yen rose against the euro, costs increased significantly when measured in euro-terms. If Toyota wished to preserve its price competitiveness in the European market, it had to absorb most of the exchange rate changes, suffering reduced or negative margins on both completed cars and key subcomponents shipped to its European manufacturing centers. Deciding to manufacture the Yaris in Japan had only exacerbated the problem.

Management Response

Toyota management was not sitting passively by. In 2001 they had started up some assembly operations in Valenciennes, France. Although a relatively small percentage of total European sales as of January 2002, Toyota planned to continue to expand its capacity and capabilities to source about 25 percent of European sales by 2004. Assembly of the Yaris was scheduled to be moved to Valenciennes in 2002. The continuing problem, however, was that it was an assembly facility, meaning that much of the expensive value-added content of th autos being assembled was still based in either Japan or the United Kingdom.

Mr. Shuhei, with the approval of Mr. Okuda, had also initiated a local-sourcing and procurement program for

FIGURE 1

Toyota Motor's European Currency Operating Structure

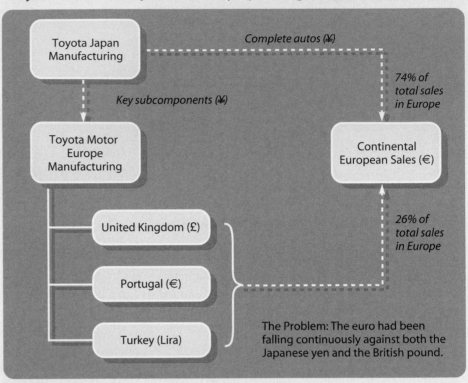

FIGURE 2

Daily Exchange Rates: Japanese Yen per Euro

FIGURE 3

Daily Exchange Rates: British Pounds per Euro

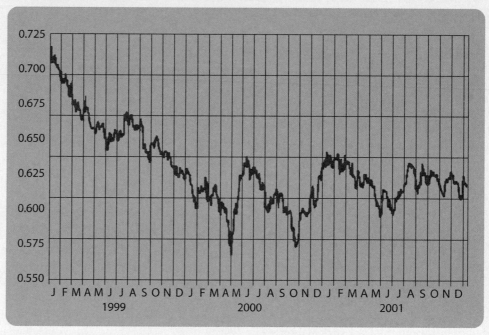

Source: © 2003 by Prof. Werner Antweiler, University of British Columbia, Vancouver, BC, Canada. Permission is granted to reproduce the above image provided that the source and copyright are acknowledged.

the United Kingdom manufacturing operations. TMEM wished to decrease the number of key components imported from Toyota Japan to reduce the currency exposure of the U.K. unit. But again, the continuing problem of the British pound's value against the euro, as shown in Figure 3, reduced even the effectiveness of this solution.

Questions for Discussion

1. Why do you think Toyota had waited so long to move much of its manufacturing for European sales to Europe?

2. If you were Mr. Shuhei, how would you categorize your problems and solutions? What was a short-term and what was a long-term problem?

3. What measures would you recommend Toyota Europe take to resolve the continuing operating losses?

Company Background

Ian J. Ward was an export merchant in difficulty. His company, Ward, Bedas Canadian Ltd., had successfully sold Canadian lumber and salmon to countries in the Persian Gulf. Over time, the company had opened four offices worldwide. However, when the Iran—Iraq war erupted, most of Ward's long-term trading relationships disappeared within a matter of months. In addition, the international lumber market began to collapse. As a result, Ward, Bedas Canadian Ltd. went into a survivalist mode and sent employees all over the world to look for new markets and business opportunities. Late that year, the company received an interesting order. A firm in Korea urgently needed to purchase lumber for the production of chopsticks.

Learning about the Chopstick Market

In discussing the wood deal with the Koreans, Ward learned that in order to produce good chopsticks more than 60 percent of the wood fiber would be wasted. Given the high transportation cost involved, the large degree of wasted materials, and his need for new business, Ward decided to explore the Korean and Japanese chopstick industry in more detail.

He quickly determined that chopstick making in the Far East is a fragmented industry, working with old technology and suffering from a lack of natural resources. In Asia, chopsticks are produced in very small quantities, often by family organizations. Even the largest of the 450 chopstick factories in Japan turns out only 5 million chopsticks a month. This compares to an overall market size of 130 million pairs of disposable chopsticks a day. In addition, chopsticks represent a growing market. With increased wealth in Asia, people eat out more often and therefore have a greater demand for disposable chopsticks. The fear of communicable diseases has greatly reduced the use of reusable chop-

sticks. Renewable plastic chopsticks have been attacked by many groups as too newfangled and as causing future ecological problems.

From his research, Ward concluded that a competitive niche existed in the world chopstick market. He believed that, if he could use low-cost raw materials and ensure that the labor cost component would remain small, he could successfully compete in the world market.

The Founding of Lakewood Forest Products

In exploring opportunities afforded by the newly identified international marketing niche for chopsticks, Ward set four criteria for plant location:

1. Access to suitable raw materials
2. Proximity of other wood product users who could make use of the 60 percent waste for their production purposes
3. Proximity to a port that would facilitate shipment to the Far East
4. Availability of labor

In addition, Ward was aware of the importance of product quality. People use chopsticks on a daily basis and are accustomed to products that are visually inspected one by one, so he would have to live up to high quality expectations to compete successfully. Chopsticks could not be bowed or misshapen, have blemishes in the wood, or splinter.

Ward needed financing to implement his plan. Private lenders were skeptical and slow to provide funds. The skepticism resulted from the unusual direction of Ward's proposal. Far Eastern companies have generally held the cost advantage in a variety of industries, especially those as labor intensive as chopstick manufacturing. U.S. companies rarely have an advantage in producing low-cost items. Further, only a very small domestic market exists for chopsticks.

However, Ward found that the state of Minnesota was willing to participate in his new venture. Since the decline of the mining industry, regional unemployment had been rising rapidly in the state. Unemployment in Minnesota's Iron Range had peaked at 22 percent. Therefore, state and local officials were anxious to attract new industries that would be independent of mining activities. Of particular help was the enthusiasm

Sources: This case was written by Michael R. Czinkota based on the following sources: Mary Clayton, "Minnesota Chopstick Maker Finds Japanese Eager to Import His Quality Qaribashi," *The Christian Science Monitor,* October 16, 1987, 11; Roger Worthington, "Improbable Chopstick Capitol of the World," *Chicago Tribune,* June 5, 1988, 39; Mark Gill, "The Great American Chopstick Master," *American Way,* August 1, 1987, 34, 78–79; "Perpich of Croatia," *The Economist,* April 20, 1991, 27; and personal interview with Ian J. Ward, president, Lakewood Forest Products.

of Governor Rudy Perpich. The governor had been boosting Minnesota business on the international scene by traveling abroad and receiving many foreign visitors. He was excited about Ward's plans, which called for the creation of more than 100 new jobs within a year.

Hibbing, Minnesota, turned out to be an ideal location for Ward's project. The area had an abundant supply of aspen wood, which, because it grows in clay soil, tends to be unmarred. The fact that Hibbing was the hometown of the governor also did not hurt. In addition, Hibbing boasted an excellent labor pool, and both the city and the state were willing to make loans totaling $500,000. Further, the Iron Range Resources Rehabilitation Board was willing to sell $3.4 million in industrial revenue bonds for the project. Together with jobs and training wage subsidies, enterprise zone credits, and tax increment financing benefits, the initial public support of the project added up to about 30 percent of its start-up costs. The potential benefit of the new venture to the region was quite clear. When Lakewood Forest Products advertised its first 30 jobs, more than 3,000 people showed up to apply.

The Production and Sale of Chopsticks

Ward insisted that to truly penetrate the international market, he would need to keep his labor cost low. As a result, he decided to automate as much of the production as possible. However, no equipment was readily available to produce chopsticks, because no one had automated the process before.

After much searching, Ward identified a European equipment manufacturer who produced machinery for making popsicle sticks. He purchased equipment from the Danish firm to better carry out the sorting and finishing processes. However, because aspen wood was quite different from the wood for which the machine was designed, as was the final product, substantial design adjustments had to be made. Sophisticated equipment was also purchased to strip the bark from the wood and peel it into long, thin sheets. Finally, a computer vision system was acquired to detect defects in the chopsticks. The system rejected more than 20 percent of the production, and yet some of the chopsticks that passed inspection were splintering. However, Ward firmly believed that further fine-tuning of the equipment and training of the new work force would gradually take care of the problem.

Given this fully automated process, Lakewood Forest Products was able to develop capacity for up to 7 million chopsticks a day. With a unit manufacturing cost of $0.03 and an anticipated unit selling price of $0.057, Ward expected to earn a pretax profit of $4.7 million in his first full year of operations.

Due to intense marketing efforts in Japan and the fact that Japanese customers were struggling to obtain sufficient supplies of disposable chopsticks, Ward was able to presell the first five years of production quite quickly. Lakewood Forest Products was ready to enter the international market. With an ample supply of raw materials and an almost totally automated plant, Lakewood was positioned as the world's largest and least labor-intensive manufacturer of chopsticks. The first shipment of six containers with a load of 12 million pairs of chopsticks to Japan was ready to be shipped.

Questions for Discussion

1. Is Lakewood Forest Products ready for exports? Using the export-readiness framework developed by the U.S. Department of Commerce and available through various sites such as http://www.tradeport.org (from "Trade Expert" go to "Getting Started" and finally to "Assess Your Export Readiness"), determine whether Lakewood's commitment, resources, and product warrant the action they have undertaken.

2. What are the environmental factors that are working for and against Lakewood Forest Products both at home in the United States and in the target market, Japan?

3. New-product success is a function of trial and repurchase. How do Lakewood's chances look along these two dimensions?

The book concludes with a chapter focusing on new horizons. Based on global research conducted by the authors, the section covers the newest developments, knowledge, and speculations about international business, as well as information about professional and employment options in the international business field.

PART
Future

7

New Horizons

Learning Objectives

- To understand the many changing dimensions that shape international business

- To learn about and evaluate the international business forecasts made by a panel of experts

- To be informed about different career opportunities in international business

Importing on the Internet

Can't find a U.S.–made snowboard at your local department store in Japan? Try the new mall on the Internet. A Portland, Oregon, firm is creating what could be described as a Japanese cybermall, an online shopping service that enables U.S. manufacturers and retailers to advertise and sell their products directly to consumers—in Japanese. The Japanese Internet service also teaches customers in Japan how to order products and services directly from the United States.

By setting up shop in local language cybermalls, U.S. firms could target potential customers around the globe without the costly headaches that often scare them away from the international marketplace. Ion Global Portland has provided Japan-specific e-business Web site development, online marketing, strategic consulting, and research services since 1995 to more than one hundred clients, including Amazon.com, British Telecom, Outpost.com, JCPenney, Nokia, and PeopleSoft. The firm created a worldwide business consulting network spanning ten countries.

Ion Global's electronic service averages 1,000 unique users per day. More than 5,000 people subscribe to its e-newsletter, according to owner Tim Clark. "We're helping companies enter the Japanese market, companies that want to take a crack without paying for major magazine ads or huge marketing campaigns," he said. The service is for companies "interested in dealing directly with customers in Japan," through catalog sales, for example, he said.

Here's how it works: A U.S. manufacturer or retailer pays a fee for a display on the Import Center site. The fee varies according to the size and complexity of the display, but runs $350 and up. Ion Global, whose staff includes fluent Japanese speakers, translates the copy into Japanese. For the Japanese consumer, the Web site is an information resource for customers who want to buy products or services "without going through middlemen or trading companies," said Mr. Clark. Access is free of charge in Japan.

The site provides information about products featured on overseas e-commerce sites that have received positive feedback from Japanese consumers. Japanese consumers visit the site both to learn about featured products and for help with composing English e-mail, interpreting sizes and units of measurement, and understanding different shipping methods.

Mickey Kerbel, president of Xtreme Inc., which makes snowboards, said he paid $345 for a one-year listing and has sold about $2,000 worth of merchandise in only a couple of months since going online. The site provides a low-cost way to gain access to some of the world's most affluent customers, said Tim Clark. Internet use in the Asia Pacific region is catching up to that of the United States. As of September 2002, Japan had close to 56 million Internet users. Some even claim that the Asia Pacific region will become the world's largest Internet market by 2006. "We're happy with the service and the list-building it has helped us with in the Japan market," said Mike Delph, management information systems manager at U.S. Cavalry, a Kentucky retailer of outdoor equipment and survival gear. He said he's amassed a large list of names through electronic mail. "We've had more responses from the (Import Center) than we have on our own English language site," said a system administrator for Blue Tech, a computer products retailer based in La Jolla, California.

Sources: http://www.nua.ie/surveys, accessed October 2, 2003; "Corporate Fact Sheet," Ion Global Web site, accessed October 2, 2003, http://www.ion-global.com; telephone interview with Tim Clark, June 25, 1999; William DiBenedetto, "Home Shopping Internetwork: Buyers Find U.S. Goods at Japanese Cybermall," *The Journal of Commerce* (January 8, 1996): 1A; Gartner's Dataquest, as cited by http://cyberatlas.internet.com, accessed October 2, 2003.

All international businesses face constantly changing world economic conditions. This is not a new situation or one to be feared, because change provides the opportunity for new market positions to emerge and for managerial talent to improve the competitive position of the firm. Recognizing change and adapting creatively to new situations are the most important tasks of the international business executive, as this chapter's opening vignette shows.

Recently, changes are occurring more frequently, more rapidly, and have a more severe impact. Due to growing real-time access to knowledge about and for customers, suppliers, and competitors, the international business environment is increasingly characterized by high speed bordering on instantaneity.[1] In consequence, the past has lost much of its value as a predictor of the future. What occurs today may not only be altered in short order but be completely overturned or reversed. For example, political stability in a country can be completely disrupted over the course of a few months. A major, sudden decline in world stock markets leaves corporations, investors, and consumers with strong feelings of uncertainty. Overnight currency declines result in an entirely new business climate for international suppliers and their customers. In all, international business managers today face complex and rapidly changing economic and political conditions.

This chapter will discuss possible future developments in the international business environment, highlight the implications of the changes for international business management, and offer suggestions for a creative response to the changes. The chapter will also will explore the meaning of strategic changes as they relate to career choice and career path alternatives in international business.

The International Business Environment

This section analyzes the international business environment by looking at political, financial, societal, and technological conditions of change and by providing a glimpse of possible future developments as envisioned by an international panel of experts.[2] The impact of these factors on doing business abroad, on international trade relations, and on government policy is of particular interest to the international manager.

THE POLITICAL ENVIRONMENT

The international political environment is undergoing a substantial transformation characterized by the reshaping of existing political blocks, the formation of new groupings, and the breakup of old coalitions.

PLANNED VERSUS MARKET ECONOMIES

The second half of the last century was shaped by the political, economic, and military competition between the United States and the Soviet Union, which resulted in the creation of two virtually separate economic systems. This key adversarial posture has now largely disappeared, with market-based economic thinking emerging as the front-runner. Virtually all of the former centrally planned economies are working on becoming market-oriented.

International business has made important contributions to this transition process. Trade and investment have offered the populace in these nations a new perspective, new choices, new jobs, and new alternatives for marketing their products and services. At the same time, the bringing together of two separate economic and business systems has resulted in new, and sometimes devastating competition, a loss of government-ordained trade relationships, and substantial dislocations and pain during the adjustment process.

Over the next five years the countries of Eastern and Central Europe will continue to be attractive for international investment due to relatively low labor cost, low-priced input factors, and large unused production capacities. This attractiveness, however, will translate mainly into growing investment from Western Europe for reasons of geographic proximity and attractive outsourcing opportunities. Particularly with the expansion of the European Union in 2004, multinational corporations will recognize the limits to growth and cost containment in their traditional countries. They are likely to move aggressively further east in search of new customers and cheaper resources—a search that will result in a substantial inflow of direct investment into Eastern Europe.

The North-South Relationship

The distinction between developed and less-developed countries (LDCs) is unlikely to change. The ongoing disparity between developed and developing nations is likely to be based, in part, on continuing debt burdens and problems with satisfying basic needs. As a result, political uncertainty may well result in increased polarization between the haves and have-nots, with growing potential for political and economic conflict. Demands for political solutions for economic problems are likely to increase. The World Trade Organization states that 2.6 billion people live on less than $2 per day.[3] Some countries may consider migration as a key solution to population-growth problems, yet many emigrants may encounter government barriers to their plans.

The developing countries of Africa continue as a very cool region for international business purposes. Given its size and diversity, it is unreasonable to expect similar economic conditions across all the nations of Africa. At any one time, some countries, their governments, their firms, and the well-being of their citizens will differ sharply from others on the same continent. Nonetheless, there is an overwhelming forecast of the growing plight of Africa. There will continue to be a lack of any realistic debate on regime change and while virtually all African governments want enhanced trade opportunities to earn their own way, they do not have the technical wherewithal to carry out such plans. Ongoing crises triggered by the HIV/AIDS pandemic and by weak infrastructure continue to inhibit the capability of many governments to run their economies. They require not just investment programs but also technical assistance on implementation procedures. International organizations need to go beyond the role of think tanks and become policy initiators. Nongovernmental organizations and private firms attend to some of the most desperate needs caused by poor world gaps, but can offer only a temporary bridging rather than a permanent filling in of such an abyss.

State-owned companies are seen mostly as inefficient, high-cost enterprises that are hotbeds of patronage and corruption. They typically are slow to adapt new technologies and, due to monopoly conditions and a lack of reward for excellence, provide a very low level of service. Similar shortcomings are likely to continue in the financial sector. Foreign investments continue to be largely in the extractive industries such as oil and gold, even though there are substantial new opportunities in other industries. There is likely to be little change until there is a sharp reduction in corruption, steep increases in transparency, and major strengthening of the judiciary so that investors and business partners can develop confidence, commitment, and trust. There must also be an emphasis on education and training since that triggers where the investments and jobs go.[4] It is not enough to expect a rising tide to raise all boats. There must also be significant effort expended to ensure the seaworthiness of the boat, the functioning of its sails, and the capability of its crew. Market-oriented performance will be critical to success in the longer run.

In addition to internal reforms, African countries must also make choices and decide on whether and how to take advantage of innovations. Decisions are often difficult, since there are very different, yet important arguments on each side. Focus on Politics provides an example of such conflicting choices.

The issue of **environmental protection** will also be a major force shaping the relationship between the developed and the developing world. In light of the need and desire to grow their economies, however, there may be much disagreement on the part of the industrializing nations as to what approaches to take. Of key concern will be the answer to the question: Who pays? For example, placing large areas of land out of bounds for development will be difficult for nations that intend to pursue all options for further economic progress. Corporations in turn are likely to be more involved in protective measures if they are aware of their constituents' expectations and the repercussions of not meeting those expectations. Corporations recognize that by being environmentally responsible, a company can build trust and improve its image—therefore becoming more competitive. For example, in the early 1990s the first annual corporate environmental report was published; now over 2,000 companies a year publish such reports.[5]

In light of divergent trends by different groups, three possible scenarios emerge. One scenario is that of continued international cooperation. The developed countries could relinquish part of their economic power to less-developed ones, thus contributing actively to their economic growth through a sharing of resources and technology. Although such cross-subsidization will be useful and necessary for the development of LDCs, it may reduce the rate of growth of the standard of living in the more developed countries. It would, however, increase trade flows between developed and less-developed countries and precipitate the emergence of new international business opportunities.

A second scenario is that of confrontation. Due to an unwillingness to share resources and technology sufficiently (or excessively, depending on the point of view), the developing and the developed areas of the world may become increasingly hostile toward one another. As a result, the volume of international business, both by mandate of governments and by choice of the private sector, could be severely reduced.

A third scenario is that of isolation. Although there may be some cooperation between them, both groups, in order to achieve their domestic and international goals, may choose to remain economically isolated. This alternative may be particularly attractive if each region believes that it faces unique problems and therefore must seek its own solutions.

Emerging Markets

Much of the growth of the global economy will be fueled by the emerging markets of the Asia Pacific region. There is also the increasing likelihood of a Free Trade Arrangement of the Americas, which will align the common economic interests of countries in South, Central, and North America. Due to substantial natural resources and relatively low cost of production, such an agreement is likely to result in an increased flow of foreign direct investment and trade activity, emanating not only from the United States, but also from Europe and Japan.

The Asia Pacific region is likely to be the hot spot in the next decade. For the industrialized nations, this development will offer a significant opportunity for exports

Focus On ⬇

Food Fight in Africa

Africa is the latest battleground in the ongoing war over genetically modified (GM) crops. GM crops grow from seeds that have had their DNA artifically changed by scientists, usually to make the plants more nutritious and resistant to disease and harsh weather conditions. Although farmers in the United States and in China have greeted the new crops enthusiastically, there has been no such fanfare in Europe where the European Union (EU) has placed a five-year moratorium on new biotech products.

Now four of the world's largest agricultural companies—Monsanto, Dupont, and Dow AgroSciences LLC from the United States and Syngenta AG of Switzerland—have announced plans to donate patent rights, seed varieties, laboratory know-how, and other forms of agricultural aid to African scientists working to create plants resistant to disease, drought, and insect damage. Proponents of GM crops argue that these donations will help bring food to the 190 million sub-Saharan Africans who are malnourished and regularly go to bed hungry. They consider the development of drought-resistant GM crops to be vital to feeding the African population. The agricultural companies support this initiative on humanitarian grounds but also acknowledge that they hope to create a market for their products in Africa. The companies are also aware of the bad publicity caused for pharmaceutical companies who appeared unwilling to help Africa battle its AIDS epidemic by supplying low-cost drugs.

Opponents of GM crops are outraged by the offer of patent rights and point out that the technology is unproven, innately dangerous, and could do untold long-term damage to people, animals, and the environment. They point to the "Green Revolution" in Asia in the 1970s that greatly increased farm yields and fed an ever increasing percentage of the population in the face of rapid population growth. At the time the programs were thought to be a major success. However, their dependence on pesticides and other poisons to lessen the effect of insects were later determined to have caused increased rates of birth defects and major environmental damage. Insects also began to become resistant to the pesticides. Now new and harsher poisons have to be used.

Opponents of GM crops argue that these seeds have not been adequately tested and pose unknown risks to the environment. They also question the motives of the agricultural companies. Although the companies are giving away the patents today, what happens as older varieties of GM crops are no longer as resistant to disease? Will the companies be as willing to give away technology in the future or will poor farmers have nothing to fall back on? Adding to the pressure on Africa is the threat that the EU will not import any genetically modified agricultural products. As a result, during a famine in southern Africa in the summer of 2002, the nation of Zambia refused to accept food aid in the form of genetically engineered corn from the United States, in order to protect its future exports.

Sources: http://www.washingtonpost.com/ac2/wp-dyn/A7970-2003Mar10, accessed September 24, 2003; Elizabeth Weise, "Bio-Food Fight Centers on Africa Critics, Backers See Continent as Battleground," *USA Today,* July 9, 2002, D6.

and investment, but it will also diminish, in the longer term, the basis for their status and influence in the world economy. While the nations in the region are likely to collaborate, they are not expected to form a bloc of the same type as the European Union or NAFTA. Rather, their relationship is likely to be defined in terms of trade and investment flows (e.g., Japan) and social contacts (e.g., the Chinese business community). A cohesive bloc may only emerge as a reaction to a perceived threat by other major blocs.

China is the leading hot prospect in international business for the coming decade. Its growth and capabilities are likely to provide for a forthcoming realignment of the world economy similar to that caused by Japan in the twentieth century. Even though there are likely to be significant conflicts between China and her major trading partners due to stiff competition, pressures for protection, and product differentiation, China will be an assertive yet collaborative actor in international business and politics.

Indigenous developments combined with persistent, heavy foreign direct investment in China from industrialized nations will continue the growth of China as a low-cost manufacturing base for the world. These investments will increase in spite of ongoing unresolved political and legal issues, which will increase risk and constrain the profitability of those investments. Nonetheless, it bears remembering that China is still a communist country and that her policies and thinking are not the same as those of highly industrialized nations. Firms in leading-edge-technology industries are likely to limit their production of sensitive materials in China.

During the coming years Chinese government officials as well as managers will discover how difficult it is to comply with agreed-upon WTO rules. Partner nations will insist, however, that adherence to such rules be relatively swift—particularly in light of large trade surpluses on the part of China. More stringent enforcement measures for intellectual property protection will be expected from the government, since the preservation of and payment for such rights will be crucial for the economic future of "innovating" nations. At the same time, investors will work on forming strong local alliances to make piracy a key issue for local companies as well. If they have a stake to protect, they will stand up for their own and their partner's rights.

The investment inflow will also provide for an increased Chinese presence in branded goods around the world. China is likely to achieve a substantial takeaway of market share from the Asian tigers, such as Taiwan, Singapore and South Korea, but also from Western brands and manufacturers. As part of this effort Chinese firms will aim to raise their own profile. For example, rather than be the supplier of goods which are then marketed internationally under a Japanese or U.S. label, Chinese firms will increasingly develop their own brand names and fight for their own name recognition, customer loyalty, and market share.[6]

India may well be the country with the second highest opportunity for global economic growth and expansion. There will continue to be major opportunities for India due to its concentration on back-office operations and service industries. The quality of India's reputation will be of ongoing concern when compared to that of chief rival China. However, competitive advantages are present in English-language use as well as engineering-based education. Unlike China, India is also more likely to concentrate on services industries, with increasing capability to add value. For example, instead of remaining confined to supporting global medical transcription services, Indian physicians increasingly can read radiology scans and furnish expert opinions.

The reputation of India's workforce continues to be enhanced through its large and successful educational system even though it remains focused on implementation rather than creativity. Limits to economic growth and influence are likely to result from political developments from the continued opaqueness of government rules, as well as ongoing enmity with Pakistan. While many experts believe that political conflict, both domestic and regional, nationalism, and class structure may temper the ability of Indian companies to emerge as a worldwide competitive force, there is strong agreement that India's disproportionately large and specialized workforce in engineering and computer sciences makes the nation a power to be reckoned with.

Overall, the growth potential of these emerging economies may be threatened by uncertainty in terms of international relations and domestic policies, as well as social and political dimensions, particularly those pertaining to income distribution. Concerns also exist about infrastructural inadequacies, both physical—such as transportation—and societal—such as legal systems. The consensus of experts is, however, that growth in these countries will be significant.

A Divergence of Values

It might well be that different nations or cultures become increasingly disparate in terms of values and priorities. For example, in some countries, the aim of financial progress and an improved quantitative standard of living may well give way to priorities based on religion or the environment. Even if nations share similar values, their priorities among these values may differ strongly. For example, within a market-oriented system, some countries may prioritize profits and efficiency, while others may place social harmony first, even at the cost of maintaining inefficient industries.

Such a divergence of values will require a major readjustment of the activities of the international corporation. A continuous scanning of newly emerging national values thus becomes imperative for the international executive.

THE INTERNATIONAL FINANCIAL ENVIRONMENT

Debt constraints and low commodity prices impose slow growth prospects for many developing countries. They will be forced to reduce their levels of imports and to exert more pressure on industrialized nations to open up their markets. Even if the markets are opened, however, demand for most primary products will be far lower than supply. Ensuing competition for market share will therefore continue to depress prices.

Developed nations have a strong incentive to help the debtor nations. The incentive consists of the market opportunities that economically healthy developing countries can offer and of national security concerns. As a result, industrialized nations may very well find that funds transfers to debtor nations, accompanied by debt-relief measures such as debt forgiveness, are necessary to achieve economic stimulation at home.

The dollar will remain one of the major international currencies with little probability of gold returning to its former status in the near future. However, some international transaction volume in both trade and finance is increasingly likely to be denominated in nondollar terms, using particularly the euro. The system of floating currencies will likely continue, with occasional attempts by nations to manage exchange rate relationships or at least reduce the volatility of swings in currency values. However, given the vast flows of financial resources across borders, it would appear that market forces rather than government action will be the key determinant of a currency's value. Factors such as investor trust, economic conditions, earnings perceptions, and political stability are therefore likely to have a much greater effect on the international value of currencies than domestic monetary and fiscal experimentation.

Given the close links among financial markets, shocks in one market will quickly translate into rapid shifts in others and easily overpower the financial resources of individual governments. Even if there should be a decision by governments to pursue closely coordinated fiscal and monetary policies, they are unlikely to be able to negate long-term market effects in response to changes in economic fundamentals.

A looming concern in the international financial environment will be the **international debt load** of the United States. Both domestically and internationally, the United States is incurring debt that would have been inconceivable only a few decades ago. For example, in the 1970s the accumulation of financial resources by the Arab nations was of major concern in the United States. Congressional hearings focused on whether Arab money was "buying out America." At that time, however, Arab holdings in the United States were $10 billion to $20 billion. Today the accumulation of foreign dollar holdings has reached much higher levels.

In 1985, the United States became a net negative investor internationally. A temporary weakening of the dollar is not to be confused with a long-term downward trend, particularly with a hands-off government policy. As a result, there are only short-term currency value advantages for new market opportunities abroad for U.S. exporters. Unless there are strong productivity gains, there will be continued losses of manufacturing capabilities and increased dependence on outsourcing. Trade deficits, soon reaching more than 5 percent of GDP, will continue to expand, particularly in the consumer goods sector. Yet, in light of highly competitive growth of the U.S. market, foreign funds will continue to finance U.S. trade deficits. While large and growing trade imbalances are unsustainable over the long term, the coming decade will still see the United States as a major market, and therefore growth engine, for the world. This debt level makes the United States the largest debtor nation in the world, owing more to other nations than all the developing nations combined. In light of ongoing trade deficits, it is projected by some that this net negative investment position will be unsustainable, and will lead to a hard landing of the U.S. currency and economy. Others argue against an unsustainable scenario, believing that there are special mitigating circumstances which let the United States tolerate this burden, such as the fact that most of the debts are denominated in U.S. dollars and that, even at such a large debt volume, U.S. debt-service requirements are only a relatively small portion of GNP.[7] Yet this accumulation of foreign debt may very well introduce entirely new dimensions into the international business relationships of individuals and nations. Once debt has reached a certain level, the creditor as well as the debtor is hostage to the loans.

Since foreign creditors expect a return on their investment, a substantial portion of future U.S. international trade activity will have to be devoted to generating sufficient funds for such repayment. For example, at an assumed interest rate or rate of return of 10 percent, the international U.S. debt level—without any growth—would require the annual payment of $260 billion, which amounts to almost 27 percent of current U.S. exports.[8] Therefore, it seems highly likely that international business will become a greater priority than it is today and will serve as a source of major economic growth for firms in the United States.

To some degree, foreign holders of dollars may also choose to convert their financial holdings into real property and investments in the United States. This will result in an entirely new pluralism in U.S. society. It will become increasingly difficult and, perhaps, even unnecessary to distinguish between domestic and foreign products—as is already the case with Hondas made in Ohio. Senators and members of Congress, governors, municipalities, and unions will gradually be faced with conflicting concerns in trying to develop a national consensus on international trade and investment. National security issues may also be raised as major industries become majority owned by foreign firms.

Industrialized countries are likely to attempt to narrow the domestic gap between savings and investments through fiscal policies. Without concurrent restrictions on international capital flows, such policies are likely to meet with only limited success. Lending institutions can be expected to become more conservative in their financing, a move that may hit smaller firms and developing countries the hardest. At the same time, the entire financial sector is likely to face continuous integration, ongoing bank acquisitions, and a reduction in financial intermediaries. Customers will be able to assert their independence by increasingly being able to present their financial needs globally and directly to financial markets, thus obtaining better access to financial products and providers.

THE EFFECTS OF POPULATION SHIFTS

The population discrepancy between less-developed nations and the industrialized countries will continue to increase. In the industrialized world, a **population increase** will become a national priority, given the fact that in many countries, particularly in Western Europe, the population is shrinking. The shrinkage may lead to labor shortages and to major societal difficulties when a shrinking number of workers has to provide for a growing elderly population.

In the developing world, **population stabilization** will continue to be one of the major challenges of governmental policy. In spite of well-intentioned economic planning, continued rapid increases in population will make it more difficult to ensure that the pace of economic development exceeds population growth. If the standard of living of a nation is determined by dividing the GNP by its population, any increase in the denominator will require equal increases in the numerator to maintain the standard of living. With an annual increase in the world population of 100 million people, the task is daunting. It becomes even more complex when one considers that within countries with high population increases, large migration flows take place from rural to urban areas.

Urbanization in taking place at different speeds on different continents. In North America, the number of city dwellers overtook the rural population before 1940. In Europe, this happened after 1950 and in Latin America at the beginning of the 1960s. Today, these three continents are almost equally urbanized; 75 percent of Europeans and Latin Americans and 77 percent of North Americans are city dwellers, according to UN estimates. A similar process is occurring in Africa and Asia, which are still mainly rural. Their proportion of city dwellers rose from 25 percent in 1975 to a little more than 37 percent in 2001.[9] The turning point, when the figures will top 50 percent, is predicted to occur around 2025. Such movements and concentrations of people are likely to place significant stress on economic activity and the provision of services but will also make it easier for marketers to direct their activities toward customers. Of key concern in some countries is **population balance**. Technology has made it possible to predict with high accuracy the gender of a child. In many countries where family growth has been restricted, parents have developed a preference for male heirs. Over time, the result has been a skewed population in which males substantially outnumber females. Particularly for younger generations, this development has led to much greater difficulties in finding a partner for marriage. In consequence, some key cultural dimensions have changed. For example, it has been reported that in the state of Haryana, India, there are just 820 girls born for every 1,000 boys. Girls of marriageable age are in such short supply that some parents are not only dropping their demands for wedding dowries (which have a centuries-old cultural tradition) but are offering a "bride price" to families of prospective mates for their sons.[10] One can also argue that over time such imbalances can drive a society to develop family models such as polyandry—in which one woman may have more than one husband. It might also be possible that societies with a large surplus of young men are more prone to engage in wars.

THE TECHNOLOGICAL ENVIRONMENT

The concept of the global village is commonly accepted today and indicates the importance of communication. Worldwide, the estimated number of people online in September 2002 was 605 million.[11] The United States and Canada have the largest number of Internet users, at more than 182 million people. However, users in the United States and Canada now represent less than a third of the global Internet community—which means that the rest of the world is catching up. Nonetheless, there is a wide digital gap around the globe, for in some nations, such as Yemen, only 17,000 users are hooked up to the Internet.[12]

For both consumer services and business-to-business relations, the Internet is democratizing global business. It has made it easier for new global retail brands—like **amazon.com**—to emerge. The Internet is also helping specialists like Australia's high sensitivity hearing aids manufacturer Cochlear to reach target customers around the

Greenpeace activists protest against Genetically Modified Organisms (GMOs) outside the US Embassy in Athens. Protesters argue that GMOs have not been proven safe, and they demand that the government force companies to label products containing GMOs so consumers can be informed about their food purchase. Food industry leaders argue that GMOs are safe, and that GMO warning labels needlessly scare consumers.

© EPA PHOTO/EPA/LOUISA GOULIAMAKI

world without having to invest in a distribution network in each country. The ability to reach a worldwide audience economically via the Internet spells success for niche marketers who could never make money by just servicing their niches in the domestic market. The Internet permits customers, especially those in emerging markets, to access global brands at more competitive prices than those offered by exclusive national distributors.[13]

Starting a new business will be much easier, allowing a far greater number of suppliers to enter a market. Small- and medium-sized enterprises, as well as large multinational corporations, will now be full participants in the global marketplace. Businesses in developing countries can now overcome many of the obstacles of infrastructure and transport that limited their economic potential in the past. The global services economy will be a knowledge-based economy and its most precious resource will be information and ideas. Unlike the classical factors of production—land, labor, and capital—information and knowledge are not bound to any region or country but are almost infinitely mobile and infinitely capable of expansion.[14] This wide availability, of course, also brings new risks to firms. For example, unlike the past, today one complaint can easily be developed into millions of complaints by e-mail.[15] In consequence, firms are subject to much more scrutiny and customer response on an international level. Overall, these new technologies offer exciting new opportunities to conduct international business.

High technology will also be one of the more volatile and controversial areas of economic activity internationally. Developments in biotechnology are already transforming agriculture, medicine, and chemistry. Genetically engineered foods, patient-specific pharmaceuticals, gene therapy, and even genetically engineered organs are on the horizon. Innovations such as these will change what we eat, how we treat illness, and how we evolve as a civilization.[16] However, skepticism of such technological innovations is rampant. In many instances, people are opposed to such changes due to religious or cultural reasons, or simply because they do not want to be exposed to such "artificial" products. Achieving agreement on what constitutes safe products and procedures, of defining the border between what is natural and what is not, will constitute one of the great areas of debate in the years to come. Firms and their managers must remain keenly aware of popular perceptions and misperceptions and of government regulations in order to remain successful participants in markets.

Even firms and countries that are at the leading edge of technology will find it increasingly difficult to marshal the funds necessary for further advancements. For example, investments in semiconductor technology are measured in billions rather than millions of dollars and do not bring any assurance of success. Not to engage in the race, however, will mean falling behind quickly in all areas of manufacturing when virtually every industrial and consumer product is "smart" due to its chip technology.

Globalization and Trade Negotiations

Globalization will continue. However, globalization issues will increasingly be understood to go far beyond the economic dimension and be much broader than "Americanization." One key question will be whether it is possible to compartmentalize globalization and whether some subcomponents can be adhered to while others are excluded. For example, if one discusses trade relations, must human rights, environmental commitments, and conservation of culture necessarily be part of such discussions? Similarly, do open trade relations with the outside require a country to simultaneously fully adhere to a market economy inside the nation? Clearly, there are linkages between all these dimensions, some of them more direct than others. The question is where to draw the boundaries between international collaboration and national sovereignty.

Trade negotiations continue to be fraught with difficulties. The differences between 148 member nations in the WTO may simply be too great to be bridged in traditional ways. It has been said that nations can be differentiated between those that feed the world, those that fight the world, and those that provide the funding for the feeding and fighting. Such a trichotomy, however, seems to be oriented along the problems of yesteryear. From the perspective of national strategy, funding, feeding, and fighting are temporary symptomatic actions that reflect the needs of the moment. More long-term may be a differentiation of countries and firms into four categories: Those who grow; those who make; those who create; those who coordinate. Each category has very distinct needs, concerns, and desires when it comes to trade and investment. For some, the purity of their agricultural production is paramount. Others require a focus on skills and manufacturing employment. Innovators insist on the protection of intellectual property rights while the coordinators place major emphasis on free and open communication.

Initially, the discovery of this wide disparity of goals will act as a damper to negotiations and reduce the simplification of trade and investment flows. There will appear to be too much contradiction to achieve closer cooperation, leading to quite substantial delays in any international agreement. However, over time, a better understanding of trade-off capabilities between national or bloc objectives, as well as the pressure emanating from new bilateral and regional negotiations, will reinvigorate the activities of multilateral institutions. To some degree, the search for differences and disagreements will be replaced by the identification of commonalities. The willingness to share burdens and to do so with those resources that are most available in each nation may then provide the forward pedal power of the trade negotiation bicycle.

A key question will be whether nations are willing to abrogate some of their sovereignty even during difficult economic times. An affirmative answer will strengthen the multilateral trade system and enhance the flow of trade. However, if key trading nations resort to the development of insidious nontariff barriers, unilateral actions, and bilateral negotiations, protectionism will increase on a global scale and the volume of international trade is likely to decline. The danger is real. Popular support for international trade agreements appears to be on the wane. The public demonstrations in Cancun during the WTO meetings there indicate that there is much ambivalence by individuals and nongovernmental organizations about trade. It is here where international business academics are, or should be, the guardians who separate fact from fiction in international trade policy discussions. Qualified not by weight of office but by expertise, international business experts are the indirect guarantors of and guides toward free and open markets. Without their input and impact, public apathy and ignorance may well result in missteps in trade policy.[17]

International trade negotiations also will be shaped by restructured composition of global trade. For example, players with exceptionally large productive potential, such as the People's Republic of China, will substantially alter world trade flows. And while governments and firms will be required to change many trading policies and practices as a result, they will also benefit in terms of market opportunities and sourcing alternatives.

Finally, the efforts of governments to achieve self-sufficiency in economic sectors, particularly in agriculture and heavy industries, have ensured the creation of long-term, worldwide oversupply of some commodities and products, many of which historically had been traded widely. As a result, after some period of intense market share competition aided by subsidies and governmental support, a gradual and painful restructuring of these economic sectors will have to take place. This will be particularly true for agricultural cash crops such as wheat, corn, and dairy products and industrial sectors such as steel, chemicals, and automobiles.

Government Policy

International trade activity now affects domestic policy more than ever. For example, trade flows can cause major structural shifts in employment. Links between industries spread these effects throughout the economy. Fewer domestically produced automobiles will affect the activities of the steel industry. Shifts in the sourcing of textiles will affect the cotton industry. Global productivity gains and competitive pressures will force many industries to restructure their activities. In such circumstances, industries are likely to ask their governments to help in their restructuring efforts. Often, such assistance includes a built-in tendency toward protectionist action.

Such restructuring is not necessarily negative. For example, since 1900, farm employment in the United States has dropped from more than 40 percent of the population to less than 3 percent.[18] Yet today, the farm industry feeds more than 290 million people in the United States and still produces large surpluses for export. A restructuring of industries can greatly increase productivity and provide new resources for emerging sectors of an economy.

Governments cannot be expected, for the sake of the theoretical ideal of "free trade," to sit back and watch the effects of deindustrialization on their countries. The most that can be expected from the executive branch and from legislators is that they will permit an open-market orientation subject to the needs of domestic policy. Even an open-market orientation will be maintained only if governments can provide reasonable assurances to their own firms and citizens that the openness applies to foreign markets as well. Therefore, unfair trade practices such as governmental subsidization, dumping, and industrial targeting will be examined more closely, and retaliation for such activities is likely to be swift and harsh.

Increasingly, governments will need to coordinate policies that affect the international business environment. The development of international indexes and **trigger mechanisms,** which precipitate government action at predetermined intervention points, will be a useful step in that direction. Yet, for them to be effective, governments will need to muster the political fortitude to implement the policies necessary for cooperation. For example, international monetary cooperation will work in the long term only if domestic fiscal policies are responsive to the achievement of the coordinated goals.

At the same time as the need for collaboration among governments grows, it will become more difficult to achieve a consensus. In the Western world, the time from 1945 through 1990 was characterized by a commonality of purpose. The common defense against the Communist enemy relegated trade relations to second place, and provided a bond that encouraged collaboration. With the common threat gone, however, the bonds diminished and the priority of economic performance increased. More often, economic security and national security were seen as competing with each other, rather than as complementary dimensions of national welfare that can operate in parallel.[19]

The response to the attacks of September 11, 2001, perhaps have galvanized a new common sense and allowed a shared vision to emerge. There are five key dimensions to this shared vision:

1. A common sense of vulnerability: What happened in New York and Washington, DC, can occur at any location around the globe.
2. A common sense of outrage: The murders did not engender moral ambivalence, at least not among international businesspeople.
3. A renewed global sense of collaboration: There appears to be a better understanding of the need to work together, to identify mutual goals, and to have a vision of a future with substantial commonalities.
4. Politics of common sense: Rigid claims in cross-national discussions are beginning to yield to more simple and direct questions. In spite of some issue-specific major disagreements, there are indications of an increased willingness to tackle the tough issues—in the international business setting, issues such as agricultural subsidies, dumping regulations, property rights, and investment rules.
5. A common set of shared concerns: Rather than emphasizing all the things that make us different and separate us, such as local concerns, special quirks, and homegrown idiosyncrasies, there seems to be a greater concentration on the issues that make us behave alike, that bring us together, and that strengthen the bonds between us.

Over time, perhaps all of these commonalities will make life better and collaboration easier.[20]

Policymakers also need a better understanding of the nature of the international trade issues confronting them. Most countries today face both short-term and long-term trade problems. Trade balance issues, for example, are short term in nature, while competitiveness issues are much more long term. All too often, however, short-term issues are attacked with long-term **trade policy measures,** and vice versa. In the

United States, for example, the desire to "level the international playing field" with mechanisms such as vigorous implementation of import restrictions or voluntary restraint agreements may serve long-term competitiveness well, but it does little to alleviate the publicly perceived problem of the trade deficit. Similarly, a further opening of Japan's market to foreign corporations will have only a minor immediate effect on that country's trade surplus or the trading partners' deficit. Yet it is the expectation and hope of many in both the public and the private sectors that instantly visible changes will occur.[21] For the sake of the credibility of policymakers, it therefore becomes imperative to precisely identify the nature of the problem and to design and use policy measures that are appropriate for its resolution.

In the years to come, governments will be faced with an accelerating technological race and with emerging problems that seem insurmountable by individual firms alone, such as pollution of the environment and global warming. As market gaps emerge and time becomes crucial, both governments and the private sector will find that even if the private sector knows that a lighthouse is needed, it may still be difficult, time-consuming, and maybe even impossible to build one with private funds alone. As a result, it becomes increasingly important for government to work closely with the business sector to identify market gaps and to devise market-oriented ways of filling them. The international manager in turn will have to spend more time and effort dealing with governments and with macro rather than micro issues.

The Future of International Business Management

Global change results in an increase in risk. One shortsighted alternative for risk-averse managers would be the termination of international activities altogether. However, businesses will not achieve long-term success by engaging only in risk-free actions. Further, other factors make the pursuit of international business mandatory.

International markets remain a source of high profits, as a quick look at a list of multinational firms shows.[22] International activities help cushion slack in domestic sales resulting from recessionary or adverse domestic conditions and may be crucial to the very survival of the firm. International markets also provide firms with foreign experience that helps them compete more successfully with foreign firms in the domestic market.

INTERNATIONAL PLANNING AND RESEARCH

Firms must continue to serve customers well to be active participants in the international marketplace. One major change that will come about is that the international manager will need to respond to general governmental concerns to a greater degree when planning a business strategy. Further, societal concern about macro problems needs to be taken into account directly and quickly because societies have come to expect more social responsibility from corporations. Taking on a leadership role regarding social causes may also benefit corporations' bottom lines, since consumers appear more willing than ever to act as significant pressure points for policy changes and to pay for their social concerns. Therefore, reputation management, or the art of building reputation as a corporate asset, is likely to gain prominence in the years ahead as the pressure on corporations to be good corporate citizens grows.[23]

Increased competition in international markets will create a need for more niches in which firms can create a distinct international competence. As a result, increased specialization and segmentation will let firms fill very narrow and specific demands or resolve very specific problems for their international customers. Identifying and filling the niches will be easier in the future because of the greater availability of international research tools and information. The key challenge to global firms will be to build and manage decision-making processes that allow quick responses to multiple changing environmental demands. This capability is important since firms face a growing need for worldwide coordination and integration of internal activities, such as logistics and operations, while being confronted with the need for greater national differentiation and responsiveness at the customer level.[24]

In spite of the frequent short-term orientation by corporations and investors, companies will need to learn to prepare for long-term horizons. Particularly in an environment of heated competition and technological battles, of large projects and slow payoffs, companies, their stakeholders, and governments will need to find avenues that not only permit but encourage the development of strategic perspectives. Figure 20.1 provides an example of such a long-term view.

FIGURE 20.1

Long-Term Planning

In our business, it's important to keep an eye on the next quarter. The one that ends midnight, December 31, 2025.

With a lot of hard work and several billion dollars, our 777 jetliner will be delivered, service-ready, in mid-1995.

And, if the market accepts our new airplane as well as it has previous Boeing jetliners, it's reasonable to expect the 777 will be part of the world air transportation system for at least the first half of the next century.

And Boeing will offer service and support for 777s as long as they're in service.

Such long-term expectations and responsibilities are at the very heart of our Company, from jetliners to spacecraft. They are the source of our most important challenges and successes.

And, they're reasons for our continuous investments in research and development, in new plants and equipment, and in talented people capable of mastering rapidly advancing technologies.

Like all businesses, we're subject to the disciplines of financial performance measurements.

But in aviation and aerospace, we have a long horizon.

After 75 years, we've learned that if you aren't in this business for the long term, you aren't likely to be in it for long.

BOEING

Governments both at home and abroad will demand that private business practices not increase public costs and that businesses serve customers equally and nondiscriminately. The concept directly counters the desire to serve first the markets that are most profitable and least costly. International executives will therefore be torn in two directions. To provide results acceptable to governments, customers, and to the societies they serve, they must walk a fine line, balancing the public and the private good.

INTERNATIONAL PRODUCT POLICY

One key issue affecting product planning will be environmental concern. Major growth in public attention paid to the natural environment, environmental pollution, and global warming will provide many new product opportunities and affect existing products to a large degree. For example, manufacturers will increasingly be expected to take responsibility for their products from cradle to grave, and be intimately involved in product disposal and recycling.

Firms will therefore have to plan for a final stage in the product life cycle, the "post-mortem" stage, during which further corporate investment and management attention are required, even though the product may have been terminated some time ago.[25]

Although some consumers show a growing interest in truly "natural" products, even if they are less convenient, consumers in most industrialized nations will require products that are environmentally friendly but at the same time do not require too much compromise on performance and value.

Worldwide introduction of products will occur much more rapidly in the future. Already, international product life cycles have accelerated substantially. Whereas product introduction could previously be spread out over several years, firms now must prepare for product life cycles that can be measured in months or even weeks. As a result, firms must design products and plan their domestic marketing strategies with the international product cycle in mind. Product introduction will grow more complex, more expensive, and more risky, yet the rewards to be reaped from a successful product will have to be accumulated more quickly.

Early incorporation of the global dimension into product planning, however, does not point toward increased standardization. On the contrary, companies will have to be ready to deliver more mass customization. Customers are no longer satisfied with simply having a product: They want it to precisely meet their needs and preferences. **Mass customization** requires working with existing product technology, often in modular form, to create specific product bundles for a particular customer, resulting in tailor-made jeans or a customized car.

Factor endowment advantages have a significant impact on the decisions of international executives. Nations with low production costs will be able to replicate products more quickly and cheaply. Countries such as China, India, Israel, and the Philippines offer large pools of skilled people at labor rates much lower than in Europe, Japan, or the United States. All this talent also results in a much wider dissemination of technological creativity, a factor that will affect the innovative capability of firms. For example, in 2002, almost half of all the patents in the United States were granted to foreign entities. Table 20.1 provides an overview of U.S. patents granted to foreign inventors.

This indicates that firms need to make nondomestic know-how part of their production strategies, or they need to develop consistent comparative advantages in production technology in order to stay ahead of the game. Similarly, workers engaged in the productive process must attempt, through training and skill enhancement, to stay ahead of foreign workers who are willing to charge less for their time. Furthermore, we

TABLE 20.1

U.S. Patents Granted to Foreign Inventors in 2002

State/Country	Totals	State/Country	Totals	State/Country	Totals
Andorra	1	Germany	11954	Peru	1
Arab Emirates	6	Greece	22	Philippines	19
Argentina	58	Guatemala	5	Poland	13
Armenia	1	Honduras	2	Portugal	12
Australia	991	Hungary	48	Romania	4
Austria	559	Iceland	15	Russian Federation	203
The Bahamas	13	India	267	Saint Kitts	2
Barbados	4	Indonesia	147	Saudi Arabia	10
Belarus	2	Israel	1108	Singapore	421
Belgium	801	Italy	1961	Slovakia	9
Bermuda	5	Jamaica	2	Slovenia	16
Bolivia	1	Japan	36340	South Africa	124
Bosnia and Herzegovina	1	Jordan	1	South Korea	4009
Brazil	112	Kazakhstan	2	Spain	358
Bulgaria	1	Kenya	1	Sri Lanka	15
Canada	3857	Kuwait	8	Sweden	1824
Cayman Islands	12	Lebanon	2	Switzerland	1532
Chile	13	Liechtenstein	17	Syria	2
China, Hong Kong	589	Lithuania	5	Taiwan	6730
China, People Rep.	390	Luxembourg	52	Thailand	61
Colombia	8	Macau	2	Tunisia	1
Costa Rica	8	Malaysia	62	Turkey	18
Croatia	12	Malta	1	Turks and Caicos	1
Cuba	9	Marshall Islands	1	USSR	1
Cyprus	1	Mexico	105	Uganda	1
Czech Rep.	29	Moldova (Rep)	1	Ukraine	28
Czechoslovakia	2	Monaco	21	United Kingdom	4197
Denmark	559	Netherlands Antilles	3	Uruguay	3
Dominican Rep.	1	Netherlands	1681	Uzbekistan	1
Egypt	5	New Guinea	1	Venezuela	32
Estonia	6	New Zealand	173	Vietnam	4
Fiji	1	Nigeria	4	British Virgin Islands	3
Finland	856	Norway	261	Yemen	1
French Polynesia	1	Pakistan	1	Yugoslavia	4
France	4421	Panama	1	Zimbabwe	1
Georgia (Rep.)	5				

Total patents issued in U.S. in 2002	184,428
Total patents issues to U.S. inventors	97,132
Total patents issued to foreign inventors	87,296
Foreign holders as a percentage of total	47.3%

Source: United States Patent and Trademark Office, Office of Electronic Information Productions/Patent Technology Monitoring Division. *Patent Counts by Country/State and Year All Patents, All Types January 1, 1977—December 31, 2002.* Washington, DC, 2003, http://www.uspto.gov.

increasingly see that an organization's ability and willingness to learn and to transfer knowledge is becoming the most critical key to multinational success. Developing the nexus between people and processes is therefore a crucial corporate activity.

An increase will occur in the trend toward strategic alliances, or partnerings, permitting the formation of collaborative arrangements between firms. These alliances will enable firms to take risks that they could not afford to take alone, facilitate technological advancement, and ensure continued international market access. These partners do not need to be large in order to make a major contribution. Depending on the type of product, even small firms can serve as coordinating subcontractors and collaborate in product and service development, production, and distribution.

On the production management side, security concerns now make it imperative to identify and manage one's dependence on international inputs. Industrial customers, in particular, are often seen as pushing for local sourcing. A domestic source simply provides a greater feeling of comfort.

Some firms also report a new meaning associated with the *made-in* dimension in country-of-origin labeling. In the past, this dimension was viewed as enhancing products, such as perfumes made in France or cars made in Germany. Lately, the made-in dimension of some countries may create an exclusionary context by making both industrial customers and consumers reject products from specific regions. As a result, negative effects may result from geographic proximity to terrorists, as has been claimed by some about textile imports from Pakistan.

The bottom line still matters. After all, money needs to be made and international business tends to be quite profitable. However, the issue of dependability of supplies is raised at many senior-management meetings, and a premium is now associated with having a known and long-term supplier. In the future, foreign suppliers may have to be recommended by existing customers or partners and be able to cope with contingencies before their products are even considered.

INTERNATIONAL COMMUNICATIONS

The advances made in international communications will also have a profound impact on international management. Entire industries are becoming more footloose in their operations; that is, they are less tied to their current location in their interaction with markets. Most affected by communications advances will be members of the services sector. For example, Best Western Hotels in the United States has channeled its entire reservation system through a toll-free number that is being serviced out of the prison system in Utah. Companies could even concentrate their communications activities in other countries. Communications for worldwide operations, for example, could easily be located in Africa or Asia without impairing international corporate activities.

For manufacturers, staff in different countries can not only talk together but can also share pictures and data on their computer screens. These simultaneous interactions with different parts of the world will strengthen research and development efforts. Faster knowledge transfer will allow for the concentration of product expertise, increased division of labor, and a proliferation of global operations.

DISTRIBUTION STRATEGIES

Innovative distribution approaches will determine new ways of serving markets. For example, television, through QVC, has already created a shopping mall available in more than 138 million homes worldwide.[26] The use of the Internet offers new distribution alternatives. Self-sustaining consumer distributor relationships emerge through, say, refrigerators that report directly to grocery store computers that they

COURTESY OF HOFFMAN-LAROCHE, INC.

Advances in telecommunications allow staff in different countries to talk together and share pictures and data on their computer screens. In the state-of-the-art video conference center at Roche's U.S. pharmaceutical headquarters in Nutley, NJ, scentists discuss research goals and results with colleagues in Basel, Switzerland.

are running low on supplies and require a home delivery billed to the customer's account. Firms that are not part of such a system will simply not be able to have their offer considered for the transaction.

The link to distribution systems will also be crucial to international firms on the business-to-business level. As large retailers develop sophisticated inventory tracking and reordering systems, only the firms able to interact with such systems will remain eligible suppliers. Therefore, firms need to create their own distribution systems that are able to respond to information technology requirements around the globe.

More sophisticated distribution systems will, at the same time, introduce new uncertainties and fragilities into corporate planning. For example, the development of just-in-time delivery systems makes firms more efficient yet, on an international basis, also exposes them to more risk due to distribution interruptions. A strike in a faraway country may therefore be newly significant for a company that depends on the timely delivery of supplies.

Companies have accepted that the international pipeline has slowed down, and that customary steps will now take longer in a new security environment. But the structure of the pipeline and the scrutiny given to the materials going through the pipeline have become important.

Firms that had developed elaborate just-in-time delivery systems for their international supplies were severely affected by the border and port closures immediately following the September 11, 2001 attacks. These firms and their service providers continue to be affected by increased security measures. Firms are also focusing more on internal security and need to demonstrate externally how much more security-oriented they have become. In many instances, government authorities require evidence of threat-reduction efforts to speed shipments along. Also, insurance companies have increased their premiums substantially for firms that are exposed to increased risk.

In the past, cargo security measures concentrated on reducing theft and pilferage from a shipment. Since September 11, additional measures concentrate on possible undesirable accompaniments to incoming shipments. With this new approach, international cargo security starts well before the shipping even begins. One result—perhaps unintended—of these changes is a better description of shipment content and a more precise assessment of duties and other shipping fees.

Carriers with sophisticated hub-and-spoke systems have discovered that transshipments between the different spokes may add to delays because of the time needed to re-scrutinize packages. While larger "clean areas" within ports may help reduce this problem, a redesign of distribution systems may lead to fewer hubs and more direct connections.

Firms with a just-in-time system are also exploring alternative management strategies, such as shifting international shipments from air to sea. More dramatically, some firms are considering replacing international shipments with domestic ones, in which truck transport would replace transborder movement altogether and eliminate the use of vulnerable ports. Future scenarios also accommodate the effects of substantial and long-term interruptions of supplies or operations. Still, any actual move away from existing just-in-time systems is likely to be minor unless new large-scale interruptions occur.

Many new positions have been created in the corporate security field, focusing on new production sites, alternative distribution methods, server mobility, and new linkages with customers. In some instances, key customers have been involved in the development of emergency procedures to keep operations going.

In spite of these measures, however, vulnerability to attack continues to be high. For example, 43 percent of all the maritime containers that arrived in the United

States in 2001 came through the ports of Los Angeles and Long Beach. There are no required secuirty standards governing the loading or transport of an intermodal container. Most are "sealed" with a 50-cent lead tag. An explosive device in a single container might well gridlock the entire flow and loading systems.[27]

INTERNATIONAL PRICING

International price competition will become increasingly heated. As their distribution spreads throughout the world, many products will take on commodity characteristics, as semiconductors did in the 1980s. Therefore, small price differentials per unit may become crucial in making an international sale. However, since many new products and technologies will address completely new needs, **forward pricing,** which distributes development expenses over the planned or anticipated volume of sales, will become increasingly difficult and controversial as demand levels are impossible to predict with any kind of accuracy.

Even for consumer products, price competition will be substantial. Because of the increased dissemination of technology, the firm that introduces a product will no longer be able to justify higher prices for long; domestically produced products will soon be of similar quality. As a result, exchange rate movements may play more significant roles in maintaining the competitiveness of the international firm. Firms can be expected to prevail on their government to manage the country's currency to maintain a favorable exchange rate. Technology also allows much more interaction on pricing between producer and customer. The success of electronic commerce providers such as e-bay (http://www.ebay.com) or http://www.priceline.com demonstrates how auctioning and bidding, alone or in competition with others, offers new perspectives on the global price mechanism.

Through subsidization, targeting, government contracts, or other hidden forms of support, nations will attempt to stimulate their international competitiveness. Due to the price sensitivity of many products, the international manager will be forced to identify such unfair practices quickly, communicate them to his or her government, and insist on either similar benefits or government action to create an internationally level playing field.

At the same time, many firms will work hard to reduce the price sensitivity of their customers. By developing relationships with their markets rather than just carrying out transactions, other dimensions such as loyalty, consistency, the cost of shifting suppliers, and responsiveness to client needs may become much more important than price in future competition.

Careers in International Business

By studying this book you have learned about the intricacies, complexities, and thrills of international business. Of course, a career in international business is more than jet-set travel between New Delhi, Tokyo, Frankfurt, and New York. It is hard work and requires knowledge and expertise. Yet, in spite of the difficulties, international business expertise may well become a key ingredient for corporate advancement. Preparing for such expertise can, however, be fraught with risk as Focus on Culture shows.

To prepare, you should be well versed in a specific functional business area and take summer internships abroad. You should take language courses and travel, not simply

Focus On ⬇

Ensuring Student Safety Abroad

After the terrorist attacks of September 11, 2001, student safety has become a more vivid concern for many universities. International outreach has long been seen as an important element in undergraduate education. Today universities must spend time and resources to ensure that those international experiences are safe. A generation ago students primarily studied abroad in Western Europe. Now they are literally scattered around the globe, often in remote and isolated places. More than 154,000 U.S. students are studying abroad for college credit, twice the number a decade ago. Varying degrees of perceived anti-American sentiment worldwide has made university administrators very security conscious.

Kroll, Inc., a New York-based global risk-management company with offices all over the world, has seen its security consulting business for colleges and universities double since September 11. It is no longer enough to simply warn students not to speak English in loud voices or not to wear clothing with U.S. logos. Today, universities are developing contingency plans for their students studying overseas with planned responses for crises ranging from the breakout of war to students being taken hostage.

Many emergency response strategies include a complete extraction plan should all students studying abroad need to be brought back to the home campus. Before September 11 only about 10 percent of universities had contingency plans for students studying abroad. Now such plans are standard fare. Also common are predeparture orientation programs where students are informed about risky conditions abroad and how those risks vary from site to site. For example, Georgetown University's Office of International Programs advises students not to visit high-risk areas such as Israel, Zimbabwe, or Indonesia while traveling abroad and will not enter into formal agreements to send students to these locations.

For universities like Georgetown, where more than half of the students study abroad, program choices are critical. High-profile cases of injuries and deaths of students while on study-abroad trips has added to the pressure on administrators to keep students safe. In 1998 a group of students on a study-abroad trip with St. Mary's College of Maryland were gang-raped when the bus they were riding in was attacked by roadway bandits in Guatemala. Several of the students sued the school, alleging negligence on the part of the professors planning the trip and claiming that the school should have been aware of a similar bus attack on a group of tourists just six months prior. Although St. Mary's officials disputed some of the students' claims they eventually settled the lawsuit for $195,000, but not before the school had received a lot of bad press.

Sources: http://www.theyhoya.com/news/012803/news2.cfm, accessed September 23, 2003; Annie Gowen, "Caution Tops Syllabus for US Students Abroad: Schools Seek Strategies to Counter Threats," *Washington Post,* June 21, 2003, B1.

for pleasure but to observe business operations abroad and gain a greater appreciation of different peoples and cultures. The following pages provide an overview of further key training and employment opportunities in the international business field.

FURTHER TRAINING

One option for the student on the road to more international involvement is to obtain further in-depth training by enrolling in graduate business school programs that specialize in international business education. A substantial number of universities in the United States and around the world specialize in training international managers. According to the Institute of International Education, the number of U.S. students studying for a degree at universities abroad rose to 154,000 students in 2002. Furthermore, American students increasingly go abroad for business and economics degrees, not just for a semester or two. At the same time, business and management are the most popular fields of study for the 583,000 international students at American universities.[28] A review of college catalogues and of materials from groups such as the Academy of International Business will be useful here.

In addition, as the world becomes more global, more organizations are able to assist students interested in studying abroad or in gathering foreign work experience.

For example http://www.iiepassport.org, http://www.studyabroad.com, http://www.overseasjobs.com, or http://www.egide.asso.fr provide rich information about programs and institutions.

For those ready to enter or rejoin the "real world," different employment opportunities need to be evaluated.

EMPLOYMENT WITH A LARGE FIRM

One career alternative in international business is to work for a large multinational corporation. These firms constantly search for personnel to help them in their international operations. Table 20.2 lists Web sites that can be useful in obtaining employment internationally.

Many multinational firms, while seeking specialized knowledge such as languages, expect employees to be firmly grounded in the practice and management of business. Rarely, if ever, will a firm hire a new employee at the starting level and immediately place him or her in a position of international responsibility. Usually, a new employee is expected to become thoroughly familiar with the company's internal operations before being considered for an international position. Reasons a manager is sent abroad include that the company expects him or her to reflect the corporate spirit, to be tightly wed to the corporate culture, and to be able to communicate well with both local and corporate management personnel. In this liaison position, the manager will have to be exceptionally sensitive to both headquarters and local operations. As an intermediary, the expatriate must be empathetic, understanding, and yet fully prepared to implement the goals set by headquarters.

It is very expensive for companies to send an employee overseas. The annual cost of maintaining a manager overseas is often a multiple of the cost of hiring a local manager. Companies want to be sure that the expenditure is worth the benefit they will receive. Failure not only affects individual careers, but also sets back the business operations of the firm. Therefore, firms increasingly develop training programs for employees destined to go abroad.

Even if a position opens up in international operations, there is some truth in the saying that the best place to be in international business is on the same floor as the chief executive at headquarters. Employees of firms that have taken the international route often come back to headquarters to find only a few positions available for them. After spending time in foreign operations, where independence is often high and authority significant, a return to a regular job at home, which sometimes may not even call on the many skills acquired abroad, may turn out to be a difficult and deflating experience. Such encounters lead to some disenchantment with international activities as well as to financial pressures and family problems, all of which may add up to significant executive stress during reentry.[29] Since family reentry angst is one reason 25 percent of expatriates quit within one year of their return, companies are increasing the attention paid to the spouses and children of employees. For example, about 15 percent of Fortune 500 firms offer support for children of employees relocated abroad.[30]

OPPORTUNITIES FOR WOMEN IN GLOBAL MANAGEMENT

As firms become more and more involved in global business activities, the need for skilled global managers is growing. Concurrent with this increase in business activity is the ever growing presence and managerial role of women in international business.

TABLE 20.2

Web Sites Useful in Gaining International Employment

AVOTEK Headhunters

http://www.avotek.com/
Nieuwe Markt 54
6511 XL Nijmegen
NETHERLANDS
Telephone: 31 24 3221367
Fax: 31 24 3240467
E-mail: avotek@tip.nl

Lists Web sites and addresses of jobs and agencies worldwide. Offers sale publications and other free reference materials.

Council on International Education Exchanges

http://www.ciee.org/
7 Custom House St., 3rd Floor
Portland, ME 04101
Telephone: (800) 40-STUDY or (207) 553-7600
Fax: (207) 553-7699
E-mail: info@councilexchanges.org

Paid work and internships overseas for college students and recent graduates. Also offers international volunteer projects, as well as teaching positions.

Datum Online

http://www.datumeurope.com/
91 Charlotte Street
London W1P 1LB
UK
Telephone: 44 171 255 1313/1314/1320
Fax: 44 (0) 171 255 1316
E-mail: admin@datumeurope.com

Online database providing all the resources to find IT, sales, and accountancy jobs across Europe.

Dialogue with Citizens

http://europa.eu.int/citizens
International Market Directorate General
MARKT A/04, C107 03/52
European Commission
Rue de la Loi, 200
B-1049 Brussels
BELGIUM
Telephone: (011) 322 299-5804
Fax: (011) 322 295-6695
E-mail: mail@europe-direct.cec.eu.int

Factsheets on EU citizens' rights regarding residence, education, working conditions and social security, rights as a consumer, and ways of enforcing these rights, etc. Easy-to-use guides that give a general outline of EU citizens' rights and the possibilities offered by the European Single Market. A Signpost Service for citizens' practical problems.

Ed-U-Link Services

http://edulink.com
PO Box 2076
Prescott, AZ 86302

(continued)

TABLE 20.2

Web Sites Useful in Gaining International Employment
(continued)

Telephone: (520) 778-5581
Fax: (520) 776-0611
E-mail: info@edulink.com

Provides listings of and assistance in locating teaching jobs abroad.

The Employment Guide's Career Web

http://www.employmentguide.com
295 Bendix Rd
Virginia Beach, VA 23452
Telephone: (877) 876-4039
E-mail: customerservice@cweb.com

Online employment source with international listings, guides, publications, etc.

Escape Artist.com Inc.

http://escapeartist.com
Suite 832-1245
World Trade Center
Panama
Republic of PANAMA
Fax: 011 507 317-0139
E-mail: headquarters@escapeartist.net

Web site for U.S. expatriates. Contains links for overseas jobs, living abroad, offshore investing, free magazines, etc.

EuroJobs

http://www.eurojobs.com
Heathfield House
303 Tarring Rd.
Worthing
West Sussex BN11 5JG
UK
Telephone: 44 (0) 1260 223144
Fax: 44 (0) 1260 223145
E-mail: medialinks@eurojobs.com

Lists vacant jobs all over Europe. Also includes the possibility of submitting CV to recruiters; employment tips and other services.

EURopean Employment Services—EURES

http://europa.eu.int/eures
Employment and Social Affairs Directorate General
EMPL A/03 BU33 02/24
European Commission
Rue de la Loi, 200
B-1049 Brussels
BELGIUM
Telephone: (011) 322 299-6106
Fax: (011) 322 299-0508 or 295-7609
E-mail: empl-eures@cec.eu.int

Aims to facilitate the free movement of workers within the 17 countries of the European Economic Area. Partners in the network include public employment services, trade unions, and

(continued)

TABLE 20.2

Web Sites Useful in Gaining International Employment
(continued)

employer organizations. The partnership is coordinated by the European Commission. For citizens of these 17 countries, provides job listings, background information, links to employment services, and other job-related Web sites in Europe.

Expat Network

http://expatnetwork.com
5 Brighton Rd.
Croyden
Surrey CR2 6EA
UK
Telephone: 44 20 8760 5100
Fax: 44 20 8760 0469
E-mail: expats@expatnetwork.com

Dedicated to expatriates worldwide, linking to overseas jobs, country profiles, health care, expatriate, gift and bookshop, plus in-depth articles and industry reports on issues that affect expatriates. Over 5,000 members. Access is restricted for nonmembers.

Federation of European Employers (FedEE)

http://www.fedee.com
Adam House
7-10 Adam Street
The Strand
London WC2 N6AA
UK
Telephone: 44 (0) 207 520 9264
Fax: 44 (0) 1359 269 900
E-mail: fedee@globalnet.co.uk

FedEE's European Personnel Resource Centre is the most comprehensive and up-to-date source of pan-European national pay, employment law, and collective bargaining data on the Web.

FlipDog.com

http://www.flipdog.com
5 Clock Tower Place
Suite 500
Maynard, MA 01754
Telephone: (877) 887-3547
E-mail: info@flipdog.com

Constitutes the Internet's largest job collection. In addition to U.S. coverage, includes approximately 82,000 vacancies abroad. One of the most comprehensive employment search engines on the Internet.

HotJobs.com Ltd.

http://hotjobs.com
406 West 31st St.
New York, NY 10001
Telephone: (212) 699-5300
Fax: (212) 944-8962
E-mail: support@hotjobs.com

Contains international job listings.

(continued)

TABLE 20.2   Web Sites Useful in Gaining International Employment
(continued)

Jobpilot

http://jobpilot.co.uk
Brook House
10 Church Terrace
Richmond
Surrey TWL0 6SE
UK
Telephone: 44 (0) 208 614-7800
Fax: 44 (0) 208 948-7322
E-mail: info@jobpilot.co.uk

"Europe's unlimited career market on the Internet."

Monster.com

http://www.monster.com
TMP Worldwide Global Headquarters
1633 Broadway
33rd Floor
New York, NY 10019
Telephone: (800) MONSTER or (212) 977-4200
Fax: (212) 956-2142

Global online network for careers and working abroad. Career resources, including message boards and daily chats.

OverseasJobs.com

http://overseasjobs.com
AboutJobs.com Network
12 Robinson Rd.
Sagamore Beach, MA 02562
Telephone: (508) 888-6889
E-mail: info@overseasjobs.com

Job seekers can search the database by keywords or locations and post a resume online for employers to view.

PlanetRecruit.com

http://planetrecruit.com
PlanetRecruit Ltd.
Alexandria House
Convent Garden
Cambridge CB1 2HR
UK
Telephone: 44 (870) 321 3 660
Fax: 44 (870) 321 3 661
E-mail: support@planetrecruit.com

One of the world's largest UK and international recruiting networks. Features accounting and finance, administrative and clerical, engineering, graduate and trainee, IT, media, new media and sales, marketing, and public relations jobs from about 60 countries.

(continued)

TABLE 20.2

Web Sites Useful in Gaining International Employment
(continued)

The Riley Guide
http://rileyguide.com
Margaret F. Dikel
11218 Ashley Drive
Rockville, MD 20852
Telephone: (301) 881-0122
Fax: (301) 984-6390
E-mail: webmaster@rileyguide.com

This is a directory of employment and career information sources and services on the Internet, providing instruction for job seekers and recruiters on how to use the Internet to their best advantage. Includes a section on working abroad, including in Europe.

SCI-IVS USA

http://sci-ivs.org
5474 Walnut Level Road
Crozet, VA 22932
Telephone: (206) 350-6585
Fax: (206) 350-6585
E-mail: sciinfo@sci-ivs.org

Through various noncommercial partner organizations worldwide and through SCE international, national and regional branch development, the U.S. branch of SCI participates in the SCI network, which exchanges over 5,000 volunteers each year in short-term (2–4 week) international group workcamps and in long-term (3–12 months) volunteer postings in more than 60 countries.

Transitions Abroad Online: Work Abroad

http://www.transitionsabroad.com
PO Box 745
Bennington, VT 05201
Telephone: (802) 442-4827
Fax: (802) 442-4827
E-mail: info@transitionsabroad.com

Contains articles from its bimonthly magazine; a listing of work abroad resources (including links); lists of key employers, internship programs, volunteer programs, and English-teaching openings.

Vacation Work Publications

http://www.vacationwork.co.uk
9 Park End Street
Oxford OX1 1HJ
UK
Telephone: 44 01865-241978
E-mail: vacationwork@vacationwork.co.uk

Lists job openings abroad, in addition to publishing many books on the topic. Has an information exchange section and a links section.

Upseek.com

http://upseek.com
Telephone: (877) 587-5627
E-mail: salesinfo@upseek.com

(continued)

TABLE 20.2

Web Sites Useful in Gaining International Employment
(continued)

A global search engine that empowers job seekers in the online job search market. Provides job opportunities from the top career and corporate sites with some European listings.

WWOOF INTERNATIONAL
http://www.wwoof.org
PO Box 2675
Lewes BN7 1RB
UK

WWOOF INTERNATIONAL is dedicated to helping those who would like to work as volunteers on organic farms internationally.

Source: Euroepan Union, http://www.eurunion.org

Research conducted during the mid-1980s[31] indicated that women held 3.3 percent of the overseas positions in U.S. business firms. By 2000, 13 percent of expatriates in U.S. corporations were women.[32] The reason for the low participation of women in global management roles seems to have been the assumption that because of the subservient roles of women in Japan, Latin America, and the Middle East, neither local nor expatriate women would be allowed to succeed as managers. The error is that expatriates are not seen as local women, but rather as "foreigners who happen to be women," thus solving many of the problems that would be encountered by a local woman manager.

There appear to be some distinct advantages for a woman in a management position overseas. Among them are the advantages of added visibility and increased access to clients. Foreign clients tend to assume that "expatriate women must be excellent, or else their companies would not have sent them."

It also appears that companies that are larger in terms of sales, assets, income, and employees send more women overseas than smaller organizations. Further, the number of women expatriates is not evenly distributed among industry groups. Industry groups that utilize greater numbers or percentages of women expatriates include banking, electronics, petroleum, publishing, diversified corporations, pharmaceuticals, and retailing and apparel.

For the future, it is anticipated that the upward trend previously cited reflects increased participation of women in global management roles.

EMPLOYMENT WITH A SMALL OR MEDIUM-SIZED FIRM

A second alternative is to begin work in a small or medium-sized firm. Very often, such firms have only recently developed an international outlook, and the new employee will arrive on the "ground floor." Initial involvement will normally be in the export field—evaluating potential foreign customers, preparing quotes, and dealing with activities such as shipping and transportation. With a very limited budget, the export manager will only occasionally visit international markets to discuss business strategies with distributors abroad. Most of the work will be done by mail, by fax, by

The Cost Per Diem in the World's Major Business Cities
(in U.S. dollars)

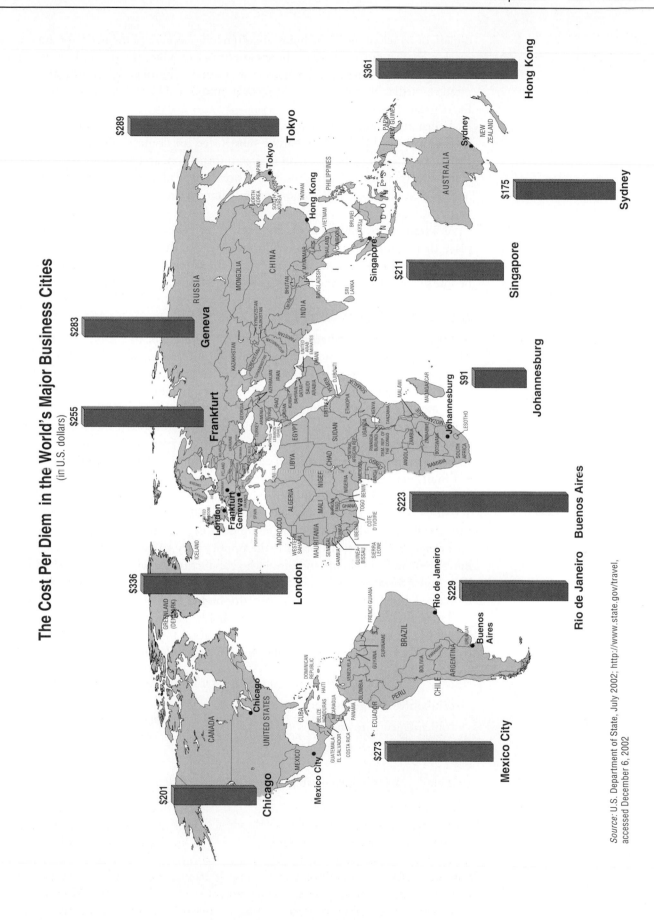

Hong Kong $361

Tokyo $289

Sydney $175

Geneva $283

Singapore $211

Frankfurt $255

Johannesburg $91

Buenos Aires $223

London $336

Rio de Janeiro $229

Chicago $201

Mexico City $273

MAP

Source: U.S. Department of State, July 2002; http://www.state.gov/travel, accessed December 6, 2002

e-mail, or by telephone. The hours are often long because of the need, for example, to reach a contact during business hours in Hong Kong. Yet the possibilities for implementing creative business transactions are virtually limitless. It is also gratifying and often rewarding that one's successful contribution will be visible directly through the firm's growing export volume.

Alternatively, international work in a small firm may involve importing; that is, finding low-cost sources that can be substituted for domestically sourced products. Decisions often must be based on limited information, and the manager is faced with many uncertainties. Often things do not work out as planned. Shipments are delayed, letters of credit are canceled, and products almost never arrive in exactly the form and shape anticipated. Yet the problems are always new and offer an ongoing challenge.

As a training ground for international activities, there probably is no better starting place than a small or medium-sized firm. Later on, the person with some experience may find work with a trading or export management company, resolving other people's problems and concentrating almost exclusively on the international arena.

SELF-EMPLOYMENT

A third alternative is to hang up a consultant's shingle or to establish a trading firm. Many companies are in need of help for their international business efforts and are prepared to part with a portion of their profits in order to receive it. Yet it requires in-depth knowledge and broad experience to make a major contribution from the outside or to successfully run a trading firm.

Specialized services that might be offered by a consultant include international market research, international strategic planning, or, particularly desirable, beginning-to-end assistance for international entry or international negotiations. For an international business expert, the hourly billable rate typically is as high as $500 for principals and $150 for staff. Whenever international travel is required, overseas activities are often billed at the daily rate of $3,000 plus expenses. Even at such high rates, solid groundwork must be completed before all the overhead is paid. The advantage of this career option is the opportunity to become a true international entrepreneur. Consultants and those who conduct their own export-import or foreign direct investment activities work at a higher degree of risk than those who are not self-employed, but they have an opportunity for higher rewards.

This concludes the text portion of this book. We hope you have worked with it, learned from it, and even enjoyed it. It is important for us to also learn from our customers. Please provide us with feedback, both praise and suggestions for improvement by contacting us:

czinkotm@georgetown.edu

ronkaii@georgetown.edu

moffettm@t-bird.edu

Thank you for being an international business student!

Summary

This final chapter has provided an overview of the environmental changes facing international managers and alternative managerial response to the changes. International business is a complex and difficult activity, yet it affords many opportunities and challenges. Observing changes and analyzing how to best incorporate them in the international business mission is the most important task of the international manager. If the international environment were constant, there would be little challenge to international business. The frequent changes are precisely what make international business so fascinating and often highly profitable for those who are active in the field.

Questions for Discussion

1. For many developing countries, debt repayment and trade are closely linked. What does protectionism mean to them?
2. Should one worry about the fact that the United States is a debtor nation?
3. How would our lives and our society change if imports were banned?
4. How have security concerns changed the way international firms do business?

Internet Exercises

1. Using the Web site of Living Abroad http://www.livingabroad. com), research several international schools that may interest you. What are the most interesting links to other Web sites concerning international issues? Why are you particularly interested in them?
2. The Web site http://www.overseasjobs.com provides valuable information for those interested in jobs overseas. What skills do international employers seem to value most? Peruse the job listings and find several jobs that you might be interested in. Also take a look at the profiles of several international companies that you might be interested in working for. What characteristics do the international firms listed here possess?

Take a Stand

It is virtually impossible to be totally protected from terrorism. However, some safety measures can be developed. For example, to reduce the exposure of students to terrorist attacks it helps to keep them all at home. Another reduction of risk can be achieved by not letting them be exposed to anyone outside their familiar groups. Say goodbye to study abroad programs, forget about international students and scholars!

For Discussion
1. Does such an approach make things better?
2. What do you propose?

PART 7 | Case 1

WHEN DIAMONDS WEEP

They may be prehistoric pieces of highly compressed carbon, but diamonds play an important role in the world economy. They are found in nature, as opposed to synthetic diamonds, which are produced in laboratories. Mining companies search for deposits deep underground, but natural diamonds are also found along riverbanks enabling anyone with a sieve and a spade to find one. In 2001, global production of natural, rough (meaning uncut and unpolished) diamonds was $7.8 billion in value and 117 million carats in weight (one carat equals 0.2 grams). As shown in Figure 1, the top five natural diamond-producing countries account for more than 86 percent of the world's rough diamond supply.

Sources: This case was prepared by Alison M. Hager under the supervision of Professor Michael R. Czinkota of Georgetown University. Finlayson, David. "Preserving diamond's integrity." *Vancouver Sun*, December 23, 2002; "A crook's best friend," *The Economist*, January 4, 2003; Reeker, Philip T. "Implementing the Kimberley Process." January 2, 2003. http://www.diamonds.net, accessed March 28, 2003; Fowler, Robert R., "Final Report of the UN Panel of Experts on Violations of Security Council Sanctions Against UNITA," (S/2000/203) March 10, 2000; "Al Qaeda Cash Tied to Diamond Trade," *Washington Post*, November 2, 2001; "Conflict and Security; Conflict Diamonds are Forever," *Africa News*, November 8, 2002; "U.S.: Blood Diamond Plan Too Soft," *Associated Press Online*, June 18, 2002; Duke, Lynne, "Diamond Trade's Tragic Flaw," *Washington Post*, April 29, 2001; Cowell, Alan, "40 Nations in Accord on 'Conflict Diamonds,'" *The New York Times*, November 6, 2002; Rory M. O'Ferrall, "De Beers O'Ferrall Calls Kimberley End of Beginning," December 2, 2002, http://www.diamonds.net, accessed March 28, 2003; Olson, Donald W., "Gemstones," U.S. Survey Minerals Yearbook, 2001, http://minerals.usgs.gov/minerals/pubs/, accessed March 28, 2003); Olson, Donald W., "Diamond, Industrial," U.S. Survey Minerals Yearbook, 2001, http://minerals.usgs.gov/minerals/pubs/, (accessed March 28, 2003); Jones, Lucy, "Diamond industry rough to regulate; Central African Republic works to monitor gem trade," *The Washington Times*, August 22, 2002, Jha, Amarendra, "Diamond Pact Hits Surat Cutters," *The Times of India*, December 28, 2002; Smillie, Ian, "The Kimberley Process: The Case for Proper Monitoring," Partnership Africa Canada, September 2002, http://www.partnershipafricacanda.org, accessed March 28, 2003; Sparshott, Jeffrey, "WTO targets 'conflict diamonds,'" *The Washington Times*, March 1, 2003, http://www.keyguide.net. http://www.debeersgroup.com.

FIGURE 1

Major Diamond-Producing Countries

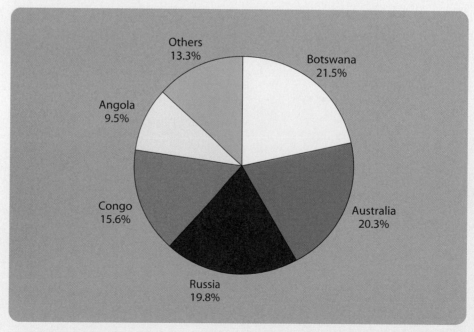

Others 13.3%
Botswana 21.5%
Angola 9.5%
Congo 15.6%
Australia 20.3%
Russia 19.8%

Source: Adapted from Donald W. Olson, "Gemstones," *U.S. Geological Survey Minerals Yearbook, 2001*, p. 19, http://minerals.usgs.gov/minerals/pubs/, accessed March 28, 2003.

From Mine to Market

Once diamonds have been excavated, they are sorted, by hand, into grades. While there are thousands of categories and subcategories based on the size, quality, color, and shape of the diamonds, there are two broad categories of diamonds—gem-grade and industrial-grade. Approximately 59 percent of the 2001 production was of gem-quality. In addition to jewelry, gem quality stones are used for collections, exhibits, and decorative art objects. Industrial diamonds, because of their hardness and abrasive qualities, are often used in the medical field, in the space program, and for diamond tools.

After the diamonds have been sorted, they are transported to one of the world's four main diamond trading centers—Antwerp, Belgium, which is the largest; New York; Tel Aviv, Israel; and Mumbai, India. Between five and ten million individual stones pass through the Antwerp trading center each day. After they have been purchased, the diamonds are sent off to be cut, polished, and/or otherwise processed. Five locations currently dominate the diamond-processing industry—India, which is the largest (processing 9 out of every 10 diamonds); Israel; Belgium; Thailand; and New York.

Finally, the polished diamonds are sold by manufacturers, brokers, and dealers to importers and wholesalers all over the world, who in turn, sell to retailers.

Global retail sales of diamond jewelry surpassed $60 billion in 2001. The United States is by far the world's leading diamond importer and market for the gems (See Figure 2). Despite the effects of the September 11, 2001 terrorist attacks, overall U.S. diamond jewelry sales for 2001 amounted to $26.1 billion, or 44 percent of the total market, down by only 1 percent from the previous year. One explanation for the smaller than expected drop was that purchases of engagement rings rose dramatically after the September 11 attacks—a trend that continued through 2001.

The total time from extraction to the time at which the diamond is sold to the end consumer is called the "pipeline" and usually takes about 2 years.

The De Beers Dynasty

For more than a century, a single company has controlled the diamond industry—De Beers. De Beers was founded in the late nineteenth century by the infamous colonial capitalist Cecil Rhodes after the discovery of the

FIGURE 2

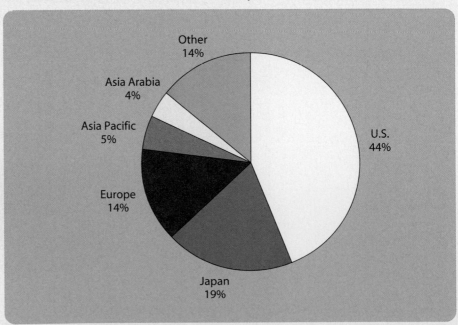

Global Retail Sales of Diamond Jewelry

Other 14%
Asia Arabia 4%
Asia Pacific 5%
Europe 14%
Japan 19%
U.S. 44%

Source: Adapted from "Conflict Diamonds," *Global Witness*, p. 3, http://www.oneworld.org/globalwitness/, accessed March 28, 2003.

Kimberley diamond fields in South Africa. In its early years, the company produced more than 90 percent of the world's diamonds. However, rival producers entered the market in the early twentieth century which challenged De Beers' preeminence. Now a privately held company with offices in London and Johannesburg, De Beers currently controls about 60 percent of the world diamond supply. Furthermore, about two thirds (by value) of the world's annual supply of rough diamonds are sorted and valued through De Beers' subsidiary Diamond Trading Company (DTC). In addition to the diamonds that De Beers acquires from the 20 mines it operates in South Africa, Namibia, and Botswana, De Beers also buys excess diamonds on the market to maintain a stable market price. All of the diamonds De Beers acquires flow into the Central Selling Organization (CSO). This organization holds ten sales each year called "sights." The only persons eligible to participate in these sales are an elite group of approximately 120 individuals and companies called "sightholders." De Beers chooses its sightholders based on their financial stability and marketing ability. At a typical "sight," the sightholders are presented with mixed "parcels" of diamonds. The parcels are packages of combined rough gem-quality and industrial diamonds, and may include stones from a number of different countries. The price of the parcels is set by De Beers, and the sightholders are not allowed to inspect or even see the parcels before they buy them.

As a result of all of these activities, DeBeers has been able to control the flow of diamonds into the world market and thus, effectively control prices. As one *Washington Post* writer put it, "De Beers is to diamonds what the Wizard was to Oz: the entity behind the curtain pulling the strings."[1]

Diamonds have long held a certain mystique. Thanks in large part to De Beers' skillful marketing efforts, diamonds have taken on an aura of rarity and eternity. Prior to the 1930s, diamond rings were rarely given as engagement rings. Today, more than 1.7 million diamond engagement rings are sold in the United States each year, and 85 percent of all American women own at least one diamond. The "A diamond is forever" campaign launched by De Beers in the in United States in the 1940s and Japan in the 1960s was such a success that it was dubbed the slogan of the century by *Advertising Age* in 2000.

Controversies Arise

Reports have recently surfaced that threaten to tarnish the diamond industry's sparkling image. The reports revealed that diamond sales finance deadly conflicts in Angola, Sierra Leone, Congo, and Liberia. The controversy around these so-called "conflict diamonds" or "blood diamonds" erupted principally because retailers can not tell consumers with certainty that their diamonds did not originate in conflict areas. According to current diamond industry estimates, conflict diamonds make up four percent of the annual global production of diamonds. However, human rights advocates disagree with that number. They argue that as many as 15 percent of all diamonds on the market could be conflict diamonds.

The History of Conflict Diamonds

During the bush war of Angola in 1992, Jonas Savimbi was head of a rebel movement called UNITA (National Union for the Total Independence of Angola). Looking for new ways to fund his army, Savimbi decided to extend his organization into the vast diamond fields of Angola. In less than one year, UNITA's diamond-smuggling network became the largest in the world—netting hundreds of million dollars a year, with which it purchased weapons. Diamonds were also a useful tool for buying friends and supporters and could be used as a means for stockpiling wealth.

Soon, warring groups in other countries like Sierra Leone, Liberia, and the Democratic Republic of Congo adopted the same strategy. For example, the RUF (Revolutionary United Front) in Sierra Leone, a group that achieved international notoriety for hacking off the arms and legs of civilians and abducting thousands of children and forcing them to fight as soldiers, has controlled the country's alluvial diamond fields since 1998.

Investigators Bring Problem to Light

For many years, illicit trading was disregarded by the majority of the diamond industry. However, in 1998, in response to its investigations of the UNITA in Angola, the U.N. Security Council issued sanctions against Angola which prevented all U.N. member states from importing from Angola any diamond that was not accompanied by a certificate of origin issued by the Angolan government guaranteeing that it had been mined legally.

Two years later, the extent of the conflict diamond problem was made public when the U.N. released a report explaining how UNITA had been able to continue dealing in diamonds despite the existence of the sanctions. The report included the names of key smugglers in the network and cities and countries through which UNITA diamonds had been known to travel. It also asserted that a lack of meaningful controls both in Angola and in the Antwerp, Belgium diamond-trading center may have actually encouraged the illegal trading activity. The problem in Angola, according to the report, was that virtually anyone in Angola could legally possess, buy, or sell diamonds within the country. There were five buying companies officially licensed by the government, but these buying companies employed many subcontractors. Because the subcontracted buyers worked on a commission basis, they had a financial incentive not to care about the origin of the diamonds. So, UNITA diamonds had no trouble finding their way into the official channels. The report also accused the Belgian authorities of failing to establish an effective import identification scheme and also of failing to monitor the activities of suspect brokers, dealers, and traders.

Since the report was released, the U.N. Security Council has imposed additional sanctions on diamond dealing in Liberia and now interdicts diamond trade from the rebel-held areas of Sierra Leone as well. However, only a few countries have enacted laws to actually implement the sanctions.

In 2002, trade statistics were circulated by several human-rights groups. The data showed that the quantity of diamond imports listed from certain countries on the books in Antwerp did not match the quantity of exports listed for those same countries (see Table 1). Furthermore, countries that did not even have working mines were reported as exporting large quantities of diamonds. Apparently, the origin of many of the diamonds entering Antwerp had been changed or disguised.

Ties to Terrorist Groups

The issue of conflict diamonds has taken on even greater policy significance after the September 11, 2001 terrorist attacks in the United States. Evidence emerged that diamonds were being used by terrorist organizations, including al Qaeda and Hezbollah, as a channel for transferring wealth around the world. Diamonds don't set off alarms at airports, they can't be sniffed by dogs, they are easy to hide, and are highly convertible to

TABLE 1   Belgian Diamond Imports Compared to Exports from Certain Countries (U.S. $ millions)

	1994	1995	1996	1997	1998	1999
Official exports from Sierra Leone	30.2	22.	27.6	10.5	1.8	1.2
Declared Belgian imports from Sierra Leone	106.6	15.3	93.4	114.9	65.8	30.4
Difference	76.4	(6.70)	65.8	104.4	64	29.2
Official exports from Cote d'Ivoire	3.1	2.9	2.4	4	3.6	4.6
Declared Beligan imports from Cote d'Ivoire	93.6	54.2	204.2	119.9	45.3	52.6
Difference	90.5	51.3	201.8	115.9	41.6	48
Official exports from Liberia	No data because of civil war, although no official exports are likely to have occurred				0.8	0.9
Declared Belgian imports from Liberia	283.9	392.4	616.2	329.2	269.9	298.8
Difference	283.9	392.4	616.2	329.2	269.1	297.9
Official exports from Guinea	28.6	34.7	35.5	46.9	40.7	40.2
Declared Belgian imports from Guinea	165.7	26.2	83.6	108.1	116.1	127.1
Difference	137.1	–8.5	48.1	61.2	75.4	86.9
Official exports from Gambia	0	0	0	0	0	0
Declared Belgian imports from Gambia	74.1	14.9	128.1	131.4	103.4	58
Difference	74.1	14.9	128.1	131.4	103.4	58

Source: Ian Smillie, "The Kimberley Process: The Case For Proper Monitoring," September 2002, http://www.partnershipafricacanada.org, accessed March 28, 2003.

cash. According to U.S. and European intelligence officials, diamond dealers working directly with men identified by the FBI as key operatives in the al Qaeda network purchased gems from the RUF rebels in Sierra Leone. The Sierra Leoneans were desperate for cash and were unable to sell directly in the diamond markets of Tel Aviv and Antwerp because of the sanctions. As a result, they sold the diamonds at a deep discount to al Qaeda middle men who smuggled the diamonds into Liberia, Monrovia, and other countries where they would eventually sell the diamonds through legitimate channels for huge profits. While the exact amount is unknown, intelligence officials believe that al Qaeda has reaped millions of dollars in virtually untraceable funds from the illicit sale of diamonds since 1998.

The Kimberley Process

On November 5, 2002, representatives from 52 countries, along with mining executives, diamond dealers, and members from advocacy groups, met in Interlaken, Switzerland to sign an agreement that they hoped would eliminate conflict diamonds from international trade. The agreement was called the Kimberley Process and took effect on January 1, 2003.

The Kimberley Process is a United Nations-backed certification plan created to ensure that only legally mined rough diamonds, untainted by conflict, reach established markets around the world. According to the plan, all rough diamonds passing through or into a participating country must be transported in sealed, tamper-proof containers and be accompanied by a government-issued certificate guaranteeing the container's contents and origin. Customs officials in importing countries are required to certify that the containers have not been tampered with and are instructed to seize all diamonds that do not meet the requirements.

The agreement also stipulates that only those countries that subscribe to the new rules will be able to trade legally in rough diamonds. Countries that break the rules will be suspended and their diamond-trading privileges will be revoked. Furthermore, individual diamond traders who disobey the rules will be subject to punishment under the laws of their own countries.

Critics speak out

Several advocacy groups have voiced concerns that the Kimberley Process remains open to abuse, and that it will not be enough to stop the flow of conflict diamonds. Many worry that bribery and forgery are

inevitable and that corrupt governments officials will render the scheme inoperable. Even those diamonds with certified histories attached may not be trustworthy.

The General Accounting Office (GAO), the investigative arm of the U.S. Congress, also voiced concerns in a 2002 report: "[T]he period after rough diamonds enter the first foreign port until the final point of sale is covered by a system of voluntary industry participation and self-regulated monitoring and enforcement. These and other shortcomings provide significant challenges in creating an effective scheme to deter trade in conflict diamonds."[2]

In response to the GAO's statement, the State Department said that it was more important to establish the accountability measures now than to debate how they could be improved. A De Beers spokesperson shared the same sentiments in a 2002 speech in London saying, "What we have now is certainly not a perfect construct, the system is not absolutely watertight, and there are still a number of outstanding anomalies. It is, however, the best compromise that could be agreed without placing intolerable burdens on the industry."[3]

The U.S. Response

In late 2002, the U.S. House of Representatives passed the "Clean Diamond Trade Act," legislation that would have fully implemented the Kimberley Process recommendations in the United States. However, the bill died when the Senate failed to act on it during the same term. In response to the bill's demise, the State Department announced in early 2003 that it would "work expeditiously with Congress to pass legislation as soon as possible."[4] Even without the legislation, the U.S. diamond industry started to implement the Kimberley plan in 2003.

In late February of 2003, the WTO Council for Trade in Goods agreed that countries could block trade in conflict diamonds despite the fact that by doing so, they would violate several articles of the GATT, because of "the extraordinary humanitarian nature of this issue."[5] Many applauded the announcement as an important step in getting U.S. legislation moving forward.

New Technologies Offer Solutions

Recently, a number of new technologies have emerged which, if adopted by the diamond industry worldwide, could change the way that diamonds are mined, traded, and sold. One emerging technology is laser engraving.

Lasers make it possible to mark diamonds—either in their rough or cut stage—with a symbol, number, or bar code that can help to identify that diamond whenever verification is necessary. Companies that adopt the technology have an interesting marketing opportunity to sell brands of diamonds. Establishing brand awareness and building equity in its name, these companies hope, will add value to the diamond and help increase consumer confidence. Sirius Diamonds, a Vancouver-based cutting and polishing company now microscopically laser engraves a polar bear logo and an identification number on each gem it processes. Another company, 3Beams Technologies of the United States, is currently working on a system to embed a bar code inside a diamond (as opposed to on its surface), which would make it much more difficult to remove.

Another option is the "invisible fingerprint" invented by a Canadian security company called Identex. The technology works by electronically placing an invisible information package on each stone. The fingerprint can include any information that the producer desires, such as the mine source and production date. The data can only be read by Identex's own scanners. Unfortunately, once the diamond is cut, the fingerprint will be lost, although it can be reapplied at any time. Clearly, this represents a major drawback to the technology because it can be abused. Nevertheless, the technology's creators believe that it will soon become an industry standard because it is a quick and cost-effective away to analyze a stone. The technology will supplement the security of paper certification, or could eventually replace it, says Identex's president Bob Jennens.

Lastly, processes are being developed to read a diamond's internal fingerprint—its unique sparkle and combination of impurities. The machine used to do this is called a Laser Raman Spectroscope (LRS). A worldwide database could identify a diamond's origin and track its journey from the mine to end consumer. However, industry expert Martin Irving is not optimistic about the chances that such a database could ever be created. There is also the problem of volume. Currently, nine out of every ten diamonds are polished in India, but there is only one LRS machine in the entire country.

Questions for Discussion

1. In light of the conflict diamond issue, would you buy a diamond? Why or why not?
2. Do you think that the Kimberley Process certification plan will help decrease the global trade in conflict diamonds? Why or why not?
3. Why do you think the diamond industry in the United States began implementing the certification scheme even before it had garnered proper legislative support?
4. Should the U.S. limit its importing of diamonds to only those countries that can effectively guarantee (e.g., through laser engravings or digital fingerprints) that they are "clean" diamonds?

Endnotes

1. Lynne Duke, "Diamond Trade's Tragic Flaw," *Washington Post*, April 29, 2001.
2. General Accounting Office, Critical Issues Remain in Deferring Conflict Diamond Trade. Washington: Government Printing Office, 2002.
3. http://www.newswire.ca/en/releases/archive/April2003/11/CO362.html.
4. http://www.state.gov/r/pa/prs/ps/wo2/1G275.htm.
5. http://www.wto.org/english/news_e/news03_3/goods_council/_zbfer03_3.htm.

For Further Exploration

Chapter 1

Cornelius, Peter and Klaus Schwab. *The Global Competitiveness Report 2002–2003*. Oxford: Oxford University Press, 2003.

Czinkota, Michael, Illka Ronkainen, and Bob Donath. *Mastering Global Markets*. Cincinnati: Thomson, 2004.

Czinkota, Michael R., and llkka A. Ronkainen. *Best Practices in International Business*. Ft. Worth, TX: Harcourt College Publishers, 2001.

Friedman, Thomas L. *The Lexus and the Olive Tree: Understanding Globalization*. New York: Farrar Straus & Giroux, 2000.

Reich, Robert. *The Future of Success: Working and Living in the New Economy*. London: Vintage Books, 2002.

Sethi, Prakash. *Setting Global Standards*. Hoboken: John Wiley & Sons, 2002.

Stieglitz, Joseph. *Globalization and Its Discontents*. New York: W.W. Norton & Company, 2003.

Chapter 2

Axtell, Roger E. *Do's and Taboos Around the World*. New York: John Wiley & Sons, 1993.

Brett, Jeanne. *Negotiating Globally: How to Negotiate Deals, Resolve Disputes, and Make Decisions Across Cultures*. New York: Jossey-Bass, 2001.

Brislin, R. W., W. J. Lonner, and R. M. Thorndike. *Cross-Cultural Research Methods*. New York: Wiley, 1973.

Cellich, Claude, and Subhash Jain. *Global Business Negotiations*. Mason, OH: Thomson Southwestern, 2003.

Copeland, Lennie, and Lewis Griggs. *Going International: How to Make Friends and Deal Effectively in the Global Marketplace*. New York: Random House, 1990.

Hall, Edward T., and Mildred Reed Hall. *Understanding Cultural Differences*. Yarmouth, ME: Intercultural Press, 1990.

Hofstede, Geert. *Cultures Consequences: Comparing Values, Behaviors, Institutions and Organizations Across Nations*. London: Sage Publications, 2003.

Kenna, Peggy, and Sondra Lacy. *Business Japan: Understanding Japanese Business Culture*. Lincolnwood, IL: NTC, 1994.

Lewis, Richard D. *When Cultures Collide*. London: Nicholas Brealey Publishing, 1996.

Marx, Elizabeth. *Breaking Through Culture Shock: What You Need to Succeed in International Business*. London: Nicholas Brealey Publishing, 1999.

O'Hara-Devereaux, Mary, and Robert Johansen. *Global Work: Bridging Distance, Culture, and Time*. San Francisco: Jossey-Bass Publishers, 1994.

Parker, Barbara. *Globalization and Business Practice: Managing Across Boundaries*. London: Sage Publications, 1999.

Terpstra, Vern, and Keith David. *The Cultural Environment of International Business*. Cincinnati: South-Western, 1991.

Trompenaars, Fons, and Charles Hampden-Turner. *Riding the Waves of Culture*. New York: Irwin, 1998.

Chapter 3

Export Quality Management: The Answer Book for Small and Medium-Sized Exporters. Geneva: United Nations Publications, 2003.

Finger, Michael J. *Institutions and Trade Policy*. Northampton, MA: Edward Elgar, 2002.

Haar, Jerry, and Anthony T. Bryan, eds. *Canadian–Caribbean Relations in Transition: Trade, Sustainable Development and Security (International Political Economy Series)*. New York: St. Martin's Press, 1999.

Krugman, Paul R., and Maurice Obstfeld. *International Economics: Theory and Policy*, 6th ed. Boston: Addison-Wesley Publishing Company, 2002.

Letterman, Gregory G. *Basics of Multilateral Institutions and Multinational Organizations: Economics and Commerce*. Ardsley, NY: Transnational, 2002.

Messerlin, Patrick A. *Measuring the Costs of Protection in Europe: European Commercial Policy in the 2000s*. Washington, DC: Institute for International Economics, 2001.

Chapter 4

Arend, Anthony Clark. *Legal Rules and International Society*. New York: Oxford University Press, 1999.

Battling International Bribery, 2000 Report. Washington, DC: The World Bank Group, 2000.

Coplin, William D. and Michael K. O'Leary, eds. *Political Risk Yearbook*. Syracuse, NY: Political Risk Services, 2001.

Foreign Policy Report 2000. Washington, DC: U.S. Department of Commerce, Bureau of Export Administration, 2000.

A Global Forum on Fighting Corruption. Washington, DC: U.S. Department of State, Bureau for International Narcotics and Law Enforcement Affairs, September 1999.

Haass, Richard N., ed. *Economic Sanctions and American Diplomacy*. New York: Council on Foreign Relations Press, 1998.

Hirschhorn, Eric L. *The Export Control and Embargo Handbook*. Dobbs Ferry, NY: Oceana Publications, 2000.

Hufbauer, Gary Clyde, Jeffrey J. Schott, and Kimberly Ann Elliott. *Economic Sanctions Reconsidered:* History and Current Policy. Washington, DC: Institute for International Economics, 2001.

Maskus, Keith E. *Intellectual Property Rights in the Global Economy*. Washington, DC: Institute for International Economics, 2000.

Organization for Economic Cooperation and Development. *The European Union's Trade Policies and Their Economic Effects.* Paris: Organization for Economic Development, 2001.

Organization for Economic Cooperation and Development. *No Longer Business as Usual: Fighting Bribery and Corruption.* Paris: Organization for Economic Development, 2000.

Trade Information Center. *Export Programs: A Business Guide to Federal Export Assistance Programs.* Washington, DC: Trade Information Center, 2000.

Chapter 5

Bhagwati, Jagdish, and Arvind Panagariya, eds. *The Economics of Preferential Trade Agreements.* Washington, DC: American Enterprise Institute, 1996.

Buckley, Peter J., and Mark Casson. *The Future of the Multinational Enterprise.* London: Macmillan, 1976.

Caves, Richard E. International Corporations: The Industrial Economics of Foreign Investment. *Economica* (February 1971): 1–27.

Dunning, John H. Trade Location of Economic Activity and the MNE: A Search for an Eclectic Approach. In *The International Allocation of Economic Activity,* edited by Bertil Ohlin, Per-Ove Hesselborn, and Per Magnus Wijkman. New York: Homes and Meier, 1977, 395–418.

Heckscher, Eli. The Effect of Foreign Trade on the Distribution of Income. In *Readings in International Trade,* edited by Howard S. Ellis and Lloyd A. Metzler. Philadelphia: The Blakiston Company, 1949.

Helpman, Elhaman, and Paul Krugman. *Market Structure and Foreign Trade.* Cambridge, MA: MIT Press, 1985.

Hymer, Stephen H. *The International Operations of National Firms: A Study of Direct Foreign. Investment.* Cambridge, MA: MIT Press, 1976.

Krugman, Paul R., and Maurice Obstfeld, *International Economics: Theory and Policy,* 5th ed., Addison-Wesley, 2000.

Linder, Staffan Burenstam. *An Essay on Trade and Transformation.* New York: John Wiley & Sons, 1961.

Maskus, Keith E., Deborah Battles, and Michael H. Moffett. Determinants of the Structure of U.S. Manufacturing Trade with Japan and Korea, 1970–1984. In *The Internationalization of U.S. Markets,* edited by David B. Audretch and Michael P. Claudon. New York: New York University Press, 1989, 97–122.

Ohlin, Bertil. *Interregional and International Trade.* Boston: Harvard University Press, 1933.

Porter, Michael. "The Competitive Advantage of Nations." *Harvard Business Review* (March–April 1990).

Porter, Michael E., "Clusters and the New Economics of Competition," *Harvard Business Review* (November–December 1998).

Ricardo, David. *The Principles of Political Economy and Taxation.* Cambridge, United Kingdom: Cambridge University Press, 1981.

Smith, Adam. *The Wealth of Nations.* New York: The Modern Library, 1937.

Vernon, Raymond. International Investment and International Trade in the Product Cycle. *Quarterly Journal of Economics* (1966): 190–207.

Wells, Louis T., Jr., A Product Life Cycle for International Trade? *Journal of Marketing* 22 (July 1968): 1–6.

Chapter 6

Agenor, Pierre-Richard, Jagdeep S. Bhandari, and Robert P. Flood. Speculative Attacks and Models of Balance of Payments Crises. *International Monetary Fund Staff Papers,* 39, 2 (June 1992) 357–394.

Bergsten, C. Fred, ed. *International Adjustment and Financing: The Lessons of 1985–1991.* Washington, DC: Institute for International Economics, 1991.

Eiteman, David K., Arthur I. Stonehill, and Michael H. Moffett. *Multinational Business Finance.* 10th ed. Boston, MA: Addison-Wesley Longman, 2004.

Evans, John S. *International Finance: A Markets Approach.* New York: Dryden Press, 1992.

Giddy, Ian H. *Global Financial Markets.* Lexington, MA: Elsevier, 1994.

Grabbe, J. Orlin. *International Financial Markets.* 2d ed. New York: Elsevier, 1991.

Handbook of International Trade and Development Statistics. New York: United Nations, 1989.

Husted, Steven, and Michael Melvin. *International Economics.* 4th ed. Reading, MA: Addison Wesley Longman, 1997.

IMF Balance of Payments Yearbook. Washington, DC: International Monetary Fund, annually.

Root, Franklin R. *International Trade and Investment.* 6th ed. Chicago: South-Western Publishing, 1990.

Chapter 7

Bank for International Settlements. *Annual Report.* Basle, Switzerland, annually.

Black Wednesday: The Campaign for Sterling. *The Economist* (January 9, 1993): 52, 54.

Commission of the European Communities. The ECU and Its Role in the Process Towards Monetary Union. *European Economy* 48 (September 1991): 121–138.

Dewey, Davis Rich. *Financial History of the United States.* 2d ed. New York: Longmans, Green, and Company, 1903.

Driscoll, David D. *What Is the International Monetary Fund?* Washington, DC: External Relations Department, International Monetary Fund, November 1992.

Eiteman, David, Arthur Stonehill, and Michael H. Moffett. *Multinational Business Finance.* 10th ed. Boston, MA: Addison-Wesley, 2004.

Federal Reserve Bank of New York. *Summary of Results of the U.S. Foreign Exchange Market Turnover Survey,* April 1995.

The Financial Times. *FT Guide to World Currencies,* February 5, 2001.

Funabashi, Yuichi. *Managing the Dollar: From the Plaza to the Louvre.* Washington, DC: Institute of International Economics, 1988.

Giddy, Ian. *Global Financial Markets.* Lexington, MA: Heath, 1993.

Goodhart, C.A.E., and L. Figliuoli. "Every Minute Counts in Financial Markets." *Journal of International Money and Finance* 10 (1991): 23–52.

Grabbe, J. Orlin. *International Financial Markets.* 2d ed. New York: Elsevier, 1991.

International Monetary Fund. *International Financial Statistics.* Washington, DC, monthly.

Morgan Guaranty. *World Financial Markets,* New York, various issues.

The New Trade Strategy. *Business Week* (October 7, 1985): 90–93.

The Paris Pact May Not Buoy the Dollar for Long. *Business Week* (March 9, 1987): 40–41.

Rivalries Beset Monetary Pact. *Business Week* (July 15, 1944): 15–16.

Tran, Hung Q., Larry Anderson, and Ernst-Ludwing Drayss. Eurocapital Markets. Ch. 8 in *International Finance and Investing.* The Library of Investment Banking, edited by Robert Lawrence Kuhn. Homewood, IL: Dow Jones-Irwin, 1990, 129–160.

Treasury and Federal Reserve Foreign Exchange Operations. *Federal Reserve Bulletin* (October 1971): 783–814.

Ungerer, Horst, Jouko J. Hauvonen, Augusto Lopez-Claros, and Thomas Mayer. *The European Monetary System: Developments and Perspectives.* Washington, DC: International Monetary Fund, 1990.

Van Dormael, Armand. *Bretton Woods.* New York: Holmes & Meier, 1978.

The Wall Street Journal. Foreign Exchange Rates, February 5, 2001, C6.

Chapter 8

The Arthur Andersen North American Business Sourcebook. Chicago: Triumph Books, 1994.

Business Guide to Mercosur. London: Economist Intelligence Unit, 1998.

Clement, Norris C., ed., *North American Economic Integration: Theory and Practice.* London: Edward Elgar Publications, 2000.

EC Commission. *Completing the Internal Market: White Paper from the Commission to the European Council.* Luxembourg: EC Commission, 1985.

The European Union: A Guide for Americans. Available at http://www.eurunion.org/infores/euguide/Chapter2.htm.

Nevaer, Louis E. V. *NAFTA's Second Decade: Assessing Opportunities in the Mexican and Canadian Markets.* Mason, OH; Thomson-Southwestern, 2003.

Ohmae, Kenishi. *The Borderless World: Power and Strategy in the Interlinked Economy.* New York: Harper Business, 1999.

Ryans, John K., Jr., and Pradeep A. Rau. *Marketing Strategies for the New Europe: A North American Perspective on 1992.* Chicago: American Marketing Association, 1990.

Schott, Jeffrey, *United States—Canada Free Trade: An Evaluation of the Agreement.* Washington, DC: Institute for International Economics, 1988.

Stoeckel, Andrew, David Pearce, and Gary Banks. *Western Trade Blocs.* Canberra, Australia: Centre for International Economics, 1990.

Sueo, Sekiguchi and Noda Makito, eds. *Road to ASEAN-10: Japanese Perspectives on Economic Integration.* Tokyo: Center for International Exchange, 2000.

Trade Liberalization: Western Hemisphere Trade Issues Confronting the United States Washington, DC: United States General Accounting Office, 1997.

United Nations. *From the Common Market to EC92: Integration in the European Community and Transnational Corporations.* New York: United Nations Publications, 1992.

Venables, Anthony, Richard E. Baldwin, and Daniel Cohen, eds. *Market Integration, Regionalism and the Global Economy.* Cambridge, England: Cambridge University Press, 1999.

Chapter 9

Addison, Tony, (Ed.). *From Conflict to Reconstruction in Africa.* Oxford: Oxford University Press, 2003.

Alon, Ilan, and Shaomin Li, (Eds.). *Chinese Economic Transition and International Marketing Strategy.* Westport, CT: Greenwood Publishing, 2003.

Duomato, Abdella, and Marsha Pripstein Posusney, (Eds.). *Women and Globalization in the Arab Middle East: Economy and Society in Transition.* Boulder, CO: Lynne Reinner Publishers, Inc., 2003.

Ericson, Richard E. *Legacies of Command: The Russian Economic Transition Experience.* London: Taylor & Francis, Inc., 2003.

Leicht, Kevin T., (Ed.). *The Future of Market Transition.* Greenwich, CT: JAI Press, 2002.

Morita, Ken. *Economic Reforms and Capital Markets in Central Europe (Transition and Development).* Burlington, VT: Ashgate Publishing Company, 2003.

Peng, Michael W. *Business Strategies in Transition Economies.* Thousand Oaks, CA: Sage, 2000.

Puffer, Sheila M., Daniel J. McCarthy, and Alexander I. Naumov. *The Russian Capitalist Experiment: From State-Owned Organization to Entrepreneurships.* Abington: Edward Elger Pub., 2000.

Studwell, Joe. *The China Dream: The Quest for the Last Great Untapped Market on Earth.* New York: Grove/Atlantic, Inc., 2003.

Chapter 10

Birn, Robin J., (ed.). *The Handbook of International Marketing Research Techniques.* London, Kogan Page, 2003.

Craig, C. Samuel, and Susan P. Douglas. *International Marketing Research: Concepts and Methods,* 2d ed. New York: John Wiley & Sons, 2000.

Churchill, Gilbert A., Jr. and Dawn Iacobucci. *Basic Marketing Research. Methodological Foundations,* 8th ed. Mason, OH: South-Western/Thomson, 2002.

Czinkota, Michael R., and Sarah McCue. *The STAT-USA Companion to International Business.* Washington, DC: U.S. Department of Commerce, 2001.

Gale Directory of Online Portable and Internet Databases. http://Library.dialog.com, accessed June 25, 2003. Published annually.

GreenBook 2003–2004, Worldwide Directory of Marketing Research Companies and

Services. New York: American Marketing Association, 2003.

Lavin, Michael. *International Business Information: How to Find It, How to Use It.* Westport, CT: Oryx Press, 2004.

Chapter 11

Cavusgil, S. Tamer, Milind R. Agarwal, and Pervez N. Ghauri, *Doing Business in Emerging Markets: Entry & Negotiation Strategies.* Thousand Oaks, CA: Sage Publications, Ltd., 2002.

Craighead's International Business, Travel and Relocation Guide to 84 Countries 2002–03, Detroit: Gale, 2002.

Culpan, Refik, *Global Business Alliances: Theory and Practice.* New York: Quorum, 2002.

Davis, Warnock. *Partner Risk: Managing the Downside of Strategic Alliances.* West Lafayette, IN: Purdue University Press, 2000.

Geroski, P. A., *Market Dynamics and Entry.* Malden, MA: Blackwell Publishers, 2002.

Holtbrügge, Dirk (Ed). *Die Internationalisierung von kleinen und mittleren Unternehmungen,* Stuttgart; ibideum, 2003.

Hoy, Frank, and John Stanworth, *Franchising: An International Perspective.* London: Routledge, 2003.

Reuer, Jeffrey J. (Ed.), *Strategic Alliances: Theory and Evidence.* Oxford: Oxford University Press, 2003.

Pena, Arranz Nieves, and Juan Carlos Fernandez de Arrovabe, *Business Cooperation.* New York: Palgrave Macmillan, 2002.

Chapter 12

Birkinshaw, Julian. *Entrepreneurship in the Global Firm.* Thousand Oaks, CA: Sage Publications, 2000.

The Economist Intelligence Unit. *151 Checklists for Global Management.* New York: The Economist Intelligence Unit, 1993.

Feist, William R., James A. Heely, Min H. Lau, and Roy L. Nersesian. *Managing a Global Enterprise.* Westport, CT: Quorum, 1999.

Grant, Robert M., and Kent E. Neupert. *Cases in Contemporary Strategy Analysis.* Oxford, England: Blackwell, 2003.

Humes, Samuel. *Managing the Multinational: Confronting the Global-Local Dilemma.* London: Prentice-Hall International (U.K.) Ltd, 1993.

Irwin, Douglas A. *Free Trade Under Fire.* Princeton, NJ: Princeton University press, 2002.

Kanter, Rosabeth Moss. *World Class.* New York: Simon & Schuster, 1995.

Kotabe, Masaaki. *Global Sourcing Strategy: R&D, Manufacturing, and Marketing Interfaces.* Greenwich, CT: Greenwood Publishing Group, 1992.

Lindsey, Brink. *Against the Dead Hand: The Uncertain Struggle for Global Capitalism.* New York: John Wiley & Sons, 2001.

Makridakis, Spyros G. *Forecasting, Planning, and Strategy for the 21st Century.* New York: Free Press, 1990.

Prahalad, C. K., and Yves L. Doz. *The Multinational Mission: Balancing Local and Global Vision.* New York: Free Press, 1987.

Rosensweig, Jeffrey. *Winning the Global Game: A Strategy for Linking People and Profits.* New York: Free Press, 1998.

Schwab, Klaus, Michael Porter, and Jeffrey Sachs. *The Global Competitiveness Report 2001–2002.* Oxford: Oxford University Press, 2002.

Scott, Allen J. *Regions and the World Economy: The Coming Shape of Global Production, Competition, and Political Order.* Oxford: Oxford University Press, 2000.

Soros, George. *George Soros on Globalization.* New York: Public Affairs, 2002.

Stieglitz, Joseph E. *Globalization and Its Discontents.* New York: W. W. Norton & Co., 2002.

Yip, George. *Total Global Strategy II.* Upper Saddle River, NJ: Prentice-Hall, 2002.

Chapter 13

Bartlett, Christopher, and Sumantra Ghoshal. *Managing Across Borders.* Cambridge, MA: Harvard Business Press, 1998.

Cairncross, Frances. *The Company of the Future.* Cambridge, MA: Harvard Business School Press, 2002.

Chisholm, Rupert F. *Developing Network Organizations: Learning from Practice and Theory.* Boston: Addison-Wesley, 1997.

Doz, Yves, Jose Santos, and Peter Williamson. *From Global to Metanational: How Companies Win in the Knowledge Economy.* Cambridge, MA: Harvard Business School Press, 2001.

Ghoshal, Sumantra, and Christopher Bartlett. *The Individualized Corporation: A Fundamentally New Approach to Management.* New York: Harper Business, 1999.

Govindarajan, Vijay, Anil K. Gupta, and C. K. Prahalad. *The Quest for Global Dominance: Transforming Global Presence into Global Competitive Advantage.* New York: Jossey-Bass, 2001.

Govindarajan, Vijay, and Robert Newton. *Management Control Systems.* New York: McGraw-Hill/Irwin, 2000.

McCall, Morgan W., and George P. Hollenbeck. *Developing Global Executives.* Cambridge, MA: Harvard Business School Press, 2002.

Pfeffer, Jeffrey, and Robert I. Sutton. *The Knowing-Doing Gap: How Smart Companies Turn Knowledge into Action.* Cambridge, MA: Harvard Business School Press, 1999.

Stewart, Thomas A. *The Wealth of Knowledge: Intellectual Capital and the Twenty-first Century Organization.* New York: Doubleday, 2001.

Chapter 14

Czinkota, Michael R., and Ilkka A. Ronkainen. *International Marketing.* Mason, OH: Thomson South-Western, 2004.

Czinkota, Michael R., Ilkka A. Ronkainen, and Bob Donath. *Mastering Global Markets: Strategies for Today's Trade Globalist.* Mason, OH: Thomson South-Western, 2004.

Czinkota, Michael R., and Jon Woronoff. *Unlocking Japan's Market.* Chicago: Probus Publishers, 1991.

Douglas, Susan P., and C. Samuel Craig, *International Marketing Research.* New York: John Wiley, 1999.

Monye, Sylvester O., ed. *The Handbook of International Marketing Communications.* Cambridge, MA: Blackwell Publishers, 2000.

Moses, Elissa. *The $100 Billion Allowance: How to Get Your Share of the Global Teen Market.* New York: John Wiley & Sons, 2000.

Ries, Laura, and Al Ries. *The 22 Immutable Laws of Branding: How to Build a Product or Service into a World-Class Brand.* New York: Harper Collins, 1999.

Schultz, Don E., and Philip J. Kitchen. *Communicating Globally: An Integrated Marketing Approach.* New York: McGraw-Hill, 2000.

U.S. Department of Commerce. *A Basic Guide to Exporting.* Washington, DC: U.S. Government Printing Office, 1996.

Yip, George S. *Total Global Strategy II.* Upper Saddle River, NJ: Prentice-Hall, 2002.

Chapter 15

Basedow, Jürgen. *Economic Regulation and Competition: Regulation of Services in the EU, Germany, and Japan.* New York: Kluwer Law International, 2002.

Cuadrado-Roura, Juan R., Luis Rubalcaba-Berjemo, John R. Bryson, and Withold J. Henisz, eds. *Trading Services in the Global Economy,* Cheltenham, Gloucestershire, United Kingdom: Edward Elgar Publishing, 2002.

Davis, Mark W., and Janelle Heinke. *Managing Services: Using Technology to Create Value.* New York: McGraw-Hill/Irwin, 2003.

Gallouj, Faiz. *Innovation in the Service Economy: The New Wealth of Nations.* Cheltenham, Gloucestershire, United Kingdom: Edward Elgar Publishing, 2002.

Johnson, Michael D., and Anders Gustafsson. *Competing in a Service Economy: How to Create a Competitive Advantage Through Service Development and Innovation.* New York: John Wiley & Sons, 2003.

Lovelock, Christopher H., and Lauren Wright. *Principles of Services Marketing and Management,* 2nd ed. Harlow, Essex, United Kingdom: Pearson Education, 2001.

Meyer, Anton, and Frank Dornach. *The German Customer Barometer.* Munich: FMG-Verlag, 2004.

Chapter 16

Helferich, Omar Keith, and Robert Cook. *Securing the Supply Chain: Management Report (2002),* Oakbrook, IL: Council of Logistics Management, 2002.

Hugos, Michael. *Essentials of Supply Chain Management.* Hoboken: John Wiley & Sons, 2002.

Pollock, Daniel. *Precipice.* Oak Brook, IL: Council of Logistics Management, 2001.

Ross, David. *Introduction to e-Supply Chain Management: Engaging Technology to Build Market-Winning Business Partnerships.* Saint Lucie, FL: Saint Lucie Press, 2002.

Schary, Philip B., and Tage Skjott-Larsen. *Managing the Global Supply Chain.* Copenhagen: Copenhagen Business School Press, 2001.

Stock, James R., and Douglas M. Lambert. *Strategic Logistics Management.* New York: McGraw-Hill, 2001

Waters, Donald. *Global Logistics and Distribution Planning: Strategies for Management.* London: Kogan Page, 2003.

Chapter 17

Brealey, Richard A., and Stewart C. Myers. *Principles of Corporate Finance.* 5th ed. New York: McGraw-Hill, 1996.

Countertrade and Offsets. A newsletter published by DP Publications Co., Fairfax Station, VA.

Directory of Organizations Providing Countertrade Services 1996–97. 7th ed. Fairfax Station, VA: DP Publications Co., 1996.

Eaker, Mark R., Frank J. Fabozzi, and Dwight Grant. *International Corporate Finance.* Fort Worth, TX: The Dryden Press, 1996.

Eiteman, David K., Arthur I. Stonehill, and Michael H. Moffett. *Multinational Business Finance.* 10th ed. Boston, MA: Addison-Wesley, 2004.

Eun, Cheol S., and Bruce G. Resnick. *International Financial Management.*

Boston, MA: Irwin McGraw-Hill, 1998.

Giddy, Ian H., *Global Financial Markets.* Lexington, MA: Elsevier, 1994.

International Buy-Back Contracts. New York: United Nations, 1991.

Jacque, Laurent L. *Management and Control of Foreign Exchange Risk.* Boston, MA: Kluwer Academic Publishers, 1996.

Madura, Jeff. *International Financial Management.* 5th ed. Cincinnati, OH: South-Western Publishing, 1998.

Martin, Stephen, ed. *The Economics of Offsets: Defence Procurement and Countertrade.* Amsterdam: Harwood Academic Publishers, 1996.

Mohring, Wolfgang. *Gegengeschaefte: Analyse einer Handelsform.* Frankfurt: M.P. Lang, 1991.

"Offsets," *Business America* 117, 9. Washington, DC: U.S. Department of Commerce, September, 1996.

Offsets in Defense Trade. Bureau of Export Administration, U.S. Department of Commerce, Washington, DC, May, 1996.

Shapiro, Alan C. *Foundations of Multinational Financial Management.* 3d ed. Upper Saddle River, NJ: Prentice Hall, 1998.

Smith, Clifford W., Charles W. Smithson, and D. Sykes Wilford. *Managing Financial Risk.* The Institutional Investor Series in Finance. New York: Harper Business, 1990.

UNCITRAL Legal Guide on International Countertrade Transactions. New York: United Nations, 1993.

Verzariu, Pompiliu, and Paula Mitchell, *A Guide on Countertrade Practices in the Newly Independent States of the Former Soviet Union.* Washington, DC: U.S. Department of Commerce, 1995.

Chapter 18

Alhashim, Dhia D., and Jeffrey S. Arpan. *International Dimensions of Accounting.* 3d ed. Boston: PWS-Kent Publishing Company, 1992.

Arpan, Jeffrey S., and Lee H. Radebaugh. *International Accounting and*

Multinational Enterprises.. New York: John Wiley & Sons, 1985.

BenDaniel, David J., and Arthur H. Rosenbloom. *The Handbook of International Mergers and Acquisitions.* Englewood Cliffs, NJ: Prentice-Hall, 1990.

Board of Directors, Enron, "Report of Investigation: Special Investigative Committee of the Board of Directors of Enron Corporation," February 1, 2002, pp. 27–28.

Bodner, Paul M. "International Taxation." In *The Handbook of International Accounting.* ed. Frederick D.S. Choi. New York: John Wiley & Sons, 1992.

Choi, Frederick D.S., ed. *The Handbook of International Accounting.* 3d ed. New York: John Wiley & Sons, 2003.

Choi, Frederick D.S., and Richard Levich. "International Accounting Diversity and Capital Market Decisions." In *The Handbook of International Accounting.* ed. Frederick D.S. Choi. New York: John Wiley & Sons, 1992.

Choi, Frederick D.S., and Gerhard G. Mueller. *International Accounting.* 2d ed. Englewood Cliffs, NJ: Prentice-Hall, 1992.

Coopers & Lybrand, *International Accounting Summaries.* 2d ed. New York: John Wiley & Sons, 1993.

Eiteman, David K., Arthur I. Stonehill, and Michael H. Moffett. *Multinational Business Finance.* 10th ed. Boston, MA: Addison-Wesley Publishing, 2004.

Goeltz, Richard K. "International Accounting Harmonization: The Impossible (and Unnecessary?) Dream," *Accounting Horizons* (March 1991): 85–88.

Haskins, M., K. Ferris, and T. Selling. *International Financial Reporting and Analysis.* Burr Ridge, IL: R. D. Irwin, 1995.

Hill & Knowlton and Korn/Ferry International, "2003 Corporate Reputation Watch Survey," 2003.

Hosseini, Ahmad, and Raj Aggarwal. "Evaluating Foreign Affiliates: The Impact of Alternative Foreign Currency Translation Methods." *Inter-*

national Journal of Accounting (fall 1983): 65–87.

McKinsey & Company, "McKinsey Global Investor Opinion Survey on Corporate Governance, 2002," July 2002.

Neuhausen, Benjamin. "Consolidated Financial Statements and Joint Venture Accounting." In *The Handbook of International Accounting.* ed. Frederick D.S. Choi. New York: John Wiley & Sons, 1992.

Nobes, Christopher, and Robert Parker. *Comparative International Accounting.* 3d ed. London: Prentice-Hall International, Ltd., 1991.

OECD, "OECD Principles of Corporate Governance," The Organisation for Economic Co-Operation and Development, 1999.

Price Waterhouse. *Corporate Taxes: A Worldwide Summary.* 1997 International ed. New York, 1997.

Tsui, J. and T. Shieh, "Corporate Governance in Emerging Markets: An Asian Perspective," in *International Finance and Accounting Handbook,* 3d ed., Frederick D.S. Choi, ed. (pp. 24.4–24.6) Hoboken, NJ: Wiley, 2004.

Chapter 19

Adler, Nancy J., and Dafna N. Izraeli, eds. *Competitive Frontiers: Women Managers in a Global Economy.* Cambridge, MA: Blackwell Business, 1994.

Austin, James. *Managing in Developing Countries.* New York: Free Press, 1990.

Biljani, Hiru. *Culture Shock! Succeed in Business: India.* New York: Graphic Arts Center Publishing Co., 2001.

Black, J. Stewart, Hal B. Gregsen, Mark E. Mendenhall, Torsten M. Kuhlmann, and Gunther K. Stahl. *Developing Global Business Leaders: Policies, Resources, and Innovation.* New York: Quorum Books, 2000.

Dalton, Maxine, Christopher Ernst, Jennifer Deal, and Jean Leslie. *Success for the New Global Manager: How to Work Across Distances, Countries, and Cultures.* New York: Jossey-Bass, 2002.

Deresky, Helen. *International Management: Managing Across Borders and Cultures.* Reading, MA: Addison-Wesley, 1997.

Harris, Philip, and Robert T. Moran. *Managing Cultural Differences.* Houston, TX: Gulf, 1996.

Hodgetts, Richard, and Fred Luthans. *International Management.* New York: McGraw-Hill, 2000.

Holley, William H., and Kenneth M. Jennings. *The Labor Relations Process.* Mason, OH: South-Western, 2000.

Lane, Henry W., Joseph J. DiStephano, and Martha L. Maznevski. *International Management Behavior.* Cambridge, MA: Blackwell Publishers, 2000.

Marquardt, Michael J., and Dean W. Engel. *Global Resource Development.* Englewood Cliffs, NJ: Prentice-Hall, 1993.

Slomp, Hans. *Between Bargaining and Politics.* Westport, CT: Praeger, 1998.

Stroh, Linda, *Globalizing People Through International Assignments.* Reading, MA: Addison-Wesley, 1999.

Chapter 20

Adler, Nancy J. *From Boston to Beijing:* Cincinnati, OH: South-Western College Publishing, 2002.

Comeliau, Christian. *Debating the Future of the Global Market Economy.* London: Zed, 2002.

Condon, Bradly. *Nafta, WTO, and Global Business Strategy: How Aids, Trade and Terrorism Affect our Economic Future.* Westport, CT: Quorum Books, 2002.

Cornelius, Peter, and Klaus Schwab, eds. *The Global Competitiveness Report 2002–2003.* Oxford: Oxford University Press, 2002.

Czinkota, Michael R., and Ilkka A. Ronkainen, eds. *Best Practices in International Business.* Fort Worth, TX: Harcourt, 2001.

Friedman, Thomas L. *The Lexus and the Olive Tree: Understanding Globalization.* Wilmington, NC: Anchor Books, 2000.

Omae, Kenichi. *The Invisible Continent: Four Strategic Imperatives of the New Economy.* New York, NY: Harperbusiness, 2001.

Sullivan, Jeremiah. *The Future of Corporate Globalization: From the Extended Order to the Global Village.* Westport, CT: Quorum Books, 2002.

Notes

Chapter 1

1. Paul R. Krugman, "What Do Undergraduates Need to Know about Trade?" AEA Papers and Proceedings, May 1993: 23–26.
2. Margaret P. Doxey, *Economic Sanctions and International Enforcement* (New York: Oxford University Press, 1980), 10.
3. WTO International Trade Statistics 2002. http://www.wto.org, accessed July 15, 2003.
4. World Investment Report 2000, United Nations Conference on Trade and Development, New York, 2000, 1, 5.
5. UN World Investment Report 2002, http://www.unctad.org, accessed July 20, 2003.
6. Eugene H. Fram and Riad Ajami, "Globalization of Markets and Shopping Stress: Cross-Country Comparisons," *Business Horizons*, January–February 1994, 17–23.
7. *Survey of Current Business* (U.S. Department of Commerce, Washington, DC), January 2002.
8. Foreign Direct Investment in the U.S., International Economic Accounts, Bureau of Economic Analysis, http://www.bea.doc.gov, accessed August 5, 2003.
9. U.S. Foreign Trade Highlights, http://www.ita.doc.gov, accessed August 5, 2003.
10. Michael R. Czinkota and Sarah McCue, *The STAT-USA Companion to International Business*, Economics and Statistics Administration (U.S. Department of Commerce, Washington, D.C.), 2001, 16.
11. OECD, Quarterly National Accounts, Paris, http://www.oecd.org, 2003.
12. *Characteristics of Business Owners*, U.S. Bureau of the Census, Washington, DC, November 5, 1997.
13. Ian Putzger, "Online and International," *Journal of Commerce Week*, November 13–19, 2000, 27–28.
14. http://www.tea.gov, accessed July 2003.
15. Michael R. Czinkota, U.S. Exports in the Global Marketplace: An Analysis of the Strengths and Vulnerabilities of Small- and Medium-Sized Manufacturers, Testimony before the Congress of the United States, House of Representatives, 107th Congress, Committee on Small Business, April 24, 2002, p. 3.
16. Charles Taylor and Witold Henisz, *U.S. Manufacturers in the Global Market Place*, Report 1058, The Conference Board, 1994.
17. Howard Lewis III and J. David Richardson, *Why Global Commitment Really Matters*, Washington, DC: Institute for International Economics, 2001.
18. Michael R. Czinkota, Ilkka A. Ronkainen, and Bob Donath, *Mastering Global Markets: Strategies for Today's Trade Globalist*, Mason, OH: South-Western, 2004.

Chapter 2

1. "Rule No. 1: Don't Diss the Locals," *Business Week*, May 15, 1995, 8.
2. Carla Rapoport, "Nestlé's Brand-Building Machine," *Fortune*, September 19, 1994, 147–156.
3. Alonso Martinez, Ivan De Souza, Fancis Liu, "Multinationals vs. Multilatinas," *Strategy and Business* (Fall, 2003): 56–67.
4. Alfred Kroeber and Clyde Kluckhohn, *Culture: A Critical Review of Concepts and Definitions* (New York: Random House, 1985), 11.
5. Geert Hofstede, "National Cultures Revisited," *Asia-Pacific Journal of Management* 1 (September 1984): 22–24.
6. Robert L. Kohls, *Survival Kit for Overseas Living* (Chicago: Intercultural Press, 1979), 3.
7. Edward T. Hall, *Beyond Culture* (Garden City, NY: Anchor Press, 1976), 15.
8. See http://www.mcdonalds.com.
9. Marita von Oldenborgh, "What's Next for India?" *International Business* (January 1996): 44–47; and Ravi Vijh, "Think Global, Act Indian," *Export Today* (June 1996): 27–28.
10. "The One Where Pooh Goes to Sweden," *The Economist*, April 5, 2003, 59.
11. "Culture Wars," *The Economist*, September 12, 1998, 97–99.
12. "Information Minister Aims to Throw Cultural Vulgarians Out of the Game," *The Washington Post*, February 2, 1999, A16.
13. "Multinational Firms Take Steps to Avert Boycotts Over War," *The Wall Street Journal*, April 4, 2003, A1, A4.
14. George P. Mundak, "The Common Denominator of Cultures," in *The Science of Man in the World*, ed. Ralph Linton (New York: Columbia University Press, 1945), 123–142.
15. Philip R. Harris and Robert T. Moran, *Managing Cultural Differences* (Houston: Gulf, 1996), 201.
16. "Euroteen Market Grabs U.S. Attention," *Marketing News*, October 22, 2001, 15.
17. David A. Ricks, *Blunders in International Business*, 3rd edition (Malden, MA: Blackwell, 2000), 4.
18. David A. Hanni, John K. Ryans, and Ivan R. Vernon, "Coordinating International Advertising: The Goodyear Case Revisited for Latin America," *Journal of International Marketing* 3, no. 2 (1995): 83–98.
19. "French Snared in Web of English," *The Washington Post*, September 27, 2000, A19; and "France: Mind Your Language," *The Economist*, March 23, 1996, 70–71.
20. "A World Empire by Other Means," *The Economist*, December 22, 2001, 65.
21. Rory Cowan, "The e Does Not Stand for English," *Global Business*, March 2000, L/22.
22. Stephen P. Iverson, "The Art of Translation," *World Trade*, April 2000, 90–92.
23. Margareta Bowen, "Business Translation," *Jerome Quarterly* (August–September 1993): 5–9.

24. "Nokia Veti Pois Mainoskampanjansa," *Uutislehti 100*, June 15, 1998, 5.

25. "Sticky Issue," *The Economist*, August 24, 2002, 51.

26. Edward T. Hall, "The Silent Language of Overseas Business," *Harvard Business Review* 38 (May–June 1960): 87–96.

27. *Statistical Abstract of the United States* (Washington, DC: U.S. Government Printing Office, 2003): 868.

28. David McClelland, *The Achieving Society* (New York: Irvington, 1961): 90.

29. *World Almanac and the Book of Facts* (Mahwah, NJ: Funk & Wagnalls, 2001), 721.

30. "Out from Under," *Marketing News*, July 21, 2003, 1, 9.

31. "Islamic Banking: Faith and Creativity," *New York Times*, April 8, 1994, D1, D6.

32. James F. Engel, Roger D. Blackwell, and Paul W. Miniard, *Consumer Behavior* (Ft. Worth, TX: Harcourt, 2001), 381.

33. Douglas McGray, "Japan's Gross National Cool," *Foreign Policy*, May/June 2002, 44.

34. Y.H. Wong and Ricky Yee-kwong, "Relationship Marketing in China: Guanxi, Favoritism and Adaptation," *Journal of Business Ethics* 22, no. 2 (1999): 107–118.

35. Earl P. Spencer, "EuroDisney—What Happened?" *Journal of International Marketing* 3, no. 3 (1995): 103–114.

36. Sergey Frank, "Global Negotiations: Vive Les Differences!" *Sales and Marketing Management* 144 (May 1992): 64–69.

37. See, for example, Terri Morrison, *Kiss, Bow, or Shake Hands: How to Do Business In Sixty Countries* (Holbrook, MA.: Adams Media, 1994) or Roger Axtell, *Do's and Taboos Around the World* (New York: John Wiley & Sons, 1993). For holiday observances, see http://www.religioustolerance.org/main_day.htm#cal and http://www.dir.yahoo.com/society_and_culture/holidays_and_observances, accessed 9/1/03.

38. James A. Gingrich, "Five Rules for Winning Emerging Market Consumers," *Strategy and Business* (second quarter, 1999): 68–76.

39. "Feng Shui Strikes Chord," available at http://www.money.cnn.com/1999/09/11/life/q_fengshui/; and "Fung Shui Man Orders Sculpture Out of Hotel," *South China Morning Post*, July 27, 1992, 4.

40. "U.S. Superstores Find Japanese Are a Hard Sell," *The Wall Street Journal*, February 14, 2000, B1, B4.

41. The results of the Gallup study are available at http://www.fortune.com.

42. Kenichi Ohmae, "Managing in a Borderless World," *Harvard Business Review* 67 (May–June 1989): 152–161.

43. Greg Bathon, "Eat the Way Your Mama Taught You," *World Trade*, December 2000, 76–77.

44. Peter McGinnis, "Guanxi or Contract: A Way to Understand and Predict Conflict Between Chinese and Western Senior Managers in China-Based Joint Ventures," in *Multinational Business Management and Internationalization of Business Enterprises*, ed. Daniel E. McCarthy and Stanley J. Hille (Nanjing, China: Nanjing University Press, 1993), 345–351.

45. Tim Ambler, "Reflections in China: Re-Orienting Images of Marketing," *Marketing Management* 4 (summer 1995): 23–30.

46. Jagdish N. Sheth and S. Prakash Sethi, "A Theory of Cross-Cultural Buying Behavior," in *Consumer and Industrial Buying Behavior*, eds. Arch G. Woodside, Jagdish N. Sheth, and Peter D. Bennett (New York: Elsevier North-Holland, 1977), 369–386.

47. Geert Hofstede, *Culture's Consequences: International Differences in Work-Related Values* (Beverly Hills, CA.: Sage Publications, 1984), Chapter 1.

48. Geert Hofstede and Michael H. Bond, "The Confucius Connection: From Cultural Roots to Economic Growth," *Organizational Dynamics* 16 (spring 1988): 4–21.

49. Simcha Ronen and Oded Shenkar, "Clustering Countries on Attitudinal Dimensions: A Review and Synthesis," *Academy of Management Journal* 28 (September 1985): 440–452.

50. "When Will It Fly?" *The Economist*, August 9, 2003, 51.

51. For applications of the framework, see Sudhir H. Kale, "Culture-Specific Marketing Communications," *International Marketing Review* 8, no. 2 (1991): 18–30; and Sudhir H. Kale, "Distribution Channel Relationships in Diverse Cultures," *International Marketing Review* 8, no. 3 (1991): 31–45.

52. Jan-Benedict Steenkamp and Frenkel ter Hofstede, "A Cross-National Investigation into the Individual and National Cultural Antecedents of Consumer Innovativeness," *Journal of Marketing* 63 (April 1999): 55–69.

53. Hong Cheng and John C. Schweitzer, "Cultural Values Reflected in Chinese and U.S. Television Commercials," *Journal of Advertising Research* 36 (May/June 1996): 27–45.

54. "Building a 'Cultural Index' to World Airline Safety," *The Washington Post*, August 21, 1994, A8.

55. "Exploring Differences in Japan, U.S. Culture," *Advertising Age International*, September 18, 1995, 1–8.

56. James A. Lee, "Cultural Analysis in Overseas Operations," *Harvard Business Review* 44 (March–April 1966): 106–114.

57. David Maxwell and Nina Garrett, "Meeting National Needs," *Change*, May/June 2002, 22–28.

58. W. Chan Kim and R. A. Mauborgne, "Cross-Cultural Strategies," *Journal of Business Strategy* 7 (Spring 1987): 28–37.

59. Mauricio Lorence, "Assignment USA: The Japanese Solution," *Sales and Marketing Management* 144 (October 1992): 60–66.

60. "Special Interest Group Operations" available at http://www.samsung.com; and "Sensitivity Kick," *The Wall Street Journal*, December 30, 1996, 1, 4.

61. Rosalie Tung, "Selection and Training of Personnel for Overseas Assignments," *Columbia Journal of World Business* 16 (Spring 1981): 68–78.

62. Simcha Ronen, "Training the International Assignee," in *Training and Career Development*, ed. I. Goldstein (San Francisco: Jossey-Bass, 1989), 426–440.

63. See for example Johnson & Johnson's credo at http://www.jnj.com/our_company/our_credo/index.htm.

64. 3M examples are adopted from John R. Engen, "Far Eastern Front," *World Trade*, December 1994, 20–24.

Chapter 3

1. Michael R. Czinkota, "The World Trade Organization: Perspectives and Prospects," *Journal of International Marketing* 3, 1 (1995), 85–92.
2. Thomas R. Graham, "Global Trade: War and Peace," *Foreign Policy* 50 (spring 1983): 124–127.
3. Edwin L. Barber III, "Investment-Trade Nexus," in *U.S. International Policy*, ed. Gary Clyde Hufbauer (Washington, DC: The International Law Institute, 1982), 9–4.
4. Remarks by Mike Moore, Director General, WTO, Geneva, June 25, 2002.
5. Jessica T. Mathews, "Power Shift," *Foreign Affairs* (January/ February 1997): 50–66.
6. Office of the United States Trade Representative: Executive Office of the President, http://www.ustr.gov/releases/2003/03/03-19.htm, accessed July 28, 2003.
7. U.S. Department of State, http://usinfo.state.gov/regional/ar/trade/nafta11.htm, accessed July 28, 2003.
8. http://www.thailand.com/exports/html/country_export_stat.htm, accessed July 29, 2003.
9. Charlene Barshefsky, "The Transatlantic Groundwork for Global Prosperity," an address before the American Council on Germany, Alexandria, VA, June 15, 2001.
10. Charlene Barshefsky, "The Transatlantic Groundwork for Global Prosperity," an address before the American Council on Germany, Alexandria, VA, June 15, 2001.
11. "South African Exports Up," http://www.winesandvines.com/headline_12_20_02_south.html, accessed July 29, 2003.
12. Joseph Quinlan, *"Drifting Apart or Growing Together? The Primacy of the Transatlantic Economy,"* Washington, DC: Center for Transatlantic Relations, 2003.
13. Bank for International Settlements (BIS), Triennial Central Bank Survey, Basel, March 2002.
14. Michael R. Czinkota, "The World Trade Organization: Perspectives and Prospects," 85–92.
15. http://www.imf.org/external/np/sec/pr/2002/pr0240.htm, accessed July 18, 2003.
16. Chris Sewell, "The World Bank Controversy Explained," Medill News Service, February 8, 2001.
17. Michael R. Czinkota and Masaaki Kotabe, "A Marketing Perspective of the U.S. International Trade Commission's Antidumping Actions—An Empirical Inquiry," *Journal of World Business* 32, 2 (1997): 169–187.
18. A. B. Bernard, and J. B. Jeusen, *Exceptional exporter performance: Cause, effect or both?* Pittsburgh, PA: Census Research Data Center, Carnegie Mellon University, 1997.
19. U.S. Department of Commerce, *National Export Strategy* (Washington, DC: U.S. Government Printing Office, October 1996).
20. Michael R. Czinkota, "Export Promotion: A Framework for Finding Opportunity in Change," *Thunderbird International Business Review*, 44, 3, (2002): 315–324.
21. http://www.irs.gov, accessed July 27, 2003.
22. Masaaki Kotabe and Michael R. Czinkota, "State Government Promotion of Manufacturing Exports: A Gap Analysis," *Journal of International Business Studies* (winter 1992): 637–658.
23. Investment Canada Act, http://investcan.ic.gc.ca, July 27, 2003.
24. Jaclyn Fierman, "The Selling Off of America," *Fortune*, December 22, 1986, 35.
25. Survey of Current Business, http://www.bea.gov and http://www.census.gov, accessed July 30, 2003.
26. "At Sanyo's Arkansas Plant the Magic Isn't Working," *Business Week* (July 14, 1986): 51–52.
27. Joseph S. Nye, "Multinational Corporations in World Politics," *Foreign Affairs* 53 (October 1974): 153–175.
28. Stephen Guisinger, "Attracting and Controlling Foreign Investment," *Economic Impact* (Washington, DC: United States Information Agency, 1987), 18.
29. Ibid., 20.
30. Victor H. Frank, "Living with Price Control Abroad," *Harvard Business Review* 62 (March–April 1984): 137–142.
31. Thomas W. Shreeve, "Be Prepared for Political Charges Abroad," *Harvard Business Review* 62 (July–August 1984): 111–118.
32. Michael R. Czinkota and Masaaki Kotabe, "America's New World Trade Order," *Marketing Management* 1, 3 (1992): 46–54.
33. Donald Manzullo and Michael R. Czinkota, "Exports and Imports: For U.S. manufacturers, it is a difficult balancing act," *The Washington Times*, May 27, 2003, A17.
34. Michael R. Czinkota, ed., *Proceedings of the Conference on the Feasibility of a Protection Cost Index*, August 6, 1987 (Washington, DC: Department of Commerce, 1987), 7.

Chapter 4

1. Quoted in Philippe Dollinger, *The German Hansa* (Stanford, CA: Stanford University Press, 1970), 49.
2. Robin Renwick, *Economic Sanctions* (Cambridge, MA: Harvard University Press, 1987), 11.
3. Margaret P. Doxey, *Economic Sanctions and International Enforcement* (New York: Oxford University Press, 1987), 10.
4. George E. Shambaugh, *States, Firms, and Power: Successful Sanctions in United States Foreign Policy* (Albany, NY: State University of New York Press, 1999), 202.
5. Gary Clyde Hufbauer, Jeffrey J. Schott, and Kimberly Elliott, *Economic Sanctions Reconsidered: History and Current Policy*, 3d ed. (Washington, DC: Institute for International Economics, 2003).
6. G. Scott Erickson, "Export Controls: Marketing Implications of Public Policy Choices," *Journal of Public Policy and Marketing* 16, 1 (spring 1997): 83.
7. Michael R. Czinkota and Erwin Dichtl, "Export Controls and Global Changes," *der markt*, 35, 3, 1996: 148–155.
8. Robert M. Springer, Jr., "New Export Law an Aid to International Marketers," *Marketing News*, January 3, 1986, 10, 67.
9. Erwin Dichtl, "Defacto Limits of Export Controls: The Need for International Harmonization," paper presented at the 2nd Annual CiMar Conference, Rio de Janeiro, August 1994.

10. Allen S. Krass, "The Second Nuclear Era: Nuclear Weapons in a Transformed World," in *World Security: Challenges for a New Century*, 2d ed., M. Klare and D. Thomas, eds. (St. Martin's Press, 1994), 85–105.

11. Craig Barrett, President Intel, Speech to the American Management Association, Spring 2002, Phoenix.

12. E. M. Hucko, *Aussenwirtschaftsrecht-Kriegswaffenkontrollrecht, Textsammlung mit Einführung*, 4th ed. (Cologne, 1993).

13. Michael R. Czinkota, "From Bowling Alone to Standing Together," *Marketing Management*, March/April 2002, 12–16.

14. Gary Clyde Hufbauer, Jeffrey J. Schott, Barbara Oegg, *Using Sanctions to Fight Terrorism*, (Washington DC, Institute for International Economics, November 2001), 1.

15. http://cornerhouse.icaap.org/briefings/19.html, accessed July 15, 2003.

16. Habib Mohsin and Leon Zurawicki, "Corruption and Foreign Direct Investment," *Journal of International Business Studies*, 33, 2:291–307.

17. George Moody, *Grand Corruption: How Business Bribes Damage Developing Countries* (Oxford: World View Publishing, 1997): 23.

18. Michael R. Czinkota, Ilkka A. Ronkainen, and Bob Donath, *Mastering Global Markets*, (Cincinnati: Thomson, 2004), 362.

19. Michael G. Harvey, "A Survey of Corporate Programs for Managing Terrorist Threats," *Journal of International Business Studies* (Third Quarter 1993): 465–478.

20. Harvey J. Iglarsh, "Terrorism and Corporate Costs," *Terrorism* 10 (1987): 227–230.

21. G. Hart and W. Rudman, *America Still Unprepared—America Still in Danger* (New York: Council on Foreign Relations, 2002), 14.

22. Gary A. Knight, Michael R. Czinkota, and Peter W. Liesch, "Terrorism and the International Firm," Proceedings: Annual meeting of the Academy of International Business, Honolulu, HI: Academy of International Business, 2003.

23. Michael Minor, "LDCs, TNCs, and Expropriations in the 1980s," *The CYC Reporter* (spring 1988): 53.

24. Shengliang Deng, Pam Townsend, Maurice Robert, and Normand Quesnel, "A Guide to Intellectual Property Rights in Southeast Asia and China," *Business Horizons* (November–December 1996): 43–50.

25. TRIPS, a more detailed overview of the TRIPS agreement, www.wto.org, February 1, 2001.

26. "Risky Returns," *The Economist*, May 25, 2000, http://www.economist.com.

27. Paul Blustein, "Kawasaki to Pay Additional Taxes to U.S.," *The Washington Post*, December 11, 1992, D1.

28. http://www.opic.gov, Washington, DC: Overseas Private Investment Corporation, May 2, 2001.

29. Federal News Service, *Hearing of the House Judiciary Committee*, April 23, 1997.

30. Surya Prakash Sinha, *What Is Law? The Differing Theories of Jurisprudence* (New York: Paragon House, 1989).

31. Michael R. Czinkota and Jon Woronoff, *Unlocking Japan's Market* (Chicago: Probus Publishing, 1991).

32. http://www.tdctrade.com/mktprof/europe/mprussia.htm, assessed June 30, 2003.

33. Timothy P. Blumentritt and Douglas Nigh, "The Integration of Subsidiary Political Activities in Multinational Corporations," *Journal of International Business Studies*, 33, 1, 2002, 57–77.

34. Michael R. Czinkota, "The Policy Gap in International Marketing," *Journal of International Marketing*, 8, 1, 2000: 99–111.

35. Bruce D. Keillor, G. Tomas M. Hult, Deborah Owens, "An Empirical Investigation of Market Barriers and the Political Activities of Individual Firms," *International Journal of Commerce and Management*, 12, 2, 2002, 89–106.

36. Michael R. Czinkota, "International Information Needs for U.S. Competitiveness," *Business Horizons* 34, 6 (November/December 1991): 86–91.

37. Najmeh Bozorgmehr and Stefan Wagstyl, "European Business Sees New Area of Potential," *Financial Times*, February 6, 2002. http://www.ft.com.

38. *International Court of Arbitration: 1999 Statistical Report* (Paris: International Chamber of Commerce, 2001).

Chapter 5

1. Adam Smith, *An Inquiry into the Nature and Causes of the Wealth of Nations* (New York: E.P. Dutton & Company, 1937), 4–5.

2. Wassily Leontief, "Domestic Production and Foreign Trade: the American Capital Position Re-Examined," *Proceedings of the American Philosophical Society*, 97, no. 4 (September 1953), as reprinted in Wassily Leontief, *Input-Output Economics* (New York: Oxford University Press, 1966), 69–70.

3. In Leontief's own words: "These figures show that an average million dollars' worth of our exports embodies considerably less capital and somewhat more labor than would be required to replace from domestic production an equivalent amount of our competitive imports. . . . The widely held opinion that—as compared with the rest of the world—the United States' economy is characterized by a relative surplus of capital and a relative shortage of labor proves to be wrong. As a matter of fact, the opposite is true." Leontief, 1953, 86.

4. If this were true, if would defy one of the basic assumptions of the factor proportions theory, that all products are manufactured with the same technology (and therefore same proportions of labor and capital) across countries. However, continuing studies have found this to be quite possible in our imperfect world.

5. For a detailed description of these theories see Elhanan Helpman and Paul Krugman, *Market Structure and Foreign Trade* (Cambridge: MIT Press, 1985).

6. This leads to the obvious debate as to what constitutes a "different product" and what is simply a cosmetic difference. The most obvious answer is found in the field of marketing: If the consumer believes the products are different, then they are different.

7. There are a variety of potential outcomes from external economies of scale. For additional details see Paul R. Krugman and Maurice Obstfeld, *International Economics: Theory and Policy*, 3rd ed. (Harper-Collins, 1994).

8. Michael E. Porter, "The Competitive Advantage of Nations,"

Harvard Business Review (March–April 1990): 73–74.

9. The term *international investment* will be used in this chapter to refer to all nonfinancial investment. International financial investment includes a number of forms beyond the concerns of this chapter, such as the purchase of bonds, stocks, or other securities issued outside the domestic economy.

Chapter 6

1. The official terminology used throughout this chapter, unless otherwise noted, is that of the International Monetary Fund (IMF). Since the IMF is the primary source of similar statistics for balance of payments and economic performance worldwide, it is more general than other terminology forms, such as that employed by the U.S. Department of Commerce.

2. All balance of payment data used in this chapter is drawn from the International Monetary Fund's *Balance of Payments Statistics Yearbook*. This source is used because the IMF presents the balance of payments statistics for all member countries on the same basis and in the same format, allowing comparison across countries.

3. The magnitude of the economic devastation in Asia is still largely unappreciated by Westerners. At a recent conference sponsored by the Milken Institute in Los Angeles, a speaker noted that the preoccupation with the economic problems of Indonesia was incomprehensible since "the total gross domestic product of Indonesia is roughly the size of North Carolina." The following speaker provided a rebuttal, noting that the last time he checked "North Carolina did not have a population of 220 million people."

Chapter 7

1. Rounding errors are solved quite simply with exchange rates. With a few notable exceptions, all active trading takes place using direct quotations on foreign currencies versus the U.S. dollar (€1.1614/$, ¥113.88/$) and for a conventional number of decimal places. These are the base rates that are then used if needed for the calculation of the inverse indirect quotes on the foreign currencies.

2. A currency trader once remarked to the authors that the spot quotes listed on such a screen were no more and no less accurate to the "true price" than the sticker price on a showroom automobile. Of course, this may no longer be true since the introduction of the Saturn, which sells at sticker price only!

3. Actually, there are a few exceptions. Panama, for example, has used the U.S. dollar for many years.

4. Bearer bonds were issued by the U.S. government up until the early 1980s, when discontinued. Even though they were called bearer bonds, a list of bond registration numbers was still kept and recorded in order to tax investors holding the bearer instruments.

Chapter 8

1. The discussion of economic integration is based on the pioneering work by Bela Balassa, *The Theory of Economic Integration* (Homewood, IL: Richard D. Irwin, 1961).

2. "U.S., Central American Nations Launch Trade Talks," *The Wall Street Journal*, January 9, 2003, A3.

3. *The European Union: A Guide for Americans* (Washington, DC: Delegation of the European Commission to the United Sttes, 2003), Chapter 2. See http://www.eurunion.org/infores/euguide/Chapter2.htm.

4. Jacob Viner, *The Customs Union Issue* (New York: Carnegie Endowment for International Peace, 1950).

5. "Japan Seeks Compensation from EU for Post-EU Expansion Tariff Rise," *Jiji Press English News Service*, July 1, 2003, 1.

6. J. Waelbroeck, "Measuring Degrees of Progress in Economic Integration," in *Economic Integration, Worldwide, Regional, Sectoral*, ed. F. Machlop (London: Macmillan, 1980).

7. "Argentina Cries Foul as Choice Employers Beat a Path Next Door," *The Wall Street Journal*, May 2, 2000, A1, A8.

8. "EU-Swiss Trade Opening Up," *World Trade*, September 2000, 20. See also http://secretariat.efta.int.

9. "The Cancun Challenge," *The Economist*, September 6, 2003, 59–61.

10. EC Commission, *Completing the Internal Market: White Paper from the Commission to the European Council* (Luxembourg: EC Commission, 1985).

11. "A Singular Market," *The Economist* (October 22, 1994): 10–16.

12. Various aspects of the 1992 Common Market are addressed in André Sapir and Alexis Jacquemin, eds., *The European Internal Market* (Oxford, England: Oxford University Press, 1990).

13. "Mega Europe," *Business Week*, November 25, 2002, 62.

14. *The European Union: A Guide for Americans* (Washington, DC: Delegation of the European Commission to the United States, 2002), ch. 2.

15. Guenther Burghardt, "The Future of the European Union," speech given at the Johns Hopkins University School of Advanced International Studies, January 23, 2001.

16. "Will France and Germany's Double Vision Give EU a Headache?" *The Wall Street Journal*, January 16, 2003, A10.

17. Economic growth effects are discussed in Richard Baldwin, "The Growth Effects of 1992," *Economic Policy* (October 1989): 248–281; or Rudiger Dornbusch, "Europe 1992: Macroeconomic Implication," *Brookings Papers on Economic Activity* 2 (1989): 341–362.

18. John F. Magee, "1992: Moves Americans Must Make," *Harvard Business Review* 67(May–June 1989): 72–84.

19. "For U.S. Small Biz, Fertile Soil in Europe," *Business Week*, April 1, 2002, 55–56.

20. "Summary of the U.S.–Canada Free Trade Agreement," *Export Today* 4 (November–December 1988): 57–61.

21. Raymond Ahearn, *Trade and the Americas* (Washington, DC: Congressional Research Service, 1997), 3–4.

22. Sidney Weintraub, *NAFTA at Three: A Progress Report* (Washington, DC: Center for Strategic and International Studies, 1997): 17–18.

23. "NAFTA's Do-Gooder Side Deals Disappoint," *The Wall Street Journal*, October 15, 1997, A19.

24. For annual trade information, see http://www.census.gov/foreign-trade/.

25. "U.S. Trade with Mexico During the Third NAFTA Year," *International Economic Review* (Washington, DC: International Trade Commission, April 1997): 11.

26. "Fox and Bush, for Richer, for Poorer," *The Economist*, February 3, 2001, 37–38.

27. "Aerospace Suppliers Gravitate to Mexico," *The Wall Street Journal*, January 23, 2002, A17.

28. "The Latin Market Never Looked so Bueno," *DSN Retailing Today*, June 10, 2002, 125–126.

29. "Retail Oasis," *Business Mexico* (April 2001): 15.

30. Lara L. Sowinski, "Maquiladoras," *World Trade* (September 2000): 88–92.

31. "The Decline of the Maquiladora," *Business Week*, April 29, 2002, 59.

32. NAFTA's Scorecard: So Far, So Good," *Business Week*, July 9, 2001, 54–56.

33. "Localizing Production," *Global Commerce* (August 20, 1997): 1.

34. "Next Stop South," *The Economist* (February 25, 1995): 29–30.

35. "Latin Trade Pact Poses Political Peril for Bush," *The Wall Street Journal*, December 31, 2002, A4.

36. "Mexico, EU Sign Free-Trade Agreement," *The Wall Street Journal*, March 24, 2000, A15.

37. "Trouble in Paradise," *The Economist*, November 23, 2002, 36–37.

38. "Caribbean Parity Enters the Picture," *World Trade*, July 2000, 46.

39. "Latin Lesson," *Far Eastern Economic Review*, January 4, 2001, 109.

40. "Recruitment Drive," *The Economist*, August 30, 2003, 25–26.

41. "The FTAA: Why is This Giant Trade Pact So Important?" *World Trade* (July 2003): 44; and "The Americas: A Cautious Yes to Pan-American Trade," *The Economist*, April 28, 2001, 35–36.

42. "Ripping Down the Walls Across the Americas," *Business Week* (December 26, 1994): 78–80; and "Free Trade Pact Looks Promising for Marketers, Advertisers," *Marketing News*, August 18, 2003, 6–7.

43. Emily Thornton, "Will Japan Rule a New Trade Bloc?" *Fortune* (October 5, 1992): 131–132.

44. Paul Krugman, "A Global Economy Is Not the Wave of the Future," *Financial Executive* 8 (March/April 1992): 10–13.

45. Michael R. Czinkota and Masaaki Kotabe, "America's New World Trade Order," *Marketing Management* 1 (summer 1992): 49–56.

46. "Afrabet Soup," *The Economist*, February 10, 2001, 77.

47. "Try, Try Again," *The Economist,*" July 13, 2002, 41.

48. Josh Martin, "Gulf States to Adopt a Single Currency," *Middle East*, May 2002, 23–25.

49. Eric Friberg, Risto Perttunen, Christian Caspar, and Dan Pittard, "The Challenges of Europe 1992," *The McKinsey Quarterly* 21, 2 (1988): 3–15.

50. "Lean, Mean, European," *The Economist*, April 29, 2000, 5–7.

51. Gianluigi Guido, "Implementing a Pan-European Marketing Strategy," *Long Range Planning* 24, 5 (1991): 23–33.

52. "TABD Uses Virtual Organization for Trade Lobbying," *Crossborder Monitor* (July 2, 1997): 1.

53. "OPEC's Joyride Was Great While It Lasted," *Business Week* (June 3, 1996): 52. See also http://www.opec.org.

54. "Are We Over a Barrel?" *Time*, December 18, 2000, B6–B11.

55. "Inside "OPEC's Backroom Deal to Keep Oil Supplies Flowing," *The Wall Street Journal*, July 29, 2003, A1, A8.

Chapter 9

1. For further explanation on these definitions, see Michael W. Peng, *Business Strategies in Transition Economies* (Thousand Oaks, CA: Sage Publications, 2000), 8–10.

2. Richard M. Hammer, "Dramatic Winds of Change," *Price Waterhouse Review* 33 (1989): 23–27.

3. Peter G. Lauter and Paul M. Dickie, "Multinational Corporations in Eastern European Socialist Economies," *Journal of Marketing* 25 (Fall 1975): 40–46.

4. Eugene Theroux and Arthur L. George, *Joint Ventures in the Soviet Union: Law and Practice*, rev. ed. (Washington, DC: Baker & McKenzie, 1989), 1.

5. *The World Factbook 1994* (Washington, DC: Central Intelligence Agency, 1994).

6. Direction of Trade Statistics, International Monetary Fund, Washington, DC, http://www.imf.org.

7. J. K. Giacobbe-Miller, D. J. Miller, W. Zhang, and V. I. Victorov, "Country and Organizational-Level Adaptation to Foreign Workplace Ideologies: A Comparative Study of Distributive Justice Values in China, Russia, and the United States." *Journal of International Business Studies*, 2003, 34, 389–406.

8. Usha C. V. Haley, "Assessing and Controlling Business Risks in China," *Journal of International Management*, 9, (2003): 237–252.

9. Harry G. Broadman, "Reducing Structural Dominance and Entry Barriers in Russian Industry," *Russian Enterprise Reform: Policies to Further the Transition, World Bank Discussion Paper No. 400* (Washington, DC: The World Bank, 1999), 15–34.

10. Thomas Wolf and Emine Guergen, *Improving Governance and Fighting Corruption in the Baltic and CIS Countries* (Washington, DC: International Monetary Fund, 2000).

11. Edward Tse, "The Right Way to Achieve Profitable Growth in the Chinese Consumer Market," *Strategy and Business* (second quarter, 1998): 10–21.

12. Mihaly Simai, *East-West Cooperation at the End of the 1980s: Global Issues, Foreign Direct Investments, and Debts* (Budapest: Hungarian Scientific Council for World Economy, 1989), 21.

13. James A. Gingrich, "Five Rules for Winning Emerging Market Consumers," *Strategy and Business* (second quarter, 1999): 19–33.

14. Michael R. Czinkota, "U.S. Manufacturers in the Global Marketplace: Market Share Changes, Vulnerabilities and Policy Changes," Testimony before the Committee on Small Business, U.S. House of Representatives, One Hundred-Eighth Congress, First Session, April 9, 2003.

15. "What's Next for the Global Economy?" *Business Week Online*, February 11, 2002, http://www.businessweek.com.

16. Johny K. Johansson, Ilkka A. Ronkainen, and Michael R. Czinkota, "Negative Country of Origin Effects: The Case of the New Russia," *Journal of International Business Studies* 25, 1 (1994): 157–176.

17. Clay Chandler, "A Golden Goose in Red China?" *The Washington Post*, August 1, 2000, E1.

18. Kiran Karande, Mahesh N. Shankarmahesh, and C. P. Rao, "Marketing to Public- and Private-Sector Companies in Emerging Countries: A Study of Indian Purchasing Managers," *Journal of International Marketing* 2, 3 (1999): 64.

19. "European Privatization: Two Half Revolutions," *The Economist* (January 22, 1994): 55, 58.

20. Oleh Havrylyshyn and Donal McGettigan, *Privatization in Transition Countries* (Washington, DC: International Monetary Fund, 1999).

21. This section based on "CelPay Puts Africa on the Wireless Map," *The Wall Street Journal*, December 2, 2002, B4; "Making the Web Worldwide," *The Economist*, September 28, 2002, 76; C. K. Prahalad and Allen Hammond, "Serving the World's Poor, Profitably," *Harvard Business Review*, 80 (September 2002): 48–59; and Dana James, "B2-4B Spells Profits," *Marketing News*, November 5, 2001, 1, 11–12.

22. A. Coskun Samli, *Entering and Succeeding in Emerging Countries: Marketing to the Forgotten Majority* (Mason, OH: Thomson-South-Western, 2004).

23. C. K. Prahalad and Stuart L. Hart, "The Fortune at the Bottom of the Pyramid," *Strategy and Business*, (first quarter, 2002): 35–47.

Chapter 10

1. David A. Ricks, *Blunders in International Business*, 3d ed. (Malden, MA: Blackwell, 2000).

2. Jan-Benedict E. M. Steenkamp, "The role of national culture in international marketing research," *International Marketing Review*, 18, 1 (2001), 30–44.

3. C. Samuel Craig and Susan P. Douglas, *International Marketing Research*, 2d ed. (New York: John Wiley & Sons, 1999).

4. For an excellent diagnostics tool see Prof. Tamer Cavusgil's "Company Readiness to Export," Michigan State University, http://globaledge.msu.edu, June 25, 2003.

5. "National Trade Data Bank," http://www.stat-usa.gov, accessed 6 June 25, 2003.

6. Michael R. Czinkota, "International Information Cross-Fertilization in Marketing: An Empirical Assessment," *European Journal of Marketing* 34, 11/12 (2000): 1305–1314.

7. Charles A. Prescott, "The New International Marketing Challenge: Privacy," *Target Marketing* 22 (no. 4, 1999): 28.

8. Ricks, *Blunders in International Business*.

9. Michael R. Czinkota, "Russia's Transition to a Market Economy: Learning About Business," *Journal of International Marketing* 5, 4 (fall 1997): 73–93.

10. Michael R. Czinkota and Masaaki Kotabe, "Product Development the Japanese Way," in M. Czinkota and M. Kotabe, *Trends in International Business: Critical Perspectives* (Oxford: Blackwell Publishers, 1998), 153–158.

11. Irvine Clarke III, "Global Marketing Research: Is Extreme Response Style Influencing Your Results?" *Journal of International Consumer Marketing*, 12, 4 (2000): 91–111.

12. C. Samuel Craig and Susan P. Douglas, "Conducting international marketing research in the twenty-first century," *International Marketing Review*, 18, (2002):80–90.

13. Janet Ilieva, Steve Baron, and Nigel M. Healey, "On-line surveys in marketing research: Pros and cons," *International Journal of Marketing Research*, 44, 3, (2002): 361–376.

14. David Luna, Laura A. Peracchio, and Maria D. de Juan, "Cross-Cultural and Cognitive Aspects of Web Site Navigation," *Journal of the Academy of Marketing Science*, 30, 4, (2002): 397–410.

15. William D. Neal, "Still got it; Shortcomings plague the industry," *Marketing News*, September 16, 2002, 37.

16. Thomas C. Kinnear and James R. Taylor, *Marketing Research: An Applied Approach*, 5th ed. (New York: McGraw-Hill, 1996).

17. Joseph Marinelli and Anastasia Schleck, "Collecting, Processing Data for Marketing Research Worldwide," *Marketing News* 31, 17 (August 18, 1997): 12, 14.

18. For details on the symposium and additional research information see http://databases.si.umich.edu/reputations, accessed June 25, 2003.

19. David A. Andelman, "Betting on the Net," *Sales and Marketing Management* (June 1995): 47–59.

20. Barry R. Shapiro, "Economic Espionage," *Marketing Management* (spring 1998): 56–58.

21. Peter Clarke, "The Echelon Questions," *Electronic Engineering Times*, March 6, 2000: 36.

22. Andrel Delbecq, Andrew H. Van de Ven, and David H. Gustafson, *Group Techniques for Program Planning* (Glenview, IL: Scott Foresman, 1975), 83.

23. William H. Davidson, "The Role of Global Scanning in Business Planning," *Organizational Dynamics* (Winter 1991): 5–16.

Chapter 11

1. Hartmut Holzmüller and Barbara Stöttinger, "Structural Modeling of Success Factors in Exporting: Cross-Validation and Further Development of an Export Performance Model," *Journal of International Marketing* 4, 2 (1996): 29–55.

2. Brendan J. Gray, "Profiling Managers to Improve Export Promotion Targeting," *Journal of International Business Studies* 28, 2 (1997): 387–420.

3. Taewon Suh, Mueun Bae, and Sumit K. Kundu, "Antecedents to smaller firms' perceived cost and attractiveness in going abroad," in *Enhancing Knowledge Development in Marketing*, (B. Money and R. Rose, eds.) Chicago: American Marketing Association, 2003.

4. S. Tamer Cavusgil, "Preparing for Export Marketing," *International Trade Forum* 2 (1993): 16–30.

5. Masaaki Kotabe, Srini S. Srinivasan, and Preet S. Aulakh, "Multinationality and Firm Performance: The Moderating Role of R&D and Marketing Capabilities," *Journal of International Business Studies*, 33, 1 (2002): 79–97.

6. Michael R. Czinkota, *Export Development Strategies* (New York: Praeger, 1982): 10.

7. Michael Kutschker and Iris Bäuerle, "Three Plus One: Multidimensional Strategy of Internationalization," *Management International Review* 37, 2 (1997): 103–125.

8. Michael Kutschker, Iris Bäuerle, and Stefan Schmid, "International Evolution, International Episodes, and International Epochs—Implications for Managing Internationalization," *Management International Review*, Special Issue 2 (1997): 101–124.

9. Kent Eriksson, Jan Johanson, Anders Majkgard, and D. Deo Sharma, "Experiential Knowledge and Cost in the Internationalization Process," *Journal of International Business Studies* 28, 2 (1997): 337–360.

10. S. Tamer Cavusgil and Shaoming Zou, "Marketing Strategy-Performance Relationship: An Investigation of the Empirical Link in Export Marketing Ventures," *Journal of Marketing* 58, 1 (1994): 1–21.

11. Michael W. Peng, *Business Strategies in Transition Economies* (Thousand Oaks: Sage Publications, 2000): 283–284.

12. Andrew McAuley, "Entrepreneurial Instant Exporters in the Scottish Arts and Crafts Sector," *Journal of International Marketing* 7, 4 (1999): 67–82.

13. Vibha Gaba, Yigang Pan, and Gerardo R. Ungson, "Timing of Entry in International Market: An Empirical Study of U.S. Fortune 500 Firms in China," *Journal of International Business Studies*, 31, 1, 39–55.

14. Masaaki Kotabe and Michael R. Czinkota, "State Government Promotion of Manufacturing Exports: A Gap Analysis," *Journal of International Business Studies* (winter 1992): 637–658.

15. Michael R. Czinkota and Michael L. Ursic, "An Experience Curve Explanation of Export Expansion," in *International Marketing Strategy* (Fort Worth: Dryden Press, 1994): 133–141.

16. Carl Arthur Solberg, "A Framework for Analysis of Strategy Development in Globalizing Markets," *Journal of International Marketing* 5, 1 (1997): 9–30.

17. Michael R. Czinkota, "A National Export Development Policy for New and Growing Businesses," in *Best Practices in International Business* (M. Czinkota and I. Ronkainen, eds.) Cincinnati: South-Western, 2001: 35–45.

18. Van Miller, Tom Becker, and Charles Crespy, "Contrasting Export Strategies: A Discriminant Analysis Study of Excellent Exporters," *The International Trade Journal* 7, 3 (1993): 321–340.

19. O.E. Williamson, *The Economic Institutions of Capitalism*, New York: Free Press, 1985.

20. Michael R. Czinkota and Masaaki Kotabe, "Entering the Japanese Market: A Reassessment of Foreign Firms' Entry and Distribution Strategies," *Industrial Marketing Management*, 29, 2000, 483–491.

21. Rajesh Chakrabarti and Barry Scholnick, "International Expansion of E-Retailers: Where the Amazon Flows," *Thunderbird International Business Review*, 44, 1, (2002): 85–104.

22. Pieter Pauwels and Paul Matthyssens, "A Strategy Process Perspective on Export Withdrawal," *Journal of International Marketing* 7, 4 (1999): 10–37.

23. Birgit Ch. Ensslinger, "Born Globals—Begriff und Bedeutung," in *Die Internationalisierung von kleinen und mittleren Unternehmungen*, (D. Holtbruegge, ed.), Stuttgart: ibidem Verlag, 2003.

24. Oystein Moen and Per Servais, "Born Global or Gradual Global? Examining the Export Behavior of Small and Medium-Sized Firms," *Journal of International Marketing*, 10, 2, (2002): 49–72.

25. Michael W. Peng and Anne Y. Ilinitch, "Export Intermediary Firms: A Note on Export Development Research," *Journal of International Business Studies* 3, 1998: 609–620.

26. Dong-Sung Cho, *The General Trading Company: Concept and Strategy* (Lexington, MA: Lexington Books, 1987): 2.

27. Lee Smith, "Does the World's Biggest Company Have a Future?" *Fortune* (August 7, 1995): 125.

28. Yoshi Tsurumi, *Sogoshosha: Engines of Export-Based Growth* (Montreal: The Institute for Research on Public Policy, 1980).

29. Atilla Dicle and Ulku Dicle, "Effects of Government Export Policies on Turkish Export Trading Companies," *International Marketing Review* 9, 3 (1992): 62–76.

30. Vanessa Bachman, Office of Export Trading Companies, U.S. Department of Commerce, Washington, DC, September 17, 2003.

31. Nancy Lloyd Pfahl, "Using a Partnership Strategy to Establish an International Trade Assistance Program," *Economic Development Review* (Winter 1994): 51–59.

32. Donald W. Hackett, "The International Expansion of U.S. Franchise Systems," in *Multinational Product Management*, ed. Warren J. Keegan and Charles S. Mayer (Chicago: American Marketing Association, 1979): 61–81.

33. Global Franchising Statistics, International Franchise Association, Washington, DC, http://www.franchise.org, accessed September 22, 2003.

34. Nizamettin Aydin and Madhav Kacker, "International Outlook of U.S.-Based Franchisers," *International Marketing Review* 7 (1990): 43–53.

35. Thomas Gross and John Neuman, "Strategic Alliances Vital in Global Marketing," *Marketing News* (June 19, 1989): 1–2. See also http://www.ti.com.

36. Iris Berdrow and Henry W. Lane, "International joint ventures: creating value through successful knowledge management," *Journal of World Business*, 38, 1, (2002): 15–30.

37. "MD-90 Airliner Unveiled by McDonnell Douglas," *The Washington Post*, February 14, 1993, A4.

38. Jordan D. Lewis, *Partnerships for Profit: Structuring and Managing Strategic Alliances* (New York: The Free Press, 1990), 85–87.

39. Joel Bleeke and David Ernst. "Is Your Strategic Alliance Really a Sale?" *Harvard Business Review* 73 (January–February 1995): 97–105.

40. Gary Hamel, Yves L. Doz, and C. K. Prahalad, "Collaborate with Your Competitors—and Win," *Harvard Business Review* 67 (January–February 1989): 133–139.

41. Vern Terpstra and Chwo-Ming J. Yu, "Piggy-backing: A Quick Road to

Internalization," *International Marketing Review* 7, (1990): 52–63.

42. Michael Z. Brooke, *Selling Management Services Contracts in International Business* (London: Holt, Rinehart and Winston, 1985), 7.

43. Richard W. Wright and Colin S. Russel, "Joint Ventures in Developing Countries: Realities and Responses," *Columbia Journal of World Business* 10 (spring 1975): 74–80.

44. Kathryn Rudie Harrigan, "Joint Ventures and Global Strategies," *Columbia Journal of World Business* 19 (summer 1984): 7–16.

45. J. Peter Killing, *Strategies for Joint Venture Success* (New York: Praeger, 1983), 11–12.

46. http://www.eads.com, accessed September 23, 2003.

47. Jeremy Main, "Making Global Alliances Work," *Fortune* (December 17, 1990): 121–126.

48. United Nations, *Guidelines for Foreign Direct Investment* (New York: United Nations, 1975), 65–76.

49. Robert E. Spekman, Lynn A. Isabella, Thomas C. MacAvoy, and Theodore Forbes III, "Creating Strategic Alliances Which Endure," *Long Range Planning* 29, 3, 1996: 346–357.

50. "Airlines Urged to Link with Foreign Carriers," *The Washington Post*, November 2, 1994, F1, F3.

51. Dennis J. Encarnation and Sushil Vachani, "Foreign Ownership: When Hosts Change the Rules," *Harvard Business Review* 63 (September–October 1985): 152–160.

52. Richard H. Holton, "Making International Joint Ventures Work" (Paper presented at the seminar on the Management of Headquarters/ Subsidiary Relationships in Trans-national Corporations, Stockholm School of Economics, June 2–4, 1980), 4.

53. John M. Mezias, "How to identify liabilities of foreignness and assess their effects on multinational corporations," *Journal of International Management*, 8, 3, (2002): 265–282.

54. Shih-Fen S. Chen and Jean-Francois Hennart, "Japanese Investors' choice of joint ventures versus wholly-owned subsidiaries in the US: The role of market barriers and firm capabilities," *Journal of International Business Studies*, 33, 1, (2002): 1–18.

Chapter 12

1. Global Business Policy Council, *Globalization Ledger*, Washington, DC: A.T. Kearney, April 2000, 3; and Jane Fraser and Jeremy Oppenheim, "What's New About Globalization?" *The McKinsey Quarterly* 2 (1997): 168–179.

2. Jonathan Sprague, "China's Manufacturing Beachhead," *Fortune*, October 28, 2002, 1192A–J.

3. The section draws heavily from George S. Yip, *Total Global Strategy II* (Englewood cliffs, NJ: Prentice Hall, 2002), Chapters 1 and 2; Jagdish N. Sheth and Atul Parvatiyar, "The Antecedents and Consequences of Integrated Global Marketing," *International Marketing Review* 18 (Number 1, 2001): 16–29; George S. Yip, "Global Strategy . . . In a World of Nations?" *Sloan Management Review* 31 (fall 1989): 29–41; Susan P. Douglas and C. Samuel Craig, "Evolution of Global Marketing Strategy: Scale, Scope, and Synergy," *Columbia Journal of World Business* 24 (Fall 1989): 47–58; and George S. Yip, Pierre M. Loewe, and Michael Y. Yoshino, "How to Take Your Company to the Global Market," *Columbia, Journal of World Business* 23 (winter 1988): 28–40.

4. Ernst Dichter, "The World Customer," *Harvard Business Review* 40 (July–August 1962): 113–122.

5. Kenichi Ohmae, *The Invisible Continent: Four Strategic Imperatives of the New Economy* (New York: Harper Business, 2001), Chapter 1; Kenichi Ohmae, *The Borderless World: Power and Strategy in the Interlinked Economy* (New York: Harper Business, 1999), Chapter 1; Kenichi Ohmae, *Triad Power—The Coming Shape of Global Competition* (New York: Free Press, 1985), 22–27.

6. Luciano Catoni, Nora Förisdal Larssen, James Nayor, and Andrea Zocchi, "Travel Tips for Retailers," *The McKinsey Quarterly* 38, 3 (2002):88–98.

7. Catherine George and J. Michael Pearson, "Riding the Pharma Roller Coaster," *The McKinsey Quarterly* 38, 4, (2002): 89–98.

8. "Paper Prices Are Driving Flurry of Industry Mergers," *The Wall Street Journal*, May 10, 2000, B4; and "Finnish Paper Concern to Buy Champion," *The Wall Street Journal*, February 18, 2000, A3, A6.

9. Stuart Crainer, "And the New Economy Winner is . . . Europe, *Strategy and Business* 6 (second quarter, 2001): 40–47.

10. Suzy Wetlaufer, "Driving Change: An Interview with Ford Motor Company's Jacques Nasser," *Harvard Business Review* 77 (March–April, 1999): 76–88.

11. "Telecommunications," *The Economist*, April 4, 2002, 102.

12. Gary Knight, "Entrepreneurship and Marketing Strategy: The SME Under Globalization," *Journal of International Marketing* 8, 2 (2002): 12–32.

13. "A Dedicated Enemy of Fashion: Nestle," *The Economist*, August 31, 2002, 51.

14. Jordan D. Lewis, *Trusted Partners: How Companies Build Mutual Trust and Win Together* (New York: The Free Press, 2000): 157.

15. Cait Murphy, "The Hunt for Globalization that Works," *Fortune*, October 28, 2002, 67–72.

16. "3 Big Carmakers to Create Net Site for Buying Parts," *The Washington Post*, February 26, 2000, E1, E8.

17. Myung-Su Chae and John S. Hill, "Determinants and Benefits of Global Strategic Planning Formality," *International Marketing Review* 17, 6 (2000): 538–562.

18. "Computing's New Shape," *The Economist*, November 23, 2002, 11–12.

19. C. Samuel Craig and Susan P. Douglas, "Configural Advantage in Global Markets," *Journal of International Marketing* 8, 1 (2000): 6–26.

20. Michael E. Porter, *Competitive Strategy* (New York: Free press, 1998), ch. 1.

21 "Europe's Car Makers Expect Tidy Profits," *The Wall Street Journal*, January 27, 2000, A16.

22. Lori Ioannou, "It's a Small World After All," *International Business* (February 1994): 82–88.

23. "Nokia Widens Gap With Its Rivals," *The Wall Street Journal*, August 20, 2002, B6.

24. Michael Porter, *Competitive Advantage* (New York: The Free press, 1987), ch. 1.

25. Robert M. Grant, *Contemporary Strategy Analysis: Concepts, Techniques, Applications* (Oxford, England: Blackwell, 2002), chapter 8.

26. George S. Yip, *Total Global Strategy II* (Upper Saddle River, NJ: Prentice-Hall, 2002), chapter 10.

27. The models referred to are GE/McKinsey, Shell International, and A. D. Little portfolio models.

28. Yoram Wind and Susan P. Douglas, "International Portfolio Analysis and Strategy: Challenge of the '80s," *Journal of International Business Studies* 12 (Fall 1981): 69–82.

29. "P&G Puts Nappies to Rest in Australia," *Advertising Age* (September 19, 1994): I-31.

30. "The Fight for Digital Dominance," *The Economist*, November 23, 2002, 61–62.

31. "Will Renault Go for Broke in Asia?" *Business Week*, February 28, 2000, and "Ford, GM Square Off Over Daewoo Motor: The Question is Why?" *The Wall Street Journal*, February 14, 2000, A1, A13.

32. "Tissue Titans Target Globally with Key Brands," *Advertising Age*, December 20, 1999, 4.

33. Richard Tomlinson, "Europe's New Computer Game," *Fortune*, February 21, 2000, 219–224.

34. Saeed Samiee and Kendall Roth, "The Influence of Global Marketing Standardization on Performance," *Journal of Marketing* 56 (April 1992): 1–17.

35. "Euroteen Market Grabs U.S. Attention," *Marketing News*, October 22, 2001, 15.

36. Aruna Chandra and John K. Ryans, "Why India Now?" *Marketing Management*, March/April 2002, 43–45.

37. Imad B. Baalbaki and Naresh K. Malhotra, "Marketing Management Bases for International Market Segmentation: An Alternate Look at the Standardization/Customization Debate," *International Marketing Review* 10, 1 (1993): 19–44.

38. Alonso Martinez, Ivan de Souza, and Francis Liu, "Multinationals vs. Multilatinas: Latin America's Great Race," *Strategy and Business*, Fall 2003, 45–58.

39. "Whirlpool's Platform for Growth," *Financial Times*, March 26, 1998, 8.

40. "Shania Reigns," *Time*, December 9, 2002, 80–85.

41. Larry Greenemeier, "Offshore Outsourcing Grows to Global Proportions," *Information Week*, February 2002, 56–58.

42. "Philips Electronics to Make China One of Three Big Research Centers," *The Wall Street Journal*, December 20, 2002, B4.

43. W. Chan Kim and R. A. Mauborgne, "Becoming an Effective Global Competitor," *Journal of Business Strategy* 8 (January–February 1988): 33–37.

44. Gary Hamel and C. K. Prahalad, "Do You Really Have a Global Strategy?" *Harvard Business Review* 63 (July–August 1985): 75–82.

45. "Nokia Widens Lead in Wireless Market While Motorola, Ericsson Fall Back," *The Wall Street Journal*, February 8, 2000, B8.

46. Andreas F. Grein, C. Samuel Craig, and Hirokazu Takada, "Integration and Responsiveness: Marketing Strategies of Japanese and European Automobile Manufacturers," *Journal of International Marketing* 9, 2 (2001): 19–50.

47. James A. Gingrich, "Five Rules for Winning Emerging Market Consumers," *Strategy and Business* (Second Quarter, 1999): 19–33.

48. "Does Globalization Have Staying Power?" *Marketing Management*, March/April 2002, 18–23.

49. Kamran Kashani, "Beware the Pitfalls of Global Marketing," *Harvard Business Review* 67 (September–October 1989): 91–98.

50. John A. Quelch and Edward J. Hoff, "Customizing Global Marketing," *Harvard Business Review* 64 (May–June 1986): 59–68; Yip, Loewe, and Yoshino, "Take Your Company to the Global Market."

51. George S. Yip and Tammy L. Madsen, "Global Account Management: The New Frontier in Relationship Marketing," *International Marketing Review* 13, 3 (1996): 24–42.

52. David B. Montgomery and George S. Yip, "The Challenge of Global Customer Management," *Marketing Management*, Winter 2000, 22–29.

53. Available at http://www.whirlpoolcorp.com.

54. John A. Quelch and Helen Bloom, "Ten Steps to Global Human Resources Strategy," *Strategy and Business* 4 (first quarter, 1999): 18–29.

55. Sharon O'Donnell and Insik Jeong, "Marketing Standardization within Global Industries," *International Marketing Review* 17, 1 (2000): 19–33.

Chapter 13

1. Lawrence M. Fischer, "Thought Leader," *Strategy and Business*, 7 (Fourth Quarter, 2002): 115–123.

2. Robert J. Flanagan, "Knowledge Management in the Global Organization in the 21st Century," *HR Magazine* 44, 11 (1999): 54–55.

3. Michael Z. Brooke, *International Management: A Review of Strategies and Operations* (London: Hutchinson, 1986); 173–174.

4. Jay R. Galbraith, *Designing the Global Corporation* (New York: Jossey-Bass, 2000), Chapter 3.

5. William H. Davidson and Philippe Haspeslagh, "Shaping a Global Product Organization," *Harvard Business Review* 59 (March/April 1982): 69–76.

6. See http://www.loctite.com/about/global_reach.html.

7. See, for example, Samuel Humes, *Managing the Multinational: Confronting the Global-Local Dilemma* (London: Prentice-Hall, 1993), Chapter 1.

8. Vijay Govindarajan, Anil K. Gupta, and C. K. Prahalad, *The Quest for Global Dominance: Transforming Global Presence into Global Competitive Advantage* (New York: Jossey-Bass, 2001), Chapters 1 and 2.

9. "How Goodyear Sharpened Organization and Production for a Tough World Market," *Business International* (January 16, 1989): 11–14.

10. Michael J. Mol, *Ford Mondeo: A Model T World Car?* (Hershey, PA: Idea Group Publishing, 2001), 1–21.

11. *3M Annual Report 2000*, pp. 1–3, 15; "3M Restructuring for NAFTA," *Business Latin America*, July 19, 1993, 6–7.

12. Philippe Lasserre, "Regional Headquarters: The Spearhead for Asia Pacific Markets," *Long Range Planning* 29 (February, 1996): 30–37, and John D. Daniels, "Bridging

National and Global Marketing Strategies Through Regional Operations," *International Marketing Review* 4 (autumn 1987): 29–44.

13. Daniel Robey, *Designing Organizations: A Macro Perspective* (Homewood, IL: Richard D. Irwin, 1982), 327.

14. Christopher A. Bartlett and Sumantra Ghoshal, *Managing Across Borders* (Cambridge, MA: Harvard Business School Press, 2002), Chapter 10.

15. See http://www.philips.com/

16. Spencer Chin, "Philips Shores Up the Dike," *EBN*, October 14, 2002, 4.

17. Milton Harris and Artur Raviv, "Organization Design," *Management Science*, 48 (July 2002): 852–865.

18. John P. Workman, Jr., Christian Homburg, and Kjell Gruner, "Marketing Organization: Framework of Dimensions and Determinants," *Journal of Marketing* 62 (July, 1998): 21–41; and Chuck U. Farley, "Looking Ahead at the Marketplace: It's Global and It's Changing," Donald R. Lehman and Katherine E. Jocz, eds., *Reflections on the Futures of Marketing* (Cambridge, MA: Marketing Science Institute, 1995), 15–35.

19. William Taylor, "The Logic of Global Business," *Harvard Business Review* 68 (March–April 1990): 91–105.

20. Mohanbir Sawhney, "Don't Homogenize, Synchronize," *Harvard Business Review* 79 (July–August, 2001): 100–108.

21. Ilkka A. Ronkainen, "Thinking Globally, Implementing Successfully," *International Marketing Review* 13, 3 (1996): 4–6.

22. Russell Eisenstat, Nathaniel Foote, Jay Galbraith, and Danny Miller, "Beyond the Business Unit," *The McKinsey Quarterly* 37 (number 1, 2001): 180–195.

23. "Country Managers," *Business Europe*, October 16, 2002, 3; John A. Quelch and Helen Bloom, "The Return of the Country Manager," *International Marketing Review* 13, 3 (1996): 31–43.

24. Rodman Drake and Lee M. Caudill, "Management of the Large Multinational: Trends and Future Challenges," *Business Horizons* 24 (May–June 1981): 83–91.

25. Joe Studwell, *The China Dream* (New York: Atlantic Monthly Press, 2002), 104–105.

26. Göran Svensson, "'Glocalization' of Business Activities: A 'Glocal Strategy' Approach," *Management Decision* 39 (number 1, 2001): 6–13.

27. Christopher A. Bartlett and Sumantra Ghoshal, "Matrix Management: Not a Structure, a Frame of Mind," *Harvard Business Review* 68 (July–August 1990): 138–145.

28. Carlos Ghosn, "Saving the Business Without Losing the Company," *Harvard Business Review* 80 (January 2002): 37–45.

29. "See Jack. See Jack Run Europe," *Fortune*, September 27, 1999, 127–136.

30. Noel Tichy, "The Teachable Point of View: A Primer," *Harvard Business Review* 77 (March–April 1999): 82–83.

31. "GE Mentoring Program Turns Underlings into Teachers of the Web," *The Wall Street Journal*, February 15, 2000, B1, B16.

32. Richard Benson-Armer and Tsun-Yan Hsieh, "Teamwork Across Time and Space," *The McKinsey Quarterly* 33, 4 (1997): 18–27.

33. David A. Griffith and Michael G. Harvey, "An Intercultural Communication Model for use in Global Interorganizational Networks," *Journal of International Marketing* 9 (number 3, 2001): 87–103.

34. "Internet Software Poses Big Threat to Notes, IBM's Stake in Lotus," *The Wall Street Journal*, November 7, 1995, A1–5.

35. Ingo Theuerkauf, David Ernst, and Amir Mahini, "Think Local, Organize. . . ." *International Marketing Review* 13, 3 (1996): 7–12.

36. C.K. Prahalad, "Globalization, Digitization, and the Multinational Enterprise," paper presented at the Annual Meetings of the Academy of International Business, November, 1999.

37. James A. Gingrich, "Five Rules for Winning Emerging Market Consumers," *Strategy & Business* (second quarter, 1999): 19–33.

38. Christopher A. Bartlett and Sumantra Ghoshal, "Tap Your Subsidiaries for Global Reach," *Harvard Business Review* 64 (November–December 1986): 87–94.

39. "The Zen of Nissan," *Business Week*, July 22, 2002, 46–49.

40. Richard I. Kirkland, Jr., "Entering a New World of Boundless Competition," *Fortune* (March 14, 1988): 18–22.

41. Michael D. White, "The Finnish Springboard," *World Trade*, January 1999, 48–49.

42. David A. Aaker and Erich Joachimsthaler, "The Lure of Global Branding," *Harvard Business Review* 77 (November/ December, 1999): 137–144.

43. Julian Birkinshaw and Neil Hood, "Unleash Innovation in Foreign Subsidiaries," *Harvard Business Review* 79 (March 2001): 131–137; and Julian Birkinshaw and Nick Fry, "Subsidiary Initiatives to Develop New Markets," *Sloan Management Review* 39 (Spring 1998): 51–61.

44. Vijay Govindarajan and Robert Newton. *Management Control Systems* (New York: McGraw-Hill/Irwin, 2000), Chapter 1.

45. Anil Gupta and Vijay Govindarajan, "Organizing for Knowledge Within MNCs," *International Business Review* 3 (number 4, 1994): 443–457.

46. William G. Ouchi, "The Relationship Between Organizational Structure and Organizational Control," *Administrative Science Quarterly* 22 (March 1977): 95–112.

47. Laurent Leksell, *Headquarters-Subsidiary Relationships in Multinational Corporations* (Stockholm, Sweden: Stockholm School of Economics, 1981), Chapter 5.

48. Henry P. Conn and George S. Yip, "Global Transfer of Critical Capabilities," *Business Horizons* 38 (January/February 1997): 22–31.

49. Anant R. Negandhi and Martin Welge, *Beyond Theory Z* (Greenwich, CT: JAI Press, 1984), 16.

50. Richard Pascale, "Fitting New Employees into the Company Culture," *Fortune* (May 28, 1984): 28–40.

51. Michael R. Czinkota and Ilkka A. Ronkainen, "International Business and Trade in the Next Decade: Report from a Delphi Study," *Journal of International Business Studies* 28, 4 (1997): 676–694.

52. Tsun-Yuan Hsieh, Johanne La Voie, and Robert A. P. Samek, "Think Global, Hire Local," *The McKinsey Quarterly* 35, 4 (1999): 92–101.

53. R. J. Alsegg, *Control Relationships Between American Corporations and Their European Subsidiaries*, AMA Research Study No. 107 (New York: American Management Association, 1971), 7.

54. Ron Edwards, Adlina Ahmad, and Simon Moss, "Subsidiary Autonomy: The Case of Multinational Subsidiaries in Malaysia," *Journal of International Business Studies* 33 (number 1, 2002): 183–191.

55. John J. Dyment, "Strategies and Management Controls for Global Corporations," *Journal of Business Strategy* 7 (spring 1987): 20–26.

56. Alfred M. Jaeger, "The Transfer of Organizational Culture Overseas: An Approach to Control in the Multinational Corporation," *Journal of International Business Studies* 14 (fall 1983): 91–106.

57. Michael Goold and Andrew Campbell, "Do You Have a Well-Designed Organization?" *Harvard Business Review* 80 (March 2002): 117–124.

Chapter 14

1. "AMA Board Approves New Marketing Definition," *Marketing News* (March 1, 1985): 1.

2. Robert Bartels, "Are Domestic and International Marketing Dissimilar?" *Journal of Marketing* 36 (July 1968): 56–61.

3. Pankaj Ghemawat, "Distance Still Matters: The Hard Reality of Global Expansion," *Harvard Business Review* 79 (September 2001): 137–147.

4. For one of the best summaries, see Country Monitor, *Indicators of Market Size for 117 Countries* (New York: EIU), 2003.

5. Philip Kotler, *Marketing Management: Analysis, Planning and Control* (Upper Saddle River, NJ: Prentice-Hall, 2003), 146.

6. James A. Gingrich, "Five Rules for Winning Emerging Market Consumers," *Strategy and Business* (second quarter, 1999): 68–76.

7. "Coke to Test Coffee in Scandinavia," *Advertising Age*, May 19, 2003, 16.

8. The World Bank, *World Development Indicators* (Washington, DC, 2003), 76.

9. Samuel Craig and Susan P. Douglas, "Conducting Market Research in the Twenty-First Century," *International Marketing Review*, 18, (2001): 80–90.

10. Van R. Wood, John R. Darling, and Mark Siders, "Consumer Desire to Buy and Use Products in International Markets: How to Capture It, How to Sustain It," *International Marketing Review* 16, 3 (1999): 231–242; and J. A. Weber, "Comparing Growth Opportunities in the International Marketplace," *Management International Review* 19 (winter 1979): 47–54.

11. "How the Chevy Name Landed on SUV Using Russian Technology," *The Wall Street Journal*, February 20, 2001, A1, A8.

12. Igal Ayal and Jehiel Zif, "Marketing Expansion Strategies in Multinational Marketing," *Journal of Marketing* 43 (spring 1979): 84–94.

13. "AOL's Big Assault on Latin America Hits Snag in Brazil," *The Wall Street Journal*, July 11, 2000, A1, A16.

14. Michael Rennie, "Born Global," *The McKinsey Quarterly* 4 (1993): 45–52.

15. Carl A. Sohlberg, "The Perennial Issue of Adaptation or Standardization of International Marketing Communication: Organizational Contingencies and Performance," *Journal of International Marketing* 10, 3 (2002): 1–21.

16. "One-Toy-Fits-All: how Industry Learned to Love the Global Kid," *The Wall Street Journal*, April 29, 2003, A1, A12.

17. Jean-Noël Kapferer, *Survey Among 210 European Brand Managers* (Paris: Euro-RSCG, 1998).

18. Davis Goodman, "Thinking Export? Think ISO 9000," *Export Today*, August 1998, 48–49.

19. *ISO Survey, 2002*, available at http://www.iso.ch.

20. "Krispy Kreme: Sweet on Britain," *USA Today*, August 12, 2003, 6A, 7A.

21. Nader Tavssoli and Jin K. Han, "Auditory and Visual Brand Identifiers in Chinese and English," *Journal of International Marketing* 10, 2 (2002): 13–28.

22. Erika Morphy, "Cutting the Cost of Compliance," *Export Today* 12 (January 1996): 14–18.

23. "Holding the Fries—At the Border," *Business Week*, December 14, 1998, 8.

24. Barry Lynn, "Germany: the Packaging Environment," *Export Today* 11 (July, 1995): 58–64.

25. Robert Gray, "Local on a Global Scale," *Marketing*, September 27, 2001, 22–23.

26. Phillip D. White and Edward W. Cundiff, "Assessing the Quality of Industrial Products," *Journal of Marketing* 42 (January 1978): 80–86.

27. Johny K. Johansson, Ilkka A. Ronkainen, and Michael R. Czinkota, "Negative Country-of-Origin Effects: The Case of the New Russia," *Journal of International Studies* 25, 1 (1994): 1–21.

28. Philip Kotler and David Gertner, "Country as Brand, Product, and Beyond: A Place Marketing and Brand Management Pespective," *Journal of Brand Management* 9 (April 2002): 249–261.

29. Ilkka A. Ronkainen, "Product Development in the Multinational Firm," *International Marketing Review* 1 (winter 1983): 24–30.

30. "For Levi's, a Flattering Fit Overseas," *Business Week* (November 5, 1990): 76–77.

31. Erin Strout, "Reinventing a Company," *Sales and Marketing Management* 152 (February 2000): 86–92.

32. International Anti-Counterfeiting Coalition, available at http://www.iacc.org.

33. Michael G. Harvey and Ilkka A. Ronkainen, "International Counterfeiters: Marketing Success Without the Cost or Risk," *Columbia Journal of World Business* 20 (fall 1985): 37–46. For worldwide piracy information, see http://www.iipa.com.

34. Matthew B. Myers and S. Tamer Cavusgil, "Export Pricing Strategy-Performance Relationship: A Conceptual Framework," *Advances in International Marketing* 8 (1996): 159–178.

35. Swee Hoon Ang, Siew Meng Leong, and Philip Kotler, "The Asian Apocalypse: Crisis Marketing for Consumers and Businesses," *Long Range Planning* 33 (February 2000): 97–119.

36. Kent B. Monroe, *Pricing: Making Profitable Decisions* (New York: McGraw-Hill, 2003), 12.

37. Johan Ahlberg, Nicklas Garemo, and Tomas Naucler, "The Euro: How to Keep Your Prices Up and Your Competitors Down," *The McKinsey*

Quarterly, 2 (1999): 112–118; and "Even After Shift to Euro, One Price Won't Fit All," *The Wall Street Journal Europe*, December 28, 1998, 1.

38. Stephen A. Butscher, "Maximizing Profits in Euroland," *Journal of Commerce*, May 5, 1999, 5.

39. Ilkka A. Ronkainen and Linda Van de Gucht, "Making a Case for Gray Markets," *Journal of Commerce*, January 6, 1987, 13A.

40. Victor H. Miesel, Harlow H. Higinbotham, Chun W. Yi, "International Transfer Pricing: Practical Solutions for Intra-Company Pricing," *International Tax Journal* 28 (fall 2002): 1–22.

41. "Multinationals Lose Half of Transfer Price Spats," *The Journal of Commerce* (September 4, 1997): 2A.

42. Mohammad F. Al-Eryani, Pervaiz Alam, and Syed H. Akhter, "Transfer Pricing Determinants of U.S. Multinationals," *Journal of International Business Studies* 21 (fall 1990): 409–425.

43. Gregory L. Miles, "Unmasking Japan's Distributors," *International Business* (April 1994): 38–42.

44. Michael R. Czinkota, "Distribution of Consumer Products in Japan," in *International Marketing Strategy: Environmental Assessment and Entry Strategies*, Michael R. Czinkota and Ilkka A. Ronkainen, eds. (Ft. Worth, TX: The Dryden Press, 1994), 293–307.

45. "American, British Companies Making Most of the Internet," February 28, 2002, http://www.cyberatlas.internet.com.

46. "Shopping for a Marketplace," *Global Business*, February 2001, 36–37.

47. Eryn Brown, "Nine Ways to Win on the Web," *Fortune*, May 24, 1999, 112–125.

48. Hope Katz Gibbs, "Taking Global Local," *Global Business*, December 1999, 44–50.

49. Richard Prem, "Plan Your e-Commerce Tax Strategy," *e-Business Advisor*, April 1999, 36.

50. Erika Morphy, "The Geography of e-Commerce," *Global Business*, November 1999, 26–33.

51. Lou Gerstner, "A Policy of Restraint," *Think Leadership*, March 1999, 1–3.

52. Amy Zuckerman, "Order in the Courts?" *World Trade*, September 2001, 26–28.

53. "Europe Lags Behind U.S. on Web Privacy," *The Wall Street Journal*, February 20, 2001, B11.

54. "Music Piracy Poses a Threat to Regional Artists," *The Wall Street Journal*, June 4, 2002, B10.

55. "Signs of Recovery," *Zenith Optimedia*, December 9, 2002, available at http://www.zenithmedia.com.

56. "Top Global Marketers," *AdAge Global*, http://www.adageglobal.com, accessed September 24, 2003.

57. Compiled from Leo Burnett, *Worldwide Advertising and Media Fact Book* (Chicago: Triumph Books, 1994).

58. "The Internet," *Advertising Age International*, June 1999, 42.

59. "Unilever, Microsoft in European Net Deal," *The Wall Street Journal*, February 2, 2000, B8.

60. Jupiter Media Matrix, Inc. in "International Global Digital Divide Narrowest for Mobile Market, *Marketing News*, July 8, 2002, 19.

61. "U.S. Multinationals," *Advertising Age International*, June 1999, 39.

62. Joseph A. Lawton, "Kodak Penetrates the European Copier Market with Customized Marketing Strategy and Product Changes," *Marketing News* (August 3, 1984): 1, 6; see also http://www.kodak.com.

63. Michael E. Porter and Mark R. Kramer, "The Competitive Advantage of Corporate Philanthropy, *Harvard Business Review* 80 (December 2002): 56–68.

64. "Business Scales World Summit," *The Wall Street Journal*, August 28, 2002, A12, A13.

Chapter 15

1. Leonard L. Berry, "Services Marketing Is Different," in *Services Marketing*, ed. Christopher H. Lovelock (Englewood Cliffs, NJ: Prentice-Hall, 1984), 30.

2. Christian Grönroos, "Marketing Services: The Case of a Missing Product," *Journal of Business & Industrial Marketing*, 13, 4y5 (1998): 322–338.

3. *Winning in the World Market* (Washington, DC: American Business Conference, November 1987), 17.

4. Olivier Furrer, Ben Shaw-Ching Liu, and D. Sudharshan, "The Relationships Between Culture and Service

Quality Perceptions: Basis for Cross-cultural Market Segmentation and Resource Allocation," *Journal of Service Research* 2, 4 (2000): 355–371.

5. Pierre Berthon, Leyland Pitt, Constantine S. Katsikeas, and Jean Paul Berthon, "Virtual Services Go International: International Services in the Marketspace," *Journal of International Marketing* 7, 3 (1999): 84–106.

6. Leonard L. Berry, Kathleen Seiders, and Dhruv Grewal, Understanding Service Convenience, *Journal of Marketing*, 66, July 2002, 1–17.

7. http://www.sitrends.org, accessed July 16, 2003.

8. http://www.cia.gov, accessed July 21, 2003.

9. International Trade Centre web page, http://www.intracen.org/servicexport, February 28, 2001.

10. Allen Sinai and Zaharo Sofianou, "Service Sectors in Developing Countries: Some Exceptions to the Rule," *The Service Economy*, July 1990, 13.

11. Masaaki Kotabe, J. Murray, and R. Javalgi, "Global sources of services and market performance: an empirical investigation," *Journal of International Marketing*, December 1998, ID-31.

12. Cliff Wymbs, "How e-commerce is transforming and internationalizing service industries," *Journal of Services Marketing*, 14, 6, 2000, 463–476.

13. Christian Grönroos, "Internationalization Strategies for Services," *Journal of Services Marketing* 13, 4y5 (1999): 290–297.

14. Terry Clark, Daniel Rajaratnam, and Timothy Smith, "Toward a Theory of International Services: Marketing Intangibles in a World of Nations," *Journal of International Marketing* 4, 2 (1996): 9–28.

15. Masao Yukawa, *The Information Superhighway and Multimedia: Dreams and Realities in Japan*, American Chamber of Commerce in Japan, Tokyo, October 12, 1994.

16. Dorothy Riddle, "Using the Internet for Service Exporting: Tips for Service Firms," *International Trade Forum*, March 1, 1999, 19–23.

17. Rosa Perez-Esteve and Ludger Schuknecht, "A Quantitative Assessment of Electronic Commerce," World Trade

Organization, Staff Working Paper ERAD 99-01, September 1999.

18. Michael R. Czinkota, "Global Giants Slow to Join Net Revolution," *The Journal of Commerce*, November 5, 1999, 9.

19. World Travel and Tourism Council, http://www.wttc.org/measure/PDF/World.pdf.

20. Dorothy I. Riddle, "Gaining Credibility Abroad as a Service Exporter," *International Trade Forum* 1 (1997): 4–7.

21. Paul G. Patterson and Muris Cicic, "A Typology of Service Firms in International Markets: An Empirical Investigation," *Journal of International Marketing* 3, 4 (1995): 57–83.

22. M. Krishna Erramilli and C. P. Rao, "Service Firms' International Entry-Mode Choice: A Modified Transaction-Cost Analysis Approach," *Journal of Marketing* 57 (July 1993): 19–38.

Chapter 16

1. Bernard LaLonde and James Ginter, "Activity-Based Costing: Best Practices," *Paper # 606*, The Supply Chain Management Research Group, The Ohio State University, September 1996.

2. Toshiro Hiromoto, "Another Hidden Edge: Japanese Management Accounting," in *Trends in International Business: Critical Perspectives*, ed. M. Czinkota and M. Kotabe (Oxford: Blackwell Publishers, 1998), 217–222.

3. http://www.pcnolan.com, accessed July 23, 2003.

4. Ling-yee Li and Gabriel O. Ogunmokum, "Effect of Export Financing Resources and Supply-Chain Skills on Export Competitive Advantages: Implications for Superior Export Performance," *Journal of World Business*, 36, 3, (2001): 260–279.

5. Perry A. Trunick, "CLM: Breakthrough of Champions, Council of Logistics Management's 1994 Conference," *Transportation and Distribution* (December 1994).

6. Richard T. Hise, "The Implications of Time-Based Competition on International Logistics Strategies," *Business Horizons* (September/October 1995): 39–45.

7. Charles C. Poirier and Stephen E. Reiter, *Supply Chain Optimization: Building the Strongest Total Business Network* (San Francisco: Berrett-Koehler Publishers, 1996).

8. Michael R. Czinkota, "Global Neighbors, Poor Relations," in *Trends in International Business*, ed. M. Czinkota and M. Kotabe (Oxford: Blackwell, 1998) 20–27.

9. Edward A. Morash and Daniel F. Lynch, "Public Policy and Global Supply Chain Capabilities and Performance: A Resource-Based View," *Journal of International Marketing*, 10, 1, (2002): 25–51.

10. International Chamber of Commerce, "Piracy soars as violence against seafarers intensifies," http://www.iccwbo.org, accessed July 23, 2003.

11. David A. Ricks, *Blunders in International Business*, 3d ed. (Cambridge: Blackwell Publishers, 2000).

12. Michael E. Porter, *The Competitive Advantage of Nations* (New York: The Free Press, 1990).

13. http://www.iata.org, accessed July 22, 2003.

14. Ian Putzger, "Pricing: Based on Volume or Weight?" *The Journal of Commerce* (February 15, 2000): 10.

15. David Hummels, "Time as a Trade Barrier," as cited in: *Logistics Management and Distribution Report*, 41, 2 (February 2002): 22–25.

16. "Survey E-Management," *The Economist* (November 11, 2000): 36.

17. Peter Buxbaum, "Timberland's New Spin on Global Logistics," *Distribution* (May 1994): 32–36.

18. U.S. Department of Commerce, *A Basic Guide to Exporting* (Washington, DC: U.S. Government Printing Office, 1992).

19. Julie Wolf, "Help for Distribution in Europe," *Northeast International Business*, January 1989, 52.

20. *International Trade Procedures* (Philadelphia: CoreStates Bank, 1995), 49.

21. International Chambers of Commerce, *Incoterms 2000* (Paris: ICC Publishing, 2000).

22. "How Exporters Efficiently Penetrate Foreign Markets," *International Business*, December 1993, 48.

23. James R. Stock and Douglas M. Lambert, *Strategic Logistics*

Management, 4th ed. (New York: McGraw-Hill, 2001): 195.

24. Huan Neng Chiu, "The Integrated Logistics Management System: A Framework and Case Study," *International Journal of Physical Distribution and Logistics Management* 6 (1995): 4–22.

25. Bernard LaLonde, Kee-Hian Tan, and Michael Standing, "Forget Supply Chains, Think of Value Flows," *Transformation*, Gemini Consulting, 3 (summer 1994): 24–31.

26. Gregory L. Miles, "Have Spares, Will Travel," *International Business* (December 1994): 26–27.

27. Charles A. Taft, *Management of Physical Distribution and Transportation*, 7th ed. (Homewood, IL: Irwin, 1984): 324.

28. Ricks, *Blunders in International Business*, 2000.

29. Elizabeth Canna, "Russian Supply Chains," *American Shipper* (June 1994): 49–53.

30. Marita von Oldenborgh, "Power Logistics," *International Business* (October 1994): 32–34.

31. Li Rongxia, "Free Trade Zones in China," *Beijing Review* (August 2–8, 1993): 14–21.

32. Kant Rao and Richard R. Young, "Factors Influencing Outsourcing of Logistics Functions," *International Journal of Physical Distribution and Logistics Management* 6 (1994): 11–19.

33. Janjaap Semeijn and David B. Vellenga, "International Logistics and One-Stop Shopping," *International Journal of Physical Distribution and Logistics Management* 10 (1995): 26–44.

34. Christopher Hobley, "Just Numbers," *European Commission's Electronic Commerce Team*, http://europa.eu.int, accessed November 2002.

35. http://www.forrester.com, accessed July 24, 2003.

36. Alexander E. Ellinger, Daniel F. Lynch, James K. Andzulis, and John J. Smith, "B-To-B-Commerce: A content Analytical Assessment of Motor Carrier Websites," *Journal of Business Logistics*, 24, 1, (2003): 199–220.

37. For more detail, see Gary A. Knight, Michael R. Czinkota, and Peter W. Liesch, "Terrorism and the International Firm," Academy of

International Business, Proceedings of the Annual Meeting, Monterey, CA, July 5–8, 2003.

38. Haw-Jan Wu and Steven C. Dunn, "Environmentally Responsible Logistics Systems," *International Journal of Physical Distribution and Logistics Management* 2 (1995): 20–38.

Chapter 17

1. Extremity-stimulus medical appliances are electrically charged sheaths that are fit over the hands, feet, or other extremities of the human subject where increased blood flow and nerve tissue regeneration is desired. This is a fictional product.

2. There are, of course, other traditional decision criteria used in capital budgeting, such as the internal rate of return, modified internal rate of return, payback period, and so forth. For the sake of simplicity, NPV is used throughout the analysis in this chapter. Under most conditions, NPV is also the most consistent criterion for selecting good projects, as well as selecting among projects.

3. A note of particular irony in this case was that the chief currency trader for Allied-Lyons had authored an article in the British trade journal *The Treasurer* only a few months before. The article had described the proper methods and strategies for careful corporate foreign currency risk management. He had concluded with the caution to never confuse "good luck with skillful trading."

4. *Trade Finance*, May 1992, 13.

5. "Current Activities of International Organizations in the Field of Barter and Barter-Like Transactions," *Report of the Secretary General*, United Nations, General Assembly, 1984, 4.

6. Jean-François Hennart and Erin Anderson, "Countertrade and the Minimization of Transaction Costs: An Empirical Examination," *The Journal of Law, Economics, and Organization*, September 2, 1993, 307.

7. Jean-François Hennart, "Some Empirical Dimensions of Countertrade," *Journal of International Business Studies* 21, 2 (Second Quarter, 1990): 243–270.

8. Abla M. Abdel-Latif and Jeffrey B. Nugent, "Countertrade as Trade Creation and Trade Diversion," *Contemporary Economic Policy* 12 (January 1994): 1–10.

9. Jong H. Park, "Is Countertrade Merely a Passing Phenomenon? Some Public Policy Implications," in *Proceedings of the 1988 Conference*, ed. R. King (Charleston, SC: Academy of International Business, Southeast Region, 1988), 67–71.

10. Hennart, "Some Empirical Dimensions of Countertrade."

11. Rolf Mirus and Bernard Yeung, "Why Countertrade? An Economic Perspective," *The International Trade Journal* 7, 4 (1993): 409–433.

12. Paul Samuelson, *Economics*, 11th ed. (New York: McGraw Hill, 1980), 260.

Chapter 18

1. This definition of the corporate objective is based on that supported by the International Corporate Governance Network (ICGN), a nonprofit organization committed to improving global corporate governance practices. Note that this definition of the corporate objective is clearly that of stockholder wealth maximization, defined previously in Chapter 17.

2. "OECD Principles of Corporate Governance," The Organisation for Economic Co-Operation and Development, 1999.

3. For example, in Germany, supervisory board audit committees must include employee representatives. However, according to U.S. law, employees are not independent.

4. This example is borrowed from "International Accounting Diversity and Capital Market Decisions," by Choi and Levich, 1992.

5. This table and the following associated discussion draws heavily on the excellent study of this subject by Philip R. Peller and Frank J. Schwitter of Arthur Andersen & Company, "A Summary of Accounting Principle Differences Around the World," in *The Handbook of International Accounting*, ed. Frederick D.S. Choi, 1992, Chapter 4.

6. Disclosure has continued to be one of the largest sources of frustration between countries. The disclosure requirements of the Securities and Exchange Commission (SEC) in the United States for firms—foreign or domestic—n order to issue publicly traded securities are some of the strictest in the world. Many experts in the field have long been convinced that the depth of U.S. disclosure requirements has prevented many foreign firms from issuing securities in the United States. The SEC's approval of Rule 144A, selective secondary market trading of private placements, is an attempt to alleviate some of the pressure on foreign firms from U.S. disclosure.

7. Frederick D.S. Choi and Gerhard G. Mueller, *International Accounting*, 2d ed. (Englewood Cliffs, NJ: Prentice-Hall, 1992), 262.

8. A. U.S. shareholder is a U.S. person (a citizen or resident of the United States, domestic partnership, domestic corporation, or any nonforeign trust or estate) owning 10 percent or more of the voting power of a controlled foreign corporation. A controlled foreign corporation (CFC) is any foreign corporation in which U.S. shareholders, including corporate parents, own more than 50 percent of the combined voting power or total value. The percentages are calculated on a constructive ownership basis, in which an individual is considered to own shares registered in the name of other family members, members of a trust, or any other related group.

Chapter 19

1. "Of Tactics and Strategy," *Global Business*, March 2000, 64; http://www.arthurandersen.com.

2. Richard D. Hays, "Expatriate Selection: Insuring Success and Avoiding Failure," *Journal of International Business Studies* 5 (summer 1974): 25–37.

3. "India's Technology Whizzes Find Passage to Nokia," *The Wall Street Journal*, August 1, 2000, B1; B12; and "Nokia's Secret Code," *Fortune*, May 1, 2000, 161–174.

4. "Ford's Brave New World," *The Washington Post*, October 16, 1994, H1, H4.

5. Christopher A. Bartlett and Sumantra Ghoshal, "What Is a Global Manager?" *Harvard Business Review* 81 (August 2003): 99–107.

7. "Waking Up Heineken," *Business Week*, September 8, 2003, 68–72; and Jan van Rosmalen, "Internationalising Heineken: Human Resource Policy in a Growing International Company," *International Management Development* (summer 1985): 11–13.

6. John A. Quelch and Helen Bloom, "Ten Steps to a Global Human Resources Strategy," *Strategy and Business* (first quarter, 1999): 18–29.

8. Floris Majlers, "Inside Unilever: The Evolving Transnational Company," *Harvard Business Review* 70 (September–October 1992): 46–52.

9. Vijay Govindarjan and Anil K. Gupta, "Building an Effective Global Business Team," *Sloan Management Review* 42 (summer 2001): 63–72.

10. Randall S. Schuler, Susan E. Jackson, Peter J. Dowling, and Denice E. Welch, "The Formation of an International Joint Venture: Davidson Instrument Panel," in *International Human Resource Management*, ed. Mark Mendenhall and Gary Oddou (Boston: PWS–Kent, 1991), 83–96.

11. "Company & Industry: Ukraine," *Crossborder Monitor* (October 23, 1996): 4; and "Middle Managers In Vietnam," *Business Asia* (May 8, 1995): 3–4.

12. Peter Lorange, "Human Resource Management in Multinational Cooperative Ventures," *Human Resources Management* 25 (winter 1986): 133–148.

13. *2002 Global Relocation Trends Survey Report* (Warren, New Jersey: GMAC Global Relocation Services, 2003); available on http://www.gmacglobalrelocation.com.

14. "People Who Need People," *The Wall Street Journal*, September 25, 2000, R8.

15. "For 'Extreme Telecommuters,' Remote Work Means Really Remote," *The Wall Street Journal*, January 31, 2001, B1, B7.

16. Carla Rapoport, "The Switch Is On in Japan," *Fortune* (May 21, 1990): 144.

17. Anders Edström and Peter Lorange, "Matching Strategy and Human Resources in Multinational Corporations," *Journal of International Business Studies* 16 (fall 1985): 125–137.

18. Elizabeth Klein, "The U.S./Japanese HR Culture Clash," *Personnel Journal* 71 (November 1992): 30–38.

19. Mirjaliisa Charles and Rebecca Marschan-Piekkari, "Language Training for Enhanced Horizontal Communication: A Challenge for MNCs," *Business Communication Quarterly* 65, 2 (2002): 9–30.

20. Rabindra Kanungo and Richard W. Wright, "A Cross-Cultural Comparative Study of Managerial Job Attitudes," *Journal of International Business Studies* 14 (fall 1983): 115–129.

21. David Ahlstrom, Gary Bruton, and Eunice S. Chan, "HRM of Foreign Firms in China: The Challenge of Managing Host Country Personnel," *Business Horizons* 44 (May 2001): 57–62.

22. Lester B. Korn, "How the Next CEO Will Be Different," *Fortune* (May 22, 1990): 157–161.

23. "The Elusive Euromanager," *The Economist* (November 7, 1993): 83.

24. Jean F. Heller, "Criteria for Selecting an International Manager," *Personnel* (May–June 1980): 18–22.

25. Robert Rosen, *Global Literacies: Lessons on Business Leadership and National Cultures* (New York: Simon & Schuster, 2000).

26. Susan Schneider and Rosalie Tung, "Introduction to the International Human Resource Management Special Issue," *Journal of World Business* 36 (winter 2001): 341–346.

27. *Compensating International Executives* (New York: Business International, 1970), 35.

28. Joel Bleeke and David Ernst, *Collaborating to Compete* (New York: John Wiley & Sons, 1993), 179.

29. Lee Smith, "Japan's Autocratic Managers," *Fortune* (January 7, 1985): 14–23.

30. "Expat Spouses: It Takes Two," *Financial Times*, March 1, 2002, 35; and Margaret A. Schaffer and David A. Harrison, "Forgotten Partners of International Assignments: Development and Test of a Model of Spouse Adjustment," *Journal of Applied Psychology* 86, 2 (2001): 238–252.

31. "Have Wife, Will Travel," *The Economist*, December 16, 2000, 70.

32. *Runzheimer Reports on Relocation*, Rochester, WI: Runzheimer International, 1997, at http//www.runzheimer.com.

33. "Global Managing," *The Wall Street Journal Europe*, January 10–11, 1992, 1, 20.

34. Jan Selmer and Alicia Leung, "Provision and Adequacy of Corporate Support to Male Spouses: An Exploratory Study," *Personnel Review* 32, 1 (2003): 9–14.

35. Linda Stroh, Arup Verma, and Stacy Valy-Durbin, "Why Are Women Left at Home: Are They Unwilling to Go on International Assignments?" *Journal of World Business* 35 (fall 2000): 238–245; and Nancy J. Adler, "Expecting International Success: Female Managers Overseas," *Columbia Journal of World Business* 19 (fall 1984): 79–85.

36. J. Stewart Black and Hal B. Gregsen, "The Right Way to Manage Expats," *Harvard Business Review* 77 (March/April 1999): 52–61; and Rosalie Tung, "Selection and Training of Personnel for Overseas Assignments," *Columbia Journal of World Business* 16 (spring 1981): 68–78.

37. Michael G. Harvey, "Dual-Career Expatriates: Expectations, Adjustment and Satisfaction with International Relocation," *Journal of International Business Studies* 28, 3 (1997): 627–658.

38. L. Robert Kohls, *Survival Kit for Overseas Living* (Yarmouth, ME: Intercultural Press, 1979), 62–68.

39. "Polar Opposites," *Global Business*, August 2000, 24.

40. C. Delia Contreras and Fabio Bravo, "Should You Accept an International Assignment?" *Chemical Engineering Progress* (August 2003): 67–76.

41. Michael G. Harvey, "A Survey of Corporate Programs for Managing Terrorist Threats," *Journal of International Business Studies* 24, 3 (1993): 465–478.

42. Mary Helen Frederick, "Keeping Safe," *International Business* (October 1992): 68–69.

43. "There's No Place Like Home," *Business Week* (October 9, 2001): 35.

44. Nancy Mueller, *Work Worldwide: International Career Strategies for the Adventurous Job Seeker* (Berkeley, CA: John Muir Publications, 2000), chapter 5.

45. Michael G. Harvey, "The Other Side of Foreign Assignments: Dealing

with the Repatriation Dilemma," *Columbia Journal of World Business* 16 (spring 1981): 79–85.

46. Raymond J. Stone, "Compensation: Pay and Perks for Overseas Executives," *Personnel Journal* (January 1986): 64–69.

47. Karen E. Thuemer, "Asia Adds Up," *Global Business* (June 2000): 51–55.

48. U.S. Department of State, *Indexes of Living Costs Abroad, Quarters Allowances, and Hardship Differentials*, January 2003, Table 3.

49. Courtesy of Thomas B. Cooke, Esq.

50. "Mexico Is Perk Paradise for U.S. Middle Managers," *The Wall Street Journal*, May 23, 2000, B1, B18.

51. "The Winds of Change Blow Everywhere," *Business Week* (October 17, 1994): 87–88; and "School Days at Work: Firms See Training as Key to Empowerment," *Crossborder Monitor* (August 3, 1994): 1, 7.

52. Industrial Democracy in Europe International Research Group, *Industrial Democracy in Europe* (Oxford, England: Clarendon Press, 1981), chapter 14; and Industrial Democracy in Europe International Research Group, *Industrial Democracy in Europe Revisited* (Oxford, England: Oxford University Press, 1993), chapter 3.

53. Erna Szabo, Felix C. Brodbeck, Deanne N. Den Hartog, and Gerhard Reber, "The Germanic Europe Cluster: Where Employees Have a Voice," *Journal of World Business* 37 (spring 2002): 55–67.

54. John Addison, "Non-Union Representation in Germany," *Journal of Labor Research* 20 (winter 1999): 73–91.

55. "EU Works Councils Get Underway," *Crossborder Monitor* (October 16, 1996): 4.

56. "Labour Disputes," *The Economist*, April 22, 2000, 96.

57. "MNCs Under Fire to Link Trade with Global Labor Rights," *Crossborder Monitor* (May 25, 1994): 1.

58. "Labor Strife in Indonesia Spotlights Development Challenge," *Crossborder Monitor* (May 25, 1994): 7.

59. "Firms Rethink Hostility to Linking Trade, Labor Rights," *The Wall Street Journal*, February 2, 2001, A12.

60. Herman Gadon, "Making Sense of Quality of Work Life Programs," *Business Horizons* 27 (January–February 1984): 42–46.

61. "Jeans Therapy," *The Wall Street Journal*, May 20, 1998, A1, A7.

62. "Hour by Hour," *Global Business* (November 2000): 25.

63. S. B. Prasad and Y. Kirshna Shetty, *An Introduction to Multinational Management* (Englewood Cliffs, NJ: Prentice-Hall, 1976), Appendix 8-A.

64. Jay Mazur, "Labor's New Internationalism," *Foreign Affairs* (January/February 2000): 79–93.

65. "Cooperation Worth Copying?" *The Washington Post*, December 13, 1992, H1, H6.

66. "Detroit Meets a 'Worker Paradise'," *The Wall Street Journal*, March 3, 1999, B1; B4.

Chapter 20

1. William Lazer and Eric H. Shaw, "Global Marketing Management: At the Dawn of the New Millennium," *Journal of International Marketing*, 8, 1, (2000): 65–77.

2. The information presented here is based largely on an original Delphi study by Michael R. Czinkota and Ilkka A. Ronkainen utilizing an international panel of experts.

3. Mike Moore, "Preparations for the Fourth WTO Ministerial Conference," Paris, October 9, 2001, http://www.wto.org.

4. "Business and Political Leaders Discuss Digital Divide," *World Economic Forum*, Davos, http://www.wforum.org, February 2, 2001.

5. "The Corporation and the Public: Open for Inspection," *World Economic Forum*, January 27, 2001, http://www.wforum.org, February 2, 2001.

6. John Pomfret, "Chinese Industry Races to Make Global Name for Itself," *The Washington Post*, April 23, 2000, H1.

7. Catherine L. Mann, "Is the U.S. Trade Deficit Still Sustainable," *Institute for International Economics*, Washington, DC, March 1, 2001.

8. "U.S. International Transactions; 2nd quarter 2003," http://www.bea.gov, September 15, 2003.

9. UN Population Division, World Urbanized Prospects, http://www.un.org/esa/population, accessed December 10, 2002.

10. John Lancaster, "The Desperate Bachelors," *The Washington Post*, December 2, 2002, A1, A17.

11. http://www.nua.ie, accessed October 2, 2002.

12. Ibid.

13. John Ouelch, "Global Village People," *Worldlink Magazine*, January/February 1999, http://www.worldlink.co.uk.

14. Renato Ruggiero, "The New Frontier," *WorldLink*, January/February 1998, http://www.worldlink.co.uk.

15. Minoru Makihara, Co-Chairman of the Annual Meeting of the World Economic Forum, Davos 2001, www.wforum.org.

16. Polly Campbell, "Trend Watch 2001," *The Edward Lowe Report*, January 2001, 1–3.

17. Michael R. Czinkota, "The Policy Gap in International Marketing," *Journal of International Marketing*, 8, 1 (2000): 99–111.

18. Labour Force Statistics, 1976–2000, Paris, OECD, 2001.

19. Michael R. Czinkota, "Rich Neighbors, Poor Relations," *Marketing Management* (spring 1994): 46–52.

20. Michael R. Czinkota, Ilkka A. Ronkainen, and Bob Donath, Mastering Global Markets: Strategies for Today's Trade Globalist, Mason, OH: Thomson, South-Western, 2004.

21. Michael R. Czinkota and Masaaki Kotabe, "The Role of Japanese Distribution Strategies," *Japanese Distribution Strategy*, M.R. Czinkota and M. Kotabe, eds. (London: Business Press, 2000): 6–16.

22. Howard Lewis III and David Richardson, *Why Global Commitment Really Matters*, Washington, DC, Institute for International Economics, 2001.

23. "The Corporation and the Public: Open for Inspection," World Economic Forum, http://www.weforum.org, February 2, 2001.

24. Benn R. Konsynski and Jahangir Karimi, "On the Design of Global Information Systems," in *Globalization, Technology, and Competition: The Fusion of Computers and Telecommunications in the 1990s*, ed. S. Bradley, J. Hausman, and R. Nolan (Boston: 1993): 81–108.

25. Michael R. Czinkota and Masaaki Kotabe, *Marketing Management* 2d ed., (Cincinnati: South-Western College Publishing, 2001), 234–235.

26. Corporate Facts, http://www.QVC.com, accessed October 2, 2003.

27. Gary Hart and Warren B. Rudman, (Stephen E. Flynn, Project Director) *America Still Unprepared—America Still in Danger*, New York, Council on Foreign Relations, December 6, 2002.

28. Institute of International Education, *Open Doors*, Internet Document, http://www.iie.org, accessed October 2, 2003.

29. Michael G. Harvey, "Repatriation of Corporate Executives: An Empirical Study," *Journal of International Business Studies* 20 (spring 1989): 131–144.

30. Joann S. Lublin, "To Smooth a Transfer Abroad, a New Focus on Kids," *The Wall Street Journal*, January 26, 1999: B1, B14.

31. Nancy J. Adler, "Women in International Management: Where are They?" *California Management Review* 26, 4 (1984): 78–89.

32. "U.S. Woman in Global Business Face Glass Borders," *Catalyst Perspective*, November 2000, http://www.catalystwomen.org.

Glossary

A

abandoned product ranges The outcome of a firm narrowing its range of products to obtain economies of scale, which provides opportunities for other firms to enter the markets for the abandoned products.

absolute advantage The ability to produce a good or service more efficiently than it can be produced elsewhere.

accounting diversity The range of differences in national accounting practices.

acculturation The process of adjusting and adapting to a specific culture other than one's own.

adaptability screening A selection procedure that usually involves interviewing both the candidate for an overseas assignment and his or her family members to determine how well they are likely to adapt to another culture.

agent A representative or intermediary for the firm that works to develop business and sales strategies and that develops contacts.

airfreight Transport of goods by air; accounts for less than one percent of the total volume of international shipments, but more than 20 percent of value.

allocation mentality The tradition of acquiring resources based not on what is needed but on what the plan makes available.

American terms Quoting a currency rate as the U.S. dollar against a country's currency (e.g., U.S. dollars/yen).

analogy A method for estimating market potential from similar products when data for the specific products do not exist.

antidumping Laws that many countries use to impose tariffs on foreign imports. They are designed to help domestic industries that are injured by competition from abroad due to imported products being sold at low prices.

antitrust laws Laws that prohibit monopolies, restraint of trade, and conspiracies to inhibit competition.

arbitration The procedure for settling a dispute in which an objective third party hears both sides and makes a decision; a procedure for resolving conflict in the international business arena through the use of intermediaries such as representatives of chambers of commerce, trade associations, or third-country institutions.

area expertise A knowledge of the basic systems in a particular region or market.

area structure An organizational structure in which geographic divisions are responsible for all manufacturing and marketing in their respective areas.

area studies Training programs that provide factual preparation prior to an overseas assignment.

arm's length price A price that unrelated parties would have reached.

autarky Self-sufficiency: a country that is not participating in international trade.

average cost method An accounting principle by which the value of inventory is estimated as the average cost of the items in inventory.

B

backtranslation The retranslation of text to the original language by a different person than the one who made the first translation.

backward innovation The development of a drastically simplified version of a product.

balance of payments (BOP) A statement of all transactions between one country and the rest of the world during a given period; a record of flows of goods, services, and investments across borders.

bank draft A financial document drawn against a bank.

barter A direct exchange of goods of approximately equal value, with no money involved.

base salary Salary not including special payments such as allowances paid during overseas assignments.

bearer bond A bond owned officially by whoever is holding it.

bilateral negotiations Negotiations carried out between two nations focusing only on their interests.

bill of lading A contract between an exporter and a carrier indicating that the carrier has accepted responsibility for the goods and will provide transportation in return for payment.

black hole The situation that arises when an international marketer has a low-competence subsidiary—or none at all—in a highly strategic market.

boycott An organized effort to refrain from conducting business with a particular country of origin or seller of goods or services; used in the international arena for political or economic reasons.

brain drain A migration of professional people from one country to another, usually for the purpose of improving their incomes or living conditions.

Bretton Woods Agreement An agreement reached in 1944 among finance ministers of 45 Western nations to establish a system of fixed exchange rates.

bribery The use of payments or favors to obtain some right or benefit to which the briber has no legal right; a criminal offense in the United States but a way of life in many countries.

Buddhism A religion that extends through Asia from Sri Lanka to Japan and has 334 million followers, emphasizing spiritual attainment rather than worldly goods.

buffer stock Stock of a commodity kept on hand to prevent a shortage in times of unexpected demand; under international commodity and price agreements, the stock controlled by an elected or appointed manager for the purpose of managing the price of the commodity.

bulk service Ocean shipping provided on contract either for individual voyages or for prolonged periods of time.

buy-back A refinement of simple barter with one party supplying technology or equipment that enables the other party to produce goods, which are then used to pay for the technology or equipment that was supplied.

C

capital account An account in the BOP statement that records transactions involving borrowing, lending, and investing across borders.

capital budget The financial evaluation of a proposed investment to determine whether the expected returns are sufficient to justify the investment expenses.

capital flight The flow of private funds abroad because investors believe that the return on investment or the safety of capital is not sufficiently ensured in their own countries.

Caribbean Basin Initiative (CBI) Extended trade preferences to Caribbean countries granting them special access to the markets of the United States.

carriage and insurance paid to (CIP) The price quoted by an exporter for shipments not involving waterway transport, including insurance.

carriage paid to (CPT) The price quoted by an exporter for shipments not involving waterway transport, not including insurance.

cartel An association of producers of a particular good, consisting either of private firms or of nations, formed for the purpose of suppressing the market forces affecting prices.

cash pooling Used by multinational firms to centralize individual units' cash flows, resulting in less spending or foregone interest unnecessary cash balances.

center of excellence The location of product development outside the home country because of an advantage of skills.

central plan The economic plan for the nation devised by the government of a socialist state; often a five-year plan that stipulated the quantities of goods to be produced.

centralization The concentrating of control and strategic decision making at headquarters.

change agent A person or institution who facilitates change in a firm or in a country.

channel design The length and width of the distribution channel.

Christianity The largest organized world religion with 1.8 billion followers; Protestantism encourages work and accumulation of wealth.

code law Law based on a comprehensive set of written statutes.

codetermination A management approach in which employees are represented on supervisory boards to facilitate communication and collaboration between management and labor.

commercial invoice A bill for transported goods that describes the merchandise and its total cost and lists the addresses of the shipper and seller and delivery and payment terms.

Commercial Service A department of the U.S. Department of Commerce that gathers information and assists U.S. business executives in conducting business abroad.

Committee on Foreign Investments in the United States (CFIUS) A federal committee, chaired by the U.S. Treasury, with the responsibility to review major foreign investments to determine whether national security or related concerns are at stake.

commodity price agreement An agreement involving both buyers and sellers to manage the price of a particular commodity, but often only when the price moves outside a predetermined range.

common agricultural policy (CAP) An integrated system of subsidies and rebates applied to agricultural interests in the European Union.

common law Law based on tradition and depending less on written statutes and codes than on precedent and custom—used in the United States.

common market A group of countries that agree to remove all barriers to trade among members, to establish a common trade policy with respect to nonmembers, and also to allow mobility for factors of production—labor, capital, and technology.

communication services Services that are provided in the areas of videotext, home banking, and home shopping, among others.

comparative advantage The ability to produce a good or service more cheaply, relative to other goods and services, than is possible in other countries.

competitive advantage The ability to produce a good or service more cheaply than other countries due to favorable factor conditions and demand conditions, strong related and supporting industries, and favorable firm strategy, structure, and rivalry conditions.

competitive assessment A research process that consists of matching markets to corporate strengths and providing an analysis of the best potential for specific offerings.

composition of trade   The ratio of primary commodities to manufactured goods in a country's trade.

concentration strategy   The market expansion policy that involves concentrating on a small number of markets.

confiscation   The forceful government seizure of a company without compensation for the assets seized.

Confucianism   A code of conduct with 150 million followers throughout Asia, stressing loyalty and relationships.

consulting services   Services that are provided in the areas of management expertise on such issues as transportation, logistics, and politics.

container ships   Ships designed to carry standardized containers, which greatly facilitate loading and unloading as well as intermodal transfers.

contract manufacturing   Outsourcing the actual production of goods so that the corporation can focus on research, development, and marketing.

contractual hedging   A multinational firm's use of contracts to minimize its transaction exposure.

contributor   A national subsidiary with a distinctive competence, such as product development.

control   Refers to legal restraints on what a foreign investor may own or control in another country.

coordinated decentralization   Direction of overall corporate strategy by headquarters while granting subsidiaries the freedom to implement strategy within established ranges.

coordinated intervention   A currency value management method whereby the central banks of the major nations simultaneously intervene in the currency markets, hoping to change a currency's value.

corporate governance   The relationship among stakeholders used to determine and control the strategic direction and performance of an organization.

corporate income tax   A tax applied to all residual earnings, regardless of what is retained or what is distributed as dividends.

corruption   Payments or favors made to officials in return for services.

correspondent banks   Banks located in different countries and unrelated by ownership that have a reciprocal agreement to provide services to each other's customers.

cost and freight (CFR)   Seller quotes a price for the goods, including the cost of transportation to the named port of debarkation. Cost and choice of insurance are left to the buyer.

cost, insurance, and freight (CIF)   Seller quotes a price including insurance, all transportation, and miscellaneous charges to the point of debarkation from the vessel or aircraft.

cost leadership   A pricing tactic where a company offers an identical product or service at a lower cost than the competition.

cost of communication   The cost of communicating electronically or by telephone with other locations. These costs have been drastically reduced through the use of fiberoptic cables.

cost of living allowance (COLA)   An allowance paid during assignment overseas to enable the employee to maintain the same standard of living as at home.

cost-plus method   A pricing policy in which there is a full allocation of foreign and domestic costs to the product.

counterpurchase   A refinement of simple barter that unlinks the timing of the two transactions, but still matches the value.

coups d'état   A forced change in a country's government, often resulting in attacks of foreign firms and policy changes by the new government.

critical commodities list   Governmental information about products that are either particularly sensitive to national security or controlled for other purposes.

cross-marketing activities   A reciprocal arrangement whereby each partner provides the other access to its markets for a product.

cross rates   Exchange rate quotations which do not include the U.S. dollar as one of the two currencies quoted.

cross-subsidization   The use of resources accumulated in one part of the world to fight a competitive battle in another.

cultural assimilator   A program in which trainees for overseas assignments must respond to scenarios of specific situations in a particular country.

cultural convergence   Increasing similarity among cultures accelerated by technological advances.

cultural risk   The risk of business blunders, poor customer relations, and wasted negotiations that results when firms fail to understand and adapt to the differences between their own and host countries' cultures.

cultural universals   Similarities in the total way of life of any group of people.

culture shock   Reactions to the psychological disorientation that most people feel when they move for an extended period of time in to a markedly different culture.

cumulative transaction adjustment (CTA)   The equity account entry on the consolidated balance sheet of multinational companies that is created to account for the translation of the foreign currency denominated balance sheets of foreign subsidiaries. Its value related to any individual foreign subsidiary only impacts the consolidated income of the company upon sale or liquidation of the subsidiary itself.

currency flows The movement of currency from nation to nation, which in turn determine exchange rates.

current account An account in the BOP statement that records the results of transactions involving merchandise, services, and unilateral transfers between countries.

current transfer A current account on the Balance of Payments statement that records gifts from the residents of one country to the residents of another.

customer involvement Active participation of customers in the provision of services they consume.

customer service A total corporate effort aimed at customer satisfaction; customer service levels in terms of responsiveness that inventory policies permit for a given situation.

customer structure An organizational structure in which divisions are formed on the basis of customer groups.

customs union Collaboration among trading countries in which members dismantle trade barriers among members and also establish a common trade policy with respect to nonmembers.

D

data privacy Electronic information security that restricts secondary use of data according to laws and preferences of the subjects.

decentralization The granting of a high degree of autonomy to subsidiaries.

deemed exports Addresses people rather than products where knowledge transfer could lead to a breach of export restrictions.

delivered duty paid (DDP) Seller delivers the goods, with import duties paid, including inland transportation from import point to the buyer's premises.

delivered duty unpaid (DDU) Only the destination customs duty and taxes are paid by the consignee.

Delphi studies A research tool using a group of experts to rank major future developments.

density Weight-to-volume ratio; often used to determine shipping rates.

deregulation Removal of government interference.

differentiation Takes advantage of the company's real or perceived uniqueness on elements such as design or after-sales service.

direct intervention The process governments used in the 1970s if they wished to alter the current value of their currency. It was done by simply buying or selling their own currency in the market using their reserves of other major currencies.

direct investment account An account in the BOP statement that records investments with an expected maturity of more than one year and an investor's ownership position of at least 10 percent.

direct involvement Participation by a firm in international business in which the firm works with foreign customers or markets to establish a relationship.

direct quotation A foreign exchange quotation that specifies the amount of home country currency needed to purchase one unit of foreign currency.

direct taxes Taxes applied directly to income.

discriminatory regulations Regulations that impose larger operating costs on foreign service providers than on local competitors, that provide subsidies to local firms only, or that deny competitive opportunities to foreign suppliers.

distributed earnings The proportion of a firm's net income after taxes which is paid out or distributed to the stockholders of the firm.

distributor A representative or intermediary for the firm that purchases products from the firm, takes title, and assumes the selling risk.

diversification A market expansion policy characterized by growth in a relatively large number of markets or market segments.

division of labor The premise of modern industrial production where each stage in the production of a good is performed by one individual separately, rather than one individual being responsible for the entire production of the good.

domestication Government demand for partial transfer of ownership and management responsibility from a foreign company to local entities, with or without compensation.

double-entry bookkeeping Accounting methodology where each transaction gives rise to both a debit and a credit of the same currency amount. It is used in the construction of the Balance of Payments.

dual pricing Price-setting strategy in which the export price and domestic price are differentiated.

dual use items Goods and services that are useful for both military and civilian purposes.

dumping Selling goods overseas at a price lower than in the exporter's home market, or at a price below the cost of production, or both.

E

eclectic Representing a collection of forces or drivers.

e-commerce The ability to offer goods and services over the Web.

economic and monetary union (EMU) The ideal among European leaders that economic integration should move beyond the four freedoms; specifically, it entails (1) closer coordination of economic policies to promote exchange rate stability and convergence of inflation rates and growth rates, (2) creation of a European central bank, and (3) replacement of national monetary authorities by the European Central Bank and adoption of the euro as the European currency.

economic exposure The potential change in the value of a firm from unexpected changes in exchange rates. Also called "operating exposure" and "strategic exposure."

economic infrastructure The transportation, energy, and communication systems in a country.

economic security Perception of a business activity as having an effect on a country's financial resources, often used to restrict competition from firms outside the country.

economic union A union among trading countries that has the characteristics of a common market and also harmonizes monetary policies, taxation, and government spending and uses a common currency.

economies of scale Production economies made possible by the output of larger quantities.

education allowance Reimbursement by company for dependent educational expenses incurred while a parent is assigned overseas.

effective tax rate Actual total tax burden after including all applicable tax liabilities and credits.

embargo A governmental action, usually prohibiting trade entirely, for a decidedly adversarial or political rather than economic purpose.

engineering services Services that are provided in the areas of construction, design, and engineering.

environmental protection Actions taken by governments to protect the environment and resources of a country.

environmental scanning Obtaining ongoing data about a country.

ethnocentric Tending to regard one's own culture as superior; tending to be home-market oriented.

ethnocentrism The regarding of one's own culture as superior to others'.

euro A single currency used by the European Union that replaced all the individual currencies of the participating member states.

Eurobond A bond that is denominated in a currency other than the currency of the country in which the bond is sold.

Eurocurrency A bank deposit in a currency other than the currency of the country where the bank is located; not confined to banks in Europe.

Eurodollars U.S. dollars deposited in banks outside the United States; not confined to banks in Europe.

Euromarkets Money and capital markets in which transactions are denominated in a currency other than that of the place of the transaction; not confined to Europe.

European Monetary System (EMS) An organization formed in 1979 by eight EC members committed to maintaining the values of their currencies within a 2 1/4 percent of each other's.

European terms Quoting a currency rate as a country's currency against the U.S. dollar (e.g., yen/U.S. dollars).

European Union An economic union between 15 leading European countries.

exchange controls Controls on the movement of capital in and out of a country, sometimes imposed when the country faces a shortage of foreign currency.

expatriate One living in a foreign land; a corporate manager assigned to a location abroad.

experiential knowledge Knowledge acquired through involvement (as opposed to information, which is obtained through communication, research, and education).

experimentation A research tool to determine the effects of a variable on an operation.

export complaint systems Allow customers to contact the original supplier of a product in order to inquire about products, make suggestions, or present complaints.

export-control system A system designed to deny or at least delay the acquisition of strategically important goods to adversaries; in the United States, based on the Export Administration Act and the Munitions Control Act.

export license A license provided by the goverment which permits the export of sensitive goods or services.

export management companies (EMCs) Domestic firms that specialize in performing international business services as commission representatives or as distributors.

export trading company (ETC) The result of 1982 legislation to improve the export performance of small and medium-sized firms, the export trading company allows businesses to band together to export or offer export services. Additionally, the law permits bank participation in trading companies and relaxes antitrust provisions.

expropriation The government takeover of a company with compensation frequently at a level lower than the investment value of the company's assets.

external economies of scale Lower production costs resulting from the free mobility of factors of production in a common market.

extraterritoriality An exemption from rules and regulations of one country that may challenge the national sovereignty of another. The application of one country's rules and regulations abroad.

ex-works (EXW) Price quotes that apply only at the point of origin; the seller agrees to place the goods at the disposal of the buyer at the specified place on a date or within a fixed period.

F

factor intensities The proportion of capital input to labor input used in the production of a good.

factor mobility The ability to freely move factors of production across borders, as among common market countries.

factor proportions theory Systematic explanation of the source of comparative advantage.

factors of production All inputs into the production process, including capital, labor, land, and technology.

factual cultural knowledge Knowledge obtainable from specific country studies published by governments, private companies, and universities and also available in the form of background information from facilitating agencies such as banks, advertising agencies, and transportation companies.

field experience Experience acquired in actual rather than laboratory settings; training that exposes a corporate manager to a different cultural environment for a limited amount of time.

FIFO Method of valuation of inventories for accounting purposes, meaning First-In-First-Out. The principle rests on the assumption that costs should be charged against revenue in the order in which they occur.

financial incentives Monetary offers intended to motivate; special funding designed to attract foreign direct investors that may take the form of land or building, loans, or loan guarantees.

financial infrastructure Facilitating financial agencies in a country; for example, banks.

financing cash flows The cash flows of a firm related to the funding of its operations; debt and equity related cash flows.

fiscal incentives Incentives used to attract foreign direct investment that provide specific tax measures to attract the investor.

fixed exchange rate The government of a country officially declares that its currency is convertible into a fixed amount of some other currency.

flextime A modification of work scheduling that allows workers to determine their own starting and ending times within a broad range of available hours.

floating exchange rate Under this system, the government possesses no responsibility to declare that its currency is convertible into a fixed amount of some other currency; this diminishes the role of official reserves.

focus group A research technique in which representatives of a proposed target audience contribute to market research by participating in an unstructured discussion.

foreign availability The degree to which products similar to those of a firm can be obtained in markets outside the firm's home country. Crucial to export determination.

foreign bond Bonds issued in national capital markets by borrowers (private companies or sovereign states) from other countries.

Foreign Corrupt Practices Act A 1977 law making it a crime for U.S. executives of publicly traded firms to bribe a foreign official in order to obtain business.

foreign currency exchange rate The price of one country's currency in terms of another country's currency.

foreign direct investment The establishment or expansion of operations of a firm in a foreign country. Like all investments, it assumes a transfer of capital.

foreign market opportunity analysis Broad-based research to obtain information about the general variables of a target market outside a firm's home country.

foreign policy The area of public policy concerned with relationships with other countries.

foreign service premium A financial incentive to accept an assignment overseas, usually paid as a percentage of the base salary.

foreign tax credit Credit applied to home-country tax payments due for taxes paid abroad.

foreign trade zones Special areas where foreign goods may be held or processed without incurring duties and taxes.

Fortress Europe Concern that the integration of the European Union may result in increased restrictions on trade and investment by outsiders.

forward contracts Agreements between firms and banks which permit the firm to either sell or buy a specific foreign currency at a future date at a known price.

forward pricing Setting the price of a product based on its anticipated demand before it has been introduced to the market.

forward rates Contracts that provide for two parties to exchange currencies on a future date at an agreed-upon exchange rate.

franchising A form of licensing that allows a distributor or retailer exclusive rights to sell a product or service in a specified area.

free alongside ship (FAS) Exporter quotes a price for the goods, including charges for delivery of the goods alongside a vessel at a port. Seller handles cost of unloading and wharfage; loading, ocean transportation, and insurance are left to the buyer.

free carrier (FCA) Applies only at a designated inland shipping point. Seller is responsible for loading goods into the means of transportation; buyer is responsible for all subsequent expenses.

free on board (FOB) Applies only to vessel shipments. Seller quotes a price covering all expenses up to and including delivery of goods on an overseas vessel provided by or for the buyer.

free trade area An area in which all barriers to trade among member countries are removed, although sometimes only for certain goods or services.

Free Trade Area of the Americas (FTAA)   A hemispheric trade zone covering all of the Americas. Organizers hope for it to be operational by 2005.

freight forwarders   Specialists in handling international transportation by contracting with carriers on behalf of shippers.

functional structure   An organizational structure in which departments are formed on the basis of functional areas such as production, marketing, and finance.

G

gap analysis   Analysis of the difference between market potential and actual sales.

General Agreement on Tariffs and Trade (GATT)   An international code of tariffs and trade rules signed by 23 nations in 1947; headquartered in Geneva, Switzerland; now part of the World Trade Organization with 148 members.

General Agreement on Trade in Services (GATS)   A legally enforceable pact among WTO participants that covers trade and investments in the services sector.

glasnost   The Soviet policy of encouraging the free exchange of ideas and discussion of problems, pluralistic participation in decision making, and increased availability of information.

global account management   Global customers of a company may be provided with a single point of contact for domestic and international operations and consistent worldwide service.

glocalization   A term coined to describe the networked global organization approach to an organizational structure.

gold standard   A standard for international currencies in which currency values were stated in terms of gold.

goods trade   An account of the BOP statement that records funds used for merchandise imports and funds obtained from merchandise exports.

government regulation   Interference in the marketplace by governments.

gray market   Marketing of products through unauthorized channels.

H

hardship allowance   A premium paid during an assignment to an overseas area that requires major adaptation.

hedge   To counterbalance a present sale or purchase with a sale or purchase for future delivery as a way to minimize loss due to price fluctuations; to make counterbalancing sales or purchases in the international market as protection against adverse movements in the exchange rate.

high-context cultures   Cultures in which behavioral and environmental nuances are an important means of conveying information.

Hinduism   With 750 million followers, a way of life rather than a religion, with economic and other attainment dictated by the caste into which its followers are born.

housing allowance   A premium paid during assignment overseas to provide living quarters.

I

implementor   The typical subsidiary role, which involves implementing strategy that originates with headquarters.

import substitution   A policy for economic growth adopted by many developing countries that involves the systematic encouragement of domestic production of goods formerly imported.

income elasticity of demand   A means of describing change in demand in relative response to a change in income.

incoterms   International Commerce Terms. Widely accepted terms used in quoting export prices.

indirect involvement   Participation by a firm in international business through an intermediary, in which the firm does not deal with foreign customers or firms.

indirect quotation   Foreign exchange quotation that specifies the units of foreign currency that could be purchased with one unit of the home currency.

indirect taxes   Taxes applied to non-income items, such as value-added taxes, excise taxes, tariffs, and so on.

information system   Can provide the decision maker with basic data for most ongoing decisions.

infrastructure shortages   Problems in a country's underlying physical structure, such as transportation, utilities, and so on.

input-output analysis   A method for estimating market activities and potential that measures the factor inflows into production and the resultant outflow of products.

insurance services   Services that are provided in underwriting, risk evaluation, and operations.

intangibility   The inability to be seen, tasted, or touched in a conventional sense; the characteristic of services that most strongly differentiates them from products.

intellectual property right (IPR)   Legal right resulting from industrial, scientific, literary, or artistic activity.

interbank interest rates   The interest rate charged by banks to banks in the major international financial centers.

intermodal movements   The transfer of freight from one mode or type of transportation to another.

internal bank   A multinational firm's financial management tool that actually acts as a bank to coordinate finances among its units.

internal economies of scale
Lower production costs resulting from greater production for an enlarged market.

internalization   Occurs when a firm establishes its own multinational operation, keeping information that is at the core of its competitiveness within the firm.

international bond   Bond issued in domestic capital markets by foreign borrowers (foreign bonds) or issued in the Eurocurrency markets in currency different from that of the home currency of the borrower (Eurobonds).

international competitiveness
The ability of a firm, an industry, or a country to compete in the international marketplace at a stable or rising standard of living.

international debt load   Total accumulated negative net investment of a nation.

international law   The body of rules governing relationships between sovereign states; also certain treaties and agreements respected by a number of countries.

International Monetary Fund (IMF)   A specialized agency of the United Nations established in 1944. An international financial institution for dealing with Balance of Payment problems; the first international monetary authority with at least some degree of power over national authorities.

International Trade Organization (ITO)   A forwardlooking approach to international trade and investment embodied in the 1948 Havana Charter; due to disagreements among sponsoring nations, its provisions were never ratified.

interpretive knowledge   An acquired ability to understand and appreciate the nuances of foreign cultural traits and patterns.

interviews   A face-to-face research tool to obtain in-depth information.

intra-industry trade   The simultaneous export and import of the same good by a country. It is of interest due to the traditional theory that a country will either export or import a good, but not do both at the same time.

intranet   A process that integrates a company's information assets into a single accessible system using Internet-based technologies such as e-mail, news groups, and the World Wide Web.

inventory   Materials on hand for use in the production process; also finished goods on hand.

inventory carrying costs   The expense of maintaining inventories.

investment income   The proportion of net income that is paid back to a parent company.

Islam   A religion that has over 1 billion followers from the west coast of Africa to the Philippines, as well as in the rest of the world and is supportive of entrepreneurism but not of exploitation.

J

joint occurrence   Occurrence of one or several shifts affecting the business environment in several locations simultaneously.

Joint Research and Development Act   A 1984 law that allows both domestic and foreign firms to participate in joint basic-research efforts without fear of U.S. antitrust action.

just-in-time inventory   Materials scheduled to arrive precisely when they are needed on a production line.

L

lags   Paying a debt late to take advantage of exchange rates.

land bridge   Transfer of ocean freight on land among various modes of transportation.

Law of One Price   The theory that the relative prices of any single good between countries, expressed in each country's currency, is representative of the proper or appropriate exchange rate value.

leads   Paying a debt early to take advantage of exchange rates.

Leontief Paradox   The general belief that the United States, as a capital-abundant country, should be exporting capital-intensive products whereas its exports are labor-intensive.

LIBOR   The London InterBank Offer Rate. The rate of interest charged by top-quality international banks on loans to similar quality banks in London. This interest rate is often used in both domestic and international markets as the rate of interest on loans and other financial agreements.

licensing   A firm gives a license to another firm to produce, package, or market its product.

licensing agreement   An agreement in which one firm permits another to use its intellectual property in exchange for compensation.

LIFO   Method of valuation of inventories for accounting purposes, meaning Last-In-First-Out. The principle rests on the practice of recording inventory by "layer" of the cost at which it was incurred.

liner service   Ocean shipping characterized by regularly scheduled passage on established routes.

lingua franca   The language habitually used among people of diverse speech to facilitate communication.

lobbyist   Typically, a well-connected person or firm that is hired by a business to influence the decision making of policymakers and legislators.

local content   Regulations to gain control over foreign investment by ensuring that a large share of the product is locally produced or a larger share of the profit is retained in the country.

location decision   A decision concerning the number of facilities to establish and where they should be situated.

logistics platform   Vital to a firm's competitive position, it is determined by a location's ease and convenience of market reach under favorable cost circumstances.

low-context cultures   Cultures in which most information is conveyed explicitly rather than through behavioral and environmental nuances.

M

Maastricht Treaty   The agreement signed in December 1991 in Maastricht, the Netherlands, in which European Community members agreed to a specific timetable and set of necessary conditions to create a single currency for the EU countries.

macroeconomic level   Level at which trading relationships affect individual markets.

management contract   An international business alternative in which the firm sells its expertise in running a company while avoiding the risk or benefit of ownership.

managerial commitment   The desire and drive on the part of management to act on an idea and to support it in the long run.

maquiladoras   Mexican border plants, with lower labor costs, make goods and parts or process food for export back to the United States.

marginal cost method   This method considers the direct costs of producing and selling goods for export as the floor beneath which prices cannot be set.

market audit   A method of estimating market size by adding together local production and imports, with exports subtracted from the total.

market-differentiated pricing   Price-setting strategy based on demand rather than cost.

market segment   Group of customers that share characteristics and behaviors.

market transparency   Availability of full disclosure and information about key market factors such as supply, demand, quality, service, and prices.

marketing infrastructure   Facilitating marketing agencies in a country; for example, market research firms, channel members.

mass customization   Working with existing product technology to create specific product bundles, resulting in a customized product for a particular customer.

materials management   The timely movement of raw materials, parts, and supplies into and through the firm.

matrix structure   An organizational structure that uses functional and divisional structures simultaneously.

maximization of shareholder value   One of the two alternative objectives of management in private companies (the alternative is *corporate wealth maximization*). The objective of shareholder value maximization is to operate the company in ways that directly reward the equity investors of the company.

media strategy   Strategy applied to the selection of media vehicles and the development of a media schedule.

mercantilism   Political and economic policy in the seventeenth and early eighteenth centuries aimed at increasing a nation's wealth and power by encouraging the export of goods in return for gold.

microeconomic level   Level of business concerns that affect an individual firm or industry.

mininationals   Newer companies with sales between $200 million and $1 billion that are able to serve the world from a handful of manufacturing bases.

minority participation   Participation by a group having less than the number of votes necessary for control.

mixed aid credits   Credits at rates composed partially of commercial interest rates and partially of highly subsidized developmental aid interest rates.

mixed structure   An organizational structure that combines two or more

organizational dimensions; for example, products, areas, or functions.

Most-Favored Nation (MFN)   A term describing a GATT clause that calls for member countries to grant other member countries the same most favorable treatment they accord any country concerning imports and exports. In the U.S. now called Normal Trade Relations (NTR).

multidomestic strategy   A business strategy where each individual country organization is operated as a profit center.

multilateral negotiations   Trade negotiations among more than two parties; the intricate relationships among trading countries.

multinational corporations   Companies that invest in countries around the globe.

N

national security   The ability of a nation to protect its internal values from external threats.

national sovereignty   The supreme right of nations to determine national policies; freedom from external control.

natural hedging   The structuring of a firm's operations so that cash inflows and outflows by currency are matched.

net errors and omissions account   Makes sure the balance of payments (BOP) actually balances.

net present value (NPV)   The sum of the present values of all cash inflows and outflows from an investment project discounted at the cost of capital.

netting   Cash flow coordination between a corporation's global units so that only one smaller cash transfer must be made.

1992 White Paper   A key document developed by the EC Commission to outline the further requirements necessary for a successful integration of the European Union.

nonfinancial incentives Nonmonetary offers intended to motivate; special offers designed to attract foreign direct investors that may take the form of guaranteed government purchases, special protection from competition, or improved infrastructure facilities.

nontariff barriers Barriers to trade, other than tariffs. Examples include buy-domestic campaigns, preferential treatment for domestic bidders, and restrictions on market entry of foreign products such as involved inspection procedures.

not-invented-here syndrome A defensive, territorial attitude that, if held by managers, can frustrate effective implementation of global strategies.

O

observation A research tool where the subjects' activity and behavior are scrutinized.

ocean shipping The forwarding of freight by ocean carrier.

official reserves account An account in the BOP statement that shows (1) the change in the amount of funds immediately available to a country for making international payments and (2) the borrowing and lending that has taken place between the monetary authorities of different countries either directly or through the International Monetary Fund.

offshore banking The use of banks or bank branches located in low-tax countries, often Caribbean islands, to raise and hold capital for multinational operations.

one-stop logistics Allows shippers to buy all the transportation modes and functional services from a single carrier.

operating cash flows The cash flows arising from the firm's everyday business activities.

operating or service lease A lease that transfers most but not all benefits and costs inherent in the ownership of the property to the lessee. Pay-

ments do not fully cover the cost of purchasing the asset or incurring the liability.

operating risk The danger of interference by governments or other groups in one's corporate operations abroad.

opportunity cost The returns foregone on any resource or asset from using it in its next best use. The principle emphasizes that most assets or resources have alternative uses that have real value.

order cycle time The total time that passes between the placement of an order and the receipt of the product.

orientation program A program that familiarizes new workers with their roles; the preparation of employees for assignment overseas.

ownership risk The risk inherent in maintaining ownership of property abroad. The exposure of foreign owned assets to governmental intervention.

P

Patent Cooperations Treaty (PCT) An agreement that outlines procedures for filing one international patent application rather than individual national applications.

pax Americana An American peace since 1945 that led to increased international business transactions.

pax Romana Two relatively peaceful centuries in the Roman Empire.

pension liabilities The accumulating obligations of employers to fund the retirement or pension plans of employees.

perestroika An attempt to fundamentally reform the Soviet economy by improving the overall technological and industrial base and the quality of life for Soviet citizens through increased availability of food, housing, and consumer goods.

perishability Susceptibility to deterioration; the characteristic of services that makes them difficult to store.

physical distribution The movement of finished products from suppliers to customers.

Plaza Agreement An accord reached in 1985 by the Group of Five that held that the major nations should join in a coordinated effort to bring down the value of the U.S. dollar.

political risk The risk of loss by an international corporation of assets, earning power, or managerial control as a result of political actions by the host country.

political union A group of countries that have common foreign policy and security policy and that share judicial cooperation.

population balance A concern in some countries where the population is being skewed by a preference for male children.

population stabilization An attempt to control rapid increases in population and ensure that economic development exceeds population growth.

portfolio investment account An account in the BOP statement that records investments in assets with an original maturity of more than one year and where an investor's ownership position is less than 10 percent.

portfolio models Tools that have been proposed for use in market and competitive analysis. They typically involve two measures—internal strength and external attractiveness.

ports Harbor towns or cities where ships may take on or discharge cargo; the lack of ports and port services is the greatest constraint in ocean shipping.

positioning The perception by consumers of a firm's product in relation to competitors' products.

preferential policies Government policies that favor certain (usually domestic) firms; for example, the use of national carriers for the transport of government freight even when more economical alternatives exist.

price controls Government regulation of the prices of goods and services.

price escalation   The establishing of export prices far in excess of domestic prices—often due to a long distribution channel and frequent markups.

primary data   Data obtained directly for a specific research purpose through interviews, focus groups, surveys, observation, or experimentation.

private placement   The sale of debt securities to private or institutional investors without going through a public issuance like that of a bond issue or equity issue.

privatization   A policy of shifting government operations to privately owned enterprises to cut budget costs and ensure more efficient services.

process structure   A variation of the functional structure in which departments are formed on the basis of production processes.

product cycle theory   A theory that views products as passing through four stages: introduction, growth, maturity, decline; during which the location of production moves from industrialized to lower-cost developing nations.

product differentiation   The effort to build unique differences or improvements into products.

product structure   An organizational structure in which product divisions are responsible for all manufacturing and marketing.

production possibilities frontier   A theoretical method of representing the total productive capabilities of a nation used in the formulation of classical and modern trade theory.

promotional message   The content of an advertisement or a publicity release.

protectionistic legislation   A trade policy that restricts trade to or from one country to another country.

proxy information   Data used as a substitute for more desirable data that are unobtainable.

punitive tariff   A tax on an imported good or service intended to punish a trading partner.

purchasing power parity (PPP)   The theory that the price of internationally traded commodities should be the same in every country, and hence the exchange rate between the two currencies of those countries should be the ratio of prices in the two countries.

Q

qualitative information   Data that are not amenable to statistical analysis, but provide a better understanding, description, or prediction of given situations, behavioral patterns, or underlying dimensions.

quality circles   Groups of workers who meet regularly to discuss issues related to productivity.

quality of life   The standard of living combined with environmental factors, it determines the level of well-being of individuals.

quality of work life   Various corporate efforts in the areas of personal and professional development undertaken with the objectives of increasing employee satisfaction and increasing productivity.

quotas   Legal restrictions on the import quantity of particular goods, imposed by governments as barriers to trade.

R

reference groups   Groups such as the family, co-workers, and professional and trade associations that provide the values and attitudes that influence and shape behavior, including consumer behavior.

reinvoicing   The policy of buying goods from one unit and selling them to a second unit and reinvoicing the sale to the next unit, to take advantage of favorable exchange rates.

reliability   Dependability; the predictability of the outcome of an action. For example, the reliability of arrival time for ocean freight or airfreight.

representative office   An office of an international bank established in a foreign country to serve the bank's customers in the area in an advisory

capacity; does not take deposits or make loans.

reverse distribution   A system responding to the need for product returns that ensures a firm can retrieve a product from the market for subsequent use, recycling, or disposal.

roll-on-roll-off (RORO)   Transportation vessels built to accommodate trucks, which can drive on in one port and drive off at their destinations.

royalty   The compensation paid by one firm to another under an agreement.

S

sanction   A governmental action, usually consisting of a specific coercive trade measure, that distorts the free flow of trade for an adversarial or political purpose rather than an economic one.

scenario building   The identification of crucial variables and determining their effects on different cases or approaches.

sea bridge   The transfer of freight among various modes of transportation at sea.

secondary data   Data originally collected to serve another purpose than the one in which the researcher is currently interested.

self-management   Independent decision making; a high degree of worker involvement in corporate decision making.

self-reference criterion   The unconscious reference to one's own cultural values.

sensitivity training   Training in human relations that focuses on personal and interpersonal interactions; training that focuses on enhancing an expatriate's flexibility in situations quite different from those at home.

service capacity   The maximum level at which a service provider is able to provide services to customers.

service consistency   Uniform quality of service.

service heterogeneity The difference from one delivery of a product to another delivery of the same product as a result of the inability to control the production and quality of the process.

services trade The international exchange of personal or professional services, such as financial and banking services, construction, and tourism.

shipper's order A negotiable bill of lading that can be bought, sold, or traded while the subject goods are still in transit and that is used for letter of credit transactions.

Single European Act The legislative basis for the European Integration.

Smoot-Hawley Act A 1930 act that raised import duties to the highest rates ever imposed by the United States; designed to promote domestic production, it resulted in the downfall of the world trading system.

social infrastructure The housing, health, educational, and other social systems in a country.

social stratification The division of a particular population into classes.

sogoshosha A large Japanese general trading company.

special economic zones Areas created by a country to attract foreign investors, in which there are no tariffs, substantial tax incentives, and low prices for land and labor.

specie Gold and silver.

spot rates Contracts that provide for two parties to exchange currencies with delivery in two business days.

standard of living The level of material affluence of a group or nation, measured as a composite of quantities and qualities of goods.

standard worldwide pricing Price-setting strategy based on average unit costs of fixed, variable, and export-related costs.

state-owned enterprise A corporate form that has emerged in non-Communist countries, primarily for reasons of national security and economic security.

straight bill of lading A nonnegotiable bill of lading usually used in prepaid transactions in which the transported goods involved are delivered to a specific individual or company.

strategic alliances A new term for collaboration among firms, often similar to joint ventures.

strategic leader A highly competent firm located in a strategically critical market.

supply-chain management Results where a series of value-adding activities connect a company's supply side with its demand side.

surveys The use of questionnaires to obtain quantifiable research information.

systems concept A concept of logistics based on the notion that materials-flow activities are so complex that they can be considered only in the context of their interaction.

T

tariffs Taxes on imported goods and services, instituted by governments as a means to raise revenue and as barriers to trade.

tax equalization Reimbursement by the company when an employee in an overseas assignment pays taxes at a higher rate than if he or she were at home.

tax policy A means by which countries may control foreign investors.

teaching services Services that are provided in the areas of training and motivating as well as in teaching of operational, managerial, and theoretical issues.

team building A process that enhances the cohesiveness of a department or group by helping members learn how to organize their work and assume responsibility for it.

technology transfer The transfer of systematic knowledge for the manufacture of a product, the application of a process, or the rendering of a service.

"tentative U.S. tax" The calculation of U.S. taxes on foreign source incomes to estimate U.S. tax payments.

terrorism Illegal and violent acts toward property and people.

theocracy A legal perspective based on religious practices and interpretations.

total cost concept A decision concept that uses cost as a basis for measurement in order to evaluate and optimize logistical activities.

tourism The economic benefit of money spent in a country or region by travelers from outside the area.

tracking The capability of a shipper to obtain information about the location of the shipment at any time.

trade creation A benefit of economic integration; the benefit to a particular country when a group of countries trade a product freely among themselves but maintain common barriers to trade with nonmembers.

trade diversion A cost of economic integration; the cost to a particular country when a group of countries trade a product freely among themselves but maintain common barriers to trade with nonmembers.

trade draft A withdrawal document drawn against a company.

trade-off concept A decision concept that recognizes linkages within the decision system.

trade policy measures Mechanisms used to influence and alter trade relationships.

trade promotion authority The right of the U.S. president to negotiate trade treaties and agreements with the U.S. congress' authority to accept or reject, but not amend.

trading blocs Formed by agreements among countries to establish links through movement of goods, services, capital, and labor across borders.

tramp service   Ocean shipping via irregular routes, scheduled only on demand.

transaction exposure   The potential for currency losses or gains during the time when a firm completes a transaction denominated in a foreign currency.

transfer prices   The prices at which a firm sells its products to its own subsidiaries and affiliates.

transfer risk   The danger of having one's ability to transfer profits or products in and out of a country inhibited by governmental rules and regulations.

transit time   The period between departure and arrival of a carrier.

translation exposure   The potential effect of a change in currency values on a firm's financial statements.

Treaty of Rome   The original agreement that established the foundation for the formation of the European Economic Community.

triangular arbitrage   The exchange of one currency for a second currency, the second for a third, and the third for the first in order to make a profit.

trigger mechanisms   Specific acts or stimuli that set off reactions.

turnkey operation   A specialized form of management contract between a customer and an organization to provide a complete operational system together with the skills needed for unassisted maintenance and operation.

U

undistributed earnings   The proportion of a firm's net income after taxes which is retained within the firm for internal purposes.

unsolicited order   An unplanned business opportunity that arises as a result of another firm's activities.

unstructured data   Information collected for analysis with open-ended questions.

V

value-added tax (VAT)   A tax on the value contributed at each stage of the production and distribution process; a tax assessed in most European countries and also common among Latin American countries.

virtual team   A team of people who are based at various locations around the world and communicate through intranet and other electronic means to achieve a common goal.

voluntary restraint agreements   Trade-restraint agreements resulting in self-imposed restrictions not covered by WTO rules; used to manage or distort trade flows. For example, Japanese restraints on the export of cars to the United States.

W

Webb-Pomerene Act   A 1918 statute that excludes from antitrust prosecution U.S. firms cooperating to develop foreign markets.

withholding taxes   Taxes applied to the payment of dividends, interest, or royalties by firms.

works council   Councils that provide labor a say in corporate decision making through a representative body that may consist entirely of workers or of a combination of managers and workers.

work redesign programs   Programs that alter jobs to increase both the quality of the work experience and productivity.

work scheduling   Preparing schedules of when and how long workers are at the workplace.

working capital management   The coordination of a firm's current assets (cash, accounts receivable, inventories) and current liabilities (accounts payable, short-term debt).

World Bank   An international financial institution created to facilitate trade.

world-class competitors   Multinational firms that can compete globally with domestic products.

World Trade Organization   The institution that supplanted GATT in 1995 to administer international trade and investment accords.

Name Index

Subject Index